THE VICTORIA HISTORY
OF THE
COUNTIES OF ENGLAND

—

A HISTORY OF
STAFFORDSHIRE

VOLUME XIV

Oxford University Press, Walton Street, Oxford OX2 6DP
Oxford New York Toronto
Delhi Bombay Calcutta Madras Karachi
Petaling Jaya Singapore Hong Kong Tokyo
Nairobi Dar es Salaam Cape Town
Melbourne Auckland

and associated companies in
Berlin Ibadan

Oxford is a trade mark of Oxford University Press

Published in the United States
by Oxford University Press, New York

British Library Cataloguing in Publication Data

A History of the county of Stafford. – (The
Victoria history of the counties of England)
Vol. 14, Lichfield
1. Staffordshire, history
I. Greenslade, M. W. (Michael Washington), *1929–*
II. University of London
Institute of Historical Research
III. Series
942.46
ISBN 0 19 722778 3

3 8014 00980 3714 ✓

Distributed by Oxford University Press until 1 January 1993
thereafter by Dawsons of Pall Mall

Printed by H Charlesworth & Co Ltd
Huddersfield, England

THE VICTORIA HISTORY
OF THE
COUNTIES OF ENGLAND

EDITED BY C. R. ELRINGTON

THE UNIVERSITY OF LONDON
INSTITUTE OF
HISTORICAL RESEARCH

INSCRIBED TO THE
MEMORY OF HER LATE MAJESTY
QUEEN VICTORIA
WHO GRACIOUSLY GAVE THE TITLE TO
AND ACCEPTED THE DEDICATION
OF THIS HISTORY

A HISTORY OF THE COUNTY OF STAFFORD

EDITED BY M. W. GREENSLADE

VOLUME XIV

LICHFIELD

PUBLISHED FOR

THE INSTITUTE OF HISTORICAL RESEARCH

BY

OXFORD UNIVERSITY PRESS

1990

CONTENTS OF VOLUME FOURTEEN

CONTENTS OF VOLUME FOURTEEN

LIST OF PLATES

Grateful acknowledgement is made to the following for permission to use material: the Bodleian Library; the British Library; the Dean and Chapter of Lichfield Cathedral; Mr. R. B. Dyott of Freeford Manor; Forsyth County Public Library, Winston-Salem, North Carolina, U.S.A.; Lichfield City Council; the Royal Commission on the Historical Monuments of England; the Staffordshire Record Office; Mr. J. E. Rackham of Lichfield; the Trustees of the William Salt Library, Stafford; and Ulster Museum, Belfast. The illustrations numbered 30–3 and 55 are from photographs by R. J. Sherlock in the possession of the Staffordshire County Planning and Development Department, to which acknowledgement is made. Photographs dated 1989 are by K. W. Sheridan.

Between pages 152 and 153

1. Lichfield Cathedral from the south-west after the demolition of the central spire in 1646. Drawing in the Bodleian Library, MS. Ashmole 1521, p. 147 (second pagination)
2. Lichfield: the city from the west *c.* 1670. Painting in the Guildhall, Lichfield
3. Lichfield: the city from the south-west in 1732. Engraving by S. and N. Buck, in Staffordshire Views, v. 138, at the William Salt Library
4. Lichfield Cathedral: view from the south-west in 1813. Water-colour drawing by J. C. Buckler, in Staffordshire Views, vi. 24, at the William Salt Library
5. Lichfield Cathedral: the Consistory Court in 1833. Drawing by J. C. Buckler, in Staffordshire Views, vi. 98, at the William Salt Library
6. Lichfield Cathedral Close: nos. 23 and 24 from the south in 1807. Drawing by J. Buckler, in Staffordshire Views, v. 157a, at the William Salt Library
7. Lichfield Cathedral Close: the courtyard of no. 23 in 1807. Drawing by J. Buckler, in Staffordshire Views, v. 157b, at the William Salt Library
8. Lichfield Cathedral Close: Vicars' Close from the west. Photograph, 1989
9. Lichfield Cathedral Close: no. 13 from the south. Photograph, 1989
10. Lichfield Cathedral Close: the Deanery from the south. Photograph, 1989
11. Lichfield Cathedral Close: St. Mary's House from the south-east. Photograph, 1989
12. Lichfield: Stowe House from the west. Photograph, 1989
13. Lichfield: Stowe Hill from the south-west. Photograph, 1989
14. Burntwood: Maple Hayes from the east. Photograph, 1989
15. Lichfield Cathedral Close: the former Bishop's Palace from the south. Photograph by Rackhams of Lichfield, 1975
16. Lichfield: no. 67 St. John Street (Davidson House). Photograph, 1989
17. Lichfield: no. 28 St. John Street (St. John's Preparatory School). Photograph, 1989
18. Lichfield: the Guildhall and Donegal House, Bore Street. Photograph, 1989
19. Lichfield: the Union Workhouse in 1843. Drawing by J. Buckler, in Staffordshire Views, v. 161, at the William Salt Library
20. Lichfield: Darwin House, Beacon Street, probably *c.* 1800. From *An Illustrated Guide to Lichfield Cathedral ... with some account of the Ancient and Loyal City of Lichfield* (Lichfield, 1897), plate between pp. 72 and 73
21. The Guild of St. Mary and St. John the Baptist, Lichfield: vignettes relating to four masters. From Lichfield Joint Record Office, D. 77/1, pp. 349, 355, 360, 365
22. John Dyott in 1573. Painting at Freeford Manor
23. Anna Seward in 1786. Painting by George Romney in Forsyth County Public Library
24. Arthur Chichester, earl (later marquess) of Donegall, *c.* 1770. Painting by Thomas Gainsborough in Ulster Museum
25. R. C. Lucas retouching his statue of Samuel Johnson in the market place, Lichfield, in 1859. Photograph in the British Library (Printed Books), Tab. 442.a.13, photographic studies by R. C. Lucas, f. [12]
26. Lichfield: the Guildhall in 1838. Drawing by J. Buckler, in Staffordshire Views, v. 164, at the William Salt Library
27. Lichfield: Minors's School in 1833, with the Crucifix Conduit. Drawing by J. Buckler, in Staffordshire Views, v. 243, at the William Salt Library
28. Lichfield: the Corn Exchange and Market Hall in 1850. Engraving in *Illustrated London News,* 12 January 1850
29. Lichfield: the railway bridge in St. John Street in 1849. Engraving in *Illustrated London News,* 14 April 1849

LIST OF MAPS, PLANS, AND OTHER FIGURES

Grateful acknowledgement is made to the following for permission to use material: the Bodleian Library; the Samuel Johnson Birthplace Museum (Lichfield City Council); the Staffordshire Record Office; and the Trustees of the William Salt Library, Stafford. Figures 6–7, 9, 11–12, 14, 17, 19–20, and 22–5 were drawn by Andrew Kirkham, Joyce Senior, and Alison Steele of the Staffordshire County Planning and Development Department from drafts prepared by M. W. Greenslade and N. J. Tringham.

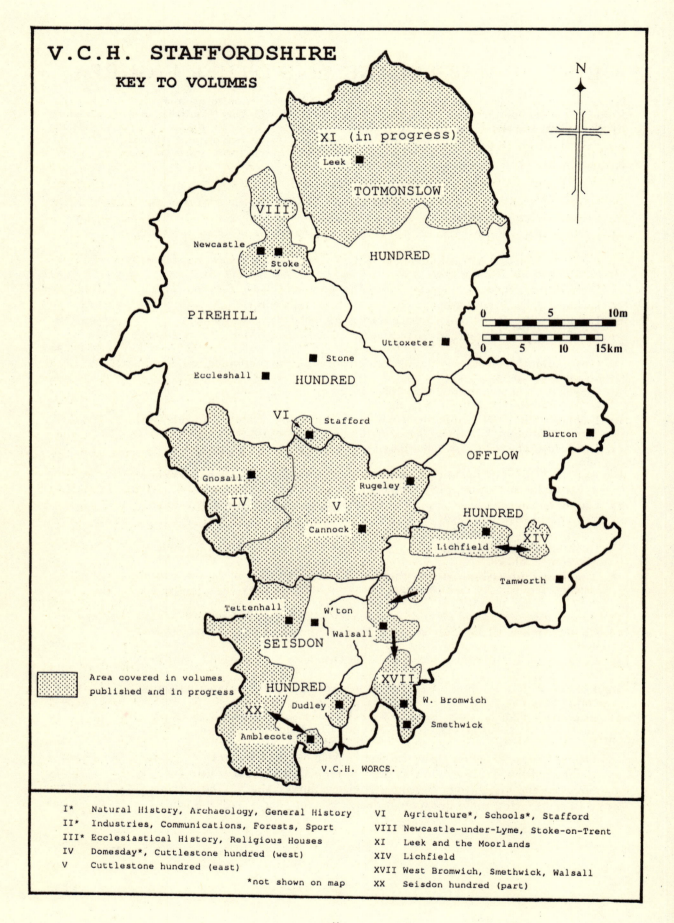

V.C.H. STAFFORDSHIRE

KEY TO VOLUMES

N

XI (in progress)

Leek

TOTMONSLOW

VIII

HUNDRED

Newcastle

Stoke

PIREHILL

Uttoxeter

0   5   10m

0   5   10   15km

Stone

Eccleshall   HUNDRED

VI   Stafford

Burton

OFFLOW

Gnosall

Rugeley

IV   V   HUNDRED

Cannock   Lichfield   XIV

Tamworth

Tettenhall   W'ton

Walsall

SEISDON   XVII

Area covered in volumes
published and in progress   HUNDRED   W. Bromwich

XX   Dudley   Smethwick

Amblecote

V.C.H. WORCS.

I*   Natural History, Archaeology, General History   VI   Agriculture*, Schools*, Stafford
II*   Industries, Communications, Forests, Sport   VIII Newcastle-under-Lyme, Stoke-on-Trent
III* Ecclesiastical History, Religious Houses   XI   Leek and the Moorlands
IV   Domesday*, Cuttlestone hundred (west)   XIV   Lichfield
V   Cuttlestone hundred (east)   XVII West Bromwich, Smethwick, Walsall
                        *not shown on map   XX   Seisdon hundred (part)

EDITORIAL NOTE

THIS volume is the tenth to appear in the Staffordshire set of the Victoria History of the Counties of England. Like its eight immediate predecessors it has been compiled under the supervision of the Staffordshire Victoria County History Committee, which represents a partnership between the university of London, the Staffordshire County Council, and the metropolitan boroughs of Dudley, Sandwell, Walsall, and Wolverhampton. The origins of the partnership are described in the Editorial Note to volume IV of the Staffordshire set, and the present membership of the Committee is set out on p. xiv below. The university of London warmly thanks the five Local Authorities for their continued support and generous financial help.

The local editorial arrangements have remained unchanged since the publication of the previous volume: the county editor is Mr. M. W. Greenslade, with Mr. D. A. Johnson and Dr. N. J. Tringham as the assistant county editors.

Many people and organizations have helped in the preparation of the present volume. Special thanks are offered to the Lichfield Conduit Lands Trust, the Swinfen Broun Charitable Trust, and the Charity of the Hospital of St. John the Baptist, Lichfield, all of which have provided generous financial assistance. Grateful acknowledgement is also made to the Dean and Chapter of Lichfield, especially the Revd. Dr. E. C. C. Hill, honorary cathedral librarian; the Revd. P. Dennison, archivist of Birmingham archdiocese; Mr. M. B. S. Exham, former registrar of Lichfield diocese; Mr. K. A. Flathers of Messrs. Sharrott, Barnes & Co., solicitors of Lichfield; Haley Sharpe Associates; Messrs. Hinckley, Birch & Exham, solicitors of Lichfield, especially Mr. R. D. Birch and Mr. R. Shipton; Mr. L. J. Livesey, Director of Staffordshire Libraries, Arts, and Archives, and members of his staff, especially Miss E. M. Hughes, Principal Area Librarian, Lichfield, and Mr. J. M. Dace, former Deputy Area Librarian; Mr. D. Martin and Mr. P. D. I. Young, successive town clerks of Lichfield; Dr. G. W. Nicholls, Curator of the Samuel Johnson Birthplace Museum, Lichfield; Mr. J. Shryane, Staffordshire County Planning and Development Officer, and members of his staff, especially Mrs. C. M. Edwards, Mr. R. A. Meeson, and Mr. A. G. Taylor; Dr. F. B. Stitt and Mr. D. V. Fowkes, successive Staffordshire County Archivists and William Salt Librarians, and members of their staff, especially Mrs. J. Hamparṭumian, archivist at the Lichfield Joint Record Office; and Mr. J. T. Thompson, Chief Executive and Secretary of the Lichfield District Council, and members of his staff. Many others who have helped are acknowledged in the lists of plates and of figures on pp. ix and xi above and in the footnotes to the articles on which their help was given.

The volume has greatly benefited from a Community Programme scheme organized by the Staffordshire Victoria History in collaboration with the William Salt Library, Stafford, and Lichfield Library. Under the scheme, which operated from 1985 to 1988, part of the *Staffordshire Advertiser* and much of the *Lichfield Mercury* were indexed. As a result a systematic use has been made of those newspapers on a scale not normally possible. Grateful acknowledgement is made of the work of the many people employed on the scheme.

STAFFORDSHIRE
VICTORIA COUNTY HISTORY COMMITTEE
as at 1 January 1990

LIST OF CLASSES OF DOCUMENTS IN THE PUBLIC RECORD OFFICE

USED IN THIS VOLUME WITH THEIR CLASS NUMBERS

Chancery

		Proceedings
C	1	Early
C	3	Series II
C	12	1758–1800
C	54	Close Rolls
C	66	Patent Rolls
C	78	Decree Rolls
C	93	Proceedings of Commissioners for Charitable Uses, Inquisitions and Decrees

		Inquisitions post mortem
C	137	Series I: Henry IV
C	138	Henry V
C	139	Henry VI
C	142	Series II
C	260	Tower and Rolls Chapel, Recorda

Court of Common Pleas

CP 25(2)	Feet of Fines, Series II
CP 40	Plea Rolls, Placita de Banco, or De Banco Rolls

Exchequer, Exchequer of Pleas

E 1	Affidavits, General 1830–75

Exchequer, Treasury of Receipt

E 40	Deeds, Series A

Exchequer, King's Remembrancer

E 134	Depositions taken by Commission
E 178	Special Commissions of Inquiry
E 179	Subsidy Rolls, etc.
E 199	Sheriffs' Accounts
E 210	Deeds, Series D

Exchequer, Augmentation Office

E 301	Certificates of Colleges and Chantries

Ministry of Education

ED 7	Elementary Education, Public Elementary Schools, Preliminary Statements

Home Office

		Census Papers
HO 107	Population Returns, 1841 and 1851
HO 129	Ecclesiastical Returns

Justices Itinerant

JUST 1	Eyre Rolls, Assize Rolls, etc.

Principal Probate Registry

		Prerogative Court of Canterbury
PROB 10	Original Wills
PROB 11	Registered Copies of Wills

Registrar General

RG 4	Non-parochial Registers
RG 9	Census Returns, 1861
RG 10	Census Returns, 1871
RG 11	Census Returns, 1881

Special Collections

SC 1	Ancient Correspondence
SC 6	Ministers' Accounts
SC 12	Rentals and Surveys, Portfolios

State Paper Office

SP 1	Henry VIII, General Series
SP 12	Elizabeth I, Domestic
SP 28	Commonwealth Exchequer Papers
SP 35	George I, Domestic

Court of Star Chamber

STAC 2	Proceedings, Henry VIII

Court of Wards and Liveries

WARD 7	Inquisitions post mortem

MAIN CLASSES OF DOCUMENTS IN THE LICHFIELD JOINT RECORD OFFICE
USED IN THIS VOLUME WITH THEIR CLASS NUMBERS

D. 15   Documents deposited by Hinckley & Birch, solicitors of Lichfield

D. 16   Lichfield Conduit Lands Trust, records

D. 20   St. Mary's, Lichfield, parish records

D. 25   Lichfield Quarter Sessions, records

D. 27   St. Michael's, Lichfield, parish records

D. 29   St. Chad's, Lichfield, parish records

D. 30   Dean and Chapter of Lichfield cathedral, records

D. 30/VC   Vicars Choral of Lichfield cathedral, records

D. 33   Lichfield City Council, records

D. 35   Lichfield City Council, records (Treasurer's department)

D. 39   St. Chad's, Lichfield, parish records (additional)

D. 52   St. Chad's, Lichfield, parish records (additional)

D. 68   Lichfield Quarter Sessions, order book 1727–58

D. 77   Lichfield City Council, records (additional)

D. 88   St. John's Hospital, Lichfield, records

D. 103   Dr. Milley's Hospital, Lichfield, records

D. 126   Lichfield Conduit Lands Trust, records (additional)

D. 127   Lichfield City Council, records (additional)

Bishop's Administrative Records
B/A/1   Bishops' Registers
B/A/3   Presentation Deeds
B/A/13   Clergy Livings
B/A/15   Tithe Awards
B/A/19   Registrars' Correspondence
B/A/21   Bishops' Temporalities

Bishop's Court Records
B/C/5   Cause Papers
B/C/11   Wills and Inventories
B/C/12   Faculties

Bishop's Visitation Records
B/V/3   Visitation Records
B/V/6   Glebe Terriers

Dean and Chapter Court Records
DC/C/1   Court Books

Peculiar Jurisdiction Records
P/C/11   Wills and Inventories

Vicars' Choral Records
VC/A/21   Temporalities

NOTE ON ABBREVIATIONS

Among the abbreviations and short titles used, the following may require elucidation. The place of publication of printed works is London, unless otherwise stated.

Abbrev. Plac. (Rec. Com.)	*Placitorum in Domo Capitulari Westmonasteriensi Asservatorum Abbreviatio* (Record Commission, 1811)
Abbrev. Rot. Orig. (Rec. Com.)	*Rotulorum Originalium in Curia Scaccarii Abbreviatio* (Record Commission, 1805, 1810)
Acts of the P.C.	*Acts of the Privy Council of England* (H.M.S.O. 1890–1964)
Alum. Cantab. to 1751; 1752–1900	*Alumni Cantabrigienses, a Biographical List to 1900*, compiled by J. Venn and J. A. Venn, *Part I, to 1751; Part II, 1752–1900* (Cambridge, 1922–54)
Alum. Oxon. 1500–1714; 1715–1886	*Alumni Oxonienses, 1500–1714; 1715–1886*, ed. J. Foster (Oxford, 1888–92)
Antiq. Jnl.	*The Antiquaries Journal*
Arch. Jnl.	*Archaeological Journal*
B.A.A.	Birmingham Archdiocesan Archives, St. Chad's Cathedral, Birmingham
BAR	British Archaeological Reports
B.L.	British Library, London
B.R.L.	Birmingham Central Library, Reference Library
Bk. of Fees	*The Book of Fees commonly called Testa de Nevill* (H.M.S.O. 1920–31)
Bodl.	Bodleian Library, Oxford
Bull. Inst. Hist. Res.	*Bulletin of the Institute of Historical Research*
C.J.	*Journals of the House of Commons*
Cal. Chanc. Wts.	*Calendar of Chancery Warrants preserved in the Public Record Office* (H.M.S.O. 1927)
Cal. Chart. R.	*Calendar of the Charter Rolls preserved in the Public Record Office* (H.M.S.O. 1903–27)
Cal. Close	*Calendar of the Close Rolls preserved in the Public Record Office* (H.M.S.O. 1892–1963)
Cal. Cttee. for Compounding	*Calendar of the Proceedings of the Committee for Compounding, etc.* (H.M.S.O. 1889–92)
Cal. Cttee. for Money	*Calendar of the Proceedings of the Committee for Advance of Money, etc.* (H.M.S.O. 1888)
Cal. Fine R.	*Calendar of the Fine Rolls preserved in the Public Record Office* (H.M.S.O. 1911–62)
Cal. H.O. Papers	*Calendar of Home Office Papers* (H.M.S.O. 1878–99)
Cal. Inq. Misc.	*Calendar of Inquisitions Miscellaneous (Chancery) preserved in the Public Record Office* (H.M.S.O. 1916–68)
Cal. Inq. p.m.	*Calendar of Inquisitions post mortem preserved in the Public Record Office* (H.M.S.O. 1904–74)
Cal. Inq. p.m. (Rec. Com.)	*Calendarium Inquisitionum post mortem sive Escaetarum* (Record Commission, 1806–28)
Cal. Inq. p.m. Hen. VII	*Calendar of Inquisitions post mortem, Henry VII* (H.M.S.O. 1898–1955)
Cal. Lib.	*Calendar of the Liberate Rolls preserved in the Public Record Office* (H.M.S.O. 1916–64)
Cal. Pat.	*Calendar of the Patent Rolls preserved in the Public Record Office* (H.M.S.O. 1891–1986)
Cal. S.P. Dom.	*Calendar of State Papers, Domestic Series* (H.M.S.O. 1856–1972)
Cal. Treas. Bks.	*Calendar of Treasury Books preserved in the Public Record Office* (H.M.S.O. 1904–62)
Cal. Treas. Bks. and Papers	*Calendar of Treasury Books and Papers preserved in the Public Record Office* (H.M.S.O. 1898–1903)
Camd. (Soc.)	Camden Society

Cat. Anct. D.	*Descriptive Catalogue of Ancient Deeds in the Public Record Office* (H.M.S.O. 1890–1915)
Census	*Census Report(s)*
Char. Dons.	*Abstract of the Returns of Charitable Donations for the Benefit of Poor Persons 1786–1788,* H.C. 511 (1816), xvi (2)
Ches. R.O.	Cheshire Record Office, Chester
Clayton, *Cathedral City*	H. Clayton, *Cathedral City, a Look at Victorian Lichfield* (Lichfield [1977])
Clayton, *Coaching City*	H. Clayton, *Coaching City, a Glimpse of Georgian Lichfield* (Didsbury [1976])
Clayton, *Loyal and Ancient City*	H. Clayton, *Loyal and Ancient City, Lichfield in the Civil Wars* (Lichfield [1987])
Close R.	*Close Rolls of the Reign of Henry III preserved in the Public Record Office* (H.M.S.O. 1902–75)
Complete Peerage	G. E. C[okayne] and others, *The Complete Peerage* (1910–59)
Cur. Reg. R.	*Curia Regis Rolls preserved in the Public Record Office* (H.M.S.O. 1922–79)
D.N.B.	*Dictionary of National Biography*
Derb. R.O.	Derbyshire Record Office, Matlock
Dugdale, *Mon.*	W. Dugdale, *Monasticon Anglicanum,* ed. J. Caley and others (1846)
Dugdale, *Warws.*	W. Dugdale, *The Antiquities of Warwickshire* (1730)
E.E.T.S.	Early English Text Society
E.H.R.	*English Historical Review*
E.P.N.S.	English Place-Name Society
Educ. Enq. Abstract	*Education Enquiry Abstract,* H.C. 62 (1835), xlii
Ekwall, *Eng. Place-Names*	E. Ekwall, *The Concise Oxford Dictionary of English Place-Names* (1960)
Erdeswick, *Staffs.*	S. Erdeswick, *A Survey of Staffordshire,* ed. T. Harwood (1844)
Feud. Aids	*Inquisitions and Assessments relating to Feudal Aids preserved in the Public Record Office* (H.M.S.O. 1899–1920)
G.E.C. Baronetage	G. E. C[okayne], *Complete Baronetage* (1900–9)
G.R.O.	General Register Office
Gent. Mag.	*The Gentleman's Magazine*
H.C.	House of Commons
H.L.R.O.	House of Lords Record Office
H.M.S.O.	Her (His) Majesty's Stationery Office
Harl. Soc.	Harleian Society
Harwood, *Lichfield*	Thomas Harwood, *The History and Antiquities of the Church and City of Lichfield* (1806)
Hist. MSS. Com.	Historical Manuscripts Commission
Hist. Parl., Commons	*History of Parliament, The House of Commons*
J.R.U.L.M.	John Rylands University Library of Manchester
Jackson, *Hist. Incidents*	J. W. Jackson, *Historical Incidents in and around Lichfield and its Ancient Charities* (Lichfield, 1936)
Jackson, *Lichfield*	J. Jackson, *History of the City and Cathedral of Lichfield* (1805)
Jennings, *Staffs. Bells*	T. S. Jennings, *A History of Staffordshire Bells* (privately printed, 1968)
Jnl. Staffs. Ind. Arch. Soc.	Staffordshire Industrial Archaeology Society, *Journal*
L.J.R.O.	Lichfield Joint Record Office (see p. xvi)
L. & P. Hen. VIII	*Letters and Papers, Foreign and Domestic, of the Reign of Henry VIII* (H.M.S.O. 1864–1932)
Laithwaite, *Conduit Lands Trust*	P. Laithwaite, *The History of the Lichfield Conduit Lands Trust* (Lichfield, 1947)
Lambourne and James, *Burntwood*	E. Lambourne and B. James, *Burntwood in Times Past* (Brinscall, Chorley, Lancs., ? 1982)

Le Neve, *Fasti*	J. Le Neve, *Fasti Ecclesiae Anglicanae* (University of London, Institute of Historical Research, 1962 and later)
Le Neve, *Fasti* (1854)	J. Le Neve, *Fasti Ecclesiae Anglicanae,* corrected and continued by T. D. Hardy (1854)
Leland, *Itin.* ed. Toulmin Smith	*The Itinerary of John Leland,* ed. L. Toulmin Smith (1906–10)
Lich. Dioc. Regy.	Lichfield Diocesan Registry
Lomax's Red Bk.	*Lomax's Red Book and Almanac for the City and County of Lichfield* (Lichfield, 1895 and later)
Lond. Gaz.	*London Gazette*
Lynam, *Church Bells*	C. Lynam, *The Church Bells of the County of Stafford* (1889)
M.A.F.F.	Ministry of Agriculture, Fisheries, and Food (Crewe Divisional Office)
Mason, *Found Ready*	S. Mason, *Found Ready: Memorials of the Rev. George Poole, B.A., late Vicar of Burntwood* (1890)
N.R.A.	National Register of Archives
Nat. Soc. *Inquiry, 1846–7*	*Result of the Returns to the General Inquiry made by the National Society, 1846–7* (1849)
O.S.	Ordnance Survey
Old Chasetown	*Old Chasetown* (Staffordshire County Council Education Department, Local History Source Book L. 38)
P.R.O.	Public Record Office, London (see p. xv)
P.R.S.	Pipe Roll Society
Parker, *Lichfield*	A. D. Parker, *A Sentimental Journey in and about the Ancient and Loyal City of Lichfield* (Lichfield, 1925)
Pevsner, *Staffs.*	N. Pevsner, *The Buildings of England: Staffordshire* (Harmondsworth, 1974)
Pitt, *Staffs.*	W. Pitt, *A Topographical History of Staffordshire* (Newcastle-under-Lyme, 1817)
Plac. de Quo Warr. (Rec. Com.)	*Placita de Quo Warranto* (Record Commission, 1818)
Plot, *Staffs.*	R. Plot, *A Natural History of Staffordshire* (Oxford, 1686)
R.D.C.	Rural District Council
Reade, *Johnsonian Gleanings*	A. L. Reade, *Johnsonian Gleanings* (priv. print. 1909–52)
Reg. Regum Anglo-Norm.	*Regesta Regum Anglo-Normannorum 1066–1154,* ed. H. W. C. Davis and others (1913–69)
7th Rep. Com. Char.	*Seventh Report of the Charity Commissioners for England and Wales,* H.C. 129 (1822), x
Rolls Ser.	Rolls Series
Rot. Litt. Pat. (Rec. Com.)	*Rotuli Litterarum Patentium* (Record Commission, 1835)
Rot. Parl.	*Rotuli Parliamentorum* [1783]
S.H.C.	Staffordshire Record (*formerly* William Salt Archaeological) Society, *Collections for a History of Staffordshire* (see p. xxi)
S.R.O.	Staffordshire Record Office, Stafford
Salop. Arch. Soc.	Shropshire Archaeological (*formerly* Archaeological and Historical) Society, *Transactions*
Salop. R.O.	Shropshire Record Office, Shrewsbury
Selden Soc.	Selden Society
Shaw, *Staffs.*	Stebbing Shaw, *The History and Antiquities of Staffordshire* (1798, 1801; reprinted with additions, Wakefield, 1976)
Sherlock, *Ind. Arch. Staffs.*	R. Sherlock, *The Industrial Archaeology of Staffordshire* (1976)
Staffs. Cath. Hist.	*Staffordshire Catholic History* (Journal of the Staffordshire Catholic History Society)
Staffs. Endowed Chars.	*Report on Charitable Endowments appropriated to purposes of Elementary Education in the County of Stafford* [Cd. 2729], H.C. (1906), xc
Staffs. Hist.	*Staffordshire History* (Stafford, 1984 onwards)
Stringer, *Lichfield*	[C. E. Stringer], *A Short Account of the Ancient and Modern State of the City and Close of Lichfield* (Lichfield, 1819)
T.B.A.S.	Birmingham and Midland Institute: Birmingham Archaeological Society, *Transactions and Proceedings*

T.S.S.A.H.S.	South Staffordshire (*originally* Lichfield, *later* Lichfield and South Staffordshire) Archaeological and Historical Society, *Transactions*
Trans. Anct. Mon. Soc.	Ancient Monuments Society, *Transactions*
Trans. R.H.S.	Royal Historical Society, *Transactions*
U.D.C.	Urban District Council
V.C.H.	*Victoria County History*
Valor Eccl. (Rec. Com.)	*Valor Ecclesiasticus* (Record Commission, 1810–34)
W.S.L.	William Salt Library, Stafford
Wesley, *Dir. Burton*	W. Wesley, *Directory of Burton-upon-Trent, Uttoxeter, Tamworth, Lichfield, and Ashby-de-la-Zouch* (Burton-upon-Trent, 1844)
White, *Dir. Staffs.* (1834; 1851)	W. White, *History, Gazetteer, and Directory of Staffordshire* (Sheffield, 1834; 1851)
Wilkins, *Concilia*	D. Wilkins, *Concilia Magnae Britanniae et Hiberniae* (1737)

ANALYSIS OF SOURCES PRINTED IN
COLLECTIONS FOR A HISTORY OF STAFFORDSHIRE
(STAFFORDSHIRE RECORD SOCIETY)
AND USED IN THIS VOLUME

ANALYSIS OF *S.H.C.* SOURCES

THE CITY OF LICHFIELD

LICHFIELD, one of the smallest of the English cathedral cities, was an ecclesiastical centre by the 7th century.[1] A town was laid out there in the 12th century, and it was incorporated and given county status by royal charters in the mid 16th century. Until the later 18th century it was among the largest and wealthiest Staffordshire towns, and with its cathedral and its position on important main roads it was also the social centre of the county.

The boundaries of the city were probably extended on the north and west in the mid 17th century, but there is no surviving perambulation before the later 18th century.[2] The area remained 3,475 a. until 1934 when it was enlarged to 3,597 a. (1,456 ha.) by the addition of part of Streethay on the east.[3] Further adjustments to the eastern boundary in 1980 reduced the area to 1,403 ha.[4] Circuit brook marks part of the northern boundary, and Darnford brook formed much of the south-eastern boundary until the changes of 1980. A large part of the city was still open country in the mid 20th century, but in the 40 years following the end of the Second World War there has been extensive residential development with a threefold increase in population. The city had little important industry before the 19th century, a fact which, when noted by James Boswell in 1776, provoked Dr. Johnson to say of his native Lichfield: 'We are a city of philosophers: we work with our heads and make the boobies of Birmingham work for us with their hands.'[5] In the later 19th century brewing and light engineering became important, and the later 20th century has seen a notable increase in light industry on several trading estates.

Lichfield is situated on the Keuper Sandstone between the high ground of Cannock Chase on the west and the valleys of the Trent and the Tame on the east. The ground within the city slopes down from 382 ft. (116 m.) in the north-west to 282 ft. (86 m.) on the sandstone shelf where the cathedral stands. The market place lies at 265 ft. (81 m.), but south and east of the city centre is a ridge which reaches 341 ft. (104 m.) at St. Michael's church on a spur at Greenhill. To the south-east the level drops to 226 ft. (69 m.) where the Tamworth road crosses the city boundary into Freeford. There is another ridge in the south-west of the city where the level reaches 423 ft. (130 m.) on the boundary at Aldershawe and Harehurst Hill.

Two pools, Minster Pool and the larger Stowe Pool, lie respectively south and east of the cathedral. Before the 18th century there was a third pool known variously as Upper, Over, and Sandford Pool; it lay west of Minster Pool, separated from it by a causeway.[6] John Leland in the 1540s noted that the pools divided the

---

[1] The following account of Lichfield was written in the later 1980s. The people named in footnotes as supplying information are warmly thanked for their help. Statements in this introductory section and in the following General History section for which sources are not given can be assumed to be based on the relevant section later in the volume.   [2] Below, boundaries and gates.

[3] *Census*, 1931.
[4] Lichfield (Parishes) Order 1980, S.I. 1980 no. 387; below, Freeford (introduction); Streethay (introduction).
[5] *Boswell's Life of Johnson*, ed. G. B. Hill, rev. L. F. Powell, ii. 464.
[6] L.J.R.O., D. 77/9/28, 37, 61; below, figs. 2 and 4; econ. hist. (agric.; fisheries).

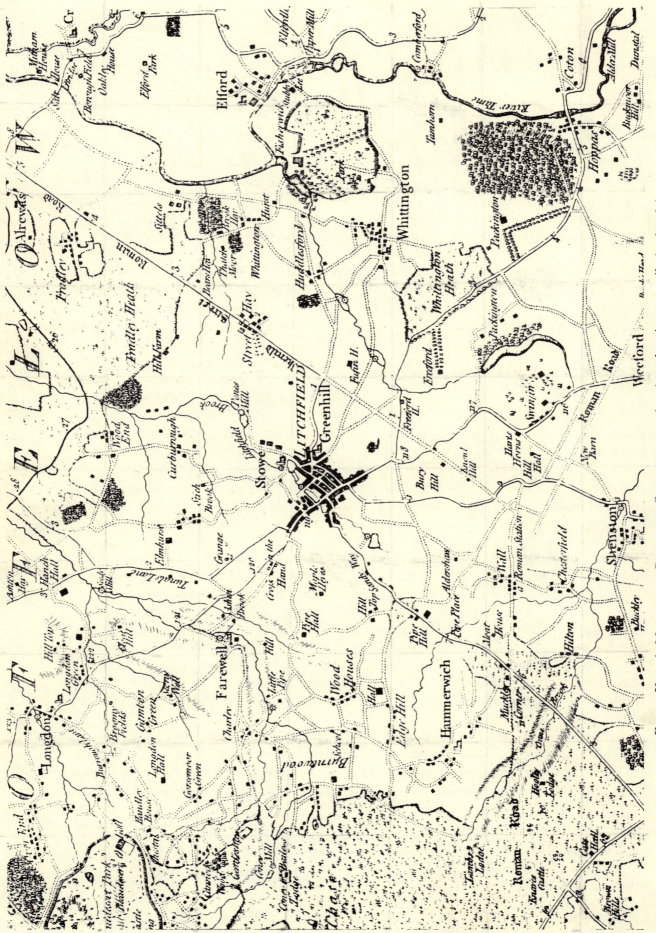

FIG. 1. YATES'S MAP OF THE COUNTY OF STAFFORD 1775 (part): scale 1 in. to 1 mile (1: 63,360)

city into north and south parts,[7] while Daniel Defoe in the 1720s described how Minster Pool 'parts Lichfield, as it were, into two cities, one is called the Town, and the other the Close'.[8] The pools were fed from the west by Leamonsley and Trunkfield brooks, but by the 1980s the brooks no longer contained sufficient water; instead water is pumped into Minster Pool from the South Staffordshire Waterworks Co.'s tunnel running from Hanch reservoir in Longdon.[9] A single stream, now covered over, runs out of Minster Pool into Stowe Pool, out of which it flows north as Curborough brook. The pools appear to be natural in origin but to have been deepened in order to drive two mills and to serve as fisheries.[10] For Celia Fiennes, visiting Lichfield in 1697, the city stood 'low and waterish', and she noted 'a great standing water ... just by the town which does often flow the grounds after rains'.[11] Horace Walpole visited Lichfield in 1743 and wrote of it that 'the bog in which the cathedral ... stands stagnates, I believe, midst beds of poppy and makes all its inhabitants as sleepy as its bishop and canons'.[12] In 1745 another traveller commented with equal sarcasm on Lichfield's situation, 'which (tho' in a bog) the inhabitants fancy to be as healthy as that of Montpellier'.[13] Upper Pool disappeared as a result of encroachment, and the area had been landscaped by the 1780s; it is now occupied by the southern part of Beacon Park. Minster and Stowe pools were landscaped in the later 18th century.[14] In 1840 a local physician denounced them as a source of disease and called for them to be filled in.[15] In the later 1850s they were dredged and turned into reservoirs by the South Staffordshire Waterworks Co.[16] Although no longer so used, they remain a striking feature of Lichfield's landscape.

The cathedral, rising above Minster Pool, has long been appreciated as an even more striking feature. In 1635 members of the city corporation described it as 'the beauty of the city'.[17] Defoe considered it 'one of the finest and most beautiful in England'.[18] Even Walpole thought it 'very fine'.[19] Henry James in 1872 forgave Lichfield for being 'stale without being really antique' because it formed 'a girdle of quietude' for a cathedral which was 'great among churches'.[20] Three visitors in 1634 noted the 'stately high spires' rising above the city.[21] For Defoe they were 'three beautiful spires, the like of which are not to be seen in one church, no not in Europe'.[22] Francis Mundy, in his poem on Needwood forest written in 1776, hailed them as the 'triumphant ladies of the vale'.[23] In the 1860s Elihu Burritt, the United States consular agent in Birmingham and a fervent admirer of Lichfield cathedral, noted how the spire of St. Mary's added a fourth to the cathedral spires: 'Lichfield looks like a little city of steeples on approaching it from any side.' Indeed, though a 'flat-footed little city', it was the 'clasp-jewel of the gold-and-green embroidered zone of the Black Country'.[24]

[7] Leland, *Itin.* ed. Toulmin Smith, ii. 100–1.

[8] D. Defoe, *Tour thro' the Whole Island of Gt. Brit.* (1927), ii. 479.

[9] *Lichfield Mercury*, 4 Aug. 1989, p. 4.

[10] *S.H.C.* 1950–1, 143–4; below, econ. hist.

[11] *Journeys of Celia Fiennes*, ed. C. Morris (1949), 111, 114.

[12] *Corresp. of Horace Walpole*, ed. W. S. Lewis, xl. 43.

[13] Hist. MSS. Com. 31, *13th Rep. IV*, p. 472.

[14] Below, econ hist. (agric.); social and cultural activities (walks).

[15] [J. C. Rawson], *Inquiry into Hist. and Influence of the Lichfield Waters* (Lichfield and London, 1840; copy in W.S.L.).

[16] Below, public services (water supplies).

[17] *Cal. S.P. Dom.* 1635, 455.

[18] Defoe, *Tour*, ii. 279.

[19] *Corresp. of Walpole*, xl. 43.

[20] H. James, *English Hours* (1960), 48; L. Edel, *Henry James: the Conquest of London, 1870–1883* (1962), 63.

[21] *Relation of a Short Survey of 26 Counties, 1634*, ed. L. G. Wickham Legg, 56.

[22] Defoe, *Tour*, ii. 279.

[23] F. N. C. Mundy, *Needwood Forest* (Lichfield, 1776), 24. Honora Sneyd, Anna Seward's protégée, was reported as calling them 'the ladies of the valley' in 1779: *Poetical Works of Anna Seward*, ed. W. Scott (Edinburgh, 1810), ii. 89; M. A. Hopkins, *Dr. Johnson's Lichfield*, 110–11.

[24] E. Burritt, *Walks in the Black Country and its Green Border-land* (1869), 341–3, 353.

GENERAL HISTORY

EARLY SETTLEMENT

FRAGMENTS of Mesolithic flints have been found on the high ground occupied by St. Michael's churchyard, and they may indicate the site of a flint industry.[1] Traces of Neolithic settlement have been discovered on the south side of the sandstone terrace occupied by the cathedral.[2] St. Michael's on its hill-top site may possibly have replaced a pagan sanctuary.[3] There have been scattered Romano-British finds in the city,[4] and it is possible that a burial discovered beneath the cathedral in 1751 was Romano-British.[5] The line of the Roman Ryknild Street runs through the south-east of the city, and the fact that it was built across existing fields suggests settlement in that area by the time of its construction.[6] The tradition of a massacre of Christians at Lichfield in the reign of Diocletian, 284–305, developed from a medieval fabrication and can no longer be accepted.[7]

Near the point south of the city where Ryknild Street crosses Watling Street is the site of *Letocetum*, the modern Wall, which originated as a 1st-century A.D. fort and developed in the 2nd century as a civilian settlement.[8] The name *Letocetum* represents the Celtic toponym *lētocaiton*, from which evolved the form *luitcoit*. Both words mean 'grey wood' and reflect the wooded character of the area. The name Lichfield is a compound of the Celtic *luitcoit* and the Anglo-Saxon *feld*, meaning 'common pasture'. It may simply be descriptive of the area at the time of the Anglian settlement *c.* 600 and mean 'common pasture in (or beside) the grey wood'. On the other hand it may indicate a Celtic settlement called *Luitcoit* and mean 'common pasture near (or belonging to) *Luitcoit*'.[9]

In the earlier or mid 7th century there was a settlement called *Caer Lwytgoed* ('town of the grey wood') in the area, and a battle was fought there involving the Welsh of Powys, who took extensive booty.[10] Its site is problematic. There is no evidence that Wall was inhabited later than the 5th century. It is possible that the fort and settlement of *Letocetum* took its name from a pre-Roman estate or administrative centre some distance away and that for local Celtic-speaking people *Luitcoit* remained the estate or centre.[11] There is no archaeological evidence that it was the later cathedral site. The earliest accounts of the establishment of the bishopric in 669 speak of Lichfield simply as a place (*locus*).[12] It may well be that in the 7th century the name Lichfield was used for an extensive area and only later came to be restricted to the cathedral and its environs.

---

[1] *T.S.S.A.H.S.* xxii. 2, 70, 72.

[2] Ibid. 2, 36–7, 42–3. For other isolated prehistoric finds see ibid. 6, 21.

[3] Below, churches.

[4] *T.S.S.A.H.S.* xxii. 2, 6; *Lichfield Mercury*, 17 Oct. 1986, p. 8.

[5] Inf. from Mr. J. Gould of Aldridge, citing *Gent. Mag.* xxi. 398.

[6] *T.S.S.A.H.S.* xxii. 97.

[7] Below, place name.

[8] Below, Wall.

[9] Below, place name.

[10] Ibid.; J. P. Clancy, *Earliest Welsh Poetry*, 89. For the dating see W. Davies, *Wales in the Early Middle Ages*, 99–101; *Mercian Studies*, ed. A. Dornier, 36–9.

[11] M. Gelling, *Signposts to the Past*, 57–9, drawing a comparison with Penkridge and with Wroxeter (Salop.).

[12] *Life of Bishop Wilfrid by Eddius Stephanus*, ed. B. Colgrave, 30–2; *Bede's Eccl. Hist. of the Eng. People*, ed. B. Colgrave and R. A. B. Mynors, 336; J. Campbell, *Essays in Anglo-Saxon Hist.* 99–119.

THE ANGLO-SAXON ECCLESIASTICAL CENTRE

There is some evidence of Romano-British Christianity in the area. A bronze bowl found at Wall bears the Christian Chi-Rho monogram.[13] A stone there, also bearing the monogram, could be 4th-century; another stone is carved with a cross.[14] Bishops and monks suffered as a result of the Welsh victory at *Caer Lwytgoed* in the earlier or mid 7th century,[15] and there may thus have been a church or monastery in the area.

In 653 Peada, the under-king of the Middle Angles and a son of Penda, king of Mercia, became a Christian on his marriage to the daughter of Oswiu, king of Northumbria. He brought back four missionaries from Northumbria, who probably worked among the Mercians as well as the Middle Angles. In 655 Oswiu took control of Mercia, establishing Peada as king of the Southern Mercians. Diuma, one of the four missionaries, was consecrated the first bishop of the Mercians, the Lindisfaras, and the Middle Angles.[16]

In 658 Wulfhere, another son of Penda, gained control of Mercia. Bishops continued to be appointed, and Wulfhere also brought Wilfrid, bishop of York, into Mercia several times between 666 and 669 to perform episcopal functions. He gave Wilfrid land in various places, and Wilfrid established *monasteria* (monasteries or minsters) there. Lichfield was one of the estates so granted. Meanwhile York was held by a rival bishop, Chad, but in 669 Archbishop Theodore deposed him in favour of Wilfrid. Impressed, however, by Chad's humility, Theodore the same year gave him the vacant Mercian bishopric. Chad's predecessors had probably been peripatetic, but Lichfield, considered by Wilfrid as suitable to become an episcopal see, was duly made Chad's see. He was received with honour by Wulfhere and was installed by Theodore and Wilfrid.[17]

Several suggestions have been put forward to explain why Lichfield commended itself to Wilfrid. If there was already a church in the area, its existence could have been one reason. There may have been a Mercian royal centre in the region, perhaps at Tamworth as there was later,[18] more probably at Bury Bank (in Stone) which was known as 'Wulfecestre' in the Middle Ages.[19] Lichfield was close to Ryknild Street and Watling Street; Ryknild Street in particular was a link with the north-east and Wilfrid's diocese. Lichfield may also have been a good base for missionary work. Woden worship in the area is attested by the place names Wednesbury and Wednesfield, while Weeford, the name of a parish south-east of Lichfield, indicates the existence there of a pagan shrine. The shrine could have been associated with the tumulus called Offlow, which lay in Weeford parish to the north of Watling Street. It may have been the burial mound of the Mercian royal family when it was still pagan and thus the focus of pagan feeling to be counterbalanced by Lichfield.[20] The tumulus was important enough to give its name to the hundred of Offlow.

[13] *T.B.A.S.* l. 50, pl. xiii; C. Thomas, *Christianity in Roman Britain to AD 500*, 123–4.

[14] *T.S.S.A.H.S.* xxvii. 27–9.

[15] Clancy, *Earliest Welsh Poetry*, 89.

[16] *Handbk. of Brit. Chron.* (1986), ed. E. B. Fryde and others, 5, 15–16, 220; *V.C.H. Staffs.* iii. 1.

[17] *Handbk. of Brit. Chron.* 16, 224; *V.C.H. Staffs.* iii. 1–3; *Life of Wilfrid*, ed. B. Colgrave, 30–3.

[18] *Hist. Essays in honour of James Tait*, ed. E. Edwards and others, 315 sqq. This reference and two in the following notes have been kindly supplied by Mr. R. A. Meeson of the Staffs. C.C. Planning and Development Dept.

[19] *Chron. of Hugh Candidus*, ed. W. T. Mellors, 146; *S.H.C.* vi (1), 9–10; Dugdale, *Mon.* vi (1), 233; Plot, *Staffs.* 406–8.

[20] Gelling, *Signposts to the Past*, 155–6, 158, 161; Ekwall, *Eng. Place-Names*, 503.

Chad's church probably stood on the site of the present cathedral. Stowe *c.* ½ mile to the north-east is traditionally the place where he preached to the people. It is probably also the site of the 'more retired dwelling place' to which he used to withdraw with a small group of companions and where he died in 672. Stowe has remained a sacred spot with its medieval church dedicated to St. Chad and its holy well bearing his name.[21] Chad was buried near the church of St. Mary, presumably the cathedral, and a considerable cult developed. In 700 a funerary church was built, probably close to the cathedral, and Chad's remains were transferred to it.[22]

Although the diocese lost its outlying parts *c.* 679, it remained extensive,[23] and with the growth of Mercia's power in the 8th century, culminating in the reign of Offa 757–96, Lichfield, as the ecclesiastical centre of the kingdom, grew in importance. The cathedral was the burial place probably of King Wulfhere (d. 674) and certainly of King Ceolred (d. 716).[24] In 787 at the council of Chelsea Offa removed part of the province of Canterbury from its archbishop and gave Bishop Hygeberht of Lichfield metropolitan authority over it. Pope Hadrian I confirmed the transfer in 788, and Lichfield thus became the centre of an archbishopric extending apparently from the Thames to the Humber. The new archbishop of Canterbury appointed in 793 was consecrated by Archbishop Hygeberht.[25] When Offa had Ethelbert, king of the East Angles, executed in 794, Hygeberht, with Offa's permission, buried the body in Lichfield cathedral in the presence of his clerks and deacons.[26] The province of Lichfield did not long survive Offa's death in 796. Although Hygeberht witnessed charters as archbishop at least until 799, in 802 Pope Leo III restored Canterbury's rights, and the council of Clovesho in 803 abolished the archbishopric of Lichfield.[27] In 822 Bishop Aethelwald organized the community at the cathedral as a body of 20 canons including a provost.[28]

It is possible that Lichfield cathedral was a literary centre in the 8th and 9th centuries, when Mercia appears to have been important in the world of culture. Offa in particular was praised as a patron of learning, and there were Mercians among the scholars who helped Alfred revive education in southern England in the late 9th century.[29] On the other hand no pre-Conquest text or manuscript, teacher or scholar can be linked without question to Lichfield. Even a 9th-century Old English homily on the life of St. Chad written in the Mercian dialect may have come from elsewhere.[30] A Mercian collection of pedigrees of English kings and lists of popes and English bishops, compiled *c.* 812, may perhaps have originated at Lichfield and may later have been kept there.[31] Ascriptions of other pre-Conquest texts to Lichfield have not been generally accepted.[32] The cathedral's sole pre-Conquest manuscript, the illuminated 8th-century gospel book known as the Lichfield Gospels or St. Chad's Gospels, did not originate at Lichfield. It was probably produced in Ireland, Iona, or Northumbria, possibly as a gift for a Mercian church or a Mercian king. It was in Wales by the early 9th century and came to Lichfield only in the 10th century.[33]

Lichfield must have suffered like the rest of Mercia at the hands of the Danish

[21] Below, churches (introduction; St. Chad's church).
[22] Below, cathedral and close.
[23] *V.C.H. Staffs.* iii. 3–4.
[24] Lichfield Cath. Libr., MS. Lichfield 22, p. 63; Bodl. MS. e Mus. 204, ff. 7–8; Bodl. MS. Ashmole 770, ff. 16v., 32; *Anglo-Saxon Chron.* ed. D. Whitelock and others, 26.
[25] *V.C.H. Staffs.* iii. 4–5.
[26] *Matthaei Paris Monachi Albanensis Angli, Historia Major,* ed. W. Wats (1684), 982.
[27] *V.C.H. Staffs.* iii. 5.

[28] Ibid. 140.
[29] Ibid. 6; K. Sisam, *Studies in Hist. of Old Eng. Literature,* 7, 133–4.
[30] *The Life of St. Chad: an Old Eng. Homily,* ed. R. Vleeskruyer (Amsterdam, 1953), 46, 61–2.
[31] *Proc. Brit. Academy,* xxxix. 289, 323–5, 329–30; Sisam, *Old Eng. Literature,* 4–6.
[32] *The Anglo-Saxons: Studies presented to Bruce Dickins,* ed. P. Clemoes, 292, 298, 310.
[33] G. Henderson, *From Durrow to Kells,* 122–9.

invaders in the late 9th century. It lay on the Danish side of Watling Street when that road was fixed as the boundary by Alfred and Guthrum between 886 and 890. There may have been some break in the episcopal succession, details of which are incomplete for the later 9th century.[34] The cathedral was presumably despoiled, and the disruption probably led to a break-up of the communal life of the canons. By 1086 its establishment had dropped from 20 canons to 5.[35]

By then it had also ceased to be the seat of a bishop and had been demoted to the status of a minster church. In 1075 the council of London gave permission for the see to be moved to Chester, in accordance with the decrees of early popes and councils banning the location of sees in small places.[36] William of Malmesbury, commenting half a century later on the transfer to Chester, described Lichfield as a mean place (*villa exigua*), isolated by the wooded nature of the district.[37] It has, however, been suggested that the real motive for the move to Chester was a desire on the part of the Norman Bishop Peter to add to his bishopric the part of Wales then being claimed by the Normans. Furthermore he had considerable property in Chester and may have had designs on the wealth of Chester abbey. If those were the intentions behind the move, they were not fulfilled, and Peter's successor Robert de Limesey transferred the see to Coventry, receiving papal approval in 1102.[38]

In fact William of Malmesbury may have exaggerated the meanness of Lichfield. It still had St. Chad's shrine, which presumably continued to attract pilgrim traffic. In 1086 Lichfield was also the name of an episcopal manor which covered much of south-east Staffordshire and may have had its origins in the estate given to the see by King Wulfhere and Wilfrid. It is, however, doubtful whether there was yet a single settlement called Lichfield. The name seems rather to have been used to describe an area in the neighbourhood of the cathedral containing several settlements. Likely places, all mentioned in documents of the 12th or 13th centuries, are Gaia north of the cathedral, probably including Beacon Street; the north end of Dam Street near a gate into the Close and a mill on the outflow of Minster Pool; Stowe, extending from the area of St. Chad's church and a nearby mill along Stowe Street and Lombard Street; 'Bech' south-east of Stowe; the high ground at Greenhill near St. Michael's church; and Sandford at a crossing of Trunkfield brook.[39] There also appears to have been an Anglo-Saxon fortification on Borrowcop Hill south of the later town centre. Before the 17th century the hill was called Burghwaycop, the Old English *burh* element suggesting a fortified place. The same element is found in Oxbury, the name of an area north of the hill by the town ditch.[40] That stretch of the ditch was known as Castle ditch,[41] presumably another reference to the hill-top fortification.

The cathedral was the focus of several roads. The route from Chester probably ran along Beacon Street and then turned east along Gaia Lane to join a road from the north running east of the cathedral. The joint route seems then to have followed Dam Street and Tamworth Street to Greenhill, although earlier the line may have run further east. At Greenhill it forked, one branch running to Burton upon Trent via Ryknild Street and the other to Tamworth along Rotten Row, so named by

[34] *Anglo-Saxon Eng.* ii, ed. P. Clemoes, 91–4.
[35] *V.C.H. Staffs.* iii. 140–1.
[36] *Letters of Lanfranc, Archbishop of Canterbury*, ed. H. Clover and M. Gibson, 77, 81.
[37] William of Malmesbury, *De Gestis Pontificum Anglorum* (Rolls Ser.), 307.
[38] C. N. L. Brooke, *The Church and the Welsh Border in the Central Middle Ages*, 11–12; *V.C.H. Staffs.* iii. 7–8.
[39] *T.S.S.A.H.S.* xxvi. 12–26. For 'Bech' see *S.H.C.* i. 93; S.R.O., D. 661/1/563 and 569.
[40] S.R.O., D. (W.) 1734/2/1/599, m. 22d.; Harwood, *Lichfield*, 513; *Eng. Place-Name Elements* (E.P.N.S.), i. 58; below, econ. hist. (agric.: fields).
[41] Below, boundaries and gates.

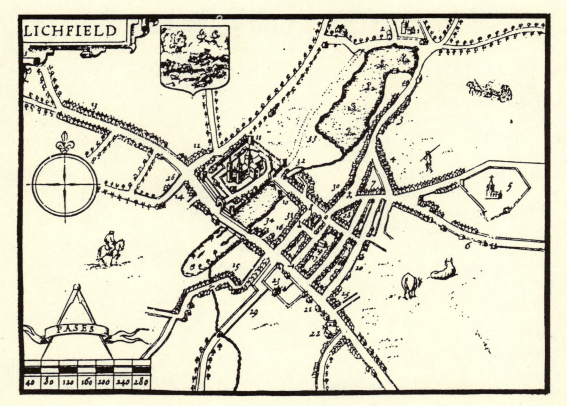

FIG. 2. LICHFIELD 1610

1 Stowe Church. 2 Stowe Mill. 3 Stowe Street. 4 Ioyles lane. 5 St. Michaels chur. 6 Rotten Rowe. 7 Tamworth stret. 8 The Chappell. 9 The Conduit. 10 Dams street. 11 St. Chads minst. 12 Iayes lane. 13 Bacon stret. 14 The Almeshouse. 15 Samford stret. 16 Sadlers street. 17 Bore street. 18 Wade street. 19 Towne Hall. 20 Frogge lane. 21 St. Iohns street. 22 St. Iohns Hospitall. 23 The Friery. 24 The Conduit. 25 The Freeschole. 26 Grey Marger lane. 27 Greenehill street. 28 Bakers lane. 29 Friers lane. 30 High Crosse. 31 Stowe Crosse. 32 Damm Mill. 33 Stowe Mere. 34 Damm Mere.

1379. It has also been suggested that there was a continuation south from Dam Street along the line of Bakers Lane and Levetts Fields.[42] The approach from the south-west evidently ran through Leamonsley and along Shaw Lane to Gaia Lane, which continued east to Stowe.[43] There may have been another route from the south-west running well south of the cathedral along the line of Friars Alley and Bore Street. Friars Alley was described in the mid 14th century as the street leading to Shrewsbury and probably continued to Wall along Chesterfield Road and Claypit Lane.[44] Another early south-west route was along the later Birmingham Road; it was described in the 13th century as the way to Aldershawe, to which it continues along Fosseway, known as the Falseway in the late 15th century.[45]

[42] *T.S.S.A.H.S.* xxii. 109; xxvi. 16, 20–3; L.J.R.O., D. 30/VC, B 110.
[43] Below, cathedral and close (the close); L.J.R.O., D. 30/VC, B 9.
[44] *T.S.S.A.H.S.* xxii. 104–6 (challenged ibid. xxv. 31 n.); Bodl. MS. Ashmole 855, p. 180; above, fig. 2.
[45] B.L. Campbell Ch. iv. 14; Bodl. MS. Ashmole 864, p. 40.

THE 12TH CENTURY

In the 12th century Lichfield was re-established as an ecclesiastical centre. Despite the removal of the see the Norman bishops rebuilt their church. Bishop Limesey, 1085–1117, allegedly used the wealth of the Coventry monks for extensive building at Lichfield. Bishop Peche, 1121–6, began further work which was probably completed by Bishop Clinton, 1129–48. Clinton also appears to have fortified the Close.[46] In the 1130s he established a chapter at Lichfield on Norman lines. It probably did not participate with the Coventry monks in the election of Clinton's successor in 1149, but it evidently took part in elections from 1161.[47] In 1176 Bishop Richard Peche re-endowed the deanery, which had been 'ruined during the time of war', presumably a reference to the rebellion of Henry II's son Henry.[48] The Close was given a piped water supply in the mid or later part of the century.[49] The first known statutes for the cathedral date from the time of Bishop Nonant, 1185–98, and are the earliest to survive for any English cathedral.[50]

Clinton held a synod at Lichfield in 1139 and another in the later 1140s.[51] The see may have returned there temporarily when Coventry priory was converted into a castle by Robert Marmion in 1143.[52] In 1157 the newly elected abbot of Chester was blessed at Lichfield, and Bishop Pucelle died there in 1184.[53] The first bishop to be buried at Lichfield after the Norman Conquest was Bishop Muschamp, who was buried there in 1208 by his own wish.[54]

Meanwhile a new town was laid out south of Minster Pool by Bishop Clinton, although Bishop Durdent may have completed it.[55] The town had a ladder plan with four rungs, the present Market Street, Bore Street, Wade Street, and Frog Lane, which linked Dam Street, Conduit Street, and Bakers Lane on one side with Bird Street and St. John Street on the other. Bore Street appears to have been the principal street, being wider than the others. At the north-east corner of the town Market Street and Bore Street were linked by a market place; a Sunday market was granted to Bishop Durdent by King Stephen in 1153. On that side the Tamworth Street and Lombard Street portion of an older settlement was grafted on to the plan, with Wade Street and Frog Lane extending across Bakers Lane. On the west side Sandford Street continued the line of Market Street beyond Bird Street. The area between Market Street and Minster Pool remained an open space. St. Mary's chapel in the market place was probably built when the town was laid out, although the earliest known mention of it was not until the late 13th century. Originally the market place surrounded the chapel on all sides, but encroachment took place on the south side. Bishop Clinton enclosed the town with a bank and ditch, and gates were set up where roads into the town crossed the ditch.

The town was described as a borough in a deed of Bishop Durdent, and it was governed as a separate manor probably from its creation. No charter has survived, but when the abbot of Burton established a borough at Abbots Bromley in 1222, he took the liberties of the Lichfield burgesses as a model. The standard rent for a burgage in Lichfield was 12d. in 1298.[56]

In addition to the market King Stephen granted Bishop Durdent a mint at

---

[46] Below, cathedral and close.
[47] *V.C.H. Staffs*. iii. 8–10, 141.
[48] Ibid. 142.
[49] Below, public services.
[50] *V.C.H. Staffs*. iii. 142.
[51] *S.H.C*. xi. 322; *Worcester Cart*. (P.R.S. N.S. xxxviii), p. 102.
[52] *V.C.H. Staffs*. iii. 8; *V.C.H. Warws*. ii. 52, 423.
[53] *Annales Cestrienses* (Lancs. and Ches. Rec. Soc. xiv), 22, 28.
[54] *V.C.H. Staffs*. iii. 11.
[55] Para. based on *T.S.S.A.H.S*. xxvi. 26–34. See also below, boundaries and gates; econ. hist. (markets and fairs); churches (St. Mary's).
[56] Below, town govt. (govt. to 1548).

Lichfield. The grant was confirmed by Duke Henry (later Henry II) in 1154 and by Richard I in 1189.[57] The mint closed down in 1198.[58] The only known surviving coin was struck during Richard's reign.[59]

Bishop Clinton may have been the founder of St. John's hospital, situated just outside the gate in St. John Street by 1208.[60] Whether that road was extended south in the mid 12th century to form a southern approach to the new town or whether such a route already existed is not clear.[61] Two crosses stood outside the gate and were known as Bishop Durdent's and Bishop Pucelle's.[62]

THE 13TH CENTURY

Lichfield finally recovered its position as a see in 1228 when Gregory IX recognized the chapter's claim to share in episcopal elections with the Coventry monks. He decreed that both chapters were to elect, meeting alternately at Coventry and Lichfield. Bishop Stavensby, 1224–38, duly abandoned the title bishop of Coventry, which had been substituted for bishop of Chester by Bishop Durdent, and he styled himself instead bishop of Coventry and Lichfield. That remained the bishops' title until Bishop Hacket, 1661–70, reversed it to Lichfield and Coventry.[63]

The chapter also increased in wealth, and the prebendal system reached, in essentials, its final form in 1255. Bishop Cornhill, 1214–23, granted the chapter the right to elect its own dean, and it did so for the first time in 1222. The authority of the dean increased, notably in the exercise of archidiaconal jurisdiction, to the exclusion of the bishop, over the cathedral and the city churches as well as over the prebendal churches and those belonging to the chapter's common fund. The cathedral dominated the religious life of the city, whose churches were simply chapels of ease in the cathedral parish. The chapter's victory in the matter of episcopal elections was symbolized in the building of a new chapter house in the 1240s. The vicars choral, first mentioned in Bishop Nonant's statutes of c. 1190, were organized by statutes drawn up in 1241, which stipulated continuous residence in Lichfield. They had their own property from the earlier 13th century and their own house from the 1240s.[64] Throughout the century the cathedral was the scene of building operations, which were completed in the 14th century and produced the plan as it is today.[65] In the town a Franciscan friary was built in the later 1230s on burgage plots on the west side of Bird Street and St. John Street.[66] By the 13th century there were burgages outside the boundary of the new town, perhaps an indication of suburban development. Property granted to the dean and chapter by Bishop Muschamp, 1198–1208, included a burgage beyond Sandford gate.[67] In the later 13th century Beacon Street, described as a suburb, contained a burgage outside the town gate.[68] There were then two half burgages nearby at Gaia and a burgage between Gaia Lane and Stowe Pool.[69] In the same period there were burgages outside Tamworth gate.[70]

[57] S.H.C. 1924, 219–20.
[58] C. Oman, Coinage of Eng. 137.
[59] G. C. Brooke, Eng. Coins, 114.
[60] V.C.H. Staffs. iii. 279.
[61] T.S.S.A.H.S. xxii. 108-9; xxvi. 23.
[62] S.H.C. 1924, 19, 52; L.J.R.O., D. 30/XXIV, f. 33v.
[63] V.C.H. Staffs. iii. 12, 61.
[64] Ibid. 143-9; below, churches (Lichfield peculiar).
[65] Below, cathedral and close.   [66] V.C.H. Staffs. iii. 268.
[67] S.H.C. 1924, p. 52.   [68] Ibid. pp. 54-8.
[69] Ibid. pp. 54-5; S.R.O., D. 948/3/15.
[70] S.H.C. 1924, pp. 196-7.

The main economic activity was retailing, and by the end of the century a three-day Whitsun fair had been added to the weekly market. The needs of the cathedral probably account for the presence of goldsmiths, glaziers, and a bellfounder. Leather working appears to have been of some importance: there was a shoemakers' quarter in the later part of the century, and tanning was in progress by 1300. There was also cloth working.

The town was important because it was on the road between London and Chester and near Ryknild Street. Henry II was at Lichfield in 1175 and 1181, and John and Henry III visited the town many times.[71] By the 1190s it was the normal stopping place in Staffordshire for the justices in eyre,[72] and forest pleas were held there in the later 13th century.[73] There was a field for judicial combat (*campum duelli*) outside the St. John Street gate in 1208; in 1203 the vill paid a fine 'pro habendo duello'.[74]

Although governed through the bishop's manorial courts, the burgesses early on developed a sense of community. In 1221 they sent two men to plead their cause over toll against the burgesses of Stafford. In 1254 'the community' nominated its bailiffs and six other citizens to represent it before the royal treasurer, using the community's seal. The seal was again in use in 1301 in a grant of land made by six men acting on behalf of the community. By the early 13th century tenants of the dean and of the prebendaries enjoyed various immunities from the bishop's manorial jurisdiction.[75]

THE LATE MIDDLE AGES

In 1291 a fire destroyed most of the town, including the churches and the friary, but the Close escaped.[76] The general rebuilding of the town may be reflected in the many grants of pavage between 1299 and 1345, although there had been earlier grants in 1285 and 1290.[77] Bishop Langton, 1296–1321, built a bridge or causeway at the west end of Minster Pool *c.* 1312, evidently replacing an earlier one; his intention may have been to ease the flow of traffic along Beacon Street and Bird Street following his closure of a right of way through the Close.[78] Work on St. Mary's continued in the 14th century when the tower was built, possibly in 1356.[79] The friary was soon rebuilt after the fire, and in 1301 it was granted a water supply from springs near Aldershawe to the south-west. The supply was later made available to the townspeople, with a conduit at the gate of the friary in Bird Street connected with others in the town.[80]

Langton carried out extensive work on the cathedral, notably the addition of the Lady Chapel, and in the Close, where he greatly strengthened the fortifications and built a new palace. The completion of a new choir at the cathedral, begun by the 1330s, was evidently delayed by the Black Death. All major medieval work on the cathedral was finished by the beginning of the 15th century, although the enrichment of the interior continued, notably under Dean Heywood, 1457–92.[81]

[71] Below, communications.
[72] *Pleas before the King or his Justices*, iii (Selden Soc. lxxxiii), p. cvi; D. Crook, *Rec. of the General Eyre*, 63 sqq.; *S.H.C.* ii (1), 30, 43.
[73] *V.C.H. Staffs.* ii. 335, 337; *Cal. Close, 1296–1302*, 396.
[74] *S.H.C.* iii (1), 101; *S.H.C.* 1924, p. 19.
[75] Below, town govt. (govt. to 1548; liberties).
[76] *Ann. Mon.* (Rolls Ser.), iii. 365; iv. 505.

[77] *Cal. Pat.* 1281–92, 172, 358; 1292–1301, 408–9; 1307–13, 440–1; 1317–21, 518–19; 1321–4, 178; 1327–30, 179; 1330–4, 28; 1334–8, 119; 1338–40, 126; 1343–5, 519.
[78] Below, street names (Bird St.); cathedral and close.
[79] Below, churches.
[80] *V.C.H. Staffs.* iii. 268; Derb. R.O., D. 2375M/130/94; below, public services (water supplies).
[81] Below, cathedral and close; *V.C.H. Staffs.* iii. 165–6.

Lichfield remained an important centre for both ecclesiastical and secular purposes. Pilgrim traffic presumably increased as a result of Langton's provision of a magnificent shrine for St. Chad's relics. By 1335 some of the saint's relics were kept in a portable shrine and his head in a painted box; there was another reliquary by 1445 containing his right arm. Pilgrims received encouragement from Dean Heywood, who secured indulgences from Canterbury in 1473 and Rome in 1482 for those attending services in the chapel of the chantry founded by him in the cathedral. Numbers of people were also brought into the town by meetings of the bishop's consistory court and by the celebration of orders in the cathedral; both were notably more frequent under Bishop Blythe, 1503–32.[82]

Assizes continued to be held at Lichfield until the 16th century.[83] In 1414, as part of an attempt to deal with a general breakdown of order, the King's Bench sat there for over three weeks as a superior eyre, with Henry V himself staying at Burton abbey and remaining in close touch with the court's proceedings.[84]

Lichfield was the assembly point for 125 Staffordshire archers in 1345 before their march to Southampton to take part in the earl of Derby's campaign in Gascony.[85] In 1402 Henry IV ordered knights, squires, and yeomen from various parts of the country to meet him at Lichfield for his campaign against Owain Glyn Dŵr.[86] During the Wars of the Roses Lancastrian troops attacked the gaol in 1459, possibly in an attempt to release prisoners taken at the battle of Blore Heath that year.[87] Richard, earl of Warwick, passed through Lichfield in 1460 on his way to meet the duke of York at Shrewsbury.[88] Before the battle of Bosworth in 1485 Lord Stanley was at Lichfield, and his younger brother Sir William Stanley received Henry Tudor there with military honours.[89]

Lichfield's importance as a trading centre was enhanced in 1307 when the three-day Whitsun fair was extended to 15 days and an eight-day fair in November was added. A four-day September fair was granted in 1337, and by 1409 there was an Ash Wednesday fair with a court of pie powder. A wide range of goods was brought into the city, and in the early 14th century there was also a flourishing wool trade.

Among the city's own products leather goods remained important. In the 17th century the saddlers' company claimed to have been in existence by the reign of Edward I and the shoemakers' since the late 1430s. Two other companies, the vintners' and the mercers', claimed to have been established in the 14th century. Quarrying was in progress in the 14th and 15th centuries, and the masons claimed to have been incorporated in the early 15th century. The carpenters, the cooks, and the barbers and surgeons traced their incorporation to Edward IV's reign. Specialist tradesmen, such as goldsmiths, bellfounders, and parchment makers, continued to work in the city.[90] Inns mentioned were the Swan in Bird Street (1362),[91] the Lion in Market Street (1440),[92] the Antelope and the Unicorn adjoining each other in Bird Street (1495),[93] the George in Bird Street, the Talbot in Beacon Street on the site of the later Angel Croft hotel, the Angel on an adjoining site to the south, the Cock also in Beacon Street, and the Star in Bore

[82] Below, cathedral and close (St. Chad's shrine; burials and monuments); N. Staffs. Jnl. of Field Studies, xix. 2; V.C.H. Staffs. iii. 165.
[83] S.H.C. vii (1), 126–7, 129; ix (1), 79; xi. 21–3; xii (1), 94, 105, 127, 132, 159; xiii. 5, 29, 45, 162, 172; xv. 120–1; J. Cockburn, Hist. of Eng. Assizes 1558–1714, 35.
[84] Henry V, ed. G. L. Harriss, 65–6.
[85] H. J. Hewitt, Organization of War under Edw. III, 42–3.
[86] Cal. Close, 1399–1402, 574.
[87] Below, town govt. (gaol).
[88] Jehan de Waurin, Receuil des Croniques et Anchiennes Istories de la Grant Bretaigne (Rolls Ser.), v. 309–10.
[89] M. Bennett, Battle of Bosworth, 92, 96.
[90] Below, econ. hist. (markets and fairs; trades and industries); guilds.
[91] Below, communications.
[92] W.S.L., H.M. Chetwynd 5.
[93] B.L. Stowe Ch. 625; Bodl. MS. Ashmole 864, p. 380; L.J.R.O., D. 30/VC, palimpsest, i, f. 13v.

Street (all 1498),[94] the Cardinal's Hat in Tamworth Street (1498, mentioned as a burgage 1350),[95] and the Eagle in Market Street (1529).[96]

The number of people visiting and passing through the city appears to have encouraged prostitution. A woman in Conduit Street was stated in 1466 to have earned 6 rials (£3) by being available day and night to members of the household of the duke of Clarence during his recent visit to Lichfield.[97] Beacon Street, probably because it was a thoroughfare on a major route, seems to have been the main area of brothels. In 1414 four brothel keepers there were presented at the manor court.[98] In 1466 a woman of Beacon Street was accused of having had with her two women recently arrived from a London brothel.[99] Probably because it was near the cathedral, the area provided the vicars choral with opportunities for fornication in the early 15th century.[1] In 1485 three brothels were recorded in Wade Street, Conduit Street, and Greenhill.[2]

The cathedral maintained its control of the three city churches, which by the 14th century were served by five chaplains appointed by five of the prebendaries. The system was modified in 1491 when a vicarage was ordained at St. Mary's, with the dean and chapter as patrons. The vicar had overall responsibility for the cathedral's parishioners in the city and had to provide a chaplain at each of the three churches, but there were still no individual parishes attached to them. St. Mary's, however, had already achieved a special prominence as the church of the guild of St. Mary and St. John the Baptist, founded in 1387 by the amalgamation of two existing guilds at St. Mary's. Admissions to the guild rose to an average of 105 a year in the later 15th century, and both men and women were eligible. The members were mainly people from Lichfield and the surrounding region, including gentry and heads of religious houses, but there were also notable people from further afield, including royalty. There was a guildhall in Bore Street by 1421. The guild had its own chaplains, who lived in a house in Breadmarket Street and helped with the services at St. Mary's; there were four of them in 1466.

The almshouse in Beacon Street later known as Dr. Milley's hospital appears to have been founded by Bishop Heyworth in or shortly after 1424. It was re-endowed for 15 almswomen in 1504 by Thomas Milley, a canon of the cathedral, and was probably rebuilt at the same time.[3] St. John's hospital was refounded and re-endowed for 13 almsmen by Bishop Smith in 1495, and as part of the refoundation he also endowed a grammar school.[4]

The guild of St. Mary and St. John the Baptist came to participate in the government of the town, and by the late 15th century it was working in association with a body called the Forty-eight, which may have represented the burgesses and commoners. The jurisdiction of the bishop, however, remained paramount, and by the early 15th century he was holding three great courts a year. There were then ten wards in the town, each with two tithingmen. Two of the wards, Stowe Street and Greenhill, were outside the gates, and by the end of the century there was also a tithingman for the part of Sandford Street beyond Sandford gate. The courts met in a moot hall, mentioned in 1308–9 and probably in Lombard Street. The bishop

[94] Below, communications; manor (estates of cathedral clergy); Bodl. MS. Ashmole 864, p. 384.
[95] Bodl. MS. Ashmole 864, p. 387; S.R.O., D. 661/2/445; Bodl. MS. Ashmole 1521, p. 29 (2nd nos.). It was described in 1665 as a messuage called the Cardinal's Cap: S.R.O., D. 661/2/490; for the Cardinal's Cap in Breadmarket St. in 1689 and the Cardinal's Hat there in 1824 see ibid. D. 661/2/114; L.J.R.O., D. 77/6/6.
[96] S.R.O., D. 661/2/417. [97] L.J.R.O., D. 30/9/3/1, f. 26v.
[98] S.R.O., D. (W.) 1734/2/1/597, m. 4.
[99] L.J.R.O., D. 30/9/3/1, f. 20.
[1] Ibid. D. 30/C.A. i, ff. 59v.–60, 121v., 128, 131.
[2] S.R.O., D. (W.) 1734/2/1/597, m. 7.
[3] V.C.H. Staffs. iii. 275–6; below, manor (other eccl. estates); chars. for the poor.
[4] V.C.H. Staffs. iii. 280–1; below, education.

had a gaol in Lichfield, possibly as early as 1164 and certainly by 1306.[5] In the later 15th century the receiver general of the bishop's temporalities used Lichfield as a centre for auditing; in 1459 he was there for three weeks and in 1463 for nineteen days.[6] In 1441 the Crown granted the dean and chapter extensive powers of self-government in the Close.[7] The city was represented at most parliaments between 1305 and 1327 and again in 1353, but it then ceased to be represented until the mid 16th century.[8]

Lichfield's position on important roads continued to attract royal visitors. Edward II was there as Prince of Wales probably in 1296 and as king in 1309, 1323, and 1326.[9] Edward III was there in 1328,[10] and in 1348 Lichfield was the scene of one of the splendid tournaments which he held after his victories at Crécy and Calais.[11] Richard II attended the enthronement of Bishop Scrope in 1386 and spent Christmas 1397 at Lichfield. In 1398 he concluded a treaty with the duke of Brittany there in May, was present at the enthronement of Bishop Burghill in September, and celebrated Christmas there with a papal nuncio and an envoy of the Eastern Emperor among his guests. He returned in 1399 on his way to London as a prisoner.[12] Henry IV was at Lichfield before and after the battle of Shrewsbury in 1403, and in 1404 he held a council there.[13] Edward IV dined with Bishop Hales at Lichfield in 1461 and made an agreement with the earl of Warwick there in 1462; in 1473 he spent over two weeks at Lichfield.[14]

FROM THE REFORMATION TO THE CIVIL WAR

The Reformation brought loss and gain to Lichfield. The status of the chapter was enhanced as a result of the dissolution of Coventry priory, despite Bishop Lee's protest that Coventry was his 'principal see and head church'. An Act of 1541 recognized Lichfield as 'the full, sole, and entire see and chapter' of the diocese.[15] Another Act of the same year reduced the size of the diocese by assigning the archdeaconry of Chester to the new diocese of Chester. The archdeaconry, however, had long enjoyed extensive administrative autonomy, and the change may not have greatly reduced the number of people coming to Lichfield on ecclesiastical business.[16] A major loss was the disappearance of pilgrim traffic following the destruction of St. Chad's shrine in 1538.[17] That year too the Franciscan friary was dissolved, the site becoming a private estate.[18] Both hospitals survived, although St. John's was threatened. Its chaplain was evidently regarded as a stipendiary priest under the Chantries Act of 1547, and his salary was appropriated by the Crown; it was, however, restored in 1550. Later attempts by the Crown to suppress the hospital were also unsuccessful.[19] The guild of St. Mary and St. John was

[5] Below, town govt. (govt. to 1548: manorial courts, community of the town; gaol).
[6] L.J.R.O., B/A/21, CC 124075, m. 11; S.R.O., D. (W.) 1734/J. 1948, m. 14d.
[7] Below, town govt. (liberties).
[8] Below, parl. representation.
[9] P.R.O., SC 1/26, no. 173; Cal. Close, 1323–7, 456, 550–2, 578; below, cathedral and close.
[10] Cal. Fine R. 1327–37, 74. He is shown at Lichfield in 1331 (ibid. 265), probably an error for Lincoln.
[11] Archaeologia, xxxi. 113–16.
[12] Below, cathedral and close.
[13] V.C.H. Staffs. i. 239–40.
[14] S.R.O., D. (W.) 1734/3/3/264; Cal. Close, 1461–8, 275; Cal. Pat. 1467–77, 396, 398–9, 405, 429–30.
[15] V.C.H. Staffs. iii. 43, 166.
[16] Ibid. 43–4.
[17] Ibid. 168.
[18] Below, manor.
[19] V.C.H. Staffs. iii. 282–3.

dissolved under the Act of 1547. Chantry and guild property in the city came into the possession of the Crown; in 1567 some of it was in decay, with the rents increasingly in arrears, and the Crown admitted that the city was thereby impoverished.[20]

The main development of the period was the city's achievement of self-government. It was incorporated by royal charter in 1548, the corporation consisting of two bailiffs and 24 brethren. In the same year Bishop Sampson conveyed his manorial rights in Lichfield to the new corporation. As a reward for the support given to Mary I by the bailiffs and citizens during the duke of Northumberland's attempt to prevent her accession, the queen issued a new charter in 1553, confirming the 1548 charter and in addition granting county status to the city with its own sheriff. The bishop had suffered another loss in 1546, when he was forced to surrender many of his estates to the Crown. They included the nearby manors of Longdon, Cannock, and Rugeley and the bishop's house at Beaudesert in Longdon, all of which passed to Sir William Paget (later Lord Paget), one of the principal secretaries of state. It is likely that Paget was instrumental in securing the charters for Lichfield. The incorporation was probably linked with the dissolution of the guild and the consequent gap in the city's government. There was extensive continuity of personnel: the first senior bailiff and half the brethren had been masters of the guild, and another six of the brethren had been guild wardens. The corporation also took over the guildhall. The city's new importance was enhanced by its once more being represented in parliament.[21]

Also linked with the guild was the new Conduit Lands Trust. In 1545 the master of the guild, Hector Beane, acting with the guild's consent and evidently sensing the coming dissolution, conveyed the guild's lands lying outside the city to eight feoffees for the maintenance of the town's water supply; any residue of income was to be used for the common good of the city. As a result Lichfield has for several centuries had both a well maintained water supply and a range of other public services.[22]

Lichfield seems to have shown little opposition to the earlier stages of the Reformation. Indeed the new corporation, despite its support of Mary in 1553, showed protestant sympathies. It sold goods belonging to the three city churches and spent part of the proceeds on taking down altars, removing 'idols and images', and providing books, including the Bible in English. In 1556 or 1557 the sheriff of the new county of Lichfield and the wives of two prominent members of the corporation gave comfort to a woman condemned to be burnt as a heretic. By contrast a large number of the cathedral clergy were deprived in 1559 or soon afterwards, and in the late 16th and early 17th century there seem to have been many Roman Catholics in the city.[23]

Despite the reduction in the size of the diocese Lichfield retained importance as a centre of ecclesiastical administration. The high proportion of lawyers among the bailiffs between 1548 and 1588[24] was presumably a reflection of the amount of business to be done. The dean and chapter wrote in 1635 of the 'multitudes of persons' coming daily to the bishop's consistory court and of the officers of the court living in the city.[25] It was as the seat of the bishop's court that the city

[20] *Cal. Pat.* 1566–9, pp. 4–6.
[21] Below, manor; town govt.; parl. representation; *V.C.H. Staffs.* iii. 51–2; *T.S.S.A.H.S.* xxii. 123–4.
[22] Laithwaite, *Conduit Lands Trust*; below, public services.

[23] Below, town govt. (govt. from 1548: the unreformed corporation); churches; Roman Catholicism.
[24] Below, econ. hist. (professions).
[25] *Cal. S.P. Dom.* 1635, 454–5.

witnessed the burning of three persons for heresy under Mary I.[26] In 1611 it was the scene of the last such burning in England, of Edward Wightman of Burton upon Trent.[27]

The number of recorded trade companies greatly increased in the later 16th and earlier 17th century.[28] Leather working continued to be important, and the tanners' company had been added to those of the shoemakers and the saddlers by 1625. Textiles too were important. The clothworkers' and weavers' company was recorded in 1552, the cappers' in 1575, and the tailors' in 1576. Capping declined in Lichfield as elsewhere in the later 16th century, but the city had over 70 tailors in 1634. Metal working was extensive. The smiths' company was recorded in 1601, with a wide range of craftsmen. The range increased in the 17th century, and in 1648 the company had 95 members. Retailers, including providers of food and drink, probably made up the largest single group of tradesmen. In the late 16th century there was even a complaint that the number of alehouses was excessive and was causing 'much decay in the place'.[29] Agriculture continued as part of the city's economy, and sheepfarming was important by the late 16th century.

In 1582 Bishop Overton stated that Lichfield 'is not the city that it hath been'. He attributed such economic decline to the city's bad government, the result of its removal from episcopal control.[30] The effects of the Reformation were more probably to blame, coupled with the decline of capping and apparently the loss of all but one of the fairs. Further economic decline probably followed the outbreak of plague in 1593, when there were over 1,100 deaths.[31] In 1622, however, three new fairs were established by royal charter. The city was also developing as a centre of communications. It was a post town on the route between London and Ireland by the later 1570s, and by the 1650s coaches between London and Chester called there, with the George and the Swan probably already the main coaching inns.[32] In the 1630s Lichfield was by far the wealthiest of Staffordshire's towns. It was assessed for ship money in 1635 at £100; Walsall came next at £25 and then Stafford at £20.[33] In 1637 Lichfield was assessed at £150, with another £10 for the Close; Stafford was assessed at £30.[34]

Edward VI was in Lichfield on 23 September 1547, when he evidently visited the cathedral.[35] Elizabeth I was at Lichfield in 1575, arriving from Kenilworth on 27 July. She appears to have stayed elsewhere and to have returned to Lichfield on 30 July; she left for Chartley, in Stowe, on 3 August. She was evidently received in the market place and entertained in the guildhall. In preparation for her visit the bailiffs had the market cross painted and the area round it paved, and the guildhall was painted and repaired. In addition work was carried out on the road leading into the city from the south. The bailiffs also paid 5s. to a William Holcroft 'for keeping Mad Richard when her Majesty was here'.[36]

[26] V.C.H. Staffs. iii. 46.
[27] Ibid. 55, 59; Clayton, Loyal and Ancient City, 7–9.
[28] For this para. see below, econ. hist.; guilds.
[29] P.R.O., PROB 11/83, f. 154v.
[30] N. Staffs. Jnl. of Field Studies, xix. 6.
[31] Below, population.
[32] Below, communications.

[33] V.C.H. Staffs. i. 288; Cal. S.P. Dom. 1635, 455.
[34] Cal. S.P. Dom. 1636–7, 493. There were separate assessments for the dean and chapter and for 29 prebends: ibid. 494.
[35] L.J.R.O., D. 30/C. A. iv, f. 145v.
[36] J. Nichols, Progresses and Public Processions of Queen Elizabeth (1821), iv (1), 72–4.

THE CIVIL WAR

Lichfield, with its strongly defended Close and its position as a focus of communications, had a strategic importance during the Civil War which resulted in three sieges of the Close, and its cathedral suffered more damage than any other.[37] The Close was garrisoned by the royalists early in 1643; the garrison, some 300 strong under the earl of Chesterfield, consisted mostly of local gentry and their retainers. A parliamentary force of 1,200 under Lord Brooke camped outside Lichfield on 1 March. On 2 March Brooke entered Lichfield and set up his headquarters in Market Street in the house of the parliamentarian Michael Biddulph of Elmhurst. The royalist troops, after fierce resistance, fell back on the Close, and an attack at once began on the south gate in Dam Street. Brooke, directing the attack from a nearby house, was shot dead, traditionally by the deaf and dumb John Dyott firing from the central tower of the cathedral. Sir John Gell came from Derby the same day to take command of the siege. He brought more troops with him, and on 3 March further reinforcements arrived under Sir William Brereton. Attacks on the west gate and on the north side of the Close were repulsed, but on 4 March a mortar was set up in the garden of Sir Richard Dyott's house in Market Street. It caused panic in the Close, and allegedly there was also a shortage of food and ammunition. Chesterfield surrendered on 5 March, and the royalist garrison was replaced by one under Colonel Russell.

Sir John Gell turned his attention to Stafford but was defeated on Hopton Heath by a royalist force on its way to relieve Lichfield. The parliamentarians then consolidated their position at Lichfield, strengthening the defences of the Close. An attempt by the royalist Col. Henry Hastings to retake the Close on 21 March was unsuccessful, but on 7 April Prince Rupert entered the city. He surrounded the Close, setting up his artillery on high ground to the north still known as Prince Rupert's Mound. Russell surrendered on 21 April, and a garrison with Col. Richard Bagot as governor took over.

Lichfield remained a royalist stronghold for the rest of the war, supported by financial levies,[38] donations, and money taken from the enemy. Bagot later claimed to have advanced money of his own as well. In July 1643 Queen Henrietta Maria passed through Lichfield on her way south from Bridlington (Yorks. E.R.). Prince Rupert passed through in March 1644 on his way to relieve Newark and again on his way back. Col. Bagot left with part of the garrison in May 1645 to reinforce the king, leaving the city defended by 100 horse and 200 foot under Major Harsnett. Defeated at Naseby in June, Charles I and the remains of his army spent the night of the 15th in and around Lichfield, Charles himself staying in the palace. Bagot, having been wounded at Naseby, returned to the Close. He died there in July and was buried in the cathedral. His replacement as governor of the garrison was his brother Hervey. Charles returned in August for two nights and again in October for one night.[39] An outbreak of plague began in July and continued into 1646. Few died in the Close, but 821 deaths were recorded in the city.

In January 1646 Sir Thomas Tyldesley was appointed governor; taken prisoner by the parliamentarians in 1644, he had escaped from Stafford to Lichfield towards the end of 1645. On 9 March Sir William Brereton captured the city and began a siege of the Close which lasted four months. He cut a trench from Stowe Pool to

---

[37] Section based on Clayton, *Loyal and Ancient City*; below, cathedral and close.   [38] e.g. records of payments by Walsall borough in Walsall Local Hist. Centre 23/13–16.   [39] Harwood, *Lichfield*, 30.

Upper Pool, building a raised defensive position or mount at each end. A third mount was built north of the Close and a fourth in Dam Street in front of the south gate. He set up his headquarters on the high ground north of the Close, defending it with more earthworks. The central spire of the cathedral was used by the royalists as a vantage point, and when they also flaunted regimental colours and officers' sashes from it on May Day, it became a symbol of resistance in the eyes of the parliamentarians. Brereton also believed that it not only contained the powder magazine but also housed 'their ladies and grandees'. He subjected it to five days' bombardment, and on 12 May it collapsed, damaging the choir and nave. One of a dwindling number of royalist garrisons, the Close continued to resist even after the fall of Oxford on 26 June and the end of royalist hopes. It finally surrendered on 10 July, and the garrison, mustering 84 officers and 700 other ranks, marched out on the 16th.

The main damage caused during the war was to the cathedral and the Close. The cathedral had been desecrated by the parliamentarians in 1643, when its glass, statuary, and organs were destroyed. The final siege left it in ruins along with the palace and many of the houses in the Close. Subsequent looting of fabric caused further destruction.[40] Beacon Street was burnt by the royalists during the final siege to deprive the attackers of cover; 52 houses there belonging to the vicars choral were destroyed, although some had been rebuilt by 1649.[41] A house in Dam Street near Minster Pool was burnt down in 1646, but it too had been rebuilt by 1649. Stowe church was occupied by the parliamentarians during the siege of 1643, and during that of 1646 the tower of St. Mary's was damaged by royalist bombardment. The market cross, with its statuary and crucifixes, was destroyed by the parliamentarians in 1643. The contents of the cathedral library were dispersed after the surrender of 1646,[42] and the Civil War has been blamed for the disappearance of the early records of the corporation. In 1658, however, Elias Ashmole (1617–92), a native of Lichfield, was pursuing his antiquarian interests by transcribing deeds in the custody of the bailiffs which have since disappeared.[43]

FROM THE RESTORATION TO THE END OF THE 18TH CENTURY

Services were again being held in the cathedral by mid June 1660, and the chapter was reconstituted in September.[44] An early problem which confronted the returning clergy was access to their houses in the Close: those not destroyed during the Civil War had been occupied by squatters, who had to be removed.[45] Work on rebuilding the ruined cathedral began in earnest with the arrival of Bishop Hacket in August 1662, and it was rededicated on Christmas Eve 1669. A new bishop's palace was built in 1687 and a new deanery in 1707.[46]

Although Presbyterians were removed from the corporation, they remained influential in the town and were active in the parliamentary election of 1667.

[40] For a view of c. 1650 see below, plate 1.
[41] L.J.R.O., VC/A/21, CC 162145, i, ff. 1–12; Bodl. MS. Ashmole 1521, p. 105; J. Ogilby, *Britannia* (1698), 11.
[42] Below, cathedral and close.
[43] Bodl. MS. Ashmole 1521, p. 179.
[44] *Elias Ashmole*, ed. C. H. Josten, ii. 780; *V.C.H. Staffs.* iii. 175.
[45] *T.S.S.A.H.S.* xxv. 37, 47–9; L.J.R.O., D. 30/LXIV, s.a. 1660 (warrant for removal).
[46] Below, cathedral and close.

Thomas Minors, a Presbyterian, established an English school in Bore Street in 1670. It may have continued to have Dissenting masters in the early 18th century, but it later came under the control of Anglicans. Support for James II, who touched for the King's Evil in the cathedral in 1687, seems to have been limited, but later the corporation and townspeople showed Jacobite sympathies.[47] A mob supporting the Pretender attacked the Whigs at a byelection in 1718, and when the Whigs captured both parliamentary seats in 1747 there were riots at the September race meeting, including an assault on the duke of Bedford.[48]

FIG. 3. REDCOURT HOUSE IN 1819

Visiting Lichfield in 1697, Celia Fiennes thought that the town had good houses and that its streets were neat and handsome.[49] For Daniel Defoe in the earlier 1720s it was 'a fine, neat, well-built, and indifferent large city', the principal town in the region after Chester. He considered that those two towns, with Coventry, were the only places of importance on the road from London to Carlisle.[50] Less enthusiastic was John Loveday, a visitor in 1732, for whom the town was 'large, but by no means compact, nor the streets wide'; the brick buildings were 'not very handsome'.[51] The use of brick as building material in preference to timber became normal from the late 17th century and was presumably in part prompted by

[47] Below, town govt. (govt. from 1548: unreformed corporation); parl. representation; education.
[48] Below, parl. representation; *T.S.S.A.H.S.* vi. 40–1.
[49] *Journeys of Celia Fiennes*, ed. C. Morris (1949), 111.

[50] D. Defoe, *Tour thro' Gt. Brit.* (1927), ii. 479.
[51] *Diary of a Tour in 1732 made by John Loveday of Caversham*, ed. J. E. T. Loveday (priv. print. Edinburgh, 1890), 7.

FIG. 4. LICHFIELD 1781

concern over the risk of fire. A fire had occurred in late 1681 or early 1682, and another evidently in 1697; in July 1697 the corporation ordered that all thatched buildings should be tiled.[52] Several town houses built in brick in the 18th century survive.[53] Two have been demolished. St. John's House (later Yeomanry House) opposite St. John's hospital was built before 1732 for Theophilus Levett, town clerk 1721–46. It replaced a house known in 1577 as Culstubbe Hall, the home of the physician Sir John Floyer in the late 17th century. It was demolished in 1925.[54] Redcourt House on the south side of Tamworth Street was built in 1766 for Lucy Porter, Dr. Johnson's step-daughter. It was demolished in 1929 or 1930.[55] Stone was used for the guildhall and St. Mary's church when they were rebuilt in the earlier 18th century.

The built-up area of the city did not expand greatly until the 19th century. Stowe House and Stowe Hill were built in the 1750s and Beacon Place in Beacon Street towards the end of the century.[56] There was also scattered settlement on or near the city boundary. Farmhouses at Knowle and Berry Hill on Ryknild Street existed by the later 18th century, the former taking its name from a nearby knoll and the latter an inhabited location in the later 14th century.[57] The Shoulder of Mutton inn at the junction of Ryknild Street and the London road had been built by 1770.[58] Sandyway on the Walsall road, already inhabited in the late 16th century, had an alehouse c. 1700.[59] The Three Tuns inn existed there by 1777.[60] There was another inn on the road in the early 19th century, the Royal Oak (later Sandyway Farm).[61] There was a hamlet called Cross o' th' Hand on the boundary with Burntwood by the later 17th century.[62] Lyncroft House on the Stafford road was built probably in the late 18th century.

Lichfield's economic activity, centred chiefly on retailing, was of only local importance.[63] Two markets were held each week, and there were four fairs, although only two were important in the 18th century. The range of goods offered for sale by Lichfield shops was limited. In 1788 Anna Seward complained that the city furnished 'nothing but clumsy necessaries' and remarked that Bath was the place to buy luxury goods, not 'plain, uninventive Lichfield'. In 1806 she claimed that a visitor would find the food at her table plain because Lichfield was 'the worst market imaginable'.[64] The manufacturing trades were confined mainly to coach-making and cloth and leather working. Tanning was the only noxious trade, and the corporation's opposition in 1761 to the establishment of a canvas manufactory by John Tunstall may have been because it was opposed to any kind of industry in the town. By 1776, however, Tunstall was making sailcloth in premises in Sandford Street. The absence of industry gave the town an air of sleepiness. Horace Walpole, comparing Wolverhampton with Lichfield in 1743, thought that the latter was 'as indolent as the former was busy',[65] and a visitor in 1782, noting the absence of industry, commented that 'the silence of the streets is interrupted only by the passage of public carriages'.[66]

Lichfield became a centre for polite society in the region. It surprised Celia

[52] S.R.O., D. 3451/2/60, 18 Mar. 1681/2, 10 Oct. 1697; L.J.R.O., D. 77/5/1, f. 78.
[53] Below, domestic buildings.
[54] L.J.R.O., D. 15/10/2/2; D. 15/10/2/61 (inventory of 1746); B.L. Harl. MS. 7022, f. 34; *Illus. Guide to Lichfield Cath. and Ancient and Loyal City of Lichfield* (Lichfield, 1897), pl. facing p. 66 (copy in Samuel Johnson Birthplace Mus.); below (20th century) and plate 3.
[55] A. L. Reade, *Reades of Blackwood Hill* (priv. print. 1906), 242–3; sale cat. 7 Nov. 1929 (copy in W.S.L., S.C. A/1/19).
[56] Below, manor (lay estates).
[57] Below, econ. hist. (agric.); S.R.O. 3764/69.
[58] L.J.R.O., D. 15/2/2, 6 May 1770.
[59] Ibid. D. 27/1/1, f. 3; W.S.L., M. 912, item 18.
[60] S.R.O., D. 615/D/240/1, deed of 27 Mar. 1777.
[61] Below, econ. hist. (agric.).
[62] Below, Burntwood, growth of settlement.
[63] For this para. see below, econ. hist.
[64] *Jnls. and Corresp. of Thomas Sedgewick Whalley*, ed. H. Wickham, ii. 25, 297.
[65] *Corresp. of Horace Walpole*, ed. W. S. Lewis, xl. 43.
[66] Derb. R.O., D. 395Z/Z1, p. 8.

Fiennes that the bishop, cathedral clergy, and an 'abundance of gentry' lived at or near Lichfield with its low-lying and watery position, rather than at Coventry with its pleasanter situation and better buildings. She wrongly thought, however, that Coventry was still, with Lichfield, the bishop's see.[67] Circumstances obliged some of the cathedral clergy to live at Lichfield, and the gentry presumably followed their lead. The city evidently lost some of its popularity in the 18th century after the bishops had abandoned their palace in the Close for their house at Eccleshall. Nevertheless Defoe thought that Lichfield was the best town in Staffordshire and the neighbouring counties for 'good conversation and good company'.[68] In the 1730s or 1740s Richard Wilkes, a physician and antiquary of Willenhall, described it as 'the most genteel place in the county'. Because there was little manufacture or commerce the inhabitants had 'more time to dress and visit', and the cathedral and 'the variety of travelling company' passing through the town were further attractions.[69] A music club promoted public concerts by the mid 1740s. Professional acting companies came to Lichfield at least from the later 1760s, and a theatre was opened in Bore Street in 1790. In addition there was a bowling green west of the town, in existence since the later 17th century, and archery was evidently a favourite pastime in the later 18th century.[70]

Although Frances, countess of Huntingdon, lived in Lichfield after she was widowed in 1701 until 1705 or later[71] and Lord Stanhope lived in the bishop's palace in 1706,[72] the nobility appear to have confined their visits largely to the race meetings which became an important feature of Lichfield's social life. First recorded when held at Alrewas in the early 1680s, the meetings were moved nearer Lichfield to Whittington heath in 1702. By the early 1740s they were held in September and lasted two days, extended to three in 1744.[73] They were accompanied by dinners, concerts, and balls. In 1733 the countess of Strafford reported that she 'never saw so much good company together in any place before'.[74] It is uncertain whether it was the wives and daughters of the visiting nobility, or those of residents, who were alluded to as 'the fair ladies of Lichfield' by Walter Chetwynd of Ingestre in 1689.[75] For the poet Isaac Hawkins Browne, Lichfield in the early 1720s was 'the Paphos of England' on account of its pretty women.[76]

The leading members of polite society lived in the Close, either being associated with the cathedral or renting houses there.[77] Gilbert Walmisley, a native of Lichfield and diocesan registrar from 1707, lived in the bishop's palace from the late 1720s until his death in 1751. He gathered a group of *literati* around him and gave encouragement to both Samuel Johnson and the actor David Garrick in their youth. Two resident prebendaries were authors: Sneyd Davies, resident from *c.* 1751 to 1769, was a poet, and Thomas Seward, resident 1754–90, edited the plays of Beaumont and Fletcher. Seward's daughter Anna (1747–1809) was a celebrated poet and was known as 'the Swan of Lichfield'.[78] The physician and scientist Erasmus Darwin lived in Lichfield between 1758 and 1780. He established a botanic society in 1778 and laid out a botanic garden at Abnalls in Burntwood.[79] Richard Greene (d. 1793), an apothecary who lived in Market Street, created a

[67] *Journeys of Celia Fiennes*, 114.
[68] Defoe, *Tour*, ii. 480.
[69] W.S.L., S. MS. 468, f. 35 (1st nos.). For the date see *S.H.C.* 4th ser. xi, p. 179, note 26.
[70] Below, social and cultural activities.
[71] L.J.R.O., D. 77/6/2, ff. 12v., 49v.; Harwood, *Lichfield*, 469; *Complete Peerage*, vi. 660.
[72] Below, cathedral and close.
[73] Below, social and cultural activities (sport).
[74] Ibid. (music; dancing assemblies); *V.C.H. Staffs.* ii. 364; Hist. MSS. Com. 78, *Hastings*, iii, p. 18.
[75] *S.H.C.* 4th ser. xi. 38.
[76] Thomas Newton, *Works* (1782), i. 22; *D.N.B.* s.v. Browne.   [77] Para. based on entries in *D.N.B.*
[78] The originator of the epithet, which is probably contemporary, is unknown: E. V. Lucas, *A Swan and her Friends*, 168, 170. For a portrait of her see below, plate 23.
[79] Below, social and cultural activities (societies).

museum there which attracted many visitors.[80] The fame of the Lichfield 'lions' spread.[81] Anna Seward was visited by the poet William Hayley in 1782,[82] the violinist Wilhelm Cramer in 1796,[83] the landscape gardener Humphry Repton,[84] the writer Walter Scott in 1807,[85] and the poet Robert Southey in 1808.[86] The resident literary circle, however, was small, and Anna Seward felt culturally isolated. She lamented the 'insensibility' of the town's leading inhabitants, and in particular the unimaginative choice of books ordered by the reading society.[87] That society was presumably the one which in 1781 ordered a copy of Fanny Burney's novel *Evelina*, published in 1778; despite the book's fame, it had not been heard of locally until Samuel Johnson brought a copy to Lichfield.[88]

As the birthplace of Samuel Johnson Lichfield was attracting visitors as early as 1801.[89] He was born in Lichfield in 1709, the son of Michael Johnson, a bookseller living in Market Street.[90] He attended schools in the city and then one in Stourbridge (Worcs.); in 1728–9 he was a student at Pembroke College, Oxford. After his father's death in 1731 he sought employment away from Lichfield. He returned after his marriage in 1735 and opened a school at Edial, in Burntwood, in 1735–6. The school failed, and in 1737 he went to London. His *Dictionary* was published in 1755. The grant of a royal pension in 1762 enabled him to travel, and he periodically visited Lichfield; his last visit was in 1784, the year of his death. In 1838 a stone statue of him, presented by the diocesan chancellor, the Revd. J. T. Law, was set up in the market square. The sculptor was R. C. Lucas.[91] A bronze statue of Johnson's biographer James Boswell, given by its sculptor Percy Fitzgerald, was set up in the square in 1908. It stands on a pedestal which is decorated with five medallions of Boswell's friends and panels depicting Boswell and Johnson together.[92]

Lichfield had some of the characteristics of a leisure town of the 18th century. Its economy supported the luxury trade of bookselling, already important in the late 17th century;[93] street lights were set up in the later 1730s;[94] and the landscape was improved by public walks and gardens.[95] It was, however, slow to develop the refinement which would have attracted more residents. Animals continued to be sold in the market square, and the popular Whitsuntide festivity of the Greenhill Bower invaded the town centre despite middle class disapproval.[96] A further distraction was the large number of public houses, 80 innkeepers being recorded in 1732.[97] Besides serving the needs of travellers and denizens, the inns accommodated troops who were frequently quartered in Lichfield.[98] In 1779 there were 70 men quartered on the George, 65 on the Swan, 34 on the Hartshorn, 30 each on the King's Head and on the Crown, and proportionate numbers on the poorer inns, so that the poorest had at least 10 each.[99] Gregory King in 1711 noted that the inhabitants were 'addicted to drinking',[1] and drunkenness was a special problem at

[80] Ibid. (museums).
[81] R. Walker, *Tour through the Northern Counties of Eng. and the Borders of Scotland* (1802), i. 107.
[82] *Gent. Mag.* ciii (2), 126.
[83] Below, social and cultural activities (music).
[84] *Poetical Works of Anna Seward*, ed. W. Scott (Edinburgh, 1810), iii. 64.
[85] *Letters of Anna Seward* (Edinburgh, 1811), iv. 337–40.
[86] Samuel Johnson Birthplace Mus., Lichfield, MS. 38/22, Anna Seward to Mary Powys, June 1808.
[87] *Letters of Anna Seward*, ii. 106–7, 204; vi. 335.
[88] *Letters of Samuel Johnson*, ed. R. W. Chapman, ii, p. 447; *D.N.B.* s.v. Arblay, Frances d'.
[89] Walker, *Tour through Northern Counties of Eng. and Borders of Scotland*, i. 104–5.
[90] Para. based on *D.N.B.*

[91] *Trans. Johnson Soc. 1986 and 1987*, 43–52; below, plate 25.
[92] *Lichfield Mercury*, 25 Sept. 1908, p. 5.
[93] Below, econ. hist. (trades and industries).
[94] Below, public services (lighting).
[95] Below, social and cultural activities (walks).
[96] Ibid. (Greenhill Bower); econ. hist. (markets).
[97] Below, econ. hist. (trades).
[98] e.g. *London Post*, 25–8 Aug. 1699; *Cal. Treas. Bks. and Papers*, 1731–4, 294; 1735–8, 71; *Public Advertiser*, 17 Apr. 1755; 26 Sept. 1762; *Universal Evening Post*, 5–8 July 1760; W.S.L., S. MS. 478/F, Lord Fielding to War Office, 20 Sept. 1794.
[99] Hist. MSS. Com. 20, *Dartmouth*, iii, p. 249.
[1] Samuel Johnson Birthplace Mus., MS. 39/13, endorsement.

the contested parliamentary elections in 1747 and 1755.[2] The demise of the Cecilian Society, a music club, *c.* 1790 was in part because its concerts had been turned into drinking sessions.[3]

Lichfield's position on the main road to the north-west of England and to Ireland made it a convenient stopping place for travellers. In 1729 the town became the centre of a turnpike network.[4] On his visit to Lichfield in 1687 James II stayed at the Deanery; he praised the workmanship of the bishop's palace, then nearing completion.[5] William III passed through Lichfield in 1690 on his way to Ireland.[6] Lichfield's position on a main road was probably the reason for its being chosen as a place to quarter French prisoners-of-war. Two Frenchmen were guarded over night at the George in 1667, before being taken to Coventry.[7] Several French officers were brought to Lichfield in 1704.[8] One on parole in 1779 gave private French lessons.[9] Large numbers of them were at Lichfield on parole during the Napoleonic Wars. Eighty arrived in January 1797, but they were taken to a gaol in Liverpool in November. Their 'graceful manners and enlightened minds' were much appreciated by Anna Seward and her friends, but other residents kept their distance.[10] In 1809, when *c.* 40 officers were quartered, the senior ones were allowed to attend the September race meeting.[11] In 1810 a party of 17, comprising three prisoners (one with a family) and black servants, who had been taken at Guadeloupe, was brought to Lichfield.[12] A French prisoner was last recorded in Lichfield in 1812.[13]

An infantry regiment was formed in 1705 by Col. Luke Lillingston at the King's Head in Bird Street. In 1751 it became the 38th regiment of foot and in 1783 the 1st Staffordshire Regiment; after reorganization in 1881 it became the 1st battalion of the South Staffordshire Regiment.[14] There was a volunteer company in Lichfield in 1745, commanded by Peter Garrick, the brother of the actor David Garrick.[15]

THE 19TH CENTURY

Between 1801 and 1901 Lichfield's population rose from just under 5,000 to nearly 8,000. The overall growth is reflected in suburban expansion and in the increasing scale of local government, public services, and economic activity.

In 1817 Lichfield was described as

an open handsome city; the houses in general are well built, the streets regular and spacious, with an excellent pavement and convenient footways, and kept very clean. The principal inhabitants are gentry, mostly persons of small independent fortunes; the remainder consist of tradesmen and artificers. The general appearance of the city affords an idea of snugness, cleanliness, and elegance, and it is

[2] Below, parl. representation.
[3] Below, social and cultural activities (music).
[4] Below, communications.
[5] *T.S.S.A.H.S.* xxvii. 62 (where the king is wrongly given as Wm. III); below, town govt. (govt. from 1548: unreformed corporation).   [6] *S.H.C.* 4th ser. xi. 41.
[7] L.J.R.O., D. 35/bailiffs' accts. 1657–1707, p. 34.
[8] *Lond. Gaz.* 14–18 Dec. 1704.
[9] Below, education (private schs.).

[10] *Swinney's Birmingham Chron.* 12 Jan. 1797; *Letters of Anna Seward*, iv. 362; v. 18.
[11] *Swinney's Birmingham Chron.* 14 Sept. 1809.
[12] S.R.O., D. 661/9/6/2/15/2.
[13] L.J.R.O., D. 29/1/2, f. 49.
[14] J. P. Jones, *Hist. of South Staffs. Regiment* (1923), 7–9, 15–16, 112.
[15] *Letters of David Garrick*, ed. D. M. Little and G. M. Kahrl, i, p. 70.

delightfully situated in a fertile spot, abounding with the most valuable produc-
tions of the agriculturalist.[16]

In the mid 1830s Lichfield was still much frequented by travellers between London
and Liverpool and between Birmingham and the West Riding of Yorkshire, and
there were five coaching inns.[17] Coaches ceased to run through the city in 1838 with
the completion of the railway between London and Liverpool via Birmingham and
Stafford. As a result the road north from Lichfield 'became like a by lane'.[18] When
the railway came to Lichfield in 1847 with the opening of the Trent Valley Railway
from Stafford to the Birmingham–London line at Rugby, the station was in
Streethay, over a mile from the city centre. A station was provided in the centre in
1849 when the South Staffordshire Railway was opened from Walsall through
Lichfield to the Midland Railway at Wychnor, in Tatenhill. Plans for a canal,
mooted from 1759, were fulfilled in 1797 when the Wyrley and Essington Canal
was opened through the south side of the city, and by 1817 there were at least six
wharfs.

Rebuilding in the town centre in the course of the century included the guildhall
(1848), St. Mary's church (1853 and 1870), and the theatre (1873), and restoration
was carried out at St. Chad's church in the 1840s and 1880s and at St. Michael's in
the 1840s and 1890s. New buildings included a corn exchange and savings bank in
Conduit Street (1849), a public library and museum in Bird Street (1859), and a
police station in Wade Street (1898). Restoration of the cathedral was carried out in
stages, beginning in the 1840s, and its completion was celebrated with a Thanksgiving Festival in 1901. The bishop's palace in the Close was enlarged in the late
1860s when Bishop Selwyn decided to move back there from Eccleshall Castle.

The suburbs of Beacon Street, Stowe Street, Greenhill, St. John Street, and
Sandford Street, established in the Middle Ages, expanded during the 19th
century. All but Beacon Street were mainly areas of artisan housing built in terraces
and courts. In the late 1860s good houses were much in demand; several houses
recently built in the suburbs had been quickly let at high rents.[19] A number of large
houses were built on the southern outskirts. A house at the junction of Tamworth
Road and Quarryhills Lane, known as Lower Borrowcop Villa in the later 1840s,
was called Freeford Villa in the 1850s. It was the home of Thomas Rowley, a
physician, and was presumably on the site of Freeford Cottage, where he was living
in 1834. He had renamed the house Quarry Lodge by 1861.[20] Berryhill House at
the north end of London Road originated as Berryhill Cottage, built by 1841 and
later enlarged.[21] Knowle Lodge at the north end of Knowle Lane had been built by
1861 when it was the home of J. P. Dyott, a solicitor; it may have been on the site of
Knowle Lane Cottage, built by 1841.[22] Knowle Hurst to the south existed as Belle
Colline by 1881.[23]

In Beacon Street Beacon Place was enlarged c. 1836, and in the course of the
century the grounds attached to it were increased from 15 a. to nearly 100 a.[24] At
the north end of Beacon Street there was a group of cottages by the 1830s around
the junction with Wheel Lane (then called Grange Lane), and the area was known

[16] Pitt, *Staffs.* i. 102.
[17] White, *Dir. Staffs.* (1834), 61; below, communications.
[18] W.S.L., S. MS. 374, p. 42.
[19] *Staffs. Advertiser*, 22 Feb. 1868, p. 4.
[20] White, *Dir. Staffs.* (1834), 160; *Slater's Nat. Com. Dir.* (1850); *P.O. Dir. Staffs.* (1850; 1854; 1860); L.J.R.O., B/A/15/Lichfield, St. Michael, no. 865; P.R.O., RG 9/1973.

[21] P.R.O., HO 107/2014 (2); L.J.R.O., B/A/15/Lichfield, St. Michael, no. 790; *Staffs. Advertiser*, 23 Aug. 1851, p. 8; [A. Williams and W. H. Mallett], *Mansions and Country Houses of Staffs. and Warws.* (Lichfield, n.d.), 17 and facing pl.
[22] P.R.O., HO 107/1008; P.R.O., RG 9/1973.
[23] Ibid. RG 11/2773; O.S. Map 6″, Staffs. LVIII. NE. (1888 edn.).
[24] Below, manor.

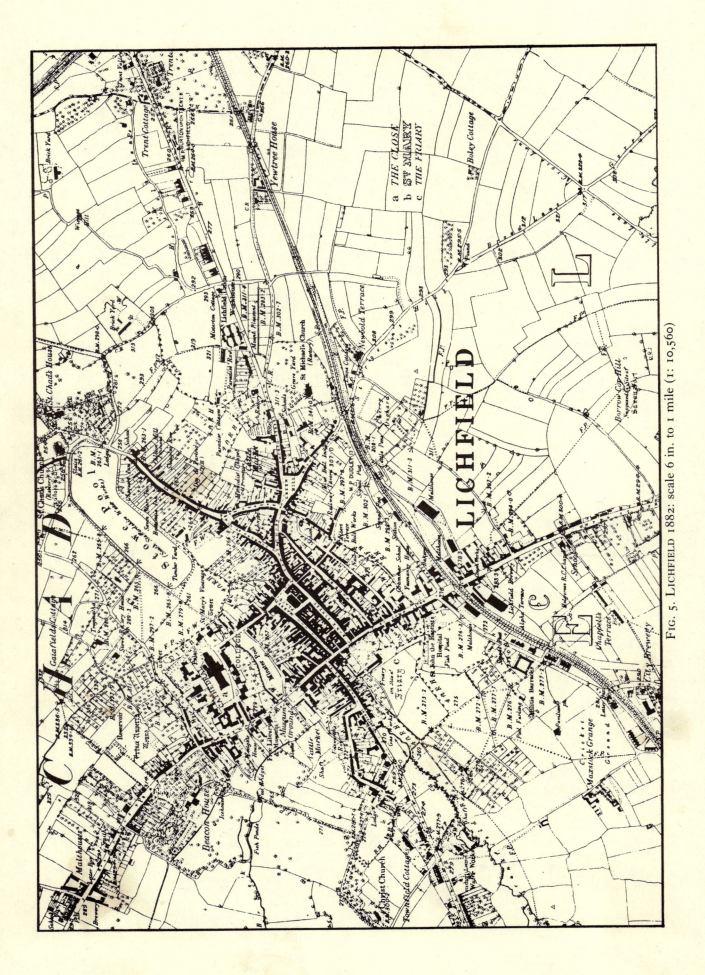

FIG. 5. LICHFIELD 1882: scale 6 in. to 1 mile (1: 10,560)

as New Town.[25] It included the Wheel inn, in existence by 1811.[26] By 1847 there were also houses along Stafford Road between Abnalls Lane and Cross in Hand Lane.[27]

The first of a number of cottages in Castle ditch running south-west from Greenhill were built in 1800. They were named Gresley Row after Sir Nigel Gresley, the Tory contestant in a byelection in 1799.[28] Trent Valley Road was built under an Act of 1832 as an extension of Church Street; it continued into Streethay, bypassing the less direct route along Burton Old Road, and from 1847 it was the link between the main line station and the city centre.[29] Paradise Row off its west end evidently existed by 1836; in 1841 it was a group of 10 cottages, with two houses to the west occupied by the owner of the row and a relative.[30] By 1847 there were two houses known as Mount Pleasant on the corresponding part of Trent Valley Road.[31] The union workhouse was opened to the east in 1840.[32] Some better-class houses were built along the road in the later 1870s.[33] In 1881 there were six households in Wissage and three in Wissage Lane.[34] In 1886 a drinking fountain and cattle trough surmounted by a lamp were erected by subscription at Greenhill as a memorial to J. J. Serjeantson, rector of St. Michael's 1868–86, in fulfilment of his long-cherished wish.[35] The fountain and trough survived in 1989, although no longer in use. In 1887 a plot of ground behind the memorial was planted and railed at the expense of Alderman R. P. Cooper.[36]

In Upper St. John Street a Roman Catholic chapel with a priest's house was opened in 1803. Rowley's Row, a terrace of 10 houses owned by Thomas Rowley, had been built to the south by 1841.[37] The area to the west was also developing. The southern end of Birmingham Road was so named by 1818. By then there was a lime works by the canal, with the Duke of Wellington inn south of the bridge, and the area round the works and a nearby timber yard was populous by the 1830s.[38] The pumping station to the east in Chesterfield Road dates from 1858.[39] The northern end of Birmingham Road, known variously as Schoolhouse Lane and St. John's Lane by the later 18th century, was called Birmingham Road by 1861.[40] A militia barracks was built there in 1854.[41] There were three houses in 1861, and over the next 20 years a number of large houses were built, some detached, some in terraces; the pair named Bonne Vue date from the late 1870s. In Chesterfield Road a terrace of six houses known as Deakin's Row and a terrace of four larger houses were also built in the late 1870s.[42] Dovehouse Fields east of Birmingham Road and north of the canal had three houses in 1851 and eight in 1861. The 30 houses making up Chappell's Terrace to the north-east had been built by 1881.[43] Shortbutts Lane linking Upper St. John Street and Birmingham Road existed in 1577; the first houses were built at the east end in the early 1890s.[44]

[25] L.J.R.O., Fecknam's Char. MSS., map of 1836; L.J.R.O., D. 29/1/3, p. 197; D. 29/1/9, p. 191.
[26] L.J.R.O., D. 77/16/5.
[27] L.J.R.O., B/A/15/Lichfield, St. Michael.
[28] Harwood, *Lichfield*, 536–7; *S.H.C.* 1933 (1), 12; S.R.O., D. 615/D/240/3; D. (W.) 1851/8/54.
[29] Below, communications.
[30] L.J.R.O., D. 29/1/9, p. 162; L.J.R.O., B/A/15/Lichfield, St. Michael; P.R.O., HO 107/1008.
[31] L.J.R.O., B/A/15/Lichfield, St. Michael; P.R.O., HO 107/2014(2).
[32] Below, parish govt.
[33] *Lichfield Mercury*, 27 Dec. 1878; L.J.R.O., D. 126/min. bk. 1856–95, pp. 358, 371.
[34] P.R.O., RG 11/2773.
[35] Lichfield Libr., St. Michael's file; inscription *in situ*.
[36] *Staffs. Advertiser*, 16 Apr. 1887, p. 7.

[37] P.R.O., HO 107/1008; L.J.R.O., B/A/15/Lichfield, St. Michael, nos. 301–10.
[38] Parson and Bradshaw, *Staffs. Dir.* (1818), 186; B.L. Maps, O.S.D. 258; J. Dewhirst, *Map of Lichfield* (1836); P.R.O., HO 107/1008; below, econ. hist. (trades and industries).
[39] Below, public services (water supplies).
[40] S.R.O., D. 342/M/T/1, 3, 7; P.R.O., HO 107/1008 and 2014 (2).
[41] Below (this section).
[42] P.R.O., RG 9/1973; RG 10/2914; RG 11/2773; L.J.R.O., D. 126/min. bk. 1856–95, p. 246; *Lichfield Mercury*, 8 Aug. 1879.
[43] P.R.O., HO 107/2014(2); P.R.O., RG 10/2914; RG 11/2773.
[44] S.R.O., D. 4566/S, bdle. 45, deed of 28 Nov. 1581; date stones of 1891 and 1893.

Leamonsley hamlet on the Walsall road evidently grew up after the opening of a fulling mill on Leamonsley brook on the city boundary in the early 1790s. In 1841 there were 13 households, including that of the tenant of the mill; in 1851 there were 27 households.[45] The Walsall road was realigned under an Act of 1832 with the new Queen Street and Walsall Road bypassing the route along Lower Sandford Street and what was later called Christchurch Lane. That lane takes its name from the church opened in 1847, and by then it had been continued south-west from the church to the new Walsall road, the old line from Lower Sandford Street having been turned into a drive for Beacon Place.[46] Houses were built along the new stretch of the Walsall road between the 1860s and 1880s.[47]

Christ Church also served the populous Lower Sandford Street, most of which became part of Christ Church parish created in 1848. New houses were built in the street in the early 19th century,[48] and the weaving shops of Sir Robert Peel's shortlived cotton manufactory there, closed by 1813, were turned into dwellings.[49] A gas works was opened in Queen Street in 1835.[50] Flower's Row off Sandford Street, consisting of 19 houses, existed by 1847, and several more terraces had been built by 1861.[51] By 1851 there was an Irish community in Sandford Street.[52]

Local government was expanded and reformed in the earlier 19th century. A body of improvement commissioners was established in 1806. It took over some of the functions of the Conduit Lands Trust, such as the provision of lighting, but the trustees continued to provide money for public services besides maintaining a water supply. A special commission was set up in 1815 to rebuild the bridge in Bird Street. In 1836 the corporation became an elected council with a mayor.[53]

Industrial development began with the expansion of cloth working when the fulling mill was built at Leamonsley in the early 1790s and Pones mill was converted into a woollen manufactory in 1809. Both were still in operation in the 1850s. Less successful was the cotton manufactory which was established in Lower Sandford Street by Sir Robert Peel in 1802. The long-established tanning industry had apparently disappeared by the 1840s. There was some expansion in metal working in the earlier 19th century, with works producing agricultural machinery and cutlery in Sandford Street. A foundry was opened in Wade Street in 1864 and another in Sandford Street in 1879; a third, belonging to the Walsall firm of Chamberlin & Hill, was opened at the north end of Beacon Street in 1890. The most striking industrial development was in brewing. Previously a trade practised by innkeepers who brewed their own ale, it was increasingly taken over by maltsters from the late 18th century. In the later 19th century they in turn were replaced by brewing companies. There were five breweries in the late 1870s, including one on the Streethay side of the city boundary.

The growth of manufacturing firms was allegedly hampered by the development of market gardening from the early 19th century, with its emphasis on seasonal labour. In the late 1840s there were c. 1,300 a. of market gardens in the city, nearly two fifths of its total acreage. The produce was sold in the towns of South Staffordshire and in Birmingham.

Lichfield's general markets declined in the course of the century, although from

[45] P.R.O., HO 107/1008 and 2014 (2).
[46] L.J.R.O., B/A/15/Lichfield, St. Chad; ibid. St. Michael; below, communications; churches.
[47] P.R.O., RG 9/1973; RG 10/2914; RG 11/2773; *Lichfield Mercury*, 3 Feb. 1882, p. 4; 3 June 1887, p. 5.
[48] S.R.O., D. 593/F/3/12/2/16, receipt of 6 Mar. 1804; L.J.R.O., D. 77/15/3, p. 10; *Lichfield Mercury*, 30 Sept. 1825, advert.

[49] S.R.O., D. 941/54; L.J.R.O., B/A/15/Lichfield, St. Chad, nos. 838–52.
[50] Below, public services.
[51] L.J.R.O., B/A/15/Lichfield, St. Mary, nos. 407–25; O.S. Map 1/500, Staffs. LII. 15. 12 (1884 edn.).
[52] Below, Roman Catholicism.
[53] Below, communications; town govt. (govt. from 1548); public services.

the 1850s there was a market hall on the ground floor of the corn exchange. Cattle markets became increasingly important, and from the late 1860s there were two smithfields. The fairs increased in number in the earlier part of the century, but they subsequently declined, leaving only the Ash Wednesday fair, which itself was little more than a pleasure fair by the later 1870s.

Lichfield retained military associations throughout the century. It had its own troop of yeomanry cavalry, which was raised in 1794 as part of a Staffordshire regiment by F. P. Eliot of Elmhurst, a keen supporter of the yeomanry movement. In 1900 it had 84 members.[54] It was in attendance when the marquess of Anglesey visited Lichfield in 1815 on his return from the Waterloo campaign, in 1839 at the visit of Adelaide, the queen dowager, and in 1843 at the visit of Queen Victoria and Prince Albert.[55] A corps of infantry volunteers was formed in 1798.[56] It was evidently re-established in 1803 and had a strength of 476 in 1806. It was probably disbanded in 1813.[57] A corps of rifle volunteers was formed in 1860 and had a strength of 84 in 1900.[58]

In September 1820 the whole Staffordshire yeomanry regiment assembled at Lichfield for six days' training on Whittington heath.[59] It assembled there again at intervals until 1833 when the Lichfield yeomanry week became an annual event, normally in the autumn or summer.[60] By 1870 the headquarters of what in 1838 had become the Queen's Own Royal Regiment was at Yeomanry House in St. John Street, the former St. John's House which was still owned by the Levetts in 1847, though then unoccupied.[61] The Prince of Wales was entertained there in 1894 during the regiment's centenary celebrations.[62] The building was taken over by the girls' high school in 1896, the yeomanry headquarters having been moved to the Friary; it was demolished in 1925.[63]

In 1853 the 1st King's Own Staffordshire Militia assembled for 28 days' training on a field in the immediate vicinity of Lichfield.[64] A barracks was opened in Birmingham Road in 1854 as a stores for the militia. There was also accommodation for the permanent staff, which in 1861 consisted of a sergeant major and nine staff sergeants with their families.[65] Nathaniel Hawthorne, visiting Lichfield in 1855, noted the large number of young soldiers newly recruited into the King's Own who were lounging about and looking 'as if they had had a little too much ale'.[66] Soon after the completion of the barracks at Whittington in 1880, the Lichfield barracks was closed.[67] It was sold in 1891 and converted into tenements known as Victoria Square.[68] The building was demolished in the late 1960s and bungalows were erected on the site.[69]

In 1817 Mary Bagot of Blithfield noted that Lichfield was 'unfrequented now except by its regular inhabitants, who form a considerable society, very different

[54] P. C. G. Webster, *Records of the Queen's Own Royal Regiment of Staffs. Yeomanry* (1870), 3; *Military Forces of Staffs. in the Nineteenth Cent.* (Stafford, 1901), 79; *D.N.B.*; W.S.L. 5/296/49.
[55] Webster, *Staffs. Yeomanry*, 39–40, 121–3, 156–7.
[56] Clayton, *Coaching City*, 48, 89–93.
[57] Ibid. 94–6; *Military Forces of Staffs.* 47–8; *V.C.H. Staffs.* i. 270; S.R.O., D. 593/F/3/12/2; W.S.L., S. 1901, pp. 88–9, 91, 154, 199–200.
[58] *Military Forces of Staffs.* 53, 70, 80.
[59] *Dyott's Diary*, ed. R. W. Jeffery, ii. 336–7; Webster, *Staffs. Yeomanry*, 59–60.
[60] Webster, *Staffs. Yeomanry*, 65 sqq.; Clayton, *Cathedral City*, 164–7; below, social and cultural activities (dancing assemblies; theatre).
[61] Webster, *Staffs. Yeomanry*, pp. vi, 114; L.J.R.O., B/A/15/Lichfield, St. Michael, no. 243.
[62] *Military Forces of Staffs.* 40–3.
[63] *Kelly's Dir. Staffs.* (1896); *Lichfield Mercury*, 17 Apr. 1925, p. 5; 1 Jan. 1926, p. 4; below, education.
[64] *Staffs. Advertiser*, 14 May 1853, p. 4; 25 June 1853, p. 4.
[65] *City and County of Lichfield Handbk.* ed. H. J. Callender (Birmingham, 1951), 36; *P.O. Dir. Staffs.* (1860); P.R.O., RG 9/1973.
[66] *Eng. Notebooks of Nathaniel Hawthorne*, ed. R. Stewart, 151.
[67] Lichfield Urban Sanitary Dist. *Rep. of M.O.H. for 1891*, 3 (copy in S.R.O., C/H/1/2/1/2); *Staffs. Advertiser*, 4 Dec. 1880, p. 6.
[68] *Staffs. Advertiser*, 16 May 1891, p. 7; Jackson, *Lichfield*, 111.
[69] *Lichfield Mercury*, 24 May 1968, pp. 1, 5.

Fig. 6

1 Lyncroft House
2 Former windmill
3 Former Midland Truant School
4 Site of Chamberlin & Hill's foundry
5 Works of Tuke & Bell
6 Former St. Chad's rectory
7 Nether Stowe
8 Stowe Hill
9 Stowe House
10 William Lunn's Homes
11 St. Michael's vicarage
12 St. Michael's Hospital, formerly Lichfield Union workhouse
13 Site of Industrial school for girls
14 Former children's homes
15 Site of quarry
16 Shoulder of Mutton inn
17 Site of gallows
18 Former Bull piece
19 Pumping station
20 Former City Brewery
21 Cricket ground
22 Victoria Hospital
23 Former Bowling Green inn
24 Site of Conduit Lands Trust waterworks and Victoria Baths
25 Site of Sandford (later Trunkfield) mill
26 Former Christ Church vicarage

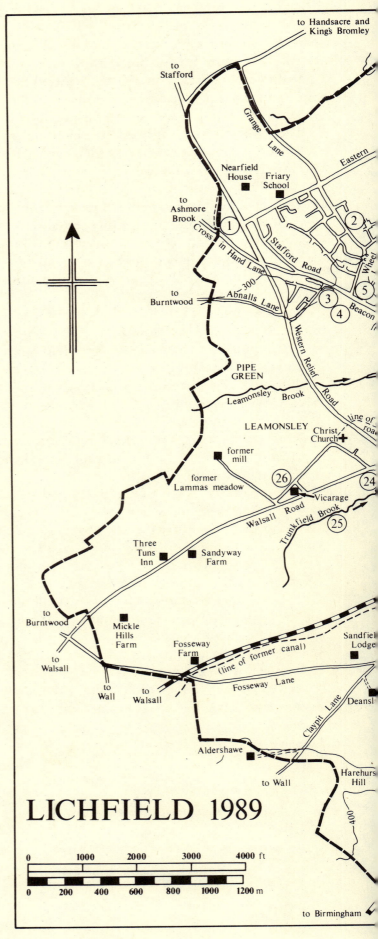

LICHFIELD 1989

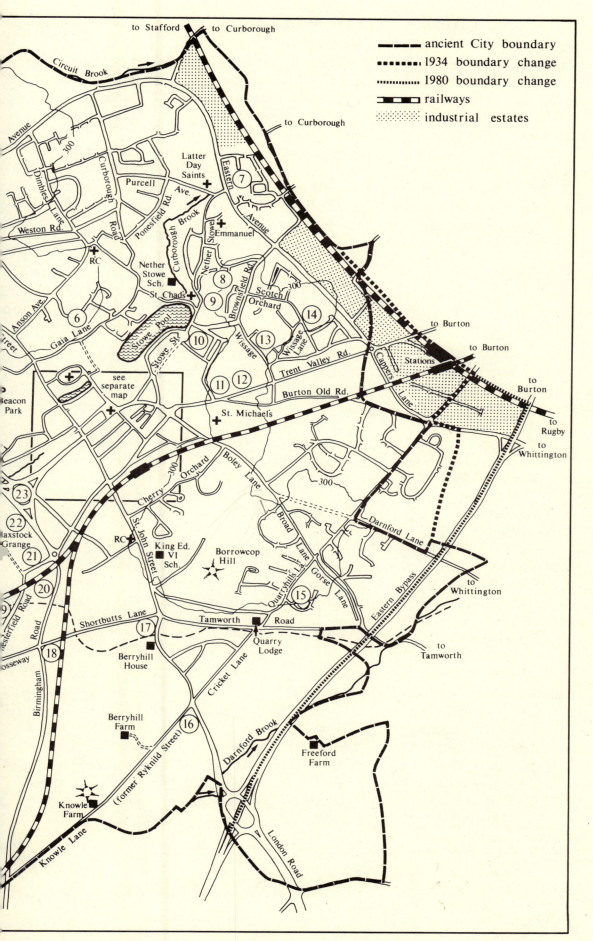

to Stafford   to Curborough

ancient City boundary
1934 boundary change
1980 boundary change
railways
industrial estates

Circuit Brook

to Curborough

Latter Day Saints
Purcell
Emmanuel
Weston Rd.
RC
Nether Stowe Sch.
St. Chads
Scotch Orchard
Stowe Pool
St. Michael's
Stowe St.
Trent Valley Rd.
Burton Old Rd.

to Burton
to Burton
Stations
to Burton
to Rugby
to Whittington

Anson Ave.
Gaia Lane
Beacon Park
see separate map

Cherry Orchard
Boley Lane
Broad Lane
Darnford Lane
Capper Lane

Eastern Avenue
Nether Stowe
Brownsfield Rd.
Wissage
Wissage Lane

Dimbles Lane
Curborough Road
Ponesfield Rd.
Curborough Brook
Ponesfield Ave.

7
8
9
10
11
12
13
14
15
16
17
18
20
21
22
23

King Ed. VI Sch.
St. John Street
RC
Borrowcop Hill
Quarryhills Lane
Gorse Lane
Eastern Bypass
to Whittington

Maxstock Grange
Chesterfield Road
Crosseway
Birmingham Road

Shortbutts Lane
Berryhill House
Tamworth Road
Quarry Lodge
Cricket Lane

to Tamworth

Berryhill Farm
(former Ryknild Street)
Darnford Brook
Freeford Farm

Knowle Farm
Knowle Lane
London Road

31

from what it was in Johnson's day'.[70] Another writer observed *c.* 1830 that it was evidently the 'quiet and retirement' of Lichfield which had for a long time attracted people of independent means as residents.[71] The disappearance of the coaching traffic in 1838 made it even quieter. In the earlier 1840s General William Dyott of Freeford found it a 'deserted city' full of 'melancholy gloom'.[72] Nathaniel Hawthorne noted in 1855 that 'the people have an old-fashioned way with them and stare at a stranger as if the railway had not yet quite accustomed them to visitors and novelty'.[73] In 1872 Henry James, for all his admiration of the cathedral, thought Lichfield 'stale without being really antique',[74] and a visitor in 1891 commented that 'there is an old-world look about this city, thoroughly English at every turn — staid, sober, and plodding'.[75]

THE 20TH CENTURY

In the 20th century, and especially in the years since the Second World War, Lichfield has developed as a residential area, with extensive light industry and a growing emphasis on tourism. There has been a corresponding growth in the city's population, which nearly tripled between 1951 and the later 1980s. Many commute to work outside the city.

In 1905 houses were being built in Frenchman's Lane, evidently the later Cherry Orchard,[76] and between 1905 and 1908 houses were built in Ivanhoe Road, a new road linking Birmingham Road and Chapel Lane.[77] About the same time houses were built at the west end of St. Chad's Road, the renamed Reservoir Road.[78] Under the Housing Acts of 1919 and the 1920s the council erected 208 houses, including the Christ Church Gardens estate off Christchurch Lane (completed 1921), Beacon Gardens off Beacon Street (1925), houses in Hobshole Lane (later Valley Road) and Trent Valley Road (1927), and the Dovehouse Fields estate west of Chapel Lane (completed 1931). There was also council building in the Dimbles area on the north side of the city which continued during the 1930s.[79] By the mid 1930s there had also been extensive private building, including houses in Stafford Road, Nether Beacon off Beacon Street, Walsall Road, and the newly laid-out Friary area.[80]

The 11½-a. Friary estate was presented to the city by Sir Richard Cooper, Bt., in 1920, primarily for building a new road to relieve traffic congestion and also to provide an open space in the city centre. The gift, in the words of a city alderman in 1928, 'let daylight into Lichfield'. That year a new road, the Friary, was opened from Bird Street to the Walsall and Birmingham roads, Sir Richard having contributed towards the building cost.[81] At the same time the clocktower of 1863 at the junction of the new road and Bird Street was re-erected on the new roundabout at the west end of the road.[82] The house on which the estate centred was

[70] Mrs. Charles Bagot [S. L. Bagot], *Links with the Past* (1901), 165.
[71] F. Calvert, *Staffs. and Shropshire* (Birmingham, 1830), 1.
[72] *Dyott's Diary*, ii. 366, 382.
[73] *Eng. Notebooks of Hawthorne*, 148.
[74] H. James, *Eng. Hours* (1960), 48.
[75] *The Antiquary*, xxiv. 147.
[76] Lichfield U.D.C. *Ann. Rep. of M.O.H. for 1905*, 8 (copy in S.R.O., C/H/1/2/1/20).

[77] Ibid. *1908*, 9 (copy in S.R.O., C/H/1/2/1/26); dates on houses.
[78] Lichfield U.D.C. *Ann. Rep. of M.O.H. for 1908*, 9; O.S. Map 6″, Staffs. LII. SE. (1903 and 1924 edns.).
[79] Below, public services.
[80] Jackson, *Hist. Incidents*, 111.
[81] *Lichfield Mercury*, 27 Apr. 1928, p. 5; 8 June 1928, p. 5.
[82] Below, public services (water supplies).

incorporated in new buildings for the girls' high school.[83] The site of the medieval friary church was excavated in 1933, and the foundations were left exposed as part of an open space.[84] The area covered by the estate formed a civil parish, which was added to St. Michael's in 1934.[85] In 1931 it had a population of one, the occupant of a gardener's cottage,[86] but that year the building of houses was begun along the new road; Friary Avenue, linking the road with Birmingham Road, was also built in the 1930s.[87] Victoria hospital was built west of the area in 1933.[88] The stretch of the Friary between the Walsall and Birmingham roads was renamed Friary Road in 1954.[89]

The outbreak of the Second World War in 1939 was followed by a suspension of building. The number of evacuees who came to Lichfield, over 2,000 at the end of 1940, caused overcrowding,[90] and a further problem was caused by Jewish tailors evacuated from London who were unable to find work.[91] There were air raids in 1940 and especially 1941; although only three people were killed and two houses destroyed, 390 houses were damaged.[92] In 1941 a British Restaurant known as the Civic Café was opened in the Methodist Hall in Tamworth Street as a wartime measure to provide cheap midday meals. At its peak it served over 450 meals a day, and by the time of its closure in 1945 it had served some 400,000 meals.[93]

With the end of the war in 1945 the council at once resumed house building, and by June 1950 it had built 301 more houses. The first privately built houses were six in Gaia Lane, begun in 1946, and 71 such houses had been completed in the city by June 1950. In 1956 the council agreed to provide 1,200 dwellings for families from Birmingham.[94] During the 1960s the north and east sides of the city between Stafford Road and Trent Valley Road were filled with new estates, private as well as council and containing high-rise blocks of flats as well as houses.[95] A new road, Anson Avenue, was built in the earlier 1960s from Beacon Street to an extension of Dimbles Lane.[96] At Leamonsley a private estate at the west end of Christchurch Lane and flats in Angorfa Close, off Walsall Road, were built in the earlier 1960s.[97] The Western Relief Road from the north end of Stafford Road to the Friary roundabout was completed in 1960.[98] In the city centre a new road continuing Birmingham Road across St. John Street to Greenhill was opened in 1955 and was named Birmingham Road in 1957.[99] A shopping precinct centring on Bakers Lane was laid out in the 1960s to the design of Shingler & Risdon of London.[1] The southern end of Stowe Street was rebuilt in the later 1960s and early 1970s; a cruck house there was converted into a centre for the elderly. The area was also pedestrianized, and the new Stowe Road was built for traffic.[2]

[83] Below, education.
[84] Below, manor.
[85] Below, parish govt.
[86] Lichfield Mercury, 30 Mar. 1934, p. 5.
[87] Ibid. 6 Mar. 1931, p. 5; 4 Jan. 1935, p. 3; O.S. Map 6", Staffs. LII. SE. (1938 edn.).
[88] Below, public services.
[89] Lichfield City Council Mins. 1953–4, p. 267.
[90] Below, public services (housing).
[91] Lichfield Charity Organization Soc. 55th Ann. Rep. for 1943 (copy in L.J.R.O., D. 77/19/1).
[92] Lichfield Mercury, 24 May 1985, p. 25.
[93] Ibid. 13 Dec. 1940, p. 5; 2 May 1941, p. 7; 13 July 1945, p. 5; Lichfield Yr. Bk. 1944, p. 8; 1946, 48 (copies in L.J.R.O., D. 33).
[94] Below, public services; Lichfield Mercury, 20 Sept. 1946, p. 8.
[95] Lichfield Mercury, 29 Nov. 1957, p. 1; 12 June 1959, p. 2; 27 Nov. 1959, p. 1; 22 July 1960, p. 2; below, manor (lay estates: Stowe Hill); public services.

[96] Lichfield Mercury, 18 Dec. 1959, p. 1; 17 Jan. 1964, p. 1; 8 Feb. 1985, advert. of house in Little Barrow Walk; Lichfield City Council Mins. 1962–3, p. 409; 1963–4, p. 609; 1964–5, p. 110.
[97] Lichfield City Council Mins. 1962–3, p. 558; 1963–4, p. 275; 1964–5, pp. 194, 473. Angorfa Close was on the site of a house called Angorfa: U. Turner, Christ Church, Lichfield, 18 (copy in W.S.L.); below, churches (Christ Church).
[98] Lichfield Mercury, 20 May 1960, p. 1.
[99] Ibid. 12 Feb. 1954, p. 4; 17 June 1955, p. 4; 30 Mar. 1956, p. 4; 16 Nov. 1956, p. 2; 21 Dec. 1956, p. 6; Lichfield City Council Mins. 1954–5, p. 271; 1955–6, p. 24; 1956–7, p. 296.
[1] L.J.R.O., D. 75; Lichfield City Council Mins. 1962–3, pp. 107, 201–2; 1963–4, pp. 609, 657; Lichfield Mercury, 31 Jan. 1964, p. 9; 20 Feb. 1987, p. 8; 10 July 1987, pp. 14, 16; below, plate 39.
[2] Lichfield Mercury, 12 Sept. 1969, p. 1; below, social and cultural activities (clubs).

LICHFIELD : central area 1989

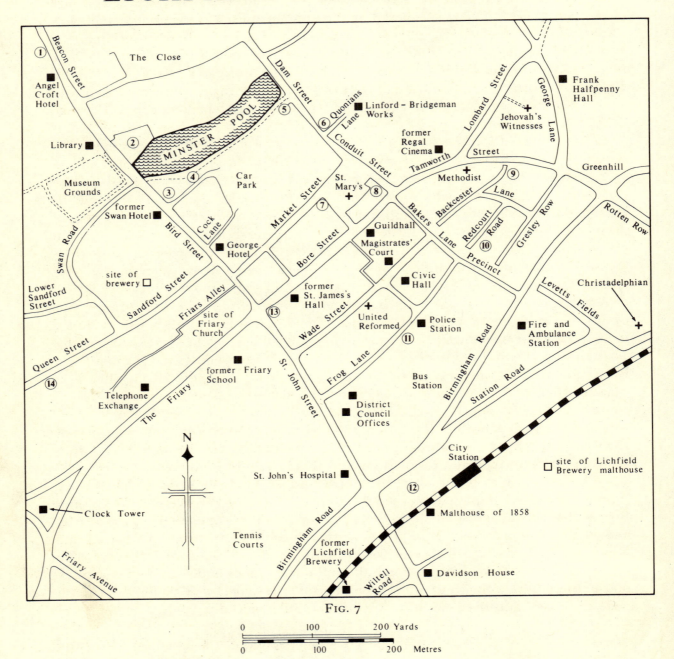

FIG. 7

0   100   200 Yards

0   100   200 Metres

① Dr. Milley's Hospital

② Garden of Remembrance

③ Arts Centre

④ Former St. Mary's School

⑤ Site of Art School

⑥ Former Dame Oliver's School

⑦ Samuel Johnson Birthplace Museum

⑧ Former Corn Exchange

⑨ Site of Redcourt House

⑩ Site of Frog Lane Boys' School

⑪ Site of Central School

⑫ Site of Flour Mill

⑬ Site of Minors's School

⑭ Site of Methodist New Connexion Chapel

34

The building of housing estates continued on the north and east sides of the city in the 1970s and 1980s,[3] and Eastern Avenue, running from Stafford Road to Trent Valley Road, was built in 1972.[4] The main growth, however, was on the south-east side. There had been some building there following the end of the Second World War. A private estate in Cricket Lane between London Road and Tamworth Road was begun in 1946,[5] and the first phase of the council's Cherry Orchard estate was finished in 1951.[6] In the earlier 1960s a private estate was built in the Minors Hill area west of Quarryhills Lane.[7] The Eastern Bypass running close to the south-east boundary from the A5 to Streethay was opened in 1971.[8] The main housing development was the Boley Park estate north-east of Broad Lane, begun by the late 1970s.[9] By 1986 it contained c. 1,700 houses with another 500 planned for 1987 and was claimed as one of the largest private estates in the country and among the top 10 in Europe.[10] A supermarket was opened there in 1984 as part of a shopping centre which was completed in 1985.[11] The Cappers Lane link road was opened north of the estate in 1984 to join Eastern Avenue and the Eastern Bypass.[12]

Several industrial estates were laid out on the east side of the city from 1946 to the 1980s. Their growth was encouraged by the building of Eastern Avenue and its extension along the Cappers Lane link road.[13] Two further commercial developments took place in the late 1980s. In 1988 the foundry of Chamberlin & Hill in Beacon Street was demolished and a Safeway supermarket was built on the site. In 1989, after Wintertons had moved their smithfield from Greenhill, the site was cleared and a W. H. Smith DIY store and a Tesco supermarket were built there.

Tourism was promoted in the 1980s. In 1986 the tourist information centre in Breadmarket Street was moved to premises in Donegal House in Bore Street, claimed as the largest and most comprehensive centre in Staffordshire.[14] The dean and chapter were active in the work. In 1980 they organized a music festival centred on the cathedral which became an annual event in 1982, with its scope later enlarged to include drama and opera.[15] The first part of the Lichfield Cathedral Visitors' Centre in the former diocesan registry in the Close was opened in 1986, and the centre was completed in 1989. A cathedral bookshop and coffee shop were opened in the Close in 1988.[16]

Lichfield rural district, formed in 1895, centred on Lichfield. At first the council met in the workhouse, its clerk's office was in Breadmarket Street, and its surveyor's office was successively in a private house, in a room in the workhouse, and from 1917 in two rooms in Mill House, Station Road. In 1917 the council bought the former grammar school and master's house in St. John Street from Dr. H. M. Morgan, the owner from 1903, and from 1920 the school was used as the council chamber and the house as offices. The premises were also used by the guardians of Lichfield poor law union until their dissolution in 1930, and the register office of Lichfield registration district was in the house until 1939.[17] With the reorganization of local government in 1974 the buildings passed to the new

[3] S.R.O., CEH/86/3, 18 Nov. 1970, 4 July 1972; CEH/282/1, 15 May 1973; CEH/282/2, 18 Sept. 1973; below, public services.

[4] Lichfield Mercury, 13 Oct. 1972, p. 1.

[5] Ibid. 25 Apr. 1947, p. 2.   [6] Below, public services.

[7] Lichfield City Council Mins. 1963–4, pp. 275, 536.

[8] Brochure for official opening, 27 Apr. 1971 (copy in W.S.L.); Lichfield Mercury, 30 Apr. 1971, p. 1.

[9] House adverts. in Lichfield Mercury, 21 Sept. 1984; 15 and 22 Feb. 1985.

[10] Lichfield Mercury, 28 Nov. 1986, p. 3.

[11] Ibid. 26 Oct. 1984, p. 26; 24 May 1985, pp. 29–31.

[12] Ibid. 17 Feb. 1984, p. 5.

[13] Below, econ. hist.

[14] Lichfield Mercury, 28 Feb. 1986, pp. 1–2.

[15] Below, social and cultural activities (music).

[16] Below, cathedral and close (houses of vicars choral; other houses).

[17] Lichfield R.D.C. The Rural Council House, Lichfield (1941; copy in W.S.L.).

Lichfield district, which in 1987 also opened offices in Frog Lane designed by Butler Wones Partnership.[18]

In 1974 the city was absorbed into Lichfield district, but in 1980 it re-emerged as a parish council which was granted city status later the same year with the chairman of the council styled a mayor. The sheriff's office survived the changes of 1974, and the sheriff continues to perambulate the city bounds every September. Several other ancient institutions and customs survive. One of the medieval manorial courts, that held on St. George's day (23 April), still meets. A court of pie powder continues to be proclaimed on Shrove Tuesday with the only surviving fair, and after the ceremony the mayor and civic party retire to the guildhall for refreshments which traditionally include simnel cake. The Greenhill Bower, with festivities dating back to the Middle Ages, is held on Spring Bank Holiday Monday. Of the numerous city companies, only the smiths' survives, and it admits among its freemen people who have given outstanding service to Lichfield. The Conduit Lands Trust, although it ceased in 1963 to be concerned with the provision of water, remains extensively involved in its second object, the promotion of the common good of the city. A similar object is pursued by the Swinfen Broun Charitable Trust. It was established in 1974, at the time of the reorganization of local government, under the will of Lt.-Col. M. A. Swinfen Broun (d. 1948) of Swinfen Hall in Weeford, who left half his residuary estate to the mayor and corporation of Lichfield.[19]

[18] *Lichfield Mercury*, 23 Oct. 1987, p. 7.

[19] *The Swinfen Broun Charitable Trust* (copy in Lichfield Libr.).

THE PLACE NAME

THE place name Lichfield occurs in a *Life* of St. Wilfrid (d. 709), written soon after the saint's death, and in the *Ecclesiastical History* of Bede (d. 731). The two surviving manuscripts of the *Life* date from the 11th century, but they preserve versions of the name that tally with those given in the earliest manuscripts of Bede, copied in the 730s and 740s. According to the *Life* Wilfrid, between 666 and 669, was given a site suitable for an episcopal see by Wulfhere, king of the Mercians. In 669 Wilfrid presented the *locum donatum sibi Onlicitfelda* (or *Anliccitfelda*) as a seat for Chad, and later in the *Life* there occurs a bishop *de Licitfelda* (or *de Lyccitfelda*).[1] The earliest manuscripts of Bede tell how Chad had his seat *in loco qui vocatur Lyccidfelth* (or *Licidfelth*) and refer to one of Chad's successors as the bishop *Lyccitfeldensi*.[2] The spelling *Licetfeld* is found in the 11th century[3] and, with the alternative *Licitfeld*, apparently survived until at least the early 12th century.[4]

The second element in the name is the Old English *feld*, generally taken to mean 'open country', either naturally treeless or cleared for agriculture.[5] The meaning of the first element has been much disputed. In the 1880s Henry Bradley suggested that Bede's *Lyccid* was an Anglicization of the early Welsh *luitcoit* (modern Welsh *llwyd goed*, 'grey wood') and that *luitcoit* itself had evolved from an earlier Celtic form *Lētocēton*, the native name of the Roman settlement at Wall, 2 miles south of Lichfield. The Latin name of the Roman settlement survived in the Antonine Itinerary of *c.* 300 as *Etocetum* and in the 7th-century Ravenna Cosmography (based on earlier material) as *Lectocetum*. Bradley proposed an amended Latin spelling *Letocetum*. He noted the *Cair Luitcoit* ('town of the grey wood') which Nennius had included in a catalogue of 28 British towns and *Caer Lwydgoed* where according to an early poem the Welsh of Powys fought a battle in the 7th century.[6]

Advances in phonology and etymology have modified and refined Bradley's theory. *Lētocaiton* has been proposed as a better rendering of the earliest Celtic form of the native name, and the spelling *Caer Lwytgoed* is now generally used for the site of the battle.[7] Linguistic evidence suggests that the native population at the time of the English settlement spoke Celtic and not Latin.[8] The *feld* in Lichfield may bear a more restricted sense than Bradley imagined: it has been argued that at the time of the English invasions *feld* meant 'common pasture', that the use of the word in an early English place name means that the land to which it refers was common pasture when the English arrived, and that *feld* became incorporated in a place name when the inhabitants of a new settlement began to put part of it under the plough.[9] It may therefore be significant that, according to the author of the Welsh poem, the booty captured by the Welsh at *Caer Lwytgoed* consisted of 1,500 cattle, 80 horses, and five bondsmen.[10] The list suggests a successful raid on a place known to control a large tract of pasture. A further trace of Celtic elements has been found in the local place name Leomansley, probably another Anglo-Celtic compound, with the Celtic *lēmo*, an elm, as part of its first element.[11]

The precise meaning of 'Lichfield' and its historical and topographical significance remain obscure. The simplest explanation is that at the time of English settlement the Celtic-speaking natives were using *Luitcoit* in its original sense, as a forest name. In that sense 'Lichfield' would be 'common pasture in (or beside) grey wood', 'grey' perhaps referring to varieties of tree prominent in the landscape.[12] The Lichfield area long remained wooded, and compound English place names in the area include references to alder, ash, and elm (Aldershawe, Ashmore Brook, Elmhurst).[13]

If the forest-name explanation is accepted the fact that Lichfield is 2 miles from Wall is

---

[1] *Life of Bishop Wilfrid by Eddius Stephanus*, ed. B. Colgrave (1927), pp. x–xi, xiii–xv, 30, 50, also noting (pp. ix–x) that, if the traditional authorship of the *Life* is accepted, the author was probably with Wilfrid at the time of Wulfhere's gift of Lichfield. And see *V.C.H. Staffs.* iii. 2. The only other modern edition of Eddius, *Eddius Stephanus: Het Leven van Sint Wilfrid*, ed. H. Moonen ('S-Hertogenbosch, 1946), uses the Latin text established by Colgrave.

[2] *Venerabilis Baedae Opera Historica*, ed. C. Plummer, i. 207, 350, giving variant spellings from early MSS.; *Bede's Eccl. Hist.* ed. B. Colgrave and R. A. B. Mynors, 336, 558, from a MS. unused by Plummer.

[3] See e.g. F. Liebermann, *Die Heiligen Englands* (Hanover, 1889), 11–12.

[4] See e.g. William of Malmesbury, *De Gestis Pontificum Anglorum* (Rolls Ser.), 16, 41, 68, 216, 277, 307–8, 311; Wm. of Malmesbury, *De Gestis Regum Anglorum* (Rolls Ser.), ii. 352–3. But see below, text on n. 24.

[5] *Eng. Place-Name Elements* (E.P.N.S.), i. 166–7.

[6] *Academy*, 30 Oct. 1886; 9 Nov. 1889; H. Bradley, *Collected Papers*, 117–19 (shortened versions of the articles). For the date of the battle see above, general hist. (Anglo-

Saxon eccl. centre).

[7] I. Williams, 'Marwnad Cynddylan', *Bull. Bd. of Celtic Studies*, vi. 134–41 (original text of the Welsh poem); I. Williams, *Canu Llywarch Hen*, 50–2 (reconstructed text); *Oxford Bk. of Welsh Verse*, ed. T. Parry, pp. 5–7 (reconstructed text in modern orthography).

[8] K. H. Jackson, *Language and Hist. in Early Britain*, 261 and n., 327.

[9] M. Gelling, 'Some thoughts on Staffs. Place-Names', *N. Staffs. Jnl. of Field Studies*, xxi. 14.

[10] The translation in J. P. Clancy, *Earliest Welsh Poetry*, 89, has been followed. The last item in the list (*phum gwriael*) has also been translated as 'five herds of [?] swine' and 'five litters [?]': D. P. Kirby, 'Welsh bards and the Border', *Mercian Studies*, 37; T. Jones, cited by J. Gould, 'Letocetum', *T.S.S.A.H.S.* v. 54.

[11] M. Gelling, 'Evidence of Place-Names', *Medieval Settlement*, ed. P. H. Sawyer, map on p. 202; *Eng. Place-Name Elements*, ii. 23.

[12] Ekwall, *Eng. Place-Names*; M. Gelling, *Signposts to the Past*, 40, 57.

[13] *T.S.S.A.H.S.* vi. 17–18; xxv. 16–17.

irrelevant. If *Luitcoit* was still being used as a settlement name when the English arrived, however, 'Lichfield' could, on the analogy of Chesterfield (Derb.),[14] be *feld* near or belonging to *Luitcoit*. The identity of such a *Luitcoit* remains unknown.[15]

The period in which the name *Lyccidfelth* was coined, and hence the date of English settlement in the area, remains conjectural. The chronology of linguistic change in Primitive Welsh, upon which a phonetic dating of the Celtic element in *Lyccidfelth* depends, is uncertain. An early date, *c.* 600, for the coinage of the name by the English assumes that there had been widespread English settlement in the area for at least two generations before the 660s; presumably Wulfhere would not have offered, and Wilfrid would not have accepted, a cathedral site in an unnamed spot that was remote and inhabited chiefly by semi-independent Britons. A coinage of *c.* 600 is possible, historically and linguistically,[16] but some linguistic anomalies remain, and they are reduced if *Lyccidfelth* is regarded instead as a formation of a later date, in the 660s.

The way in which the *Life* describes the gift may help to elucidate the early development of the place name. The prefix *on-* (or *an-*)[17] attached to the name suggests that what the *Life* records is the king's gift of a place 'in Lichfield' and that 'Lichfield', like some other English place names, may have originated as an area name that was later restricted to the principal place in the area.[18] It that were so, *Lyccidfelth* would presumably be the late 7th-century form of an already existing area name, increasingly used to describe merely the cathedral itself and its immediate environs.

Past etymologies have fostered myth and confusion. Some explanations of the first element in 'Lichfield' were eccentric,[19] but two were widely canvassed and seriously considered. One suggested a derivation from the Old English *līc* (Middle English *lich*), 'a corpse', and the other from Old English words for 'stream' or 'bog' (*laec, lece, lic*).[20] Both were etymologically unsound because they were based on post-Conquest developments of the place name. Lichfield appears as 'Licefelle' and 'Lecefelle' in Domesday[21] and as 'Licefeld' in a document written in the late 1140s.[22] Variations on the last spelling are found at least until the end of the 12th century.[23] By the 1120s, however, the form 'Lichefeld' had appeared.[24] That, with its variations 'Lichesfeld' and 'Licheffeld', was the spelling favoured by the king's clerks.[25] By the mid 13th century it had triumphed, and at that point the first known attempts to explain 'Lichfield' were made. The first element was

taken to be 'lich' or 'liches' and the place name to mean 'the field of corpses', which needed an explanation.[26]

The view apparently held at Lichfield in the 13th century was that the corpses resulted from a battle. Far more influential was a conjecture made by Matthew Paris (d. 1259) of St. Albans abbey. According to him the name, *campus cadaverum*, commemorated the slaughter of 999 Christians, martyred under the emperor Diocletian, 284–305. He linked Lichfield, possibly for the first time, with the fabrications that were accumulating round the figure of St. Alban, the British protomartyr.

All that is known of the historical St. Alban is his name. Geoffrey of Monmouth invented a St. Amphibalus as Alban's supposed catechist, whose converts, according to a later 12th-century *Life* of St. Alban, were massacred in Wales. Matthew Paris identified the place of the massacre as Lichfield. His identification was accepted by at least one 14th-century hagiographer at St. Albans, by John Lydgate in 1439, and by the Warwick antiquary John Rous (d. 1491). Rous's version was preserved by John Leland, and passed into the general currency of antiquarian writing. It seems that it was only then that it aroused any attention at Lichfield.

The story was not taken seriously in medieval Lichfield. There is no evidence of any cult of the martyrs; the story is not mentioned in the surviving cathedral chronicles or in Leland's account of his visit to the city *c.* 1540. In 1549, however, the newly formed city corporation chose to make the alleged massacre the design of its seal. For over a century the Lichfield martyrs featured regularly in the city's official art: on successive corporation seals, in paintings in St. Mary's church, and in a stone bas-relief carved for the guildhall. Attempts were made to use local toponyms to support the story. In the 1570s it was claimed that Boley and Spearhill, alluding to bows and spears,[27] preserved folk memories of the massacre, and in the 1680s land at Elmhurst known as Christianfield was regarded as its site. In 1651 the story of the martyrs, as told by local people, explained to the Quaker George Fox his vision of blood flowing through the streets of Lichfield.

Amphibalus had already been dismissed as a fabrication in 1639 by Archbishop Ussher, who remarked that only the people of Lichfield still believed the massacre story. The fictitious saint was the sole link between Lichfield and the story of a mass martyrdom of early Christians and Ussher's case against him was generally regarded as unanswerable. Nevertheless, some of those who favoured the *lich* derivation of the

[14] *Eng. Place-Name Elements*, ii. 231.
[15] Above, general hist. (early settlement).
[16] Jackson, *Language and History*, 225, 261 and n., 325, 327–8, 329 n., 332–4, 557, 563, 647.
[17] The reading 'in Licitfelda' in *Historiae Britannicae Scriptores XV*, ed. T. Gale (Oxford, 1691), 59, makes sense but has no MS. authority.
[18] J. Campbell, *Essays in Anglo-Saxon Hist.* 112–13.
[19] For some suggestions see *T.S.S.A.H.S.* xxviii. 13.
[20] *Eng. Place-Name Elements*, ii. 10, 22–4.
[21] *V.C.H. Staffs.* iv. 42–3.
[22] *Worcester Cartulary* (P.R.S N.S. xxxviii), p. 102.

[23] *Hist. and Mun. Doc. of Ireland* (Rolls Ser.), 5 ('Licifelt'), 15 ('Licefeld'), 18 ('Licifield'); Gelling, *Signposts*, 54.
[24] Wm. of Malmesbury, *De Gestis Regum*, i. 79, 85, 100.
[25] e.g. *S.H.C.* i. 3, 38, 53, 108, 115, 121; ii (1), 30, 43, 57, 59, 101.
[26] For the rest of this section see *T.S.S.A.H.S.* xxviii. 1–13.
[27] 'Boley' probably means 'wood where logs are obtained' and 'Spearhill' probably derives either from the felling of wood for spear-shafts or from a surname Spere: inf. from Dr. M. Gelling.

place name continued to explain it by stories of Christian martyrdom. The most elaborate version of the story came as late as 1819, following the discovery of human and other remains at Elmhurst a few years earlier. A variant, possibly based on a misinterpretation of the design of the 16th- and 17th-century corporation seals, claimed that the corpses of the place name were those of the army of three Christian kings, defeated at Lichfield by Diocletian. Various spots were suggested as the resting place of the Christian dead, Elmhurst, St. Michael's churchyard, Borrowcop Hill, and the site of the cathedral. The theory, repeated in the 19th century, that all place names containing the element *lich* marked the sites of battlefields revived the view apparently adopted at Lichfield in the 13th century.

The 'stream' or 'bog' derivation was canvassed from the later 17th century. It was pointed out that the suggested derivation was topographically sound, suiting the marshy nature of the city's site, was a rational explanation, and did away with Amphibalus. It found some support among Staffordshire historians, but is etymologically impossible.

POPULATION

IN 1327 there were 108 people in Lichfield assessed for tax amounting to £8 2s. 6d. The number assessed was the highest in the county, but Stafford, with an assessed population of 77, had the higher assessment of £11.[28] Lichfield had 1,024 people assessed for poll tax in 1377.[29] In 1525 there were 391 people liable for tax,[30] while 286 appeared on a muster roll of 1539.[31] In 1563 there were stated to be 400 households in the city.[32] Over 1,100 people died during an outbreak of plague in 1593.[33]

The Protestation Returns of 1642 listed 706 men. Most were grouped by ward, with 89 in Beacon Street, 116 in Bird Street and Sandford Street, 75 in Saddler (otherwise Market) Street, 60 in Conduit Street and Dam Street, 62 in Bore Street, 46 in St. John Street, 28 in Wade Street, 62 in Tamworth Street, 71 in Stowe Street, and 61 in Greenhill.[34] During a further outbreak of plague in 1645-7 there were at least 801 deaths.[35] In 1664 there were 296 householders assessed for hearth tax, with a further 242 too poor to pay.[36] The figures do not include the inhabitants of the Close, where 35 people were assessed in 1666.[37] The detailed census made in 1695 by Gregory King (1648–1712), a native of Lichfield and a pioneer English statistician, recorded 2,833 people in the town and 205 in the Close.[38] The figures given by John Snape in 1781 were respectively 3,555 and 216.[39]

Between 1801 and 1901 Lichfield's population rose from 4,842 to 7,902. In the city centre, covered by St. Mary's parish, there was a decline at the end of the century; from 2,422 in 1801 and 2,382 in 1811, the population had risen to 2,832 by 1881 but had dropped to 2,281 by 1901. The population of the Close rose, with some fluctuation, from 200 in 1801 to 249 in 1901. That of the north part of the city, covered by St. Chad's parish, nearly doubled, from 1,183 in 1801 to 2,057 in 1901, though there was some fluctuation after 1851, with a peak of 2,205 in 1881. The biggest growth was in the south, in St. Michael's parish, where the population tripled from 1,037 to 3,308.[40] The decline in the north and centre after 1881 and a slowing then in the rate of growth in the south were largely the result of the closing of two foundries, a brewery, and a barracks.[41]

During the 20th century the population has more than tripled. It had reached 8,616 by 1911, and although dropping to 8,393 by 1921, it had risen to 8,507 by 1931. It was 10,619 in 1951, 14,087 in 1961, and 22,660 in 1971. In 1987 it was estimated as 28,310.[42]

BOUNDARIES AND GATES

THE limits of the medieval town were marked by a ditch, presumably dug when the town was established in the mid 12th century: Bishop Clinton, 1129–48, is credited with having fortified the town by surrounding it with an embankment. A ditch was recorded in 1208 and probably earlier.[43] On the east of the town the ditch ran from Stowe Pool to the junction of Lombard Street and Stowe Street.[44] From that point it ran south across the end of Stowe Street, along what later became George Lane, across Tamworth Street, and then along the later

[28] *S.H.C.* vii (1), 214, 235–6.
[29] Ibid. 4th ser. vi. 2.
[30] *N. Staffs. Jnl. of Field Studies*, xiv. 45.
[31] *S.H.C.* N.S. iv. 222–6.   [32] *S.H.C.* 1915, 152.
[33] *T.S.S.A.H.S.* xxii. 126; L.J.R.O., D. 27/1/1, ff. 5–7.
[34] H.L.R.O., H.G. 10 (1–2).
[35] Harwood, *Lichfield*, 306; *Elias Ashmole*, ed. C. H. Josten, ii. 389; *S.H.C.* 4th ser. v, p. 73; *Cal. S.P. Dom.* 1645–7, 520.
[36] *S.H.C.* 1950–1, 183 (based on P.R.O., E 179/375/2).
[37] *S.H.C.* 1923, 239–40.
[38] B.L. Harl. MS. 7022, ff. 1–42; *Earliest Classics: Graunt and King*, ed. P. Laslett, 90–1; *D.N.B.*
[39] Above, fig. 4.
[40] *V.C.H. Staffs.* i. 329; Census, 1901.
[41] Lichfield Urban Sanitary Dist. *Rep. of M.O.H. for 1891*, 3 (copy in S.R.O., C/H/1/2/1/2).
[42] Census, 1911–71; Staffs. C.C. *Small Area Population Estimates mid 1987*.
[43] H. Wharton, *Anglia Sacra* (1691), i. 434; *S.H.C.* 1924, pp. 19, 165.
[44] Much of its line in the late 18th century can be followed on fig. 4, above; by then, however, Stowe Pool no longer extended as far west as formerly.

Gresley Row south-west to St. John Street. It crossed that street at a point north of St. John's hospital and ran north-west to the present Friars Alley.[45] It then turned north to Trunkfield brook, following it downstream across Sandford Street and continuing north presumably in the form, once more, of a ditch. 'Gneybon' ditch was recorded in that area in the earlier 13th century,[46] and further north 'le Ellerendych' ran east to a point in Beacon Street where Dr. Milley's hospital was later built opposite the north-west corner of the Close.[47] Land on the north side of Upper Pool certainly lay within the town: a cross by the Beacon Street gate, described in 1360 as lately erected, marked 'the end of the town',[48] and the archdeacon of Chester's house on the corner of Beacon Street and Shaw Lane was described in 1448 as being outside the Close but in the town.[49] The Close itself formed the north-east part of the town, and the Close ditch on the north and east presumably served as the town boundary.

The line of the ditch between Tamworth Street and St. John Street became known as Castle ditch, probably taking its name from an Anglo-Saxon fortification on Borrowcop Hill to the south-east.[50] By the earlier 1340s the eastern part of Castle ditch was used as a lane.[51] In 1781 there were houses along the lane.[52] What remained of Castle ditch survived apparently until 1849.[53] The stretch of ditch north-east of Tamworth Street as far as Stowe Street had been converted into George Lane by the later 16th century.[54]

Gates were set up where roads crossed the ditch. Tamworth Street gate and Sandford Street gate were recorded c. 1200;[55] St. John Street gate in 1208, when it was called Culstubbe gate after the name of the nearby marsh;[56] Beacon Street gate in the mid 13th century;[57] and Stowe Street gate in the later 13th century.[58] Geoffrey de porta, who made a grant of land in the Beacon Street area in the mid 13th century, may have been a gatekeeper.[59] The gateways were probably of simple wooden construction, intended chiefly to control the entry into the town of goods liable to pay toll rather than for defence. No substantial structures are shown on Speed's 1610 plan of Lichfield, and stone gateways would have made defensive sense only if there was also a stone wall between them.

The ditch presumably marked the extent of the town when established in the mid 12th century, but a burgage outside the Sandford Street gate was recorded in a charter of Bishop Muschamp, 1198–1208, and there were burgages outside three other gates in the later 13th century.[60] The townspeople evidently had some rights in the agricultural land which surrounded the town and which in the early 14th century was known as the territory of Lichfield.[61] The jurisdiction of the town court, however, did not extend to that land, and in 1330 presentments relating to a settlement at Gaia beyond the Beacon Street gate were made at Longdon manor court.[62] The corporation established for the town in 1548 probably acquired legal rights to the surrounding land, but the line of the boundary at that date is uncertain: the charter of incorporation states merely that the limits of the city and its suburbs 'should extend as far as in times past they have been reputed and considered to extend'. Mary I's charter of 1553 repeated the formula.

The first known statement of the boundary which included the surrounding land is in a perambulation of the later 18th century.[63] Perambulations of townships adjoining the city made in 1597[64] show that on the east and south Lichfield's boundary was much as it was in the 18th century but that on the north and west the area of the city was less extensive. An increase in area at the expense of Curborough and Elmhurst township on the north and of Pipehill township on the west probably resulted from a dispute with Lord Paget over the city's boundary, apparently settled in 1657.[65] In the 20th century small adjustments have been made to the eastern boundary.[66]

STREET NAMES

THE streets listed below are those within the gates of the medieval town. Surviving streets are given under their modern names. Derivations are taken from *English Place-Name Elements* (E.P.N.S.) and *Middle English Dictionary*, ed. H. Kurath and S. M. Kuhn.[67]

Backcester Lane. Back Lane (1861);[68] Backcester Lane (1900).[69] Originally part of Wade Street, the street presumably derives its modern name from association with the adjacent Bakers Lane. *Bakers Lane.* Baxter Street (1295), Baxter Lane (1413);[70] Bakers Lane (1610);[71] Peas Porridge

---

[45] Harwood, *Lichfield*, pl. facing p. 483.
[46] L.J.R.O., D. 30/VC, B 26.
[47] *V.C.H. Staffs.* iii. 276 n. 5.
[48] L.J.R.O., D. 30/XXV, f. 26; D. 30/VC, palimpsest, i, f. 4v.
[49] Ibid. D. 30/C.A. iv, f. 16v.; L.J.R.O., B/A/1/10, f. 36.
[50] Above, general hist. (Anglo-Saxon eccl. centre).
[51] Bodl. MS. Ashmole 855, p. 186.   [52] Above, fig. 4.
[53] L.J.R.O., D. 20/5/1, 17 Dec. 1849.
[54] Below, street names.
[55] Bodl. MS. Ashmole 1521, p. 36 (2nd nos.).
[56] *S.H.C.* 1924, p. 19; below, street names (St. John Street).
[57] L.J.R.O., D. 30/VC, B 65; above, general hist. (the 13th century).   [58] *S.H.C.* 1924, p. 207.

[59] W.S.L. 55/84/52. [60] *S.H.C.* 1924, pp. 52, 55, 196, 208.
[61] S.R.O., D. 948/3/18, 23, 30; W.S.L., H.M. uncat. 15/8.
[62] S.R.O., D. (W.) 1734/2/1/598, m. 6.
[63] Harwood, *Lichfield*, 356–8.
[64] S.R.O., D. (W.) 1734/2/3/112D.
[65] L.J.R.O., D. 35/bailiffs' accts. 1657–1707, pp. 1, 3.
[66] Above, introduction.
[67] Thanks are offered to Dr. Margaret Gelling for commenting on this article in draft.
[68] P.R.O., RG 9/1972.
[69] O.S. Map 1/2,500, Staffs. LII. 15 (1902 edn.).
[70] L.J.R.O., D. 30/VC, B 113; Bodl. MS. Ashmole 855, p. 197.   [71] Above, fig. 2.

Lane (1698).[72] The original name is derived from Old English *baecestre*, a baker. The name Peas Porridge Lane was still used in 1812,[73] but Bakers Lane was preferred as an alternative in 1761 and was the name given on Snape's plan of 1766.[74]

Beacon Street. Bacoune, Bacunne, Baucune Street (later 13th century);[75] Bacone Street (1307);[76] Beacon Street (1806).[77] The original name, still in use as Bacon Street in 1836,[78] is presumably derived from the word for pig meat. The early 19th-century change to Beacon Street is evidently a polite emendation.

Bird Street. Newebrugge Street (1368);[79] Brigge Street (1400);[80] Brugge Street (1411);[81] Byrd Street (1506);[82] Bryd Street (1518);[83] Bird Street (1669).[84] The earliest recorded name refers to a new bridge built *c.* 1312 at the west end of Minster Pool.[85] The bridge probably replaced an earlier one: a messuage in a street towards the bridge end was recorded in 1281.[86] The spelling Byrd (later Bird) may have been a family name.

Bore Street. Bord Street (1331);[87] Bor Street (1414);[88] Bore Street (1506);[89] Boar Street (1707).[90] The spelling Bore Street was again favoured in 1800.[91] Presumably the name is derived from Middle English *bord* and refers to the boards used for the sale of goods in the market place.

Breadmarket Street. Wommones Chepyng (1388);[92] Breadmarket Street otherwise Womens Cheaping (1689).[93] The earlier name means women's market, evidently a part of the market place where women sold goods. Womens Cheaping was the standard name in 1781, but since the early 19th century the name Breadmarket Street has been preferred.[94]

Butcher Row, see Cook Row.

Cardons Lane. Kardones Lane (1367);[95] Cardons Lane (1498).[96] Named after the Cardon family which held land in the area in the late 13th century,[97] the lane ran west off Beacon Street on the north side of the later Angel Croft hotel.[98] It was known as Guard Lane in 1770.[99] As Cardons Lane once again, it was closed in 1805 when the land was granted by the corporation to

Samuel Barker, a Lichfield banker who lived in the house which later became the hotel.[1]

Chapel Lane. Gutter Lane (1498);[2] Chapell Lane (early 16th century);[3] Gutter Lane otherwise Chappell Lane (1649).[4] The lane lay on the south side of St. Mary's church and was presumably created by the encroachment of buildings on the market place. In the early 19th century Gutter Lane ran between Chapel Lane and Bore Street.[5] The name Gutter Lane is evidently an alternative for *le pendes* or *le pendis*, names recorded in 1316–17 and 1414 as the boundary of land in the Chapel Lane area,[6] and 'the little lane called the Pentes' was recorded in 1476–7.[7] The word means the projecting eaves of a row of buildings.

Cock Alley. Wroo Lane (1335);[8] Slurkockes Lane (1372);[9] Slorecokes Lane otherwise Wroo Lane (early 16th century);[10] Cokke Lane (1522);[11] Cocke Lane (1645);[12] Cock Alley (1882).[13] The lane probably existed in 1308 when Henry and Nicholas de le Wroo witnessed a Lichfield charter.[14] The lane ran east from Bird Street on the north side of the George hotel. Its original name is presumably derived from Middle English *wro*, meaning a corner and referring to the sharp angle in the lane as it turned towards Minster Pool. The alternative name is probably derived from a personal by-name: Reynold Schirloc held land in the area in 1313.[15]

Conduit Street. Cundu' Street (1365–6);[16] Cundyth Street (1386).[17] A conduit stood at the junction of Bore Street and Conduit Street in 1482.[18] In 1386 and 1407 Conduit Street stretched from Bore Street to the dam over Minster Pool.[19] Part of the southern stretch was then known also as Cook Row. In the late 18th century all of the street from Bore Street to the north side of the market place was known as Butcher Row, itself a later name of Cook Row, and the stretch further north was regarded as part of Dam Street.[20] The southern stretch was still known as Butcher Row in 1836, but the name had reverted to Conduit Street by 1851.[21]

Cook Row. Cocus Row (1365–6);[22] Coke Row

[72] L.J.R.O., D. 77/6/1, f. 83.
[73] Ibid. D. 126/min. bk. 1741–1856, p. 177.
[74] Ibid. D. 126/Plan of Lichfield, 1766, by John Snape; S.R.O., D. 615/D/230/2/19, deed of 18 July 1761.
[75] *S.H.C.* 1924, pp. 54, 265; 1939, 90.
[76] S.R.O., D. 661/1/637.
[77] L.J.R.O., VC/A/21, CC 17529, plan 14.
[78] J. Dewhirst, *Map of Lichfield* (1836).
[79] L.J.R.O., D. 30/VC, B 83.
[80] Ibid. D. 30/VC, palimpsest, i, f. 17.
[81] S.R.O. 3764/77.
[82] S.R.O., D. (W.) 1734/2/1/597, m. 21d
[83] Ibid. m. 14.
[84] W.S.L., S.D. Pearson 855.
[85] S.R.O., D. (W.) 1734/J. 2057, mm. 4 (section relating to livery of pence), 5 (necessary expenses).
[86] Bodl. MS. Ashmole 855, p. 213.
[87] *S.H.C.* 1921, 9.
[88] S.R.O., D. (W.) 1734/2/1/597, m. 3.   [89] Ibid. m. 21d.
[90] L.J.R.O., D. 77/9/16.
[91] *Aris's Birmingham Gaz.* 2 June 1800.
[92] Bodl. MS. Ashmole 855, p. 193.
[93] S.R.O., D. 661/2/114.
[94] Stringer, *Lichfield*, 145; above, fig. 4.
[95] B.L. Stowe Ch. 92.
[96] Bodl. MS. Ashmole 864, p. 379.
[97] Ibid. 855, p. 183.
[98] L.J.R.O., VC/A/21, CC 17529, plan 14; above, fig. 2.

[99] L.J.R.O., D. 15/10/2/27, deed of 6 Aug. 1770.
[1] Ibid. D. 15/10/2/27, deed of 27 Nov. 1812; D. 77/5/3, f. 28.
[2] Bodl. MS. Ashmole 864, p. 384.
[3] L.J.R.O., D. 30/VC, palimpsest, i, f. 29v.
[4] Ibid. VC/A/21, CC 162145, ii, f. 37.
[5] Ibid. CC 17529, plan 18.
[6] Bodl. MS. Ashmole 855, p. 186; S.R.O., D. (W.) 1734/2/1/597, m. 1.
[7] Harwood, *Lichfield*, 329.
[8] L.J.R.O., D. 30/VC, B 121.
[9] Ibid. B 91.
[10] Ibid. D. 30/VC, palimpsest, i, f. 18.
[11] S.R.O., D. (W.) 1734/2/1/597, m. 28d.
[12] W.S.L. 329/30.
[13] O.S. Map 1/500, Staffs. LII. 15. 7 (1884 edn.). It was unnamed in 1900: O.S. Map 1/2,500, Staffs. LII. 15 (1902 edn.).
[14] S.R.O. 3764/50.
[15] L.J.R.O., D. 30/K 1.
[16] Bodl. MS. Ashmole 855, p. 180.
[17] L.J.R.O., D. 30/VC, B 53.
[18] Below, public services (water supplies).
[19] L.J.R.O., D. 30/VC, B 53.
[20] Above, fig. 4.
[21] J. Dewhirst, *Map of Lichfield* (1836); White, *Dir. Staffs.* (1834), 157; (1851), 523.
[22] Bodl. MS. Ashmole 855, p. 179.

(later 14th century);[23] Bocherrowend (1549).[24] The row was that stretch of Conduit Street on the east side of St. Mary's church.

Culstubbe Street, see St. John Street

Dam Street. Dom Street (1344);[25] Dam Street (1362).[26] The name is derived from a dam or causeway which gave access from the Close to the town at the east end of Minster Pool.[27] By the late 18th century the name was used for the whole of the street running north from the market place, part of which had formerly been known as Conduit Street.

Friars Alley. Friers Lane (1610);[28] Friers Alley (1781).[29] The alley runs along the north side of the site of the Franciscan friary.

Frog Lane. Frogemerc Street (1297);[30] Froge-mere Street (1315);[31] Frog Lane (1439);[32] Throgmorton Street otherwise Throgge Lane (1596);[33] Frogg Lane otherwise Froggmorton Lane (1664).[34] The earliest names incorporate the Middle English words for frog and for marsh or mere and suggest an area of water-logged land.

George Lane. Yolls Lane (1575);[35] Joles Lane (1599);[36] Joyles Lane (1610);[37] George Lane (1730).[38] The lane follows the line of the town ditch. Its earlier name is probably derived from the Christian name Joel or Juel; it was renamed presumably after George I or II. The earlier name persisted, as Joyles Lane, in the early 19th century.[39]

Guard Lane, see Cardons Lane.

Gutter Lane, see Chapel Lane.

Joles Lane, see George Lane.

Lombard Street. Lumbard otherwise Stowe Street (1633);[40] Lumber, Lumberd Street (later 1640s, 1650s);[41] Lombard Street (1707).[42] The street was formerly that part of Stowe Street which lay within the town gate. The present name is evidently derived by analogy from Lombard Street in London.

Market Street. Robe Street (1336);[43] Saddler Street (1439);[44] Robe Street otherwise Saddler Street (1487);[45] Market Street (1766).[46] The word robe presumably refers to cloth working or selling, as saddler refers to leather working. See also Rope Street.

Pentes Lane, see Chapel Lane.

Quonians Lane. Quoniames Lane (1327);[47] Ko-nyames Lane (1362);[48] Quonyans Lane (1654).[49]

The name Quoniames is recorded in 1283 in Quoniames well[50] and is possibly derived from the Latin word *quoniam*.

Robe Street, see Market Street.

Rope Street. So recorded in 1382–3;[51] last recorded in 1502.[52] The street lay off Bird Street[53] and was possibly a corruption of or an alternative name for Robe Street, or part of it: tithingmen for Rope Street presented at the manor court in 1414, but in the later 15th century their place was taken by tithingmen for Saddler Street (the later name of Robe Street).[54]

Saddler Street, see Market Street.

St. John Street. Culstubbe Street (1297);[55] Seyntiones Street (1411);[56] St. John Street (1695).[57] The original name was taken from the nearby Culstubbe marsh[58] and was derived from Middle English words *collen*, to pull, and *stubbe*, a tree-stump. The later name refers to the hospital of St. John the Baptist established by the early 13th century.[59] In the early 18th century it was normal to distinguish the parts of the street on either side of the town gate as St. John Street within the bars and St. John Street without the bars.[60] The name Upper St. John Street for the latter was in use by the earlier 19th century.[61]

Sandford Street. Sondford Street (1294);[62] Sandford Street (1405).[63] The street was named after a ford over Trunkfield (formerly Sandford) brook. The description Sandford Street beyond the water (*ultra aquam*) was in use by 1485 for the western continuation.[64]

Stowe Street. So recorded in the later 13th century,[65] and a burgage *in vico de Stowe* was recorded in 1258.[66] The street leads to St. Chad's church at Stowe. It originally stretched on either side of the town gate,[67] but that part within the gate was known as Lombard Street in the earlier 17th century.

Tamworth Street. So recorded in 1311.[68] The street is part of the road to Tamworth.

Throgge Lane, Throgmorton Street, see Frog Lane.

Wade Street. So recorded in 1297.[69] The name is presumably derived from Old English *waed*, a ford, suggesting an area of waterlogged land.

Women's Cheaping, see Breadmarket Street.

Wroo Lane, see Cock Lane.

Yolls Lane, see George Lane.

[23] L.J.R.O., D. 77/1, f. 16.
[24] *Cal. Pat.* 1548–9, 391.
[25] L.J.R.O., D. 30/VC, B 59.
[26] B.L. Stowe Ch. 91.
[27] Above, introduction.
[28] Above, fig. 2.
[29] Above, fig. 4.
[30] L.J.R.O., D. 30/VC, B 8.
[31] Ibid. B 66.
[32] *Cal. Close*, 1435–41, 268.
[33] S.R.O., D. 661/4/11/10.
[34] W.S.L., S.D. Pearson 1391.
[35] L.J.R.O., D. 88/rental of Jan. 1574/5, s.v. Rolleston.
[36] S.R.O., D. 661/2/364.
[37] Above, fig. 2.
[38] L.J.R.O., D. 77/9/35.
[39] Ibid. D. 88/lease bk. 1804–22, ff. 11v., 74.
[40] S.R.O., D. 661/2/147.
[41] W.S.L. 350B/30; L.J.R.O., D. 15/11/14/7.
[42] L.J.R.O., D. 77/9/30.
[43] Ibid. D. 30/VC, B 89.
[44] *Cal. Close*, 1435–41, 268.
[45] Bodl. MS. Ashmole 855, p. 201.
[46] L.J.R.O., D. 126/Plan of Lichfield, 1766.
[47] Ibid. D. 30/VC, B 86.
[48] Ibid.
[49] W.S.L. 333/30.
[50] *S.H.C.* 1924, p. 267.
[51] Bodl. MS. Ashmole 855, p. 189.
[52] B.R.L. 435125.
[53] L.J.R.O., D. 30/C.A. i, f. 95.
[54] S.R.O., D. (W.) 1734/2/597.
[55] L.J.R.O., D. 30/VC, B 8.
[56] B. H. Putnam, *Procs. before J.P.s*, p. 309.
[57] L.J.R.O., D. 77/6/1, f. 58.
[58] Below, econ. hist. (agric.).
[59] *V.C.H. Staffs.* iii. 279.
[60] L.J.R.O., D. 77/6/2, f. 12.
[61] White, *Dir. Staffs.* (1834), 154.
[62] S.R.O., D. 661/1/584.
[63] S.R.O. 3005/133.
[64] Ibid. D. (W.) 1734/2/1/597, m. 7d.
[65] Ibid. D. 948/3/10.   [66] *S.H.C.* 1924, p. 49.
[67] L.J.R.O., D. 30/VC, palimpsest, i, ff. 45v., 47.
[68] S.R.O., D. 948/3/22.
[69] L.J.R.O., D. 30/VC, B 8.

DOMESTIC BUILDINGS

FIFTY or more surviving houses in the city, in addition to those in the Close, retain at least part of their timber-framed structure.[70] They are generally of two storeys or of two storeys with attics. Most of the street fronts in the central area, as in Market Street, Bore Street, Lombard Street, and Greenhill, are jettied at each floor, and the roof lines are of continuous gables with ridges at the same level as that of the main roof. The gables either rise from just above the jetty, as at nos. 11 and 13 Market Street, or rest upon a section of wall, as at no. 16 Market Street. Where the framing is exposed the gables are usually the area of most elaborate decoration, in square panels with shaped braces. Several houses have herring-bone studding to the first floor, such as Lichfield House (the Tudor Café) in Bore Street.[71] The survival of original framing to the ground floor is not common, but where it occurs it is undecorated. The few houses with close studding, such as those in Vicars' Close[72] and no. 11 Lombard Street, or with cruck framing, such as no. 11 Greenhill, may be earlier than most of the box-framed buildings, which are probably of the later 16th and earlier 17th century. A number of that period in Stowe Street were demolished in the 1960s.[73]

Despite its local availability there is no evidence for the widespread use of ashlar in domestic buildings. The fact that there were a few specific references to stone houses in the late Middle Ages and the 16th century is probably itself an indication that they were exceptional. A notable example was the house on the corner of Beacon Street and Shaw Lane occupied by the archdeacons of Chester.[74] The present distribution of timber-framed buildings suggests that timber remained the usual walling material until the late 17th century, when it was displaced by brick. As early as around the end of the 15th century brick was used for major work such as St. John's hospital, nos. 23 and 24 the Close, a house on the site of no. 19 the Close, and the clerestory of St. Chad's church at Stowe. In 1670 it was used for Minors's School.[75] Its general use for houses may have begun with the building in 1682 of the house for the headmaster of the grammar school, no. 45 St. John Street, now part of the offices of Lichfield District council.[76] Built of dark red brick, it is, of two storeys with attics and has bracketed eaves and a hipped roof. The front is of four bays, and the plan is roughly square, with the stairs at the centre. The interior was rearranged in the 18th century; original fittings, mostly plank-built

doors, survive only on the upper floors. The Deanery (1707) is also of brick, but, like the bishop's palace, a stone building of 1687, it belongs more to the country-house tradition than to town architecture.

The notable feature of Lichfield houses in the earlier 18th century is the occurrence of baroque elements in the decoration of the street façades. The most elaborate is that of Donegal House in Bore Street, which was built in 1730 for James Robinson, a mercer, probably to the design of Francis Smith of Warwick.[77] The front is of five bays and three storeys on a basement, and the ends are marked by pilasters which support a heavily moulded cornice. The central doorway has a segmental pediment on Tuscan columns and supports the cill and architrave of the central window on the first floor. The window has a triangular pediment which similarly runs into the architrave of the corresponding window on the second floor. That has a shaped head flanking a prominent keystone which runs into the cornice. The other windows are without architraves, but they have elaborately shaped stone heads with tabled keystones; those on the two upper floors also have aprons below the cills. Several original panelled rooms and an original staircase survive.

Elements of the Donegal House elevation occur on several other houses but nowhere else with such richness. Less elaborate shaped window heads are features of nos. 8–10 Bird Street, no. 17 Bird Street, and no. 15 Market Street. The use of stone architraves to emphasize the central bay can be seen at nos. 37–39 Lombard Street, no. 20 Beacon Street, and nos. 12–14 Conduit Street where the second-floor keystone rises into a heavily moulded cornice. Concurrently there was a plainer style which continued the late 17th-century tradition of plain fronts with dentil cornices below steeply pitched roofs, such as that at nos. 24–26 Bore Street.

After the mid 18th century the most fashionable element of Lichfield house fronts was the venetian window, which was either centrally placed over the entrance, as at no. 73 St. John Street, or used to light the principal rooms on the ground and first floors, as at no. 67 St. John Street (Davidson House) and Darwin House in Beacon Street.[78] The latter, dating from c. 1760, has two other features which were common in Lichfield at the time and may have continued for the rest of the century, namely a string course which continues the line of the first-floor cills and a shallow cornice supported on curved brackets. By the later 18th century roof pitches

---

[70] Many have been recorded: S.R.O., Mf. 121. Mr. A. G. Taylor of the Staffs. C.C. Planning and Development Dept. is thanked for commenting on this section and providing additional material.
[71] Below, plate 18.   [72] Below, plate 8.
[73] National Monuments Rec. of Royal Com. on Hist. Monuments, photographic colln.; above, general hist.
[74] L.J.R.O., D. 30/XXIV, f. 30; D. 30/C.A. i, ff. 65v.– 66; D. 88, rentals of 1555–6 and Jan. 1574/5; below, manor (estates of cathedral clergy).

[75] V.C.H. Staffs. iii. 278, 286; below, cathedral and close; churches; education.
[76] L.J.R.O., D. 126/acct. bk. 1663–1805, accts. 1681–2, 1682–3; V.C.H. Staffs. vi. 160; above, general hist. (20th century).
[77] Reade, Johnsonian Gleanings, ix. 104; L.J.R.O., D. 77/3/1, f. 6v.; date stone on south side; below, plate 18. It is ascribed to Smith on stylistic grounds by Professor A. H. Gomme of Keele University in a personal communication.
[78] Below, plates 16 and 19.

FIG. 8

were generally low, as a result of the use of slate instead of tile, and even if not hidden by a parapet they are hardly visible from the street.

Sophisticated neo-classical decoration is not common in the city. It appears first at the George hotel in Bird Street, which has been described as one of the best late 18th-century hotel buildings in the country.[79] It has a front of three storeys and eleven bays. The five central bays are rusticated on the ground floor, where they incorporate the former carriage entrance, and they have pilasters extending up the second and third floors, marking the assembly room within.

The simplest of styles was used for most houses in the early 19th century. Cornices surviving from that period are shallow and moulded; there are no architraves to the windows, most of which do not have a keystone; the entrance is framed by a wooden doorcase which usually has a plain fanlight. Stuccoed brickwork, which was used at Westgate House in Beacon Street probably in the later 18th century, was occasionally used for architectural effect in the early 19th century. Examples are the former National Westminster Bank on the corner of Bird Street and the Friary and no. 28 St. John Street, now St. John's preparatory school, which also has a ground-floor colonnade along the street front.[80] Lichfield is unusual in having no regency terraces; even a designed pair of houses, such as nos. 48–50 Beacon Street, is uncommon. The Gothic Revival of the 19th century made little impact on the city's domestic architecture. There is a terrace of cottages with Gothic-style windows in Levetts Fields, built by the mid 1830s, and Minster Cottage in Minster Pool Walk is a small Gothic villa of the 1840s in painted stucco with ornamental bargeboards.[81] The multi-coloured brick style of the mid and later 19th century, which was used in the Corn Exchange of 1850,[82] was not adopted for houses in Lichfield.

In the four main streets of the town centre (Market Street, Bore Street, Wade Street, and Frog Lane) it is noticeable that there is no planned rear access to individual properties. Many still have service passages, usually at the side of the site and so leaving the maximum clear frontage for the house or shop. A few passages are wide enough for a cart, but most are sufficient only for a pedestrian.

COMMUNICATIONS

THE Roman Ryknild Street ran through the south-east part of the present city, where its line is preserved by modern roads.[83] The name was used in the mid 1270s and in 1442, but in the 14th and early 15th century the road was called Stony Street.[84] Before the boundary changes of 1934 and 1980 much of the city boundary followed the line of the road. North-east of Lichfield the line is followed by the Burton road which was of importance by the 12th century as part of the route between the south-west and the north-east of the country. It was used in 1175

[79] Pevsner, *Staffs.* 193. [80] Below, plate 17.
[81] J. Dewhirst, *Map of Lichfield* (1836); L.J.R.O., B/A/15/Lichfield, St. Mary, no. 177.
[82] Below, econ. hist. (markets and fairs).
[83] *T.S.S.A.H.S.* xix. 1–4.
[84] Bodl. MS. Ashmole 855, pp. 182, 189; L.J.R.O., D. 30/VC, B 16, 101, 112; S.R.O., D. (W.) 1734/2/1/598, mm. 22, 30.

and 1181 by Henry II and on many occasions by John and Henry III, all of them staying at Lichfield.[85] It is indeed probable that Ryknild Street continued to be important after the Romano-British period and therefore influenced the choice of Lichfield as the site for an episcopal seat in the later 7th century.[86] Further south it crossed Watling Street near Wall.

The medieval route from London to Chester and the north-west also ran through Lichfield, bringing Henry III there many times.[87] It approached the city from the south over Longbridge, mentioned in the 14th century and presumably then a causeway across marshy ground by Darnford brook.[88] In 1575 the city bailiffs paid for two days' work at Longbridge 'to cast down the way' in preparation for Elizabeth I's visit to Lichfield.[89] Its course from the city's southern boundary to the bridge was realigned c. 1700. During a law suit of the 1740s Richard Dyott of Freeford stated that originally the road ran across 'low and loamy land' to the west and was adequate so long as carriage was mainly by packhorse. With the increase of inland trade, 'particularly the pot trade from Burslem in Staffordshire and the manufactures between Manchester and London and other places', the road became 'cut and galled' by wheeled traffic. It had a further disadvantage in that it 'went with an elbow'. The adjoining Old field, which was used for grazing sheep, was higher ground, and 'people gradually left the old road and went directly over the higher ground ... and by degrees made that the common road'.[90]

In the north of the city the route followed Beacon Street, described as the road to Stafford in the later 13th century,[91] and Cross in Hand Lane. It branched off to follow the lane running along the north-west boundary which was still known as Old London Road in 1835. The cross with the hand which stood at the fork by the 15th century was probably a direction post.[92] In 1770 the course of the road was straightened to avoid the hollow way in Cross in Hand Lane by means of a new line to the east, the present Stafford Road.[93]

In 1729 Lichfield became the hub of a system of turnpike roads. A trust was established that year to administer the Staffordshire section of the London–Chester road, the Lichfield–Burton road, the Lichfield–Birmingham road as far as Shenstone, and the Lichfield–Walsall road

as far as Muckley Corner on Watling Street.[94] The road branching from the London–Chester road and continuing to High Bridges at Handsacre in Armitage was also included. Originally its route through the city followed Wheel Lane and Grange Lane, but under an Act of 1783 the route was changed to Stafford Road and Featherbed Lane on the north-western boundary.[95] The Lichfield–Tamworth road was turnpiked in 1770.[96] The sections of the turnpike roads through the city centre were exempted from the jurisdiction of the turnpike trustees, who in 1757 declared them to be 'the streets within the bar gates'.[97] The Lichfield Improvement Act of 1806 gave the improvement commissioners control of those streets and of the streets in the suburbs; in 1833 the suburbs were defined by the trustees as extending to the Wheel inn in Beacon Street on the north, the Roman Catholic chapel in St. John Street on the south, St. Michael's lich gates on the east, and the brook in Queen Street on the west.[98] The Lichfield part of the London–Chester road was disturnpiked in 1870, along with Featherbed Lane. The Shenstone road was disturnpiked in 1875, the Burton and Muckley Corner roads in 1879, and the Tamworth road in 1882.[99]

A tollhouse had been established by the early 1730s on the corner of Beacon Street and Wheel Lane with gates across each road.[1] People coming into the city from a short distance outside objected to having to pay tolls there, and in 1766 an attempt was made to replace the house and gates with two others on the city boundary.[2] The attempt was unsuccessful, but in 1782 the gates were removed and replaced by others further north outside the city.[3]

The bridge in Bird Street was at first too narrow for coaches, which had to go round by Bore Street, Lombard Street, Stowe Street, and Gaia Lane. The bridge was widened by the Conduit Lands trustees in the late 1760s so that coaches could use Bird Street.[4] It remained unsatisfactory, and the approach along Bird Street was still narrow. The 1806 Act empowered the improvement commissioners to rebuild the bridge. They lacked the funds to do so, and in 1815 another Act established a special commission to rebuild it.[5] Work began in 1816 to the design of Joseph Potter the elder and was finished in 1817. To raise the necessary money a tollgate was erected near the junction of Beacon

[85] V.C.H. Staffs. ii. 275; R. W. Eyton, Court, Household, and Itin. of Hen. II, 193, 242; Rot. Litt. Pat. (Rec. Com.), itin. of John; Cal. Chart. R. 1226–57, 213, 370; Close R. 1234–7, 141–2, 501–2, 569–71; Cal. Lib. 1251–60, 6–7.
[86] Above, general hist. (Anglo-Saxon eccl. centre).
[87] V.C.H. Staffs. ii. 275, 277; Cal. Chart. R. 1226–57, 472; Close R. 1237–42, 330; Cal. Lib. 1240–5, 252, 323; 1251–60, 388–92.
[88] L.J.R.O., D. 30/VC, B 38; below, econ. hist. (agric.).
[89] J. Nichols, Progresses and Public Processions of Queen Elizabeth (1821), iv (1), 73.
[90] S.R.O., D. 661/2/801, pp. 12–13; L.J.R.O., D. 44/4; below, econ. hist. (agric.).
[91] S.H.C. 1924, pp. 55, 57.
[92] J. Ogilby, Britannia (1675), pl. between pp. 44 and 45; Bodl. MS. Ashmole 1521, p. 86; S.R.O., D. (W.) 3222/191/21, p. 6; below, Burntwood, growth of settlement.
[93] Above, fig. 1; L.J.R.O., D. 15/2/2, 6 May, 17 June 1766, 6 Apr. 1773. For a proposal for a similar line in 1748 see ibid. 7 Jan., 4 Feb. 1747/8.

[94] S.H.C. 4th ser. xiii. 97–8.
[95] Above, fig. 1; L.J.R.O., D. 15/2/3, 2 Dec. 1783.
[96] S.H.C. 4th ser. xiii. 110.
[97] L.J.R.O., D. 15/2/2, 6 Dec. 1757.
[98] Clayton, Coaching City, 65–6; L.J.R.O., D. 15/2/4, 6 Apr. 1833.
[99] Annual Turnpike Acts Continuance Act, 1868, 32 & 33 Vic. c. 90; 1875, 38 & 39 Vic. c. 194; 1878, 41 & 42 Vic. c. 62; 1879, 42 & 43 Vic. c. 46; L.J.R.O., D. 15/2/5, 1 Mar. 1870, 7 Sept. 1875, 10 June, 16 Dec. 1879.
[1] S.R.O., D. 603/K/5/19, f. 90; L.J.R.O., D. 15/2/1, 23 June, 6 Dec. 1744.
[2] S.R.O., D. 603/K/5/19, ff. 88–90; L.J.R.O., D. 15/2/2, 5 Apr., 6 May, 17 June 1766.
[3] L.J.R.O., D. 15/2/3, 6 Nov. 1781, 5 Mar. 1782; below, Curborough and Elmhurst, introduction.
[4] Clayton, Coaching City, 10; L.J.R.O., D. 126/min. bk. 1741–1856, pp. 28, 30; acct. bk. 1663–1805, accts. 1768–9, 1769–70, 1770–1.
[5] 55 Geo. III, c. 29 (Local and Personal).

Street and Gaia Lane; it was still in use in 1824.[6] In addition Bird Street was widened.[7]

Other road improvements were carried out under an Act of 1832.[8] On the Muckley Corner road Queen Street (so named by 1841) and its Walsall Road extension were built to bypass the curve along Lower Sandford Street and through Leomansley; one aim was to make access to the city easier for coal carts.[9] On the Burton road Trent Valley Road and its continuation into Streethay replaced the route along Burton Old Road and part of the former Ryknild Street.[10] Several relief roads have been built in the 20th century.[11]

Lichfield was a post town on the route between London and Ireland by the later 1570s.[12] It was on the route of coaches between London and Chester in the late 1650s.[13] James Rixam, who was junior bailiff in 1656–7, operated as a carrier between Lichfield and London in 1662, and in 1681 William Old ran a service to London and back every three weeks.[14] The main coaching inns were the Swan and the George, both in Bird Street. The Swan existed as an inn by 1362, although the present building dates from the late 18th century; the London coach called there by 1662. It was closed as an hotel in 1988.[15] The George existed by 1498, and it too is a late 18th-century building.[16]

In the earlier 1790s the three principal inns were the George, the Swan, and the Talbot on the corner of Bird Street and Bore Street. Converted from a private house between 1760 and 1772, the Talbot, unlike the other two, catered only 'for gentlemen on horseback'. The London–Chester and London–Liverpool mail coaches passed through in each direction every day. Another coach between London and Liverpool also passed through daily in each direction, while the Royal Chester coach from London called every other weekday and returned on the following days. There was a coach running from Birmingham to Sheffield and back six days a week, and another from Birmingham to Manchester and back three days a week. A waggon left for London from the Goat's Head in Breadmarket Street every Monday.[17]

In the mid 1830s Lichfield was still much frequented by travellers, both on the route between London and Liverpool (rather than Chester) and on that between Birmingham and the West Riding of Yorkshire. The coaching inns were the George, the Swan, the Talbot, the Old Crown in Bore Street, in existence by 1722, and the King's Head in Bird Street, known as such by 1694 but in existence as the Antelope by 1495 and later called the Bush. Carriers operated from the King's Head, the Goat's Head, the Turk's Head in Sandford Street, the Scales in Market Street, the Dolphin and the Woolpack, both in Bore Street, and the Coach and Horses and the Lord Nelson, both in St. John Street.[18]

The railways put at end to Lichfield's long-distance coaches, even before there was a railway through the city. The last such coach through Lichfield, the Chester mail, was discontinued in 1838. Instead coaches were introduced that year running to the railway station at Stafford and to the unfinished London–Birmingham line at Denbigh Hall near Bletchley (Bucks.).[19] In 1841 there were omnibuses to Birmingham, Rugeley, and Tamworth, and although in 1844 there were still coaches to Birmingham, Wolverhampton, Stafford, and Uttoxeter, by 1850 there were only omnibuses. One ran to Birmingham, and the others ran from the George and the Swan to Lichfield's two railway stations.[20] The Birmingham omnibus ceased running c. 1870, and by 1912 the George omnibus served City station and that from the Swan Trent Valley station.[21]

The first Lichfield motor bus, running to Whittington, was introduced in 1913 by Jones & Co., a firm of motor-car hirers in Bird Street. By 1916 there was a service to Tamworth from Market Square, and in the earlier 1920s motor buses ran from Lichfield to many parts of the county.[22] A service was introduced between Lichfield and Walsall in 1927 and one between Lichfield and Hanley in 1931.[23] The omnibus from the Swan ceased to operate in 1923, and that from the George evidently stopped running soon afterwards.[24] Buses were transferred from Market Square to a bus station in the Friary opened in 1952 as a temporary measure; the Walsall buses continued to use a terminus out-

[6] Clayton, *Coaching City*, 73–6 and pl. between pp. 44 and 45; *Lichfield Mercury*, 14 July 1815; 6 Sept. 1816; 19 and 26 Dec. 1823; 2 Jan. 1824; 1 Apr., 4 Nov. 1825; L.J.R.O., D. 15/2/13.

[7] Stringer, *Lichfield*, 111; S.R.O., D. 4566/98, deed of 7 Aug. 1817.

[8] *S.H.C.* 4th ser. xiii. 98.

[9] L.J.R.O., D. 15/2/4, 3 July, 7 and 24 Aug., 18 Sept. 1832, 6 Apr., 7 May 1833, 2 Dec. 1834, 2 May 1837; P.R.O., HO 107/1008; *Dyott's Diary*, ed. R. W. Jeffery, ii. 158.

[10] L.J.R.O., D. 15/2/4, 2 Dec. 1834, 7 Apr. 1835, 2 May 1837, 6 Mar. 1838; S.R.O., D. 661/11/2/3/1/13, 11 June 1836; *Dyott's Diary*, ed. Jeffery, ii. 197; J. Dewhirst, *Map of Lichfield* (1836).

[11] Above, general hist.

[12] *S.H.C.* 1950–1, 188; *Issues of the Exchequer* (Rec. Com.), 359.

[13] *S.H.C.* 1934 (1), 52; W.S.L., S. MS. 370/viii/1, pp. 131, 134–5, 137 (transcr. of advertisements in *Mercurius Politicus* 1657–9); *Life, Diary, and Corresp. of Sir Wm. Dugdale*, ed. W. Hamper, 139–41, 146–7.

[14] *Elias Ashmole*, ed. C. H. Josten, iii. 851; T. DeLaune, *Present State of Lond.* (1681), 418.

[15] Below, manor (estates of cathedral clergy); W.S.L., S.

MS. 370/viii/1, p. 162 (transcr. of advertisement in *The Kingdome's Intelligencer*, 15–22 Sept. 1662); *Lichfield Mercury*, 11 Nov. 1988, p. 21.

[16] Bodl. MS. Ashmole 864, p. 383; above, domestic buildings.

[17] *Univ. Brit. Dir.* iii (1794), 609. For the Talbot 1760–72 see Clayton, *Coaching City*, 25–7, based on L.J.R.O., D. 22/1/1–27.

[18] White, *Dir. Staffs.* (1834), 61, 162; Pigot, *Nat. Com. Dir.* (1835). For the Old Crown see also *Lond. Gaz.* 1–4 Sept. 1722, and for the King's Head S.R.O., D. (W.) 1851/8/41; B.L. Stowe Ch. 625; L.J.R.O., D. 15/11/14/1.

[19] Clayton, *Coaching City*, 20–1, 86–7; *Dyott's Diary*, ed. Jeffery, ii. 271, 273, 275; L.J.R.O., D. 15/2/4, 1 May 1838; *Staffs. Advertiser*, 14 Apr. 1838.

[20] Pigot, *Nat. Com. Dir.* (1841); Wesley, *Dir. Burton* (1844), 27–8; *P.O. Dir. Staffs.* (1850).

[21] *P.O. Dir. Staffs.* (1868; 1872); *Kelly's Dir. Staffs.* (1912).

[22] *Kelly's Dir. Staffs.* (1912; 1916; 1924); L.J.R.O., D. 54/1.

[23] *Lichfield Mercury*, 22 Apr. 1927, p. 4; 27 Feb. 1931, p. 1.

[24] Ibid. 12 Oct. 1923, p. 5; 29 Feb. 1924, p. 1; *Kelly's Dir. Staffs.* (1924).

side City station.[25] A permanent station was opened in the new stretch of Birmingham Road opposite the station *c.* 1964.[26]

In 1759 a canal was proposed from Minster Pool or Stowe Pool to the Trent at Weston (Derb.), but the scheme came to nothing.[27] In the 1760s and 1770s there were two other schemes, also unsuccessful, for canals via Lichfield linking Birmingham and the Black Country with the Trent and Mersey Canal, completed in 1777.[28] There was, however, a wharf on the Trent and Mersey at King's Bromley which served the city, and the opening of the canal greatly reduced the cost of carriage between Manchester and Lichfield.[29] The stretch of the Coventry Canal east of the city was completed in 1788, and by 1817 there was a wharf on the Burton road on the Streethay–Whittington boundary.[30] The Wyrley and Essington Canal, opened from the Birmingham Canal near Wolverhampton to the Coventry Canal at Huddlesford in Whittington in 1797, ran through the south side of the city. By 1799 cheap coal was being sold at a wharf provided by the corporation.[31] In 1817 it was stated that an average of 606 boats a year were unloading 10,302 tons of goods at the six or more wharfs in the city; the two busiest were those on either side of London Road.[32] The Lichfield stretch of the canal was closed in 1954, but for many years previously it had been used only by maintenance boats. Part of it was filled in soon after its closure.[33]

The Trent Valley Railway from Stafford to the Birmingham–London line at Rugby was opened along the north-east boundary of the city in 1847, with a station and station master's house north of the Burton road on the Streethay side of the boundary. The railway's distance from the city centre seems to have been the result of geographical considerations rather than local opposition.[34] In 1849 the South Staffordshire Railway from Walsall to the Midland Railway at Wychnor, in Tatenhill, was opened through Lichfield. It had a station, City, east of St. John Street and another, Trent Valley Junction, near the point in Streethay where it crossed the Trent Valley Railway.[35] City station was rebuilt in 1884 when the line from Birmingham to Sutton Coldfield was extended to join the South Staffordshire line at Lichfield.[36] The bridge by which the railway crosses St. John Street dates from 1849. It was designed by Thomas Johnson of Lichfield to evoke a city gate, with battlements, heraldic decoration, and side towers containing multi-arched pedestrian ways. It was extensively altered when the track was widened for the line from Birmingham; the pedestrian ways were removed in 1969.[37]

The two stations in Streethay were replaced in 1871 by a single Trent Valley station where the lines cross. Low Level and High Level platforms served the Trent Valley and the South Staffordshire lines respectively.[38] The Trent Valley station of 1847 was retained as the station master's house; it was demolished in 1971.[39] The High Level was closed in 1965; its buildings had been burnt down some years before and had not been replaced. The Low Level buildings were demolished in 1969 and rebuilt on a modest scale.[40] The line to Walsall was closed for passengers in 1965 and for freight in 1984, although it continued to serve an oil depot at Brownhills.[41] In 1988 the Trent Valley High Level platforms were reopened for passengers and the service between Birmingham and Lichfield City was extended there.[42]

THE CATHEDRAL AND THE CLOSE

THE CATHEDRAL. The cathedral church of St. Mary and St. Chad, built of dark red sandstone, comprises a Lady Chapel of three bays with a three-sided east end, an aisled choir of eight bays, a central tower and spire, north and south transepts each of two bays, an aisled nave of eight bays, and two west towers with spires.[43] A two-storeyed building, formerly a chapel, stands in the angle of the south choir aisle and south transept. A chapter house with a library above stands beyond the north choir aisle, from which it is approached through a vestibule.

[25] *Lichfield Mercury*, 23 May 1952, p. 3.
[26] *Lichfield City Council Mins.* 1963–4, pp. 99, 182, 377, 482, 527.
[27] *T.S.S.A.H.S.* xxiii. 109–11; W.S.L., M. 727.
[28] C. Hadfield, *Canals of W. Midlands* (1969), 20, 63, 70; *V.C.H. Staffs.* ii. 292 n.; W.S.L., S. MS. 370/viii/5, pp. 276–9 (transcript of letter in *Lond. Chron.* 8–11 Mar. 1766).
[29] S.R.O., D. 593/F/3/12/2/4, receipt of 5 Aug. 1777 and King's Head receipts; D. 593/F/3/12/2/7, receipts of 13 May, 21 July, 21 Sept. 1786; Hadfield, *Canals of W. Midlands*, 36.
[30] Below, Streethay, introduction.
[31] *T.S.S.A.H.S.* i. 29–30.
[32] L.J.R.O., D. 35/St. Michael's poor rate bk. 1817.
[33] *T.S.S.A.H.S.* i. 38–9.
[34] C. R. Clinker, *Railways of W. Midlands 1808–1954*, 18; Clayton, *Cathedral City*, 22–4; Laithwaite, *Conduit Lands Trust*, 30; L.J.R.O., B/A/15/Streethay, no. 102.
[35] Clinker, *Railways of W. Midlands*, 19. For the site of Trent Valley Junction station see Clayton, *Cathedral City*,

46 (based on O.S. Map 1″, sheet 62 NW., 1857 edn.: inf. from Mr. Clayton).
[36] Clinker, *Railways of W. Midlands*, 43; *Lichfield Mercury*, 18 July 1884, p. 7; 7 Nov. 1884, p. 5.
[37] Sherlock, *Ind. Arch. Staffs.* 179–80; below, plate 29.
[38] C. R. Clinker, *Clinker's Reg. of Closed Passenger Stations and Goods Depots*, 8, 166, 178.
[39] *Lichfield Mercury*, 30 May 1969, p. 5; Clayton, *Cathedral City*, 27.
[40] Clinker, *Closed Passenger Stations*, 75; *Lichfield Mercury*, 8 Aug. 1969, p. 1; 15 Aug. 1969, p. 1; 12 Sept. 1969, p. 5; 16 Oct. 1970, p. 1.
[41] *Lichfield Mercury*, 23 Mar. 1984, p. 5; Clinker, *Closed Passenger Stations*, 75.
[42] *Lichfield Mercury*, 9 Sept. 1988, pp. 13, 58; 2 Dec. 1988, p. 5.
[43] This section is concerned only with the history of the cathedral as a building. For an account of its institutional history see *V.C.H. Staffs.* iii. 140–99. Dr. Warwick Rodwell, consultant archaeologist to the dean and chapter, is thanked for his help.

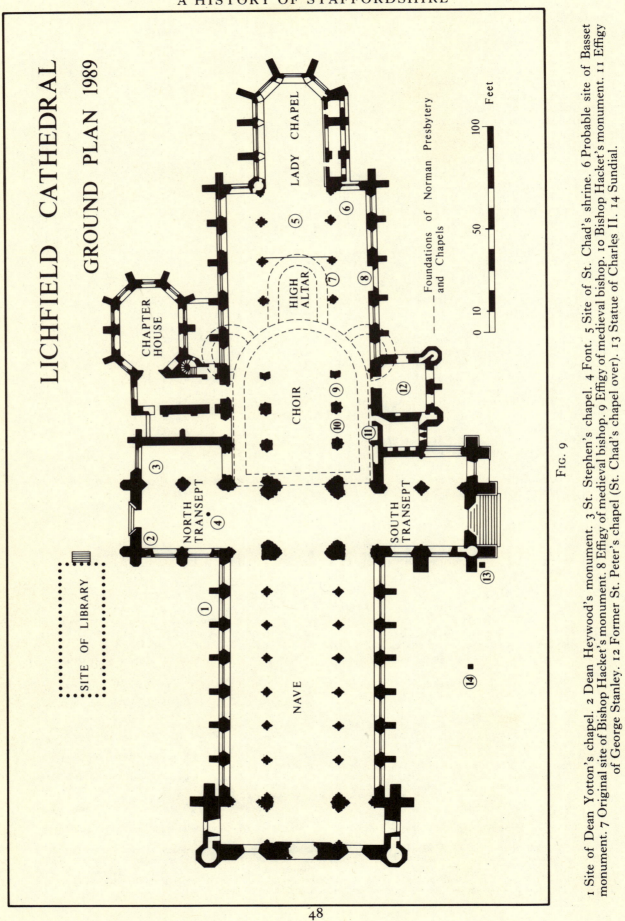

LICHFIELD CATHEDRAL
GROUND PLAN 1989

SITE OF LIBRARY

CHAPTER HOUSE

NORTH TRANSEPT

NAVE

CHOIR

HIGH ALTAR

LADY CHAPEL

SOUTH TRANSEPT

Foundations of Norman Presbytery and Chapels

Feet

0   10   50   100

FIG. 9

1 Site of Dean Yotton's chapel. 2 Dean Heywood's monument. 3 St. Stephen's chapel. 4 Font. 5 Site of St. Chad's shrine. 6 Probable site of Basset monument. 7 Original site of Bishop Hacket's monument. 8 Effigy of medieval bishop. 9 Effigy of medieval bishop. 10 Bishop Hacket's monument. 11 Effigy of George Stanley. 12 Former St. Peter's chapel (St. Chad's chapel over). 13 Statue of Charles II. 14 Sundial.

The cathedral established by St. Chad, bishop 669–72, was presumably the church dedicated to St. Mary near which he was buried. In 700 his remains were transferred to a funerary church, apparently dedicated to St. Peter.[44] The two churches probably stood near each other. The cathedral may have been in the area later occupied by a side chapel on the north side of the presbytery of the Norman cathedral. The site of the chapel, which corresponds to part of the present north choir aisle, was believed in the 18th century to be the burial place of two Mercian kings.[45] The funerary church may have stood where there was later a side chapel on the the south side of the Norman presbytery; that chapel was replaced in the earlier 13th century by one with an altar dedicated to St. Peter,[46] a name possibly significant in view of the likely dedication of the Saxon funerary church. Nothing survives of either church apart from a decorated cross-shaft set into the foundations on the north side of the nave.[47] It is not known when the churches were incorporated into one cathedral building.

Bishop Limesey, 1085–1117, is reported to have used money obtained from Coventry priory for constructing 'great buildings' at Lichfield, perhaps even before he moved the see to Coventry in 1102.[48] His successor Robert Peche, 1121–6, was reportedly also the initiator of 'great buildings' at Lichfield. Their work was probably completed by Bishop Clinton, 1129–48. The Norman church was cruciform in plan and had an apsidal presbytery extending from the central crossing to about the middle of the fourth bay of the present choir. A shrine of St. Chad presumably stood near the high altar. A narrow ambulatory or processional way round the presbytery provided access to the two side chapels already noted and to an elongated apsidal chapel at the east end. In the later 12th century, possibly the 1160s, the eastern chapel was replaced by a three-bayed rectangular chapel which extended nearly as far as the first bay of the present choir. An altar stood in line with the second bay, and under it was buried a font apparently used as a relic container. The chapel was encased, possibly in the 1170s, in a large square-ended presbytery which had a row of four chapels at its east end. The new work was evidently intended to provide greater freedom of movement around an improved shrine of St. Chad. A new choir of seven bays was built to the west in the 1190s, totally encasing the presbytery. The outer wall of the choir was misaligned on the north. Possibly the fault occurred because work at the east end was commenced before the demolition of the side chapel. That chapel, as already noted, may have been a place of special religious significance because of royal burials and its removal postponed on that ac-

count until it was reached by the new work. The later stages of the work were probably completed by Bishop Muschamp, 1198–1208, who was the first post-Conquest bishop to be buried at Lichfield.[49] The chapel on the south side of the choir was replaced by a single-storeyed, three-bayed chapel with a doorway through the easternmost bay almost opposite the Norman high altar. The chapel was presumably intended for use as a sacristy. The Easter sepulchre recorded in Bishop Nonant's statutes of c. 1190 was probably a movable structure.[50]

The rebuilding of the Norman cathedral was begun in the early 13th century with the construction of a clerestory in the choir and of a central tower. The tower had a lantern with windows set above an arcade and later obscured by vaulting. Work on both transepts was under way in Bishop Cornhill's time, 1215–23, and continued in the 1230s: royal grants of timber and stone for the new work were made in 1221, 1231, 1235, and 1238. Henry III was at Lichfield in 1235, 1237, and 1241; he evidently admired the high wooden roof of the 'new work' there, carved and painted to resemble stonework, and in 1242 he ordered the construction of a similar roof for his chapel at Windsor.[51] The north transept was presumably completed, or nearing completion, in 1241 when Bishop Pattishall was buried there.[52] The north doorway was decorated externally with figures, including in the outer moulding on the east a tree of Jesse and on the west St. Chad and the apostles.[53] The south transept, finished about the same time, had a window designed to represent St. Catherine's wheel.[54]

The chapel off the south choir aisle was rebuilt in the 1230s or 1240s, presumably at the direction of Dean Mancetter who was buried there in 1254. It comprised two storeys and a crypt; on the ground floor there was an altar, dedicated to St. Peter, set on a dais along the east wall.[55] A south-west turret incorporated a deep pit which may have been a well, and stairs in a south-east turret led to a barrel-vaulted crypt. The upper storey may have accommodated relics of St. Chad. Access to it was presumably by a staircase from the south choir aisle and through what had formerly been a window in the aisle wall. There may also have been a balcony in front of the entrance, from which the relics could be displayed. Not long after the chapel was finished, a ground-floor chamber was added to the west; it was originally entered through a doorway near the south-west turret. Three large wall cupboards in the chamber were presumably used for storing either relics or muniments. In the mid 1250s and the 1340s St. Peter's chapel was used for transacting business, which probably included sittings of the consistory court.[56]

[44] Above, general hist. (Anglo-Saxon eccl. centre).
[45] Ibid.; *T.S.S.A.H.S.* xxviii. 61.
[46] Below (this section).
[47] *T.S.S.A.H.S.* xxii. 62 and pl. I.
[48] Para. based on *V.C.H. Staffs.* iii. 143; *Arch. Jnl.* lxix. 1–24; Friends of Lichfield Cath. *50th Ann. Rep.* (1987), 10–14.
[49] Above, general hist. (the 12th century).

[50] Dugdale, *Mon.* vi (3), 1256.
[51] *V.C.H. Staffs.* iii. 149.
[52] Below (burials and monuments).
[53] A. B. Clifton, *Cathedral Church of Lichfield* (Lichfield, 1898), 48–9.
[54] W.S.L., Staffs. Views, vi. 42; below, fig. 10.
[55] *S.H.C.* 1924, p. 19.
[56] Ibid.; Bodl. MS. Ashmole 794, f. 102v.

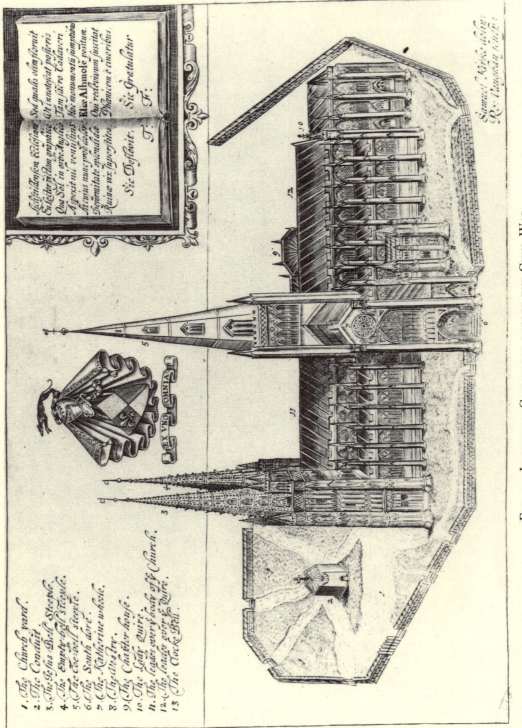

Fig. 10. Lichfield Cathedral before the Civil War

The long vestibule which leads off the north side of the choir predates the chapter house to which it provides access. Its original purpose is uncertain. The chapter may have met there, although one of the transepts was a more likely venue. A newel staircase at the vestibule's south-east corner gave access to an upper storey, later an annexe to a library over the chapter house. The chapter house was built in the 1240s and is an elongated octagon with a ten-celled roof vaulted from a central pillar.[57] It has an upper chamber, now the library, which in the early 14th century was given a tiled floor, still in existence.[58]

The rebuilding of the nave dates from the time of Bishop Meuland, 1257–95. It was presumably directed at least in part by Thomas le Waleys, recorded as the master of the fabric in 1268 and as master of the work in the 1270s. The work, which was probably completed by 1285, involved raising the pitch of the Norman roof so that the new roof covered or cut across the windows of the lantern tower. Work on the west front began shortly afterwards.[59] The front was designed as a screen with tiers of statues. The lowest order contained the twelve apostles, with the four evangelists and Moses and Aaron in the porch of the central doorway; a figure of the Virgin and Child was placed against the centre pillar of the doorway with one of Christ above. The second order of figures depicted kings of either Israel and Judah or of England, with St. Chad in the centre. Above, flanking the west window, were two rows apparently of prophets, prophetesses, and judges. In a niche over the window stood a statue of Christ. Figures of patriarchs covered the face of the north and south towers.[60] The two west spires and the central spire were finished probably by 1323.[61] Above the west doorway inside the cathedral a text praising Oswiu, king of Northumbria, traditionally regarded as the cathedral's founder, and later royal benefactors was written possibly to mark the completion of the west end; it was still visible in the early 18th century.[62]

Meanwhile, at the instigation of Bishop Langton, 1296–1321, work on the Lady Chapel at the east end of the cathedral had been started, probably c. 1315.[63] It was unfinished at Langton's death in 1321, when he left money for its completion. The design, a rectangle of three bays with a three-sided east end, is unusual in England but has French parallels. The architect may have been William Franceys, possibly a Frenchman, who was recorded as the bishop's mason at Lichfield in 1312–13.[64] He may other-wise have been known as William de Eyton, recorded as the cathedral's master mason in 1322. The chapel was evidently finished by 1336 when two keepers of its fabric were appointed. Figures of the ten wise and foolish virgins were placed on pillars in the chapel.[65] Three small chambers on its south side were probably designed as sacristies for chantry chaplains serving at the chapel altar. Vaults underneath the chambers were entered by a stair at the west end of the westernmost chamber. Externally there were recesses, presumably for tombs, against two of the chambers, and possibly also against the easternmost chamber, although in the early 18th century there was a doorway there into the Close.[66]

William de Eyton was possibly responsible for the first stages of the construction of a new choir. He died probably during the winter of 1336–7, and in 1337 the chapter engaged as consultant William of Ramsey, the king's master mason,[67] then working at St. Paul's, London. His appointment was probably recommended by Gilbert de Bruera, a canon of Lichfield who in 1335 became dean of St. Paul's.[68] In 1337 Philip de Turvill, a canon who had been Bishop Langton's commissary, left 300 marks for 'the new work between the choir and the Lady Chapel' and gave a statue of Our Lady for her altar.[69] Ramsey died in 1349, and the completion of the new choir was probably interrupted by the effects of the Black Death. Work had been resumed by 1352 and included the construction of a stone staircase and stone balcony to the upper storey of St. Peter's chapel. A stone screen, which formed the reredos behind the high altar and had niches for statues, may have been completed in the later 14th century.[70]

The south transept was apparently refurbished: in 1346 a vicar choral was given permission to be buried there before the cross which he had provided.[71] Historical notes on the kings of England and on Lichfield cathedral and its bishops were painted on folding panels at the doorway of the south transept. The panels may have been made during the time of Bishop Northburgh, 1321–58, the last bishop listed on them.[72] In 1378 his successor, Bishop Stretton, improved St. Chad's shrine, which had been given by Bishop Langton.[73]

Further work on the fabric took place in the 1380s. It included the decoration of the middle part of the choir with statues set against the pillars; on one side were figures of St. Peter, the Virgin Mary, and St. Mary Magdalene, and on the other St. James, St. Philip, and St. Christo-

[57] V.C.H. Staffs. iii. 149–50.
[58] Antiquity, lxiii. 292–3.
[59] S.R.O., D. (W.) 1734/J. 1636; V.C.H. Staffs. iii. 150; S.H.C. 1924, p. 265.
[60] T.S.S.A.H.S. xxviii. 57–8; [J. C. Woodhouse and J. Newling], Short Account of Lichfield Cathedral (Lichfield, 1823 edn.), 103–11. For a 1736 drawing of St. Chad's statue see Bodl. MS. Top. Eccl. d. 6, f. 13v.
[61] V.C.H. Staffs. iii. 150, 157.
[62] T.S.S.A.H.S. xxxiii. 57.
[63] Para. based on V.C.H. Staffs. iii. 157.
[64] S.R.O., D. (W.) 1734/J. 2057, m. 5 (section relating to cost of ditch towards Gaia).
[65] T.S.S.A.H.S. xxviii. 61.
[66] Ibid. 61–2.
[67] V.C.H. Staffs. iii. 158.

[68] J. Harvey, Eng. Medieval Architects (1984), 242; Le Neve, Fasti, 1300–1541, Coventry and Lichfield, 52; ibid. St. Paul's, London, 5.
[69] Sede Vacante Wills (Kent Arch. Soc. Records Branch, iii), 117; Cal. Pat. 1313–17, 616.
[70] T.S.S.A.H.S. xxviii. 61. Removed by Wyatt c. 1790, parts of the screen were later incorporated in the sedilia on either side of the high altar and in monuments to Bp. Lonsdale and Dean Howard: H. E. Savage, The Sedilia (Lichfield, 1914), 3–4.
[71] Bodl. MS. Ashmole 794, f. 95.
[72] B.L. Cott. MS. Vesp. E. xvi, ff. 26, 34; T. Dingley, Hist. from Marble, ii (Camd. Soc. [1st ser.], xcvii), 327; V.C.H. Staffs. iii. 174 n.
[73] Below (St. Chad's shrine).

pher.[74] At the beginning of the 15th century, when the rebuilding of the cathedral was finished, the duties of the keeper of the fabric were given statutory confirmation.[75] A scene showing the Trinity flanked by two censing angels was painted on the wall of the south choir aisle, probably in the mid 15th century; traces of it were restored in 1979.[76] Dean Heywood, 1457–92, paid for covering the walls and ceiling of the chapter house with frescoes, one of which partly survives over the doorway. He also gave money for the glazing of the chapter-house windows with pictures of the apostles and glazing the windows in the vestibule.[77] In 1543 the chapter arranged for the regilding of the reredos.[78]

The main impact of the Reformation on the fabric was the destruction of St. Chad's shrine in 1538.[79] Statues on the high altar and elsewhere inside the cathedral were removed in 1548.[80] It seems that in contrast the west front, which Leland in the earlier 1540s had described as 'the glory of the church', was not defaced.[81] Erdeswick in the 1590s remarked that it was 'exceedingly finely cut' with statues of prophets, apostles, and kings of Judah and of England.[82] The cathedral was severely damaged during the parliamentarian siege and occupation in 1643, and the siege of 1646 brought down the central spire. Lead and other materials were stripped away, and in 1649 it was reported that 'a great part of the roof is uncovered'. What lead remained was taken away by parliamentary order in 1651.[83] Many of the statues on the west front were badly damaged.[84]

In 1660 only the chapter house and the 'vestry' (probably St. Peter's chapel) were still roofed. The dean and chapter immediately set about restoring the fabric, and following the arrival of Bishop Hacket in August 1662 work proceeded energetically. Most of the cathedral had been reroofed by September 1665 and the central spire was complete by April 1666; glass was placed in the west window later the same year. The cathedral was rededicated on Christmas Eve 1669.[85] Choir stalls for the prebendaries and others were paid for by donors whose names were placed over the seats.[86] A pulpit was given in 1671 by Francis Bacon, prebendary of Ryton,[87] and an elaborate reredos, based on the design of one in the Chapel Royal at Whitehall, was installed c. 1678. The generosity of Catherine (d. 1674), wife of Sir Richard Leveson of Trentham, in restoring the cathedral fabric was recorded in an inscription over the south doorway. Henry Webb, the diocesan registrar, paid for the restoration of the entrance to the choir in 1680.[88] A statue of Charles II, attributed to Sir William Wilson, was placed in the central niche of the apex of the west front; it may have been covered with bronze.[89] The duke of York (later James II) paid for the glazing of the west window.[90]

In the 1770s the roofs were found to be in a dangerous state.[91] Their pitch was lowered and the lead covering replaced with slate. A restoration took place between 1788 and 1795 under the direction of James Wyatt. His principal object was to enlarge the choir, so that it could contain the whole congregation. The late 17th-century reredos and the medieval stone screen which separated the choir from the Lady Chapel were removed. The elongated choir was made easier to keep warm by blocking the arcades and by cutting off the nave east of the crossing with a high stone screen, the base of which was made with material from the redundant medieval screen. An altar was set up at the east end of the former Lady Chapel. The former high altar and possibly its rails were taken to St. Chad's church at Stowe, which was presented in 1812 with a copy of Rubens's Crucifixion, originally the centre piece of the reredos.[92] Wyatt had the pews removed from the nave, which ceased to be used for services, and the pulpit was taken to Elford church in 1789.[93] Two vestries, one for the vicars choral and the other for the choristers, were fitted out against the screen at the west end of the choir. Wyatt also replaced some of the stone vaulting in the nave with plaster, raised the roofs of the aisles, and rebuilt much of the central spire. The restoration was completed by the insertion of painted glass in the east window. That glass was removed in 1803, when the window and six others in the Lady Chapel were filled with panels of mid 16th-century stained glass from the dissolved Cistercian abbey of Herckenrode (Belgium). Some of the glass was also placed in the south window of the south transept and in windows in the south and north choir aisles.[94] Shortly after 1811 Dean Woodhouse had glass depicting the founders and patrons of the cathedral inserted in the north transept window.[95] The south transept window was given glass depicting Old and New Testament figures in 1813.[96] Dean Woodhouse was also responsible in 1814 for removing the 17th-century choir stalls and re-ordering the choir.[97] The font in the early 19th century was at the west end of the north nave aisle.[98]

[74] T.S.S.A.H.S. xxviii. 63.
[75] V.C.H. Staffs. iii. 165.
[76] Harwood, Lichfield, 112; Friends of Lichfield Cath. 42nd Ann. Rep. (1979), 8–9, 11.
[77] Lichfield Cath. Libr., MS. Lichfield 4, f. 32.
[78] V.C.H. Staffs. iii. 168.
[79] Below (St. Chad's shrine).
[80] L.J.R.O., D. 30/C.A. iv, f. 148.
[81] Leland, Itin. ed. Toulmin Smith, ii. 102.
[82] Erdeswick, Staffs. 281. For what is evidently a pre-Civil War view of the front see V.C.H. Staffs. iii, pl. facing p. 148.
[83] V.C.H. Staffs. iii. 174.
[84] W.S.L., Staffs. Views, vi. 13; D. Defoe, Tour thro' the Whole Island of Gt. Brit. (1927), ii. 481.
[85] V.C.H. Staffs. iii. 175–6.
[86] Shaw, Staffs. i. 258.
[87] Harwood, Lichfield, 67.
[88] Shaw, Staffs. i. 258; S.H.C. 1920 and 1922, 33.
[89] V.C.H. Staffs. iii. 175–6; W.S.L., S. MS. 374, p. 355.
[90] V.C.H. Staffs. iii. 176 n.
[91] Para. based on V.C.H. Staffs. iii. 186–9.
[92] Below, churches.
[93] Harwood, Lichfield, 67 n. It was removed from Elford in 1848 and placed in the later 19th cent. in Whittington church, where it remains: inf. from the Revd. Dr. E. C. C. Hill, cathedral librarian.
[94] Archaeologia, cviii. 189–226.
[95] [Woodhouse and Newling], Short Account of Lichfield Cathedral (1811 edn.), 55–9. It was removed to Lichfield guildhall in 1893.
[96] Ibid. (1823), 48.
[97] Ibid. 8; Erdeswick, Staffs. 290.
[98] Dugdale, Mon. vi (3), pl. facing p. 1238.

Many of the medieval statues on the west front were removed in 1744 or 1749. Those of the second row were refashioned in 1820 and 1821 by Joseph Harris of Bath in the form of pre- and post-Conquest kings of England.[99]

Sydney Smirke restored the south aisle of the nave between 1842 and 1846.[1] The work of opening out the choir was begun by Smirke in 1856 and continued from 1857 by George Gilbert (later Sir Gilbert) Scott. New furnishings included a metal screen made by Skidmore of Coventry between the crossing and the choir, Minton pavement tiles inside the altar rails, an alabaster reredos, and oak stalls and a bishop's throne carved by William Evans of Ellastone, uncle of the novelist George Eliot.[2] A new pulpit and lectern were provided in the nave, as well as an alabaster font given by the wife of Dean Howard. The cathedral was reopened in 1861. Visitors were afterwards allowed free access to the nave and transepts, but admission to other parts was by leave of the verger on payment of a contribution to the fabric fund.[3]

During the remainder of the 19th century plaster work in various parts of the cathedral was replaced by stone. Between 1877 and 1884 the empty niches on the west front were given new statues and existing ones were remodelled. Most of them were carved by Robert Bridgeman of Lichfield, but that of Queen Victoria on the north side of the central window was carved by her daughter, Princess Louise.[4] The statue of Charles II in the apex was replaced by one of Christ and survived in the late 1980s near the south doorway of the cathedral. In 1893 the north transept window was replaced with glass depicting Christ's genealogy, donated by James Hardwick of Hints. New glass depicting bishops of the early Church was inserted in the south transept window in 1895; it was given by Bishop Lonsdale's nephew, A. P. Heywood-Lonsdale.[5] Also in 1895 ten statues of virgin saints were placed in the Lady Chapel.[6] A service of thanksgiving in 1901 marked the completion of the restoration.

St. Peter's chapel had been used as the canons' vestry in the early 18th century.[7] In 1797 it was fitted out as the bishop's consistory court, formerly in the north transept.[8] A triple seat for the judge's use with a later 17th-century canopy, which survives in the chapel, evidently comprises Bishop Hacket's throne and two other seats refashioned after the stalls were removed from the choir in 1814. The court continued to

meet there until 1876, when the chapel became a vestry again.[9] It was used by the vergers in the late 1980s. The vault underneath the chapel was used as a charnel house in the early 18th century; it was reserved in 1797 as the burial place of the Paget family of Beaudesert in Longdon.[10] The upper chamber was dedicated in 1897 as St. Chad's chapel and in the late 1980s was a place for private prayer.[11]

The north-east corner of the south transept was used as a vestry by the vicars choral in the earlier 18th century and the south-east corner as the dean's consistory court.[12] The court continued to meet there until the abolition of the dean's probate jurisdiction in 1858.[13] In 1926 both parts were dedicated as St. Michael's chapel in memory of Staffordshire men who had died during the First World War. In 1960 it became the regimental chapel of the Staffordshire Regiment.[14] St. Stephen's chapel in the north transept on the east side was used as the bishop's consistory court in the late 17th century.[15] The court remained there until the chapel was opened out during restoration work c. 1790; it moved first to the chapter house and in 1797 to St. Peter's chapel.[16] The font given by Mrs. Howard was moved from the west end of the nave to the north transept in 1982.[17]

The space between the vestibule and the north transept was enclosed c. 1860 in order to create vestries for the vicars choral and the choristers, replacing those at the west end of the choir.[18] Two upper storeys were added as vestries in the early 1980s.

St. Chad's shrine. Bede described the saint's shrine as a wooden coffin in the shape of a little house, with an aperture in its side through which pilgrims could put their hands to take out some of the dust.[19] In the Norman cathedral the shrine probably stood behind the high altar, in the apse of the presbytery. A light was maintained before it in the later 12th century.[20] In the early 14th century some of the relics were placed in a costly shrine commissioned in Paris by Bishop Langton.[21] It presumably stood in the space between the high altar and the Lady Chapel, then still under construction. In 1378 Bishop Stretton arranged for it to be moved to 'a marble place next to the Lady Chapel'.[22] The move probably entailed placing the shrine on a marble table. When its ornaments were listed in 1445, it was apparently in the form of an oblong chest with the narrower sides facing east and

[99] T.S.S.A.H.S. xxviii. 58; Erdeswick, Staffs. 281 n.; [Woodhouse and Newling], Short Account of Lichfield Cathedral (1823), 105–11.
[1] Para. based on V.C.H. Staffs. iii. 194–5; J. Hewitt, Handbk. for Lichfield Cathedral (Lichfield, 1875), 54–9.
[2] Staffs. Advertiser, 4 June 1887, p. 6.
[3] Lich. Dioc. Yr. Bk. (1881), 96.
[4] C. Harradine, Hand Guide to Lichfield Cathedral containing a detailed account of the sculpture on the West Front (Lichfield, 1891; copy in W.S.L.).
[5] Clifton, Cath. Church of Lichfield, 71, 74–5.
[6] Ibid. 101.
[7] T.S.S.A.H.S. xxviii. 61–2.
[8] L.J.R.O., D. 30/C.A. ix, ff. 7v., 14; Gent. Mag. lxx (1), 17.
[9] L.J.R.O., D. 30/C.A. xiv, p. 51; below, plate 5.
[10] T.S.S.A.H.S. xxviii. 61–2.
[11] Clifton, Cath. Church of Lichfield, 106–7.

[12] B. Willis, Survey of Cathedrals (1727), pl. before p. 371.
[13] V.C.H. Staffs. iii. 74; J. G. Lonsdale, Recollections of the Internal Restoration of Lichfield Cathedral (Lichfield, 1884), 7 (copy in W.S.L.).
[14] Hist. of Naval and Military Monuments, Memorials, and Colours (1967), 18–19 (copy in W.S.L.).
[15] L.J.R.O., D. 30/plan of bishop's palace and the cathedral c. 1685.
[16] Ibid. D. 30/C.A. viii, f. 118.
[17] Lichfield Cath. Libr., chapter mins. 1979–82, p. 242.
[18] J. G. Lonsdale, Recollections of Work done in and upon Lichfield Cathedral 1856–94 (Lichfield, 1895), 7, 18 (copy in W.S.L.).
[19] Bede's Eccl. Hist. of the Eng. People, ed. B. Colgrave and R. A. B. Mynors, 346.
[20] S.H.C. 1924, p. 165.
[21] V.C.H. Staffs. iii. 157.
[22] Bodl. MS. Ashmole 794, f. 173v.

west. A gilt statue of St. Chad and other statues stood on the south side, and there was also a statue of the Virgin Mary and a silver-gilt statue of a man brandishing a sword, possibly a representation of St. Michael the Archangel.[23]

By 1345 there were also relics of the saint in a portable shrine. It was made in the form of a church with transepts and a bell tower and may have been a model of the cathedral itself. It too was adorned with statues in 1445. One of St. Chad stood on the face of one of the transepts, with a gold statue of St. Catherine above, and a statue of the Virgin Mary stood on the face of the other transept. The bell tower contained or was surmounted by an enamelled gilt crucifix.

The saint's head was kept in a painted wooden box in 1345. By 1445 it was encased in a gilt reliquary, possibly in the form of a mask or a complete head which could be opened up to reveal the skull, and a mitre was hung over it. The reliquary was kept in its own chapel, probably the chamber over St. Peter's chapel off the south choir aisle. The saint's right arm was by then kept in a separate silver-gilt reliquary, probably made in the form of an arm: at one end was the model of a hand in the act of giving a blessing.[24]

The reliquaries were destroyed in 1538 in the general attack on pilgrimage shrines. The statues, jewels, and other ornaments were seized by the Crown; the cathedral was granted for its own uses the shrine itself, presumably the marble fabric behind the high altar.[25] The saint's bones were smuggled away by Canon Arthur Dudley. Some were taken to Flanders in 1669, and by 1671 were in Liège; others remained in England and are now kept in the Roman Catholic cathedral in Birmingham.[26]

SIDE ALTARS. St. Mary's altar was recorded in the early 1220s.[27] Statutes of 1241 mention five chaplains serving the cathedral's principal altars.[28] Those altars probably included the four at the east end of the choir before the construction of the Lady Chapel; the fifth may have been the high altar, or else St. Chad's altar which is known to have been in the nave in 1325.[29] A list of chantries made in 1335[30] records the altars of the Virgin Mary, St. Chad, St. John, St. Radegund, St. Catherine, St. Thomas, St. Peter (in the chapel off the south choir aisle), St. Stephen (in the north transept and in existence by

1241),[31] St. Andrew (probably in the north choir aisle),[32] and St. Nicholas (probably in the south choir aisle).[33] St. Kenelm's altar was recorded in 1466.[34] A chantry at the altar of St. Blaise, evidently in the choir, was founded by Dean Heywood, 1457–92. He adorned the altar with an alabaster 'table', probably a reredos, on which scenes of the saint's life were depicted.[35] In 1468 he founded a chantry at the altar of Jesus and St. Anne. The altar stood in its own chapel in a loft, which lay across the north choir aisle next to the choir screen. Its furnishings included statues of the Risen Christ and of St. Anne, a pair of organs, and choir stalls.[36] In 1499 there was an altar of St. George,[37] and there was presumably an altar in the chapel built on to the north side of the nave by Dean Yotton (d. 1512).[38] There may also have been a chapel in the chamber over the vestibule leading to the chapter house; in the early 18th century the chamber was known as St. Peter's chapel and had wall paintings which included one of the saint's crucifixion.[39]

BURIALS AND MONUMENTS. Bishop Geoffrey Muschamp (d. 1208) was the first post-Conquest bishop to be buried in the cathedral.[40] The site is unknown. Of his successors William Cornhill (d. 1223) was buried in the south choir aisle[41] and Hugh Pattishall (d. 1241) in the north transept before the altar of St. Stephen.[42] Both Roger Weseham (d. 1257) and Roger Meuland (d. 1295) were buried in the cathedral.[43] Meuland's burial site may have been in the choir on the south side of the high altar: a tomb there drawn by William Dugdale before the Civil War may have been his.[44] Walter Langton (d. 1321) was first buried at the east end of the choir, presumably beyond St. Chad's shrine and near the Lady Chapel. In 1360 his body was moved by his successor Robert Northburgh to an elaborate canopied tomb of white stone on the south side of the high altar.[45] Northburgh himself was presumably buried in the cathedral, but there is no record of the site. Robert Stretton (d. 1385) was buried in St. Andrew's chapel.[46] John Burghill (d. 1414) directed that he should be buried in the Lady Chapel,[47] as did Reynold Boulers (d. 1459).[48] John Hales (d. 1490) chose to be buried near the west door, and Geoffrey Blythe (d. 1532) before the image of St. Chad, possibly a reference to the statue on the saint's shrine

[23] Shrewsbury Public Libr., MS. 2.
[24] Ibid.; *S.H.C.* vi (2), 207.
[25] *V.C.H. Staffs.* iii. 168 (where the figure of £400 given as the income of the shrine at the Reformation in fact refers to the whole revenue of the cathedral).
[26] *Staffs. Cath. Hist.* ix. 12–15; H. Foley, *Rec. of Eng. Province of Society of Jesus*, ii. 232; M. Hodgetts, *St. Chad's Cathedral, Birmingham* (1987), 10–11, 18.
[27] *S.H.C.* 1924, p. 15.
[28] Below, churches (parochial organization to 1491).
[29] *S.H.C.* 1924, p. 331.
[30] Bodl. MS. Ashmole 794, ff. 48–9.
[31] *T.S.S.A.H.S.* xxviii. 62.
[32] L.J.R.O., D. 30/C.A. ii, f. 5v.
[33] Lord Basset (d. 1390), whose tomb was in that aisle, left money to the altar: *Cat. Anct. D.* v, A 11372; below (burials and monuments).
[34] Lichfield Cath. Libr., MS. Lichfield 4, f. 21v.
[35] Ibid. ff. 21, 32; H. E. Savage, *Thomas Heywode, Dean*

(Lichfield, 1925), 9–10.
[36] Savage, *Heywode*, 11–18; *V.C.H. Staffs.* iii. 165; Lichfield Cath. Libr., MS. Lichfield 4, ff. 22v., 31; MS. Lichfield 5, ff. 22v.–23.
[37] L.J.R.O., D. 30/C.A. iii, f. 36v.
[38] *T.S.S.A.H.S.* xxviii. 58.   [39] Ibid. 62–3.
[40] Above, general hist. (the 12th century).
[41] Shaw, *Staffs.* i. 246.
[42] *T.S.S.A.H.S.* xxviii. 62.
[43] H. Wharton, *Anglia Sacra* (1691), i. 447; *Annales de Wigornia* (Rolls Ser.), 525.
[44] Willis, *Survey of Cathedrals*, 387; B.L. Loan MS. 38, f. 8.
[45] Wharton, *Anglia Sacra*, i. 449; B.L. Loan MS. 38, f. 6 (reproduced in Shaw, *Staffs.* i, pl. xxvi).
[46] Wharton, *Anglia Sacra*, i. 449; B.L. Loan MS. 38, f. 3 (reproduced in Shaw, *Staffs.* i, pl. xxiii).
[47] Willis, *Survey of Cathedrals*, 389.
[48] P.R.O., PROB 11/4, f. 122v.

behind the high altar.[49] Blythe was the last bishop to be buried in the cathedral until 1670. Only two effigies of medieval bishops survived the Civil War; both are now in the south choir aisle.[50] One is of the 13th century; the other is 14th-century.

A monument to Dean Heywood (d. 1492) contained effigies of him in his vestments and as a cadaver; only the second survives. In the early 18th century it was in a wall in the south choir aisle; it was moved in 1877 to the north-west corner of the north transept.[51] Dean Boleyn (d. 1603) was buried at the entrance to the choir.[52] A monument to Ralph, Lord Basset (d. 1390), formerly stood at the east end of the south choir aisle, and one to George Stanley (d. 1509) of Hammerwich survives in the wall of the same aisle.[53] A medieval effigy survives in the wall of the south choir aisle[54] and two others in the wall of the south nave aisle. A monument to William, Lord Paget (d. 1563), his eldest son Henry (d. 1568), and their wives was erected in 1577 on the site of St. Chad's shrine. It was commissioned by Henry's brother Thomas, Lord Paget, from the Flemish sculptor Jan Carlier. Unusually for English monuments of that time the material used was marble and the figures were in a kneeling, not recumbent, position. It was destroyed during the Civil War.[55] Robert Master (d. 1625), chancellor of Lichfield diocese, and his wife Catherine were commemorated in a monument at the east end of the south choir aisle, also destroyed during the Civil War.[56]

Bishop John Hacket (d. 1670) was buried on the south side of the high altar. When the choir arches there were blocked in the late 18th century, his monument was set against the wall of the south choir aisle. It was moved in 1979 to a position under a choir arch near the west end of the aisle.[57] Of later bishops buried in the cathedral or its graveyard, Richard Smalbroke (d. 1749) and James Cornwallis (d. 1824) are commemorated by wall tablets in the south transept; Henry Ryder (d. 1836) by a life-size figure sculpted by Sir Francis Chantrey in the north choir aisle; George Selwyn (d. 1878) by an effigy in one of the chambers on the south side of the Lady Chapel decorated with scenes reflecting the bishop's work with Maoris in New Zealand and miners in Lichfield diocese; and Edward Woods (d. 1953) by a bronze bust of 1958 by Jacob Epstein, first placed in the north choir aisle and in 1989 at the north end of the vestibule leading to the chapter house.[58] Augustus Legge (d. 1913) has no memorial in the cathedral. In contrast, John Lonsdale (d. 1867), although buried at Eccleshall, has an effigy with medieval canopies in the north choir aisle.

There are wall tablets to Dean Lancelot Addison (d. 1703) at the west end of the south nave aisle and Dean John Woodhouse (d. 1833) in the north transept. Dean Henry Howard (d. 1868) is commemorated by an effigy with medieval canopies in the south choir aisle. A wall tablet in the south transept to John Saville (d. 1803), vicar choral, has verses by his friend Anna Seward. The young daughters of William Robinson, prebendary of Pipa Parva, are commemorated at the east end of the south choir aisle in a sculpture by Chantrey dated 1817. Other monuments include those to Lady Mary Wortley Montagu (d. 1789), the writer, at the west end of the north nave aisle, Andrew Newton (d. 1806), founder of Newton's College in the Close, in the south transept, and Sir Charles Oakeley (d. 1826), governor of Madras, in the north transept. There are memorial busts of the actor David Garrick (d. 1779) and Dr. Samuel Johnson (d. 1784) in the south transept. Naval and military memorials are chiefly in the south transept.[59]

PLATE. Inventories of 1345 and 1445 list the cathedral's plate, as well as vestments and other liturgical artefacts, often with a note of their donors.[60] In 1549 the dean and chapter divided surplus plate among themselves, and what remained was mostly seized by the Crown in 1553. Replacements were acquired during Mary I's reign and later, but their seizure was ordered by the Privy Council in 1579.[61] The earliest surviving plate comprises a chalice, two flagons, a paten, and a paten cover, all of 1662; a ciborium given in 1670 by Lucy, dowager countess of Huntingdon; a paten and almsdish of 1701; and a chalice and paten of 1702.

BELLS. A scheme for ringing the cathedral bells was included in Bishop Nonant's statutes of c. 1190. It mentioned at least two great bells, as well as a 'sweet bell' and its 'companion', presumably bells with a light timbre. A reference to the smallest bell 'in the church' may suggest that the others were in an external bell tower.[62] There was a belfry 'in the close' by 1315, when it was burnt down.[63] A belfry mentioned in 1385 may have been the cathedral's south-west tower: a great bell called Jesus, made in London and given by Dean Heywood, was consecrated in a belfry 'on the south side of the cathedral' in 1477.[64] There were evidently bells in the central tower, which was presumably the 'great belfry' badly damaged in 1537.[65]

In 1553 the Crown allowed the cathedral to keep its 12 bells.[66] In the earlier 17th century a great bell (evidently the Jesus bell) hung in the south-west tower and there was a bell (or bells)

[49] Willis, *Survey of Cathedrals*, 390–1. Blythe died on 19 January 1531/2: L.J.R.O., D. 30/C.A. iv, f. 93v.
[50] *T.S.S.A.H.S.* xxviii. 59.
[51] Ibid.
[52] Shaw, *Staffs.* i. 246.
[53] *T.S.S.A.H.S.* xxviii. 59–60.
[54] Ibid. 60.
[55] *Trans. Anct. Mon. Soc.* xxix. 124–36.
[56] Shaw, *Staffs.* i. 248; B.L. Loan MS. 38, f. 5.
[57] *T.S.S.A.H.S.* xxviii. 59–60.
[58] *Lichfield Mercury*, 27 June 1958, p. 1; 21 Apr. 1989, p. 47.

[59] *Hist. of Naval and Military Monuments, Memorials and Colours* (1967).
[60] *S.H.C.* vi (2), 207–13; Shrewsbury Public Libr., MS. 2.
[61] *V.C.H. Staffs.* iii. 168–9.
[62] Dugdale, *Mon.* vi (3), 1256–7; *V.C.H. Staffs.* iii. 142. Mrs. Lucy Smith of Lichfield is thanked for her help with this section.
[63] Wharton, *Anglia Sacra*, i. 447.
[64] L.J.R.O., D. 30/C.A. i, f. 2v.; Lichfield Cath. Libr., MS. Lichfield 4, ff. 28, 31v.–32.
[65] Bodl. MS. Ashmole 770, f. 66v.
[66] *V.C.H. Staffs.* iii. 168.

in the central tower.[67] The Jesus bell was melted down in 1653,[68] and most of the other bells were presumably destroyed about the same time. One at least was saved: in 1661 the chapter clerk recovered 'a stolen bell' at Coventry.[69] It is possibly the small, medieval bell which survived in the central tower in the late 1980s. A peal of six was placed in the south-west tower in the 1670s. The bells proved unsuitable and were recast in 1688 as a peal of ten by Henry Bagley of Ecton (Northants.). Three of the new bells were recast by Bagley in the early 1690s.[70] No. 9 was recast by Abraham Rudhall of Gloucester in 1758, and the treble and the tenor by Thomas Rudhall in 1764; the tenor was again recast in 1813 by Thomas Mears of London. All ten were recast in 1947 by John Taylor & Co. of Loughborough.[71]

ORGANS. In 1482 Dean Heywood gave a 'great organ' to be placed on the choir screen.[72] In 1639 Robert Dallam agreed to build an organ, which, if built, was presumably destroyed or dismantled during the Civil War.[73] At the Restoration Bishop Hacket commissioned a new organ from Bernard Smith, evidently completed in 1669. It was known as 'the Ladies' Organ' because its cost was met by ten women, including Anne, duchess of York, and Frances, duchess of Somerset.[74] A small organ for use in the Lady Chapel was made probably in the 1660s. It fell into private hands and c. 1900 was presented to Lichfield museum by Bishop Selwyn's widow Harriet. It was restored to working order in 1954 and returned to the cathedral.[75] A 'great organ' was built by Thomas Schwarbrook (d. c. 1753). It was replaced in 1789 by one built by Samuel Green. The present organ, made by George Holdich, was given in 1860 by Josiah Spode of Hawkesyard Park in Armitage and was placed in the north transept aisle; it was enlarged in 1884.[76]

CLOCKS AND SUNDIAL. There was a cathedral clock in 1401 when a keeper was appointed by the chapter at 20s. a year.[77] A keeper was still employed in the late 16th century.[78] The clock may then have been in the south-west tower, where it evidently was in the earlier 17th century.[79] There was a clock on the west front of the south-west tower in the later 18th century. Its

dial was removed in 1823.[80] A clock was installed in the south-west tower in 1891, with a dial at the west end of the south nave aisle.[81]

A sundial near the south doorway of the cathedral was removed in 1781 and re-erected in 1785 at the west end in order to regulate the clock on the tower.[82] It was removed in 1881 and passed into private hands. It was returned to the cathedral in 1929 and placed on a pedestal in its present position south of the nave.[83]

BOOKS AND ARCHIVES. A brick library was built beside the north transept in the late 15th century.[84] Its small manuscript collection was catalogued in 1622.[85] When the Close was surrendered to parliamentarian forces in 1646, the terms of surrender stipulated that the library's contents were to be preserved.[86] None the less they were dispersed, and in 1663 the chapter recovered books from Shrewsbury.[87] The library was restocked by Frances, duchess of Somerset (d. 1674), who left it nearly 1,000 books belonging to her late husband William Seymour, duke of Somerset, the recorder of Lichfield.[88] Between 1680 and 1682 Dean Smalwood had ten cases made for the books, each case bearing a wooden boss with the donor's arms, including his own.[89] The library was further augmented by Dean Addison (d. 1703).[90]

In 1757 the chapter ordered the demolition of the library in order to improve the aspect of the Close; the adjoining chapter clerk's house, which was timber-framed, was also demolished because it was a fire risk to the cathedral.[91] The books and the cases were moved in 1763 to the chamber over the chapter house.[92] The cases were replaced by smaller ones in the later 19th century. After a bequest by Frederick Martin, a canon of Lincoln cathedral, of over 2,000 books in 1865, the library was extended by opening a doorway into the adjoining room over the vestibule.[93]

The library's greatest possession is the 8th-century St. Chad's gospel book. It is periodically displayed in the chapter house, as a memorial to Bishop Stretton Reeve (d. 1981).

In the earlier 17th century the cathedral's archives were kept in the chamber over the chapter house.[94] A chest of drawers dated 1663 in the present library annexe was presumably

[67] Above, fig. 10.
[68] *V.C.H. Staffs.* iii. 174.
[69] L.J.R.O., D. 30/LXIV.
[70] W.S.L., S. MS. 24 (i) (modifying *V.C.H. Staffs.* iii. 176).
[71] Lynam, *Church Bells*, 18; Friends of Lichfield Cath. *47th Ann. Rep.* (1984), 17–18.
[72] Lichfield Cath. Libr., MS. Lichfield 4, f. 31.
[73] L.J.R.O., D. 30/P 1.
[74] R. Greening, *Organs of Lichfield Cathedral* (Lichfield, 1974), 5 (copy in W.S.L.); *V.C.H. Staffs.* iii. 176; Shaw, *Staffs.* i. 249–50.
[75] Greening, *Organs*, 6–8; *Lichfield Mercury*, 23 Oct. 1953, p. 4; 2 July 1954, p. 2.
[76] Greening, *Organs*, 8–15.
[77] L.J.R.O., D. 30/C.A. i, f. 58.
[78] Ibid. D. 30/bk. of miscellanea, f. 105.
[79] Above, fig. 10.
[80] W.S.L., Staffs. Views, vi. 81; W.S.L., transcr. diary of Anne Bagot, p. 33.
[81] *Lichfield Mercury*, 7 Aug. 1891, p. 8.
[82] L.J.R.O., D. 30/X, 1772–85, 31 Aug. 1781; D. 30/C.A.

viii, f. 105; W.S.L. 196/42/77.
[83] L.J.R.O., D. 30/C.A. xix, p. 296.
[84] *V.C.H. Staffs.* iii. 166; B.L. Add. MS. 5829, f. 2v.
[85] *Medieval and Renaissance Studies*, ii (1950), 151–68.
[86] Clayton, *Loyal and Ancient City*, 124.
[87] L.J.R.O., D. 30/LXIV, s.a. 1663.
[88] Harwood, *Lichfield*, 109; below, town govt. (govt. from 1548: corporation officers).
[89] L.J.R.O., D. 30/Z 12, where the books are recorded as those of Frances's father Rob. Devereux, earl of Essex; Shaw, *Staffs.* i. 261, where the unrecorded donor of a book case is identifiable from his surviving boss as Sir Thos. Thynne, Bt., who succeeded to the baronetcy in 1680 and became Viscount Weymouth in 1682: G.E.C. *Baronetage*, ii. 103.
[90] Inf. from the Revd. Dr. E. C. C. Hill.
[91] L.J.R.O., D. 30/C.A. viii, f. 35v.; *Gent. Mag.* xxix. 4.
[92] L.J.R.O., D. 30/C.A. viii, f. 47. For a view in 1812 see Bodl. G.A. Staffs. 4°, 6, facing p. 107.
[93] Lonsdale, *Recollections of Work*, 20.
[94] *Relation of a Short Survey of 26 Counties, 1634*, ed. L. G. Wickham Legg (1904), 57.

made to store documents. The archives were moved to the upper storey of St. Peter's chapel, probably in 1763 to make room for the transfer of the library that year. They were moved in 1896 to the library annexe.[95] In 1973 most of the archives were deposited in the Lichfield Joint Record Office.[96]

THE CLOSE. The cathedral stands on a sandstone platform which runs east–west. Formerly the land sloped downwards on its north side as it still does on the south, and the constricted nature of the site was noted by William of Malmesbury.[97] According to a late 13th-century description, the cathedral lay between Lemansyche and Way Clife, evidently two roads.[98] The former may have been an early name for Gaia Lane, along the north side of the Close: Shaw Lane, the extension of Gaia Lane on the west side of Beacon Street, points towards Leamonsley. Way Clife may have been the road along the south side of the cathedral: the foundations of houses there are built up against a steep bank, evidently the 'cliff'. The Close covers 16 a., including land reclaimed out of Minster Pool on the south and a ditch on the other three sides.[99] From the mid or later 12th century a supply of fresh water was piped from springs at Pipe in Burntwood.[1] The Close became self-governing in 1441.[2]

There were presumably houses for clergy around the Anglo-Saxon cathedral. The surviving distribution of houses[3] may have originated in part under Bishop Clinton, who reorganized the cathedral clergy as a secular chapter, probably in the 1130s, and created the new town of Lichfield on a grid pattern of streets.[4] In the late 13th century the bishop's house and those of the cathedral clergy occupied sites whose size reflected the status of the occupant: the bishop's site, 320 ft. by 160 ft. in the north-east corner, was twice the size of the adjoining deanery, and the canons had 'places' half the size of the deanery.[5] By modern measurement the frontage of the bishop's site is c. 240 ft. and of the dean's c. 120 ft.; the frontage of a canonical plot should therefore be 60 ft. That is the width of three sites on the north side of the Close, although houses on the south side have 50-ft. frontages.

Bishop Langton, 1296–1321, built a new palace in the north-east corner and converted a canonical house in the north-west corner into a common residence for the vicars choral. It seems that he also built some canonical houses,[6]

evidently including one in the south-west corner and probably one in the south-east. As part of his work on fortifying the Close with a stone wall and gates, he stopped a right of way which evidently ran along the road south of the cathedral.[7]

Houses for canonical residence were conferred by the bishop,[8] but other houses were assigned by the dean and chapter. In 1328 the chapter agreed that if a house was available, Robert Mavesyn, a layman, and his family should have it,[9] and in 1329 it converted a house to hold 'feasts and other necessities'.[10] Of nine houses listed in 1380–1, eight were occupied by canons and one by a laywoman, Maud, the widow of Sir Richard de Stafford.[11] In 1411 Bishop Burghill assigned a site nearly opposite the south door of the cathedral to the chantry priests for their common residence. At the end of the century two canons built themselves substantial brick houses on the sites of the later nos. 23 and 24, and a similar house was built by a canon on the site of the later no. 19 in the early 16th century. Also in the early 16th century a house west of the deanery on the north side of the Close was replaced by a common residence for the cathedral choristers. The Reformation caused a change in the use of only one house, that of the chantry priests, which passed into lay ownership.

During the Civil War the strategic importance of the Close was recognized by both royalist and parliamentarian forces which in turn garrisoned and besieged it.[12] The palace and several houses, especially on the north side, were badly damaged,[13] and the Commons ordered the demolition of the walls in 1646, repeating the order in 1647.[14] Because of the abolition of the cathedral chapter there were no clergy to repair the houses, which were quarried for building materials by 'poor and pilfering people' or abandoned to squatters. Pigs rooted in the graveyard, and by 1660 there were several alehouses.[15]

At the Restoration Bishop Hacket considered the palace beyond repair and chose to occupy a house on the south side of the Close, later the site of no. 19. A new palace was built on the old site in 1687. Other houses were restored by their occupants. Anthony Scattergood, Hacket's chaplain and prebendary of Prees, spent £300 in the later 1660s on rebuilding his house,[16] and Sir Walter Littleton, the diocesan chancellor, restored no. 24. The dean rebuilt the deanery in 1707. When Daniel Defoe visited the Close in the earlier 1720s he was impressed by the 'great

[95] Harwood, *Lichfield*, 96; L.J.R.O., D. 30/C.A. xv, p. 365.
[96] Inf. from Mrs. Jane Hamparṭumian, archivist at L.J.R.O.
[97] William of Malmesbury, *De Gestis Pontificum Anglorum* (Rolls Ser.), 307; inf. from Mr. R. A. Meeson of the Staffs. C. C. Planning and Development Dept.
[98] Dugdale, *Mon.* vi (3), 1242. [99] *V.C.H. Staffs.* i. 329.
[1] Below, public services (water supplies).
[2] Below, town govt. (liberties).
[3] Details of individual houses are given below.
[4] *V.C.H. Staffs.* iii. 141; above, general hist. (the 12th century).
[5] Dugdale, *Mon.* vi (3), 1242 (where the measurements of the palace are wrongly printed: Wharton, *Anglia Sacra*, i. 459).

[6] Wharton, *Anglia Sacra*, i. 447.
[7] *Cal. Pat.* 1348–50, 56; below (ditch).
[8] e.g. L.J.R.O., B/A/1/1, ff. 2, 22v., 51v.
[9] Bodl. MS. Ashmole 794, f. 20v.
[10] Ibid. f. 33.
[11] *S.H.C.* xvii. 168 (date corrected by *S.H.C.* 4th ser. vi. 3 n.); *S.H.C.* 1917–18, 83; Le Neve, *Fasti, 1300–1541, Coventry and Lichfield*, 27, 30, 35, 39, 43, 49, 54, 69.
[12] Above, general hist. (the Civil War).
[13] *T.S.S.A.H.S.* xxv. 35–47.
[14] *C.J.* iv. 633; v. 250.
[15] L.J.R.O., D. 30/dean and chapter rental, 1660; *T.S.S.A.H.S.* xxv. 37, 47–9.
[16] Bodl. MS. Tanner 44, f. 121; MS. Tanner 131, f. 68; Harwood, *Lichfield*, 242.

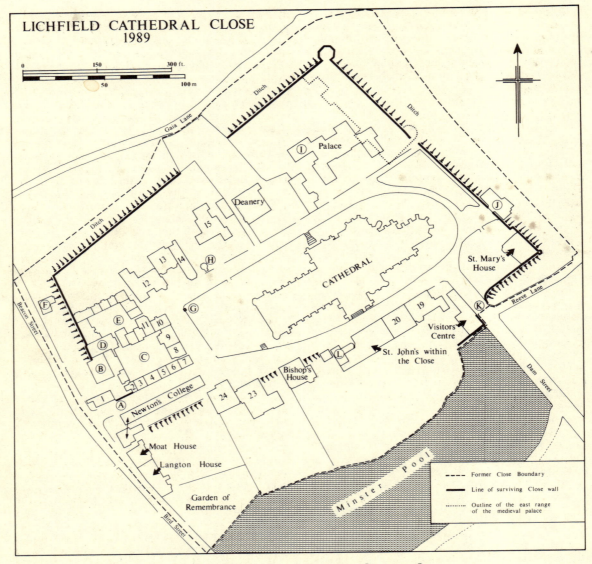

FIG. 11. LICHFIELD CATHEDRAL CLOSE 1989

A Site of west gate. B Darwin House. C Former lower courtyard of the vicars choral. D Former common hall of the vicars choral. E Vicars' Close (former upper courtyard of the vicars choral). F Dimble House. G Former Conduit (1786). H Former Conduit (1803). I Chapel. J Selwyn House. K Site of south-east gate. L The Refectory.

The numbers are those of the houses in the Close.

many very well-built houses'.[17] A number of them were then let to laymen, as bishops chose not to live at Lichfield and few canons took up permanent residence. An Act of 1706 was unsuccessful in encouraging residence, and under cathedral statutes of 1752 canons were required to be in residence only one month or two months a year.[18] When letting houses in the 18th century canons normally reserved the right to occupy the house, or a part of it, during their term of residence.[19] The vicars choral also let their surplus houses to lay tenants by the earlier 17th century.[20]

In the late 1730s the chapter voiced its concern about the kind of tenant coming to live in the Close.[21] Some were tradesmen, despite a ban on their admittance by Dean Kimberley in 1717.[22] A glover was living there in 1728, a weaver in 1730 and 1743, and a tailor in 1754. A printer had his works in the Close in 1752, and there was a joinery and chairmaking business at least between 1755 and 1762. Private schools

[17] D. Defoe, *Tour thro' the Whole Island of Gt. Brit.* (1927), ii. 479.
[18] *V.C.H. Staffs.* iii. 181–2.
[19] L.J.R.O., D. 30/XXXIII, f. 17; *Letters of Anna Seward* (Edinburgh, 1811), iii. 48.

[20] *V.C.H. Staffs.* iii. 185; *T.S.S.A.H.S.* xxv. 41–3; L.J.R.O., D. 30/C.A. vii, ff. 131v., 143.
[21] L.J.R.O., D. 30/Ee 4, answers to Bp. Smalbroke's articles of enquiry, 1738.
[22] *V.C.H. Staffs.* iii. 183.

were run in the later 18th century.[23] In contrast, tenants of high social standing occupied the more substantial houses, especially the palace, and through their influence the Close became a centre of polite society in the 18th century. The chapter responded by improving the Close. Orders to repair the pavements were made in 1718 and 1721, and by the late 1740s a man was employed to keep the walks clean.[24] By the late 18th century a line of trees had been planted as a walk along the north and east sides.[25] The removal in 1757 of the library and chapter clerk's house on the north side of the cathedral was ordered partly for aesthetic reasons, and in 1786 the conduit north-west of the cathedral was demolished because it was considered unsightly.[26] The demolition of the south-east gate of the Close in the mid 18th century was intended to make access easier for coaches.[27] In the late 18th century there was a fashion for whitewashing the exterior of houses.[28]

By the earlier 18th century the houses on the south and east sides of the lower courtyard of the residence of the vicars choral had been remodelled to face the cathedral and the road from Beacon Street; later in the century houses on the west side were remodelled to front Beacon Street. At the east end of the Close the future Selwyn House was built in 1780 by a canon, and other houses were built in the west ditch of the Close in the 18th century. The construction in 1800 of Newton's College on the south side of the road from Beacon Street required the demolition of the medieval west gate and of a house which adjoined no. 24. The approach road, which had formerly been only some 15 ft. across, was widened; it was also lowered in order to provide a less steep gradient into the Close.[29]

An Act of 1797 under which the residentiary chapter was reorganized to comprise the dean and six canons was intended to make residence more attractive, and each residentiary was assigned a particular house.[30] Residence was required for only part of the year, and houses continued to be let to lay tenants. The Act, however, encouraged residentiaries to make repairs and improvements.[31] The Cathedrals Act of 1840 reduced the number of residentiaries to four, freeing two houses of which one, the future Bishop's House, was assigned to the chapter clerk and the other became the vicarage of St. Mary's, Lichfield.[32] By the late 19th century it seems that canons normally resided the whole year. New terms of residence made in 1937 confirmed that pattern.[33]

In 1989 the resident chapter still comprised the dean and four canons, each of whom was a dignitary. The precentor, whose office had formerly been attached to the first residentiaryship, lived in no. 23; the chancellor, formerly the second residentiary, lived in no. 13, having moved out of no. 12 when it was taken over by the Cathedral school in 1942; the treasurer, whose office was revived in 1905 and was assigned the prebends once held by the fifth residentiary, lived in no. 24; and the custos, whose office carrying responsibility for the cathedral building was created in 1937 and assigned the prebends once held by the fourth residentiary, lived in no. 20. Nearly all the houses in the Close, including the palace, were owned by the dean and chapter. The exceptions were Bishop's House and no. 6 (the bishop's chauffeur's house), which were the property of the Church Commissioners, and St. John's within the Close and no. 20, owned by the trustees of Lichfield Theological College.[34]

Royal visitors to Lichfield in the 12th and 13th centuries[35] presumably stayed in the Close. Edward II came to Lichfield several times. In 1309 the bishop had rooms prepared for him, presumably in the palace,[36] and in 1323 he stayed in the palace and the queen in the deanery.[37] In 1386 Richard II in the company of several magnates attended the enthronement of Bishop le Scrope.[38] He kept Christmas at Lichfield in 1397, staying until mid January.[39] He returned in May 1398, when he made a treaty with John, duke of Brittany,[40] and in September the same year on the occasion of the enthronement of his confessor, John Burghill. That ceremony was also attended by the archbishops of Canterbury, York, and Dublin, four English bishops, the dukes of York and Exeter, and several earls, and the king gave a feast in the palace to which all the cathedral clergy were invited.[41] Returning for Christmas in 1398, Richard lodged in the palace and received as guests a papal nuncio and an envoy of the Eastern Emperor, Manuel II. Tournaments, proclaimed as far away as Oxford, were held daily, probably up to Epiphany 1399, and a banqueting hall was built next to the great hall of the palace.[42] Within the year Richard was again in Lichfield as the prisoner of Henry Bolingbroke, earl of Lancaster (later Henry IV),

[23] Reade, *Johnsonian Gleanings*, iv. 173, 140; A. L. Reade, *Reades of Blackwood Hill* (priv. print. 1906), 130 n.; *Aris's Birmingham Gaz.* 14 Apr. 1755; W.S.L., Broadsheets 33/25; S.R.O., D. 593/F/3/12/3/1B, pp. 20–1; below, education.
[24] L.J.R.O., D. 30/X, 1709–26, 25 July 1718 and 16 June 1721; D. 30/C.A. viii, ff. 21v., 23.
[25] Above, fig. 4.
[26] Above (cathedral: books and archives); below, public services (water supplies).
[27] Below (ditch).
[28] *Letters of Anna Seward*, iii. 71, 342; iv. 147–8; *Poetical Works of Anna Seward*, ed. W. Scott (Edinburgh, 1810), iii. 161.
[29] *Letters of Anna Seward*, v. 393; L.J.R.O., Newton's College MSS., plan of proposed building.
[30] 37 Geo. III, c. 20 (Priv. Act); Stringer, *Lichfield*, 207, 210, 213.
[31] *V.C.H. Staffs.* iii. 182; *Letters of Anna Seward*, vi. 300;

Recollections of Sophia Lonsdale, ed. V. Martineau, 23.
[32] *V.C.H. Staffs.* iii. 190.
[33] Ibid. 195–6.
[34] Inf. from Mr. L. J. Ainsley, cathedral administrator.
[35] Above, communications.
[36] *Cal. Chanc. Wts.* 289–90; S.R.O., D. (W.) 1734/J. 2057, m. 1 (section relating to forinsec expenses).
[37] Bodl. MS. Ashmole 794, f. 6v.
[38] Wharton, *Anglia Sacra*, i. 450.
[39] *Chron. Mon. Sancti Albani* (Rolls Ser.), iii. 224; *Cal. Pat. 1396–9*, 258, 292.
[40] B.L. Cott. MS. Jul. B. vi, no. 58.
[41] L.J.R.O., D. 30/C.A. i, ff. 52v.–53; Wharton, *Anglia Sacra*, i. 451.
[42] *Historia Vitae et Regni Ricardi Secundi*, ed. G. B. Stow (Univ. of Pennsylvania, 1977), 151; *Cal. Pat. 1399–1401*, 107; *V.C.H. Oxon.* iv. 63; Bodl. MS. Ashmole 1521, p. 20 (2nd nos.).

en route from Chester to London. Richard spent St. Bartholomew's day (24 August), a Sunday, incarcerated in the archdeacon of Chester's house in Beacon Street, whence he apparently attempted an escape.[43]

Later royal visitors included Charles I three times in 1645 when the Close was a royalist garrison,[44] James II in 1687, William III in 1690,[45] Princess Victoria in 1832 and again as queen in 1843,[46] and Queen Adelaide, the widow of William IV, in 1839.[47] Maundy money was distributed in the cathedral by Elizabeth II in 1988.[48]

DITCH, WALL, AND GATES. The Close is protected on the south by Minster Pool and on the other three sides by a deep man-made ditch. According to a 14th-century Lichfield chronicler Bishop Clinton, 1129–48, fortified the castle (*castrum*) of Lichfield.[49] The work may have included the construction of a wall and gates, strengthening the Close. The Close was described as a *castellum c.* 1200, and by the 14th century the mill in Dam Street on the south side of the Close was known as Castle mill.[50] Two gates were recorded in the early 1290s.[51] One was presumably at the south-east corner guarding the approach from the town over Minster Pool dam. The other was evidently at the west end: a house was mentioned in the later 13th century on the north side of a gate towards Gaia.[52]

In 1299 Bishop Langton was licensed to wall the Close in stone and crenellate it.[53] He also rebuilt the gates, which may have already been of stone. To meet the cost he was granted murage in Lichfield for seven years.[54] The work was unfinished at his death in 1321. In 1322, during the crisis involving Thomas, earl of Lancaster, the chapter under royal pressure ordered the immediate clearance of the ditch and the completion of the west tower of the south-east gate.[55]

The fortification comprised corner towers and interval towers along the wall. An octagonal tower at the north-east corner was incorporated in Langton's palace; its base survived in the late 1980s. At the south-east corner there was a parapet along the top of the wall and a projecting turret, which survive as part of the later St. Mary's House. The south-west tower was recorded in 1312–13 and was shown on Speed's

1610 map of Lichfield; it had been demolished by 1661.[56] The north-west tower had a statue of Bishop Walter, presumably Walter Langton, in the 1390s;[57] the tower was evidently another Civil War casualty. Three interval towers were placed on the east wall, two of them incorporated in Langton's palace and the third on the site of the later Selwyn House.[58] The Dean's Tower, so called in 1315, apparently stood on the west wall; it had been demolished by 1661.[59]

The gate built by Langton at the south-east corner of the Close had two towers. The eastern one, whose base was excavated in the late 1980s, was a half-octagon with 12-ft. sides. The western tower was presumably of similar dimension. The gate had a portcullis in 1376.[60] There was a drawbridge, still in existence in the earlier 18th century, which crossed the outflow of water from Minster Pool, and also a wicket for pedestrians.[61] The gate was removed in the mid 18th century in order to improve access for coaches into the Close.[62] A northward extension of the eastern tower was used as a porter's lodge in the early 17th century. After being damaged in the Civil War, it was rebuilt and in 1666 was assessed for tax on four hearths.[63] By 1734 the porter or verger lived in a house at the west gate, and the former lodge was demolished between 1812 and 1836.[64]

The west gate was completed by the chapter in the time of Bishop Northburgh, 1322–58.[65] It was in the form of a tall block with side windows.[66] It was decorated with coats of arms, and there was a statue of the Virgin Mary by 1530.[67] The gate was demolished in 1800 to make room for Newton's College.[68] Traces of its stonework survive on the north side of the road from Beacon Street. A house, evidently at the north-west corner of the gate, was let in 1661 to James Barrow, a tailor. He converted a dungeon underneath the house into a cellar for his own use and was ordered by the chapter to dig another dungeon of the same size with a hole to provide light.[69] In 1734 the house was occupied by the verger; it was rebuilt in 1835 and survives as no. 1 the Close.[70]

There is no evidence that the Close ditch ever contained water. It was dry in the 1590s, and evidently in the mid 1550s.[71] By the mid 17th century it was called the Dimple or Dimble, a name meaning a deep hollow filled with trees or bushes.[72]

[43] *Hist. Vitae et Regni Ricardi Secundi*, 156; *Archaeologia*, xx (1824), 175–6; L.J.R.O., D. 30/C.A. i, f. 56v.
[44] Above, general hist. (the Civil War).
[45] Ibid. (Restoration to end of 18th cent.).
[46] *Dyott's Diary*, ed. R. W. Jeffery, ii. 144–5, 377.
[47] L.J.R.O., D. 30/C.A. x, p. 393.
[48] *Lichfield Mercury*, 8 Apr. 1988, suppl.
[49] Wharton, *Anglia Sacra*, i. 434; *S.H.C.* 4th ser. xi. 8.
[50] Below, econ. hist. (mills).
[51] *S.H.C.* vi (1), 272.
[52] *S.H.C.* 1924, p. 244.
[53] *Cal. Pat.* 1292–1301, 409.
[54] *S.H.C.* 1924, pp. 141–2.
[55] *Cal. Close*, 1318–23, 424; Bodl. MS. Ashmole 794, f. 2v.
[56] *T.S.S.A.H.S.* xviii. 64; L.J.R.O., D. 30/bk. of miscellanea, f. 67; D. 30/XXXI, f. 57; above, fig. 2.
[57] *V.C.H. Staffs.* iii. 276 n.
[58] Stringer, *Lichfield*, 210; below, fig. 12.
[59] *S.H.C.* 1924, p. 96; L.J.R.O., D. 30/bk. of miscellanea, f. 67; D. 30/XXXI, f. 57.

[60] Bodl. MS. Ashmole 794, f. 162.
[61] Stringer, *Lichfield*, 209–10.
[62] Ibid. 210; Harwood, *Lichfield*, 295.
[63] L.J.R.O., D. 30/C 33; *T.S.S.A.H.S.* xxv. 45, 47; *S.H.C.* 1923, 240.
[64] Bodl. G.A. Staffs. 4°, 7, facing p. 295; J. Dewhirst, *Map of Lichfield* (1836); below (next para.).
[65] Wharton, *Anglia Sacra*, i. 447.
[66] Bodl. G.A. Staffs. 4°, 7, facing p. 293; below, plate 2.
[67] Harwood, *Lichfield*, pl. facing p. 293; L.J.R.O., D. 30/C.A. iv, f. 65v.
[68] Harwood, *Lichfield*, 11.
[69] L.J.R.O., D. 30/XXXII, ff. 5, 10v.; D. 30/Ii 4, 11 Oct. 1664; above, fig. 4.
[70] L.J.R.O., D. 30/XXXV, f. 116v.; D. 30/27, specification for new house.
[71] Ibid. D. 30/bk. of miscellanea, f. 67; Erdeswick, *Staffs.* 280–1.
[72] L.J.R.O., D. 30/LIV, f. 97; *Eng. Place-Name Elements* (E.P.N.S.), i. 137.

THE PALACE. In the late 13th century the bishop's house was in the north-east corner of the Close.[73] In 1310–11 the 'old hall', presumably part of his house, stood west of a new house or palace being built for Bishop Langton.[74] Langton's palace stretched along the east wall of the Close and was enclosed by its own wall. Nothing remains above ground, but its layout can be reconstructed from building accounts of 1304–14[75] and a plan of 1685.[76]

Work on the palace started shortly before 1304 and was probably finished in 1314 when Langton was at Lichfield.[77] Walter the carpenter[78] and Hugh de la Dale, a mason,[79] were responsible for a palace whose great hall, 100 ft. by 56 ft., was the fifth or sixth largest in England at the time.[80] Resting on a stone vault and entered at first floor level, the hall was probably aisled, with columns supporting an elaborately carved wooden roof, admired in 1634 for its gilt carvings.[81] Paintings of the coronation, marriages, wars, and funeral of Edward I decorated the walls; they were still visible in the 1590s.[82] There were probably windows in the north and south gable ends and evidently along the west side which overlooked a garden. The bishop's private quarters lay north of the hall. To the south what was called the Lady's Chamber in 1685 was possibly a reception room. Its name may have derived from decoration with emblems of the Virgin, to whom Langton's devotion is suggested by his inauguration of work on the cathedral's Lady Chapel. Although the chamber occupied the normal position of the buttery and pantry, it is unlikely to have been used for that purpose because access from the free-standing kitchen south of the hall was by a passage under the chamber and up a stair into the hall. The passage led at ground level past a chapel, whose east end was a tower protruding from the Close wall. The chapel may have had two storeys: a lower one with access from the passage for the use of servants, and an upper one with access from the Lady's Chamber for the bishop's use. The kitchen opened into a service courtyard in which there was a stable-block. Other outbuildings there included a bakehouse, a granary, a hay barn, a salthouse, a 'dressours' (where meat was dressed), a dovecot, and a pinfold. At the south end of the courtyard was a gateway which faced the main, south-east entrance of the Close. The palace grounds were entered through a gateway in the south-west corner of an inner courtyard. Chambers over the gateway were apparently approached by an external staircase and included an oriel window.

The gateway was part of a long range of chambers for members of the bishop's household. On the north side of the courtyard was a private garden evidently created for Langton by Walter the gardener.

There was a warden of the palace in 1306–7 when his daily wage was 1½d., reduced to 1d. by the mid 15th century.[83] In 1461 Bishop Hales engaged William the plumber to maintain and repair the lead on the palace roof. He was given a plot of land against the outer wall of the palace, on which he was to build a house. William was still paid his fee in 1476.[84] In 1479 the bishop employed the palace warden, John Paxson, to maintain the lead; Paxson was also the cathedral sacrist.[85] The warden in the mid 1520s was William Blythe, presumably a relative of Bishop Blythe.[86]

In 1638 Bishop Wright complained that the palace was unsuitable as a residence because parts were occupied by 'maltsters and others'.[87] It was severely damaged during the Civil War. A report in 1671 noted that all the timber work of the hall and of the chambers at its north end had been destroyed and that only the stone vault remained; the long range of chambers in the inner courtyard also lacked its roof. What remained of the fabric had been used as a quarry when Bishop Hacket, 1661–70, renovated a house on the south side of the Close as his residence.[88] The only fragment of the medieval palace which survives above ground is the base of a column found in the early 20th century and set up in the garden.[89]

By 1672 Bishop Wood was suing Hacket's son and executor, Sir Andrew Hacket, for compensation for Hacket's additional damage to the palace,[90] and in 1684 Wood was ordered to pay £2,600 and Hacket £1,400 towards the cost of rebuilding. Wood was suspended from office in the same year, and the responsibility for carrying out the work fell to Archbishop Sancroft, who delegated the task to Dean Addison. The site was cleared and a new palace built on an east–west alignment across the inner courtyard. Work began in May 1686 and was completed by October 1687. The architect was Edward Pierce (or Pearce). Of brick with stone dressings, the palace comprised on the ground floor a central hall and parlour with a drawing room on the east and a chapel on the west. A bakehouse, brewhouse, and pigsty were built in the north-west corner of the grounds, the rest of which was laid out as gardens and a cherry orchard. After his reinstatement Bishop Wood refused to live there, preferring Eccleshall Castle. His succes-

[73] Dugdale, *Mon.* vi (3), 1242.
[74] S.R.O., D. (W.) 1734/J. 2057, mm. 4 (section relating to cost of new wall), 9 (forinsec expenses). The building is first described as *palacio* in 1447–8: L.J.R.O., B/A/21, CC 124078, m. 1.
[75] S.R.O., D. (W.) 1734/J. 2057, mm. 1–9.
[76] Below, fig. 12. Dr. John H. Harvey is thanked for his help with the following para.
[77] L.J.R.O., B/A/1/1, f. 117.
[78] S.R.O., D. (W.) 1734/J. 2057, mm. 1 (cost of new work), 7 (cost of houses).
[79] Ibid. m. 9 (forinsec expenses); Bodl. MS. Ashmole 1527, f. 39v.
[80] M. Wood, *Eng. Medieval House* (1965), 45–6, 62–6.
[81] *Relation of a Short Survey of 26 Counties, 1634*, ed. L. G.

Wickham Legg, 58.
[82] Erdeswick, *Staffs.* 281–2.
[83] S.R.O., D. (W.) 1734/J. 2057, m. 9 (wages); L.J.R.O., B/A/21, CC 124078, m. 1.
[84] S.R.O., D. (W.) 1734/3/2/5; L.J.R.O., B/A/21, CC 123984, m. 6d.
[85] P.R.O., SC 6/Hen. VII/1846, m. 5.
[86] S.R.O., D. (W.) 1734/3/2/11, m. 1; D. (W.) 1734/3/2/12, m. 1.
[87] *Cal. S.P. Dom.* 1638–9, 119.
[88] S.R.O. 547/1, ff. 107–8; L.J.R.O., palace building accts., H. Archbold and J. Allen to Sir A. Hacket, 10 July 1671.
[89] L.J.R.O., D. 85/2/2, p. [3].
[90] Para. based on *T.S.S.A.H.S.* xxvii. 57–63.

sors followed suit, and the palace was let to tenants: Lord Stanhope, later earl of Chesterfield, by 1706;[91] Rebecca, widow of Sir Wolstan Dixie, in 1727;[92] Gilbert Walmisley (d. 1751), the bishop's registrar;[93] Canon Thomas Seward (d. 1790) and his daughter Anna (d. 1809);[94] Sir Charles Oakeley (d. 1826), former governor of Madras, and then his widow Helena (d. 1838);[95] and the Revd. John Hinckley (d. 1867), vicar of Sheriffhales and of Woodcote (Salop.).[96] The palace became the bishop's residence when Bishop Selwyn moved in, evidently in the late 1860s. He added a chapel at the north-west corner in 1868 and front wings in 1869.[97] Apart from the years 1922 to 1931 when Bishop Kempthorne exchanged accommodation with theological college students from Selwyn House, the palace remained the bishop's home until 1953. That year Bishop Reeve moved into Bishop's House on the south side of the Close, and the palace was vested in the dean and chapter. Since 1954 it has been occupied by the Cathedral school.[98]

THE DEANERY. The dean's house occupies its ancient site west of the bishop's palace. The hall of the medieval house apparently projected east from a north–south range 148 ft. long.[99] The house was badly damaged during the Civil War and was assessed for tax on only two hearths in 1666.[1] Dean Wood, 1663–71, dismantled what remained of the hall with the intention of re building it, and the house was sufficiently habitable in 1687 to accommodate James II.[2] In the early 18th century Dean Binckes built a new deanery. The southern part of the long range was taken down, because it was ruinous and obscured the view from the new palace. A front was built at a right-angle to the remaining portion of the range with a central doorway flanked by three windows on either side.[3] The building was completed in 1707.[4] The doorway was moved to its present position on the east side of the house in 1807–8, when internal remodelling also took place.[5] Additions and further alterations were made in 1876 and 1893.[6] The northern part of the medieval range, which had been converted into outbuildings, was demolished in 1967.[7]

THE HOUSES OF THE VICARS CHORAL. In 1315 Bishop Langton gave the vicars choral land at the west end of the Close previously held by a canon; the grant excluded a dovecot and a barn.[8] In the 16th century it was believed that Langton had given the vicars the site of two canonical houses.[9] Possibly he later gave them the property reserved in 1315: Darwin House on the west side of the vicars' lower courtyard stands partly on land known in the 18th century as the Dovehouse.[10] The vicars built their houses college-style around two courtyards with a common hall presumably at the west end of the central range. The upper courtyard was known as Vicars' Close in the late 1980s and the houses there have their own sequence of numbers.[11] The houses in the lower courtyard, which were remodelled in the 18th century to face the cathedral and the road from Beacon Street, are numbered as part of the sequence in the Close.

The first vicars to occupy the site apparently built their own chambers or houses, although it was subsequently the dean and chapter who assigned them to new vicars and authorized exchanges.[12] The common hall, mentioned in 1321, had a solar at its north end in 1334.[13] A common kitchen was recorded in 1329.[14] The vicars, however, continued as before to dine daily with the resident canons. In 1390 their dining rights were withdrawn and they had to provide themselves with a dining hall, the earlier common hall presumably being too small.[15] It was probably to meet the need that the vicars in 1399–1400 were granted, presumably by Bishop Burghill, the 'new house' which Richard II had had built in the palace grounds in 1398.[16] Material from it was probably used to enlarge the common hall. The hall was rebuilt and the houses repaired at the charge of Thomas Chesterfield, a canon of Lichfield 1425–52.[17]

In 1474 Dean Heywood rebuilt the south side of the lower courtyard. The new work included a two-storeyed block comprising a chamber called *le drawth* for infirm vicars, a chapel where the vicars could study and pray and where infirm vicars could hear mass, a muniment room for documents and treasures, and other small buildings (*domicule*). The walls were plastered and the windows glazed. The block had its own entrance gate on the road from Beacon Street.[18] The gable end of a chamber over a latrine, on the north side of the west gate of the Close, survived in the early 19th century.[19]

The Civil War appears to have left the vicars' houses relatively undamaged. Of the 20 houses listed in 1649, only two in the lower courtyard

[91] Jackson, *Lichfield*, 208; below, Roman Catholicism.
[92] Reade, *Johnsonian Gleanings*, vi. 112 n.
[93] *V.C.H. Staffs.* iii. 189.
[94] Ibid. 189–90.
[95] *D.N.B.*; W.S.L., S. MS. 384, p. 217.
[96] Reade, *Johnsonian Gleanings*, vii. 166–7.
[97] *V.C.H. Staffs.* iii. 79; Pevsner, *Staffs.* 188; below, plate 15.
[98] *Lichfield Mercury*, 24 July 1953, p. 7; 26 Mar. 1954, p. 3; below (other houses: Selwyn House).
[99] H. E. Savage, *Dr. Binckes, in Convocation and the Deanery* (Lichfield, 1929), 21–2.
[1] *T.S.S.A.H.S.* xxv. 44; *S.H.C.* 1923, 240.
[2] Savage, *Binckes*, 22; above, general hist. (Restoration to end of 18th cent.).
[3] Savage, *Binckes*, 21–2 and frontispiece.
[4] Bodl. MS. Rawl. D. 1481, p. 87.
[5] Savage, *Binckes*, 22–3; L.J.R.O., D. 30/XLIII, ff. 48v.–49; below, plate 10.

[6] Savage, *Binckes*, 23.
[7] Inf. from Mr. N. Hastilow, formerly architectural adviser to the dean and chapter.
[8] L.J.R.O., D. 30/K 2.
[9] Wharton, *Anglia Sacra*, i. 447.
[10] L.J.R.O., VC/A/21, CC 164146A, p. 341.
[11] Below, plate 8.
[12] e.g. Bodl. MS. Ashmole 794, ff. 18, 40v., 54.
[13] Ibid. ff. 1v., 48.
[14] Ibid. f. 34v.
[15] *V.C.H. Staffs.* iii. 153, 156; L.J.R.O., D. 30/XIII, ff. 37v.–38.
[16] Bodl. MS. Ashmole 1521, p. 20 (2nd nos.).
[17] *V.C.H. Staffs.* iii. 164; Le Neve, *Fasti, 1300–1541, Coventry and Lichfield*, 18, 60.
[18] Lichfield Cath. Libr., MS. Lichfield 4, f. 27.
[19] *T.S.S.A.H.S.* xxv. 41 (no. 6); W.S.L., Staffs. Views, v. 166; L.J.R.O., VC/A/21, CC 17529, plan 14.

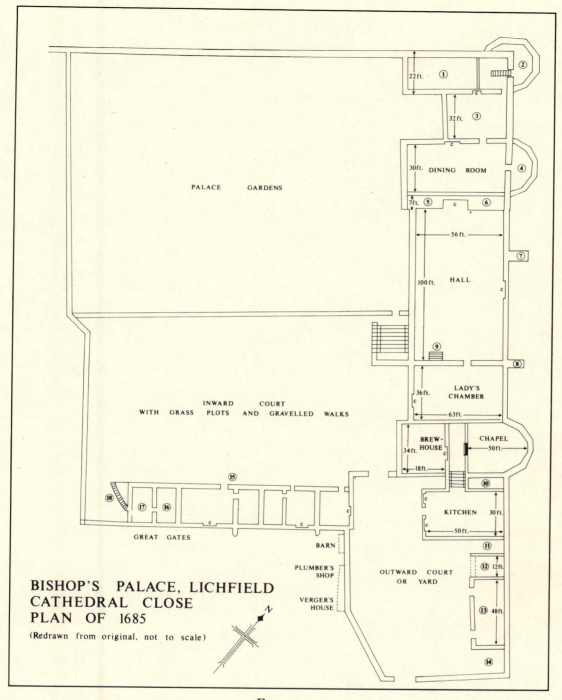

PALACE GARDENS

22 ft. ① ② ③ 32 ft.

30 ft. DINING ROOM ④

7 ft. ⑤ c ⑥

56 ft. ⑦

100 ft. HALL

INWARD COURT
WITH GRASS PLOTS AND GRAVELLED WALKS

⑨ ⑧

36 ft. LADY'S CHAMBER

63 ft.

BREW-HOUSE CHAPEL
34 ft. 50 ft.

18 ft. ⑩

KITCHEN 30 ft.

50 ft.

⑪

⑫ 12 ft.

⑬ 48 ft.

⑭

⑮
⑱ ⑰ ⑯
c c c

GREAT GATES

BARN

PLUMBER'S SHOP

VERGER'S HOUSE

OUTWARD COURT OR YARD

BISHOP'S PALACE, LICHFIELD
CATHEDRAL CLOSE
PLAN OF 1685
(Redrawn from original, not to scale)

N

FIG. 12

1 Lodging or other room. 2 Tower, 52 ft. high, each edge 13 ft. on the outside. 3 Bishop's lodging room. 4 Second tower, each edge 10 ft. 5 & 6 Pantry. 7 & 8 Buttery [i.e. buttress] made out into the Dimples. 9 Stairs into the passage under the Lady's Chamber. 10 Open ground for a sough for the rain water from the roofs of the chapel and kitchen. 11 Open ground for pens for poultry etc. 12 Coach-house with folding doors. 13 Stables. 14 Where [there] was the dunghill. 15 Lodging rooms for the bishop's gentlemen, 20 ft. high. 16 Porter's chamber [over gateway]. 17 Gatehouse chamber [over gateway]. 18 Stairs up side of buttress. c chimney.

The names for the various parts of the palace are those given in the original plan, but the spelling has been modernized. In addition to the measurements here shown in diagramatic form, the plan gives the thickness of the inner wall of the east range from the north end to the brewhouse as 6 ft.

The plan gives additional information relating to the cellars and roofs: hall, 'roof leaded, cellar[e]d under all with stone arches'; dining room, chambers 1 and 3, and Lady's Chamber, 'roof leaded, cellar[e]d under with timber work'; chapel, 'roof leaded'; brewhouse, 'roof[e]d shorewise only [i.e. a lean-to roof] and tiled'; kitchen, 'roof tiled, not cellar[e]d under but as low at least as the cellars'; coach-house and stables, 'roof tiled'; lodging rooms for the bishop's gentlemen, 'all chamber[e]d over, but the chamber floors were all lay[e]d with plaster'.

near the Close gate together with the latrine were described as completely ruined; the common hall was also badly damaged.[20]

In the early 18th century most of the houses were considered to be in good repair. Half of the 20 recorded in 1706 were occupied by tenants,[21] and wealthy tenants may have been responsible in the early 18th century for remodelling in brick the houses in the lower courtyard. By 1732 houses along the southern range there had been remodelled to front outwards and not into the courtyard,[22] and two houses at the west end of that range (nos. 2 and 3 the Close, formerly one house, and no. 4) were heightened and provided with fronts of five bays. The eastern range of the same courtyard was similarly remodelled in the 18th century. The vicars took down their common hall in 1756 and built a new one at the west end of the central range, presumably the site of the one it replaced. The new hall, 46 ft. by 25 ft. and 30 ft. high, was at first-floor level, approached by an oak staircase from the east, and had an oriel window facing Beacon Street.[23] At the east end was a new muniment room.[24] The completion of the hall in 1757 was marked by a concert of music and dancing, and the hall's use for public assemblies continued until the late 18th century.[25] By 1800 it had been divided, the west end being converted into flats.[26] Part of the ceiling decoration survives, but the staircase was removed c. 1979 when no. 4 Vicars' Close was remodelled.

In 1758 Erasmus Darwin, the physician, converted a timber-framed house on the west side of the lower courtyard into a large brick house with a front facing Beacon Street.[27] The house, later known as Darwin House, has a central doorway and venetian windows and was originally approached from Beacon Street by a bridge across the ditch.[28] The bridge was later replaced by a double flight of stone steps. Houses on the west side of the upper courtyard were remodelled in 1764 as a three-bayed house faced with brick.[29]

In 1988 the house at the south-east corner of the lower courtyard (no. 7 the Close) was converted into offices, and in the same year the ground floor of no. 9 was opened as a bookshop and coffee shop.

Later rebuilding and the frequent subdivision and amalgamation of houses have obscured the original structures. The most complete row of medieval building is along the north side of the upper courtyard, where the timber-framed houses are all of one bay; they are jettied to the south and have a tall chimney-stack against their north wall. The east side of the courtyard and the eastern half of the central range are also timber-framed, and three timber-framed houses survive at the east end of the south range of the lower courtyard.

OTHER HOUSES. There was a house in the north-west corner of the Close in the early 14th century.[30] A house on the site of no. 12 was damaged during the Civil War, but it was still inhabited in 1666 when assessed for tax on three hearths.[31] It was assigned to the second residentiary in 1797. The central range and cross wing of the present house may be 17th-century in date and the brickwork of the lower floors is 18th-century. The house was extensively remodelled in the early 19th century by the Lichfield architect Joseph Potter the elder.[32] In 1865 a third storey was added and most of the windows were altered.[33] In 1942 the house, which had been occupied by the chancellor, was opened as a preparatory school, known as St. Chad's Cathedral school and later as Lichfield Cathedral school.[34] The school still used the house in 1989.

A house on the site of nos. 13 and 14 was assigned in 1527 by Bishop Blythe as a residence for the cathedral choristers and their master. A gatehouse was built in front of the house in 1531 by Dean Denton, whose arms and rebus were engraved over the archway.[35] By the 1580s the choristers were no longer living in common, and the house was let.[36] In the 1620s the gatehouse was fitted up as a song school by Michael East, the master of the choristers, who lived in an adjoining building, probably the gatehouse of the neighbouring canonical house.[37] The common hall of the choristers' house ran east–west, with a parlour in the west crosswing and service rooms and entry in the east; part of the fabric survived in the late 1980s in the upper storey of no. 13.

By the 17th century the east wing had been enlarged as a kitchen range, and in 1666 the house was assessed for tax on 10 hearths.[38] It may have been divided in the earlier 18th century, when the western part (the later no. 13), comprising the former common hall and parlour, was given a brick front with canted bays and a central staircase.[39] In 1772 the lessee of both parts, John Daniel, was permitted to demolish the gatehouse,[40] and he probably extended south the eastern part (the later no. 14). A staircase and entrance hall were installed in the former service area in the earlier 19th century. The internal divisions of both parts of the

[20] T.S.S.A.H.S. xxv. 37–8, 41–4; Harwood, Lichfield, 266.
[21] L.J.R.O., D. 30/C.A. vii, f. 131v.
[22] Below, plate 3.
[23] L.J.R.O., D. 30/C.A. vii, f. 235v.; L.J.R.O., VC/A/21, CC 17529, plan 14, nos. 8–9; Parker, Lichfield, 32–3; below, plate 20.
[24] L.J.R.O., D. 30/C.A. vii, ff. 235v., 238v.; L.J.R.O., VC/A/21, CC 17529, plan 14, no. 9.
[25] Harwood, Lichfield, 291–2; Shaw, Staffs. i. 308; Aris's Birmingham Gaz. 5 Nov. 1764; 3 Apr. 1780; 25 Dec. 1797.
[26] L.J.R.O., VC/A/21, CC 164146B, p. 256.
[27] L.J.R.O., D. 15/8/3/2, deed of 8 Aug. 1760; D. 30/XXXVIII, f. 3v.; A. Seward, Memoirs of the Life of Dr. Darwin (1804), 14–15; D. King-Hele, Erasmus Darwin, 17–18.
[28] Below, plate 20.
[29] L.J.R.O., VC/A/21, CC 17529, plan 14, no. 10; date stone on house.
[30] L.J.R.O., D. 30/K 2.
[31] T.S.S.A.H.S. xxv. 44; S.H.C. 1923, 240.
[32] L.J.R.O., D. 15/8/1/2; D. 30/XLV, f. 156v.; Lichfield Cath. Libr., MS. Lichfield 79, p. 147; Bodl. G.A. Staffs. 4°, 6, facing p. 161.
[33] L.J.R.O., B/A/13/III Lichfield, 2nd canonry.
[34] V.C.H. Staffs. iii. 196–7.
[35] Ibid. 164–5; Gent. Mag. lii. 559.
[36] V.C.H. Staffs. iii. 172–3; L.J.R.O., D. 30/bk. of miscellanea, f. 67v.
[37] L.J.R.O., D. 30/L 5; T.S.S.A.H.S. xxv. 43–4.
[38] S.H.C. 1923, 239.
[39] Below, plate 9.
[40] V.C.H. Staffs. iii. 189; L.J.R.O., D. 30/X, 1772–85, 31 July 1772.

house were altered during the 19th century.[41] In 1924 a library to house the collection of Dean Savage was opened in no. 14.[42] It was moved to the back of the house in 1975 when the dean and chapter's office was established in the front.[43] In the late 1980s no. 13 was occupied by the chancellor.

In 1367 there was a house on the plot where no. 15 was later built.[44] In the mid 17th century its gatehouse adjoined that of the choristers' house.[45] The house was damaged during the Civil War and may have been demolished soon afterwards: the central range of no. 15 and a short east wing are 17th-century and perhaps date from the Restoration. It was assigned to the fourth residentiary in 1797. Piecemeal extensions to the north and west were made in the late 18th century, and in the early 19th century a new staircase and west and south-west wings, each of one room, were added.[46] A kiosk in the south-west corner of the garden, used from the mid 1980s for the sale of refreshments, was built in 1803 as a water conduit for the Close.[47]

Selwyn House, in the ditch on the east side of the Close, was built in 1780 for Canon James Falconer.[48] It appears to incorporate a brick building, possibly of the earlier 18th century. It principal elevation is to the Close, with two lower floors facing the ditch. It was enlarged in the early 19th century and was given an iron balcony on the north. In 1908 it became a hostel for students of Lichfield Theological College and was named Selwyn Hostel in memory of a previous resident, Harriet Selwyn (d. 1907), the widow of Bishop Selwyn. In 1922 the students moved into the palace, and the house was the bishop's residence until 1931, when the students moved back.[49] After the closure of the college in 1972, Selwyn House was divided into flats.

St. Mary's House incorporates an early 14th-century house built into the south-east corner of the Close wall, perhaps by Bishop Langton. The house was originally either L-shaped or built round a courtyard, with a first floor hall reached on the west side by an external staircase. A further three storeys were reached by an internal staircase inside a defensive turret projecting from the south-east corner; the top storey gave access to the parapet of the Close wall. There is a 15th-century window on the south side of the house.[50] In 1626 the house, formerly occupied by the prebendary of Freeford, was known as

'the old palace'.[51] As it stood outside the grounds of the medieval palace, the reason for the name is uncertain. It was remodelled internally in 1710 by its occupant, Canon Walter Horton,[52] and again in 1804–5,[53] following its appropriation to the third residentiaryship in 1797. Under the Cathedrals Act of 1840 that residentiaryship was abolished, but the house remained occupied by the holder until his death in 1845. It became the vicarage for St. Mary's, Lichfield, apparently in 1851 and so remained until 1965 when it was converted into diocesan offices.[54]

No. 19 stands on the site of a brick house built in the early 16th century by George Strangeways, archdeacon of Coventry.[55] In 1662 that house was chosen as a residence by Bishop Hacket, who spent some £800 restoring and adding to it. When the work was completed in 1667 the house contained a dining room and a gallery and 34 or 35 other rooms; there was a stable for 16 horses in the south-east corner of the garden.[56] Hacket apparently tried to secure the house as the bishop's palace but after his death in 1670 it once more became a canonical house.[57] In the later 18th century it was occupied by Charles Howard (d. 1771), a proctor in the consistory court, who improved the garden behind the house with a grotto of shells and fossils.[58] In 1797 the house was assigned to the diocesan registrar. It then comprised a central range with wings at either end; at the back the ground floor, which extended beyond the Close bank, was supported by arches.[59] It was demolished in 1799, and William Mott, the deputy diocesan registrar, built a new house.[60] It continued to be occupied by the registrar or his deputy until 1987, when on the retirement of Mr. M. B. S. Exham as registrar it passed to Lichfield Diocesan Board of Finance which sold it that year to the dean and chapter.[61]

Mott fitted out Hacket's stable as a muniment room.[62] A new stable was added on the north side of the room, and part of it was converted into the chapter clerk's office in 1925.[63] The office was moved in 1975 to no. 14 the Close. Most of the diocesan records were deposited in the Lichfield Joint Record Office in 1968 and the remainder in 1984. The whole building was converted as the Lichfield Cathedral Visitors' Study Centre, the first part in 1986 and the second in 1989.[64]

[41] L.J.R.O., D. 15/11/14/80; Lichfield Cath. Libr., Savage Papers, B 4/4/1/12.
[42] V.C.H. Staffs. iii. 197.
[43] Inf. from Mr. S. T. Bridgewater, former cathedral administrator.   [44] S.H.C. N.S. x (2), 121–2.
[45] T.S.S.A.H.S. xxv. 44.
[46] L.J.R.O., D. 30/XLIV, ff. 178v.–179; Bodl. G.A. Staffs. 4°, 6, facing p. 163.
[47] Below, public services (water supplies).
[48] L.J.R.O., B/A/21, CC 123942–3; L.J.R.O., D. 30/X, 1772–85, 11 Aug. 1780.
[49] Lichfield Mercury, 29 Mar. 1907, p. 5; 27 Mar. 1908, p. 5; L.J.R.O., D. 85/2/3, pp. 44–5.
[50] Below, plate 11.
[51] L.J.R.O., D. 30/C 33.
[52] Plaque on north side of house. For views of 1799 see Bodl. G.A. Staffs. 4°, 6, facing p. 163.
[53] L.J.R.O., D. 30/XLII, ff. 122v.–123.
[54] Below, churches.   [55] B.L. Harl. MS. 3839, f. 40.
[56] Bodl. MS. Tanner 45, f. 18; MS. Tanner 131, f. 68;

L.J.R.O., palace building accts., certification of 26 June 1672.
[57] V.C.H. Staffs. iii. 177; L.J.R.O., D. 30/XXXIII, f. 17; D. 30/C.A. vii, f. 154.
[58] Reade, Johnsonian Gleanings, iv. 106–7, 112–14; Poetical Works of Anna Seward, i, p. cviii; W.S.L., S. MS. 478, Lady Holte to Chas. Howard, 1774.
[59] Bodl. G.A. Staffs. 4°, 7, facing p. 295 (front and back views).
[60] Bodl. MS. Top. Staffs. C 1, f. 68v.; Harwood, Lichfield, 295. For a view of it as part of the aspect of the south side of the Close in 1817 see Bodl. G.A. Staffs. 4°, 7, facing p. 293.
[61] Inf. from Mr. M. B. S. Exham.
[62] Harwood, Lichfield, 295. For an external view in 1812 see Bodl. G.A. Staffs. 4°, 7, facing p. 297. The muniments were badly stored: W. D. Bruce, Acct. of the present deplorable state of Eccl. Courts of Record (1854), 37–40.
[63] L.J.R.O., D. 30/C.A. xix, 1–2.
[64] Inf. from Mr. Exham and Canon A. N. Barnard, cathedral chancellor.

The site of no. 20 was also acquired by Bishop Hacket. In 1666 he built a stone house there, possibly as a banqueting hall.[65] An oak panel dated 1669, bearing his arms and those of the diocese, was placed over the fireplace in the house; it was moved, probably in the early 19th century, to the entrance hall of the palace, where it remains.[66] In 1692 the house was used as the diocesan registrar's office and muniment room.[67] Having moved the registry to no. 19, William Mott bought the house in 1803. He let it to Richard Wright, who used it until 1806 to display items from the museum of his grandfather, Richard Greene.[68] The house was demolished in 1819.[69] It was rebuilt in 1833 by Mott's son John, also deputy diocesan registrar.[70] In 1871 the house was acquired for the principal of Lichfield Theological College.[71] The college was closed in 1972,[72] and in the late 1980s the house was occupied by the cathedral custos.

There was a canonical house west of the site of no. 20 in the early 15th century.[73] In 1798 it was let to William Mott, who bought it in 1803.[74] His son John probably rebuilt it when he built no. 20 in 1833, and in 1872 it too was acquired by the theological college.[75] After the college's closure the house was let to the trustees of St. John's hospital, who demolished it and in 1981 built an almshouse, called St. John's within the Close, to the design of W. Hobbiss & Partners of Birmingham.[76]

Land further west was assigned in 1411 by Bishop Burghill as the site for a residence, later known as New College, for the 13 cathedral chantry priests.[77] The building, constructed in 1414 and improved in 1468, comprised a range of chambers round a central courtyard. The hall stood at the south-east corner with a kitchen and a buttery at its west end; there was a chapel in the west range. After the dissolution of the chantries in 1548, the college was sold to London speculators, and by 1564 it was owned by the archdeacon of Stafford, Richard Walker (d. 1567). Walker was also master of Lichfield grammar school, and it was presumably as a result of his endowment of the school that the college was acquired by Lichfield corporation.[78] An extension at the south end of the west range was mentioned in a lease of c. 1590 to Edward

Noble and his wife Isabel. In 1666 the property was assessed for tax on 16 hearths.[79] It was later divided into separate houses: there were three in 1708 and four in 1755.[80] One was demolished in 1817, and the others were let by the corporation in 1819 to William Mott for 10,000 years.[81] The site was acquired by Lichfield Theological College in 1872, and a library and student rooms were built on it. A chapel was added in 1885.[82] In 1980 the chapel was converted into an educational and social centre, known as the Refectory.[83]

There was a house on the site of Bishop's House in 1411,[84] and two lengths of ashlar wall at basement level may survive from it. By the late 18th century the house had a gabled range facing the Close and a rear wing. It was remodelled internally in 1796 by the lessee, J. F. Mucklestone, the subchanter; he also built a stable and a coach house to the east.[85] The house was assigned to the sixth residentiary in 1797. Under the Cathedrals Act of 1840 the house and stable were assigned to the chapter clerk, but the coach house was assigned to the occupier of no. 24, the fifth residentiary, whose own coach house had been demolished in 1800.[86] In the later 19th century a large block was added south-east of the house and both main elevations were rebuilt. The house became the bishop's residence in 1953.

The south and west walls of no. 23 contain the remains of a courtyard house built in red brick by Henry Edial, prebendary of Gaia Minor 1480–1520.[87] The brickwork was decorated with dark headers representing a cross and St. Peter's keys on the west chimney stack and St. Laurence's gridiron on the south wall.[88] The house, which was assigned to the first residentiary in 1797, was extensively remodelled c. 1812;[89] the courtyard was roofed over to form a spacious hall with a staircase in Tudor Gothic style. The staircase was renewed c. 1900. Part of the house was apparently occupied in 1891 as St. Werburga's Home, established that year as a layworkers' training and retreat house run by deaconesses; the first residentiary canon was the warden.[90] In the late 1980s the house was occupied by the precentor.

The predecessor of no. 24 was in ruins in 1461 when it was assigned to Thomas Milley, preben-

[65] L.J.R.O., palace building accts., H. Archbold and J. Allen to Sir A. Hacket, 10 July 1671; Bodl. G.A. Staffs. 4°, 6, facing p. 66; Stringer, *Lichfield*, 209.
[66] L.J.R.O., D. 85/2/3, f. 2v.
[67] Ibid. D. 30/XXXIII, f. 17; D. 30/C.A. vii, f. 154; Jackson, *Lichfield*, 205–6.
[68] L.J.R.O., Theol. Coll. deeds, deed of 7 July 1803; *Aris's Birmingham Gaz.* 27 June 1803; below, social and cultural activities (museums).
[69] Stringer, *Lichfield*, 209.
[70] W.S.L., S. MS. 371 (iv), 38; below, econ. hist. (professions).
[71] P.R.O., RG 10/2914; E. C. Inman, *Hist. of Lichfield Theological College 1857–1927*, 25–6.
[72] Inf. from the trustees of the Theological College.
[73] Dugdale, *Mon.* vi (3), 1254.
[74] L.J.R.O., Theol. Coll. deeds, deeds of 1 Jan. and 21 July 1798, 19 July 1803.
[75] Inman, *Lichfield Theol. Coll.* 28.
[76] *Lichfield Mercury*, 10 Apr. 1981, p. 19; below, chars. for the poor.
[77] Para. based on *T.S.S.A.H.S.* xxvi. 36–43.

[78] Harwood, *Lichfield*, 211; *V.C.H. Staffs.* vi. 159. Walker is wrongly described as dean in *T.S.S.A.H.S.* xxvi. 37.
[79] *S.H.C.* 1923, 239.
[80] L.J.R.O., D. 77/9/51, deed of 19 Apr. 1708; S.R.O., D. 546/3/1/1.
[81] L.J.R.O., D. 77/5/3, ff. 63v., 94v.; D. 77/9/51, deed of 29 Dec. 1819.
[82] Inman, *Lichfield Theol. Coll.* 28, 42.
[83] Inf. from Canon G. M. Smallwood, former cathedral custos.
[84] Dugdale, *Mon.* vi (3), 1254.
[85] Bodl. G.A. Staffs. 4°, 6, facing p. 162; L.J.R.O., D. 30/papers re Revd. R. Foote's house, Aug. 1797.
[86] *Lond. Gaz.* 12 Mar. 1841, p. 664; below (Newton's College).
[87] B.L. Harl. MS. 3839, f. 40; Le Neve, *Fasti, 1300–1541, Coventry and Lichfield*, 43; below, plate 7 (the house is identifiable as no. 23 by reference to Bodl. G.A. Staffs. 4°, 6, facing p. 161).
[88] Below, plate 6.
[89] L.J.R.O., D. 30/XLIV, f. 94.
[90] *Lich. Dioc. Mag.* xii. 2, 22, 91; *Staffs. Advertiser*, 10 Jan. 1891, p. 3; *V.C.H. Staffs.* iii. 87.

dary of Hansacre and later archdeacon of Coventry. He rebuilt it in red brick over stone vaults which abutted the Close bank; the north-west corner of the house appears to incorporate the base of a stone tower which was presumably part of a wall built on the bank. The house rises to three storeys on the south side; some of its exterior brickwork and stone dressings survive.[91] It was assessed for tax on 10 hearths in 1666, when it was occupied by Sir Walter Littleton, the diocesan chancellor.[92] It had been damaged during the Civil War, and Littleton restored it at a cost of over £500.[93] Alterations in the 18th century included the addition of a staircase against the south-west chimney stack and a Gothick triple window on the north side. The house was assigned to the fifth residentiary in 1797. It was remodelled c. 1814 when part of the south wall was rebuilt and most of the windows altered.[94] In the late 1980s the house was occupied by the treasurer, who was also archdeacon of Lichfield.

A house which adjoined no. 24 on the north-west was demolished in 1800, along with no. 24's coach house, the west gate of the Close, and part of a house in the ditch, to make room for Newton's College.[95] The college was established by Andrew Newton as an almshouse for the widows and unmarried daughters of clergy, primarily of those who had served in Lichfield cathedral. Newton (d. 1806), the son of a Lichfield brandy and cider merchant, gave it an endowment of £20,000.[96] The college building comprises a range of 16 dwellings with a central doorway, designed by Joseph Potter the elder and built in brick with stone facings on the south side of the road from Beacon Street. The first almswomen moved in probably towards the end of 1803.[97] A house, also designed by Potter, was built soon afterwards at the south-west corner of the range in Beacon Street and provided a further four dwellings.[98] Two dwellings at the west end of the range were demolished in 1929, and a garden was laid out over the site. At the same time the other dwellings in the range were adapted for nine residents and the Beacon Street house was converted into three flats.[99] Because of a lack of eligible almswomen, the college trustees transferred the building to the dean and chapter in 1988.[1]

There was formerly a house in the south-west angle of the Close wall, probably incorporating a defensive turret like that at St. Mary's House. In 1311 a house there was assigned to Geoffrey de Blaston, archdeacon of Derby, whose 'tower' near Minster Pool was recorded in 1312. The house then had a hall with a solar and a cellar at one end and a separate kitchen and bakehouse; work on another solar and cellar at the other end had recently been started by Bishop Langton. As the previous occupant had been the bishop's nephew, Walter of Clipston, Langton was probably responsible for building all of the house.[2] Both the house and the tower were destroyed during the Civil War.[3]

Moat House in the south-west part of the Close ditch was built in the earlier 18th century by Thomas Ames. In the early 19th century it was occupied by Henry Chinn, a lawyer.[4] It is adjoined on the south by Langton House, built probably in the mid 18th century. Dimble House in the north-west corner of the ditch was built probably in the late 18th century.[5]

MANOR AND OTHER ESTATES

MANOR. An episcopal estate covering much of south-east Staffordshire was entered in Domesday Book under the heading *LICHFIELD*. It may have been given to St. Wilfrid by King Wulfhere in the late 660s as an endowment for the new diocese.[6] The town of Lichfield, created in the mid 12th century, became known as the manor of Lichfield, and the remaining part of the Domesday estate was by the mid 13th century called the manor of Longdon.[7] Lichfield manor was held by the bishop until 1548 when Bishop Sampson was forced to grant his lordship in the town, but not in the Close, to the corporation established by Edward VI earlier that year.[8] In 1582 Bishop Overton tried to reclaim the lordship.[9] He was evidently unsuccessful, and in 1598 he quitclaimed his rights to Elizabeth I, who later the same year confirmed the corporation as lord of the manor. Elizabeth's grant was made at the request of Robert Devereux, earl of Essex, as part of an arrangement whereby the corporation was to grant Essex a lease of the manor for life. Essex died in 1601 before the lease could be made, but his son, also Robert (d. 1646), became lessee in 1604.[10] A fee farm of £50 payable to the bishop under the 1548 grant was vested in the Ecclesiastical Commissioners in 1867. It was redeemed by Lichfield city council for £400 in 1971.[11]

[91] L.J.R.O., B/A/1/12, f. 130v.; B.L. Harl. MS. 3839, f. 40; Le Neve, *Fasti*, 15, 44 (s.v. Thos. Mills).
[92] *S.H.C.* 1923, 239.
[93] *Cal. S.P. Dom.* 1676–7, 13; Harwood, *Lichfield*, 308; *T.S.S.A.H.S.* xxv. 46.
[94] L.J.R.O., D. 30/XLIV, f. 174v.
[95] Harwood, *Lichfield*, 163; *Lond. Gaz.* 12 Mar. 1841, p. 664; Guildhall Libr., London, MS. H 9.4, no. 16, 14 and 15 Feb. 1800; above, fig. 4.
[96] L.J.R.O., Newton's College MSS.; *Letters of Anna Seward*, v. 155; *Staffs. Advertiser*, 18 Jan. 1806.
[97] L.J.R.O., D. 15/6/3/1; *Staffs. Advertiser*, 30 July 1803.
[98] L.J.R.O., D. 15/6/3/2.
[99] Ibid. Newton's College MSS., building corresp. 1927–30.
[1] Inf. from Mr. Ainsley, cathedral administrator.
[2] L.J.R.O., B/A/1/1, f. 51v.; *T.S.S.A.H.S.* xviii. 64.
[3] L.J.R.O., D. 30/XXXI, f. 57; D. 30/LIV, f. 98; *T.S.S.A.H.S.* xxv. 46.
[4] L.J.R.O., D. 30/XXXV, f. 113v.; D. 30/XLV, f. 82.
[5] *Aris's Birmingham Gaz.* 5 Sept. 1803.
[6] *V.C.H. Staffs.* iii. 2; iv. 42–3.   [7] *S.H.C.* v (1), 108.
[8] Harwood, *Lichfield*, 336.
[9] *Acts of P.C.* 1581–2, 447–8.
[10] Harwood, *Lichfield*, 338–42.
[11] Inf. from the Church Commissioners.

ESTATES OF THE CATHEDRAL CLERGY. Land in the Gaia Lane area of Lichfield was included in the endowment of the cathedral prebend of Gaia, in existence probably by the mid 12th century; the prebend was divided into two prebends, Gaia Major and Gaia Minor, before 1279.[12] In 1498 the prebend of Freeford's property in Lichfield included the Angel in Beacon Street on the south side of the later Angel Croft hotel.[13] It was rebuilt in the early 16th century, but was destroyed in the Civil War.[14] In the later 1270s a house outside the Close was annexed to Wolvey prebend.[15] Known by 1438 as Pool Hall, it stood in Beacon Street on the site of Westgate House.[16] Evidently destroyed during the Civil War, it was rebuilt by 1670 and again in the later 18th century, possibly by the lessee, Peter Garrick.[17] The prebend of Hansacre had a tenement in Beacon Street by 1393, as did Weeford prebend in 1548.[18]

An estate called Bispells south of the Tamworth road on the boundary with Freeford originated as land belonging to the prebend of Bishopshull in Lichfield cathedral. It was acquired, evidently on lease, by Anthony Dyott of Freeford in 1610.[19] It covered 43 a. in 1847 when it was sold by the Ecclesiastical Commissioners to William Dyott of Freeford.[20] It remained part of the Dyott estate in the late 1980s.

By 1176, and apparently before 1135, the dean had an estate at Deanslade on the city's southwestern boundary with Wall.[21] There was a house there by 1560, and in 1649 the estate comprised 60 a.[22] When sold by the Ecclesiastical Commissioners in 1920 it comprised 85 a.[23] In the late 1980s most of the land was part of the estate of Aldershawe Hall in Wall. The farm buildings date from the later 19th century.

A house on the corner of Beacon Street and Shaw Lane was annexed to the archdeaconry of Chester, evidently in 1272.[24] It may have been the stone house recorded in that area in the late 13th century;[25] in the later 16th century the archdeacon's stone-built house was described as 'magnificent'.[26]

The vicars choral received grants of houses, land, and rent charges from the early 13th century and became the largest clerical landowners in the town.[27] A rental of 1497–8[28] shows

the extent of their property, which included the Swan in Bird Street (acquired in 1362),[29] two inns in Beacon Street, the Talbot on the site of the later Angel Croft hotel[30] and the Cock, and a house in Beacon Street called White Hall on the north side of Dr. Milley's hospital. By 1592 the vicars also had in Beacon Street an inn called the Lamb, on the site of the later Westgate Cottage opposite the entrance to the Close.[31] The house to the north was built c. 1790 for George Addams, a wine merchant;[32] it became the Angel Croft hotel c. 1930.[33] White Hall was rebuilt in the earlier 18th century as the Coach and Horses inn but was again a private house in 1806 when it was occupied by a wine merchant, John Fern; in 1848 another wine merchant, Henry Hewitt, was living there.[34] Either Fern or Hewitt built the present house. The house at Stowe with an orchard which Bishop Meuland in 1261 assigned for the use of aged or infirm vicars may have been the house at Stowe given to the vicars by the dean and chapter in the 1240s. It was apparently destroyed during the Civil War.[35] In the early 19th century the vicars held nearly 320 a. of land in Lichfield; it was transferred to the Ecclesiastical Commissioners in 1872.[36]

Grants were made to the cathedral's common fund of a house in Lichfield by Bishop Peche in 1176 and of land at Femley Pits on the city's southern boundary by Ernulf, a canon, in the early 13th century.[37] In the late 1840s, besides their property in the Close, the dean and chapter owned 11 a. in Lichfield, with a further 79 a. assigned to the cathedral's fabric fund.[38]

Several chantries and obits in the cathedral were endowed with houses and land in Lichfield.[39] It is not known what happened to the property at the Dissolution.

Tithe in Lichfield was included in Bishop Peche's re-endowment of the deanery in 1176. When the endowments were reorganized in 1192, the tithe, evidently from the cathedral *parochia*, was assigned to the prebends of Freeford, Hansacre, Gaia Major, Stotfold, and Weeford.[40] The prebendaries shared among themselves the great tithe from certain fields in Lichfield and in the out-townships. In the late 1640s the grain was divided by the drawing of lots, the resulting portions being called pound parts and mark parts.[41] The precise manner of

12 V.C.H. Staffs. iii. 141, 144.
13 Bodl. MS. Ashmole 864, p. 379; L.J.R.O., VC/A/21, CC 17529, plan 14.
14 L.J.R.O., D. 30/VC, palimpsest, i, f. 8; D. 30/LV, f. 47.
15 Ibid. D. 30/XXIV, f. 17v.; S.H.C. 1924, p. 245.
16 L.J.R.O., D. 30/VC, B 84; L.J.R.O., B/A/15/Lichfield, St. Chad, no. 734.
17 Ibid. D. 30/XXXII, f. 8; D. 30/XXXVII, f. 28v.; D. 30/XXXVIII, f. 39.
18 Ibid. D. 30/C.A. iv, f. 154; Bodl. MS. Ashmole 855, p. 180.
19 S.R.O., D. 661/2/113 and 426; J. Dewhirst, Map of Lichfield (1836).
20 Lond. Gaz. 2 July 1847, p. 2415.
21 S.H.C. 1924, p. 240.
22 L.J.R.O., D. 30/C.A. iv, f. 28v.; D. 30/LIV, f. 62.
23 Eccl. Com. sale cat., 3 Mar. 1920, lot 61 (copy in S.R.O., D. 4566/E).
24 S.H.C. 1924, p. 57; Harwood, Lichfield, 280 n.
25 Dugdale, Mon. vi (3), 1242.
26 L.J.R.O., D. 30/C.A. iv, f. 16v.; Bodl. MS. e Mus. 204, f. 49.
27 L.J.R.O., D. 30/VC, B 1–142; S.H.C. 1924, p. 47.
28 Bodl. MS. Ashmole 864, pp. 377–406.
29 Ibid. 1521, p. 27 (2nd nos.).
30 L.J.R.O., VC/A/21, CC 17529, plan 14, no. 32; L.J.R.O., D. 15/10/2/27.
31 Ibid. D. 27/1/1, f. 4; ibid. VC/A/21, CC 162111, deed of 12 Mar. 1810; CC 17529, plan 14. It is shown as 'Landi' inn on fig. 4, above.
32 Shaw, Staffs. i. 347; L.J.R.O., D. 15/10/2/27, deed of 4 Aug. 1790.
33 Kelly's Dir. Staffs. (1928; 1932).
34 Aris's Birmingham Gaz. 2 Mar. 1747; H. S. Ward, Lichfield and its Cathedral (Lichfield, 1893), 24 (copy in W.S.L.); L.J.R.O., VC/A/21, CC 17529, plan 14, no. 35; L.J.R.O., B/A/15/Lichfield, St. Chad, no. 726.
35 L.J.R.O., D. 30/XXIV, ff. 16, 29; Dugdale, Mon. vi (3), 1261; V.C.H. Staffs. iii. 148, 180.
36 L.J.R.O., VC/A/21, CC 17529; V.C.H. Staffs. iii. 193.
37 S.H.C. 1924, pp. 53, 67.
38 L.J.R.O., B/A/15/Lichfield, St. Chad, St. Michael.
39 e.g. S.H.C. 1924, pp. 51–2, 72–3, 109, 134–5; L.J.R.O., D. 30/C.A. i, ff. 65v.–66, 95–95v.; ii, f. 18.
40 Below, churches (parochial organization to 1491).
41 L.J.R.O., D. 30/LV, ff. 7–8, 50, 54, 80, 110.

the distribution is obscure. The prebendaries of Freeford and Gaia Major also took great tithe from other land in Lichfield, and the prebendary of Weeford took tithe from the produce of gardens in Beacon Street and Wade Street.[42] Other prebendaries who took tithe from land or gardens in Lichfield in the late 1640s were those of Bishopshull, Bishops Itchington, Gaia Minor, and Prees or Pipa Minor.[43] No tithe of wool or lambs was taken,[44] apparently because it was a custom by the 1620s that such tithe could be demanded only if the sheep had been kept for 28 days or more on the land which owned the tithe: prebendal land was so intermingled that graziers could easily avoid payment by moving their flocks about.[45] In 1694 small tithes were assigned to the vicar of St. Mary's, Lichfield.[46]

The great tithes were commuted in the late 1840s. In respect of the 739 a. from which the pound and mark parts were drawn, a rent charge of £143 13s. 9d. was awarded to the Ecclesiastical Commissioners (Freeford £26 10s. 2d., Hansacre £29 16s. 9d., and Weeford £86 6s. 10d.) and one of £40 4s. 1d. to the dean and chapter as appropriators of Stotfold prebend. A further £449 7s. 10d. was awarded to the Ecclesiastical Commissioners in respect of the following prebends: Bishopshull £90 from 34 a., Bishops Itchington £11 5s. from 36 a., Curborough £1 2s. 6d. from 8½ a., Freeford £211 2s. 10d. from 954 a., Gaia Major £62 8s. from 272½ a., Gaia Minor £5 0s. 8d. from 96½ a., Hansacre £2 10s. from 26 a., Prees £21 from 83 a., and Weeford £54 18s. 10d. from 263 a. The dean and chapter as appropriators of Stotfold prebend were awarded a rent charge of £20 10s. from 76 a. The vicar of St. Mary's was awarded a rent charge of £275 7s. 9d. for small tithes.[47]

OTHER ECCLESIASTICAL ESTATES.

The endowments of the medieval almshouse of St. John the Baptist, Lichfield, included land and houses in the town.[48] A survey made in the early 1720s listed 149 a. west of the almshouse bounded by Trunkfield brook and the Walsall and Birmingham roads, 21½ a. in Dovehouse field and adjacent fields, 40 a. on the south side of Ryknild Street opposite Knowle Farm, 17 a. between Borrowcop Hill and the Tamworth road, 19½ a. along the north side of the Tamworth road at a place called the Quarry in the angle of Quarryhills Lane and Gorse Lane, and 17 a. on the east side of Gorse Lane stretching down to Darnford brook.[49] The almshouse retained much of the land until 1921, when it was sold together with houses to various buyers.[50]

At its re-endowment in 1502–4 the almshouse

for women in Beacon Street later called Dr. Milley's hospital had property in Lichfield comprising a house in Bird Street, one in Wade Street, two in Sandford Street, 7 cottages and 2 crofts also in Sandford Street, 2 a. at Borrowcop, and land called Godcroft near Beacon Street.[51] By 1821 the Borrowcop land had been lost, but more houses had been built in Sandford Street and the hospital also had 4 houses in Stowe Street. All the land was sold in 1921 and 1923.[52]

Bishop Peche, 1161–82, gave a messuage in Lichfield to Bordesley abbey (Worcs.)[53] and two houses to St. Thomas's priory near Stafford.[54] Bishop Nonant, 1188–98, gave a house in Lichfield as a lodging for the abbot of Buildwas (Salop.), and before c. 1200 the abbey apparently had a messuage in the Close.[55] The nuns of Henwood priory (Warws.) held land called Mary ridding in Lichfield in the later 13th century.[56] By 1283 the nuns of Farewell priory had a house in Quonians Lane; in 1399 they also had five tenements and other parcels of land elsewhere in the town.[57] The priory was dissolved in 1527, and its estates were given to the dean and chapter, who in 1550 let them at fee farm to William, Lord Paget, lord of Longdon.[58] Canwell priory was given land in Lichfield by Ralph, Lord Basset, of Drayton (d. 1390).[59]

In 1467 Bevis Hampton gave land called Pownes fields to Halesowen abbey (Worcs.) as the endowment of a chantry in the abbey church. The land was presumably part of the Pones Mill estate, divided in 1302.[60] At the Dissolution the property passed, under the style of 'the manor of Lichfield', to Sir John Dudley, who transferred it to his brother Andrew. In 1546 Andrew conveyed the so called manor to Hugh Lee, a clerk of the royal armoury at Greenwich.[61] Lee was succeeded in 1576 by his grandson Hugh (later Sir Hugh) Wrottesley, who held the estate at his death in 1633.[62] Nothing further is known about it.

The guild of St. Mary and St. John the Baptist owned extensive property in the city until the Reformation.[63]

LAY ESTATES.

BEACON PLACE on the west side of Beacon Street was built in the late 18th century by George Hand, a proctor of the consistory court, who was living in the Close in 1781.[64] He died at Beacon Place in 1806, and his widow Ann lived there until her death in 1826. The house, standing in grounds of 15 a., was sold by trustees in 1827 to Thomas Hinckley, a Lichfield attorney.[65] By 1828 the property had been divided between him and his brother

[42] Ibid. D. 30/LV, ff. 48, 54, 111.
[43] Ibid. ff. 9, 57, 65, 84.   [44] Ibid. f. 111.
[45] *C.J.* i. 631.   [46] Below, churches.
[47] L.J.R.O., B/A/15/Lichfield, St. Chad, St. Mary, St. Michael.   [48] *V.C.H. Staffs.* iii. 279–80, 282.
[49] L.J.R.O., D. 88/hosp. land, plans nos. 1–3.
[50] Annotated copy of 1921 sale cat. in S.R.O., D. 4363/A/5/14.
[51] *V.C.H. Staffs.* iii. 276; L.J.R.O., D. 103/6/28/1 and 2.
[52] *7th Rep. Com. Char.* 383–4; L.J.R.O., D. 103/2/5, 12 Jan. and 9 Mar. 1921; D. 103/2/6, 14 Dec. 1921; 10 Jan. 1923.   [53] *Cal. Chart. R.* 1257–1300, 66.
[54] *S.H.C.* viii (1), 133–4.
[55] *V.C.H. Salop.* ii. 53; *S.H.C.* 1924, p. 190.
[56] *S.H.C.* 1924, p. 346.
[57] Ibid. p. 267; S.R.O., D. (W.) 1734/2/3/55D.
[58] *V.C.H. Staffs.* iii. 224; L.J.R.O., D. 30/C 29.
[59] *V.C.H. Staffs.* iii. 215.
[60] *Cal. Pat.* 1467–77, 16; *Archaeologia*, lii (2), 626; below (lay estates: Pones Mill).
[61] *L. & P. Hen. VIII*, xiii (2), p. 191; xiv (1), p. 252; xxi (2), p. 245.
[62] *S.H.C.* N.S. vi (2), 298; *V.C.H. Staffs.* xx. 27, 225.
[63] Below, guilds.
[64] Shaw, *Staffs.* i. 347; W.S.L., M. 883.
[65] Reade, *Johnsonian Gleanings*, iv. 195, 197; S.R.O., D. 4566/E, abstract of title of Arthur Hinckley, pp. 1–16; L.J.R.O. D. 77/22/10, sale partics. of Beacon Place.

Richard, also an attorney, and both lived at Beacon Place. In his will of that year Thomas left his half share to Richard. By 1836 Thomas had gone mad and was in confinement; he died in 1837.[66] In 1835 Richard married, as her third husband, Ellen Jane, daughter of J. C. Wood-house, dean of Lichfield 1807–33. She was living with her sister at Maple Hayes, in Burntwood, and she and Richard made their home there while Beacon Place was being extended and refurbished. They had moved to Beacon Place by April 1837. General William Dyott of Freeford noted their sumptuous style of living and commented that they had made Beacon Place into 'a superb residence' and 'one of the best houses in the neighbourhood'; he attributed the improvements to Mrs. Hinckley's taste and money.[67] The work was designed by Sydney Smirke and included the addition of two wings.[68] The house was renamed Beacon House.[69] In 1848 the grounds covered 36 a.[70]

Richard Hinckley died in 1865 and his wife in 1870. The Beacon House estate passed to Richard's nephew, Arthur Hinckley, who continued to live at Stowe Hill. In 1881 he sold Beacon House to S. L. Seckham, who moved there from Hanch Hall in Longdon. The house became known as Beacon Place again.[71] At the end of the century the gardens and park covered nearly 100 a.; there were three drives, with lodges in Beacon Street, Sandford Street, and Walsall Road.[72] Seckham moved to Whittington Old Hall c. 1897, and Beacon Place was let.[73] He died in 1901, and Beacon Place passed, subject to his widow's life interest, to their son Gerald.[74] In 1922 he sold it with 10 a. to the War Department, which had taken it over as offices during the First World War.[75] During the Second World War it was used by the Royal Army Service Corps. It stood empty from the later 1950s, and after being bought by the city council it was demolished in 1964. The site was let to a private developer, and houses were built over it in the later 1960s.[76] Much of the land formerly attached to the house has been incorporated in Beacon Park.

THE FRIARY originated as a house of Franciscan friars, established c. 1237.[77] In 1309 the friars occupied 3½ burgages,[78] presumably along St. John Street and Bird Street and bounded on the north by Friars Alley. The original precinct probably extended on the west as far as the town ditch, beyond which an area of land was later added. The friary was dissolved in 1538 and its site granted in 1544 to Gregory Stonyng, master of St. Mary's guild in 1536–7 and one of the first two bailiffs of the corporation in 1548–9.[79] In 1580–1 the estate was held by his son Edward (d. 1611). Edward's son Henry sold the estate to Thomas Clayton, who was succeeded in 1613 by his infant daughter Ursula.[80] In 1636 she married John Hill of Little Pipe in Farewell, a barrister of Gray's Inn.[81] The estate covered 10½ a. in 1638.[82] Hill, town clerk by 1660,[83] was succeeded in 1667 by his son John, who sold the estate to Zachary Johnson (d. 1669), rector of Seal (Leics., later Derb.). Zachary was succeeded by his nephew Richard Johnson (d. probably in the late 1690s), who left the estate in trust as the endowment for an almshouse at Seal.[84] Tenants in the 18th century included Michael Rawlins (d. 1754), son of a former town clerk, John Rawlins;[85] Thomas Cobb, political agent for Lord Anson and Lord Gower, from 1754;[86] and William Inge of Thorpe Constantine (d. 1785), a magistrate for both Lichfield and Staffordshire.[87]

In 1891 the trustees of Richard Johnson's charity sold the estate, then 11½ a., to the tenant John Godfrey-Fausett (d. 1893). In 1894 it was sold to Harry Tichborne Hinckes of Tettenhall (d. 1895), whose nephew and heir Ralph Tichborne Davenport (later Hinckes) sold it in 1907 to Col. Henry Williams, the tenant. In 1920 Williams sold it to Sir Richard Cooper, Bt., M.P. for Walsall, who gave it to the city later the same year for the purpose of laying out a new road and developing the area.[88]

The friary church, cloisters, refectory, and most of the domestic buildings were destroyed at the Dissolution.[89] The site of the church was excavated in 1933, and the foundations were left exposed.[90] A four-column portico was set up by the council in 1937 as an entrance to the site.[91] The only domestic buildings which survived were the west range and a house at its southern

[66] S.R.O., D. 661/11/2/3/1/13, 22 Aug. 1836; D. 4566/E, abstract of Arthur Hinckley, p. 25; Pigot & Co. *New Com. Dir.* [1829], 714*.
[67] Clayton, *Cathedral City*, 7; S.R.O., D. 150/1/135; D. 661/11/2/3/1/13, 12 Feb. and 22 Aug. 1836, 13 Apr. and 10 May, 23 Sept. 1837; *Dyott's Diary*, ed. R. W. Jeffery, ii. 283, 309.
[68] [A. Williams and W. H. Mallett], *Mansions and Country Seats of Staffs. and Warws.* (Lichfield, n.d.), 12.
[69] S.R.O., D. 150/1/132; P.R.O., HO 107/1008.
[70] L.J.R.O., B/A/15/Lichfield, St. Chad.
[71] S.R.O., D. 4566/D, Beacon Place bdle., abstract of title of S. L. Seckham; *Kelly's Dir. Staffs.* (1884).
[72] [Williams and Mallett], *Mansions and Country Seats*, 12 and pl. facing p. 13; S.R.O., D. 4566/D, Beacon Place bdle., copy of sale cat. 1897.
[73] *Lomax's Red Bk.* (1896), 17; (1897), 23; *Kelly's Dir. Staffs.* (1900); *Lichfield Mercury*, 28 Jan. 1898, p. 4; S.R.O., D. 4566/D, Beacon Place bdle., sale cat. 1897.
[74] S.R.O., D. 4566/D, Beacon Place bdle., will of S. L. Seckham, 1898; *Lomax's Red Bk.* (1904), 23.
[75] Jackson, *Historical Incidents*, 111; S.R.O., D. 4566/D, Beacon Place bdle., deed of 12 Dec. 1922.
[76] *Lichfield Mercury*, 11 Mar. 1960, p. 6; 18 Sept. 1964, p. 8; 26 May 1967, p. 17.

[77] *V.C.H. Staffs.* iii. 268 (where the text on nn. 3 and 10 should be ignored: it is based on *Cal. Pat.* 1247–58, 651, where Luffield priory (Northants.) is wrongly identified as Lichfield priory).
[78] *T.S.S.A.H.S.* xviii. 62.
[79] *V.C.H. Staffs.* 269–70; Harwood, *Lichfield*, 415, 418.
[80] Harwood, *Lichfield*, 490–1; P.R.O., C 142/320, no. 59; C 142/338, no. 95.
[81] L.J.R.O., D. 27/1/1, f. 87v.; *S.H.C.* v (2), 175.
[82] Harwood, *Lichfield*, pl. facing p. 483.
[83] L.J.R.O., D. 77/4/6/1, f. 3.
[84] Ibid. D. 20/1/1, f. 169; *S.H.C.* v (2), 175; Harwood, *Lichfield*, 486; J. Nichols, *History and Antiquities of County of Leicester*, iii, p. *988.
[85] Shaw, *Staffs.* i. 321; A. L. Reade, *Reades of Blackwood Hill* (priv. print. 1906), 229.
[86] *S.H.C.* 4th ser. vi. 124–5; Harwood, *Lichfield*, 486.
[87] *Gent. Mag.* lv (1), 158; Shaw, *Staffs.* i. 409.
[88] *Lichfield Mercury*, 19 Aug. 1938, p. 4; S.R.O., D. 4566/J, abstract of title to Friary estate, 1920; above, general hist.
[89] *V.C.H. Staffs.* iii. 270.
[90] *Lichfield Mercury*, 23 Feb. 1934, p. 5; *Lomax's Red Bk.* (1935), 17.
[91] *Lichfield Mercury*, 5 Feb. 1937, p. 5; 12 Feb. 1937, p. 3.

end. The northern end of the range was demolished when a new road was cut across the site in the later 1920s. The house was presumably 'the inn called le Bishop's Lodging or le Great Chamber', used as a guest house by the friars and included in the 1544 sale to Stonyng.[92] Built of sandstone probably in the early 16th century, the house together with the south end of the west range is L-shaped with a wing on the west.[93] The house was remodelled by Stonyng and further improved in the late 18th century by William Inge.[94] It was taken over by the girls' high school in 1921 and incorporated in new buildings opened in 1928.[95]

A rent of £3 from a house and 1 a. in Lichfield was part of the *PENDEREL GRANT* settled on trustees by Charles II in 1675. The grant provided pensions for members of the Penderel family and their descendants as a reward for helping him to escape after the battle of Worcester in 1651.[96] The rent was redeemed in 1914.[97]

A mill at Nether Stowe was held c. 1180 by Gilbert Poun, a chamberlain of Bishop Peche,[98] and in 1242–3 Robert Poun held an estate there called *PONES MILL* as ⅙ knight's fee.[99] Robert's heir may have been Geoffrey, son of Gilbert Poun, who held land in the area in the later 13th century.[1] By 1285 Ralph Poun held the estate, recorded in 1298 as 1/15 knight's fee, and in 1299 it comprised the mill, a messuage, and 39 a.[2] In 1302 Ralph's son Robert granted the mill to Robert, lord of Pipe in Burntwood.[3] The rest of the estate is probably identifiable as the land called Pownes fields given to Halesowen abbey in 1467.[4]

Two houses at Stowe, *STOWE HOUSE* and *STOWE HILL*, were built in the 1750s by Elizabeth Aston, daughter of Sir Thomas Aston of Aston, in Runcorn (Ches.).[5] In 1752, while living in the Close, she bought 9 a. on Stowe Hill from her sister Magdalen, who had inherited the land from her husband Gilbert Walmisley, the diocesan registrar (d. 1751).[6] Elizabeth had built three houses there by 1756.[7] She herself lived in the house later known as Stowe Hill.[8] The house to the south-west later known

as Stowe House appears to have been occupied by Thomas Hinton, perpetual curate of the nearby St. Chad's (d. 1757).[9] In 1770 and 1771 it was occupied by Thomas Day, author of *Sandford and Merton*.[10] It became the home of Elizabeth's sister Jane, who probably moved there on the death of her husband Francis Gastrell, vicar of Frodsham (Ches.), in 1772. In 1776 Samuel Johnson, a friend of both sisters, described her as living 'at the lower house on Stow Hill'.[11] The third house was standing empty in 1777,[12] and only two were mentioned by Anna Seward in 'Lichfield: an elegy', written in 1781:[13]

We mark the villa, rising near the lake,
And fairer she, that 'midst the verdant brake,
From sultry gleams, and wintry tempest shrill,
Stands softly curtained on the eastern hill.

When Elizabeth died in 1785, Stowe Hill passed to Magdalen Walmisley, then living in Bath, and Stowe House to Jane Gastrell. Magdalen at once moved to Stowe Hill, and when she died in 1786, that too passed to Jane.[14] She let it to Lady Carhampton, presumably Judith, widow of the 1st earl of Carhampton, but in 1788 it stood empty.[15] Jane died in 1791, and in 1792, under the terms of her will, both houses were sold.[16]

Stowe House, so called by then, was bought by John Walker Wilson, who sold it to Fairfax Moresby in 1793. Moresby went to live there, but it was let by 1817.[17] That year Moresby sold it to Richard Gresley, who moved there from Kenilworth (Warws.).[18] In 1830 he sold it with 10 a. to William Gresley, assistant curate at St. Chad's from 1829 and prebendary of Wolvey in the cathedral from 1840. He was still living at Stowe House in 1843.[19] By 1848 the 40-a. estate was owned and occupied by Richard Greene, a Lichfield banker. His bank collapsed in 1855, and in 1856 the house and 24 a. were offered for sale.[20] The estate was bought by Charles Holland, M.D., who changed the name of the house to St. Chad's House and lived there until his death in 1876.[21] As Stowe House it was sold that

[92] *V.C.H. Staffs.* iii. 270. The Chester Franciscan friary also had a bishop's lodging: *V.C.H. Ches.* iii. 173 n.
[93] Harwood, *Lichfield*, pl. facing p. 482; Bodl. MS. G.A. Staffs. 4°, 8, facing p. 481; W.S.L., Staffs. Views, v. 245b.
[94] Harwood, *Lichfield*, 486; Jackson, *Lichfield*, 61.
[95] Below, education.
[96] S.R.O., D. 590/699A; *Salop. Arch. Soc.* 4th ser. vii. 33.
[97] Inf. from Mr. K. S. P. Swayne, of Fowler, Langley & Wright, solicitors of Wolverhampton.
[98] *S.H.C.* 1924, p. 229.   [99] *Bk. of Fees*, ii. 969.
[1] S.R.O., D. 661/1/525.
[2] Ibid. D. (W.) 1734/J. 2268, f. 1v.; *Feud. Aids*, v. 8; *S.H.C.* vii (1), 60.
[3] *S.H.C.* 1911, 58–9. For the later hist. of the mill see below, econ. hist. (mills; trades and industries).
[4] Above (other eccl. estates).
[5] Reade, *Johnsonian Gleanings*, v. 245.
[6] L.J.R.O., D. 15/11/14/91, deed of 18 Aug. 1752; *V.C.H. Staffs.* iii. 189.
[7] L.J.R.O., D. 15/11/14/92, faculty of 27 Apr. 1756.
[8] Reade, *Johnsonian Gleanings*, v. 249–50.
[9] Harwood, *Lichfield*, 507; *Gent. Mag.* lv (2), 497, where Ric. Greene of Lichfield states (1785) that Hinton built the house.
[10] Below, education.
[11] Reade, *Johnsonian Gleanings*, v. 252–4; *Boswell's Life of Johnson*, ed. G. B. Hill, revised L. F. Powell, ii. 469–70, 540.
[12] L.J.R.O., D. 15/11/14/91, will of Eliz. Aston 1777.
[13] *Poetical Works of Anna Seward*, ed. W. Scott (Edinburgh, 1810), i. 92. Only 2 houses are shown on a view of Stowe c. 1785 in Shaw, *Staffs.* i. 344.
[14] Reade, *Johnsonian Gleanings*, v. 249–52.
[15] L.J.R.O., D. 15/11/14/92, deed of 29 Sept. 1792; *Complete Peerage*, iii. 23–4.
[16] Reade, *Johnsonian Gleanings*, v. 252.
[17] L.J.R.O., D. 15/11/14/91, abstract of title of Fairfax Moresby, pp. 25–9, 31–6; W.S.L., S. MS. 384, p. 73; Parson and Bradshaw, *Staffs. Dir.* (1818), 175.
[18] *S.H.C.* N.S. i. 116; L.J.R.O., D. 15/11/14/96, draft deed Jan. 10 Geo. IV.
[19] W.S.L. 11/344/5/50; 11/344/11/50; 11/344/26/50; *Dyott's Diary*, ed. R. W. Jeffery, ii. 192, 354, 366; *S.H.C.* N.S. i. 116, 150; Le Neve, *Fasti* (1854), i. 642.
[20] L.J.R.O., B/A/15/Lichfield, St. Chad; Clayton, *Cathedral City*, 90–7.
[21] *P.O. Dir. Staffs.* (1860; 1872); S.R.O., D. 4566/K, acct. of estate of late Chas. Holland.

year to W. F. Gordon, who moved there from Stoke upon Trent and was still living there in 1900.[22]

In 1902 Stowe House was bought by Nelly Thorpe, the widowed daughter of A. J. Mundella, the Liberal politician. Soon after settling there she fell ill, and her daughter Dorothea moved there with her husband G. R. Benson.[23] A Liberal politician and a man of letters, Benson (1864–1945) was created Baron Charnwood in 1911. He was elected to Lichfield city council in 1904 and was mayor 1910–11; he also served on Staffordshire county council and was chairman of Staffordshire quarter sessions from 1929. A pillar of the Johnson Society, he was its president 1934–5.[24] Mrs. Thorpe died in 1919, but Lord and Lady Charnwood remained at Stowe House until 1933. Their son John, who married in 1933 and was sheriff of Lichfield 1933–4, remained at the house until c. 1937.[25] It was taken over by the army at the beginning of the Second World War, but from 1940 until 1944 it was occupied by Belmont School, evacuated there from Hassocks (Suss.).[26] In 1945 it was bought with 14 a. by the city council, which sold the house to the county council in 1948 but retained most of the land. In 1951 work began on the conversion of the house into a home for nurses at Victoria and St. Michael's hospitals. It remained a nurses' home until 1969 when it was bought by Birmingham Regional Hospital Board and turned into a management training centre.[27]

The house is of brick with white-painted dressing. Alterations have obscured the plan of the original house. The main front is on the west and has five bays. The wide central bay breaks forward and contains a pedimented entrance. The south-east corner of the house was altered early in the 19th century when a large drawing room was built there; it projects south from the main block and ends in a canted bay. A ballroom, which has been divided into bedrooms, was built against the north-east corner early in the 20th century, and much of the elaborate 18th-century style decoration of the older rooms probably dates from that time. The original service wing was to the north; it was demolished when the house was made into a nurses' home and new kitchens were built on the site.[28]

Stowe Hill was bought in 1792 by Phoebe Simpson, who had moved there from Wickersley (Yorks. W.R.) by 1798. A member of the Rider family of Lichfield, she was the widow of Stephen Simpson, a younger son of Stephen Simpson, a Lichfield attorney.[29] She died in 1816 at what was then known as Stowe Hill House, which passed to William Harding of Breck House near Liverpool.[30] At first he let the house,[31] but in 1821 he sold it to Frances Dorothy Furnivall, who was still living there in 1854.[32] The estate covered 17 a. in 1848.[33] The next owner was Arthur Hinckley, who moved there in 1859 and died in 1889.[34] The estate was bought by F. H. Lloyd, a South Staffordshire iron and steel master, who moved to Stowe Hill from Wood Green, Wednesbury, and remained there until his death in 1916.[35] A Birmingham firm bought the estate in 1955. In 1956 the house and 7 a. were put up for sale, while a further 12 a. between Netherstowe and Brownsfield Road were advertised as building land.[36] The house was bought in 1978 by Mr. and Mrs. P. L. Rule.[37]

The house is also of brick with white-painted dressings. The entrance front, which is on the north, is of five bays, and the garden front has a large central semicircular bow. On the west there is a lower service wing, while on the east a 19th-century conservatory with a segmented front extends across the width of the house.[38] There are many mid 18th-century fittings, including the main staircase. The grounds include a grotto, built partly from medieval stonework, and a sunken fernery. The 18th-century stables backing on Netherstowe were converted into a house in 1959.[39] Part of the brick boundary wall survives in the same road.

[22] S.R.O., D. 4566/K, notice of sale of Stowe House 1876 and draft conveyance 3 Oct. 1876; *Eggington and Brown's Lichfield Almanack* (1877), 43; *Lomax's Red Bk.* (1901), 23.
[23] Lady Charnwood [D. M. Benson], *An Autograph Collection*, 260–1; Lady Charnwood, *Call Back Yesterday*, 73; *Lichfield Mercury*, 11 July 1919, p. 4; *Lomax's Red Bk.* (1903), 23; (1904), 27; *D.N.B.* Suppl. s.v. Mundella.
[24] *Lichfield Mercury*, 9 Feb. 1945, p. 5.
[25] Ibid. 11 July 1919, p. 4; inscription on south-west window in St. Chad's church; L.J.R.O., D. 29/51/1, p. 94; *Lomax's Red Bk.* (1934), 19, 23, 29, 49; (1938), 39.
[26] L.J.R.O., D. 77/19/14; inf. from Mr. W. J. Wilson, tutor warden at Stowe House (1986).
[27] *Lichfield Mercury*, 2 Aug. 1946, p. 2; L.J.R.O., D. 77/19/14.
[28] Below, plate 12; *Lichfield Mercury*, 12 Sept. 1952, p. 5; 5 Mar. 1971, p. 7.

[29] L.J.R.O., D. 15/11/14/92, deed of 29 Sept. 1792; S.R.O., D. 170/161; Reade, *Johnsonian Gleanings*, iv. 150–1, 164.
[30] L.J.R.O., D. 15/11/14/92, deed of 7 Apr. 1821; *Lichfield Mercury*, 9 Feb. 1816.
[31] Parson and Bradshaw, *Staffs. Dir.* (1818), 177.
[32] L.J.R.O., D. 15/11/14/92, deed of 7 Apr. 1821; *P.O. Dir. Staffs.* (1854).
[33] L.J.R.O., B/A/15/Lichfield, St. Michael.
[34] *Lichfield Mercury*, 1 Feb. 1889, p. 5; S.R.O., D. 3309/3.
[35] S.R.O., D. 3309/3; *Lichfield Mercury*, 7 Jan. 1916, p. 5.
[36] *Lichfield Mercury*, 29 Apr. 1955, p. 5; 18 Nov. 1955, p. 7; 2 Nov. 1956, p. 1.
[37] Inf. from Mrs. Rule.
[38] Below, plate 13.
[39] *Lichfield Mercury*, 21 Aug. 1959, p. 2.

TOWN GOVERNMENT

GOVERNMENT TO 1548. Lichfield was described as a borough in a deed of Bishop Durdent, 1149–59,[40] and on the occasion of a general eyre in 1199 the town was represented by its own jurymen as 'a borough, vill, and liberty'.[41] No charter of liberties has survived, but 'the liberties of the free burgesses of Lichfield' were taken as a model by the abbot of Burton when he established a borough at Abbots Bromley in 1222.[42] A custom recorded in 1221 related to the protection of a wife's marriage portion.[43] Another custom was the exemption of burgesses from pleas under the writ of *mort d'ancestor*: three such pleas were stayed at an assize in 1226 because of 'the liberty of the borough of Lichfield'.[44] Burgesses paid no entry fine when taking up a burgage[45] and, according to a survey of the bishop's estates made in 1298, no heriot was taken.[46] The bishop governed the town through a manor court whose competence was confined to the area within the town ditch and the suburbs. In addition the burgesses developed informal powers of self-government.[47] Certain privileges were enjoyed by the tenants of the dean and cathedral prebendaries, and in 1441 the Close became self-governing.[48]

The value of the town to the bishop may be gauged by the £12 6s. 8d. for which the escheator accounted as the farm of Lichfield in the six months following the death of Bishop Nonant in March 1198.[49] By 1298 the town was valued at £25, made up of £14 6s. 8d. for burgage rents (each worth 12d. a year), £6 13s. 4d. for the tolls of the markets and of the fairs, and £4 for the profits of the manor court. Castle mill (in Dam Street) and Stowe mill were valued at £33 6s. 8d.[50] The income in 1308–9 was greater. The market tolls then produced £10 18s. 4½d. and the fair tolls £6, while profits from the court totalled £8 11s. 8d. Burgage rents were the same as in 1298, but a further 4s. 4d. came from encroachments. The bishop's bailiff also accounted for Castle mill and Stowe mill, and the sale of corn ground at them was worth £43 13s. 5d., against which £4 4s. 5d. was set for their upkeep. Other expenses in 1308–9 included £41 10s. for the salaries of the bishop's officers, so that the profit that year was £30 19s. 11d.[51]

A rental of 1435 assessed the burgage rents at £19 6s. ¾d.[52] In 1447–8 the actual rent collected was only a little over £12, with a further 5s. 4d.

from encroachments; court profits totalled £8 5s. 8d. and the market and fair tolls were let for £5. After the senior bailiff's expenses had been met, the profit was £16 17s. By that date the mills were no longer the bailiff's responsibility but were accounted for separately by a lessee who paid £40 a year.[53] In 1541–2 the burgage rents were a little under £12 and court fines £2 10s. 8d; expenses, however, were not great, and there was a profit of £21.[54]

In 1312–13 the senior bailiff answered to the reeve of Longdon manor for the town's finances.[55] By the mid 15th century both the bailiff and the lessee of the Lichfield mills accounted directly to the bishop's receiver general, who stayed at Lichfield for the annual audit of the accounts of all the episcopal manors.[56]

MANORIAL COURTS AND OFFICERS. In the early 1160s the owner of a shop in the town had his possession of it confirmed by the bishop on condition that he attended the bishop's court three times a year when pleas were held and at other times when summoned.[57] That court is most likely to have been one for the town alone, as there were later three great courts for the town, while Longdon manor had only two each year.[58] There was a town court styled the *dernmoot* in the earlier 13th century when a man abjured his rights to a burgage in it (*in placito Lichiffeldie quod vocatur dernemoth*),[59] and around 1250 the bishop forced the tenants of the dean and of the cathedral prebendaries to attend the *dernmoot* twice a year as well as the portmoot, evidently the small court.[60] There is no later mention of the court. *Dern* means secret or private,[61] and the *dernmoot* may have been a court which was not open to all the town's inhabitants. Such an explanation, however, conflicts with the nearest etymological equivalent, the *dernhundred* of some Irish towns which was apparently a full assembly.[62] The name may signify the exclusion of men outside the town, in particular the men of Longdon manor whose own courts were also held in Lichfield, at least in the early 14th century.[63] The *dernmoot* may have been the occasion of a view of frankpledge; at the *quo warranto* inquiry of 1293 the bishop claimed a view in Lichfield along with pleas of the Crown, infangthief, waif, and pleas of withernam.[64]

[40] *S.H.C.* 1924, p. 87.   [41] P.R.O., JUST 1/800, m. 3.
[42] A. Ballard and J. Tait, *Brit. Borough Charters, 1216–1307*, 18.
[43] *Bracton's Note Bk.* ed. Maitland, iii, pp. 715–16.
[44] W.S.L., M. 5/6; *Abbrev. Plac.* (Rec. Com.), 102.
[45] e.g. B.L. Add. MS. 46460, f. 57; S.R.O., D. (W.) 1734/2/1/597, mm. 5–6, 18.
[46] S.R.O., D. (W.) 1734/J. 2268, f. 1.
[47] Below (manorial courts; community of the town).
[48] Below (liberties).
[49] *S.H.C.* ii (1), 59, 63–4; *V.C.H. Staffs.* v. 53.
[50] S.R.O., D. (W.) 1734/J. 2268, f. 1.
[51] *T.S.S.A.H.S.* xviii. 62–4.
[52] W.S.L., S. MS. 335(i), m. 5.
[53] L.J.R.O., B/A/21, CC 124078, m. 1; S.R.O., D. (W.) 1734/3/2/9.
[54] S.R.O., D. (W.) 1734/J. 1949, mm. [1–2]. The calcula-

tion of the profit, however, omits the expense of the livery paid to the receiver general with which the bailiff was burdened.
[55] *T.S.S.A.H.S.* xviii. 65; S.R.O., D. (W.) 1734/J. 2057, m. 5.
[56] L.J.R.O., B/A/21, CC 123984, m. 15; CC 124075, m. 11.
[57] *S.H.C.* iii (1), 186.
[58] For the Longdon courts see S.R.O., D. (W.) 1734/2/1/598 sqq.
[59] W.S.L., S.D. Cornford 71 (calendared in *S.H.C.* 1921, 28, where the suggested date is too early).
[60] *S.H.C.* 1924, pp. 171–3.
[61] *Middle Eng. Dict.* ed. H. Kurath and S. M. Kuhn, 1006–7.
[62] *Borough Customs*, i (Selden Soc. xviii), 321.
[63] Below.
[64] *Plac. de Quo Warr.* (Rec. Com.), 710–11.

Court records survive only from the early 15th century. There were then three great courts: two were held on Mondays near the feasts of St. Hilary (13 January) and St. George (23 April) and the third on the feast of St. Mary Magdalen (22 July).[65] In 1414 each court was styled a view of the great portmoot of Lichfield, but by the 1470s the Hilary and St. George's courts were known as views of the borough or of the free borough (or of the free burgesses), and the Magdalen court as a view of tithingmen. The tithingmen represented wards in the town and made presentments relating to offences such as assaults, gossiping, and failure to attend the watch. Their presentments at the Magdalen court were heard by a sworn jury of burgesses styled the Twelve, which at the other two great courts made its own presentments relating to nuisances such as the defects of gutters, encroachments on manorial land, and the lighting of fires in public places. The courts did not consider felonies, which were tried by county J.P.s.[66]

In the early 15th century there were two tithingmen each for Beacon Street, Bird Street, St. John Street, Market Street (then known as Rope Street), Bore Street, Wade Street, Conduit Street (evidently including Dam Street), Stowe Street, Tamworth Street, and Greenhill. By 1494 the Bird Street tithingmen were also responsible for Sandford Street as far west as Trunkfield brook, and there was an additional single tithingman for that part of the street beyond the brook.[67] The tithingmen were evidently chosen by their ward at an occasion called a drinking, recorded in 1494 and 1507 when both men and women were fined for failure to attend.[68] The election was probably by majority decision, as was the custom in 1645,[69] and the 18th-century practice of making every inhabitant contribute to the cost of the drinking[70] may have been followed in the Middle Ages.

The Twelve[71] were probably chosen by the bishop's bailiffs. In the years for which records of all three great courts survive (1506 and 1536), the Twelve were drawn from a pool of at least 30 men; in both years eight continued in office from the Hilary court to the St. George's court, but none to the Magdalen court.[72] The fact that their names were written on the court rolls may indicate official recognition of their standing in the town, and special consideration was ac-

corded them by the steward, who in the 1520s and 1530s gave them breakfasts on court days.[73]

There was evidently a small court by the mid 13th century.[74] It was held on Mondays, weekly in the 15th century but possibly less frequently in the mid 1520s when the senior bailiff attended only 15 courts a year.[75] The court dealt with pleas of debt and trespass and breaches of the assize of bread and of ale. A court of pie powder was held at the time of the Ash Wednesday fair by 1464.[76]

The great courts were held before the bishop's steward, who was also responsible for the other episcopal estates in Staffordshire.[77] In 1531 what was probably the honorific office of high steward was held by George Talbot, earl of Shrewsbury.[78] With the alienation of some of the bishop's estates to Sir William Paget in 1546, a steward for the town alone was appointed, and in 1547 that office was held by John Otley, a Staffordshire J.P.[79]

The bishop's chief resident officer was the bailiff. That title was used in the 1160s; in the earlier 13th century the preferred style was reeve.[80] The title bailiff was again normally used in the mid 13th century when Peter of Colchester is the first recorded office-holder known by name.[81] From the late 13th century two bailiffs held office together,[82] but only one was responsible for drawing up accounts.[83] The senior bailiff's fee in 1308–9 was 15s. for his robe. By the later 1440s it was 20s. together with 6s. 8d. for collecting rents, and both sums were still paid in 1542.[84]

Two constables were chosen at the St. George's court in the 15th and early 16th century.[85]

Lichfield men were presented at a general eyre in 1199 for selling wine against the assize, and in 1203 the town was fined by the king for not observing the assize of bread. In the early 13th century the assize of bread and ale was kept by the bishop's officers.[86] By 1485 presentments relating to the assize were made at the manor court by four jurors, presumably pairs of tasters for bread and ale; they were styled clerks of the market in 1547.[87]

An official styled the warden of the fields, responsible for impounding stray animals, was recorded in 1501 and 1520, when he reported to the manor court.[88] There was a pinfold in Dam Street near the gate of the Close, but by 1476 it

[65] S.R.O., D. (W.) 1734/2/1/597. There is no record of a Magdalen court in a year when the feast fell on a Sunday.
[66] B. H. Putnam, *Procs. before J.P.s*, pp. 277, 299, 304, 309–10, 331.
[67] S.R.O., D. (W.) 1734/2/1/597, mm. 3, 17.
[68] Ibid. mm. 17, 25.
[69] W.S.L. 329/30.
[70] Lichfield Libr., Conduit St. and Dam St. dozeners' bk. 1720–1877, entry preceding 22 July 1740.
[71] The number actually empanelled was sometimes more: S.R.O., D. (W.) 1734/2/1/597, mm. 12d. (fifteen), 18d., 20d., 21, 24, 29 (all fourteen).
[72] Ibid. mm. 18d., 20d., 21, 35–6.
[73] Ibid. D. (W.) 1734/3/2/10, m. 1; D. (W.) 1734/3/2/11, m. 1; D. (W.) 1734/3/2/12, m. 1; D. (W.) 1734/3/2/13, m. 4; B.R.L. 433125.
[74] *S.H.C.* 1924, p. 172.
[75] S.R.O., D. (W.) 1734/2/1/597; D. (W.) 1734/3/2/10, m. 1; D. (W.) 1734/3/2/11, m. 1.
[76] Ibid. D. (W.) 1734/J. 1948, m. [5].
[77] Ibid.; D. (W.) 1734/J. 1949, m. [1]; D. (W) 1734/J.

2057, m. 1; L.J.R.O., B/A/21, CC 124078, m. 1.
[78] Bodl. MS. Ashmole 1521, pp. 153–4.
[79] S.R.O., D. (W.) 1734/J. 2243; Harwood, *Lichfield*, 336; *S.H.C.* 1912, 322; *V.C.H. Staffs.* iii. 51.
[80] *S.H.C.* iii (1), 186; *S.H.C.* 1939, 87; S.R.O., D. (W.) 1734/2/1/760, m. 129.
[81] *S.H.C.* 1924, pp. 76, 175.
[82] *Sel. Bills in Eyre, 1292–1333* (Selden Soc. xxx), 48–9; L.J.R.O., D. 30/VC, B 32, 36, 87, and 112; below (community of the town).
[83] L.J.R.O., B/A/21, CC 124075, mm. 4–5; S.R.O., D. (W.) 1734/3/2/5, m. [3]; W.S.L., S. MS. 335(i), m. 5.
[84] *T.S.S.A.H.S.* xviii. 62–4; L.J.R.O., B/A/21, CC 124078, m. 1; S.R.O., D. (W.) 1734/J. 1949, m. [1].
[85] S.R.O., D. (W.) 1734/2/1/597, mm. 1–2, 7, 20, 26; below, public services (policing).
[86] *S.H.C.* iii (1), 45, 101; *S.H.C.* 1924, p. 172.
[87] S.R.O., D. (W.) 1734/2/1/597, m. 7; D. (W.) 1734/J. 2243.
[88] Ibid. D. (W.) 1734/2/1/597, mm. 15, 26d.

had been removed, probably to Beacon Street.[89] Another pinfold stood at Greenhill in 1498.[90]

There was a moot hall where courts for both the town and Longdon manor were held by 1308.[91] It probably stood in Lombard Street, where there was a building called the Moot Hall in 1708.[92] When the bishop surrendered Longdon manor to Sir William Paget in 1546, the Longdon courts were transferred to Longdon Green.[93] The town courts may have continued in the moot hall, but they were evidently moved to the guildhall when the newly established corporation acquired the manor of Lichfield in 1548.

THE COMMUNITY OF THE TOWN. A representative element in the government of the town is indicated in 1221 when the burgesses of Lichfield disputed with those of Stafford over the exaction of toll: the case was pleaded before royal justices, and Lichfield sent two representatives.[94] In 1284 'the community of the city of Lichfield' sent the king a letter, evidently in response to a summons for representatives to appear before the treasurer at Westminster; William the taverner and Ralph de Barton described as 'our bailiffs' and six 'citizens' were nominated.[95] The community was recorded again in 1301 when six men acting on its behalf made a grant of land next to an aqueduct in the town, the tenant paying the community 2s. a year for the aqueduct's maintenance. What was presumably the community's seal was appended to that grant, and a portion of it survived in 1658; the impression was of a bishop, presumably St. Chad, flanked on the left and evidently on the right by an angel, with the cathedral behind.[96] Further evidence of the community is the grant of pavage to the burgesses and 'goodmen' of Lichfield in 1285 and 1290 and again in 1345.[97] Similarly a deacon was retained in office by the dean and chapter in 1333 at the request of the community of the town.[98] The community was again mentioned in 1450 when its cattle were in the care of the town's common herdsman.[99]

Corporate identity among the burgesses was strengthened by membership of the guild of St. Mary and St. John the Baptist, formed in 1387.[1] Its purpose was not only 'to maintain divine service and works of charity' but also 'to suppress vice and evil deeds ... so that peace, tranquillity, concord, and unity should be promoted',[2] and accordingly it came to participate in the government of the town. The master of the guild often had experience as one of the Twelve,[3] and in 1406 he took precedence over

the town bailiffs in the witness list of a charter.[4] In 1486 the master and his brethren in consultation with Sir Humphrey Stanley of Pipe in Burntwood, himself several times master, made ordinances for 'the unity, peace, and welfare of the community'.[5] The ordinances in part regulated the conduct of a body called the Forty-eight, which was associated with the guild in governing the town and which possibly represented the town's burgesses and commoners. Members of the Forty-eight along with the guild master had to swear to maintain concord amongst themselves, and any dispute between guild members was to be heard by the master and his brethren on pain of expulsion from 'the worshipful election and fraternity of the city'; the master and brethren were also to settle disputes between members and their servants. The master, brethren, and the Forty-eight were to hold meetings in the guildhall or elsewhere when there was business to discuss; a fine was to be imposed on any member of the Forty-eight who was absent, and after three absences the member was to be expelled. The ordinances also concerned matters relating to public order in the town.[6] It was made clear that there was no intention to abrogate the jurisdiction of the bishop's manor court,[7] and presumably the aim was to provide a means of more immediate supervision than the annual Magdalen court. The guild was evidently still helping to maintain public order in the early 16th century when guild constables were recorded.[8]

The guild also gave corroboration to public transactions. As early as 1389 a meeting of the guild approved and registered a deed concerning property in Lichfield, apparently itself unconnected with the guild.[9] The ordinance of 1532 reconstituting St. Mary's vicarage was sealed with the guild seal in the guildhall by the master acting with the consent of the brethren and 'all the inhabitants' of the city.[10]

There is no evidence that the master acted in opposition to the bailiffs or that the guild strove for independence from the bishop, to whom the town remained subject. A dispute with the bishop's officers over the collection of tolls in the early 16th century was settled by agreement, the bishop being urged to be 'a good lord'.[11] In 1547 the Twelve at the Magdalen court complained that neighbouring gentlemen were overburdening the town's common pasture with sheep. The bishop's steward, John Otley, who was one of the chief offenders, was asked to help so that he should have the gratitude of 'the poor community'.[12]

[89] Ibid. D. (W.) 1734/2/1/598, m. 44; below, govt. from 1548 (manorial cts.).
[90] Bodl. MS. Ashmole 864, p. 388; L.J.R.O., D. 30/VC, palimpsest, i, f. 40r. and v.
[91] T.S.S.A.H.S. xviii. 62–3.
[92] L.J.R.O., D. 77/9/1, f. 10v.
[93] S.R.O., D. (W.) 1734/2/1/606, m. 38; D. (W.) 1734/2/1/607, m. 4.
[94] Rolls of Justices in Eyre (Selden Soc. lix), 496.
[95] P.R.O., E 210/1206 (calendared in Cat. Anct. D. iii, p. 549).
[96] Bodl. MS. Ashmole 855, p. 190.
[97] Above, general hist. (late Middle Ages).
[98] Below, churches (parochial organization to 1491).
[99] Below, econ. hist. (agric.).

[1] Below, guilds.
[2] T.S.S.A.H.S. xxvii. 39.
[3] Ibid. 45 n.
[4] L.J.R.O., D. 30/VC, B 112.
[5] Gild of St. Mary, Lichfield (E.E.T.S., extra ser. 114), 11–13; Harwood, Lichfield, 406–7, 410; T.S.S.A.H.S. xxvii. 44–5; below, Burntwood, manors.
[6] Below, public services (policing).
[7] Gild of St. Mary, 12, sections 4 (where 'furrers' is probably a form of 'afferrers', i.e. jurors) and 5.
[8] L.J.R.O., D. 30/C.A. iv, f. 97v.
[9] Bodl. MS. Ashmole 855, p. 202.
[10] L.J.R.O., D. 30/C.A. iv, f. 97.
[11] S.R.O., D. (W.) 1734/2/2/42.
[12] Ibid. D. (W.) 1734/J. 2243.

Although the burgesses associated with each other to protect and promote their interests, they did so without acquiring formal power of self-government. Such power might have been sought if Lichfield had been more important economically. The Lichfield Forty-eight were last mentioned in 1538.[13] They may have been in mind when in 1553, shortly after the town had been incorporated, there was an unsuccessful attempt to replace the corporation with a ruling council of 48. It was to be made up of equal numbers of burgesses and commoners and styled the Common Hall or Common Council of the bailiffs, burgesses, and commonalty of Lichfield.[14]

GOVERNMENT FROM 1548. Lichfield was incorporated by a charter of Edward VI granted in 1548.[15] It was to be governed by two bailiffs, chosen annually on St. James's day (25 July), and 24 burgesses or brethren. Later the same year Bishop Sampson granted the manor of Lichfield to the corporation for a fee farm rent of £50.[16] In 1553 Mary I granted a new charter in consideration of 'the diligent industry and faithful service' given by the bailiffs and citizens during the recent rebellion,[17] possibly involving the arrest of servants of the duke of Northumberland.[18] The most significant addition to the city's privileges under the charter was the creation of the county of Lichfield with a sheriff.[19] In 1598 the method of choosing the bailiffs was altered by agreement with Bishop Overton, who had tried to reclaim Lichfield manor. The corporation was to present the names of at least two candidates to the bishop, who was to choose one of them to be the senior bailiff, announcing his choice at the guildhall by noon on St. James's day.[20]

The corporation was reorganized in 1622 by a charter of James I which reduced the number of brethren to 21. The bailiffs were in future to be drawn from the brethren only, with the bishop choosing the senior bailiff on St. James's day as previously. Refusal to take up the office of bailiff or of sheriff of the county was punishable by a fine. At least one bailiff was to be present when the corporation made any decision. The charter was reissued in 1623 with a clause guaranteeing the independence of the Close, shortly after James had granted a separate charter to the dean and chapter extending their privileges.[21]

A charter granted by Charles II in 1664 did not alter the composition of the corporation. In 1684 the attorney general brought a writ of quo

warranto against the city as part of Charles's attack on corporations, and the 1664 charter was surrendered. The brethren continued to meet, and they paid at least £20 towards the cost of a new charter, which was granted by James II in 1686 and reconstituted the corporation as a mayor and 12 aldermen.[22] It was annulled by James in October 1688, and the 1664 charter was restored.[23]

No further changes were made to the composition of the corporation until 1835. The Municipal Corporations Act of that year established a corporation of 18 councillors, of whom 6 were to be aldermen, under a mayor. The councillors were to be elected from two wards, North and South.[24] The first mayor of the reformed council was elected, along with the sheriff, in January 1836; thereafter both were chosen at the council's November meeting. Under the Representation of the People Act, 1948, the date of the council elections and mayor-making was changed in 1949 to May. The electoral divisions were reorganized in 1968, when six wards were created: Leomansley, Chadsmead, Curborough, Stowe, Central, and St. John's. There was no increase in the number of councillors.[25]

In 1974, under the Local Government Act of 1972, the city lost its self-governing status and was absorbed into the newly created Lichfield district. It is represented on the district council by 15 councillors, chosen from the six wards created in 1968. Those councillors also acted as a body of charter trustees who preserved the city's offices of dignity by electing annually a mayor and a sheriff; they also had custody of the civic regalia.[26] The trustees were superseded in 1980 by a parish council with 30 councillors representing the six wards.[27] The parish was granted city status in November the same year, with the chairman of the parish council, elected at the council's May meeting, styled a mayor.[28]

Lists of bailiffs, mayors, sheriffs, recorders, stewards, and town clerks from 1548 to 1805 are printed in T. Harwood's *The History and Antiquities of the Church and City of Lichfield*.[29] The lists are continued to 1972 in *City and County of Lichfield: Municipal Year Book 1972–74*.[30] Mayors and sheriffs since 1836 are listed on boards in the guildhall.

MANORIAL COURTS AND OFFICERS. From the 18th century the manor courts fell into disuse. The small court may have been discontinued after 1730 when it ceased to be recorded in the court books,[31] and the Hilary great court was last held

[13] *Gild of St. Mary*, 14; Harwood, *Lichfield*, 417.
[14] Harwood, *Lichfield*, 342–4.
[15] *Cal. Pat.* 1547–8, 386–7. All the royal charters discussed here, except that of 1548, survive and are in L.J.R.O. An English translation of the charters, including that of 1548, was made in 1803 by Stephen Simpson, the town clerk: L.J.R.O., D. 77/2/1. An English abstract is printed in Harwood, *Lichfield*, 335–50.
[16] Above, manor.
[17] *Cal. Pat.* 1553–4, 50–2. A similar formula was used in ten other Marian charters granted to towns: *Worcs. Hist. Soc.* N.S. viii. 4 n.
[18] *Acts of P.C.* 1552–4, 308.
[19] Below (county of the city).
[20] Harwood, *Lichfield*, 339–40.

[21] Below (liberties).
[22] *Cal. S.P. Dom.* 1684–5, 141, 255; L.J.R.O., D. 35/bailiffs' accts. 1657–1707, pp. 97, 101.
[23] *Cal. S.P. Dom.* 1687–9, 283.
[24] 5 & 6 Wm. IV, c. 76; *Lond. Gaz.* 7 Dec. 1835, pp. 2348–9.
[25] L.J.R.O., D. 77/5/4; D. 127/council min. bks.; 11 & 12 Geo. VI, c. 65.
[26] The Charter Trustees Order 1974, S.I. 1974, no. 176.
[27] The Lichfield (Parishes) Order 1980, S.I. 1980, no. 387.
[28] Charter of 4 Nov. 29 Eliz. II.
[29] pp. 419–39.
[30] pp. 21–30 (copy in Lichfield Libr.).
[31] L.J.R.O., D. 77/6/4, p. 74.

in 1741.[32] The main business of the Magdalen great court (the presentment by tithingmen of assaults) was taken over by the city's J.P.s, who in 1727 further encroached on the court by ordering the tithingmen to attend quarter sessions and report on street cleansing.[33] The Magdalen court did little business from the 1840s and was last held in 1885.[34] The St. George's court was retained as the occasion when manorial officers were chosen. It ceased to be held after 1885 but was revived in 1889.[35] It was still held as a ceremonial event in the late 1980s. A court of pie powder continues to be proclaimed at the time of the Ash Wednesday fair.[36]

By the 1640s the tithingmen were styled dozeners, a word derived from their Latin name *decenarii*.[37] They continued to represent wards in pairs, except that three dozeners were together responsible for Bird Street and Sandford Street, and that by 1658 there was only one dozener for Beacon Street and one for Wade Street.[38] From the mid 19th century they rarely attended the Magdalen court; only one was listed in 1869, and none from 1870.[39] They were still chosen for Tamworth Street in 1875 and for Conduit Street and Dam Street in 1877.[40] By 1748 the dozeners carried halberds as symbols of office.[41]

The jury formerly known as the Twelve continued to receive the dozeners' presentments as well as making its own. In the 18th century up to 20 men were usually empanelled, with occasionally more at the Magdalen court; as men were often chosen in their absence they were evidently selected by rota. With little business to be done, it became customary to adjourn the courts to a date a month or two ahead when the jury reassembled for a dinner at the house of the foreman, generally an innholder. The adjournment of the Hilary court was usually to early March, that of the St. George's court to June, and that of the Magdalen court to October.[42] By the mid 18th century the meeting of the adjourned St. George's court was styled the Burgage Jury, after the burgage holders whose court it was, and that of the Magdalen court the Tinsel Jury, a name meaning a fine.[43] The dinners were at least partly paid for by the bailiffs, evidently as a continuation of the payment for the breakfasts of the Twelve on court days in the Middle Ages. Payment was stopped in 1695, but from the later 1750s the bailiffs paid 10s. towards each dinner.[44] In 1837 the reformed council agreed to pay 3 guineas to the meeting of the St. George's

court and 2 guineas to that of the Magdalen court.[45] Each court received 3 guineas when the payments were stopped in 1885. Payment for the St. George's court was revived in 1889.[46]

The appointment of the clerks of the market was discontinued in 1885, but two constables were chosen at the St. George's court when it was revived in 1889.[47] By the mid 17th century two pinners were chosen at the court, one responsible for the city portion of St. Chad's parish and the other for that of St. Michael's.[48] From 1718 the former was paid 10s. a year by the corporation, which let ½ a. of land in Sedy field known as pinner's baulk, evidently as an endowment of the office.[49] From 1895 each pinner was paid 10s.[50] By the early 1950s the payment was 15s., and its equivalent, 75p, was still paid in the late 1980s.[51] Four commoners were recorded in 1645 and were chosen at the St. George's court by the mid 1690s. They were responsible for checking that townspeople did not overpasture the commons and the fallow fields.[52] In the mid 1740s they were denounced as young tradesmen who went out on summer evenings rounding up horses and asses found on the waste or in lanes, impounding them, and extracting from their owners money which they then spent on ale.[53] The commoners were still chosen in 1889.[54]

There was a pinfold in Beacon Street by 1645, near the corner of the later Anson Avenue.[55] In 1809 the improvement commissioners ordered its removal, and in 1810 a new one was set up at the junction of Beacon Street and Cross in Hand Lane.[56] The construction of houses at Greenhill in the earlier 19th century caused the removal of a pinfold there, possibly on the site of the pinfold recorded in the later Middle Ages. It was probably moved to a site at the junction of Broad Lane and Darnford Lane, where it stood in 1882. It survived there in the mid 1930s.[57]

COMMISSION OF THE PEACE. A commission was established by the charter of 1548, with the two bailiffs as justices. Mary I's charter of 1553 added a recorder and a steward to the commission, which was empowered to hear all felonies, including murder, and to deliver the gaol. Both bailiffs were required to sit, together with the recorder or the steward; under the charter of 1622 only one bailiff had to sit. A further extension of the commission was made by the charter of 1664 to include the retiring bailiffs for the year after they had left office. From the later

[32] Ibid. p. 192; D. 77/5/2, f. 40v.
[33] Ibid. D. 68, ff. 5v.–6, 55v., 79v., 114.
[34] Ibid. D. 77/6/6.
[35] *Lichfield Mercury*, 26 Apr. 1889, p. 5.
[36] Below, econ. hist. (markets and fairs).
[37] W.S.L. 350B/30.
[38] Ibid. 329/30; 330/30; 334/30.
[39] L.J.R.O., D. 77/6/6–7.
[40] Ibid. D. 77/6/9; Lichfield Libr., Conduit St. and Dam St. dozeners' bk. 1720–1877.
[41] L.J.R.O., D. 68, f. 114. For a drawing of some of them in 1819 see Bodl. G.A. Staffs. 4°, 8, facing p. 398.
[42] L.J.R.O., D. 77/6/4–5.
[43] Ibid. D. 35/bailiffs' accts. 1704–94, pp. 199 sqq.; *Eng. Dialect Dict.* ed. J. Wright, vi (1905), 158.
[44] L.J.R.O., D. 35/bailiffs' accts. 1704–94, pp. 169 sqq.
[45] Ibid. D. 77/5/4, ff. 71v., 77.
[46] Ibid. D. 35/council ledger bk. 1884–99, pp. 165, 167;

cash bk. 1885–1900, p. 154.
[47] *Lichfield Mercury*, 26 Apr. 1889, p. 5.
[48] W.S.L. 329/30; L.J.R.O., D. 77/6/1–6.
[49] L.J.R.O., D. 35/bailiffs' accts. 1704–94, pp. 63, 73, 79, 118, 125; D. 77/5/1, f. 204; D. 77/9/29.
[50] Ibid. D. 35/council ledger bk. 1884–99, p. 355.
[51] *City and County of Lichfield Abstract of Accts. 1953*, 10; inf. from the town clerk.
[52] W.S.L. 329/30; L.J.R.O., D. 77/6/1–5.
[53] S.R.O., D. 661/2/802, p. 32.
[54] *Lichfield Mercury*, 26 Apr. 1889, p. 5.
[55] W.S.L. 329/30; L.J.R.O., VC/A/21, CC 17529, plan 15; J. Snape, *Plan of Lichfield, 1781.*
[56] L.J.R.O., D. 35/improvement com. min. bk. 1806–9, 19 Oct. 1807; D. 77/5/3, f. 44v.; L.J.R.O., B/A/15/Lichfield, St. Chad.
[57] L.J.R.O., D. 77/5/4, f. 88v.; D. 77/15/3, p. 56; O.S. Map 6″, Staffs. LII. SE. (1883, 1938 edns.).

17th century the recorders were noblemen, and it is unlikely that any attended. From the early 19th century, however, the recorders were local gentlemen who did attend on occasion.[58] By the later 17th century the steward was normally a lawyer. He probably attended when important cases were heard; in the early 19th century capital offences were tried only in his presence.[59] The Municipal Commissioners in 1833 acknowledged the integrity and impartiality of the magistrates but doubted their competence.[60] Petty sessions were held weekly by 1834.[61] Under the Municipal Corporations Act of 1882 the recorder became sole judge of the quarter sessions.[62] The sessions were abolished by the Courts Act, 1971.[63] Sessions were held in the guildhall until 1867 when new premises were built in Wade Street on the site of the former gaol.[64] They were rebuilt in 1963.[65]

COURT OF RECORD. A court of record was established by the 1548 charter to meet weekly on Thursdays and deal with pleas relating to debts or damages of 40s. or over. Its competence was widened by the 1553 charter to include sums of less than 40s. Records of the court which survive for the 1660s and from 1696 show that it was held in the guildhall before the bailiffs and the town clerk.[66] Little business was done from the 1730s, and none from 1836 when recourse to the new county court was preferred. The court was formally abolished in 1857.[67] Under the 1548 charter the corporation was allowed to keep the fines imposed by the court in return for a fee farm of 20s. to the Crown. The farm was redeemed in 1874.[68]

THE UNREFORMED CORPORATION. There was a close connexion between the first members of the corporation and the dissolved guild of St. Mary. Gregory Stonyng, the senior bailiff nominated in the 1548 charter, and half the 24 brethren had been masters of the guild, and a further 6 had been guild wardens.[69] The junior bailiff nominated in 1548 was Mark Wyrley, a lawyer who had been the bishop's bailiff in the town in 1541–2.[70]

Power was evidently concentrated in a small group of men, often bound by family ties.[71] Henry Bird, a baker, who was listed third among the brethren nominated in the 1548 charter, was senior bailiff in 1551–2 and sheriff in 1561–2. Nicholas Bird, also a baker, who was listed twenty-third in 1548, was senior bailiff on four occasions between 1559 and 1588 and sheriff in 1556–7; he was second in a list of the brethren

made in 1583. Other members of the Bird family who held office were Henry Bird the younger, a baker, who was junior bailiff and senior bailiff in the later 1560s, and John Bird, another baker, who was junior bailiff in 1577–8. Humphrey Lowe, a mercer who was listed twelfth in 1548, was sheriff in 1554–5, junior bailiff in 1556–7, and senior bailiff in 1564–5 and 1573–4. In 1583 he headed the list of brethren. Simon Biddulph, another mercer, was not nominated in 1548, although he had been a warden of the guild in 1546; none the less he was junior bailiff in 1553–4 and three times senior bailiff betweeen 1562 and 1576. His son, also Simon, had a similar career as junior bailiff in 1581–2 and three times senior bailiff between 1588 and 1606. Others who held the office of senior bailiff three times before 1600 were John Burnes, an upholsterer, and John Chatterton, styled gentleman;[72] those who held it twice were William Hawrytt, an innholder, Thomas Rowe, a butcher, John Snape, a husbandman, Thomas Whitmore, a baker, and William Wightwick, a tanner. James Weston, a lawyer and diocesan registrar who was listed third among the brethren in 1583, held office only once, as junior bailiff in 1562–3; he was, however, a Lichfield M.P. in 1584–5.[73] John Dyott, another lawyer, was three times junior bailiff between 1558 and 1573 but never senior bailiff. The leading families intermarried. Humphrey Lowe's son Michael married one of the elder Simon Biddulph's daughters,[74] and Lowe's sister married James Weston,[75] himself John Dyott's son-in-law.[76]

There is evidence of Protestant sympathies among the earliest brethren. About 1550 the corporation ordered the removal of 'idols and images' and altars from St. Mary's church.[77] In 1556 or 1557 the sheriff, Nicholas Bird, and a group of women who included Simon Biddulph's wife Margaret and Humphrey Lowe's wife Joan gave comfort to Joyce Lewes of Mancetter (Warws.), when she was burnt as a heretic in Lichfield.[78]

It seems that supporters of parliament against Charles I achieved prominence under the patronage of Robert Devereux, earl of Essex (d. 1646). From 1604 Essex held a lease of Lichfield manor for life, and the Lichfield waits wore his badge.[79] The town clerk nominated in the 1622 charter, Michael Noble, had puritan sympathies, and he and Devereux's half-brother were Lichfield's M.P.s in the Long Parliament.[80] Between 1648 and 1659 Richard Drafgate, probably a former agent of Devereux, was twice senior bailiff, sharing office in 1656–7 with

[58] 1st Rep. Com. Mun. Corp. H.C. 116, App. III, p. 1927 (1835), xxv; below (corporation officers).
[59] 1st Rep. Com. Mun. Corp. p. 1927; White, Dir. Staffs. (1834), 76; below (corporation officers).
[60] 1st Rep. Com. Mun. Corp. p. 1931.
[61] White, Dir. Staffs. (1834), 71.
[62] 45 & 46 Vic. c. 50.
[63] L.J.R.O., D. 25/1/5.
[64] Staffs. Advertiser, 28 Mar. 1868, p. 7; O.S. Map 1/500, Staffs. LII. 15. 13 (1884 edn.); below (gaol).
[65] Date stone on building.
[66] W.S.L. 300–328/30; L.J.R.O., D. 77/7.
[67] L.J.R.O., D. 77/7/3–6; White, Dir. Staffs. (1851), 492, 494.
[68] L.J.R.O., D. 127/council min. bk. 1866–82, p. 185.

[69] Harwood, Lichfield, 413–19.
[70] Ibid. 419; S.R.O., D. (W.) 1734/J. 1949, m. [1].
[71] Para. based on Harwood, Lichfield, 418–24; S.H.C. iii (2), 28.
[72] For the Chatterton family see below, Fisherwick, manors (Horton); Streethay, estates (Fulfen).
[73] S.H.C. 1917–18, 376.
[74] P.R.O., PROB 11/62, f. 102; PROB 11/66, f. 193.
[75] S.H.C. 1917–18, 382.
[76] Ibid. v (2), 117.
[77] Below, churches.
[78] B.L. Harl. MS. 421, ff. 69, 70v., 71.
[79] Above, manor; below, social and cultural activities (music).
[80] Below, parl. representation.

James Rixam (or Rixom), a Presbyterian who was a town carrier.[81] Another Presbyterian, Thomas Minors, a mercer who was Lichfield's M.P. 1654–60, was in turn both junior and senior bailiff, and his brother-in-law, William Jesson, junior bailiff.[82] At the Restoration both Minors and Jesson, despite their wealth, were dismissed from the corporation.[83]

Charles II's charter of 1664 did not alter the composition of the corporation. The surrender of the charter in 1684 was generally believed to be intended to bring the town under the control of George Legge, Lord Dartmouth, one of the leading favourites at court. He had married in 1667 a Lichfield heiress, Barbara, daughter of Sir Henry Archbold, the diocesan chancellor 1675–82; her elder sister Mary had married as her second husband the Lichfield physician John Floyer, knighted in 1685. According to Dartmouth's rival Thomas Thynne, later Viscount Weymouth, Floyer worked on Dartmouth's behalf in Lichfield, 'endeavouring to frame that corporation anew by leaving out some of the best men in it, that it may solely depend on that family'. The town clerk, John Rawlins, supported Thynne and delayed the issue of a new charter.[84] The new corporation established by James II in 1686, although reduced in size, took its members exclusively from the retiring brethren, and the first mayor, Thomas Hammond, was the retiring senior bailiff. Hammond was appointed a J.P. for life, as was Floyer. No record of the meetings of the mayor and aldermen has survived, and it is uncertain to what extent the brethren supported the king. James visited Lichfield in 1687, when he touched for the King's Evil in the cathedral, and it was evidently on that visit that the corporation gave him 'a present' of £107 10s.[85] None the less the entire corporation and Floyer were removed from office in stages during 1688.[86] When Charles II's charter was restored in October 1688 most of the men appointed in 1686 regained power.[87]

Meetings of the corporation, for which records survive from 1679, were styled the Common Council until 1688 when the name Common Hall was adopted.[88] They were held frequently but at irregular intervals, the only fixed occasion being St. James's day when the bailiffs and sheriff were chosen. Business was confined generally to the oversight of corporate and manorial property and the administration of trust funds, including that of the grammar school. Although public works received less

attention, chiefly because they were supported financially by the Conduit Lands trustees,[89] the brethren were concerned to promote the town's welfare. They supported the creation of the Lichfield turnpike trust in 1729,[90] used a gift of money to abolish market tolls in 1741,[91] and landscaped parts of the town in the late 18th century.[92]

The corporation was poorer than the Conduit Lands trust, which in 1545 had acquired many of the endowments of the medieval guild of St. Mary and St. John the Baptist. Under the 1548 charter the corporation was permitted to acquire land worth up to £20 a year, raised to £100 by the 1622 charter. Land acquired under the charter is not readily distinguishable from land which the corporation held as lord of Lichfield manor or as the trustee of various charities. Income from 'city lands', presumably corporate property, was £3 13s. 5d. in 1577–8; by the late 1650s it was apparently a little over £13.[93] In the later 1760s revenue from both corporate and charity land was some £140.[94] In 1776 the corporation held 270 a. of inclosed land in Curborough and Elmhurst, Farewell, King's Bromley, Aldridge, and Mayfield and 58½ a. of common land and 6 a. of Lammas meadow in Lichfield.[95] The chief items of manorial revenue were burgage rents, tolls from markets and fairs, and the profits of the mills and the fisheries of the town's pools. Burgage rents produced £20 in 1577–8, and in 1674 they were valued, together with fines for encroachments on the streets, at £29.[96] In the later 1760s they produced only £12.[97] The tolls from markets and fairs were let for £20 a year in 1696, and the lease was renewed in 1716 for the same rent.[98] The corporation extinguished market tolls from Christmas 1741, except for pickage and for tolls other than those on corn when a market day coincided with a fair. It was able to do so because of a gift of £500 from Sir Lister Holte, newly elected as one of Lichfield's M.P.s. Of that sum £400 was invested and its income spent on paving, an expense previously met out of the market tolls; the remaining £100 was spent on the guildhall.[99] The corporation still received tolls from the two fairs; they produced nearly £5 in the earlier 1740s but only around £2 from later in the decade.[1] Stowe mill was let in 1717 for £38 a year and the malt mill in Dam Street in 1718 for £22.[2] The corporation also received the fines for refusal to serve as sheriff; they amounted to as much as 100 guineas when five men were fined in 1778.[3]

[81] Harwood, *Lichfield*, 341 (where 'Drascut' is probably a variant of Drafgate), 426–7; below, protestant nonconformity (Presbyterians).
[82] Harwood, *Lichfield*, 426–7, 479; *S.H.C.* 1920 and 1922, 96, 99–101.
[83] Bodl. MS. Tanner 44, ff. 108, 125.
[84] *Hist. Parl., Commons, 1660–90*, i. 385; Reade, *Johnsonian Gleanings*, viii. 49–50; W. A. Shaw, *Knights of Eng.* ii. 260.
[85] Harwood, *Lichfield*, 476–7; L.J.R.O., D. 35/bailiffs' accts. 1657–1707, p. 105.
[86] *Hist. Parl., Commons, 1660–90*, i. 386.
[87] L.J.R.O., D. 77/5/1, ff. 4, 14v., 19; Harwood, *Lichfield*, 429.
[88] L.J.R.O., D. 77/5/1.
[89] Below, public services (water supplies).
[90] L.J.R.O., D. 77/5/1, f. 259v.

[91] Below.
[92] Below, social and cultural activities (walks).
[93] Harwood, *Lichfield*, 382; L.J.R.O., D. 35/bailiffs' accts. 1657–1707, pp. 1–2.
[94] L.J.R.O., D. 35/bailiffs' accts. 1704–94, pp. 298–304.
[95] Ibid. D. 77/8/1.
[96] Ibid. D. 35/bailiffs' accts. 1657–1707, pp. 232–42; Harwood, *Lichfield*, 382.
[97] L.J.R.O., D. 35/bailiffs' accts. 1704–94, pp. 298, 302.
[98] Ibid. D. 77/9/23.
[99] Ibid. D. 77/5/2, f. 39v.
[1] Ibid. D. 35/bailiffs' accts. 1704–94, pp. 158, 168, 173, 185, 190.
[2] Ibid. D. 77/9/61 and 63.
[3] Ibid. D. 35/bailiffs' accts. 1704–94, p. 404; below (county of the city).

A lease of manorial revenue for seven years in 1664 was probably made in order to raise capital. The lessee paid £200 cash, 20s. a year, and the £50 fee-farm rent which the corporation owed the bishop for the manor; the lessee also agreed to clean the streets, pay the millers' wages, and repair the mills.[4] A policy of financial retrenchment was undertaken in 1695.[5] The appointment of Nicholas Deakin as chamberlain by 1737 may have been an attempt to impose stricter financial control. He took over responsibility for the accounts from the town clerk and was still in office in 1743.[6] By 1809 a treasurer was employed.[7] A rate was levied in 1816 and again in 1820.[8]

Although under the 1622 charter the corporation had a complement of 21 brethren, there were only 17 in 1696 and 15 in 1720.[9] In 1793 there were 16.[10] The low number was presumably deliberate and helped to concentrate power. No family came to dominate the corporation, however, and the offices of both senior and junior bailiff seem to have been held by the brethren according to seniority. No man ever retained office from one year to another, and only a few were senior bailiff more than twice. The brethren fostered a sense of community among themselves and of superiority over others by attention to ceremonial. They wore gowns which were probably modelled on the scarlet gown worn by the master of St. Mary's guild in the earlier 16th century.[11] In the late 17th century the gowns were evidently of heavy, good-quality cloth: the brethren permitted themselves to attend church on Sunday without them in the hot summer of 1705 and when it rained.[12] From 1622, if not before, the bailiffs had maces carried before them, even in the Close although it lay outside their jurisdiction.[13] A sword was placed by their seat in St. Mary's church, where they attended services with the brethren, who also had their own seats there. It was presumably at St. Mary's too that the customary St. James's day sermon was preached after the new bailiffs and sheriff had been chosen.[14] The brethren made solemn public appearances in their gowns in the late 17th and the 18th century, and presumably earlier, when walking the fairs and at times of public rejoicing, such as that for the military victories in 1702 when a bonfire was lit in the market square and a hogshead of ale provided.[15] In 1695, however, expenditure at the walk, presumably on food and drink, was stopped,[16] and in the late 18th century only the bailiffs joined in the procession at the Whitsuntide inspection of the watch.[17]

Concerned for its dignity, the corporation in

1705 allowed three members to resign because they had been reduced to poverty, and in 1708 it dismissed another who was facing bankruptcy. At a meeting in 1720 when new members were chosen, one evidently unsuitable candidate was rejected on the nod.[18] In 1696 the brethren forced the dismissal of John Matlock, a writing master at the grammar school, who besides being 'a turbulent person' had acted 'very unhandsomely' towards them.[19]

The corporation promoted good relations with the nobility by patronizing the race meetings on Whittington heath[20] and by organizing public feasts called buck-eatings. The deer were provided free by local noblemen and eaten at feasts held at the corporation's expense. The cost was limited to £10 a year in 1679.[21] In 1718 it was resolved that up to 50 guests were to be invited to eat a buck given by Lord Weymouth, provided that the cost did not exceed £5.[22] In 1727 a buck was given by Lord Weymouth and another by Lord Uxbridge, the recorder; one buck was eaten at the George, with musicians playing and probably with the sheriff in attendance, and the other was eaten at the gaol, with the corporation providing drink for the gaoler and the prisoners.[23] By 1734 the feasts had become ordinaries, for which the participants paid a small fee. A feast at the guildhall in 1734 cost each guest 12d., as did feasts in 1737, one at the guildhall and the other at the Bowling Green inn.[24] A guinea fee paid in 1799 to the gamekeepers of Lord Dartmouth, then recorder, and of Sir Nigel Gresley suggests that buck-eatings still took place, although the corporation no longer financed them.[25]

THE REFORMED COUNCIL. The Municipal Commissioners visited Lichfield in December 1833. They received no co-operation from the unreformed corporation, which had challenged the commissioners' powers and forbidden the town clerk to show them the corporation records. As a result the commissioners took evidence from local inhabitants, notably the antiquary Thomas Harwood.[26] The commissioners' chief complaint referred to the corporation's party bias.[27] A minority of the corporation had wished to cooperate with the commissioners. The group was led by Charles Stringer, the junior bailiff, and Charles Simpson, the town clerk, and included Thomas Adie, the only member of the corporation to be returned as a councillor at the elections which followed the passing of the Municipal Corporations Act of 1835.[28] The elections returned a Radical majority. Besides Adie, a plumber and glazier, councillors in-

4 L.J.R.O., D. 77/9/59.
5 Ibid. D. 77/5/1, f. 63.
6 Ibid. D. 77/5/2, ff. 31, 45v.
7 Treasurer's acct. 1809–16 (loose sheet in L.J.R.O., D. 25/1/2).
8 Ibid. D. 25/1/2, ff. 170v.–171, 233.
9 Ibid. D. 77/5/1, ff. 67, 216.
10 Univ. Brit. Dir. iii (1794), 610–12.
11 Gild of St. Mary, 15.
12 L.J.R.O., D. 77/5/1, ff. 16v., 124v., 270.
13 Below (liberties; city seals).
14 Below (city seals); churches.
15 L.J.R.O., D. 77/5/1, ff. 113, 116v.; D. 77/5/2, f. 84v.
16 Ibid. D. 77/5/1, f. 63.
17 Below, social and cultural activities (Greenhill Bower).
18 L.J.R.O., D. 77/5/1, ff. 122, 139, 216.
19 Ibid. f. 64.
20 Below, social and cultural activities (sport).
21 L.J.R.O., D. 77/5/1, f. 4.
22 Ibid. f. 206.
23 Ibid. D. 35/bailiffs' accts. 1704–94, p. 97.
24 Ibid. D. 77/5/2, ff. 15, 27.
25 Ibid. D. 35/bailiffs' accts. 1794–1835, pp. 26, 44.
26 Staffs. Advertiser, 14 and 28 Dec. 1833; 1st Rep. Com. Mun. Corp. H.C. 116, App. III, p. 1925 (1835), xxv; L.J.R.O., D. 77/5/3, ff. 223v.–224.
27 1st Rep. Com. Mun. Corp. pp. 1929–32.
28 L.J.R.O., D. 77/5/3, f. 225; D. 77/5/4, f. 17v.

cluded Joseph Potter the elder, an architect, Richard Harris, an auctioneer, William Weldhen, a coachmaker, William Standly and Thomas Walton, both chemists, John Proffitt, a hat maker, and Thomas Rowley, a physician.[29] Rowley, who had become a Congregationalist in 1823 and became an Anglican in 1841,[30] was chosen mayor.

In 1836 the council inherited £22 in cash and a debt of £260 from the unreformed corporation. It increased the rent of the market stallages and of the fisheries of the pools, and it cut expenditure.[31] It also sold property. Land and cottages in St. John Street were sold in 1838 for over £580; land in Paradise fields on the north side of Trent Valley Road was sold in 1839 for £381 as the site for the Lichfield union workhouse; and the former workhouse in Sandford Street was sold in 1840-1 for £740.[32] In 1842 the council raised £735 by the sale of stock which the corporation had bought from the proceeds of the lease in 1819 of the New College in the Close.[33] A borough rate was levied from 1846.[34] The mayor was voted a salary of £60 and the treasurer one of £10 in 1836.[35]

Elections in 1843 produced a Conservative council.[36] The Liberals were returned in 1853, and Rowley became mayor again. They kept control until 1881, when a Conservative majority was returned.[37] The council was controlled by Conservatives or by Independents until its abolition in 1974.[38] The first woman councillor, Mrs. Daisy Stuart Shaw, was elected for South Ward in 1919; she became the first woman mayor in 1927.[39]

The Labour and Co-operative Party first contested an election in 1919, when two candidates stood in North Ward. None stood from 1925.[40] The first Labour supporter to be elected was Frank Halfpenny at a byelection in South Ward in 1937, although he did not stand on a party ticket. Official Labour candidates were not elected until 1946, when two were successful in North Ward. In 1949 Halfpenny, standing as a Labour candidate, lost his seat, but he was re-elected for North Ward in 1953; in 1965 he became the first Labour mayor.[41]

IMPROVEMENT COMMISSIONERS AND URBAN SANITARY AUTHORITY. A body of improvement commissioners was established by an Act of 1806 to pave, clean, light, watch, and maintain the town's streets. Besides *ex officio* members, the commissioners included everyone owning or occupying land worth £20 a year.[42] The commissioners levied a rate, received gratuities of £40 from the corporation and £60 from the Conduit Lands trustees,[43] and sold annuities.[44] In 1836 they transferred their powers to the reformed council.[45] The council acted as commissioners until an Act of 1872 gave it powers as an urban sanitary authority.[46]

CORPORATION OFFICERS. The recordership was established by the 1553 charter. The recorder in 1583 was Thomas Egerton, who was solicitor general; he later became lord chancellor and was created Viscount Brackley.[47] Sir Simon Weston, nominated as recorder in the 1622 charter, was the son of James Weston, the diocesan registrar and a Lichfield M.P.; in the 1620s Simon was himself M.P. for Lichfield and then for Staffordshire.[48] The recordership was later held by William Seymour, duke of Somerset (d. 1660), presumably because he was brother-in-law of Robert Devereux, earl of Essex (d. 1646), lessee for life of Lichfield manor.[49] The recorder named in the 1664 charter was Thomas Wriothesley, earl of Southampton and high constable of England (d. 1667). He was followed by two other dukes of Somerset, William Seymour (d. 1671) and John Seymour (d. 1675).[50] The corporation next chose Thomas Osborne, earl of Danby, lord treasurer of England.[51] The choice offended Thomas Thynne, later Viscount Weymouth, a descendant of the Devereux family. After Danby was impeached in 1679, the corporation tried to conciliate Thynne and promised him the recordership when it next became vacant; in fact in 1684 they chose George Legge, Lord Dartmouth, and he was confirmed in office by the charter of 1686.[52] After Danby was restored to favour he once more became recorder, apparently in 1688, and retained the office until his death, as duke of Leeds, in 1712. The corporation then fulfilled its promise to Weymouth, although by a majority of only one; he remained recorder until his death in 1714.[53] The choice of recorder evidently reflected the political character and needs of the corporation, and throughout the rest of the 18th century the recorders were noblemen.[54] After the death of Henry, earl of Uxbridge, in 1743, the corporation was allegedly persuaded by Theophilus

[29] Ibid. D. 77/5/4, ff. 16–21; *Dyott's Diary*, ed. R. W. Jeffery, ii. 376.
[30] L.J.R.O., D. 112/1/1, pp. 27, 40.
[31] Ibid. D. 35/bailiffs' accts. 1794–1835, p. 407; *Abstract of Accts. of Treasurer of Borough Fund of City of Lichfield* (Lichfield, 1836; copy in W.S.L.).
[32] L.J.R.O., D. 35/borough fund acct. bk. 1836–68, pp. 46, 48, 54, 56, 92, 94, 106.
[33] Ibid. p. 130; D. 35/bailiffs' accts. 1794–1835, pp. 229, 232.
[34] Ibid. D. 35/borough fund acct. bk. 1836–68, pp. 198, 208, 218.
[35] Ibid. D. 77/5/4, ff. 35, 51v.
[36] W.S.L., Broadsheets 11/16–19; S.R.O., D. 661/11/2/3/1/16, entry for 7 Nov. 1843.
[37] *Staffs. Advertiser*, 5 Nov. 1853, p. 4; L.J.R.O., D. 77/7/7.
[38] Election results are reported in *Lichfield Mercury*.
[39] *Lichfield Mercury*, 7 Nov. 1919, p. 4; 11 Nov. 1927, p. 5.
[40] Ibid. 31 Oct. 1919, p. 3; 3 Nov. 1922, p. 5; 6 Nov. 1925, p. 5.
[41] Ibid. 12 Mar. 1937, p. 5; 8 Nov. 1946, p. 4; 13 May 1949, p. 7; 8 May 1953, p. 7; 20 May 1966, p. 5.
[42] 46 Geo. III, c. 42 (Local and Personal).
[43] L.J.R.O., D. 35/bailiffs' accts. 1794–1835, pp. 324, 328; below, public services (water supplies).
[44] L.J.R.O., D. 35/improvement com. min. bk. 1806–9, 31 July and 21 Aug. 1806; D. 77/15/5, pp. 9–10.
[45] Ibid. D. 77/15/3, pp. 19–21.
[46] *P.O. Dir. Staffs.* (1872; 1876).
[47] W.S.L., S. MS. 413, f. 16v.; *D.N.B.*
[48] *S.H.C.* 1920 and 1922, 34–5.
[49] *Complete Peerage*, xii (1), 69–73.   [50] Ibid. 75, 131–3.
[51] Hist. MSS. Com. 78, *Hastings*, ii, p. 327; *D.N.B.*
[52] Hist. MSS. Com. 20, *11th Rep. V, Dartmouth*, p. 122; *Complete Peerage*, vii. 508; xii (2), 585–6.
[53] L.J.R.O., D. 77/5/1, f. 161; Hist. MSS. Com. 22, *11th Rep. VII*, p. 26; Harwood, *Lichfield*, 438.
[54] Harwood, *Lichfield*, 438.

Levett, the town clerk, to choose John Leveson-Gower, Lord (later Earl) Gower, in preference to Uxbridge's heir, who had recently dismissed Levett as steward of Yoxall manor.[55] In the early 19th century the recorders were local gentlemen.[56] After 1835 lawyers were appointed, and in 1836 the council voted a salary of 60 guineas.[57]

The office of steward was mentioned in the 1553 charter, and in 1583 it was held by Richard Broughton.[58] From the later 17th century the steward was normally a barrister with a salary of 40s., raised to £5 in 1705 and to 5 guineas in 1727.[59] A salary of 15 guineas was paid in the earlier 19th century.[60] The office was evidently abolished in 1835.[61]

The office of town clerk, so called in the 1553 charter, was earlier mentioned in the 1548 charter under the style of steward. The charter of 1622 confirmed Michael Noble in office for life and laid down that his successors were to be chosen from the brethren and were to hold office during the corporation's pleasure. The clerk appointed in 1688, Richard Wakefield, was the son-in-law of John Rawlins, clerk from 1667 to his death in 1685.[62] Wakefield was succeeded in 1721 by Theophilus Levett, whose appointment was opposed by one of the city's M.P.s, Walter Chetwynd, a Whig, probably on political grounds. Levett remained in office until his death in 1746.[63] The next clerk, Joseph Adey (d. 1763), was followed in 1764 by his nephew, Charles Simpson. Charles retired in 1792 and was replaced by his son Stephen (d. 1825), who was in turn succeeded by his son Charles.[64] By 1826 the clerk received a salary of £21.[65]

Charles Simpson retained office as town clerk under the reformed council.[66] Under the Municipal Corporations Act, however, he had to relinquish his post as clerk to the justices of the peace and was awarded as compensation an annuity of £71 6s. 8d. for life.[67] Simpson was politically active and was agent for the Liberal parliamentary candidate in 1841.[68] As a consequence he was dismissed when the Conservative council held its first meeting in 1844. Simpson regarded his dismissal as taking effect as soon as the motion had been passed and apparently walked out of the council chamber with the minute book; he also retained the council seal, and a replacement had to be made.[69] He was awarded a life pension of £50 18s. 2d.[70] which he retained on his reinstatement when the Liberals regained control in 1853.[71] Standing unsuccessfully as a Liberal parliamentary candidate in 1874,[72] he remained clerk until 1887 when he was again dismissed. The council had found him increasingly difficult to work with because of his eccentric behaviour and advanced age. Once again Simpson regarded his dismissal as taking immediate effect and abruptly stopped taking the minutes, which were continued by a councillor. The council had difficulty in recovering the seal and muniments, and it was over a year before Simpson handed them over.[73] He died aged 90 in 1890.[74]

THE GUILDHALL. The corporation from its establishment in 1548 evidently met in the hall in Bore Street formerly used by St. Mary's guild. It was the tenant in 1549, and it presumably bought the hall from the London speculator to whom the Crown had sold it that year.[75] By the later 17th century the council chamber occupied the upper storey, and there were various rooms underneath, including in the early 1670s a tailor's warehouse and in 1696 a shop.[76] The royal arms and those of the city were painted in the hall in 1677, at the expense of the Conduit Lands trustees.[77] By 1707 the fabric was so ruinous that the corporation decided to rebuild the hall and engaged Joseph Moseley and John Pilsworth. The money was again provided by the Conduit Lands trustees.[78] The work was apparently restricted to internal repairs,[79] but the hall was later given a new front. When the corporation renegotiated the lease of the rooms underneath the hall in 1732, it reserved the right to insert stairs from the street in front of them and to erect a new façade.[80] Structural work continued in the late 1730s and mid 1740s, the Conduit Lands trustees bearing most of the cost.[81] The new façade was rusticated on the ground floor with two doorways on the left and two windows on the right; the upper storey had pedimented windows and above was a parapet in which a sculptured stone panel bearing the city arms was set in 1744, at the cost of Lord Gower, recorder of Lichfield.[82] Access to the council chamber was by internal stairs leading up from the right-hand doorway; the left-hand doorway led to an uncovered passage

[55] S.R.O., D. 603/K/5/1, f. 1; L.J.R.O., D. 77/5/2, f. 46v.
[56] Harwood, *Lichfield*, 438; Stringer, *Lichfield*, 97.
[57] L.J.R.O., D. 77/5/4, f. 30.
[58] *S.H.C.* iii (2), 28.
[59] Harwood, *Lichfield*, 382, 438; L.J.R.O., D. 77/5/1, ff. 112v., 126v., 249v.
[60] L.J.R.O., D. 35/bailiffs' accts. 1794–1835, pp. 284, 292.
[61] White, *Dir. Staffs.* (1834), 77, lists a steward, but White, *Dir. Staffs.* (1851), 493, does not.
[62] *Cal. S.P. Dom.* 1667, p. 15; 1687–9, p. 334; L.J.R.O., D. 77/5/1, f. 14; P.R.O., PROB 11/382, ff. 177–8.
[63] P.R.O., SP 35/27, nos. 31, 37, 47; SP 35/62, no. 12; Reade, *Johnsonian Gleanings*, iv. 190.
[64] *Cal. H.O. Papers*, 1760–5, p. 477; Reade, *Johnsonian Gleanings*, iv. 145, 163–9.
[65] L.J.R.O., D. 35/bailiffs' accts. 1794–1835, p. 300.
[66] Ibid. D. 77/5/4, f. 23.
[67] Ibid. ff. 39v., 47v.
[68] *Lichfield Mercury*, 25 Apr. 1890, p. 8; 20 Feb. 1891, p. 5.
[69] L.J.R.O., D. 77/5/4, ff. 176v., 177v.; Lichfield Libr., inventory of contents of mus. and art gallery [? 1976].
[70] *Lichfield Mercury*, 25 Apr. 1890, p. 8.
[71] L.J.R.O., D. 127/council min. bk. 1853–66, p. 1.
[72] *Lichfield Mercury*, 25 Apr. 1890, p. 8.
[73] *Staffs. Advertiser*, 17 Mar. 1888, p. 6; L.J.R.O., D. 127/council min. bk. 1882–87, pp. 154–5.
[74] *Lichfield Mercury*, 25 Apr. 1890, p. 8.
[75] *Cal. Pat.* 1549–51, 96.
[76] L.J.R.O., D. 35/bailiffs' accts. 1657–1707, pp. 59, 64, 103, 158; Reade, *Johnsonian Gleanings*, ix. 61.
[77] L.J.R.O., D. 16/5/1, entry for 8 Dec. 1676; D. 126/acct. bk. 1663–1805, s.a. 1676–7, and loose accts. 1677.
[78] Ibid. D. 77/5/1, f. 132; D. 126/acct. bk. 1663–1805, 8 Dec. 1707.
[79] Ibid. D. 35/bailiffs' accts. 1704–94, pp. 11–12.
[80] Ibid. D. 77/5/1, f. 270v.; D. 77/9/1, f. 31.
[81] Ibid. D. 77/5/2, f. 40; D. 126/acct. bk. 1663–1805, accts. 1738–9, 1743–4, 1744–5; min. bk. 1741–1856, p. 6.
[82] Ibid. D. 77/5/2, f. 52; J. Edmondson, *Complete Body of Heraldry*, i (1780); below, plate 26.

to the gaol. In 1742 the corporation created additional rooms at the rear by converting a house which seems formerly to have been part of the gaol.[83] The hall was rebuilt in 1846–8 to the design of Joseph Potter the younger, the Conduit Lands trustees once more financing the work. The building is in a Gothic style with a plate-traceried north window of five lights. Internally a hammerbeam roof was inserted and a passage along the east side was made at first floor level.[84] The walls were wainscotted in 1852–3.[85] The stone panel of the city arms was removed and later placed in Museum Grounds in Bird Street. In 1893 early 19th-century glass from the north transept of the cathedral, with a new panel depicting Queen Victoria, was inserted in the north window.[86]

Donegal House, adjoining the guildhall on the west, was built in 1730.[87] It was bought by the council in 1910 for conversion into offices.[88] When the council was abolished in 1974, the ownership of the guildhall passed to Lichfield district council which in 1987 let it to the revived city council on a 999-year lease at a peppercorn rent. The mayor's parlour remained in Donegal House, also owned since 1974 by the district council.[89]

COUNTY OF THE CITY. Lichfield was created a county separate from Staffordshire by the charter of 1553 with effect from St. Thomas's day (21 December) that year. The sheriff chosen that day was to hold office until the following Michaelmas; thereafter the sheriff was to be chosen on the day after Michaelmas. Under the charter of 1622 he was to be chosen on St. James's day (25 July) and was not to be a bailiff or one of the brethren. Lichfield remained a county until reunited with Staffordshire by the Local Government Act of 1888; it was one of only four counties of cities not to be made a county borough.[90]

The first sheriff was Gregory Stonyng, the senior bailiff nominated in the 1548 charter; and the next three sheriffs were also original members of the corporation. Within a few years it was customary for a junior member of the corporation to be chosen sheriff, later becoming junior bailiff.[91] That practice continued until the charter of 1622. In the early 19th century it was alleged that the sheriff had to spend between £60 and £80 to fulfil his duties.[92] A fine was imposed on those who refused to serve: £30 in the 1680s, it was £20 in the 1740s, 20 guineas in the early 1770s, and 30 guineas in the early 19th century. From the later 18th century it was common for more than one fine to be taken:

three men were fined in 1771 and 1772, five in 1778, and generally two or three from the 1780s.[93] The practice appears to have been a deliberate policy by the corporation to raise revenue; it was criticized by the Municipal Commissioners in 1833, and in 1834 the fine was reduced to 10 guineas. It was soon restored to 30 guineas, however, after five men had preferred to pay the reduced fine rather than serve.[94] The first woman sheriff was Councillor Mary Halfpenny, chosen in 1968.[95] The shrievalty survives as an office of dignity. Since the establishment of the parish council in 1980, the sheriff has been chosen at the council's May meeting.

Under the 1548 charter an annual perambulation of the city's bounds was made on 1 May by the bailiffs accompanied by the sheriff of Staffordshire. After the county of Lichfield was created in 1553, the sheriff of Lichfield headed the perambulation and the date was moved to the feast of the Nativity of the Virgin Mary (8 September). The perambulation was still held in the late 1980s.

The sheriff was empowered by the 1553 charter to hold a monthly county court on Thursdays; the senior bailiff was to act as escheator, and the profits were to be shared with the corporation. No records have survived. In 1841 the court dealt with the recovery of debts under 40s.[96] It probably met in the guildhall, where the weekly court of record was held. In 1867 it was moved to the new magistrates' court in Wade Street.[97]

The office of county coroner, held by the town clerk, was established by the 1553 charter. The Local Government Act of 1888 transferred his powers to the Staffordshire coroner.[98]

LIBERTIES. By the early 13th century the Lichfield tenants of the dean and of the cathedral prebendaries enjoyed certain privileges which set them apart from the bishop's tenants in the town.[99] They were not answerable in the bishop's manor court for breaking the assize of bread and ale, and they could recover any distress taken for such offences; nor were they required to attend the manor court for offences committed on prebendal land, as the relevant prebendary punished them.[1] Prebendal tenants were in the same tithings as their neighbours and attended the town's view of frankpledge, but they were not fined if they defaulted. They were liable for service as tithingmen and tasters, and they also helped to maintain the watch; they were excused, however, the guard of robbers who had taken refuge in a church. They did not have to pay dues to the bishop but had to

[83] L.J.R.O., D. 68, f. 73v.; D. 77/5/2, f. 40. For an early 19th-century view of the interior see Bodl. G.A. Staffs. 4°, 8, facing p. 478.

[84] L.J.R.O., D. 126/min. bk. 1741–1856, pp. 345–7, 352–4, 374, 378, 385; W.S.L., Staffs. Views, v. 163; below, plate 18.

[85] L.J.R.O., D. 126/min. bk. 1741–1856, pp. 433, 436, 448, 453.

[86] Lichfield Mercury, 2 June 1893, p. 4; plaque underneath window.

[87] Above, domestic buildings.

[88] L.J.R.O., D. 127/council min. bk. 1909–14, pp. 56, 172; 1919–24, p. 141C.   [89] Inf. from the town clerk.

[90] 51 & 52 Vic. c. 41, s. 31 and 3rd sched.

[91] Harwood, Lichfield, 418–25.

[92] 1st Rep. Com. Mun. Corp. p. 1927.

[93] L.J.R.O., D. 35/bailiffs' accts. 1704–94; 1794–1835.

[94] Ibid. D. 77/5/1, ff. 7, 10v.; D. 77/5/3, f. 230; 1st Rep. Com. Mun. Corp. pp. 1931–2.

[95] Lichfield Mercury, 24 May 1968, p. 5.

[96] Pigot, Nat. Com. Dir. (1841), 27.

[97] L.J.R.O., D. 127/council min. bk. 1866–82, p. 30.

[98] 51 & 52 Vic. c. 41.

[99] Para. based on S.H.C. 1924, pp. 171–6.

[1] For refs. to 13th-cent. prebendal courts see ibid. pp. 17, 55, 173, 345.

contribute to expenses incurred when the king or justices came to Lichfield. No restrictions were placed on their freedom to buy and sell goods in the town, but they were required to use the bishop's mill. The privileges were upheld by arbitrators in 1252. They were tested in 1317 when the tenants of the prebendary of Freeford in Sandford Street, required to contribute to a levy for the repair of Sandford Street gate, successfully protested that they were obliged to meet only royal financial demands.[2]

Probably as a result of an attack on the Close in 1436, the Crown in 1441 granted the dean and chapter extensive powers of self-government. No royal officer was to be allowed into the Close, where the dean and chapter were to have the return and execution of all writs and were to be J.P.s.[3] In 1531 Sir Anthony Fitzherbert, a justice of King's Bench, issued a writ against Canon David Pole and it was executed by the janitor of the Close. Fitzherbert interfered again in 1532, when he ordered the arrest of a felon who had taken refuge in a canon's house.[4] The events evidently caused the chapter later in 1532 to warn the subchanter and sacrist against endangering the privileges of the Close when they planned to ask a Staffordshire J.P. to issue a warrant against a canon.[5] The incorporation of the town in 1548 did not affect the independence of the Close.

The privileges of the Close were extended by James I in 1623. The dean and resident canons remained J.P.s, and to their number were added the bishop, the bishop's vicar general, and Robert Devereux, earl of Essex (d. 1646), lessee for life of Lichfield manor. The J.P.s had to take an oath of fidelity to the cathedral. The Close was exempted from the jurisdiction of all town officers, although the bailiffs were allowed to have their maces carried before them when they attended services in the cathedral. The vicars choral and the cathedral officers (the two chapter clerks, the two clerks of the fabric, the bailiff of the liberty, and the collector of pensions) were exempted from jury service in the town. No one living in the Close was to lose civic rights, and conversely no craftsman working at the cathedral was to be refused permission to live in the town.[6] The corporation resisted the restriction of its authority, and in particular it sought to tax residents of the Close. In 1638, after a dispute over the payment of ship money, the solicitor general declared that the Close was in neither the town nor the county of Lichfield.[7] With the abolition of the cathedral chapter in 1649, the privileges were no longer enforced. They were re-established, with difficulty, at the Restoration.[8] The Close remained a liberty until 1836 when it was added to Lichfield under the 1835 Municipal Corporations Act.[9]

Even before the grant of self-government in 1441 the dean and chapter maintained a watch for the Close. The last watchman died in 1956.[10] The Close had its own stocks in the mid 18th and earlier 19th century.[11]

GAOL AND HOUSE OF CORRECTION. There may have been a gaol at Lichfield in 1163–4 when the sheriff of Staffordshire received an allowance for escorting prisoners from Lichfield.[12] There was certainly a gaol in 1306, when it was repaired at the bishop's expense in readiness for the arrival of justices of trailbaston.[13] The mention in 1309 of three stalls around the gaol suggests that it stood in the market place.[14] In 1459 the gaol needed repair after it had been attacked by the men of Henry Percy, earl of Northumberland. He was a supporter of the Lancastrian cause, and possibly the attack was an attempt to release prisoners following the Yorkist victory at Blore Heath that year.[15] By the 16th century the gaol probably stood behind the guildhall, with an entrance passage from Bore Street along the east side of the hall: fragments of 16th-century and earlier stonework survive there as part of a building which is mostly 18th-century.

In 1728 the corporation ordered the construction of a cage 8 ft. square and as deep as possible under the floor of a dungeon, presumably in the gaol.[16] In the earlier 1740s extra accommodation for prisoners was provided in a house in Wade Street behind the gaol.[17] New cells were built in 1801.[18] They were probably the 14 cells, each 9 ft. by 6 ft., mentioned in 1832, when there were also 6 day rooms and 5 open yards. Although there was room in 1832 for 50 prisoners, only 13 had been held at any one time that year; they were guarded by a gaoler and a turnkey, who were both resident.[19] There were only three prisoners early in 1848, when conditions were considered unsuitable and a recommendation was made that they should be sent to the county gaol at Stafford. By 1853 the corporation was paying for the maintenance of its prisoners at Stafford.[20] The Lichfield gaol, however, was not closed until 1866.[21] Most of the site was used for the construction in 1867 of a magistrates' court,[22] but four cells were incorporated into the guildhall and in 1986 they were opened as part of a small museum.[23]

[2] Ibid. pp. 176–7.
[3] Cal. Pat. 1441–6, 31–2.
[4] L.J.R.O., D. 30/C.A. iv, ff. 93, 94v.
[5] Ibid. f. 98.
[6] V.C.H. Staffs. iii. 173.
[7] Ibid. 173–4.
[8] Lichfield Cath. Libr., MS. Lichfield 22, pp. 35–9.
[9] 5 & 6 Wm. IV, c. 76.
[10] Below, public services (policing).
[11] Below (punitive instruments).
[12] S.H.C. i. 38.
[13] S.R.O., D. (W.) 1734/J. 2057, m. 9.
[14] T.S.S.A.H.S. xviii. 63.
[15] L.J.R.O., B/A/21, CC 124075, m. 4; V.C.H. Staffs. i. 243–4.

[16] L.J.R.O., D. 35/bailiffs' accts. 1704–94, p. 102; D. 77/5/1, f. 253.
[17] Ibid. D. 68, f. 73v.
[18] Ibid. D. 35/bailiffs' accts. 1794–1835, pp. 56, 58.
[19] Returns of Places of Confinement which do not come under the Gaol Act, H.C. 485, p. 64 (1833), xxviii; Returns of Gaols, 1833, H.C. 484, p. 34 (1833), xxviii.
[20] Staffs. Advertiser, 19 Feb. 1848, p. 8; L.J.R.O., D. 25/1/3, 6 Jan. 1855; D. 127/council min. bk. 1853–66, pp. 6, 25.
[21] 28 & 29 Vic. c. 126.
[22] L.J.R.O., D. 127/council min. bk. 1853–66, p. 462; 1866–82, p. 7.
[23] Lichfield Mercury, 2 May 1986, p. 11.

Prisoners were shackled in the 17th and 18th centuries.[24] In 1728 it was proposed to provide work for the prisoners.[25] There was apparently no work in 1818, and a handmill for grinding corn was installed in 1823–4; by 1833 work also included the heading of pins.[26]

Debtors were consigned to the gaol by the sheriff. In 1645 fetters for them included 4 neck collars, 4 pairs of bolts, 5 pairs of shackles, a chain, and a clog and chain. The same equipment was recorded in 1674.[27] Debtors were evidently kept in a separate chamber, first mentioned in 1657.[28]

The gaoler was paid a salary of £50 a year in the late 1780s,[29] raised to £60 in 1836 when his duties included the care of the guildhall.[30] In 1839 the gaoler's wife was appointed matron at a salary of £5.[31]

In 1681 the corporation considered building a house of correction, but the idea was apparently not carried out.[32] Part of the gaol was used as a house of correction in 1725, but that year the corporation assigned instead part of the workhouse in Sandford Street, with the workhouse master acting as governor.[33] In 1803 the corporation ordered the conversion of a room under the guildhall into a house of correction, to be maintained by the three city parishes.[34] It contained a cell in 1821.[35]

PUNITIVE INSTRUMENTS.

The murderers of a royal forester were hanged at Lichfield in 1175, Henry II himself having tried them there.[36] A gallows was built, or possibly repaired, at the bishop's expense in 1532–3.[37] In 1650 there was a gallows on the west side of the London road near its junction with Shortbutts Lane.[38] The gallows there fell down c. 1700, its foundations undermined by people digging for sand, but it was re-erected.[39] It was used, apparently for the last time, in 1810 when three forgers were hanged.[40]

There was a pillory in 1305, and it stood on the north side of the market square in 1402–3.[41] In the later 18th century it stood at the northwest corner of the market house, but seems to have been set up only when required.[42] A cuck-stool was mentioned in 1485 and was used to punish harlots as well as scolds.[43] In the early 18th century it was customary to set up the stool on land off Bird Street, presumably on the edge of Minster Pool so that duckings could take place. In 1734 a stool had to be retrieved out of Stowe Pool.[44] Stocks were recorded in the late 1680s when they too had to be pulled out of one of the pools.[45] In the later 18th century they formed part of the pillory in the market square.[46] Stocks kept in the guildhall in 1895 are probably those in the museum opened there in 1986.[47] There were also stocks in the Close. They stood at the west end of the cathedral near the conduit in 1749 and were moved in 1823 to the south side of the cathedral.[48] A whipping stock stood next to the pillory in the 18th century.[49] A scold's bridle was bought by the Conduit Lands trustees in 1666–7, and one was still in use in 1781.[50] One kept in the guildhall in 1856 is probably that displayed in the museum there.[51] A branding iron was available in 1701.[52]

CITY SEALS, ARMS, INSIGNIA, AND PLATE.

The right to use a common seal was granted to the corporation by the charter of 1548. One was designed in 1549, and a drawing of it was made at a heraldic visitation in 1583. It depicted three dismembered bodies with weapons and the profile of a man's head above. Legend, Roman: SIGILLVM COMMVNI BALLIVORVM ET BVRGENSIVM DE LICHFEILD 1549.[53] The iconography refers to the legend of a massacre of Christians at Lichfield in the Roman period or later,[54] and its choice by the corporation may have been intended to break with the cult of St. Chad, while at the same time displaying protestant zeal.[55] The seal was remodelled when the corporation was reorganized in 1622. An impression of 1625 also showed three dismembered bodies but with three trees in the background and the man's head in the centre. Legend, Roman: SIGILLVM COMMVNI BALLIVORVM ET BVRGENSIVM CIVITATIS LYCHFELD.[56] A new matrix, 2⅜ in. in diameter, was made in 1688; it added a banner and a crown to the design and omitted the man's head. Legend,

[24] *Lond. Gaz.* 1–4 July 1689; L.J.R.O., D. 35/bailiffs' accts. 1704–94, pp. 134, 593; D. 77/10/3.
[25] L.J.R.O., D. 68, f. 8v.
[26] *Returns of Gaols, 1818*, H.C. 135, p. 43 (1819), xvii; *Rep. to Sec. of State, pursuant to Gaol Act*, H.C. 104, p. 274 (1824), xix; *Returns of Places of Confinement*, 64; *Lichfield Mercury*, 15 Aug. 1823.
[27] L.J.R.O., D. 15/5/1/2; D. 77/10/3.
[28] Ibid. D. 35/bailiffs' accts. 1657–1707, p. 3.
[29] J. Howard, *Acct. of Lazarettos* (1789), 174.
[30] L.J.R.O., D. 77/5/4, f. 42v.
[31] Ibid. f. 109v.
[32] *Cal. Treas. Bks.* 1681–5 (1), 307, 322.
[33] L.J.R.O., D. 77/5/1, f. 243.
[34] Ibid. D. 77/5/3, f. 18v.
[35] *Returns of Gaols, 1821*, H.C. 400, pp. 50–1 (1821), xxi.
[36] *Gesta Regis Henrici Secundi Benedicti Abbatis* (Rolls Ser.), i. 94.
[37] S.R.O., D. (W.) 1734/3/2/13, m. 4d.
[38] Ibid. D. 661/2/243; J. Ogilby, *Britannia* (1675), pl. between pp. 42 and 43.
[39] L.J.R.O., D. 77/6/1, ff. 73, 121; *S.H.C.* 4th ser. vi, pl. facing p. 118.
[40] *Staffs. Advertiser*, 2 June 1810.

[41] *S.H.C.* vii (1), 166; Bodl. MS. Ashmole 855, p. 185.
[42] L.J.R.O., D. 35/bailiffs' accts. 1794–1835, p. 70; below, fig. 16.
[43] P.R.O., SC 6/Hen. VII/1846, m. 5; below, public services (policing).
[44] L.J.R.O., D. 35/bailiffs' accts. 1704–94, p. 128; D. 77/9/1, f. 6.
[45] Ibid. D. 35/bailiffs' accts. 1657–1707, p. 114.
[46] Below, fig. 16.
[47] *Trans. N. Staffs. Field Club*, xxx. 151; above (gaol).
[48] L.J.R.O., D. 30/C.A. viii, f. 22; W.S.L., S. MS. 374, p. 355.
[49] L.J.R.O., D. 25/1/1, f. 135v.; D. 68, ff. 7v., 16v.
[50] Ibid. D. 35/bailiffs' accts. 1704–94, p. 445; D. 126/acct. bk. 1663–1805, acct. 1666–7.
[51] *Arch. Jnl.* xiii. 266.
[52] L.J.R.O., D. 35/bailiffs' accts. 1657–1707, p. 182; *Cal. S.P. Dom.* 1700–2, 414.
[53] What may be a worn example of the seal survives as B.L. Detached Seals clv. 1 (illustrated in *S.H.C.* 1913, pl. facing p. 300).
[54] Above, place name.
[55] *T.S.S.A.H.S.* xxviii. 8.
[56] Bodl. MS. Ashmole 855, p. 190.

FIG. 13. CITY OF LICHFIELD: SEAL OF 1549

Roman: SIGILLVM COMMVNE CIVITATIS DE LICH-FEILD AN NO DOMINI 1688.[57] A wafer matrix with the same device and legend was used by the city council in the late 1980s.

The city arms in 1610 represented the three dismembered bodies, one of them wearing a crown, with trees behind.[58] In the 18th century the design retained the bodies but altered the background to a hill surmounted by trees, a tower (or castle) flying a pennon, and the cathedral with a pennon flying from each of its three spires.[59] In addition to the pictorial design, a heraldic device of chevrons on a checky field was also used as arms by the late 17th century; it was authorized in 1950 by the College of Arms together with two supporters, St. Chad on the

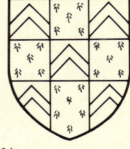

THE CITY OF LICHFIELD.
Checky of nine gold and ermine, in each of the gold squares a chevron gules.

FIG. 14

right side and a robed master of St. Mary's guild on the left, and a crest above.[60]

Gilt or silver maces to be carried before the bailiffs by serjeants-at-arms were authorized by the charter of 1622. Described in 1634 as black staves tipped with silver,[61] the maces were apparently lost or removed during the Commonwealth. Two maces were presumably made at the time of the 1664 charter, but only one survives. The other was missing in 1690 when the corporation, concerned that 'the grandeur of the city' was impaired by the possession of only one mace, decided to have another one made. An order was placed with Peter (later Sir Peter) Floyer of London, who was also to regild the existing mace; he was paid £55 19s. for both jobs in 1690.[62]

The churchwardens of St. Mary's, the civic church, provided a sword for the bailiffs' seat in church in 1657–8. It was known as the church sword in 1690–1, and the maces were placed on either side of it when the bailiffs attended services. In 1868 the mayor, Rowland Crosskey, an ironmonger by trade, gave a new sword, still used in the late 1980s.[63]

When the corporation was reconstituted in 1686 under a mayor, he was allowed to have a sword carried before him, and one was given by the recorder, Lord Dartmouth.[64]

[57] Birch, *Cat. of Seals in Brit. Museum*, ii. 105.
[58] Above, fig. 2.
[59] Edmondson, *Complete Body of Heraldry*, i (1780); W.S.L., S. MS. 16, p. 25; J. Snape, *Plan of Lichfield, 1781*.
[60] Plot, *Staffs.* map; C. W. Scott-Giles, *Civic Heraldry of Eng. and Wales* (1953), 333–4.
[61] *Relation of a Short Survey of 26 Counties, 1634*, ed. L. G. Wickham Legg, 58.

[62] L.J.R.O., D. 35/bailiffs' accts. 1657–1707, p. 126; D. 77/5/1, f. 32; W. T. Prideaux, *List of Wardens of Company of Goldsmiths since 1688* (1936), 2.
[63] L.J.R.O., D. 20/4/1, 1657–8 acct.; D. 35/bailiffs' accts. 1657–1707, pp. 124, 134; T. Moseley, *Lichfield Corp. and St. Mary's Church*, 3 (copy in L.J.R.O., D. 77/9/11); P.O. *Dir. Staffs.* (1868).
[64] Harwood, *Lichfield*, 349; Dartmouth arms on scabbard.

A silver drinking bowl with a cover, made in 1666, was presented by Elias Ashmole, a native of Lichfield, in 1667.[65] The bowl has three roundels, each depicting a dismembered body. A silver bowl and two silver cups with covers were given in 1900 by the sons of a former mayor, H. H. Hewitt (d. 1893).[66] The bowls and the cups were displayed in St. Mary's Centre in the late 1980s along with the 1686 sword and 1690 mace. The 1664 mace is kept in the guildhall.

A mayor's badge and chain were presented in 1873 by Richard Dyott of Freeford, the city's M.P. The intention was to provide regalia for the mayor to wear at a reception held at the guildhall for the shah of Persia. The badge is a painting on porcelain of the city's pictorial arms used in the 18th century. A matching badge and chain for the mayoress was presented in 1935 by the wife of Thomas Moseley, for whom it had been made during her husband's term of office in 1934. A sheriff's badge and chain, showing the city's heraldic arms, was presented by S. L. Seckham in 1895. A matching badge and chain for the sheriff's lady was presented in 1935 by Harold Graham, then sheriff.[67]

The mayor wore a ceremonial gown by 1851.[68] The custom was evidently abandoned but was revived in 1913 when Robert Bridgeman, on becoming mayor that year, provided a scarlet gown.[69] The sheriff has worn a gown since 1899.[70] In 1902 the mayor and sheriff were provided with cocked hats.[71]

PARISH GOVERNMENT AND POOR RELIEF

FROM the 16th century the part of the city within the ditch, except for the Friary estate, made up St. Mary's parish. The southern part of the city was in St. Michael's parish and the northern part in St. Chad's; both those parishes also included a large area outside the city. The Close formed a separate parish. The Friary remained extra-parochial until under an Act of 1857 it became a parish. In 1934 it was added to St. Michael's.[72]

St. Mary's church had a single warden in 1457.[73] In 1490 property for the maintenance of a lamp there was given to 'special wardens' of the church, and there were two churchwardens in the mid 16th century.[74] In the earlier part of the century they apparently presented their accounts to the guild of St. Mary and St. John the Baptist; in the 1630s the accounts were passed by the city bailiffs, the vicar, and others and in 1679 by the bailiffs and the vicar alone.[75] By 1733 one of the churchwardens was appointed by the vicar and the other by the parishioners.[76] Sidesmen existed by the 1630s; by 1714 two were elected.[77] Surveyors of the highways were mentioned in 1637–8, and by the later 1690s two were appointed by the bailiffs.[78] In 1728 there was a complaint that several parishioners were refusing to carry out their statute labour on the roads, either personally or by substitute, and the corporation ordered the bailiffs to enforce the law.[79]

There were two parish clerks in 1466. One of them, William Sumner, was accused not only of moral failings and neglecting his duties but also of acting in an unclerical way: his manner was refined, his shoes were pointed, his hair was styled and flowing, he wore no belt, and his expression was supercilious.[80] Two clerks were being maintained by the guild at the time of its suppression.[81] The clerk's chamber, mentioned in 1630–1, was taken down in 1635–6.[82] In the 18th century the clerk was appointed by the vicar.[83] A sexton was appointed by the parishioners in 1760, 1771, and 1821.[84]

St. Michael's church had keepers of the fabric and lights c. 1300,[85] and there were two churchwardens in 1463.[86] They apparently presented their accounts to the guild in the earlier 16th century, and later in the century they accounted to the bailiffs.[87] By 1731 the curate appointed one of the wardens and the parishioners the other.[88] Sidesmen existed by 1596–7.[89] In 1637 seven were elected, one being for Greenhill and the rest for places outside the city, but thereafter the Greenhill appointment was dropped.[90] By the later 1690s two highway surveyors were appointed by the bailiffs, evidently for the city portion of the parish.[91] There was a parish clerk in the mid 1550s.[92] In the 18th and earlier 19th century the office was held with that of sexton and appointments were made by the vicar of St. Mary's.[93] The vestry met in the chancel of St.

[65] *Elias Ashmole*, ed. C. H. Josten, i. 156 and facing pl.; iii. 1045–7. Josten dates the presentation day to 1666; the bailiffs' letter of thanks gives it as Thurs. 17 Jan. 1666, which, by modern reckoning, was in 1667.
[66] *Lichfield Mercury*, 16 Mar. 1900, p. 8.
[67] Inscriptions on reverse of badges; *Staffs. Advertiser*, 14 June 1873, p. 7.
[68] Official Bower Programme, 1923, p. 7 (copy in L.J.R.O., D. 77/20/8, between pp. 78 and 79).
[69] *Lichfield Mercury*, 8 Mar. 1918, p. 3.
[70] L.J.R.O., D. 127/council min. bk. 1899–1902, p. 20.
[71] Ibid. p. 240.
[72] *Lichfield Mercury*, 30 Mar. 1934, p. 5.
[73] *Gild of St. Mary, Lichfield* (E.E.T.S. extra ser. 114), 19, 23.
[74] Bodl. MS. Ashmole 855, p. 191; *S.H.C.* 1915, 170.
[75] *Gild of St. Mary*, 14; L.J.R.O., D. 20/4/1.

[76] L.J.R.O., D. 20/4/3.
[77] Ibid. D. 20/4/1, 1634–5; D. 20/4/2.
[78] Ibid. D. 20/4/1; D. 77/7/1–3 and 5.
[79] Ibid. D. 77/5/1, f. 258.
[80] Ibid. D. 30/9/3/1, ff. 17v., 21.
[81] Below, guilds.   [82] L.J.R.O., D. 20/4/1.
[83] Ibid. D. 30/9/1/10–12, 14–15.
[84] Ibid. D. 20/4/3–4; D. 30/9/1/8/13.
[85] Below, churches.   [86] Bodl. MS. Ashmole 855, p. 194.
[87] *Gild of St. Mary*, 14; *T.S.S.A.H.S.* vii. 12.
[88] L.J.R.O., D. 27/5/1, f. 2; B.R.L. 320888, no. 224.
[89] L.J.R.O., B/C/5/Exhibits/Lichfield, St. Michael.
[90] Ibid. D. 27/1/2, lists at end.
[91] Ibid. D. 77/7/1–3 and 5.
[92] L.J.R.O., B/C/5/Exhibits/Lichfield, St. Michael, churchwardens' accts.
[93] L.J.R.O., D. 27/1/4, p. 254; D. 30/9/1/8/16–19.

Michael's in the mid 18th century; a meeting room was built in the angle between the chancel and the south aisle in the mid 1780s.[94]

In 1346 a 'keeper or syndic or proctor' led the 'parishioners' of Stowe in resistance to the demand by the prebendary of Gaia Major for a tithe of the stone quarried for work on St. Chad's church.[95] The St. Chad's churchwardens, of whom there were two by the mid 16th century, apparently accounted to the guild earlier in the century.[96] By 1740 it was customary for the curate of St. Chad's to choose a warden for the city portion of the parish; there was a separate warden for the 'country' portion, presumably chosen by the inhabitants of Curborough and Elmhurst, who were appointing by 1755. There were also two sidesmen. In 1829 the vestry decided that it was 'essentially necessary that the parishioners should in future appoint one churchwarden'. They duly did so, with the curate appointing another. There was no mention of Curborough and Elmhurst, but from 1830 there was a warden appointed by the curate, another appointed by the parishioners, and a third for Curborough and Elmhurst. The last was variously styled sidesman and churchwarden from 1851 until 1865 when two sidesmen were appointed instead.[97] By the 1690s two highway surveyors were appointed for the parish by the bailiffs.[98] By the earlier 18th century a parish clerk was appointed by the vicar of St. Mary's, the office being combined with that of sexton.[99]

In the Close the clerk of the cathedral was also sexton in the 1690s.[1]

POOR RELIEF. Each parish organized its own poor relief. There were two overseers for St. Mary's in 1642.[2] By the late 1690s the bailiffs appointed two overseers for each of the three city parishes.[3] It was the custom by the later 1730s for the parishioners of St. Chad's to submit six names.[4] The dean and chapter appointed two overseers for the Close; in 1833 they were the chapter clerk and the senior verger.[5] The parts of St. Michael's and St. Chad's outside the city organized their poor relief separately from the rest of their respective parishes.[6]

In the 1770s there were several unsuccessful schemes for co-operation between the three city parishes in administering relief. One of the St. Mary's churchwardens issued a pamphlet in 1775 urging the union of all three for relief purposes and the building of a single workhouse.[7] In 1777 a St. Mary's committee recommended the extension of its workhouse so that it could take in the paupers of the other two parishes.[8] In the same year the St. Chad's vestry set up a committee to discuss the idea of a single workhouse with the other two parishes. It was stressed that there was to be no question of a union with St. Mary's or of any contribution towards the St. Mary's poor.[9]

The St. Mary's committee of 1777 also recommended the establishment of a committee of nine besides the churchwardens and overseers to organize relief in the parish, helped by a salaried overseer.[10] In 1788, after complaints of irregularities, the vestry appointed a committee of 25, including the churchwardens and overseers, to inspect the overseers' accounts and supervise relief; it worked through a subcommittee of six appointed monthly.[11] In 1818 the vestry ordered that the overseers' accounts were to be certified quarterly by a small committee. It also required the master of the workhouse to submit a monthly return to the vestry giving details of inmates and the amount spent on them; if they were employed, details were to be given of any income, which was to be paid into the parish funds.[12] The governor of the workhouse appointed in 1826 also acted as assistant overseer.[13] A select vestry was established for St. Mary's in 1820[14] and one for St. Michael's in 1827.[15]

In 1691 the corporation let a house on the south side of Sandford Street east of the bridge over Trunkfield brook to Francis Burditt of London and others as a linen manufactory where the poor of the city would be employed and paid a wage; the corporation carried out the necessary repairs and alterations. There was a proviso that the liberties of the city tradesmen were not to be infringed.[16] The manufactory lasted only until 1696.[17] The building was later let for other purposes, although it continued to be called the workhouse. It seems to have been used for the poor in 1701–2 when the bailiffs spent 6d. 'in removing Mrs. Ward to the workhouse'.[18]

In 1724 the corporation decided to give the occupants notice to quit so that it could turn the building into a workhouse for the city, and in 1725 it carried out extensive repairs.[19] A master had been appointed by December that year, and the Conduit Lands trustees bought two stocking frames for use at the workhouse. The corporation assigned part of the building as a house of correction with the master of the workhouse acting as governor.[20] Poor from St. Mary's parish were occupying part of the workhouse by

[94] S.R.O., D. 593/F/3/12/3/1B, pp. 28–9; below, churches.
[95] Bodl. MS. Ashmole 794, f. 97.
[96] S.H.C. 1915, 174; Gild of St. Mary, 14.
[97] L.J.R.O., D. 29/4/1; W.S.L., M. 871.
[98] L.J.R.O., D. 77/7/1–3 and 5.
[99] Ibid. D. 30/9/1/8/8–9, 37–8.
[1] Ibid. D. 35/bailiffs' accts. 1657–1707, pp. 147, 157.
[2] P.R.O., SP 28/194, no. 677.
[3] L.J.R.O., D. 77/7/1–5.
[4] Ibid. D. 77/7/6, ff. 2–3; W.S.L., M. 871.
[5] V.C.H. Staffs. i. 298–9; L.J.R.O., D. 30/X, 1726–58; Ann. Rep. Com. Poor Laws, H.C. 44, p. 269A (1834), xxviii (1). [6] Below, Burntwood; Curborough; Streethay; Wall.
[7] Copy in L.J.R.O., D. 77/16/3.

[8] L.J.R.O., D. 20/4/3.
[9] Ibid. D. 29/4/1, 19 June 1777. [10] Ibid. D. 20/4/3.
[11] Ibid. D. 29/4/4, 22 and 24 Apr., 8 May 1788.
[12] Ibid. 14 May, 7 Nov. 1818.
[13] Ibid. 26 Apr. 1826, 7 Apr. 1830.
[14] Ibid. D. 20/6/9–10.
[15] Ibid. D. 35/St. Michael's vestry min. bk. 1827–47.
[16] Ibid. D. 35/bailiffs' accts. 1657–1707, pp. 142–3; D. 77/5/1, f. 40; D. 77/9/10; above, fig. 4.
[17] L.J.R.O., D. 77/5/1, f. 67.
[18] Ibid. D. 35/bailiffs' accts. 1657–1707, pp. 168, 180.
[19] Ibid. 1704–94, pp. 88–9, 92–3; D. 77/5/1, f. 237v.
[20] Ibid. D. 77/5/1, f. 243; D. 126/acct. bk. 1663–1805, acct. 1725–6 and reverse pages, 26 Aug. and 19 Dec. 1725.

1728, and that year the corporation gave St. Michael's permission to put its poor in the lower part at a rent of 4d. a year, with the right to take in a garden and erect a pigsty.[21]

In 1740 St. Michael's and St. Chad's decided to establish their own workhouse. St. Mary's continued to occupy the Sandford Street building at a rent of 5s. a year, paying the corporation £5 5s. back rent in 1741–2.[22] In 1743 and 1744 the Conduit Lands trustees made two payments of £15 to St. Mary's towards the cost of repairing and furnishing the workhouse.[23] In 1738–9 the parish had received £1 5s. 8d. for work done at the workhouse with a further 12s. for linen cloth and 2s. 2d. for cabbage cloth; £33 7s. was received in 1744 for tammy made at the house.[24] In that year the parish entered into an agreement with John Phillips for farming the poor in the workhouse at 14d. each a week.[25]

In 1777 a parish committee recommended the extension of the workhouse as a house of industry under a salaried master and mistress who were to be husband and wife. Work was to be done both in the house and elsewhere; women were to do spinning for the clothiers of the area. Adults were to be allowed to keep 2d. in every shilling earned, while children were to have 'some gratuity out of their wages'. The master was to be 'a person of some education' so that he could spend at least four hours a day teaching the children, and he was also to superintend the workroom. He was to have 'a boy or two' to help in the house and the garden, and his wife was to be allowed some girls to help her on the domestic side; children would thereby become better qualified for going out to service.[26] A salaried master was duly appointed.[27] In August 1795 a little blanketing was being made in the house for the use of the inmates, of whom there were 41.[28] In the year ending Easter 1803 the inmates earned £60 5s. 11d. towards their maintenance, chiefly by working on stock provided by a cotton manufacturer, probably Sir Robert Peel who had a works in Sandford Street.[29] Between February and May 1805 the parish received £3 8s. 1d. for work done in the house, and in July there were 35 inmates.[30] In 1831, to save the cost of a charwoman, the select vestry ordered that women in receipt of weekly pay who were capable of work were to be used to clean the workhouse.[31] In 1832 it instructed that all children from the workhouse who had been put out

to nurse 'at Meat's of Chorley' (in Farewell) were to be brought into the workhouse.[32] It decided in 1833 to have a uniform of grey cloth made for able-bodied male inmates.[33]

The parish also maintained poorhouses. In 1778 it paid for work on poorhouses in Stowe Street.[34] In 1822 the select vestry ordered six men and one woman to quit the parish houses which they occupied; the woman lived in Sandford Street. One of the men had been given his house the previous year for himself, his wife, and their five children, along with an allowance of 5s. a week for his family and an advance of £3 to buy materials for his trade as a woolcomber. In the event two of the other men were allowed to remain, one of them rent free.[35]

In 1740 St. Michael's and St. Chad's agreed to rent or buy a house and convert it into a joint workhouse.[36] One had been established at Greenhill by 1741 when St. Chad's appointed six trustees or governors for it.[37] The Conduit Lands trustees provided £30 for furniture.[38] In 1746 the St. Chad's vestry found that poor of the parish lately turned out of the workhouse were being maintained more cheaply on outdoor relief, and it ordered that they were not to be sent back to Greenhill.[39] Later the same year it ordered that several paupers were to receive outdoor relief and were not to go into the workhouse.[40] St. Chad's appointed no workhouse trustees that year but did so in 1747.[41]

There continued to be a workhouse at Greenhill, but by 1780 different premises there were being used, evidently by St. Michael's alone.[42] There was a fire in 1790, and perhaps as a result St. Michael's no longer had a workhouse in 1795 and was still without one in the early 1800s.[43] By 1811 it again had a workhouse at Greenhill, occupying part of the former White Hart public house, which had been converted into two dwellings.[44] In 1827 the workhouse consisted of a parlour and a kitchen on the ground floor, four chambers on the first floor, and two attic chambers.[45] That year the St. Michael's select vestry drew up a scheme for the transfer of the inmates to the St. Mary's workhouse, but the St. Mary's vestry rejected the plan. St. Michael's then appointed a master for Greenhill who agreed to farm the poor at 3s. 9d. each a week for those aged over 14 and 3s. for those under 14, inclusive of three meals a day, coal, and candles.[46] By 1833 the 3s. 9d. had risen to 4s.[47] Meanwhile, in

[21] Ibid. D. 77/5/1, f. 256v.
[22] Ibid. D. 35/bailiffs' accts. 1704–94, pp. 152 sqq.; 1794–1835, p. 361.
[23] Ibid. D. 20/6/1–2.
[24] Ibid. D. 126/min. bk. 1741–1856, p. 6; acct. bk. 1663–1805, accts. 1742–3, 1743–4.
[25] Ibid. D. 20/6/2.
[26] Ibid. D. 20/4/3.
[27] Ibid. D. 20/6/3, 26 Feb. 1779.
[28] Sir F. M. Eden, State of the Poor (1797), ii. 652.
[29] Harwood, Lichfield, table between pp. 380 and 381; below, econ. hist. (trades and industries).
[30] L.J.R.O., D. 77/20/8, printed reps. of overseers between pp. 14 and 15.
[31] Ibid. D. 20/6/9, f. 133v.
[32] Ibid. f. 149v.
[33] Ibid. f. 153.
[34] Ibid. D. 20/6/3.
[35] Ibid. D. 20/6/9, ff. 13v., 25v.–28.

[36] Ibid. D. 29/4/1, 16 Mar. 1739/40.
[37] Ibid. 31 Mar. 1741.
[38] Ibid. D. 126/acct. bk. 1663–1805, acct. 1739–40.
[39] Ibid. D. 29/4/1, 2 Mar. 1745/6.
[40] Ibid. 6 July 1746. [41] Ibid. 21 Apr. 1747.
[42] S.R.O., D. 593/F/3/12/1/9 and 11; D. 593/F/3/12/3B, pp. 182–3.
[43] L.J.R.O., D. 126/acct. bk. 1663–1805, acct. 1789–90; Eden, State of Poor, ii. 652; Harwood, Lichfield, table between pp. 380 and 381.
[44] St. Michael's Church Lands records (at Hinckley, Birch & Exham, solicitors of Lichfield), acct. bk. 1811–1980, p. iii; S.R.O., D. (W.) 1851/10/7, plan of St. Michael's par., no. 20.
[45] L.J.R.O., D. 35/St. Michael's vestry bk. 1827–47, pp. 13–14.
[46] Ibid. D. 20/4/4, 14 Aug. 1827; D. 35/St. Michael's vestry bk. 1827–47, pp. 6–11 with loose sheet.
[47] Ann. Rep. Com. Poor Laws, p. 266A.

1830 the vestry ordered that those in receipt of outdoor pay had to attend divine service every Sunday unless they were ill.[48]

The St. Chad's overseers took a lease of a house in Stowe Street in 1781 and turned it into a workhouse, described in 1819 as an old and inconvenient building.[49] There were six inmates c. 1803.[50] A new governor of what was called the Stowe house of industry was elected by the parishioners in 1816.[51] In the earlier 1830s the workhouse poor were farmed at 3s. 6d. each a week.[52]

St. Chad's was the only one of the three parishes to be maintaining any poorhouses in 1776.[53] A house adjoining the churchyard was used as a poorhouse in 1781.[54] A range of cottages called Littleworth west of the church was maintained by the churchwardens in 1758, presumably for the benefit of the poor.[55] There was evidently some rebuilding in 1790 when 3,000 bricks were delivered to Littleworth.[56] In 1848 three of the cottages were held by the overseers of Stowe and the fourth by the overseers of Curborough and Elmhurst. From c. 1850 the Curborough and Elmhurst overseers charged a rent of 6d. a week for their cottage; the other three were given rent free to the poor by the churchwardens, usually to widows and spinsters. The Curborough and Elmhurst cottage was pulled down in 1912 after standing empty for 10 years. From 1913 a rent of 3d. a week was charged for the other three as new tenants came in.[57] The two nearest the church were made into a single dwelling in 1932.[58] In 1934 the parochial church council decided to repair the cottages and charge 3s. a week for the larger and 2s. for the smaller. Electric lighting was installed in 1935. In 1944 the cottages were let to the Beacon Street boy scouts.[59] They were rebuilt in the later 1940s as a single house for the caretaker of St. Chad's well.[60] By 1984 the house was used as a day centre for the unemployed.

The injunctions to the Lichfield cathedral clergy at the royal visitations of 1547 and 1559 included orders enjoining hospitality to the poor and the maintenance of all existing alms and doles.[61] Chapter accounts, which survive from the 1660s, show numerous payments to the poor, including money for the support and education of the children of two deceased vicars. Widow Morgill received 2s. 6d. a month from 1668 to 1674, with the stipulation in 1671 that she must attend prayers daily.[62] In 1694 Bishop Lloyd decreed that, in accordance with the 1559 injunction concerning hospitality, £13 a year was to be levied at the rate of 5s. a week from the commons of the dean (1s. 8d. a week) and the four residentiary canons (10d. a week); the 5s. was to be distributed to the poor of the Close every Thursday after morning prayers.[63] Although the chapter accounts do not record such payments until 1693–4, the bishop may merely have been confirming by statute an existing arrangement: in 1693 5s. a week was already being distributed to the poor at the cathedral in bread. By 1738 the £13 was known as bread money.[64] In 1694 Lloyd also ordered that the offertory money received at the cathedral was to be distributed weekly to needy Anglicans of both the city and the Close.[65] By 1738 the poor were further provided with 'an hospitality not to be named',[66] perhaps a public lavatory. In 1773 the dean and chapter, faced with a great increase in the number of poor living in the Close and the need to levy a poor rate, assigned both the bread money and the offertory money to the overseers in the hope of keeping down or avoiding rates. They recommended that their successors should continue the practice.[67] From 1799 part of the bread money was given to the cathedral choristers, and by the later 19th century they received all of it.[68]

A rate was regularly levied by 1807.[69] In 1832 the amount raised was £102 6s. 8d., with a further £37 1s. in donations and offerings; £205 18s. was spent on poor relief.[70] Early in 1833 the Close, which had no workhouse, was giving weekly pay to 9 women and 5 men, all former domestic servants, and to 10 children. One of the men, who had a wife and three children and had earlier been the dean's coachman, received 8s. a week and had his rent paid.[71]

The Lichfield poor law union, covering the city and a large surrounding area, was formed in 1836.[72] At first the St. Mary's parish workhouse and that at Rugeley were retained as the union's workhouses.[73] In 1840 a workhouse, designed in a Tudor style by G. G. Scott and W. B. Moffatt, was opened for the union in Trent Valley Road. Casual wards were added in 1874 and an infirmary in 1893. The building, much altered, is now St. Michael's hospital.[74]

There have been several other sources of relief. In the Middle Ages alms were distributed

48 L.J.R.O., D. 35/St. Michael's vestry bk. 1827–47, 22 Nov. 1830.
49 S.R.O., D. 593/F/3/12/1/9; D. 615/E(x)/6, f. 16; Eden, *State of Poor*, ii. 652; Stringer, *Lichfield*, 153.
50 Harwood, *Lichfield*, table between pp. 380 and 381.
51 *Lichfield Mercury*, 27 Dec. 1816.
52 *Ann. Rep. Com. Poor Laws*, p. 266A.
53 L.J.R.O., D. 25/1/1, f. 92v.
54 L.J.R.O., VC/A/21, CC 164146A, pp. 296–8.
55 Ibid. D. 29/4/1, regular entries from 10 Dec. 1758.
56 Ibid. Nov. 1790.
57 Ibid. D. 29/4/2, pp. 7–26.
58 *St. Chad's Mag.* Apr. and Sept. 1932 (copies in W.S.L.).
59 L.J.R.O., D. 29/5/1, pp. 101, 104, 110–11, 161, 171.
60 Below, churches.
61 L.J.R.O., D. 30/bk. of miscellanea, ff. 97v.–98, 101v.–102.
62 L.J.R.O., D. 30/LXIV; D. 30/I 4, 13 Oct. 1671.
63 *Statuta et Consuetudines Ecclesiae Cathedralis Lich-*
fieldiae (priv. print. 1863), 108–9.
64 L.J.R.O., B/V/3, Lloyd's cath. visitation 1693, f. 23; D. 30/Ee 4, answers to articles of inquiry, 1738.
65 *Statuta et Consuetudines*, 108–9.
66 L.J.R.O.. D. 30/Ee 4, answers to articles of inquiry, 1738.
67 Ibid. D. 30/X, 1772–85, 21 May 1773.
68 Ibid. D. 30/IX, ff. 18, 27, 36v.; D. 30, vol. of cath. accts. 1875–1908.
69 W.S.L., S. MS. 341.
70 L.J.R.O., D. 30/8/28.
71 *Ann. Rep. Com. Poor Laws*, p. 269A.
72 Poor Law Com. Order 1836 forming the union (copy in L.J.R.O., D. 77/16/3).
73 S.R.O., D. 458/A/G/49, pp. 19, 24, 306; L.J.R.O., D. 20/6/10, 24 Jan. and 1 Feb. 1837.
74 *N. Staffs. Jnl. of Field Studies*, ii. 106; *Lichfield Mercury*, 20 Oct. 1893, p. 3; below (Soc. for Suppression of Mendicity); below, public services (medical services); below, plate 19.

in the Close. On one occasion, in or shortly before 1293, a distribution at the house of Adam de Walton, the precentor, drew a great crowd of beggars. When the door was opened, the beggars rushed in, and during the attempt to keep order one of them was struck to the ground by a servant and trampled to death in the crush.[75] Bishop Langton paid William Tabard of Lichfield to bake and brew for the poor for 10 weeks at the beginning of 1312.[76] In 1312–13 large quantities of wheat, mixed corn, barley malt, oat malt, eggs, and probably herrings were distributed at the bishop's expense by Alexander the porter, presumably at the gates of the palace.[77] When Langton's body was translated to a new tomb in 1360, 1,600 poor were given 1d. each.[78] In 1466 a woman living in Stowe Street, whose husband was seldom at home, survived by sending a boy to the Close to beg on her behalf.[79] In 1550–1 the vicars gave oatmeal and salt to the poor, perhaps in the form of porridge.[80]

The endowments of some obits and chantries in the cathedral provided for annual distributions to the poor.[81] Funerals at the cathedral were sometimes accompanied by gifts of food, cash, and clothing. By will proved 1369 Robert Portjoy, a vicar choral, left 1d. each to 20 poor women keeping vigil round his corpse and 100s. in bread for the poor on the day of his funeral. Canon Nicholas Lichfield (d. 1375) provided a gown and a hood for each of six men praying round his corpse. Canon Thomas Milley (d. 1505) left 50s. to be distributed in bread to the poor on the day of his funeral and 50s. for a further distribution on the day of his trental. William Wrixham (d. 1505), another of the cathedral clergy, left 20s. to be given to the poor on the day of his funeral and another 20s. on the day of his trental.[82]

The 1622 charter to the city laid down that the market tolls and customs should be used by the corporation primarily for the relief of the poor.[83] In the later 17th century the corporation made payments to various needy people. From 1718 £2 a year was assigned for poor travellers, and from the late 1770s until the end of the century larger sums were disbursed to travellers.[84]

The Conduit Lands trustees made numerous charitable payments. In the later 17th century they paid for the apprenticing of many poor children, including girls. Eleven boys were apprenticed in 1667. In 1673 Catherine Johnson was paid £3 10s. towards the apprenticing of her son Michael (father of Samuel Johnson) to Richard Simpson, a London stationer, with a

further 10s. for the cost of the journey to London. She received payments of £3 for each of two other sons, Benjamin (also apprenticed to Simpson) in 1676 and Andrew in 1677.[85] In 1713 the trustees paid Francis Deakin £5 towards the cost of books for his son John, who was at Christ's College, Cambridge.[86] They again made several payments for apprenticing in the mid 1720s.[87] They also spent money on weekly pay and grants in kind for the poor between 1724 and 1742; 'decayed tradesmen' were among the beneficiaries, including 'Mr. Johnson', presumably Michael Johnson, who received 10 guineas in 1731. In 1757, when corn was dear and many householders were in need, the trustees bought wheat and rye which they resold to the poor at a much reduced price; in February 270 families benefited, in March 321, and in April 327.[88]

Medical help too was provided. In 1699 the Conduit Lands trustees paid George Hector £5 for attending nine people; he set several broken bones and cured a scrofulous neck tumour.[89] In 1727 and 1728 a total of £16 4s. 6d. was paid to 'Mr. Hammond for physic given to poor inhabitants this very sickly time'.[90] Erasmus Darwin provided the poor with medical help as well as food and other assistance during his time in Lichfield from 1756 to 1781.[91] In 1828 J. T. Law, master of St. John's hospital and chancellor of the diocese, abolished pew rents in the hospital chapel and asked those who had been paying to give the money instead for the provision of medical help for the poor who suffered accidents or sudden illness.[92]

A Society for the Suppression of Mendicity was established in 1820, and in 1823 it claimed to have saved the city from being infested with beggars. In the previous 12 months it had relieved 1,943 people, chiefly labourers travelling in search of work and sailors going from port to port. Relief was normally confined to food and lodging, but in exceptional cases money was given to enable people to return to their homes. By 1827 the society's expenditure exceeded subscriptions, and it appealed to the three city parishes for help, pointing out that it was saving expense to the ratepayers. The St. Mary's select vestry refused to subscribe, and the other two parishes, having at first promised help, followed suit. The society was then wound up. It was revived in 1828, and St. Mary's relented and subscribed £5.[93] The society had its own lodging house by 1827; the premises were at the east end of Tamworth Street in the earlier 1830s.[94] The society again lapsed, but in

[75] S.H.C. vi (1), 272; Le Neve, Fasti, 1300–1541, Coventry and Lichfield, 7.
[76] S.R.O., D. (W.) 1734/J. 2057, m. 4.
[77] Ibid. m. 5; T.S.S.A.H.S. xviii. 66.
[78] H. Wharton, Anglia Sacra (1691), i. 449.
[79] L.J.R.O., D. 30/9/3/1, f. 16.
[80] Ibid. D. 30, 16th-cent. acct. bk. of vicars choral.
[81] Below, chars. for the poor.
[82] Bodl. MS. Ashmole 794, ff. 129, 154v.; L.J.R.O., D. 30/C.A. iii, ff. 83, 113.
[83] L.J.R.O., D. 77/2/1, p. 58.
[84] Ibid. D. 35/bailiffs' accts. 1657–1707; 1794–1835.
[85] Ibid. D. 16/3/6; D. 16/5/1, accts. 1671–2, 1672–3, and mins. 12 Dec. 1698; D. 16/5/2, Jan. 1705/6; D. 126, memo. bk. 1661–79, p. 8 and reverse pages; acct. bk. 1663–1805, accts. 1674–5 (note following), 1675–6 (note following),

1695–6, 1697–8, 1698–9.
[86] Ibid. D. 126, acct. bk. 1663–1805, acct. 1712–13; Alum. Cantab. to 1751, i (2), 25.
[87] L.J.R.O., D. 126, acct. bk. 1663–1805.
[88] Ibid. D. 20/4/3.
[89] Ibid. D. 16/5/1, items of Dec. 1698 and Jan. 1698/9; D. 126, acct. bk. 1663–1805.
[90] Ibid. D. 126, acct. bk. 1663–1805.
[91] A. Seward, Memoirs of the Life of Dr. Darwin (1804), 5–6.
[92] Staffs. Advertiser, 6 Dec. 1828.
[93] Lichfield Mercury, 31 Oct. 1823; 27 Oct. and 3 Nov. 1826; 30 Nov. 1827; L.J.R.O., D. 20/6/9, ff. 78, 90, 92; D. 35/St. Michael's vestry bk. 1827–47, p. 5.
[94] Lichfield Mercury, 7 Sept. 1827; White, Dir. Staffs. (1834), 96; S.R.O., D. 615/M/3/8.

1869 a new one was formed. In its first year it relieved 473 people and the streets were cleared of 'professional' beggars. Persons seeking relief were referred by the police to the society's subscribers, who received tickets according to the amount of their subscription. If thought suitable by a subscriber, the applicant was given a ticket exchangeable only through the police, a restriction which was thought to discourage all but a few. Relief took the form of supper, bed, and breakfast in the society's lodging house, the meals consisting of 8 oz. of bread and 2 oz. of cheese.[95] The completion of the casual wards at the workhouse in 1874 removed the need to consider claims from tramps.[96] The society was wound up for lack of support in the late 1870s but was quickly replaced by a similar society which continued until c. 1909.[97]

In 1820 the corporation received subscriptions to a fund for supplying soup to the poor of the city.[98] A soup kitchen was set up on the initiative of Richard Greene at the time of the cholera outbreak of 1849, although the city itself escaped. The first distributions appear to have been in January 1850 when over 50 gallons of strong soup were distributed three times a week to an average of 446 families, consisting of 758 adults and 1,046 children. The soup was given free to the aged, the sick, and those receiving poor relief, while those earning less than 15s. a week paid $\frac{1}{4}d$. a pint.[99] Subscriptions amounted to £166 8s. 2d. in 1856–7.[1] In the mid 1870s the kitchen was in Wade Street, and it continued in

existence until c. 1902.[2] A kitchen for invalids was established in 1870. During the season November 1874 to April 1875 it was at Mrs. Blakeman's in Market Street and was open every Tuesday, Thursday, and Saturday. Its activities were taken over by the Lichfield nursing institution in 1882 and by the Victoria nursing home, opened in 1899.[3]

In the 1880s a group of ladies arranged for the Parchments, a cottage near Stowe Pool, to be used as a place where poor girls of the city and its neighbourhood could be given work.[4] By 1896 a Lichfield branch of the South Staffordshire Association for the Help and Training of Friendless Girls was maintaining a refuge in Beacon Street. Girls of good conduct were sent to be trained as domestic servants at a school opened in 1895 at Brereton, in Rugeley.[5] It was commented that Lichfield being a garrison town, 'there was much to do'.[6] Two houses in Beacon Street were bought in 1908 and opened as a refuge and training home for poor girls of the area. Named Beacon Holme, it was run by the Lichfield Ladies' Association for the Care of Friendless Girls and staffed until c. 1920 by sisters from the Community of St. Peter at Horbury (Yorks. W. R.).[7] By the later 1930s the number of girls at the home had dwindled, and it was closed in 1939.[8] It was reopened for a time shortly after the outbreak of the Second World War.[9]

An account of the endowed charities for the poor is given below in a separate section.

PARLIAMENTARY REPRESENTATION

LICHFIELD was represented by two members in the parliament of 1305, in most parliaments between 1311 and 1327, and in that of 1353.[10] It then ceased to be represented until some time during the 1547–52 parliament when two members were again sent.[11] It was made a one-member constituency by the Instrument of Government in 1653 but regained its second member in 1659.[12] It became a one-member constituency again in 1867.[13] In 1885 the city was merged into the Lichfield parliamentary division, which covered much of south-east Staffordshire.[14] The constituency was reduced to Lichfield and Tamworth in 1951. Lichfield

became part of the new Mid-Staffordshire constituency in 1983.[15]

The electorate numbered between 17 and 30 in the mid 16th century and over 300 in 1685.[16] In 1701 the House of Commons resolved that the electorate consisted of the corporation, burgage holders, 40s. freeholders, and freemen who paid scot and lot (i.e. those who were enrolled as members of one of the city's trade companies and who were resident).[17] In 1761 there were 520 voters, of whom 21 were members of the corporation, 216 burgage holders, 122 freeholders, and 161 freemen. Almost all the freeholders and over half the burgage holders

[95] *Staffs. Advertiser*, 21 Aug. 1869, p. 7; 4 Sept. 1869, p. 4; 18 Sept. 1869, p. 7; 3 Sept. 1870, p. 6; 24 Apr. 1875, p. 7; L.J.R.O., D. 77/20/5, p. 52.
[96] *Staffs. Advertiser* (S. Staffs. edn.), 17 Feb. 1877, p. 7; S.R.O., D. 458/A/G/57.
[97] *Eggington & Brown's Lichfield Yr. Bk.* (1879), 20; *Meacham's Lichfield Almanack* (1881), 11; *Lomax's Red Bk.* (1909), 93; *Lichfield Mercury*, 16 Jan. 1880, p. 5.
[98] S.R.O., D. 593/F/3/12/2/32, receipts of 18 and 21 Feb. 1820.
[99] *Staffs. Advertiser*, 26 Jan. 1850, p. 3; 2 Feb. 1850, p. 3; *Lichfield Soup Kitchen: 3rd Rep. Cttee. of Management* (1852; copy in W.S.L.).
[1] L.J.R.O., D. 121.
[2] *Eggington's Lichfield Almanack* (1875); *Lomax's Red Bk.* (1902), 77.
[3] *Eggington's Lichfield Almanack* (1875); *P.O. Dir. Staffs.* (1876), showing a Wm. Blakeman as a confectioner in Market St.; below, public services (medical services).

[4] Jackson, *Lichfield*, 22 (2nd nos.).
[5] *Staffs. Advertiser*, 12 Dec. 1896, p. 7.
[6] *Recollections of Sophia Lonsdale*, ed. V. Martineau, 178.
[7] *8th Rep. Lichfield Diocesan Trust, 1910*, 31 (copy in S.R.O., D. 4566/98); Jackson, *Lichfield*, 22 (2nd nos.); *Kelly's Dir. Staffs.* (1916).
[8] *Lichfield Mercury*, 3 Mar. 1939, p. 7.
[9] Ibid. 14 Feb. 1941, p. 4.
[10] S.H.C. 1917–18, 18, 24, 26–7, 29–30, 39, 41, 50–1, 95.
[11] Ibid. 321.
[12] Ibid. 328 sqq.; 1920 and 1922, 3 sqq., 95, 105.
[13] Representation of the People Act, 1867, 30 & 31 Vic. c. 102.
[14] Redistribution of Seats Act, 1885, 48 & 49 Vic. c. 23.
[15] *Dod's Parl. Companion* (1951; 1984).
[16] *Hist. Parl., Commons, 1509–58*, i. 187; *1660–90*, i. 383.
[17] Harwood, *Lichfield*, 366; *1st Rep. Com. Mun. Corp. H.C.* 116, App. III, p. 1926 (1835), xxv.

lived outside the city; many had evidently been provided with their voting qualification by the Whig alliance of Earl Gower and the Anson family.[18] In 1799 the electorate numbered 556 and the non-residents remained numerous; of the burgage holders 46 were resident and 164 non-resident, of the freeholders 121 and 91 respectively, of the freemen 77 and 1, and of the annuitants (voters who held rents charged on burgage property) 1 and 35. The other electors were the members of the corporation (then numbering 16), 2 cathedral vicars choral, a cathedral canon, and the vicar of St. Mary's.[19] The electorate was increased to 861 by the 1832 Reform Act and to 1,320 by the 1867 Reform Act. In 1885 the electorate of the Lichfield parliamentary division was 8,842.[20]

Little is known of the members returned in the 14th century. William of Lichfield, who attended the 1313 parliament, is probably identifiable as William the taverner, the representative in 1320 and town bailiff in 1308–9,[21] and Stephen le Blount, in the 1326–7 parliament, was probably the Stephen Blund who was the bishop's steward in the early 1320s.[22] The two members elected to the 1547–52 parliament were both dependants of Sir William Paget (later Lord Paget) of Beaudesert in Longdon, who controlled the representation until his death in 1563; the only burgess known to have been elected during that period, in 1553 and 1554, was Mark Wyrley, one of the bailiffs named in the city's 1548 charter of incorporation.[23] Most other members in the 16th and earlier 17th century owed their promotion to connexions at court or with local peers; several were lawyers, such as members of the Weston and Dyott families.[24]

The two members in the Short Parliament of 1640 were Richard Dyott of Freeford, a royalist, and Sir Walter Devereux, the natural son of the earl of Essex (d. 1601) and a parliamentarian. Devereux was chosen for the Long Parliament later in 1640, with the puritan town clerk, Michael Noble, as his colleague. Devereux died in 1641 and was succeeded by a royalist, Sir Richard Cave, who was chosen apparently at the wish of Prince Rupert. Cave was removed by resolution of the House of Commons in 1642 and replaced by Michael Biddulph of Elmhurst, a supporter of parliament.[25] From 1654 to 1660 Lichfield was represented by a Presbyterian mercer, Thomas Minors. He was joined in the parliament elected in 1659 by Daniel Watson of Burton upon Trent. In 1660 Watson was elected with Michael Biddulph's son, also Michael, but was unseated later the same year on petition and replaced by Minors.[26]

At the 1661 election the Lord Treasurer,

Thomas Wriothesley, earl of Southampton and recorder of Lichfield from 1664, promoted his kinsman, Sir Henry Vernon, Bt., of Hodnet (Salop.).[27] The members chosen, however, were Colonel John Lane of Bentley, a royalist, and Michael Biddulph's brother Sir Theophilus Biddulph, then of Greenwich (Kent).[28] Lane died in 1667 and was succeeded by Richard Dyott, who had the support of the Presbyterians in the city; it was on that account that Bishop Hacket described Dyott as 'true to the king but not to the Church' and tried to prevent his election.[29] In 1675 the corporation agreed to a request from Thomas Thynne, later Viscount Weymouth, to work for the election of his cousin Daniel Finch, a prominent Tory and son of the Lord Chancellor.[30] At a byelection in 1678 following Richard Dyott's death, however, Sir Henry Lyttelton, Bt., a court candidate, was elected. The corporation invited Lyttleton to stand again at the general election in February 1679, when he was elected with Sir Theophilus Biddulph's son Michael (later Sir Michael). Finch, however, was returned at an election in August 1679, having been advised by Thynne to canvass in person because of the strong prejudice against the court. To ensure his election Thynne had 'fixed the sheriff'.[31] Finch's colleague Sir Michael Biddulph refused to stand at the 1685 election and the corporation promoted the candidature of Elias Ashmole. He withdrew under royal pressure to make way for Richard Leveson, a court supporter favoured by Lord Dartmouth.[32] It was alleged at the time that Dartmouth, who had married a Lichfield heiress, aimed at controlling the city.[33]

The Dartmouth interest collapsed at the Revolution, and in 1689 Sir Michael Biddulph stood again and was returned with Robert Burdett, a Tory.[34] Burdett was returned in 1690 with a fellow Tory, Richard Dyott of Freeford; in 1695 his colleague was Sir Michael Biddulph. The victors in 1698 were Dyott and Biddulph, who stood together in January 1701 when Biddulph was defeated by William Walmesley, a Whig. In November 1701 Dyott and Biddulph were returned unopposed, as they were again in 1702. Dyott and a fellow Tory, Sir Henry Gough, were returned in 1705, and a Tory, John Cotes, and Sir Michael Biddulph in 1708.[35] The corporation showed its Tory sympathies when it greeted Henry Sacheverell in 1710, and at an election later that year the Tories Dyott and Cotes defeated Biddulph and Walmesley.[36] At the election for the first Hanoverian parliament in 1715 Dyott and Cotes were defeated by a Whig, Walter Chetwynd of Grendon (Warws.), and a moderate Tory, Samuel Hill of Shenstone. At a byelection in 1718 Chetwynd was displaced

[18] S.R.O., D. 661/19/4/2; below (this section).
[19] S.R.O., D. 661/19/4/3.
[20] Brit. Parl. Election Results, 1832–1885, ed. F. W. S. Craig, 185–6; 1885–1918, 388.
[21] S.H.C. 1917–18, 30, 39; Shaw, Staffs. i. 30; T.S.S.A.H.S. xviii. 62–3.
[22] S.H.C. 1917–18, 50; 1924, p. 354.
[23] Ibid. 1917–18, 321 sqq.; Hist. Parl., Commons, 1509–58, i. 187.
[24] S.H.C. 1917–18, 364 sqq.; 1920 and 1922, 3 sqq.
[25] Ibid. 1920 and 1922, 58, 70–1.

[26] Ibid. 99–101, 105, 107–8, 112.
[27] Cal. Treas. Bks. vii (3), 1561–2; Hist. Parl., Commons, 1660–90, iii. 638.   [28] S.H.C. 1920 and 1922, 118.
[29] Ibid.; Bodl. MS. Tanner 45, f. 214v.
[30] L.J.R.O., D. 77/5/1, f. 4.
[31] Hist. Parl., Commons, 1660–90, i. 382–5.
[32] Ibid. 385–6; S.H.C. 1950–1, 215–27.
[33] Above, town govt. (govt. from 1548: unreformed corporation).   [34] Hist. Parl., Commons, 1660–90, i. 386–7.
[35] S.H.C. 1920 and 1922, 173 sqq.
[36] Ibid. 205, 210; L.J.R.O., D. 77/5/1, f. 148.

by a Tory, William Sneyd of Bishton in Colwich; it was then alleged that Whig supporters were 'barbarously beaten and abused and their lives endangered by a very great mob with papers in their hats resembling white roses', the Pretender's emblem. After a petition Sneyd was unseated in favour of Chetwynd.[37] Whigs continued to be elected until 1734, when two Tories, Sir Rowland Hill and George Vernon, were returned unopposed. Vernon was nominated by John, Baron Gower, of Trentham, who then dominated the political scene in Staffordshire, and he was again returned in 1741 together with a fellow Tory, Sir Lister Holte, Bt.[38]

In 1744 Gower deserted the Tories and allied himself in government with the Whigs. His new allies in Staffordshire were Admiral Lord Anson and Thomas Anson of Shugborough, and together they determined to take control of Lichfield from the corporation and the neighbouring gentry.[39] In preparation for the election of 1747 they purchased at least 13 burgages and gave bribes, spending an estimated £20,000 to secure the election of Gower's son Richard Leveson-Gower and of Thomas Anson, and causing Lady Anson, Thomas's sister-in-law, to characterize Lichfield as 'the borough of Guzzledown'. Party politics even spread to the racecourse at Whittington where rival Whig and Tory meetings were held between 1748 and 1753.[40] Richard Leveson-Gower died in 1753, and at a byelection in November that year the Gower candidate Henry Vernon was defeated by a local Tory, Sir Thomas Gresley, Bt., of Drakelow (Derb.). The corporation was active on Gresley's behalf and allegedly interfered with the poll. Over 100 men, most of them 'foreigners', were admitted to the butchers' company the night before the election and claimed the right to vote as freemen;[41] other freemen were improperly allowed to vote; and additional burgage voters had been created by the drawing up of a new rental. Moreover, as access to corporation records was refused, it was difficult for the Gower candidate to challenge intending voters. Gresley had also made a show of strength by entering the city at the head of a band of 200 gentlemen and 500 freemen wearing blue and white ribbons. Gresley died in December 1753, and his election was in any event disallowed by the House of Commons in January 1754. At the general election later that year the Gower-Anson candidates, Thomas Anson and Granville Leveson-Gower, triumphed, principally because of their grip on the burgage and freehold vote.

Accounts kept for the 1747–54 elections by the Whig agent, Thomas Cobb, showed that 72 votes had been acquired since 1747 at a cost of £7,894 9s. 4d. spent on buying property. The property was also regarded as a financial investment, in contrast with the large sums of money

that had formerly been paid out to alehouse keepers. Expenditure on drink, however, was still necessary. In preparation for a byelection in 1755 it was decided to centralize the entertainment of voters at Cobb's house, the Friary, to which each alehouse keeper would be asked to send a hogshead of ale: 'we think a hogshead from every house will be as much as can be drank by all our friends that are voters from this time to the end of the election if the tap is kept open every day.' In 1761 fourteen publicans were still demanding the payment of bills, then totalling £389 16s.

Despite its control of the electorate the Gower-Anson interest was again challenged in 1761 when the election of a local Tory, John Levett of Wychnor in Tatenhill, son of a former town clerk, was proclaimed after a scrutiny. Levett was unseated after a petition by his Whig opponent Hugo Meynell, who replaced him as M.P.[42] Whigs were thereafter returned unopposed until 1799 and included from 1768 to 1795 Thomas Gilbert, poor-law reformer and land agent to the Gowers.[43]

The corporation remained firmly Tory, much to the annoyance of Anna Seward, a Whig, who complained that she lived among 'a set of violent Tories who believe that the Royal and the Great can do no wrong'.[44] The corporation put up its own candidate, Sir Nigel Gresley, Bt., at a byelection in 1799, but he was defeated by Sir John Wrottesley, Bt., who stood in the Gower interest and was able to draw on the votes of non-resident annuitants.[45] It may have been a consequence of the corporation's frustration that in 1801 it arranged for the admission of 386 freemen. The new freemen were known as 'guinea pigs' because each paid as his admission fee to a trade company a guinea provided by the corporation; the companies did not benefit financially because the guineas were returned to the corporation.[46] In the event the Whig candidates at the 1802 election, Thomas Anson and Sir John Wrottesley, were returned unopposed. There were no contests at later elections until 1826, when Sir Roger Gresley, Bt., stood unsuccessfully as a Tory.[47] In 1825 Thomas, Viscount Anson (later earl of Lichfield), had taken over the Gower interest in Lichfield and bought up all the vote-carrying property of George Granville Leveson-Gower, marquess of Stafford. Anson retained George Vernon, the sitting M.P., as the partner for Sir George Anson until 1831, when an independent Whig, Sir Edward Scott, Bt., took his place.[48] Whig, and later Liberal, M.P.s continued to be returned until 1865, when Richard Dyott of Freeford, a Conservative, was elected. In 1868, after Lichfield had become a one-member constituency, Dyott defeated the Liberal candidate, and Conservatives held the seat for as long as the city retained its own M.P.[49] Reform rendered the Anson

[37] *Hist. Parl., Commons, 1715–54*, i. 319.
[38] *S.H.C.* 1920 and 1922, 225 sqq.
[39] This and next para. based on *S.H.C.* 1920 and 1922, 250 sqq.; *S.H.C.* 4th ser. vi. 115–35.
[40] Below, social and cultural activities (sport).
[41] L.J.R.O., D. 77/4/3, entry for 23 Nov. 1753.
[42] *S.H.C.* 4th ser. vi. 129–31.
[43] *S.H.C.* 1920 and 1922, 287 sqq.; 1933 (1), 2, 8, 12.

[44] Lichfield Libr., Anna Seward MSS. letter 13.
[45] *S.H.C.* 1933 (1), 15–17.
[46] White, *Dir. Staffs.* (1834), 76.
[47] *S.H.C.* 1933 (1), 18, 22, 26, 38, 44, 48, 56.
[48] Ibid. 69, 71; S.R.O., D. 661/11/2/3/1/11, 31 May 1825.
[49] *Brit. Parl. Election Results, 1832–1885*, 185–6; *Lichfield Mercury*, 20 Feb. 1891, p. 5.

property in Lichfield useless for electoral purposes, and the earl of Lichfield started selling off his burgages in 1882. More burgages were offered for sale by his son in 1894 and 1902.[50]

Liberals represented the Lichfield parliamentary division from 1885 to 1923, when Frank Hodges, general secretary of the miners' federation, won the seat for the Labour party. Hodges was defeated by a Conservative in 1924, and from 1929 the constituency was represented by a National Labour supporter, J. A. Lovat-Fraser. After his death in 1938 the National Labour candidate was defeated by the official Labour candidate, C. C. Poole, who was re-elected in 1945.[51] Another Labour candidate, Julian Snow, was elected in 1950 and represented the constituency until his retirement in 1970. A Conservative, J. A. d'Avigdor-Goldsmid, was then elected, retaining the seat in February 1974 but losing it to a Labour candidate, B. J. Grocott, in the October election that year. It was regained for the Conservatives in 1979 by John Heddle, who at the elections of 1983 and 1987 held the Mid-Staffordshire constituency.[52]

PUBLIC SERVICES

WATER SUPPLIES. The Close was supplied with water from springs at Pipe, in Burntwood, from the mid or later 12th century.[53] Between c. 1140 and c. 1170, in return for 15s. 4d. paid by the canons, Thomas of Bromley granted the cathedral two springs for making a conduit. It has been suggested that the name Pipe was derived from the conduit; if so, the system existed c. 1140 when Pipe was mentioned as a place.[54] The system may, however, have been copied from that at Christ Church, Canterbury, which dated from about the later 1150s; Walter Durdent, bishop of Coventry 1149–59, was previously prior of Christ Church. About 1259 William Bell of Pipe granted a third spring next to the conduit head for 12s. The pipes ran from the conduit head near Maple Hayes to a conduit in the Close, a distance of 1½ mile. The conduit presumably stood north-west of the cathedral, its site in the 17th century.

In 1280 the dean and chapter gave the archdeacon of Chester, Jordan of Wombourne, permission to run a side pipe to his house in Beacon Street; it was to be used only when he was in residence and removed when he ceased to be archdeacon.[55] In 1293 a dispute involving Thomas of Abnall, through whose land the pipes ran, was settled in favour of the dean and chapter. Thomas acknowledged their right to an uninterrupted supply and also access over his land to maintain the pipes.[56] By 1300 there was a piped supply into the canons' houses in the Close, and Bishop Langton's statutes of that year noted that some canons had an abundant supply while others had less than they should. The statutes directed that the canons were to use water in moderation and that the aqueduct was to be inspected every month by three or four canons chosen by the chapter.[57]

In the 1480s the supply was cut off by Sir Humphrey Stanley, lord of Pipe, who smashed the aqueduct. When the dean and chapter repaired it, Stanley's wife smashed it again. She also broke down the door of the conduit head and damaged the cistern. The dean and chapter petitioned Henry VII, who in 1489 ordered Stanley to stop interfering with the supply.[58] The water was also used by the townspeople of Lichfield: at an episcopal visitation of the cathedral in 1516 or 1517 the dean stated that women fetching water from the conduit in the Close were causing scandal to the residents.[59] In 1531 the chapter decided that the vicars and chantry priests should be allowed to have water from the aqueduct at a place in the Close called Moses' Head and that the choristers should have it straight from the aqueduct.[60]

By the 1630s the conduit was known as Moses and was surmounted by a stone cross. The dean and chapter then entered into contracts for the laying of 10 yd. of new lead pipes a year where the existing ones were broken or inadequate.[61] The system suffered as a result of the Civil War: 'the cisterns of lead were taken and sold, the pipes of lead digged up and cut off.'[62] At her death in 1671 Elizabeth Hinton, a widow living in the Close, left £10 towards the restoration of 'the late ruined waterwork'.[63]

The dean and chapter made an agreement in 1697 for a new conduit to replace Moses. The cistern was to have a capacity of 30 hogsheads, and 50 hogsheads a day were to be conveyed from the conduit head through pipes of alder wood and lead. The dean and chapter made an agreement in 1705 for the laying of 200 yd. of wooden pipes, but in 1708 they began replacing the wooden pipes. They contracted for the laying of 1,500 yd. of lead pipes, and in addition all the wooden pipes were to be checked and only those in a sound condition retained. Fourteen inhabitants of the Close, besides the dean and chapter and vicars choral collectively and the

[50] S.R.O., D. 4363/A/5/1, 3–4.
[51] *Brit. Parl. Election Results, 1885–1918*, 388; *1918–1949*, 464.
[52] Ibid. *1950–1970*, 490; *Dod's Parl. Companion* (1971 and later edns.).
[53] Para. based on *Antiq. Jnl.* lvi (1), 74–6. Thanks for help with this section are offered to Mr. J. Martin of the S. Staffs. Waterworks Co. and Mr. H. G. Sims who formerly worked for the company.   [54] Below, Burntwood, manors.
[55] *S.H.C.* 1924, p. 317; *V.C.H. Staffs.* iii. 142.

[56] L.J.R.O., D. 30/bk. of miscellanea, ff. 53–54v.
[57] Dugdale, *Mon.* vi (3), 1261.
[58] L.J.R.O., B/A/1/12, f. 171v.; D. 30/Oo 2.
[59] *S.H.C.* 4th ser. vii. 2.
[60] L.J.R.O., D. 30/C.A. iv, f. 76v.
[61] Ibid. D. 30/6/5/1; D. 30/XXXI, f. 24; *Cal. S.P. Dom.* 1638–9, 119; above, fig. 10.
[62] *Antiq. Jnl.* lvi (1), 77.
[63] A. L. Reade, *Reades of Blackwood Hill* (priv. print. 1906), 267 n.

bishop, agreed to subscribe annually towards the cost for seven years. In 1720 a further agreement was made for the replacement of the remaining wooden pipes.[64]

There was a shortage of water by the 1760s, and in 1769 the chapter ordered the conduit to be stopped up at 9 o'clock each night until the supply improved.[65] In 1774 it forbade anyone except its own plumber to turn off the water supply.[66] In general the dean and chapter claimed the right to cut off the supply to existing houses and to connect new ones solely at its own discretion.[67]

A brick conduit head was built at Maple Hayes c. 1780 to replace the existing head, which probably dated from the 13th century. It remained in use until 1821 when the old head was brought back into operation in order to improve the supply.[68] Meanwhile in 1786 the conduit in the Close was demolished because it was considered unsightly, and a reservoir and stone-encased pump were erected on the same site north-west of the cathedral.[69] The new system proved inadequate. On his death in 1800 Richard Bailye of the Close left the dean and chapter £50 to build a conduit of the same capacity as the old one but standing in the south-west corner of the garden of no. 15. A brick conduit was duly built there in 1803.[70] By 1812, however, the supply had again become inadequate, the shortage being blamed on the increase in the population of the Close following the opening of Newton's College in 1803.[71]

In 1876 it was agreed that the Close should be connected to the town supply, with the water being metered. Many residents preferred the supply from Maple Hayes, especially for drinking water, and it continued in use until 1969. It was then abandoned because of the cost of maintenance and the expense of law suits against farmers who damaged the pipes during ploughing.[72] From the mid 1980s the conduit was used as a kiosk for the sale of refreshments.

The town had its own water supply from the Middle Ages. In the 1270s there was an aqueduct in the 'high street', perhaps connected to the Close supply and running down Conduit Street, a name which included Dam Street in the later 14th century.[73] In June 1301 the community of the town granted land next to the aqueduct in Lichfield at a rent of 2s. to be used for the maintenance of the aqueduct.[74] In July 1301 Henry Bellfounder granted the Francis-

cans of Lichfield springs at Foulwell near Aldershawe with the right to build a stone conduit head there and to pipe the water to the friary about ½ mile away.[75] There were two conduits in the friary precinct in 1538, one in the cloister and the other 'at the revestry door'.[76] Henry stipulated that the friars were not to give any water away without his consent, but a public conduit was built in Bird Street south of the friary gate; it became known as Crucifix conduit from the crucifix which surmounted it.[77] By 1482 the supply had been extended along Bore Street to a conduit at the junction with Conduit Street and thence along Tamworth Street to a conduit at the junction with Lombard Street. The latter became known as Stone Cross conduit from the stone cross which stood there by the later 13th century. Cross (or Market Cross) conduit in the market place was mentioned in the 1540s and was served by a branch pipe running along Breadmarket Street.[78] In the 15th century there was a public cistern at the junction of Conduit Street and Quonians Lane.[79] After the dissolution of the friary the watercourse within the precinct remained in private hands, but in 1550 the owner of Foulwell granted the spring there to the corporation at a rent of 4d. a year.[80] By the earlier 17th century a pipe ran from the Friary watercourse to the Weston family's home in St. John Street.[81]

In 1545 Hector Beane, the master of the guild of St. Mary and St. John the Baptist, acting with its consent, granted guild lands at Great Wyrley in Cannock, Norton Canes, Little Wyrley in Norton Canes, and Wall to eight feoffees, who were to use the income to maintain Lichfield's water supply.[82] The conduits and watercourses were to be kept in repair by two wardens appointed annually on the feast of the Conception of St. Mary (8 December) from among the most substantial townsmen by the feoffees and six such townsmen. The wardens were to account at the end of their year of office to the constables and the six townsmen (later known as sidesmen). Any residue of income was to be used for the common weal of the town by the six townsmen with the consent of the feoffees. A new deed of feoffment was to be made every 21 years.

The Conduit Lands Trust supplied the city with water until the 20th century. The trustees had taken over the payment of the Foulwell rent by the late 1660s.[83] By 1666 they were appoint-

[64] L.J.R.O., D. 30/6/5/2; D. 30/Nn 22. For a view of the conduit in 1782 see Bodl. G.A. Staffs. 4°, 7, facing p. 297.
[65] L.J.R.O., D. 30/X, 1758–72, 20 Nov. 1767.
[66] Ibid. D. 30/C.A. viii, f. 77.
[67] Ibid. D. 30/6/5/2, case of 1812, pp. 3–4.
[68] Antiq. Jnl. lvi (1), 77–9; L.J.R.O., D. 30/6/5/7.
[69] Antiq. Jnl. lvi (1), 79; V.C.H. Staffs. iii. 189; W.S.L., Staffs. Views, vi. 17.
[70] Reade, Johnsonian Gleanings, iv. 176–7; viii. 162; V.C.H. Staffs. iii. 189.
[71] L.J.R.O., D. 30/6/5/2, case of 1812, p. 5.
[72] Antiq. Jnl. lvi (1), 73, 79; Express & Star, 25 June 1969; L.J.R.O., D. 126/min. bk. 1856–95, pp. 306, 310.
[73] S.H.C. 1924, p. 29.
[74] Above, town govt. (govt. to 1548: community of the town).
[75] V.C.H. Staffs. iii. 268 (where the date of the grant is wrongly given as 1310).
[76] F. A. Hibbert, Dissolution of the Monasteries, 253–4.

[77] V.C.H. Staffs. iii. 268; Harwood, Lichfield, 484, 489–91, and pl. facing p. 483.
[78] S.R.O., D. (W.) 1734/2/1/760, m. 123; L.J.R.O., D. 126/acct. bk. 1663–1805, acct. 1694–5; Harwood, Lichfield, 488, 495; Leland, Itin. ed. Toulmin Smith, ii. 100 (mentioning only the conduit outside the friary and 'another about the market place'); Lichfield Libr., Plan of Lichfield, 1766, by John Snape; above, figs. 2, 4. For the stone cross see e.g. S.H.C. 1924, p. 208; Bodl. MS. Ashmole 855, p. 186; above, fig. 2 (calling it high cross).
[79] L.J.R.O., D. 30/XXV, f. 22; Bodl. MS. Ashmole 864, pp. 386–7.
[80] Harwood, Lichfield, 489–92. The 1550 grant is in L.J.R.O., D. 126/misc. envelope.
[81] Harwood, Lichfield, 484 and pl. facing p. 483.
[82] L.J.R.O., D. 77/16/1, printed in Laithwaite, Conduit Lands Trust, 77–8. It is wrongly dated 1546 ibid. 9.
[83] L.J.R.O., D. 126/acct. bk. 1663–1805.

ing a plumber to maintain the conduit heads, pipes, cisterns, and cocks; the appointment was for life at a salary of £6 a year, raised to £10 in 1774.[84] The trust's first private connexion was in 1707 when the trustees agreed that pipes should be laid from Crucifix conduit along St. John Street with branches to the house of the master of the grammar school, that of the master of St. John's hospital, and that of Dorothy Hawkes. The three agreed to pay the cost of laying the new pipes and a further 1s. a year to the corporation for 99 years. The master of St. John's agreed to pay half the cost of raising and enlarging Crucifix conduit, the trust paying the rest. It was stipulated that the supply was to be solely for the families of the three people.[85] The public system was extended in the earlier 1770s. A new line was laid along Bird Street and Beacon Street to a cistern at the pinfold in Beacon Street, with a branch along the eastern end of Sandford Street. Another was laid along Market Street, Dam Street, and Butcher Row (otherwise Conduit Street), and the pipes in St. John Street were extended south. A new line was laid parallel to the existing line in Bore Street and was continued along Tamworth Street and Greenhill to a reservoir in St. Michael's churchyard.[86] There was an immediate demand for private connexions, and in 1774 the trustees decided that those should be from the new pipes rather than the old system. As part of an attack on waste they insisted in the 1780s that people with a private connexion had to make small reservoirs with cocks and pumps similar to those in the public supply. In 1798 they ordered that there was to be no private connexion unless there was also a pump to provide a supplementary supply; their plumber was to be allowed to inspect the pump once a month. People with a private connexion were forbidden to enlarge or alter their reservoirs or pipes without permission under pain of having the supply cut off.[87] In the early 1790s a reservoir was constructed in George Lane, taking its supply from two springs at Greenhill.[88]

Repairs were regularly carried out at the four conduits, which were also embellished. In 1666 sixpence was spent on 'hewing the windows at Stone Cross conduit' and 12s. on gilding a brass vane and painting six doors for the conduits.[89] A dial was set on Stone Cross conduit in 1675, and the city arms were placed on Crucifix conduit in 1677.[90] In 1703 £1 10s. was paid for drawing, painting, and gilding three dials on Stone Cross conduit, and the next year a globe and vane there were gilded and coloured.[91] In 1706 Butcher Row conduit was gilded and coloured.[92] In 1708, when Crucifix conduit was enlarged for the new private connexions, it was redecorated.[93] Stone Cross conduit was rebuilt in 1750 and Crucifix conduit in the late 1750s.[94] In 1792 the trustees ordered the removal of all but Crucifix conduit and the erection of pumps instead.[95] Stone Cross conduit was still standing in 1795 and that in the market place in 1803, but by 1806 only Crucifix conduit survived.[96] In 1827 the trustees ordered the rebuilding of its dome.[97] In 1863 it was adapted as the base of a clock tower designed in a Romanesque style by Joseph Potter the younger, but the conduit continued in use. In 1927 the tower was sold to the corporation, which re-erected it at the west end of the new road across the Friary in 1928. Its five bells were recast that year by E. D. Taylor of Loughborough (Leics.).[98]

By the early 19th century the supply was diminishing while the population was rising, and the trustees made various attempts to improve the supply and to find new sources. In 1805 the lead pipes between Aldershawe and Crucifix conduit were replaced by cast-iron pipes with a 3-in. bore.[99] An Act of 1815 empowered the trust to supply water from a spring at Pipe Green; after surveys had been carried out, the scheme was abandoned.[1] A new reservoir was built at Greenhill in 1820.[2] Between 1826 and 1831 the pipes between Aldershawe and the conduit were replaced with 4-in. bore lead pipes.[3] The regulations regarding private connexions were reiterated in 1838, with additional stipulations that public reservoirs were to have priority, that an annual acknowledgement was to be paid for a private tap, and that the water was not to be connected to water closets.[4] In 1844 the charge for a tap was 5s., and the same sum was fixed for water closets in 1857.[5] Meanwhile the trust's income had been greatly increased by mining royalties from 1842 and by payments from canal and railway companies for land taken. Such money, however, had to be

[84] Ibid. D. 16/3/3; D. 16/5/4, receipt of 10 Apr. 1768; D. 126/min. bk. 1741–1856, p. 58; acct. bk. 1663–1805, accts. 1774–5, 1775–6.
[85] Ibid. D. 77/9/15.
[86] Ibid. D. 16/5/6–9; D. 126/min. bk. 1741–1856, pp. 27, 30–1, 40–2, 50, 53; acct. bk. 1663–1805, accts. 1767–8, 1769–73; Laithwaite, *Conduit Lands Trust*, pl. facing p. 30 (based on T. Richardson, Plan of soughs and drains of Lichfield, 1779, in the possession of Mr. J. Martin of the S. Staffs Waterworks Co.; copy in L.J.R.O.).
[87] Laithwaite, *Conduit Lands Trust*, 21; L.J.R.O., D. 126/min. bk. 1741–1856, front end-paper and pp. 53–4, 75, 78, 84, 139–40.
[88] L.J.R.O., D. 126/min. bk. 1741–1856, pp. 108, 110, 114, 116; acct. bk. 1663–1805, accts. 1790–1, 1791–2.
[89] Ibid. bound accts. 1663–1715.
[90] Ibid. D. 16/5/1, accts. 1674–5; D. 126/loose accts., bills, etc., acct. of 1677.
[91] Ibid. D. 16/5/3, bill of 6 Dec. 1703; D. 126/acct. bk. 1663–1805, acct. 1703–4.
[92] Ibid. D. 126/acct. bk. 1663–1805, acct. 1705–6.
[93] Ibid. accts. 1706–7, 1707–8; accts., bills, etc., bill of 1708.

[94] Ibid. meeting of 15 Dec. 1747 and accts. 1749–50, 1757–8, 1758–9.
[95] Ibid. min. bk. 1741–1856, p. 123.
[96] Ibid. D. 16/5/11, bill of July 1795; D. 16/5/18/15. For views of the market place conduit in the early 1780s, of Stone Cross conduit in 1793, and Crucifix conduit c. 1800 and in 1833 see Bodl. G.A. Staffs. 4°, 8, facing pp. 455, 478, 489; below, plate 27.
[97] L.J.R.O., D. 126/min. bk. 1741–1856, pp. 250–1.
[98] Ibid. acct. bk. 1805–65, accts. 1862–5; misc. envelope, deed of 24 Aug. 1927; Laithwaite, *Conduit Lands Trust*, 50–2; Jennings, *Staffs. Bells*, 109; inscription on the tower.
[99] L.J.R.O., D. 16/5/17; D. 16/5/18/21; D. 16/5/21; D. 126/min. bk. 1741–1856, p. 152; acct. bk. 1663–1805, acct. 1804–5.
[1] Ibid. D. 16/5/35; D. 126/min. bk. 1741–1856, pp. 192, 196, 206, 212, 220–4; acct. bk. 1663–1805, acct. 1814–15; 55 Geo. III, c. 27 (Local and Personal).
[2] L.J.R.O., D. 16/5/32A; D. 126/min. bk. 1741–1856, pp. 215–16, 218; acct. bk. 1805–85, acct. 1820.
[3] Ibid. D. 126/min. bk. 1741–1856, pp. 243–5, 260–1.
[4] Ibid. pp. 305–6.
[5] Ibid. p. 336; min. bk. 1856–95, pp. 7–8.

held by the Charity Commissioners until required for capital expenditure.[6]

In 1853 a 21-year lease was taken of Trunkfield mill, but it was not until 1855, after a new deed of feoffment, that it was decided to start pumping water from there. By then the supply was down to an average of 18,000 gallons a day, a decrease of over 20,000 gallons a day compared with a few years before.[7] In 1868 the Trunkfield site was yielding 160,000 gallons a day and Aldershawe 15,000. The water was pumped to Crucifix conduit and distributed from there to 57 public pumps, 13 standpipes and public taps, 30 fire hydrants, and 343 houses. The supply, however, was not continuous in all parts of the city.[8] It was also inadequate to meet all demands: in 1871 a request for an extension of the supply to Leamonsley was refused.[9] In 1862 the charge for a private tap was reduced to 6d. in the case of houses paying less than £10 rent,[10] and in 1873 a new tariff was introduced. The domestic rate varied from 1s. to 10s. according to rent paid, and the commercial rate was fixed at 2d. for every 1,000 gallons.[11]

Land had meanwhile been bought east of Trunkfield. In 1875 a new works was opened capable of supplying 300,000 gallons a day from a well there, and a reservoir was built on the high ground at Beecroft east of Beacon Street.[12] The Aldershawe supply continued in use; in 1878 the lead piping from the spring to Crucifix conduit was replaced by iron piping.[13] By the 1920s the new works had become inadequate for the growing demand, and the trustees set about installing new plant. In 1928, before the work was completed, the supply was found to be contaminated by sewage from Trunkfields farm. Rather than become involved in heavy expenditure, the trustees decided in 1930 to close the works and take a supply from the South Staffordshire Waterworks Co.[14]

That company had been formed under an Act of 1855 to supply much of south and south-east Staffordshire, including Lichfield. The supply, drawn from the Lichfield area, was inaugurated in 1858. There was a pumping station at Sandfields in the south-west of the city, and Minster and Stowe pools, leased from the council in 1855, were drained and turned into reservoirs. There was opposition to the establishment of the company from the city, fearful for its exist-

ing supply, and in the event the company's tunnelling drained many wells in Lichfield. Until 1930 the company supplied only the outlying parts of the city.[15] In 1923 its supply was linked with that of the Conduit Lands trust for fire purposes by means of a main laid by the trustees down St. John Street to the company's main at Gallows wharf in London Road. In 1930 a valve was opened into that main, and the whole of the city was supplied by the company. The trust's works was closed, and the Aldershawe main was diverted into one of the company's headings.[16] Minster and Stowe pools were handed back to the council in 1970.[17]

In 1963 the Conduit Lands Trust sold its share in the water undertaking to the company,[18] but although no longer concerned with supplying water it continued to function as a charity. As provided in the 1545 feoffment, the trustees have been extensively involved in public works, including education. That involvement continued even after responsibility for some of the amenities provided by the trust had passed to the improvement commissioners established under an Act of 1806. Besides paying £50 towards the cost of obtaining the Act, the trustees paid the commissioners £60 a year; they also contributed towards individual projects.[19] In 1837 the reformed council, having taken over the commissioners' powers, petitioned parliament for the transfer of the trust's powers as well, claiming that the trustees 'fritter away their income in ill-advised expenses instead of supplying the city with water'. The trustees retaliated by suspending payment of the £60. The council abandoned the scheme, and in 1838 payment was resumed, including the £60 due for 1837.[20] Payment continued until 1844, but thereafter money was granted or lent for specific projects.[21] In 1855 the council again resolved to take measures to secure the transfer of the trust's powers to itself, both because it considered that the trustees were not carrying out their duties properly and because they were anyway closely identified with the community.[22] A scheme of management drawn up by the Charity Commissioners in 1871 ended the rivalry by giving the council a majority representation on the trust.[23] In 1900 the number of wardens was reduced from two to one.[24] A further reorganization in 1982 reduced the num-

[6] L.J.R.O., D. 16/4/4; D. 126/min. bk. 1741–1856, pp. 322–3, 330–1, 341–2, 504, 526; *Staffs. Advertiser*, 4 Apr. 1868, p. 6; Laithwaite, *Conduit Lands Trust*, 31.
[7] L.J.R.O., D. 126/min. bk. 1741–1856, pp. 441–4, 458–9, 472, 492, 504, 507, 511, 526, and back end-paper; acct. bk. 1805–85, accts. 1854, 1855, 1857.
[8] *Staffs. Advertiser*, 8 Aug. 1868, p. 7.
[9] L.J.R.O., D. 126/min. bk. 1856–95, pp. 210–11, 218, 262.
[10] Ibid. p. 204.
[11] Ibid. pp. 255, 261.
[12] Ibid. pp. 186–7, 197, 217, 237, 299, 302–3, 306, 308, 316; waterworks acct. 1873–99; *Staffs. Advertiser*, 8 Aug. 1868, p. 7.
[13] L.J.R.O., D. 126/min. bk. 1856–95, pp. 340–2, 354, 359.
[14] Laithwaite, *Conduit Lands Trust*, 34–5; *Lichfield Mercury*, 22 June 1928, p. 5; 6 July 1928, p. 7; 14 Sept. 1928, p. 5; 16 Aug. 1929, p. 9.
[15] A. Feeny, *S. Staffs. Waterworks Co.* (Birmingham, 1880), 17–27, 31–3 (copy in W.S.L.); Clayton, *Cathedral City*, 72–86; Sherlock, *Ind. Arch. Staffs.* 180–1; *S.H.C.* 1950–1, 202–4; *Staffs. Advertiser*, 8 Nov. 1856, p. 5; 4 Apr. 1868, p. 6; 8 Aug. 1868, p. 7; Lichfield U.D.C. *Ann. Rep. of M.O.H. for 1905*, 6, 9 (copy in S.R.O., C/H/1/2/1/20); below, plate 30.
[16] Laithwaite, *Conduit Lands Trust*, 35–6; *Lichfield Mercury*, 16 Nov. 1923, p. 8.
[17] *Lichfield Mercury*, 8 May 1970, p. 6.
[18] Inf. from Mr. J. Martin.
[19] Lichfield Conduit Lands, *Gifts and Donations* (copy in L.J.R.O., D. 126/misc. envelope).
[20] L.J.R.O., D. 77/5/4, ff. 63–4; D. 126/min. bk. 1741–1856, pp. 289, 295.
[21] Ibid. D. 77/15/4, pp. 84–5, 104–5; D. 126/min. bk. 1741–1856, pp. 330–1; acct. bk. 1805–85, acct. 1843–4; Lichfield Conduit Lands, *Gifts and Donations*; Laithwaite, *Conduit Lands Trust*, 41.
[22] L.J.R.O., D. 127/council min. bk. 1853–66, p. 109.
[23] *Lichfield Conduit Lands Trust: Scheme, Dec. 19th, 1871* (Lichfield, 1872; copy in L.J.R.O., D. 126/min. bk. 1856–95).
[24] Laithwaite, *Conduit Lands Trust*, 82.

ber of trustees from 14 to 12, consisting of three ex-officio members (the rector of St. Michael's, the mayor, and the chairman of Lichfield district council), three nominees of the city council, one nominee of the district council, and five co-opted members. Nominated and co-opted trustees were required to have been resident for five years in the area of the city as it was before the local government reorganization of 1974. The trust's income is mainly from investments, nearly all its lands having been sold.[25]

Wells, both public and private, were another source of water. St. Mary's well in Breadmarket Street opposite the west end of St. Mary's church existed in the late Middle Ages, and it may have been the well for the neglect of which the inhabitants of Bore Street were presented at the manor court in the 1650s.[26] In the mid 17th century there were other public wells in St. John Street,[27] in Bird Street and Sandford Street ward,[28] and in Beacon Street ward, which had a common well in Gaia Lane in 1704.[29] In the 18th century the Conduit Lands trustees paid for the conversion of several public wells into pumps. In 1737 they voted 30s. to the inhabitants of Wade Street towards the expense of turning their street well into a pump, the well being dangerous to children and to persons passing at night.[30] In 1768 the trustees decided to erect a pump at the well at the bottom of Stowe Street; Dr. Johnson, on a visit to Lichfield in 1769, wrote how 'in Stowe Street where I left a draw well I have found a pump'. He also found 'the lading well' in George Lane 'shamefully neglected'; in 1770 the trustees installed a pump in George Lane.[31] In the mid 1780s they employed John Sharrot to maintain 16 street pumps at the rate of 3s. a pump each year.[32] In 1875 the trustees decided to replace street wells with standpipes.[33] The continuing existence of private wells was a cause of complaint by the sanitary inspector in 1904, the public supply being within reasonable distance. In 1948 there were 41 houses dependent on outside standpipes, and two houses on the edge of the city were served by wells. By 1959 only three properties were without a piped supply.[34]

SEWERAGE, SCAVENGING, AND WASHING PLACES. A common muckhill was mentioned in 1535, apparently at Stowe Hill, and there was one on waste ground in Quonians Lane in the earlier 18th century.[35] In the earlier 18th century people who failed to clean the portion of the street in front of their houses were liable to prosecution at quarter sessions.[36] By the 1730s the corporation was also paying a man to clean the streets.[37] In 1778 a scavenger was appointed at quarter sessions for each of 14 streets, but from 1780 the court appointed a single scavenger for the whole city. He was at first paid by the Conduit Lands trustees, who from 1798 shared the cost with the corporation.[38] In 1784 the trustees paid six labourers to remove ice from the streets, and in 1814 they spent £15 on removing snow from the streets and snow and ice from the pumps.[39]

In 1774 a brick sewer was constructed from the Hartshorn inn along St. John Street and thence along Bore Street and Breadmarket Street, with side extensions into Tamworth Street and Market Street; it continued through the market place and along Dam Street to discharge into a reservoir at the end of Quonians Lane. There were four cesspools at intervals along it. It was laid by a number of inhabitants with the agreement of the corporation, and the Conduit Lands trustees agreed to keep it in repair.[40] It evidently replaced a similar system: an open channel existed in Dam Street in the early 18th century, and the bailiffs paid for the repair of a sough in St. John Streeet in 1736 and for the cleaning of the common gutter in 1767.[41]

Responsibility for drainage and cleaning the streets passed to the improvement commissioners in 1806. After failing to retain an unpaid scavenger for the whole city, they appointed scavengers for different parts late in 1806 to hold office for a year. Several scavengers bought their appointment, presumably because they were allowed to keep the scourings and soil. Occupiers of houses were still expected to sweep the adjoining footways. New appointments of scavengers were made in 1807 and 1808; it was stipulated in 1808 that they had to sweep the streets on Tuesdays and Saturdays between 8 a.m. and 5 p.m.[42] In 1815 a single scavenger was again appointed for the whole city; he was allowed to retain what he cleared away and was to be paid a salary assessed on performance.[43]

The commissioners replaced the open channels with underground culverts. In 1807 they entered into a contract for the building of culverts in St. John Street below the Bars, Bird Street, Bore Street, Conduit Street, and Dam

[25] Lichfield Conduit Lands: Scheme 30th July, 1982.
[26] Harwood, Lichfield, 478 n.; L.J.R.O., D. 30/VC, palimpsest, i, f. 27; W.S.L. 339/30.
[27] Harwood, Lichfield, 485 and pl. facing p. 483; W.S.L. 335/30.
[28] W.S.L. 337/30.
[29] W.S.L. 333/30; 350A–B/30; L.J.R.O., D. 77/6/2, f. 35v.
[30] L.J.R.O., D. 126/acct. bk. 1663–1805, acct. 1737–8 and reverse pages, 16 Dec. 1737.
[31] Ibid. acct. 1770–1; min. bk. 1741–1856, pp. 30, 34; Letters of Samuel Johnson, ed. R. W. Chapman, i, p. 229.
[32] L.J.R.O., D. 126/min. bk. 1741–1856, p. 84; acct. bk. 1663–1805, accts. 1784–7.
[33] Ibid. min. bk. 1856–95, p. 308.
[34] Lichfield U.D.C. Ann. Rep. of M.O.H. for 1904, 11 (copy in S.R.O., C/H/1/2/1/18); 1910 (ibid. C/H/1/2/1/30); City of Lichfield, Ann. Rep. of M.O.H. for 1948 (ibid. C/H/1/2/2/24); 1959 (ibid.).
[35] Harwood, Lichfield, 324; L.J.R.O., D. 77/9/41.
[36] L.J.R.O., D. 68, ff. 5v., 29, 46v.–48v.
[37] Ibid. D. 35/bailiffs' accts. 1704–94, pp. 122, 132, 135.
[38] Ibid. D. 25/1/1, ff. 97, 116, 121, 135; D. 35/bailiffs' accts. 1794–1835, pp. 24–122 passim; D. 126/min. bk. 1741–1856, pp. 74, 124, 141; acct. bk. 1663–1805.
[39] L.J.R.O., D. 126/acct. bk. 1663–1805, acct. 1783–4; acct. bk. 1805–85, acct. 1813–14; min. bk. 1741–1856, p. 191.
[40] Ibid. D. 77/5/2, f. 177; D. 126/min. bk. 1741–1856, p. 69; Laithwaite, Conduit Lands Trust, 44 and plan facing p. 34.
[41] J. L. Clifford, Young Samuel Johnson, 23; L.J.R.O., D. 35/bailiffs' accts. 1704–94, pp. 134, 311.
[42] L.J.R.O., D. 35/improvement com. min. bk. 1806–9, 3 and 10 July, 6, 20, 27 Nov., 4 Dec. 1806, 29 June and 2 Dec. 1807, 21 Nov. and 5 Dec. 1808; 1818–28, 16 Dec. 1824.
[43] Ibid. D. 77/15/5, pp. 43–6.

Street and in 1816 into another for Wade Street, Tamworth Street, and Sandford Street and from Gresley Row to Wade Street.[44] In 1832 they made an agreement with the architect Thomas Johnson for the laying of a covered sewer from Crucifix conduit along Bore Street, Tamworth Street, Lombard Street, and Stowe Street to Curborough brook by St. Chad's churchyard; much of the cost was met by the Conduit Lands trustees.[45] The council extended the sewer to the Ponesfield area further down the brook in the late 1830s.[46] In 1854 it made an agreement for the construction of a sewer in Beacon Street emptying into a drain near the Fountain inn.[47] Minster Pool ceased to be used for the discharge of sewage from the Close when it became a reservoir for the South Staffordshire Waterworks Co. in the later 1850s.[48]

By the mid 1860s sewage disposal was becoming a serious problem. Water closets discharging into the sewers were being introduced, but there was not enough water available to flush the sewers adequately. In addition Curborough brook was becoming polluted. In 1871 Samuel Keen, Lord Lichfield's tenant at Curborough farm,[49] complained to the council and to Lord Lichfield about damage to stock and pasture and to his family's health. The council covered the course of the brook by the farm, and Lord Lichfield paid for Keen's children to be sent away to school in order to remove them from the unhealthy atmosphere. The council bought the leasehold of 39 a. in Curborough in 1877 and laid out a sewage farm there, with new sewers in the town. Pollution continued, and in 1878 Lord Lichfield secured an injunction against the council restraining them from turning untreated sewage into the brook. He also received a reimbursement of the school fees, while Keen was granted compensation. The council bought the freehold of the land and attempted to make improvements to the sewage farm. In 1883 the owner of the nearby Wood End farm in King's Bromley complained that sewage was being deposited on his land. The council bought Wood End and extended the sewage farm. None the less pollution of the area continued and cattle were still harmed. The problem was caused by the amount of rainwater flowing into the sewers with resultant flooding at the sewage farm, by the difficulty of dealing with effluent from the breweries, and by the heaviness of the soil at the farm which prevented easy drainage. In 1891 Lord Lichfield obtained a writ of sequestration, which was held in suspense while the corporation carried out extensive improvements, including the completion of a system of separate sewers for surface water and sewage, the installation of six tanks at the sewage farm, and the purchase of yet another farm at Curborough.[50] Sewerage was extended to various suburban areas in the later 1890s.[51]

The widespread introduction of water closets in place of midden privies came in the early 20th century. There were some 1,674 by 1912 and only 30 middens. By then all new houses, other than those beyond the water mains and sewers, had to be provided with water closets. By 1890 house refuse was collected once a week by corporation carts and dumped in a disused brick pit outside the city. Collections were twice a week by 1910. A refuse destructor was erected in Curborough Lane in 1912.[52]

In 1651 all the butchers were fined by the manor court for washing at the conduits, and Thomas Minors was fined for washing clothes at one of the conduits.[53] A fine of 20s. was fixed in 1654 for the washing of hemp in any running water within the manor.[54] In 1667–8 the Conduit Lands trustees paid for a public proclamation against the washing of small clothes at the conduits. Authorized washing places existed by the bridge in Sandford Street and by the mill in Dam Street by the mid 1660s, and the Conduit Lands trustees regularly paid for their repair.[55] In 1692 they agreed to have the washing place at the mill repaired and covered after the corporation had been presented in 1691 for failing to repair it.[56] The bailiffs were presented in 1711 for not repairing the washing stock there, but in 1711–12 they mended the stock in Sandford Street.[57]

PAVING. Several grants of pavage were made to the townsmen and to the bishop between 1285 and 1345.[58] In 1472–3 the manorial bailiff paid a paviour and his gang for work on the causeway at New Bridge,[59] but by 1535 the guild was responsible for paving throughout the town and employed the bellman to do the work.[60] In the mid 17th century the corporation was evidently employing a paviour: in 1651 James Denston was presented at the manor court for failing to

[44] Ibid. D. 35/improvement com. min. bk. 1806–9, 7 Aug. 1806 sqq.; D. 77/15/5, pp. 10–12, 45–9.
[45] Ibid. D. 35/improvement com. min. bk. 1828–35, Jan.–Oct. 1832; D. 77/15/5, pp. 175–84; D. 126/min. bk. 1741–1856, p. 266.
[46] Ibid. D. 77/15/12.
[47] Ibid. D. 77/5/6, ff. 31–2.
[48] Clayton, Cathedral City, 76, 83; above (water supplies).
[49] In a detached part of Farewell and Chorley, later transferred to Alrewas.
[50] Staffs. Advertiser, 30 Sept. 1865, p. 5; 20 July 1872, p. 6; 30 Nov. 1878, p. 5; 25 Apr. 1891, p. 2; 21 Nov. 1891, p. 5; Lichfield Mercury, 28 Dec. 1877, retrospect; 13 Dec. 1878; 27 Dec. 1878, retrospect; 2 Jan. 1880, retrospect; T. Wardle, On Sewage Treatment (n.d., preface dated 1893), 336–40; Lichfield Urban Sanitary Dist. Rep. of M.O.H. for 1890, 7 (copy in S.R.O., C/H/1/2/1/1); 1891, 7 (copy ibid. C/H/1/2/1/2); 1892, 7–8 (copy ibid. C/H/1/2/1/3); 1893 (copy ibid. C/H/1/2/1/4); L.J.R.O., D. 127/council

min. bk. 1882–7, p. 113; 1887–8, p. 29; 1891–4, p. 167.
[51] Lichfield U.D.C. Ann. Rep. of M.O.H. for 1896, 9 (copy in S.R.O., C/H/1/2/1/7); 1899, 8 (copy ibid. C/H/1/2/1/10).
[52] Lichfield Urban Sanitary Dist. Rep. of M.O.H. for 1890, 7; Lichfield U.D.C. Ann. Rep. of M.O.H. for 1902, 12 (copy in S.R.O., C/H/1/2/1/14); 1910, 10 (copy ibid. C/H/1/2/1/30); 1912, 9 (copy ibid. C/H/1/2/1/34); Lichfield Mercury, 23 May 1913, p. 5.
[53] W.S.L. 331/30.
[54] Ibid. 330/30.
[55] L.J.R.O., D. 126/acct. bk. 1663–1805.
[56] Ibid. D. 77/6/1, f. 33; D. 126/loose accts., bills, etc., meeting of 8 Dec. 1692.
[57] Ibid. D. 35/bailiffs' accts. 1704–94, p. 36; D. 77/6/1, f. 31v.
[58] Above, general hist. (late Middle Ages).
[59] W.S.L., S. MS. 335 (i), m. 5d.
[60] Harwood, Lichfield, 325.

pave the streets within the city and was ordered to carry out the work on pain of a fine.[61] In 1664 the corporation made the maintenance of the streets in the city a charge on a seven-year lease of manorial revenues.[62] By the end of the century it was again employing a salaried paviour.[63]

Paving was financed from the toll on corn at the markets until 1741 when the corporation decided to invest £400 out of a gift of £500 from one of the city's M.P.s and spend the income on paving.[64] The Conduit Lands trustees also contributed towards the cost of paving, notably in the later 18th century; in 1770 alone they spent some £400 on Stowe Street, St. John Street, and the Bird Street bridge.[65] In the earlier 1790s the marquess of Stafford, Lord Granville Leveson-Gower, and Thomas Anson contributed extensively towards paving.[66]

Responsibility for paving passed from the corporation to the improvement commissioners in 1806.[67] The Conduit Lands trustees, however, continued to contribute towards paving, and on several occasions in the earlier 19th century their payments amounted to around half their total expenditure for the year.[68] At a public meeting in 1823 J. L. McAdam advocated the macadamizing of the streets, and despite controversy extensive macadamizing was carried out by the commissioners.[69]

LIGHTING. In December 1735 the inhabitants of Lichfield petitioned the Conduit Lands trustees for a system of lighting, and the trustees began to erect lamps in the streets. A lamplighter was appointed at a salary of £4 a year. Lamps were provided for private houses at an annual charge, fixed at 7s. 6d. a lamp in 1746. An oil room containing a cistern was built in 1740. In 1767–8 there were 34 public lamps and 32 private. In 1768–9 the number of lamps rose to 82, of which 51 were public; the total in 1773–4 was 103. The season for lighting was normally from Michaelmas to Lady Day but was sometimes extended into April. In 1791 the trustees decided to make it eight months instead of six. The lamplighter's salary, which rose steadily with the growing number of lamps, was £20 by 1792–3; from 1803 he had an assistant, paid £6.[70] In the later 1760s half the cost of the salary

and the oil was met by Lord Gower.[71] A new oil house was formed in 1798 by partitioning off part of the fire engine house at the guildhall.[72] For a single season, 1798–9, the trustees tried the experiment of employing a contractor, William Couldery, who lit 134 lamps from 10 September to 10 April at 13s. a lamp; the agreement specified 150.[73]

In 1806 the improvement commissioners took over responsibility for lighting. In October they made an agreement with T. S. Couldery of London for lighting 250 lamps from 13 October to 10 April (except for five days each month around full moon) at 13s. 3d. a lamp; the lamps were to be lit until 2 a.m., but lighting-up time varied according to the time of year. The agreement also specified that the 1807–8 season was to begin on 10 September, and Couldery was then to receive 14s. 9d. a lamp. From 1810 the lamps were unlit for seven days a month, but the payment for each one had risen to 16s.[74] By 1832–3 the number to be lit was 268 at 13s. each.[75]

Proposals were made to the commissioners in 1823 and 1827 for lighting the city with gas.[76] In 1833 they contracted with William Evans of Derby for a season's lighting by olefiant gas. He was to provide the new lamps required, taking the old ones in exchange, and was to be paid £2 2s. for each lamp lit from 22 September to 22 April, except for seven days at each full moon. He erected 123 new lamps. The contract was renewed in 1834.[77] From 1835 coal gas was supplied by the Lichfield Gas Light Co., formed that year. The agreement was for a sufficient quantity of lamps to be lit from the first Saturday in September to the last Saturday in April (except for seven days at full moon) at the rate of £2 5s. a lamp. By 1851 there were 160 public lamps, including 21 in the Close.[78] The gas works was in Queen Street and remained in operation until 1956.[79]

In 1882 the council decided to continue with gas rather than change to electricity.[80] There were several unsuccessful private schemes for supplying the city with electricity. The council had its own scheme in 1900 but abandoned it in 1901.[81] Meanwhile in 1894 a private house in Lichfield was lit by electricity, and in 1899 Jones & Co. installed electric lighting in its emporium

[61] W.S.L. 331/30.
[62] Above, town govt. (govt. from 1548: unreformed corporation).
[63] L.J.R.O., D. 35/bailiffs' accts. 1657–1707, pp. 175–6, 192; 1704–94, *passim*; D. 77/5/1, ff. 91, 265; D. 77/5/2, ff. 15, 218; W.S.L., H.M. uncat. 15/7.
[64] Above, town govt. (govt. from 1548: unreformed corporation). [65] L.J.R.O., D. 126/acct. bk. 1663–1805.
[66] S.R.O., D. 593/F/3/12/1/13 and 15; D. 593/F/3/12/2/9; D. 593/F/3/12/4/6.
[67] Above, town govt. (govt. from 1548: improvement com.).
[68] L.J.R.O., D. 126/min. bk. 1741–1856, pp. 177–8, 351, 355, 358; acct. bk. 1805–85, accts. 1811–12, 1817–18, 1842, 1844, 1846.
[69] *Lichfield Mercury*, 5 and 12 Dec. 1823; 19 Mar., 14 and 21 May, 24 Sept., 8 Oct. 1824; 7 Jan. 1825; 15 and 22 Dec. 1826; L.J.R.O., D. 35/improvement com. min. bk. 1818–28, 2 Mar., 20 July, 14 Dec. 1826, 27 Feb. 1828; 1828–35, 23 Dec. 1828, 10 Oct. 1829, 17 Aug. 1833.
[70] L.J.R.O., D. 16/5/6, lamp bill 1767–8; D. 126/acct. bk. 1663–1805, accts. and reverse pages; acct. bk. 1805–85,

acct. 1805–6; min. bk. 1741–1856, pp. 10, 27, 115–17, 120, 149.
[71] S.R.O., D. 593/F/3/12/1/2–4.
[72] L.J.R.O., D. 16/5/11, Bramall's bill 1797–8; D. 126/acct. bk. 1663–1805, acct. 1803–4.
[73] Ibid. D. 16/5/11, Couldery's bill 1798–9; D. 126/min. bk. 1741–1856, p. 141; acct. bk. 1663–1805, acct. 1798–9.
[74] Ibid. D. 35/improvement com. min. bk. 1806–9, 17 July 1806 sqq.; D. 77/15/5, pp. 2–6, 20–5.
[75] Ibid. D. 77/15/5, pp. 186–92.
[76] Ibid. D. 35/improvement com. min. bk. 1818–28, 1 Jan. 1824, 9 Aug. 1827.
[77] Ibid. 1828–35, 6 May 1835; D. 77/15/5, pp. 201–10, 218–25; White, *Dir. Staffs.* (1834), 94.
[78] L.J.R.O., D. 77/15/5, pp. 239–46; S.R.O., D. 941/4; White, *Dir. Staffs.* (1851), 485–6.
[79] *Lichfield Mercury*, 23 Dec. 1955, p. 5.
[80] L.J.R.O., D. 127/council min. bk. 1882–7, p. 25.
[81] Ibid. pp. 28–9, 61; 1897–9, p. 181; 1899–1902, pp. 126–7, 191; 1 Edw. VII, c. 38 (Local); 5 Edw. VII, c. 114 (Local); 5 Edw. VII, c. 160 (Local); *Lichfield Mercury*, 1 Oct. 1926, p. 5.

in Bird Street.[82] Although a scheme of 1910 for generating electricity for the cathedral proved impracticable,[83] the bishop's palace had its own supply from 1914, with a dynamo under the northeast tower of the Close.[84] The council's scheme was revived in 1913 but shelved on the outbreak of war. A council committee was set up in 1923, and it was decided to take a supply from Walsall corporation's undertaking. It was switched on in 1926, with a transforming station in Wade Street and a switch house in London Road.[85]

POLICING. Guild ordinances of 1486 specified policing duties of the manorial constables. People involved in fights were to be arrested and taken to the gaol. Their release was conditional on their finding surety and, in the case of bloodshed, paying 20d. to the guild's common chest and 4d. to the constables; for lesser disturbances the fine was 12d. to the chest and 4d. to the constables. Night walkers and other unruly persons were to be taken into custody until released by the master of the guild and his brethren, who were to warn offenders to behave on pain of being expelled from the city or imprisoned. Harlots were to be put on the cuckstool and, after being 'shamed', were to leave the city on pain of imprisonment. Scolds were to be warned in the name of the guild, and if they persisted after two warnings, they were to be put on the cuckstool.[86] By the early 16th century the guild had its own constables.[87]

A watch was maintained in the town in the early 13th century.[88] By the early 15th century it was customary for a watch to be maintained at the Whitsun fair, the principal fair when presumably there was a special risk of disorder. By 1421 the watch was inspected on the first two days of the fair by the bishop's steward and bailiff at Greenhill, probably the site of the fair. A lodge or bower made of birch trees was erected there for the two officials, the watch was provided with ale, and the bishop's minstrels played.[89] The steward and other manorial officials still attended on both days in the 1470s, but by the beginning of the 16th century the inspection was held on the first day only.[90] In 1518 the watch, drawn from the various wards, was described as going on watch around the town, and in 1532 the gates of the town were guarded during the fair.[91] The Green-

hill inspection was still carried out in 1542, but it had evidently become purely ceremonial by the late 17th century.[92]

A curfew and a day bell at the fourth hour were rung at St. Mary's in 1466 by ancient custom.[93] A day bell was still rung in the later 17th century and an evening bell in the later 1830s, although in 1817 it was evidently rung only during the winter and early spring.[94] The St. Mary's curfew was revived in 1924 and was still rung in 1929.[95]

In 1727 the corporation ordered the establishment of a night watch from Michaelmas to Lady Day in place of the crier's perambulation with his bell. Four able men were to be hired to keep watch from 11 p.m. to 4 a.m. and to go from house to house knocking on each door every two hours; each watchman was to be assigned to a particular part of the city. The watch was to be paid by the constables, the money being raised by a special rate on each ward. From Lady Day to Michaelmas the crier was still to go round.[96] In the earlier part of 1777 the Conduit Lands trustees paid the watch.[97] In 1784 there was a proposal by 'the gentlemen of Lichfield', presumably the corporation, that the sergeants of the Staffordshire Regiment living in Lichfield should form a watch with an equal number of local people to patrol the city from 10 p.m. to 6 a.m. at 2s. each a night. One sergeant protested vehemently to Major Sneyd in the hope that he would never allow the sergeants 'to be accoutred with lanterns and staffs and to march through the streets of Lichfield in that low station of a watchman'.[98] From the 1780s the corporation employed night watchmen during the September races, normally four paid 2s. a night each.[99] In 1806 the responsibility passed to the improvement commissioners, and from 1827 watchmen were appointed for the spring race meeting as well. The appointment of watchmen for the races was discontinued after the September meeting of 1834 in order to save money.[1] The patrol of the city was mentioned in January 1817, but in 1833 the commissioners were not exercising their power to appoint night watchmen, the city being 'orderly and quiet'.[2]

The corporation appointed 'a special constable and police officer' for the city in 1825; he was paid 30s. a week in 1832 when he was also appointed gaoler at £12 a year.[3] Special con-

[82] Clayton, *Cathedral City*, 167; *Lichfield Mercury*, 6 Oct. 1899, p. 5.
[83] L.J.R.O., D. 77/20/8, cathedral appeal pamph. 1924, between pp. 94 and 95.
[84] Ibid. D. 85/2/3, pp. 41–2.
[85] *Lichfield Mercury*, 16 July 1926, p. 5; 1 Oct. 1926, p. 5; 18 June 1976, p. 10; L.J.R.O., D. 127/electric lighting cttee. bk.
[86] *The Gild of St. Mary, Lichfield* (E.E.T.S. extra ser. 114), 12–13.
[87] Above, town govt. (govt. to 1548: community of the town).
[88] Ibid. (liberties).
[89] Ches. R.O., DCH/O/8, m. 2, decayed rents section (where the illegible words have been deduced from L.J.R.O., B/A/21, CC 124078, m. 1); L.J.R.O., B/A/21, CC 124075, m. 4.
[90] L.J.R.O., B/A/21, CC 123984, m. 6d.; B.R.L. 435125.
[91] S.R.O., D. (W.) 1734/2/1/597, m. 14; D. (W.) 1734/3/2/13, m. 4d.
[92] Ibid. D. (W.) 1734/J. 1949, m. 1; below, social and

cultural activities (Greenhill Bower).
[93] L.J.R.O., D. 30/9/3/1, ff. 17v., 21, 25v.
[94] Ibid. D. 20/4/1, 1669–70, 1672–3; D. 20/4/2, 25 Mar. 1683; W.S.L., S. MS. 374, p. 288; Mrs. Charles Bagot [S. L. Bagot], *Links with the Past* (1901), 167.
[95] L.J.R.O., D. 20/5/3, 24 Jan. 1924, 18 Feb. 1929; *Lichfield Mercury*, 4 Jan. 1924, p. 4.
[96] L.J.R.O., D. 68, f. 5; D. 77/5/1, f. 252.
[97] Ibid. D. 35/bailiffs' accts. 1704–94, pp. 455, 467, 493, 541, 563; D. 126/acct. bk. 1663–1805, acct. 1776–7.
[98] S.R.O., D. 603/K/9/13, Serjant to Sneyd, 17 Nov. 1784.
[99] L.J.R.O., D. 35/bailiffs' accts. 1704–94, pp. 455, 491 sqq.; 1794–1835, pp. 22–94 *passim*.
[1] Ibid. D. 35/improvement com. min. bk. 1806–9, 15 and 28 Aug. 1806; 1818–28, 28 May 1827; 1828–35, 6 Jan. 1829, 17 Nov. 1834.
[2] *Lichfield Mercury*, 17 Jan. 1817; *1st Rep. Com. Mun. Corp.* H.C. 116, p. 1928 (1835), xxv.
[3] *Lichfield Mercury*, 23 Sept. and 28 Oct. 1825; L.J.R.O., D. 77/5/3, f. 212.

stables were employed that year, and in 1833 the two manorial constables were noted as part of the police force.[4] In 1836 the council ordered the conversion of the magistrates' room on the ground floor of the guildhall into a police office.[5] In the later 1830s the two serjeants at mace were also paid as constables, and there were two police officers in 1841.[6] In 1844 the city's police force was amalgamated with the Staffordshire county force,[7] but in 1847 the council appointed four watchmen to patrol the city and suburbs from 10 p.m. until 6 a.m. between December and March.[8] In 1848 the police station was on the north side of Bore Street near its junction with Conduit Street.[9] In 1851 the police force consisted of a superintendent and six constables, four of them paid by the council.[10] It was evidently in that year that the George IV inn next to the guildhall was converted into the police station.[11] The city had its own force once more from c. 1860 until 1889 when it was taken over by the county force.[12] The station was then moved into the guildhall.[13] A new station was opened in Wade Street in 1898 and remained in use until 1971 when it was replaced by the new divisional headquarters in Frog Lane.[14]

In 1772 the bailiffs bought a hue-and-cry board for the display of the lists of offenders at large which Sir John Fielding, the Bow Street magistrate, began circulating that year to civil authorities.[15] By 1816 the city had an association for the prosecution of felons, which was still in existence in 1826.[16]

The watchman of the Close was mentioned in the late 13th century and the janitor in 1321. In the mid 1350s there was a subjanitor paid 4d. a week and a keeper of the west gate. The janitor was also known as the serjeant.[17] His office had developed into that of verger and constable by the late 17th century.[18] In 1523 the chapter ordered that the gates of the Close were not to be opened before the seventh hour in the morning except for bringing in ale and other goods, when only one gate to be opened.[19] In 1715 it ordered the verger to shut the gates at 10 p.m., leaving the wicket at the south gate open until 11 p.m.[20] In 1664 a watchman was employed in the Close for six weeks during a time of plague, and during the outbreak of 1665 two watchmen guarded the gates for nine weeks.[21] An instance

of sanctuary in the Close, probably the last, occurred in 1532 when a thief took refuge there.[22]

In 1825 there was a specially appointed constable besides the usual constable in the Close.[23] The inhabitants of the Close established a night watch for six months from December 1830 to protect themselves 'against nightly depredations'. Four watchmen were appointed to patrol in pairs from 9 p.m. to 5 a.m., each pair working on alternate nights. The dean and chapter paid half the cost from the fabric fund, and the other half was met by a rate on the inhabitants. The watch, evidently reduced to the winter months from 1831, was still maintained in 1839.[24] From 1876, in reaction to nocturnal thefts in Lichfield and the neighbourhood, the dean and chapter appointed a night watchman for the Close, supported by contributions from the inhabitants.[25] He had the authority of a constable evidently from 1880.[26] Albert Haycock, sworn as watchman in 1912, continued to hold the office until his death in 1956, although for some time he had been too ill to carry out his duties. He patrolled the Close from 9.30 p.m. to 4.30 a.m., calling out the time and the state of the weather. He had full powers of arrest and exercised them on occasion, but he never used the handcuffs, whistle, and truncheon provided.[27]

FIRE PRECAUTIONS. Arrangements for fire fighting are recorded from the 17th century, with the Conduit Lands trustees playing a prominent part. Several wards were presented at the manor court in the 1650s for not having a hook and a ladder.[28] Buckets were stored in St. Mary's. The number dwindled from 36 in 1629 to 11 in 1668, and in 1669 five dozen were bought by the trustees. They were included among the goods for which the churchwardens were responsible, but they were maintained by the trustees.[29] On three occasions in the 18th century the trustees bought two dozen buckets, while in 1751 they bought a dozen and the Sun Fire Office bought another dozen.[30] In 1724 the trustees ordered the purchase of 12 fire hooks of the kind used in London and 4 ladders 30 or 40 ft. long. They took over responsibility for hooks and ladders from the wards in 1782.[31] In 1697,

[4] L.J.R.O., D. 35/bailiffs' accts. 1794–1835, p. 362; *1st Rep. Com. Mun. Corp.* p. 1928.
[5] L.J.R.O., D. 77/5/4, f. 38.
[6] Ibid. ff. 40v., 54; D. 35/boro. fund acct. bk. 1836–68, pp. 1, 5, 9, 11, 27, 39; P.R.O., HO 107/1008.
[7] L.J.R.O., D. 126/misc. envelope, annotated copy of Lichfield Conduit Lands, *Gifts and Donations*.
[8] Ibid. D. 77/15/4, p. 110.
[9] L.J.R.O., B/A/15/Lichfield, St. Mary, no. 256.
[10] White, *Dir. Staffs.* (1851), 494.
[11] S.R.O., C/PC/1/8/1; L.J.R.O., D. 88, deed of 20 Sept. 1855.
[12] *Staffs. Advertiser*, 12 May 1888, p. 6; S.R.O., C/PC/1/8/1; S.R.O., Q/ACp 1/4, pp. 81, 85; L.J.R.O., D. 127/council min. bk. 1888–91, pp. 54–5.
[13] *Kelly's Dir. Staffs.* (1892).
[14] *Lomax's Red Bk.* (1899), 14; *Lichfield Mercury*, 2 Apr. 1971, p. 6.
[15] L.J.R.O., D. 35/bailiffs' accts. 1704–94, pp. 353, 355, 359, 367, 373, 382, 393; L. Radinowicz, *Hist. of Eng. Criminal Law*, iii. 49–54.

[16] *Lichfield Mercury*, 10 May and 6 Dec. 1816; 24 Nov. 1826.
[17] *S.H.C.* vi (1), 272; Bodl. MS. 794, ff. 2v., 91v., 95v.
[18] L.J.R.O., D. 30/LIV, f. 98; D. 30/8/13/4; *S.H.C.* 4th ser. v, p. 271.   [19] L.J.R.O. D. 30/C.A. iv, f. 8v.
[20] Ibid. D. 30/X, 1709–26, 2 Dec. 1715.
[21] Ibid. D. 30/LXIV.   [22] *V.C.H. Staffs.* iii. 161.
[23] L.J.R.O., D. 30/8/28.
[24] Ibid.; D. 30/C.A. x, pp. 191–2, 347; D. 30/box 12.
[25] Ibid. D. 30/8/32.
[26] Ibid. D. 127/council min. bk. 1866–82, p. 357.
[27] *Lichfield Mercury*, 1 June 1956, pp. 6–7.
[28] W.S.L. 333/30; 339/30; 350A/30, ff. 7–8; 350B/30.
[29] L.J.R.O., D. 20/4/1–2; D. 126/bound accts. 1663–1715, acct. 1668–9; acct. bk. 1663–1805, accts. 1684–5, 1703–4.
[30] Ibid., D. 16/5/5, bill and notice of despatch 1768; D. 126/acct. bk. 1663–1805, accts. 1724–5, 1726–7, 1750–1, 1768–9, 1776–7, and reverse pages, 11 Dec. 1724; min. bk. 1741–1856, p. 27.
[31] Ibid. D. 126/min. bk. 1741–1856, pp. 76, 84, 111.

probably after a bad fire, the corporation ordered that all thatched buildings in the built-up part of the city were to be tiled within six months on pain of a fine of 10*s*. a month.[32]

A fire engine was brought from London at the trustees' expense in 1667, and they also paid for materials for a building to house it.[33] There was a second and larger engine by 1684.[34] By 1691 there were four new engines besides the old engine; one was known as the Bachelors engine and another as the Virgins.[35] A barn in Wade Street was rented as an engine house from 1690.[36] By 1695 there was a second engine house in the market place adjoining St. Mary's, to which the Wade Street engines were moved in 1734.[37] In 1736 the trustees fitted up part of the Roundabout House in the north-east corner of the market place as an engine house.[38] It was apparently about then that Richard Dyott bought the city a new engine,[39] and the trustees bought another in 1745.[40] In 1779 the Bachelors engine was converted from 'a squirt into a perpetual stream'.[41] Having leased land in Quonians Lane in 1774 for building an engine house, the trustees in 1779 instead converted two rooms under the guildhall leased from the corporation.[42] In order to improve the water supply in case of fire the trustees in 1782 ordered the fitting of a cock with a suction pipe at each conduit and the provision of two carts for carrying water to the engines.[43]

Fire precautions were not included among the responsibilities of the improvement commissioners in 1806 but remained in the hands of the trustees. In 1808 they repaired a treadle engine, a little engine, and a squirt engine.[44] The engine house at the guildhall was replaced in 1825 by one in Quonians Lane, also leased from the corporation.[45] In 1850 there were four engines, a small hand engine which was out of repair, 24 iron buckets and a number of useless leather buckets, a water cart, three old fire hooks, and four lengths of hose. Extra equipment was bought, including 24 iron buckets and two lengths of hose.[46] In 1860 the trustees decided to sell all the engines except the treadle engine and also to give up the tenancy of the engine house.[47]

Insurance companies also kept engines in the city. The Birmingham Fire Office had an engine there in 1850, and one was presented to the council by an insurance company in 1857.[48] The Lancashire Insurance Co., which had amalgamated with the Birmingham Fire Office, had an engine at Lichfield in 1871, probably the engine specially built by the company for Lichfield and its neighbourhood, which in 1875 was kept in Bore Street opposite St. James's Hall. It was moved to the Swan *c.* 1880. By then the company maintained a brigade of eight at Lichfield.[49]

There was public agitation in 1872 for improved fire precautions, notably the provision of a public engine and the establishment of a brigade.[50] In 1873, after a serious fire in Breadmarket Street, the council took over responsibility for fire fighting. It bought an engine and established a brigade, fitting up a building at the east end of Sandford Street as a fire station.[51] The Conduit Lands trustees contributed towards the cost of the new engine and also resolved to repair their own engine and hand it over, with an annual allowance, to the brigade; it was still kept in working order in 1884. The Royal Society for the Protection of Life from Fire presented the city with a fire escape in 1876, and the Conduit Lands trustees granted the council £50 to provide a shed for it in the market place.[52] In 1886 the council took over the control and maintenance of the Lancashire Insurance Co.'s engine in return for a payment of £50 by the company.[53] The south bay of the market hall at the Corn Exchange was turned into a station for both engines in 1888, and the insurance company's engine was still there *c.* 1894.[54] A steam fire engine was presented to the city in 1898 by A. O. Worthington of Maple Hayes in Burntwood, and the former police station at the guildhall was converted into a fire station.[55] A motor fire engine was bought in 1922, with the rural district council contributing half the cost

[32] Ibid. D. 77/5/1, f. 78; S.R.O., D. 3451/2/60, 10 Oct. 1697 (collection at Pattingham 'for the sufferers at Lichfield').
[33] L.J.R.O., D. 126/acct. bk. 1663–1805, accts. 1666–7, 1667–8.
[34] Ibid. D. 35/bailiffs' accts. 1657–1707, p. 100; D. 126/acct. bk. 1663–1805, accts. 1684–5, 1687–8, 1688–9.
[35] Ibid. D. 126/acct. bk. 1663–1805, acct. 1690–1; loose accts., bills, etc., bills of 1693, 1697, 1702.
[36] Ibid. acct. bk. 1663–1805, accts. 1689–90, 1690–1, 1693–4.
[37] Ibid. accts. 1694–5, 1733–4; loose accts., bills, etc., bills of 1695, 1697, 1700, 1704; S.R.O., D. 4566/M, will of Sam. Mousley, 14 May 1733.
[38] L.J.R.O., D. 126/acct. bk. 1663–1805, accts. 1735–6 sqq. and reverse pages, 13 Dec. 1735; T. Richardson, Plan of soughs and drains of Lichfield, 1779 (in the possession of Mr. J. Martin of the S. Staffs. Waterworks Co.; copy in L.J.R.O.); Bodl. G.A. Staffs. 4°, 8, facing p. 455; below, econ. hist. (markets and fairs).
[39] L.J.R.O., D. 126/acct. bk. 1663–1805, reverse pages, 17 Dec. 1736; Shaw, *Staffs.* i. 336.
[40] L.J.R.O., D. 126/acct. bk. 1663–1805, accts. 1743–4, 1744–5, and meetings 15 Dec. 1746 and 15 Dec. 1747.
[41] Ibid. acct. 1778–9; min. bk. 1741–1856, p. 66.
[42] Ibid. D. 35/bailiffs' accts. 1704–94, p. 424; D. 77/5/2, ff. 176v., 196; D. 126/min. bk. 1741–1856, pp. 54–5, 66, 72; acct. bk. 1663–1805, acct. 1779–80.

[43] Ibid. D. 126/min. bk. 1741–1856, p. 75; acct. bk. 1663–1805, acct. 1782–3.
[44] Ibid. D. 16/5/20, Acton's bill, Bonell's bill.
[45] Ibid. D. 16/5/37, Genders' bill and corp. receipt for rent; D. 16/5/39, Crompton's bill and corp. receipt for rent. [46] Ibid. D. 126/min. bk. 1741–1856, pp. 414–20.
[47] Ibid. 1856–95, pp. 80–3.
[48] *Staffs. Advertiser*, 23 Mar. 1850, p. 4; 16 May 1857, p. 5.
[49] Ibid. 11 Nov. 1871, p. 7; *Eggington's Lichfield Almanack* (1875); *Lichfield Mercury*, 30 Apr. 1880, p. 5; *Meacham's Lichfield Almanack* (1881).
[50] *Staffs. Advertiser*, 10 Aug. 1872, p. 7; L.J.R.O., D. 127/council min. bk. 1866–82, p. 149.
[51] L.J.R.O., D. 127/council min. bk. 1866–82, pp. 160, 167–8; *Staffs. Advertiser*, 8 Feb. 1873, p. 6; 15 Mar. 1873, p. 7; *Eggington's Lichfield Almanack* (1875); O.S. Map 1/500, Staffs. LII. 15. 12 (1884 edn.).
[52] L.J.R.O., D. 126/min. bk. 1856–95, pp. 249–50, 310; acct. bk. 1805–85, accts. 1872–6; *Staffs. Advertiser*, 13 May 1876, p. 7; *Lichfield Mercury*, 25 July 1884, p. 5.
[53] *Lichfield Mercury*, 12 Feb. 1886, p. 8; 16 Aug. 1889, p. 5.
[54] *Lomax's Red Bk.* (1889), 47; (1894), 59; L.J.R.O., D. 127/council min. bk. 1888–91, pp. 12–13.
[55] L.J.R.O., D. 127/council min. bk. 1897–9, pp. 60, 103–4, 126, 179–80, 195; *Lichfield Mercury*, 25 Feb. 1898, p. 5.

and towards its maintenance.[56] In 1936 the city and the rural district formed a joint fire brigade and bought a second engine.[57] The fire station was moved to Friary Road during the Second World War. The county council became the fire authority in 1948 and opened a new station in Birmingham Road in 1963.[58]

MEDICAL SERVICES. Medical practitioners are recorded in Lichfield from the early 14th century.[59] In 1767 the corporation subscribed 20 guineas to the Staffordshire General Infirmary opened at Stafford the previous year. It thereby became one of the trustees of the infirmary, with the right to recommend two in-patients a year and any number of out-patients. It ceased to be a trustee after 1834.[60] St. Mary's parish subscribed 2 guineas a year from 1802 and was entitled to recommend the same number of patients; from 1811 to 1831 it subscribed 3 guineas (5 guineas in 1814). St. Michael's subscribed 5 guineas from 1812 but reduced its subscription to 3 guineas in 1819 to be in line with St. Mary's; it ceased to subscribe after 1822. St. Chad's subscribed 3 guineas from 1815 to 1841.[61]

A dispensary for the poor, supported by subscription, existed at Lichfield by 1803.[62] In 1831 the St. Mary's select vestry voted the dispensary £10 a year to supply medicine to the poor of the parish. It also voted £5 a year for a physician to give occasional advice to the poor and £5 for a surgeon to be in attendance on them. At the same time the vestry stopped its annual subscription to the infirmary at Stafford as it considered the dispensary competent to provide the same assistance.[63] The St. Michael's vestry was employing a parish surgeon in the mid 1830s.[64] The dispensary was in Tamworth Street in the earlier 1830s.[65] By 1850 it was in Wade Street and then had a physician, Thomas Rowley, two surgeons, and a dispenser. There were some 500 patients a year, besides midwifery cases. Donations and subscriptions amounted to some £150 a year.[66] Rowley had also established a self-supporting dispensary in St. John Street.[67] The Wade Street dispensary was still in operation in 1861[68] and is probably identifiable with the Lichfield dispensary of 1868. The subscribers to

that dispensary were allowed to recommend patients, who paid 6d. or 18d. according to the type of recommendation. In 1875 it became a provident dispensary with benefit members paying 3d. a month and subscribers providing further income. Those qualifying for membership were shopkeepers and tradesmen whose house rent did not exceed £10 a year, indoor apprentices earning up to 18s. a week, childless married couples earning jointly up to 23s. a week, and married couples who had children and earned up to 27s. a week.[69] In 1877-8 the Lichfield provident dispensary had 781 benefit members, and it was still in existence in 1946.[70]

A nursing institution was formed in 1879. It was supported by subscriptions and donations and maintained a nurse who worked under a lady superintendent. In 1888 the nurse visited some 12 poor a day. In 1882 the institution took over an invalids' kitchen established in 1870. The two moved from Dam Street to Bore Street c. 1891 and to Bird Street c. 1894.[71]

Both were taken over by the Lichfield Victoria nursing home, opened in 1899 in Sandford House, no. 15 Sandford Street, as a memorial to Queen Victoria's reign. It was intended for the poor of the city and depended on subscriptions and donations. Part of the initial outlay was met from the funds established to mark the queen's jubilees of 1887 and 1897 and the funds of the nursing institution. The scheme was originated by Canon M. H. Scott, vicar of St. Mary's 1878–94 and archdeacon of Stafford from 1888 until his death in 1898. One of the two wards was named after him and the other after Mary Slater of Haywood House, Bore Street (d. 1898), who left most of her residuary estate to the nursing association.[72] In 1910 the nursing home was enlarged by the addition of a third public ward, two private wards, and an operating theatre. An adjoining house left to the trustees by George Martin of Sandyway (d. 1908) was converted into nurses' quarters and offices. The nursing home was renamed the Lichfield Victoria nursing home and cottage hospital.[73] That was in turn renamed the Victoria hospital, Lichfield, in 1932,[74] and in 1933 the hospital moved into a new building in the Friary, designed by T. A. Pole of London.[75] A maternity wing was added in 1941, and a patients' day

[56] *Lichfield Mercury*, 14 July 1922, p. 5; 28 July 1922, p. 6; 5 Jan. 1923, p. 5.
[57] Ibid. 10 July 1936, p. 6; 29 Oct. 1987, p. 22; *Kelly's Dir. Staffs.* (1936).
[58] *Lichfield Mercury*, 25 Sept. 1964, p. 9; inf. from Assistant Divisional Officer N. Cliffe.
[59] Below, econ. hist. (professions).
[60] S.R.O., D. 685/12/1; L.J.R.O., D. 35/bailiffs' accts. 1704–94, p. 309; D. 77/5/2, f. 137; *V.C.H. Staffs.* vi. 234.
[61] S.R.O., D. 685/12/1; L.J.R.O., D. 35/St. Michael's overseers' bk. 1807–20, p. 248.
[62] W.S.L., S. MS. 478, Jones to Baxter, 30 Aug. 1803; L.J.R.O., D. 35/bailiffs' accts. 1794–1835, p. 260.
[63] L.J.R.O., D. 20/6/9, ff. 131v., 132, 135v.
[64] Ibid. D. 35/St. Michael's vestry min. bk. 1827–45, 25 Mar. 1836.
[65] S.R.O., D. 615/M/3/8 (1832); White, *Dir. Staffs.* (1834), 96.
[66] *Slater's Nat. and Com. Dir.* (1850), Staffs. pp. 34, 37; White, *Dir. Staffs.* (1851), 508 (giving the address as Wade

St.); P.R.O., RG 9/1972.
[67] *Staffs. Advertiser*, 28 Mar. 1863, p. 5; White, *Dir. Staffs.* (1851), 508.
[68] P.R.O., RG 9/1972.
[69] *Staffs. Advertiser*, 26 Dec. 1868, p. 4; 26 Dec. 1974, p. 7.
[70] *Staffs. Advertiser*, 26 Dec. 1868, p. 4; 9 Feb. 1878, p. 5; *Lomax's Red Bk.* (1936), 101; L.J.R.O., D. 77/19/3.
[71] *Staffs. Advertiser*, 9 Dec. 1882, p. 4; 23 June 1888, p. 2; *Lomax's Red Bk.*(1886), 27; (1892), 65; (1895), 65.
[72] *Lichfield Mercury*, 28 July 1899, p. 5; *Lomax's Red Bk.* (1899), 5, 7, 14–15. For Scott, brother of Sir Gilbert Scott, see *Lich. Dioc. Mag.* (1898), 96–8; M. Scott, *The Force of Love: a memoir of the Ven. M. H. Scott* (1899).
[73] *Lichfield Mercury*, 9 May 1909, p. 5; 22 July 1910, p. 4; 29 Feb. 1952, p. 3.
[74] Victoria Hosp., Lichfield, *Ann. Rep.* 5 (copy in S.R.O., D. 4108, box L).
[75] *Lichfield Mercury*, 16 June 1933, p. 4; 23 and 30 June 1933, p. 5.

room, separate from the main building, was opened in 1958. In 1983 there were 36 general beds.[76]

The Sandford Street premises were bought by Staffordshire county council in 1934 and reopened as a clinic. That year too the Lichfield Orthopaedic and Aftercare clinic, a voluntary organization, moved there. Since its opening in 1923 it had occupied the house in Station Street formerly attached to the City flour mill.[77] In 1985 the Sandford Street building was used as county council offices.

In 1940 the former workhouse in Trent Valley Road became St. Michael's hospital. At first a general hospital, in 1984 it was a 135-bed hospital for the elderly.[78]

An isolation hospital was opened in 1890 at Wood End farm in King's Bromley, bought by the corporation a few years before to extend its sewage farm. The hospital was run jointly by Lichfield urban sanitary authority and Lichfield rural sanitary authority. By 1899 the farmhouse was used mainly for cases of scarlet fever, while cases of smallpox, diphtheria, and typhoid fever were treated in two cottages nearby. In 1904 a separate iron building was erected for smallpox cases. A new ward was added to the main block in 1910.[79] In 1941 the hospital was replaced by Wissage hospital, opened in the former girls' industrial school and closed in 1949.[80]

About the beginning of 1889 the corporation bought a carriage for conversion into an ambulance, it being illegal to use hired vehicles for carrying infectious cases. The converted vehicle was still in use in 1893 when the medical officer of health recommended the provision of a proper ambulance.[81] Lichfield was later included in the area served by the rural district council's ambulance service. A motor ambulance was bought by the rural district council in 1927 and kept at its offices in St. John Street. That vehicle was replaced by a new ambulance in 1935 and a new garage was built at the council offices.[82] In 1948 the service passed into the control of Staffordshire county council, which used a garage at Stowe House as the ambulance station until a new station was opened in Birmingham Road in 1963.[83]

About 1775 George Chadwick, a physician, appears to have begun using his house in St. John Street for the reception of lunatics. In 1778 he was licensed by quarter sessions to receive up to 10 patients there. Erasmus Darwin and a justice inspected the house in 1779 and found conditions good; there were eight patients, drawn from Staffordshire, Worcestershire, and Leicestershire and including one woman. In 1787 Chadwick was charging an entrance fee of 1 guinea, £17 for the first year, and £14 for the second year if the patient was not troublesome. Although the annual licence continued to be for 10 patients, there were 14 by 1788, and in addition Chadwick's wife was then confined to her room as a lunatic. A peak of 23 patients was reached in 1808. In 1811 the inspectors reported that patients in close confinement were kept in dirty conditions with insufficient straw; Chadwick protested that the inspection was made on a Saturday morning a few hours before the rooms were due to be cleaned. Although more favourable reports followed, numbers dropped to 9 in 1814, and that year the licence was not renewed.[84] Chadwick was probably a relative of the John Chadwick who ran an asylum at Abbots Bromley in succession to his father and died in the mid 1790s. His medicines for treating insanity passed to S. Bakewell, evidently a relative by marriage, who advertised them in 1797 and was then living in Lichfield.[85]

In July 1817 a licence for an asylum in a house adjoining George Chadwick's was granted to Thomas Rowley, a surgeon living in St. John Street. He had already received a criminal lunatic in January, and in July he had seven other patients, several of whom had been inmates of Chadwick's asylum.[86] Rowley transferred the asylum to a house at Sandfields apparently in 1818.[87] In 1820 two pauper lunatics were admitted from the workhouse in St. Mary's parish and another from Derbyshire; the St. Mary's vestry agreed in 1822 to allow Rowley 9s. a week for each pauper from the parish.[88] Although he continued to own the asylum, by 1826 it was run by Samuel Heighway, who had 13 patients in 1827 and was still superintendent in 1836.[89] In 1841 the superintendent was Samuel Smith, with 32 patients.[90] By 1846 there were 44 patients, 38 of them paupers. Inspectors that year found the establishment unsatisfactory; in particular the dormitories outside the house, which were occupied by the paupers, were cold and damp. Rowley was notified accordingly, and

[76] Ibid. 16 May 1941, p. 4; 27 June 1958, p. 1; 4 July 1958, p. 1; E. J. Leighfield, 'Reminiscing' (TS. hist. for 50th anniversary of Lichfield Victoria hosp. 1983; copy in Lichfield Libr.).
[77] Staffs. C.C. Record for 1933, 546; 1934, 12; Lichfield Mercury, 20 July 1934, p. 6; 30 Sept. 1938, p. 6; 17 Mar. 1939, p. 5.
[78] E. J. Leighfield, 'St. Michael's Hosp., Lichfield' (TS. hist. c. 1978; copy in Lichfield Libr.); City of Lichfield, Ann. Rep. of M.O.H. for 1948 (copy in S.R.O., C/H/1/2/2/24); Lichfield Mercury, 21 Sept. 1984, p. 10.
[79] Staffs. Advertiser, 8 Sept. 1888, p. 5; 29 Dec. 1888, p. 6; 10 Jan. 1891, p. 5; Lichfield Mercury, 25 Apr. 1899, p. 6; Lichfield Urban Sanitary Dist. Rep. of M.O.H. for 1891, 7 (copy in S.R.O., C/H/1/2/1/2); Lichfield U.D.C. Ann. Rep. of M.O.H. for 1898, 8 (copy ibid. C/H/1/2/1/9); 1904, 6 (copy ibid. C/H/1/2/1/18); 1910, 6 (copy ibid. C/H/1/2/1/30); O.S. Map 6", Staffs. LII. NE. (1887, 1902, 1924 edns.).
[80] Lichfield Mercury, 7 Mar. 1941, p. 7; Lichfield R.D.C. Ann. Rep. of M.O.H. for 1947, 9–10; 1949, 8 (copies in

S.R.O., C/H/1/2/2/25).
[81] L.J.R.O., D. 127/council min. bk. 1888–91, p. 38; 1891–4, p. 191.
[82] Lichfield R.D.C. Ann. Rep. of M.O.H. for 1927, 18; 1934, 4; 1935, 8 (copies in S.R.O., C/H/1/2/2/25).
[83] Ibid. 1948, 6; Lichfield Mercury, 24 Sept. 1963, p. 1; inf. from Mr. W. J. Wilson, tutor warden at Stowe House (1986).
[84] L.J.R.O., D. 25/1/1, ff. 98 sqq.; D. 25/1/2, ff. 7–137 passim; D. 25/3/3; D. 27/1/4, burial of 22 June 1799; W. Ll. Parry-Jones, Trade in Lunacy, 124.
[85] Aris's Birmingham Gaz. 9 Oct. 1797; Univ. Brit. Dir. ii (1793), 382; Staffs. Advertiser, 19 Nov. 1808.
[86] L.J.R.O., D. 25/1/2, f. 183; D. 25/3/3; Parson and Bradshaw, Staffs. Dir. (1818), 178.
[87] White, Dir. Staffs. (1834), 96, 160; L.J.R.O., D. 25/3/3, rep. of 1820; S.R.O., D. 615/M/3/5.
[88] L.J.R.O., D. 20/6/9, ff. 4, 28; D. 25/3/3.
[89] White, Dir. Staffs. (1851), 508; L.J.R.O., D. 20/6/10, 19 Apr. 1836; D. 25/3/3.
[90] P.R.O., HO 107/1008.

he sold the asylum. The reception of paupers then ceased and the worst buildings were abandoned. Even so, subsequent inspections revealed fluctuating standards. By 1854 the asylum was owned and run by Dr. H. Lynch with two classes of patient, the first class being charged £80 a year and upwards and the second £50. There were 11 private patients in 1855; there were also 13 paupers, again occupying outside buildings, and the inspectors recommended that they should be brought into the house. On further visits in December they found the place so dirty, cold, and neglected that in 1856 the lunacy commissioners urged the withdrawal of the licence and the asylum duly closed.[91] The house, known as Sandfields Lodge, dates from the 18th century, with additions of the early 19th century, but part is incorporated in the adjoining Sandfields House, dating from c. 1860.[92]

Hawthorn House in Burton Old Road, in the late 1980s a home for 60 mentally handicapped adults, was opened in 1968. It consists of two houses, Hawthorn House and the Hollies, the second of which was originally for children.[93]

Sir John Floyer, who practised as a physician in Lichfield from 1676, and the Conduit Lands trustees, of whom Floyer was one, promoted a chalybeate spring at Stowe north-west of St. Chad's Well. From 1695 the trustees paid for work at the spring and its approach, and they paid 10s. rent for it from 1698.[94] There was mention in 1717 of people resorting to Stowe 'to drink the waters and other diversion there to take'.[95] In 1725 the trustees built a brick 'cover or little house over the spaw well at Stowe'.[96] After Sir John's death in 1734 the spring's popularity declined, although the trustees were still paying the rent in the early 1760s. By the 1780s the spring again enjoyed a temporary popularity.[97] An attempt was made to promote it in the early 19th century. In 1818 its water was analysed and declared similar to that of Tunbridge Wells. The claim was repeated in 1824 by William Simpson of Stowe, who advertised the spring as open from 7 a.m. until 2 p.m. daily.[98] The brick structure survived until 1968, though latterly as a tool shed, and it was then demolished and the site built over.[99]

BATHS. As part of his general promotion of cold bathing Sir John Floyer built a bath at Unett's Well at Abnalls in Burntwood. The Conduit Lands trustees gave £10 towards the cost in 1700, and in 1701 Sir John took a 99-year lease of the site from the lord of Pipe. He agreed to spend £30 on building a bath house with two baths to be called St. Chad's Bath. There was to be a keeper supported by gratuities.[1] The two baths were in use by midsummer, the upper being for women and the lower for men. They were separated by a wall, and each had a changing room attached.[2] In 1703 Sir John assigned the lease to the Conduit Lands trustees but retained the appointment of the keeper, who was to pay the trustees 5s. a year to cover the rent. Sir John stipulated that the poor of the city and the Close were to be admitted free and that the other inhabitants were to pay. The trustees were still paying the rent in the early 1760s.[3] Only one bath house remained in 1770.[4] In 1780 the lord of Pipe let it to Erasmus Darwin, and he incorporated it in the botanic garden which he had laid out at Abnalls. It was restored in 1889-90 by A. O. Worthington of nearby Maple Hayes and survived in the later 1980s.[5]

About the mid 1780s James Falconer, prebendary of Ufton Decani and a resident of the Close, built two cold baths near Parchment House north of Stowe Pool. He may have been influenced by his nephew, Dr. William Falconer of Bath, who was an authority on cold-water cures. The baths still existed in 1826.[6]

In 1824 a group including Stephen Simpson, the town clerk, tried unsuccessfully to establish hot, cold, and vapour baths in the city, to be supported by subscription.[7] The Conduit Lands trustees, urged on by the council, had plans for building baths from 1844,[8] and in 1880 they gave permission for the cooling pond at their waterworks off Walsall Road to be used as a public bathing place.[9] In 1885 Bishop C. J. Abraham, precentor of the cathedral, being anxious that the choristers should learn to swim, put a proposal for a public swimming bath to the Conduit Lands trustees. They agreed to provide a site, and in 1886 Abraham formed a committee, which raised £200 from the dean and chapter, Abraham himself, Bishop Selwyn's widow,

[91] *Further Rep. Com. Lunacy*, H.C. 858, pp. 103–4, 315 (1847–8), xxxii; *10th Rep. Com. Lunacy*, H.C. 258, pp. 22–3, 34 (1856), xviii; *11th Rep. Com. Lunacy*, H.C. 157, p. 44 (1857 Sess. 2), xvi; *Staffs. Advertiser*, 28 Oct. 1854, p. 1; L.J.R.O., B/A/15/Lichfield, St. Michael, no. 516; P.R.O., HO 107/2014 (2). Mr. L. Smith of Moseley, Birmingham, is thanked for his help with references to the commissioners' reports.
[92] S.R.O., Mf. 121, nos. 193–5; *Staffs. Advertiser*, 22 Mar. 1862, p. 8. Mrs. E. Holdcroft and Miss C. Holdcroft of Sandfields Lodge are thanked for their help.
[93] Inf. from Staffs. C.C. Social Services Dept.
[94] L.J.R.O., D. 126/acct. bk. 1663–1805; above, fig. 4. For Floyer see below, econ. hist. (professions).
[95] L.J.R.O., D. 77/9/63, lease of 18 June 1717.
[96] Ibid. D. 126/acct. bk. 1663–1805, acct. 1724–5 and end pages, 11 Dec. 1724; Bodl. G.A. Staffs. 4°, 8, facing p. 510.
[97] *Gent. Mag.* lv (2), 497; L.J.R.O., D. 126/acct. bk. 1663–1805.
[98] *Lichfield Mercury*, 9 Oct. 1818; 9 Apr. 1824; Stringer, *Lichfield*, 158–9.
[99] Clayton, *Coaching City*, 41.

[1] L.J.R.O., D. 16/2/54; D. 126/acct. bk. 1663–1805, acct. 1699–1700.
[2] Sir J. Floyer, *Hist. of Cold Bathing* (1709), 16–26.
[3] L.J.R.O., D. 16/2/55; D. 126/acct. bk. 1663–1805.
[4] Below, plate 42.
[5] S.R.O., D. 150/1; D. King-Hele, *Doctor of Revolution*, 110; [A. Williams and W. H. Mallett], *Mansions and Country Seats of Staffs. and Warws.* (Lichfield, n.d.), 58; below, Burntwood, growth of settlement.
[6] *T.S.S.A.H.S.* xii. 49–52; *Lichfield Mercury*, 17 Feb. 1826. The building is shown on a map of 1786 but not by J. Snape, *Plan of Lichfield, 1781*.
[7] Clayton, *Cathedral City*, 17–19 (based on L.J.R.O., D 77/23/12).
[8] L.J.R.O., D. 126/min. bk. 1741–1856, pp. 331, 342; min. bk. 1856–95, pp. 120, 366; D. 127/council min. bk. 1866–82, pp. 4, 84, 315; *Lichfield Conduit Lands Trust: Scheme, Dec. 19th, 1871* (Lichfield, 1872), 22–3 (copy in D. 126/min bk. 1856–95); *Lichfield Mercury*, 6 Sept. 1878, supplement (annotated copy in L.J.R.O., D. 77/20/5, between pp. 16 and 17).
[9] L.J.R.O., D. 126/min. bk. 1856–95, pp. 387, 389.

and Mrs. Bridgeman of the Close. The trustees promised £300, and in 1887 they leased a site adjoining the waterworks to the comittee at a nominal rent. Later that year the Victoria Baths, built 'with a view to economy rather than architectural style', were opened as a memorial of Queen Victoria's jubilee.[10] On the expiry of the lease in 1908 the trustees took over the running of the baths, extending them in 1914.[11] In 1928 the water was found to be polluted and the baths were closed.[12] After being refurbished they were reopened in 1933 on lease to the council.[13] The baths continued in use until 1977 when they were replaced by a pool at the Friary Grange sports centre in Eastern Avenue.[14]

HOUSING. In the late 1880s Sophia Lonsdale, daughter of H. G. Lonsdale, vicar of St. Mary's 1830–51, stated that the city's slums were worse than anything which she had seen in London.[15] Old houses in Bakers Lane were condemned as unfit in 1891 and demolished in 1892. The medical officer of health commented in 1891 that there were others not much better in Greenhill and George Lane.[16] A block of houses in Cotton Shop Yard off Lombard Street was condemned in 1897. That year the medical officer of health noted the shortage of small tenements and the consequent overcrowding among the poor.[17] In 1904 the council demolished 14 cottages which it had bought in St. John Street and built 14 new cottages on the site, 'a much needed addition to the dwellings of the working classes in the city', but in 1914 there was still a lack of cheap houses for the poor.[18]

The council built 208 houses under the Housing Act of 1919 and the various Acts of the 1920s and another 168 under the Acts of the 1930s.[19] The Christ Church Gardens estate off Christchurch Lane was completed in 1921 and the Beacon Gardens estate off Beacon Street in 1925.[20] Houses in Hobshole Lane (later Valley Lane) were finished in 1927, and 22 were then being built nearby in Trent Valley Road.[21] The Dovehouse Fields estate west of Upper St. John Street was completed in 1931.[22] The main area of building in the 1930s was in the north-east

part of the city. Houses had already been built in the Dimbles (later Dimbles Hill) in the late 1920s, and work continued there and in Curborough Road, Leyfields, Ponesfield Road, and Stychbrook Gardens.[23] By the outbreak of the Second World War in 1939 the council owned 404 houses, about one in six of the total in the city.[24] The Ministry of Health gave permission for the completion of the 60 houses being built on the Ponesfield estate, provided that priority was given to workers at the R.A.F. station at Fradley in Alrewas.[25] Early in the war overcrowding resulted from the number of evacuees from West Bromwich, Birmingham, and elsewhere, notably London. Most of those from West Bromwich soon returned home, but at the end of 1940 there were 610 evacuees billeted in the city under official arrangements and 1,536 others who had found their own accommodation.[26]

Slum clearance was carried out in 1934, mainly in Wade Street. In 1935 fifty-three houses were demolished or scheduled for demolition, notably in the area between Church Street and Rotten Row, while 114 were condemned in 1937. Sixty-four in Sandford Street and Stowe Street were scheduled for demolition in 1939, and in 1940 the Ministry gave permission for the clearance of the 23 worst. Otherwise clearance was halted by the war.[27]

During the war new sites were bought and laid out in Curborough Road and Stowe Street, and with the end of the war in 1945 work was resumed on the Ponesfield estate and started in Stowe Street. Work also began on 50 prefabricated bungalows in Anglesey Road near the junction of Weston Road with Curborough Road, and the first was occupied in 1946.[28] The St. Michael Road estate between Stowe Street and Church Street was begun that year.[29] The Weston Road estate was in progress by 1947, and the first part of the Cherry Orchard estate was finished in 1951.[30] By June 1950 the council had built 301 houses since the end of the war and a further 87 were in progress; private builders had completed 71, with 19 under construction.[31] The council owned 1,038 dwellings by 1955.[32] Twelve houses in clearance areas

[10] Ibid. D. 77/19/38, deed of 3 May 1887; D. 126/ min. bk. 1856–95, pp. 442, 444–5, 449, 451–2, 460, 469; *Staffs. Advertiser*, 9 July 1887, p. 5; *Lichfield Mercury*, 15 July 1887, p. 5; 8 May 1914, p. 8; *Kelly's Dir. Staffs.* (1888).
[11] *Kelly's Dir. Staffs.* (1908); *Lichfield Mercury*, 8 May 1914, p. 8; L.J.R.O., D. 126/acct. bk. 1901–16, pp. 290, 296, 300, 304, 310, 312, 314.
[12] *Lichfield Mercury*, 14 Sept. 1928, p. 5; 11 Oct. 1929, p. 5; above (water supplies).
[13] *Lichfield Mercury*, 12 May 1933, p. 5; Laithwaite, *Conduit Lands Trust*, 63.
[14] *Lichfield Mercury*, 14 Jan. 1977, p. 10.
[15] *Recollections of Sophia Lonsdale*, ed. V. Martineau, 166.
[16] Lichfield Urban Sanitary Dist. *Rep. of M.O.H. for 1891*, 8 (copy in S.R.O., C/H/1/2/1/2); *1892*, 8 (ibid. C/H/1/2/1/3).
[17] Lichfield U.D.C. *Ann. Rep. of M.O.H. for 1897*, 9–10 (S.R.O., C/H/1/2/1/8); *Lichfield Mercury*, 27 May 1898, p. 8.
[18] Lichfield U.D.C. *Ann. Rep. of M.O.H. for 1895*, 10 (S.R.O., C/H/1/2/1/6); *1896*, 9–10 (ibid. C/H/1/2/1/7); *1902*, 9 (ibid. C/H/1/2/1/14); *1903*, 11 (ibid. C/H/1/2/1/16); *1904*, 8 (ibid. C/H/1/2/1/18); *1913*, 8 (ibid. C/H/1/2/1/36); *Municipal Jnl.* xiv, 20 Jan. 1905.

[19] *Lichfield City Council Yr. Bk.* (1940), 29 (copy in L.J.R.O., D. 33).
[20] Plaques *in situ*.
[21] *Lichfield Mercury*, 16 Sept. 1927, p. 6.
[22] Ibid. 15 May 1931, p. 6; plaque *in situ*.
[23] *Lichfield Mercury*, 10 Feb. 1928, p. 5; 5 Jan. 1934, p. 6; 14 Dec. 1934, p. 8; 4 Jan. 1935, p. 3; 11 Oct. 1935, p. 5; 10 July 1936, p. 6; 11 Feb. 1938, p. 2; *St. Chad's, Lichfield, Par. Mag.* Apr. 1931 (copy in W.S.L.); O.S. Map 6", Staffs. LI. SE. (1938 edn.).
[24] *Lichfield City Council Yr. Bk.* (1940), 29; *Lichfield Mercury*, 8 Feb. 1946, p. 3.
[25] *Lichfield Mercury*, 10 Nov. 1939, p. 5.
[26] Ibid. 3 July 1942, p. 2.
[27] Ibid. 5 Jan. 1934, p. 6; 14 Dec. 1934, p. 8; 4 Jan. 1935, p. 3; 3 Jan. 1936, p. 5; 10 Apr. 1936, p. 5; 8 Jan. 1937, p. 3; 30 Sept. 1938, p. 6; 18 Aug. 1939, p. 5; 3 July 1942, p. 2; W.S.L. 387/37.
[28] *Lichfield Mercury*, 13 Apr. 1945, p. 7; 9 Nov. 1945, p. 5; 8 Feb. 1946, p. 3.
[29] Ibid. 15 Feb. 1946, p. 7; 10 May 1946, p. 2.
[30] Ibid. 13 June 1947, p. 2; S.R.O., CEH/1, 9 May 1951.
[31] *Lichfield Mercury*, 11 Aug. 1950, p. 5.
[32] *Lichfield City Council Yr. Bk.* (1955–6), 30.

were demolished in 1953; in 1959 fifty were demolished.[33]

In 1956, at the request of the Ministry of Housing, the council agreed with Birmingham city council and Staffordshire county council that it would provide 1,200 dwellings for families from Birmingham. The first, a house in Windmill Lane, was occupied in 1957, and 191 dwellings had been built by June 1962. By 1970 the council had let 837 houses, maisonettes, and flats under the agreement, all of them in the north of the city. Work had then begun on a 200-a. site on which 1,400 dwellings were to be built by the council and private builders; some 300 of the council's 700 were intended for Birmingham families.[34] The council's peak year for building was 1966–7, when 440 dwellings were erected, and by 1971 it owned 2,727 dwellings.[35]

The council's 500th dwelling to be built after the war was a four-room flat in a three-storey block in Friday Acre off Dimbles Lane, completed in 1953.[36] Plans for high-rise blocks were in hand by 1956, and the first, a five-storey block in Dimbles Lane, was opened in 1959.[37] By the mid 1980s many of the blocks had become dilapidated, with damp a particular problem. The district council, by then the housing authority, modernized some and sold others.[38] The four eight-story blocks in Hobs Road near the junction of Eastern Avenue and Trent Valley Road, built in 1962 and containing 128 flats, were sold in 1984 to Regalian Properties, which refurbished them, renamed them the Towers, and in 1985 began selling them.[39] Andrews House in Swan Road off Bird Street, an eight-

storey block of 64 flats built in 1965, was sold in 1987 to Coventry Churches Housing Association for conversion into 59 flats for the elderly. The work was completed in 1989.[40] The district council opened the nearby Sandford House, a block of 60 flats for the elderly, in 1987.[41]

Nearfield House in Stafford Road in the north-east corner of the city, which dates from 1911, was opened as an old people's home by the county council in 1951.[42]

POST OFFICES AND TELEPHONE SERVICE. Lichfield was a post town on the route between London and Ireland by the 1570s.[43] There was a local foot post c. 1680; it operated to Cannock in 1698, but that service had been discontinued by 1703.[44] The post office was in Sandford Street in 1779.[45] It occupied the parlour of a house in the same street in 1804, having moved there evidently in 1800.[46] By 1818 it was in Bird Street.[47] It was still there in the earlier 1850s but had moved to Bore Street by 1860.[48] It was transferred in the late 1870s to larger premises on the south side of the same street which had been a girls' boarding school.[49] In 1905 it moved to a new building in Bird Street south of Minster Walk.[50] That was replaced in 1968 by a post office in the Baker's Lane shopping precinct.[51]

The National Telephone Co. opened an exchange in Wade Street in 1897.[52] The exchange in the Friary dates from 1938.[53]

Public gardens, libraries, and museums are treated elsewhere.[54]

ECONOMIC HISTORY

AGRICULTURE. Open fields surrounded the city.[55] On the west Pool field, mentioned in 1298, stretched north-west from Sandford mill pool.[56] An acre at 'Sondflad' in 1315 probably lay to the east on the south side of Lower Sandford Street; a field there was called Burgess

field in the early 16th century and Town field in 1654.[57] Parnel (later Parnells) field, mentioned in 1549, lay north of the street.[58] Further north Shaw field on the south side of Shaw Lane was recorded in 1336[59] and Hungerhill field on rising ground to the west in 1317.[60] Smith field, men-

[33] *Lichfield Mercury*, 19 Nov. 1954, p. 4; City of Lichfield, *Ann. Rep. of M.O.H. for 1959* (copy in S.R.O., C/H/1/2/2/24).
[34] *Lichfield Mercury*, 28 Dec. 1956, p. 7; 12 June 1970, p. 8.
[35] *Lichfield City Council Yr. Bk.* (1966–7), 30; (1967–8), 30; (1971–2), 34.
[36] *Lichfield Mercury*, 17 Apr. 1953, p. 5.
[37] Ibid. 12 Oct. 1956, p. 7; 27 Nov. 1959, p. 1; 11 Dec. 1959, p. 1.
[38] Ibid. 18 Jan. 1985, p. 5; 14 Feb. 1986, p. 8; 28 Aug. 1987, p. 1; 3 Feb. 1989, p. 15.
[39] Ibid. 15 June 1984, p. 1; 17 May 1985, p. 5; 20 Sept. 1985, p. 3; 2 May 1986, pp. 22–3; 15 Aug. 1986, p. 10; *Lichfield City Council Mins. 1963–1964*, 180.
[40] *Lichfield City Council Mins. 1964–1965*, 456; *Lichfield Mercury*, 28 June 1985, p. 1; 8 Nov. 1985, p. 1; 17 Oct. 1986, p. 2; 6 Feb. 1987, p. 1; 8 Jan. 1988, p. 1; 22 Jan. 1988, p. 2; 24 Feb. 1989, p. 7; 14 Apr. 1989, p. 11.
[41] *Lichfield Mercury*, 8 May 1987, p. 6; 1 May 1987, p. 3.
[42] Ibid. 29 June 1951, p. 4; W.S.L., Sale Cat. C/3/19.
[43] Above, communications.
[44] Plot, *Staffs.* 277; W.S.L., M. 912, no. 22.
[45] T. Richardson, Plan of soughs and drains of Lichfield,

1779 (in the possession of Mr. J. Martin of the S. Staffs. Waterworks Co.; copy in L.J.R.O.).
[46] L.J.R.O., D. 77/21/16; Guildhall Libr., London, MS. H 9.4, no. 16.
[47] Parson and Bradshaw, *Staffs. Dir.* (1818), 167.
[48] *P.O. Dir. Staffs.* (1854; 1860).
[49] Ibid. (1876), 163, s.v. Bishop; *Staffs. Advertiser*, 18 Aug. 1877, p. 4; 22 June 1878, p. 4; (S. Staffs. edn.), 25 Aug. 1877, p. 5; O.S. Map 1/500, Staffs. LII. 15. 12 (1884 edn.).
[50] *Lichfield Mercury*, 23 June 1905, p. 5; below, plate 36.
[51] *Lichfield Mercury*, 8 Mar. 1968, p. 1.
[52] *Lichfield Mercury, Special Issue*, Apr. 1972 (bound between issues of 21 and 28 Apr. in Lichfield Libr. set).
[53] Date on building.
[54] Below, social and cultural activities.
[55] Their positions are indicated mostly by the survival of names in an 1806 land survey: L.J.R.O., VC/A/21, CC 17529, plans 7–13.
[56] Ibid. D. 30/VC, B 9; J. Dewhirst, *Map of Lichfield* (1836).
[57] L.J.R.O., D. 30/VC, B 26; D. 30/VC, palimpsest, i, f. 26; W.S.L. 333/30; S.R.O., D. 150/1/2.
[58] *Cal. Pat.* 1549–51, 15.
[59] L.J.R.O., D. 30/VC, B 17.
[60] S.R.O., D. 948/3/30 and 36.

tioned in the late 13th century, lay on the north side of Shaw Lane.[61]

Lincroft field on the west side of Wheel Lane was mentioned in 1305[62] and Sely or Sedy field on the east side of Grange Lane in 1351.[63] Ley or Legh field, mentioned in 1298, lay further east chiefly in the angle of lanes leading to Elmhurst and Curborough.[64] To the south-west on the north side of Gaia Lane lay Gay field, mentioned in the 1320s.[65] There were selions in a field on Stowe Hill in 1383[66] and to the south-east in Wissage field in the later 13th century.[67]

Bolley (later Boley) field, mentioned in the later 13th century, lay south-east of St. Michael's churchyard along Boley Lane and Darnford Lane as far as Ryknild Street.[68] North-east of the field there were selions in the early 16th century at Spearhill in the angle made by Burton Old Road and Ryknild Street.[69] Farthing field south of Darnford Lane on the east side of Ryknild Street was recorded in 1387.[70]

Selions were recorded in 1325 beside the town ditch east of Upper St. John Street in a field called Oxbury,[71] known as Castleditch field by 1550.[72] To the south there was open-field land near Borrowcop Hill by the later 13th century when Burway field was recorded; selions on 'Burweycop' were mentioned in 1444, and an inclosed field there was known as Burway or Borrowcop field in 1719.[73] To the west between Upper St. John Street and Birmingham Road lay South field, recorded in the mid 13th century and known as Dovehouse field by the early 16th century.[74] It presumably stretched as far south as Shortbutts Lane where there was arable called the Shortbutts in 1408.[75] A field on Berry Hill was presumably open when recorded in 1329, there being selions in it in 1463.[76] Longbridge field south-east of Ryknild Street near the London road was recorded in 1352.[77]

Merstal field, so called in the later 13th century but known as Redlake field by the later 1470s, lay between Birmingham Road and Chesterfield Road.[78] Sand field further west in the present Sandfields area existed in 1325.[79] To the north, stretching up to Trunkfield brook, lay Trumpe (later Trunk) field, recorded in 1658.[80]

The open fields were evidently inclosed piecemeal mainly in the 17th and early 18th century. In 1698 the corporation considered reserving some inclosures as grazing land for cattle belonging to the poor, but changed its mind on the matter.[81] Early in 1700 five freeholders and leaseholders headed by Richard Dyott of Freeford, having agreed to inclose their land, gave their tenants-at-will notice to quit that year's fallow on Lady Day. The names of ten tenants were listed, all of them evidently sheepmasters who were especially opposed to inclosure.[82] There was also opposition from a Thomas Shaw, who was presented at the manor court in 1702 for declaring 'that he would be one of the first that should set fire to the rails and stoops about the inclosures in this manor, and that those knaves and fools that set them up ... would go to the devil for it'.[83]

There was open meadow called Trump meadow along Trunkfield brook in 1397.[84] In the early 18th century part of Lammas meadow on the city's western boundary north of the Walsall road was regarded by the poor as yearlong common, although in fact only seasonal rights existed. The meadow covered nearly 14 a. when it was inclosed by Act in 1815; over half of it then belonged to the marquess of Stafford and the rest to the corporation.[85]

Areas of marsh lay close to the town. Waterlogged land around Upper Pool west of Bird Street was known as 'the moggs', a name implying persistent dampness.[86] The place-name is recorded from 1498,[87] but the word was a personal name in the mid 13th century, and in 1344 Nicholas Mogge held Mogges place, a tenement in the Bird Street area.[88] Stowe Moggs, so called in the late 18th century,[89] was an area of marsh west of Stowe Pool. Both moggs were enlarged as land was reclaimed from the pools. Encroachments were recorded in the mid 15th century at the west end of Stowe Pool, and they were still being made there in the earlier 17th century.[90] Swan piece (later Swan Moggs), gained out of Upper Pool on its southern side, was recorded in 1672–3; the land was drained under the terms of a lease of 1800.[91] There was marsh at Culstubbe beyond St. John Street gate in 1298.[92] Marsh in the Sandford Street area in the earlier 14th century may have lain east of Sandford mill pool, where there was marsh in the earlier 19th century.[93]

Areas of barren land on the higher ground

[61] S.H.C. 1924, pp. 318, 350.
[62] S.R.O., D. 661/1/641; D. 948/3/18, 23, and 36.
[63] Ibid. D. 948/3/51; S.R.O. 3764/79.
[64] S.H.C. 1939, 90–3, 98.
[65] S.R.O., D. 948/3/35, 37, and 58.
[66] L.J.R.O., D. 30/VC, B 78.
[67] Ibid. D. 30/XXIV, f. 32; S.R.O., D. 661/1/556.
[68] S.R.O., D. 661/1/561–2; D. 948/3/4; L.J.R.O., D. 30/VC, B 25.
[69] L.J.R.O., D. 30/VC, palimpsest, ii, f. 17v.
[70] Bodl. MS. Ashmole 855, p. 188.
[71] S.R.O. 3764/56; L.J.R.O., D. 30/VC, B 128.
[72] S.R.O., D. 661/2/365; S.R.O. 3005/134.
[73] S.H.C. 1924, p. 208; S.R.O., D. 239/M/2800; D. 661/2/365; D. (W.) 1734/3/2/1, m. 22 (cancelled entry).
[74] S.R.O. 3764/49 and 54; L.J.R.O., D. 30/VC, B 7; D. 30/VC, palimpsest, i, f. 25.
[75] L.J.R.O., D. 30/XXIV, f. 8v.
[76] S.R.O. 3764/58; Bodl. MS. Ashmole 855, p. 194.
[77] L.J.R.O., D. 30/VC, B 38.
[78] S.H.C. 1924, p. 347; Harwood, Lichfield, 327.
[79] S.R.O. 3764/57; Dewhirst, Map of Lichfield.
[80] W.S.L. 334/30; Dewhirst, Map of Lichfield.
[81] L.J.R.O., D. 77/5/1, f. 90.
[82] S.R.O., D. 661/1/82. For the sheepmasters see below (this section).
[83] L.J.R.O., D. 77/6/1, f. 127v.
[84] Ibid. D. 88/hosp. land, plan no. 1, item 39; S.R.O., D. (W.) 1734/2/1/599, m. 37.
[85] L.J.R.O., D. 77/9/33; S.R.O., D. 615/M/3/4; 55 Geo. III, c. 27 (Local and Personal).
[86] Eng. Dialect Dict. ed. J. Wright, iv (1903), 193.
[87] Bodl. MS. Ashmole 864, p. 380. The name was used in 1340 for land at Aldershawe in Wall: H. Sanders, Hist. and Antiquities of Shenstone (1794), 283.
[88] W.S.L. 55/84–5/52; B.L. Add. Ch. 73329.
[89] Above, fig. 4.
[90] L.J.R.O., B/A/21, CC 123984, m. 6; CC 124078, m. 1; ibid. D. 77/9/3.
[91] Ibid. D. 35/bailiffs' accts. 1657–1707, p. 63; D. 77/9/28, 37, and 42.
[92] S.R.O., D. (W.) 1734/J. 2268, f. 1.
[93] Bodl. MS. Ashmole 855, p. 180; Dewhirst, Map of Lichfield.

west and south of the town were known as moors. Pipe moor, which presumably lay near the boundary with Pipehill, was recorded as common pasture in 1298. Encroachments were made on it in the early 14th century, and it is probably the later Pipe green which was private pasture in the 18th century.[94] To the east near the upper reaches of Trunkfield brook lay Halle moor, mentioned in 1283.[95] Wibbilde or Wibbelle moor, recorded c. 1200 and surviving in 1440, lay near Knowle on the city's southern boundary.[96] Hye moor, recorded as pasture in 1298, lay west of the London road near Longbridge brook.[97]

Leamonsley common, an area of common pasture on the city's western boundary, stretched south and east from Leamonsley mill pool to the Walsall road. Marsh common lay south of Shortbutts Lane. Their inclosure was first considered by the corporation in 1793. A meeting to discuss the matter was held in 1814, and in 1815 an Act was passed authorizing their inclosure.[98] Leamonsley common, covering 33 a., was bought by John Atkinson of Maple Hayes in Burntwood. Marsh common, covering 14½ a., was drained at the expense of the inclosure commissioners and offered for sale in 1816, when most of it was bought by the marquess of Stafford.[99] The Act also authorized the inclosure of 4 a. at Femley Pits near the city's southern boundary, and of land where the town bull had traditionally been pastured. Called Bull pieces, that land lay in two parts, 3 a. on the west side of Marsh common and 2 a. on Berry Hill.[1] In 1801 the inhabitants of Greenhill had customary pasture rights in St. Michael's churchyard.[2]

Pipe green on the city's western boundary south of Abnalls Lane was excluded from the Act of 1815 because it was owned by the inhabitants of Beacon Street in trust for the poor of that street. In 1791 the trust made an agreement with John Hartwell, who was about to build a mill at Leamonsley on the southern edge of the green; it assigned him 2 r. to cut a water course which was needed to supply the mill pool but also helped to drain the green. In return Hartwell agreed to pay 10s. a year to the curate of St. Chad's for the distribution of bread to the poor of Beacon Street on Christmas day. A meeting of Beacon Street residents in August 1793 restricted access to the green: it was to be closed between 12 February and 1 May each year, no person was to pasture more than two head of cattle at any time, and for each head a fee of 3s. 6d. was to be taken, half to be used for draining and improving the green and half to be given to the poor. Each Christmas St. Chad's vestry was to appoint an organizing committee comprising a treasurer, an inspector to open and close the green and to control access to it, and three other members. In 1803 John Atkinson, then negotiating the purchase of the Maple Hayes estate, was given right of access across the green to Maple Hayes in return for £2 2s. a year, to be distributed in bread by the curate of St. Chad's to the poor of Beacon Street on Christmas day.[3] The trust still owned the green in the later 1980s, when it covered 26 a.

Inclosed fields called Old Field and New Field bounded by London Road, Cricket Lane, and Tamworth Road were bought by Anthony Dyott of Freeford from Ralph Jarman of Lichfield in 1610. New Field, east of Ryknild Street, was probably cultivated as part of the Dyott estate, while Old Field was let.[4] Crops were occasionally grown in Old Field, as in the 1630s,[5] but because the soil was sandy the land was normally used as a sheepwalk by the tenants of Freeford. Cattle owned by Lichfield townspeople were also pastured there by the common herdsman, as were horses and asses belonging to the poor of the city.[6] The grazing land became popularly known as Oldfield Common, although the Dyotts maintained that they owned it and that no right of common in fact existed.[7] Richard Dyott inclosed 146 a. in the 1690s and in the early 18th century, but left 40 a. uninclosed at the southern end of the field as a gesture to those who had customarily used the land as pasture. His son Richard inclosed a further 29 a. in the later 1720s, making for several years an annual gift of £5 worth of bread for the poor of Lichfield. Later he sent £5 worth of grain to be baked, but in response to criticism of the grain's quality he stopped the gift and refused to allow the common herdsman on his land.[8] The herdsman, however, still grazed the remaining 11 a. of uninclosed land in the mid 18th century. The lord of Swinfen, in Weeford, and his tenants also claimed rights of pasture in Old Field and in 1745 challenged the Dyotts' inclosures there. The challenge was unsuccessful, but Richard Dyott and John Swinfen of Swinfen agreed in 1793 to an exchange which gave Swinfen the uninclosed land in Old Field.[9]

The inclosure of open-field land and the conversion of moorland to arable resulted in the creation of several small farms in the south-west of the city. A 20-a. holding at Knowle was bought by John Burnes in 1660; in the early 18th century Richard Burnes leased an adjoining 37 a. from St. John's hospital, and in 1785 John Burnes bought 35 a. on Harehurst Hill west of the Lichfield–Shenstone road from Phineas Hussey of Little Wyrley.[10] Knowle Farm was built on Ryknild Street in the later 18th century

[94] S.R.O., D. (W.) 1734/J. 2057, mm. 1–2; J. 2268, f. 1; below (this section).
[95] L.J.R.O., D. 30/VC, B 34; W.S.L., H.M. 40/8, deed of 4 Dec. 1728.
[96] L.J.R.O., D. 30/XXIV, f. 16v.; D. 30/VC, B 1 and 92.
[97] S.R.O., D. (W.) 1734/J. 2268, f. 1; L.J.R.O., VC/A/21, CC 17529, plan 7.
[98] L.J.R.O., D. 77/5/2, f. 250; S.R.O., D. 593/K/1/3/2, Jos. Simpson to Jas. Loch, 30 July 1814; D. 615/M/3/4; 55 Geo. III, c. 27 (Local and Personal).
[99] Lichfield Mercury, 29 Sept. and 22 Dec. 1815; S.R.O., D. 593/F/3/12/2/29, receipt of 27 Apr. 1816.

[1] S.R.O., D. 593/K/1/3/4, Wm. Feary to Jas. Loch, 4 Feb. 1816; D. 615/M/3/4.
[2] Below, churches.
[3] L.J.R.O., D. 45.
[4] S.R.O., D. 661/2/112–13, 132, 134.
[5] Ibid. D. 661/2/139.
[6] Ibid. D. 661/2/801; D. 661/2/802, pp. 8, 10. For the herdsman see below (this section).
[7] S.R.O., D. 661/2/801, pp. 2, 7, 47.
[8] Ibid. p. 7; D. 661/2/802, pp. 9–11; L.J.R.O., D. 44/4.
[9] S.R.O., D. 661/2/800; D. 661/2/801, p. 7; D. 661/2/805.
[10] L.J.R.O., D. 15/10/1/26; D. 15/11/14/9; D. 88/hosp. land, plan no. 2.

and was extended in the early 19th century. There was evidently a farmhouse on Berry Hill in 1761; it was replaced by the present Berryhill Farm, a small brick house of the late 18th or early 19th century. In 1851 the attached farm covered 46 a.[11] George Houldcroft, the keeper of the Royal Oak inn (later Sandyway Farm) on the Walsall road, was also a farmer at the time of his death in 1812.[12] He evidently leased nearby land from St. John's hospital and may have built the small brick farmhouse (the original Sandyway Farm) which stands south-east of the former inn. The farm covered 43 a. in 1921. Fosseway Farm to the south-west, built probably in the early 19th century, was also owned by St. John's hospital, and in 1921 the attached farm covered 21 a.[13] Mickle Hills farm to the north-west covered 80 a. in 1800, and the present farmhouse was built about that time.[14] Closer to the city centre were two more farms owned by St. John's hospital in the later 19th century: Trunkfields, which occupied buildings previously used as a water mill, and Maxstock Grange. In 1921 the farms covered respectively 47 a. and 26 a.[15] A large farm had been created by the mid 18th century out of inclosed land in Old Field and New Field on the boundary with Freeford. It was managed as part of the estate of the Dyotts of Freeford.[16]

Wheat, barley, rye, oats, and peas were grown in the later 17th century.[17] The principal crops at the end of the 18th century were wheat, barley, oats, turnips, and clover, giving way to root crops and vegetables with the growth of market gardening from the early 19th century.[18] Land called 'le gylden' (the golden) was recorded in the Castle ditch area in 1550.[19] The name probably indicates the cultivation of saffron, and in 1650 Saffron croft was recorded in the Greenhill area and Saffron garden in Beacon Street.[20] The crop was presumably used as a dye by Lichfield clothworkers.

Cattle belonging to townspeople were grazed under the supervision of the common herdsman, who with his wife was presented at Longdon manor court in 1450 for illegally driving the cattle of 'the community of Lichfield' into Freeford.[21] In the earlier 18th century the herdsman took the cattle out at 6 a.m., having announced his departure by horn, and returned at 5 p.m.; the fields used for grazing were known collectively as the herdsman's walk, and the herdsman was allowed the first three days' grazing after cropping.[22] The herdsman's fee in 1645 was 12d. a quarter for every beast that he tended.[23] As a result of inclosure the only part of the walk to survive in the earlier 18th century was Sand field,[24] and the herdsman was last listed as an officer of Lichfield manor in 1731.[25] It was a custom in the 18th century that he kept a bull 'for the use of the town', grazing it on the land called Bull pieces on the south side of the city. A town bull was still kept in the mid 18th century.[26] There was a swineherd in 1506, probably with similar duties to the herdsman's.[27]

Sheep farming was important by the 16th century. In 1547 the manor court complained that gentlemen kept large flocks of sheep on the town's common land, although they had no grazing rights. The chief offender, with a flock of 280, was John Otley, the bishop's steward. His bad example encouraged others, and Otley was asked to withdraw his flock.[28] The demand for pasture also led some townspeople in the late 16th century to drive their sheep over the city's boundary to Elmhurst and Pipehill.[29] By the mid 17th century sheep were herded in flocks managed by sheepmasters, who owned or leased land on which they grazed their own sheep and, for a fee, sheep belonging to others. The customary stint was five sheep for each acre of fallow held by the sheepowner; masters who needed additional fallow rented it at 4d. an acre. They regularly overstinted, as in 1651 when 10 masters were fined for illegally grazing 1,400 sheep.[30] There was a sheepcot on Berry Hill in 1547, one on Borrowcop Hill in 1553, and one at Deanslade on the boundary with Wall in the earlier 17th century.[31]

Swans were kept by the bishop in the early 14th century, presumably on the pools. A flock of 21 was fed during the winter of 1309–10, and special pens were constructed as nesting areas in 1310.[32] Ownership of the birds passed to the corporation as lord of the manor from 1548. In 1704 the lessee of Swan piece, waste land which had been reclaimed from Upper Pool, was required to allow the swans to make their nests there. The corporation still provided winter food in 1803.[33] There were several dovecots in the Close in the Middle Ages. One stood in the grounds of the bishop's palace in 1298, and another at the west end of the Close in 1315.[34] There was a newly built dovecot near the cathedral in 1327.[35] Other dovecots were presumably indicated by land in Hungerhill field called

[11] Ibid. D. 27/1/4, p. 164; *Staffs. Advertiser*, 23 Aug. 1851, p. 8.
[12] L.J.R.O., P/C/11, Geo. Houldcroft (1812).
[13] Annotated copy of 1921 sale cat. in S.R.O., D. 4363/A/5/14.
[14] L.J.R.O., D. 88/deed of 29 Dec. 1800.
[15] Ibid. deeds of 28 May 1861, 24 June 1921; annotated sale cat. 1921; below (mills).
[16] Below, Freeford, econ. hist.
[17] *S.H.C.* 4th ser. v, pp. 145, 179, 280; S.R.O., D. 603/E/2/67; D. 4566/9, deed of 10 Aug. 1694.
[18] Pitt, *Staffs.* i. 97, 102; below (nurseries).
[19] S.R.O., D. 661/2/365.
[20] Ibid. D. 603/E/2/67; L.J.R.O., D. 30/LIV, f. 88.
[21] S.R.O., D. (W.) 1734/2/1/603, m. 36, Freeford section.
[22] L.J.R.O., D. 77/5/1, f. 5; D. 77/6/4, p. 121; S.R.O., D. 661/2/802, p. 8.
[23] Articles made by Lichfield manor court, 28 Apr. 1645, item 32 (transcr. in L.J.R.O., D. 121, TS. 'The Manor of Lichfield').

[24] S.R.O., D. 661/2/802, p. 24.
[25] L.J.R.O., D. 77/6/4, p. 82.
[26] S.R.O., D. 661/2/802, p. 29.
[27] Ibid. D. (W.) 1734/J. 2057, mm. 1–2, 4–5.
[28] Ibid. D. (W.) 1734/J. 2243.
[29] Ibid. D. (W.) 1734/2/1/612, mm. 61d., 74; D. (W.) 1734/2/1/674, m. 6.
[30] Ibid. D. 661/2/802, p. 8; W.S.L. 331/30, ct. of 22 July 1651; Articles made by Lichfield manor court, 1645, item 10.
[31] S.R.O., D. 661/2/332 and 444; L.J.R.O., D. 30/LIV, f. 62.
[32] Ibid. D. (W.) 1734/J. 2057, mm. 1–2, 4–5.
[33] L.J.R.O., D. 35/bailiffs' accts. 1704–94, e.g. pp. 521, 551, 589; 1794–1835, e.g. pp. 4, 40, 76; D. 77/9/28; D. 77/9/37, deed of 16 May 1704.
[34] S.R.O., D. (W.) 1734/J. 2268, f. 1; L.J.R.O., D. 30/K 2.
[35] Bodl. MS. Ashmole 794, f. 18.

'Duffehowshey' in 1339 and by Dovehouse field, recorded in the early 16th century.[36] There was a goosehouse in Wade Street in 1495.[37] Land on Borrowcop Hill called 'cunnigrey' in the early 16th century suggests the existence at some time of a rabbit warren.[38]

Crops and other produce were grown on 694.7 ha. (1,716 a.) of the 953.8 ha. (2,357 a.) of farming land returned for St. Michael's civil parish in 1984. Barley was the most important grain crop, covering nearly 288 ha., with wheat covering 119.4 ha. Market gardens covered 241.4 ha. No sheep or pigs were returned, but there were 207 head of cattle, mostly dairy cows. Of the 14 farmers and smallholders who made returns, 9 cultivated holdings of 10 ha. or less and only 2 cultivated more than 200 ha.[39]

The Staffordshire Agricultural Society, founded in 1800 with Richard Dyott of Freeford as president, met in Lichfield and its membership was drawn mainly from South Staffordshire. In 1812 it was absorbed into the Staffordshire General Agricultural Society, whose meetings also took place in Lichfield; that society was dissolved c. 1826. The Lichfield (later Lichfield and Midland Counties) Agricultural Society was formed in 1838; it continued to meet until 1953 and was dissolved in 1956.[40] A farmers' club held monthly meetings in Lichfield in the earlier 1840s.[41]

NURSERIES AND MARKET GARDENS.

In 1731 land south-west of St. Michael's church called Cherry Orchard and planted with cherry and other fruit trees was occupied by William Bramall (d. 1759), possibly a commercial gardener.[42] His son John, who was a steward of the Lichfield Friendly Society of Florists and Gardeners in 1769, ran a nursery at Cherry Orchard. He was described as a gardener in 1779, when he advertised his stock of hedging shrubs, fruit trees, grass seed, flowers, and asparagus plants at his nursery; he visited South Staffordshire towns and Birmingham on market days to take orders. In the 1780s he was engaged by the corporation to plant trees on Borrowcop Hill and the island in Stowe Pool.[43] He died in 1807 and was succeeded in business by his son John, who in 1810 had premises in Bore Street. John had left Lichfield by 1819.[44] By the 1830s Cherry Orchard had been converted into plots for market gardens.

In 1800 Thomas Clerk of Market Street advertised the construction of forcing houses and the laying out of lawns, parks, pleasure gardens, and plantations.[45] In 1807 he took a lease of 2½ a. south of Chapel Street off Upper St. John Street for conversion into a nursery. He was still in business in 1826 when he advertised the sale of 30,000 ornamental evergreens, American and other flowering shrubs, and fruit trees. In the 1830s the nursery was run by John Clerk, who was in business as a florist and nurseryman in Market Street in 1850.[46]

Market gardening became important in Lichfield in the early 19th century.[47] Potatoes, asparagus, and gooseberries were grown by Thomas Cartmail in the Castle Ditch area in 1814.[48] Market gardens covered c. 24 a. in the southern part of the city in 1817, and by the 1830s several arable fields had been turned into garden plots, especially on the south and west sides of the city, as well as in Cherry Orchard.[49] In the late 1840s there were c. 1,300 a. of market gardens, of which 550 a. were planted with potatoes, 300 a. with peas, 160 a. with onions, and 150 a. with cabbages, turnips, carrots, broccoli, and other vegetables. As many as 70 market gardeners were listed in 1846, each making journeys out of Lichfield two or three times a week to sell produce in South Staffordshire towns and in Birmingham.[50]

The ready supply of labour was allegedly because the men were content to have summer work only, supporting themselves during the winter with doles from the city's many charities.[51] Children augmented the workforce. In 1810 the rules of a charity school established the previous year were amended to allow for holidays of two weeks for sowing potatoes, two weeks for lifting them, and three weeks for harvesting corn. Holidays for boys at the school in 1833 were a week on each of those occasions, with further time off if requested by parents.[52]

In 1830 the diocesan chancellor, the Revd. J. T. Law, promoted a scheme for letting plots of land on which the poor could grow food, especially potatoes. He himself offered plots at 1s. 6d. a rood and received over 180 applicants. The scheme was inspired by a similar one in Somerset promoted by his father G. H. Law, the bishop of Bath and Wells.[53] In 1835, at Law's instigation, the Lichfield Florist Society established a cottagers' prize to encourage labourers in the cultivation of their gardens. Four prizes ranging from £5 to £1 were to be awarded

[36] S.R.O., D. 661/2/531; above (this section: fields).
[37] Bodl. MS. Ashmole 1521, p. 25 (2nd nos.).
[38] L.J.R.O., D. 88/undated memo. of leases.
[39] M.A.F.F., agric. returns 1984.
[40] V.C.H. Staffs. vi. 94; Dyott's Diary, ed. R. W. Jeffery, i. 335; ii. 302; Lichfield Mercury, 27 Jan. 1956, p. 4.
[41] Staffs. Advertiser, 3 Feb. 1844, p. 1.
[42] S.R.O., D. 4566/S/58, deed of 3 Feb. 1730/1; L.J.R.O., P/C/11, Wm. Bramall (1759); ibid. D. 27/1/4, p. 150; above, fig. 4.
[43] Aris's Birmingham Gaz. 18 Oct. 1779; S.R.O., D. 4566/S/48, deed of 15 Feb. 1802; below, social and cultural activities (walks).
[44] L.J.R.O., P/C/11, John Bramall (1809), Ann Bramall (1819); L.J.R.O., D. 27/1/5, burial of 19 Feb. 1807; Aris's Birmingham Gaz. 26 Nov. 1810.
[45] Aris's Birmingham Gaz. 29 Sept. 1800.

[46] L.J.R.O., D. 15/11/14/62; S.R.O., D. (W.) 1851/10/7, no. 301; Lichfield Mercury, 20 Oct. 1826; P.O. Dir. Staffs. (1850).
[47] Lichfield Mercury, 21 June 1816.
[48] S.R.O., D. 593/F/3/12/2/27, receipt of 9 Sept. 1814.
[49] Ibid. D. (W.) 1851/10/7; L.J.R.O., D. 35/St. Michael's par. rate bk. 1817.
[50] Guide to City of Lichfield (1848), 17–18 (copy in W.S.L.); L.J.R.O., D. 15/5/1/8.
[51] Schs. Inquiry Com. [3966–VII], p. 223, H.C. (1867–8), xxviii (7).
[52] S.R.O., D. 4566/99, Frog Lane sch. acct. bk. 1809–81, entry for 10 Apr. 1810; min. bk. 1833–40, entry for 24 Dec. 1833.
[53] J. T. Law, The Poor Man's Garden (1830; copy in W.S.L.); Ann. Rep. Com. Poor Laws, H.C. 44, p. 268A (1834), xxviii (1).

annually to labourers living in the city and earning not more than 18s. a week. The aim was to promote habits of industry in labourers' families and to give their children a knowledge of gardening which would enable them to earn a livelihood. The scheme continued until 1859 when the society decided to abandon it.[54]

Although threatened by foreign competition and improved methods of transport from the 1870s, market gardening in Lichfield remained important.[55] Eleven gardeners were listed in 1880 and 12 in 1900.[56] In 1910 there were market gardens and allotments in several parts of the city, notably in the Birmingham Road area and at Gaia Fields north of Gaia Lane.[57] In 1984 market gardens covered 241.4 ha. (597 a.) of the farming land returned for St. Michael's civil parish. Of that acreage 65.8 ha. produced potatoes, 41.2 ha. cabbages, 35.2 ha. peas, 31.5 ha. cauliflowers, 26.8 ha. parsnips, 16.2 ha. brussels sprouts, and 12.1 ha. lettuces. Fruit grown on 3.8 ha. included strawberries, raspberries, blackcurrants, and gooseberries. A further 5.6 ha. were devoted to nursery trees and plants, and nearly 1.1 ha. to flowers.[58]

MILLS. In 1086 the bishop's manor of Lichfield included two mills held in demesne and a third associated with one of the subinfeudated members of the manor. The first two were probably on the same site as two later mills, one on the outflow from Minster Pool at the north end of Dam Street and the other at Stowe on the outflow from Stowe Pool near St. Chad's church.[59] There was a mill in Lichfield belonging to the bishop in 1183.[60] In 1252 the settlement of a dispute between the bishop and the dean and chapter stipulated that the bakers and brewers in the city who were tenants of the canons and of the martiloge had to use the bishop's mill; others could do so if they wished.[61] In 1298 the bishop's demesne in the city included two mills, one on Minster Pool known as Castle mill in the 14th and 15th centuries, and one at Stowe. They were the most important item in the bishop's income from the town in 1298; their value was then £33 6s. 8d., while in 1308–9 the net profit from them was £39 9s.[62]

In the early 14th century Castle mill ground malt only,[63] and it came to be known as the malt mill.[64] In 1670 it consisted of a corn mill and a malt mill, and it was described as a corn mill in 1696.[65] By 1716 it had been converted into an oil mill.[66] In 1731 the corporation ordered the lease of the malt mill to Joseph Willett, a millwright of Erdington (Warws.), for conversion into a wheat, rye, and malt mill; he was also to turn part of the building into a house.[67] By 1808 the mill had been renamed Union mill.[68] It remained in use as a corn mill but was demolished in 1856 when Minster Pool was turned into a reservoir by the South Staffordshire Waterworks Co.[69]

Stowe mill ground wheat and mixed corn in the early 14th century.[70] In the early 1460s it consisted of two mills under one roof called Stowe mill and Gay mill, and Gay mill was still in operation in 1520.[71] Stowe mill consisted of a wheat mill and two corn mills in 1670 and of three corn mills in 1696 and 1717.[72] In 1737 the corporation ordered the lease of Stowe mills to Thomas Torte of Birmingham for rebuilding as an iron manufactory.[73] The rebuilt mill was advertised for letting in 1745 as a building of three bays with a smithy adjoining. There were three water wheels, 'one entirely new, designed for a tossing hammer and a tilting hammer; and the other two wheels might be used for any other work whatsoever.'[74] The mill was again advertised in 1752 and was then stated to be 'capable of being converted into bolting mills, paper mills, or any branch in the iron way'.[75] In 1753 the corporation entered into an agreement for rebuilding it as a three-storey sack flour mill.[76] In 1785 Stowe mill was a small T-shaped building, which continued in use as a corn mill. It was demolished in 1856 when Stowe Pool was turned into a reservoir by the South Staffordshire Waterworks Co.[77]

Pones mill on Curborough brook at Nether Stowe was held c. 1180 by Gilbert Poun and descended with an attached estate until 1302 when it was granted to Robert of Pipe.[78] It then descended with Pipe manor in Burntwood and was included in the Hercy family's moiety of the manor on John Stanley's death in 1514. In 1565 it passed to Christopher Heveningham, who in 1570 granted it to Simon Biddulph of Lichfield.[79] It remained with the Biddulph family of Elmhurst at least until the mid 18th century:

[54] Lichfield Libr., Florist Soc. min. bk. 1816–92, 3 Dec. 1835, 26 July 1859.
[55] V.C.H. Staffs. vi. 126; Staffs. Advertiser, 23 June 1888, p. 2.
[56] Kelly's Dir. Staffs. (1880; 1900).
[57] S.R.O., D. 3573/Lichfield 1, pp. 17–19; 2, passim.
[58] M.A.F.F., agric. returns 1984.
[59] V.C.H. Staffs. iv. 42; T.S.S.A.H.S. xxvi. 15.
[60] S.H.C. i. 108.
[61] S.H.C. 1924, pp. 172–3.
[62] Above, town govt. (govt. to 1548). For the name Castle mill see T.S.S.A.H.S. xviii. 62–6; S.R.O., D. (W.) 1734/2/1/598, m. 44; D. (W.) 1734/3/2/5.
[63] T.S.S.A.H.S. xviii. 62, 64, 66.
[64] L.J.R.O., B/A/21, CC 124078, m. 1; L.J.R.O., D. 30/XVIII, f. 3.
[65] L.J.R.O., D. 35/bailiffs' accts. 1657–1707, p. 246; D. 77/9/60.
[66] Ibid. D. 77/6/3, f. 112v.; D. 77/9/61.
[67] Ibid. D. 77/5/1, ff. 267v., 269v.
[68] Ibid. D. 35/bailiffs' accts. 1794–1835, p. 112; D. 35/im-

provement com. min. bk. 1806–9, 15 June and 10 Aug. 1807; D. 77/9/62.
[69] Parson and Bradshaw, Staffs. Dir. (1818), 185; White, Dir. Staffs. (1851), 523; Staffs. Advertiser, 8 Nov. 1856, p. 5; above, public services (water supplies). For views of 1798 and 1814 see Bodl. G.A. Staffs. 4°, 8, facing p. 503; Bodl. MS. Top. Staffs. C. 1, f. 68v.
[70] T.S.S.A.H.S. xviii. 62, 64, 66.
[71] S.R.O., D. (W.) 1734/3/2/5 and 7–9; D. (W.) 1734/J. 1948, m. [6]; W.S.L., S. MS. 335 (i), m. 7.
[72] L.J.R.O., D. 35/bailiffs' accts. 1657–1707, p. 246; D. 77/9/60 and 63.   [73] Ibid. D. 77/5/2, f. 23v.
[74] Aris's Birmingham Gaz. 29 Apr. 1745.
[75] Ibid. 11 May 1752.
[76] L.J.R.O., D. 77/5/2, ff. 79–80; D. 77/9/63.
[77] Shaw, Staffs. i. 344; Parson and Bradshaw, Staffs. Dir. (1818), 185; White, Dir. Staffs. (1851), 523; Staffs. Advertiser, 8 Nov. 1856, p. 5; below, plate 56.
[78] Above, manor (lay estates).
[79] W.S.L., S. MS. 326/2, m. 4; below, Burntwood, manors.

in 1744 Sir Theophilus Biddulph granted a 21-year lease of the mill to Thomas Gilbert of Darnford mill in Streethay.[80] By 1809 it had been turned into a woollen manufactory.[81]

Sandford mill on Trunkfield brook at Leamonsley existed by 1294.[82] It belonged to St. John's hospital, and in 1339 Bishop Northburgh assigned the 20s. rent from the mill towards the provision of clothing and other necessities for the brethren.[83] A rent of 20s. was still paid in 1535.[84] In 1658 the miller was fined for building a new mill which encroached on the highway, and the manor court ordered him to pull down as much of it as stood on the highway.[85] By the mid 19th century it was known as Trunkfield mill and was still a corn mill.[86] In 1853 it was let to the Conduit Lands trustees, who erected a pumping engine nearby.[87] They converted the mill to steam power and let it in 1857 to James Meacham, who worked it as a bone mill.[88] He gave up the tenancy in 1872, and the mill was disused by 1882.[89] In 1921 the building and the pool were part of Trunkfields farm, owned by St. John's hospital.[90] The pool had been drained by the mid 1930s.[91]

There was a windmill in Gay field in 1343.[92] By 1574 there was one in Stowe Hill field, evidently on the east side of the later Brownsfield Road; it had been pulled down by 1649.[93] Land in Castleditch field was described in 1606 as the site of a former windmill.[94] There was a windmill east of Grange Lane by 1807. Known as Grange mill by 1818, it was converted to steam power in 1857 and continued in use until the earlier 1870s. In 1905 the tower, which is of brick with an embattled parapet, became part of Windmill House, built by Sir Thomas Blomefield, Bt.[95]

There was a horse mill in Bakers Lane in 1611, but it had gone out of use by 1636.[96]

In 1860 Albion flour mill in Stowe Street, described as newly erected, was offered for sale with a house and shop following the bankruptcy of the milling firm of Oldfield & Clarke. In the early 1870s it was run by Stephen Keene and in

1877 by John Benton, who had a bakery attached. It was disused in 1882.[97] The City flour mill in Station Road was built in 1868 by J. C. Richardson, who ran it with an adjoining bakery until c. 1913. The mill remained in operation until 1962 when it became a warehouse. That was closed in 1967, and the building was demolished to make way for a service depot of the Kenning Motor Group. The adjoining house, where an infant welfare centre had been opened in 1917, was made into offices by Kennings.[98]

FISHERIES. The bishop as lord of Lichfield manor had the fishing of the town's pools. In 1298 the fishery was valued at 66s. 8d. a year, with a further 2s. for the fishery of the bays of the pools.[99] There was a keeper of the fishpools by the early 14th century.[1] In 1420 the fishery of Stowe Pool was let for 50s., that of Sandford (later Upper) Pool for 40s., and the fishery of eels in Middle (later Minster) Pool for 20s. In 1521 the three fisheries were let together for 66s. 8d.[2] The bishop evidently reserved the right to take fish for himself: perch, tench, pike, and eels were supplied to Bishop Hales when in Staffordshire in 1461, and in 1501–2 Bishop Arundel employed a fisherman to catch fish which were sent to him in London.[3]

The pools passed to the corporation with the manor in 1548. In 1697 Celia Fiennes remarked that the fishing was good but was the privilege of the magistrates only, by whom she presumably meant the members of the corporation.[4] In the later 17th century the corporation employed a fisherman who caught fish by net from a boat and was responsible for keeping the pools free of weeds.[5] In 1696 the Minster Pool fishery was let for 30s. a year, and in 1701 that of Stowe Pool for £5 and 'a good dish of fish' at each quarter sessions or 6s. 8d.[6] Both fisheries seem to have been let until the later 18th century when the corporation resumed direct control, restocking Minster Pool with carp, tench, and perch in 1765 and in the 1770s.[7] A new boat was bought

[80] S.R.O., D. 661/1/799; D. (W.) 1738/C/5/6; D. (W.) 1851/8/30; L.J.R.O., D. 29/4/1, p. 11.
[81] Below (trades and industries).
[82] S.R.O., D. 661/1/519–20 and 584; Lichfield Libr., Plan of Lichfield, 1766, by John Snape.
[83] V.C.H. Staffs. iii. 280.
[84] Valor Eccl. (Rec. Com.), iii. 141.
[85] W.S.L. 334/30.
[86] L.J.R.O., D. 126/min. bk. 1741–1856, p. 442; P.R.O., HO 107/2014 (2); White, Dir. Staffs. (1851), 523.
[87] Above, public services (water supplies).
[88] Staffs. Advertiser, 21 Feb. 1857, p. 1; L.J.R.O., D. 126/min. bk. 1856–95, p. 18.
[89] P.O. Dir. Staffs. (1860; 1868); O.S. Map 6″, Staffs. LII. SW. (1887 edn.).
[90] Annotated copy of 1921 sale cat. in S.R.O., D. 4363/A/5/14.
[91] Jackson, Hist. Incidents, 111.
[92] Bodl. MS. Ashmole 1527, f. 20v.
[93] W.S.L., S. MS. 326/2, m. 4; L.J.R.O., VC/A/21, CC 164145, i, f. 63; S.R.O., D. (W.) 1851/10/7, no. 1057.
[94] P.R.O., E 178/7203.
[95] Jnl. Staffs. Ind. Arch. Soc. ix (1), 35; W. A. Seaby and A. C. Smith, Windmills in Staffs. (Staffs. County Mus. 1980), 11, 20; Parson and Bradshaw, Staffs. Dir. (1818), 185; H. Asher, Guide to Lichfield (Lichfield, 1892), 29 (copy in W.S.L.); P.O. Dir. Staffs. (1868; 1872); Jackson, Hist. Incidents, 114; L.J.R.O., D. 35/bailiffs' accts. 1794–1835,

p. 108. For Blomefield see Lichfield Mercury, 27 July 1928, p. 3.
[96] Harwood, Lichfield, 384; P.R.O., E 178/7203.
[97] P.O. Dir. Staffs. (1860; 1872); Kelly's Dir. Staffs. (1880); Staffs. Advertiser, 26 May 1860, p. 8; Lichfield Mercury, 9 Nov. 1877; 6 June 1879; O. S. Map 6″, Staffs. LII (1883 edn.).
[98] Lichfield Mercury, 30 Oct. 1914, p. 4; 8 Nov. 1968, p. 11; 15 Nov. 1968, p. 15; P.O. Dir. Staffs. (1868; 1872; 1876); Kelly's Dir. Staffs. (1880 and later edns.); Lomax's Red Bk. (1914), 45; (1915), 47; Lichfield R.D.C. Ann. Rep. of M.O.H. for 1917, 15; 1921, 8 (copies in S.R.O., C/H/1/2/2/25); S.R.O., D. 3573/Lichfield 2, p. 31; above, public services (medical services: orthopaedic clinic); below, plate 31.
[99] S.R.O., D. (W.) 1734/J. 2268, f. 1.
[1] L.J.R.O., D. 30/N 15.
[2] Ches. R.O., DCH/O/8, m. 2; S.R.O., D. (W.) 1734/3/2/10, m. 1.
[3] Medieval Fish, Fisheries, and Fishponds in Eng. ed. M. Aston (B.A.R. Brit. Ser. clxxxii, 1988), 29; B.R.L. 435125.
[4] Journeys of Celia Fiennes, ed. C. Morris (1949), 111.
[5] L.J.R.O., D. 35/bailiffs' accts. 1657–1707, pp. 4, 67, 86, 127, 140, 147, 158.
[6] Ibid. D. 77/5/1, f. 103; D. 77/9/24, deed of 21 July 1696.
[7] Ibid. D. 35/bailiffs' accts. 1704–94, pp. 299, 345, 357, 367.

for 10 guineas, and a boathouse, probably on Minster Pool, was built or repaired in 1769.[8] In 1777 the corporation began the major task of cleaning Stowe Pool, which had become clogged with weeds.[9]

Fishing in both pools was allowed for permit holders from 1778 at a guinea a year, but their number was limited in 1793 to 12; the fee was raised to £5 by 1804.[10] Members of the corporation presumably did not have to pay. In July 1805 they bound themselves not to fish in Minster Pool before Lady Day or allow anyone to fish there after that date unless in their company.[11] The Stowe Pool fishery was again let from 1810. A three-year lease in 1842 restricted the lessee to fishing with bait only.[12] In 1855 both Minster Pool and Stowe Pool were let to the South Staffordshire Waterworks Co. and were subsequently used as reservoirs until 1970, when they passed back to the city.[13] In the later 1980s fishing in Stowe Pool was permitted by licence from Lichfield district council, and Minster Pool was then used for stocking purposes.[14]

In 1298 St. John's hospital owned a fishery in the pool of Sandford mill.[15]

MARKETS AND FAIRS. In 1153 King Stephen granted the bishop a Sunday market at Lichfield.[16] The vill was fined in 1203 for changing the day to Friday,[17] and by 1293 the market day was Wednesday.[18] There was a market on Saturday as well as Wednesday by the early 17th century, but the charter of 1622 replaced them by markets on Tuesday and Friday.[19] By the earlier 18th century hawkers were setting up stalls on waste ground south of Minster Pool to avoid market tolls.[20] Toll on corn, however, was abolished in 1741 as a result of a gift from one of the city's M.P.s.[21] The Friday market was the principal market in the 1780s,[22] and the Tuesday market lapsed in the 1840s.[23] The Friday market too declined in the later 19th century because of competition both inside and outside the city.[24] It was, however, still held in the late 1980s, along with a Saturday market which was

started in the mid 20th century, later discontinued, and revived in 1978.[25] A Monday market was started in 1957 but ceased later in the year for lack of support.[26] In the 1980s a market was also held in Market Street during the Greenhill Bower festivities.[27] The city council then remained responsible for the markets but paid the district council to run them.[28]

The market has long been held in the area on the north side of St. Mary's church. Originally the whole area round the church formed the market place, but encroachment had taken place on the south side by c. 1500.[29] In the later Middle Ages different parts of the market place were used for particular commodities. Cloth Cheaping, mentioned from 1312, lay on the south side, probably being the Wool Cheaping of 1330.[30] Women's Cheaping, mentioned in 1388, was becoming known as Breadmarket Street by the late 17th century.[31] The salt market was on the north side at the beginning of the 15th century,[32] and Butcher Row had become the name of the stretch of Conduit Street on the east side by the mid 16th century.[33] In the earlier 19th century a pot market was held in the space beyond the east end of St. Mary's.[34] In the 1780s, to avoid friction between local people and dealers buying for resale elsewhere, the markets were opened at 11 a.m. but outsiders were not allowed to buy before noon.[35]

A market cross stood north of St. Mary's in the late Middle Ages.[36] Dean Denton, 1522–33, surrounded it with eight arches and roofed it, making a structure 'for poor market folks to stand dry in'. The building was topped with eight statues of apostles, two brass crucifixes on the east and west sides, and a bell.[37] It was destroyed by the parliamentarians in 1643, and a market house was built in the 1650s. Part at least of the cost was met with £41 10s. 'British money' collected at Lichfield in the mid 1640s. Though intended for the relief of the army in Ireland, the money remained in the hands of the collectors, who in 1652 gave it to the corporation towards the erection of a market house.[38] The building evidently consisted of an upper storey

[8] Ibid. pp. 307, 325, 371.
[9] Ibid. pp. 395, 399, 405.
[10] Ibid. pp. 398, 406, 588; 1794–1835, p. 77; ibid. D. 77/5/2, f. 250.
[11] Ibid. D. 77/5/3, f. 25v.
[12] Ibid. D. 77/9/54; Aris's Birmingham Gaz. 29 Oct. 1810.
[13] Above, public services (water supplies).
[14] e.g. Lichfield Mercury, 25 Sept. 1987, p. 56; 16 Oct. 1987, p. 7.
[15] L.J.R.O., D. 30/VC, B 9.
[16] Reg. Regum Anglo-Norm. iii, no. 456.
[17] S.H.C. iii (1), 93, 101.
[18] Plac. de Quo Warr. (Rec. Com.), 711.
[19] L.J.R.O., D. 77/2/1, ff. 57–8.
[20] [J. Rawson], Inquiry into Hist. and Influence of the Lichfield Waters (Lichfield and London, 1840), 12 (copy in W.S.L.).
[21] Above, town govt. (govt. from 1548).
[22] Above, fig. 4.
[23] Pigot, Nat. Com. Dir. (1841), Staffs. p. 27; Wesley, Dir. Burton (1844), 27; P.O. Dir. Staffs. (1850); White, Dir. Staffs. (1851), 484; Rep. Com. Mkt. Rights and Tolls (C. 6268-II), p. 94, H.C. (1890–1), xxxviii.
[24] Rep. Com. Mkt. Rights, 92–5; below (cattle markets).
[25] Lichfield Handbook (1951), 48; S.H.C. 1950–1, 210; Lichfield Mercury, 9 June 1978, pp. 1, 15; 2 Nov. 1979, p. 13.

[26] Lichfield Mercury, 12 July 1957, p. 2; 15 Nov. 1957, p. 2.
[27] Lichfield Dist. Official Guide [1982], 93.
[28] Lichfield Mercury, 22 Feb. 1985, p. 2.
[29] Above, street names (Chapel Lane).
[30] L.J.R.O., D. 30/VC, B 29, deeds of 10 Apr. 1312 and 25 Feb. 1329/30; D. 30/VC, palimpsest, i, f. 36v.; D. 30/XXIV, f. 36v.
[31] Above, street names.
[32] Bodl. MS. Ashmole 1527, ff. 20v.–21; L.J.R.O., D. 30/C.A. i, f. 60v.
[33] Above, street names. For what may be a reference to a shambles see L.J.R.O., D. 30/VC, B 122, deed of 21 Dec. 1343.
[34] Stringer, Lichfield, 146; J. Rawson, Public Bank for Savings and Public Improvement of Lichfield (Lichfield, 1849), 35 (copy in W.S.L.); Bodl. MS. Top. Staffs. C. 1, f. 93; L.J.R.O., B/A/15/Lichfield, St. Mary.
[35] Agrarian Hist. of Eng. and Wales, vi, ed. G. E. Mingay, 197.
[36] L.J.R.O., D. 30/VC, palimpsest, i, f. 27.
[37] Leland, Itin. ed. Toulmin Smith, ii. 100; B.L. Harl. MS. 2043, f. 24 (transcribed in Shaw, Staffs. i. 323); Harwood, Lichfield, pl. facing p. 453.
[38] Harwood, Lichfield, 454–5; S.H.C. 4th ser. i, p. xl; L.J.R.O., D. 35/bailiffs' accts. 1657–1707, p. 5; above, general hist. (Civil War).

on an open arcade: in 1668 the Conduit Lands trustees' expenditure on repairs to it included payment for 15 piers and 4 windows, and in 1701 the corporation made a lease of rooms 'over the market cross'. There was also a market bell on the building: a renewal of the lease in 1716 reserved to the corporation the right to ring it.[39] The market house was rebuilt at the trustees' expense in the early 1730s. The new building was single-storeyed with two arched openings on each of its four sides.[40] A market bell was provided by the corporation in 1756–7.[41] The market house was again taken down in 1789,[42] and in the earlier 1790s the Roundabout House to the east and the former fire engine house adjoining it were also demolished.[43] A subscription for a new market house was opened in the mid 1790s, with the corporation contributing £10, the marquess of Stafford £50, and the Conduit Lands trustees £100. The new building, completed in 1797, stood on the site of the Roundabout House and was designed apparently by a Mr. Statham; it was a stone building with arched openings and was surmounted by a balustrade.[44] The market place was enlarged in 1835 by the demolition of a range of houses in the north-east corner; the corporation paid £200 towards the cost, and the Conduit Lands trustees contributed £550 to a public subscription.[45] In 1848 it was decided to build a combined market hall and corn exchange,[46] and the market house was pulled down in 1849.[47]

The Corn Exchange, a two-storeyed brick building in Conduit Street designed in a Tudor style by Johnson & Son of St. John Street, was erected by a company formed for the purpose and was opened in 1850. The arcaded ground floor was a market hall, and the upper floor, with an octagonal north end, housed the corn exchange; a savings bank in the same style was built at the Bore Street end of the building. The market hall was let to the corporation and was used as a butter and poultry market; doors and glazing had been added by 1889. The upper floor was also used as an assembly hall.[48] The whole building was bought by the corporation in 1902. The ground floor continued as a market hall, and the upper floor, after being occupied by the War Office from 1916, became the Lichfield City Institute in 1920.[49] In the mid 1970s shops were built on the ground floor and the upper floor was converted into a restaurant.[50]

The 1622 charter authorized the sale of cattle, sheep, horses, poultry, and pigs at the markets.[51] A livestock market was held in 1669–70, and in 1674 John Lambe paid the corporation 3s. 4d. for the swine market in Tamworth Street.[52] In the late 18th century cattle, sheep, and pigs from the area around Lichfield were occasionally offered for sale at the Friday market.[53] A sheep and cattle auction on ground opposite St. Michael's church was advertised in 1811; Greenhill may in fact have been used for a livestock market much earlier.[54] In 1824 there was a move among the local graziers, farmers, and butchers for the establishment of a weekly or fortnightly market at Greenhill dealing in cattle, sheep, and pigs.[55] In September 1838 the corporation agreed to hold a cattle and sheep market on the first Monday of each month; the sheep were to be sold in the market place and the cattle in Bore Street and the other streets used during the fairs.[56] The market was being held by August 1839 when it was described as new and thinly attended.[57] It was moved to Greenhill under a council order of 1844 and was still being held on the north side of Church Street in 1864.[58] In 1870 Winterton & Beale owned a smithfield there, described as new, with sales on the first and third Mondays of the month.[59] Another smithfield on ground north of the Swan hotel had lapsed before August 1869 when it was reopened for a monthly market by a Mr. Gillard, possibly the Charles Gillard who was a Lichfield auctioneer in 1841 and 1851.[60] By 1875 sales were held every alternate Monday at both smithfields and were by auction.[61] A new smithfield was built at the Swan by Public (later Lichfield) Cattle Sales Co. formed in 1876,[62] and in 1883 Thomas Winterton began building

[39] L.J.R.O., D. 77/9/23; D. 126/acct. bk. 1663–1805, payments 12 Aug.–27 Nov. 1668.
[40] L.J.R.O., D. 126/acct. bk. 1663–1805, accts. 1731–2, 1733–4, and reverse pages, 14 Dec. 1732, 15 Dec. 1733; Bodl. G.A. Staffs. 4°, 8, facing p. 455; Shaw, *Staffs.* i. 323; below, fig. 16.
[41] L.J.R.O., D. 35/bailiffs' accts. 1704–94, pp. 223, 237.
[42] Ibid. pp. 532, 534, 537, 541, 547; D. 77/5/2, f. 219v.
[43] Ibid. D. 16/2/56; D. 35/bailiffs' accts. 1704–94, pp. 589, 592, 596; D. 77/5/2, f. 248; Bodl. G.A. Staffs. 4°, 8, facing p. 455; Stringer, *Lichfield*, 138.
[44] L.J.R.O., D. 35/bailiffs' accts. 1704–94, pp. 595–6; 1794–1835, pp. 10, 22; D. 77/5/2, f. 250; S.R.O., D. 593/F/3/12/2/9, receipt of 6 May 1796; L.J.R.O., D. 126/min. bk. 1741–1856, pp. 133, 138, 140; acct. bk. 1663–1805, acct. 1797–8; W.S.L., Staffs. Views, v. 174; Stringer, *Lichfield*, 138.
[45] L.J.R.O., D. 35/bailiffs' accts. 1794–1835, p. 396; D. 35/improvement com. min. bk. 1828–35, 23 Mar. 1835; D. 77/5/3, ff. 238–9; D. 126/min. bk. 1741–1856, pp. 280, 293; acct. bk. 1805–85, accts. 1835, 1838; Bodl. MS. Top. Staffs. C. 1, f. 93; Rawson, *Public Bank for Savings*, 15–18; J. Dewhirst, *Map of Lichfield* (1836).
[46] *Staffs. Advertiser*, 12 Feb. 1848, p. 4.
[47] White, *Dir. Staffs.* (1851), 485.
[48] *Staffs. Advertiser*, 19 Jan. 1850, p. 7; White, *Dir. Staffs.* (1851), 485; P.O. Dir. Staffs. (1860); Clayton, *Cathedral City*, 71–2; *Rep. Com. Mkt. Rights*, 93; L.J.R.O., D.

77/15/4, p. 105; below, plate 28.
[49] L.J.R.O., D. 127/council min. bk. 1899–1902, p. 274; *Lichfield Mercury*, 1 Oct. 1920, p. 8.
[50] *Lichfield Mercury*, 30 Nov. 1973, p. 7; 24 June 1977, p. 7.
[51] L.J.R.O., D. 77/2/1, pp. 57–8.
[52] Ibid. D. 35/bailiffs' accts. 1657–1707, pp. 51, 234.
[53] Shaw, *Staffs.* i. 323; Pitt, *Staffs.* i. 102.
[54] *Staffs. Advertiser*, 2 Feb. 1811; *T.S.S.A.H.S.* xxii. 111. It was evidently used for the Whitsun fair in the 15th century: below.
[55] *Lichfield Mercury*, 14 May 1824.
[56] L.J.R.O., D. 77/5/4, f. 94v.
[57] *Dyott's Diary*, ed. R. W. Jeffery, ii. 298.
[58] *Staffs. Advertiser*, 23 Jan. 1844, p. 1; *Guide to City of Lichfield* (1848), 44 (copy in W.S.L.); L.J.R.O., D. 77/14/3, memo. 1900; St. Michael's Church Lands records (at Hinckley, Birch & Exham, solicitors of Lichfield), min. bk. 1836–1903, pp. 90, 101.
[59] *Harrod & Co.'s Dir. Staffs.* (1870), 916, 921; *Rep. Com. Mkt. Rights*, 95; O.S. Map 1/500, Staffs. LII. 15. 8 and 9 (1884 edn.).
[60] *Staffs. Advertiser*, 14 Aug. 1869, p. 7; 4 Sept. 1869, p. 4; below (trades and industries).
[61] *Eggington's Lichfield Almanack* (1875); P.O. Dir. Staffs. (1876); *Eggington & Brown's Yr. Bk. for Lichfield* (1879), 85.
[62] *Staffs. Advertiser*, 26 Aug. 1876, p. 2; 16 June 1877, p. 7; *Kelly's Dir. Staffs.* (1880).

a covered market in Church Street.[63] There was a street market for horses once a month by 1879, and it was evidently still held in 1889. By then the smithfields were selling cheese, poultry, bacon, and potatoes, to the detriment of the general Friday market.[64] An annual wool sale was started at the Greenhill smithfield in 1884 with some 4,000 fleeces advertised, and by 1892 some 32,000 were pitched there.[65] The Swan smithfield was closed c. 1906.[66] In 1927 the Church Street smithfield dealt in cattle, sheep, pigs, wool, and potatoes on alternate Mondays and in horses on the first Friday of the month.[67] A livestock market was held there every Monday from 1935.[68] In 1988 Wintertons moved the smithfield to their new Lichfield Auction Centre at Fradley in Alrewas. The Church Street site was then cleared to make way for new commercial development.[69]

In 1293 the bishop claimed a fair at Lichfield on the Tuesday, Wednesday, and Thursday of Whit week by immemorial right.[70] A fair was held in 1305, presumably at that time.[71] In 1307 the king granted the bishop a fair at Lichfield on Whit Monday and the 14 days following and another on the morrow of All Saints and the seven days following (2–9 November).[72] In 1337 a third fair was granted on the eve and feast of the Exaltation of the Cross (13 and 14 September) and the two days following.[73] There was a fair on Ash Wednesday by 1409, with an accompanying court of pie powder by 1464.[74] By the early 15th century the Whitsun fair was evidently held at Greenhill.[75] It seems that by 1622 only the Ash Wednesday fair survived, and the charter of that year stated that by ancient custom it began on Shrove Tuesday and continued until the following Friday.[76]

By the early 16th century a toll of 4d. was charged on every cart carrying merchandise to or from 'the fair', probably the Ash Wednesday fair, and 3d. on every horse; 'any worshipful man's household stuff' was to be free. Tolls on salmon, herrings, eels, salt fish, stockfish, oil, and honey were taken in kind. The Lichfield smiths paid little, and pewterers and cooks were also favoured. Mercers, grocers, and artificers from Coventry were charged simply 'a franchise penny' when they traded from shops and not from stalls in the streets. It was customary for the smiths to set up their stalls by the market cross, along with pedlars and hardware men; the salmon stalls were by the conduit. The tolls were confirmed by agreement between the bishop and townsmen c. 1509.[77] A

further agreement in 1531 laid down a more detailed system. The burgesses retained their ancient freedom from tolls. Other inhabitants had to pay ½d. a yard for their booths and stalls at the Ash Wednesday fair but not on other occasions. They also had to pay 2d. for every cartload of goods brought for sale at the Ash Wednesday fair. At that fair outsiders were to be charged 1d. a yard for stalls selling salmon, salt fish, eels, oil, honey, 'and such other victual', and ½d. a yard for those selling wool, onions, garlic, wooden dishes, ropes, horse harness, and things of small value. On other occasions outsiders were to be charged ½d. a yard for any stall. Townsmen who took advantage of their lower rates to sell outside goods were to be charged 2d. a yard. People carrying non-Lichfield goods out of the town for resale were to pay 2d. on every cart and apparently ½d. on every horse. Buyers of horses, oxen, and cows four years old had to pay 1d. a beast and ½d. on younger beasts. The charge for a pig a year old was ¼d. and for a boar 1d. Sheep were toll free, as were carts and horses simply carrying goods through the town.[78]

The tolls give an indication of the commodities traded at the fairs in the earlier 16th century. An earlier indication may be provided by the list of goods chargeable under a grant of pavage and murage made to the bishop in 1299.[79] In 1367 Halesowen abbey (Worcs.) bought 6,000 red herring and two barrels of herring prepared in stock at the Ash Wednesday fair.[80] Salmon was bought at the Ash Wednesday fair of 1453 for the duke of Buckingham.[81] Commodities bought there in the mid 1520s for Sir Henry Willoughby of Wollaton Hall (Notts.) included eels, herring, salmon, mussels, honey, oil, and currants. Fish was bought for him at the Whitsun fair in 1522, and fish, honey, oil, figs, sugar loaves, lemon conserve, and a 'scummer' (a fire shovel or a cooking ladle) at one of the fairs in 1527.[82] A London stock-fish monger complained to Thomas Cromwell in 1532 about the illegal export from Ireland to Lichfield of a quantity of salmon, herring, other fish, oil, and honey.[83]

The 1622 charter confirmed the Ash Wednesday fair and added three others, on 1 May (or if that day was a Sunday, on 2 May) and the day following, on the Friday before the feast of St. Simon and St. Jude (28 October) and the day following, and on the Friday after the Epiphany (6 January).[84] In 1681 the corporation ordered that tanners were not to bring leather up into the

[63] Lichfield Mercury, 14 Aug. 1970, p. 13.
[64] Eggington & Brown's Yr. Bk. for Lichfield (1879), 85; Rep. Com. Mkt. Rights, 94.
[65] Lichfield Mercury, 27 June 1884, p. 5; 3 June 1887, p. 4; 12 May 1893, p. 4.
[66] Lomax's Red Bk. (1906), 87.
[67] Min. of Agric. and Fisheries, Mkts. and Fairs in Eng. and Wales (Pt. II. Midland Mkts.) (1927), 12, 17, 56–8, 138.
[68] Lichfield Mercury, 27 Dec. 1935, p. 1; S.H.C. 1950–1, 206.
[69] Lichfield Mercury, 11 Dec. 1987, pp. 26, 39; 30 Dec. 1988, pp. 20–1; 27 Jan. 1989, pp. 5, 9; above, general hist. (20th cent.).
[70] Plac. de Quo Warr. (Rec. Com.), 711.
[71] S.R.O., D. (W.) 1734/J. 2057, m. 7.

[72] Cal. Chart. R. 1300–26, 78.
[73] Ibid. 1327–41, 424.
[74] Rot. Parl. iii. 631; above, town govt. (govt. to 1548: manorial courts).
[75] Below, social and cultural activities (Greenhill Bower).
[76] L.J.R.O., D. 77/2/1, p. 56; Shaw, Staffs. i. 139.
[77] S.R.O., D. (W.) 1734/J. 2268, f. 33.
[78] Bodl. MS. Ashmole 1521, pp. 153–4.
[79] Below (trades and industries).
[80] Soc. of Antiquaries Libr., London, MS. 535.
[81] Camd. Misc. xxviii (Camd. 4th ser. xxix), 15.
[82] Hist. MSS. Com. 69, Middleton, pp. 340, 342, 351, 373, 380, 387.
[83] N. Staffs. Jnl. of Field Studies, xix. 2; L. & P. Hen. VIII, v, p. 722.
[84] L.J.R.O., D. 77/2/1, pp. 56–7.

guildhall for sale during the fairs, but it permitted them to sell it in the entry under the hall.[85] The Ash Wednesday fair (known as the Old Fair by the late 17th century) and the May fair were held in the market place by the early 18th century, and probably earlier.[86] The Epiphany fair had lapsed by 1735 but may have been revived c. 1790.[87] The autumn fair was called the goose fair by the later 1740s.[88] As a result of the change in the calendar in 1752 the date of the May fair was moved to 12 May and that of the goose fair to the first Friday in November.[89] The goose fair was still held in the late 18th century, but in 1829 it was described, like the Epiphany fair, as 'little more than nominal'.[90]

In 1815 at the instigation of local farmers two fairs were introduced, on the first Monday in July and the first Monday in November.[91] The May fair in 1817 was noted as having a large number of cows, heifers, and horses and a record number of clothiers' stalls.[92] In the mid 1820s the Ash Wednesday fair was dealing in sheep, cattle, horses, cheese, and bacon.[93] In 1838 the corporation agreed to establish a wool fair in the market place and the surrounding streets as part of the July fair. One was held in 1839, but it was not a success and does not appear to have been repeated.[94] The July and November fairs were evidently held at Greenhill in the later 1840s but were discontinued soon afterwards owing to the competition of the monthly cattle markets.[95] In 1852 a fair dealing in cheese, bacon, geese, and onions was started in the market place on the first Monday of October; it was still held in the late 1870s.[96] In December 1863 the corporation ordered that cattle for the Ash Wednesday and May fairs were to be driven to Greenhill and were not to stand in Bore Street, Bird Street, or elsewhere. It also ordered that the Ash Wednesday fair was to be held on Shrove Tuesday only.[97] In 1868 the fair was proclaimed on Shrove Tuesday and held on Ash Wednesday. The cattle fair at Greenhill was average, but the cheese fair was well supplied; there was a pleasure fair in the evening.[98] The May fair evidently lapsed in the late 1870s, although the mayor continued to proclaim it, after giving a breakfast, until 1892.[99]

By the later 1870s the Ash Wednesday fair

was little more than a pleasure fair.[1] Because it disturbed the Ash Wednesday service in St. Mary's, the council changed the day to Shrove Tuesday in 1890.[2] In the late 1980s a fair with a court of pie powder was still proclaimed in the market place by the town crier in the presence of the mayor and a civic party, but only a pleasure fair is held, continuing for the rest of the week. After the proclamation the mayor and the civic party return to the guildhall for simnel cake; the provision of 'simnels and wine' at the Ash Wednesday fair was recorded in 1747.[3]

TRADES AND INDUSTRIES. The Middle Ages. The needs of the cathedral and its clergy may have fostered some of Lichfield's earliest trades. Three vintners trading in 1199 included Samson the vintner, who witnessed a charter of Bishop Muschamp.[4] A later vintner was William the taverner, who was the bishop's bailiff in the town in 1308–9. During his term of office he supervised the purchase and transport of wine from Bristol, Worcester, and Bridgnorth.[5] Two goldsmiths, Hugh and Robert, were recorded in 1203–4, and another two, Godfrey of Stafford and William Young, in the later 13th century.[6] Stephen of Knutton, a goldsmith, may have been living in Lichfield in 1320.[7] In the mid 15th century two goldsmiths were enrolled as members of the guild of St. Mary and St. John the Baptist, and in 1466 a goldsmith held land in Market Street.[8] Master Michael the bellfounder was recorded in the later 13th century. His son, Henry Bellfounder, continued the trade and is presumably identifiable as the Master Henry Michel of Lichfield who in 1313 cast a great bell for Croxden abbey.[9] Two men who were probably bellfounders acquired land in Lichfield in 1332–3, and Richard and Simon Belzetter, recorded respectively in 1372 and 1395–6, may on the evidence of their name have cast bells.[10] Hamon the illuminator held land in Lichfield in 1298, and a painter was admitted to St. Mary's guild in 1416 and another in the 1470s.[11] A clockmaker was recorded in the earlier 1470s.[12] There were parchment makers in the 15th century, and Henry the bookseller was recorded in the early 16th century.[13]

Lichfield's principal trades, however, were

[85] Ibid. D. 77/5/1, f. 6v.
[86] Ibid. D. 20/4/3, 1725–6 sqq.; D. 35/bailiffs' accts. 1704–94, pp. 136, 143; D. 77/5/1, f. 6v.; D. 77/9/23.
[87] Shaw, Staffs. i, table facing p. 1 of introduction; L.J.R.O., D. 35/bailiffs' accts. 1704–94, p. 475; Univ. Brit. Dir. iii (1794), 609; above, fig. 4.
[88] L.J.R.O., D. 35/bailiffs' accts. 1704–94, pp. 175, 286, 292, 313, 475.
[89] Aris's Birmingham Gaz. 23 Oct. 1752; 9 Apr. 1753.
[90] L.J.R.O., D. 35/bailiffs' accts. 1704–94, p. 475; Pigot, Nat. Com. Dir. (1829), 714; above, fig. 4.
[91] Wolverhampton Chron. 21 June and 12 July 1815; Lichfield Mercury, 3 Nov. 1815; White, Dir. Staffs. (1834), 62.
[92] Lichfield Mercury, 16 May 1817.
[93] Ibid. 5 Mar. 1824; 18 Feb. 1825; 10 Feb. 1826; 22 Feb. 1828.
[94] L.J.R.O., D. 77/5/4, f. 94v.; Staffs. Advertiser, 6 July 1839; 4 July 1840.
[95] Wesley, Dir. Burton (1844), 27; Guide to City of Lichfield (1848), 43–4; White, Dir. Staffs. (1851), 484–5.
[96] Staffs. Advertiser, 9 Oct. 1852, p. 8; 8 Oct. 1853, p. 4; 1 Oct. 1861, p. 2; 23 Jan. 1864, p. 1; Eggington & Brown's Yr. Bk. for Lichfield (1879), 85.

[97] L.J.R.O., D. 127/council min. bk. 1853–66, pp. 393–4; Staffs. Advertiser, 23 Jan. 1864, p. 1.
[98] Staffs. Advertiser, 29 Feb. 1868, p. 5.
[99] Eggington & Brown's Yr. Bk. for Lichfield (1879), 85; Lichfield Mercury, 13 May 1892, p. 8.
[1] Lichfield Mercury, 8 Mar. 1878.
[2] Ibid. 15 Sept. 1889, p. 5; 10 Jan. 1890, p. 5; 17 Jan. 1890, p. 4.
[3] L.J.R.O., D. 35/bailiffs' accts. 1704–94, p. 176.
[4] Ibid. D. 30/XXIV, f. 16v.; S.H.C. iii (1), 45.
[5] T.S.S.A.H.S. xviii. 63.
[6] S.H.C. iii (1), 122; S.H.C. 1924, pp. 207, 352.
[7] Ibid. 1911, 92.
[8] L.J.R.O., D. 77/1, pp. 88, 106; S.R.O., D. 948/3/66.
[9] S.H.C. 1924, pp. 252, 346–7; C. Lynam, Abbey of St. Mary, Croxden, Staffs. p. vi.
[10] L.J.R.O., D. 30/VC, B 75 and 111; S.R.O. 3764/69; Bodl. MS. Ashmole 855, p. 184.
[11] Bodl. MS. Ashmole 855, p. 213; L.J.R.O., D. 77/1, pp. 58, 137.
[12] S.H.C. 1928, 211.
[13] Cal. Pat. 1436–41, 84; L.J.R.O., D. 30/VC, palimpsest, i, f. 32; below, guilds (religious guilds).

retailing, the wool trade, and the production of leather goods. A market was granted in 1153, and a fair was held by the late 13th century.[14] The range of commodities which came into the town is probably indicated by a list of goods on which tolls were to be levied under a grant of pavage and murage to the bishop in 1299: they included horses, cattle, pigs, sheep, and goats; corn, meal, onions, garlic, honey, and oil; meat, cheese, butter, and a variety of fish; salt; hides, skins, fleeces, and wool; cloth and silk; web, canvas, and hemp; dyestuffs; tallow; coal; millstones; timber and tan bark; and iron and metal products.[15] There may have been trading links with France in the mid 1260s when a merchant from Amiens, Walter de Spany or Espaigny, was resident in Lichfield.[16] Cloth may have been produced locally as early as the late 12th century when there was a dyer in the town, and another dyer was recorded in 1298, when there was also a fuller holding land in the Sandford area.[17] Merchants came from London in 1305 and 1306 to buy wool, and in 1327 Lichfield wool merchants were ordered to send representatives to York to discuss with the king matters relating to the wool trade.[18] Part of the market place was known as Cloth Cheaping by 1312 and as Wool Cheaping by 1330.[19] At least some of the wool may have come from the Peak District where the dean and chapter had estates: in the late 14th century wool received as tithe was evidently sold in Lichfield, and in 1598 there was a wool house in the Close.[20] There was a shoemakers' quarter (sutoria) in the town in the later 13th century,[21] and tanners were recorded in the late 13th and early 14th century.[22] Saddlers recorded in the later 14th century presumably worked in Saddler (later Market) Street.[23] Among those assessed for the 1380 poll tax[24] were 12 tailors, 11 shoemakers, 2 glovers, 2 weavers, 2 fullers, and 2 skinners; providers of food and drink comprised 8 bakers, 3 butchers, 2 millers, a cook, and a fisherman, and retailers 4 mercers, 2 drapers, a spicer, and a chapman. Cottagers and labourers, however, made up the largest group and indicate Lichfield's close dependance on agriculture.

Glass may have been made on land north of Fosseway which was called Glascroft in 1215.[25] Adam the glazier witnessed a deed relating to land at Leamonsley in the earlier 13th century,[26] and William the glazier, son of John the glazier, was evidently living in the Sandford Street area

in the late 13th century.[27] William was presumably the William 'le verrer' who in 1311–12 supplied or made glass for the great hall of Bishop Langton's new palace in the Close and did work for the bishop at Eccleshall.[28] There was another William the glazier in Lichfield in 1349, whose son John Glaswright was living there in 1395.[29]

Land west of Beacon Street called Soperscroft in 1498 may indicate that soap was made there.[30] In 1506–7 a man was presented in the manor court for polluting Upper Pool in the same area with soap water, presumably a result of soap manufacture.[31] A presentment for pollution with soap water in Bore Street was made in 1522.[32]

Stone used in the early 14th century for the construction of Bishop Langton's palace in the Close came from Freeford, evidently the quarry on the city's south-eastern boundary at Quarryhills Lane, still worked in the early 19th century.[33] Along with other quarries it presumably also provided stone for the cathedral. There was a quarry in Lincroft field between Beacon Street and Wheel Lane by 1356; it was extended that year when Hugh de Norburgh, knight, granted the two wardens of the cathedral fabric adjoining land measuring 60 ft. by 40 ft. The enlarged quarry was evidently that known as the great quarry in 1498. The area was still worked in the mid 17th century.[34] A stonebreaker, William son of Geoffrey, who granted land in Streethay to Hugh the mason in the mid 14th century, may have worked a quarry at Stowe; a quarry there was certainly worked in the mid 1470s and evidently lay in the grounds of the later Stowe Hill House.[35]

There was a tiler in Lichfield in the early 13th century and a tilehouse at Greenhill in the early 16th century.[36] Tiles may have been made at the kiln house in Beacon Street, recorded in 1402.[37] Robert Bird, a brickmaker, was living in Stowe Street in 1466.[38] Brick buildings survive from around the end of the 15th century and include houses in the south-west corner of the Close and the east range of St. John's hospital in St. John Street.

THE 16TH AND 17TH CENTURIES. Men indicted for a disturbance in the town c. 1509 included 19 cappers, 11 tailors, 6 weavers, 4 shearmen, 3 glovers, 2 dyers, a corviser, and a skinner; 3 spurriers, 3 smiths, and 3 cutlers; 4 bakers and

[14] Above (markets).
[15] S.H.C. 1924, pp. 141–2.
[16] Cal. Pat. 1258–66, 431, 518.
[17] S.H.C. iii (1), 114; S.R.O., D. (W.) 1734/J. 2268, f. 4; L.J.R.O., D. 30/XXIV, f. 30v.
[18] S.R.O., D. (W.) 1734/J. 2057, mm. 7–8; Cal. Close, 1327–30, 237.
[19] Above (markets).
[20] V.C.H. Staffs. iii. 155; L.J.R.O., DC/C/1/1, 24 July 1598.   [21] L.J.R.O., D. 30/VC, B 2.
[22] S.R.O., D. 661/1/584; D. 661/2/532; D. 948/3/33; S.H.C. 1939, 93, 97.
[23] B. H. Putnam, Procs. before J.P.s, 276; S.H.C. 1939, 99; Bodl. MS. Ashmole 855, p. 195.
[24] S.H.C. xvii. 161–8, 180–1 (date corrected by S.H.C. 4th ser. vi. 3 n.).
[25] Bodl. MS. Ashmole 1527, f. 35; W.S.L., S. MS. 326/2, m. 6; L.J.R.O., B/A/15/Lichfield, St. Michael, nos. 591–3.
[26] L.J.R.O., D. 30/B 26.

[27] S.R.O. 938/48; S.R.O., D. 661/1/584; D. 661/2/519.
[28] Ibid. D. (W.) 1734/J. 2057, m. 4, 'cost of great hall' and 'livery of pence' sections.
[29] L.J.R.O., D. 30/VC, B 26 and 34.
[30] Bodl. MS. Ashmole 864, p. 380.
[31] S.R.O., D. (W.) 1734/2/1/597, mm. 18, 22d.
[32] Ibid. m. 27d.
[33] L.J.R.O., D. 30/VC, palimpsest, ii, f. 20; Harwood, Lichfield, 561; above, cathedral and close.
[34] L.J.R.O., D. 30/VC, B 134; L.J.R.O., VC/A/21, CC 162145, i, f. 37; Bodl. MS. Ashmole 864, p. 392.
[35] L.J.R.O., B/A/21, CC 123984, m. 6d.; L.J.R.O., VC/A/21, CC 162145, i, f. 56; S.R.O., D. 661/1/649; D. 3309/3.
[36] L.J.R.O., D. 30/VC, palimpsest, i, f. 43v.; S.H.C. iv (1), 54.
[37] S.R.O. 3764/76; L.J.R.O., VC/A/21, CC 162145, i, f. 9.
[38] L.J.R.O., D. 30/XVIII, f. 23v.

4 butchers.[39] Out of the 61 men who between 1548 and 1604 served as bailiff 19 were providers of food and drink (including 8 bakers and 5 innkeepers), 14 were cloth and leather workers (including 6 cappers and 4 tanners), 12 were retailers (of whom 8 were mercers), but only 2 were metal workers (one a goldsmith and the other a pewterer). Of the rest as many as 10 were lawyers.[40] Membership of the city's craft guilds, or companies, also gives some indication of the relative importance of different trades, although the evidence is patchy. There were some 70 tailors in 1634,[41] compared with 27 shoemakers and curriers in 1626[42] and 16 saddlers in 1629;[43] metal workers were especially numerous, with 95 members of the smiths' company in 1648.[44] There are no contemporary figures for the other companies.

Capping in Lichfield suffered as part of a national decline in the later 16th century. A petition to the queen by the Lichfield cappers in 1575 was supported by Lord Paget, and in 1584 the meagreness of the town's contribution to the relief of Nantwich (Ches.) after a fire was blamed on the decay of capping.[45] It seems that in the later 17th century woollen cloth was worked chiefly by feltmakers.[46] Cloth was dyed in Sandford Street, where there was a dyehouse in 1664 owned by Richard Grimley and one in 1679 owned by the Smaldridge family.[47]

A silkweaver lived in Stowe Street in 1632, and Richard Riley had three looms in his shop, possibly at Greenhill, at his death in 1674, one of them for weaving tiffany, a thin, transparent silk.[48] Bone-lace weavers were recorded in Lichfield in 1669, 1678, and 1695.[49] In the mid 1650s the manor court banned the washing of hemp and flax in Leamonsley brook and other watercourses, and a tow or flax dresser was one of the squatters in the Close in 1660.[50] It was presumably locally grown flax that was used in the linen manufactory in operation in Sandford Street between 1691 and 1696.[51]

A tanner, John Blount, who was junior bailiff in 1589–90, and his son George, also a tanner, had land in Sandford Street in 1587.[52] The tanhouse of William Tunckes, who had leather, tanned skins, and bark worth £200 at his death in 1668,[53] was probably in Sandford Street since Thomas Tunckes certainly worked as a tanner there in the early 18th century. Other 17th-century tanners included John Mathew who had hides and calf skins worth £120 in his tanhouse

at his death in 1608, and Francis Chaplain who had leather worth £224 at his death in 1671.[54] The kinds of leather goods manufactured in the 16th and 17th centuries are indicated by the existence of two trade companies, one for shoemakers and curriers and another for saddlers, bridlecutters, horse-collar makers, glovers, whittawers, and makers of breeches.[55]

Michael Johnson, a Lichfield bookseller and father of Samuel, bought skins and hides in various parts of England and in Scotland and Ireland, using the best to make parchment in a manufactory which he established c. 1697. He was evidently still working the manufactory, which stood east of the Close on a site later occupied by Parchment House, in 1725.[56]

Thomas Thacker, who had 350 calf and sheep skins at his death in 1646, was probably a fellmonger. Another Thomas Thacker had over £50 worth of fleeces together with curing equipment at his death in 1659.[57] John Bailey (d. 1682), a fellmonger, was living in Saddler Street in the 1650s. His son John may have continued the trade, and he, Francis Bailey, and another John Bailey were among the sheepmasters who opposed the inclosure of the town's open fields c. 1700.[58]

A goldsmith, Thomas Marshall, was a member of the corporation in 1548.[59] Nicholas Collins and John Gladwin, both members of the London company of goldsmiths, worked in Lichfield in the 1570s. Collins died there in 1589 and was evidently succeeded in his business by George Collins, recorded as a goldsmith in 1596.[60] The smiths' company contained a wide range of craftsmen.[61]

Among the distributive trades mercers included Humphrey Lowe (d. probably 1583), a member of the corporation in 1548, his son John (d. 1588),[62] and Simon Biddulph (d. 1580), a member of the corporation by 1553.[63] The goods in Thomas Deakin's shop at his death in 1660 show him to have been a mercer of moderate wealth; those of a chapman, Michael Riley, were listed in 1671. John Greene, a haberdasher of hats, was recorded in 1666.[64] John Burnes (d. 1600) and his son Thomas (d. 1610) were upholsterers. The upholsterer named John Burnes who bought a share of the Aldershawe estate in Wall in 1621 was probably Thomas's son.[65]

An apothecary named George Curitwell (or Curitall) was bailiff in 1594–5, 1599–1600, and 1609–10.[66] John Parker had an apothecary's

[39] P.R.O., SP 1/231, f. 100.
[40] Harwood, *Lichfield*, 419–23; below (professions).
[41] L.J.R.O., D. 77/4/7/1, f. 45v.
[42] Chetham's Libr., Manchester, Mun. A. 6.56A, f. 2.
[43] L.J.R.O., D. 77/4/5/2, f. 4.
[44] Ibid. D. 77/4/6/1, ff. 97v., 99.
[45] Hist. MSS. Com. 9, *Salisbury*, ii, p. 116; *Cal. Pat.* 1575–8, p. 9; *Acts of P.C.* 1575–7, 36; P.R.O., SP 12/270, ff. 169–70.
[46] W.S.L. 281/30; B.R.L., Elford Hall MSS. nos. 348, 366; S.R.O., D. 603/E/2/74; D. 615/D/246, deed of 23 Mar. 1659/60; *S.H.C.* 4th ser. v, p. 248.
[47] L.J.R.O., D. 29/3/1, entry for 1664 levy; *S.H.C.* 4th ser. v, pp. 282–3.
[48] S.R.O., D. 661/1/799, pp. 1–2; *S.H.C.* 4th ser. v, pp. 232–3.
[49] W.S.L. 283/30; L.J.R.O., D. 30/8/14 and 16; S.R.O., D. 4045/8/7/2.
[50] W.S.L. 330/30; 348/30; *T.S.S.A.H.S.* xxv. 49.

[51] Above, parish govt. (poor relief).
[52] S.R.O. 3005/134; Harwood, *Lichfield*, 422.
[53] *S.H.C.* 4th ser. v, pp. 172–3.
[54] Ibid. pp. 48, 190–1. [55] Below, guilds.
[56] Reade, *Johnsonian Gleanings*, iii. 26–8, 89–94, 119.
[57] *S.H.C.* 4th ser. v, pp. 67, 117.
[58] *S.H.C.* 1939, 151; W.S.L., S.D. Pearson 990; L.J.R.O., P/C/11, John Bailey (1682), Thos. Bayley (1707); S.R.O., D. 661/1/82.
[59] Harwood, *Lichfield*, 418–19.
[60] *T.S.S.A.H.S.* iii. 15; P.R.O., PROB 11/73, ff. 311v.–312; L.J.R.O., D. 77/11/1, f. 57.
[61] Below, guilds.
[62] P.R.O., PROB 11/66, f. 193; 11/73, ff. 124v.–125.
[63] Below, Curborough and Elmhurst, estates (Elmhurst).
[64] *S.H.C.* 4th ser. v, pp. 119–20, 155, 188–9.
[65] Ibid. p. 48; L.J.R.O., D. 27/1/1, ff. 14v., 31v.; below, Wall, manor.
[66] Harwood, *Lichfield*, 423–4.

shop at the sign of the Naked Boy in Saddler Street at his death in 1654.[67] The goods of the apothecary Samuel Newboult at his death in 1661 included a wide range of ointments and spices.[68]

A bookbinder, John Marten, was recorded in the early 16th century, and a man of the same name was a bookseller in the later 16th century.[69] Thomas Milner, a bookbinder, was recorded in 1561.[70] Richard Gladwin (d. 1663) was working as a stationer and bookbinder by 1637, and in 1639 Richard Ford was engaged to bind a service book from St. Mary's church.[71] Edward Milward was a bookseller at the time of his death, probably in 1681.[72] William Bailey of Market Street (d. 1715) had established himself as a bookbinder by 1682 and was selling books by 1688 when he became a member of the corporation. Although he had been apprenticed to the trade in Wolverhampton, he may have been related to members of the Bailey family already noted as fellmongers in Lichfield from the mid 17th century.[73] Michael Johnson (d. 1731) was apprenticed in 1673 to Richard Simpson, a London bookseller and stationer, at the expense of the Conduit Lands trustees. His brother Benjamin was apprenticed to Simpson in 1675, also at the trustees' expense.[74] Michael was established in Lichfield as a bookseller by 1683 and travelled to sell in neighbouring towns. He probably kept his stock in the Market Street house which he bought and rebuilt in 1707, having previously been the lessee.[75]

A brickmaker named Alan Carter was recorded in the later 16th century. In the 1570s some of the bricks for Lord Paget's new house at Beaudesert in Longdon were supplied by a Lichfield man called Marson, who also supplied gutters and crest tiles.[76] Denis Napper was recorded as a brickmaker in 1616, and the probate inventory of a man of the same name in 1660 included 1,500 bricks, 3,000 tiles, 20 dozen gutters, and 6 dozen crest tiles kept at his house, as well as 2,500 unbaked bricks at the 'clay pits'.[77] Late 17th-century brickmakers included William Tranter, Edward Merrey, and Thomas Marklow.[78]

THE 18TH AND EARLIER 19TH CENTURY. While Lichfield's older trades remained important, new ones developed in response to particular needs, especially those of the leisured classes. In 1826 out of 307 resident parliamentary voters the cloth and leather trades accounted for 90 (mainly tailors and shoemakers), food and drink for 54 (mainly victuallers, maltsters, and butchers), building for 25, and metal for 22. Distributive traders such as grocers, mercers, and druggists numbered only 14. A group comprising 17 gardeners (probably market gardeners), 8 yeomen, and a farmer, represented an agricultural element in the economy.[79] By 1851 the manufacturing trades had declined in comparison with retailing. Of the tradesmen listed in 1851 only 46 were cloth and leather workers and only 17 metal workers, but 128 people were involved in the food and drink trade (of whom 73 were innkeepers, brewers, and maltsters) and 71 worked in the distributive trades.[80]

Charles Howard, who in 1709 rented land at Stowe Moggs for tenters, built a fulling mill at Stowe in or shortly before 1710. He was still working as a clothmaker at his death in 1717.[81] A fine worsted cloth called tammy was made in the mid 1720s, probably by John Hartwell, a member of the dyers' and clothworkers' company in 1726. He was in business as a woollen draper when he died in 1759.[82] Robert Hartwell (d. 1765) and his brother John (d. 1771), probably John's sons, were described as weavers,[83] and they may have owned the dyehouse which in 1766 stood on the north side of Lombard Street at its junction with Stowe Street.[84] The younger John's heir was his nephew Charles Gregory of Lombard Street, who had tenters at Stowe Moggs in 1771 and at his death in 1782.[85] A third John Hartwell, a manufacturer of tammy and saddlecloth in 1783, was ordered by the corporation in 1787 to remove his tenters, presumably at Stowe Moggs where he still some tenters in 1797.[86]

In the early 1790s John Hartwell built a fulling mill on Leamonsley brook on the Burntwood boundary; it was known as Leamonsley mill by 1816.[87] He died in 1798 and the business passed to his widow Mary.[88] Operations had ceased by 1809. In that year Mary let the mill, described as lately a fulling, carding, and spinning mill, and a warehouse and weaving shop on the south side of Lombard Street near the junction with George Lane, to a group of cotton manufacturers.[89] Both the mill and the Lombard Street premises were subsequently run by John Henrickson, a cotton spinner who

[67] W.S.L., S.D. Pearson 532, 600; *S.H.C.* 4th ser. v, pp. 13, 101–2.
[68] *S.H.C.* 4th ser. v, pp. 157–9.
[69] P.R.O., SP 1/231, f. 98; Birmingham Bibliog. Soc. *Working Papers for an Hist. Dir. of W. Midlands Book Trade to 1850*, i. 12.
[70] *S.H.C.* 1938, 49.
[71] S.R.O., D. 4566/S/30, deed of 8 Apr. 1637; Lichfield Cath. Libr., MS. Lichfield 22, pp. 89–90; *S.H.C.* 4th ser. v, p. 138.
[72] P.R.O., PROB 11/366, ff. 225v.–226.
[73] Reade, *Johnsonian Gleanings*, iv. 179; ix. 93–4; S.R.O., D. 1042/1, p. 32; L.J.R.O., D. 77/5/1, f. 19.
[74] Above, parish govt. (poor relief).
[75] Reade, *Johnsonian Gleanings*, iii. 5–10, 95–6; iv. 4, 17.
[76] *S.H.C.* n.s. ix. 157; *V.C.H. Staffs.* ii. 255.
[77] B.R.L. 380097; *S.H.C.* 4th ser. v, pp. 121–2.
[78] L.J.R.O., B/A/21, CC 123828; S.R.O., D. 1042/1, pp. 46, 49.
[79] S.R.O., D. 615/P(P)/1/7/2.

[80] White, *Dir. Staffs.* (1851), 518–27.
[81] Reade, *Johnsonian Gleanings*, iv. 105; L.J.R.O., D. 27/1/3, burial of 26 Nov. 1717; D. 35/bailiffs' accts. 1704–94, pp. 19, 31, 33; D. 77/9/22.
[82] L.J.R.O., D. 27/1/4, p. 154; D. 77/3/1; L.J.R.O., P/C/11, John Hartwell (1760); W.S.L., S. MS. 370/viii/2, p. 798.
[83] L.J.R.O., D. 29/1/1, f. 141; D. 77/3/1, p. 36; L.J.R.O., P/C/11, Rob. Hartwell (1765), John Hartwell (1771).
[84] Lichfield Libr., Plan of Lichfield, 1766, by John Snape.
[85] L.J.R.O., D. 27/1/4, burial of 4 Apr. 1782; D. 35/bailiffs' accts. 1704–94, pp. 338, 356, 418, 436, 450.
[86] Ibid. D. 35/bailiffs' accts. 1704–94, p. 596; 1794–1835, p. 31; D. 77/5/2, f. 229; *Bailey's Brit. Dir.* (1784), 400.
[87] L.J.R.O., D. 77/5/2, f. 243; S.R.O., D. 150/1/104; *Lichfield Mercury*, 15 Mar. 1816.
[88] S.R.O., D. 150/1/108, pp. 10, 15.
[89] Ibid. D. 615/M/3/8; L.J.R.O., D. 62/1.

went bankrupt in 1815, and in 1818 by Thomas Dicken, a cotton spinner and probably the Thomas Dicken of Alrewas who was one of the 1809 group.[90] By 1834 the mill had been let to Daniel Green, a worsted spinner, who lived there. He was still working it in the earlier 1850s, but by 1859 it was occupied by James Johnson, another worsted spinner.[91] Mary Hartwell had died in 1833, and the mill was sold that year to Thomas Adie. On his death in 1859 it passed to his widow Ann. When she died in 1860 her daughter Caroline sold it to the South Staffordshire Waterworks Co., which immediately sold it to Samuel Pole Shawe of Maple Hayes in Burntwood. James Johnson relinquished his tenancy and the mill was closed. In 1861 two servants from Maple Hayes and their families were living in parts of the premises.[92]

Another woollen manufactory was established at Pones mill in 1809 or earlier by Thomas Morgan, son of a Lichfield bookseller. He was still running it in 1817.[93] By 1827 the mill was owned by Thomas Hitchcock and John Sultzer, both of whom had business connexions with the hosiery trade in Leicester. It then produced carpets and knitting yarns.[94] Hitchcock lived in the millhouse and evidently ran the mill; he was still living there in 1841. In 1848 Sultzer alone was recorded as the mill owner.[95] In 1850 the mill, possibly still owned by Sultzer, produced lace and also silk trimmings for coaches.[96] In the late 1980s the buildings were occupied as two houses, Netherstowe House (North) and (South). The southern range was probably the mill and comprises two adjoining blocks which date from the late 17th or early 18th century; they are of brick on substantial stone footings of earlier date. The northern range of c. 1800 was probably the millhouse; it is a three-storey block of brick four bays wide, with a hipped roof, sash windows, and a front door set in a pilaster case under a decorative fanlight.[97]

Thomas Bailey, a jersey comber and weaver, was working in Lichfield in 1794.[98] There were weaving shops in Sandford Street in the early 1800s and a dyehouse in 1814.[99] Three woolcombers were listed in 1818, besides a mop and horse-rug manufacturer, James Binns, in Stowe Street. He was still there in 1841 but had been succeeded by 1851 by Joseph Binns, a wool carder and maker of mops and mop yarn.[1]

John Hartwell (d. 1798) produced cotton saddlecloth, probably in 1776 and certainly by 1793.[2] In 1809 his fulling mill at Leamonsley and his workshop in Lombard Street were let to cotton manufacturers.[3] Cotton yarn was still made at the Lombard Street premises in 1835, under the direction of Samuel Wiggen (or Wiggin).[4] A small cotton manufactory was established by 1802 in Sandford Street by Sir Robert Peel, whose brother Joseph ran it in 1803; it survived in 1809 and possibly in 1813. Workers lived in a nearby row of 14 houses, used also as weaving shops.[5] The manufactory probably supplied the stock worked by the inmates of St. Mary's parish workhouse in Sandford Street in 1803.[6] Calico was printed, probably at the Peel works, by 1803, and three calico workers were recorded in 1804, at least one of them living in Sandford Street.[7]

A sailcloth merchant, John Tunstall, attempted to establish a canvas manufactory in 1761 but was thwarted by the corporation, possibly because it opposed industry in the town. By 1776, however, he was making sailcloth and streamers for ships evidently in premises at the west end of Sandford Street.[8] His son Bradbury ran the manufactory by 1784, and in 1793 he was working as a hemp and flax dresser.[9] The business was described as considerable in 1811, and Bradbury was still running it in 1829.[10] A flax shop owned by William Sherratt was burnt down in 1776, and Thomas Sherratt was in business in 1793 as a hemp and flax dresser.[11] It is not known where they had their premises. Two flax dressers were listed in 1818, one at Greenhill and the other in Tamworth Street.[12] Rope Walk recorded on the north side of Lombard Street in 1781 was presumably used at some time for making rope, and a rope manufactory in Sandford Street was closed in 1809.[13] Two ropemakers were listed in 1818, one in Lombard Street and the other in St. John Street. The Lombard Street ropemaker, Joseph Howis, was still in business in the earlier 1830s.[14]

Leather working remained important, especially in the Sandford Street area where a tan-

[90] *Lichfield Mercury*, 3 and 17 Nov., 22 Dec. 1815; 15 Mar. 1816; Parson and Bradshaw, *Staffs. Dir.* (1818), 185.

[91] White, *Dir. Staffs.* (1834), 161; (1851), 519; *P.O. Dir. Staffs.* (1854); L.J.R.O., B/A/15/Burntwood, no. 619; ibid. Lichfield, St. Chad, no. 726, giving the tenant as Joseph Green; P.R.O., HO 107/980 and 2014 (2); S.R.O., D. 150/1/108, p. 29.

[92] S.R.O., D. 150/1/107-9; D. 4566/F, Maple Hayes sale 1884; P.R.O., RG 9/1973.

[93] *Aris's Birmingham Gaz.* 4 June 1810; *Lichfield Mercury*, 31 Jan. 1817; L.J.R.O., D. 109/title deeds of nos. 27-31 Wade St., declaration of Jane Frost, 28 Nov. 1882.

[94] *Lichfield Mercury*, 9 Mar. 1827; Pigot & Co. *New Com. Dir. for 1822-3*, Leics. p. 216; S.R.O., D. 4566/S, deed of 16 June 1826.

[95] L.J.R.O., D. 77/15/12; L.J.R.O., B/A/15/Lichfield, St. Chad, no. 454; P.R.O., HO 107/1008.

[96] *P.O. Dir. Staffs.* (1850), 275.

[97] Description supplied by Mr. A. G. Taylor, Staffs. C.C. Planning and Development Dept.

[98] Reade, *Johnsonian Gleanings*, iv. 176.

[99] L.J.R.O., D. 15/8/5/4; D. 77/5/3, f. 64v.; D. 77/21/16.

[1] Parson and Bradshaw, *Staffs. Dir.* (1818), 169, 174, 176;

Pigot, *Nat. Com. Dir.* (1841), Staffs. p. 31; White, *Dir. Staffs.* (1851), 519.

[2] *Boswell: the Ominous Years 1774-1776*, ed. C. Ryskamp and F. A. Pottle, 291-2; *Univ. Brit. Dir.* iii (1794), 608.

[3] Above (this section).

[4] S.R.O., D. 615/M/3/8; D. 615/P(P)/1/9, s.n. S. Wiggen; L.J.R.O., D. 77/3/1, p. 41; White, *Dir. Staffs.* (1834), 156.

[5] L.J.R.O., D. 29/1/2, ff. 33, 41v., 43; D. 29/1/3, p. 1; S.R.O., D. 941/54; Harwood, *Lichfield*, 510; *Aris's Birmingham Gaz.* 5 Dec. 1803.

[6] Above, parish govt.

[7] *Staffs. Advertiser*, 14 May 1803; L.J.R.O., D. 25/1/2, f. 23; D. 29/1/2, f. 34v.

[8] L.J.R.O., D. 77/5/2, f. 110; D. 88/deeds of 8 Nov. 1788 and 30 Aug. 1803; *V.C.H. Staffs.* ii. 222.

[9] *Bailey's Brit. Dir.* (1784), 400; *Univ. Brit. Dir.* iii. 611.

[10] T. Pennant, *Journey from Chester to London* (1811), 155; Pigot, *Nat. Com. Dir.* (1829), 716.

[11] W.S.L., S. 1902/i, p. 63; L.J.R.O., D. 77/4/1/2.

[12] Parson and Bradshaw, *Staffs. Dir.* (1818), 173, 175.

[13] L.J.R.O., D. 77/5/3, f. 42; above, fig. 4.

[14] Parson and Bradshaw, *Staffs. Dir.* (1818), 174, 176; White, *Dir. Staffs.* (1834), 160.

house and tanyards were worked by Thomas Tunckes in the early 18th century.[15] In 1776 there was a tanhouse on Trunkfield brook west of the Turk's Head inn in Sandford Street and two tanyards further downstream on the north side of the street.[16] A tanyard offered for sale in 1825 with 49 handlers (or pits), 39 vats, and 6 lime vats was probably in Sandford Street, and there were still tanpits in 1848 on the south side of Sandford Street and of Queen Street, although by then they were probably disused.[17] Waste land north of Quonians Lane was let by the corporation in 1711 to Thomas Bailey, a tanner, and the lease was renewed in 1741 in favour of Francis Bailey, also a tanner.[18] In 1766 there was a tanyard on the north side of Stowe Street on the stream leading to Stowe Pool and another on the south side of the mill in Dam Street. The former survived in 1830 and the latter probably in 1834, when the corporation considered action against the tenant of a skinhouse who claimed the privilege of washing skins in Minster Pool.[19]

Saddlemaking presumably used much of the locally produced leather, but the trade declined from the early 19th century as Walsall became the main centre in Staffordshire for the manufacture of saddles.[20] Frances Purden & Son was making saddles, harnesses, horse-collars, and sponge boots for horses in Bird Street in 1818. The son was presumably Thomas Purden who was listed as a saddler in Bird Street in 1834, when he was one of five saddlers in the city; in 1851 he was one of three.[21] There were still three saddle and harness makers in Lichfield in 1880.[22]

A coachmaker named John Lamb was working in the town in 1710 and 1727.[23] By the later 18th century there were two coachmakers, William Butler in Bore Street and James Butler in Wade Street. James, who took over William's firm in 1766, was still in business in 1779, when he also advertised as a house painter.[24] A coach works owned by Charles Holmes in 1810 may have occupied the Butler premises in Wade Street; certainly the partnership of Holmes & Turnor operated from Wade Street in 1816.[25] Known as Holmes & Butcher by 1829, the partnership was evidently dissolved in 1848 and the works was continued by William Holmes.[26] In 1860 Arthur and Herbert Holmes worked as

coach and harness makers in St. John Street, possibly on the north side of St. John's hospital where John Heap had a coach works in 1848. By 1864 they had moved their premises to Bird Street, evidently on the corner with Bore Street.[27] As Holmes & Co. the business continued there until c. 1918.[28] In 1818 William Weldhen was making coaches and coach harnesses, evidently on the east side of Upper St. John Street where he had a workshop and showroom in 1847.[29] Premises there were in the hands of John Weldhen in 1864. The business was sold in 1890 to John Hall, a coachmaker based in Gaia Lane.[30] Hall continued the St. John Street works until c. 1918.[31]

The metal trades appear to have declined in importance. Although Stowe mill was rebuilt as an iron manufactory c. 1740, there is no evidence that it was in fact so used, and in 1753 it was converted into a flour mill.[32] A few nailers were recorded in the early 19th century, and several tinplate workers and a locksmith were listed in 1818. There was a nail manufacturer in Sandford Street in 1829.[33] By 1826 agricultural implements were made in Sandford Street by Samuel Gregory, who advertised his newly invented chaff-cutting machine that year and was still in business in 1840.[34] In 1834 James Barlow was making cutlery, also in Sandford Street.[35]

Although Anna Seward complained in 1788 about the poor range of goods available in Lichfield, shopkeepers in 1793 included 13 grocers and drapers, a fruiterer and poulterer, a confectioner, a pastry cook, a tea dealer, a haberdasher, and a china and glass dealer. There were also four apothecaries and druggists.[36] In 1834 the distributive trades included 17 shopkeepers, 12 grocers and tea dealers, 5 confectioners, 3 poulterers, 7 milliners and dressmakers, 5 linen and woollen drapers, and 3 china and glass dealers. The numbers were much the same in 1851.[37]

Of the food and drink trades brewing was the most important, producing beer mainly for local consumption. William Bonniface, the landlord of the George in Farquhar's play The Beaux' Stratagem (1707), extolled the ale which he brewed as being 'smooth as oil, sweet as milk, clear as amber, and strong as brandy'.[38] Lichfield ale had a national reputation by 1769 and was praised by James Boswell in 1776.[39] It was

[15] L.J.R.O., D. 77/6/3, f. 153; D. 88/lease bk. 1712–27, deed of 23 Oct. 1724.
[16] Lichfield Libr., Plan of Lichfield, 1766.
[17] Lichfield Mercury, 14 Jan. 1825; L.J.R.O., B/A/15/ Lichfield, St. Mary, nos. 371, 373.
[18] L.J.R.O., D. 77/9/41.
[19] Ibid. D. 77/5/3, f. 229v.; Lichfield Libr., Plan of Lichfield, 1766; S.R.O., D. 615/M/3/7.
[20] V.C.H. Staffs. ii. 235.
[21] Parson and Bradshaw, Staffs. Dir. (1818), 177; White, Dir. Staffs. (1834), 160; (1851), 526.
[22] Kelly's Dir. Staffs. (1880).
[23] S.R.O., D. 4566/S/54, deed of 1 Jan. 1709/10; D. 4566/S/58, deed of 9 Mar. 1726/7.
[24] Aris's Birmingham Gaz. 11 Aug. 1766; 16 Feb. 1767; 8 Nov. 1779.
[25] Ibid. 26 Mar. and 10 Sept. 1810; Lichfield Mercury, 9 Feb. 1816.
[26] Pigot, Nat. Com. Dir. (1829), 714*; Staffs. Advertiser, 15 Jan. 1848, p. 1; L.J.R.O., B/A/15/Lichfield, St. Mary, no. 534.
[27] P.O. Dir. Staffs. (1860; 1864); L.J.R.O., B/A/15/

Lichfield, St. Mary, no. 462; O.S. Map 1/500, Staffs. LII. 15. 12 (1884 edn.).
[28] Kelly's Dir. Staffs. (1916; 1924).
[29] Parson and Bradshaw, Staffs. Dir. (1818), 182; L.J.R.O., B/A/15/Lichfield, St. Michael, no. 250.
[30] P.O. Dir. Staffs. (1864); Lomax's Red Bk. (1886), 56; Lichfield Mercury, 12 Sept. 1890, p. 4.
[31] Kelly's Dir. Staffs. (1916; 1924).
[32] Above (mills).
[33] Parson and Bradshaw, Staffs. Dir. (1818), 168, 170–1, 173, 177–8, 180; Pigot, Nat. Com. Dir. (1829), 716; L.J.R.O., D. 29/1/3, pp. 177, 179, 200.
[34] Lichfield Mercury, 10 Feb. 1826; L.J.R.O., D. 109/Lowe's Char./draft affidavits 1841.
[35] White, Dir. Staffs. (1834), 154.
[36] Univ. Brit. Dir. iii. 610–12; above, general hist. (Restoration to end of 18th century).
[37] White, Dir. Staffs. (1834), 157–61; (1851), 518–27.
[38] Act I, sc. i.
[39] P. Russel and O. Price, England Displayed (1769), ii. 68; Boswell: the Ominous Years, ed. Ryskamp and Pottle, 290–1.

usually brewed by innkeepers, of whom 80 were recorded in 1732, 56 in 1776, and 55 in 1818; there were also 17 beerhouse keepers in 1818. A brewing trade in which maltsters produced ale for retailing had developed in Lichfield by the end of the 18th century: there were 9 maltsters in 1793 and 17 in 1818.[40] In 1834 there were 3 brewers and 19 maltsters, most of them at Greenhill and in Lombard Street and Tamworth Street.[41]

John Newton (d. 1754), who traded as a brandy and cider merchant in the East Midlands and parts of Yorkshire, was based in Lichfield and was probably a member of a King's Bromley family which had property in Barbados.[42] David Garrick, the actor, and his brother Peter went into business as wine merchants in 1739 evidently in their Beacon Street house. It was continued by Peter (d. 1796) and was run in 1818 by Charles Hewitt and in 1834 and 1851 by Henry Hewitt. It passed in the 1860s to the Griffith family, already wine merchants in Beacon Street.[43] John Fern, the lessee of the Swan, and George Addams were in business as wine merchants in 1793. They both lived in Beacon Street, Fern in White Hall and Addams in what became the Angel Croft hotel.[44] Fern's business was continued after his death in 1801 by his youngest son Robert, who went bankrupt in 1802.[45] Addams's business was taken over by George Dodson, who by 1812 had vaults behind a house (later called Cathedral House) on the north side of the Angel Croft. Dodson died in 1833 and was succeeded in business by Philip and Thomas Griffith.[46] By 1841 the firm was run by John and Arthur Griffith.[47]

Bookselling and printing was one of the main specialist trades catering for the leisured classes in Lichfield. After the bookseller William Bailey died in 1715, his business was evidently continued by John and Richard Bailey, recorded as booksellers in the mid 18th century. Richard's son William (d. 1785) was a printer as well as an apothecary.[48] After Michael Johnson's death in 1731, his son Nathaniel ran the bookselling business until his own death in 1737. It was then taken over by Michael's widow Sarah. After her death in 1749 the business was carried on by the Johnson family's servant Catherine Chambers (d. 1767).[49] What remained of Michael John-

son's stock of books was possibly bought on Catherine's death by a man named Major Morgan who was trading as a bookseller and printer in Lichfield in 1764. He ran his business from a shop in Market Street opposite Johnson's house.[50] Morgan died in 1802, and the business was continued by his son William (d. 1844).[51] Another late 18th-century bookseller and printer was John Jackson, in business by 1776, possibly operating from his house in what is now Friars Alley off Bird Street. He died probably in 1815, leaving his printing press to his son William, who is not known to have continued the trade.[52] Richard Greene, an apothecary and the founder of a museum in his house in Market Street, had a printing press probably in 1781 and certainly in 1784.[53] By 1810 Thomas Lomax had a printing works in Tamworth Street; he moved that year to premises at the corner of Bird Street and Market Street. The business was continued by his son Alfred, who became a noted publisher of religious books.[54]

The *Lichfield Mercury*, first issued in 1815, was printed on a press owned by its proprietor, James Amphlett, initially in Bore Street and later in Market Street. By 1823 the press was again in Bore Street, but in 1824 it was moved to premises at the east end of Sandford Street. A further move to the house which later became the Samuel Johnson Birthplace Museum took place in 1830. The paper was closed in 1833, although later revived.[55]

An increased emphasis on personal fashion created a demand for service trades and goods. In 1753 the Market Street apothecary Richard Greene was advertising his toothpaste in pots costing 6*d.* and 1*s.*; he had agents elsewhere in Staffordshire and the Midlands and in Liverpool.[56] Thomas Twyford was working in 1793 as a dentist, perfumerer, and toyseller; he was still working as a dentist in 1810.[57] William Roberts was working as a dentist in Bore Street in 1834.[58] There was a hatmaking business by 1744, and the Trigg family, in business from 1760, still made hats in 1900 at premises in Market Street.[59] There were three peruke makers in the later 1760s and one in 1771,[60] and in the later 1770s Anna Seward claimed that hairdressers ran about the city all morning, as Lichfield grew 'more fine and fashionable every

[40] *S.H.C.* 1950–1, 191; *Univ. Brit. Dir.* iii. 610–12; Parson and Bradshaw, *Staffs. Dir.* (1818), 30.

[41] White, *Dir. Staffs.* (1834), 62, 157, 160.

[42] T. Newton, *Works* (1782), i. 7, 55; Shaw, *Staffs.* i. 147.

[43] W.S.L., S. MS. 370(i), 301; *Lichfield Official Handbk.* (1906), 58–9; (1910), 63–4; Parson and Bradshaw, *Staffs. Dir.* (1818), 189; White, *Dir. Staffs.* (1834), 161; (1851), 527.

[44] *Univ. Brit. Dir.* iii. 610–11; L.J.R.O., VC/A/21, CC 17529, plan 14; L.J.R.O., D. 15/10/2/27, deed of 4 Aug. 1790.

[45] L.J.R.O., P/C/11, John Fern (1801), Ann Bradburne (1838).

[46] Ibid. D. 15/10/2/27, deeds of 27 Nov. 1812 and 10 Sept. 1834; W.S.L., S. MS. 384, p. 78.

[47] Pigot, *Nat. Com. Dir.* (1841), Staffs. p. 31; L.J.R.O., B/A/15/Lichfield, St. Chad, no. 730.

[48] Birmingham Bibliog. Soc. *Working Papers for an Hist. Dir. of W. Midlands Bk. Trade to 1850*, i. 5; Reade, *Johnsonian Gleanings*, iv. 179–80; ix. 228–9.

[49] Birm. Bibliog. Soc. *Working Papers*, i. 10; Reade, *Johnsonian Gleanings*, iii. 101, 168 n.

[50] Birm. Bibliog. Soc. *Working Papers*, ii. 6; Reade, *Johnsonian Gleanings*, iii. 168 n.

[51] *Staffs. Advertiser*, 25 Dec. 1802; L.J.R.O., D. 109/title deeds to nos. 27–31 Wade St., declaration of Jane Frost.

[52] Birm. Bibliog. Soc. *Working Papers*, iii. 8, 21; L.J.R.O., P/C/11, John Jackson (1816).

[53] *Jnls. and Corresp. of Thomas Sedgewick Whalley*, ed. H. Wickham, i. 326; S.R.O., D. 593/F/3/12/2/6, election receipts 1784.

[54] *Aris's Birmingham Gaz.* 1 Jan. and 15 Oct. 1810; A. J. Bull, *House of Lomax 1810–1969* (copy in W.S.L.); *V.C.H. Staffs.* iii. 75; L.J.R.O., B/A/15/Lichfield, St. Mary, no. 218.

[55] Below, social and cultural activities (newspapers).

[56] *Aris's Birmingham Gaz.* 19 Mar. 1753.

[57] Ibid. 30 Apr. 1810; *Univ. Brit. Dir.* iii. 611.

[58] White, *Dir. Staffs.* (1834), 155.

[59] *Aris's Birmingham Gaz.* 10 Dec. 1744; *Eggington's Lichfield Almanack* (1875), advertisement; *Kelly's Dir. Staffs.* (1900).

[60] *Aris's Birmingham Gaz.* 30 Sept. 1765; L.J.R.O., VC/A/21, CC 164146A, pp. 41, 47, 94.

day'.[61] Three hairdressers were recorded in 1793, one in 1801, another in 1812, and seven in 1818.[62] There were eight in 1834 and 1851.[63] There was an umbrella repairer in Gresley Row in 1829 and 1834, and an umbrella maker in St. John Street in 1851.[64]

Watchmakers were recorded in 1741, 1764, 1780, and 1793.[65] By 1818 there were five watch and clock makers, including William Vale in Bore Street, still working in 1841.[66] Edmund Vale, evidently William's successor, was a brass founder employing 15 men and 5 boys in 1861 and was one of five clockmakers in Lichfield in 1864.[67] Charles Thornloe was in business as a brass founder and clockmaker in Tamworth Street in 1834. He moved to Bore Street shortly before 1886, when the firm was taken over by John Salloway.[68] His great-nephew J. M. S. Salloway continued the business as a jeweller in the late 1980s.

William Evans made and repaired trumpets, horns, and bugles in 1800, presumably for the soldiers based in Lichfield.[69] Charles Allport was a maker of musical instruments in St. John Street in 1850; he also made guns, continuing a trade established by John Allport in the early 1840s.[70]

In 1765 a Mr. Laine advertised his skill in painting portraits in miniature on bracelets, rings, and snuffboxes, and a miniaturist was working in Tamworth Street in 1839.[71] In 1861 a photographer, William Andrews, had a studio in Dam Street, and by 1864 William Nicholls had one in Tamworth Street. Both were still working in 1872, but only Nicholls in 1876.[72]

A Birmingham auctioneer was using a Lichfield inn for business in 1797, and auction rooms were opened in Sandford Street by W. Harris in 1800.[73] By 1834 Richard Harris had auction rooms in Breadmarket Street, and what were probably the same premises were occupied by Ratcliffe Harris in 1848. Charles Gillard was an auctioneer in Bird Street in 1841, moving to Bore Street by 1851.[74] He may have been the Mr. Gillard who in 1869 reopened the smithfield near the Swan hotel. Another smithfield, at Greenhill, was run in 1870 by the auctioneers Winterton & Beale.[75]

The rebuilding of Lichfield in the 18th century provided work for brickmakers, notably members of the Marklow (later Marklew) family, John (d. 1717), William (fl. 1738), and Denis (d. 1753). In 1734 the corporation granted Denis Marklew a 21-year lease of land at Berry Hill. He was to make bricks there for only the first 14 years of the lease and then restore the land for agricultural use.[76] In the earlier 1740s Marklew also dug clay at Femley Pits near the city's southern boundary. A brickmaker, John Bond, dug clay at Femley Pits in the early 1790s.[77] In 1778 the corporation let land at Quarryhills Lane to Thomas Cheatam for three years to make bricks, but not tiles.[78] A brick kiln at Lincroft was used by the architect Joseph Potter the elder in the early 19th century, and by 1830 there was a kiln on the east side of the lane to Curborough.[79] A brickworks on Wissage Hill in the early 1820s may have been run by George Gilbert, recorded as a brickmaker at Greenhill in 1818.[80] In the 1840s John Gilbert, also of Greenhill, dug clay at Wissage to make bricks, pipes, tiles, and quarries. He was presumably related to Elias Gilbert, who by 1841 had a brickworks west of the Stafford road over the Burntwood boundary.[81]

A stone cutter, William Thompson of St. John Street, was presented at the manor court in 1758 for obstructing the road with stone and marble blocks. He may have been the 'Mr. Tompson' who worked on the north-west spire of the cathedral in 1766.[82] Another stone cutter, Thomas Thompson, was living in Bore Street in 1777.[83] In 1818 two stone and marble cutters were living in St. John Street, Joseph Johnson and Samuel Hayward, the latter also making statues.[84] In 1851 the same or another Joseph Johnson was working as a stone and marble mason in both Frog Lane and Beacon Street and George Johnson as one in St. John Street.[85] In 1848 Richard Hamlet had a stoneyard off Dam Street,[86] and John Hamlet worked on the restoration of the cathedral in the late 1850s.[87] Thomas Denstone worked as a carver and gilder in Dam Street in 1829 and 1841, and his premises had evidently been taken over by William Strickland by 1851.[88]

[61] Samuel Johnson Birthplace Mus., Lichfield, MS. 38/7, Anna Seward to Mary Powys (undated letter).
[62] Univ. Brit. Dir. iii. 611; Parson and Bradshaw, Staffs. Dir. (1818), 29; L.J.R.O., D. 29/1/2, f. 40; D. 88/lease bk. 1804–22, f. 44v.
[63] White, Dir. Staffs. (1834), 158; (1851), 524.
[64] Ibid. (1834), 161; Pigot, Nat. Com. Dir. (1829), 716; P.R.O., HO 107/2014 (2).
[65] S.H.C. 4th ser. xi. 86–7; Aris's Birmingham Gaz. 7 Aug. 1780; Univ. Brit. Dir. iii. 610; L.J.R.O., VC/A/21, CC 164146A, p. 36.
[66] Parson and Bradshaw, Staffs. Dir. (1818), 172, 176, 179, 181; L.J.R.O., D. 109/Lowe's Char./draft affidavits 1841.
[67] P.R.O., RG 9/1972; P.O. Dir. Staffs. (1864).
[68] White, Dir. Staffs. (1834), 161; Kelly's Dir. Staffs. (1884); Lichfield Mercury, 22 Jan. 1886, p. 4.
[69] Aris's Birmingham Gaz. 28 Apr. 1800.
[70] P.O. Dir. Staffs. (1850), 276; Lomax's Red Bk. (1886), 49; (1913), 58; P.R.O., HO 107/2014 (2).
[71] Aris's Birmingham Gaz. 30 Dec. 1765; W.S.L., M. 869/4.
[72] P.R.O., RG 9/1972; P.O. Dir. Staffs. (1864 and edns. to 1876).
[73] Aris's Birmingham Gaz. 4 and 11 Sept. 1797; 1 Dec. 1800.

[74] White, Dir. Staffs. (1834), 156; (1851), 521; L.J.R.O., B/A/15/Lichfield, St. Mary, no. 243.
[75] Above (markets).
[76] Reade, Johnsonian Gleanings, iv. 69, 71; B.R.L. 381700, pp. 73, 92; L.J.R.O., D. 77/5/2, f. 13.
[77] L.J.R.O., D. 35/bailiffs' accts. 1704–94, pp. 152, 158, 578.
[78] Ibid. D. 77/5/2, f. 193.
[79] S.R.O., D. 593/F/3/12/1/17 and 20–6; D. 593/F/3/12/2/34, receipt of 22 July 1822; D. 615/M/3/6–7.
[80] Ibid. D. 593/F/3/12/2/34, receipt of 24 July 1822; ibid. D. (W.) 1851/10/7, no. 1065; Parson and Bradshaw, Staffs. Dir. (1818), 172.
[81] L.J.R.O., D. 15/8/5/5; below, Burntwood, econ. hist. (other industries).
[82] L.J.R.O., D. 77/6/4, p. 374; Aris's Birmingham Gaz. 29 Sept. 1766.
[83] L.J.R.O., D. 27/1/4, burial of 4 Oct. 1777.
[84] Parson and Bradshaw, Staffs. Dir. (1818), 173–4; S.R.O., D. (W.) 1851/8/55.
[85] White, Dir. Staffs. (1851), 526.
[86] L.J.R.O., B/A/15/Lichfield, St. Mary, no. 165.
[87] J. G. Lonsdale, Recollections of the Internal Restoration of Lichfield Cathedral (Lichfield, 1884), 12 (copy in W.S.L.).
[88] Pigot, Nat. Com. Dir. (1829), 716; (1841), Staffs. p. 31; White, Dir. Staffs. (1851), 521.

There was a bonehouse evidently on the north side of the Wyrley and Essington Canal west of Chesterfield Road by 1806. The miller, Thomas Wood, was ordered that year to stop production following a complaint by the vicar of St. Mary's that the works was 'a noisome and offensive building and a great nuisance to the inhabitants of the city'. He was still in business in 1818 and the bonehouse remained there in 1836.[89] In 1847 a bonehouse south of the canal on the west side of Birmingham Road was run by Richard and James Brawn.[90] Between 1857 and 1872 James Meacham ran Trunkfield mill as a bonemill.[91]

In 1818 John and Richard Brawn were in business as limemasters with works on the north side of the Wyrley and Essington Canal where it met Birmingham Road. They were recorded as coal, lime, and timber merchants in 1834.[92] Richard and James Brawn ran the business in 1847, and John Brawn worked as a lime burner there in 1872.[93] Two coal merchants ran businesses in 1818 from a wharf where the canal met Upper St. John Street. One of them, Thomas Robinson, still traded there in 1851.[94]

THE LATER 19TH AND THE 20TH CENTURY. The growth of industrial firms in Lichfield had apparently been hampered by the development from the early 19th century of market gardening with its emphasis on seasonal labour: in 1888 the vicar of St. Mary's, Canon M. H. Scott, expressed the hope that new lines of business and manufacture might be introduced to give the labouring and artisan classes more opportunity of earning regular wages.[95]

Some new industries had already been established, especially in metal working and light engineering. In 1864 Frederick Symonds ran an iron and brass foundry on the south side of Wade Street. In 1882 Symonds also had a nail and bolt works on the north side of Frog Lane. He closed the Frog Lane works, and probably that in Wade Street too, in 1890.[96] Perkins & Sons, a firm based in Yoxall, had established an iron foundry in Sandford Street by 1879.[97] The firm became Woodroffe & Perkins Ltd. in 1904, and in 1923 it was bought by the engineering firm of Tuke & Bell Ltd. of Beacon Street and renamed the Lichfield Foundry Ltd. The Sandford Street works was closed in 1983.[98] Chamberlin & Hill, a Walsall firm of iron and brass

founders established in 1890, set up a foundry in 1898 in Beacon Street opposite Wheel Lane. Production was concentrated on high-quality castings for use in the textile and mining industries. The works was rebuilt in 1953 and closed in 1986.[99] It was demolished in 1988 and was replaced that year by a Safeway supermarket.[1] Tuke & Bell Ltd., established in London in 1912, moved to Lichfield in 1918 and occupied a site on the corner of Beacon Street and Wheel Lane. It concentrated on the production of sewage purification plant and parts for refuse vehicles, but by the late 1920s it also assembled motor cars. It ceased to manufacture parts for refuse vehicles in 1950 but continued to design and make sewage treatment equipment. In 1986 ownership was vested wholly in the firm's employees as shareholders.[2]

Charles Bailey, who sold agricultural implements in St. John Street by 1868, made tools in a works at St. John's wharf on the Wyrley and Essington Canal by 1872 and was still in business in the mid 1890s.[3] By 1899 Perkins & Sons had a works making agricultural implements in Frog Lane, presumably on the site of the former nail and bolt works; it was still in operation in 1912.[4]

John Lester established himself as a bicycle maker in 1889 with premises in Tamworth Street, and by 1897 he was advertising his own make, the 'Lester'. His firm survived until 1913.[5] Bicycles were also assembled at the turn of the century by Auckland and Co. in Bore Street.[6]

The most important industry from the later 19th century was brewing. By 1848 the wine merchants John and Arthur Griffith had established a brewery in their Beacon Street premises behind Cathedral House. They had a malthouse to the south on the site of the later Lichfield library, and the 1858 malthouse which survives by the railway on the east side of Upper St. John Street was probably theirs too.[7] The venture was unsuccessful because demand was still met by Lichfield innkeepers.[8] In 1864 John, Henry, and William Gilbert formed the Lichfield Malting Co., based in Tamworth Street, and in 1866 a malthouse was built on the north side of the railway south of Birmingham Road.[9] The firm was merged with the Griffiths' brewery in 1869 to form the Lichfield Brewery Co.[10] In 1873 the new company opened a brewery, designed by

[89] L.J.R.O., D. 35/improvement com. min. bk. 1806-9, 7 Aug. and 15 Oct. 1806, 8 Jan. 1807; Parson and Bradshaw, Staffs. Dir. (1818), addenda facing p. i; S.R.O., D. 615/M/3/5; B.L. Maps, O.S.D. 258; J. Dewhirst, Map of Lichfield (1836).
[90] L.J.R.O., B/A/15/Lichfield, St. Michael, no. 497.
[91] Above (mills).
[92] Parson and Bradshaw, Staffs. Dir. (1818), 169; White, Dir. Staffs. (1834), 161; B.L. Maps, O.S.D. 258.
[93] L.J.R.O., B/A/15/Lichfield, St. Michael, nos. 468, 472; P.O. Dir. Staffs. (1872).
[94] Parson and Bradshaw, Staffs. Dir. (1818), 170, 178; White, Dir. Staffs. (1851), 527.
[95] Staffs. Advertiser, 3 Mar. 1888, p. 7.
[96] P.O. Dir. Staffs. (1864); Lichfield Mercury, 2 May 1890, p. 4; O.S. Map 1/500, Staffs. LII. 15. 12 and 13 (1884 edn.).
[97] Eggington & Brown's Year Bk. (1879), 202; O.S. Map 1/500, Staffs. LII. 15. 12 (1884 edn.).
[98] Kelly's Dir. Staffs. (1924); inf. from Mr. P. E. Sankey of

Tuke & Bell Ltd.
[99] Lomax's Red Bk. (1898), 25; S.H.C. 1950-1, 208; Lichfield Mercury, 10 Jan. 1986, p. 1; inf. from the late M. M. Hallett, former managing director.
[1] Lichfield Mercury, 9 Dec. 1988, p. 21.
[2] Ibid. 6 Sept. 1918, p. 2; Kelly's Dir. Staffs. (1928); V.C.H. Staffs. ii. 153; inf. from Mr. P. E. Sankey.
[3] P.O. Dir. Staffs. (1868; 1872; 1876); Kelly's Dir. Staffs. (1880 and edns. to 1896).
[4] Lomax's Red Bk. (1899), 29; Kelly's Dir. Staffs. (1900; 1912).
[5] Lomax's Red Bk. (1897), 50; (1905), 34; (1913), 12; Kelly's Dir. Staffs. (1892).
[6] Lomax's Red Bk. (1897), 36; (1901), 4.
[7] Staffs. Advertiser, 17 Feb. 1849, p. 1; L.J.R.O., B/A/15/Lichfield, St. Chad, nos. 730, 736.
[8] Lichfield Official Handbk. (1906), 59.
[9] P.O. Dir. Staffs. (1864); Staffs. Advertiser, 17 Nov. 1866, p. 4; Lichfield Mercury, 4 Apr. 1902, p. 5.
[10] Staffs. Advertiser, 3 July 1869, p. 7.

George Scamell of Westminster, beside the railway line on the west side of Upper St. John Street.[11] A large malthouse on the opposite side of Upper St. John Street south of the station was built about the same time. The company was bought by Samuel Allsopp & Sons of Burton upon Trent in 1930 and brewing at Lichfield evidently ceased in 1931. The malthouse was destroyed by fire in 1950.[12]

The City Brewery Co. was established in 1874 with premises, also designed by George Scamell, on the south side of the railway between Birmingham Road and Chesterfield Road. After a fire in 1916 the brewery was closed, and the company was taken over in 1917 by Wolverhampton and Dudley Breweries Ltd. A malthouse survived on the site in the late 1980s.[13]

In 1874 John and Arthur Griffith again opened a brewery, on the north side of Sandford Street. John died in 1886, and the brewery was taken over by Harold Jackson and c. 1898 by Sydney Oldham. In 1924 it was owned by Davenport's C. B. Ltd., who still ran it in 1940.[14]

The Trent Valley Brewery Co. was established in 1875. It opened a brewery, again designed by George Scamell, in 1877 just over the city boundary in Streethay.[15] The company amalgamated with the Lichfield Brewery Co. in 1891. The brewery was demolished in 1970.[16]

The firm of A. W. and W. A. Smith, established by 1877, had a brewery at the corner of Beacon Street and Wheel Lane. It was evidently later acquired by the Lichfield Brewery Co., which sold the site in 1918 to the engineering firm of Tuke & Bell.[17]

A works producing soda water, lemonade, and mineral water was established in Church Street by John Simms in 1840 and was still in operation in 1951.[18] In 1931 the Lichfield Aerated Water Co., a subsidiary of Ind Coope & Allsopp, opened a works at the Lichfield Brewery Co. premises in Upper St. John Street. The company was taken over by Burrows & Sturgess of Derby in 1935, and a new works was opened in Birmingham Road. As the Birmingham Chemical Co. the firm produced essences and fruit juice compounds for the food trade. The company retained its Upper St. John Street offices; the name Wiltell Road there is taken from the firm's motto 'Quality Will Tell'.[19]

When Alfred Lomax retired in 1901, his printing and publishing business, based at the corner of Bird Street and Market Street since 1810, was transferred to F. H. Bull and E. Wiseman who traded as A. C. Lomax's Successors. In 1942 the firm was bought from Bull's widow by the directors of the *Lichfield Mercury*; it remained a separate printing works until its closure in 1969.[20] The *Lichfield Mercury*, revived in 1877, was printed in the Bird Street premises of its proprietor Frederic Brown, who had taken over a printing works owned in 1850 by Francis Eggington.[21] The paper was printed there until the mid 1960s, when printing was transferred to Tamworth.[22]

James Hamlet was working in Sandford Street as an ecclesiastical stone and marble mason between 1864 and 1872, probably continuing the business of Richard Hamlet in Dam Street in 1848. There were two other stone masons in 1868 and 1872, of whom John Matthewson of Sandford Street also worked marble.[23] Robert Bridgeman, who came to work on the cathedral in 1877 as foreman of a Peterborough firm of stonemasons, established his own stonemason's business in Lichfield in 1879. His first premises were off Dam Street, later the site of the School of Art; by 1882 he had moved to Quonians Lane. The works produced goods in wood and stone which were marketed in many parts of the country and abroad. The firm had a workforce of over 200 in 1914. On his death in 1918 Robert was succeeded by his son Joseph, who was in turn succeeded by his son Charles in 1950. In 1968 Charles sold the firm to Linfords, based in Cannock, which as Linford-Bridgeman still owned the Quonians Lane premises in 1986.[24]

A tradesmen's association was established in Lichfield in 1896; it changed its name to a chamber of trade in 1912.[25] In the late 1920s and again in the later 1930s commercial development in Lichfield was promoted by the city council and a chamber of commerce.[26] In 1945 the council bought Trent Valley House (formerly in Streethay but since 1934 in Lichfield) and 16 a. around it, and opened the Trent Valley Trading Estate there in 1946. By the early 1950s factories there produced roller bearings, electrical equipment, dairy machinery, plastics, and furniture.[27] A factory making pre-stressed concrete blocks was opened in 1945 in Dovehouse Fields next to the railway east of Birmingham Road.[28] The Trent Valley Estate was extended north in the early 1960s and again after Eastern

[11] Ibid. 16 Mar. 1872, p. 4; 5 Apr. 1873, p. 6; below, plate 32.

[12] *Lichfield Mercury*, 25 July 1930, p. 10; 27 Oct. 1950, p. 5.

[13] Ibid. 27 Oct. 1916, p. 5; 19 Oct. 1917, p. 2; A. Barnard, *Noted Breweries of Gt. Britain and Ireland*, iv. 117–23; below, plate 33.

[14] *Lichfield Mercury*, 7 Jan. 1887, p. 5; *Lichfield Official Handbk.* (1906), 59–60; *Kelly's Dir. Staffs.* (1888 and edns. to 1940); O.S. Map 1/500, Staffs. LII. 15. 12 (1884 edn.).

[15] Barnard, *Noted Breweries*, iv. 128; *Staffs. Advertiser* (S. Staffs. edn.), 28 Apr. 1877, p. 4; Sherlock, *Ind. Arch. Staffs.* 78.

[16] *Lichfield Mercury*, 6 Feb. 1891, p. 5; Sherlock, *Ind. Arch. Staffs.* 75.

[17] *Staffs. Advertiser*, 12 May 1877, p. 7; *Lichfield Mercury*, 6 Sept. 1918, p. 2.

[18] A. Williams, *Sketches in and around Lichfield and Rugeley* (Lichfield, 1892), 423; *City and County of Lichfield Handbk.* ed. H. J. Callender (Birmingham, 1951).

[19] *Lichfield Mercury*, 14 Aug. 1931, p. 5; 6 Dec. 1935, p. 3; *750th Anniversary of Lichfield Cathedral* (1946), 30 (copy in W.S.L.).

[20] Bull, *House of Lomax 1810–1969*; above (previous section).

[21] *P.O. Dir. Staffs.* (1850 and later edns.); S.R.O., D. 4566/98, corresp. re 38 Bird St.; below, social and cultural activities (newspapers).

[22] Inf. from the *Lichfield Mercury* office.

[23] *P.O. Dir. Staffs.* (1864; 1868; 1872).

[24] *Lichfield Mercury*, 8 Mar. 1918, p. 3; inf. from Mr. Charles Bridgeman and Mr. J. Linford.

[25] *Lichfield Mercury*, 3 May 1901, p. 8; 10 May 1912, p. 4.

[26] Ibid. 8 Jan. 1937, p. 5.

[27] Ibid. 13 Sept. 1946, p. 7; 11 Oct. 1946, p. 4; *S.H.C.* 1950–1, 207, 209.

[28] *Lichfield Mercury*, 21 Aug. 1964, p. 11.

Avenue was opened in 1972.[29] A further expansion of light industry to the south was started in 1981 with the opening of the Britannia Enterprise Park. As part of the Boley Park Industrial Estate, it was further added to in the mid and late 1980s.[30]

PROFESSIONS.
Apart from the cathedral clergy, lawyers have been the main group of professional men in the city since the 16th century, their business initially generated by the ecclesiastical courts. They acquired a body of wealthy clients as Lichfield developed in the 18th century as a place of residence for polite society, and they also served the needs of various charitable and public trusts.

The corporation's first bailiffs in 1548, Mark Wyrley and Gregory Stonyng, were lawyers, and eight other lawyers were bailiffs in the period to 1588.[31] They included John Dyott (d. 1578), a barrister,[32] Richard Martin, diocesan registrar by 1551,[33] and James Weston (d. 1589), diocesan registrar by 1562 and M.P. for Lichfield 1584–5.[34] The Martin family were lawyers for several generations: Edward Martin, a bachelor of laws and master of the guild of St. Mary and St. John the Baptist in 1512–13,[35] John (d. 1635), Simon (d. 1681), and Simon's son, also Simon (d. 1688).[36] Other members of the Weston family too were lawyers: James's brother Robert (d. 1573) was chancellor of both Lichfield and Exeter dioceses, James's son Simon became recorder of Lichfield, and another son James was admitted to the Inner Temple.[37]

There were ten lawyers in 1793, six of them proctors in the bishop's consistory court and four attorneys.[38] In 1834 there were four proctors and ten attorneys, and in 1851 two proctors and eleven attorneys.[39] Of the proctors listed in 1793 William Mott had been articled in 1774 as a clerk to William Buckeridge, a proctor; he became deputy diocesan registrar in 1781 and registrar to the dean and chapter in 1799, retaining both offices until his death in 1826.[40] His son John, articled in 1798, succeeded him as deputy diocesan registrar and was still in office in 1854.[41] Thomas Hinckley, another proctor recorded in 1793, evidently had a civil practice as well: he was practising as an attorney in 1784 and was steward of Longdon manor between 1794 and 1809.[42] He died in 1817, and his sons Arthur, Thomas, and Richard continued the practice, evidently from an office in Market Street.[43] Thomas the younger succeeded his father as steward of Longdon manor and remained steward until 1825; he retired probably after buying Beacon Place in 1827. His brother Richard retired evidently on his marriage in 1835.[44] In 1850 the practice was managed by Thomas Hodson from an office in no. 13 the Close.[45] Arthur Hinckley (d. 1862) remained senior partner and was joined in 1857 by Frederick Hinckley (d. 1907).[46] Some time between 1860 and 1864 the practice moved to premises in Bird Street.[47] In 1941 Hinckley, Brown & Crarer amalgamated with Birch & Birch, a practice which had been established in Lichfield in 1841 by George Birch (d. 1899). The new firm retained the Bird Street premises until 1958, when it moved to Birch's house at no. 20 St. John Street. The firm of Hinckley, Birch & Exham, formed in 1962, continued in practice there in the late 1980s.[48]

Two of the four attorneys recorded in 1793 were Charles Simpson and his son Stephen, both of them in turn town clerk. Stephen's son, Charles, was also town clerk 1825–44 and 1853–87. Based in Tamworth Street in 1834, Charles had moved to St. John Street by 1848.[49]

Another long-lived practice was established by Henry Chinn, who in 1798 was articled as a clerk to William Jackson, a proctor, transferring himself later the same year to George Hand of Beacon Place.[50] Hand died childless in 1806, and Chinn continued the practice, admitting his son Thomas in 1816.[51] The Chinns evidently used as their office Langton House in Beacon Street.[52] The practice survived in the family until the death of Alan Chinn in 1919.[53]

A physician (*medicus*) named William of Southwell made a grant of land in the town in 1308, and another named John of Southwell was recorded in 1313.[54] Robert the leech and John Leech were recorded respectively in 1372 and 1443.[55] A surgeon named Robert Sale, otherwise

[29] *Lichfield Handbk.* (Lichfield, c. 1960), 24 (copy in Lichfield Libr.); *Lichfield District Official Guide* (1979), 97; above, general hist. (20th century).

[30] *Lichfield Mercury*, 16 Oct. 1981, p. 11; 17 Feb. 1984, p. 19; 29 July 1988, p. 9.

[31] Harwood, *Lichfield*, 419–22.

[32] Below, Curborough and Elmhurst, estates (Stychbrook).

[33] Harwood, *Lichfield*, 418–19.

[34] Ibid. 421; *S.H.C.* 1917–18, 381–2. His will is in P.R.O., PROB 11/73, ff. 380v.–381.

[35] Harwood, *Lichfield*, 412.

[36] Reade, *Johnsonian Gleanings*, iv. 118, 120–2; *Elias Ashmole*, ed. C. H. Josten, iv. 1591; L.J.R.O., P/C/11, Simon Martin (1681).

[37] Erdeswick, *Staffs.* 165 and preceding pedigrees; *Cal. of Inner Temple Recs.* ed. F. A. Inderwick (1896), i. 395; above, town govt. (govt. from 1548: corporation officers).

[38] *Univ. Brit. Dir.* iii. 610.

[39] White, *Dir. Staffs.* (1834), 156, 160; (1851), 521, 526.

[40] L.J.R.O., B/A/19, articles of agreement, 29 Sept. 1774; L.J.R.O., Theological Coll. deeds, will of Wm. Smalbroke (proved 1797); Mott tablet in south choir aisle of Lichfield cathedral.

[41] L.J.R.O., B/A/19, articles of agreement, 21 July 1798; White, *Dir. Staffs.* (1834), 87; *P.O. Dir. Staffs.* (1854).

[42] *Bailey's Brit. Dir.* (1784), 400; S.R.O., D. (W.) 1734/2/1/753–5.

[43] Reade, *Johnsonian Gleanings*, vii. 166–7; Parson and Bradshaw, *Staffs. Dir.* (1818), 183.

[44] S.R.O., D. (W.) 1511(34)/5/12; D. (W.) 1734/2/1/755–6; above, manor (lay estates: Beacon Place).

[45] *P.O. Dir. Staffs.* (1850); Lichfield Cath. Libr., Savage papers, B 4/4/1/12.

[46] Reade, *Johnsonian Gleanings*, vii. 167; *Lichfield Mercury*, 12 Apr. 1907, p. 5.

[47] *P.O. Dir. Staffs.* (1860; 1864).

[48] *Lichfield Mercury*, 30 June 1899, p. 5; inf. from Mr. R. D. Birch of Hinckley, Birch & Exham.

[49] White, *Dir. Staffs.* (1834), 156; L.J.R.O., B/A/15/ Lichfield, St. Mary, no. 461; above, town govt. (govt. from 1548: corporation officers).

[50] L.J.R.O., B/A/19, deposition of Geo. Hand, 22 Jan. 1806.

[51] Ibid. articles of 13 Nov. 1816; above, manor (lay estates: Beacon Place).

[52] Parson and Bradshaw, *Staffs. Dir.* (1818), 170; White, *Dir. Staffs.* (1834), 160; L.J.R.O., D. 30/lease bk. 15, f. 82.

[53] *Lichfield Mercury*, 24 Jan. 1919, p. 4.

[54] S.R.O. 3764/50; W.S.L. 55/92/52.

[55] L.J.R.O., D. 30/XXIV, f. 41; *S.H.C.* n.s. iii. 166.

Plymun', was living in Lichfield in the early 16th century.[56] At least four surgeons were recorded in the 1660s,[57] and from 1676 John (later Sir John) Floyer (d. 1734) practised as a physician in Lichfield. Floyer wrote on cold bathing, asthma, and the rate of the pulse, and it was on his advice that Samuel Johnson was taken to London in 1712 to be touched for the evil by Queen Anne.[58] At his birth in 1709 Johnson had benefited from the ministrations of a 'man-midwife', George Hector, son of Edmund Hector, a Lichfield surgeon (d. 1709). George was also a surgeon and was paid by the Conduit Lands trustees to attend the poor. He was still in Lichfield in 1719 but later moved to Lilleshall (Salop.), his son Brooke Hector (d. 1773) continuing the Lichfield practice as a physician. George's brother Benjamin was a surgeon in Lichfield and was living there apparently in 1741.[59] Erasmus Darwin, physician and naturalist, practised in Lichfield from 1756 to 1781. In 1762 he advertised a course of anatomical lectures: the body of a malefactor about to be executed at Lichfield was to be taken to Darwin's house in Beacon Street, and the course would begin the day after the execution and continue 'every day as long as the body can be preserved'.[60] In the 1770s George Chadwick, a physician, opened a lunatic asylum in his house in St. John Street; it was closed in 1814.[61]

Cary Butt, who died at Pipe Grange in Pipehill in 1781, practised in Lichfield as a surgeon. His practice was continued by his son-in-law Thomas Salt, one of four surgeons in Lichfield in 1793. Thomas, who died in 1817, was probably the 'Mr. Salt' from whom the later medical writer Shirley Palmer learnt the rudiments of medicine.[62] William Rowley, recorded as an apothecary in 1793, was described as a surgeon at his death in 1797. His son Thomas, also a surgeon, owned a lunatic asylum from 1817 and was later physician to the two dispensaries in the city.[63] Thomas (d. 1863) was prominent in local affairs and was twice mayor.[64] There were six surgeons in Lichfield in 1818 and seven in 1851.[65]

Only one physician, Trevor Jones, was recorded in 1793. He was still practising in 1829, along with two others.[66] Richard Wright (d.

1821), grandson of the apothecary Richard Greene, practised as a physician in 1818.[67] There were three physicians in 1834, including Thomas Rowley and James Rawson, both of whom were still practising in 1851.[68]

A banker named John Barker was nominated to the Conduit Lands Trust in 1762 and was treasurer of the Lichfield turnpike trust by 1766.[69] He died in 1780, and his bank was continued by his widow Catherine.[70] She was banker to the Lichfield and Staffordshire Tontine Society, established in 1790 with benefits payable to members after seven years.[71] Her son Samuel became a partner in the bank in 1792 but retired in 1799, the year after the bank's principal clerk, John Barker Scott, became a partner.[72] Scott, who was probably John Barker's nephew,[73] continued the bank after Catherine's death in 1803, and in 1814 he admitted as partners his brother Robert, then of London, and James Palmer and William Guest Bird, both of Lichfield. The bank was then run as J. B. Scott & Co. and had its premises in Market Street, probably on the north side where the premises were in 1848. Bird left the partnership in 1818, and J. B. Scott died in 1819.[74] Robert Scott died in 1827, and his interest passed to his son-in-law, Richard Greene, later of Stowe House.[75] The day-to-day management of the bank was the responsibility of James Palmer, who died in 1850 leaving it in debt. Greene continued the bank, but it failed in 1855.[76]

The Lichfield Savings Bank was established in 1818 and opened every Friday in the National school in Frog Lane. By 1827 it had 722 individuals and 6 friendly societies as depositors. Premises for it were built in 1849 at the corner of Bore Street and Conduit Street. It closed in 1880.[77]

A Lichfield branch of the National Provincial Bank was established in 1834, and in 1838 it acquired the clients of the Rugeley, Tamworth, and Lichfield Joint Stock Bank which closed its Lichfield branch that year. The branch in 1848 was in Bird Street, at what later became the corner with the Friary.[78] Following the 1970 merger of the National Provincial Bank and the Westminster Bank, the Bird Street branch was

---

[56] P.R.O., SP 1/231, f. 98.
[57] L.J.R.O., D. 88/rental of 1662, p. [2]; *S.H.C.* 1936, 147, 150; *S.H.C.* 4th ser. v, p. 149.
[58] *D.N.B.*; R. Simms, *Bibliotheca Staffordiensis* (Lichfield, 1894), 172–3.
[59] Reade, *Johnsonian Gleanings*, viii. 7–8; A. L. Reade, *Reades of Blackwood Hill* (priv. print. 1906), 152–3; Laithwaite, *Conduit Lands Trust*, 80.
[60] D. King-Hele, *Doctor of Revolution*, 37–140, *passim*.
[61] Above, public services (medical services).
[62] Reade, *Johnsonian Gleanings*, iv. 130, 133; viii. 116; *Univ. Brit. Dir.* iii. 610; *D.N.B.* s.v. Palmer, Shirley.
[63] S.R.O., D. 593/B/1/26/24, abstract of title of Wm. Rowley's executor; L.J.R.O., D. 29/1/2; above, public services (medical services).
[64] *Staffs. Advertiser*, 28 Mar. 1863, p. 5.
[65] Parson and Bradshaw, *Staffs. Dir.* (1818), 189; White, *Dir. Staffs.* (1851), 526.
[66] *Univ. Brit. Dir.* iii. 610; Pigot, *Nat. Com. Dir.* (1829), 715.
[67] Parson and Bradshaw, *Staffs. Dir.* (1818), 188; below, social and cultural activities (museums).

[68] White, *Dir. Staffs.* (1834), 160; (1851), 520.
[69] Laithwaite, *Conduit Lands Trust*, 80; *Aris's Birmingham Gaz.* 1 Sept. 1766.
[70] L.J.R.O., B/A/19, papers re John Barker, copy will, 1780; *Univ. Brit. Dir.* iii. 609.
[71] Printed rules of soc. (copy in L.J.R.O., D. 121); *Aris's Birmingham Gaz.* 20 Nov. 1797.
[72] S.R.O., D. (W.) 3222/467; L.J.R.O., B/A/19, papers re John Barker, copy case and opinion on bankruptcy, 1821.
[73] His mother's maiden name was Barker: S.R.O., D. 1011/1/5, no. 53; *Staffs. Advertiser*, 1 Dec. 1821.
[74] *Staffs. Advertiser*, 15 Jan. 1803; 11 Dec. 1819; S.R.O., D. (W.) 1851/8/57A; L.J.R.O., P/C/11, Mary Scott (1822); ibid. B/A/15/Lichfield, St. Mary, no. 203.
[75] *Staffs. Advertiser*, 21 May 1825; 28 July 1827; Clayton, *Cathedral City*, 90–2.
[76] Clayton, *Cathedral City*, 92–5.
[77] *Lichfield Mercury*, 14 Dec. 1827; 20 Feb. 1880, p. 5; J. Rawson, *Public Bank for Savings and Public Improvement of Lichfield* (Lichfield, 1849; copy in W.S.L.); date stone on 1849 building; below, plate 28.
[78] L.J.R.O., B/A/15/Lichfield, St. Mary, no. 347.

closed in 1974 and business transferred to premises in the market square, originally opened in 1952 as a branch of the Westminster Bank.[79]

A bank was opened in Dam Street by Stevenson, Salt & Co. of Stafford in 1857, following the collapse of Greene's bank. In 1866 the company was taken over by Lloyds Bank, which still occupied the premises in the late 1980s.[80]

The London and Midland Bank opened a branch at nos. 21 and 23 Market Street in 1892; it was moved to new premises at the corner of Market and Dam Streets in 1972.[81] A branch of Barclays Bank was opened at no. 15 Market Street in 1952; it was moved to Breadmarket Street in 1973.[82]

Joseph Potter (d. 1842) practised as an architect in Lichfield from the late 1780s, when he was employed by James Wyatt to supervise alterations to Lichfield cathedral. He had a considerable practice throughout Staffordshire, for which he became county surveyor, and in neighbouring counties. The practice, which by 1814 was run from a house on the north side of St. John's hospital, was continued by his son Joseph (d. 1875). By 1845 the younger Joseph was living at Pipehill and apparently had his office there.[83] Thomas Johnson (d. 1853), who worked as an architect in Tamworth Street in 1829, was a son-in-law of the architect James Trubshaw of Little Haywood in Colwich, with whom he was for a time in partnership. By 1834 Johnson was living in the later Davidson House in Upper St. John Street.[84] Johnson's son, also Thomas (d. 1865), continued the practice.[85]

GUILDS

RELIGIOUS GUILDS. There were guilds attached to all three town churches before the Reformation. The brothers of St. Chad at Stowe existed c. 1300, and the guild of St. Chad with land at Stowe was mentioned in 1365. It may still have been in existence in 1431.[86] There was a guild of St. John the Baptist attached to St. Mary's church in 1353. It had both men and women as members, and its chaplain was the chantry priest serving the altar of St. John the Baptist.[87] There was also a guild of St. Mary in the mid 14th century, and that too had a male and female membership.[88] In the earlier 16th century there was a guild of St. Michael with land adjoining St. Michael's churchyard.[89]

The two guilds attached to St. Mary's were amalgamated in 1387. That year Richard II licensed seven petitioners to found a guild of St. Mary and St. John the Baptist at Lichfield for a fee of £30. Bishop Scrope added his licence.[90] The petitioners were also given permission by the king to acquire property worth up to £10 a year for the maintenance of the guild and the support of its chaplain. In part satisfaction the king in 1392 licensed a grant of property in Lichfield to the guild.[91] Gifts of other lands followed.[92] By 1477 the guild held extensive property in Lichfield and in nearby parts of Staffordshire. In the city it had 12 burgages, including the White Hart in Saddler Street, 22 cottages, 4 shops, a tenement, a garden, 6 barns, and over 20 a. in the open fields.[93]

The members of the new guild appointed a master and four wardens and drew up ordinances for running the guild. The master and wardens were to be elected at an annual meeting of the brothers and sisters on the feast of the Conception of St. Mary (8 December) or in the week following. The electors were to be a committee consisting of six brethren chosen by the retiring master, three others chosen by those six, and the retiring wardens. Those elected had to live in Lichfield during their term of office, and anyone elected who refused to serve was to be expelled from the guild. The master and wardens were to issue livery each year ready for the Nativity of St. Mary (8 September), and on that day or within the week a feast attended by the brothers and sisters was to be held if the masters and wardens thought fit. New members were to be admitted at the discretion of the master and wardens, with whom an admission fee was to be agreed.[94] Most of the fees were paid in cash, and in the early 16th century they were normally between 20d. and 3s. 8d. Occasionally they took the form of land or goods; thus a parchment maker admitted in the early 15th century gave the parchment for a missal.[95] Other ordinances dealt with the standard disputes between members and the relief of members who became destitute.

Annual admissions in the earlier 15th century averaged 31 and rose to an average of 105 in the later part of the century, reaching 160 in the last

[79] Lichfield Mercury, 28 Nov. 1952, p. 7; 28 Sept. 1984, p. 14.
[80] R. S. Sayers, Lloyds Bank in the Hist. of English Banking, 34, 311; inf. from Mr. P. A. Pullin, assistant manager.
[81] H. Asher, Guide to Lichfield City (Lichfield, 1892), 21; inf. from the bank.
[82] Lichfield Mercury, 31 Oct. 1952, p. 7; inf. from the bank.
[83] H. Colvin, Biog. Dict. Brit. Architects, 654; L.J.R.O., D. 126/min. bk. 1741–1856, p. 353; S.R.O., D. 615/E(x)/6, no. 50.
[84] Colvin, Biog. Dict. Brit. Architects, 840; Pigot, Nat. Com. Dir. (1829), 714*; White, Dir. Staffs. (1834), 155; L.J.R.O., B/A/15/Lichfield, St. Michael, nos. 252–3.

[85] Staffs. Advertiser, 13 May 1865, p. 4.
[86] L.J.R.O., D. 30/XXIV, ff. 32v.–34, 47.
[87] Ibid. D. 30/VC, B 11; Cal. Pat. 1354–8, 412.
[88] S.H.C. 4th ser. xiii. 19.
[89] J.R.U.L.M., Ryl. Ch., Phillipps 126; Cal. Pat. 1569–72, pp. 348, 397–8, 405.
[90] S.H.C. 4th ser. xiii. 19; T.S.S.A.H.S. xxvii. 39–40.
[91] Cal. Pat. 1385–9, 380; 1391–6, 118.
[92] e.g. Bodl. MS. Ashmole 855, pp. 195–202.
[93] L.J.R.O., D. 126/cartulary (partially transcribed in Harwood, Lichfield, 326–34).
[94] S.H.C. 4th ser. xiii. 19 sqq.
[95] T.S.S.A.H.S. xxvii. 40; Harwood, Lichfield, 399–402.

two decades. In the 16th century the annual average was 93.[96] At least 167 members of the earlier guild of St. Mary were admitted posthumously into the new guild, and posthumous admissions continued, becoming particularly numerous in the earlier 16th century.[97] Besides Richard II and his queen, Anne, who head the list of members, many notable persons were admitted, including Henry VII in 1487 and his queen in 1494. Local gentry and the heads of religious houses in the Midlands figure prominently; leading inhabitants of several English towns also appear.[98]

In 1389 a full assembly was held in a private house.[99] A guildhall in Bore Street by 1421 may have been the 'Stayvethall' (or 'Staynethall') for which an ornament worth £3 was given c. 1406.[1] By the late 15th century the guild was participating in the government of the town, and the master was assisted by a group called the Forty-eight.[2]

The guild ordinances provided that there should be as many chaplains as was thought necessary by the worthier brethren.[3] A new chaplain was to be admitted by the master and wardens after the existing chaplains had checked his suitability. St. Mary's being the guild church, the chaplains were expected to help with the daily services and to be present at the mass of St. Mary and the anthem 'Salve Regina' each day. It was laid down that one of the guild chaplains was to be appointed clerk by the master and wardens with an annual remuneration of 6s. 8d.; he had to present an account of the guild's income and expenditure to the master and wardens when required. As stipulated in the ordinances, the guild chaplains lived in a house called the Priests' Hall which stood in Breadmarket Street opposite the south-west corner of the church. It was given to the guild by Adam Ingestre at the time of its foundation.[4] By 1389 the guild had bought a chalice and a vestment.[5] There were four guild priests in 1466, although one of them was then stated to be serving a cure in the Close and neglecting his duty of celebrating at St. Mary's.[6]

The guild was dissolved evidently in 1548.[7] Its lands then lay mainly in Lichfield with some in other parts of Staffordshire; property at Great Wyrley in Cannock, at Norton Canes, including Little Wyrley, and at Wall had been conveyed to trustees in 1545 for the maintenance of Lichfield's water supply.[8] The guild's net annual income was just over £41 in 1548. The guild was then supporting four priests, a deacon, two parish clerks, and two children to sing and celebrate daily in St. Mary's; the church's vestments included 'six copes for children'. The priest who acted as clerk to the guild received a stipend of £6 6s. 8d. and the other three priests one of £5 13s. 4d. each. A sum of £4 13s. 4d. was paid to the poor. The guild had 12 oz. of silver-gilt plate, ornaments worth 3s. 2d., and household stuff in the guildhall worth £1 17s. 8d. One of the priests died in November 1548; the rest received pensions of £5 13s. 4d. each, and one of them was vicar of St. Mary's in the 1550s. Various smaller pensions were granted to four other 'incumbents' of the guild and to a chorister.[9] The Crown soon began to sell the guild's property piecemeal. In 1549, for example, two London speculators bought the chaplains' house, and another bought the guildhall.[10] It was alleged in 1571 that some of the property in Lichfield was still being concealed from the Crown.[11]

The guild seal in use in 1545 depicted the Virgin and Child.[12]

CRAFT GUILDS. There is no contemporary evidence that there were craft guilds in Lichfield in the Middle Ages, but their existence in that period is suggested by a list of what were styled trade companies, drawn up probably in the 1650s. The list records those Lichfield companies whose members had been loyal to Charles I, giving the dates of origin and incorporation claimed by each company and a trick of their arms. In order of alleged age the companies were as follows: saddlers, in existence in Edward I's reign; vintners, incorporated in Edward III's reign and granted arms in 1427–8; mercers, established in 1393–4; masons, incorporated in the reign of Henry IV; shoemakers, incorporated in 1438–9; carpenters, established in 1477; barbers and surgeons, incorporated in Edward IV's reign; cooks, incorporated in the same reign; joiners, incorporated in 1570–1; painters and stainers, of 'great antiquity' but not incorporated until 1580; smiths, incorporated in Elizabeth I's reign; and butchers, incorporated in 1605. Three companies, the bakers, the farriers, and the glaziers, were described simply as ancient.[13] Of those listed the shoemakers are known from other evidence to have existed as a company in 1561,[14] the bakers in 1576,[15] the saddlers in 1594,[16] the smiths in 1601,[17] the mercers in 1623,[18] and the butchers in 1641.[19] The masons and carpenters were recorded as a

[96] *The Church in Pre-Reformation Society*, ed. C. M. Barron and C. Harper-Bill, 161.
[97] L.J.R.O., D. 77/1, pp. 255 sqq. (with the admissions from the earlier guild on pp. 312–15).
[98] *T.S.S.A.H.S.* xxvii. 41–2.
[99] Bodl. MS. Ashmole 855, p. 202.
[1] *T.S.S.A.H.S.* xxvii. 45 n.
[2] Above, town govt. (govt. to 1548: community of the town).
[3] *S.H.C.* 4th ser. xiii. 25–6, where *probabiliores* is wrongly given as *prohabiliores*.
[4] Harwood, *Lichfield*, 478; *Cal. Pat.* 1548–9, 420; L.J.R.O., D. 30/VC, palimpsest, i, f. 28; L.J.R.O., VC/A/21, CC 17529, plan 18.
[5] H. F. Westlake, *Parish Guilds of Mediaeval Eng.* 225.
[6] L.J.R.O., D. 30/9/3/1, f. 17.
[7] The guild register gives the names of a master and

wardens for 1549, but no new members are listed: *S.H.C.* 4th ser. xiii. 21 n.
[8] P.R.O., SC 12/29/1; above, public services (water supplies).
[9] *S.H.C.* 1915, 170–1; Harwood, *Lichfield*, 14, 455–6.
[10] *Cal. Pat.* 1548–9, 392, 420; above, town govt. (govt. from 1548: guildhall).
[11] *Cal. Pat.* 1569–72, pp. 397–8, 405.
[12] For impressions of that year see L.J.R.O., D. 77/16/1; P.R.O., E 40/13437.   [13] W.S.L., S. MS. 195/1.
[14] Chetham's Libr., Manchester, Mun. A. 6.56A, f. 41.
[15] Harwood, *Lichfield*, 355.
[16] L.J.R.O., D. 77/4/1/1, ff. 39–42.
[17] *Gild of St. Mary, Lichfield* (E.E.T.S., extra ser. 114), 45–57.
[18] *Trans. R.H.S.* N.S. vii. 109–25.
[19] L.J.R.O., D. 77/4/1/1, ff. 32–6.

single company in 1698.[20] Four companies were omitted from the 1650s list, presumably because their members were disloyal to the Crown, the clothworkers and weavers recorded in 1552,[21] the cappers in 1575,[22] the tailors in 1576,[23] and the tanners in 1625.[24]

The last recorded admission of a capper was in 1708 and of a tanner in 1753.[25] There were only two members of the mercers' company in 1786 and it became extinct c. 1797.[26] The bakers' and the clothworkers' companies still existed in 1833.[27] Although the 1835 Municipal Corporations Act took away the economic privileges of trade companies, the members of four Lichfield companies continued to meet for social purposes: butchers at least until 1865,[28] shoemakers at least until 1870,[29] tailors at least until 1880,[30] and smiths until 1896.[31] The smiths' company was revived in 1943 when the eldest son of one of the last members successfully claimed admittance and was enrolled in the presence of the mayor. In the late 1980s the company held its annual feast in February. Beside admitting freemen of its own craft, the revived company also admits as honorary freemen those who have given outstanding service to the city.[32]

Allied crafts were often included in one company. The saddlers were members of what in 1594 was styled the company of glovers, whittawers (workers in fine leather), and saddlers; the style varied in the 17th and 18th centuries and included bridle cutters, horse-collar makers, skinners, fellmongers, and makers of breeches.[33] The style of the mercers' company in 1623 included grocers, woollen drapers, linen drapers, silkmen, hosiers, salters, apothecaries, and haberdashers.[34] The shoemakers were members of what was more usually known as the company of corvisors and curriers.[35] The style of the smiths' company in 1601 included goldsmiths, ironmongers, cardmakers (makers of wire brushes used in combing wool), pewterers, plumbers, cutlers, and spurriers; by 1630 braziers and nailers had been added to the company's name. In addition ironmongers, locksmiths, tinplate makers, and watchmakers were admitted in the 17th century.[36] The butchers and the chandlers in 1641 together formed a company.[37]

Ordinances made in the late 16th and early 17th century gave details of the conditions for membership and of the government of the companies.[38] Freedom was open to the eldest son of a freeman, to an apprentice of seven years'

standing, and to others who paid an entrance fee, normally £10. A widow who carried on her husband's trade was eligible for membership.[39] Each company was governed by one or more masters or wardens, chosen annually on or near a feast day: clothworkers, four masters or wardens at Corpus Christi; tailors, one master and two wardens within a month of the Nativity of St. John the Baptist (24 June); mercers, a master and two wardens on the Wednesday after the feast of St. James the apostle (25 July); butchers, two wardens on Lammas day (1 August); shoemakers, two wardens on the feast of St. Crispin and St. Crispian (25 October); tanners, two wardens at Martinmas (11 November); saddlers, two masters on St. Clement's day (23 November); bakers, two wardens on St. Clement's day; smiths, one master and two wardens on the Friday after St. Clement's day, changed in 1630 to the Wednesday; cappers, one master and two wardens on St. Catherine's day (25 November). The revived company of smiths installs its master at a mayoral court held on the last Tuesday in February.[40]

The ordinances also stated rules for the manufacture and sale of goods. From their records it is known that the tailors in 1659 investigated 'foreigners' working in the city, and that the smiths in 1701–2 acted against a man selling scythes and another selling candlesticks.[41] The decline of the mercers' company suggests that restrictive practices were abandoned in the distributive trades in the 18th century. Self regulation also took place. In 1676 the butchers agreed not to sell on Sundays,[42] and in 1766 Lichfield tradesmen imposed a ban on Sunday trading.[43]

The companies also had an important social function, providing members with convivial meetings. The election of officers was an occasion for feasting, which also took place at other times: the shoemakers had an additional feast at Corpus Christi in the later 16th century,[44] as did the tailors in the 17th century.[45] There is no evidence that any company had its own common hall, and the feasts were held at inns in the 18th century, and presumably earlier; the guildhall, however, may also have been a venue, and the tailors had a feast there in 1803.[46] Minstrels played at the shoemakers' feasts in the later 16th century,[47] and payments to musicians, including trumpeters, drummers, and boy choristers, were regularly made by the tailors and the smiths in the 17th and earlier 18th century.[48] The smiths' company bought a ceremonial cup for £20 1s. in 1708–9; it was presumably the silver cup sold in

[20] Ibid. D. 77/5/1, f. 90.
[21] S.R.O., D. 4566/M.
[22] Acts of P.C. 1575–7, 36.
[23] Gild of St. Mary, 25–32.
[24] L.J.R.O., D. 77/4/1/1, ff. 44–9.
[25] Ibid. D. 77/3/1, pp. 12, 32.
[26] W.S.L., M. 849; 7th Rep. Com. Char. 437.
[27] 1st Rep. Com. Mun. Corp. H.C. 116, App. III, p. 1927 (1835), xxv.   [28] L.J.R.O., D. 77/4/3.
[29] Chetham's Libr., Mun. A. 6.56c.
[30] L.J.R.O., D. 77/4/7/4.
[31] Lichfield Mercury, 24 Sept. 1943, p. 2.
[32] Ibid.; inf. from Mr. J. M. S. Salloway, hon. clerk.
[33] L.J.R.O., D. 77/4/1/1, f. 39; D. 77/4/5/1.
[34] Trans. R.H.S. N.S. vii. 109–25.
[35] Chetham's Libr., Mun. A. 6.56A, ff. 2, 5, 42v.

[36] Gild of St. Mary, 46, 60; L.J.R.O., D. 77/4/6/1.
[37] L.J.R.O., D. 77/4/1/1, f. 32.
[38] Para. based on ibid. D. 77/4/1/1; D. 77/4/2; S.R.O., D. 4566/M; Gild of St. Mary, 25–76; Trans. R.H.S. N.S. vii. 109–25.
[39] e.g. L.J.R.O., D. 77/4/5/2, ff. 2, 4; D. 77/4/6/1, f. 196; D. 77/4/7/2, f. 10.
[40] Inf. from Mr. Salloway.
[41] L.J.R.O., D. 77/4/6/1, f. 172v.; D. 77/4/7/1, f. 21.
[42] Ibid. D. 77/4/3, 18 July 1676.
[43] Aris's Birmingham Gaz. 17 Nov. 1766.
[44] Chetham's Libr., Mun. A. 6.56A, ff. 42 sqq.
[45] L.J.R.O., D. 77/4/7/1, ff. 4, 40v.
[46] Ibid. D. 35/bailiffs' accts. 1704–94, p. 72.
[47] Chetham's Libr., Mun. A. 6.56A, ff. 42 sqq.
[48] L.J.R.O., D. 77/4/6/1–2; D. 77/4/7/1–2.

1737.[49] Members' wives had their own meetings or were allowed to join their husbands after dinner; in 1786 the saddlers' company allowed married members to bring a substitute companion.[50] In the earlier 17th century the tailors paid 1s. or 2s. to 'the women',[51] and in 1701–2 the smiths spent 2s. on March beer (strong ale) for the women's wassail.[52] The shoemakers required attendance at the marriage and burial of a brother or sister member in the early 17th century,[53] and in the late 17th and early 18th century the smiths had their own funeral pall.[54]

Members were notified of meetings by a summoner or beadle: one was recorded for the smiths in 1672,[55] the shoemakers in 1681,[56] the cappers in 1695,[57] and the tailors in 1697.[58] Both the smiths and the shoemakers provided their summoner with a uniform and a badge of office.[59]

The companies' chief source of revenue was admission fees; other income included fines for breaching company rules and, for the smiths' company in the late 17th and early 18th century, a charge of 2s. 6d. each time the company's funeral pall was used.[60] The smiths also operated or participated in a lottery in 1757.[61] Most expenditure went on feasting, but a proportion of the fines and other income was normally assigned for poor relief. Payments to 'the poor man's box' were stipulated in ordinances made for the clothworkers in 1552,[62] the saddlers in 1594,[63] and the butchers in 1641.[64] The 1601 ordinances of the smiths' company required that half of the fines should be distributed to the city's poor. New ordinances in 1630 omitted that provision, but in the late 17th and early 18th century the smiths made regular payments of up to 5s. a year to poor travellers.[65]

Freedom of a company conferred the right to vote in parliamentary elections, and both the Whigs and the Tories arranged for large numbers of new freemen to be enrolled at election time. The smiths' company was often used for the purpose, and the resulting accumulation of capital from admission fees was distributed among members, £80 in 1747, £40 in 1753, and £186 in stages between 1799 and 1801. No distribution was made after the admission of 125 freemen to the company in April 1801 because a corrupt method of paying entrance fees had been employed.[66]

CHURCHES

THERE were Christians, probably with a church, at the Romano-British settlement at Wall, and it is possible that Christianity persisted in the area. Bishops and monks suffered as a result of a Welsh victory at *Caer Lwytgoed* (either Wall itself or a place in the neighbourhood) in the earlier or mid 7th century. There may thus have been a church or monastery there. The relationship between Wall, *Caer Lwytgoed*, and Lichfield, however, is obscure. A cathedral was established at Lichfield in 669 as the seat of Chad, the newly appointed bishop. A later tradition that a church had been built there in 656 or 657 by King Oswiu was evidently based on the mistaken assumption that the creation of the bishopric of the Middle Angles, Lindisfaras, and Mercians mentioned by Bede coincided with the establishment of the see of Lichfield. Chad's cathedral and the funerary church built in 700 stood on or near the site of the present cathedral.[67]

At Stowe, ½ mile north-east of the cathedral, is the church of St. Chad, recorded c. 1190.[68]

Stowe, a name evidently meaning a holy place or a church,[69] has long been identified as the 'more retired dwelling place' not far from Chad's cathedral to which the saint used to go with a few companions for reading and prayer and at which he died.[70] A holy well near Stowe church is traditionally associated with Chad's devotions and mortifications.[71] In the late 12th century special honour was paid to a statue of the saint in the church,[72] and for one 13th-century canon of the cathedral Stowe was 'that sacred spot'.[73] When in 1321 the cathedral chapter decided to join the Lichfield Franciscans in prayers for the sick Bishop Langton, it was to Stowe that both groups processed for a service.[74] A 13th-century topographer, who claimed that Stowe was the place where Chad preached to the people, wrote that there were two minsters at Lichfield, a western and an eastern.[75] The first was the cathedral, and the second was presumably Stowe. The local importance of Stowe church in the early Middle Ages was evidently reflected in the size of the Norman building. It has even

[49] Ibid. D. 77/4/6/1, f. 120; D. 77/4/6/2, acct. for 23 Nov. 1737.
[50] Ibid. D. 77/4/5/1, f. 1v.
[51] Ibid. D. 77/4/7/1, ff. 4–15.
[52] Ibid. D. 77/4/6/1, f. 172v.
[53] Chetham's Libr., Mun. A. 6.56A, f. 16.
[54] L.J.R.O., D. 77/4/6/1, ff. 115v., 123, 181v.
[55] Ibid. f. 186v.
[56] Chetham's Libr., Mun. A. 6.56A, f. 7v.
[57] L.J.R.O., D. 77/4/1/1, f. 22v.
[58] *Gild of St. Mary*, 42.
[59] L.J.R.O., D. 77/4/6/1, ff. 115v., 120, 136v., 174; Chetham's Libr., Mun. A. 6.56A, ff. 8, 10, 38v.
[60] L.J.R.O., D. 77/4/6/1.
[61] Ibid. D. 77/4/6/2, entry for 23 Nov. 1757.
[62] S.R.O., D. 4566/M.   [63] L.J.R.O., D. 77/4/1/1, f. 39v.

[64] Ibid. f. 35v.
[65] Ibid. D. 77/4/6/1; *Gild of St. Mary*, 47–55, 59–76.
[66] L.J.R.O., D. 77/4/6/2; above, parl. representation.
[67] Above, general hist.; cathedral and close.
[68] *Statutes of Lincoln Cathedral*, ed. H. Bradshaw and C. Wordsworth, ii (1), 19–20, printing Bp. Nonant's Lichfield statutes. The version in Dugdale, *Mon.* vi (3), 1256, is incorrect at that point.
[69] *Eng. Place-Name Elements* (E.P.N.S.), ii. 159.
[70] *Bede's Eccl. Hist. of Eng. People*, ed. B. Colgrave and R. A. B. Mynors, 336–44.
[71] Below (St. Chad's church).
[72] *Statutes of Lincoln Cathedral*, ii (1), 19–20.
[73] *S.H.C.* 1924, p. 51.
[74] Bodl. MS. Ashmole 794, f. 1.
[75] Dugdale, *Mon.* vi (3), 1242.

been suggested that Stowe church stands on the site of Chad's cathedral and that his more retired dwelling place was on or near the site of the church of St. Michael at Greenhill, ½ a mile south of Stowe.[76] There is, however, no evidence that Chad was ever the object of any special cult at St. Michael's, and Stowe remains the likely site of his oratory.

St. Michael's at Greenhill is first recorded c. 1190,[77] but it stands on a much older religious site. A crouched burial, a type more common before than after the Conquest, has been found in its large graveyard, formerly 7 a. in extent and possibly an early Christian burial ground serving a wide area.[78] The church occupies a prominent hilltop site within view of Ryknild Street, and the site and the dedication to the psychopomp St. Michael suggest an early cemetery chapel, perhaps replacing a pagan sanctuary. The size of the graveyard led, from the late 16th century, to speculations about its origin. It was suggested, for example, that it had been the burial place of early Christians, victims of a supposed massacre of the followers of the apocryphal St. Amphibalus.[79] Another suggestion made it a Mercian tribal necropolis.[80] Its size may merely reflect its function as the principal graveyard for the city and the neighbourhood.

A third medieval church, St. Mary's in the market place, is not certainly recorded until 1293.[81] According to a note of 1713 in its churchwardens' accounts an ancient inscription in the tower stated that the foundation stone had been laid in 856.[82] The inscription, if it was not merely a product of antiquarian guesswork, had probably been misread, perhaps as a result of damage. Architectural evidence suggests that a tower was built in the 14th century, so that the date may have been MCCCLVI, not DCCCLVI. The church was probably established when the new town was laid out in the mid 12th century. It may have been served by Thomas the priest (also called Thomas the chaplain) who held a burgage in Lichfield granted to St. Thomas's priory near Stafford c. 1175. At its dissolution in 1538 the priory had a burgage near St. Mary's 'over against Bore Street'.[83] The church was referred to as the chapel church in 1329, a usage which persisted into the 20th century.[84] The usual name at least until the early 17th century was the chapel of St. Mary in the market place.[85]

There has been public worship in the chapel of St. John's hospital in St. John Street since the mid 13th century.[86] The Franciscan friary established on the west side of Bird Street and St. John Street in or shortly before 1237 and dissolved in 1538, had a large church, and in the 1530s townspeople were attending services there.[87] About 1400 three of the friars were celebrating obits, probably for the souls of townspeople.[88] No new church was built in Lichfield until 1847 when Christ Church was built to serve the Leamonsley area.

PAROCHIAL ORGANIZATION TO 1491. In the Middle Ages the cathedral, like most other secular cathedrals, dominated the religious life of the city. It was variously described as the mother church, the great church, the major church, and simply the church of Lichfield.[89] Lichfield, however, was unique among English cathedral cities in the arrangements made for the pastoral care of its inhabitants. Although there were three city churches, they had no parishes. Instead the city was part of the parochia[90] of the cathedral, and its churches were chapels of ease served by cathedral clergy. The system was a similar though more elaborate version of the arrangements found in the parishes of the Mercian minsters which survived the Norman Conquest and developed into collegiate churches.[91]

The boundaries of the late Anglo-Saxon parochia are indicated by the places which c. 1190 owed the cathedral the due or dues of 'wax scot, which is called plough alms'.[92] They were the prebends of Pipa Major (taking its name from Pipe, in Burntwood),[93] Weeford, Freeford, Hints 'and all the chapels' (later Hansacre prebend),[94] Wyrley, Bishopshull (taking its name from land in Lichfield later known as Bispells),[95] Stotfold, Curborough, Gaia, and Harborne, the vill of Lichfield, and the manor of Longdon. All lay within the large Domesday manor of Lichfield, which covered an even wider area.[96] It may be that in the 11th century the parochia coincided with the manor.

By the later Middle Ages, and probably by the end of the 13th century, the parochia had been reduced. Parishes had been formed on the outer fringes, with their churches appropriated to prebends in the cathedral. What remained in the parochia was more or less the area later covered by the Lichfield parishes of St. Mary, St. Mich-

[76] V.C.H. Staffs. iii. 140; Harwood, Lichfield, 504; H. P. R. Finberg, 'The Archangel Michael in Britain', Millénaire Monastique du Mont Saint-Michel, iii, ed. M. Baudot (Paris, 1971), 460.
[77] Statutes of Lincoln Cathedral, ii (1), 19–20.
[78] T.S.S.A.H.S. xvi. 58–61; xxii. 71.
[79] Ibid. xxviii. 2, 9.
[80] H. E. Savage, Church Heritage of Lichfield (Lichfield, 1914), 7–9.   [81] Rot. Parl. i. 100.
[82] L.J.R.O., D. 20/4/2, inside end cover. Harwood, Lichfield, 455, wrongly gives the date as 855.
[83] S.R.O. 938/25–6 and 29; S.H.C. viii (1), 133–4; V.C.H. Staffs. iii. 260–1, 266.
[84] L.J.R.O., D. 30/B 93; D. 30/C 31; W.S.L. 335/30; Parker, Lichfield, 2.
[85] L.J.R.O., B/A/1/2, f. 190v.; L.J.R.O., D. 30/9/3/1, f. 15v.; Bodl. MS. Ashmole 1521, pp. 89–90; S.H.C. 4th ser. xiii. 25; Shaw, Staffs. i. 138.
[86] Below (St. John's hosp.).

[87] V.C.H. Staffs. iii. 268–70.
[88] S.R.O., D. 603/ADD/A/1928.
[89] e.g. Bodl. MS. Ashmole 855, p. 182; S.H.C. 1924, pp. 15, 47, 319.
[90] Used here in the sense of the territory of an early medieval minster, to distinguish it on the one hand from the diocese and on the other from the later parishes.
[91] V.C.H. Staffs. iii. 298–331; iv. 13–14, 128. For a cathedral city where parishes developed in the 12th century see e.g. Winchester in the Early Middle Ages, ed. M. Biddle (Winchester Studies, i), 332; Chartulary of Winchester Cathedral, ed. A. W. Goodman, p. lix.
[92] Statutes of Lincoln Cathedral, ii (1), 19. Wax scot and plough alms were two separate dues in the pre-Conquest church: F. Barlow, Eng. Church 1000–1066 (1979), 162.
[93] Below, Burntwood (manors).
[94] S.H.C. 1915, 16, 128, 197.
[95] Above, manor (estates of cath. clergy).
[96] Above, manor.

ael with its out-townships, and St. Chad with its single out-township. The parochial organization was not based on the three churches. It was instead founded on prebendal estates, with a number of prebendal parishes served by stipendiary chaplains. By the 14th century the city was divided in the main between five such parishes attached to the prebends of Freeford, Hansacre, Longdon, Stotfold, and Weeford. Those five prebends were then the core of the cathedral's prebendal system; indeed they may have developed from the estates held by the five canons at Lichfield in 1086.[97] In addition all other prebendaries holding property in the city were supposed to make provision for the spiritual needs of the inhabitants of that property.[98]

Already in the late 12th century there was a short-lived parochial subdivision of the Lichfield area. When Bishop Peche re-endowed the deanery in 1176, his grants included 'a tithe of the rent from Lichfield and of the parish within the borough and without',[99] and c. 1190 Lichfield was described as consisting of 'the dean's parish' and the rest of the vill.[1] That division is not found again, and the extent of the dean's parish is not known. The parish disappeared in 1192 when Bishop Nonant granted the dean the church of Adbaston in place of all his other endowments.[2] Lichfield, however, remained within the peculiar jurisdiction of the dean until the 19th century.[3]

By the 14th century the three city churches were served by five chaplains appointed by the prebendaries of Freeford, Hansacre, Longdon, Stotfold, and Weeford. In 1241 there were five chaplains performing weekly courses of duty in the cathedral and holding special rights and responsibilities regarding the celebration of mass at the high altar.[4] There is no indication that they performed duties in the city churches, but it is likely that they were the predecessors of 'the five parochial chaplains' who by the 1330s were responsible for licensing a deacon at St. Mary's.[5] In the mid 14th century 'the chaplains of the prebendaries in the city of Lichfield' were serving the three city churches. Though appointed by the five prebendaries, they swore obedience to the dean. Three of them celebrated daily at St. Mary's, one at St. Michael's, and one at Stowe. Each Saturday they went to the chapter house at the cathedral to receive instructions for the following week's services from the subchanter and the other vicars choral. One chaplain acted as hebdomadary, or duty chaplain for the week, with another as his deputy. On 14 festivals each year the chaplains took part in processions at the cathedral; whenever the por-

table shrines of St. Chad were carried in procession, two of the chaplains carried one.[6]

No chaplain or prebendary had exclusive responsibility for any one city church. Although later tradition sometimes attached Stowe to Weeford prebend and St. Michael's to Freeford prebend,[7] there is no evidence that the two prebendaries were ever patrons of those churches or that their chaplains had any special rights or duties in them. In 1460 and 1461 the chaplain of the prebendary of Weeford was celebrating mass at St. Michael's and the chaplain of the prebendary of Longdon celebrated at Stowe. It was his course of duties 'in the three chapels of Lichfield' that the Weeford chaplain allegedly disrupted because he frequently went to Weeford on Sundays to hold services there.[8] The chaplains had some duties outside Lichfield. In 1384 the chapter ordered that the Weeford, Hansacre, and Freeford chaplains were to go in procession to those places on Rogation days.[9]

The chaplains were stipendiaries with no security of tenure. In the 14th century the chapter was swift to repress any signs of independence among them,[10] and there is no evidence that they were allowed to hold leases of prebendal land or tithes. Presumably one reason for the canons' caution was that elsewhere such leases had sometimes enabled stipendiaries to become de facto vicars.[11] It was perhaps a similar caution that kept the chapter from laying down a standard stipend. In the 15th century the chaplains apparently claimed dining rights at the Lichfield guild chaplains' house. One of them complained in 1466 that the senior guild chaplain would not let him become a messmate there, 'contrary to the statute of the place'. There was in fact no such provision in the guild's statutes.[12]

By the earlier 14th century the prebendary of Gaia Major, whose prebend covered much of the city's northern suburb, was providing a chaplain for his parishioners. In 1335 his vicar choral stated that a chaplain had been dismissed when he became infirm and that the parishioners were then being tended by a priest who also served a chantry in the cathedral.[13] In addition the priest held burial services at St. Michael's, presumably for Gaia parishioners.[14] He sometimes celebrated mass in the chapel of John Clarel, archdeacon of Stafford and prebendary of Prees.[15] In 1401 and the later 1420s the chapter ordered the prebendary of Gaia Major to repress the sexual misconduct reported in his prebend, apparently one of the areas where vicars choral kept mistresses.[16] The growth of the suburb may explain why Gaia Major was

---

[97] V.C.H. Staffs. iii. 141; above, general hist.
[98] L.J.R.O., D. 30/C 32.
[99] 'decimam cense de Lich' et de parochia tam infra burgum quam extra': Lichfield Cath. Libr., MS. Lichfield 28, f. 217v.
[1] Statutes of Lincoln Cathedral, ii (1), 19.
[2] V.C.H. Staffs. iii. 141.
[3] Below (Lichfield peculiar).
[4] Dugdale, Mon. vi (3), 1242.
[5] Below (this section).
[6] Bodl. MS. Ashmole 794, ff. 91, 126, 134, 200v.–201.
[7] Bodl. MS. Ashmole 1521, p. 87; V.C.H. Staffs. iii. 279.

[8] L.J.R.O., D. 30/9/3/1, f. 3.
[9] Bodl. MS. Ashmole 794, ff. 200v.–201.
[10] Ibid. ff. 91, 126, 134, 177–8, 200v.–201; L.J.R.O., D. 30/C.A. i, f. 23v.
[11] See e.g. F. Barlow, Durham Jurisdictional Peculiars, 35.
[12] L.J.R.O., D. 30/9/3/1, f. 16; S.H.C. 4th ser. xiii. 19–26.
[13] Bodl. MS. Ashmole 794, f. 49.
[14] 'celebrat pro corpore presenti': ibid. For such masses see Reg. of John de Grandisson, ed. F. C. Hingeston-Randolph, i. 132; Hereford Breviary, ii (Henry Bradshaw Soc. xl), 43.
[15] Bodl. MS. Ashmole 794, f. 49. For Clarel see Le Neve, Fasti, 1300–1541, Coventry and Lichfield, 19, 48.
[16] L.J.R.O., D. 30/C.A. i, ff. 59v.–60, 121v., 128, 131.

named instead of Longdon as one of the five prebends at the core of the prebendal system in 1426[17] and why a chapter decree of 1486 restricting burials in the Close was aimed at the parishioners of Gaia Major.[18]

Other clergy serving in the city included chantry chaplains at the three churches[19] and the chaplains of the guild of St. Mary and St. John the Baptist founded at St. Mary's in 1387. The guild ordinances provided that there should be as many guild chaplains as the leading brethren thought necessary, and required them to help the parochial chaplains with the services at St. Mary's.[20] By then there was also a deacon at St. Mary's supported by donations from the parishioners and from members of the guild.[21] He was probably a successor of Adam, a deacon at St. Mary's in 1293,[22] and of William Heringes, a deacon whom the chapter allowed to remain at the church in 1333 after 'the community of the town' had petitioned on his behalf, although he lacked a licence from the five chaplains.[23] About 1406 there were 10 chaplains at St. Mary's, presumably the five parochial chaplains and five guild chaplains or other stipendiaries. The three clergy then at St. Michael's and the two at Stowe may have been chantry chaplains.[24] In 1466 there were four guild chaplains and three or four other stipendiaries at St. Mary's in addition to the five parochial chaplains.[25]

A commission for the dean's visitation in 1356 was directed to the five parochial chaplains; four were described as serving the city parishioners of the prebends of Hansacre, Longdon, Stotfold, and Weeford, and the fifth as serving the 'entire' prebend of Freeford, presumably both inside and outside the city. The chaplains were to ensure that all clergy with chantries, chaplaincies, or clerical income in the city, all priests and minor clergy serving at St. Mary's or in Freeford prebend, and the wardens of the goods of each chapel were present at the visitation. Each of the five prebends was to provide from its city parishioners three or four trustworthy men, clergy or laymen, to make presentments. On the morning of the visitation the five chaplains were to bring to the deanery a list of all those who would be appearing before the visitor.[26]

A second commission for the same visitation was sent to the prebendaries of Bishopshull, Gaia Minor, Longdon, Stotfold, and Weeford and to their vicars and parish priests. It evidently related only to areas outside the city, except that it included the churches of St. Michael and Stowe. Clergy officiating within the jurisdictions or parishes of the five named prebends were to be summoned before the visitor to show their licences and ordination papers. Five or six trustworthy persons were to be sent from each parish or township, and two or three from each hamlet. The various wardens were to bring their accounts, and everybody was to be ready to make the necessary presentments. The visitation

was planned to last six days. On 3 October the visitor was due to deal with the city parishioners, lay and clerical, of the prebends of Hansacre, Longdon, Stotfold, and Weeford, all the parishioners of the prebend of Freeford, and the clergy, funds, fabric, and furnishings of St. Mary's, Lichfield, and of the chapel or chapels of Freeford. That was to be followed by visitations of the extramural portion of Weeford prebend, at Weeford chapel (4 October), the extramural portion of Stotfold prebend and the clergy, funds, fabric, and furnishings of St. Michael's, Lichfield, at St. Michael's (5 October), the extramural portion of Longdon prebend at Longdon church (6 October), the prebend of Bishopshull and the clergy, funds, fabric, and furnishings of Stowe church at Stowe (7 October), and the prebend of Gaia Minor, also at Stowe (8 October). The prebend of Gaia Major was apparently not visited.[27]

The pattern of the visitation reveals two main distinctions, one between the city and the area outside, the other between the parishioners and the three city churches. The three churches were not associated with any parishioners but were treated for visitation purposes merely as buildings with their own staff, income, and possessions.

The arrangements for the dean's visitations in the 1460s show that the city churches were still not regarded as parish churches. The visitations covered parishioners living 'within the city and the suburbs', the suburbs being streets such as Beacon Street and Stowe Street outside the town ditch and the gates. Presentments were made by street. In 1466 Ashmore Brook was evidently included with the city and suburbs. Penances were not necessarily performed in the church where the offender worshipped; rather it seems that the publicity of the penance was related to the seriousness of the offence. A woman from Stowe Street who had smeared wax from church candles on the floor to the danger of those treading on it was ordered to do penance at Stowe, but a man from Saddler Street who maltreated his wife and kept three concubines at Curborough had to do penance at the cathedral and all three city churches.[28]

PAROCHIAL ORGANIZATION FROM 1491. By the later 15th century the system was breaking down. The canons who held the five prebends were not necessarily residentiaries, and those who did not reside left the appointment of their chaplains to their vicars choral or the lessees of their prebendal estates. It was claimed that vicars and lessees sometimes made bad choices, that canons whose prebends included property in the *parochia* did not normally employ chaplains to serve their parishioners, and that for lack of a priest people had died without receiving the last rites.[29]

[17] Ibid. f. 112v.
[18] Below (the cathedral as a city church).
[19] Below (under the individual churches).
[20] Above, guilds.
[21] *S.H.C.* 4th ser. xiii. 26.
[22] *Rot. Parl.* i. 100.   [23] Bodl. MS. Ashmole 794, f. 45.
[24] S.R.O., D. 603/ADD/A/1928. The date has been supplied by Dr. R. N. Swanson of Birmingham University.
[25] L.J.R.O., D. 30/9/3/1, ff. 15v., 19.
[26] Ibid. D. 30/9/3/3.   [27] Ibid. D. 30/9/3/3/4.
[28] Ibid. D. 30/9/3/1, ff. 2, 15v.–17v., 19–26v.
[29] Ibid. D. 30/C 32.

In 1491 a vicarage was ordained at St. Mary's with the dean and chapter as patrons.[30] The time was presumably chosen deliberately since there was then a vacancy in the see, and the leading spirit behind the ordination was probably the dean, Thomas Heywood. The vicar was to be at least an M.A. and able to preach, and he was to reside in Lichfield. He was to be responsible for all the canons' parishioners in the *parochia* who were not already being served by a perpetual curate. He had to provide and pay a chaplain to help him at St. Mary's, with another for St. Michael's and a third for Stowe. In return he

that he had based his claim to collate on forgeries, and they collated their own candidate, while expressing their willingness to submit the matter to arbitration. Blythe made a new presentation in 1530, and again the chapter rejected his claim. The dispute was settled by arbitration later in 1530 on terms unfavourable to the dean and chapter. The 1491 ordination was cancelled, and the vicarage was annexed to the prebend of Pipa Parva, thus putting it in the bishop's gift. Reginald Hospys, the man collated by the chapter in 1529, resigned the vicarage and was admitted to Pipa Parva.[32] His resignation of the

TABLE: Endowment of the Vicarage of St. Mary's, Lichfield

Prebendary contributing	Basis of contribution	Amount		
		£	s.	d.
Freeford	Possession of greatest number of parishioners	6	13	4
Hansacre	Second largest number of parishioners	5	13	4
Weeford	Third largest number of parishioners	5	13	4
Longdon		5	6	8
Stotfold		5	6	8
Gaia Major	A number of parishioners in the city	1	0	0
Bishops Itchington	Twelve households at most		6	8
Gaia Minor	Six households		3	4
Wolvey	One household			6
Curborough	Three households		1	8
The Dean	Two households at Elmhurst		1	0
Prees	One household			6
Dernford	One household			6
Ufton*	One household at Chorley			6
Bishopshull	Nine poor households		3	0
Pipa Parva**	Six households at Pipehill and Wall		3	0
Total		30	14	0

Source: L.J.R.O., D. 30/C 32.
*Whether Ufton Decani or Ufton Cantoris is not stated.
**To begin payment when he had recovered the great tithes.

was to receive a stipend of £30 14s. from the dean and 15 canons, who were charged according to the number of parishioners which each had in the *parochia*; most of the money came from the holders of the five prebends. The vicar was also assigned the oblations and small tithes from two newly built houses, Lea Grange in Curborough and Elmhurst and a house at Stychbrook, since it was not known in which prebendal parish they stood. He was required to swear fidelity and obedience to the dean and chapter, who were also to be the final arbiters in any dispute which he might have with a canon. In addition he and the curates were made responsible for collecting Easter offerings and paying them to the relevant canons.

In 1502, after the death of the first vicar, Bishop Arundel presented to the vicarage. He asserted that the collation was his by right, and he ordered the dean and chapter to induct the new vicar. They did so, apparently without protest.[31] When Bishop Blythe collated in 1529, however, the chapter resisted him. They stated

prebend in 1531 and Blythe's death in January 1531/2[33] put an end to the settlement. In May 1532 the three keepers of the spiritualities of the vacant see, two of whom were Lichfield canons,[34] revived the ordination of 1491. They denounced Blythe's scheme as having deprived many people of divine service and pastoral care for two years and declared that the reordination of the vicarage would do away with the 'unsettled and absurd' system of pastoral care in the city.[35]

The ordination of 1491 and its revival in 1532 was evidently intended to be merely a simplification of the medieval system without any attempt at coherent reform, perhaps because of the risk of episcopal interference. The canons continued to think in terms of prebendal parishes. In 1512 during a vacancy in the deanery the chapter held a visitation of Lichfield and its suburbs and of the hamlets of Elmhurst, Curborough, and Streethay, but it was treated as a visitation of the five prebends, then taken to be Freeford, Hansacre, Weeford, Longdon, and

[30] No copy of the ordination survives, but the reordination of 1532 (below) claimed to be a revival of the 1491 arrangements. Support is lent to the claim by the fact that in 1491 the first vicar was ordered to reside constantly at Lichfield according to the terms of the ordination (L.J.R.O., D. 30/C.A. iii, f. 4), a requirement repeated in 1532.

[31] L.J.R.O., B/A/1/13, f. 215; L.J.R.O., D. 30/C.A. iii, f. 60v. [32] Ibid. D. 30/C.A. iv, ff. 60v.–62, 70. [33] Ibid. ff. 82, 93v. [34] Richard Strete, archdeacon of Salop, and David Pole, prebendary of Tachbrook: Le Neve, *Fasti, 1300–1541, Coventry and Lichfield*, 18, 59. The third keeper was the dean of the Court of Arches. [35] L.J.R.O., D. 30/C 32.

Bishopshull.[36] In 1531 the parish in which St. John's hospital lay remained officially that of 'the parochial or prebendal church of Freeford in the city of Lichfield'.[37] In the earlier 17th century people still tended to be identified by the prebend in which they lived rather than by the church which they attended. The chapter continued to maintain that the cathedral was the sole parish church of the area and that the other city churches were merely chapels of ease. In 1606 it supported the defence put forward by a suspected papist, Sir John Heveningham of Pipe Hall in Burntwood, who, accused of failing to attend services at Stowe, pointed out that he had worshipped at the cathedral and that Stowe was not a parish church.[38]

In addition the 1491 and 1532 arrangements left the question of boundaries vague. It was stated in 1563 that the city of Lichfield contained three parochial churches or chapels with cure which, 'having no certain limits, bounds, wards, or number of householders appointed to any of them particularly, do serve the whole city confusedly'.[39] Outside the city the hamlets in Burntwood immediately west of the city were disputed between Stowe and St. Michael's in the 16th and 17th centuries. Stowe claimed 'two great streets called Beacon Street and Stowe Street and two lanes called Gay Lane and Shawfield Lane' as within its parish, but outside the city it seems to have relied on prebendal boundaries to support its claims. George Boleyn, dean 1576–1603, secured some agreement about boundaries, but the details are not known.[40] Probably the main pressure for the adoption of sure boundaries came from lay authorities, as a result of the increasing use of ecclesiastical parishes as units of local government.

The stipend of the vicar of St. Mary's was, at over £30, generous by the standards of the late 15th century.[41] Out of it, however, he had to pay three chaplains, and by the later 16th century inflation had reduced its value. There was no vicarage house, and in 1604 the vicar was a non-resident pluralist.[42] Several of the vicars were given prebends in the cathedral to augment their stipend.[43] Bishop Morton tried to solve the problem in 1621 and 1626 by promoting Bills to annexe Freeford prebend, which was in his gift, to the vicarage of St. Mary's and to make St. Mary's a parish church. The 1626 Bill proposed that the vicarage should be held with the prebend and that a house in the Close known as 'the old palace' should become the vicarage house. The incumbent was to reside in Lichfield for most of the year. The Bill also proposed a reform of the rules governing the collection of small tithes in Lichfield. That proposal was

unpopular in the city, and the Bill was amended, apparently omitting it. It was then abandoned, probably because Morton did not think the Bill worthwhile as amended.[44]

In 1646, following the surrender of the royalist garrison in the Close, parliament appointed a lecturer to serve the cathedral. He was moved in 1647 and was probably not replaced.[45] In 1648 parliament reorganized the parochial system in the city. Two ministers were to be appointed by the committee for plundered ministers and approved by the assembly of divines. Each was to have a stipend of £150 paid from the cathedral's sequestrated property and a house from that property.[46]

The first two ministers, Francis Tallents and Richard Cleyton, were succeeded in 1651 by William Langley, who preached at St. Mary's, and John Butler, who preached at Stowe. Langley was suspended in 1654 for preaching on Christmas Day, administering the sacrament according to the Book of Common Prayer, and refusing to work with Butler because he had not been episcopally ordained. Langley and the city authorities petitioned the Council of State for the restoration of his salary, but he was not reinstated, although he was still living in the city in 1655. Butler had moved to St. Mary's by 1656 and continued there, with the £150 salary, until his ejection in 1662.[47] He was succeeded at Stowe by Thomas Miles, whose appointment was approved in August 1656; the previous December the Council of State had granted a £50 augmentation to the minister at Stowe. Miles continued there until he too was ejected in 1662.[48]

St. Michael's was presumably served during the Commonwealth by one of the city ministers. Children were baptized there throughout the period. Thomas Hubbock, who was curate before the Civil War and again in 1668, apparently remained in Lichfield for at least part of the intervening period: in 1650 and 1651 the churchwardens paid him for preparing some accounts. A Mr. Smith was paid for a sermon in 1654.[49]

The Restoration brought a return to the arrangements of 1532. In 1693 William Baker, the vicar of St. Mary's and prebendary of Wolvey, complained during Bishop Lloyd's visitation of the cathedral that although he had cure of souls throughout the city 'and for 7 miles about it' and was obliged to employ three curates, he still received only £30 a year and the scanty surplice fees of St. Mary's.[50] In his cathedral statutes of 1694 Lloyd rebuked the chapter for setting a bad example to lay impropriators in the diocese. The dean and the prebendaries named in the ordination of 1532 were instructed to make no further

[36] Ibid. D. 30/C.A. iii, f. 105v.
[37] Ibid. C.A. iv, f. 72v.
[38] Bodl. MS. Ashmole 1521, pp. 87, 89.
[39] S.H.C. 1915, 152.
[40] Bodl. MS. Ashmole 1521, pp. 85–7, 91.
[41] M. Bowker, Secular Clergy in Dioc. of Lincoln 1495–1520, 142.
[42] S.H.C. 1915, 85, 152; L.J.R.O., D. 30/C 33.
[43] S.H.C. 1915, 170–1, 176–8.
[44] L.J.R.O., D. 30/C 33; C.J. i. 605, 631, 819, 821, 832.
[45] W. A. Shaw, Hist. Eng. Ch. 1640–60, ii. 329, 340;

V.C.H. Staffs. iii. 174–5, which wrongly states that there was a minister at the cathedral in 1655.
[46] Harwood, Lichfield, 458–9.
[47] Ibid. 459; S.H.C. 1915, 171, 178–9; Calamy Revised, ed. A. G. Matthews, 94; Cal. S.P. Dom. 1654, 8; 1655, 194; 1658–9, 33, 41; W. Langley, The Persecuted Minister (1656), epistle dedicatory to pt. i and pp. 109, 114.
[48] S.H.C. 1915, 174, 180; Cal. S.P. Dom. 1655–6, 52.
[49] S.H.C. 1915, 172, 179.
[50] L.J.R.O., B/V/3, cathedral visitation 1693, f. 17; Le Neve, Fasti (1854), i. 642.

leases of any part of 'the rectory or rectories' of St. Mary's, St. Michael's, and St. Chad's without a clause transferring the small tithes, Easter offerings, and oblations to the bishop for the benefit of the vicar of St. Mary's. The £30 stipend was to continue until all the rectorial property had been granted on new leases.[51] In addition the statutes as a matter of course described the three city churches as parish churches.[52]

ST. MARY'S. The vicarage of St. Mary's remained in the gift of the dean and chapter, although the precise identity of the patrons remained obscure. In 1791 it was impossible to decide whether, besides the dean, they were the residentiary chapter, the full chapter, or the canons listed in the ordination of 1532 as having prebendal property in the three city parishes.[53] In practice presentations were made by the dean and residentiaries.[54]

On a vacancy in 1965 a priest in charge was appointed instead of a vicar since the future of the church had become uncertain with the decline of population in the city centre. In 1979 the benefice was united with that of St. Michael's as the benefice of St. Mary with St. Michael. The dean and chapter were the patrons, and the rector of St. Michael's, who was already priest in charge of St. Mary's, was appointed the first rector of the new benefice. The two parishes, however, remained distinct. The east end of St. Mary's was retained for regular worship, but the rest of the building was converted into St. Mary's Centre, opened in 1981.[55]

When in 1694 the vicar was assigned all small tithes in St. Mary's, St. Michael's, and St. Chad's as leases of prebendal property fell in, he retained his £30 stipend pending new leases.[56] The value of the small tithes diminished with inclosure and the consequent extension of arable and decline of pasture, and in 1739 Bishop Smalbroke ordered that the vicar was to have the stipend as well as the tithes. At the same time he stipulated that the vicar was to increase the stipends of the three curates at St. Mary's, St. Michael's, and St. Chad's to £30.[57] About 1830 the vicar's average annual income, after the deduction of £60 permanent payment (presumably to St. Michael's and St. Chad's), was £458, out of which he paid his curate £135; there was no vicarage house.[58] From 1838 he received a rent charge of £17 1s. for the commuted small tithes of Fulfen, from 1847 one of £209 14s. for

the small tithes of St. Michael's parish, and from 1848 rent charges of £20 for all the tithes of St. Mary's and £135 for the small tithes of St. Chad's.[59] A house in the south-east corner of the Close became the vicarage house evidently in 1851 on the admission of George Hodson as vicar; his predecessor H. G. Lonsdale, vicar since 1830, had lived at Lyncroft House in Stafford Road.[60] The house in the Close remained the vicarage until the resignation of the last vicar in 1965, and it then became diocesan offices.[61]

In 1331 John de la Bourne, a chaplain, was licensed to endow a chantry in St. Mary's with three houses and 12 a. in Lichfield. The chantry chaplain was to celebrate daily for the royal family, Bishop Northburgh and his successors, three canons of Lichfield, and Bourne's parents, friends, and benefactors. Already a benefactor of St. John's hospital, Bourne granted it the right of presentation to the chantry, and the first priest was instituted in 1332. In 1345 Northburgh granted the prior and brethren of St. John's the right to present one of their own number, and the king confirmed the grant in 1346. In 1352 the bishop appointed William de Couton to the chantry, with a pension of 20s., on his resignation as prior of the hospital.[62] The chantry at the altar of St. John the Baptist in St. Mary's, which in 1356 was licensed to receive a house and 16 a. in Lichfield, was probably the same chantry; the altar seems to have been in the north chapel.[63] The prior and brethren of St. John's were still presenting to Bourne's chantry in 1384.[64] No mention was made of it at the Reformation, but the priest named Richard Hill, who was then celebrating in St. Mary's and receiving rent given for the purpose from land in the prebend of Freeford, was presumably a chantry priest.[65]

In 1490 Robert Worth, a Lichfield spicer, and his wife Joan gave half a burgage and a garden in Wade Street to maintain a lamp before the high altar in St. Mary's.[66]

The guild of St. Mary and St. John the Baptist, which was attached to St. Mary's, was formed in 1387 by the amalgamation of two existing guilds. The guild chaplains, of whom there were four in 1466, were expected to help with the daily services in the church and to be present at the mass of St. Mary and the anthem 'Salve Regina' each day.[67]

About 1550 several items belonging to the church, notably vestments, had been sold by the corporation and the proceeds spent not only on

[51] *Statuta et Consuetudines Ecclesiae Cathedralis Lichfieldiae* (priv. print. 1863), 95–8; *V.C.H. Staffs.* iii. 180.
[52] *Statuta et Consuetudines*, 94–5.
[53] L.J.R.O., D. 30, case for counsel's opinion, 1791, p. 13.
[54] Ibid. D. 30/9/1/6/47; D. 30/X 11 and 14; D. 30/C.A. viii, ff. 67, 110v.
[55] *Short Account of Parish Church of Lichfield dedicated to St. Mary* (5th edn.), 16 (copy in Lichfield Libr.); St. Mary's Centre, *Lichfield Heritage and Treasury Exhibition*, 2; *Lichfield Mercury*, 27 Aug. 1971, p. 1; *Lich. Dioc. Dir.* (1979); *Lond. Gaz.* 2 Aug. 1979, p. 9798; below (this section: architectural description).
[56] Above (parochial organization from 1491).
[57] *V.C.H. Staffs.* iii. 184; *Statuta et Consuetudines*, 134–5.
[58] *Rep. Com. Eccl. Revenues* [67], pp. 486–7, H.C. (1835), xxii.

[59] L.J.R.O., B/A/15/Fulfen; ibid. Lichfield, St. Chad; Lichfield, St. Mary; Lichfield, St. Michael.
[60] P.R.O., HO 107/2014 (2); P.R.O., RG 9/1973; L.J.R.O., B/A/3, Lichfield, St. Mary; White, *Dir. Staffs.* (1834), 155; (1851), 520; Pigot, *Nat. Com. Dir.* (1835); *P.O. Dir. Staffs.* (1850).
[61] *Lich. Dioc. Dir.* (1965; 1966; 1967); *Par. Ch. of Lichfield dedicated to St. Mary*, 16.
[62] *V.C.H. Staffs.* iii. 279–80, 287; Harwood, *Lichfield*, 456 n., 541–2.
[63] *Abbrev. Rot. Orig.* (Rec. Com.), ii. 243; *Cal. Pat. 1354–8*, 412; below (archit. description).
[64] *S.H.C.* n.s. x (2), 154.
[65] *S.H.C.* 1915, 171; *Cal. Pat. 1572–5*, p. 409.
[66] Bodl. MS. Ashmole 855, p. 191.
[67] Above, guilds.

repairs and new furnishings but also in taking down the altars, removing 'idols and images', and setting up the scriptures.[68] In 1641–2 the churchwardens removed the communion table and rails. There was a table again by 1662–3 when new mats were placed by it and seats were removed from the chancel. In 1664–5 new rails and a new table were bought.[69] In 1642 the dean licensed a lecture at St. Mary's every Friday.[70] A weekly lecture supported by subscriptions was begun in 1656 and was still preached in 1659–60.[71]

By the early 1680s there were several endowed sermons. William Thropp, by deed or will of 1631, left a rent charge of 6s. 8d. for a sermon on Mid-Lent Sunday. William Hawkes by will of 1631 left a rent of 13s. 4d. for an afternoon sermon on the Sunday before Palm Sunday and another on Palm Sunday. Humphrey Matthew, a Lichfield tanner, by deed of 1645, gave a rent of 10s. for a sermon on the first Sunday after New Year's day. Thomas Minors (d. 1677) left a rent of 10s. for a sermon on St. Thomas's day (21 December). In addition Elizabeth Lovatt had given 10s. a year for a sermon on the first Sunday of Lent, and Michael Nickins 13s. 4d. for an annual sermon. The Revd. John Deakin of Rugeley (d. 1727) left £20 which produced 10s. a year for a sermon at St. Mary's on the second Wednesday in Lent. About 1820 money was still paid in respect of Hawkes's, Matthew's, and Deakin's endowments, and in the 1960s, under a Scheme of 1955, 10s. sermon money was still paid.[72] From 1725 to 1772 the Conduit Lands trustees provided £10 a year for a sermon at St. Mary's on the afternoon of sacrament Sunday, the second Sunday in the month. For at least part of that time the stipend covered sermons on Low Sunday and Trinity Sunday also. Initially the preacher was the curate, later the master at the grammar school, and finally the vicar.[73]

Several gifts were made in the 17th century for the repair of the church. By deed of 1615 John Utting of Lichfield gave the income from a house and garden; in the early 19th century it amounted to £8 a year. By 1673 Mary Dilkes had left 5s. a year. In the later 17th century George Dawes left a 10s. rent charge for the repair of the church. All were paid in 1820; Dawes's charity was still paid c. 1880.[74] In 1773 the churchwardens received £30 from an unnamed benefactor, the interest to be used for the administration of Holy Communion at St. Mary's every Christmas Day.[75]

On Census Sunday 1851 the congregation was 422 in the morning, with a further 130 Sunday school children, and 585 in the evening.[76] An offertory collection was begun in 1868.[77] A parish room in Wade Street was used for services from c. 1876 until the late 1920s and was still used as a parish room in 1933.[78] A monthly parish magazine was started in 1893.[79] A parochial church council began to meet in 1898, continuing until 1914; it was revived in 1920.[80]

A club under the direction of the parish clergy was formed for Sunday school teachers and boys in the first class of the Sunday school by R. P. Ross, curate in the later 1860s. In 1871 it was enlarged to include the choir, and later the same year membership was opened to the whole parish. The entrance fees were 1s. for Sunday school children, 1s. 6d. for Sunday school teachers and choir boys not in the Sunday school, and 2s. for the rest. Cricket and football clubs were formed as branches of the club, with members paying 6d. a month. The club was still in existence in 1878.[81] There was still a St. Mary's football team in 1921 when it played a revived St. Michael's club.[82]

The present church of St. Mary is of sandstone and dates from the later 19th century, having replaced a church opened in 1721. The 18th-century church was a rebuilding of a medieval church which consisted of an aisled chancel, an aisled nave, and a west tower with a spire. That church may itself have been a rebuilding, after the fire of 1291, of a church built for the new town c. 1150. The tower, mentioned in 1414,[83] was probably built in the 14th century: north and south windows in the present tower, blocked and much restored, appear to be of that date. An inscription formerly in the tower may have borne the date 1356.[84] A south door was mentioned in 1414, and the north door probably existed by then.[85] In the later 15th century Dean Heywood gave money towards extensive work on the church: £21 for the construction of columns in the nave, £15 13s. 4d. for building a rood loft over the entrance to the choir, £16 6s. 8d. for building a new rood loft 'in the north part', and £8 for glazing 'the principal window', presumably the east window.[86] The north part was presumably the chapel on the north side of the chancel which later became the burial place of the Dyotts of Freeford. It was evidently the 'St. John's choir' of the late 16th century, a name suggesting a survival from St. John's chantry and the guild.[87] The spire existed by 1594 when it was blown down.[88] It evidently fell

[68] *S.H.C.* N.S. vi (1), 177; *S.H.C.* 1915, 170.
[69] L.J.R.O., D. 20/4/1.
[70] Harwood, *Lichfield*, 458.
[71] L.J.R.O., D. 20/4/1.
[72] *7th Rep. Com. Char.* 439; L.J.R.O., D. 20/4/1–2, lists of church rents at beginning of each; S.R.O., Chars. Index; below, chars. for the poor (chars. for city; chars. for St. Mary's). For the Nickins family, owners of Culstubbe Hall in St. John Street, see L.J.R.O., D. 15/10/2/2.
[73] L.J.R.O., D. 126/acct. bk. 1663–1805; D. 126/min. bk. 1741–1856, p. 29.
[74] *7th Rep. Com. Char.* 418, 438–9. For Dawes see below (St. Chad's); L.J.R.O., D. 29/1/2.
[75] L.J.R.O., D. 20/4/3.
[76] P.R.O., HO 129/377/1/14.   [77] L.J.R.O., D. 20/4/5.
[78] *Lich. Dioc. Ch. Cal.* (1877; 1928); *P.O. Dir. Staffs.*

(1872); L.J.R.O., D. 27/5/3.
[79] *Lichfield Mercury*, 29 Dec. 1893, p. 4.
[80] L.J.R.O., D. 20/5/2–3.
[81] St. Mary's Club min. bk. 1871–8, in the possession of Sharrott, Barnes & Co., solicitors of Lichfield.
[82] *St. Michael's, Lichfield, Par. Mag.* Sept. 1921 (copy in L.J.R.O., D. 27/9/7).
[83] S.R.O., D. (W.) 1734/2/1/597, m. 1d.
[84] Above, churches (introduction).
[85] S.R.O., D. (W.) 1734/2/1/597, m. 1d.; L.J.R.O., D. 20/4/1.
[86] Lichfield Cath. Libr., MS. Lichfield 4, f. 20v.
[87] P.R.O., PROB 11/73, ff. 380v.–381; Bodl. MS. Rawl. D. 1481, f. 102; below, Freeford (church). For mention of both chancel aisles see L.J.R.O., D. 20/4/1, 1662–3.
[88] Shaw, *Staffs.* i. 138.

again *c.* 1626, and in 1629–30 money was spent on 'topping the steeple', repairing the battlements and pinnacles of the tower, and erecting a new weathercock.[89] The 'steeple top' was rebuilt in 1668 and four windows were inserted in it. Further work was carried out on the tower in the early 1680s, and it was extensively repaired in 1699 and 1700.[90]

A gallery was erected at the west end of the nave in 1630 by William Hawkes, who directed that those occupying it should each pay 1*s.* On the corners of the gallery were paintings showing Diocletian's army and the preaching of St. Amphibalus, with quotations from scripture below. A second gallery was built by the parishioners in 1635–6, and there too the occupants paid 1*s.* each.[91] The grammar school had its own gallery by the earlier 1660s. A new vestry was built in 1662–3 and its predecessor was let. A sundial was bought in 1639–40.[92]

A brief had been issued by March 1716 'towards the damage of St. Mary's, Lichfield, computed at £4,966 and upwards'.[93] During divine service on the following Easter Sunday part of the spire fell down. Members of the congregation were so alarmed that they broke through the windows to escape; the preacher was lame and simply put the pulpit cushion over his head.[94] A few weeks later the parishioners decided to remove the spire as the first stage of repairing the church. In the event there was a complete rebuilding, and the new church was opened in 1721.[95] In 1717 a subscription was raised locally, and preference in the choice of seats in the new church was given to those who had subscribed most. The Conduit Lands trustees gave £100, with another £184 in the later 1720s for further work. The corporation gave £100, and Edward Chandler, the newly appointed bishop, promised four payments of £30 'if I live to continue as bishop so long'.[96] The church was designed by Francis Smith of Warwick in a Classical style. Built of brick, it consisted of a chancel, an aisled nave with north, south, and west galleries, and a west tower, which, without its spire, was retained from the previous church, though encased.[97] The new building was 12 ft. shorter at the east end than its predecessor.[98] In 1739 a number of people,

including the bishop and the dean, promised to subscribe varying sums towards the cost of an altarpiece and other 'ornaments' in order to relieve the parishioners of the expense; 'an able and experienced architect' to be chosen by the parishioners was to decide what ornaments were needed. Subscriptions were still being received in the mid 1750s, but the altarpiece was installed *c.* 1743. It filled the whole of the east wall and depicted the rising sun with the pelican in her piety above.[99] Extensive repairs were carried out in 1806 by Joseph Potter the elder and again in the earlier 1820s when in addition the exterior was covered in stucco.[1]

In 1853 the tower was lowered and remodelled in a Gothic style and a spire was added. The work, for which a subscription was raised, was a memorial to Henry Gylby Lonsdale, vicar 1830–51, who was buried below the tower. The architect was G. E. Street, who also submitted a design for rebuilding the body of the church.[2] The rebuilding eventually took place between 1868 and 1870 with James Fowler of Louth (Lincs.), a native of Lichfield, as architect. It was carried out as a memorial to Lonsdale's brother John, bishop of Lichfield 1843–67; the bishop's son, Canon John Gylby Lonsdale, was vicar 1866–78, and he and his family met much of the cost, towards which a subscription was also raised. The new church, built in a Gothic style, consisted of a chancel with a chapel for the Dyott family on the north side and a vestry and organ chamber on the south, an aisled nave of four bays, and the tower and spire of 1853. The lower part of the tower was dilapidated by 1868 and was almost completely rebuilt.[3]

The conversion of the church into St. Mary's Centre was carried out between 1978 and 1981 to the design of the firm of Hinton Brown Langstone of Warwick. The cost was met by donations from charities, public bodies, and individuals. The chancel and its aisles were retained as a church. The rest of the building was divided into two floors. On the ground floor a day centre for the elderly and a coffee shop were opened in the nave, with offices, kitchens, and lavatories in the aisles and an entrance hall and gift shop at the west end of the north aisle. The nave can be opened into the chancel for

[89] L.J.R.O., D. 20/4/1.
[90] Ibid.; D. 20/4/2; D. 126/acct. bk. 1663–1805.
[91] Bodl. MS. Ashmole 853, f. 85v.; L.J.R.O., D. 20/4/1, 1635–6; Stringer, *Lichfield*, 6–7; below, chars. for the poor (St. Mary's). For the supposed massacre of Christians locally under Diocletian and for St. Amphibalus see above, place name.
[92] L.J.R.O., D. 20/4/1.
[93] Ibid. D. 20/3; W. A. Bewes, *Church Briefs*, 305; S.H.C. 1938, 242.
[94] Lichfield Cath. Libr., MS. Lichfield 22, p. 118; L.J.R.O., D. 20/4/2, 1715–16.
[95] L.J.R.O., D. 20/1/2, note on inside front cover; D. 20/4/2.
[96] Parker, *Lichfield*, 3–4; L.J.R.O., D. 20/4/2, 21 Sept. 1721; D. 126/acct. bk. 1663–1805, accts. 1717–18, 1718–19, 1725–6, 1727–8, and reverse pages, 26 Aug. 1725, 15 Dec. 1727; D. 126/loose accts., bills etc., 9 Dec. 1717.
[97] L.J.R.O., D. 20/4/3, 11 Apr. 1732; D. 20/4/4, rep. of 10 Jan. 1831 by Thos. Johnson; Lichfield Libr., printed appeal for contributions towards restoration of St. Mary's, 1868; Bodl. MS. G.A. Staffs. 4°, 8, facing p. 478; Shaw, *Staffs.* i. 323; S.H.C. 1942–3, pl. facing p. 130; T.S.S.A.H.S. ii. 67;

below, fig. 16. The north and south galleries were mentioned in 1792 and the west gallery in 1803: L.J.R.O., D. 20/4/4.
[98] *Staffs. Advertiser*, 23 Apr. 1870, p. 7. That probably accounts for the belief in the earlier 19th century that the open space adjoining the east end was consecrated ground: Stringer, *Lichfield*, 146; J. Rawson, *Public Bank for Savings and Public Improvement of Lichfield* (Lichfield, 1849), 33 (copy in W.S.L.).
[99] Deed of 14 July 1739 on display at St. Mary's Centre; L.J.R.O., D. 20/4/3; D. 77/5/2, f. 52; D. 126/min. bk. 1741–1856, p. 6; D. 126/acct. bk. 1663–1805, acct. 1742–3; *Recollections of Sophia Lonsdale*, ed. V. Martineau, 25; T.S.S.A.H.S. ii. 67.
[1] L.J.R.O., D. 20/4/4; *Staffs. Advertiser*, 23 Apr. 1870, p. 7.
[2] L.J.R.O., D. 20/5/1; D. 77/20/8, subscription list between pp. 14 and 15; L.J.R.O., B/C/5/1853/Lichfield, St. Mary; Lichfield Cath. Libr., Moore and Hinckes drawings, xvi, no. 1; *Staffs. Advertiser*, 4 Jan. 1868, p. 4; 23 Apr. 1870, p. 7.
[3] *Staffs. Advertiser*, 23 Apr. 1870, p. 7; L.J.R.O., D. 20/5/1; Lichfield Libr., printed appeal and printed list of subscribers.

large church services and is also used for meetings. The upper floor is occupied by a Lichfield heritage exhibition over the body of the church and a treasury in the tower. The civic regalia and plate are on display in the treasury together with church plate, including pieces from St. Mary's and the cathedral, and plate belonging to the Staffordshire Regiment.[4]

In 1552 the church goods included a silver-gilt chalice and paten.[5] The plate now consists of a silver-gilt chalice of 1637 given in 1873 by Canon Lonsdale, a silver-gilt chalice and paten of 1671 given that year by Sir Theophilus Biddulph of Elmhurst, a silver-gilt flagon and lid of 1731 given by Richard Wakefield, a former town clerk,[6] a silver-gilt flagon, lid, and paten of 1736, a silver paten of 1736, a silver-gilt christening bowl of 1742 given in 1743 by Sarah Adey, two silver-gilt collecting plates of 1743 given by Capt. Michael Rawlins, a silver alms-dish of 1870 given by James Fowler, the architect of the rebuilt church, and a silver chalice of 1878.[7]

There were three bells in 1552.[8] In 1629 there were four, including a little bell. The great bell was recast in 1634 at Walsall by Thomas and Richard Clibury and Thomas Hancox.[9] In 1670 or 1671 a peal of six was cast by a bellfounder named Keene, evidently in the Close.[10] Two of the bells were recast by Henry and William Clibury at Wellington (Salop.) in 1673.[11] Several, including the little bell, were recast in 1711–12.[12] The present peal of eight was cast by Abraham Rudhall of Gloucester; he cast eight in 1726 but recast the eighth bell in 1734.[13]

The church had a clock by 1628, and a new clock and chimes were installed in 1676.[14] By the later 18th century there was a clock projecting from the west face of the tower over Bread-market Street.[15] In 1929, after the existing clock had ceased to work, it was replaced by an old clock from the cathedral, and a subcription was raised for a dial on the north face of the tower. It was still in operation in the later 1980s.[16]

The church had a pair of organs in 1552.[17] An organ built by Flight & Robson was installed by subscription in 1826 and a salaried organist appointed.[18] In 1835 the choir consisted of three men, each paid £5 a year, and six boys, each paid £2 2s.[19] The present organ was on show at the Great Exhibition of 1851 and was later

bought for the church by Canon Lonsdale. It was enlarged in 1907.[20]

The registers date from 1566.[21]

No evidence has been found that St. Mary's ever had a graveyard attached. There were some burials inside the church, but otherwise parishioners were buried in the graveyards of St. Michael's and St. Chad's.[22]

St. Mary's, having been the guild church in the later Middle Ages, became Lichfield's civic church. The bailiffs and the corporation had their own seats there, and the churchwardens provided a sword for the bailiffs' seat in the later 1650s.[23] In the earlier 17th century the corporation's muniments were kept in a chest in one of the aisles.[24] The corporation contributed towards the repair of the church in the late 17th century and towards its rebuilding in the 18th.[25] In 1825 it subscribed 50 guineas to the fund for the new organ, and in 1830 it agreed to subscribe 5 guineas for the maintenance of the organ and choir.[26] New civic seats were installed in 1945, the gift of the Bridgeman family and the late Mrs. Herbert Russell; they were made by the local firm of Robert Bridgeman & Sons.[27] It was presumably at St. Mary's that the customary sermon on St. James's day (25 July) was preached after the election of the bailiffs and sheriff.[28] The church has continued to be used for civic services since the opening of St. Mary's Centre.

St. Mary's was also the church used by the grammar school. Besides the gallery for the boys, there was a schoolmaster's seat in 1682–3. In the 1680s the churchwardens paid a William Kiss to keep the boys quiet during services and sermons.[29] A scholars' bell was rung in the later 17th century.[30]

ST. CHAD'S. By 1734 the curacy of St. Chad's church at Stowe was a perpetual curacy in the nomination of the vicar of St. Mary's.[31] The benefice was declared a rectory in 1867.[32] It remained in the gift of the vicar of St. Mary's until the union of the benefices of St. Mary's and St. Michael's in 1979. The patronage of St. Chad's was then transferred to the dean and chapter.[33]

By will of 1680 Thomas Bearcroft, rector of Walton upon Trent (Derb.), left a £10 rent

[4] St. Mary's Centre, *Lichfield Heritage and Treasury Exhibition*; inf. from Mr. J. M. S. Salloway of Lichfield.
[5] *S.H.C.* N.S. vi (1), 177.
[6] Below, chars. for the poor (chars. for city).
[7] *T.B.A.S.* lxxiii. 12–15, 16–19, 54–5, and pl. 4; L.J.R.O., D. 20/1/3; inf. from Mr. Salloway.
[8] *S.H.C.* N.S. vi (1), 177.
[9] L.J.R.O., D. 20/4/1.
[10] Ibid. 1670–1, 1673–4; D. 126/bound accts. 1663–1715, 15 and 24 Feb. 1670/1.
[11] Ibid. D. 16/5/1, 1672–3; D. 20/4/1, 1673–4.
[12] Ibid. D. 20/4/2.
[13] Ibid. D. 20/4/3; Lynam, *Church Bells*, 18.
[14] L.J.R.O., D. 16/5/1, 1674–5; D. 20/4/1, 1627–8, 1675–6.
[15] Shaw, *Staffs.* i. 323; below, fig. 16.
[16] *Lichfield Mercury*, 25 Jan. 1929, p. 5; 14 Nov. 1986, p. 7.
[17] *S.H.C.* N.S. vi (1), 177.
[18] L.J.R.O., D. 20/4/1, 8 Apr. 1822 sqq.; *Lichfield Mercury*, 14 and 28 Apr., 5 and 26 May, 21 July 1826.
[19] L.J.R.O., D. 20/5/1.

[20] St. Mary's Centre, *Lichfield Heritage and Treasury Exhibition*; *Lich. Dioc. Mag.* (1907), 186.
[21] L.J.R.O., D. 20/1.
[22] Ibid. D. 20/4/4; below (St. Michael's); Freeford, churches.
[23] Above, town govt. (city seals, arms, insignia, and plate).
[24] *Cal. S.P. Dom.* 1629–31, 248; *Acts of P.C.* 1629–30, pp. 376–7.
[25] L.J.R.O., D. 35/bailiffs' accts. 1657–1707, pp. 100, 125, 132, 189; above (this section).
[26] L.J.R.O., D. 35/bailiffs' accts. 1794–1835, pp. 292, 338; D. 77/5/3, f. 185.
[27] T. Moseley, *Lichfield Corp. and St. Mary's Church* (copy in L.J.R.O., D. 77/9/11).
[28] L.J.R.O., D. 77/5/1, f. 92.
[29] Ibid. D. 20/4/2.
[30] Ibid. D. 20/4/1, 1672–3; D. 20/4/2, 29 Sept. 1682.
[31] Ibid. D. 30/9/1/6/45/1.
[32] *Lond. Gaz.* 30 Apr. 1867, p. 2530.
[33] Ibid. 2 Aug. 1979, p. 9798; *Lich. Dioc. Dir.* (1987–8).

charge from Longway farm in Elmhurst to augment the stipend of 'the orthodox preaching minister' at Stowe.[34] A grant of £200 was made from Queen Anne's Bounty in 1729 to meet a legacy of £200 from Mrs. E. Palmer.[35] In 1739 Bishop Smalbroke ordered that the stipend paid to the curate by the vicar of St. Mary's was to be increased to £30 a year.[36] The living was valued at £35 a year in 1803.[37] Further grants were made from Queen Anne's Bounty of £200 in 1810, £600 in 1811, £400 in 1812, and £400 in 1824.[38] The incumbent's average net income c. 1830 was £90 a year. Henry White, incumbent since 1805, was also sacrist of the cathedral, vicar of Dilhorne, vicar of Chebsey, and perpetual curate of Pipe Ridware, and he had an assistant curate to whom he paid £35 a year.[39] The income in 1884 was £338 17s. 8d., consisting of £30 rent from Morrey farm in Yoxall, bought by the governors of Queen Anne's Bounty in 1734, £23 11s. rent from land near Ashmore Brook in Burntwood bought by the governors in 1813, a £25 rent charge for commuted great tithes in Elmhurst granted in 1842 by Dean Howard, £226 1s. 6d. from tithe rent charges granted by the Ecclesiastical Commissioners, the rent charge given by Thomas Bearcroft, by then £9, £13 11s. 6d. from Queen Anne's Bounty, £2 from the letting of the churchyard, fees of £8 17s., and 16s. 8d. from two endowed sermons.[40]

A rectory house was built in Gaia Lane in 1869. The 1½-a. site and half the cost were given by the Ecclesiastical Commissioners.[41] A new house was built in the Windings on part of the site in 1976; its predecessor was sold and converted into flats.[42]

The executors of Bishop Weseham (d. 1257) established a chantry at Stowe, endowing it with a rent charge of 5s. 3d. from property in Lichfield.[43] More property was later granted to the chantry, including a house for the chaplain near St. Chad's. The endowments passed to the vicars choral, and by 1311 the property was so neglected that the chantry had lapsed. In that year the dean and chapter intervened and appointed a chaplain. The vicars protested that they needed the property, and an agreement was reached whereby they were allowed to keep it and the chaplain was appointed as one of the vicars choral. At each subsequent vacancy they were to present one of their number not already holding cure of souls to the dean and chapter for appointment to the chantry. He was to swear to celebrate daily at Stowe and was to receive a stipend from the vicars.[44] In 1335 the chantry priest stated that he was too busy with his cathedral duties and too infirm to serve the chantry regularly, especially in the winter; he also complained that he was not receiving the stipend from his fellow vicars, with which he could otherwise have paid a priest to serve the chantry. The dean and chapter promised to help him but ordered him meanwhile to carry out the duty.[45] The chantry may have lapsed by 1431 when the dean and chapter searched their registers for evidence about its foundation and endowment at the request of the 'masters or wardens' of St. Chad's chapel at Stowe.[46] If it had lapsed, it was revived as a cursal mass. The vicars were still presenting one of their number in 1538.[47] It may have been the priest's service described in 1549 as having a stock of sheep let for 5s. to support a priest singing mass for all Christian souls.[48]

In 1408 Thomas Parker, a canon of the cathedral, and three other clergy were licensed to found a chantry in St. Chad's and endow it with 14 houses and 70 a. in Lichfield. A chaplain was to celebrate daily at the altar of St. Catherine at the east end of the north aisle for Parker, for Margery, widow of Richard Walton, and for Richard's soul. The foundation was evidently in fulfilment of Richard's wishes.[49] The dean and chapter were the patrons, but on several occasions they instituted candidates nominated by others: a chaplain instituted in 1433 was the nominee of one of the clergy involved in the foundation in 1408.[50] The value of the chantry was given as £10 7s. 8d. net a year in 1546 and £11 8s. 3d. in 1548, and the priest's salary as £9 7s. 2d. and £10 18s. 3d. respectively. At its suppression the chantry had silver-gilt plate and some ornaments, worth in all 1s. 10d. The priest was assigned a pension of £6.[51]

By the 14th century there was a guild attached to St. Chad's.[52] A cottage worth 2s. a year in 1549 had been left to maintain lights in the church and such similar items as the parishioners thought fit.[53]

There was an anchoret at Stowe in the earlier 1440s, and the bishop provided him with firewood and coal.[54] Two bequests of money were made to an anchoret there in the 1460s.[55] An anchoret named John Mede was living at Stowe in 1504.[56] A cottage in the churchyard called 'the ancker's house' was sold by the Crown in 1571.[57]

In 1645 Humphrey Matthew, a Lichfield tanner, gave a 10s. rent charge for a sermon at St.

[34] L.J.R.O., D. 39/1/8; D. 39/4/1.
[35] C. Hodgson, *Account of Augmentation of Small Livings by Governors of Bounty of Queen Anne* (1826), 152, 358.
[36] Above (St. Mary's).
[37] L.J.R.O., D. 30/9/1/10/1.
[38] Hodgson, *Bounty of Queen Anne* (1845), p. ccxcvi.
[39] *Rep. Com. Eccl. Revenues* [67], pp. 486–7, H.C. (1835), xxii; L.J.R.O., D. 39/1/12.
[40] L.J.R.O., D. 29/1/2; D. 39/1/4–8; below, Curborough and Elmhurst (estates: tithes).
[41] *Lich. Dioc. Ch. Cal.* (1870), 75; *Lond. Gaz.* 6 Feb. 1866, pp. 663–4; 22 Mar. 1867, pp. 1857–8; 3 Dec. 1869, p. 6842; L.J.R.O., D. 29/1/2.
[42] Inf. from the rector, the Revd. Prebendary J. A. Widdas.
[43] *S.H.C.* 1924, p. 317.

[44] Ibid. pp. 318–19; L.J.R.O., D. 30/XXIV, f. 32; Harwood, *Lichfield*, 280–1.
[45] Bodl. MS. 794, ff. 49–50v.
[46] L.J.R.O., D. 30/XXV, f. 29.
[47] Ibid. D. 30/C.A. iv, ff. 12v., 121v.
[48] *S.H.C.* 1915, 174.
[49] *Cal. Pat.* 1405–8, 395; L.J.R.O., D. 27/9/2; D. 30/C.A. i, f. 144.
[50] L.J.R.O., D. 30/C.A. i, f. 144; iii, f. 92v.; iv. f. 26v.
[51] *S.H.C.* 1915, 174; Harwood, *Lichfield*, 14.
[52] Above, guilds.
[53] *S.H.C.* 1915, 174.
[54] S.R.O., D. (W.) 1734/3/2/1, mm. 22, 26.
[55] L.J.R.O., D. 30/XVIII, ff. 3, 14v.
[56] *V.C.H. Staffs.* iii. 137.
[57] P.R.O., C 66/1088, m. 18.

Chad's on Low Sunday. Before 1674 William Jackson left rent of 6s. 8d. for a sermon on Whit Sunday or Trinity Sunday. Both sums were still paid in 1884.[58] In the later 17th century George Dawes left a rent charge of 10s. for the repair of the church; it was still paid in 1954.[59] In the late 18th century, apart from endowed sermons, there was a sermon only once a month on sacrament Sundays. A sermon was therefore preached in the cathedral every Sunday morning for the benefit of the parishioners of Stowe.[60] By 1812 there were evening prayers with a sermon every Sunday, and that year Henry White introduced a morning service as well.[61] Easter communicants averaged some 66 in the earlier 1830s.[62] On Census Sunday 1851 the congregation was 260 in the morning, with a further 130 Sunday school children, and 500 in the afternoon, with 131 Sunday school children.[63] William Fuller, rector 1894–1918, stated at the time of his resignation that St. Chad's had for many generations 'stood for Evangelical doctrine and practice'.[64]

In 1833 lending libraries consisting mainly of religious books were being run from St. Chad's in Sandford Street and Beacon Street.[65] The distribution of an almanac began in 1854, and it evidently developed into a parish magazine.[66] There were football and cricket clubs attached to the church by 1885. That year the members made it a rule that all of them should belong to the curate's bible class and that persistent bad language during play should be punished by expulsion. A large number of young men started to attend the class every week, and many also attended church services and Sunday evening lectures. It was claimed that there was a marked change in language and conduct which spread to other clubs in the city.[67] A youth club was started in 1886 by the rector, John Graham, and three assistants.[68] A St. Chad's Sick and Benefit Society was established in 1891.[69] Richard Arblaster of Longdon Green (d. 1873) left £100 to St. Chad's, the income to be used to provide 'kneelings' for the poor, to heat the church, and to meet other expenses of divine service; the legacy became payable after the death of his widow in 1893.[70] A surpliced boys' choir was formed in 1893.[71]

No. 20 Gaia Lane was used as a parish room from 1928 until 1933 or later.[72] Land was bought in Curborough Road as the site for a church hall evidently in 1942. In 1960, with the development of the Wheel Lane area, a new site

was bought in the Leasowe, and the foundation stone of the hall there was laid in 1963. The other site was sold.[73]

Mission centres had been opened in St. Chad's schoolroom in Stowe Street and in Cross in Hand Lane by 1871. The mission at the school continued until c. 1903. The other was replaced c. 1874 by a mission room in Beacon Street, which continued until its replacement c. 1903 by a room in Gaia Lane, itself closed c. 1906.[74] The parish room in Gaia Lane was apparently used as a mission room also.[75]

St. Chad's church consists of a chancel with a north vestry, an aisled and clerestoried nave of five bays with a south porch, and a west tower.[76] It is built of sandstone except for the nave clerestory, which is of brick. The plan of the nave and aisles is notable for aisles of the same width as the nave, and it has probably been little changed since the 12th century.[77] The 12th-century nave, from which a blocked window survives at the west end, was tall, and its steeply pitched roof probably continued over the aisles, though pierced over the south aisle by five steeply pitched transeptal roofs. In the 13th century the arcades were rebuilt, beginning with that on the south, and a new south doorway was inserted; a late medieval door survives. The chancel too was rebuilt in the 13th century. Its east end was rebuilt or extended in the 14th century, the date of the east window and the first windows on the north and south. Most of the aisle windows appear to have been renewed in that period, and the transeptal roofs in the south aisle had been removed by then. The tower was added in the same century.[78] There was formerly a building against its north side; it was removed in the early 18th century, but its roof line can still be seen. It was probably an anchoret's cell, although the antiquary William Stukeley stated in 1736 that it was St. Chad's oratory.[79] The windows at the western end of the chancel were remodelled in the 15th century. Clerestories were added to the chancel and the nave c. 1500.

There was a north door by the 1780s.[80] In 1790 it was agreed that the vestry spoiled the appearance of the church and that a new vestry should be built in the tower, the old one being replaced by a pew. The seating was irregular and out of repair, and it was decided to provide new pews. It was also agreed that the roof should be rebuilt. The work was carried out to the design of Joseph Potter the elder, and Jane Gastrell of

[58] 7th Rep. Com. Char. 408–9, 443; L.J.R.O., P/C/11, Alice Simpson (1674); above (this section: incumbent's income); below, chars. for the poor (chars. for city).
[59] S.R.O., D. 4566/M, abstract of will of Geo. Dawes; L.J.R.O., D. 29/6/2, char. com. to G. F. Taylor, 30 Aug. 1954.
[60] Below (the cathedral as a city church).
[61] L.J.R.O., D. 29/1/2; D. 29/7/3, p. 40.
[62] Ibid. D. 29/1/2.
[63] P.R.O., HO 129/397/1/13.
[64] L.J.R.O., D. 77/20/8, p. 7.
[65] Ibid. D. 29/1/2.
[66] Ibid. The set of magazines for 1930 is numbered vol. lxxx (copy in W.S.L.).
[67] Lich. Dioc. Mag. (1885), 27.
[68] Ibid. (1886), 52.
[69] Staffs. Advertiser, 4 Jan. 1896, p. 5.

[70] L.J.R.O., D. 29/4/2, p. 2.
[71] Lichfield Mercury, 1 May 1953, p. 2.
[72] L.J.R.O., D. 29/5/1, pp. 46, 55, 58, 89.
[73] Ibid. pp. 149–51, 153–4, 156; D. 39/2/3.
[74] Lich. Dioc. Ch. Cal. (1872; 1873; 1875; 1904; 1905; 1906). For the mission room at Elmhurst see below, Curborough and Elmhurst.
[75] L.J.R.O., D. 29/5/1, pp. 46, 55, 58, 89.
[76] For a view in 1842 see below, plate 57.
[77] For the enlargement of the N. aisle in the late 1840s see below.
[78] For the quarrying of stone for work on the church in the mid 1340s see above, par. govt. (St. Chad's: churchwardens).
[79] Gent. Mag. clv (2), 95; W.S.L., Staffs. Views, v. 194, 200.
[80] L.J.R.O., D. 27/9/2.

Stowe House met over half the cost.[81] The altar removed from the cathedral about that time was brought to St. Chad's;[82] the present altar rails are of the later 17th century and may also have come from the cathedral. In 1812 Richard Wright, a Lichfield surgeon, presented the church with a copy of Rubens's 'Crucifixion', formerly the centre piece of the cathedral's reredos, and it was placed over the altar. It had been removed by 1859, and in 1875 it was in the vestry.[83] In the later 1980s it hung in the south-west corner of the church. In 1824 a gallery was erected by subscription to provide more free seats.[84]

A restoration of the interior was carried out by Thomas Johnson of Lichfield in 1841. He did further work in 1848 and 1849, notably the rebuilding and enlarging of the north aisle. Most of the cost was raised by subscription. In 1852 the gallery was taken down.[85] The chancel was restored in 1856 to the design of Ewan Christian; its clerestory was removed, and a vestry was built on the north side.[86] The tower and the exterior of the church were restored in the later 1880s with J. O. Scott as architect; a turret was added to the tower. An appeal was launched for the restoration 'as a diocesan monument to St. Chad'.[87] In the mid 1890s the pulpit and reading desk on the north side of the chancel arch were replaced by a pulpit on the south side. At the same time the organ, moved when the gallery was taken down, was transferred from the south-west corner of the nave to the east end of the north aisle, and a choir vestry was formed next to it. Between then and 1905 the box pews were gradually replaced.[88] A reredos was erected in 1897 in memory of Canon John Graham, incumbent 1854–93.[89] In 1925 the 15th-century font was moved from its position in the nave near the south door to a baptistery formed at the west end of the south aisle at the expense of Lord Charnwood, who lived at Stowe House.[90] A statue of St. Chad was placed over the south porch in 1930 by Lady Blomefield in memory of her husband, Sir Thomas Blomefield of Windmill House (d. 1928).[91] In 1949 a screen was erected across the tower arch in memory of Alderman J. R. Deacon (d. 1942) by his widow; it was made by his firm, J. R. Deacon Ltd.[92] The east end of the south aisle was formed into a Lady chapel in 1952 as a memorial to the fallen of the Second World War.[93]

The monuments in the church include two in the south wall of the chancel with Johnsonian connexions. One is to Lucy Porter (d. 1786), Dr. Johnson's step-daughter. Below it is a memorial to Catherine Chambers (d. 1767), servant to Michael Johnson and his family. It was erected in 1910 after her tomb and that of Lucy Porter had been discovered during work on the chancel floor.[94]

In 1552 the church goods included a silver-gilt chalice and paten. A latten cross, a brass holy-water stock, a wooden sepulchre, a vestment, and several cloths had been sold by the corporation and the proceeds used in taking down altars and repairing the church.[95] The plate now consists of a silver-gilt chalice and paten dated 1634 and given by John Hammersley, a silver flagon and lid of 1751 evidently given by Elizabeth Rutter, two silver collecting plates made and acquired in 1798, a silver bread plate of 1835 given in 1836 by Thomas Heywood to mark his appointment as parish clerk, an office held by his father and grandfather, and a silver chalice of 1865.[96]

In 1552 there were three bells and a sanctus bell.[97] One of the three was presumably the bell once thought to be dated 1255 but in fact probably cast at Nottingham c. 1500. It forms one of a peal of four. Of the other three bells, one was cast in 1665 by William Clibury at Wellington (Salop.) and two in 1664 and 1670, apparently by Thomas Clibury of Wellington.[98]

The registers date from 1635; there are few entries between 1640 and 1654.[99]

The churchyard was enlarged by ⅛ a. in the early 1780s, part of the cost being met by Lord Gower and George Anson.[1] There were further additions of ¼ a. in 1828, ⅓ a. in 1937, ⅓ a. in 1958, and nearly ½ a. in 1969.[2] A house adjoining the churchyard north-west of the church was let to the parish by the vicars choral in 1781 and used as a poorhouse. By the later 1830s it was occupied by the sexton. The Ecclesiastical Commissioners, having acquired most of the property of the vicars choral in 1872, conveyed the house to the rector in 1885.[3] It was still occupied by the sexton in the 1950s but no longer stands.[4]

St. Chad's well further north-west of the church was in the 16th century traditionally associated with the saint: John Leland described it as 'a thing of pure water', with a stone in the

[81] Ibid. D. 29/4/1, 25 July, 23 Sept. 1790, 10 Apr. 1792; L.J.R.O., B/C/5/1799/Lichfield, St. Chad.
[82] Shaw, *Staffs.* i. 260.
[83] L.J.R.O., D. 29/1/2; D. 29/4/1, 1813–14; D. 29/4/2, p. 80; D. 29/7/1, p. 77; Lichfield Cath. Libr., Moore and Hinckes drawings, xvi, no. 6; J. Hewitt, *Handbk. for Lichfield Cathedral* (Lichfield, 1875), 48.
[84] *Lichfield Mercury*, 25 July 1823; L.J.R.O., D. 29/4/1.
[85] L.J.R.O., D. 29/4/1.
[86] Ibid. D. 29/4/2, p. 74.
[87] *Lich. Dioc. Mag.* (1885), 27, 79; (1886), 71; (1887), 72.
[88] Ibid. (1894), 125; (1905), 136; H. Clayton, *St. Chad's Church, Lichfield* (1972; copy in W.S.L.); L.J.R.O., B/C/5/1894/Lichfield, St. Chad; B/C/12/Lichfield, St. Chad; D. 29/4/1; S.R.O., D. 4566/99, min. bk. of restoration cttee. 1894–9. [89] Tablet in chancel.
[90] *T.B.A.S.* lxviii. 20; P. Laithwaite, *Story of Church of St. Chad, Lichfield*, 16 (copy in Lichfield Libr.); L.J.R.O., B/C/12/Lichfield, St. Chad; D. 29/5/1, pp. 17, 20.
[91] *St. Chad's Par. Mag.* Feb. 1931; Aug. 1933.

[92] Inscription on screen; Laithwaite, *Church of St. Chad*, 17.
[93] Clayton, *St. Chad's Church.*
[94] L.J.R.O., D. 29/7/3; D. 39/1/13.
[95] *S.H.C.* N.S. vi (1), 178; *S.H.C.* 1915, 173–4.
[96] *T.B.A.S.* lxxiii. 10–11, 30–1, 38–9, 44–5, 52–3.
[97] *S.H.C.* N.S. vi (1), 178; *S.H.C.* 1915, 173.
[98] Jennings, *Staffs. Bells*, 18, 20, 59–61; Lynam, *Church Bells*, 19 and plates 1–3; *Trans. Old Stafford Soc.* 1952–3, 7.
[99] L.J.R.O., D. 29/1.
[1] Ibid. D. 29/4/1, 6 Apr. 1779 and accts. for 1781–2; L.J.R.O., VC/A/21, CC 164146A, pp. 296–8.
[2] Ibid. D. 29/4/1, 29 May, 12 July 1828, 12 and 26 Feb., 7 Mar. 1829; Lich. Dioc. Regy., Bp.'s Reg. H, pp. 625–45; Reg. W, pp. 7, 601; Reg. X, pp. 335–9; Reg. Y, pp. 131–4.
[3] L.J.R.O., D. 29/4/1; D. 29/6/1; *Lond. Gaz.* 6 Feb. 1885, p. 528; *V.C.H. Staffs.* iii. 193; above, par. govt. (poor relief).
[4] *Lichfield Mercury*, 1 May 1953, p. 2; 11 Mar. 1955, p. 4; 6 May 1960, p. 6.

bottom on which according to tradition St. Chad used to stand naked and pray.[5] In the earlier 18th century the water was thought to be good for sore eyes.[6] The churchwardens of St. Chad's paid for the cleaning of the well in the late 1820s. In the 1830s the supply of water was improved under the supervision of James Rawson, a local physician, and at his instigation an octagonal stone structure was built over the well.[7] After the water had dried up in the early 1920s, the well was lined with brick and a pump was fitted to the spring which fed it. In 1923 the rector held a service to inaugurate the pump.[8] An annual Roman Catholic pilgrimage to the well, drawing support from all over the Midlands, was started in 1922 and continued into the 1930s.[9] There was an Anglican pilgrimage in 1926.[10]

By 1941 the well was derelict, and Bishop Woods appointed a commission to consider the future of the site. A scheme for restoration was drawn up by Frederick Etchells of West Challow, in Letcombe Regis (Berks.). A trust was established and an appeal launched. The nearby Littleworth cottages were demolished and a caretaker's house was built on the site. The foundation stone was laid by the Princess Royal in 1947, and the house was opened in 1949 by the duchess of Gloucester as patron of the Friends of Lichfield Cathedral. It was later occupied as a curate's house and by 1984 was a centre for the unemployed. The well had been restored by the early 1950s. The octagonal building was replaced by an open structure with a tiled roof which in the later 1980s was covered with a vine.[11]

ST. MICHAEL'S. By 1728 the curacy of St. Michael's was a perpetual curacy in the nomination of the vicar of St. Mary's.[12] The benefice was declared a rectory in 1867.[13] It remained in the gift of the vicar of St. Mary's until 1979 when the two benefices were united as the benefice of St. Mary with St. Michael. The dean and chapter became the patrons, and the rector of St. Michael's was appointed the first rector. The two parishes, however, remain distinct.[14]

In 1739 Bishop Smalbroke ordered that the stipend paid to the curate by the vicar of St. Mary's was to be increased to £30 a year.[15] Meanwhile in 1729 a grant of £200 was made from Queen Anne's Bounty to meet gifts of £100 from Henry Raynes and £100 from Mrs.

E. Palmer; there were further grants of £200 in 1756, £200 in 1810, and £1,000 in 1812.[16] The living was valued at £45 in 1803.[17] The incumbent's average net income c. 1830 was £137 a year, but there was no glebe house.[18] In 1842 the Ecclesiastical Commissioners granted an augmentation of £17 a year.[19] The income in 1884 was £337, consisting of £40 rent from Morrey farm at Yoxall, £29 from land in Shenstone and at Ashmore Brook in Burntwood and elsewhere in St. Michael's parish, £190 from commuted tithes, a £44 stipend from the Ecclesiastical Commissioners, £7 from Queen Anne's Bounty, £12 from the letting of the churchyard for grazing, and fees averaging £25.[20] In 1858 a house for the incumbent was built in Trent Valley Road on a site opposite the church given by the earl of Lichfield; it was of brick in a Tudor style.[21] It was demolished after a new house was built to the south-west in St. Michael Road in the mid 1970s.[22] The new house remains the rectory house for the combined benefice.

Under the will of Robert de Hulton (d. 1273) his executors founded a chantry in St. Michael's for the souls of Robert, his wife Hawise, and their forebears buried in the churchyard. As the endowment they conveyed 7 a. and 5s. rent to Robert's son Robert, who substituted 10s. rent from Morughale (in Streethay) and Lichfield and added other rents and a meadow near Wychnor bridge in Tatenhill. The executors presented the first chaplain but granted Robert and his heirs the presentation of future chaplains, evidently to the precentor of the cathedral for institution.[23] Lettice, widow of Henry Bendy, gave land in Longdon to the chantry.[24] The chaplain was still celebrating in St. Michael's in 1394, but the chantry and its endowments were later annexed to the chantry of St. Radegund in the cathedral.[25]

In 1344 William Walton of Lichfield gave 3 a. in Lichfield for 200 years to a group described as parishioners of the chapel of St. Michael and to William Meys, keeper of the lights and fabric of the chapel. The gift was made to provide a light in the chapel on feast days for William during his lifetime, and after his death for his soul and the souls of his wife Margaret, Master Adam Walton, and Isabel de Rokeby. It was also for the support of a chaplain celebrating on 6 February, the morrow of the feast of St. Agatha. The land was worth £11 8s. 3d. net in 1549.[26] Walton also gave a 3s. rent from a burgage in

[5] Leland, *Itin.* ed. Toulmin Smith, ii. 99.
[6] *Diary of a Tour in 1732 made by John Loveday of Caversham*, ed. J. F. T. Loveday (Edinburgh, 1890), 9.
[7] *Gent. Mag.* clv (2), 96; L.J.R.O., D. 29/4/1, accts. 1828–9; W.S.L., Staffs. Views, v. 200; below, plate 57.
[8] L.J.R.O., D. 29/5/1, p. 3; D. 29/7/3, p. 31.
[9] *Lichfield Mercury*, 30 June 1922, p. 5; *St. Chad's Par. Mag.* July 1930; July 1932; P. Laithwaite, *Hist. of St. Chad's Church, Lichfield, Staffs.* (1938), 28 (copy in Lichfield Libr.).
[10] W.S.L. Broadsheets 4/47.
[11] L.J.R.O., D. 29/5/1, pp. 218, 223–4; D. 52/2.
[12] Ibid. D. 30/9/1/6/50.
[13] *Lond. Gaz.* 6 Dec. 1867, p. 6709.
[14] Above (St. Mary's).
[15] Ibid.
[16] C. Hodgson, *Account of Augmentation of Small Livings*

by *Governors of Bounty of Queen Anne* (1826), 152, 357.
[17] L.J.R.O., D. 30/9/1/10/1.
[18] *Rep. Com. Eccl. Revenues* [67], p. 487, H.C. (1835), xxii.
[19] *Lond. Gaz.* 13 Sept. 1842, pp. 2246–8.
[20] L.J.R.O., D. 27/5/3. For Morrey farm see above (St. Chad's: incumbent's income).
[21] *Annals of Dioc. of Lichfield, 1859*, 62 (copy in W.S.L.).
[22] Lich. Dioc. Regy., Bp.'s Reg. Y, pp. 178–9, 190, 218; inf. from the rector, the Revd. C. M. Savage.
[23] *S.H.C.* 1924, pp. 29–30; S.R.O., D. (W.) 1734/2/1/760, mm. 128–129d.
[24] *S.H.C.* 1924, p. 196.
[25] S.R.O., D. (W.) 1734/2/1/760, m. 129; *S.H.C.* 1915, 158.
[26] L.J.R.O., D. 30/C 34 (summarized, with errors, by Harwood, *Lichfield*, 515–16); *S.H.C.* 1915, 172.

Lichfield to the Hulton chantry priest.[27]

In 1344 William Story of Morughale, in fulfilment of his father's will, gave 4d. rent from land there to maintain a lamp in St. Michael's.[28] In 1349 Maud Atwall gave land in Lichfield for lights in St. Michael's and for a priest to celebrate on the feast of St. Mark (25 April). The rent from the land was 3s. 4d. in 1549. In 1508 Thomas Chatterton gave 12d. rent from land in Fulfen in Streethay to maintain two tapers before the statue of Our Lady and St. Catherine in St. Michael's. Before 1548 a John Atkin gave land by then worth 4s. 8d. a year for an obit there. In 1549 what was called the priest's service was stated to have been endowed by William Allen and his wife Joan with land in Lichfield then let for 12s.[29]

There was a guild of St. Michael in the early 16th century.[30]

In 1693 the precentor stated that the rectorial prebendaries had neglected the spiritual needs of St. Michael's until the arrival in 1683 of Dean Addison, who frequently preached and catechized there.[31] In 1694 Bishop Lloyd, finding that there was no regular preaching at the church, ordered that, pending the proper endowment of St. Mary's vicarage, the dean and other prebendaries whose predecessors had been party to the agreement of 1532 should preach in the afternoon at St. Michael's, in person or by a substitute, on those Sundays when they preached at the cathedral in the morning. The dean and the residentiary canons were also to preach twice a year at St. Michael's, in person or by a substitute.[32] About 1720 the prebendaries began asking leave to drive up to the church door in bad weather. The parishioners would not grant permission, and in 1723 the prebendaries refused to attend in person until permission was granted. Instead, to the annoyance of the parishioners, they sent one of the vicars choral, providing him with a set of printed sermons for the whole year. Bishop Chandler intervened in 1724, and the permission was evidently given.[33] In the late 18th century there was a sermon only once a month on sacrament Sunday, and a sermon was therefore preached in the cathedral every Sunday morning for the benefit of the parishioners of St. Michael's.[34]

In 1785 the vestry voted £1 1s. a quarter for 'a person to teach the singers to sing'.[35] Rules were drawn up for a society of singers in 1820. The men were to receive £2 12s. each a year and the boys £1 1s.; anyone absent from divine service, except by reason of illness, was to be fined 6d. a time.[36] On Census Sunday 1851 the congregation was 150 in the morning, with a further 85 Sunday school children, and 270 in the evening, with 85 Sunday school children.[37] A parochial library existed by 1856, and from 1860 it was housed in the school built that year.[38] A parish magazine was started in 1887.[39] On winter Saturday evenings in the earlier 1890s 'free and easies' were held in the boys' schoolroom for the working men of Greenhill. They began in January 1890, when there was also a Sunday evening meeting devoted to 'sacred melody and reading'.[40] The parish hall in St. Michael Road was opened in 1953 on a site given by F. D. Winterton.[41]

About 1300 Geoffrey le Wyte of Lichfield gave St. Michael's 4d. rent from his house near the church; the keepers of the fabric and lights had the right to distrain for it.[42] By the early 1530s the churchwardens received £4 5s. 8d. from 11 tenants of property in Lichfield and Fulfen,[43] but in 1585-6 there were only five tenants and the income was £2 19s. In 1732 it was £7 3s. 6d.[44] By will of 1765 John Deakin of Lichfield left rents for beautifying St. Michael's. The rents amounted to £38 15s. in 1784, and in 1797 the vestry decided to use them to meet the cost of replacing the pulpit, desk, and seats.[45] St. Michael's Church Lands trust (later St. Michael's Church trust) was established in 1811. The churchwardens vested the property, all of it still in Lichfield and Fulfen, in six trustees. The appointment of future trustees lay with the vestry. The long leases were replaced by annual tenancies, and by c. 1820 the income had risen to £125 2s. There was, however, a debt of £880, the residue of loans raised to compensate the tenants for the surrender of their leases and to pay for repairs and improvements.[46] Some of the land was sold in 1855, and the proceeds with other funds were used to pay off the creditors at 10s. in the £.[47] It was stated in 1868 that the income of the trust combined with pew rents was sufficient to keep the church and churchyard in repair so that no church rate was levied in the parish.[48] In 1983 the trust's income was £1,160.32, derived entirely from investments.[49]

St. Michael's church stands within a large churchyard on a hilltop site on the south side of the road to Burton. It is built of sandstone and consists of a chancel with a south vestry and organ chamber, an aisled and clerestoried nave of four bays with a north porch, and a west tower with a recessed spire.[50] In the 13th century it consisted only of a chancel and a nave; a

[27] S.R.O., D. (W.) 1734/2/1/760, m. 129.
[28] L.J.R.O., D. 27/4/2.
[29] S.H.C. 1915, 172-3; Cal. Pat. 1549-51, 126-7; 1556-9, p. 3.
[30] Above, guilds.
[31] V.C.H. Staffs. iii. 179 n.
[32] Statuta et Consuetudines Ecclesiae Cathedralis Lichfieldiae (priv. print. 1863), 97-8.
[33] V.C.H. Staffs. iii. 184.
[34] Below (the cathedral as a city church).
[35] L.J.R.O., B/C/5/Exhibits/Lichfield, St. Michael, 'Copies of Orders', p. 5.
[36] Ibid. D. 35/St. Michael's overseers' bk. 1807-20, p. 17.
[37] P.R.O., HO 129/377/1/16.
[38] S.R.O., D. 4566/99, managers' min. bk. 1840-58, 3 Mar. 1856; Staffs. Advertiser, 9 June 1860, p. 4.

[39] Vol. xxvii is for 1913 (copy in L.J.R.O., D. 27/9/7).
[40] Lichfield Cath. Libr., Harradine scrapbk. p. 86; S.R.O., CEH/88/1, 25 Oct. 1893.
[41] Lichfield Mercury, 6 Mar. 1953, p. 5.
[42] L.J.R.O., D. 27/4/2.
[43] Harwood, Lichfield, 523-4.
[44] T.S.S.A.H.S. vii. 11-12.
[45] Harwood, Lichfield, 516; L.J.R.O., D. 27/5/1, f. 8; below (this section).
[46] 7th Rep. Com. Char. 439-41.
[47] St. Michael's Church Trust records (in the possession of Hinckley, Birch & Exham, solicitors of Lichfield), min. bk. 1836-1903, pp. 3-71, passim.
[48] Staffs. Advertiser, 28 Mar. 1868, p. 7.
[49] Inf. from Mr. M. B. S. Exham.
[50] For a view in 1841 see below, plate 56.

lancet window survives at the west end of the nave, opening into the later tower. A south aisle was added in the 14th century, and it was perhaps then that all but one of the six side windows in the chancel were rebuilt and the clerestories added. Later, probably in the 15th century, a north aisle, with a north porch, and a tower and spire were added and an east window was inserted.[51] The spire was blown down in 1594; in 1601 money was spent on 'topping' and repairing the tower and making a weathercock.[52]

In the later 18th century a family mausoleum was built in the angle of the chancel and the south aisle by the earl (later marquess) of Donegall, who lived at Fisherwick from c. 1760 until his death in 1799.[53] A gallery was erected at the west end of the nave for the singers c. 1780, although three of the seats were reserved for letting to help towards the cost.[54] In 1784 a faculty was granted for a vestry room on a plot of ground at the south-east end of the church, so that vestry meetings would no longer have to be held in the church.[55] There was a vestry (presumably a robing room) in the north-west corner of the church in 1786, but by 1797 it was in the base of the tower.[56] In 1798 and 1799 the pulpit and desk on the south side of the chancel arch were rebuilt and new pews were installed. In the south aisle a door was blocked and a new one built to the west opposite the north door. It was apparently then that all but one of the windows on both sides of the chancel and those in the north aisle were replaced by two-light Decorated windows.[57] An organ was installed in the gallery in 1816; it was replaced by subscription in 1825.[58]

The nave was restored in 1842 and 1843 to the design of Thomas Johnson of Lichfield.[59] Much of the inspiration came from the banker Richard Greene, a churchwarden and also the secretary of the Lichfield Society for the Encouragement of Ecclesiastical Architecture, founded in 1841. He contributed £100 towards the appeal in 1841 to supplement the rate levied for the work; other contributions included £50 from the Hon. H. E. J. Howard, dean of Lichfield, and £25 from Queen Adelaide, the queen dowager. The work included the reroofing of the nave, the repair of the side aisles and the nave clerestory, the reintroduction of Perpendicular windows in the north aisle, the rebuilding of the

north porch, and the remodelling of the south aisle with new buttresses and a south door in place of a window. The gallery was removed. The mausoleum and the vestry room were replaced by a stokehold over which a clergy vestry was built with doors into the chancel and the south aisle; an organ loft was built over the vestry.

In 1845 and 1846 the chancel was restored to the design of Sydney Smirke. The east window was turned into a three-light window, all the side windows became single lancets, and the clerestory was removed. The whole was plastered. A recessed 13th-century tomb of a civil lawyer was uncovered in the north wall.[60]

In the late 1870s a stone pulpit was erected, and in the mid 1880s new seating was installed.[61] Extensive work was carried out in 1890 and 1891 to the design of J. O. Scott. The chancel was restored and refurbished, largely at the expense of the rector, C. E. Hubbard. The plaster was removed and the stonework renewed. The jambs and tracery of the medieval east window were uncovered and restored. It was not until 1897 that enough money was available for new glass, depicting the Ascension, to be inserted. The tower was repaired and the internal lancet window unblocked.[62] In 1906 the spire, damaged by a storm, was restored and a new vane erected.[63] A new vestry in the south-east angle of the church was dedicated in 1923.[64] The stone pulpit was replaced by one of oak in 1926. A baptistery was formed at the west end of the south aisle in 1958, the font of 1669 being moved there from a position near the north door. In 1980 a kitchen and lavatories were installed in the base of the tower.[65]

In the centre of the nave is a floor slab commemorating Samuel Johnson's father Michael (d. 1731), his mother Sarah (d. 1759), and his brother Nathaniel (d. 1737), all of whom were buried in the church. It was placed there in 1884 to mark the centenary of Johnson's own death. The inscription on it is that composed by Johnson for an earlier stone which he ordered a few days before he died; that stone was removed when the church was repaved in the late 1790s.[66]

In 1552 the church possessed a silver-gilt chalice and paten. Some of the church's possessions, including several brass items, had been sold by the corporation to buy a bible in

[51] Shaw, *Staffs.* i, pl. facing p. 338; W.S.L., Staffs. Views, v. 142, 212–13, 218, 223.
[52] Shaw, *Staffs.* i. 138; Harwood, *Lichfield*, 528.
[53] L.J.R.O., D. 30/6/2/3/2; W.S.L., Staffs. Views, v. 218; *Evening Mail*, 7–10 Mar. 1800 (copy in D. 27/9/3). For burials of the family at St. Michael's from 1763 see L.J.R.O., D. 27/1/4, pp. 184, 202, 234, and 22 Nov. 1780 and 17 Feb. 1783; D. 27/1/5, p. 78; below, plate 56.
[54] L.J.R.O., B/C/5/Exhibits/Lichfield, St. Michael, 'Copies of Orders', pp. 10–11; L.J.R.O., D. 27/3/1; D. 27/9/2.
[55] Ibid. D. 27/3/2.
[56] Ibid. D. 27/3/3; D. 27/9/2.
[57] Ibid. D. 27/3/3; D. 27/5/1, ff. 61v., 62, 64, 66v.; W.S.L., Staffs. Views, v. 213, 218–20, 223.
[58] L.J.R.O., D. 27/5/1, f. 102; *Lichfield Mercury*, 19 Nov. 1824; 25 Feb., 4 Mar. 1825.
[59] This para. and the next based on W. E. Foster, *Hist. of St. Michael's, Lichfield* (1951), 6 (copy in Lichfield Libr.); J. A. C. Baker, *Short Hist. of St. Michael's Church, Lichfield*, 12–13 (copy in W.S.L.); *First Rep. of Lichfield Soc. for Encouragement of Eccl. Archit.* (Rugeley, 1843), 22–3 (copy

in W.S.L.); *V.C.H. Staffs.* iii. 193; L.J.R.O., D. 27/3/9–10; D. 27/5/2; D. 27/9/5; D. 30/St. Michael's chancel, 1845; W.S.L., S. MS. 478, Greene, 3 Jan. 1842; W.S.L., Staffs. Views, v. 214, 217, 222, 224–5; Lichfield Cath. Libr., Moore and Hinckes drawings, xvi, nos. 3 and 5.
[60] The tomb was evidently visible in the 1790s: Shaw, *Staffs.* i. 340.
[61] L.J.R.O., D. 27/3/14–15; D. 27/5/3.
[62] Ibid. D. 27/3/4; D. 27/3/15; D. 27/3/18; D. 27/5/3; *Lichfield Mercury*, 5 Sept. 1890, p. 8; *Lich. Dioc. Ch. Cal.* (1891), 158; *Lich. Dioc. Mag.* (1891), 179; (1897), 166.
[63] *Lich. Dioc. Mag.* (1906), 147.
[64] *Staffs. Advertiser*, 13 Jan. 1923, p. 4.
[65] Baker, *St. Michael's*, 16; *Lichfield Mercury*, 26 Aug. 1960, p. 3; L.J.R.O., B/C/12/Lichfield, St. Michael.
[66] L.J.R.O., D. 27/1/3, entry between those for Sept. and Oct. 1731, and burials of 7 Dec. 1731, 5 Mar. 1736/7, 23 Jan. 1759; Samuel Johnson Birthplace Mus., MS. 22/3; Harwood, *Lichfield*, 520–1 (stating that the repaving was in 1796; 1797 or 1798 is more likely: above); Shaw, *Staffs.* i. 327, 340.

FIG. 15. CHANCELLOR LAW'S TOMB IN 1864

English, the Book of Common Prayer, and the Paraphrases of Erasmus and to repair the church.[67] In 1651 the plate included a double and a single flagon.[68] A flagon, three plates, and a basin were bought in 1683.[69] At some date a silver-gilt chalice and paten of 1684 were acquired. They were sold with a pewter flagon and plates in 1852 to a Birmingham firm in part payment for a new set of plate. The chalice and paten of 1684 were bought the same year by St. Clement's, Oxford, and attempts in 1892 and 1923 to recover them for St. Michael's were unsuccessful.[70]

There were three bells in 1552.[71] A peal of six was cast by Abraham Rudhall of Gloucester in 1722 or 1723.[72] The third and fourth bells were recast in 1919 by James Barwell Ltd. of Birmingham.[73] A clock was installed in the tower c. 1814.[74]

The registers date from 1574.[75] There are few entries between 1642 and 1655.

The large churchyard around St. Michael's has long been the main burial ground for the city, and from early times it evidently served a wide area.[76] Formerly 7 a. in extent, it was extended by 2 a. in 1944.[77] Its wall and hedge were mentioned in 1586. Besides the lich gate on the north side, a south gate and a south stile were mentioned in 1710.[78] The main approach from the north was planted in 1751 with elms, felled in 1958 as unsafe.[79] On the north side is the mausoleum of J. T. Law, chancellor of the diocese 1821–54 (d. 1876), and his wife Lady Charlotte (d. 1866). Erected by 1864, it was originally surmounted by a clock with two dials, which was lit at night and was intended to remind those on their way to Trent Valley station both of the time of day and of the shortness of their time on earth.[80]

Since St. Mary's had no graveyard, most of its parishioners were buried at St. Michael's.[81] In 1886 the vicar of St. Mary's agreed to conduct the funerals of his parishioners in St. Michael's churchyard, but he stressed that by ancient custom the duty was the rector's.[82] From 1888 an annual collection was taken at St. Mary's towards the cost of maintaining St. Michael's churchyard. At first £10 a year was paid to St.

[67] *S.H.C.* N.S. vi (1), 178; *S.H.C.* 1915, 171–2.
[68] L.J.R.O., D. 27/4/1.
[69] Ibid. B/C/5/Exhibits/Lichfield, St. Michael.
[70] Ibid. D. 27/3/11; D. 27/5/2–3; *Lichfield Mercury*, 2 Feb. 1923, p. 4; 9 Mar. 1923, p. 4.
[71] *S.H.C.* N.S. vi (1), 178.
[72] Lynam, *Church Bells*, 18; L.J.R.O., B/C/5/Exhibits/ Lichfield, St. Michael, 1722–3, 1726–7. The bells are dated 1722; payments for their installation are dated March 1722/3. Jennings, *Staffs. Bells*, 81, states that the tenor was recast in 1730.
[73] *St. Michael's, Lichfield, Par. Mag.* June 1945 (copy in L.J.R.O., D. 27/9/7).
[74] L.J.R.O., D. 27/5/1, f. 100; D. 126/acct. bk. 1805–85, accts. 1813–14; St. Michael's Church Trust, acct. bk.

1811–1980, ff. 151–2.
[75] L.J.R.O., D. 27/1.
[76] Above, churches (introduction).
[77] Harwood, *Lichfield*, 515; *T.S.S.A.H.S.* xvi. 59–60; Lich. Dioc. Regy., Bp.'s Reg. W, p. 491; X, pp. 76–7. Part was taken for the widening of the Burton road in 1821: L.J.R.O., D. 15/2/4, 6 Feb., 3 July 1821.
[78] L.J.R.O., B/C/5/Exhibits/Lichfield, St. Michael.
[79] L.J.R.O., D. 27/2/4, memo. among 1779 entries; *Lichfield Mercury*, 10 Jan. 1958, p. 1; 1 Aug. 1958, p. 9.
[80] *Staffs. Advertiser*, 10 Mar. 1866, p. 4; 26 Feb. 1876, p. 7; 18 Jan. 1879, p. 3, reprinting an article on Lichfield from *The Builder*.
[81] L.J.R.O., D. 20/1. Some were buried at Stowe.
[82] Ibid. D. 20/5/1, note of 14 Sept. 1886.

Michael's, but the sum dwindled and payment ceased in 1920. In 1922 and 1924 St. Mary's paid £3 3s.[83] In 1933 the two churches collaborated in the purchase of the land later used to extend the churchyard.[84] By the 1980s the old part was maintained by the city council.[85]

The pasture of the churchyard was being let each year by the 1530s.[86] By 1801 it was the custom that only parishioners living at Greenhill had the right of pasture in the churchyard, for which they paid the churchwardens a stated sum, but of the 40 or more people entitled only 11 exercised the right.[87] In 1774 a meeting of parishioners ordered the construction of a separate gate for cows and wagons.[88] The vestry decided in 1801 that only sheep should be grazed, since the pasturing of cattle was a cause of damage and a desecration. The residents of Greenhill were empowered to choose two of their number to help the churchwardens and to look after the residents' rights.[89] Cows, however, continued to be grazed, and one killed a child in the churchyard in 1809.[90] The order of 1801 was repeated in 1811, when it was decided to lease a field where those claiming the right to pasture cows could put in one beast under the supervision of one of themselves and one of the churchwardens. The rent was to be paid out of the rent of the churchyard, any deficiency being met by those benefiting. The churchyard itself was let for 10 years to a single tenant at £30 a year for sheep only.[91] Rent from the churchyard was £12 in 1884.[92]

CHRIST CHURCH. Christ Church, Leamonsley, was consecrated in 1847. The ¾-a. site was given in 1844 by Richard Hinckley of Beacon House, his wife Ellen Jane, and Hugh Woodhouse, formerly of Beacon House. The cost of building the church was met by Ellen, and she and her husband gave £150 stock as a repair fund. Richard Hinckley also gave a house in Christchurch Lane and further stock to produce £30 a year for the minister. The Ecclesiastical Commissioners made a grant of £100 a year.[93] The first perpetual curate, T. A. Bangham, 1847–76, was nominated by the vicar of St. Michael's.[94] In 1848 a parish covering much of the west side of the city and including Leamons-

ley, Lower Sandford Street, and Sandfields, was formed out of St. Michael's and St. Chad's parishes with the bishop as patron.[95] The perpetual curacy was styled a vicarage in 1868, and the bishop remains the patron.[96] In 1860 the Ecclesiastical Commissioners assigned the incumbent tithe rent charges from St. Michael's and St. Chad's parishes amounting to £163 17s. 6d.[97] They granted £600 in 1868 towards the cost of enlarging the vicarage house.[98] In 1947 the house was divided, the rear portion being leased, and in 1957 a new house was completed on the opposite side of Christchurch Lane.[99]

On Census Sunday 1851 the congregation was 100 in the morning and 210 in the evening, each time with 90 Sunday school children.[1] In 1871 the vicar was licensed to perform divine service at the ragged school in Lower Sandford Street.[2] In the later 1870s a mission room was opened in the same street.[3] It was replaced in the later 1880s by a room over the entrance to Flower's Row on the north side of Sandford Street which remained in use until 1919.[4] There was a parish lending library in the later 1880s,[5] and a parish magazine was started in 1889.[6] In the early 20th century Christ Church Working Men's Club met in the mission room.[7] A hut used by Christ Church Boys' Club from 1938 was conveyed to the parish in 1947 for use as a parish hall as well as club premises for boys and girls.[8] A new hall, the Martin Heath Memorial Hall, north-west of the church was opened in 1964. The cost was met from the Martin Heath Memorial Fund established under the will of Edith Mary Heath, of Angorfa, Walsall Road, daughter of George Martin; she died in 1952, leaving her residuary estate to Christ Church. She had served as vicar's warden from 1931 to 1951 in succession to her husband Samuel. The hall was enlarged in 1984.[9]

In 1885 Richard Hinckley's nephew Arthur Hinckley, of Stowe Hill, established a trust to administer the income from £1,000 stock placed at his disposal by Richard before his death in 1865. It was to be used for church purposes, the maintenance of the Hinckley family tombstones at Christ Church, and distributions to the poor of the parish. It was stipulated that if ritualistic practices were introduced, the trustees could withhold the money spent on the church as long

[83] Ibid. D. 20/4/5; D. 20/5/1, Easter vestry 1904, 1907, 1917; D. 20/5/2, 18 May 1922, 20 May 1924; D. 27/5/3–4.
[84] Ibid. D. 20/5/2, 24 Feb. 1933, 11 Dec. 1933.
[85] Inf. from Mr. Savage.
[86] Harwood, *Lichfield*, 324, 522.
[87] L.J.R.O., D. 27/5/1, f. 12.
[88] L.J.R.O., B/C/5/Exhibits/Lichfield, St. Michael, 'Copies of Orders', pp. 9–10.
[89] L.J.R.O., D. 27/5/1, f. 12.
[90] Ibid. D. 27/1/5, burial of 31 Mar. 1809.
[91] Ibid. D. 27/5/1, ff. 24, 25v.–26, 87.
[92] Above (this section: incumbent's income).
[93] Lich. Dioc. Regy., Bp.'s Reg. O, pp. 16–31; *Lond. Gaz.* 5 May 1848, pp. 1742–3. Help with this section was kindly given by Mr. E. W. Beddows of Walsall Road, Lichfield.
[94] L.J.R.O., B/A/3/Lichfield, Christ Church; U. Turner, *Christ Church, Lichfield* (priv. print. 1985), 24 (copy in W.S.L.).
[95] *Lond. Gaz.* 18 Feb. 1848, pp. 625–6.
[96] *Lich. Dioc. Ch. Cal.* (1869); *Lich. Dioc. Dir.* (1988–9).
[97] *Lond. Gaz.* 30 Oct. 1860, pp. 3913, 3919–21.

[98] Ibid. 14 Aug. 1868, p. 4520.
[99] Turner, *Christ Church*, 15–16; *Lichfield Mercury*, 19 Apr. 1957, p. 1; inf. from the late Miss Ursula Turner.
[1] P.R.O., HO 129/377/1/18.
[2] Lich. Dioc. Regy., Bp.'s Reg. 33, p. 179.
[3] *Lich. Dioc. Ch. Cal.* (1878); docs. at Christ Church, parcel 21, lease of 5 Mar. 1900; O.S. Map 1/500, Staffs. LII. 15. 12 (1884 edn.).
[4] *Lich. Dioc. Ch. Cal.* (1888; 1917–18); Turner, *Christ Church*, 4; *Staffs. Advertiser*, 28 Sept. 1894, p. 4; S.R.O., D. 4566/C, sale cat. 1921; L.J.R.O., D. 103/2/5, 24 Sept. 1919, 14 Jan. 1920; O.S. Map 1/2,500, Staffs. LII. 15 (1902).
[5] Christ Church par. accts. 1886–7, 1887–8 (copy in S.R.O., D. 4566/C).
[6] Vol. x is for 1898 (copy at Christ Church).
[7] Christ Church par. accts. 1903–4, 1905–6 (copy in S.R.O., D. 4566/C).
[8] Docs. at Christ Church, parcels 2 and 22.
[9] Ibid. parcels 4 and 5; *Lichfield Mercury*, 29 Feb. 1952, p. 3; 6 June 1952, p. 8; 21 Dec. 1984, p. 2; Turner, *Christ Church*, 16, 18.

as such practices continued. The income of the Hinckley (Christ Church) Trust in 1985 was £1,252, which was spent on church needs.[10]

The church is a building of red sandstone and was designed in a Decorated style by Thomas Johnson of Lichfield. Originally it consisted of a chancel, a nave, and a west tower containing a gallery and a bell cast in 1845 by C. and G. Mears of London.[11] North and south transepts were added to the chancel in 1887 to the design of Matthew Holding of Northampton. It was intended to build north and south aisles as well, but a single bay only was built on each side adjoining the transepts. The work on the north side was paid for by S. L. Seckham of Beacon Place, churchwarden 1885–7 and 1892–6, and the cost of the south side was met by subscription and the proceeds from a bazaar; £200 was given by A. O. Worthington of Maple Hayes in Burntwood, churchwarden 1897–1918.[12] The southern extension consists, as planned, of an organ chamber and a clergy and choir vestry. The northern extension is occupied by a Lady chapel, which was refurbished in memory of J. B. Lane (d. 1947) by his widow and dedicated in 1950.[13] A chancel screen was presented in 1888 by Kinbarra, wife of S. L. Seckham,[14] and in 1897, to mark the church's golden jubilee, canvas panels painted by J. D. Batten were placed on the chancel ceiling.[15] The sanctuary was refurbished in 1906 with an alabaster reredos and marble paving to the design of G. F. Bodley; they were presented in memory of Sarah Cox by her husband and daughters.[16] The clock in the tower was presented in 1913 by A. O. Worthington in memory of his wife Sarah.[17] The churchyard was enlarged in 1895 and 1929.[18]

THE CATHEDRAL AS A CITY CHURCH.

After the establishment of the cathedral in the later 7th century it was presumably used as the principal baptistery for the Lichfield area. The cult of St. Chad may also have made its precincts the principal burial ground for a time: a late Anglo-Saxon graveyard lay on the south side of the cathedral.[19] It is probable, however, that there were burials at St. Michael's and at Stowe before the Conquest, and it is clear that by the 1190s the canons claimed no monopoly of Lichfield baptisms or burials for the cathedral. The cathedral's primacy in that respect was maintained by a demand that all fees, with the

apparent exception of mortuaries, should be paid to the sacrist.[20]

The cathedral statutes of 1294 laid down that every member of a canonical household was entitled to be buried in the cathedral graveyard.[21] Some townsmen from outside the Close continued to be buried within the cathedral precincts, but by the later 15th century the chapter regarded the practice as one to be discouraged. In 1486 it decreed that no outsiders, 'especially parishioners of the prebend of Gaia Major', were to be buried in the cathedral graveyard unless they were cathedral servants or members of a canon's household.[22] The decision was an episode in the chapter's struggle to emphasize the privacy and dignity of the Close. Even when distinguished people were buried in the cathedral itself, the chapter became increasingly anxious not to seem obsequious. In 1532, after the cathedral clergy had recently twice gone in procession into the town to meet funeral cortèges and escort them to the cathedral, the chapter ruled that in future no cortège and no visitor, however distinguished, was to be met outside the Close. To do so dishonoured the cathedral and was contrary to the practice of other cathedrals and collegiate churches.[23] The first surviving parish register for the cathedral, dating from 1661, shows that by the late 17th century it was the inhabitants of the Close who were baptized and buried there but that fashion drew some couples from far afield to be married in the cathedral.[24] In the late 1980s an area north-east of the cathedral was used for the interment of ashes.

As in other cathedrals, an early-morning weekday service for the laity was introduced at the Reformation. Ordered by the injunctions of the royal visitation of 1559, it was a brief service of prayers intended for the boys of the grammar school 'and all other well-disposed people and artificers' who would be at work at the time of matins later in the morning. It continued until the Civil War and was revived by Bishop Lloyd in 1694. Still held in the mid 18th century, it was later abandoned.[25]

Sermons were more common at the cathedral after the Reformation than in the other Lichfield churches. It was even stated in 1604 that none of the city clergy preached.[26] Many of the cathedral sermons were probably not intended for townspeople. Dean Collingwood, 1512–21, had preached to the people for half an hour every

[10] Turner, *Christ Church*, 17–18; inf. from Hinckley, Birch & Exham, solicitors of Lichfield, who act as clerk to the trust.

[11] Pevsner, *Staffs.* 190; Lynam, *Church Bells*, 19; Lich. Dioc. Regy., Bp.'s Reg. O, pp. 19–24; docs. at Christ Church, parcel 16, faculty of 9 July 1885.

[12] *Staffs. Advertiser*, 4 June 1887, p. 5; 31 Dec. 1887, p. 7; *Lich. Dioc. Mag.* (1888), 80, 149, 163; Turner, *Christ Church*, 4, 25.

[13] Inscription in the chapel; Turner, *Christ Church*, 13.

[14] Turner, *Christ Church*, 4; Burke, *Land. Gent.* (1894), ii. 1815.

[15] Turner, *Christ Church*, 6–7; *Kelly's Dir. Staffs.* (1900).

[16] Tablet in the chancel; *Lichfield Mercury*, 14 Dec. 1906, p. 4; 21 Dec. 1906, p. 4.

[17] *Lichfield Mercury*, 10 Oct. 1913, p. 5; *Staffs. Advertiser*, 11 May 1918, p. 5; Turner, *Christ Church*, 9, 25.

[18] Turner, *Christ Church*, 15; *Lich. Dioc. Mag.* (1895), 189; Lich. Dioc. Regy., Bp.'s Reg. U, p. 27; W, pp. 289, 342.

[19] *T.S.S.A.H.S.* xxii. 37–8.

[20] *Statutes of Lincoln Cathedral*, ed H. Bradshaw and C. Wordsworth, ii (1), 19–20.

[21] *V.C.H. Staffs.* iii. 150.

[22] L.J.R.O., D. 30/C.A. ii, f. 14.

[23] Ibid. C.A. iv, ff. 95v.–96.

[24] *Lichfield Cathedral Reg.* (Staffs. Par. Reg. Soc. 1973–4), 2. The registers of baptisms and burials to 1984 and of marriages to 1836 are in L.J.R.O., D. 102. Those of baptisms and burials to 1744 and of marriages to 1754 are printed in the Staffs. Par. Reg. Soc. volume.

[25] *V.C.H. Staffs.* iii. 173, 180, 186; C. Wordsworth, *Notes on Mediaeval Services in Eng.* 8–9.

[26] *S.H.C.* 1915, 152.

1. The cathedral from the south-west after the demolition of the central spire in 1646

2. The city from the west *c.* 1670

3. The city from the south-west in 1732

LICHFIELD

4. View from the south-west in 1813

5. The Consistory Court in 1833

LICHFIELD CATHEDRAL

6. Nos. 23 and 24 from the south in 1807

7. The courtyard of no. 23 in 1807

LICHFIELD CATHEDRAL CLOSE

8. Vicars' Close from the west

9. No. 13 from the south

10. The Deanery from the south

11. St. Mary's House from the south-east, showing the corner turret

LICHFIELD CATHEDRAL CLOSE

13. LICHFIELD: Stowe Hill from the south-west

15. LICHFIELD CATHEDRAL CLOSE: the former Bishop's Palace from the south

12. LICHFIELD: Stowe House from the west

14. BURNTWOOD: Maple Hayes from the east

16. No. 67 St. John Street (Davidson House)

17. No. 28 St. John Street (St. John's Preparatory School)

18. The Guildhall and Donegal House, Bore Street, with Lichfield House (the Tudor Café) on the right

LICHFIELD

19. The Union Workhouse in 1843

20. Darwin House, Beacon Street, probably *c.* 1800, with the hall of the vicars choral on the left

LICHFIELD

(a) John Jenens (Gennings), 1535–6

(b) Gregory Stonyng, 1536–7

(c) Richard Watwode, 1538–9

(d) John Balle, 1540–1

21. THE GUILD OF ST. MARY AND ST. JOHN THE BAPTIST, LICHFIELD:
vignettes relating to four masters

22. JOHN DYOTT in 1573

23. ANNA SEWARD in 1786

24. ARTHUR CHICHESTER, EARL (LATER MAR-
QUESS) OF DONEGALL, c. 1770

25. R. C. LUCAS retouching his statue of
Samuel Johnson in the market place,
Lichfield, in 1859

26. The Guildhall in 1838

27. Minors's School on the corner of Bore Street and St. John Street in 1833, with the Crucifix
Conduit on the right

LICHFIELD

28. The Corn Exchange and Market Hall in 1850, with the Savings Bank on the left

29. The railway bridge in St. John Street in 1849

LICHFIELD

30. The South Staffordshire Waterworks Co.'s pumping station at Sandfields in 1965

31. The City Flour Mill, Station Road, in 1965

LICHFIELD

32. The former Lichfield Brewery, Wiltell Road, off St. John Street, in 1966

33. The malthouse of the former City Brewery off Birmingham Road in 1965

LICHFIELD

34. The United Reformed Church, Wade Street

35. The Methodist Church, Tamworth Street

36. The Arts Centre, Bird Street, with the former post office on the right

LICHFIELD

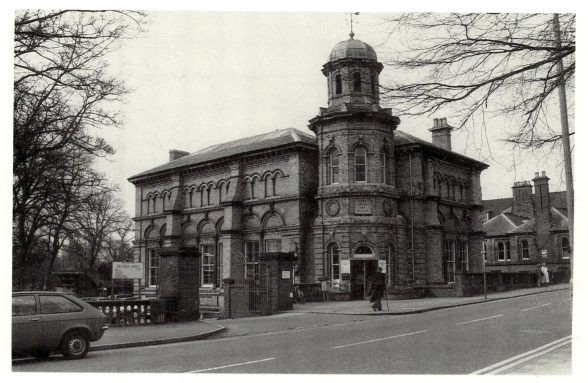

37. Lichfield Library, Bird Street

38. The former Friary School, with the foundations of the medieval Franciscan church in the foreground

LICHFIELD

39. LICHFIELD: Bakers Lane shopping precinct

40. BURNTWOOD: Sankey's Corner, Chase Terrace, with the former Chase Cinema on the left
and Burntwood Library and Lambourne House on the right

41. Christ Church from the south-east in 1839

Cold Bath, near Lichfiel

R Greene Fecit 1770.

42. The bath house at Abnalls in 1770

BURNTWOOD

43. View from the north-east in the 1680s

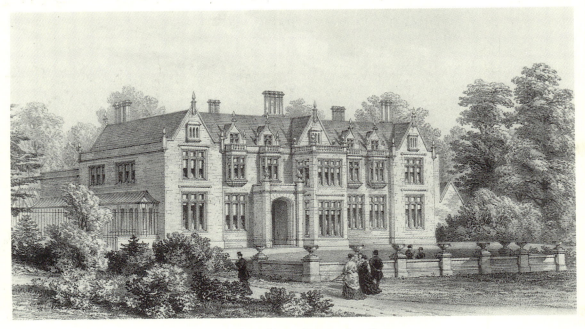

44. View from the east in 1874

ELMHURST HALL

45. View from the south in the 1680s

46. View from the south-east in the 1790s

47. View from the north-east in 1786, with a marquee by the lake

FISHERWICK HALL

48. FREEFORD: the hall from the west in the 1790s

49. BURNTWOOD: Edial Hall from the south-east in 1824

50. Tomb slabs of Thomas Streethay (d. 1521) and his wife Elizabeth (d. 1500) and of John Streethay (d. 1523) and his wife Anne (d. 1534), formerly in St. Michael's church, Lichfield

51. The hall from the south-west in the 1790s

STREETHAY

52. The church from the south-east *c.* 1870, with Robert Gordon, incumbent 1858–90, and his family

53. The interior in 1859, looking east

HAMMERWICH: CHURCH OF ST. JOHN THE BAPTIST

54. Wall Hall from the south in 1961

55. The Roman bath house from the west, with the church of St. John the Baptist in the background

WALL

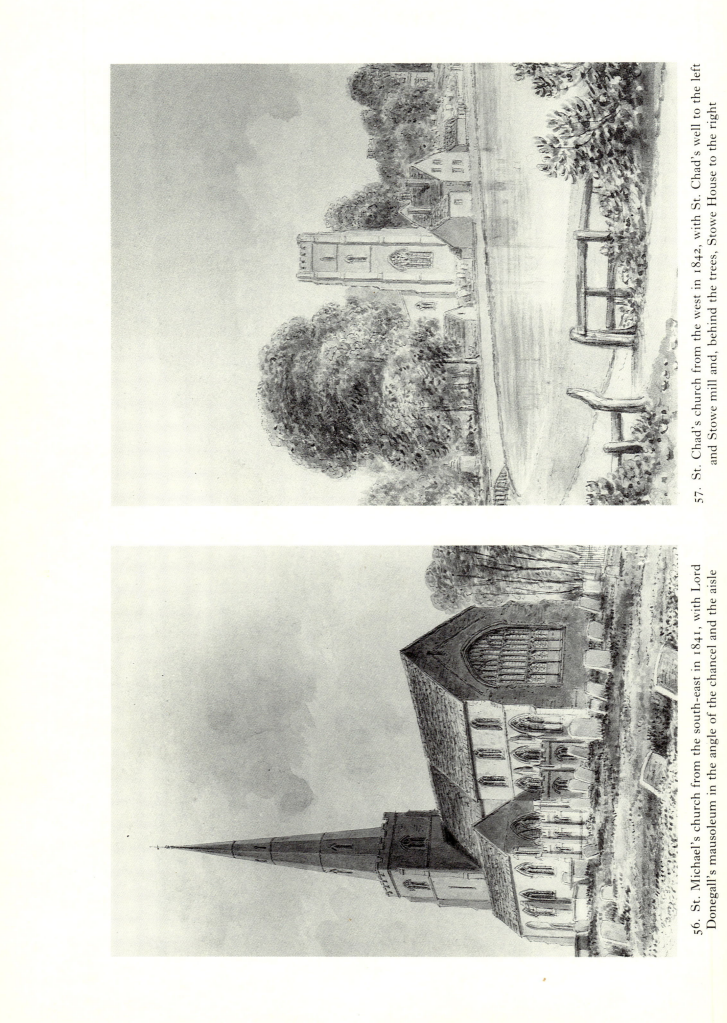

57. St. Chad's church from the west in 1842, with St. Chad's well to the left and Stowe mill and, behind the trees, Stowe House to the right

56. St. Michael's church from the south-east in 1841, with Lord Donegall's mausoleum in the angle of the chancel and the aisle

Sunday, but it was stated in 1575 that he was the first and only dean to do so. By the early 17th century there were civic services in the cathedral, and they presumably included a sermon. In 1635 Archbishop Laud found that there were too many pews in the nave and forced their removal. From 1548 there was a divinity lecturer at the cathedral, obliged to lecture there three times a week. The post lapsed in the reign of Mary I, and despite an injunction of 1559 ordering the appointment of a lecturer, it may not have been revived until after 1583. In 1759 the chapter reminded the lecturer that constant residence was obligatory. By the 1850s his duties were limited to preaching on certain saints' days.[27] It was stated in 1791 that until lately a sermon had been preached in the nave of the cathedral every Sunday morning for the benefit of the parishioners of St. Michael's and of Stowe, who otherwise had only a sermon once a month on sacrament days apart from endowed sermons.[28]

James Wyatt's restoration of the cathedral between 1788 and 1795 evidently had the effect of keeping people away from services. He threw the choir and Lady chapel together, blocked up arches, and erected a screen between the choir and the nave, to create what was virtually a small self-contained church isolated from the rest of the building. Sydney Smirke and George Gilbert Scott opened the building out again in 1856–61.[29] From the mid 19th century there was a great increase in the number of services, including communion services, and a wider use was made of the cathedral.[30] The congregation on Census Sunday 1851 was 135 in the morning and 224 in the afternoon.[31] The wider use of the building continued in the 20th century but the number of sung services declined.[32]

ST. JOHN'S HOSPITAL. The chapel of St. John's hospital in St. John Street has been open for public worship since the mid 13th century.[33] The hospital then lay in the prebend of Freeford, and at some time between 1224 and 1238 the prebendary, Simon of London, granted the prior and brethren permission to establish a chantry in the hospital. Simon's parishioners were to be permitted to attend divine service in the hospital on holy days, and the hospital was allowed one small bell to summon them. The chantry was eventually established in 1259 by the executors of Ralph of Lacock, the last subdean of the cathedral.

Simon of London was careful to protect the rights of his prebend. The hospital's lay brethren, servants, and other inmates were to make their confessions to the prebendal chaplain, unless he licensed them to go elsewhere. All offerings at the chantry mass were to be paid to the prebendal chaplain. The bodies of all who died in the hospital, including the prior and brethren, were to be buried in the prebendal church, and the prior and brethren and their servants were to attend divine service in that church on the great feasts. It has been generally assumed that the church was St. Michael's in Lichfield, but it may in fact have been Hammerwich chapel, which was within Freeford prebend.[34]

In spite of the agreement the hospital had by 1257 secured the right of burying its habited brethren and sisters and other inmates dying there. In accordance with his will Ralph of Lacock was buried at the hospital by permission of the dean and chapter, but the prior and brethren promised that they would not use the permission as a precedent.[35] Remains of a medieval graveyard have been found at St. John's, and in the mid 1340s there was a preaching cross or open-air pulpit in the graveyard from which Dean FitzRalph preached. Burials still took place in the precincts in the earlier 19th century.[36] Since the 1970s the ground by the south wall of the chapel has been used as a garden of remembrance where the ashes of people closely associated with the hospital are interred.[37]

By the 15th century the hospital had become an almshouse, under a master who was in orders. Until the 19th century the masters were often non-resident, and services in the chapel were presumably conducted by the hospital chaplain. Statutes of 1927 made the master the chaplain.[38] The chapel was used by the parishioners of St. Mary's during the rebuilding of their church between 1716 and 1721 and during further work in 1845.[39] The parishioners of St. Michael's worshipped there when their church was being restored in 1842–3.[40] Pew rents were abolished in 1828.[41] On Census Sunday 1851 there was an attendance of 123 at matins and 168 at evensong.[42] By 1868 services were held on Wednesday and Friday as well as Sunday.[43] Since the later 1920s they have been Anglo-Catholic in character. There are marriage and baptismal registers dating from 1914 and 1941 respectively.[44]

The chapel is described with the rest of the hospital buildings in another volume.[45] In 1984 a stained glass window depicting Christ in majesty, to a design by John Piper, was installed in place of the plain east window of the chapel. The cost was met by a bequest from Samuel Hayes, a resident of the hospital, and by the hospital trustees.[46]

[27] H. Wharton, *Anglia Sacra* (1691), i. 455–6; *V.C.H. Staffs.* iii. 167, 173, 183, 192.
[28] L.J.R.O., D. 30, case for counsel's opinion, 1791, f. 2.
[29] Above, cathedral and close.
[30] *V.C.H. Staffs.* iii. 192, 195.
[31] P.R.O., HO 129/377/1/15.   [32] *V.C.H. Staffs.* iii. 196.
[33] First two paras. based on *V.C.H. Staffs.* iii. 144–5, 279; *S.H.C.* 1924, p. 203.
[34] Below, Hammerwich, church.
[35] *V.C.H. Staffs.* iii. 279; *S.H.C.* 1924, pp. 320–1.
[36] *V.C.H. Staffs.* iii. 279 and n.; *Lichfield Mercury*, 14 Oct. 1825.

[37] Tablet on S. wall; memorial stones in the garden of remembrance dating from 1971 onwards; inf. from the master.
[38] *V.C.H. Staffs.* iii. 280–5, 287–8.
[39] L.J.R.O., D. 20/4/2 and 5.
[40] Ibid. D. 27/3/9.
[41] Above, par. govt. (poor relief).
[42] P.R.O., HO 129/377/1/18.
[43] *Staffs. Advertiser*, 28 Mar. 1868, p. 7.
[44] *V.C.H. Staffs.* iii. 285.   [45] Ibid. 286.
[46] H. Clayton, *St. John's Hosp. Lichfield* (n.d. but 1984; copy in W.S.L.); *Lichfield Mercury*, 29 June 1984, p. 45.

THE LICHFIELD PECULIAR. From the 13th to the 19th century ecclesiastical jurisdiction in Lichfield and its neighbourhood was exercised not by the bishop but by the dean of the cathedral and, during vacancies in the deanery, by the chapter. About 1190 the dean had the power to discipline clergy in the city 'by appeal'.[47] Possibly he already held the archidiaconal jurisdiction there which he possessed by 1241,[48] but it is more likely that it was acquired in the intervening half century when his privileges and influence had grown generally.[49] In the mid 13th century the chapter was drawing to itself rights of ecclesiastical supervision in the Lichfield area exercised a few years earlier by individual canons,[50] and the dean was the principal beneficiary. By the later 13th century his position in relation to both bishop and chapter was unusually strong for an English dean. He established his claim that he not only had ordinary jurisdiction over the lands and churches of the cathedral clergy but that he was also their visitor.[51] He had no rival as the principal dignitary in the chapter, Lichfield being unusual among English cathedral chapters in giving no special place of honour to the archdeacons of the diocese.[52] In some cathedrals jurisdiction over the city was the responsibility of the subdean; at Lichfield the post apparently had no such function, and in any case it disappeared in 1257.[53]

The extent of the dean's jurisdiction within the city was occasionally challenged. In 1393 Thomas Walton, prebendary of Freeford, claimed jurisdiction over people living in the portion of the city within his prebend. Bishop Scrope, called in to arbitrate, upheld the dean's rights over the whole city. The decision was used as a precedent in 1531, when it was decided, against a later prebendary of Freeford, John Blythe, that probate of the will of John Browne of Greenhill, in Freeford prebend and outside the bars of the city, belonged to the dean. Thomas Fitzherbert, prebendary of Weeford 1513–19, also seems wrongly to have believed that the dean's jurisdiction over the city stopped at the bars.[54]

The only serious episcopal challenge to the authority of the dean and chapter in the city seems to have been that made by Bishop Northburgh, 1321–58, as part of his general assault on the chapter's privileges. During a vacancy in the deanery in 1324 he asserted that he, not the chapter, possessed ecclesiastical jurisdiction in the city when the deanery was vacant. He ordered the chapter's commissaries, who had excommunicated three townsmen and suspended a Lichfield priest, to withdraw the sentences immediately or appear before his court.[55] He failed to break the chapter's resistance, and when in 1428 Bishop Heyworth and the chapter reached a composition allowing episcopal visitation of the cathedral, it included the provision that prebendal churches and those of the common fund were to be exempt from episcopal visitation save in cases of scandalous neglect.[56] Episcopal attempts to secure the patronage of St. Mary's in 1529–30 and the 1620s failed.[57]

The only place in the city over which the dean failed to maintain jurisdiction was St. John's hospital. In the earlier 13th century the hospital was subject to the jurisdiction of the prebendary of Freeford, but by the 1250s it had passed into that of the dean and chapter. It was to them that in 1257 the prior and brethren of St. John's addressed a petition to be allowed to bury Ralph of Lacock, the subdean. They promised that such permission would not be to the prejudice of the cathedral or its chaplains and that they would not seek any further burial rights without the assent of the dean and chapter. In 1259, however, the founders of Lacock's chantry at the hospital vested the appointment of its priest in the bishop. In 1323 Bishop Northburgh asserted his right to appoint the prior of the hospital against the brethren's claim, and he carried out several visitations of St. John's. Bishop Smith's statutes of 1495 reforming the hospital vested the appointment of the master in the bishop. In the early 1530s Dean Denton claimed ordinary jurisdiction over St. John's and sent his commissary to visit it. Bishop Blythe excommunicated the master, who had co-operated with Denton, and successfully maintained his episcopal rights.[58]

In 1471 the parochial chaplain serving St. Mary's prevented a collector for St. Anthony's hospital in London from taking a collection on the first Sunday of Lent. The collector retaliated by claiming that his privileges included the right to forbid the use of bells, candles, and the processional cross in recalcitrant churches. He was promptly taken before Dean Heywood and forced to apologize for violating the dean's jurisdiction.[59]

In June and July 1326 what was described as 'the chapter of the city of Lichfield' met at least once a week to deal with ecclesiastical cases, most of them concerning sexual misdemeanours.[60] It was presumably the court of the dean's Lichfield jurisdiction. The normal day of meeting seems to have been Saturday, the day after the chapter met,[61] and the court appears to have been held by the chapter clerk.[62] It may have been convened only in the aftermath of a visitation, or it may have met regularly, as needed, on Saturday. The parochial chaplains had to attend the cathedral that day,[63] and they were thus available to give evidence if necessary. It seems

[47] Wilkins, *Concilia*, i. 497.
[48] Ibid. 499–500.
[49] *V.C.H. Staffs.* iii. 143–5.
[50] e.g. over St. John's hosp.: above.
[51] K. Edwards, *Eng. Secular Cathedrals in the Middle Ages* (1967), 132, 142, 147.
[52] *V.C.H. Staffs.* iii. 142.
[53] Ibid. 144; Edwards, *Eng. Secular Cathedrals*, 153–4.
[54] L.J.R.O., D. 30/C.A. i, ff. 36v.–37; C.A. iv, ff. 78v.–80.
[55] *V.C.H. Staffs.* iii. 155; *S.H.C.* 1924, p. 348.

[56] *V.C.H. Staffs.* iii. 163.
[57] Above (parochial organization from 1491).
[58] *V.C.H. Staffs.* iii. 279–81; *S.H.C.* 1924, p. 320. And see above (St. John's hosp.).
[59] L.J.R.O., D. 30/9/3/1, f. 29v.
[60] Ibid. D. 30/9/3/2/7.
[61] *V.C.H. Staffs.* iii. 145.
[62] The R. Bernard who held at least two of the courts was the chapter clerk: J. C. Cox, *Notes on Churches of Derb.* iv. 489; *S.H.C.* 1924, p. xxi.
[63] Above (parochial organization to 1491).

to have been the only ecclesiastical body which dealt with the city as a whole.

The dean's peculiar, covering the parishes of St. Mary, St. Michael, and St. Chad with the out-townships, continued in existence until 1846. All peculiar and exempt jurisdictions in the diocese, with the exception of the cathedral and its Close, were then transferred to the bishop.[64] The dean and chapter retained the power to grant probate and administration of wills within the area of the former peculiar until such rights were abolished in 1858.[65]

ROMAN CATHOLICISM

THE large number of Lichfield cathedral clergy deprived along with the bishop in 1559 or soon afterwards included the dean, the precentor, and the chancellor.[66] Although the treasurer took the Oath of Supremacy, he resigned in 1560. In 1582 Bishop Overton complained of the lax administration of the dean's peculiar jurisdiction in Lichfield, where there were evidently many Roman Catholics.[67] A puritan survey of 1604 found 'many popish' there. One of the Roman Catholic martyrs of the Elizabethan period, St. Edmund Gennings, was born at Lichfield in 1567 of a protestant family. Having been converted, he was ordained abroad in 1590 and returned to Lichfield. He was captured in London and executed in 1591.

Four papists were listed in St. Mary's parish in 1705, all 'of a mean condition', and a 'very poor' widow in the Close was also recorded as a papist. In 1706 there were two papists in the Close, a German and a Frenchman who were servants of Lord Stanhope; a charwoman in Stowe Street was a reputed papist. The bailiffs and justices certified in the earlier 1740s that there were no papists in the city 'save only two or three women'.[68] In 1767 four women in St. Mary's parish were returned as papists and two in St. Chad's. There were 19 in St. Michael's parish, which included the Roman Catholic centre at Pipe Hall in Burntwood. All 19 were farmers and servants except Miss Teresa Wakeman, described as a young lady of fortune and therefore probably living in the city; she had a resident priest, the Franciscan Thomas Hall, also known as Laurence Loraine. Thirteen Roman Catholics took the oath of allegiance at Lichfield quarter sessions in 1778 under the terms of the Catholic Relief Act of that year; six appear to have been among those listed in St. Michael's in 1767.[69] About a dozen people from Lichfield attended the chapel at Pipe Hall in the early 1790s.

The chapel was closed when Thomas Weld sold the hall in 1800. He gave the vestments and other items belonging to the chapel and £200 to Thomas Clifford of Tixall. Clifford raised a further £400 and bought a house on the corner of Bore Street and Breadmarket Street occupied by a Roman Catholic baker. It provided lodgings for a priest, and a chapel was formed by throwing two rooms together. John Kirk, who had been the priest at Pipe Hall from 1788 to 1792, was appointed to Lichfield by the vicar apostolic of the Midland District in 1801 with a stipend of £60 a year.[70]

Kirk considered the house inconvenient and meanly situated. In particular the sanctuary of the chapel was directly over the baker's oven, and the heat was almost unbearable. In 1802 he bought land in Upper St. John Street and built a chapel and house there, completed in 1803. Subscriptions were raised from the Catholic nobility, gentry, and clergy.[71] The chapel was originally dedicated to SS. Peter and Paul, but when it was enlarged in 1834 the dedication was changed to Holy Cross. At the time of the founding of the Lichfield mission there were 60 adult communicants.[72] By 1810 there were 75 communicants. The numbers included Catholics of the Tamworth area, for whom Kirk was responsible until the later 1820s, and also French émigrés and prisoners of war.[73] By 1841 the Lichfield congregation averaged c. 90, some of them people travelling from Liverpool to London; in summer numbers were increased by 'hundreds of Irish'. Most of the congregation were very poor. On Census Sunday 1851 attendances at Holy Cross were 70 in the morning and 20 in the afternoon; it was claimed that the average morning attendance was 100 with 20 Sunday school children in addition, while the evening attendance averaged 50.[74] There was by then an Irish community in Sandford Street, still in existence in 1888 when the poor attended by the superintendent of the Lichfield nursing association included 'the lowest Irish in Sandford Street'.[75] Kirk died in 1851, aged 91, and was buried in the chapel. Joseph Parkes, his assistant for 10 years, succeeded him.

The size of the congregation was greatly increased by the Irish who settled in the mining area around Chasetown, in Burntwood, in the later 19th century; Chasetown became a separate mission in 1883.[76] The priest at Holy Cross was appointed chaplain to Roman Catholics at Whittington barracks, opened in 1880; the Whittington salary and offertories brought in nearly £96 in 1892 out of the Lichfield mission's total income of just under £216. In 1894 the Holy Cross congregation numbered 210, with another

[64] V.C.H. Staffs. iii. 74.
[65] Ibid. 94.
[66] This section is based on Staffs. Studies, ed. P. Morgan (Keele, 1987), 129–39.
[67] V.C.H. Staffs. iii. 53.
[68] Harwood, Lichfield, 309.
[69] L.J.R.O., D. 25/1/1, f. 99.
[70] Cath. Mag. v. 321 (reprinted in Staffs. Cath. Hist. xiv).
[71] B.A.A., C. 1665.
[72] Ibid. C. 1662.
[73] Cath. Mag. v. 323–4; Staffs. Cath. Hist. xx. 20; for the prisoners of war see also above, general hist.
[74] Staffs. Cath. Hist. viii. 30 (wrongly given as vol. vii in Staffs. Studies, 138, n. 40).
[75] Staffs. Advertiser, 23 June 1888, p. 2; Recollections of Sophia Lonsdale, ed. V. Martineau, 187–8.
[76] Below, Burntwood, Roman Catholicism.

19 Catholics in the workhouse and 8 in the Truant school; at Whittington barracks there were a further 267.

In 1967 a church dedicated to SS. Peter and Paul was opened on the corner of Dimbles Lane and Dimbles Hill to serve the growing residential area in the north of the city. It has continued to be served from Holy Cross. The Roman Catholics attached to the two churches numbered 1,800 in the mid 1980s, with another 100 at Whittington barracks. A parish hall, built in the garden of the Holy Cross presbytery, was opened in 1955.[77] In 1987 Holly Cottage in Chapel Lane near Holy Cross became the presbytery. The other house remained in use for meetings and office purposes.[78]

The church of Holy Cross is a brick building in a Gothic style with an entrance front and turret of Tixall stone in a mixed Romanesque and Gothic style.[79] Fearing possible hostility in a cathedral city, Kirk originally built the chapel and the house under the same roof to give the overall impression simply of a dwelling house. In 1834, however, the entrance front was added, giving the building the appearance of a chapel; it was designed by Joseph Potter of Lichfield (probably Joseph the younger).[80] The sanctuary was built at the same time. An organ and gallery had been installed in 1823. A transept (liturgically north, in fact south-west) was added in 1895, and it was evidently then that the altarpiece, a painting of the Crucifixion by the Flemish artist Nicolaes de Bruyn (d. 1656), was removed. It had probably come from the Pipe Hall chapel.[81] In 1922 a new altar was consecrated in memory of Kirk and of Hugh McCarten, the priest in charge of the mission 1882–1911.[82]

The church of SS. Peter and Paul was designed in a modern style by Gwilliam & Armstrong of Sutton Coldfield (Warws.). It is built of blue brick and has seating for the congregation on three sides of a centrally placed altar.[83]

PROTESTANT NONCONFORMITY

DISSENT from the established Church developed in Lichfield in the 1650s. In 1669 Bishop Hacket complained that Dean Wood, 1664–71, was 'a professed favourer of nonconformists' and that 'puritanism has spread excessively in our city, not only by his sufferance but by his furtherance'.[84] Dean Addison, 1683–1703, in contrast was a vigorous upholder of the established Church, and in 1684 he reported to Archbishop Sancroft that he had 'so thoroughly practised the nonconformist dissenters as to bring them all to holy communion except three or four Anabaptists and one Quaker'.[85] Presbyterians, however, retained a meeting house, which was still open in 1743 when the corporation claimed that there was not 'any Quaker or above two dissenters from the established Church of England, under any denomination whatsoever'.[86] Congregationalists were active at the beginning of the 19th century, and their meetings caused Anna Seward in 1809 to deplore the end of Lichfield's 'happy exemption from the ravings of religious enthusiasm'.[87] Besides chapels for Wesleyan, New Connexion, and Primitive Methodists and for Congregationalists, there were also in the 1820s and 1830s several meeting places registered for unidentified congregations.[88] The challenge to the Church of England was met notably by Henry Lonsdale, vicar of St. Mary's 1830–51, who according to his daughter found 14 'flourishing dissenting chapels firmly established in Lichfield and fairly emptied the lot'.[89] The claim was exaggerated, but the number of nonconformists attending evening services on Census Sunday in 1851 was only 263, compared with 1,957 worshippers at the afternoon and evening Church of England services in the city.[90]

BAPTISTS. Francis Silvester and Robert Prittie of Lichfield were among the signatories of a letter of advice sent to Oliver Cromwell by Baptist churches in the Midlands in 1651. By 1654 there was a Baptist minister in the city, Thomas Pollard, but apparently only three or four Anabaptists were living there in the mid 1680s.[91] They probably attended meetings led by Lawrence Spooner, a Baptist who held a conventicle at his house in Curborough in 1683.[92] It was almost certainly Spooner who gave hospitality to two Baptists visiting Lichfield in 1690. The city congregation then included Particular Baptists.[93] An Anabaptist named Thomas Fullelove or Fullelowe was living in St. Mary's parish in the mid 1720s; he joined the saddlers' trade company in 1726.[94] There was probably a Baptist congregation in

[77] Lichfield Mercury, 4 Feb. 1955, p. 5.
[78] Inf. from the Very Revd. Canon K. J. Good, parish priest of Holy Cross.
[79] The church is not orientated: the altar is at the south-west end.
[80] Cath. Mag. v. 322 and frontispiece (a view of the church drawn by Joseph the younger).
[81] B.A.A., B. 11620; C. 1665 (wrongly given as C. 1662 in Staffs. Studies, 138, n. 30); Cath. Mag. v. 322; Kelly's Dir. Staffs. (1896; 1940).
[82] Staffs. Advertiser, 23 Sept. 1911, p. 9; 16 Dec. 1922, p. 5; plaque by the altar.
[83] Lichfield Mercury, 7 July 1967, p. 14.
[84] A. G. Matthews, The Congregational Churches of Staffs.

(n.d.; preface 1924), 71; below (Friends; Presbyterians).
[85] Matthews, Cong. Churches, 79–80.
[86] Harwood, Lichfield, 309.
[87] Jnls. and Corresp. of Thomas Sedgewick Whalley, ed. H. Wickham, ii. 327–8 (calling them Methodists); T.S.S.A.H.S. xiii. 58–9.
[88] S.H.C. 4th ser. iii. 55, 59, 62, 68, 70, 83–4.
[89] Recollections of Sophia Lonsdale, ed. V. Martineau, 24.
[90] P.R.O., HO 129/377/1/13–16, 18, and 20.
[91] Matthews, Cong. Churches, 35–6, 80.
[92] Below, Curborough and Elmhurst, nonconformity.
[93] Matthews, Cong. Churches, 80.
[94] L.J.R.O., D. 20/1/2, list of births of dissenters' children; D. 77/3/1.

Lichfield in 1861 when a Baptist minister was living in Gresley Row.[95]

CHRISTADELPHIANS. In 1870 the recently appointed headmistress of St. Chad's school was forced to resign because of her Christadelphian beliefs. Thomas Sykes, who had formed a small Christadelphian community at Bourton on the Water (Glos.), moved to Lichfield in 1874. By 1885 eight Christadelphians were meeting in each other's houses, and in 1890 a meeting room was opened above Sykes's shop in Tamworth Street. In 1902 the vicar of St. Mary's, C. N. Bolton, denounced the sect as heretical, and a public meeting followed at which the members defended their beliefs. Their numbers increased, and from 1903 meetings were held in St. James's Hall in Bore Street. After the hall was converted into a cinema in 1912, the society of over 40 members built its own hall in Station Road; it was opened in 1914 and extended in 1959.[96] The society still met there in the late 1980s.

CONGREGATIONALISTS, LATER UNITED REFORMED CHURCH. In 1790 Congregationalists met in Tunstalls Yard at the west end of Sandford Street, using a barn owned by Bradbury Tunstall, a sailcloth manufacturer and a sympathizer. Meetings ceased in 1796 but were restarted in 1802, and by 1808 there were sufficient numbers to constitute a church.[97] A brick chapel was opened in Wade Street in 1812, and a house for the minister, paid for mostly by a Miss Newnham of Birmingham, was added behind it in 1813. A gallery was added at the north end of the chapel in 1815, and side galleries were erected in 1824 and 1837.[98] There was a Sunday school by 1837.[99] On Census Sunday 1851 there were attendances of 115 in the morning and 120 in the evening, with 26 Sunday school children in the morning.[1] A hall was built in Frog Lane behind the chapel in 1932.[2] The chapel remained in use in the late 1980s.

FRIENDS. The Quaker George Fox visited Lichfield after his release from Derby gaol in 1651.[3] As the result of a vision he walked barefoot through the streets and the market place crying 'Woe unto the bloody city of Lichfield'. No one hindered him, and he afterwards concluded that he had been sent by God to 'raise up' the blood of the 999 Christian martyrs who had, according to legend, been slain in the Lichfield area under the emperor Diocletian.[4] In 1655 two Quakers, Alexander Parker and Thomas Taylor, held a meeting in a house belonging to Humphrey Beeland. Many of their hearers were 'rude and brutish people', but others were 'very tender and much convinced'. A disputation between a Quaker and the Muggletonian Thomas Tomkinson took place at a Lichfield inn, apparently in the late 1670s.[5]

The Lichfield converts probably met at the house of William Reading of Lynn in Shenstone. He became a Quaker in 1654 and held meetings at his house by the early 1670s. The meeting place was moved to Chesterfield, also in Shenstone, in the early 1680s. The opposition of the Church of England prevented the Quakers from meeting in the city, and in 1684 Dean Addison reported that there was only one Quaker there. An unsuccessful attempt was made in 1703–4 to secure a meeting place in the city, evidently in a building occupied by a Friend, Richard Palmer. His son William was also a Friend, and when chosen constable of Lichfield manor in 1716 he refused to take the oath of office. William attended the Chesterfield meeting until it failed through lack of support in the 1720s.

In 1816 a house in Sandford Street was registered for worship by Quakers.[6] The meeting, organized as part of the North Warwickshire monthly meeting, was discontinued in 1829.[7]

METHODISTS. *Wesleyan*. Although John Wesley passed through or near Lichfield in 1755, 1756, and 1777, he did not preach there.[8] A house at Gallows wharf, where the London road crossed the Wyrley and Essington Canal, was registered for worship by protestant dissenters in 1811. It was almost certainly for Wesleyan Methodists: the registration was witnessed by Joshua Kidger, presumably the J. Kedger who in 1813 registered a Wesleyan chapel in Lombard Street.[9] That chapel, on the south side of the street, was actually built in 1814 or 1815[10] and was presumably used by the Methodist John Kidger of Belton (Leics.) who ministered in Lichfield between 1815 and 1818.[11] A Sunday school had been established by 1823.[12] In 1826 the congregation was served by ministers from neighbouring circuits, still the practice in the earlier 1840s.[13] On Census Sunday 1851 there were attendances of 22 in the morning and 41 in the evening, with 51 Sunday school children in the morning. It was claimed that during the winter months the evening congregation numbered up to 130 people.[14] A new chapel, built to

[95] P.R.O., RG 9/1973.

[96] Jackson, *Hist. Incidents*, 80–1; inf. from Mr. O. Keyte, church librarian.

[97] *T.S.S.A.H.S.* xiii. 53–7; L.J.R.O., D. 25/1/1, f. 169; D. 112/1/1, pp. 3–4, 9; above, econ. hist. (trades and industries).

[98] L.J.R.O., D. 112/1/1, pp. 19–20, 23; *Lichfield Mercury*, 5 Mar. 1824; *Trans. Cong. Hist. Soc.* iii. 44–5; above, plate 34.

[99] L.J.R.O., D. 112/7/1.

[1] P.R.O., HO 129/377/1/14.

[2] Jackson, *Hist. Incidents*, 68.

[3] This and next para. based on *Staffordshire Studies*, ed. P. Morgan (Keele, 1987), 105–12.

[4] Above, place name.

[5] *D.N.B.* s.v. Tomkinson.

[6] *S.H.C.* 4th ser. iii. 39.

[7] Friends' Meeting House, Bull Street, Birmingham, North Warws. Monthly Meeting min. bk. 1827–38.

[8] *Jnl. of John Wesley*, ed. N. Curnock, iv. 109, 185; vi. 174.

[9] *S.H.C.* 4th ser. iii. 23, 32.

[10] Stringer, *Lichfield*, 153; White, *Dir. Staffs.* (1834), 90; O.S. Map 1/500, Staffs. LII. 13. 8 (1884 edn.).

[11] *Wesleyan Methodist Mag.* (Mar. 1826), 145–9.

[12] *Lichfield Mercury*, 19 Dec. 1823.

[13] Ibid. 13 Oct. 1826; Wesley, *Dir. Burton* (1844), 26.

[14] P.R.O., HO 129/377/1/14.

the design of Thomas Guest of Birmingham, was opened in Tamworth Street in 1892.[15] It remained in use in the late 1980s. The former chapel was used as the Sunday school until 1902 when a school was built behind the Tamworth Street chapel.[16] From 1921 to 1979 it was used by the Lichfield Afternoon Women's Institute, which in 1980 sold it to the Jehovah's Witnesses.[17]

A Wesleyan chapel was established in Wade Street in or shortly before 1815. It was still in use in 1837.[18]

New Connexion. In 1826 Bradbury Tunstall registered as a chapel for worship by New Connexion Methodists the Sandford Street barn formerly used by the Congregationalists.[19] It was replaced by a chapel built on the south side of Queen Street in 1833.[20] On Census Sunday 1851 there were attendances of 32 in the morning and 45 in the evening, with 16 Sunday school children in the morning.[21] The chapel was sold in 1859, the congregation having disbanded.[22]

Primitive. A Primitive Methodist missionary preached at Greenhill on Whit Monday 1820, and possibly as a consequence a blacksmith's outhouse in St. Chad's parish was registered for worship in November that year. It was presumably replaced by a schoolroom in St. Mary's parish registered for worship in 1831. In 1836 the Darlaston and Birmingham circuits provided two missionaries for the Lichfield area, and a chapel was opened in George Lane in 1848.[23] The attendance there on Census Sunday 1851 was 23 in the afternoon and 57 in the evening; no morning service was held that day, but it was stated that normally there was an attendance of 60, with 51 Sunday school children.[24] The chapel was closed in 1934 and reopened the following year as a Salvation Army hall.[25] It was later bought by Frank Halfpenny, a city councillor, and in 1958 given by him to the Lichfield and Tamworth Constituency Labour Party, which named it Frank Halfpenny Hall. It was sold in 1984 to the Swinfen Broun Charitable Trust, which later let it to the Pre-School Playgroup Association.[26]

PRESBYTERIANS. Thomas Minors (d. 1677), a mercer who was M.P. for Lichfield 1654–60 and a prominent member of the corporation at that time, was also a leading Presbyterian. Among his protegés were John Butler, minister at St. Chad's in 1651 and minister at St. Mary's by 1656, and Thomas Miles, Butler's successor at St. Chad's.[27] Both Butler and Miles were ejected in 1662, and Miles evidently formed a Presbyterian congregation, holding services in a Curborough farmhouse; some 40 people presented for non-attendance at St. Chad's in 1665 were possibly members of that meeting. Miles was licensed as a Presbyterian teacher in 1672, but nothing further is known of him.[28]

The Presbyterians remained powerful in the city after the Restoration. Bishop Hacket complained that 'the Presbyterians of the city do what they list, come not to the holy communion, baptize in hugger-mugger, are presented for their faults but no order taken with them', and Dean Wood allotted prominent seats in the cathedral to Thomas Minors and his brother-in-law William Jesson.[29] Presbyterian influence extended in 1667 to the election as M.P. of Richard Dyott, who Hacket believed was completely under their control.[30] In July 1669 Minors and Jesson were summoned before the Privy Council for holding a conventicle in Minors's house. They moved the meeting to a farmhouse at Elmhurst, where a conventicle later the same month lasted most of the day. According to Hacket it was attended by some 80 people, of whom the ringleader was a Lichfield carrier named James Rixam (or Rixom), a man 'no way fit for that trust, being a transcendent schismatic'. Minors and Jesson subsequently appeared before the Council but were discharged.[31]

Five houses in Lichfield were licensed for Presbyterian worship in 1672; they included Minors's house and that of John Barker, another mercer who was later one of the trustees of the English school in Bore Street established under Minors's will.[32] By 1695 a Presbyterian minister, Robert Travers, was working in the area, with a chapel at Longdon Green. He baptized at Lichfield in 1700, and there was a meeting house in the city by 1707.[33] It was burnt down during riots in 1715 but had been rebuilt by 1718.[34] In 1720 Travers was living in the house of Elizabeth Jesson, possibly in Saddler Street.[35] In 1738 his own house in Lichfield was licensed for worship.[36] He may still have been active in 1747,

[15] Above, plate 35.

[16] *Staffs. Advertiser*, 15 Aug. 1891, p. 7; *Lichfield Mercury*, 22 Apr. 1892, p. 5; *Lomax's Red Bk.* (1903), 11.

[17] *Lichfield Mercury*, 2 Nov. 1979, p. 18; 1 Feb. 1980, p. 16; below (other denominations).

[18] P.R.O., RG 4/3297.

[19] *Lichfield Mercury*, 22 Sept. 1826; *S.H.C.* 4th ser. iii. 79; Bodl. G.A. Staffs. 4°, 6, plan of Lichfield after p. vii.

[20] L.J.R.O., D. 15/2/4; L.J.R.O., B/A/15/Lichfield, St. Chad; S.R.O., D. 941/6/1 (naming 12 trustees in 1834).

[21] P.R.O., HO 129/377/1/20.

[22] S.R.O., D. 941/6/7 and 9.

[23] J. Petty, *Hist. of Primitive Methodist Connexion* (1864), 114, 492–3; *S.H.C.* 4th ser. iii. 50, 77, 100.

[24] P.R.O., HO 129/377/1/13.

[25] *Lomax's Red Bk.* (1934), 34; (1935), 99; below (other denominations).

[26] *Lichfield Mercury*, 22 Feb. 1985, p. 10; inf. from Mr. D. Y. Mathison of Lichfield Labour Party.

[27] *Calamy Revised*, ed. A. G. Matthews, 94, 350; above, town govt. (govt. from 1548: unreformed corporation); parl. representation; churches (parochial organization from 1491).

[28] *Trans. Cong. Hist. Soc.* iii. 34–6; Matthews, *Cong. Churches*, 93.

[29] Matthews, *Cong. Churches*, 71–2.

[30] Bodl. MS. Tanner 45, ff. 214v., 278.

[31] Matthews, *Cong. Churches*, 72–5; Bodl. MS. Tanner 44, f. 125; below, Curborough and Elmhurst, nonconformity.

[32] Matthews, *Cong. Churches*, 91; Harwood, *Lichfield*, 479.

[33] S.R.O., D. 4119, pp. [11, 51, 56]; *Jnl. of United Reformed Church Hist. Soc.* iii, no. 7 (1985), 268–78.

[34] S.R.O., D. 4119, p. [61]; *Flying Post*, 16–19 July 1715 (transcr. in W.S.L.).

[35] S.R.O., D. 4119, pp. [10, 49]; Reade, *Johnsonian Gleanings*, vii. 159.

[36] L.J.R.O., D. 68, f. 52v.

but by April 1748 the congregation was served by Samuel Stubbs.[37] The Lichfield chapel was closed in 1753,[38] but the congregation continued to meet at Longdon Green.

OTHER DENOMINATIONS. There was a meeting room for Latter Day Saints (Mormons) in Sandford Street in 1861.[39] Nothing further is known about it. The present Mormon church in Purcell Avenue was registered in 1972.[40] Between 1972 and 1977 the headquarters of the Mormons' English church was in Lichfield.[41]

In 1887 the Salvation Army took a year's lease of part of the Corn Exchange in which to hold services. In 1935 the former Primitive Methodist chapel in George Lane was acquired for the same purpose.[42]

A group of Open Brethren was established in Lichfield shortly before or during the First World War. The members met in a room in the former militia barracks in Victoria Square, and there was a Sunday school. The group ceased to meet in the late 1930s.[43]

Jehovah's Witnesses have met in Lichfield at least from 1956. Their Kingdom Hall in Lombard Street, registered in 1980, occupies the former Wesleyan chapel.[44] A Pentecostalist church was formed in 1961 and met in Frank Halfpenny Hall in George Lane until 1969, when the Emmanuel Pentecostal church in Nether Stowe was opened. Its name was later changed to the Emmanuel Christian Centre, and the congregation still met there in the late 1980s.[45] A Spiritualist church was formed in Lichfield in 1986; members at first met in the Friary school and later in Cruck House in Stowe Street.[46] A group of Brethren formed the Lichfield Christian Centre in 1986; they met first in rooms in Bore Street and later in Cruck House.[47]

SOCIAL AND CULTURAL ACTIVITIES

GREENHILL BOWER. The festivities at Greenhill associated by the 15th century with the inspection of the watch during the Whitsun fair included the erection of a bower for the bishop's steward.[48] The practice continued after the transfer of the manor to the corporation in 1548, but the inspection seems to have become entirely ceremonial by the late 17th century.[49] The first detailed description of the festivities dates from the 1790s.[50] On Whit Monday the sheriff, bailiffs, and town clerk processed from the guildhall to the bower at Greenhill, accompanied by the two manorial constables, ten armed men, eight morris dancers, a fool, and a band of musicians playing drums and fifes. At the bower the town crier proclaimed the opening of the manor's court of array, and read through the list of suitors. The ceremony of calling the court having been completed, the constables and armed men, with the dancers and musicians, returned to the city centre, and in each street or ward the party was led by the ward's dozeners (tithingmen) past each house, over which a volley was fired as a salute. The

FIG. 16. THE BOWER PROCESSION PASSING THROUGH THE MARKET PLACE IN THE LATER 18TH CENTURY

[37] *Trans. Cong. Hist. Soc.* iii. 41; S.R.O., D. 615/D/265, Travers to Swinburne, 2 Apr. 1748.
[38] Matthews, *Cong. Churches*, 110.
[39] *Harrison, Harrod & Co.'s Dir. Staffs.* (1861).
[40] G.R.O. Worship Reg. no. 73201.
[41] *Truth Will Prevail. The Rise of the Church of Latter-day Saints in the Brit. Isles, 1837–1987*, ed. V. B. Bloxham, J. R. Moss, and L. C. Porter, 426.
[42] *Staffs. Advertiser* (S. Staffs. edn.), 30 July 1887, p. 4; *Lichfield Mercury*, 7 June 1935, p. 4.

[43] Inf. from Mr. D. Budge of Lichfield United Reformed Church.
[44] *Lichfield Mercury*, 27 Jan 1956, p. 5; G.R.O. Worship Reg. no. 75505.
[45] *Lichfield Mercury*, 5 Dec. 1969, p. 7; inf. from Mr. D. Danks, an elder.   [46] Inf. from a church member.
[47] Inf. from a church member.
[48] Above, public services (policing).
[49] *Journeys of Celia Fiennes*, ed. C. Morris (1949), 164–5.
[50] Shaw, *Staffs.* i. 316–17.

dozeners, carrying pageants (puppets on the end of poles), and all the householders of the ward then returned to the bower, where they were provided with a cold collation; anyone failing to attend was fined 1*d*. Meanwhile the constables' party returned to inspect the next ward. After all the wards had been inspected, everyone assembled in the market square where the town clerk delivered an oration. The pageants were then deposited in the tower of St. Mary's church.

Certain aspects of the festivities, such as the procession, the morris dancing, and the bower itself may have derived from earlier folk customs. In 1698 Celia Fiennes referred to the occasion as the Green Bower; the main attractions were then the dressing of the dozeners' pageants (which she called 'babys') with garlands, and the procession to Greenhill. Besides the bailiffs' bower there were then smaller ones in which fruit and sweetmeats were sold.[51] In the 1730s or 1740s Richard Wilkes, the antiquary, noted how people flocked from the neighbouring villages to see 'this gaudy show'; each ward had its own mawkin (doll) or a posy of flowers carried in the procession, with the city drummers providing music.[52] Possibly the pageants were originally effigies of saints, but by the early 19th century trade emblems were used.[53] Anna Seward described the festivities in 1795 as 'our grotesque Whitsun Monday anniversary'; in her youth the day had been enjoyed by all ranks of society, but it had become 'the vulgar jubilee of the town and its environs'.[54] Thomas Harwood, the historian of the city, a few years later thought it 'an idle and useless ceremony, adapted for the amusement of children'.[55] It was also expensive. In 1705 the cost, borne by the corporation, was apparently only £7 7*s*.; it rose to £27 in 1793, £37 in 1798, and £40 in 1802.[56] After the 1806 festivities the corporation ordered that on the grounds of expense and inconvenience there was to be in future no bower or procession, although the inspection continued to be held.[57]

In response to popular demand the celebrations had been revived by 1811. The expense was met by subscribers, notably the city's M.P.s and General William Dyott of Freeford, and there was a management committee.[58] In 1825 the corporation agreed to make an annual donation of 10 guineas, but that was withdrawn by the first elected council in 1836.[59] By 1851 relations had improved and the mayor attended

the celebrations in his robe of office.[60] The restored procession included a Maid Marian and, from 1850 or earlier, a knight whose armour was hired from London.[61] Tableaux were introduced in the 1870s, and a bower queen was first crowned in 1929.[62] Pageants were still carried in procession in the 1880s. Cakes were distributed free in the early 20th century; they were reduced in size and confined to children in 1922 and stopped altogether in 1939.[63]

Menageries and circuses were added to the festivities in the early 19th century, and in 1827 there was a fireworks display at the Bowling Green inn. From the early 19th century theatricals performed by travelling companies became a regular feature.[64] Trains later brought large numbers of day trippers from the Black Country, the East Midlands, and the Potteries; 20,000 were thought to have come in 1850.[65] In the late 1980s the Bower, held on Spring Bank Holiday Monday, continued to attract large crowds.

FOLK CUSTOMS. A boy bishop received a customary 5*s*. from the bishop on Holy Innocents' day (28 December) in 1306.[66] Copes for use by boys on that feast day were kept in the cathedral sacristy in the mid 1340s.[67] It was still a custom to appoint a boy bishop in the earlier 16th century.[68]

There was a maypole at Greenhill in 1674, and the 'new post' set up there by the corporation in 1702–3 was presumably a replacement.[69] The Greenhill wakes were mentioned in 1828, when they were held on Monday and Tuesday, 20 and 21 October.[70]

Morris dancers were paid by the Whig agent in Lichfield at a parliamentary election in 1761, and dancing at election time remained a custom in the earlier 19th century.[71] Morris men also danced at Christmas 'masquerades' in the late 18th and early 19th century.[72] They danced at the Greenhill Bower festivities until the late 19th century, when they were replaced by boys from the Truant school in Beacon Street; the boys still danced in 1907.[73] A group called the Lichfield Morris Men was formed in 1979 to perform dances particular to Lichfield. It resumed dancing at the Bower and also stages mumming plays at Christmas time.[74] A ladies' group, the Three Spires Ladies' Morris, was formed in 1981 to perform clog dances.[75] The Ryknild Rappers were formed in 1988 to per-

[51] *Journeys of Celia Fiennes*, 164–5.
[52] W.S.L., S. MS. 468, p. 3. For the date see *S.H.C.* 4th ser. xi. 179 (note 26).
[53] Harwood, *Lichfield*, 352.
[54] *Letters of Anna Seward* (Edinburgh, 1811), iv. 82, 196.
[55] Harwood, *Lichfield*, 354.
[56] *Lichfield Mercury*, 2 May 1823; L.J.R.O., D. 35/bailiffs' accts. 1704–94, p. 585; 1794–1835, pp. 38, 64.
[57] L.J.R.O., D. 77/5/3, f. 30; D. 77/6/5.
[58] S.R.O., D. 593/F/3/12/1/22–6; *Lichfield Mercury*, 3 May 1816; Official Bower Programme, 1923 (copy in L.J.R.O., D. 77/20/8, between pp. 78 and 79).
[59] L.J.R.O., D. 35/bailiffs' accts. 1794–1835, p. 284; D. 77/5/3, f. 150v.; D. 77/5/4, f. 40v.
[60] Official Bower Programme, 1923, p. 7.
[61] Ibid.; Stringer, *Lichfield*, 88; *Illus. London News*, 25 May 1850, p. 364.
[62] Parker, *Lichfield*, 63; L.J.R.O., D. 107, min. bk. 1924–47, pp. 67, 69, 75.

[63] Official Bower Programme, 1923, p. 4; L.J.R.O., D. 107, min. bks. 1904–10, 1910–23, 1924–47.
[64] *Lichfield Mercury*, 1 June 1827; below (theatre; circuses).
[65] *Illus. London News*, 25 May 1850, p. 364; Lichfield Cath. Libr., Harradine scrapbk. p. 22.
[66] S.R.O., D. (W.) 1734/J. 2057, m. 9.
[67] *S.H.C.* vi (2), 202.
[68] *V.C.H. Staffs.* iii. 164.
[69] L.J.R.O., D. 35/bailiffs' accts. 1657–1707, pp. 185, 232.
[70] *Staffs. Advertiser*, 25 Oct. 1828.
[71] S.R.O., D. 593/F/3/12/1/7; D. 593/F/3/12/2/6, receipt of 1 Apr. 1784; D. 593/F/3/12/2/9, receipt of 16 Jan. 1795; D. 593/F/3/12/4/5, Cobb's acct.; D. 615/P(p)/1/11, entry for July 1831; *S.H.C.* 4th ser. vi. 124.
[72] S.R.O., D. 593/F/3/12/1/9–10, 24–6.
[73] *Jnl. Eng. Folk Dance and Song Soc.* viii (2), 84.
[74] Inf. from Mr. Nigel Moss, a member.
[75] Inf. from Mrs. Sheila Dalrymple, a member.

form traditional sword dances.[76] A week-end festival of folk dance and music was started in 1975 and continued to be held in the later 1980s.[77]

Well dressing took place in Lichfield on Ascension day in the early 19th century, the ceremony being conducted by a clergyman with children carrying green boughs; the gospel was read at each well and pump visited, and doors of houses were decorated with the boughs.[78] The decoration of houses alone was revived in the Close in the 1920s and still took place in the later 1980s.[79] Cathedral choristers wassailed at Christmas in 1800, and the custom continued in the later 19th century.[80]

SPORT. A tournament was held at Lichfield in the presence of Edward III in 1348.[81] Daily tournaments took place when Richard II spent Christmas at Lichfield in 1398.[82] There was a tennis court in the grounds of the Franciscan friary before its dissolution, probably in an enclosed yard between the church and cloister.[83]

Bear baiting took place in the early 19th century at Greenhill, which was probably the traditional site for the sport.[84] A bull was brought by travelling showmen in 1827 and baited at Greenhill, Sandyway, and other places in the city. The baitings aroused disapproval and were probably not repeated.[85]

A main of cocks was held at the Talbot inn in 1704, with a team of gentlemen from Staffordshire, Derbyshire, Warwickshire, and Leicestershire matched against a team from Worcestershire, Shropshire, and Wales.[86] In the later 1740s mains were held at the Swan, where a pit was mentioned in 1800.[87] Mains in the early 19th century normally took place during the horse-race meetings.[88] In 1828 the city bailiffs closed the Swan pit, and despite initial resistance cock fighting there probably ceased.[89] A cock fight attracting competitors from Walsall and Dudley was held in 1851, probably in a pit south of Gresley Row.[90]

Hare coursing promoted by Lichfield innkeepers took place at Freeford in 1829.[91] A hare-coursing club had been established by the landlord of the Swan by 1876, with meetings held on estates around Lichfield. The club still existed in 1891.[92]

By the early 1680s horse races were held in September on Fradley heath in Alrewas northeast of Lichfield, with the corporation from 1686 awarding a prize of a silver tankard of 'about 6 pounds'.[93] In 1702 the races were moved to Whittington heath south-east of the city. The corporation continued its patronage, awarding the tankard initially for a four-year period only but probably continuing it after 1706. From 1716 the corporation awarded a plate worth £10, increased to 10 guineas by 1729 and still given in 1737.[94] In the early 1740s the meeting was held in the first week of September and lasted two days, extended to three in 1744. It became one of the leading meetings in the Midlands and had a notable effect on the city's social life, with well-attended public breakfasts and dinners, balls, and concerts taking place. The races became involved in party politics in 1747, and a rival September meeting, organized by Tories, was held between 1748 and 1753.[95] The line of the course was apparently altered in the early 1740s to give spectators a better view of the racing.[96] In 1766 the landlord of the Red Lion in Dam Street advertised his intention to set up a viewing stand and a booth at the course, and a grandstand was erected by subscription in 1773.[97] From the 1780s the meeting declined, and a third day's racing was sustained only with money raised by Lichfield inhabitants. The opening of a new stand in 1803 suggests a revival in the meeting's popularity, but in 1842 General William Dyott of Freeford, a trustee of the races, noted that the racing that year was 'not deserving description'. The meeting was overshadowed by one at Wolverhampton but managed to survive until 1895.[98]

In the early 18th century a race was held in March, apparently on land near the Swan.[99] A March hunt meeting on the Whittington course had been established by 1818 and was held under the auspices of Lord Anson from 1823 or earlier.[1] It did not find favour with General Dyott, who noted that it failed to attract people of quality; he described the 1836 meeting as 'a wretched affair', which included a hurdle race, 'a new fashioned sport much in vogue with the foxhunters'.[2]

[76] Inf. from Mr. Moss.
[77] Inf. from Mrs. Penny McLennan, chairman of Staffordshire Folk which runs the festival.
[78] Pitt, *Staffs.* i. 100; Stringer, *Lichfield*, 133; Harwood, *Lichfield*, 509.
[79] W.S.L., S. MS. 341; *Lomax's Red Bk.* (1934), 19; *Lichfield Mercury*, 9 May 1986, p. 3.
[80] Harwood, *Lichfield*, 284; Guildhall Libr., London, MS. H 9.4, no. 16, 27 Dec. 1800; W.S.L., CB/Lichfield/27, ff. 47–8.
[81] Above, general hist. (late Middle Ages).
[82] Above, cathedral and close.
[83] *Letters relating to the Suppression of Monasteries* (Camd. Soc. [1st ser.], xxvi), 275.
[84] Bodl. G.A. Staffs. 4°, 8, facing p. 536.
[85] *Lichfield Mercury*, 19 and 26 Oct. 1827.
[86] W.S.L., S. 1902i, f. 61.
[87] *Aris's Birmingham Gaz.* 17 Feb. 1746; 13 Apr. 1747; 28 Apr. 1800.
[88] *Lichfield Mercury*, 1 Sept. 1815; 5 Mar. 1824; 4 Mar. and 12 Aug. 1825; 9 Mar. and 24 Aug. 1827.
[89] *The Register. Literary, Scientific, and Sporting Jnl.* 20 Sept. 1828 (copy in W.S.L.).

[90] *Staffs. Advertiser*, 12 Apr. 1851, p. 6; 26 Apr. 1851, p. 3; L.J.R.O., B/A/15/Lichfield, St. Michael, no. 188a.
[91] S.R.O., D. 661/11/2/3/1/11, 16 Feb. 1829.
[92] *Staffs. Advertiser*, 28 Oct. 1876, p. 6; 12 Oct. 1878, p. 2; 3 Oct. 1891, p. 3; L.J.R.O., D. 77/20/8, pp. 12, 17.
[93] *V.C.H. Staffs.* ii. 364; *T.S.S.A.H.S.* vi. 39–44; L.J.R.O., D. 77/5/1, f. 15v.
[94] L.J.R.O., D. 77/5/1, ff. 111, 184, 192v., 260v., 266v.; D. 77/5/2, ff. 12, 13v., 24v.
[95] *V.C.H. Staffs.* ii. 365; *T.S.S.A.H.S.* vi. 42; below (music; dancing assemblies).
[96] S.R.O., D. 603/K/4/3, f. 26.
[97] *Aris's Birmingham Gaz.* 15 Sept. 1766; *V.C.H. Staffs.* ii. 365.
[98] *V.C.H. Staffs.* ii. 365–6; *T.S.S.A.H.S.* vi. 43; S.R.O., D. 661/11/2/3/1/16, 20 Sept. 1842.
[99] Bodl. MS. Top. Staffs. C 1, f. 33.
[1] *Lichfield Mercury*, 27 Nov. 1818; 29 Jan. 1819; 19 and 26 Mar., 24 Sept. 1824; S.R.O., D. 661/11/2/3/1/11, 19 Mar. 1823.
[2] S.R.O., D. 661/11/2/3/1/11, 15 Mar. 1826; *V.C.H. Staffs.* ii. 366; *T.S.S.A.H.S.* vi. 13–14.

Pony races were held on a field near the Shoulder of Mutton inn on the London road in October 1812.[3]

Bowls were played at the Bowling Green inn, built west of the Friary apparently in the 1670s;[4] a clubhouse which survived there in the later 1980s may have been that which existed in 1796.[5] The present Lichfield Bowling Club which uses the green was formed apparently in the 1840s.[6] A club established in 1901 using a green on the north side of the Swan was named the Swan Bowling Club in 1922. In 1962 it was re-formed as the Lichfield City Club and moved to a green laid out by the city council in Beacon Park. It continued to play there in the late 1980s under the name of the Lichfield Crown Green Bowling Club.[7] The Museum Bowling Club had been formed by 1922, playing on a green in Museum Grounds.[8] It still played there in the late 1980s. The Trent Valley Bowling Club, with a green behind the Trent Valley inn over the Lichfield boundary in Streethay, was formed in 1929. It still played on that green in the late 1980s.[9]

Archery butts stood in Castle ditch in the late 17th century.[10] They were at the Bowling Green inn by the early 1770s, when there was a society of Gentlemen Archers.[11] There were also butts on the east side of Beacon Street south of Wheel Lane in 1776.[12] An archery society still existed in 1824.[13] It was revived in 1846 under the presidency of J. S. Manley of Manley Hall in Weeford, and by 1850 it had 118 members. Competition meetings were held in July and August, using butts on land near St. John's hospital.[14] The society survived until at least 1914.[15] It was revived in 1965, with butts on the rugby football ground in Boley Lane; in 1968 the butts were moved to playing fields off Gaia Lane and in 1980 to Christian Fields off Eastern Avenue, where a clubhouse was opened in 1986.[16] On the occasion of a national competition hosted by the Lichfield society in 1987, butts were set up in Beacon Park.[17]

A cricket club was established in or shortly before 1817, and there was a Lichfield team in 1830.[18] Lichfield Cricket Club was formed apparently in 1844. In 1862 it used a ground off the Stafford road.[19] It later acquired a ground on the north side of Chesterfield Road. From 1873 that ground was also used by the newly formed county club, whose secretary from 1874 was H. S. Chinn, a Lichfield solicitor.[20] There was little enthusiasm for the sport, and an attempt to popularize it by the introduction in 1878 of a week-long festival was not a success. The last festival was held in 1883, when the county club left Lichfield and Chinn resigned as secretary.[21] The city club survived and continued to play on the Chesterfield Road ground in the late 1980s. A club for tradesmen was formed in 1861.[22] A cricket club was set up as a branch of St. Mary's Church Club probably in 1871, and in 1872 it played a match against another Lichfield team, the 'Hearts of Oak'. By 1885 St. Chad's church had a cricket club too.[23] The Lichfield Wednesday Cricket Club, evidently for tradesmen, was revived in 1912, and a club for artisans was formed the same year.[24]

A football club was also formed as a branch of St. Mary's Church Club probably in 1871, and St. Chad's church had a football club by 1885.[25] Lichfield Football Club was formed in 1874 and played on the cricket club ground in 1876 according to both London Association and Rugby Union rules.[26] It was re-formed as the City Football Club in 1890 and is probably identifiable as the Lichfield Phoenix Football Club in existence by 1908 and renamed the City Club in 1913.[27] Other clubs before the First World War included one for artisans, formed in 1912, and one for tradesmen, formed in 1913.[28] The present Lichfield Football Club was formed in 1966; it first played on a pitch in Beacon Park and from 1970 on one in Shortbutts Lane.[29] Lichfield Rugby Football Club was formed in 1925. It played on various sites before a permanent ground was acquired in Boley Lane in 1961. A new ground was opened off the Tamworth road over the city boundary in 1985.[30]

Lawn tennis tournaments were held on the cricket club ground during the week of the cricket festival between 1878 and 1883 and continued there in the late 1880s.[31] Lichfield County Lawn Tennis Club had been formed by 1890, and by 1900 it had courts on the north side of Birmingham Road near St. John's hospital.[32] The club still played there as Lichfield Lawn Tennis Club in the late 1980s. The present Friary Lawn Tennis Club was formed in 1937 with courts in the Dell between Christchurch

[3] Clayton, *Coaching City*, pl. facing p. 55.
[4] L.J.R.O., D. 88/lease bk. 1712–27, deed of 29 Oct. 1726.
[5] Ibid. D. 88/deed of 15 Apr. 1796.
[6] *Staffs. Advertiser*, 28 July 1888, p. 4.
[7] L.J.R.O., D. 83/6, 5 Mar. 1962; D. 83/7, pp. 137, 141; inf. from Mr. A. Riley, a member.
[8] *Lichfield Mercury*, 24 Nov. 1922, p. 4.
[9] Inf. from Mr. R. Smith, a member.
[10] L.J.R.O., D. 77/6/2, f. 119v.; D. 77/9/1, f. 15v.
[11] W.S.L., S. 1902i, f. 63.
[12] L.J.R.O., D. 77/8/1, p. 7.
[13] *Lichfield Mercury*, 8 Oct. 1824.
[14] Soc. of Lichfield Archers, *Laws and Regulations* (Lichfield, 1850; copy in W.S.L.); *Staffs. Advertiser*, 12 July 1851, p. 4.
[15] *Recollections of Sophia Lonsdale*, ed. V. Martineau, 110.
[16] *Lichfield Mercury*, 4 Apr. 1986, p. 61.
[17] Ibid. 14 Aug. 1987, p. 60.
[18] Ibid. 11 Apr. 1817; Clayton, *Cathedral City*, 12.
[19] *Staffs. Advertiser*, 3 May 1862, p. 4; *Lichfield Mercury*, 11 Apr. 1919, p. 3.

[20] W. G. Watson, *Staffs. Cricket* (Stafford, 1924), 68, 70, 82.
[21] Ibid. 88–96.
[22] Printed appeal 29 Nov. 1861 (copy in L.J.R.O., D. 121).
[23] St. Mary's Club min. bk. 1871–8 (in possession of Sharrott, Barnes & Co., solicitors of Lichfield); above, churches.
[24] *Lichfield Mercury*, 24 May 1912, p. 4; 21 June 1912, p. 8.
[25] Above, churches.
[26] *Staffs. Advertiser*, 14 Oct. 1876, p. 7.
[27] *Lichfield Mercury*, 25 Apr. 1890, p. 6; 15 May 1908, p. 6; 18 July 1913, p. 7.
[28] Ibid. 2 Aug. 1912, p. 8; 1 Aug. 1913, p. 5.
[29] Inf. from the secretary, Mr. B. Gilbert.
[30] *Lichfield Mercury*, 1 Mar. 1985, pp. 21–3; inf. from Mr. Adrian Goldstone, a member.
[31] W.S.L., D. 1929/1/111, pp. 68–9, 71; *Staffs. Advertiser*, 28 July 1888, p. 2.
[32] *Lichfield Mercury*, 2 Jan. 1891, p. 4; O.S. Map 1/2,500, Staffs. LII. 15 (1902 edn.).

Lane and the Walsall road. The club was a successor to the Christ Church Lawn Tennis Club which had played since the 1920s on courts in Christchurch Lane; the vicarage was built on the site in 1957.[33] In 1985 the Friary Club moved to a site off the Tamworth road shared with the Rugby Football Club.[34]

There was a roller skating rink at the Corn Exchange in 1877. By 1912 there was a rink in Beacon Street, apparently in a disused maltings; it had been closed by 1916.[35] There was an athletic club by 1888; it was dissolved in 1911.[36] A bicycling club was formed in 1881 and was one of two or three such clubs in 1904.[37] The Friary Grange Sports Centre attached to Friary Grange (later Friary) school in Eastern Avenue and open to the public out of school hours incorporates a sports hall and a swimming pool opened in 1977.[38]

WALKS, GARDENS, AND PARK. A building called the Temple in 1694 probably stood on Borrowcop Hill: a path to it passed by an orchard called Cherry Garden (later Cherry Orchard) on the west side of Sturgeon's Hill.[39] In the early 1720s there was an arbour on top of the hill.[40] In 1750 the corporation apparently replaced it with a summerhouse, which may have been the cruciform building which stood there by 1776.[41] In 1756 the corporation ordered the planting of a line of trees along the path to the summit[42] and engaged a nurseryman, John Bramall, to plant more trees in 1783, probably in connexion with a fête champêtre held that year.[43] By 1805 the building had been replaced by one of brick with two arches each side and seats around it from which the view could be admired; the cost was met by public subscription.[44] It was restored in the mid 1980s under the government's Community Programme Scheme.

In 1772 New Walk was laid out on the south side of Minster Pool between Dam Street and Bird Street, with a gate at either end, and in 1782 the Conduit Lands trustees ordered the removal of a lamp at the north end of Cock Lane to a position along the walk.[45] In 1773 the corporation decided to fashion the pool's northern bank as a serpentine, and by 1776 there was an island in the pool at its west end.[46] In 1789 an island in Stowe Pool was planted with fir trees by John Bramall, who carried out further planting in 1792; the island survived in 1802.[47] A walk around Stowe Pool was laid out c. 1790.[48] On the pool's north side stood a willow tree habitually visited by Samuel Johnson. The tree was blown down in 1829 and from it was planted another which survived until itself blown down in 1881. A third tree was planted from it but was felled in 1956 because it was unsafe. A fourth tree, planted from it in 1957, survived in the late 1980s.[49] A botanic garden north of the pool in the grounds of Parchment House was laid out probably in the early 1780s by John Saville, a vicar choral of the cathedral. It soon became a visitors' attraction.[50]

Beacon Park lying west of Bird Street and Beacon Street originated in land reclaimed out of Upper Pool; in the late 18th century there were lines of trees there and what may have been ornamental pools.[51] The area was chosen as the site of the free library and museum, opened in 1859, and a public garden (known as Museum Grounds) was laid out to the south.[52] A drinking fountain in the garden was given by Thomas Rowley in 1863, and in 1871 J. T. Law, the diocesan chancellor, presented an ornamental fountain.[53] The figures of lions around Law's fountain were given by R. P. (later Sir Richard) Cooper, a city alderman, probably in the late 1880s.[54] In 1892 the Conduit Lands trustees agreed to supply water to the fountain three times a week in the summer without charge.[55] East of the fountain is a statue of Edward VII, presented in 1908 by Robert Bridgeman, then sheriff.[56] West of the fountain is a bronze statue of Commander E. J. Smith, captain of the liner *Titanic*, sunk in 1912; it was carved by Lady (Kathleen) Scott, widow of Capt. Robert Scott, the Antarctic explorer, and unveiled in 1914. The cost was met by a national subscription, and the statue was placed in Lichfield because the city was both the centre of the diocese in which Smith was born and conveniently placed for visitors travelling between London and Liverpool.[57] Set by the east wall of the garden are the remains of a sculpture of the city's coat of arms taken from the pediment of the 18th-century guildhall.[58] A Crimean War cannon and a First World War German gun which had been placed in the grounds were removed for scrap metal in

[33] Inf. from Mrs. Mabel Wickham, a member.
[34] *Lichfield Mercury*, 12 Apr. 1985, p. 60; 14 June 1985, p. 72.
[35] *Staffs. Advertiser* (S. Staffs. edn.), 14 Apr. 1877, p. 5; *Kelly's Dir. Staffs.* (1912); S.R.O., D. 4566/99, Lichfield Group Managers' min. bk. 1913–16, p. 249.
[36] *Lichfield Mercury*, 28 Dec. 1888, p. 6; 5 May 1911, p. 5.
[37] Ibid. 26 Aug. 1881, p. 4; L.J.R.O., D. 107, min. bk. 1904–10.
[38] *Lichfield Mercury*, 14 Jan. 1977, pp. 1, 10; 21 Jan. 1977, pp. 1, 12.
[39] L.J.R.O., D. 77/6/1, f. 53.
[40] Ibid. D. 88/hosp. land, plan no. 3.
[41] Ibid. D. 77/8/1, before p. 1; W.S.L., S. 630 (ii), between pp. 112 and 113.
[42] L.J.R.O., D. 77/5/2, f. 91v.
[43] Ibid. D. 35/bailiffs' accts. 1704–94, p. 463; Bodl. MS. Top. Staffs. C 1, f. 83v.
[44] Jackson, *Lichfield*, 43.
[45] L.J.R.O., D. 35/bailiffs' accts. 1704–94, p. 349; D.

[46] 77/5/2, f. 166v.; D. 126/min. bk. 1741–1856, p. 76; above, fig. 4.
[46] L.J.R.O., D. 35/bailiffs' accts. 1704–94, p. 415; D. 77/5/2, f. 172; D. 77/8/1, p. 1; above, fig. 4.
[47] L.J.R.O., D. 35/bailiffs' accts. 1704–94, pp. 535, 537, 597; 1794–1835, p. 64.
[48] Ibid. D. 35/bailiffs' accts. 1704–94, pp. 533, 589, 591.
[49] Shaw, *Staffs.* i. 346; *Lichfield Mercury*, 26 Apr. 1929, p. 6; 20 Apr. 1956, p. 4; 27 Sept. 1957, p. 4.
[50] Shaw, *Staffs.* i. 346; *Letters of Anna Seward*, ii. 181; v. 79.   [51] Above, fig. 4.
[52] W. H. Crompton, *Illus. Plan of the City and Close of Lichfield, 1862*; below (libraries).
[53] L.J.R.O., D. 126/min. bk. 1856–95, pp. 212, 217; D. 127/council min. bk. 1853–66, p. 360; 1866–82, pp. 115, 124.
[54] *Kelly's Dir. Staffs.* (1888; 1896).
[55] L.J.R.O., D. 126/min. bk. 1856–95, pp. 511, 514.
[56] *Lomax's Red Bk.* (1909), 15, 17.
[57] *Lichfield Mercury*, 31 July 1914, p. 5.
[58] Above, town govt. (govt. from 1548: guildhall).

1940.[59] A recreation ground was opened on nearly 5 a. west of the library in 1891.[60] The ground was extended north in 1944 with 11½ a. given by Lt.-Col. M. A. Swinfen Broun.[61]

The War Memorial Garden on the east side of Bird Street beside Minster Pool was laid out in 1920 and contains a monument and sundial made by the Lichfield firm of Robert Bridgeman & Sons. The stone balustrade along the street was formerly at Moxhull Hall in Wishaw (Warws.).[62] A Memorial Garden dedicated to Lichfield citizens who died in the Second World War and 'later struggles for freedom' was laid out on the south side of Minster Pool in 1955.[63]

MUSIC. The bishop's minstrels played at the Whitsuntide inspection of the watch at Greenhill in 1421,[64] and in 1449 histriones (either minstrels or dramatic performers) from Lichfield entertained Sir William Vernon, possibly when he was visiting his manor of Wall.[65] A fiddler was enrolled as a member of St. Mary's guild in 1488–9.[66] Minstrels played for the shoemakers' company at their feasts in the later 16th century.[67] The Lichfield waits were mentioned in 1572 when they travelled to Wollaton Hall (Notts.) to play for the Willoughby family.[68] Praised by visitors who heard them at the Swan in 1634, the waits then wore the badge of Robert Devereux, earl of Essex, who held a life interest in Lichfield manor.[69] Trumpeters and drummers played at the feasts of the smiths' company in the late 17th century and in the later 1730s,[70] and drummers played at the Greenhill Bower festivities in the earlier 18th century.[71] In 1686 Richard Dyott at the age of 19 formed a society of bell-ringers called the Loyal Youths, with himself as master. They met weekly and apparently rang both the cathedral's bells and those of St. Mary's church. Each ringer wore a flannel waistcoat edged with black buttons and a black silk cap. The society still existed in 1690.[72]

An orchestra was hired from Leicester to play for a ball in the guildhall during the 1714 race meeting. Tomson and Powell who sang at a concert during the 1733 meeting and Festener who played the German flute on the same occasion were probably professionals.[73] In 1746 Musgrave Heighington, the composer, performed for the city's music club,[74] and in 1796

Wilhelm Cramer, the violinist, played privately for Anna Seward and her guests at supper parties on four consecutive evenings.[75] The pianist and composer Muzio Clementi (d. 1832) lived at Lyncroft House on the Stafford road c. 1830, but he is not known to have performed publicly in the city.[76] The violinist Nicolo Paganini (d. 1840) played in Lichfield in 1833.[77]

Interest in music was fostered by a music club which by 1739 met in the vicars' hall in the Close.[78] It promoted public concerts, including by 1745 one annually on St. Cecilia's day (22 November). It was known as the Cecilian Society by 1752, when the feast-day concert was accompanied by a dinner, both taking place at the King's Head in Bird Street.[79] Concerts at other times of the year were held in the guildhall, until they were transferred to the newly decorated vicars' hall in or soon after 1756. A subscription ticket for five concerts in February and March 1767 cost 5s., with non-subscribers paying 2s. a concert.[80] A high standard was apparently maintained, and performers included the vicar choral John Saville, a principal singer at music festivals throughout the country. From the earlier 1780s he was accompanied by his daughter, Elizabeth Smith, also a singer.[81]

A dispute arose between performing and non-performing members as the meetings turned into eating and drinking sessions, with music taking second place; it was settled by agreement in 1790. The performers were to decide matters relating to the society's musical life, such as the purchase of scores and instruments, the choice of music to be played, and the restriction on the number of flutes, horns, and oboes to be used at a time. The number of non-performing members was fixed at a maximum of 60, and admittance to the feast-day concert and dinner was to be by ticket only. The landlord was barred from membership and forbidden to invite outsiders to attend the concert, the venue of which was transferred from the King's Head to the Swan.[82] The society seems to have lost support. A drive in 1817 to attract new members and revive the society's 'harmonic festivities' suggests that it had ceased to promote concerts, and in 1816 and 1817 subscription concerts were instead advertised as under the patronage of the dean and chapter.[83] The society was dissolved in 1837[84] but had been revived by 1849, possibly in con-

[59] Lichfield Mercury, 10 May 1940, p. 5; 14 June 1940, p. 5.
[60] Staffs. Advertiser, 25 July 1891, p. 2.
[61] Lichfield Mercury, 10 Dec. 1943, p. 7; 11 Aug. 1944, p. 5.
[62] Ibid. 22 Oct. 1920, p. 5; Lichfield Official Guide (1927), 24–5.
[63] Lichfield Mercury, 7 Oct. 1955, p. 3.
[64] Above, public services (policing).
[65] W.S.L. 50/A 2/56.
[66] L.J.R.O., D. 77/1, p. 210.   [67] Above, guilds.
[68] Hist. MSS. Com. 69, Middleton, 421.
[69] Relation of a Short Survey of 26 Counties, 1634, ed. L. G. Wickham Legg, 59.
[70] Above, guilds.
[71] Above (Greenhill Bower).
[72] W.S.L., S. MS. 24 (i), at back of MS.; S.R.O., D. 661/2/173.
[73] Hist. MSS. Com. 19, 11th Rep. IV, Townshend, p. 230;

Hist. MSS. Com. 78, Hastings, iii, p. 18.
[74] W.S.L., S. MS. 24 (iv); D.N.B. For the club see below.
[75] Letters of Anna Seward, iv. 288–9; D.N.B.
[76] M. Unger, Muzio Clementis Leben (Langensalza, Germany, 1914), 270–2.
[77] S.R.O., D. 3019/203/30/64.
[78] W.S.L., S. MS. 24 (iv).
[79] Aris's Birmingham Gaz. 11 Nov. 1745; 27 Nov. 1752; 2 Dec. 1754.
[80] Ibid. 14 Sept. 1747; 26 Aug. 1751; 13 Jan. 1766; 26 Jan. 1767; Letters of Anna Seward, i. 37–8, 69.
[81] Letters of Anna Seward, i. 37–8, 69; Jnls. and Corresp. of Thos. Sedgewick Whalley, ed. H. Wickham, i. 414, 448–9, 490–1; ii. 12, 28, 52; Gent. Mag. liv (1), 48, 453–4.
[82] Printed acct. of agreement and new rules, 17 May 1790 (copy in L.J.R.O., D. 127).
[83] Lichfield Mercury, 27 Dec. 1816; 17 and 24 Jan. 1817.
[84] W.S.L., S. MS. 374, p. 398.

nexion with the formation by 1848 of the Lichfield Choral Society.[85] Nothing further is known about either society.

The Lichfield Amateur Musical Society was formed in 1852 and at first gave performances in the Corn Exchange; from 1853 the concerts took place in the guildhall. Three performances a year were given in the later 1860s at a cost of 10s. to subscribers, and the players practised twice weekly in the bandroom of Yeomanry House in St. John Street.[86] The society lapsed in 1874 but was revived in 1878 and re-formed in 1881 as the Lichfield Musical Society, still in existence in 1942.[87] The Lichfield Operatic Society was formed in 1895, dissolved in 1911, and revived in 1942.[88] It still existed in the late 1980s.

A militia band gave public concerts in 1800, one of them accompanied by a firework display.[89] A bandstand was erected in Museum Grounds by John Gilbert, a city councillor, in 1893 to mark the marriage of the duke of York to Princess May of Teck (later George V and Queen Mary).[90] Bands which played at the 1905 Bower festivities included the Lichfield Volunteer Band and a drum and fife band from Whittington barracks. Lichfield City Band was formed in 1910 and survived in 1937. A new city band was formed in 1985.[91]

A diocesan festival of parish choirs, the first of its kind in the country, was held in the cathedral in 1856 under the auspices of the Diocesan Choral Association. The festival was held every three years, growing in size until in 1880 there were over 1,800 singers. In 1883 the number of singers was limited to 1,000.[92] The festival was last held in 1912.[93] A music festival promoted by the dean and chapter and using the cathedral as the principal venue was held in 1980. It was held annually from 1982, lasting 10 days. Drama was added in 1986 and opera in 1987.[94]

DANCING ASSEMBLIES. Balls were held during the race meetings from the 1730s; in the later 1770s they took place in the guildhall under the management of the race stewards.[95] By the early 19th century they were less well patronized than before. General William Dyott remarked that the autumn race ball in 1821 was not

'attended by the neighbouring nobility and gentry, as was the custom twenty years ago', and that that of 1842 attracted only 'a thin attendance, and not a fag or rag of quality'.[96]

Subscription balls were held in the vicars' hall during the winters of 1779–80 and 1780–1, usually about the time of a full moon. A subscription ticket cost 10s. 6d. and individual tickets 3s. 6d. in 1797–8.[97] The George was then the usual venue.[98] Subscription balls were still held there in the late 1870s.[99]

Balls were held by 1820 for the Staffordshire Yeomanry when they assembled annually for a week's training on Whittington heath. They were still held in the early 1860s.[1]

By the late 1830s there was an annual county ball in January.[2] In the late 1870s it was held in St. James's Hall in Bore Street, which remained the venue until the hall's conversion into a cinema in 1912. The balls were then transferred to the George; they ceased during the First World War and were not revived.[3]

THEATRE. The *histriones* from Lichfield who entertained Sir William Vernon in 1449 were either dramatic performers or minstrels.[4] Lord Warwick's players, who evidently performed in the city on the occasion of Elizabeth I's visit in 1575, were presumably actors under the patronage of Ambrose Dudley, earl of Warwick.[5] George Farquhar's play *The Beaux' Stratagem* (1707) is set in Lichfield, where the author had been stationed on military duty. His play *The Recruiting Officer* (1706) was performed by amateurs in Lichfield in 1727, probably in a room in the bishop's palace; the part of Serjeant Kite was played by David Garrick, then aged ten, making his first stage appearance.[6] Professional companies played in the city at least from the later 1760s. One led by Roger Kemble came in 1770 and performed *The Recruiting Officer*, probably in the guildhall; the cast included William Siddons, the future husband of Kemble's daughter Sarah.[7] A company led by Samuel Stanton included Lichfield in its provincial circuit in 1776 and in the 1780s.[8]

In 1790 a theatre designed by John Miller of London was built in Bore Street on the site of

[85] Lichfield Libr., Amateur Musical Soc. scrapbk. 1852–72, accts. (at front) of Cecilian Soc. 1849–51; S.R.O., D. 4566/99, Boys' Nat. sch. min. bk. 1840–58, 6 Nov. 1848; *Staffs. Advertiser*, 9 Jan. 1849, p. 4.

[86] W.S.L. 360–61/36; ibid. broadsheets 34/4; *Recollections of Sophia Lonsdale*, ed. V. Martineau, 46.

[87] *Lichfield Mercury*, 18 Oct. 1878, p. 4; 30 Sept. 1881, p. 5; 19 June 1942, p. 4; Lichfield Libr., Amateur Mus. Soc. min. bk. 1860–74; Lichfield Mus. Soc. scrapbks. 1881–97.

[88] *Lichfield Mercury*, 21 July 1911, p. 5; 28 July 1911, p. 5; 19 June 1942, p. 4.

[89] Guildhall Libr., London, MS. H 9.4, no. 16.

[90] *Lichfield Mercury*, 4 Apr. 1902, p. 5.

[91] L.J.R.O., D. 107, min. bk. 1904–10; 1924–47, p. 166; *Lichfield Mercury*, 24 June 1910, p. 4; 7 June 1985, p. 10.

[92] *Lichfield Mercury*, 25 May 1883, p. 5; 22 June 1888, p. 8; 27 June 1890, p. 8.

[93] *Lich. Dioc. Mag.* 1912, 112–13.

[94] *Lichfield Mercury*, 29 May 1987, p. 23; 27 May 1988, p. 4.

[95] Hist. MSS. Com. 78, *Hastings*, iii, pp. 3, 18; *Order for regulating the balls, 1776* (copy in W.S.L., S. MS. 341).

[96] S.R.O., D. 661/11/2/3/1/11, 13 Sept. 1821; D. 661/11/2/3/1/16, 20 Sept. 1842.

[97] *Aris's Birmingham Gaz.* 18 Oct. and 8 Nov. 1779; 31 Jan., 2 Oct., and 4 Dec. 1780; 6 Nov. 1797.

[98] Ibid. 3 Nov. 1800; 28 Nov. and 26 Dec. 1803; 5 and 26 Nov. 1810; *Lichfield Mercury*, 17 Nov. 1815; 9 Feb. 1816; *Staffs. Advertiser*, 3 Jan. 1829.

[99] *Staffs. Advertiser*, 12 Jan. 1878, p. 1.

[1] Ibid. 4 Oct. 1862, p. 8; *Dyott's Diary*, ed. R. W. Jeffery, i. 336.

[2] S.R.O., D. 661/11/2/3/1/16, 12 Jan. 1843; *Staffs. Advertiser*, 5 Jan. 1839; 18 Jan. 1840.

[3] *Staffs. Advertiser*, 19 Jan. 1878, p. 4; Clayton, *Cathedral City*, 161.

[4] Above (music).

[5] J. Nichols, *Progresses and Public Processions of Queen Elizabeth* (1821), iv (1), 74; *D.N.B.* s.v. Dudley, Ambrose.

[6] J. L. Clifford, *Young Samuel Johnson*, 97–8.

[7] *Aris's Birmingham Gaz.* 5 Jan. 1767; Clayton, *Coaching City*, 45–6, 54; R. Manvell, *Sarah Siddons*, 10–14, 18–19.

[8] *Boswell: the Ominous Years 1774–1776*, ed. C. Ryskamp and F. A. Pottle, 292, 297; L.J.R.O., D. 35/bailiffs' accts. 1704–94, pp. 446, 468, 512, 538.

the White Hart inn. The cost was probably met by subscription, and in 1793 ownership was vested in a body of shareholders.[9] James Miller, a theatrical manager from Worcester, was licensed to perform in the theatre for 60 days from 10 September 1791, but by the mid 1790s licences were for only 14 days, presumably an indication that longer runs were unprofitable.[10] Companies generally played for a week or less, usually at the time of the race meetings.[11] Players included Isabella Mattocks in 1797, Edmund Kean in 1809 (when still nationally unknown), William Betty (the Young Roscius) in 1807 after his voice had broken and again in 1816, and Dorothea Jordan in 1810.[12]

The theatre, known as the Theatre Royal by 1859, was demolished in 1871.[13] It was replaced in 1873 by St. James's Hall, which had an assembly room with a stage, and a separate dining room.[14] The hall became the usual venue for theatricals, concerts, and dances.[15] It was converted into a cinema in 1912. In 1949 it became the David Garrick theatre, under the management of R. F. Cowlishaw and his wife Joan. The theatre's second producer, in its opening year, was Kenneth Tynan, who produced Farquhar's *The Beaux' Stratagem*. Because of financial difficulties the theatre was closed soon after Joan Cowlishaw's death in 1953, and the building reverted to use as a cinema.[16]

George Stevens gave a performance in Lichfield of his humorous monologue 'Lecture on Heads' in 1773.[17] From the early 19th century theatricals, pantomimes, and comic routines were performed during the Greenhill Bower festivities by companies such as Richardson's and Holloway's.[18] Popular performances also took place when the Staffordshire Yeomanry assembled for its annual training week.[19] An amateur group, first recorded in 1853, played regularly for charity until dissolved c. 1890.[20] A group called the Lichfield Amateur Players was formed in the early 1940s and continued to give performances as the Lichfield Players in the later 1980s.[21] In 1946 Dorothy L. Sayers's play *The Just Vengeance*, commissioned by the dean and chapter and with music by Antony Hopkins, was performed in the cathedral in the presence of Queen Elizabeth.[22]

CIRCUSES AND OTHER ENTERTAINMENTS. Exhibitions of wild beasts were held in 1751 and 1796,[23] and in the early 19th century they were a feature of the Greenhill Bower festivities.[24] In 1823 an exhibition at the Bower was accompanied by shows of giants and dwarfs, a display of horsemanship, and a camera obscura. Wombwell's menagerie advertised its attendance at the Bower in 1824 and 1826, as did Mr. Adams's Olympic Circus in 1826; the circus had previously been in Lichfield during the 1824 September race meeting.[25] Day's menagerie and Biddall's exhibition, apparently a circus, were attractions at the 1873 Bower.[26]

A troupe of Prussian acrobats performed in the guildhall in 1765.[27] Conjurors visited Lichfield in 1768, and in 1780 a conjuror named Herman Boaz gave shows in the guildhall.[28] In 1794 a Signor Rosignol performed bird imitations there.[29] The Chevalier D'Éon demonstrated his skill in 'the art of attack and defence with a single rapier' in Lichfield in 1795 at what was one of his last public performances.[30]

An exhibition of automata was held at the George in 1816. In 1823 a revolving panorama and a cosmorama, through which pictures were displayed, were shown at the theatre in Bore Street.[31]

CINEMAS. 'Animated pictures', including films of recent disasters, were an attraction at the 1909 Shrove Tuesday fair.[32] Films were shown in St. James's Hall from 1910, and in 1912 the hall was converted into the Palladium cinema.[33] Renamed the Lido in 1937, the cinema was burnt down in 1942 but was immediately rebuilt to ensure continued entertainment for United States soldiers passing through the nearby Whittington barracks. It remained a cinema until 1949 and then became a theatre until 1953.[34] The building reopened as the Adelphi cinema, which closed in 1959.[35] The Regal cinema in Tamworth Street was opened in 1932.

[9] Clayton, *Coaching City*, 46–7; S.R.O., D. (W.) 1851/8/54; printed share certificate (copy in L.J.R.O., D. 77/20/7, between pp. 22 and 23). For a view in 1820 see Bodl. G.A. Staffs. 4°, 8, facing p. 492.
[10] L.J.R.O., D. 25/1/1, ff. 176, 186, 209v., 218.
[11] Ibid. D. 25/1/2, ff. 13v., 24, 34, 45, 57, 69; W.S.L. broadsheets 35/2; *Aris's Birmingham Gaz.* 12 June, 30 Oct., 13 Nov., 27 Nov. 1797; *Swinney's Birmingham Chron.* 7 Sept. 1797; 4 Sept. 1800; 11 Aug. 1803.
[12] *Aris's Birmingham Gaz.* 12 June 1797; *Letters of Anna Seward*, vi. 363–6; *Swinney's Birmingham Chron.* 20 Sept. and 11 Oct. 1810; *Lichfield Mercury*, 6 Sept. 1816; W.S.L., S. 1901, pp. 92–3.
[13] L.J.R.O., D. 77/20/5, p. 83.
[14] *Staffs. Advertiser*, 11 Oct. 1873, p. 6.
[15] L.J.R.O., D. 77/20/5, pp. 28, 96–7, 104; above (dancing assemblies).
[16] *David Garrick Memorial Theatre, Lichfield, 1949–53* (Lichfield, 1953; copy in W.S.L.); below (cinemas).
[17] *Letters of David Garrick*, ed. D. M. Little and G. M. Kahrl, ii, pp. 899–900.
[18] *Staffs. Advertiser*, 7 June 1873, p. 7.
[19] Ibid. 1 June 1872, p. 7; W.S.L., S. 1902i, f. 65.

[20] Balance sheet for performance, 1853 (copy in W.S.L.); *Lichfield Mercury*, 9 Nov. 1894, p. 8.
[21] Inf. from the chairman, Mrs. P. Gibson.
[22] *750th Anniversary of Lichfield Cath.* (1946), 32 (copy in W.S.L.); *Lichfield Mercury*, 21 June 1946, pp. 4–5.
[23] *Gent. Mag.* xxi. 378–9; *Letters of Anna Seward*, iv. 346.
[24] W.S.L., transcr. diary of Anne Bagot, pp. 10, 164.
[25] S.R.O., D. 661/11/2/3/1/11; *Lichfield Mercury*, 23 May 1823; 28 May and 3 Sept. 1824; 12 and 19 May 1826.
[26] *Staffs. Advertiser*, 7 June 1873, p. 7.
[27] *Aris's Birmingham Gaz.* 11 Nov. 1765.
[28] Ibid. 10 Apr. 1780; W.S.L., H.M. 24/3.
[29] L.J.R.O., D. 35/bailiffs' accts. 1704–94, p. 588; *Aris's Birmingham Gaz.* 24 July 1780.
[30] *Letters of Anna Seward*, iv. 75–6; *D.N.B.*
[31] *Lichfield Mercury*, 20 Dec. 1816; 21 Nov. 1823.
[32] L.J.R.O., D. 77/20/7, p. 11.
[33] *Lichfield Mercury*, 4 Nov. 1910, p. 4; 27 Dec. 1912, p. 4.
[34] Ibid. 22 Jan. 1937, p. 1; 6 July 1943, p. 7; *Garrick Memorial Theatre*, p. [1].
[35] *Lichfield Mercury*, 30 Oct. 1959, p. 1.

It became a bingo hall in 1974, and films have since been shown regularly in the Civic Hall in Wade Street, opened the same year.[36]

ARTS CENTRE. The former post office in Bird Street was opened as an Arts Centre in 1970 and extended in 1972 and in 1976. It provides a venue for a wide range of activities and includes an art gallery; it also has a restaurant and bar.[37]

FREEMASONS AND FRIENDLY SOCIETIES. An Ancient Lodge of Freemasons was established at the Scales inn in 1784 and still met in 1813. A Lodge of Moderns was formed in 1787 at the Three Crowns inn in Breadmarket Street and still met c. 1809. In the earlier 1830s the Three Crowns was the meeting place of St. John's Lodge, closed in 1850 but revived in 1865.[38] In the later 1970s the lodge moved to Tamworth, where it still met in the late 1980s. The Elias Ashmole Lodge was established in 1972; it too met in Tamworth in the late 1980s.[39]

Despite its name the Friendly Society of Florists and Gardeners, in existence by 1769, does not appear to have been a benefit society.[40] The earliest such society recorded in the city was the Lichfield Friendly Society, formed in 1770; it met at the Three Crowns in 1790.[41] There was a female society by 1773; its rules were confirmed in 1794. By custom in the 1770s its members walked in procession to hear a sermon in the cathedral on St. Peter's and St. Paul's day (29 June). A dinner and ball were held later in the day in the guildhall.[42] There were, in addition, five other friendly societies in the later 1790s: the Original Friendly, the Golden Tankard, the Old Crown Club, the Young Men's Friendly, and the Junior Friendly.[43] The Royal Oak Friendly Society had been formed by 1808.[44] A benefit club which met at the Three Crowns was dissolved in or shortly before 1827, when a new club, the Young Man's Independence, was formed at the same inn.[45] The Lichfield Friendly Institution, formed in 1833, drew membership from within 10 miles of the city boundary, an area reduced by 1862 to a five-mile radius from the city centre. The institution was dissolved in 1876.[46]

The benefit functions of the friendly societies

were apparently taken over by lodges of Oddfellows, of which the earliest in Lichfield were the Loyal Brunswick Independent Lodge of Oddfellows, formed in 1812,[47] the Loyal Wellington Lodge, formed by 1816, and the Loyal Independent Lodge George IV, formed in 1821.[48] The Manchester Unity of Oddfellows established a district at Lichfield in 1842, and three lodges were formed in the city that year. The Loyal Brunswick Lodge joined the unity in 1867.[49] In 1876 there were 10 registered lodges of Oddfellows, 5 of Oddsisters, one of Free Gardeners, and a court of Foresters; the recorded membership of six of the lodges was then 690.[50]

A Rechabite tent was established in Market Street in 1911.[51]

CLUBS, COFFEE HOUSES, AND NEWSROOMS. A gentlemen's drinking club known as the Court of Truth met weekly at the George in 1735; it moved to Harrison's coffee house in 1739 but returned to the George in 1740.[52] A gentlemen's club called the Lichfield Club was opened in 1879; it met at no. 24 Bird Street until its dissolution in 1934.[53] A working men's club, organized by the rector of St. Michael's, was opened in Church Street in 1878; its premises comprised a coffee house and a reading room. A temperance society, the Lighthouse Lodge of the Independent Order of Good Templars, was formed there in 1893.[54] A soldiers' club was established at no. 17 Bird Street (later the Lichfield Mercury offices) in 1900 for the use of men stationed at Whittington barracks; it was closed in 1928, and the premises were taken over by a Conservative club.[55] A coffee house and newsroom in Breadmarket Street in 1818 was managed as part of the Three Crowns inn.[56] In 1850 there was a temperance house in Tamworth Street and by 1868 one in Market Street, possibly in the same premises as the coffee house recorded there in 1904.[57]

The Lichfield Afternoon Women's Institute was formed in 1917. From 1921 it met in the former Wesleyan Methodist hall in Lombard Street, which it sold in 1980.[58] In the late 1980s the institute met in the Arts Centre in Bird Street, as did the Lichfield Evening Women's Institute, formed in 1967.[59] The Lichfield Townswomen's Guild was formed in 1959 and met in St. Mary's Centre in the late 1980s.[60]

[36] Ibid. 15 July 1932, p. 5; 5 July 1974, p. 12; 23 Nov. 1984, p. 10; R. James and J. E. Rackham, *Lichfield Then and Now* (Lichfield, 1988), 50.
[37] Inf. from the administrator; above, plate 36.
[38] F. W. Willmore, *Hist. of Freemasonry in Province of Staffs.* (1905), 44–5, 64, 112; *Kelly's Dir. Staffs.* (1932; 1936; 1940).
[39] Inf. from the Provincial Grand Lodge of Staffs., Wolverhampton. [40] Below (societies).
[41] Printed rules of soc. 1790 (copy in L.J.R.O., D. 77/18/9).
[42] *Aris's Birmingham Gaz.* 5 July 1773; 4 July 1774; 3 July 1775; printed rules of soc. 1794 (copy in B.R.L., 540458).
[43] L.J.R.O., D. 25/1/1, ff. 197v., 199v., 204–5.
[44] Ibid. D. 25/1/2, f. 63v.
[45] *Lichfield Mercury*, 6 July 1827.
[46] Lichfield Friendly Institution, *Rules and Regulations* (Lichfield, 1833; copy in W.S.L.); *Rep. Chief Registrar of Friendly Socs. 1876*, *App. P*, H.C. 429-I, p. 178 (1877), lxxvii; L.J.R.O., D. 77/5/3, f. 216v.; D. 77/18/11.

[47] *Staffs. Advertiser*, 10 Feb. 1877, p. 7.
[48] *Lichfield Mercury*, 19 July 1816; 1 Aug. 1823.
[49] Ibid. 14 Oct. 1910, p. 8.
[50] *Rep. Chief Reg. Friendly Socs. 1876*, 403–4.
[51] *Lichfield Mercury*, 22 Dec. 1911, p. 5.
[52] R. B. Adam, *Glimpse of Club Life in Lichfield, England, 1735–40* (Buffalo, New York, priv. print. 1924; copy in Samuel Johnson Birthplace Mus.).
[53] *Staffs. Advertiser*, 26 Oct. 1878, p. 4; *Lomax's Red Bk.* (1935), 11; S.R.O., D. 3573/Lichfield 1, p. 72.
[54] *Lichfield Mercury*, 4 Oct. 1878, p. 4; 24 Feb. 1893, p. 5.
[55] Ibid. 23 Mar. 1900, p. 5; 6 Apr. 1928, p. 1; *Kelly's Dir. Staffs.* (1932).
[56] Parson and Bradshaw, *Staffs. Dir.* (1818), 170, 187.
[57] *Slater's Nat. and Com. Dir.* (1850), Staffs. p. 36; *P.O. Dir. Staffs.* (1868); *Kelly's Dir. Staffs.* (1880 and later edns.).
[58] Inf. from the secretary, Mrs. M. Lockwood; above, protestant nonconformity.
[59] Inf. from the president, Mrs. Audrey Holmes.
[60] *Lichfield Mercury*, 16 Jan. 1959, p. 1.

Recreational clubs were organized by the parish churches in the later 19th and early 20th century.[61] Social clubs were opened in Weston Road in 1953, in Purcell Avenue in 1968, and on the Boley Park housing estate in 1984.[62] Cruck House in Stowe Street, a timber-framed building, was opened by the council as an old people's centre in 1971.[63]

The Lichfield Newsroom was opened in 1832 in a room in a house in Market Street owned by the Revd. J. T. Law, the diocesan chancellor.[64] It was intended for the use of gentlemen living in and around the city, as well as army officers temporarily stationed there. Members paid an annual subscription of 30*s*., which was reduced to 25*s*. in 1836. The room was open on weekdays between 9 a.m. and 9 p.m. (10 p.m. from 1835); there was a selection of London and provincial newspapers, but no magazines. From 1837 the enterprise was in debt, chiefly because Law, who had acted as chairman, secretary, and treasurer, devoted less time to it. In August 1841 there were 55 members, and in December that year 45. In January 1842 the institution was moved to a room at the Swan. It remained there until 1845, when Law again rented it a room in his house; he also paid its debts and in 1848 gave it an endowment of £150. The abolition of newspaper tax removed much of the original purpose of the newsroom, and its membership further declined. By drawing on capital the newsroom survived at Law's house until 1867, when it moved to a cheaper room elsewhere in Market Street. In 1872 it moved to a room in the market square, and in 1875 to one in Tamworth Street. By then there were fewer than 20 members. In 1879 those who remained joined the newly opened Lichfield Club in Bird Street and wound up the newsroom.

LIBRARIES. It was the intention of the Revd. John Deakin, master of Rugeley grammar school (d. 1727), to establish a lending library in Lichfield. He wished his books to be kept by members of his family resident in the city, or otherwise by someone chosen by the vicar of St. Mary's church, and to be loaned to anyone living in Lichfield or within fives miles of it. His wishes, however, seem not to have been followed.[65] In 1810 the Birmingham booksellers Thomson & Wrightson, who had opened a branch in Bird Street, announced their intention of setting up a circulating library with a stock of 1,000 books.[66] There was a circulating library in Frog Lane in 1818, run by a Mrs. Shaw,[67] and Henrietta Shaw managed one in St. John Street in 1834, when there was another in Bird Street run by Sarah Goodwin.[68] There were parochial lending libraries from the earlier 19th century.[69]

The Lichfield permanent subscription library was established in 1817 or 1818, in a building at the corner of Beacon Street and the road into the Close.[70] It was in debt by 1832 when the Revd. J. T. Law, the diocesan chancellor, rescued it, providing new premises in his house in Market Street.[71] In 1847 the library, which was open on working days from 12 noon until 4 p.m., had a stock of *c*. 2,000 books and periodicals; by 1851 it had a further 250 titles.[72] In 1882 it was moved to an upper room in the newly built art school in Dam Street.[73] It was probably closed in 1896, when the city council took over the art school.[74]

Lichfield council adopted the Free Libraries and Museums Act in 1857, and opened a library in Bird Street in 1859. Built of yellow brick in an Italianate style, it was designed by Bidlake & Lovatt of Wolverhampton.[75] The figure of an armed sailor on the building by the entrance was given *c*. 1905 by Robert Bridgeman, after it had been rejected by York city council which had commissioned it for a Boer War memorial.[76] The library was extended north in 1974 over the stack room of the Lichfield Joint Record Office.[77]

The record office had been established in 1959 under an agreement between the diocese, the city, and the county council, in the basement of the former probate court adjacent to the library, and the stack room was built in 1968 to house the diocesan and city records. Documents were read by the public in the library until 1981 when the ground floor of the probate court became the search room. In 1989 part of the former Friary school building was being converted into new premises for the library and the record office.[78]

MUSEUMS. Natural and historical artefacts were collected from the 1740s by Richard Greene, an apothecary, in his house in Market Street. He allowed inspection by the public and in 1773 printed a catalogue. The museum became one of the city's principal attractions for visitors. The collection was sold in parts after his death in 1793.[79] Some items were bought by his grandson, Richard Wright, who from 1803 displayed them in the former diocesan registry in the Close. In 1806 they were moved to

[61] Above, churches (St. Mary's; St. Chad's; St. Michael's; Christ Church).

[62] *Lichfield Mercury*, 25 Sept. 1953, p. 4; 29 Nov. 1968, p. 15; 7 Dec. 1984, p. 17.

[63] Ibid. 2 Apr. 1971, p. 5; *T.S.S.A.H.S.* i. 14 sqq.

[64] Para. based on Lichfield Libr., Lichfield Newsroom min. bks. 1832–43; 1843–79.

[65] L.J.R.O., P/C/11, John Deakin (1727); below, chars. for the poor (city: chars. of Francis and John Deakin).

[66] *Swinney's Birmingham Chron.* 4 Jan. 1810.

[67] Parson and Bradshaw, *Staffs. Dir.* (1818), 187.

[68] White, *Dir. Staffs.* (1834), 90, 160.

[69] Above, churches (St. Chad's; St. Michael's; Christ Church).

[70] Parson and Bradshaw, *Staffs. Dir.* (1818), 187; *Lichfield Mercury*, 14 Feb. 1817; L.J.R.O., D. 30/27.

[71] W.S.L., transcr. diary of Anne Bagot, p. 124a; L.J.R.O., D. 30/XLIX, f. 132; O.S. Map 1/500, Staffs. LII. 15. 12 (1884 edn.). For a view of the house in 1833 see W.S.L., Staffs. Views, v. 158.

[72] *Cat. of Bks. belonging to Permanent Libr. Lichfield, 1847* and *Supplement to Cat. of Bks. 1851* (copies in W.S.L.).

[73] S.R.O., D. 4566/12, papers re 14 Market St.; *Staffs. Advertiser*, 2 Sept. 1882, p. 4; 23 Dec. 1882, p. 5.

[74] *Kelly's Dir. Staffs.* (1896; 1900).

[75] *Illus. London News*, 24 Oct. 1857; *Staffs. Advertiser*, 12 Feb. 1859, p. 4; above, plate 37.

[76] Inf. from Mr. C. W. Bridgeman of Lichfield.

[77] Inf. from Mrs. J. Hampartumian, archivist at L.J.R.O.

[78] Inf. from Mrs. Hampartumian; below, education.

[79] *T.S.S.A.H.S.* xviii. 79; *D.N.B*; R. Warner, *Tour through the Northern Counties of Eng. and the Borders of Scotland* (1802), i. 107.

premises next to Wright's house at the north end of Dam Street. He died in 1821, and the items were sold.[80]

A museum was established in the Bird Street library in 1859. In 1958 it was moved to the former probate court on the north side of the library. It was closed in 1970 and its contents put into store.[81]

The Samuel Johnson Birthplace museum in the market square occupies a house built apparently in 1707 by Johnson's father, Michael.[82] The premises were bought in 1887 by James Johnson of Southport (Lancs.) in order to preserve the house in which Dr. Johnson was born. Under James Johnson's will the house was sold to the city in 1900, the money being given by John Gilbert, and in 1901 a museum devoted to the life and works of Samuel Johnson was opened.[83] The museum contains an extensive library of manuscripts and books, including over 1,000 books collected by the Revd. Dr. Peter Hay Hunter of Edinburgh and given by his widow in 1911.[84] The museum was run by the city council until 1974, when its management was transferred to a trust. In 1982 the restored city council regained control.[85] The museum is the headquarters of the Johnson Society, founded in 1910.[86]

Davidson House in Upper St. John Street was opened in 1938 as a museum for the South Staffordshire Regiment and is named after the donor, Brig.-Gen. C. S. Davidson. In 1963 the museum was moved to Whittington barracks, where there was already a North Staffordshire regimental museum. A combined museum for the Staffordshire Regiment was opened there in 1969.[87]

St. Mary's Centre was opened by a trust in 1981 in part of the redundant church of St. Mary.[88] It includes an exhibition of items relating to Lichfield's history.

SOCIETIES AND ANTIQUARIAN PURSUITS.

The Friendly Society of Florists and Gardeners held an auricula and polyanthus show at the Chequers inn in Lombard Street in 1769, when one of the stewards was the nurseryman John Bramall.[89] Autumn shows were held in the late 18th and early 19th century.[90] The society was reorganized in 1816 as the Lichfield Florist Society, and its early members included John Hewitt, precentor of the cathedral, and William Buck, head gardener at Elford Hall. There were twice-yearly shows, and exhibits included melons and gooseberries. Dahlias were shown for the first time in 1835. By the mid 1850s the autumn show was normally held out of doors, with a band providing music.[91] Known as the Floral and Horticultural Society by 1868, it still existed in 1920.[92] There may have been a connexion with the Lichfield Floral and Horticultural Reading Society, established in 1841 with the purpose of circulating relevant publications among members.[93] In 1875 John Graham, rector of St. Chad's, established a cottagers' flower show to encourage gardening by the working classes; it was still held in 1877.[94]

The Lichfield Botanical Society was formed in 1778 by Erasmus Darwin to promote a translation of the botanical works of Linnaeus. In the late 1770s Darwin created a botanic garden at Abnalls in Burntwood, which was maintained after he left Lichfield in 1781 by a fellow member of the society.[95]

The Lichfield Society for the Encouragement of Ecclesiastical Architecture was formed by 1841, and until 1852 it met in a room in J. T. Law's house in the Market Street.[96] Nothing further is known of it.

Richard Greene, besides forming a museum from the 1740s, collected manuscripts of local interest and made notes on the city's history from corporation archives, parish records, cathedral muniments, and elsewhere. He contributed articles on Lichfield's history and antiquities to the *Gentleman's Magazine*.[97] He was also responsible for placing a plaque on a house in Dam Street to mark the spot where the parliamentary commander Lord Brooke had been killed in 1643 while preparing to mount an assault on the royalist garrison in the Close.[98] A plaque on Brooke House in Dam Street in the late 1980s is probably the original, although the façade of the house has been changed. In 1795 John Jackson, a Lichfield bookseller and printer, published anonymously his *History of the City and County of Lichfield* and *History and Antiquities of the Cathedral Church of Lichfield*, both based on original research. They were revised and reprinted under his own name in 1805 as a single volume, *History of the City and Cathedral of Lichfield*. His intention in writing was partly to meet the need for a guide book for visitors to the cathedral and the city. In 1806 Thomas Harwood, headmaster of Lichfield grammar school 1791–1813, published *The History and Antiquities of the Church and City of Lichfield*, also based on considerable original research.[99] Charles Stringer, a house painter,[1] published

[80] *T.S.S.A.H.S.* xviii. 81–2; Lichfield Cath. Libr., misc. papers, Hen. Wright to F. P. Eliot, 4 Oct. 1806; L.J.R.O. VC/A/21, CC 17529, plan 22, no. 1.
[81] *Staffs. Advertiser*, 12 Feb. 1859, p. 4; *Lichfield Mercury*, 11 July 1958, p. 3; 14 Nov. 1986, p. 5.
[82] Reade, *Johnsonian Gleanings*, iv. 13–19.
[83] *Dr. Samuel Johnson and his Birthplace* (Lichfield, 1933), 16–17 (copy in W.S.L.); L.J.R.O., D. 127/council min. bk. 1899–1902, pp. 76–8, 174.
[84] *Staffs. Advertiser*, 23 Sept. 1911, p. 10
[85] Inf. from the curator, Dr. G. W. Nicholls.
[86] *Lichfield Mercury*, 19 Aug. 1910, p. 5.
[87] Ibid. 7 Oct. 1938, p. 3; inf. from Maj. R. D. W. McLean of the Staffs. Regiment; above, plate 16.
[88] Above, churches.
[89] *Garden Hist.* xvi (1), 18.

[90] *Swinney's Birmingham Chron.* 10 Aug. 1797; 10 May 1810; *Aris's Birmingham Gaz.* 30 July 1810.
[91] Lichfield Libr., Florist Soc. min. bk. 1816–92.
[92] L.J.R.O., D. 77/20/8, pp. 34–5; *Staffs. Advertiser*, 25 July 1868, p. 7; Jackson, *Hist. Incidents*, 110.
[93] Printed rules of soc. 1841 (copy in L.J.R.O., B/A/19, Haworth bdle. 1840–3).
[94] *Staffs. Advertiser* (S. Staffs. edn.), 28 July 1877, p. 7.
[95] *Letters of Erasmus Darwin*, ed. D. King-Hele, 109–11; below, Burntwood, growth of settlement.
[96] *V.C.H. Staffs.* iii. 193; Lichfield Libr., Lichfield Newsroom min. bk. 1843–79, entry for 6 Dec. 1852.
[97] *D.N.B.*
[98] Jackson, *Lichfield*, 53 n.
[99] *S.H.C.* 4th ser. xi. 123.
[1] Parson and Bradshaw, *Staffs. Dir.* (1818), 180.

anonymously his *Short Account of the Ancient and Modern State of the City and Close of Lichfield* in 1819. It included several woodcuts by the author, who from the 1780s made numerous sketches of buildings and street scenes in the city and the Close.[2]

Samuel Pegge, who became a prebendary of Lichfield in 1757, made notes on the history of the cathedral as part of his collection of Staffordshire material.[3] In 1811 the dean, John Chappell Woodhouse, and Canon John Newling published anonymously their *Short Account of Lichfield Cathedral; more particularly of the Painted Glass with which its Windows are adorned*.[4]

The South Staffordshire Archaeological and Historical Society was formed (as the Lichfield Archaeological and Historical Society) in 1957.[5] It is a publishing society and also arranges lectures, given in the late 1980s in St. Mary's Centre and in Tamworth. The Lichfield Civic Society, established in 1961, monitors the city's architectural heritage and its natural environment.[6] It still existed in the late 1980s.

NEWSPAPERS. The *Lichfield Mercury and Midland Chronicle* was first published in July 1815 by James Amphlett.[7] Until then Amphlett had published the newspaper at Stafford as the *Staffordshire Mercury*, which he had established

in 1814.[8] He sold the *Lichfield Mercury* in 1821 to John Woolrich of Lichfield, and in 1825 it was acquired by a consortium of local gentlemen, who described themselves as moderate Liberals. The paper, which came out on Fridays, was edited by George Hinde, who later became its proprietor. It was discontinued in 1833.[9]

The *Lichfield Advertiser* was started in 1865 but apparently ceased publication the following year.[10] The *Lichfield Chronicle* was being published in 1877, when one of its proprietors, Frederic Brown, a printer, severed his links with it.[11] He established a rival Friday paper, the *Lichfield Mercury*, first printed in September 1877 from premises at nos. 36–8 Bird Street.[12] Brown died in 1901 and the paper's ownership passed to his brother Edward, who sold it to W. H. Smith & Son in 1905.[13] The paper was later acquired by Allison & Bowen, owners of the *Staffordshire Chronicle*. On Richard Bowen's death in 1933 it was bought by a syndicate. The Bird Street premises were demolished in 1972, and a new office was opened at no. 17 Bird Street.[14]

Frederic Brown was a Conservative,[15] and between 1883 and 1897 there was a rival Liberal paper, the *Lichfield Herald*.[16] A Saturday paper, the *Lichfield Times and South Staffordshire Advertiser*, was started in 1926 and was still published in 1954.[17]

EDUCATION

THERE was presumably a school connected with Lichfield cathedral from early times. About 1190 the subchanter ran a song school, which eventually evolved into the present Lichfield Cathedral school. The duties of the cathedral's chancellor *c.* 1190 included the supervision of a school or schools;[18] whether or not he was expected to provide for teaching grammar, there is no evidence later that the chapter employed or supported a grammar master.

Master Peter, schoolmaster of Lichfield, heard a tithe case for the bishop's commissary general in 1272.[19] Master Matthew, school-

master of Lichfield, is recorded in 1312–13,[20] and Ralph, schoolmaster, in 1335.[21] William Bishop, schoolmaster, was admitted to the Lichfield guild of St. Mary and St. John the Baptist in 1440.[22] There was a grammar master, John Mercer, in the town in 1461,[23] and a schoolmaster, Ralph Gydnall, in 1466.[24] A schoolhouse at Greenhill was mentioned in the late 1320s.[25] It has been asserted that there was a school attached to St. John's hospital before 1495 and that the noted grammarian Robert Whittinton attended it as a boy in the 1480s,[26] but there seems to be no authority for either

[2] *T.S.S.A.H.S.* iv. 27–46. W.S.L. has photographic reproductions of the originals which are in Bodl. Libr.

[3] W.S.L., S. MS. 302; *D.N.B.*

[4] The authors are identified in the 8th edn. (post 1864).

[5] *Lichfield Mercury*, 27 Sept. 1957, p. 3 (correcting date given in *S.H.C.* 4th ser. xi. 151).

[6] Soc. brochure (copy in W.S.L.).

[7] Incomplete sets in W.S.L., Lichfield Libr., and B.L. Newspaper Libr., Colindale.

[8] *S.H.C.* 4th ser. vi. 196–7.

[9] W.S.L., S. MS. 374, p. 357; *Lichfield Mercury*, 16 Sept. 1825; 6 June 1879, p. 5.

[10] Copies in B.L. Newspaper Libr. and Lichfield Libr.

[11] Printed handbills (copies in L.J.R.O., D. 77/20/5, between pp. 84 and 85).

[12] Incomplete but complementary sets in B.L. Newspaper Libr. and Lichfield Libr.

[13] *Lichfield Mercury*, 13 Dec. 1901, p. 4; S.R.O., D. 4566/98, corresp. re 38 Bird St.

[14] *Lichfield Mercury*, 28 Apr. 1933, p. 4; *Special Issue*, Apr. 1972 (bound between issues of 21 and 28 Apr. in Lichfield Libr. set); inf. from the *Lichfield Mercury* office.

[15] S.R.O., D. 4566/98, corresp. re 38 Bird St., F. Brown to Hinckley, Hodson & Brown, Feb. 1893.

[16] *Kelly's Dir. Staffs.* (1888); incomplete sets in B.L. Newspaper Libr.

[17] Set in B.L. Newspaper Libr.

[18] Dugdale, *Mon.* vi (3), 1256–7; Wilkins, *Concilia*, i. 498–9; *Lincoln Cathedral Statutes*, ed. H. Bradshaw and C. Wordsworth, ii (1), 17, 20, 23.

[19] Lichfield Cath. Libr., MS. Lichfield 28, ff. 297 (*magister scolarum Lich'*), 297v. (*rector scolarum Lich'*), calendared in *S.H.C.* 1924, pp. 360–1. For the terminology see N. Orme, *Educ. and Soc. in Med. and Renaissance Eng.* 49–50.

[20] S.R.O., D. (W.) 1734/J. 2057, m. 5.

[21] L.J.R.O., D. 30/VC, B 10, deed of 25 Mar. 1335.

[22] Harwood, *Lichfield*, 403.

[23] L.J.R.O., D. 30/9/3/1, f. 3v.

[24] Ibid. f. 25v.

[25] Bodl. MS. Ashmole 855, pp. 180, 187.

[26] *D.N.B.* s.v. Whittington, Rob., citing Stringer, *Lichfield*, 112. Stringer's statement was evidently taken from Harwood, *Lichfield*, 439, who cites no evidence.

statement. In 1495 it was stated that, contrary to canon law, there was no established grammar school at the cathedral or in the town and no free instruction in grammar.[27]

A free grammar school was established in 1495 by Bishop Smith. An English school for poor boys was built in 1670 by Thomas Minors, and in the 1670s a charity founded by Humphrey Terrick was paying for poor children to be taught. In the early 18th century there were said to be two charity schools in the town, one for 30 boys, the other for 18 girls; all were given clothes.[28] The boys' was evidently Minors's school. The girls' was probably the charity school apparently taught or organized by a Mrs. Matlock to which the cathedral chapter subscribed £8 a year between 1713 and 1726,[29] rather than one of the dame schools which the corporation supported from Terrick's charity in the late 17th and early 18th century.[30]

Dame schools are found occasionally from the mid 17th century. A schoolmistress and her pupils were allotted seats in St. Mary's in 1649.[31] In 1675 a room in a tailor's shop was called 'the schoolhouse' and was furnished as such.[32] Dean Addison inspected the various 'petty' schools in the town in 1684, making sure that the children were taught the Catechism.[33] Two dame-school teachers are connected with Samuel Johnson. Ann Oliver was his first teacher; the cottage in Dam Street which was pointed out as hers c. 1800 now dates mainly from the early 19th century but incorporates parts of an earlier timber-framed structure. It has been suggested that Tom Brown, Johnson's second teacher, was a shoemaker who supplemented his earnings by keeping a school. He may in fact have been Thomas Brown, master of Minors's school.[34]

In the 1770s Lichfield was the scene of two educational experiments conducted by members of Erasmus Darwin's circle. Thomas Day, an admirer of Rousseau, took Stowe House in 1770 and there attempted, unsuccessfully, to educate a foundling girl on Rousseauesque lines in the hope of turning her into a perfect wife for himself.[35] In 1779 Darwin and Josiah Wedgwood, the potter, collaborated briefly in having their sons taught at home in modern subjects.[36] The Darwin circle produced two influential didactic books for children. Richard Lovell Edgeworth and his wife Honora wrote *Practical Education; or Harry and Lucy*, initially for their own children, and Edgeworth published it at Lichfield in 1780. It inspired Day to write *Sandford and Merton*.[37]

At the beginning of the 19th century Madras schools for girls and boys were established in Lichfield, and in mid century a system of parochial day schools emerged. There were a number of Sunday schools. The Madras school for boys in Frog Lane, opened in 1809, was both a day and a Sunday school. Day boys were obliged to attend on Sundays, and any other Lichfield boys were freely admitted then.[38] A Sunday school was established at St. Chad's in 1821. It had over 100 pupils in 1833 and still flourished in 1846–7, when over 200 children were being taught by voluntary helpers.[39] There was a Sunday school attached to the Congregational chapel in Wade Street in 1821 and one at the Methodist chapel in Lombard Street in the mid 1820s.[40] In 1833 there were three Sunday schools in the city, apart from that at St. Chad's. Two, both mixed, lay in the city part of St. Chad's parish; one had over 70 pupils, the other, founded in 1831, had over 100. At St. Michael's there was a Sunday school for girls, partly supported by the income from a small legacy, with 70 pupils and with a lending library attached to it. Although it was said that a Sunday school for boys was being formed, in 1846–7 there was still only a girls' Sunday school, at which a paid mistress taught 60 pupils.[41] A Sunday school existed at Christ Church by 1850 and may have been founded in 1847.[42]

Public education, especially at the elementary level, was mainly an Anglican preserve. When a privately funded high school for girls was established in 1892 its promoters were Anglicans who intended it as an Anglican foundation. It became a maintained county school in 1916 and the grammar school followed suit under a Scheme of 1920;[43] otherwise local authority schools were not started in the city until after the Second World War.

No school board was formed in Lichfield school district. In 1877 the city council set up an attendance committee for the urban part of the district and the guardians one for the rural part.[44] The guardians provided attendance officers,[45] but not the city council; the mayor claimed that 80 per cent of the city's children already went to school.[46] In the mid 1880s, however, the chairman of the city's attendance committee was complaining to a Royal Commission about the

[27] L.J.R.O., B/A/1/13, f. 167.
[28] M. G. Jones, *Char. School Movement*, 370; [T. Cox], *Compleat Hist. of Staffs.* (1730), 159.
[29] L.J.R.O., D. 30, cath. offertory bk. 1713–26.
[30] The mistress to whom Terrick's char. was paid 1710–25 was Sarah Mason: L.J.R.O., D. 35/bailiffs' accts. 1704–94, pp. 31, 38; L.J.R.O., D. 77/5/1, f. 240.
[31] Ibid. D. 20/4/1, 1649 accts.
[32] S.H.C. 4th ser. v, pp. 245–6.
[33] Bodl. MS. Tanner 131, f. 89.
[34] Bodl. G.A. Staffs. 4°, 8, facing p. 503; A. L. Reade, *Reades of Blackwood Hill* (priv. print. 1906), 246–7; Reade, *Johnsonian Gleanings*, i. 30–3; iii. 77–80; viii. 108; ix. 56–7; plaque on Dam St. cottage; below (Minors's sch.).
[35] D.N.B.; S. H. Scott, *Exemplary Mr. Day*, 69–79.
[36] *Letters of Erasmus Darwin*, ed. D. King-Hele, 99; *Letters of Josiah Wedgwood*, ed. K. E. Farrer (priv. print. 1903), ii. 430–1, 440–2, 445–6.
[37] D. Clarke, *Ingenious Mr. Edgeworth*, 89–90, 246–7; R.

L. Edgeworth, *Memoirs*, ed. M. Edgeworth (1820), ii. 334–6.
[38] S.R.O., D. 4566/99, Frog Lane boys' sch. acct. bk. 1809–81, introductory pages.
[39] *Lichfield Mercury*, 21 Oct. 1825; *Educ. Enq. Abstract*, 880; Nat. Soc. *Inquiry, 1846–7*, Staffs. 6–7.
[40] *Lichfield Mercury*, 12 Oct. 1821; 19 Dec. 1823; 30 Dec. 1825.
[41] *Educ. Enq. Abstract*, 880; Nat. Soc. *Inquiry, 1846–7*, Staffs. 6–7.
[42] Below (primary and secondary schs: Christ Church sch.).
[43] *V.C.H. Staffs.* vi. 161; below (primary and secondary schs: Friary sch.).
[44] *Staffs. Advertiser* (S. Staffs. edn.), 13 Jan. 1877, p. 7; 19 May 1877, p. 7; 23 June 1877, p. 7.
[45] Ibid. (S. Staffs. edn.), 23 June 1877, p. 7; 14 July 1877, p. 4.
[46] Ibid. (S. Staffs. edn.), 19 May 1877, p. 7.

difficulty of dealing with truancy at Lichfield, and by 1887, when the city eventually appointed an attendance officer, average attendance in city schools was only 74 per cent.[47] In 1889 attendance was 81 per cent, and in autumn 1891, after the introduction of free elementary education, it rose to 86 per cent.[48]

A Lichfield schools managers' council, set up in 1887, rarely met.[49] It was superseded in 1902 by a committee of managers, to which two managers were elected from each public elementary school, with the mayor as an *ex officio* member. It was a consultative, co-ordinating, and fund-raising body. The county council became the local education authority for the city in 1903, and by 1907 the committee of managers was negotiating with it over the provision of new schools.[50]

In 1909 Graham (later Sir Graham) Balfour, the county council's director of education, suggested that Lichfield's voluntary elementary schools should be grouped under a joint board of management and should then be graded. Individual schools would retain their own managers. The city's Roman Catholic school refused to co-operate but the six Anglican elementary schools agreed to the proposal. In 1910 a board of managers of the Lichfield group of voluntary schools was formed; it comprised managers from each school and representatives of the city and county councils. The Lichfield grouping was the only one of any significance in Staffordshire.[51] In 1913 the six schools were graded into infants', intermediate, and senior departments.[52] There were further reorganizations in 1921, following the 1918 Education Act, and in 1928, after the Hadow Report.[53] By the 1930s the county council was having to cajole some of the schools to stay open; only the Depression postponed plans to build county elementary schools in the city. After the 1944 Education Act the group lost any remaining importance. In 1945 the diocese of Lichfield decided that it could no longer promise financial support for all Church schools, and between then and 1948 those in the city concluded that they must take controlled status or close. Meetings of the group managers became sparsely attended and in 1951 the group was wound up.[54] In the late 1980s there were 9 primary schools and 3 secondary schools in Lichfield. Virtually all were housed in post-war buildings.

LICHFIELD CATHEDRAL SCHOOL. For the cathedral song school of the late 12th century the precentor, who chose the choristers, had overall responsibility. His deputy, the subchanter, ran the school, and instruction was given by a subordinate, evidently the song school master.[55] The boys presumably lived at home or lodged in the Close; the 'alumnus' who was lodging with the vicar choral Alan of Ashbourne in 1322 may have been one of them.[56] From 1265 they were given various endowments for their maintenance. By 1496 they were required to live in the Close, and in or shortly after 1527 they began to live in common in a house on the site of the present nos. 13 and 14.[57] From 1520 the master of the choristers was paid £2 13s. 4d. a year and 3s. a year for each boy. He taught them pricksong and descant, and was allowed to charge fees for giving them private organ lessons.[58] He could also supplement his salary by taking part in concerts which they gave. In 1523 he was made custodian of the cathedral's music books.[59] In 1524 some at least of the boys were expected to be able to read lessons at matins.[60]

Injunctions of 1547 and 1559 gave the master responsibility for choosing and managing the boys.[61] By 1582 the choristers' house in the Close was let and they were once more living at home or in lodgings. They were taught in a room in the Close; from the 1620s it was a schoolroom built by Michael East (d. 1648), the master, on the gatehouse of their former house.[62] Probably nothing was taught save music. Elias Ashmole became a chorister and began to spend part of his time at what he later called the music school merely to improve his musical skills; previously he had attended the city's grammar school.[63] In 1649, after the cathedral's establishment had been disbanded, Michael East's son Michael, who had been a vicar choral, lived next door to what had been the choristers' house and had the use of the schoolroom;[64] he may have kept a private music school there. In 1660 the cathedral was once more employing choristers, and by 1663 its music school had been re-established.[65] The cathedral statutes of 1694 gave the master of the choristers a stipend of £10 a year but restored his earlier subordination to the precentor.[66] The singing or music school[67] remained in its 17th-century schoolroom until 1772, when the gatehouse was de-

[47] S.R.O., CEH/88/1, 7 Nov. 1889; L.J.R.O., D. 117/14, 29 July and 28 Nov. 1887; *Lichfield Mercury*, 13 May 1887; *Staffs. Advertiser*, 17 Sept. 1887, p. 6.
[48] S.R.O., CEH/88/1, 7 Nov. 1889, 7 Nov. 1891.
[49] L.J.R.O., D. 117/14, 29 July 1887–13 Jan. 1902 *passim*. The body was later known as the Lichfield School Managers' Assoc.: ibid. 13 Jan. 1902.
[50] Ibid. 13 Jan. 1902 sqq.
[51] *Staffs. Advertiser*, 30 July 1910, Suppl.; 5 Apr. 1913, p. 10; *Staffs. C.C. Record for 1910*, 84; G. Balfour, *Ten Years of Staffs. Education, 1903–1913* (Stafford, 1913), 66, 92–3; Staffs. C.C. *Order for Grouping*, 1 Jan 1910 (copy in S.R.O., D. 4566/N, envelope of misc.).
[52] S.R.O., D. 4566/99, Lichfield Group Managers' min. bk. 1913–16, pp. 2–3, 11, 34, 118, 133.
[53] Ibid. min. bk. 1916–24, pp. 123–6, 178, 184; *Staffs. C.C. Record for 1921*, 223–4; *1928*, 591.
[54] S.R.O., D. 4566/N, Lichfield Group Managers' min. bk. 1934–48, pp. 44, 48–9, 74–5, 133, 253–5; min. bk. 1948–51, pp. 3, 38–9, 45–6.

[55] Dugdale, *Mon.* vi (3), 1256–7; Wilkins, *Concilia*, i. 498–9; *Lincoln Cathedral Statutes*, ii (1), 17, 20, 23.
[56] Bodl. MS. Ashmole 794, f. 3v.
[57] *V.C.H. Staffs.* iii. 149, 156, 163 n., 164–5.
[58] L.J.R.O., D. 30/C.A. iii, f. 124v. Contrary to the implication in *V.C.H. Staffs.* iii. 164, it is not clear that the mastership was a new post in 1520, and there is no evidence that the master was expected to teach anything but music.
[59] L.J.R.O., D. 30/C.A. iii, ff. 137v., 138v.
[60] Ibid. iv, f. 9.   [61] *V.C.H. Staffs.* iii. 166.
[62] Ibid. 172–3; *T.S.S.A.H.S.* xxv. 38, 44; above, cathedral and close (close: other buildings).
[63] *Elias Ashmole*, ed. C. H. Josten, ii. 312–13.
[64] *T.S.S.A.H.S.* xxv. 38, 44.
[65] L.J.R.O., D. 30/LXIV, accts. for 1660; *V.C.H. Staffs.* iii. 180.
[66] *Statuta et Consuetudines Ecclesiae Cathedralis Lichfieldiae* (priv. print. 1863), 38, 73, 82.
[67] e.g. L.J.R.O., D. 30/Bb 11, vicars' presentments 1706, 1723, 1726, 1730.

molished. Thereafter it used the anteroom of the cathedral library. In 1802 the vicars choral offered the older boys the use of a room in their hall for singing practice.[68]

In the early 19th century, apparently for the first time, the chapter began to make some regular provision for teaching the boys the elements. In the 18th century the chapter had preferred to take its choristers from poorer families, although such boys sometimes had little schooling. In 1810 the subchanter asserted that the ability to read was 'not *absolutely* necessary to learn the rudiments of singing'.[69] When, however, in 1809 Dean Woodhouse helped to establish a Madras school for boys in Frog Lane the choristers were sent to it.[70] A new regime was established for the choir school in 1817 or 1818, with the help of a gift from Woodhouse. In 1818 one of the lay vicars was being paid to teach the boys the elements; the cathedral organist was responsible for their musical education.[71] In 1866 the choristers had a schoolmaster, who was allowed to take up to 14 probationers in addition to 10 choristers; all were taught free.[72] The arrangements depended on the goodwill of the chapter, which pointed out in 1867 that it was not obliged by the cathedral statutes to provide a school.[73] In 1879 the master was living and presumably teaching in part of the former choristers' house; government and diocesan inspectors had found the school satisfactory.[74]

In 1880 the chapter decided to build the choristers a schoolroom in Stone Yard off Dam Street.[75] From 1892 the master took boarders, which enabled the chapter to draw choristers from a wider area. The school remained small: in 1905 or 1906 there were 17 boys, of whom 6 were boarders. The school buildings then comprised two houses in Dam Street, occupied by the master and the boarders, and the schoolroom. The boys had a playing field and the exclusive use of the public swimming baths one afternoon a week.[76] A new two-storeyed schoolhouse was opened in Stone Yard in 1913.[77] By the late 1930s there were 36 boys (two sets of 18 choristers) at the school.[78] In 1942 the school was reopened in no. 12 the Close as a day and boarding preparatory school called St. Chad's cathedral school.[79] Fee-paying non-choristers were admitted. From 1955 the school also occupied the bishop's palace. Girls were admitted from 1975. A department for boys and girls aged 4–7 was opened in 1978. In 1981 it moved into the building in Pool Walk formerly occupied by St. Mary's C.E. infants' school. It moved in 1989 to the Broadhurst Building, designed by the Duval Brownhill Partnership and erected behind no. 12 the Close.

The dean and chapter owned the school until 1981, when it became fully independent and changed its name to Lichfield cathedral school. In 1989 there were some 180 children. About 25 places in the preparatory department were reserved for choristers and probationers, who received scholarships from the dean and chapter.

KING EDWARD VI COUNTY COMPREHENSIVE SCHOOL.

The school, in Upper St. John Street, was formerly Lichfield grammar school, founded in 1495. It became a mixed comprehensive school in 1971. Its history is treated in another volume.[80]

MINORS'S SCHOOL.

Thomas Minors, a Presbyterian mercer, built a school in 1670.[81] The schoolhouse, a four-bayed, two-storeyed brick building, stood at the corner of Bore Street and St. John Street.[82] The schoolroom was on the ground floor at the west end of the building.[83] Minors maintained the school until his death in 1677, and by will gave the building as a school for 30 poor boys of the city, to be chosen by trustees and taught without charge to read English 'until they can well read chapters in the Bible'.[84] The schoolmaster was to have half the house, and the garden, rent free. For his salary he was to have the income from c. 9 a. at Leamonsley, which were to be rack rented. Repairs to the house were to be paid for by rack renting the rooms over the schoolroom and with 13s. 4d. of a £1 rent charge. The remaining 6s. 8d. was to be spent on coal for the schoolroom. Another rent charge of 6s. 8d. was to provide wine and cakes for the trustees at their annual school inspection.[85]

By will dated 1686 William Jesson, Minors's brother-in-law, left a £1 rent charge to buy bibles for pupils. By will dated 1727 Joan Parker left £20, the interest on which was to be paid to the master.[86] An early 18th-century survey claimed, probably mistakenly, that the boys were clothed as well as taught.[87]

Minors may have hoped[88] to keep his school independent of the city's Anglican establishment. A tradition of Dissent may have survived

[68] Ibid. D. 30/L 6; D. 30/X, 1772–85, 31 July 1772; D. 30/C.A. ix, pp. 50–1; above, cathedral and close.
[69] Lichfield Cath. Libr., MS. Lichfield 91.
[70] S.R.O., D. 4566/99, Frog Lane boys' sch. acct. bk. 1809–81, 25 July 1809.
[71] *V.C.H. Staffs.* iii. 186; *Digest of Returns to Sel. Cttee. on Educ. of Poor*, H.C. 224, p. 857, (1819), ix (2).
[72] *V.C.H. Staffs.* iii. 193.
[73] L.J.R.O., D. 30, return to Eccl. Com. Aug. 1867.
[74] *Rep. Cath. Com. Lichfield* [C. 4238], App. p. 3, H.C. (1884–5), xxi.   [75] L.J.R.O., D. 30/C.A. xiv, p. 248.
[76] Ibid. D. 30, cath. accts. 1875–1908, entries from 1903–4; C. Hobley, *Cath. Sch., Lichfield, Reg. 1838–1905* (Lichfield, 1906), 4–7, 15 (copy in Lichfield Cath. Libr.).
[77] *Lomax's Red Bk.* (1914), 18; inscription on building.
[78] *V.C.H. Staffs.* iii. 196.
[79] Rest of para. and following para. based on *V.C.H.*

Staffs. iii. 196–7; E. E. F. Walters, *St. Chad's Cath. Sch., Lichfield, the first fifteen years* (Lichfield, 1981; copy in W.S.L. 45/86); *Lichfield Mercury*, 23 June 1989, p. 10; Lichfield cath. sch. prospectus; inf. from the head master.
[80] *V.C.H. Staffs.* vi. 159–61.
[81] Harwood, *Lichfield*, 426–7, 479–80; above, protestant nonconformity.
[82] *Staffs. Advertiser*, 16 May 1914, p. 4; above, plate 27.
[83] *7th Rep. Com. Char.* 401.
[84] Harwood, *Lichfield*, 479–80; [W. T. Mynors], *A Lichfield Worthy of the 17th Cent.: Thos. Minors* (Lichfield, 1929; reprinted from *Lichfield Mercury*, 19 and 26 Apr., 3 and 10 May 1929).
[85] *7th Rep. Com. Char.* 401–2.   [86] Ibid. 402.
[87] [T. Cox], *Compleat Hist. of Staffs.* (1730), 159.
[88] See e.g. [Mynors], *Lichfield Worthy*, 16; *S.H.C.* 4th ser. ii. 29–31, 37.

for 50 years: in 1700 the master, Thomas Brown, failed to subscribe[89] (although few schoolmasters at Lichfield seem to have subscribed), and in 1718 the son of Mr. Harrison, 'the English schoolmaster at Lichfield', was baptized by a Presbyterian minister.[90] By the mid 18th century, however, the school was Anglican,[91] and so remained until it closed in 1876.[92]

Brown may be the Lichfield schoolmaster of that name who died in 1717, plausibly identified as the Tom Brown who taught Samuel Johnson and published a writing book.[93] If so, Johnson was probably a private pupil. John Clifford, master 1758–1805,[94] took such pupils. Richard Dyott of Freeford sent his son William to 'Clifford's school' at Lichfield in the later 1760s. In 1780 Clifford advertised as a writing master who took boarders, and in the late 1780s Henry Salt, son of a Lichfield surgeon, went to Minors's school.[95] Clifford's income from the endowments of the English school was £16 10s. in 1786.[96] Another John Clifford, probably his son, master by 1818 and in 1844, was in 1821 occupying the whole of the schoolhouse rent free and received c. £30 a year from the school lands.[97]

In 1801 or 1802 the Conduit Lands trustees paid £25 towards repairing the schoolhouse.[98] The establishment of a Madras school for boys in 1809 reduced the demand for places at Minors's, but by 1821 it was again full. The Lichfield philanthropist Andrew Newton (d. 1806) left it £3,333 6s. 8d. stock in reversion, which it received in 1825; c. 1813 his executors paid nearly £200 for repairs to the schoolhouse.[99]

In 1826 the school's trustees decided to increase to 60 the number of free places, to teach writing and arithmetic as well as reading, to convert upper rooms into a second schoolroom, to increase the master's salary by £30, and to engage an undermaster. In 1828 an undermaster was engaged at £30 a year.[1] In 1844 the building was repaired and more school accommodation was provided, perhaps by enlarging the schoolrooms.[2]

An undermaster was employed until at least 1844,[3] but from 1845 his place seems to have been taken by trainees from the diocesan training school, and in 1848 school hours were adjusted to meet their requirements. In 1847 the master of Minors's was retained by the training school as its master of method.[4] In 1851–2 he was being helped at Minors's by three or four trainees and was able to divide the school into four classes. The arrangement probably continued until the training school closed in 1863.[5] In 1846 a night school was being held.[6]

Trustees in the 1840s could afford to enforce residence qualifications strictly.[7] In 1851–2 there were 30 free boys and 43 paying 2d. a week; by 1857 the number of fee-payers had risen to 60, and the trustees raised the fee to 8d. a week. By 1860 fees were once more 2d. a week. An inspector gave the school a very favourable report in 1851–2, and Sylvanus Biggs, master from c. 1858 to 1876, was highly regarded in the city. His later claim that during his mastership there were usually 100–150 pupils perhaps exaggerated the numbers, but fees of 9d. or 1s. a week c. 1870 support his assertion that most of the boys were middle-class.[8] The inspector in 1865 for the Taunton Commission thought it a 'very good' school, popular with small tradesmen,[9] but recommended that it be affiliated to the grammar school.[10] The Endowed Schools Commission pressed for amalgamation, the Minors trustees admitting that the schoolhouse, despite being picturesque, was no longer suitable.[11] A Scheme of 1876 wound up Minors's and transferred most of its endowments to a reorganized grammar school,[12] where there were to be four Minors scholarships for boys from public elementary schools in the city.[13] The schoolroom end of Minors's schoolhouse was pulled down for road widening in or shortly after 1902,[14] and what remained was demolished in 1914.[15]

PRIMARY AND SECONDARY SCHOOLS.

School of industry for girls, later *girls' National school.* In 1806 Dean Proby and other inhabitants of the Close established a school of industry for 24 girls, who were clothed and were

[89] L.J.R.O., D. 30/subscription bk. 1660–1753, f. 53, where the subscription is made out but not signed.
[90] S.R.O., D. 4119, p. [61].
[91] L.J.R.O., D. 15/6/2/1.
[92] Ibid. D. 15/6/2/3 and 4.
[93] *Boswell's Life of Johnson,* ed. G. B. Hill, revised L. F. Powell, i. 43; Reade, *Johnsonian Gleanings,* i. 30–3; iii. 78–80; ix. 64.
[94] Inscription on Clifford's gravestone in St. Chad's churchyard, Lichfield (inf. from Mrs. C. Stanton of Tamworth); L.J.R.O., P/C/11, John Clifford (1806).
[95] *Dyott's Diary,* ed. R. W. Jeffery, i, p. xi; *Aris's Birmingham Gaz.* 16 Oct. 1780; J. J. Halls, *Life and Corresp. of Hen. Salt* (1834), i. 9–10.
[96] Harwood, *Lichfield,* 371–2.
[97] L.J.R.O., D. 15/6/2/2, pp. 54–63; *7th Rep. Com. Char.* 402; Parson and Bradshaw, *Staffs. Dir.* (1818), 170; Wesley, *Dir. Burton* (1844), 28.
[98] L.J.R.O., D. 126/min. bk. 1741–1856, pp. 132, 143; acct. bk. 1663–1805, 2 Nov. 1801 or 4 Jan. 1802.
[99] L.J.R.O., D. 15/6/2/2, pp. 13, 108; D. 77/18/3; *7th Rep. Com. Char.* 402–3; *Staffs. Advertiser,* 18 Jan. 1806.
[1] L.J.R.O., D. 15/6/2/2, pp. 19–22.
[2] Ibid. pp. 29–31; *Guide to City of Lichfield* (Lichfield, 1848), 41 (copy in W.S.L.).

[3] *Educ. Enq. Abstract,* 880; Wesley, *Dir. Burton* (1844), 28.
[4] L.J.R.O., D. 15/6/2/3, 4 Jan. 1848; Lichfield Dioc. Bd. of Educ. *9th Ann. Rep.* (Lichfield, 1848), 8 (copy in W.S.L.).
[5] G. Griffith, *Free Schs. and Endowments of Staffs.* (1860), 97; J. R. Lindley, 'Hist. of Educ. in Lichfield' (TS. of 1942 in Lichfield Libr.), p. 114.
[6] L.J.R.O., D. 15/6/2/3, 28 Sept. 1846.
[7] Ibid. 30 Nov. 1846, 29 Aug. 1847.
[8] Lindley, 'Hist. of Educ.', pp. 114–16; *Staffs. Advertiser,* 2 May 1857, p. 4; Griffith, *Free Schs.* 97; Jackson, *Hist. Incidents,* 3 (2nd nos.).
[9] *Rep. Schs. Inquiry Com. vol. viii* [3966–VII], pp. 161, 165, 223 n., H.C. (1867–8), xxviii (7).
[10] Ibid. *vol. xv* [3966–XIV], p. 428, H.C. (1867–8), xxviii (12).
[11] See e.g. L.J.R.O., D. 15/6/2/4, 3 Mar. 1873, 26 Feb., 20 July and 21 Dec. 1874, 21 July 1875; [Mynors], *Lichfield Worthy,* 20–1. [12] *V.C.H. Staffs.* vi. 161.
[13] *Staffs. Endowed Chars.* 86–7.
[14] L.J.R.O., D. 77/20/8, p. 46; D. 127/council min. bk. 1899–1902, p. 259.
[15] *Staffs. Advertiser,* 16 May 1914, p. 4; 30 May 1914, p. 7.

taught reading and needlework. In 1809 the subscribers decided to enlarge the school to take 40 girls and to adopt the Madras system.[16] By 1810 Dean Woodhouse had fitted up a barn in Quonians Lane as a schoolroom. The list of subscribers was extended to the city. The corporation subscribed from 1811, and there were grants from Andrew Newton's executors and the diocesan branch of the National Society. The marquess of Stafford, whose wife had subscribed since 1809, let the barn and an adjoining cottage for the schoolmistress to the school in 1813 at a nominal rent and kept them in repair. By 1814 there were 60 pupils, of whom 40 were clothed, and the new schoolroom had been extended. Andrew Bell, the creator of the Madras system, had visited the school.[17] In 1818 the mistress received c. £40 a year for teaching 60–100 girls. In the early 1830s 64 poor girls were taught, of whom 40 were clothed.[18] There were 48 day and Sunday pupils in 1846–7.[19] In 1849 the school's managers and those of the Frog Lane boys' school bought the Frog Lane schoolhouse and an adjoining house, where new boys' and girls' National schools were opened in 1850. The girls' school was closed in 1873.[20]

Frog Lane boys' school. The school, initiated by Dean Woodhouse,[21] supported by subscriptions and by donations from the Conduit Lands trustees and the executors of Jane Gastrell of Stowe House,[22] and assisted by William Vyse, one of the residentiary canons and an early supporter of Bell's system,[23] was opened in 1809 in a converted barn in Frog Lane, with an adjoining house for the master. The school, an early example of a provincial school on the Madras system, was a day and Sunday school for boys aged 6–12. The master also ran a night school. Attendance at the Sunday school, free to all city boys, was compulsory for boys at the day school; the Sunday curriculum seems to have been restricted to religious intruction. The day boys, who were nominated by the subscribers, received a free education, free haircuts, and each year a pair of shoes. Bell visited the school to advise on teaching and discipline. In the early years attendance was c. 100–150. When a diocesan branch of the National Society was formed in 1812 the school was held out as a model.[24] Among its supporters was Sir Charles Oakeley, Bt., tenant of the bishop's palace 1810–26, who as governor of Madras had encouraged Bell's educational experiments in India.[25] Gifts totalling £220 were received from Andrew Newton's executors in 1810 and 1817, and a legacy of £100 from Mary Brown in 1816.

The school was enlarged in 1820. In the 1820s and 1830s numbers apparently ranged from c. 80 to c. 110.[26] A school lending library was established in 1838.[27] The need for economies ended free haircuts in 1836, and an increase in numbers and the need to pay an assistant master ended the distribution of shoes in 1840.[28] From 1844 the boys had to pay 2d. a week; two or more brothers attending together were given reductions.[29] Moves in the 1840s to merge the school with Minors's school and the National school for girls and to build a large new school on a different site foundered owing to opposition from the managers of the girls' school.[30]

In 1849 the managers bought the site and buildings, previously leased, and co-operated with the girls' school in building new adjoining National schools for boys and girls, a plain brick building designed by Richard Greene, a Lichfield banker, and opened in 1850.[31] The lending library was transferred in 1856 to St. Michael's parochial library, from which the older boys might borrow books.[32] In 1861 there were over 120 boys.[33] The girls' school was closed in 1873,[34] and the boys took over their schoolroom. Frog Lane was under government inspection by 1869 and received an annual grant from 1871.[35] In 1876 average attendance was c. 100. Two classrooms were added in 1877; most of the cost was met from the proceeds of the sale of Minors's schoolhouse.[36]

Under Isaac Humphreys, master 1876–1901, average attendance doubled, assistant masters were employed, the library was re-established, and a football team was formed. It used a playing field at Paradise off Trent Valley Road acquired for the city's day and Sunday schools in 1879. Weekly fees were increased from 3d. to 6d. in 1882 without opposition, and when free elementary education was introduced in 1891 over 80 parents promised regular voluntary con-

[16] Nat. Soc. *2nd Ann. Rep.* (1814), 135–6.
[17] S.R.O., D. 593/F/3/12/2/21, receipt of 9 Dec. 1808; D. 593/F/3/12/2/35, receipts of 12 Oct. 1822; D. 593/F/3/12/4/8, no. 61; L.J.R.O., D. 35/bailiffs' accts. 1794–1835, pp. 152, 162, 166, 178, 182, 250, 324, 396; D. 77/5/3, f. 45; D. 109/Lowe's char., deeds of 2 and 3 Mar. 1810, 1 Jan. 1813; Nat. Soc. *2nd Ann. Rep.* (1814), 134–6.
[18] *Educ. of Poor Digest,* H.C. 224, p. 866 (1819), ix (2); *Educ. Enq. Abstract,* 880; White, *Dir. Staffs.* (1834), 96, 156.
[19] Nat. Soc. *Inquiry, 1846–7,* Staffs. 6–7.
[20] Below (Frog Lane boys' sch.).
[21] Para. based on S.R.O., D. 4566/99, acct. bk. of Frog Lane boys' sch. 1809–81; Nat. Soc. *2nd Ann. Rep.* (1814), 133–5.
[22] For Jane Gastrell see above, manor (lay estates: Stowe House and Stowe Hill).
[23] *Gent. Mag.* lxxxvi (1), 275; A. Bell, *Madras School* (1808), 96, 98, 211.
[24] *Staffs. Advertiser,* 29 Feb. 1812.
[25] *Some Acct. of Services of Sir Chas. Oakeley, Bt.,* ed. H. Oakeley (priv. print. 1829), 123–4 (copy in W.S.L.); *D.N.B.*

s.v. Oakeley, Chas.; R. and C. C. Southey, *Life of Bell* (1844), i. 135 n.
[26] S.R.O., D. 4566/99, acct. bk. 1809–81.
[27] Ibid. Frog Lane sch. managers' min. bk. 1833–40, 5 Feb. and 7 May 1838.
[28] Ibid. 4 July 1836, 13 Jan. 1840.
[29] Ibid. managers' min. bk. 1840–58, 5 Feb. 1844.
[30] Ibid. 21 July 1842, 10 May, 13 June, and 12 July 1843, 4 Mar. and 1 Apr. 1844, 5 and 22 Feb. 1849.
[31] Ibid. 25 Apr., 14 Sept., and 8 Dec. 1849, 14 Apr. 1851; S.R.O., D. 812/3/126–8; *Staffs. Advertiser,* 16 Mar. 1850, p. 4.
[32] S.R.O., D. 4566/99, managers' min. bk. 1840–58, 4 Feb. and 3 Mar. 1856.
[33] Ibid. acct. bk. 1809–81, printed circular at end.
[34] *Staffs. Endowed Chars.* 84.
[35] Log bk. 1869–98 (at Nether Stowe sch.), p. 2; S.R.O., D. 4566/99, acct. bk. 1809–81, 30 Dec. 1871.
[36] Log bk. 1869–98, pp. 60, 77, 91–2, 96–9, 102; S.R.O., D. 4566/99, managers' min. bk. 1872–97, 9 June, 12 July, 31 Aug., 3 Sept. and 23 Oct. 1877; acct. bk. 1809–81, accts. for 1877–8.

tributions.[37] The buildings, however, were inadequate: the school was closed in 1913 and the boys were moved to a new Church of England Central school in the same street.[38]

St. Mary's schools, Sandford Street. An infants' school was established by subscription in 1825 in a new schoolroom in Sandford Street west of Trunkfield brook.[39] It was still there in 1834[40] but was probably closed when the former parish workhouse, further east in the same street, was converted into a parochial school for St. Mary's in or shortly after 1841. The new school seems originally to have been intended for girls and infants, but by 1844 boys were admitted. In 1851 there were schools for boys, girls, and infants, with a master, two mistresses, and an attendance of over 200.[41] By 1860 the schools were for girls and infants only.[42] In 1863 the children were moved to the schoolroom of the former diocesan training school in Pool Walk.[43]

British school. A British school was established in Sandford Street in 1827 and later that year had *c.* 60 pupils, who were taught the elements. It was supported by subscriptions and fees of 3*d.* a week. It still existed in 1830.[44]

St. Chad's, Stowe, C.E. (Controlled) primary school, St. Michael Road, formerly *Stowe Street Endowed school*. In 1833 Frances Furnivall of Stowe Hill built a school in Stowe Street and employed a mistress to teach poor children on the lines advanced by Samuel Wilderspin, a pioneer of the infant-school system. In 1843 she conveyed in trust the schoolhouse, a stable converted to house two schoolmistresses, a playground and 1½ a. adjacent, and £1,000 stock. The trustees were to elect up to 150 children from St. Mary's parish and from the city part of the parishes of St. Michael and St. Chad, to be admitted from the age of two. There were to be two classes: one for boys and girls under 8, paying 1*d.* a week, the other for girls aged 8–15, paying 2*d.* Teaching was to be Anglican.[45] In 1851 there were *c.* 120 pupils.[46] From 1855 the school was subject to government inspection. A classroom was added in 1882.[47] Average attendance was *c.* 90 in the later 1880s but was over 130 by 1900.[48] Stowe became a junior mixed and infants' school in 1921.[49]

The Second World War halted plans to close the school, but the school building remained dilapidated and overcrowded.[50] In 1950 the school took controlled status.[51] It was still overcrowded in 1953, when there were 161 on the roll.[52] An extension was added in the late 1950s.[53] The school moved into new buildings in St. Michael Road in 1974, and the Stowe Street buildings were taken over by the Lichfield Educational Assessment Centre. In 1989 they housed Stowe Special Unit.[54]

St. Joseph's R.C. (Aided) primary school, Cherry Orchard. Concerts of sacred music at the Roman Catholic chapel were advertised in 1827 to help raise money for schooling poor children of the congregation. In 1841 there was no day or Sunday school at the church but the priest, John Kirk, paid for the education of a few children in Lichfield and Tamworth. A school was built at Holy Cross church, Chapel Lane, in 1844. It was a girls' school, with a mistress, in 1850. In 1850–1 an average of 20 Sunday school pupils attended Sunday morning services at Holy Cross.[55] The school seems subsequently to have lapsed.[56] There was a day school at the church by 1872.[57] In 1875 a certificated mistress was appointed and the school, St. Joseph's, came under government inspection. Later that year an evening school was added; its subsequent history is unknown. An assistant mistress was appointed in 1883. In the earlier 1890s the school had an average attendance of 70 or 80. Non-Catholics were attending the school by the late 1880s, and of 95 children in May 1899 only 39 were Catholics.[58] Hugh McCarten, priest at Lichfield 1882–1911, extended the school premises, largely at his own expense.[59]

In the 1920s and 1930s the school had an average attendance of 100–110.[60] It had two rooms: a schoolroom of 1899 adjoining the church, and a room for infants in the church.[61] It became a primary school in 1948. In 1955 the infants were moved to a room in the new parish hall. They remained there until 1958, when the first stage of a new school in Cherry Orchard was opened. From then until 1972 the school was on two separate sites. There were 165 on the roll in 1966 and 192 in 1969. The Cherry Orchard buildings were extended in 1966 and 1972; later in 1972 the Holy Cross premises

[37] Log bk. 1869–98, pp. 66, 125, 127–8, 149, 158, 162, 178–80, 185, 251; log bk. 1898–1913 (at Nether Stowe sch.), pp. 52, 56; S.R.O., D. 4566/99, min. bk. 1872–97, 17 and 30 July 1891.
[38] Log. bk. 1898–1913, pp. 119–20, 164, 182, 225; S.R.O., D. 4566/99, Lichfield Group Managers' min. bk. 1910–12, pp. 4–5, 10–11.
[39] W.S.L., transcr. diary of Anne Bagot, p. 47; S.R.O., D. 615/M/3/7; S.R.O., D. (W.) 1851/6/6, p. 60.
[40] White, *Dir. Staffs.* (1834), 96.
[41] S.R.O., D. 812/3/129; L.J.R.O., D. 88/deed of 23 Apr. 1845; L.J.R.O., B/A/15/Lichfield, St. Mary, no. 380; Wesley, *Dir. Burton* (1844), 28; White, *Dir. Staffs.* (1851), 508, 521.
[42] *P.O. Dir. Staffs.* (1860).
[43] Below (St. Mary's sch., Pool Walk).
[44] *Lichfield Mercury*, 14 Dec. 1827; 8 Jan. 1830.
[45] L.J.R.O., D. 52/1/3; D. 52/1/5 (summarized in *Staffs. Endowed Chars.* 85); White, *Dir. Staffs.* (1834), 96; above, manor (lay estates: Stowe House and Stowe Hill). For Wilderspin see *D.N.B.*
[46] White, *Dir. Staffs.* (1851), 508.
[47] S.R.O., D. 4566/99, spring-file, copy deed of 6 Mar.

1843, annexe of 2 Mar. 1855; *Lichfield Mercury*, 26 Feb. 1960, p. 9. [48] *Kelly's Dir. Staffs.* (1888; 1900).
[49] *Staffs. C.C. Record for 1921*, 223–4.
[50] L.J.R.O., D. 52/1, letters of 15 Apr. 1948, 20 Jan. 1949; D. 52/1/1, 21 Oct. 1936–21 May 1941 *passim*; D. 52/1/3; *Lichfield Mercury*, 26 Feb. 1960, p. 9.
[51] L.J.R.O., D. 52/1, letters of 28 Oct. and 14 Nov. 1950.
[52] Ibid. D. 52/1/3.
[53] *Lichfield Mercury*, 24 Sept. 1971, p. 6.
[54] S.R.O., CEH/84/2, Apr. and Nov. 1974; inf. from Staffs. C.C. Educ. Dept.
[55] *Staffs. Studies*, ed. P. Morgan (Keele, 1987), 134, and sources cited there; *Slater's Nat. and Com. Dir.* (1850), Staffs. p. 33.
[56] No school is mentioned in dirs. of the 1860s.
[57] *P.O. Dir. Staffs.* (1872).
[58] Log bk. 1875–1900 (at the school), pp. 1, 10, 118, 207, 303, 426, 483.
[59] Ibid. pp. 369, 486, 490, 495; B.A.A., B 12435, B 12447, B 12482; *Staffs. Advertiser*, 23 Sept. 1911, p. 9.
[60] Log bk. 1927–75 (at the school), prelim. pages.
[61] Lindley, 'Hist. of Educ.' p. 160.

were closed and some of the pupils of St. Joseph's were moved to SS. Peter and Paul primary school, Dimbles Hill.[62]

Christ Church C.E. (Controlled) primary school, Christchurch Lane. By 1850 Richard Hinckley and his wife, the founders of Christ Church, were supporting a Sunday school in a schoolroom which they had built on the south side of Christchurch Lane. Traditionally the school dates from 1847, the year of the church's consecration.[63] In 1861 Richard gave the schoolroom, and his wife £1,100 stock, to endow an Anglican day school, independent of government. Pupils aged 3–14 were to be taught the elements, the girls knitting and plain sewing. They were to attend Christ Church twice every Sunday. Fees of 1d. or 2d. a week were to be charged according to age.[64] A teacher's house was bought in 1875 with help from the National Society, to which the school became affiliated.[65] From 1877, contrary to its founders' intentions, it received a government grant.[66] Classrooms were added in 1885 and 1891, but the building was condemned in 1908.[67] Nevertheless it remained in use until 1910, when a mixed and infants' school for 252 children was opened on the north side of Christchurch Lane with the help of the Hinckley Trust and the Conduit Lands trustees.[68] The old buildings were converted into private houses.[69] Christ Church became a junior mixed and infants' school in 1913[70] and took controlled status in 1950.[71] New classrooms were added in the late 1950s and an assembly hall in 1967.[72]

St. Michael's C.E. (Controlled) primary school, Sturgeons Hill. In 1858 an infants' school was opened in a converted barn opposite the gates of St. Michael's churchyard. Within a year there were 80 pupils. A night school also taught young men and boys the elements twice a week in winter; in 1859–60 it had 40 pupils.[73] A new infants' and Sunday school was opened nearby in Church Lane (later Church Street) in 1860; money was raised by subscription, and there were grants from government and the National Society. The building, Elizabethan in style, comprised a large schoolroom and a classroom.

There was a bell tower with a small room for the parochial library.[74] A house was bought for the mistress in 1862. In 1869, with grants from government and the National Society, a boys' school was built on a site adjoining the building of 1860, which became a girls' and infants' school.[75]

By the later 1880s the schools were overcrowded.[76] Thomas Rowley (d. 1863), a Lichfield physician, left £500, received in 1887, for new buildings,[77] which were in fact paid for in 1889 by A. P. Allsopp, M.P. for Taunton, a former parishioner.[78]

The boys' and girls' schools were merged in 1891–2 to form a mixed school with senior and junior departments.[79] Average attendance *c.* 1899 was 160 mixed and 107 infants.[80] In 1921 St. Michael's became a junior mixed and infants' school and in 1930 it had 291 on its books.[81] It took controlled status in 1950.[82] New buildings in Sturgeons Hill were opened in 1966, but some of the children were still using the Church Street buildings in 1974.[83]

Ragged school. In 1858 or 1859 T. A. Bangham, the incumbent of Christ Church, rented two or three adjoining cottages in Lower Sandford Street, and by 1861 had converted one of them into a schoolhouse, where he kept a night school for 30 children. He and his successor, W. H. H. Fairclough, ran a mixed ragged school there, taught by a mistress, until 1878 or 1879.[84]

St. Mary's school, Pool Walk. The girls and infants of St. Mary's schools in Sandford Street moved into the schoolroom of the former diocesan training school in Pool Walk in 1863. By 1869 attendance sometimes exceeded 200, and in that year a classroom was added. In 1876, as numbers continued to rise, the infants were moved to a new school in Wade Street.[85] In 1897 there was room for all the girls on the school's books, but in 1904–5 and 1906–7 attendance was over 170 and the building was once more overcrowded.[86] In 1913 Pool Walk became a higher standard girls' school. The girls were moved to the Central school in 1921, and Pool Walk became an infants' school.[87] It took con-

[62] Log bk. 1927–75, pp. 52–3, 63, 69, 76, 132–3, 172, 226–7, 238–9; *Lichfield Mercury*, 18 July 1958, p. 1.
[63] S.R.O., D. 4566/C, copy conveyance 9 Mar. 1910; *P.O. Dir. Staffs.* (1850); *Lichfield Mercury*, 17 Mar. 1972, p. 8.
[64] S.R.O., D. 4566/C, copy conveyance 9 Mar. 1910.
[65] Ibid. Christ Church terrier 1884, pp. 8–9.
[66] *Staffs. Endowed Chars.* 83.
[67] S.R.O., D. 4566/C, case for counsel's opinion 1908; ibid. valuation of sch. premises 9 Dec. 1909; *Kelly's Dir. Staffs.* (1896).
[68] S.R.O., D. 4566/99, Lichfield Group Managers' min. bk. 1910–12, p. 79; *Staffs. Advertiser*, 8 Oct. 1910, p. 7; Laithwaite, *Conduit Lands Trust*, 56.
[69] *Lichfield Mercury*, 17 Mar. 1972, p. 9.
[70] Ibid. 12 Apr. 1968, p. 13.
[71] S.R.O., CEH/85/1, 6 June 1950.
[72] Ibid. 2 Dec. 1958, 7 July 1959; CEH/85/2, 19 June 1967; *Lichfield Mercury*, 6 Feb. 1987, p. 24.
[73] *Annals of Dioc. of Lichfield, 1859* (Newcastle-under-Lyme, 1859), 62–3; *Staffs. Advertiser*, 14 Apr. 1860, p. 7.
[74] *Staffs. Advertiser*, 9 June 1860, p. 4.
[75] Ibid. 2 Aug. 1862, p. 4; L.J.R.O., D. 27/7/2; S.R.O., CEH/88/1, 25 Aug. 1865–8 June 1869 *passim*.

[76] S.R.O., CEH/88/1, newspaper cutting of 13 May 1887; *Kelly's Dir. Staffs.* (1888).
[77] S.R.O., CEH/88/1, 20 Apr. 1868, 8 June 1869; S.R.O., Charities Index; *Staffs. Endowed Chars.* 84–5.
[78] S.R.O., CEH/88/1, 14 Dec. 1886–3 June 1889 *passim*; L.J.R.O., D. 27/7/3; *Staffs. Advertiser*, 15 June 1889, p. 7.
[79] S.R.O., CEH/88/1, 20 Nov. 1891, 11 Feb. and 13 Apr. 1892.
[80] *Kelly's Dir. Staffs.* (1900).
[81] S.R.O., D. 4566/99, Lichfield Group Managers' min. bk. 1924–34, p. 162; *Staffs. C.C. Record for 1921*, 223–4.
[82] S.R.O., CEH/88/3, 6 July 1950.
[83] Ibid. CEH/88/3 and 4.
[84] P.R.O., RG 9/1972; L.J.R.O., D. 103/2/4, p. 22; D. 103/3/2, accts. from 1858–9 to 1879–80; *P.O. Dir. Staffs.* (1864; 1868; 1872); *Eggington's Lichfield Almanack* (1875); *Eggington & Brown's Lichfield Almanack* (1877), 28.
[85] Log bk. 1863–78 (at Nether Stowe sch.), pp. 20, 242, 257–9, 261–2, 356, 362, 385, 394, 409.
[86] Log bk. 1878–1904 (at Nether Stowe sch.), p. 360; log bk. 1904–21 (at Nether Stowe sch.), pp. 21, 48, 52.
[87] Ibid. 1904–21, pp. 117–18, 210; S.R.O., D. 4566/99, Lichfield Group Managers' min. bk. 1916–24, pp. 176–8.

trolled status in 1951 and was closed in 1981. The building was used by Lichfield cathedral school from 1981 to 1989.[88]

Beacon Street school, later *Springfield infants' school*. In 1871 St. Chad's parish decided to raise a voluntary rate for a parish school, and in 1875 Lord Lichfield gave a site in Beacon Street; Charlotte Stripling, a parishioner, paid for a schoolroom, and the school was opened in 1876. In 1881 a classroom was added. Part of the site was let, providing a small income.[89] By 1901 the school was for girls and infants and had 93 on its books.[90] In 1913 it became an infants' school.[91] It took controlled status in 1950.[92] The name was changed in 1958, and the school was closed in 1982.[93] A private nursery school took over the building in 1988.[94]

St. Mary's infants' school, Wade Street. In 1876 the infants at the Pool Walk school were transferred to a new schoolroom in Wade Street. Average attendance was over 150 in the later 1880s but had declined by almost a third by 1900. The school was closed in 1913, and the children were moved to the new Central school in Frog Lane. The Wade Street building remained in use as a parish room.[95]

Friary school, Eastern Avenue, formerly *Lichfield high school for girls, the Friary school*, and *Friary Grange school*.[96] In 1892 a committee led by Sophia Lonsdale opened Lichfield high school for girls in rented premises in Market Street, with two mistresses, a pupil-teacher, and 15 pupils. The school, a fee-paying Anglican establishment, took day girls and boarders aged eight[97] and above, and there was a kindergarten for boys and girls up to eight. By 1896 there were 60 pupils and eight teachers,[98] and that year the school moved to Yeomanry House in St. John Street.

By 1907 there were 89 pupils, but in that year the headmistress left to start a school at Derby, taking with her several teachers and nearly all the boarders, leaving only 66 pupils; in 1911 there were only 47, all day girls. From 1912 the school received an annual grant from the county council. In 1916 St. John's school, another girls' private school in Lichfield, merged with it to become a maintained secondary school with 99 pupils. By 1919 there were 169 pupils and 10 full-time mistresses. In 1918 a staff hostel was opened in Beacon Street, and in 1919 an adjacent house, Beaconhurst, was acquired as an extra boarding house.

In 1920 the Friary estate was given to the city. The city council let the Friary building to the county council for use by the high school, which moved into it in 1921. Beaconhurst became the staff hostel, and the boarders moved to a rented house, Nether Beacon. In 1925 the county council bought the Friary and some of its land. The school was renamed the Friary school in 1926 and stopped taking boarders. A large new building, including an assembly hall, a refectory, laboratories, and an art room, was added in 1928.[99] During the 1930s numbers increased both in the main school and in the preparatory department, which took boys and girls up to 10.

Under the 1944 Act the school became a secondary grammar school for girls. The preparatory department was closed in 1948, making the Friary a single-sex school. By 1954 there were 415 pupils. A boarding house for *c.* 30 girls was opened in Westgate House, Beacon Street, in 1953.

In 1971 the school became a mixed comprehensive. The first stage of a large school in Eastern Avenue, named Friary Grange, was opened in 1973 and the older pupils were moved to it. The buildings included a sports centre serving both the school and the city. Westgate House was closed in 1981, and the school once more ceased to take boarders. It remained split between two sites until 1987, when the Friary site was closed and the Eastern Avenue school was renamed the Friary.[1] The western end of the buildings on the original Friary site became Lichfield College in 1987.[2] The eastern end was being converted into a public library and record office in 1989.

Central school, later *Lichfield Church of England secondary school*, Frog Lane. A school for 270 boys and 140 infants was opened in 1913 in Frog Lane, replacing the existing Frog Lane boys' school and the Wade Street infants' school. It consisted of a marching hall for infants and eight classrooms. The boys' department was for senior boys only. The infants' department was closed in 1921, and the Central school became a mixed senior school. In 1925–6 average attendance was 330. From 1928 age, not standard, governed admission, children being admitted at 11. From 1931 the school took the older children from the village schools at Elmhurst and Weeford. The building was, however, unsatisfactory as a senior school: it was overcrowded and lacked an assembly hall and rooms for practical or scientific work. The school had no playing field.[3] Under the 1944 Act it became a secondary modern school. Despite extensions in 1948 and 1950 it remained overcrowded; in the mid 1950s some classes were being held in buildings elsewhere in the city. In 1964 the 350 pupils were

[88] S.R.O., CEH/87/1, 28 Nov. 1951; CEH/87/2, 8 July 1981.
[89] L.J.R.O., D. 39/3/1, annotated copy of deed of 1 July 1875; *Staffs. Advertiser*, 19 Aug. 1871, p. 4; *Staffs. Endowed Chars.* 82–3; C. E. Graham, *Memoir of Rev. John Graham* (1899), 41.
[90] L.J.R.O., D. 93/2, p. 1.
[91] Ibid. pp. 139–40.
[92] S.R.O., CEH/84/1, 6 Oct. 1950.
[93] L.J.R.O., D. 93/3, prelim. pages; *Lichfield Mercury*, 23 July 1982, p. 1.
[94] *Lichfield Mercury*, 10 June 1988, p. 15.
[95] St. Mary's girls' and infants' sch. log bk. 1863 78 (at

Nether Stowe sch.), p. 448; S.R.O., D. 3573/Lichfield 2, p. 85; S.R.O., D. 4566/99, Lichfield Group Managers' min. bk. 1910–12, p. 85; *Kelly's Dir. Staffs.* (1888; 1896; 1900); *Staffs. Advertiser*, 5 Apr. 1913, p. 10.
[96] Account based on H. Mullins, *Hist. of Friary School, Lichfield* (Rugeley, 1981); inf. from Staffs. C.C. Educ. Dept.
[97] *Staffs. Advertiser*, 5 Dec. 1891, p. 1.
[98] Ibid. 18 July 1896, p. 7.
[99] Above, plate 38.
[1] *Lichfield Mercury*, 18 Sept. 1987, p. 1.
[2] Below (further and adult. educ.).
[3] Log bk. 1913 38 (at Nether Stowe sch.), pp. 5–6, 49, 105, 149, 190 2; *Staffs. Advertiser*, 5 Apr. 1913, p. 10.

transferred to the new Nether Stowe school and the Frog Lane building was closed.[4]

Willows county primary school, Anglesey Road, formerly *Curborough Road county primary school*,[5] was opened in former R.A.F. buildings off Curborough Road in 1948.[6] It was a junior and infants' school until 1957, and thereafter an infants' school. It was named Willows in 1957 or 1958. The children were transferred to Chadsmead infants' school in 1961. A new junior and infants' school was then established in the Willows premises. New buildings were opened in 1970 replacing the earlier accommodation. They were extended in 1974 and a nursery unit was added in 1976.

Chadsmead county junior school, Friday Acre, was opened in 1956.

Kings Hill school, Kings Hill Road, was opened in 1958 as a mixed secondary modern school. It stood near King Edward VI grammar school and shared the same playing fields.[7] The schools were merged in 1971, the Kings Hill building becoming the Bader Hall of the new King Edward VI comprehensive school.[8]

Chadsmead county infants' school, Friday Acre, was opened in 1961, adjoining the junior school.

Nether Stowe county high school, St. Chad's Road, a mixed comprehensive secondary school, was opened in 1964 and substantially extended in 1969.[9]

Scotch Orchard county primary school, Stowe Hill, was opened in 1964[10] and extended in 1974.

Charnwood county primary school, Purcell Avenue, was opened in 1970 as junior and infants' schools sharing a single site.[11] They were merged in 1981.

SS. Peter and Paul R.C. (Aided) primary school, Dimbles Hill, was opened in 1972.[12]

FURTHER AND ADULT EDUCATION.
Itinerant lecturers offering courses of subscription lectures on astronomy, chemistry, and popular science visited Lichfield in the later 18th and earlier 19th century.[13] Lectures on agricultural chemistry and on the telegraph drew large audiences at the Corn Exchange in the 1850s.[14] The Revd. J. G. Cumming, headmaster of the grammar school 1855–8, gave courses of free public lectures on science.[15]

A mechanics' institute recorded in 1837 may have been the mutual improvement society which in 1850 was said to have failed because it became 'a political organ'.[16] A Lichfield Reading and Mutual Instruction Society was established in 1850 to provide young men with 'economical' means of self-improvement. For 10s. a year it offered them a reading room, a circulating library, lectures, and evening classes. In 1851 it had *c.* 140 members and over 700 books. It was dissolved in 1859, and its books were given to the newly opened free library in Bird Street.[17]

A similar body, the Lichfield Working Men's Association, had been formed in 1854. During its first 15 months 375 men joined it. By 1856 it had rooms in Tamworth Street and was holding classes in singing, reading and writing, and English history. There were lectures, some open to the public, and a library of *c.* 350 books.[18] The committee of management, made up of clergy and gentry, organized public readings, concerts, exhibitions, and fêtes.[19] An early attempt to form a drawing class under a master from Birmingham School of Art was apparently unsuccessful,[20] but subsequently classes were held, and in 1868 several members passed Society of Arts examinations.[21] By then, however, the association's lectures were usually poorly attended,[22] and in 1888 there were only *c.* 30 members, the association depending financially on subscriptions from middle-class supporters. It was amalgamated that year with St. Mary's Men's Society, in existence by 1878.[23] Its failure may have been because some people believed it to be politically biased.[24] The St. Mary's society, renamed the Scott Institute in 1898 in memory of Archdeacon M. H. Scott, vicar of St. Mary's 1878–94,[25] kept the Tamworth Street premises until 1920. It was then replaced by the City Institute, which was non-parochial and non-denominational, with rooms in the former Corn Exchange. The institute was dissolved in the early 1970s.[26]

[4] Log bk. 1938–60 (at Nether Stowe sch.), pp. 99–100, 113, 126, 146, 193–4, 215–16, 219–20; Staffs. C. C. Record for 1933, 731–2; Lichfield Mercury, 7 Jan. 1949, p. 2; 3 July 1964, p. 1.
[5] Rest of section based on S.R.O., Survey of School Recs. 1979; inf. from Staffs. C.C. Educ. Dept.
[6] Lichfield Mercury, 7 Jan. 1949, p. 2.
[7] Ibid. 5 Sept. 1958, p. 1; Staffs. C.C. Building for Educ. in Staffs. 1950 to 1963 (1964), 15.
[8] M. Stanton, 'Educ. Development in Lichfield' (TS., 1972), chap. 4 (copy in Lichfield Libr.). The building of the former grammar sch. was named Johnson Hall. Group Capt. Douglas Bader had officially opened Kings Hill sch. in 1959: Lichfield Mercury, 3 July 1959, p. 1.
[9] Inf. from the sch.
[10] Lichfield Mercury, 4 Sept. 1964, p. 1.
[11] Ibid. 17 Apr. 1970, p. 1; 30 Oct. 1970, p. 1.
[12] Ibid. 1 Sept. 1972, p. 11.
[13] W.S.L., H.M. 24/3, 27 Apr. 1773; Poetical Works of Anna Seward, ed. W. Scott (Edinburgh, 1810), iii. 319;

Lichfield Mercury, 4 Apr., 6 June, 10 Oct. 1817; 16, 23, and 30 Jan., 5 Feb. 1824.
[14] Staffs. Advertiser, 25 June 1853, p. 4; 12 Feb. 1859, p. 4.
[15] Ibid. 5 May 1855, p. 4; 23 May 1857, p. 4; 1 May 1858, p. 4; V.C.H. Staffs. vi. 160–1.
[16] Staffs. Advertiser, 3 June 1837; 16 Mar. 1850, p. 6.
[17] Ibid. 19 Jan. 1850, p. 4; 16 Mar. 1850, p. 6; 14 May 1859, p. 4; White, Dir. Staffs. (1851), 504.
[18] Staffs. Advertiser, 19 Jan. 1856, p. 2.
[19] Ibid. 9 Jan. 1858, p. 4; 6 Feb. 1858, p. 4; 13 Mar. 1858, p. 4; 19 Feb. 1859, p. 4; 22 Feb. 1868, p. 7; C. E. Graham, Memoir of Rev. John Graham (1899), 54–5.
[20] Staffs. Advertiser, 19 Jan. 1856, p. 2; 9 Jan. 1858, p. 4.
[21] Ibid. 18 July 1868, p. 4; 1 Aug. 1868, p. 7.
[22] Ibid. 22 Feb. 1868, p. 7.
[23] Ibid. 26 Oct. 1878, p. 4; 26 May 1888, p. 7; 30 June 1888, p. 5.   [24] Ibid. 30 Sept. 1882, p. 4.
[25] Lomax's Red Bk. (1899), 14. For Scott see above, public services (medical services: Victoria hosp.).
[26] Lichfield Mercury, 1 Oct. 1920, p. 8; 30 Apr. 1971, p. 13.

In 1873 there was a mutual improvement society attached to the Congregational chapel in Wade Street. It was dissolved in 1877. A similar body was formed at the chapel in 1884, but no more is known of it.[27] A Wesleyan Mutual Improvement Guild was established in 1892;[28] no more is known of it.

Society of Arts examinations were held at Lichfield in 1868, and in 1874 there were newly formed art classes in the city, run in connexion with the Science and Art Department.[29] Science classes were added in 1875.[30] Classes were held at St. Michael's school and the subscription library in Market Street.[31] An Art School building 'in the half-timbered style' was erected by public subscription in 1882 to the design of H. E. Lavender of Walsall. It stood on the corner of Dam Street and Pool Walk, with the school of art occupying rooms on the ground floor. A large room on the first floor was let to the subscription library. In 1883 the first art classes were held in the building.[32]

By early 1891 the city council had adopted the Technical Instruction Act, and from 1892 university extension lectures were given at the Art School.[33] In 1896 the city council bought the building from the school's trustees with money provided by the Conduit Lands Trust, which also provided an annual subsidy for the school.[34] In 1898–9 what had become Lichfield Science, Art, and Technical School enrolled 132 students for evening classes.[35] The building was still generally known as the School of Art,[36] but by 1913 there were only seven art students and two art classes a week. Most of the evening classes dealt with general subjects such as elementary science and many of the pupils were schoolchildren.[37] In 1916 the building was requisitioned by the army, and until 1919 classes were held in the public library and museum and in the Central school, Frog Lane. In 1938 there were almost 300 students, including 75–90 attending art classes.[38] The institution became Lichfield Art, Commercial, and Technical School in 1940 and Lichfield Evening Institute and School of Art, with two separate principals, in 1946.[39] The building was abandoned in 1950 because of

subsidence and was demolished in 1954. The school moved temporarily to Frog Lane and in 1952 to new premises in Cherry Orchard.[40] It became Lichfield School of Art and Evening Institute, under a single principal, in 1963, Lichfield School of Art and Adult Education in 1982, and Lichfield College in 1985. In 1987 it moved into the western end of the former Friary school.[41]

PRIVATE SCHOOLS AND SPECIALIST TEACHERS. Middle-class day and boarding schools began to appear in the city in the mid 18th century. There were generally about 7–10 open at any one time between c. 1820 and the early 1870s, declining by 1900 to 2, the average during most of the 20th century.[42] In the 19th century their pupils were generally the sons and daughters of shopkeepers, tradesmen, and farmers.[43]

Some, such as the earliest known girls' boarding school, advertised by Abra Maria Harris in 1755 as about to be established in Bore Street,[44] were ephemeral or stillborn. Most did not outlive their founder's death, retirement, departure from Lichfield, or bankruptcy. Among the longer lived was a girls' school established in the Close by Mrs. Sarah Eborall in 1830 and transferred to a house in Lombard Street by her daughter Eliza Eborall in 1849.[45] Marian Evans (the novelist George Eliot) visited two of her cousins boarding at the school in 1840 and two of her nieces in 1859.[46] In or shortly before 1863 the school was taken over by the Misses Crockett, who continued it until the 1890s.[47]

The longest lived private school seems to have been one established as a boys' school in Lombard Street by Thomas Newbolt before 1841.[48] Newbolt moved to Wade Street c. 1845,[49] and by 1855 his classical, commercial, and mathematical academy had passed to Weldon Underwood, who was running it in 1862.[50] He was succeeded soon afterwards by W. S. Metcalfe, who kept the school in 1872.[51] By 1875 the master of what had become known as Meredith House school was E. H. Reynolds, minister of

[27] L.J.R.O., D. 112/1/1, 2 Oct. 1873; *Staffs. Advertiser*, 28 Oct. 1876, p. 7; *Lichfield Mercury*, 3 Oct. 1884, p. 4.
[28] *Lichfield Mercury*, 7 Oct. 1892, p. 8.
[29] *Staffs. Advertiser*, 18 July 1868, p. 4; 1 Aug. 1868, p. 7; *Lichfield Ind. and Loan Exhibition, 1874. A Guide.* (copy in W.S.L.).
[30] *Staffs. Advertiser*, 28 Oct. 1876, p. 7.
[31] Ibid. 2 Sept. 1882, p. 4; *P.O. Dir. Staffs.* (1876).
[32] *Staffs. Advertiser*, 2 Sept. 1882, p. 4; 23 Dec. 1882, p. 5; 27 Jan. 1883, p. 4; *Kelly's Dir. Staffs.* (1884), wrongly giving date of building as 1880; plaque on site.
[33] L.J.R.O., D. 127/council min. bk. 1888–91, p. 240; 1891–4, pp. 46, 141–2; *Lichfield Mercury*, 9 Sept. 1892, p. 4; *Lomax's Red Bk.* (1893), 5.
[34] L.J.R.O., D. 127/council min. bk. 1894–7, pp. 224–7; *Lichfield Mercury*, 30 Oct. 1896, p. 4; 6 Nov. 1896, p. 4; Laithwaite, *Conduit Lands Trust*, 56.
[35] L.J.R.O., D. 127/council min. bk. 1897–9, p. 260; *Lomax's Red Bk.* (1899), 13.
[36] See e.g. *Kelly's Dir. Staffs.* (1916).
[37] *Staffs. Advertiser*, 5 Apr. 1913, p. 10; *Lichfield Mercury*, 16 Sept. 1938, p. 2; 18 July 1958, p. 1.
[38] S.R.O., D. 4566/99, Lichfield Group Managers' min. bk. 1913–16, p. 257; 1916–24, pp. 2, 6, 10, 51, 78; *Lichfield Mercury*, 16 Sept. 1938, p. 2.
[39] *Lichfield City Council Yr. Bk. 1940*, 45; *1941*, 45; *1946*,

43; *1947*, 45 (copies in L.J.R.O., D. 33).
[40] *Lichfield Mercury*, 6 Jan. 1950, p. 4; 3 Feb. 1950, p. 3; 10 Oct. 1952, p. 5; 29 Oct. 1954, p. 4.
[41] *Lichfield City Council Yr. Bk. 1963–4*, 41; Staffs. C.C. Educ. Cttee. *Lichfield Coll. Prospectus, 1988–1989*, 2–3.
[42] e.g. Parson and Bradshaw, *Staffs. Dir.* (1818), 170, 188; Pigot, *Dir. Birmingham* (1829), 84; White, *Dir. Staffs.* (1834), 156; Pigot, *Nat. Com. Dir.* (1841), Staffs. p. 28; *P.O. Dir. Staffs.* (1850 and edns. to 1876); *Kelly's Dir. Staffs.* (1880 and edns. to 1940).
[43] e.g. *Rep. Schs. Inquiry Com. vol. xv* [3966–XIV], p. 427, H.C. (1867–8), xxviii (12).
[44] *Aris's Birmingham Gaz.* 6, 13, and 20 Jan. 1755.
[45] *Lichfield Mercury*, 1 Jan. 1830; *Staffs. Advertiser*, 30 June 1849, p. 1.
[46] L. and E. Hanson, *Marian Evans & George Eliot*, 32, 216; G. S. Haight, *George Eliot*, 304.
[47] *Staffs. Advertiser*, 11 July 1863, p. 8; *P.O. Dir. Staffs.* (1864 and edns. to 1876); *Kelly's Dir. Staffs.* (1880 and edns. to 1892).
[48] Pigot, *Nat. Com. Dir.* (1841), Staffs. p. 28.
[49] *Staffs. Advertiser*, 26 Sept. 1857, p. 1, stating that Wade St. sch. had been established 'upwards of twelve years'.
[50] Ibid. 13 Jan. 1855, p. 1; 5 July 1862, p. 1.
[51] *P.O. Dir. Staffs.* (1864; 1868; 1872).

the Wade Street Congregational chapel.[52] In 1877 he was succeeded by Sylvanus Biggs, who had been master of Minors's school.[53] Biggs ran a preparatory school at Meredith House until c. 1893, when it was taken over by Rose Barry.[54] She kept the school until her death in 1946, running it as a girls' day and boarding school, with a kindergarten and a preparatory department for boys.[55] The school remained at Meredith House as a girls', boys', and preparatory school until c. 1955. It then moved to no. 28 St. John Street where, as St. John's preparatory school, it remained in the late 1980s.[56]

The earliest known writing master in the city seems to have been Gregory King, who taught writing, palaeography, and arithmetic there in 1669, besides working as a herald painter.[57] John Matlock, a scrivener living in Sandford Street in 1695, was running 'a great writing-school' there in 1714 and also worked as a surveyor and cartographer. He died in 1720, and the school was continued by his brother Robert and Robert's son Richard, and later by Robert's son Matthew, described in 1749 as a writing master. John or Robert added a schoolroom to the family's house in Sandford Street, where Matthew was still living in 1761. In 1748 the house was said to be very much out of repair, and the school may already have been in decline. No more is known of it.[58] Richard Kidger, who opened an academy in 1827 and was still running it in 1844, seems to have considered himself to be primarily a writing master.[59] An unnamed teacher of penmanship apparently had great success when he visited Lichfield in 1836.[60]

Of drawing masters[61] the only one of distinction was the landscape painter and watercolourist John Glover (1767–1849), who taught at Lichfield with success from 1794 to 1805, his pupils including Henry Salt, the artist and traveller.[62]

Teaching French was the speciality of a girls' boarding school opened in the Close in 1766 by Mr. and Mrs. Latuffière, who had kept a French academy at Reading (Berks.). They had moved to Derby by 1775. Their school was evidently highly regarded.[63] A French officer living on parole in Lichfield taught some of the Darwin and Wedgwood children French in Erasmus Darwin's house in 1779.[64] M. Wahast was teaching French and Italian in 1824,[65] and M. and Mme Suingle, natives of Tours, advertised French lessons in 1825.[66] In the later 1840s a Mr. Prochownick taught French and German in Lichfield one day a week.[67]

The earliest dancing teachers are known merely because they taught boys who became famous. Elias Ashmole probably took dancing lessons from a Rowland Osborne, and Johnson had a few lessons.[68] A Mr. Lariviere offered classes in the guildhall in 1780.[69] Some time before 1810 one Webster taught dancing and posture in the room in which Johnson was born.[70] A Mr. Bemetzrieder advertised classes twice a week at the Swan in 1825.[71] In 1856 the Parisienne Mme Apolline Zuingle, professor of dancing and perhaps a relative of the Suingles, settled at Brooke House in Dam Street, and for at least 15 years taught dancing, callisthenics, and drill.[72] Less exotic figures included the Mr. Bennett whose young pupils held a ball at the Talbot in 1823; he was probably the W. B. Bennett who in 1851 worked as a dancing master, piano tuner, newsagent, and county court bailiff.[73]

By the early 16th century some of the lay vicars of the cathedral were supplementing their stipends by giving music lessons, and in the earlier 17th century the organist taught keyboard music.[74] In the 18th and 19th centuries the vicars were well paid and apparently had no financial need to teach,[75] but a few did: Samuel Spofforth gave organ lessons from the 1820s to the 1850s;[76] Mark Allen taught from the late 1840s to the late 1860s and in 1851 was in business with the organist at St. Mary's, selling sheet music and pianos;[77] Samuel Pearsall gave singing lessons from the 1850s to the 1870s.[78] Directories record five music teachers in the city

[52] Eggington's Lichfield Almanack (1875); P.O. Dir. Staffs. (1876).
[53] Staffs. Advertiser, 6 Jan. 1877, p. 1; 5 Jan. 1878, p. 1; above (Minors's sch.).
[54] Kelly's Dir. Staffs. (1892); Lichfield Mercury, 31 Aug. 1894, p. 4; 22 Feb. 1946, p. 5.
[55] Kelly's Dir. Staffs. (1896 and edns. to 1940); Lomax's Red Bk. (1940), 52; Lichfield Mercury, 22 Feb. 1946, p. 5.
[56] City and County of Lichfield Handbk. ed. H. J. Callender (Birmingham, 1951), 49; Lichfield Mercury, 30 Oct. 1987, p. 6; inf. from Mr. R. Shipton, of Hinckley, Birch & Exham, solicitors of Lichfield.
[57] D.N.B.
[58] L.J.R.O., P/C/11, John Matlock (1720); S.R.O., D. 615/D/230/2/15; S.R.O., D. 1778/V/1209, Hen. Rathbone to Fra. Mauries, 15 Nov. 1714; Reade, Johnsonian Gleanings, iii. 87; viii. 35; above, town govt. (govt. from 1548: unreformed corporation).
[59] Lichfield Mercury, 29 Dec. 1826; Pigot, Dir. Birmingham (1829), 84; White, Dir. Staffs. (1834), 156; Pigot, Nat. Com. Dir. (1841), Staffs. p. 28; Wesley, Dir. Burton (1844), 28.
[60] W.S.L., S. 1902/i, f. 65.
[61] e.g. adverts. in Lichfield Mercury, 10 May 1816; 13 July 1827.
[62] D.N.B. s.v. Glover; V.C.H. Leics. iii. 228–9; Letters of Anna Seward (Edinburgh, 1811), v. 194; J. J. Halls, Life and Corresp. of Hen. Salt (1834), i. 14; S.H.C. 1942–3, pp. xlviii–xlix.

[63] L.J.R.O., D. 30/C.A. viii, f. 55v.; P. Laithwaite, 'Palace to Let' (TS. in Samuel Johnson Birthplace Mus.), pp. 60, 100, 106; Aris's Birmingham Gaz. 7 Oct. and 18 Nov. 1765, 20 Jan. 1766; S. Markham, John Loveday of Caversham, 444; Letters of Josiah Wedgwood, ed. K. E. Farrer (priv. print. 1903), ii. 117–18; M. Butler, Maria Edgeworth, 51–2, 55–6.
[64] Letters of Wedgwood, ii. 441–2, 445–6, 449–51, 471.
[65] Lichfield Mercury, 23 July 1824.
[66] Ibid. 23 Sept. 1825.
[67] Staffs. Advertiser, 15 Jan. 1848, p. 1.
[68] Elias Ashmole, ed. C. H. Josten, ii. 313; Reade, Johnsonian Gleanings, x. 48.
[69] Aris's Birmingham Gaz. 13 Mar. 1780.
[70] L.J.R.O., D. 77/20/7, p. 15.
[71] Lichfield Mercury, 11 Feb. 1825.
[72] P.R.O., RG 9/1972; Staffs. Advertiser, 5 July 1856, p. 1; 22 July 1871, p. 1.
[73] Lichfield Mercury, 12 Dec. 1823; White, Dir. Staffs. (1851), 519.
[74] L.J.R.O., D. 30/C.A. iii, f. 124v.; V.C.H. Staffs. iii. 164, 173; Ashmole, ed. Josten, ii. 313.
[75] V.C.H. Staffs. iii. 185–7, 192–3.
[76] Pigot, Dir. Birmingham (1829), 86; Pigot, Nat. Com. Dir. (1841), Staffs. p. 30; White, Dir. Staffs. (1851), 520.
[77] Staffs. Advertiser, 20 Jan. 1849, p. 1; White, Dir. Staffs. (1851), 518–19; P.O. Dir. Staffs. (1868).
[78] P.O. Dir. Staffs. (1850); Staffs. Advertiser, 12 July 1856, p. 1; 11 Jan. 1862, p. 1; 15 July 1871, p. 1.

in 1835, six in 1860, and four in 1876, but from the 1880s only one or two at any one time.[79] They included John Gladman, who gained his musical expertise with yeomanry and militia bands and taught in Lichfield from the mid 1870s until shortly before his death in 1933.[80]

OTHER EDUCATIONAL INSTITU-TIONS. *Workhouse school*, later *Lichfield Child-ren's Homes (Wissage)* and *the Poplars*. From 1837 until 1877 the guardians employed a mis-tress to teach the children living in the union workhouse.[81] Thereafter workhouse children were generally sent to St. Michael's school.[82] By 1896 the workhouse was overcrowded and gov-ernment policy was increasingly in favour of removing children from workhouses.[83] The guardians already boarded out orphans and deserted children,[84] and in 1897 they sent Roman Catholic children to orphanages at Birmingham and Coleshill (Warws.) and all others to the district schools at Wigmore, West Bromwich.[85] In 1904 there were 31 Lichfield union children at Wigmore, but the schools were overcrowded, and in 1905 the union was asked to remove its children. The boys were placed in a rented house in Tamworth Street and attended a local school; the girls were sent to a Dr. Barnardo's Home at Ilford (Essex).[86] In 1909 the union opened children's homes at Wissage, with the children attending local schools.[87] When the homes were transferred to the county council in 1930 they could take 31 boys and 34 girls.[88] In 1989 the establishment, renamed the Poplars and under the county council's social services department, was used partly as a 10-bed family centre, housing chil-dren in care, partly for 16 mentally handicapped children and young adults.[89]

Diocesan Training School for Masters and *Com-mercial School*. In 1839 the diocesan board of education established training and commercial schools for boys in a rented house on the corner of Bird Street and Pool Walk. In 1840 it bought the adjoining house in Bird Street and built a single-storeyed schoolhouse in an Elizabethan style behind the second house to the design of Thomas Johnson of Lichfield. The new institu-tion was intended for the sons of farmers and tradesmen. The commercial school, mainly for day boys, was to include in its curriculum subjects such as book keeping and technical drawing. The staff were also to train teachers for National and commercial schools; the trainees would be boarders and be given teaching prac-tice at a local school. Finance was by fees, subscriptions, and grants from the three archidi-aconal boards of education in the diocese.[90]

The commercial school had over 60 pupils in 1840. In 1842 there were 42, of whom six were boarders.[91] A boy who left in 1847 later recalled that his parents had sent him there for 'the best education the local towns could afford'.[92] It seems, however, to have been wound up in the late 1840s, possibly to provide more room for the teacher training school.[93]

The training school had originally found it difficult to attract pupils. Only 14 enrolled dur-ing its first three years: trainees being boarders had to pay £26 or £30 a year compared with the 5 guineas paid by the day boys of the commer-cial school. The boarding fees were reduced and scholarships offered. In 1844 there were 16 trainees, more than could be easily housed.[94] In the late 1840s there were at times over 20 trainees, but because there was insufficient money to bring the premises up to the govern-ment's standard for a teachers' training college neither the school nor its pupils were eligible for government grants. By 1853 applications for places were becoming fewer.[95]

In 1853 the diocese of Worcester offered the Lichfield diocesan board a share in its diocesan training school at Saltley, in Aston (Warws., later Birmingham), which had government rec-ognition. The proposal aroused strong feelings of diocesan patriotism and was rejected.[96] A new system of scholarships was introduced, and in 1858 there were 20 trainees. As early as 1844 almost all had been destined for National schools, and in 1858 Bishop Lonsdale declared that the training school's chief function was to produce village schoolmasters.[97] By then, how-ever, village schoolmasters were beginning to need certificates, and subscribers were increas-ingly reluctant to support the Lichfield school. In 1863 it was closed, the schoolhouse of 1840 was handed over to St. Mary's girls' and in-fants' school, and the diocese took a share in Saltley.[98]

[79] Pigot, *Nat. Com. Dir.* (1835), 418; *P.O. Dir. Staffs.* (1860; 1876); *Kelly's Dir. Staffs.* (1880 and edns. to 1928).
[80] *P.O. Dir. Staffs.* (1876); *Kelly's Dir. Staffs.* (1880 and edns. to 1928); *Lichfield Mercury*, 10 Feb. 1933, p. 4.
[81] S.R.O., D. 458/A/G/49, pp. 24, 41; 58, p. 411.
[82] Ibid. 58, pp. 417, 465; 66, p. 63; 69, p. 328; *Staffs. Adver-tiser* (S. Staffs. edn.), 25 Aug. 1877, p. 5; 8 Oct. 1887, p. 5.
[83] S.R.O., D. 548/A/G/69, pp. 140, 149–50, 199–200; *28th Ann. Rep. Local Govt. Bd. 1898–99* [C. 9444], p. 142, H.C. (1899), xxxvii.
[84] *Recollections of Sophia Lonsdale*, ed. V. Martineau, 171.
[85] S.R.O., D. 458/A/G/69, pp. 270, 283, 307, 318–19, 338, 348, 370–1, 392–3, 406; ibid. 70, pp. 9–10, 37, 83. For Wigmore schools see *V.C.H. Staffs.* xvii. 45.
[86] S.R.O., D. 458/A/G/75, pp. 54, 176–7, 389, 419, 435–7.
[87] Ibid. 79, pp. 53, 81, 234, 259–60; S.R.O., D. 4566/99, Lichfield Group Managers' min. bk. 1913–16, p. 48; *Lich-field Mercury*, 6 Aug. 1909, p. 5.
[88] *Staffs. C. C. Record for 1930*, 767.
[89] Inf. from the dept.
[90] S.R.O., D. 4566/98, abstract of title 1839, deeds of 23
Apr. 1839 and 24 June 1840, plans and contract 1840; W.S.L., Staffs. Views, v. 189; H. E. J. Howard, *Charge delivered at Triennial Visitation of Peculiars of Cathedral Church of Lichfield, 1840* (Lichfield, 1840), 14–16, 19 (copy in W.S.L.); Lich. Dioc. Bd. of Educ. *3rd Ann. Rep.* (Lich-field, 1842), 26 (copy in W.S.L.).
[91] Howard, *Charge*, 16, 19; *3rd Ann. Rep.* 7.
[92] L.J.R.O., D. 77/20/5, p. 102.
[93] e.g. *P.O. Dir. Staffs.* (1850), 275; White, *Dir. Staffs.* (1851), 508.
[94] Howard, *Charge*, 15, 19; Lich. Dioc. Bd. of Educ. *3rd Ann. Rep.* 6–7; *5th Ann. Rep.* (Lichfield, 1844), 8–10, 32 (copy in W.S.L.).
[95] Lich. Dioc. Bd. of Educ. *9th Ann. Rep.* (Lichfield, 1848), 7–9, 13 (copy in W.S.L.); *14th Ann. Rep.* (Lichfield, 1853), 8, 13 (copy in W.S.L.).
[96] *Staffs. Advertiser*, 1 Oct. 1853, p. 7; 16 Feb. 1856, p. 3.
[97] Ibid. 27 Mar. 1858, p. 7; *5th Ann. Rep.* 9–10.
[98] *Staffs. Advertiser*, 4 June 1887, p. 7; *Lich. Dioc. Ch. Cal.* (1864), 199; (1865), 161. *V.C.H. Staffs.* iii. 78, wrongly implies that it was closed in 1861.

Lichfield Theological College, the Close. The early history of the college, opened in 1857, is treated in another volume. It was closed in 1972.[99]

Industrial school for girls, Wissage, later *Wissage remand home* and *Chadswell assessment centre*. In 1887 Sir Smith Child, Bt., of Stallington Hall in Stone, gave the county £1,000 to establish an industrial school for girls. The magistrates bought land at Wissage and began to build a school, which was completed by Staffordshire county council and opened in 1889. In the early 1920s the number of girls declined and the school was closed in 1925.[1] The building remained empty until 1935, when it was refurbished and opened by the Staffordshire Association for Mental Welfare as a day centre for up to 60 children.[2] From 1941 to 1949 the building was used as an isolation hospital.[3] In 1950 the county council took it over as a remand home for boys, and later the council's social services department managed it as Chadswell assessment centre. It was closed in 1982, the building was demolished, and the site built over.[4]

Midland Truant school, later *Beacon school*. In 1893 the boroughs of Burton upon Trent, Walsall, and West Bromwich built an industrial school for boys on 8 a. at the north end of Beacon Street. The Renaissance-style buildings, in brick with Bath stone dressings, were designed by R. Stevenson of Burton. Since 1926 Walsall has had sole responsibility for the school, as a residential school for children with special educational needs. In 1989 there were only 20–30 children, from Walsall and Sandwell, and closure in 1989 or 1990 was proposed.[5]

Special Schools. In 1951 the former Frog Lane school was converted into an occupational centre for backward and handicapped children. It was still so used in the early 1960s.[6] Lichfield Educational Assessment Centre, Purcell Avenue, was opened in 1972 for children with learning, emotional, speech, or communication problems, and from 1974 it also used the buildings of the former Stowe Street school.[7] Rocklands school, Wissage Road, was opened in the later 1960s as a junior training centre for severely handicapped children and in 1972 became a day school for children with severe learning difficulties.[8] Saxon Hill school, Kings Hill Road, a day and residential school for physically handicapped children, was opened in 1979.[9] Queen's Croft school, Birmingham Road, for children with mild or moderate learning difficulties, was opened in 1980.[10]

CHARITIES FOR EDUCATION. By will dated 1652 Humphrey Terrick devised to the corporation a house in Tamworth Street, the rent to be used for teaching poor children to spell and read. In 1656 his father conveyed the house to the corporation.[11] By the early 1670s the rent was £3, which the corporation paid each year to a master or mistress, evidently of a dame school. From 1709–10 the number of children to benefit was eight.[12] The charity lapsed in 1742; the tenant paid no rent and allowed the house to fall into ruin. In 1764 the corporation let the site at £3 a year to a tenant who agreed to build a new house, and in 1767 the charity was revived, the corporation paying £3 a year for teaching eight boys to read and write. In 1769 it recovered the rent arrears 1742–64, invested the money, and in 1780 used it to buy £100 stock. In 1795 the charity again lapsed.[13] Part of the rent that accumulated was used to buy further stock. From 1809 the corporation paid the charity's income, generally £9 a year, to the boys' school in Frog Lane, to which, in return, it nominated five or more boys. In the early 1850s the money was divided between the boys' and girls' schools in Frog Lane, and in the mid 1860s £5 a year was given to the Pool Walk girls' school. From 1863, when the lease of the Tamworth Street house fell in and the rent was raised, grants were also made to the grammar school for scholarships. Under Schemes of 1876 the endowment was handed over to the grammar school and two Terrick's scholarships of £8 a year were established for boys from elementary schools in the city.[14]

The Conduit Lands trustees made both regular and *ad hoc* grants to the grammar school from the 17th century, and later the trust extended its support to other schools and to further education. The Conduit Lands Educational Foundation, under Schemes of 1871 and 1901, promoted secondary and higher education. Under a Scheme of 1982 one of the Conduit Lands Trust's main objects is the advancement of the education of people under the age of 25 living, or with parents living, within the 1974 city boundaries.[15]

[99] *V.C.H. Staffs.* iii. 77–8; above, cathedral and close.
[1] S.R.O., CES/2/1 and 12; *Staffs. Advertiser*, 22 Oct. 1887, p. 6; 28 Mar. 1896, p. 5; *Staffs. C. C. Record for 1889*, 63–4, 71; *1890*, 36; *1924*, 543; *1925*, 543; see also J.R. Lindley, 'Hist. of Educ. in Lichfield' (TS. of 1942 in Lichfield Libr.), pp. 204–5.
[2] *Lichfield Mercury*, 18 Oct. 1935, p. 10; 29 Nov. 1935, p. 6.
[3] Above, public services (medical services).
[4] *Lichfield Mercury*, 20 July 1951, p. 7; 15 Mar. 1985, p. 1; inf. from the dept.
[5] *V.C.H. Staffs.* xvii. 254–5; *Staffs. Advertiser*, 13 Jan. 1894, p. 3; *Lichfield Mercury*, 5 May 1989, p. 1; 6 Oct. 1989, p. 1.
[6] *Lichfield Mercury*, 3 Aug. 1951, p. 8; 15 July 1960, p. 3; inf. from Staffs. C.C. Educ. Dept.
[7] *Lichfield Mercury*, 17 July 1987, p. 8; 6 Jan. 1989, p. 11; inf. from Staffs. C.C. Educ. Dept.

[8] Inf. from the school and from Staffs. C.C. Social Services Dept.
[9] *Lichfield Mercury*, 18 May 1979, p. 11.
[10] Ibid. 27 Mar. 1981, p. 14.
[11] *7th Rep. Com. Char.* 403.
[12] L.J.R.O., D. 35/bailiffs' accts. 1657–1707, pp. 71, 97, 128, 135, 159, 177; 1704–94, pp. 2, 14, 20, 31, 38; D. 77/5/1, f. 240.
[13] Ibid. D. 35/bailiffs' accts. 1704–94, pp. 314–15, 321, 323, 329, 331; D. 77/9/2, pp. 9–10; *7th Rep. Com. Char.* 403.
[14] *7th Rep. Com. Char.* 403–4; White, *Dir. Staffs.* (1834), 96; (1851), 507; *Rep. Schs. Inquiry Com. vol. xv* [3966–XIV], p. 428, H.C. (1867–8), xxviii (12); *Staffs. Endowed Chars.* 86–7.
[15] S.R.O., Charities Index; Laithwaite, *Conduit Lands Trust*, 53–6; *Lichfield Conduit Lands: Scheme, 30th July 1982*, 13.

In 1877, after some agitation to direct more of the revenue of city charities to educational purposes, two scholarships of £30 a year were established at the grammar school from Lowe's and Wakefield's charities. They were for boys from elementary schools in the city.[16] By the 1880s the trustees of the Municipal Charities were distributing £100 a year from Mousley's charity among the city's elementary schools. The grant, later £120, was discontinued after the 1902 Education Act.[17]

CHARITIES FOR THE POOR

BY the 19th century Lichfield was plentifully endowed with charities. They were in general carefully preserved, and those that had been endowed with land had extended their activities as their incomes grew. Trustees' motives in adding to the number of beneficiaries were not always altruistic. Charity money bought parliamentary votes in the 18th century,[18] and in the early 1840s the Tory trustees of Lowe's Charity and the Radical trustees of the Lichfield Municipal Charities apparently used the distribution of charities for party purposes.[19] Nevertheless, the Charity Commissioners who visited Lichfield in 1821 found little to criticize, and in 1828 the city's record was compared favourably with that of other places where augmented charity revenues had led to corruption and embezzlement.[20]

By the 1860s, however, there were complaints that there were too many charities and that the traditional distributions of food, cash, and clothing were having a degrading effect on the poor. In 1865 T. H. Green found Lichfield 'the great seat of superfluous charities' in Staffordshire; the £600 a year said to be handed out in doles and gratuities encouraged idleness in 'an ill-conditioned surplus population'.[21] An inspector at an inquiry into the city's charities in 1868 was shocked to hear that in St. Mary's parish, containing 1,200 householders, 600 or 700 women applied each year to a clothing charity.[22] In 1885 the mayor claimed that a scheme to relieve distress by offering work on the roads at 2s. 6d. a day, more than was paid in other Midland towns, had been met with curses by the unemployed, who expected to be given charity. A Charity Commission inquiry into the Municipal Charities in 1888 heard calls for fewer doles, a greater emphasis on medical and educational provision, and popular representation on the trust. A Scheme of 1891 followed those lines.[23] Further modifications have since been made.

The local agitation of the 1880s also led to the formation in 1889 of a Lichfield branch of the Charity Organization Society. It opened an office in Dam Street, where it remained in the 1940s. In 1940 it established there a citizens' advice bureau for the Lichfield area.[24]

ALMSHOUSES AND ALMSHOUSE CHARITIES. *St. John's Hospital.* The men's almshouse in St. John Street known until 1989 as St. John's hospital was founded as a hospital, probably in the earlier 12th century. By the later 15th century it was an almshouse, and it was re-established and re-endowed as such in 1495 and 1496. Its institutional and architectural history to 1970 are treated in another volume;[25] the history of its chapel as a place of public worship is treated above.[26] In 1981 its trustees opened an almshouse in the Close on the site of the former theological college. The building included five flats for married couples and seven for single men, a common room, and a guest room. The new almshouse was called the hospital of St. John the Baptist within the Close, and the master of St. John's hospital was given the pastoral care of the almsfolk.[27] In 1989 the trustees decided that the word 'hospital' might cause confusion, and that in future the St. John Street building would be known as St. John's without the Bars. The building of 1981 was already known simply as St. John's within the Close.[28]

Dr. Milley's Hospital. The women's almshouse in Beacon Street, known until the 19th century as the women's hospital and since then as Dr. Milley's hospital, was established probably in 1424 or shortly afterwards; it was re-endowed, and probably rebuilt, in 1502–4 by Thomas Milley, a canon of the cathedral. Its institutional and architectural history to 1970 are treated in another volume.[29] In 1985–7 the building was restored, modernized, and extended; the number of flats was increased from 8 to 10, and a common room was added.[30]

William Lunn's Homes, formerly *Lunn's Almshouses.* In 1654 William Lunn gave two houses in Stowe Street as almshouses for six

[16] L.J.R.O., D. 53/2/7, pp. 1–5; *Staffs. Advertiser* (S. Staffs. edn.), 9 June 1877, p. 7; 7 July 1877, p. 7.

[17] L.J.R.O., D. 117/14, 10 Oct. 1887; *Staffs. Endowed Chars.* 86.

[18] S.R.O., D. 593/F/3/12/3/2, poll bk. of 1761, comments of Markley Bellison and Jas. Wildman; S.R.O., D. 661/17/1; L.J.R.O., D. 16/5/4, order of 20 Dec. 1753.

[19] L.J.R.O., D. 109/Lowe's Char., draft affidavits etc. 1841.

[20] [J. Wade], *Acct. of Public Chars. in Eng. and Wales,* 400; *D.N.B.* s.v. Wade, John.

[21] *Schs. Inquiry Com.* viii. 223, 228.

[22] *Staffs. Advertiser,* 28 Mar. 1868, p. 7; cf. *Early Victorian Eng.* ed. G. M. Young, ii. 332, citing no source.

[23] *Staffs. Advertiser,* 31 Jan. 1885, p. 5; 23 June 1888, pp. 2, 4; 20 June 1891, p. 7.

[24] Jackson, *Hist. Incidents,* 17–18 (2nd nos.); *Recollections of Sophia Lonsdale,* ed. V. Martineau, 165–70, 176; Lichfield Char. Organization Soc. *53rd, 55th, 56th Ann. Rep.* (copies in L.J.R.O., D. 77/19/1).

[25] *V.C.H. Staffs.* iii. 279–89.

[26] Above, churches (St. John's hosp.).

[27] H. Clayton, *St. John's Hosp., Lichfield* (n.d. but 1984; copy in W.S.L.); *Lichfield Mercury,* 23 Oct. 1981, p. 14; inf. from Mr. R. D. Birch, of Lichfield, former steward of the hospital.

[28] *Lichfield Mercury,* 3 Feb. 1989, p. 5. The word 'hospital' was retained in the title of the trust.

[29] *V.C.H. Staffs.* iii. 275–8.

[30] *Lichfield Mercury,* 22 Nov. 1985, p. 5; 30 Jan. 1987, p. 12; 3 Apr. 1987, p. 9.

poor widows, with 2 a. in Long Furlong as endowment.[31] The charity may not have become effective until 1667, when Edward Lunn conveyed the property in trust.[32] By 1762 the trustees were under the supervision of the city bailiffs. The almshouses then comprised six two-roomed cottages with gardens. In 1868 the almswomen were given clothes by the trustees and most of them received from the parish each week 1s. or 1s. 6d. and a loaf.[33] The charity was administered with the Municipal Charities from 1899 and was merged with them in 1908. In 1959 the almshouses were replaced on the same site by a terrace of six old people's bungalows known as William Lunn's Homes. Three more bungalows were opened on the site in 1982, and another four in 1985.[34]

Newton's College, the charitable foundation of Andrew Newton in the Close, is treated above.[35]

Buckeridge's Almshouses. The Revd. George Buckeridge (d. 1863), master of St. John's hospital, gave T. A. Bangham, incumbent of Christ Church, two adjacent cottages in Lower Sandford Street to be used as parish almshouses. The transaction was informal, and although Buckeridge's heirs did not contest the gift, they did not formally renounce their rights in the property. Bangham collected money to establish an endowment fund for the almshouses, which he intended should be named after Richard Hinckley, his church's principal benefactor, but he died in 1876 with the project unrealized. He and his successors chose as tenants aged parishioners charged nominal rents in accordance with Buckeridge's wishes. By 1908 the cottages had become uninhabitable, and the vicar sold them. The money received was invested, and the income from what was known as the Buckeridge Bequest was used for charitable purposes among Anglicans in the parish.[36]

Other Almshouses. There was an almshouse in Stowe Lane in 1343–4.[37] At some time in the later Middle Ages there was a 'domus emosinalis' in Wade Street, presumably an almshouse.[38]

Fecknam's Charity. John Fecknam or Feckenham (d. 1585), innkeeper and twice senior bailiff, gave by will the reversion of 21 a. in Lichfield to augment the income of St. John's and Dr. Milley's. Each received £14 in 1786, £37 16s. a year from 1827 to 1835, and £99.22 in 1988.[39]

Saturford's (later *Wightwick's*) *Charity.* By will dated 1586 George Saturford bequeathed his leases and the income from them to St. John's and Dr. Milley's, with Dr. Milley's to be given preference. His executor, Matthew Wightwick, later stated that the leases had been valued at £50 and instructed his own executor, Alexander Wightwick, to give that sum to the almsfolk. Instead Alexander and his descendants kept the money and paid £1 16s. a year to Dr. Milley's and £1 4s. a year to St. John's. In 1815 John Wightwick gave the £50 and a £10 donation to the feoffees of Dr. Milley's, who used the £60 as capital and paid £1 4s. a year to St. John's as Wightwick's Charity. The payment was redeemed in 1983.[40]

Charities of Walton, Salt, Allen, and Cressett. The corporation was apparently obliged to pay the interest on Jane Walton's £20 loan charity (1572) to the almswomen of Dr. Milley's and the interest on Walter Salt's £30 loan charity (1599) to the inmates of Dr. Milley's and St. John's. By the late 1650s it paid 30s. a year to Dr. Milley's as Walton's Charity and 24s. to each almshouse as Salt's Charity.[41] By deed or will of 1604 Anne Allen gave the corporation £15 to provide annual payments of 9s. to Dr. Milley's and 9s. to other poor widows. In the late 1650s the corporation instead paid 5s. to Dr. Milley's, 4s. to St. John's, and 9s. to other poor.[42] In 1692 it paid £5 to Dr. Milley's as the interest on Mr. Cressett's £100, an otherwise unknown benefaction. By the early 19th century it was making annual payments of £9 4s. to Dr. Milley's and £1 8s. to St. John's, evidently including the four charities.[43]

St. John's hospital also benefited under Phoebe Simpson's Charity.[44]

BENEFACTIONS ASSOCIATED WITH CATHEDRAL CHANTRIES AND OBITS.

The ordination of some chantries and obits in the cathedral provided for annual distributions of money or food to the poor, evidently of Lichfield:[45] *Bishop Muschamp* (d. 1208), 6s. 8d., later history unknown;[46] *Dean Mancetter* (d. 1254), 20s. in bread, still distributed in 1535 but in memory of Master Peter of Radnor;[47] *Dean Mancetter*, a further 20s. in bread or other food, still distributed in 1548;[48] *William de Burton* (will dated 1268), prebendary of Gaia Major, 6s. to the most needy, paid until the late 1320s, revived in 1338, later history unknown;[49] *Canon*

[31] Harwood, *Lichfield*, 507, citing inscription formerly in St. Chad's church.
[32] W.S.L., M. 849; *Char. Dons.* 1158–9. *7th Rep. Com. Char.* 404, cites a deed of 1762 stating that Wm. Lunn executed the 1667 conveyance, and regards that as the foundation of the char.
[33] *7th Rep. Com. Char.* 404; *Staffs. Advertiser*, 28 Mar. 1868, p. 7.
[34] *Lichfield Mercury*, 26 Sept. 1958, p. 6; 21 Aug. 1959, p. 1; 28 Aug. 1959, p. 1; inf. from the Clerk, Lichfield Municipal Charities.   [35] Above, cathedral and close.
[36] S.R.O., D. 4566/C, Buckeridge Almshouses papers and printed copies of Christ Church par. accts. 1909–10, 1924; S.R.O., Charities Index.
[37] Bodl. MS. Ashmole 1521, p. 30 (2nd nos.).
[38] L.J.R.O., D. 30/VC, palimpsest, i, f. 30.
[39] L.J.R.O., Fecknam's Char. MSS.; S.R.O., Charities Index; *7th Rep. Com. Char.* 392–3; Harwood, *Lichfield*, 420–2, 472; inf. from Hinckley, Birch & Exham, solicitors

of Lichfield.
[40] *7th Rep. Com. Char.* 385–6; *V.C.H. Staffs.* iii. 277; inf. from Mrs. B. W. Moore, steward of the hospital.
[41] L.J.R.O., D. 35/bailiffs' accts. 1657–1707, inside front cover. For the loan chars. see below (city chars.).
[42] L.J.R.O., D. 35/bailiffs' accts. 1657–1707, inside front cover, and p. 3; Harwood, *Lichfield*, 373; *7th Rep. Com. Char.* 393–4.
[43] L.J.R.O., D. 35/bailiffs' accts. 1657–1707, p. 146; *7th Rep. Com. Char.* 393–4.   [44] Below (parochial chars.).
[45] e.g. Bodl. MS. Ashmole 794, f. 61–61v.
[46] L.J.R.O., D. 30/XXIV, f. 17; *S.H.C.* 1924, p. 52.
[47] L.J.R.O., D. 30/I 8; *S.H.C.* 1924, p. 113; *Valor Eccl.* (Rec. Com.), iii. 51, 138.
[48] *Valor Eccl.* iii. 139; *S.H.C.* 1915, 157, giving sum distributed in 1548 as 20d.; *S.H.C.* 1924, p. 18.
[49] Bodl. MS. Ashmole 794, ff. 38, 60v.–61v., 63v.; *S.H.C.* 1915, 166, listing Burton's obit in 1548 but not mentioning a dole.

Nicholas de Lega (d. 1268), acknowledged in mid 14th century to include provision for annual distribution to poor, details and later history unknown;[50] *Master Ralph de Chaddesden*, cathedral treasurer, established in 1276, 20s., still paid in 1347;[51] *Master Peter of Radnor*, cathedral chancellor, established in 1277, 12s. in bread, still distributed in 1548;[52] chantry at St. Nicholas's altar established by *Bishop Langton* in 1319, details unknown, 3d. distributed in 1548;[53] *Master William de Bosco*, cathedral chancellor, established in 1325, 7s. in bread, peas, or beans, still distributed in 1535;[54] *Master John de Kynardessey* (d. 1332 or 1333), prebendary of Eccleshall, details unknown, 1s. 4d. given to almsfolk in 1548;[55] *Roger le Mareschall*, prebendary of Dernford, established in 1335, 10s., later history unknown;[56] *John Colman and Margery his wife*, details unknown, probably mid 15th century, 3s. 4d. distributed annually 1538–48;[57] chantry of Jesus and St. Anne established by *Dean Heywood* in 1468, dole to 12 men, probably still distributed in 1548;[58] *John Meneley*, prebendary of Offley 1452–80, details unknown, 5s. 10d. to almswomen in 1504, 4s. to the poor and the Lichfield Franciscans in 1535.[59]

Dean Yotton (d. 1512) stipulated that the priest of his chantry should be a graduate in civil law or divinity; if the former he was to give free legal aid to poor people brought before the bishop's consistory court, if the latter he was to preach four times a year without charge in nearby churches. The only recorded priest had degrees in both subjects.[60]

Only one obit charity survived the Reformation, that of *Bishop Meuland*. In 1265 he arranged that when he died one third (£6 13s. 4d.) of a pension which he had acquired for the cathedral from the church of Wigan (Lancs.) should be used each year to endow his obit. Of that £6 13s. 4d. the sacrist was to distribute £3 6s. 8d. in bread to the poor after the service. Meuland died in 1295, and the bread dole existed c. 1300. By 1535 the sacrist was distributing it on St. Thomas's day (21 December).[61] In the early 18th century the dole was apparently still worth £3 6s. 8d. By 1878, however, only £1 was being spent on bread, which was distributed annually among all householders in the Close on St. Thomas's day as St. Thomas's Dole.[62] The pension was commuted in 1958.[63] By then the origins of the dole had been forgotten. The distribution continued: the head verger

bought bread rolls on St. Thomas's day and delivered them to all the houses in the Close. In the early 1970s the tradition was brought to an end. The charity was revived in 1988: after a service in the cathedral on 21 December the congregation was given bread rolls in the Close refectory.[64]

CITY CHARITIES. *Loan Chests.*[65] Under the will of John Harewood (d. 1389), prebendary of Gaia Minor,[66] his executors established a £20 fund for the poor of Lichfield. By the 1450s the money was kept in St. Mary's church. In 1457, under the will of Master George Radcliffe, treasurer of the cathedral 1435–49 and archdeacon of Chester 1449–54,[67] his executors added £20 to the fund. Harewood's money was kept in a chest known variously as Our Lady's alms chest and Harewood's coffer. Radcliffe's bequest was put into another chest in St. Mary's known as Radcliffe's coffer. The rules for Harewood's coffer have not survived. Radcliffe's beneficiaries, who were to be poor men living in the city and its suburbs, were to receive interest-free loans of up to 20s. for up to six months and had to leave in the chest pledges made of metal and worth at least 3s. 4d. more than the sum borrowed. A pledge not redeemed within six months was to be sold and the amount of the loan was to be returned to the coffer. If the sale realized more than the amount of the loan half the surplus was to go to the defaulting borrower and half to augment the capital of the charity. The master of the guild of St. Mary and St. John the Baptist, the cathedral sacrist, the chapelwarden of St. Mary's, and a priest chosen by the guild each had a key to one of the coffer's four locks. The rules were similar to those for loan chests at Oxford and Cambridge; the coffer was one of the few medieval loan chests in England outside the two universities.[68] In 1485 Dean Heywood found that only £13 remained in the two Lichfield chests. He recovered £20, gave £7 himself, had the entire £40 placed in Radcliffe's coffer, and in 1486 stipulated a strict observance of Harewood's and Radcliffe's rules and careful supervision by the guild. The later history of the charity is unknown.

Corporation Loan Charities. In the later 16th and earlier 17th century the corporation administered various charities designed or adapted to provide interest-free or low-interest loans, any interest being distributed among the poor. Most

[50] Bodl. MS. Ashmole 794, ff. 122v., 136; *S.H.C.* 1915, 157; 1924, p. 334 n.
[51] Bodl. MS. Ashmole 794, f. 103; *S.H.C.* 1924, p. 115.
[52] *S.H.C.* 1915, 166; 1924, p. 114; *Valor Eccl.* iii. 135; *V.C.H. Staffs.* iii. 269.
[53] *S.H.C.* 1915, 157; 1924, pp. 191–2.
[54] Ibid. 1924, p. 331; *Valor Eccl.* iii. 137.
[55] *S.H.C.* 1915, 158; Le Neve, *Fasti, 1300–1541, Coventry and Lichfield*, 34–5, 37, 46.
[56] Bodl. MS. Ashmole 794, f. 50v.; Le Neve, *Fasti*, 32; *S.H.C.* 1915, 167, recording obit of an otherwise unknown Thos. Marshall but no dole.
[57] *S.H.C.* xi. 235; *S.H.C.* 1915, 165.
[58] H. E. Savage, *Thos. Heywode, Dean* (Lichfield, 1925), 11–12; *S.H.C.* 1915, 156, 167.
[59] *Valor Eccl.* iii. 139, 154; Le Neve, *Fasti*, 48; Harwood, *Lichfield*, 513.
[60] H. Wharton, *Anglia Sacra* (1691), i. 454; *S.H.C.* 1915,

[59] *D.N.B.* s.v. Siddall, Hen.
[61] L.J.R.O., D. 30/I 8; *S.H.C.* 1924, p. 164; *Valor Eccl.* iii. 138; Wharton, *Anglia Sacra*, i. 441.
[62] L.J.R.O., D. 30/Nn 20; *Hist. of Church and Manor of Wigan*, i (Chetham Soc. N.S. xv), 30 n.; iii (Chetham Soc. N.S. xvii), 672.
[63] Inf. from Mr. M. B. S. Exham, former chapter clerk.
[64] Lichfield Cathedral Libr., act bk. of hebdomadary chapter 1969–74, p. 897; Friends of Lichfield Cathedral, *50th Ann. Rep.* (1987), 14–15 (copy in cathedral libr.); *Lichfield Cathedral News Sheet, 25th Dec. 1988* (copy in cathedral libr.).
[65] Para. based on *Gild of St. Mary, Lichfield* (E.E.T.S., extra ser. 114), 18–24.
[66] Le Neve, *Fasti, 1300–1541, Coventry and Lichfield*, 42.
[67] Ibid. 12–13.
[68] M. Rubin, *Charity and Community in Med. Cambridge*, 282–8; *Bull. Inst. Hist. Res.* xvii. 113.

loan charities seem to have been lost or absorbed into general corporation funds in the mid 17th century. Unless otherwise stated, all that is known is the name of the benefactor and the amount of the gift.[69]

Richard Skeffington, probably Sir Richard (d. 1647), second son of Sir William Skeffington, Bt., of Fisherwick, gave £80, all or some of which remained in 1658.[70]

Richard Caldwell (d. 1584), a London physician and a native of Staffordshire, gave £40 in 1582, to be lent interest-free for five-year periods to eight residents of Lichfield. Nothing is known of the charity after c. 1620, and it had been lost by 1690. Caldwell's similar charity for Burton upon Trent, supervised by the Lichfield bailiffs, was extant in the 1660s.[71]

Jane Walton gave £20 in 1572, the interest to be paid to the almswomen of Dr. Milley's hospital. By the late 1650s the capital apparently formed part of the corporation's general funds, and loans had ceased.[72]

Walter Salt left £30 in reversion to be lent for three-year periods to three inhabitants of Lichfield. The bailiffs were to pay 54s. a year interest to the almsfolk of Dr. Milley's and St. John's from the time of Salt's death. By the late 1650s the capital apparently formed part of the corporation's general funds, and loans had ceased.[73]

John Burnes, probably the upholsterer who was three times senior bailiff and died in 1600, gave £10, to be lent for three-year periods to poor tradesmen. It had been lost by 1690.[74]

At unknown dates Richard Blount gave £3 or £10, all or some of which remained in 1658;[75] a person called Needeman gave £6 13d. 4d.; a Mr.[76] or Mrs. Howard gave £30; Robert Ball gave £12, of which £4 was distributed to the poor; the corporation gave £33 4s.

The Virginia Lottery Money, evidently a prize won in one of the lotteries run by the Virginia Company between 1612 and 1621, provided £25.[77]

John Utting, probably the John Utting who gave property to St. Mary's church in 1615,[78] gave £26 13s. 4d.

Walter Wrottesley, who gave £150 and later added £50 more, was presumably Walter Wrottesley (d. 1630), squire of Wrottesley, in Tettenhall, whose first wife inherited lands in and around Lichfield.[79] In 1630 the corporation lent the £200 for six months to Sir Walter Heveningham (d. 1636) of Pipe Hall, in Burntwood. It had been lost by 1690.[80]

William Sale, residentiary canon of the cathedral and former master of St. John's hospital, by will proved 1588 bequeathed £20 to provide £5 loans for four-year periods to four poor artificers, interest-free.[81]

At an unknown date a Mr. Cowper gave £10.

William Hawkes, by will dated 1631, endowed three charities. One bequest, of £40 to the poor, was evidently used for loans. It had been lost by 1690.[82]

Sir John King, who died in the Close in 1637, bequeathed £20 to the corporation for the poor.[83] The money was evidently used for loans.

The Charities of the Biddulph Family. By deed of 1579 confirmed by will proved 1580 Simon Biddulph of Lichfield settled £40 in trust to provide £6 13s. 4d. loans to six Lichfield tradesmen. His trustees were still granting loans in 1631.[84] No more is known of the charity.

His son Simon (d. 1632), of Lichfield, bequeathed £5 a year to the city's poor, to be distributed on Good Friday and Christmas Eve. He was perhaps confirming, and augmenting to £5, a dole established by the earlier Simon. Two of his own sons later charged land at Hammerwich with the £5. The charity, sometimes wrongly attributed to Sir Theophilus Biddulph, Bt. (d. 1683), of Elmhurst, was 20 years in arrear in 1728 when, following a Chancery decree, the Biddulphs paid the corporation £100. The money was distributed among c. 600 poor in doles of 1s.–10s. In the early 1820s the owner of the land at Hammerwich distributed £5 in 1s. doles on Good Friday and the Friday before Christmas to Lichfield poor, chiefly widows. In 1908 the charity, then known as the Biddulphs' Charity, was merged with the Municipal Charities.

By deed of 1731 or 1737 Sir Theophilus Biddulph, Bt. (d. 1743), of Elmhurst, settled the rents of three houses in Greenhill in trust for the poor. The income in 1786 was £1 5s. The charity was apparently unknown c. 1820. New trustees were appointed in 1845, and in 1868 the survivor distributed the rents, £10 1s. 6d., among 60 Greenhill poor, mainly women, in 2s. 6d. doles. The charity lapsed in 1879 but was

[69] Details based on a 17th-century catalogue printed by Harwood, *Lichfield*, 375–6. Harwood's assertion that the catalogue (mostly in the form 'X gave £Y') is of loan charities is correct where it can be checked. The order here is that of the catalogue.
[70] L.J.R.O., D. 35/bailiffs' accts. 1657–1707, pp. 2, 5; Shaw, *Staffs.* i. 336, providing the donor's Christian name; *S.H.C.* 1920 and 1922, 48–9.
[71] P.R.O., C 93/43, no. 24; W.S.L. 1/64–95/23; W. Munk, *Roll of Royal Coll. of Physicians* (1878), i. 59–61.
[72] L.J.R.O., D. 35/bailiffs' accts. 1657–1707, inside front cover, and p. 3; *7th Rep. Com. Char.* 393–4. For its later hist. see above (almshouse chars.).
[73] *7th Rep. Com. Char.* 393–4. For its later hist. see above (almshouse chars.). It is presumably the loan charity with identical terms said in the 18th century to have been given by a Wm. Salt on 'Jan. 18, 1600': Harwood, *Lichfield*, 375.
[74] P.R.O., C 93/43, no. 24; above, econ. hist. (trades and industries).

[75] L.J.R.O., D. 35/bailiffs' accts. 1657–1707, p. 2; Shaw, *Staffs.* i. 336. The Ric. Blount who endowed a similar charity at Stafford by will proved 1575 did not mention Lichfield in his will: P.R.O., PROB 11/57, ff. 365–7; *V.C.H. Staffs.* vi. 270.
[76] Shaw, *Staffs.* i. 336.
[77] C. L'E. Ewen, *Lotteries and Sweepstakes*, 70–88.
[78] Above, churches (St. Mary's).
[79] *S.H.C.* n.s. vi (2), 279, 284, 289, 295.
[80] P.R.O., C 93/43, no. 24; Harwood, *Lichfield*, 385; below, Burntwood (manors).
[81] *Wolverhampton Antiquary*, i. 65–7; *V.C.H. Staffs.* iii. 287; vi. 270–1.
[82] P.R.O., C 93/43, no. 24; *7th Rep. Com. Char.* 416–17; below (this section).
[83] *D.N.B.*; J. Lodge, *Peerage of Ireland* (1789), iii. 222.
[84] This and next para. based on P.R.O., PROB 11/62, f. 103v.; L.J.R.O., D. 77/11/1; D. 130/Finney's Charity acct. bk. 1689–1805, at rear; *7th Rep. Com. Char.* 417–18.

revived shortly before 1888. It was administered with the Municipal Charities from 1899 and was merged with them in 1908.[85]

Maddocke's Charity. By deed of 1586 Humphrey Maddocke, a Lichfield mercer, charged 4 a. at Curborough with 13s. 4d. a year for 119 years; the land was then to be rack rented. The 13s. 4d. and the subsequent rack rent were to be distributed on Good Friday among the poorest householders in the city. About 1820 the net annual income, £6 13s. 8d., was distributed on Good Friday in 1s. or 2s. doles. The charity was merged with the Municipal Charities in 1858.[86]

Michael Lowe's Charity. By will proved 1594 Michael Lowe of Timmor, in Fisherwick, confirmed an earlier grant of houses and 45 a. land in Lichfield to provide 12 respectable poor men each year with a coat, a cap, a waggon load of coal (or other fuel of equal value), and 12s.[87] By the later 17th century the income was sufficient to permit an increase in the number of beneficiaries. In the late 1680s 16 men received the charity each year; in the 18th century there were generally over 20 a year, and sometimes over 30.[88] Occasionally the trustees tried to ensure that recipients attended church on formal occasions wearing their caps and coats and did not sell or alter their coats. From 1751 hats were given instead of caps.[89] The estate amounted to 57 a. in 1820. Rack renting was gradually introduced from 1808; the rent increased from £21 in 1796 to £66 in 1820 and £200 in 1868, when 71 men each received a coat, a hat, coal, and 7s.[90] A Scheme of 1877, modified in 1906, diverted £30 a year to educational purposes; one of 1886 limited the number of poor men receiving coat, hat, coal, and 7s. to 50, but allowed the trustees also to give pensions of 3s.–6s. a week to up to 10 men and to support provident clubs, societies, and institutions.[91] In 1978–9 the charity had an income of over £30,000. It was amalgamated with nine other Lichfield charities in 1980 to form Michael Lowe's and Associated Charities.[92]

Smith's Charity. From the charity which Henry Smith, a London merchant, eventually established by declaration of trust dated 1627 Lichfield was assigned £18 a year for its poor. It received its first payment in 1632. In 1641 Smith's trustees charged the £18 on Fradswell manor, in Colwich; by 1673 it was being levied instead on Drayton Bassett manor. The charity was distributed at Lichfield by the parish officers of St. Mary's, though not restricted to that parish. In early years gifts were of clothes, cash,

and bread, and until 1671 there were also payments for apprenticing. Thereafter the money was spent solely on clothes, and from the 18th century the only clothes distributed were flannel petticoats or lengths of flannel, given to poor women at the beginning of winter. There were 94 beneficiaries in 1820, 139 in 1851, 105 in 1897, and 61 in 1967.[93] In 1980 the charity became part of Michael Lowe's and Associated Charities.

Budd's Charity. By will, probably dated 1627, Margaret Budd left a 24s. rent charge on a house in Sandford Street to the bailiffs and churchwardens, to be distributed to 12 poor widows on Good Friday and St. Thomas's day (21 December). About 1820 the owner of the house distributed the dole himself on Good Friday and Christmas Eve, as had previous owners.[94] No more is known of the charity.

Hawkes's Bread Charity. By will of 1631 William Hawkes, senior bailiff in 1626–7, left the corporation two 13s. 4d. rent charges, one for sermons at St. Mary's on Care (or Carl) Sunday (the Sunday before Palm Sunday) and on Palm Sunday, the other for bread for poor who attended them. In 1650 his trustees gave the corporation 1½ a. in Lichfield in lieu of the charges. The bread dole was still worth 13s. 4d. in the early 18th century, but by 1786, when the income from the land was £2 10s., all save the 13s. 4d. for sermons was distributed in bread. There was no distribution from 1806 until 1820, when £50 of accumulated arrears was given to the poor in blankets and other necessaries.[95] From 1835 the charity was one of the Municipal Charities.

Collins's Charity. By will dated 1637 George Collins, presumably the man who was twice senior bailiff, left a rent charge on land at Pipe in Burntwood to provide four poor Lichfield women with gowns together costing at least £3 on All Saints' day (1 November). After the two trustees named by Collins had died the city bailiffs were to choose the beneficiaries. By the early 18th century £3 had become the amount of the rent charge. In the early 19th century the funds of the charity were allowed to accumulate, and distributions of gowns were infrequent.[96] From 1835 the charity was one of the Municipal Charities.

Nevill's Charity. By will proved 1639 John Nevill, citizen and grocer of London and a native of Lichfield, left the corporation a £6 rent charge on houses in London for bread, to be distributed every Sunday after morning service.

[85] W.S.L., M. 849 (which dates Sir Theophilus's deed 10 Mar. 1736); Scheme of 27 June 1899 (which dates it 10 Mar. 1730); *Staffs. Advertiser*, 4 Apr. 1868, p. 6; 23 June 1888, p. 2.
[86] L.J.R.O., D. 130/Maddocke's Charity acct. bk. 1858–95; *7th Rep. Com. Char.* 415–16; *Staffs. Advertiser*, 4 Apr. 1868, p. 6.
[87] P.R.O., PROB 11/83, ff. 148v.–155; L.J.R.O., D. 109/Lowe's Charity feoffments, deeds of 1571 and 1636; *7th Rep. Com. Char.* 405–6.
[88] L.J.R.O., D. 109/Lowe's Charity acct. bks. 1687–1768, 1769–1844.
[89] Ibid. acct. bk. 1687–1768, entries for 1726, 1727, 1729, 1736, 1740, 1750, and order of 30 Nov. 1725 on back end papers.
[90] Ibid. acct. bk. 1769–1844; *7th Rep. Com. Char.* 406–7;

Staffs. Advertiser, 28 Mar. 1868, p. 7.
[91] L.J.R.O., D. 109/Lowe's Charity, Scheme of 1886, Order of 1906.
[92] Ibid. acct. bk. 1967–82.
[93] L.J.R.O., D. 20/7/3; D. 109/Smith's Charity acct. bk. 1851–1968; Lichfield Cathedral Libr., MS. Lichfield 22, pp. 73–4 (2nd nos.); *7th Rep. Com. Char.* 408; *8th Rep. Com. Char.* H.C. 13, pp. 660–4 (1822), xviii; W. K. Jordan, *Chars. of London 1480–1660*, 117–22; *Staffs. Advertiser*, 28 Mar. 1868, p. 7.
[94] *7th Rep. Com. Char.* 416; Reade, *Johnsonian Gleanings*, ix. 62.
[95] L.J.R.O., D. 20/1/2, inside front cover; Harwood, *Lichfield*, 369, 425; *7th Rep. Com. Char.* 416–17.
[96] L.J.R.O., D. 35/bailiffs' accts. 1704–94, p. 7; Harwood, *Lichfield*, 424–5; *7th Rep. Com. Char.* 408.

Half was to go to the poor of Stowe Street, half to other poor in the city. In the late 18th century the corporation paid the money to a baker who sent weekly supplies of bread to St. Mary's and St. Chad's. The parish clerk of St. Chad's was sent each week 12 penny loaves which he distributed in Stowe Street; c. 1800, however, the overseers of St. Mary's ended his supply. About 1820 the sexton of St. Mary's gave penny loaves every Friday to the poor of his parish, save for four Fridays a year when he gave them to the almswomen of Dr. Milley's hospital.[97] From 1835 the charity was one of the Municipal Charities.

Perkins's Charity. Mary Perkins (d. 1643) of Lichfield gave by will a rent charge of £4 for charitable uses. Her son John Perkins and granddaughter Ruth Bayley by wills proved 1685 and 1713 provided for its payment.[98] No more is known of it.

Matthew's Charity. For many years before 1645 Ann, wife of Humphrey Matthew, a Lichfield tanner, gave six poor widows a cloth waistcoat each year. By deed of 1645, at her request, her husband settled 6 a. in Lichfield to endow her charity. The corporation was to have the land after the Matthews had died; it was to spend 20s. of the income on sermons at St. Mary's and St. Chad's, 2s. on managing the charity, and the rest on waistcoats for poor widows on St. Thomas's day (21 December). By the late 1650s the corporation was paying for the sermons and was distributing six waistcoats marked with red letters each year as Mrs. Ann Matthew's Gift. The charity continued in that form until the early 18th century, when its income began to increase. In 1705 two gowns were given besides the waistcoats, and by 1745, when the charity was being attributed to Humphrey Matthew, it was distributed in gowns, coats, and money. About 1820 between 30 and 50 poor widows a year were each given a gown and 2s. 6d.[99] From 1835 it was one of the Municipal Charities.

Ruins of the Minster Charity. In 1651 parliament ordered that £1,200 raised by the sale of materials from the derelict cathedral should be used for poor relief. Of that sum the corporation was given £40 in 1657 and a further £20 in 1659; the money was put out on loan and the interest paid to the overseers. In 1690 it was claimed, probably incorrectly, that £100 in all had been received.[1] In the early 18th century the bailiffs distributed £5 a year in coal to the poor, but after complaints of irregularities it was decided in 1717 that the charity should be distributed instead by the churchwardens and overseers. The money was divided evenly between the three parishes until 1743, when, following an alleged increase in the number of poor

in St. Mary's parish, its share was raised to £2 and the shares of St. Michael's and St. Chad's reduced to 30s. each.[2] In the late 18th and early 19th century the charity was distributed in bread on St. Thomas's day (21 Dec.) by the overseers.[3] From 1835 it was one of the Municipal Charities.

Dilkes's Charity. By will proved before 1673 Mary Dilkes, apparently of Lichfield, left two rent charges on a house in Conduit Street, 10s. for distribution among 30 poor widows on Lady day, and 5s. for repairs to St. Mary's. The 5s. was regularly paid, and until 1817 the owners of the house distributed 10s. to widows, latterly in 1s. doles. The marquess of Stafford, who bought the house in 1819, was said in 1820 to be willing to revive the charity.[4] He apparently did not do so.

Minors's Charity. By will dated 1677 Thomas Minors, founder of Minors's school, bequeathed a 10s. rent charge for an annual sermon in St. Mary's. If the authorities forbade the preacher to speak, the 10s. was to be distributed among 10 poor Lichfield widows. In 1786 it was stated that the money was given to 10 widows, and had been for many years. The charity had been lost by 1821.[5]

Marshall's Charity. By will proved 1681 Thomas Marshall of Lichfield devised in trust 1½ a. in Lichfield, the rent to be distributed at Christmas among the city's poor. In 1737 there was a dispute between the trustees, and part of the rent, then 22s. 6d., was withheld. The charity had been lost by 1786.[6]

Finney's Charity. By will proved 1689 William Finney, citizen and tallow chandler of London, devised land in Lichfield and Mavesyn Ridware worth £31 6s. 8d. a year to Lichfield corporation and provided for the purchase of further land to raise the total rental to £37; land at Yoxall was bought. Every year 22 poor men and 10 poor widows were each to be given a wainload of coals, 1s., and a cloth gown with W. F. on the sleeve; the men were to be given caps, the women cash to buy themselves headcloths. Recipients were to be Anglicans, with preference for Finney's kin. The first distribution took place in 1690. In 1738 the estate was 63 a. and the income £37 16s. 8d. By c. 1820 the rent income was £219 and the corporation had increased the number of beneficiaries. Between 1815 and 1820 from 79 to 263 men and women a year received 6s. for coal and 1s. cash, the balance between the sexes reflecting that laid down by Finney. The men were also given a hat and a coat with W. F. on the sleeve, and the women, all aged widows, a gown, a cap, and a handkerchief. Recipients did not normally benefit more than once every two years. The corporation diverted surplus funds to good

[97] *7th Rep. Com. Char.* 414–15; J. and G. F. Matthews, *Year Bks. of Probates,* ii. 347; Harwood, *Lichfield,* 462.
[98] Reade, *Johnsonian Gleanings,* ix. 59, 61, 64.
[99] L.J.R.O., D. 35/bailiffs' accts. 1657–1707, pp. 2–3, 70, 148, 159, 177, and notes inside front cover; 1704–94, pp. 3, 7, 167; *7th Rep. Com. Char.* 408–10.
[1] L.J.R.O., D. 35/bailiffs' accts. 1657–1707, pp. 2, 4, and notes inside front cover; *Cal. S.P. Dom. 1653–4,* 407; Shaw, *Staffs.* i. 336, 338; *7th Rep. Com. Char.* 413; *V.C.H. Staffs.* iii. 174.

[2] L.J.R.O., D. 77/5/1, f. 200; D. 77/5/2, f. 43.
[3] Ibid. D. 35/bailiffs' accts. 1704–94, pp. 585, 595; 1794–1835, p. 72; *7th Rep. Com. Char.* 414.
[4] *7th Rep. Com. Char.* 418; *Char. Dons.* 1158–9, calling her Ann Dilkes.
[5] W.S.L., M. 849; *7th Rep. Com. Char.* 434.
[6] L.J.R.O., P/C/11, Thos. Marshall (1681); S.R.O., D. 4566/M, 'Acct. of Mr. Marshall's will'; *Char. Dons.* 1158–9; *7th Rep. Com. Char.* 434.

causes; in 1819, for example, it spent £50 of the charity's money on blankets for the poor.[7] From 1835 the charity was one of the Municipal Charities.

Hinton's Charity. By will dated 1685 Roger Hinton of Castle Church charged his estate there with annuities for the poor of various places in Staffordshire; the poor of Lichfield were to receive £12 a year. The charity was established in 1692, after Chancery proceedings.[8] Lichfield was receiving its £12 by 1703. Initially the money was distributed in doles of up to 10s.; later, smaller gifts were made to larger numbers. From 1703 to 1724 the beneficiaries included the almswomen of Dr. Milley's hospital.[9] It had been directed in 1692 that the entire income of the estate was to be divided among the places concerned, but it was not until the early 19th century that the charity received the full economic rent. Between 1805 and 1820 Lichfield received £336 12s. 6d. in irregular instalments. There were routine distributions to the poor in 1807–12 and 1814, and in 1821 the vicar and churchwardens of St. Mary's distributed an accumulated £140 throughout the city in 10s. and £1 doles. By 1889, when Lichfield received £31, the mayor received the money and handed it over to the ministers of all denominations in the city for distribution.[10] In 1955 Lichfield's share of the charity was made part of the Municipal Charities, which in 1988 received £58.93 from Hinton's Charity.[11]

Ashmole's Charity. By 1757 the corporation was distributing £2 2s. a year among the poor as the interest on £60 given for charitable uses by Elias Ashmole (d. 1692). The charity was not established by will, and no deed has been found. In 1678 Ashmole wrote that for over 20 years he had given £5 a year to the poor of the city; the corporation perhaps accumulated the £60 from those gifts. In 1765 it reduced its payments to £2 a year. Until 1805 the charity was distributed in 2s. doles to poor women. Nothing was paid in 1806. There was a distribution to both men and women in 1807; thereafter no payments were made to the poor for at least 13 years.[12] From 1835 the charity was one of the Municipal Charities.

Charities of Francis and John Deakin. By will of unknown date Francis Deakin the younger, a Lichfield fellmonger, left a £1 rent charge to buy 6d. loaves for poor householders of the city on the Wednesday after Ash Wednesday. The Revd. John Deakin of Rugeley bequeathed the city £20; of the interest 10s. was to be used to augment Francis's bread dole and 10s. for a sermon at St. Mary's on the same day.[13] A Revd. John Deakin, master of Rugeley grammar school, died in 1727; his will made no bequest of

£20 to the city, but it asked his father and brother Francis, both of Lichfield, to use his books and other goods, valued after his death at £20, to establish a free library at Lichfield, and they presumably preferred instead to extend an existing family charity.[14] The corporation used the £20 to buy another £1 rent charge. About 1820 the vicar of St. Mary's was distributing 30s. in 6d. loaves after the sermon to poor householders chosen for life from the three city parishes, preference being given to widows.[15] No more is known of the charities.

Mousley's Charity. Samuel Mousley (d. 1733), twice senior bailiff, left houses, barns, land in Lichfield, Curborough and Elmhurst, £100 cash, and the residue of his personal property, which probably amounted to another £100, to the corporation, the income to be distributed among the poor. About 1820 the gross annual income was £225, although the net income was sometimes much less. It was distributed in cash payments of 10s., and occasionally of £1 or £2, and £5 a year was subscribed to the Lichfield dispensary.[16] From 1835 the charity was one of the Municipal Charities.

Wakefield's Charity. By will proved 1733 Richard Wakefield, town clerk of Lichfield 1688–1721, left the reversion of his Lichfield property, the income to be distributed annually by the constables, churchwardens, and overseers among the Lichfield poor not in receipt of parish relief. The life tenant died in 1754, and in 1755 the estate was conveyed to trustees who were to distribute the income themselves to the poor at Michaelmas. Recipients were not to have received parish relief for six months. In 1820 the net income of the estate, then 48 a., was £185, and 472 beneficiaries received between £1 and 5s.[17] Management of the charity was transferred in 1914 to the Municipal Charities, with which in 1955 the charity was merged.[18]

Taylor's Charity. By will Cary Butt (d. 1781) of Pipe Grange in Pipehill devised in trust for sale 3 a. in Lichfield which he had acquired from Catherine Taylor. Part was already charged with a payment of up to 10s. for the Lichfield poor. In 1783, when Butt's trustees sold the land, the rent charge was said to be 15s., payable to the poor at Christmas. The origins of the charge are unknown. Taylor's conveyance to Butt did not mention it, but she was later alleged to have been anxious to secure its payment. About 1820 the solicitor to Butt's trustees was distributing the 15s. income of what had become known as Mrs. Taylor's Charity among deserving poor, giving preference to Mrs. Taylor's kin.[19] No more is known of the charity.

Bolton's Charity. By deed or will before 1799 a Mrs. Bolton gave £50, the interest to be given

[7] L.J.R.O., D. 130/Finney's Char. acct. bk. 1689–1805; *Wills proved in P.C.C.* xi (Index Libr. lxxvii), 97; *7th Rep. Com. Char.* 410–13.
[8] *7th Rep. Com. Char.* 418–19.
[9] L.J.R.O., D. 20/7/1 and 2.
[10] *7th Rep. Com. Char.* 419–24; *Staffs. Advertiser*, 2 Feb. 1889, p. 7.
[11] Inf. from the Clerk, Lichfield Municipal Charities.
[12] *7th Rep. Com. Char.* 431; *Elias Ashmole*, ed. C. H. Josten, iv. 1570, 1828–32.
[13] *7th Rep. Com. Char.* 415.

[14] L.J.R.O., P/C/11, Revd. John Deakin (1727); *Rugeley Par. Reg.* i (Staffs. Par. Reg. Soc. 1928), p. xiv; *V.C.H. Staffs.* v. 163, which wrongly gives John's Christian name as James and where, on n. 60, 'p. 23' should read 'p. 289'.
[15] *7th Rep. Com. Char.* 415.
[16] Ibid. 424–7; Harwood, *Lichfield*, 431, 465.
[17] *7th Rep. Com. Char.* 427–31; Harwood, *Lichfield*, 369; A. L. Reade, *Reades of Blackwood Hill* (priv. print. 1906), 228–9.
[18] L.J.R.O., D. 130/2/4/1 and 2; Scheme of 30 Sept. 1955.
[19] Reade, *Johnsonian Gleanings*, iv. 124, 126; *7th Rep. Com. Char.* 432.

to 20 poor widows of the city at Christmas. The charity may still have existed in 1806, but no more is known of it.[20]

Slaney's Charity. By deed of 1827 Richard Slaney of Uttoxeter, an ex-convict who had been transported and had returned to England,[21] gave £700 to St. Mary's, St. Michael's, and St. Chad's, the income to be equally divided among the parishes for clothes 'with an appropriate badge' for up to 12 aged and indigent men.[22] The badging requirement seems to have been ignored. In the 1840s and 1850s St. Mary's spent the money on shoes, in 1868 all parishes distributed boots, and in the early 20th century St. Chad's gave clothes and shoes.[23] In 1922 the charity was converted into three separate parochial endowments.[24] In 1980 the charity, reunited, became part of Michael Lowe's and Associated Charities.

Lichfield Municipal Charities. The Municipal Corporations Act of 1835 transferred the management of charities which had been administered by the unreformed corporations to bodies of municipal charity trustees. Lichfield Municipal Charities, comprising the charities of John Allington, Elias Ashmole, Walter Chetwynd and Richard Plumer, George Collins, William Finney, Humphrey Matthew, Samuel Mousley, and John Nevill, William Hawkes's bread charity, and the Ruins of the Minster Charity, were further regulated by an Order of 1843. The existing forms of benefaction were in general preserved. Except for Mousley's Charity (for the city alone) and Chetwynd and Plumer's Charity (for the parishes of St. Michael and St. Chad) the beneficial area of the Municipal Charities became the city, its suburbs, and the Close. In 1858 the Municipal Charities trustees took over the management of Maddocke's Charity. In 1888 an inquiry revealed that for many years the Order of 1843 had not been observed. The town clerk, Charles Simpson, steward and treasurer of the Municipal Charities since 1848, had ignored it and had not told trustees of it. It had escaped notice in 1868 during an earlier inquiry into Lichfield charities. The trustees had made grants to schools and to deserving institutions, had reserved a certain amount of money each year for cases of sickness, and had then allotted fixed sums to the four districts into which they divided the city, for distribution among the poor. A Scheme of 1891 provided that of the 15 trustees 5 were to be directly elected by ratepayers, 3 were to be appointed by the city council, and 7 were to be co-opted. The first elections of trustees were held in 1891 and produced much working-class excitement. In 1908 direct election was abolished and the number of trustees was reduced to 13: the mayor, 2 co-opted trustees, 6 appointed by the city council, 2 ap-

pointed by the board of guardians, and 1 each from the Lichfield branch of the Charity Organization Society and the Lichfield nursing home. The charities of the Biddulphs and Sir Theophilus Biddulph, and Lunn's almshouses were merged with the Municipal Charities. From 1908 to 1955 the trustees were empowered to use the income of Chetwynd and Plumer's Charity and Mousley's Charity for educating poor children. In 1955 the charities of Rowland Muckleston, Luke Robinson, and Richard Wakefield, and the Lichfield share of Roger Hinton's Charity were merged with the Municipal Charities. The main object of the 13 trustees (the mayor, 6 appointed by the city council, and 6 co-opted) was to be support for Lunn's almshouses and the almspeople. Under the Scheme the trustees replaced the almshouses in 1959 with William Lunn's Homes, which they later extended. A Scheme of 1982 increased the number of trustees to 14 (the mayor, 3 appointed by the city council, 2 appointed by the district council, and 8 co-opted) and confirmed that the city on the eve of the 1974 reorganization of local government was the beneficial area of the Municipal Charities. In 1988 the income of the charities was £91,259, the expenditure £23,559.[25]

Passam's Charity. By will proved 1860 Elizabeth Passam of Lichfield bequeathed £1,000, to be invested in stock. The income was to be distributed among poor widows and families living in Lichfield in sums not exceeding 10s. on 24 January, the anniversary of the death of her brother Thomas Passam, by whose wish the bequest was made.[26] In 1980 the charity became part of Michael Lowe's and Associated Charities.

John Foster Haworth and Blanche Susan Haworth Charity Fund. By will proved 1867 Margaret Haworth, formerly of the Close, left the reversion of £2,000 to the dean of Lichfield for a fund for the very poor of the city, preference being given to consumptives and chimney-sweeping boys. The life interest expired in 1888, and the first grants were made in 1889. In the mid 1980s the income of £150 was used for grants to Dr. Milley's hospital and for small payments to its almswomen and other elderly women. In 1989 the charity became part of Michael Lowe's and Associated Charities.[27]

Michael Lowe's and Associated Charities. In 1980 the charities of Michael Lowe, Jesson Mason, Elizabeth Passam, Elizabeth Preest, Alice Simpson, Phoebe Simpson, and Richard Slaney, Turnpenny's Charity, the charity known as Mrs. Richard Hinckley's Memorial, and the Lichfield portion of Henry Smith's Charity were amalgamated to produce a fund for the general or individual relief of residents of the city. In the year 1988–9 the combined charity

[20] Shaw, *Staffs.* i. 337; Harwood, *Lichfield*, 373.
[21] *Staffs. Advertiser*, 28 Mar. 1868, p. 7; and see L.J.R.O., D. 29/4/2, p. 32.
[22] L.J.R.O., D. 109/Slaney's Charity, deed of 8 May 1827.
[23] Ibid. D. 20/7/5; D. 29/4/2, pp. 32–4, 55; *Staffs. Advertiser*, 28 Mar. 1868, p. 7.
[24] L.J.R.O., D. 109/Slaney's Charity, Scheme of 28 Feb. 1922.
[25] *Staffs. Advertiser*, 28 Mar. 1868, p. 7; 4 Apr. 1868, p. 6;

23 June 1888, pp. 2, 4; 11 Oct. 1890, p. 7; 18 Oct. 1890, p. 3; 20 June 1891, p. 7; inf. from the Clerk, Lichfield Municipal Charities.
[26] S.R.O., Charities Index; *Staffs. Advertiser*, 1 Dec. 1860, p. 4.
[27] S.R.O., D. 4566/G, Haworth Charity papers; inf. from the Clerk's office, Michael Lowe's and Associated Charities. For Marg. Haworth see e.g. *P.O. Dir. Staffs.* (1850), 276; White, *Dir. Staffs.* (1851), 520.

had an income of £69,621, of which £15,424 was distributed in fuel grants, £294 in pensions, and £14,275 in other grants. Haworth's Charity was amalgamated with the charity in 1989.[28]

PAROCHIAL CHARITIES. ST. MARY'S. *Hawkes's Gallery Charity*. When William Hawkes paid for a gallery in St. Mary's church in 1630 he stipulated that those who took sittings in it should pay a 1s. entry fee, to be given to poor communicants on Palm Sunday and Low Sunday. Four shillings was distributed in bread in 1634 and 6s. in 1635.[29] The charity presumably ended when the church was demolished and rebuilt in the early 18th century.

Thropp's Charity. By deed or will of 1631 William Thropp, presumably the mercer of that name who died in 1632, gave a £1 rent charge to pay 6s. 8d. for a sermon at St. Mary's on Mid-Lent Sunday and the distribution then of 13s. to 13 poor widows. The distributor was paid 4d. The charity apparently still existed in the 1680s but had been lost by 1786.[30]

Allington's Charity. John Allington (d. 1642), thrice bailiff, bequeathed rent charges in trust to the two senior freemen of the Lichfield mercers' company for a weekly bread dole for the poor of St. Mary's. According to a 17th-century inscription formerly in St. Mary's church the rent charges amounted to £5 6s. In the 17th and early 18th century 2s. a week was distributed in bread. In 1786 the total rent charge was said to be only £4.[31] Bread continued to be distributed at the church every Sunday until c. 1797, when the mercers' company became extinct and the charity lapsed. In 1818 Chancery transferred the management to the corporation and ordered the revival of the dole. Accumulated funds went in the costs of obtaining the decree. In 1821 the Charity Commissioners, accepting that the rent charges totalled £4, noted that the corporation had received no money since 1818 and had not revived the dole. It was later revived as one of the Municipal Charities, and in 1843 its beneficial area was extended to cover the city, its suburbs, and the Close.[32]

Edward Finney's Charity. By 1651 Edward Finney the elder, probably the senior bailiff of 1636–7, had established a bread dole at St. Mary's endowed with 1s. a month. Apparently it still existed c. 1715.[33] No more is known of it.

John Matthews's Charity. By deed or will John Matthews (d. in or before 1669), perhaps the junior bailiff of 1650–1, gave the minister and churchwardens of St. Mary's a 10s. rent charge on property at Little Wyrley, in Norton

Canes, for distribution among 10 poor widows. In 1671 and 1672 the property was conveyed to John Darlaston the younger and his wife. Darlaston and his father covenanted to pay the corporation 10s. a year, which would be given to St. Mary's for distribution.[34] The charity survived in the 1690s and early 1700s, latterly as Mr. Darlison's Gift.[35] No more is known of it.

Robinson's Charity. By will proved 1767 Luke Robinson of Lichfield left £300, the interest to be distributed among the poor of St. Mary's at Christmas. About 1820 the charity's £18 income from stock was distributed annually among poor chosen for life. From 1858 to 1897 the charity was given in 10s. doles, no longer to recipients chosen for life; later it was distributed in cash or coal. In 1908 its management was transferred to the Municipal Charities. The beneficial area remained St. Mary's parish until 1955, when the charity was merged with the Municipal Charities.[36]

Edge's Charity. By will proved 1777 Richard Edge, a Lichfield mercer, left his friend and former apprentice James Wickins £30, the interest to be used to buy 2d. white loaves for distribution by the churchwardens of St. Mary's on 23 or 24 December among the poor of the parish. The bread was to be bought from bakers in Conduit Street or Dam Street. Wickins kept the money and used the interest (24s. in 1786) to buy 1d. loaves which he distributed at his house on Christmas morning among aged persons from the three city parishes, giving priority to parishioners of St. Mary's. About 1817 he gave the £30 to the vicar of St. Mary's, who c. 1820 was paying 30s. interest to the churchwardens for distribution among poor parishioners on Christmas morning.[37] No more is known of the charity.

Hector's Charity. In 1778 Mary Hector (d. 1783) of Lichfield gave £50 to endow an annual Lady day distribution by the St. Mary's churchwardens to 20 poor widows of the parish. The charity was not established until 1834; previously the interest on the capital was paid into St. Mary's general church account. In 1856 the bank in which the £50 had been deposited failed, and the charity came to an end.[38]

ST. MICHAEL'S, CITY PORTION. *Bailey's Charity*. By will dated 1735 Elizabeth Bailey of Lichfield devised land in Abbots Bromley, the income to be divided equally between St. Michael's parish and the township of Newton, in Blithfield, for distribution among their poor at Easter. St. Michael's annual share c. 1820 was £2 10s., which the churchwardens distributed after con-

[28] Inf. from the Clerk.
[29] L.J.R.O., D. 20/4/1, 1633–4, 1634–5; Harwood, *Lichfield*, 462, wrongly giving the name as Fowkes.
[30] L.J.R.O., D. 20/4/2, inside front cover; D. 27/1/1, f. 78; Harwood, *Lichfield*, 374; *Char. Dons.* 1158–9.
[31] L.J.R.O., D. 20/1/2, inside front cover; Harwood, *Lichfield*, 371, 424–5, 462, 464; Shaw, *Staffs.* i. 334–5.
[32] *7th Rep. Com. Char.* 437–8; *Staffs. Advertiser*, 23 June 1888, p. 2.
[33] L.J.R.O., D. 20/1/2, inside front cover; D. 20/4/1, 1650–1; Harwood, *Lichfield*, 424–6, 462. Shaw, *Staffs.* i. 337, gives the endowment as 12s. a month.
[34] L.J.R.O., D. 20/4/1, 1669–70; Harwood, *Lichfield*, 427;

7th Rep. Com. Char. 439.
[35] L.J.R.O., D. 35/bailiffs' accts. 1657–1707, pp. 148, 159, 177; 1704–94, pp. 2, 7.
[36] Ibid. D. 130/2/3/1 and 2; *7th Rep. Com. Char.* 431–2; Scheme of 30 Sept. 1955 (copy in possession of the Clerk, Lichfield Municipal Charities).
[37] L.J.R.O., P/C/11, Ric. Edge (1777); Harwood, *Lichfield*, 370; *7th Rep. Com. Char.* 438.
[38] L.J.R.O., D. 15/6/1; W.S.L., M. 849; *7th Rep. Com. Char.* 438–9; B. Robinson, *Geneal. Memoirs of Family of Brooke Robinson* (priv. print 1896), 109–10 (copy in W.S.L.); Reade, *Johnsonian Gleanings*, ii. 76 n.; iv. 173, 175–6.

sulting the vicar.[39] The land was sold in 1947 or 1948 and the money was invested. In 1978 St. Michael's received £3.25 for its poor.[40]

Gregory's Charity. Greenwood Gregory, the son of a Lichfield dyer and alive in 1721,[41] left the churchwardens a £1 rent charge on a house in Lombard Street for a Christmas distribution to the poor of Greenhill. The charity existed by 1786. In the early 1820s the churchwardens distributed the money, a few shillings at a time, to poor parishioners.[42] The £1 was still being received in 1884, but by 1989 the charity was extinct.[43]

Mason's Charity. By will proved 1823 Jesson Mason of Lichfield left £800, the interest to be used to provide coats, hats, gowns, and caps at Christmas for the poor of Greenhill and St. John Street. Clothing was distributed until the beginning of the Second World War and clothing vouchers were then given until the 1960s. Thereafter small cash grants were made. In the 1970s there was an income of £80–£100 from stock.[44] In 1980 the charity became part of Michael Lowe's and Associated Charities.

ST. CHAD'S, CITY PORTION. *Turnpenny's Charity.* A person called Turnpenny bequeathed a 6s. 8d. rent charge to provide a bread dole for the poor of Beacon Street.[45] The benefactor was probably Zachary Turnpenny (d. 1672), subchanter of the cathedral, who lived in Beacon Street.[46] By 1786 the dole was being distributed on Ascension Day, probably, as c. 1820, in 1d. loaves handed out by the churchwardens.[47] The otherwise unknown 6s. 8d. paid in the late 18th century by the heirs of John Fletcher to provide a bread dole for the poor of St. Chad's parish was probably Turnpenny's Charity.[48] In the 1930s bread rolls were distributed to poor parishioners on Ascension Day.[49] In 1980 the charity became part of Michael Lowe's and Associated Charities.

Charity of Alice Simpson or Thomas Green. By will proved 1674 Alice Simpson devised her house in Stowe Street to her cousin William Holmes subject to a 10s. rent charge, to be distributed on St. Thomas's day (21 Dec.) among five poor widows of Stowe Street and five of Beacon Street.[50] Holmes and his heirs concealed the charity, and it did not become effective until either 1696 or 1736, when Thomas Green, who had bought the house, agreed to honour Simpson's wishes. The 10s. was to be distributed by the incumbent and parish offic-

ers; if insufficient widows applied, the number was to be made up by poor householders. About 1820 the money was handed out at Christmas in 1s. doles.[51] By 1918 poor widows living near the two streets were also eligible for the doles.[52] In 1980 the charity became part of Michael Lowe's and Associated Charities.

Christopher Lowe's Charity. By will proved 1705 Christopher Lowe, a Lichfield innkeeper, left £5 to provide a 5s. distribution at Christmas among five of the poorest householders in Beacon Street not in receipt of parish relief. The charity had been lost by 1786.[53]

Preest's Charity. By will proved 1838 Elizabeth Preest of the Close, a servant of the Revd. T. H. White, left £100 in reversion to St. Chad's to provide Christmas gifts of a woollen cloak and 1s. 6d. to poor women who attended the church most regularly.[54] The money was lent to a maltster who went bankrupt, but £76 was recovered from his estate and in 1849 was invested in stock. In the later 19th century cloaks and shawls were given.[55] In 1980 the charity became part of Michael Lowe's and Associated Charities.

CHRIST CHURCH. *Mrs. Richard Hinckley's Memorial.* By deed of 1881 the trustees under the will of T. A. Bangham (d. 1876), incumbent of Christ Church, gave £225 stock, the income to be divided annually between two poor parishioners, who were not to benefit in consecutive years.[56] In 1980 the charity became part of Michael Lowe's and Associated Charities.

Martin Heath Memorial Fund. By will proved 1952 Edith Mary Heath (née Martin) left the residue of her estate to the vicar and churchwardens of Christ Church. Part was to be used to endow an annual New Year's gift of £1 each to 12 poor parishioners, six men and six women, aged 60 or more.[57] The gifts were being distributed in the 1980s.

THE CLOSE. *Muckleston's Charity.* By will proved 1897 Rowland Muckleston, rector of Dinedor (Herefs.), who had been born in the Close, established a charity for its poor. Its endowment in 1902 was £2,850 stock, and £65 of its £71 income was then being distributed in pensions for five people. In 1919 its management was transferred to Lichfield Municipal Charities. The beneficial area remained unchanged until 1955, when the charity was merged with the Municipal Charities.[58]

[39] *7th Rep. Com. Char.* 442.
[40] L.J.R.O., D. 27/8/3, Order of 9 May 1947; inf. from the rector of St. Michael's.
[41] L.J.R.O., P/C/11, Chas. Gregory (1721).
[42] W.S.L., M. 849; Shaw, *Staffs.* i. 338; *7th Rep. Com. Char.* 442.
[43] L.J.R.O., D. 27/5/3; inf. from the rector.
[44] Ibid. D. 109/Mason's Charity; S.R.O., Charities Index.
[45] *7th Rep. Com. Char.* 442–3.
[46] L.J.R.O., D. 35/bailiffs' accts. 1657–1707, p. 66; *Lichfield Cathedral Reg.* (Staffs. Par. Reg. Soc. 1973–4), 9; S.H.C. 1936, 146. [47] *7th Rep. Com. Char.* 442–3.
[48] Harwood, *Lichfield*, 374.
[49] L.J.R.O., D. 29/4/2, p. 36; D. 29/6/2; S.R.O., Charities Index; *St. Chad's Par. Mag.* May 1930 (copy in W.S.L.).
[50] L.J.R.O., P/C/11, Alice Simpson (1674); Shaw, *Staffs.* i. 338.

[51] *7th Rep. Com. Char.* 443–4, dating Green's agreement 1696. W.S.L., M. 849, and *Char. Dons.* 1158–9, date it 1736.
[52] L.J.R.O., D. 29/4/2, pp. 37–8.
[53] Reade, *Johnsonian Gleanings*, i. 35; Harwood, *Lichfield*, 374, wrongly giving the bequest as £5 5s.
[54] L.J.R.O., P/C/11, Eliz. Preest (1838); *Staffs. Advertiser,* 12 Apr. 1834.
[55] L.J.R.O., D. 29/1/2; D. 29/4/2, pp. 28–30, 55; D. 29/6/2, notes on Preest's Charity.
[56] Christ Church, Lichfield, parcel 2; S.R.O., Charities Index.
[57] S.R.O., Charities Index; *Lichfield Mercury*, 6 June 1952, p. 8; above, churches (Christ Church).
[58] S.R.O., D. 4108, box L; R. Simms, *Bibliotheca Staffordiensis* (Lichfield, 1894), 319–20; *Repton Sch. Reg. 1557–1905*, ed. G. S. Messiter, 86; Scheme of 30 Sept. 1955.

OTHER PAROCHIAL CHARITIES. *Chetwynd and Plumer's Charity.* In 1726 or 1727[59] Walter Chetwynd and Richard Plumer, the city's M.P.s, gave the corporation £400 for the poor, to be divided equally between the city portions of St. Michael's and St. Chad's. Over £300 was used in 1730 to buy 32 a. in Mayfield. The remaining money was left at interest, yielding £1 12s. a year until 1753 and £1 8s. a year thereafter. In the 19th century the Mayfield rental was £30–£40 a year. The corporation paid money on request to the churchwardens of the two parishes, who generally used it to apprentice poor boys. From 1835 the charity was one of the Municipal Charities. The Order of 1843 regulating the Municipal Charities widened the potential range of benefactions while retaining the original beneficial area, and was confirmed in 1891. The beneficial area was extended to the city in 1908.[60]

Phoebe Simpson's Charity. By deed of 1807 Phoebe Simpson of Stowe Hill gave £400 stock, the income to be divided equally between St. John's hospital and the three city parishes. The hospital's share was to be divided equally among the almsmen, and the money for the city parishes was to be given to their poor. About 1820 the charity's income, £20, was paid to the vicar of St. Mary's, who gave the overseers of the other two parishes their shares.[61] The charity lapsed in 1855 but was revived in 1869 and the arrears were recovered. By the 1940s the income was distributed in small Christmas gifts to the poor and the almsmen.[62] In 1980 the charity became part of Michael Lowe's and Associated Charities.

[59] Harwood, *Lichfield*, 536, gives 1726, perhaps supported by L.J.R.O., D. 35/bailiffs' accts. 1704–94, p. 93; W.S.L., M. 849 and Harwood, *Lichfield*, 372, give 1727.
[60] *7th Rep. Com. Char.* 435–7; *S.H.C.* 1920 and 1922, 225, 231–2; *Staffs. Advertiser*, 4 Apr. 1868, p. 6; 23 June 1888, p. 2; inf. from the Clerk, Lichfield Municipal Charities.
[61] *7th Rep. Com. Char.* 434–5; above, manor (lay estates: Stowe Hill).
[62] L.J.R.O., D. 29/1/2 and 12; D. 109/Phoebe Simpson's Charity; *Staffs. Advertiser*, 28 Mar. 1868, p. 7.

OUTLYING TOWNSHIPS

BY the late 17th century the Lichfield parishes of St. Michael and St. Chad covered a large area outside the city. Besides the townships treated below, the area included Haselour and Statfold some miles east of the city which were claimed as part of St. Michael's. Both had become independent by the 1830s[1] and are reserved for treatment in a future volume.

BURNTWOOD

THE urban parish of Burntwood was formerly a township in the north-west of the parish of St. Michael, Lichfield.[2] In 1929 the name of the civil parish was changed from Burntwood, Edial, and Woodhouses to simply Burntwood.[3] Besides those three early hamlets the parish includes Chasetown and Chase Terrace, which grew up as mining villages in the later 19th century. Since the 1960s, following the closure of the last mine, there has been extensive residential development around Burntwood itself and in Chasetown and Chase Terrace, along with some industrial growth, and in 1974 the parish was designated an urban parish. The east and north-west parts remain agricultural.

The township originally covered 4,417 a.[4] In 1879 an area of 8 a. around the present Ashmore Brook House was added from Curborough and Elmhurst.[5] In 1929 an area of 613 a. around Abnalls and Ashmore Brook was transferred to Farewell and Chorley, and in 1934 one of 93 a. covering Pipe Grange farm, Hilltop farm, and the fishponds at Maple Hayes was added to Wall. Burntwood was thus reduced to 3,719 a. (1,506 ha.).[6] In 1980 nearly 251 a. (101.2 ha.) in the corner of the parish south of Lichfield Road at Edial were transferred to Hammerwich.[7] This article covers the parish as it was constituted before the boundary changes of the 20th century.

Several streams form stretches of the parish boundary. On the north-west the boundary runs along Big Crane brook and follows it through Biddulph's Pool, evidently formed in 1734.[8] Further south the brook is joined by Little Crane brook and becomes Crane brook, mentioned in 1300.[9] The area below the confluence was formerly occupied by Norton bog, but c. 1798 Crane brook was dammed to form Norton Pool, a reservoir for the Wyrley and Essington Canal. The pool was renamed Chasewater in 1956 and is now part of a pleasure park.[10] The boundary runs through the middle of it.

On the north the boundary follows a stream known in the early 19th century as Dry or Bye brook to its confluence with Redmoor brook and then runs along the line of the former mill stream taken off Redmoor brook for Coney mill.[11] It then turns east along Chorley Road as far as the bridge over Maple brook (formerly Chestall brook); the bridge existed by 1597 when it was known as Maple bridge.[12] The boundary follows Maple brook as far as Creswell Green. Parts of the former boundary on the north-east followed Bilson brook (formerly Bourne brook).[13] On the south-east a short stretch of the boundary follows the upper reaches of Leamonsley (or Pipe) brook.[14] Much of the pre-1980 southern boundary was formed by Black brook (formerly Hammerwich Water).[15]

The ground rises from around 300 ft. (91 m.) along the eastern boundary to 500 ft. (152 m.) in the south-west along Chasewater and 650 ft. (198 m.) in the north-west where it rises steeply on the edge of Cannock Chase. There is some

[1] White, *Dir. Staffs.* (1834), 358–9, 379.
[2] This article was written mainly in 1986–7. The Revd. J. F. Molyneux, parish priest of St. Joseph's, Chasetown, 1978–87, and others named in footnotes are thanked for their help.
[3] Below, local govt. For the boundaries between the three hamlets in the early 19th century see S.R.O., D. (W.) 3222/191/25.
[4] *Census*, 1881.
[5] Ibid. 1891; P.R.O., RG 10/2914; RG 11/2773; below, Curborough and Elmhurst, introduction.
[6] *Census*, 1931, 1951; Staffs. Review Order, 1934, p. 64 and map 7 (copy in S.R.O.).
[7] The Lichfield (Parishes) Order 1980, S.I. 1980 no. 387; inf. from the Chief Executive, Lichfield District Council.

[8] Below, econ. hist. (park, warrens, and fisheries).
[9] *S.H.C.* v (1), 178.
[10] C. Hadfield, *Canals of W. Midlands* (1985), 96; below, social and cultural activities.
[11] S.R.O., D. (W.) 3222/191/20–2; D. 4045/8/8/3.
[12] Ibid. D. (W.) 1734/J. 2057, m. 3; D. (W.) 1734/2/1/601, m. 19; D. (W.) 1734/2/3/112D; W.S.L., S. MS. 326/2, m. 5; J.R.U.L.M., Ryl. Ch. Phillipps 126, dorse.
[13] S.R.O., D. (W.) 1734/2/1/379, m. 1d.; D. (W.) 1734/2/1/380, m. 4; D. 833/3/1, deed of 23 Dec. 1745; J.R.U.L.M., Ryl. Ch. Phillipps 126.
[14] S.R.O., D. (W.) 3222/191/20; D. (W.) 1734/2/3/112D; *Gent. Mag.* lv (2), 496.
[15] Below, Hammerwich, introduction.

BURNTWOOD 1987

N

| 0 | 500 | 1,000 Yards |
| 0 | 500 | 1,000 Metres |

site of Coney Mill

Maple

Chorley Road

Coney Lodge Farm

Redmoor Brook

Green Lane Farm

School

BONEY HAY

Kingsdown Road

Rugeley Road

Springlestyche Lane

Ironstone Road

600

School

Castle Farm

Meg Lane

CHASE TERRACE

Rake Hill

Nag's Head Inn

St. John's

M

Cross St.

Redwood Drive

Slade Avenue

Morley Road

600

Biddulph's Pool

to Cannock

Cannock Road

Princess Street

New Street

Water Street

site of No. 5 Pit

School

Sankey's Corner

Bridge Cross Road

School

Elder Lane

School

to Norton Canes

Big Crane Brook

site of No. 3 Pit

Emmanuel

Library and Council Offices

Oakdene Road

Springhill Road

Memorial Institute

M

Recreation Centre

High Street

School

Cannock Road

Cannock School

CHASETOWN

School

Vicarage

School

Chase Road

site of Ball Inn

site of No. 4 Pit

Hill St.

Elim

RC

Norton Lane

Union Street

New St.

site of No. 2 Pit

Queen Street

M

500

Church Street

School

site of Gasworks

St. Anne's

Sailing Centre

Chasewater

Fig. 17

196

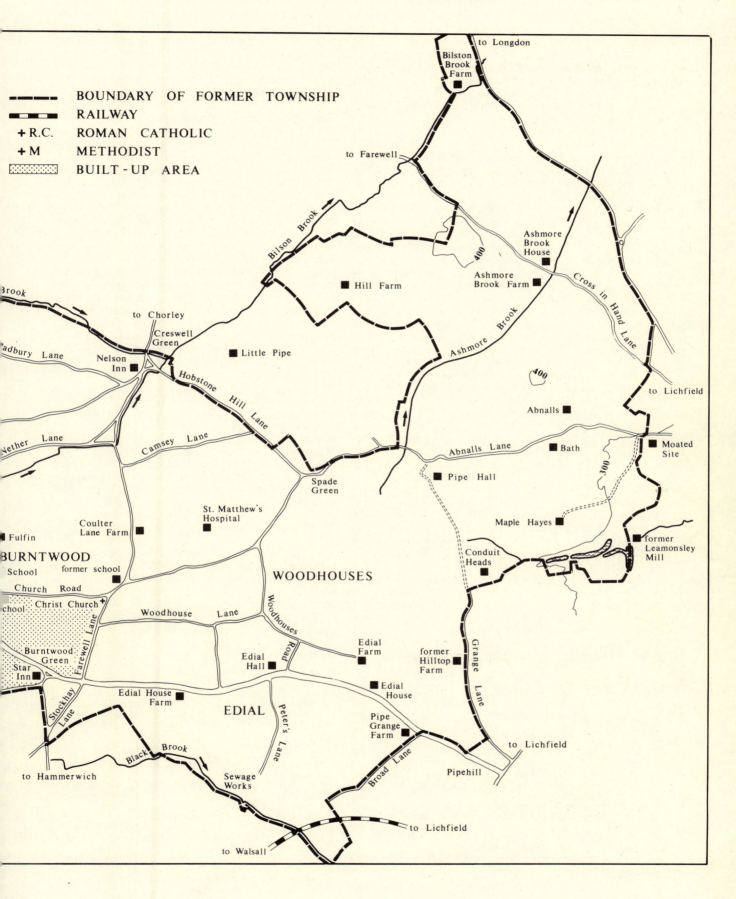

BOUNDARY OF FORMER TOWNSHIP
RAILWAY
+R.C.   ROMAN CATHOLIC
+M   METHODIST
BUILT-UP AREA

to Longdon

Bilston Brook Farm

to Farewell

Bilson Brook

Hill Farm

Ashmore Brook House

Ashmore Brook Farm

Cross in Hand Lane

to Chorley

Creswell Green

Padbury Lane

Nelson Inn

Little Pipe

Hobstone Hill Lane

Ashmore Brook

400

to Lichfield

Abnalls

400

Nether Lane

Camsey Lane

Abnalls Lane

Bath

300

Moated Site

Spade Green

Pipe Hall

Fulfin

Coulter Lane Farm

St. Matthew's Hospital

Maple Hayes

former Leamonsley Mill

BURNTWOOD

School   former school

Conduit Heads

Church Road

WOODHOUSES

Christ Church +

Woodhouse   Lane

Woodhouses Road

Burntwood Green

Star Inn

Farewell Lane

Edial Hall

Edial Farm

former Hilltop Farm

Grange Lane

Edial House

Stockhay Lane

Edial House Farm

EDIAL

Peter's Lane

Pipe Grange Farm

to Lichfield

to Hammerwich

Black Brook

Sewage Works

Broad Lane

Pipehill

to Lichfield

to Walsall

197

undulation in the east where the level rises to 401 ft. (122 m.) north-west of Abnalls but falls again to Ashmore brook, with a similar rise and fall to Bilson brook. Hobstone Hill to the north-west of Woodhouses rises to 489 ft. (149 m.).

Most of the area overlies the Keuper Sandstone, and on the east Cross in Hand Lane and Abnalls Lane are cut deeply through it. There is an area of Bunter Upper Mottled Sandstone in the south part of Chasetown. The Eastern Boundary Fault of the Cannock Chase Coalfield runs down the western edge of the parish. There is extensive Boulder Clay in the west part of the parish, which remained heathland until its inclosure in 1861.[16]

Sixty people were assessed for hearth tax in 1666.[17] In 1801 the population was 582, and it increased steadily to 749 in 1841 and 781 in 1851.[18] With the development of mining, numbers rose to 1,632 in 1861, 4,525 in 1871 (but including 549 in the lunatic asylum opened in 1864), 6,270 in 1881, and 7,113 in 1891; many of the newcomers were Irish.[19] The slowing down in the rate of growth was due at least in part to a depression in the coal trade: the master at the school in Chasetown recorded in January 1877 and April 1882 that the depression was causing families to leave the area in search of employment elsewhere.[20] The population was 8,195 in 1901, 8,636 in 1911, and 9,302 in 1921. After the boundary change of 1929 the reduced parish had a population of 8,883 in 1931. Numbers had risen to 10,750 by 1951 and 12,085 by 1961. The rapid growth of the area as a residential district in the 1960s brought the population to 23,088 in 1971. It had risen to 26,186 by 1981.[21]

GROWTH OF SETTLEMENT. The whole township lay within the part of Cannock forest which became Cannock Chase in the 13th century. The eastern side had the earlier settlement and was known as Pipe c. 1140.[22] The name may have derived from the conduit south of Pipe Hall which supplied water to Lichfield Close or simply from the watercourse (Leomansley or Pipe brook) which rises near the conduit.[23] A manor house evidently existed at Pipe by the mid 12th century.[24] There was settlement at Abnalls and Ashmore Brook and probably Edial by the later 13th century and at Woodhouses by

the mid 15th century. Burntwood itself was not recorded as a hamlet until the later 16th century and was never part of Pipe manor. The north-east part of the township was known as Childerhay by 1298,[25] with the area further west around Spade Green known as Childerend Pipe and Childerhay End in the later 16th century.[26]

The name Burntwood was in use by 1298 when the bishop had 300 a. of common pasture in 'Brendewode'.[27] The spelling Brundwood became normal in the later 16th century and was itself superseded by the modern spelling in the 17th century.[28] It has been suggested that the name derives from the burning of a heath in Cannock forest by the vill of Hammerwich; a presentment of the incident was made at the forest proceedings in 1262.[29] It may, however, derive simply from the clearance of woodland by burning for agricultural purposes. There was settlement at Burntwood by 1570,[30] and in 1600 a blacksmith of Burntwood was licensed to keep an alehouse there.[31] The hamlet probably centred on the green at the junction of Norton Lane and Cannock Road. Norton Lane was mentioned in 1449.[32] Cannock Road was formerly Cannock Street, mentioned in 1698, the name being changed in the early 20th century.[33] The green was apparently known as Hanley green in the late 17th century, but it was called Burntwood green in 1724. A house which stood there in the early 17th century was occupied as the Star inn by 1790; it has since been rebuilt.[34] It may have taken its name from Star Lane (later Hammerwich Road) leading south from the green and so named by 1453.[35] A beerhouse known as the Three Horseshoes stood on the south side of the green by 1770 and was still there in the mid 19th century.[36] 'Stok' Lane mentioned in 1437[37] may have been Stockhay Lane, which runs south-west from the green. By 1775 there was settlement further west on the edge of the heath in Norton Lane and in the northern end of what was later called Chase Road. The former Ball inn, which stood in Chase Road by 1824, may already have been there in 1775.[38]

There was also scattered early settlement north of the green up to the parish boundary. There were buildings in what is now Church Road by 1775,[39] and in 1769 a school was

[16] V.C.H. Staffs. i, map before p. 1; Geol. Surv. 1", drift, sheet 154 (1922 edn.). For a band of red marl S. of Boney Hay used for brickmaking see below, econ. hist.
[17] S.H.C. 1923, 162–4.
[18] V.C.H. Staffs. i. 323.
[19] P.R.O., RG 9/1973; RG 10/2914–15; RG 11/2773–4; Census, 1881, 1891.
[20] S.R.O., CEL/85/1, pp. 249, 332.
[21] Census, 1901–81. The figure for 1981 refers to the parish as constituted before the boundary change of 1980.
[22] V.C.H. Staffs. iii. 223.
[23] Eng. Place-Name Elements (E.P.N.S.), ii. 65; E. Ekwall, Eng. River-Names, 327; above, Lichfield, public services.
[24] Below, manors.
[25] S.R.O., D. (W.) 1734/J. 2268, f. 4v.; D. (W.) 1734/2/3/112D; W.S.L. 132/8/xxii/47.
[26] W.S.L., S. MS. 326/2, mm. 5–6; S.R.O., D. (W.) 1734/J. 2042–4.
[27] S.R.O., D. (W.) 1734/J. 2268, f. 1.
[28] Ibid. D. (W.) 1734/2/1/609, m. 18; D. (W.)

[29] S.H.C. v (1), 136 (where 'vills' should read 'vill'); Burntwood: a town guide (1985 edn.), 5.
[30] S.R.O., D. (W.) 1734/2/1/609, m. 19; below, local govt.
[31] S.H.C. 1935, 205.
[32] S.R.O., D. (W.) 1734/2/1/603, m. 29.
[33] B.R.L. 338243; O.S. Map 6", Staffs. LII. SW. (1902 and 1924 edns.).
[34] Deeds in possession of Sharrott, Barnes & Co., solicitors of Lichfield; B.R.L. 338243; L.J.R.O., B/A/15/Burntwood, nos. 223–4; L.J.R.O., D. 27/1/3, ff. 20, 22.
[35] Below, Hammerwich, introduction.
[36] S.R.O., D. (W.) 1511(34)/33, Longdon; L.J.R.O., B/A/15/Burntwood, no. 258; White, Dir. Staffs. (1834), 105; (1851), 115; P.O. Dir. Staffs. (1850).
[37] S.R.O., D. (W.) 1734/2/1/600, m. 8; D. (W.) 1734/2/1/603, m. 7.
[38] Above, fig. 1; W.S.L. 47/1/45, f. 34.
[39] Above, fig. 1.
1734/2/1/614, mm. 35d., 36d.

opened nearby at the southern end of Coulter Lane, itself mentioned in 1670.[40] A church was opened in 1820 at the junction of Church Road and Farewell Lane (known as Chorley Road until 1974).[41] Coulter Lane Farm probably dates from c. 1800. Creswell Green on the boundary at the northern end of Coulter Lane was an inhabited area by 1380 when Henry of Cressewalle was assessed for tax.[42] There was evidently settlement in the Padbury Lane area to the south-west by 1298 when John of Padbury held land in Pipe.[43] Padbury Way was mentioned in the early 16th century, and there were buildings in Padbury Lane by 1775.[44] The Nelson inn at Cresswell Green existed by 1824.[45]

Fulfen on Rugeley Road to the west was an inhabited area by the 1530s; Fulfen Way was mentioned in 1446.[46] Cottages had been built at Fulfen by 1577 as encroachments on the waste.[47] The Nag's Head inn at the junction of Rugeley Road and Nether Lane existed by 1799 and probably by 1775.[48] A farm occupied the site of Green Lane Farm near the junction of Green Lane and Rugeley Road by 1700, and by 1753 there were two small farmsteads there.[49] West of Rugeley Road there was settlement by 1775 in the Rake Hill area.[50] There was waste called Rackhill in 1597, and Rakehill Lane was mentioned in 1670.[51] The road now called Rake Hill was known as Stephen's Hill in the early 19th century.[52] Castle Farm in Meg Lane dates from c. 1700. The nearby Springlestyche Lane was mentioned in 1597 as Springlesuch Lane.[53]

Boney Hay west of Ogley Hay Road became a populous area in the later 19th century. It evidently derives its name from waste called 'le Burnehew' in 1361.[54] The area was known as Burnehey and Bornehay by the 16th century, and in 1571 there was a house there.[55] Coney Lodge and Coney mill on the heath to the north-west evidently existed by the 17th century.[56]

Twenty-nine people in Burntwood were assessed for hearth tax in 1666.[57] The hamlet and its outlying area had a population of 426 in 1841 and 483 in 1851.[58] Nailing had by then become important.[59] With the development of coalmining on the west side of the heath in the 1850s and the inclosure of the heath in 1861 the landscape was transformed. New centres of population

developed rapidly. Old roads were realigned or obliterated and new ones were laid out. In particular a new road had been made by 1859 north-west from Burntwood green to the boundary at Biddulph's Pool whence it continued to Cannock.[60]

The village of Chasetown, at first known simply as Cannock Chase, developed on either side of an existing road running north across the heath; at first the road was called Rugeley Road, but by 1881 it had become High Street. Colliery Road, renamed Church Street by 1881, gave access to the mine opened at its west end in 1852.[61] There was initially no housing for miners near the pits on either side of the boundary with Hammerwich, and many settled in and around Burntwood hamlet and in Hammerwich.[62] Three pairs of cottages were built on the north side of Colliery Road c. 1854, and the adjoining Uxbridge Arms existed by 1856.[63] In 1858 building plots were advertised along Rugeley Road and Lichfield Road (Queen Street by 1881), 'situations where houses are very much in demand'.[64] An Anglican mission centre was started in the late 1850s, with a church from 1865; there was a school by 1859. The Queen's hotel in Lichfield Road was being used for meetings by Wesleyan Methodists in 1860.[65] Two shopkeepers, three beer retailers (besides the landlord of the Uxbridge Arms), a builder, a drill owner, a shoemaker, and a market gardener were listed at the village of Cannock Chase in 1860.[66] A new road (later Edwards Road) linked Rugeley Road and Lichfield Road by 1861.[67] After the inclosure of that year terraces of houses were built along both sides of those two main roads.[68] By 1867 the village was known as Chasetown.[69] The credit for devising the name is variously given to George Poole, vicar of Burntwood, and his wife and to Elijah Wills, master of the boys' department at the school.[70] New Street and Union Street were so named by 1881, and by 1883 building extended to Hill Street and beyond.[71] New houses were built further north along High Street in the early 20th century.[72] In 1902 a clock with three gas lamps was erected at the junction of High Street and Queen Street as a memorial to local people killed in the Boer War. It was knocked down by a lorry

[40] S.R.O., D. (W.) 1734/2/1/747, p. 116; below, education.
[41] Burntwood Libr., Burntwood par. council mins., roads and street lighting cttee. mins. 24 Apr. 1974; below, churches.
[42] S.H.C. xvii. 178
[43] S.R.O., D. (W.) 1734/J. 2268, f. 2v.
[44] J.R.U.L.M., Ryl. Ch. Phillipps 126; above, fig. 1.
[45] W.S.L. 47/1/45, f. 30; S.R.O., D. 4045/7/2.
[46] Below, manors; J.R.U.L.M., Ryl. Ch. Phillipps 126.
[47] S.R.O., D. (W.) 1734/2/1/612, m. 14d.
[48] Ibid. D. 4045/7/2; above, fig. 1.
[49] Deeds kindly made available by Mr. and Mrs. C. Gooch of Green Lane Farm.
[50] Above, fig. 1.
[51] S.R.O., D. (W.) 1734/2/1/747, p. 116; D. (W.) 1734/2/3/112D.
[52] S.R.O., D. (W.) 1821/5.
[53] Ibid. D. (W.) 1734/2/3/112D.
[54] Ibid. D. (W.) 1734/2/1/598, m. 19
[55] Ibid. D. (W.) 1734/2/3/112D; W.S.L., S. MS. 326/2, m. 5; J.R.U.L.M., Ryl. Ch. Phillipps 126.
[56] Below, econ. hist.
[57] S.H.C. 1923, 163.
[58] P.R.O., HO 107/980; HO 107/2014 (2).
[59] Below, econ. hist.
[60] S.R.O., Q/RDc 102C; Staffs. Advertiser, 1 Oct. 1859, p. 8.
[61] P.R.O., RG 9/1973; RG 10/2914; RG 11/2773; below, econ. hist.
[62] S.R.O., D. 603/M/6/1, Landor to Beer 5 Mar. 1850; P.R.O., HO 107/2014 (2).
[63] S.R.O., D. 603/M/6/2, Landor to Beer 7 Aug. 1853, Woodhouse to Landor 15 Apr. 1854, Woodhouse to Beer 18 Apr. 1854; D. 1456/7, p. 15; ibid. Q/RDc 99.
[64] Staffs. Advertiser, 18 Sept. 1858, p. 8; 23 Oct. 1858, p. 8; W.S.L., Sale Cat. F/5/17.
[65] Below, churches; prot. nonconformity; education.
[66] P.O. Dir. Staffs. (1860).
[67] Staffs. Advertiser, 19 Oct. 1861, p. 8.
[68] P.R.O., RG 10/2914.
[69] Lond. Gaz. 5 Feb. 1867, p. 625.
[70] Mason, Found Ready, 48; The Blackcountryman, ix (2), 26.
[71] P.R.O., RG 11/2773; O.S. Map 6″, Staffs. LI. SE. (1888 edn.); LVII. NE. (1887 edn.).
[72] O.S. Map 6″, Staffs. LI. SE. (1921 edn.); date stones of 1915 and 1916; below, churches.

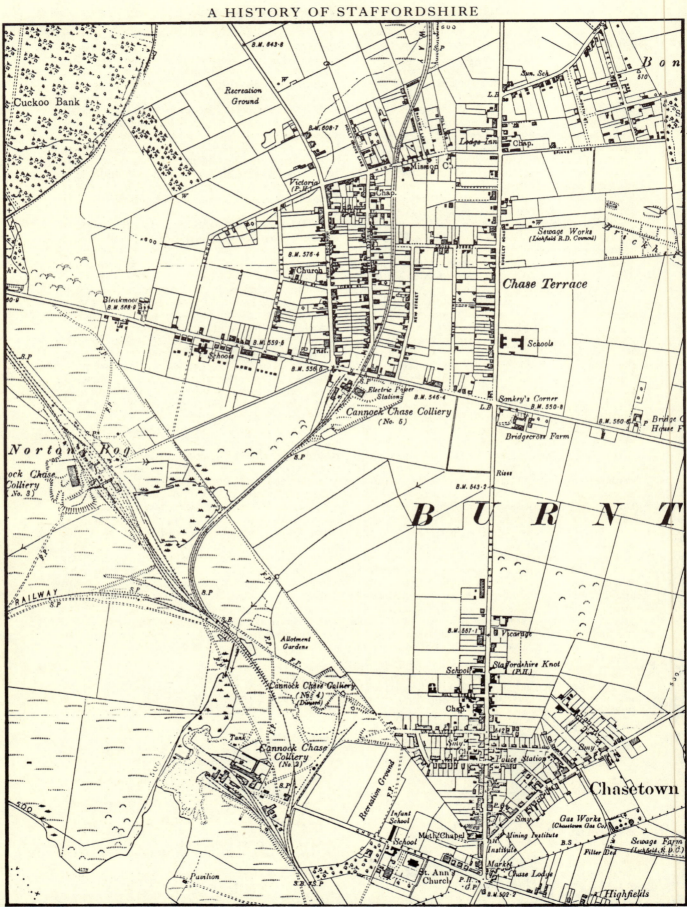

FIG. 18. CHASETOWN AND CHASE TERRACE 1915: scale 6 in. to 1 mile (1:10,650)

in 1967. It was replaced by a new clock in 1969, but that too was damaged in 1979 and no longer stands.[73]

By the early 1860s mining had spread north, with new mines on the south side of Cannock Road.[74] There was a beer retailer at Biddulph's Pool by 1864.[75] A new mining village known by 1870 as Chase Terrace developed in the area north of Cannock Road and west of Rugeley Road. Two Oaks inn, in the road called High Street by 1870, existed by 1868 and probably by 1864.[76] Building land near the inn was advertised in 1868 and 1870 and in Ironstone Road in 1868; Ironstone Road itself was an old road across the heath. Building plots in a new road leading off Ironstone Road were advertised in 1871.[77] The same year 101 plots were advertised fronting on Cannock Road, Rugeley Road, and other roads then being made. It was stressed that houses were in great demand and rents high; many of the miners employed in the nearby pits had to walk many miles to work.[78] A Primitive Methodist chapel was opened in Prince's (by 1915 Princess) Street in 1870 and a school in Cannock Road in 1875.[79] On the east side of Rugeley Road Boney Hay was already a predominantly mining community in 1861, and it continued to develop as such over the next two decades.[80] In 1884 the Chase Terrace area had a population of nearly 2,000.[81] Chase Terrace itself continued to expand. Cross Street and New Street had been formed by 1900 and Water Street by 1915; by then the corresponding side of Rugeley Road had been built up.[82] By 1928 the population of the area was 3,350.[83]

Several farms were formed after the 1861 inclosure. Bridge Cross farm, south-east of the crossroads on the Cannock and Rugeley roads, dated from 1864; Byrdes Crosse, a place name found in 1578, was probably an early form of Bridge Cross.[84] Thomas Sankey was evidently the first occupant of the farm, and by 1900 the area round the crossroads was known as Sankey's Corner.[85] Bridge Cross House Farm further east on the north side of the main road had been built by 1866, with Morlings Farm to the north-east and Spinney Farm at Boney Hay by 1883.[86]

A large number of houses were built between the two World Wars, notably along the Cannock road, Springhill Road, and the northern stretch of High Street, Chasetown.[87] Parks were laid out. That at the southern end of High Street, Chasetown, was opened in 1923 as a war memorial. The ornamental gateway was erected by miners' subscriptions in memory of Arthur Sopwith, general manager of the Cannock Chase Colliery Co. 1873–1918.[88] Burntwood park at the junction of Cannock Road and Elder Road was opened in 1931 and Chase Terrace park between High Street and Cross Street in 1932.[89]

Soon after the Second World War the Oakdene estate east of Chasetown was begun, and it was still expanding in 1958, when it was the largest council estate in Lichfield rural district.[90] The last mine in the area was closed in 1959, but between 1961 and 1971 the population nearly doubled as Burntwood became an overspill area for people from Birmingham and the Black Country. The western side of the parish developed as a predominantly residential district with both council and privately built housing.[91] Building continued in the 1980s; council estates have included one of 26 houses and flats on derelict ground between Queen Street and High Street in Chasetown completed in 1986 and the Rake Hill estate begun that year.[92] There has been industrial development on the mining sites south-west of Sankey's Corner and also in Chasetown and Burntwood, but most of the working population are commuters whose employment is outside the area.[93] Sankey's Corner has become the commercial and administrative centre, with the development of an industrial estate, the opening of the Burntwood Town Shopping Centre and the market in 1970, and the completion of the library and the parish council offices in 1987.[94]

The hamlet of Edial developed along the stretch of the Lichfield road east of Burntwood known by 1409 as Edial Lane.[95] A house in the area passed to the Kynchall family in 1299; the place from which they took their name evidently lay around the junction of Lichfield Road and Broad Lane where the late 18th-century Pipe Grange Farm stands.[96] Broad Lane, so called in

---

[73] Lambourne and James, *Burntwood*, 36; Burntwood Libr., Burntwood par. council mins. 19 Apr. 1967, 5 Feb. 1969, and environmental cttee. mins. 5 Sept. 1979.
[74] Below, econ. hist.
[75] *P.O. Dir. Staffs.* (1864).
[76] *Staffs. Advertiser*, 17 Oct. 1868, p. 8; 7 May 1870, p. 8; *P.O. Dir. Staffs.* (1864; 1868); S.R.O., Q/RDc 102c.
[77] *Staffs. Advertiser*, 14 Apr. 1868, p. 8; 17 Oct. 1868, p. 8; 7 May 1870, p. 8; 9 Dec. 1871, p. 8; S.R.O., D. (W.) 3222/191/20–1.
[78] *Staffs. Advertiser*, 8 Apr. 1871, p. 8; 10 June 1871, p. 8; 28 Oct. 1871, p. 8.
[79] O.S. Map 6″, Staffs. LI. SE. (1921 edn.); below, prot. nonconformity; education.
[80] P.R.O., RG 9/1973; RG 10/2914; RG 11/2774; *Staffs. Advertiser*, 23 Mar. 1872, p. 8; *Lichfield Mercury*, 2 Sept. 1881, p. 5.
[81] *Lich. Dioc. Mag.* (1884), 139.
[82] O.S. Map 6″, Staffs. LI. SE. (1902 and 1921 edns.); date stone of 1893 in Cross St.; Lichfield R.D.C. *Ann. Rep. of M.O.H. 1914*, 27 (copy in S.R.O., C/H/1/2/2/25).
[83] *Lichfield Mercury*, 12 Oct. 1928, p. 5.
[84] Inscription on the former farmhouse, now Bridge Cross

Working Men's Club; S.R.O., D. (W.) 1734/2/1/612, m. 29.
[85] P.R.O., RG 10/2914; *Staffs. Advertiser*, 28 Feb. 1874, p. 1; *P.O. Dir. Staffs.* (1868; 1872); O.S. Map 6″, Staffs. LI. SE. (1902 edn.); above, plate 40.
[86] *Staffs. Advertiser*, 28 Feb. 1874, p. 1; O.S. Map 6″, Staffs. LI. SE. (1888 edn.).
[87] O.S. Map 1/2,500, Staffs. LI. 16 (1947 edn.).
[88] Lambourne and James, *Burntwood*, 42; *Lichfield Mercury*, 13 Apr. 1923, p. 4; 4 May 1923, p. 5; below, econ. hist. (coal mining).
[89] *Lichfield Mercury*, 5 June 1931, p. 6; 15 July 1932, p. 9.
[90] Ibid. 3 Nov. 1950, p. 3; 4 Apr. 1952, p. 4; 4 Mar. 1955, p. 2; *Cannock Chase Courier*, 9 Jan. 1958, pp. 6–7.
[91] *Lichfield Mercury*, 6 Aug. 1971, p. 17; *The Blackcountryman*, ix (3), 55, 58; Burntwood Libr., par. council mins.
[92] *Lichfield Mercury*, 14 Nov. 1986, p. 7; 2 Jan. 1987, p. 13.
[93] *Burntwood: a town guide* (1985 edn.), 5; Lambourne and James, *Burntwood*, 3.
[94] *Lichfield Mercury*, 31 July 1970, pp. 10–12; below, social and cultural activities; econ. hist.; local govt.
[95] S.R.O., D. 150/1/186 and 196; D. (W.) 1734/1/4/3A; 1734/2/1/760, m.97; W.S.L., S. MS. 326/2, m. 6; *S.H.C.* vii (1), 232; x (1), 110; *S.H.C.* 1939, 81–2.
[96] S.R.O., D. (W.) 1734/2/1/599, m. 32d.; 603, m. 41.

1453, may be the Kynchall Lane of 1412.[97] An inn kept by the Webbs of Edial at least between 1417 and 1466 was probably the inn in the township mentioned in 1496.[98] A predecessor of Edial House Farm existed by the later 17th century and probably earlier, and the Edial Hall demolished in 1809 probably dated from the late 17th century.[99] Edial Farm was built as a small house in the later 18th century and was extended twice in the 19th century; it has farm buildings of the late 18th and early 19th century.[1] Edial House originated in the late 18th century as a small brick cottage. It was enlarged by the addition of a new block towards Lichfield Road in the early 19th century and another to the east late in the century; it was further enlarged to the west in the later 20th century.[2] Forge Lane was so named by 1616.[3] Peter's Lane existed by 1725.[4] A stretch of the railway opened in 1849 from Walsall to Wychnor via Lichfield[5] runs across the area south of Broad Lane. In 1666 sixteen people in Edial were assessed for hearth tax.[6] The population was 98 in 1841 and 76 in 1851.[7]

The rest of the parish lay within the hamlet of Woodhouses and included small settlements at Abnalls and Ashmore Brook. In 1666 at least 17 people in Woodhouses were assessed for hearth tax.[8] The population was 225 in 1841 and 222 in 1851.[9]

Woodhouses presumably originated as a clearing in the woodland, and the place name 'Wodehousleye' is found in the area in 1374.[10] Woodhouse green was mentioned in 1433.[11] Settlement spread along Woodhouses Road, with two open fields to the east extending to the township boundary along Grange Lane.[12] There was a farm at Hilltop on the Woodhouses side of Grange Lane by the early 17th century; the name Hilltop was in use in 1693.[13] Woodhouse Lane, formerly called Pinfold Lane and Green Lane, was probably the road described in 1656 as the common road from Pipe-Woodhouses to Cannock heath.[14] A county lunatic asylum was opened in 1864 on Hobstone Hill north-west of Woodhouses.[15] A way at Hobbestone mentioned in 1392 may have been the Hobbestone Lane of 1571 and the Hobstone Hill Lane which runs south-east from Cresswell Green along the par-

ish boundary.[16] Spade Green on the boundary further south-east was mentioned in 1538 and was an inhabited area by 1690 when Spade Green House was mentioned.[17] Thirteen poplars were planted at Spade Green to commemorate the battle of Waterloo; the last was cut down in 1930.[18]

Abnalls on the road from Lichfield to Chorley was an inhabited area in 1275,[19] but its name, probably Old English in origin and meaning Abba's nook of land,[20] suggests earlier settlement. The moated site on the Lichfield side of the boundary may have been that of the medieval manor house.[21] The road, now Abnalls Lane, was known as Pipe Lane at least between 1464 and 1683.[22] The point where it goes over the boundary was described in 1597 as 'the place where the broken cross in Pipe Lane stood'; a ditch at Broken Cross was mentioned in 1467.[23] There was a farm at Maple Hayes south of Abnalls by the early 18th century; the present house there dates from c. 1790.[24]

The grounds of what was formerly the home farm of Maple Hayes on the south side of Abnalls Lane contain the remains of the botanic garden laid out by Erasmus Darwin in the late 1770s. The $7\frac{1}{2}$-a. site on an east-facing slope was described by Anna Seward as 'a little, wild, umbrageous valley, a mile from Lichfield, amongst the only rocks which neighbour the city so nearly. It was irriguous from various springs, and swampy from their plenitude.' It included a spring called Unett's Well and the bath built over the spring by Sir John Floyer in 1701, 'the only mark of human industry which could be found in the tangled and sequestered scene'. There Darwin 'widened the brook into small lakes' and also 'taught it to wind between shrubby margins'. He planted a variety of trees and plants, 'uniting the Linnean science with the charm of landscape'.[25] Darwin left Lichfield in 1781, and William Jackson, a fellow member of the Lichfield Botanical Society and a proctor of the bishop's consistory court, then looked after the garden until his death in 1798.[26] In 1799 Darwin conveyed the lease to his son Erasmus, although he successfully opposed his son's plan to build himself a cottage there.[27] The younger Erasmus's widow Elizabeth conveyed the lease in 1804 to John Atkinson, who the

[97] Ibid. D. (W.) 1734/1/4/3A.
[98] Ibid. D. (W.) 1734/2/1/598, mm. 34, 54, 55d., 72; D. (W.) 1734/2/1/601, mm. 14 sqq.; D. (W.) 1734/2/1/602, m. 26; D. (W.) 1734/2/1/603, mm. 51, 59; D. (W.) 1734/2/1/604, m. 16d.
[99] Below, manors.
[1] Mr. and Mrs. W. B. Wort of Edial Farm are thanked for their help.
[2] Sir Eric and Lady Pountain of Edial House are thanked for their help.
[3] S.R.O., D. (W.) 1734/2/1/613, m. 67.
[4] Ibid. D. 150/4/4.
[5] Above, Lichfield, communications.
[6] S.H.C. 1923, 164.
[7] P.R.O., HO 107/980; HO 107/2014 (2).
[8] S.H.C. 1923, 161–2. At least two people, Walter Heveningham of Pipe Hall and Henry Sprott of Ashmore Brook, were included under Chorley.
[9] P.R.O., HO 107/980; HO 107/2014 (2).
[10] S.R.O., D. (W.) 1734/2/1/598, m. 27.
[11] Ibid. D. (W.) 1734/2/1/602, m. 20.
[12] Above, fig. 1; below, econ. hist.
[13] P.R.O., PROB 11/413, ff. 341v.–342; below, manors.

[14] S.R.O., D. (W.) 3222/191/25; L.J.R.O., D. 15/11/14/137, deed of 17 Nov. 1656; O.S. Map 6", Staffs. LII. SW. (1887 edn.).
[15] Below, public services.
[16] S.R.O., D. (W.) 1734/2/1/599, m. 24; W.S.L., S. MS. 326/2, m. 6; O.S. Map 6", Staffs. LII. SW. (1902 edn.).
[17] S.R.O., D. (W.) 1734/2/1/606, m. 25; D. 150/5/13, f. 48; W.S.L., S. MS. 326/2, m. 6.
[18] Lichfield Mercury, 7 Feb. 1930, p. 5.
[19] S.H.C. 1924, pp. 264–5.
[20] Place-Names of Glos. (E.P.N.S.), iii. 210.
[21] Below, manors.
[22] S.R.O., D. 150/6/1; D. (W.) 1734/2/1/598, m. 40.
[23] Ibid. D. (W.) 1734/2/1/598, m. 49; D. (W.) 1734/2/3/112D.
[24] Below, manors.
[25] A. Seward, Memoirs of the Life of Dr. Darwin (1804), 125–32; Letters of Anna Seward (Edinburgh, 1811), ii. 311–12; D. King-Hele, Doctor of Revolution, 110–12; S.R.O., D. 150/3/1; above, Lichfield, public services.
[26] Letters of Erasmus Darwin, ed. D. King-Hele, 110.
[27] Ibid. 314; King-Hele, Doctor of Revolution, 273; S.R.O., D. 150/3/2.

same year had bought Maple Hayes.[28] The site was advertised for letting in 1823 as the Abnalls 'with the Bath and fruit trees'.[29] Terraces and low banks there may indicate former garden features. The deeply cut stream along the south side is fed by at least two springs, and several pools formed by damming it survive. The larger spring is enclosed by the bath.

By the late 13th century there was settlement at Ashmore Brook, which lies on the road from Lichfield to Farewell mentioned in 1292.[30] The route of the London–Chester road formerly followed the lane as far as the Lichfield–Burntwood boundary and there branched off along the boundary.[31] By the later 17th century a hamlet on the boundary by the fork was known as Cross o' th' Hand. It took its name from 'the cross with the hand' mentioned in the later 15th and early 16th century, evidently a direction post. A post stood there in 1675, but it had gone by 1728 when the highway surveyors of St. Chad's parish were presented for not erecting 'a hand to direct travellers' at Cross o' th' Hand.[32]

To the north the boundary follows the line of the London–Chester road to a point beyond the bridge over Bilson brook; a bridge existed by 1597.[33] Bilston Brook farm in the north-eastern tip of the township was held by Thomas Bilson in 1580 and 1592, and his grandfather had held it before him.[34] The grandfather was probably the Thomas Bilston who was described as of Longdon Way c. 1540.[35] The farmhouse has a timber-framed cross wing which probably dates from the 17th century.[36] Hill farm to the south-west existed by the earlier 18th century.[37]

SOCIAL AND CULTURAL ACTIVITIES.

In the Middle Ages the inhabitants of Burntwood held their wake on the Sunday after Michaelmas.[38] A mid-October race meeting on the heath was started in 1835; the course, just under a mile round, was in the Ball's Mount and Spring Hill area west of Burntwood hamlet. The last meeting was held in 1854.[39] In 1896 land known as the old Burntwood racecourse, 12 a. in extent and fronting on the Lichfield–Cannock and Rugeley–Brownhills roads, was sold as 100 building plots.[40]

What became known as the Chase Wakes originated in the wakes at Chasetown held to celebrate the opening of St. Anne's church in September 1865. They became an annual event held on the third Monday, Tuesday, and Wednesday in September. In the mid 1870s they were transferred to the first Monday, Tuesday, and Wednesday.[41] A flower show was introduced on the Tuesday and Wednesday in 1868.[42] In 1877 a group of leading inhabitants started an athletics meeting on the Wednesday in a field in Church Street near the Colliery school, the aim being to keep people occupied 'at a time when, being out of harness, there is a tendency to give way to extravagant and pernicious practices'. From 1878 the meeting was held on the Tuesday also, and the sports became the central event of the wakes. In 1879 the proceedings on both days began with a procession which 'perambulated the country from Brownhills to Burntwood' and consisted of 'a cavalcade of inhabitants representing various characters in picturesque and grotesque costumes'.[43] A fun fair had been added by 1883. The date had by then been changed to the second Tuesday and Wednesday in August, evidently in order to coincide with the school holidays.[44] In 1919 the wakes were moved from Church Street to the Cannock Chase Colliery Co.'s sports ground on the east side of High Street, Chasetown. With the decline of coal mining in the area support for the wakes dwindled, and they ceased in 1959. In 1970 they were revived by Burntwood parish council on the same site, and they continue to be held on the first Saturday in August.[45]

The High Street ground was also used by the colliery company's football team, formed c. 1875. In the 1935–6 season it won the Walsall and District League Championship, the Fazeley Charity Cup, and the Walsall Senior Cup.[46] In the early 1930s there was a Princess Street Albion Football Club in Chase Terrace.[47] Chasetown Football Club originated in 1954 as Chase Terrace Old Scholars Youth Club, adopting the new name in 1972. Its pitch was on the High Street ground until 1983 when it opened the Scholars ground and clubhouse at the west end of Church Street. The facilities are also used by a number of other sports and social clubs.[48] By 1868 Chasetown had a cricket club, probably the colliery cricket club in existence by 1870 with a ground apparently in Church Street.[49] In 1883 a cricket match was played between

[28] S.R.O., D. 150/3/3; below, manors.
[29] *Lichfield Mercury*, 18 Apr. 1823.
[30] *S.H.C.* 1939, 90, 107–8; *Select Bills in Eyre 1292–1333* (Selden Soc. xxx), 48–9.
[31] Above, Lichfield, communications.
[32] S.R.O., D. (W.) 1734/2/1/598, mm. 39, 48; L.J.R.O., D. 29/3/1; D. 77/6/4, pp. 40, 119, 130; D. 77/9/6–7; J. Ogilby, *Britannia* (1675), 45 and pl. preceding; T. H. White, *The Marigold Window* (1849), 175.
[33] S.R.O., D. (W.) 1734/2/3/112D.
[34] Ibid. D. (W.) 1734/2/1/607, m. 2; D. (W.) 1734/2/1/738, pp. 129–30, 139; D. (W.) 1734/2/1/739, pp. 244–5; D. (W.) 1734/2/1/740/1, pp. 114, 118, 156.
[35] Ibid. D. (W.) 1734/2/1/739, pp.244–5; below, econ. hist. (agric.: fields).
[36] It has not been possible to gain admission to the house in order to make a detailed architectural survey.
[37] Below, manors.
[38] Bodl. MS. Ashmole 1521, p. 86.
[39] *V.C.H. Staffs.* ii. 367; C. H. Gregory, *Burntwood Past and Present* (Lichfield, 1953); W.S.L. 7/63/42.

[40] *Lichfield Mercury*, 16 Oct. 1896, p. 4; *Staffs. Advertiser*, 7 Nov. 1896, p. 4.
[41] Lambourne and James, *Burntwood*, 5; *Staffs. Advertiser*, 8 Sept. 1877, p. 4; *Lichfield Mercury*, 5 Sept. 1879, p. 5; S.R.O., CEL/85/1, pp. 23, 53, 84, 218, 232; CEL/85/3, pp. 207–8.
[42] *Staffs. Advertiser*, 19 Sept. 1868, p. 6; 8 Sept. 1877, p. 4.
[43] Ibid. 8 Sept. 1877, p. 4; *Lichfield Mercury*, 6 Sept. 1878; 5 Sept. 1879, p. 5.
[44] *Lichfield Mercury*, 17 Aug. 1883, p. 5; S.R.O., CEL/85/1, pp. 218, 305; CEL/85/3, pp. 185, 388.
[45] Lambourne and James, *Burntwood*, 5; *Lichfield Mercury*, 13 Aug. 1971, p. 9; 18 Aug. 1972, p. 9; 10 Aug. 1973, p. 9.
[46] *The Blackcountryman*, ix (2), 26; *Old Chasetown*, 80–1.
[47] Cannock Libr., Local Hist. Photographic Survey, 32PRI.
[48] Inf. from Mr. D. Shelton, manager of Chasetown F.C.
[49] *Staffs. Advertiser*, 15 Aug. 1868, p. 2; 25 June 1870, p. 2; S.R.O., CEL/85/1, pp. 153, 200, 32.

Burntwood and Hammerwich, evidently under the auspices of the respective incumbents; the Burntwood club was probably attached to the Burntwood Young Men's Friendly Society.[50] St. Matthew's cricket club dates from 1897.[51] There was a lawn tennis club at Chasetown by 1888.[52] In 1963 the National Coal Board leased the sports ground in High Street, Chasetown, to Burntwood parish council, which opened a swimming bath there in 1969; the present recreation centre includes squash courts and a table tennis room added in 1975 and a sports hall added in 1980.[53]

By the summer of 1899 Norton Pool was attracting local people and others from further away with a steamer and other boats provided on weekdays by Donaldson & Sons, apparently of the Uxbridge Arms in Church Street.[54] In 1956 the pool, having been taken over by Brownhills urban district council, was renamed Chasewater and opened to the public. The development of the pool and the adjoining land as a sailing centre and pleasure park was continued from 1966 by Aldridge-Brownhills urban district council and after further local government reorganization in 1974 by Walsall borough council and Staffordshire county council.[55] The premises of Chase Sailing Club and Staffordshire Schools Sailing Centre are situated on the Chasetown shore. In 1986 reclaimed mining land on the same shore was opened as a park of 50 a. whose facilities include several sports pitches.[56]

Chasetown had a cinema by 1915, the Palace de Luxe near the junction of High Street and Church Street. It was closed in the early 1920s and reopened in 1933 as the Plaza, which was advertised for sale in 1957. In 1987 the building was used by a car-spraying business. The Chase Cinema at Sankey's Corner was opened in the mid 1930s and was a bingo hall by 1987.[57]

There was a Chasetown brass band by 1868, probably the colliery company's band which by the late 1870s played at the athletic sports meeting and led the processions.[58] By 1893 it was performing at the Lichfield Greenhill Bower, and it was regularly engaged by the Bower committee in the earlier 20th century.[59] Having won second prize in a competition in 1919, it became known as the Cannock Chase Colliery Silver Prize Band.[60] A Chasetown

Temperance Brass Band was formed in 1897, and in the summer of 1899 it gave sacred concerts on Sundays on the dam of Norton Pool on the Hammerwich side of the boundary.[61] A drum and fife band was formed at Christ Church, Burntwood, in 1886 with 24 members,[62] and there was a brass band attached to Boney Hay mission room, opened in 1893.[63] Chase Terrace had a choral society in 1882.[64]

J. R. McClean (d. 1873) established a free lending library for the colliery company's employees, with the books kept at the Colliery school and available on Tuesday evenings.[65] By 1881 Chasetown had a reading room which was considered superior to that at Lichfield 'for variety and judicious selection of publications'.[66] In 1899 a reading room for young people was opened over two shops in Eastgate Street, Chase Terrace, with upwards of 30 members and a subscription of 2d. a week.[67] When the county council established its circulating library service in 1916, the first centres included three council schools in Burntwood, Chasetown, and Chase Terrace; the Roman Catholic school in Chasetown was added later in the year.[68] A branch library was built at Sankey's Corner in 1955 and was enlarged to house a children's section in 1965.[69] Rebuilding began in 1984. Part of the new building was in use in 1986, and the whole was opened in 1987. The name was changed from Chase Terrace Library to Burntwood Library.[70]

A working men's institute was built in 1888 on a site given by the colliery company at the southern end of High Street, Chasetown. The idea for an institute developed out of a bible class run for the young men of the neighbourhood by Catherine Sopwith, wife of the general manager of the colliery company, Arthur Sopwith. The building originally consisted of a reading room and a billiard room and was lit by electricity generated by the company. The cost of building, some £700, was met by donations and fund-raising events. A hall for entertainments was added within a few years; the billiard room was enlarged shortly before the First World War and again in 1939. Before the nationalization of the coal industry in 1947 the institute bought the freehold of the site from the colliery company.[71] The institute was closed in 1986 after the trustees had tried unsuccessfully

[50] Mason, Found Ready, 109.
[51] Burntwood: a town guide (1985 edn.), 7.
[52] L.J.R.O., D. 77/16/3, p. 179.
[53] Lichfield Mercury, 15 Mar. 1968, p. 1; 22 Aug. 1969, pp. 6, 17; 29 Aug. 1969, p. 15; 31 Oct. 1975, p. 8; 18 Aug. 1989, p. 11; inf. from the Town Manager and Clerk to Burntwood Town Council.
[54] Lichfield Mercury, 30 June 1899, p. 7; 28 July 1899, p. 3; 18 Aug. 1899, p. 8. A James Donaldson kept the Uxbridge Arms: Kelly's Dir. Staffs. (1896; 1900).
[55] Lichfield Mercury, 18 May 1956, p. 5; Chasewater Study: Rep. of Survey (July 1984), 8 (copy in Staffs. C.C. Planning and Dev. Dept.). Mr. R. L. Gilbert of the Countryside Div., Planning and Dev. Dept., is thanked for his help.
[56] Lichfield Mercury, 13 June 1986, p. 13; 10 Oct. 1986, p. 15.
[57] O.S. Map 1/2,500, Staffs. LVII. 4 (1919 edn.); Kelly's Dir. Staffs. (1916; 1924; 1936); Old Chasetown, 74–5; The Blackcountryman, ix (3), 58; Lambourne and James, Burntwood, 38; Lichfield Mercury, 11 Jan. 1957, p. 1; inf. from Mr. C. Daker of Chasetown; above, plate 40.
[58] Staffs. Advertiser, 19 Sept. 1868, p. 6; Lichfield Mercury, 6 Sept. 1878; 5 Sept. 1879, p. 5.
[59] Lichfield Cath. Libr., Harradine scrapbook, p. 109; L.J.R.O., D. 107, min. bks. 1904–47.
[60] Lambourne and James, Burntwood, 35.
[61] Old Chasetown, 66, 88; Lichfield Mercury, 30 June 1899, p. 7.   [62] S.R.O., D. 4520/4, pp. 10, 12.
[63] Old Chasetown, 88.
[64] Staffs. Advertiser, 11 Feb. 1882, p. 7.
[65] Jnl. Staffs. Ind. Arch. Soc. ix (2), 59.
[66] Lichfield Mercury, 2 Sept. 1881, p. 5.
[67] Ibid. 25 Aug. 1899, p. 8.
[68] S.R.O., CC/B/24/1, pp. 7, 14–15.
[69] Walsall Observer, 15 June 1973; Express & Star, 20 Dec. 1982; Lichfield Mercury, 15 June 1984, p. 3.
[70] Lichfield Mercury, 15 June 1984, p. 3; 28 Feb. 1986, p. 3; 5 Dec. 1986, p. 8; 3 Apr. 1987, p. 9; Midweek Mercury, 19 Aug. 1987, p. 1; above, plate 40.
[71] Lichfield Mercury, 10 Feb. 1888, p. 4; 8 Mar. 1968, p. 16; Staffs. Advertiser, 28 Apr. 1888, p. 5; Kelly's Dir. Staffs. (1892).

to raise money for refurbishing it.[72] The building was subsequently demolished.

In 1921 a village institute was opened in wooden premises in Rugeley Road, Burntwood, as a memorial to local people killed in the First World War. There too the cost was met by donations and fund-raising events; W. W. Worthington of Maple Hayes contributed £100. A new building was opened in 1935 and extended in 1948, 1956, and 1957. It was rebuilt in 1971.[73] The Morley Road Social Centre in Burntwood was opened in the early 1970s.[74] A women's institute was started at Burntwood in 1922.[75]

The boy scout movement was introduced into the area in 1914. A troop was formed at Chasetown, meeting in an upstairs room at the Uxbridge Arms. Another troop was formed at Chase Terrace, meeting first in private houses and then at the Cannock Road school. A building in Ironstone Road was bought for it in 1928; extended in 1935, the building remained the headquarters in the 1980s, when there were also groups at Boney Hay and Burntwood.[76]

There was a friendly society at Burntwood by 1799, from which year the overseers paid 'club money' on behalf of certain poor.[77] It was probably the Burntwood Friendly Society which owned a meadow in the Boney Hay area in 1815.[78] A new Burntwood Friendly Society was founded in 1831 and was meeting at the Star in 1876.[79] The Burntwood Female Friendly Society was formed in 1835 and also met at the Star; it still existed in 1849 but not in 1876.[80] The Loyal Star of Hope Lodge of Oddfellows was founded in 1872 and met at the Star in 1876.[81] A Young Men's Friendly Society was formed in connexion with Christ Church, Burntwood, in 1883.[82] In 1894 the Pink Friendly Society, evidently for women was meeting at the Star.[83]

Chasetown had six registered friendly societies in 1876: the Engineers' Lodge of Oddfellows, founded in 1861 and meeting at the White Lion; the United Adult and Juvenile Independent Friendly Society, founded in 1862 and meeting at the Staffordshire Knot; the Court McClean of the Ancient Order of Foresters, founded in 1862 and meeting at the Uxbridge Arms; the McClean Cannock Chase Colliery Lodge of Oddfellows, founded in 1867 and meeting at the Colliery school; the Chasetown Primitive Methodist Benevolent Society, attached to Zion's Hill chapel and registered in 1868; and the Pride of the Chase Lodge of United Free Gardeners, founded in 1876 and meeting at the Staffordshire Knot.[84] A Female Friendly Society in association with the Primitive Methodist chapel at Chase Terrace was formed apparently in 1883,[85] while a Chasetown Female Benevolent Society was meeting at the no. 3 board school in 1888.[86] In 1899 there were two other female societies, the Victoria at Chasetown and one associated with the Methodist New Connexion chapel at Chase Terrace.[87]

The Rechabite movement was introduced into the area in the earlier 1890s by A. H. Atkins, assistant master at the no. 1 board school in Burntwood, and his wife Edith, a draper. Atkins established a tent for men and another for juveniles at Chasetown; his wife established a female tent there and a juvenile tent at Burntwood. About 1920, after her husband's death, Edith founded a mixed tent at Burntwood named after him and was running that and the Burntwood juvenile tent in the late 1930s. She was still living in 1941 when her son F. H. Atkins, also a staunch Rechabite, died.[88]

MANORS AND OTHER ESTATES.

There was a manor of *PIPE* by 1135, the tenant having been enfeoffed with ⅛ knight's fee by the bishop of Coventry.[89] It was also known as Great Pipe, as distinct from Little Pipe, a detached part of the parish of St. Chad, Lichfield.[90] Held as ¼ fee by the 1240s and assessed at 1 hide c. 1255, Pipe remained a member of the bishop's manor of Longdon, which in 1546 passed to the Paget family (successively Barons Paget, earls of Uxbridge, and marquesses of Anglesey). Pipe was still a member of Longdon manor in the 1850s.[91] It covered Edial and Woodhouses but did not include Burntwood, which grew up on part of the waste of Longdon manor.[92]

The bishop's tenant in 1167, and apparently in 1135, was Henry of Pipe, who witnessed a deed c. 1150.[93] William of Pipe may have held the manor in 1199.[94] Richard of Pipe held it in 1242–3 and he or another Richard in 1284–5.[95] Sir Robert, son of Richard of Pipe, held it in 1293 and died evidently in 1306; he was a royal commissioner and tax collector in Staffordshire and bailiff and steward of the bishop.[96] He was succeeded by his son Thomas Pipe (Sir Thomas

[72] *Lichfield Mercury*, 9 May 1986, p. 1; 30 May 1986, p. 2; 15 July 1988, p. 11.
[73] Ibid. 4 Jan. 1935, p. 5; 10 Sept. 1948, p. 5; 11 Jan. 1957, p. 7; 21 Aug. 1970, p. 9; *Lichfield Dist. Official Guide* [early 1980s], 22; Lambourne and James, *Burntwood*, 37.
[74] Inf. from the Centre.
[75] *Lichfield Mercury*, 10 Mar. 1922, p. 8.
[76] Ibid. 25 Oct. 1935, p. 6; 21 Mar. 1958, p. 6; Lambourne and James, *Burntwood*, 43; *Burntwood: a town guide* (1985 edn.), 25.
[77] S.R.O., D. 4045/7/2.
[78] Ibid. D. (W.) 3222/191/20.
[79] *Rep. Chief Registrar of Friendly Socs. 1876, App. P*, H.C. 429-1, p. 397 (1877), lxxvii.
[80] *Rules of the Burntwood Female Friendly Soc.* (Lichfield, 1849; copy in W.S.L.). It does not appear in *Rep. Chief Registrar 1876*.
[81] *Rep. Chief Registrar 1876*, 398; *Staffs. Advertiser* (S. Staffs. edn.), 21 July 1877, p. 4.
[82] Mason, *Found Ready*, 109–10.

[83] *Lichfield Mercury*, 13 July 1894, p. 8.
[84] *Rep. Chief Registrar 1876*, 398; *Staffs. Advertiser*, 11 Aug. 1877, p. 7.   [85] *Lichfield Mercury*, 16 June 1899, p. 7.
[86] L.J.R.O., D. 77/16/3, p. 195.
[87] *Lichfield Mercury*, 14 July 1899, p. 3; 15 Sept. 1899, p. 8.
[88] Ibid. 1 Feb. 1935, p. 5; 14 Feb. 1941, p. 8; *Kelly's Dir. Staffs.* (1896; 1924; 1940).   [89] *S.H.C.* i. 147.
[90] e.g. ibid. 47 (1167); S.R.O., D. (W.) 1734/J. 2268, f. iv. (1298); D. (W.) 1734/2/1/624, m. 12 (1575); D. (W.) 1734/2/1/752, pp. 162–3 (1769).
[91] *Bk. of Fees*, ii. 968; Shaw, *Staffs.* i, app. to Gen. Hist. p. xvi; *V.C.H. Staffs.* iii. 51–2; below, local govt.
[92] S.R.O., D. 150/4/16–18.
[93] *Pipe R. 1167* (P.R.S. xi), 53; *S.H.C.* i. 147; iii (1), 185.
[94] *S.H.C.* iii (1), 34.
[95] *Bk. of Fees*, ii. 968; *Feud. Aids*, v. 23.
[96] *S.H.C.* vi (1), 139, 295; vii (1), 60, 153; *S.H.C.* 1939, 86, 91–2, 106–7; *Cal. Pat. 1292–1301*, 164, 517, 612; 1301–7, 16; S.R.O., D. (W.) 1734/J. 2268, f. iv.; Bodl. MS. d.d. Weld c. 1/1; L.J.R.O., D. 30/VC, B 6.

by 1311), who was summoned to a council at Westminster in 1324 and was a royal commissioner in Staffordshire and Shropshire in 1327. He was dead by 1329.[97]

In 1332 Pipe was held by his widow Margaret.[98] Her son James Pipe granted the manor to her in 1334–5, and in 1337–8 she assigned it to Sir Richard Stafford, a son by her first husband, Edmund Stafford, Baron Stafford (d. 1308).[99] In the earlier 1340s James Pipe unsuccessfully sued Sir Richard for the manor, claiming that he had made the grant to his mother while under age.[1] Sir Richard was M.P. for the county in 1341, a soldier, and a diplomat.[2] He was succeeded in 1380 by his son Edmund, bishop of Exeter 1395–1419, keeper of the privy seal 1389–96, and lord chancellor 1396–9 and 1401–3.[3] On Edmund's death in 1419 a life interest in Pipe passed to his nephew Thomas Stafford (d. 1425).[4]

The manor then passed to Edmund's great-niece Maud, wife of Thomas Stanley of Elford.[5] On Thomas's death in 1463 their son Sir John succeeded. Several times sheriff and M.P. for Staffordshire, he was living at Pipe in 1458. In 1461 he settled the manor in trust for his third wife Elizabeth and their son Humphrey, then aged about six.[6] After Sir John's death in 1476 Humphrey's right was challenged by his half-brother John, and the dispute was settled in Humphrey's favour in 1490–1.[7] Knighted by Henry VII at the battle of Bosworth in 1485 and created a banneret at the battle of Stoke in 1487, Sir Humphrey, who lived at Pipe, was three times sheriff and several times M.P. for Staffordshire. He died in 1504 and was buried in Westminster Abbey.[8] His son and heir John, who also lived at Pipe, died in 1514, leaving two infant daughters and coheirs, Elizabeth and Isabel.[9]

By 1522 Elizabeth was the wife of Sir John Hercy of Grove (Notts.) and Isabel of Walter Moyle of Buckwell in Boughton Aluph (Kent). Each couple had a moiety of Pipe. Isabel died there, and her husband held the moiety until his death in 1558. Their daughter Mary married Erasmus Heveningham of Heveningham (Suff.).

Erasmus died in 1559, evidently at Pipe Hall, and on Mary's death her son Christopher Heveningham succeeded to the moiety. In 1565 Sir John Hercy and Elizabeth conveyed the other moiety to Christopher and his wife Dorothy. Christopher Heveningham died at his manor of Aston, in Stone, in 1574 and was succeeded by his son Walter, a minor.[10] Walter, who was sheriff in 1609–10 and was knighted in 1619, died at Pipe Hall in 1636.[11] His heir was his grandson Walter Heveningham.[12] Pipe had been sequestrated by 1648 because of the younger Walter's Roman Catholicism, and Robert Pargiter of Greatworth (Northants.) then stated that he had bought the manor from Walter.[13] In 1658 Walter was described as of Pipe Hall.[14] He lived at both Pipe and Aston and died in 1691.[15]

Under a settlement of 1691 Pipe passed to his daughter Bridget and her husband Sir James Simeon, Bt., of Brightwell Baldwin (Oxon.).[16] The settlement replaced one of 1688 in favour of Walter's nephew Christopher Heveningham, who received instead an annuity of £50 and unsuccessfully challenged Sir James's right.[17] Bridget died in 1692 and Sir James in 1709. He was succeeded by his son Edward, who died unmarried in 1768.[18] Pipe passed to his great-nephew Edward Weld of Lulworth Castle (Dors.), who was succeeded by his brother Thomas in 1775.[19] In 1800 Thomas sold the manor to Samuel Pipe Wolferstan of Statfold, a distant relative who claimed descent from Sir Richard Stafford.[20] Samuel was succeeded in 1820 by his son Stanley, who sold Pipe Hall farm, 226 a. in 1844, to S. P. Shawe of Maple Hayes in 1859.[21] Stanley Pipe Wolferstan's son Francis, who succeeded in 1867, sold Pipe manor to Shawe's son and heir Henry in 1868.[22] In 1884 Henry sold much of the Maple Hayes estate, including Pipe manor and Pipe Hall farm, to A. O. Worthington, and on Worthington's death in 1918 the manor and farm passed to his son William, who died in 1949. The farm was still part of the Maple Hayes estate in 1986.[23]

The lord of the manor surnamed of Pipe in the mid 12th century presumably had a house

[97] L.J.R.O., B/A/1/1, f. 49; S.R.O., D. (W.) 1721/1/1, f. 292; D. (W.) 1734/J. 2057, m. 3; Shaw, *Staffs.* i. 163; *S.H.C.* vii (1), 232; *S.H.C.* 1917–18, 41, 46, 82; *Cal. Fine R.* 1327–37, 40, 149.
[98] *S.H.C.* x (1), 110; *Complete Peerage*, xii (1), 173.
[99] Erdeswick, *Staffs.* 236.
[1] *S.H.C.* xi. 100, 121, 157; xii (1), 22, 26.
[2] *S.H.C.* 1917–18, 82–5.
[3] *Cal. Inq. p.m.*, xv, p. 619; *D.N.B*; *Handbook of Brit. Chron.* (1986), 87, 95.
[4] S.R.O., D. (W.) 1734/2/1/601, m. 19; *S.H.C.* 1917–18, 132; P.R.O., C 138/36, no. 22; C 139/15, no. 18.
[5] *S.H.C.* iii (1), 51–2; *S.H.C.* 1910, 315–16; 1917–18, 132; Shaw, *Staffs.* i. 353.
[6] *S.H.C.* 1917–18, 203–4, 228–9, 277 n.; S.R.O., D. 150/1/322; D. (W.) 1734/2/1/760, m. 118.
[7] Shaw, *Staffs.* i. 354; P.R.O., CP 40/918, m. 330.
[8] *S.H.C.* iii (2), 52 n.; *S.H.C.* 1917–18, 277–8; W. A. Shaw, *Knights of Eng.* ii. 23–4; Shaw, *Staffs.* i. 354; P.R.O., C 142/28, no. 11; S.R.O., D. (W.) 1734/2/1/604, m. 34.
[9] Shaw, *Staffs.* i. 354; *L. & P. Hen. VIII*, i (1), pp. 218, 682; P.R.O., C 142/30, no. 68; S.R.O., D. (W.) 1734/2/1/605, m. 5d.
[10] *S.H.C.* iii (2), 52; v (2), 173; xiii. 242; *S.H.C.* 1925, 24–30; Shaw, *Staffs.* i. 354; S.R.O., D. 150/4/1; P.R.O., C

142/167, no. 83.
[11] *S.H.C.* 1925, 33–5, 42.
[12] P.R.O., C 142/444, no. 88.
[13] *Cal. Cttee. for Compounding*, iii. 1865; *Cal. Cttee. for Money*, iii. 1327–8, 1415.
[14] S.R.O., D. 4556/B, deed of 25 Mar. 1658.
[15] *S.H.C.* 1925, 42.
[16] S.R.O., D. 150/1/4; *S.H.C.* 1925, 44; *Staffs. Cath. Hist.* xxii. 25; *V.C.H. Oxon.* vii. 129–30.
[17] S.R.O., D. 150/1/1; D. 150/1/3; D. 150/1/8; D. 150/1/43, pp. 77–87; D. 1229; *S.H.C.* 1925, 47–53.
[18] G.E.C. *Baronetage*, iv. 93; *S.H.C.* 1925, 44.
[19] Burke, *Land. Gent.* (1882), ii. 1712.
[20] S.R.O., D. 1527/24, 28 Oct. sqq. esp. 26 Nov. (refs. kindly supplied by Mr. D. G. Brown of Tamworth); D. 4556/B, deed of 8 Apr. 1800; Erdeswick, *Staffs.* 237.
[21] Burke, *Land. Gent.* (1882), ii. 1775; L.J.R.O., B/A/15/Burntwood; S.R.O., D. 4566/F, Maple Hayes papers, abstract of title 1883.
[22] Burke, *Land. Gent.* (1882), ii. 1775; S.R.O., D. 150/1/17.
[23] S.R.O., D. 4566/F, H. C. Shawe corresp., Maple Hayes file, Shawe to Hinckley, Hodson & Co. 18 Apr. 1884; Maple Hayes sale cat. 1883, p. 5 (copy in D. 4566/F); *Lichfield Mercury*, 27 June 1884, p. 5; *Kelly's Dir. Staffs.* (1888 and edns. to 1940); inf. from Mr. R. Brookes of Pipe Hall Farm.

there, and in 1299 Sir Robert Pipe dated a deed from Pipe.[24] In 1371 the bishop licensed the performance of a marriage in the chapel within the manor of Pipe, presumably a chapel in the manor house.[25] The hall of Pipe was mentioned in 1436.[26] Walter Heveningham was assessed for tax on 15 hearths there in 1666.[27] By the earlier 1690s Pipe Hall was occupied as a farmhouse by the Bates family, still the tenants in 1778 and probably in 1781.[28] It was rebuilt c. 1770,[29] and in the early 19th century there were minor extensions and some internal remodelling. Two rooms on the first floor appear to have been once connected by an open arcade of three arches, and they probably formed the Roman Catholic chapel in use until 1800.[30] North-west of the house are timber-framed farm buildings whose walls have been much undercut in brick; they include a 17th-century barn.

An estate at Pipe in 1167 was described as the land of three canons.[31] It may have been the land given to the canons and lay brothers of Farewell by Bishop Clinton c. 1140. Soon afterwards the bishop made a grant, probably of the same estate, to the nuns of Farewell at the request of three hermits and brothers. The grant included land at Pipe. Henry II, probably in 1155, confirmed the nuns in their possession of a carucate of land at Pipe assarted from Cannock forest.[32] That may be the origin of the *AB-NALLS* estate which was within the nuns' manor of Farewell by the early 14th century. When the priory was suppressed in 1527, its estates included land at Ashmore Brook, Pipe, Abnalls, and Burntwood. Later in 1527 the Crown granted the priory's possessions to the dean and chapter of Lichfield, who in 1550 granted Farewell manor to William, Lord Paget.[33]

A house and virgate at Abnalls were held of Farewell priory by Roger of Abnall (Abenhale) in 1318 or 1319,[34] probably in succession to Thomas of Abnall who was a tenant of the priory in the earlier 1290s.[35] Roger was still alive in 1327 but had probably been succeeded by Amy (or Amice) of Abnall by 1333.[36] In 1357 the estate, consisting of a messuage, a mill, a carucate, and other land in Abnalls, Pipe, Elm-

hurst, and Lichfield, was held by Nicholas Taverner, described as parson of Stretton.[37] Probably by 1378 a house and $\frac{1}{2}$ virgate in Abnalls had passed from him to Aymer Taverner, a prominent citizen of Lichfield also known as Aymer Lichfield.[38] Aymer probably died in 1399.[39] The Abnalls estate was held in the early 15th century by William Newport, who made it his home. He was knighted in 1400 and was three times sheriff and three times M.P. for the county.[40] He evidently died in 1415 or 1416, and Abnalls passed to Sir William Lichfield, Aymer's heir and kinsman, who was living there in 1417.[41] In 1421 he made a settlement of what was called the manor of Abnalls.[42] The manor then descended with his share of Freeford, passing in 1537 to the Wingfield family.[43] The Wingfields conveyed the manor in 1566 to Sir Edward Littleton of Pillaton, in Penkridge,[44] who at his death in 1574 was holding it of Thomas, Lord Paget, as of the manor of Farewell.[45] The Wingfields retained some property in Abnalls which passed with their Freeford estate to Jane Kniveton c. 1600.[46] In 1609 Sir Edward Littleton's son Sir Edward conveyed a house and land in Great and Little Abnalls and elsewhere in the area to Thomas Sprott of Ashmore Brook, whose family had held another house and land at Abnalls at least since the earlier 16th century.[47]

Abnalls then descended with the Ashmore Brook estate until the earlier 19th century. It appears then to have been divided, part becoming the home farm of Maple Hayes[48] and part being sold to Thomas Smith of Lichfield, probably in the 1830s. In 1844 his devisees owned a 56-a. farm centring on Abnalls Cottage on the north side of Abnalls Lane.[49] That house was rebuilt in 1848.[50] It was the home of William Gresley, prebendary of Wolvey in Lichfield cathedral, in the earlier 1850s,[51] and in the mid 1850s R. C. Chawner moved there from Wall, remaining until his death in 1870. His widow and daughter lived there until about the mid 1880s, when they moved to Edial House.[52] By the later 1880s it was the home of H. C. Hodson, diocesan registrar from 1878, who became noted for his kennels of pure-bred bloodhounds there.

[24] S.R.O., D. (W.) 1734/1/4/3A.
[25] S.H.C. N.S. viii. 57.
[26] S.R.O., D. (W.) 2/1/603, m. 2.
[27] S.H.C. 1923, 161.
[28] S.R.O., D. 150/4/8–10, 12; D. 150/5/18–19; L.J.R.O., D. 126/acct. bk. 1663–1805, accts. 1714–15, 1717–18, 1723–4, 1735–7; Staffs. Studies, ed. P. Morgan (Keele, 1987), 131; Shaw, Staffs, i. 355; below, Roman Catholicism.
[29] Staffs. Cath. Hist. xiv. 321; Shaw, Staffs. i. 355.
[30] Below, Roman Catholicism.
[31] S.H.C. i. 48.
[32] V.C.H. Staffs. iii. 222–3.
[33] Ibid. 166, 224.
[34] S.R.O., D. (W.) 1734/2/3/52; D. (W.) 1734/J. 2039; W.S.L., S.D. Pearson 1136.
[35] L.J.R.O., D. 30/G4, m. 1.
[36] S.H.C. vii (1), 232; x (1), 110.
[37] Ibid. xi. 169.
[38] S.R.O., D. (W.) 1734/2/1/378, m. 1; D. (W.) 1734/2/3/55; D. (W.) 1734/J. 2039; S.H.C. xv. 61; S.H.C. 1917–18, 142–3.
[39] J.C. Cox, Notes on Churches of Derb. iii. 487.
[40] S.H.C. xvii. 10, 15–16, 19–20, 29–30, 35; S.H.C. 1912, 280; 1917–18, 169–71; E. Powell, 'Public Order and Law Enforcement in Shropshire and Staffs. in the early 15th

cent.' (Oxford Univ. D. Phil. thesis, 1979), pp. 198, 275.
[41] P.R.O., C 138/19, no. 27; S.R.O., D. (W.) 1734/2/1/601, m. 14d.; D. (W.) 1734/J. 2051; S.H.C. xvii. 62.
[42] P.R.O., C 139/122, no. 35.   [43] Below, Freeford.
[44] S.H.C. xi. 284; xvii. 210–11, 215–16; S.R.O., D. (W.) 1734/2/1/387, m. 19d.
[45] P.R.O., C 142/172, no. 119.
[46] S.H.C. xviii (1), 6–7, 10, 13–14, 21.
[47] S.H.C. N.S. iv. 11–12; below (Ashmore Brook).
[48] B.L. Maps, O.S.D. 258; L.J.R.O., B/A/15/Burntwood; Maple Hayes sale cat. 1883, pp. 4–5 (copy in S.R.O., D. 4566/F).
[49] S.R.O., D. (W.) 1851/8/46, sale partics. of Ashmore Brook and Abnalls 1834; D. 4363/P/1/2; L.J.R.O., B/A/15/Burntwood, apportionment, p. 2.
[50] Date on the house.
[51] White, Dir. Staffs. (1851), 515; P.O. Dir. Staffs. (1854); Le Neve, Fasti (1854), i. 642; L.J.R.O., B/A/15/Burntwood, pencil note on no. 752.
[52] Clayton, Cathedral City, 79; Staffs. Advertiser, 17 Sept. 1870, p. 4; Kelly's Dir. Staffs. (1884; 1888); Lichfield Mercury, 10 Jan. 1890, p. 8; 5 May 1893, p. 8; S.R.O., D. 4566/F, Maple Hayes corresp. file, Chawner to [Shawe] 7 Aug. 1883; below, econ. hist. (coalmining); Wall, manor and other estates (Wall Hall).

He died in 1924; Mrs. E. M. R. Hodson lived there in the 1930s.[53] The house was divided into two in 1948.[54] The medieval house may have occupied the moated site on the south side of Abnalls Lane just inside the Lichfield city boundary.[55]

An estate in *ASHMORE BROOK* held by Thomas of Hamstead (d. by 1254) was probably that held of the bishop in 1298 by another Thomas of Hamstead as $\frac{1}{8}$ knight's fee. It was later held by Nicholas of Hamstead.[56] It eventually passed to Roger Fordiave, who was succeeded in 1420 or 1421 by his daughter Margaret and her husband John Sprott; the inheritance included four messuages in the area which were held of Farewell priory.[57] In 1510 Ashmore Brook was the home of Thomas Sprott, who died in 1531 and was then serjeant of Lichfield cathedral. He held what was described as a capital messuage at Ashmore Brook of the bishop as $\frac{1}{8}$ knight's fee, along with three messuages in Abnalls, Burntwood, and Hammerwich and other property in the area. He was succeeded by his son Edward.[58] In 1571 Edward was living in the capital messuage, which had an estate of 85 a. attached to it; he had a second house at Ashmore Brook with 74 a. attached. Both were held of the former episcopal manor of Longdon, and he held two other houses in the area, one of them at Abnalls, as tenant of Farewell manor.[59] Edward died in 1591.[60] His heir was his son Roger, who was living at Ashmore Brook in 1598.[61] Thomas Sprott, probably Roger's son, had the estate in 1604, and he was succeeded by his nephew Thomas, evidently by 1611; Thomas had already acquired the nearby Bilston Brook farm in 1605.[62] He died in 1655, having made a settlement in 1654 at the time of the marriage of his grandson and heir Henry Sprott to Ann, daughter and heir of Thomas Lokier of the Marsh, in Barrow (Salop.). Ashmore Brook House, the capital messuage, was settled on Henry for life with remainder to Ann for life as jointure. The second house at Ashmore Brook was settled for life on Henry's mother Dorothy Saunders, who was the remarried widow of Thomas's son Edward, killed at the battle of Marston Moor in 1644.[63] Henry died in 1673 with a son Thomas as his heir; his widow Ann lived until 1721. Thomas was succeeded in 1710 by his son Henry, who lived at

the Marsh and died in 1744 with his brother Samuel, a physician of Ludlow, as his heir.[64]

Samuel Sprott died in 1760, and the Ashmore Brook estate passed to Henry's three daughters, Ann the wife of James Moseley, Elizabeth the wife of William Toldervy, and Dorothy the wife of John Ashwood. Ann Moseley's heir was her son Walter, of Leaton in Bobbington, who also succeeded Elizabeth Toldervy under her will of 1794. Dorothy's share passed on her death in 1783 to her daughter Dorothy, who married Sir Henry Hawley of Leybourne Grange (Kent) and also died in 1783, leaving a son Henry; her husband continued to hold her share of Ashmore Brook by the courtesy.[65]

In 1812 Walter Moseley, Sir Henry Hawley, and Henry Hawley sold Ashmore Brook House, his other house at Ashmore Brook, and Abnall House (so named by 1654) to John Atkinson of Maple Hayes; the property was subject to payments to the lord of Longdon.[66] Atkinson sold Ashmore Brook House in 1838 to Richard Hinckley and Maryanne Woodhouse, both of Beacon House, Lichfield. Hinckley bought his share for the benefit of his wife Ellen, Maryanne's sister, to whom the other share passed on Maryanne's death in 1843.[67] In 1844 the farm attached to the house covered 159 a.[68] Hinckley died in 1865, and on Ellen's death in 1870 what was then known as Ashmore Brook farm passed to her granddaughter Ellen, the wife of the Revd. F. W. Vernon of Hilton. She died in 1899, and her trustees sold the farm to A. O. Worthington of Maple Hayes.[69] It was still part of the Maple Hayes estate in 1986.[70]

Ashmore Brook Farm consists of a late-medieval central range with a cross wing at either end. The central range was originally a two-bayed open hall. A chimney stack and an upper floor were inserted in the earlier 17th century. In 1666 Henry Sprott was assessed for tax on eight hearths in the house.[71] The service cross wing at the west end was reconstructed in the 18th century, a staircase being built into the angle between its southward projection and the hall range. The wing was extended northwards in the 19th century. The eastern cross wing, which includes another staircase, was rebuilt early in the 19th century and remodelled later in the century. Most of the external timber walling has been rebuilt in brick. The house originally

[53] *Kelly's Dir. Staffs.* (1888 and later edns.); *Lichfield Mercury,* 11 Apr. 1924, p. 5.
[54] C. H. Gregory, *Burntwood Past and Present* (Lichfield, 1953).
[55] *V.C.H. Staffs.* i. 364.
[56] S.R.O., D. (W.) 1734/J. 2268, m. iv.; *S.H.C.* iv (1), 131; vi (1), 167.
[57] S.R.O., D. (W.) 1734/2/1/378, m. 14d.; D. (W.) 1734/2/1/379, m. 6; D. (W.) 1734/2/3/55; W.S.L., S. MS. 326, m. 5.
[58] W.S.L., S. MS. 36/8; P.R.O., E 150/1037; Bodl. MS. Ashmole 1521, p. 85; L.J.R.O., D. 30/C.A. iv, f. 81v.
[59] W.S.L., S. MS. 326, m. 5; S.R.O., D. (W.) 1734/J. 2039.
[60] P.R.O., PROB 11/78, ff. 68v.–69v.
[61] S.R.O., D. 150/4/2; D. (W.) 1734/2/3/112d; *S.H.C.* 1935, 14.
[62] P.R.O., C 3/410, no. 37; S.R.O., D. (W.) 1734/2/1/740/1, pp. 114, 118, 156, 188, 197; *S.H.C.* n.s. iii. 26.

[63] S.R.O., D. 833/3/1, deed of 16 Aug. 1654 and abstract of settlements; D.(W.) 1734/2/1/744, p. 86; P.R.O., PROB 11/261, ff. 294v.–295; P.R.O., E 134/19 Geo. II Trin./3.
[64] Shrewsbury Public Libr., MS. 4078, p. 951; Salop. R.O. 3898/Rg/3, burial 1 Feb. 1709/10; P.R.O., E 134/19 Geo. II/Trin. 3; S.R.O., D. 833/3/1, deed of 10 July 1734. The first two references were kindly supplied by Dr. P. A. Stamper of the Shropshire V.C.H.
[65] Shrewsbury Public Libr., MS. 4078, p. 951; S.R.O., D. 150/1/110, 113–15, 118; D. 833/3/4, deed of 19 Nov. 1779.
[66] S.R.O., D. 150/1/118 and 121; D. 833/3/1, deed of 16 Aug. 1654.
[67] Ibid. D. 150/1/132; 1/135; 1/142, pp. 6–7; above, Lichfield, manor (lay estates: Beacon Place).
[68] L.J.R.O., B/A/15/Burntwood.
[69] S.R.O., D. 150/1/137, 140–2, 144.
[70] Inf. from Mr. and Mrs. P. F. Broome of Ashmore Brook Farm.
[71] *S.H.C.* 1923, 161.

stood within a moat fed by Ashmore brook, three sides of which survived in the 1840s.[72]

The second house, on the opposite side of the road, had a 216-a. farm attached in 1795.[73] The site of the house, which was moated, was a detached portion of Curborough and Elmhurst until 1879.[74] The farm was owned and occupied by Thomas Worthington in 1844 when it covered 48 a.[75] By 1861 it was occupied by William Taylor, who sold it c. 1890 to Thomas Bailye. In 1982 Bailye's grandson Kenneth Bailye sold the house to Ian Herman, who in turn sold it to J. W. L. Fielding in 1985. Mr. Bailye moved to the nearby Rowan Cottage, which then became the farmhouse for what had become known as Ashmore Brook Dairy farm.[76] The former farmhouse, known as Ashmore Brook House in 1987, is a brick house of three storeys, which was described in 1795 as just erected.[77] Its main front faces south, and there is a back service wing. The south arm of the moat, fed by Ashmore brook, survives.

In 1680 *EDIAL HALL* was the home of Thomas Hammond, who was junior bailiff of Lichfield in 1679–80, senior bailiff in 1685–6, and mayor in 1686–7. In 1702 he had a small estate adjoining the hall and property elsewhere, including Lichfield. He was succeeded that year by his son Thomas.[78] In 1716 the younger Thomas sold the hall to William Fettiplace Nott, husband of his sister Sarah and steward of Lichfield from 1699 until his death in 1726.[79] His heir was his son Fettiplace, senior bailiff of Lichfield in 1752–3 and 1759–60 and steward 1762–9; he died in 1775.[80] The hall was occupied as a school by Samuel Johnson c. 1736 and was advertised for letting in 1750; it was occupied by Thomas Ashmole in 1773.[81] In his will Fettiplace directed that the hall should be sold with other property to meet his legacies and the debts of his son, another Fettiplace.[82] In 1776 or 1777 the hall and the adjoining farm were bought by Benjamin Robinson, who sold them in 1779 to John Fern, a Lichfield wine merchant.[83] In 1801 Fern was succeeded in the Edial property and in the wine business by his son Robert.[84] By 1806 Robert was bankrupt, and his assignees that year conveyed the hall and farmhouse to Richard Greenhough, a Lichfield maltster.[85] The hall was the home of the Revd.

E. P. Waters by 1805, and he was running a school there in 1807.[86] The hall was demolished in 1809.[87]

In 1811 Greenhough sold the property to two brothers, Henry and Francis Styche.[88] It was probably the same Henry Styche who in 1834 was living at what was called Edial Hall and was farming there in 1841.[89] By 1851 he had been succeeded by his son Henry; the farm was 29 a. in extent in 1844.[90] The younger Henry, who was unmarried, was succeeded c. 1870 by John Styche, who farmed at Edial Hall until c. 1880.[91] In 1896 the farm, then of 22 a., was bought by Daniel Hulme.[92] John Mayer was farming there in 1916 and 1933, but the farm was owned by George Mayer of the Chetwynd Arms at Brocton, in Baswich. Under the terms of his will it was put up for sale in 1933.[93] In 1978 it was bought by Harry Wharmby and his wife, who also owned the Angel Croft hotel in Lichfield.[94]

The building demolished in 1809 was a double-pile brick house surmounted by a cupola; it dated from c. 1700.[95] The present Edial Hall, formerly Edial Hall Farm, is a brick house of the earlier 18th century with two bays of a 17th-century roof at its western end. It was presumably the farmhouse described in 1779 as 'adjoining and being heretofore part of' Edial Hall.[96] There was still a tradition in the Styche family in the earlier 20th century that when the family bought the property in 1811 the living quarters of the hall had recently been demolished and that what then stood had been used mainly as servants' quarters and harness rooms.[97] Two ranges of timber-framed farm buildings survive; they date probably from the 17th century, though they were underbuilt and extended in brick in the 19th century.

The house known as *EDIAL HOUSE FARM* by 1896[98] dates from the early 19th century, but an estate centring on an earlier house existed by the 17th century and probably by the 16th: in 1571 Fabian Orme of Overton Grange in Hammerwich held a house and land in Edial called Stokehay, a name preserved in Stockhay Lane south-west of Edial House farm. The estate descended with Overton Grange until 1628 when George Orme sold it to Simon Jasson of Lichfield.[99] Simon was living at Edial when he died in 1653.[1] His heir was his son

72 L.J.R.O., B/A/15/Burntwood, no. 804.
73 Salop. R.O. 515/2, pp. 251–3.   74 Above, introduction.
75 L.J.R.O., B/A/15/Burntwood; Lichfield, St. Chad.
76 P.R.O., RG 9/1974; *Kelly's Dir. Staffs.* (1888; 1892; 1896); inf. from Mr. K. Bailye.
77 Salop R.O. 515/2, p. 253.
78 Reade, *Johnsonian Gleanings*, vi. 40, 132–3, 146; Laithwaite, *Conduit Lands Trust*, 79.
79 Reade, *Johnsonian Gleanings*, vi. 142, 146; *Trans. N. Staffs. Field Club*, lxvi. 88.
80 Reade, *Johnsonian Gleanings*, vi. 146–7.
81 Below, education; *Aris's Birmingham Gaz.* 29 Oct. 1750; L.J.R.O., D. 27/1/4, f. 256.
82 Reade, *Johnsonian Gleanings*, vi. 134–5, 147; S.R.O., D. 237/28, deed of 15 May 1779; D. 615/D/262, deed of 26 Mar. 1776.
83 S.R.O., D. 150/5/15–17; D. 237/28, deed of 15 May 1779.
84 Ibid. D. 237/28, deeds of 3 and 4 Jan. and 24 June 1802; L.J.R.O., P/C/11, John Fern (1801); above, Lichfield, econ. hist. (trades and industries).
85 S.R.O., D. 237/28, deed of 9 July 1806.
86 *Staffs. Advertiser*, 4 May 1805; *S.H.C.* n.s. i. 149; T. H.

White, *The Marigold Window* (1849), 211; R. Simms, *Bibliotheca Staffordiensis*, 508 (for T. H. White); *Alum. Oxon. 1715–1886*, iv. 1507.
87 Reade, *Johnsonian Gleanings*, ii. 81.
88 *Trans. N. Staffs. Field Club*, lxvi. 89.
89 White, *Dir. Staffs.* (1834), 105; P.R.O., HO 107/980.
90 P.R.O., HO 107/2014 (2); L.J.R.O., B/A/15/Burntwood.
91 P.R.O., RG 9/1974; RG 10/2915; *P.O. Dir. Staffs.* (1872; 1876); *Kelly's Dir. Staffs.* (1880).
92 *Staffs. Advertiser*, 7 Nov. 1896, p. 4.
93 *Kelly's Dir. Staffs.* (1916; 1932); *Trans. N. Staffs. Field Club*, lxvi. 86; W.S.L., Sale Cat. E/3/15.
94 *Lichfield Mercury*, 9 Nov. 1979, p. 10. Mr. and Mrs. Wharmby are thanked for their help.
95 Shaw, *Staffs.* i. 355; above, plate 49.
96 S.R.O., D. 237/28, deed of 15 May 1779.
97 *Trans. N. Staffs. Field Club*, vi. 89.
98 S.R.O., D. 615/E(s)/3/19.
99 W.S.L., S. MS. 326/2, m. 5; S.R.O., D. (W.) 1734/2/3/112D; D. 4566/S, bdle. 30, deed of 8 Nov. 1628; below, Hammerwich, estates.
1 S.R.O., D. 4566/S, bdle. 30, will of 25 May 1653.

Simon, who in 1656 bought a second house and more land at Edial from Humphrey Anson; that was the only house mentioned in his will of 1667.[2] He was assessed for tax on six hearths at Edial in 1666.[3] Simon died in 1667 or 1668 with a son Sebastian, a minor, as his heir.[4] Sebastian had moved from Edial to Walcot, in Charlbury (Oxon.), by 1704.[5] He died in 1710 or 1711, leaving two houses and land in Edial to his nephew Sebastian Jasson, then a minor but of age by 1716.[6] The younger Sebastian, who was living at Hill Top in Pipehill by 1718, sold the two houses and the land attached in 1721 to Theophilus Levett, town clerk of Lichfield from 1721 until his death in 1746.[7]

Levett's heir was his son John, who died unmarried in 1799. His Edial property evidently passed to his brother, the Revd. Richard Levett, and on Richard's death in 1802 to the next brother, Thomas, of Packington Hall in Weeford.[8] In that year Thomas owned a 107-a. farm in Edial.[9] He died in 1820 with a son Theophilus as his heir. Theophilus was succeeded in 1839 by his son John, who owned the house and 157 a. in 1841.[10] John was succeeded in 1853 by his son Theophilus and he in 1899 by his son Basil, whose brother Berkeley succeeded in 1929.[11] In 1937 Berkeley sold the farm to J. E. Hammersley.[12] F. Hammersley was farming there in 1962.[13] In 1987 the farm was owned by Mr. E. Howdle.

Thomas Bird of Lichfield and his wife Isabel probably held a house at *FULFEN* in the early 16th century: besides a house their holding in Longdon manor consisted of 48 a. in Burntwood called 'Fulfennes' and a plot recently taken from the waste between Fulfen and the heath. Isabel was the daughter and heir of a branch of the Bird family living at Ashmore Brook. The house had formerly been held by Henry Bytheway and later by John Verror, while Fulfennes had been held by David Bird and later by Agnes Bird.[14]

A house, a cottage, and land at Fulfen were conveyed in 1537 by John Leeke to Humphrey Cotton and his wife Anne.[15] A Humphrey Cotton held a house and pasture in Fulfen and Childerhay in 1571 and was still alive in 1577.[16] William Cotton had succeeded by 1597 and was living at Fulfen in 1602.[17] A Thomas Cotton was living in Burntwood in 1609.[18] Another William Cotton was occupying a house called Fulfen in 1664 and was assessed for tax on three hearths in

Burntwood in 1666.[19] He died in 1669 or 1670 with an infant son William as his heir.[20]

The estate later passed to George Ball, whose son Richard succeeded in 1717 or 1718 to what was then called Fulfin House.[21] In 1765 the house and estate were held by Elizabeth Ball of Castle Bromwich (Warws.). She died unmarried in 1769 with her cousin James Birch as her heir. He was succeeded by his son George, and he by his son Thomas, who added Reynardson to his surname on the death of his father-in-law in 1812. As Maj.-Gen. Thomas Birch Reynardson he held the Fulfen estate in 1821.[22] In 1844 it was a 103-a. farm.[23]

Reynardson died in 1847, and in 1848 his widow Etheldred Anne sold Fulfin House to John Mann of Cleat Hill in Longdon.[24] By 1851 it was occupied by John Tudor, who had moved there from a farm in Church Road and farmed at Fulfen until his death c. 1872; his son Charles was farming 179 a. there in 1881.[25] The property was later owned by J. T. Kent, who was farming there by the 1920s and from whom it was compulsorily purchased in 1946 for St. Matthew's hospital. The land was farmed by the hospital authorities, but the house was left unoccupied. In 1951 the Ministry of Health sold the house and 17 a. to J. R. Fletcher, a Burntwood butcher, whose widow Mrs. M. Fletcher sold the house in 1984 to Mr. and Mrs. M. J. Hogan.[26]

The main block of the house known as Fulfin is of two bays and probably dates from the 16th century. It was originally timber framed and jettied on all four sides; there are also remains of two first-floor oriel windows. It seems too small to have been the house occupied by the Cotton family in the 16th and 17th centuries. Positioned on a hill on the edge of Cannock Chase, it may have been built as a hunting lodge or a standing from which spectators could watch the hunting. In the 17th century a chimney stack was built around the central truss, and in the 18th century a short brick wing was added on the north side. A little later the main block was cased in brick and much of the timber walling was removed. The wing was extended along the whole of the north side in the 19th century.

The house known as *HILL HOUSE* or *HILL FARM* by the later 18th century was owned in 1742 with an attached farm by John Dyott of Lichfield. By 1769 it had passed to his nephew

[2] Ibid. and will of 23 Apr. 1667.
[3] *S.H.C.* 1923, 164.
[4] S.R.O., D. 4566/S, bdle. 34, deed of 24 Mar. 1676/7.
[5] Ibid. deed of 26 Mar. 1704.
[6] Ibid. bdle. 30, will of 21 Dec. 1710.
[7] Ibid. deeds of 7 Jan. 1719/20, 3 Feb. 1720/1; bdle. 34, deed of 18 Nov. 1718; Reade, *Johnsonian Gleanings*, iv. 182, 184–5, 190.
[8] Reade, *Johnsonian Gleanings*, iv. 190–1.
[9] L.J.R.O., D. 15/10/2/46.
[10] Burke, *Land. Gent.* (1952), 1517; S.R.O., D. 4566/12, papers in case of Levett v. Ashmall 1859.
[11] Burke, *Land. Gent.* (1952), 1517; [D. R. Haszard], *The Levetts of Staffs.* 11 (copy in W.S.L.).
[12] S.R.O., D. 4566/9, S. J. A. D. Levett corresp., file 1938–45, 4 Feb. 1938.
[13] Burntwood Libr., Burntwood par. council mins. 5 Sept. 1962.
[14] J.R.U.L.M., Ryl. Ch. Phillipps 126.
[15] *S.H.C.* xi. 275–6; S.R.O., D. (W.) 1734/2/1/747, p. 116.

[16] W.S.L., S. MS. 326/2, m. 6; S.R.O., D. (W.) 1734/2/1/612, m. 22.
[17] *S.H.C.* xvi. 175; *S.H.C.* 1935, 309, 420.
[18] S.R.O., D. (W.) 1734/2/1/740B, p. 27.
[19] B.R.L., Homer 95; *S.H.C.* 1923, 165.
[20] S.R.O., D. (W.) 1734/2/1/747, p. 116.
[21] Ibid. p. 66.
[22] Burke, *Land. Gent.* (1882), ii. 1347 (which gives Thomas as George's eldest son; but see Burntwood, education); P.R.O., PROB 10/2523, will of Eliz. Ball, 1770. Warw. Jan.
[23] L.J.R.O., B/A/15/Burntwood.
[24] Burke, *Land. Gent.* (1882), ii. 1347; S.R.O., D. (W.) 3222/272.
[25] White, *Dir. Staffs.* (1851), 515; L.J.R.O., B/A/15/Burntwood; P.R.O., HO 107/2014 (2); P.R.O., RG 10/2914; RG 11/2774; S.R.O., D. 4045/7/3; below, econ. hist. (other industries: brick making).
[26] *Lichfield Mercury*, 20 July 1951, p. 2; inf. from Mrs. Fletcher and Mrs. Hogan.

Simon Dyott of Birmingham.[27] Simon was still alive in 1771, but by 1778 he had been succeeded by his son Joseph, a London factor.[28] Joseph sold the farm in 1784 to John Barker, a Birmingham brassfounder.[29] Barker sold it in 1800 to Thomas Ashmall of Farewell Hall.[30] On Ashmall's death in 1802 the farm passed to his son John, who died in 1839. In his will John directed that Hill farm should be sold, and in 1841 it was bought by James Palmer, who added to it his adjoining farm at Little Pipe.[31] Palmer died in 1850, having directed that his property was to be sold for the benefit of his son and two daughters. The original part of Hill farm was sold in 1854 to S. P. Shawe of Maple Hayes, who bought the Little Pipe portion also in 1855.[32] In 1890 his son Henry sold the 212-a. Hill farm to A. O. Worthington of Maple Hayes, and in 1986 the farm was still part of the Maple Hayes estate.[33]

The house dates from the 18th century and originally consisted of a three-bayed block facing south and a low rear wing. In the earlier 19th century the wing was enlarged and heightened to three storeys and another wing was added on the east. The entrance was moved to the east front of the east wing.

MAPLE HAYES takes its name from land called 'Mabbley hays' which by 1498 was divided into four crofts, one of them in Pipe park.[34] By 1728 a farm called Pipe or Maple Hayes farm was owned by William Jesson of Lichfield.[35] A Mr. Jasson had been assessed for poor rate on 'Mapel Hey' in 1674,[36] but it is not clear whether that was a farm or simply a piece of land. There appears to have been a farm by the early 18th century: a Robert Watson was living at Maple Hayes in 1704 and a Robert Beardmore in 1724.[37]

William Jesson died in 1732,[38] and his property was divided between his two sisters, Elizabeth, the wife of Fowke Hussey of Little Wyrley in Norton Canes, and Anna Maria, the wife of Thomas Mason of Newcastle under Lyme. In 1735 Elizabeth settled the reversion of her share on her daughter Sybilla, who in 1783, with her husband Thomas Ware Cooper, sold it to her nephew, Phineas Hussey.[39] The other half was held in 1750 by Thomas Mason, Anna Maria having died; the reversion lay with their son Jesson, who had succeeded by 1772.[40] In 1785 Phineas Hussey and Jesson Mason made an exchange whereby Mason secured the whole of Maple Hayes farm.[41] He sold it in 1786 to George Addams, a Lichfield wine merchant.[42] Addams had rebuilt the house by 1796, but he sold the estate in 1804 to John Atkinson of Bank House, Manchester.[43]

Atkinson was living at Maple Hayes by 1812, and he built up a collection of paintings and other works of art there.[44] He was sheriff of Staffordshire in 1828–9.[45] He let the house in 1834, and in 1838 he was living in Boulogne.[46] In 1839 he sold the freehold portion of the estate, including the house, to Sir Thomas Fremantle, Bt., of Swanbourne (Bucks.), later Baron Cottesloe; the leasehold portion was bought by Sir James Fitzgerald, Bt., of Wolseley Hall in Colwich, husband of Sir Thomas Fremantle's sister Augusta.[47] Sir James died later in 1839, and Maple Hayes became Augusta's home until the later 1840s.[48] In 1851 she and her brother sold the house and 180 a. to Samuel Pole Shawe of Hints Hall, who moved to Maple Hayes and considerably enlarged the estate.[49] He died in 1862, leaving the estate to his third wife Mary for life with reversion to his son by his second marriage, Henry Cunliffe Shawe. Mary continued to live at Maple Hayes until her death in 1882.[50]

In 1884 Henry, then of Weddington Hall (Warws.), sold the house and 455 a. of the 1,010-a. estate to Albert Octavius Worthington, a partner in the Burton upon Trent brewing firm of Worthington & Co.[51] He continued to buy property in the area, including more of the Maple Hayes estate in 1885 and 1890.[52] He was succeeded in 1918 by his son William Worthington Worthington, who died in 1949 with a grandson and minor, Charles Worthington, as his heir.[53] Most of the estate, c. 1,540 a., was sold in 1950 to a trust, which still owned c. 1,400 a. in 1986.[54] The house was bought with 24 a. by Staffordshire county council in 1951 and opened as a boarding annexe for Lichfield grammar school in 1953.[55] In 1981 the house

[27] S.R.O., D. 150/1/45–6.
[28] Ibid. D. 150/1/49–50.
[29] Ibid. D. 150/1/55.   [30] Ibid. D. 150/1/67.
[31] Ibid. D. 150/1/73; D. 150/1/74, pp. 54, 59–63; D. 150/1/122; White, *Dir. Staffs.* (1834), 105; L.J.R.O., B/A/15/Burntwood.
[32] S.R.O., D. 150/1/77; D. 150/1/94.
[33] Ibid. D. 4566/F, Maple Hayes papers, deed of 7 May 1890; inf. from Mrs. S. Hammersley of Hill Farm.
[34] Bodl. MS. Ashmole 864, p. 391; L.J.R.O., D. 30/VC, palimpsest, ii, f. 2.
[35] S.R.O., D. 150/1/18.
[36] Ibid. D. 150/7/1.
[37] L.J.R.O., D. 27/1/3, burial of 14 June 1704, baptism of 9 Apr. 1724.
[38] S.R.O., D. 150/4/5.
[39] Ibid. D. 3697/7/1; D. 3697/7/8; D. 3697/7/10.
[40] Ibid. D. 150/5/15; D. 3697/7/13.
[41] Ibid. D. 3697/7/10.
[42] Ibid. D. 150/1/21; *Univ. Brit. Dir.* iii (1794), 612.
[43] S.R.O., D. 150/1/24 and 26.
[44] Ibid. D. 150/1/118; Lichfield Cath. Libr., Harradine scrapbook, p. 46.
[45] *S.H.C.* 1912, 292.
[46] S.R.O., D. 150/1/132, p. 1; D. 4363/P/1/2; *Staffs.*

Advertiser, 29 Apr. 1837, p. 1; above, Lichfield, manor (lay estates: Beacon Place).
[47] S.R.O., D. 150/1/42–3; Burke, *Peerage* (1871), 450; *Complete Peerage,* iii. 461.
[48] S.R.O., D. 150/1/39; W.S.L. 94/32/76; L.J.R.O., B/A/15/Burntwood; *Guide to City of Lichfield* (1848), 48; *P.O. Dir. Staffs.* (1850).
[49] S.R.O., D. 4566/F; White, *Dir. Staffs.* (1851), 514, wrongly giving Samuel as John.
[50] Burke, *Land. Gent.* (1894), ii. 1830–1; S.R.O., D. 4566/F, will of S. P. Shawe 1859 and copy of Maple Hayes Estate sale cat. 1883, p. 3.
[51] S.R.O., D. 4566/F; *Lichfield Mercury,* 27 June 1884, p. 5; A. Barnard, *Noted Breweries of Gt. Brit. and Ireland,* i. 413, 415; above (Pipe manor).
[52] S.R.O., D. 150/1/159; D. 4566/F; above (Ashmore Brook; Hill Farm); below (Hilltop); below, Wall, manor (Hill Top farm; Pipe Grange).
[53] Burke, *Land. Gent.* (1952), 2795.
[54] *Lichfield Mercury,* 14 Apr. 1950, p. 4; 9 June 1950, p. 5; inf. from Mr. J. L. L. Savill, agent to the Trustees of the Maple Hayes Estate.
[55] *Lichfield Mercury,* 2 June 1950, p. 3; 4 Aug. 1950, p. 5; 20 Nov. 1950, p. 7; *V.C.H. Staffs.* vi. 161; S.R.O., D. 553/10, p. 51.

and land were bought by Dr. E. N. Brown, who opened a school for dyslexic children there in 1982.[56] The home farm in Abnalls Lane, which included the site of Darwin's botanic garden, was sold in 1951 to Capt. T. W. Matthews and bought from him in 1978 by Mr. E. J. Foster.[57]

The house originally consisted of a three-storeyed central block of five bays facing east and flanked by recessed single-storeyed wings of three bays. In 1802 it had a hall, dining parlour, drawing room, breakfast parlour, kitchen, and butler's pantry on the ground floor, five chambers on the first floor, and six attics.[58] It was enlarged by A. O. Worthington. In 1884–5 each wing was raised to two storeys and given a canted bay window on the east front.[59] In 1895 a new block was added at the south-west corner to house a library and a billiard room.[60] The long two- and three-storeyed service range on the north side is also late 19th-century.[61] After W. W. Worthington's succession in 1918[62] the principal rooms on the east front were fitted with panelling in an early 18th-century style; the room on the north-west corner was given rich 18th-century-style plasterwork. Parkland survives to the south and east with a boundary belt and the southern part of a string of ornamental pools.[63]

The great tithes were commuted in 1844 for the following rent charges: to the Ecclesiastical Commissioners £343 in respect of the prebend of Weeford in Lichfield cathedral, £19 0s. 7d. in respect of the prebend of Pipa Minor, £13 8s. 11½d. in respect of the prebends of Hansacre and Freeford, and £2 16s. in respect of the prebend of Gaia Minor; to the dean and chapter £4 9s. 8d. in respect of the prebend of Stotfold appropriated to them in 1803; to the Revd. J. A. Cotton £1 7s. in respect of the 5-a. Hobstone Piece; and to Stanley Pipe Wolferstan of Statfold £3 in respect of 20 a. owned by himself. The small tithes were held by the vicar of St. Mary's, Lichfield, to whom they had been granted by Bishop Lloyd in 1694; they were commuted for a rent charge of £132 15s. Parts of the area were partially or completely exempt from tithe, in some cases in return for a prescriptive payment.[64]

In 1311 John de la Bourne, a chaplain, and Reynold le Bedel of Lichfield received royal licence to grant St. John's hospital in Lichfield 10½ a. and £10 rent in Lichfield and Pipe. Adam Eton and John Wilmot, chaplains, granted it property in Pipe in 1349.[65] In 1844 the hospital owned 82 a. in Burntwood, including a 14-a. farm at Hilltop.[66] In 1921 what was called Hilltop farm, covering 21 a., was sold to W. W. Worthington[67] and became part of the Maple Hayes estate. The farmhouse, which was derelict in 1986, dates from the early 17th century. It is timber framed, but the walls have been infilled or replaced with brick and stone. It has a three-roomed plan, with an internal stack which has an ovolo-moulded fireplace surround. The roof was renewed in the 19th century.

The vicars choral of Lichfield cathedral owned land in Edial and Woodhouses in 1535.[68] In 1844 they owned a scattered estate of 42 a. in the area.[69] They transferred all their property outside the Close to the Ecclesiastical Commissioners in 1872.[70]

The property of St. Radegund's chantry, founded in the cathedral in 1242, formed a manor which by 1338 included a capital messuage in Pipe called Mossland. Half the messuage was then held by Richard Fordiave, but by 1357 the whole was held by Adam Eyton, chaplain, who had conveyed it to Richard Arley by 1359.[71] William Kynchall held a plot of land in Pipe of the chantry in 1357.[72] In 1461 the chantry's property included three messuages and land in Edial; it had a messuage and land in Edial and a messuage and land in Woodhouses in 1482.[73] By the 1530s the estate in the area seems to have consisted only of land in Moss field in Edial.[74] The chantry's property sold by the Crown to two London speculators in 1549 included rents totalling 4s. 5d. from six holdings in Edial.[75] They were sold to William, Lord Paget, in 1550.[76] In 1571 six tenants held of Thomas, Lord Paget, 18 a. in Moss field which had formerly belonged to the chantry.[77]

In the early 16th century St. Catherine's chantry in the cathedral owned 1 a. in Kynchall moor in the Edial area.[78]

The endowments of the Holy Trinity chantry in Longdon church, founded in 1528, included rent from lands in Edial and Woodhouses. It was sold by the Crown to speculators in 1571.[79]

[56] *Lichfield Mercury*, 18 Sept. 1981, p. 1; 18 Dec. 1981, p. 10; below, educ.
[57] Inf. from Mr. Foster.
[58] L.J.R.O., D. 88, sale partics. of estates near Lichfield 1802, p. 1. For a view of 1803 see Bodl. G.A. Staffs. 4°, 7, facing p. 374; for a view of 1989 see above, plate 14.
[59] Date on rainwater heads on E. and S. fronts and on bow window on S. front; S.R.O., D. 4566/F, Maple Hayes file, H. C. Shawe corresp. 31 July 1884.
[60] Date on rainwater heads.
[61] O.S. Map 1/2,500, Staffs. LII. 14 (1902 edn.).
[62] The attribution of the work to W. W. Worthington has been supplied by Dr. E. N. Brown. For interior views in A. O. Worthington's time see [A. Williams and W. H. Mallett], *Mansions and Country Seats of Staffs. and Warws.* (Lichfield, n.d.), pl. facing p. 58.
[63] L.J.R.O., B/A/15/Burntwood.
[64] Ibid.; *V.C.H. Staffs.* iii. 182; above, Lichfield, churches (parochial organization from 1491).
[65] *V.C.H. Staffs.* iii. 279–80; *Cal. Pat.* 1313–17, 367.

[66] L.J.R.O., B/A/15/Burntwood.
[67] L.J.R.O., D. 88, deed of 24 June 1921; S.R.O., D. 4363/A/5/14, pp. 10–11.
[68] *Valor Eccl.* (Rec. Com.), iii. 136.
[69] L.J.R.O., B/A/15/Burntwood.
[70] *V.C.H. Staffs.* iii. 193.
[71] S.R.O., D. (W.) 1734/2/1/760, mm. 68–9, 127; *S.H.C.* 1939, 115; *V.C.H. Staffs.* iii. 149. In 1338 there was other property in Elmhurst (in St. Chad's, Lichfield), Longdon, and Whittington.
[72] S.R.O., D. (W.) 1734/2/1/760, m. 68.
[73] Ibid. mm. 109, 123.
[74] *S.H.C.* 1939, 105; *Valor Eccl.* iii. 140.
[75] *Cal. Pat.* 1548–9, 391.
[76] *S.H.C.* 1939, 111.
[77] W.S.L., S. MS. 326/2, mm. 5–6.
[78] J.R.U.L.M., Ryl. Ch. Phillipps 126, dorse.
[79] *L. & P. Hen. VIII*, xxi (1), p. 464; *Valor Eccl.* iii. 151; *S.H.C.* 1915, 181; *Cal. Pat.* 1569–72, 398; P.R.O., E 40/14618; W.S.L., S.D. Pearson 1147.

ECONOMIC HISTORY. AGRICULTURE. Several open fields lay around Woodhouses and Edial. Pipe field on the east, mentioned in 1358, adjoined Edial Lane (the Lichfield road) and extended into Pipehill. It was still an open field in 1705.[80] Woodhouses field was bounded by Woodhouses Road and Grange Lane. Mentioned in 1519, it had evidently been divided by 1578 when Woodhouses Great field was recorded; Little field, an open field adjoining it and also bounded by Grange Lane, was recorded between 1608 and 1663.[81] Great field contained closes by the mid 18th century and was finally inclosed in 1777.[82] Moss field at Edial adjoined Woodhouses Great field. Mentioned in 1462, it was still an open field in 1608 but had been inclosed by the 1690s.[83]

Ashmore Brook had its own open fields. 'Le Rudyng' there, evidently an assart, contained selions in 1342.[84] In 1426 John Sprott took possession of a headland in Ashmore Brook field; its bounds included John's furlong called Twentylands.[85] In the later 16th century the Sprotts' Ashmore Brook estate included 2 a. in Twentylands field and 2 a. in Middle field.[86] Earlier in the century the family claimed right of way across the two fields when going between Ashmore Brook and Longdon. About 1540 Edward Sprott complained that Thomas Bilston of Longdon Way had inclosed one of the fields, thus forcing him to make a long detour. Bilston complained that Sprott had broken down his hedges and driven an ox cart across his land.[87] Thomas Sprott's estate at Ashmore Brook in 1654 included land called the Great Twentylands.[88]

A survey of 1298 recorded 300 a. of common pasture in Burntwood.[89] One of 1597 recorded a heath of 800 a. in Burntwood and Hammerwich where the freeholders and copyholders of Longdon, Burntwood, Hammerwich, Ashmore Brook, Farewell, Childerhay, Edial, and Woodhouses had grazing rights.[90] Piecemeal inclosure of the waste was in progress by the mid 12th century when assarted land in Pipe formed part of Farewell priory's estate.[91] There was assarting at Ashmore Brook in the mid 13th century.[92] In 1298 two plots of 'new land' in the wood of 'Pipemore' (one of 4 a. and one of 10 a.) were held of the bishop, with four more in 'Kinghalemore' (one of ½ a., two of 1½ a., and one of 2¼ a.[93] In the later 16th century there was extensive inclosure of parcels of waste for arable and for building cottages.[94] None the less a large area of heath survived in the western part of the township until the later 19th century. In 1861 the remaining 1,840 a. of common were inclosed under an Act of 1857.[95]

Of the bishop's nine free tenants at Pipe in 1298, only the prior of St. John's hospital in Lichfield owed labour services, which consisted of carriage of mill stones and could be commuted for a payment of 6d. Four neifs and a cottar held land in Pipe; the neifs owed the same services as those of Streethay and Morughale, and the cottar owed carriage of mill stones.[96] In the earlier 17th century Sir Walter Heveningham exacted labour services as lord of Pipe. In leases between 1625 and 1635 he specified from one to twelve days' work a year, including ploughing, carting, and harvesting, to be done within a given distance of Pipe or Edial at two days' notice.[97]

Barley, oats, and rye were being grown on a farm at Woodhouses in 1605, and barley, French wheat and barley, peas, and oats on a farm in Norton Lane in 1653.[98] Corn, barley, peas, oats, and beans were recorded on farms in Burntwood in the later 1670s.[99] A turnip field in Woodhouses was mentioned in 1777.[1] The main crops in the township in the late 1860s were turnips, barley, and wheat.[2] The machinery at Hill farm north of Woodhouses in 1871 included a turnip slicer and a turnip pulper, while in 1874 the 240-a. Bridge Cross farm south-east of Chase Terrace was growing turnips and barley.[3] Potatoes too were grown: potato setting in the spring and picking in the autumn caused extensive absenteeism among the boys at the Colliery school in Chasetown from its early days in the 1860s.[4] In 1984 the main crops in Burntwood parish were barley (161.8 ha. officially recorded), wheat (66.1 ha.), and potatoes (28.4 ha.).[5]

There was a market gardener living at Woodhouses in 1851.[6] James Hastilow of Castle farm was listed as a market gardener in the 1860s.[7] Four market gardeners were recorded in Burntwood in 1870, one of them also the landlord of the Nag's Head at Fulfen, and there was

[80] S.R.O., D. (W.) 1734/2/1/605, m. 21d.; D. (W.) 1734/2/1/612, m. 36; D. (W.) 1734/2/1/656, m. 8; D. (W.) 1734/2/1/760, m. 118; D. 4566/B, deeds of 9 and 10 Mar. 1704/5.
[81] Ibid. D. 150/1/323; D. (W.) 1734/2/1/613, m. 31d.; D. (W.) 1734/2/1/631, f. 6; D. 4566/B, deed of 2 Jan. 1634/5 and unexecuted deed of 1663.
[82] Ibid. D. 150/1/327A; D. 4566/S, bdle. 35, deed of 12 May 1752; L.J.R.O., D. 88, plan of Woodhouses field 1777.
[83] S.R.O., D. (W.) 1734/2/1/610, m. 3; D. (W.) 1734/2/1/613, m. 31d.; D. (W.) 1734/2/1/760, m. 118; D. 4566/B, unexecuted deed of 1663; D. 4566/S, bdle. 33, deed of 23 June 1693; L.J.R.O., B/A/15/Burntwood, no. 638; Reade, Johnsonian Gleanings, vi. 132.
[84] B.L. Add. Ch. 73223.
[85] S.R.O., D. (W.) 1734/2/1/380, m. 3.
[86] Ibid. D. (W.) 1734/J. 2039, 2042-4.
[87] P.R.O., C 1/951, nos. 80-1; C 1/1063, nos. 66-7.
[88] S.R.O., D. 833/3/1.
[89] Above, growth of settlement.
[90] S.R.O., D. (W.) 1734/2/1/112D.

[91] Above, manors.
[92] B.L. Add. Ch. 73219, 73221.
[93] S.R.O., D. (W.) 1734/J. 2268, f. 2v.
[94] S.H.C. 1926, 90-2; S.R.O., D. 150/4/2; D. (W.) 1734/2/1/612, mm. 14, 23, 31; D. (W.) 1734/2/1/621, f. 8; D. (W.) 1734/2/1/625, f. 8.
[95] 20 Vic. c. 5 (Local and Personal); S.R.O., Q/RDc 102.
[96] S.R.O., D. (W.) 1734/J. 2268, ff. 2v., 3v.; below, Streethay, econ. hist.
[97] S.R.O., D. 4566/B, deeds of 18 Jan. 1624/5, 1 Oct. and 20 Nov. 1634, 2 Jan. 1634/5.
[98] S.H.C. 4th ser. v, pp. 45, 86-8.
[99] Ibid. pp. 263, 265-6, 268.
[1] L.J.R.O., D. 88, plan of Woodhouses field 1777.
[2] P.O. Dir. Staffs. (1868).
[3] S.R.O., D. 4566/F, Hill Farm, sale cat. 1871; Staffs. Advertiser, 28 Feb. 1874, p. 1.
[4] S.R.O., CEL/85/1.
[5] M.A.F.F., agric. returns 1984.
[6] P.R.O., HO 107/2014 (2).
[7] Ibid. RG 9/1973; Harrison, Harrod & Co. Dir. Staffs. (1861), 256.

another at Chasetown.[8] Horticulture accounted for 3.2 ha. in Burntwood parish in 1984. Most of it was concerned with fruit: 2 ha. were devoted to strawberries and 1 ha. to raspberries, blackcurrants, gooseberries, and other small fruit. Vegetables were grown on the remaining 0.2 ha.[9]

Sheep, mentioned in the Pipe area in 1503,[10] were evidently important by then. In 1537 the holder of the Fulfen estate had common of pasture for 300 sheep as well as 200 cattle on Cannock Chase and in 'Luffule' wood and Pipe.[11] On a farm at Woodhouses in 1605 there were 80 wethers and hogs and 16 ewes and lambs, valued at £20, besides 7 cows and 3 calves valued at £12.[12] On a farm in Burntwood in 1677 4 cows, 3 heifers, and a yearling calf were valued at £8 16s. 8d.; 20 sheep, a fat hog, and two stalls of bees were together worth £6.[13] Bees were mentioned at Woodhouses in 1671 and at Burntwood in 1678.[14]

Sheep farming remained important in Burntwood, with farmers grazing their flocks on the heath until its inclosure in 1861.[15] Animals offered for sale at Maple Hayes in 1803 included 51 fat sheep, 104 ewes, 126 hoggets, and 3 rams; there were also 15 cows in calf, 3 barren cows, 10 heifers, 10 stirks, 11 yearling cows, and a bull.[16] In 1809 the warrener at the lodge north-west of Boney Hay kept a farm where there were 78 ewes, wethers, and lambs, 6 cows and heifers in calf, 2 stirks, and 3 calves.[17] The stock offered for sale at Pipe Hall farm in 1821 included some 100 Leicester ewes and theaves in lamb, some 100 ewe and wether hogs, and 120 fat sheep besides an unspecified number of Longhorn cattle.[18] Sheep for sale at Maple Hayes in 1829 consisted of 103 Leicester ewes in lamb, 71 ewe and wether hogs, and 2 Leicester rams; the other animals were 6 cows, 3 horses, and 20 pigs.[19] At Hill farm in 1871 there were 100 sheep, 11 cattle, 4 horses, and upwards of 21 pigs, and stock offered for sale at Edial in 1893 included 201 Shropshire sheep and 21 head of cattle.[20] In 1984 the livestock officially recorded in Burntwood parish consisted of 629 cattle and calves, 1,410 pigs, 3,636 sheep and lambs, and 93 hens and pullets with 3 cocks and cockerels for breeding.[21]

PARK, WARRENS, AND FISHERIES. By 1498 the lord of Pipe had a park south-east of Pipe Hall.[22] A piece of land south of the hall called the Park was measured at 26 a. in 1689.[23] By 1690 the park had evidently been divided into three, the great park, the little park, and 'the park next the house or conygrey'.[24] In 1844 three fields south and south-east of the hall were known as Little, Middle, and Great Park.[25]

The prioress of Farewell had a warren at Ashmore Brook in 1418; land there was known as the Conigree in the mid 17th century.[26] At Edial in 1608 there were closes called the Cunnyngryes, a name which survived as the Conigrees in 1704.[27] A warren with a lodge north-west of Boney Hay was destroyed in the attack on the Cannock Chase warrens by local inhabitants in the winter of 1753–4, but it was subsequently restocked.[28] The Mr. Derry whose farming stock was advertised for sale in 1809 after his death was succeeded as warrener there by James Derry. James was living at the lodge in 1822 and was still warrener in 1851 when he was also farming 8 a. attached to the lodge.[29] The warren evidently survived until the inclosure of 1861.[30] The lodge survives as Coney Lodge Farm and contains a roof truss, perhaps of the 17th century, which was once part of a small timber-framed building. By the later 18th century the house was of brick and two bays long, and it was extended in the 19th century.[31]

Sir Humphrey Stanley had a fishery at Pipe in 1490, when he accused Thomas Godsale of Lichfield of stealing pike, tench, roach, and perch from it.[32] In 1734 John Biddulph leased 3 a. of boggy ground along Big Crane brook on the north-west boundary of Burntwood to make two pools, one of them for fish. A pool called Biddulph's Pool survives there; in the early 19th century it was also known as Lichfield heath pool.[33]

MILLS. A mill at Ashmore Brook belonging to the lord of Pipe in 1286 and evidently still in use in 1330[34] may have been Abnalls mill, which was in decay in 1420.[35] A millward was living at Abnalls in 1340,[36] and a mill formed part of the estate centring on Abnalls which was held by Nicholas Taverner in 1357.[37] There may have been a mill on Leamonsley brook on or near the site of the late 18th-century fulling mill on the Burntwood-Lichfield boundary: in 1427 there was a Mill Lane in the area.[38]

There was a mill in Burntwood in 1690 called

[8] J. G. Harrod & Co. *Dir. Staffs.* (1870), 764, 808.
[9] M.A.A.F., agric. returns 1984.
[10] S.R.O., D. (W.) 1734/2/1/604, m. 32.
[11] *S.H.C.* xi. 275–6.
[12] *S.H.C.* 4th ser. v, p. 45.   [13] Ibid. pp. 265–6.
[14] Ibid. pp. 195, 267–8.
[15] S.R.O., D. (W.) 3222/191/30.
[16] *Staffs. Advertiser*, 15 Jan. 1803.
[17] Ibid. 11 Mar. 1809.
[18] *Lichfield Mercury*, 16 Feb. 1821.
[19] *Staffs. Advertiser*, 24 Jan. 1829.
[20] S.R.O., D. 4566/F, Hill Farm, sale. cat. 1871; *Lichfield Mercury*, 17 Feb. 1893, p. 4.
[21] M.A.F.F., agric. returns 1984.
[22] Bodl. MS. Ashmole 864, p. 391; L.J.R.O., D. 30/VC, palimpsest, ii, f. 2; iii, f. 1.   [23] S.R.O., D. 150/6/4.
[24] Ibid. D. 150/5/13, ff. 54, 57, 96.
[25] L.J.R.O., B/A/15/Burntwood, nos. 709–11.
[26] S.R.O., D. 833/3/1, deed of 16 Aug. 1654; D. (W.) 1734/2/1/379, m. 4.

[27] *S.H.C.* 1934 (2), 43; S.R.O., D. 4566/S, bdle. 30, deed of 1 Feb. 1655/6; bdle. 34, deeds of 24 Mar. 1676/7 and 26 Mar. 1704.
[28] D. Hay and others, *Albion's Fatal Tree*, 190, 229–30, 235; above, fig. 1.
[29] *Staffs. Advertiser*, 11 Mar. 1809; White, *Dir. Staffs.* (1834), 104; (1851), 514; S.R.O., D. 4045/7/2; W.S.L. 47/1/45, ff. 28, 59; L.J.R.O., B/A/15/Burntwood; P.R.O., HO 107/2014 (2).
[30] W.S.L. 47/12/45; 47/13C/45.
[31] Mr. M. J. Chatterton of Coney Lodge Farm is thanked for his help.
[32] P.R.O., CP 40/913, m. 337.
[33] W.S.L. 47/11/45, pp. 11–12.
[34] *S.H.C.* vi (1), 167; S.R.O., D. (W.) 1734/2/1/598, m. 6.
[35] S.R.O., D. (W.) 1734/3/2/1, mm. 1, 7, 13, 17; W.S.L., S. MS. 326/2, m. 5.
[36] L.J.R.O., D. 30/G 4, m. 16.   [37] Above, manors.
[38] S.R.O., D. (W.) 1734/2/1/602, m. 9; above, Lichfield, econ. hist. (trades and industries).

New Pool mill; it probably stood on Redmoor brook north of Boney Hay where there was a new pool in 1597.[39] Coney mill stood on Redmoor brook in that area in 1775. It was still in use in 1824 but had ceased to work by the mid 1830s. A house survived there, and the site of the pool became arable.[40]

There was a mill at Edial in 1666.[41]

MARKETS. By 1869 an open-air market was held on Fridays behind the Uxbridge Arms in Church Street, Chasetown. It was still an outdoor market in 1900, but a market hall existed there in 1915.[42] In the 1920s an open-air market was held in the yard of the Victoria public house in Ironstone Road, Chase Terrace.[43] In 1970 the Graysin Group started a Saturday market on the car park behind the new shopping centre on the north side of Cannock Road at Sankey's Corner. It was held on Fridays also by 1986. That year permission was given on a trial basis for 16 stalls two days a week in front of the centre, and in 1988 the market was made permanent.[44] An open-air market by Burntwood recreation centre was held on Thursday evenings during the summer in 1982 and 1983. Local traders protested, and permission was withheld in 1984.[45]

COALMINING. Coal pits, probably west of Hobstone Hill, were mentioned in the early 1650s,[46] and c. 1700 an inhabitant of Edial was dealing in coals.[47] Thomas Fairley, who went to live in the Burntwood area in 1768, was described as a collier in 1770.[48]

In the early 1840s the 1st marquess of Anglesey was investigating the possibility of large-scale mining along the Eastern Boundary Fault of the Cannock Chase Coalfield in the vicinity of Norton Pool. Boring had been carried out by 1847 near the eastern dam of the pool on the Hammerwich side of the boundary.[49] That year conditions for leasing the minerals in the area were drawn up, but potential investors were deterred by the lack of transport.[50] In 1849 the marquess sank a pit (known as the Marquess)

near the dam, and the first coal was drawn in December.[51] The Anglesey Branch Canal, incorporating a feeder from Norton Pool, was cut in 1850 to link the pit with the Wyrley and Essington Canal in Ogley Hay.[52] In May 1852 the Shallow Coal was reached in a second pit, the Uxbridge, nearby on the Burntwood side of the boundary; also called the Cathedral, it became known as the Fly from the speed of winding.[53] By October some 200 tons of coal a day were being sold from the colliery, and Lord Anglesey's agent wrote of 'the quantity of boats always waiting at Hammerwich for loading'.[54] In the same year a railway was built from the colliery to the South Staffordshire Railway[55] and offices were built near the Uxbridge pit.[56] A new pit was opened evidently in the earlier part of 1854; later known as no. 4, it lay north-east of the Uxbridge (no. 2).[57]

Lord Anglesey advertised the colliery for letting in 1853.[58] In 1854 he made an agreement with Richard Croft Chawner of Wall, chairman of the South Staffordshire Railway Co. and of the South Staffordshire Waterworks Co., and John Robinson McClean, engineer and lessee of the railway and engineer of the waterworks. They were to have a lease of the colliery and of mineral rights under 2,000 a. on Cannock Chase for 31 years. Lord Anglesey died before the lease was signed, but Chawner and McClean had already been given possession. A retrospective lease from 1854 was made by the 2nd marquess in 1858.[59] Meanwhile the original Hammerwich pit ceased working in 1856.[60] To raise additional capital and extend operations the two lessees formed the Cannock Chase Colliery Co. in 1859. They held most of the ordinary shares, and McClean, the principal shareholder, was appointed managing director.[61] On his death in 1873 his son Frank was appointed in his place; he resigned in 1877 after a disagreement with the board of directors over policy.[62]

A new pit (no. 3, also known as the Preference and as the Plant) was being sunk in 1859 south of the Cannock road near the parish boundary.

[39] L.J.R.O., D. 110; S.R.O., D. (W.) 1734/2/3/112D, bounds of Burntwood and Hammerwich.
[40] Above, fig. 1; W.S.L. 47/1/45, ff. 28, 59; L.J.R.O., B/A/15/Burntwood.
[41] S.H.C. 1923, 164.
[42] S.R.O., CEL/85/1, pp. 109, 115, 150, 249; O.S. Map 1/2,500, Staffs. LVII. 4 (1902 and 1919 edns.).
[43] Lichfield Mercury, 31 July 1970, p. 12.
[44] Ibid. 17 Apr. 1970, p. 9; 7 Feb. 1986, p. 2; 7 Nov. 1986, p. 11; 18 Mar. 1988, p. 3.
[45] Ibid. 10 Feb. 1984, p. 12; 24 Feb. 1984, p. 2; 27 Apr. 1984, p. 13; 7 Feb. 1986, p. 2.
[46] S.R.O., D. 150/6/8.
[47] W.S.L., M. 912, item 30.
[48] S.R.O., D. 4045/8/1/27.
[49] Ibid. D. 603/M/5/5, George to Landor, 5 Nov. 1847; D. 603/M/6/3, Wm. Stott's reps. 1842, 1844; D. 603/M/6/4, conditions for letting mines 1847; V.C.H. Staffs. ii. 69–70, 77–9. The following account corrects some of the details given ibid. 79 and in V.C.H. Staffs. v. 62.
[50] D. G. Brown, 'Econ. Dev. of Marquess of Anglesey's Cannock Chase Estate 1842–1891' (Wolverhampton Polytechnic M.A. thesis, 1985), 39–40.
[51] S.R.O., D. 603/M/5/3, draft letter 12 Apr. 1849; D. 603/M/6/1, Landor to Anglesey, 6 Dec. 1849; Landor to Beer, 6 Dec. 1849; statement of expenditure at Hammerwich colliery 1849 to 1850; S.R.O., Q/RDc 99.

[52] Below, Hammerwich, introduction.
[53] S.R.O., D. 603/M/5/5, Landor to Landor, 31 May 1852; S.R.O., Q/RDc 102C; G. Barrow and others, Memoirs of Geol. Surv., Geol of Country around Lichfield, 83 n.; Jnl. Staffs. Ind. Arch. Soc. ix (2), 10; The Blackcountryman, ix (3), 56.
[54] S.R.O., D. 603/M/6/2, Landor to Beer, 13 Oct. 1852.
[55] Below, Hammerwich, introduction.
[56] The Blackcountryman, ix (3), 56.
[57] S.R.O., D. 603/M/6/2, Hammerwich Collieries, statement of prospects Dec. 1852; D. 603/M/7/1/10, Woodhouse to Landor, 13 June 1853; Landor to Landor, 18 July 1853; S.R.O. 1456/7, pp. 13–14; Jnl. Staffs. Ind. Arch. Soc. ix (2), 4, 11.
[58] S.R.O., D. 603/M/6/2, summary of tenders 1853–4; Landor to Beer, 7 Aug. 1853; Jnl. Staffs. Ind. Arch. Soc. ix (2), 2.
[59] S.R.O., D. 603/M/6/2, Woodhouse to Landor, 15 Apr. 1854; Woodhouse to Beer, 18 Apr. 1854; D. 603/M/8/1/1; D. 603/M/8/2/2; D. 4426/3/1; The Blackcountryman, ix (2), 44; J. Marshall, Biog. Dict. Railway Engineers, 146; below, Wall, manor (Wall Hall).
[60] S.R.O. 1456/2, p. 13; 1456/3.
[61] Ibid. 1456/2, pp. 3, 5; D. 4426/1/4 and 6; D. 4426/3/2 and 3.
[62] S.R.O. 1456/2, pp. 155, 239; 1456/9, section V; D.N.B. 1901–11, s.v. McClean, Frank.

It evidently began production in 1861.[63] No. 5, north-east of no. 3, was being sunk in 1861, and the Deep Coal was evidently reached early in 1863.[64] The company's four pits were employing nearly 2,000 men and boys in 1865 and produced 12,000 tons a week during the winter; each had its branch railway.[65] In 1867 the main railway was extended as the Cannock Chase & Wolverhampton Railway to join lines in Cannock and Norton Canes; the colliery, already connected with the South Staffordshire Railway, was thus given a connexion with the London & North Western Railway at Rugeley.[66] In the same year Lord Anglesey granted a new lease.[67] By then the company was extending its operations into Cannock.[68]

In 1883 Arthur Sopwith, engineer and general manager of the company from 1873, introduced electricity at no. 2 pit. A claim that it was the first in the world to be so lit has been refuted in favour of a pit at Hamilton (Lanarks.), lit in 1882. The supply had been extended to no. 3 by 1907. A power station was opened at no. 5 in 1908, and by 1912 all the company's pits except one in Cannock were supplied.[69] Sopwith was succeeded by his son Shelford in 1918.[70]

No. 4 pit was disused by 1883.[71] In 1907 no. 2 was employing 251 men underground and 95 above, and nos. 3 and 5 together had 684 underground and 322 above.[72] Work stopped at no. 5 some time c. 1919.[73] No. 2 ceased to be a drawing pit in 1923; instead an inclined ropeway known as the Drift took the coal up to the canal. Production there stopped in 1940.[74] No. 3 was reconstructed as the centre of the colliery in the 1920s and continued in operation until 1959.[75] With its closure mining in Burntwood came to an end. Workshops opened there in 1924 and reorganized in 1957 have continued as the National Coal Board's area workshops.[76]

OTHER INDUSTRIES. There was a locksmith at Edial in 1624[77] and a pinmaker at Woodhouses in 1663.[78] A buckle maker settled at either Edial or Woodhouses in 1772.[79] Nailing was the most important metal industry. A nailer named John Tymnis or Tymons was living at Burntwood in 1651 and 1664,[80] and another named Richard Biddulph died there in 1670.[81] There were several references to nailers at Burntwood in the 18th century.[82] There was a nailshop at Woodhouses in 1819, and the seven in Burntwood in the earlier 1820s stood mainly west of the green and around Rake Hill.[83] By 1841 there was an extensive domestic industry, employing women and children as well as men. It was concentrated around Burntwood itself, and in 1851 the main areas were the green, the Cannock road, Ball Lane, Commonside, and Ranter's Row.[84] Nailing was still important in 1861, although numbers were declining and in some families sons were becoming miners instead.[85] By 1881 there were only four nailers in Burntwood, with a fifth at Woodhouses.[86] Former nailers' cottages still stand in Farewell Lane and Rake Hill.[87]

A presentment of brickmaking on the waste at Burntwood was made at the Longdon manor court in 1713.[88] A band of red marl south of Boney Hay in the area of the present Slade Avenue has been used for brickmaking. A map of the earlier 1820s shows Brick kiln slade, Brick kiln pits, and Brick kiln bank on the heath there. In 1860 it was the site of a disused brickworks which may have been the brickworks in Burntwood belonging to Lord Anglesey in 1854.[89] A brickmaker named Samuel Cheetham was living at Spade Green in 1806 and was described as a brickmaker of Woodhouses in 1813.[90] Another brickmaker named William Robinson was living at Woodhouses in the earlier 1830s.[91] In 1841 Elias Gilbert had a brickworks west of Lincroft Cottage, his house on Stafford Road on the boundary with Lichfield. He was still running it with a farm in 1861, and in 1871 both were in the hands of his widow Mary.[92] John Tudor of Fulfin House worked as a brickmaker as well as a farmer in the 1860s.[93] There was a brickyard on the north side of Springlestyche Lane in 1882.[94] Bricks are said to have been made at some time before 1918 from a band of marl south of Queen Street in Chasetown.[95]

Walter Heveningham had a quarry near Pipe Hall in the 1680s: under an agreement of 1685 'sound, hard quarrell stone' from it was to be used for making a sough at the conduit head nearby.[96] Fines were imposed at the Pipe manor court in 1777 for quarrying stone at Edial and in

[63] *Staffs. Advertiser*, 1 Oct. 1859, p. 8; S.R.O. 1456/2, pp. 8–9, 38; 1456/7, p. 13; S.R.O., D. 603/M/8/2/6; D. 4426/1/4, p. 3.
[64] S.R.O. 1456/4–5; 1456/7, p. 15; D. 603/M/8/2/6; *Jnl. Staffs. Ind. Arch. Soc.* ix (2), 12; *Old Chasetown*, 8.
[65] *Jnl. Staffs. Ind. Arch. Soc.* ix (2), 13.
[66] Ibid. 56; Brown, 'Cannock Chase Estate', 88–92; *V.C.H. Staffs.* ii. 318.
[67] S.R.O., D. 4426/3/4–5.
[68] *Jnl. Staffs. Ind. Arch. Soc.* ix (2), 14, 63.
[69] Ibid. 18, 25–6; *Cannock Advertiser*, 24 Aug. 1961, p. 1; S.R.O. 1456/9, corresp. 1873–6, pp. 8, 10.
[70] *Jnl. Staffs. Ind. Arch. Soc.* ix (2), 21, 33, 36.
[71] O.S. Map 6″, Staffs. LI. SE. (1888 edn.).
[72] *Jnl. Staffs. Ind. Arch. Soc.* ix (2), 24.
[73] Ibid. 33, 63.
[74] Ibid. 36, 38; *Old Chasetown*, 18–19.
[75] *Jnl. Staffs. Ind. Arch. Soc.* ix (2), 38; *Lichfield Mercury*, 6 Feb. 1959, p. 6; *Cannock Advertiser*, 13 Apr. 1961, p. 1.
[76] *Jnl. Staffs. Ind. Arch. Soc.* ix (2), 38; *Old Chasetown*, 26; *Cannock Chase Courier*, 25 May 1961, pp. 8–9.
[77] L.J.R.O., D. 27/1/1, f. 62.
[78] *S.H.C.* 4th ser. v, p. 136.   [79] S.R.O., D. 4045/8/1/3.

[80] Ibid. D. (W.) 1734/2/1/743, p. 223; Lichfield Guildhall, deed of 21 Apr. 1664.
[81] S.R.O., D. 4045/8/1/18, 33, and 64; D. 4045/8/7/10.
[82] *S.H.C.* 4th ser. v, p. 187.
[83] S.R.O., D. 603/H/5/5; D. 4045/7/2, 10 and 19 Apr., 29 June 1819; D. (W.) 1821/5.
[84] P.R.O., HO 107/980 and 2014 (2); L.J.R.O., B/A/15/ Burntwood.   [85] P.R.O., RG 9/1974.
[86] Ibid. RG 11/2774.
[87] Lambourne and James, *Burntwood*, 26.
[88] S.R.O., D. 603/J/7/6/1.
[89] S.R.O., D. (W.) 1821/5; D. 603/H/5/24; S.R.O., Q/RDc 102c; Barrow and others, *Geol. of Country around Lichfield*, 147; O.S Map 6″, Staffs. LI. SE. (1888 edn.).
[90] L.J.R.O., D. 29/1/2, f. 37; D. 29/1/3, p. 3.
[91] White, *Dir. Staffs.* (1834), 105.
[92] P.R.O., HO 107/980 and 2014 (2); P.R.O., RG 9/1973; RG 10/2915; L.J.R.O., B/A/15/Burntwood, no. 762.
[93] *P.O. Dir. Staffs.* (1860 and edns. to 1872); P.R.O., RG 9/1973; above, manors.
[94] O.S. Map 6″, Staffs. LII. SW. (1887 edn.).
[95] Barrow and others, *Geol. of Country around Lichfield*, 142.   [96] L.J.R.O., D. 16/5/1.

Pinfold (later Woodhouse) Lane in Wood-houses.[97] Stone was quarried on the waste at Hobstone in the mid 1780s, and a quarry south of Camsey Lane in the same area was being worked at the beginning of the 20th century.[98] There was a gravel pit straddling the boundary with Hammerwich by Norton Pool in the earlier 1840s[99] and another on the Slade Avenue site in the early 1880s.[1] The inclosure award of 1861 assigned just under 3 a. at Ball's Mount west of Burntwood to the highway surveyors as a quarry for stone and gravel for road repair. A gravel pit there was being worked in 1921, and at some earlier date building sand was dug to the west at Spring Hill.[2]

Industrial estates were established from the 1960s on the site of no. 5 pit south of Cannock Road at Chase Terrace, off Queen's Drive on the south side of Chasetown, and off New Road in Burntwood.[3]

LOCAL GOVERNMENT. MANORIAL GOVERNMENT. Manorially Edial and most of Woodhouses were within Pipe manor, but Burntwood, a later settlement which grew up on the waste of Longdon manor, was never part of Pipe manor.[4] By 1293 Pipe attended Longdon manor's view of frankpledge, held at Lichfield.[5] It presented with Wall by 1297, and by 1327 the tithing of Pipe and Wall was represented by four frankpledges; there were three from 1452.[6] From 1494 the tithing was styled Pipe (evidently Pipehill), Wall, Edial, and Woodhouse (Wood-housen or Woodhouses from the later 16th century).[7] Burntwood had been added to the name by 1570.[8] Between 1559 and 1563 the tithing was sometimes called Pipe cum membris, also the name of the constablewick, and that style was used regularly from 1576.[9] In the late 1630s the tithing broke into three separate tithings, each with one frankpledge. One tithing covered Burntwood, Edial, and Woodhouses, another Wall, and the third Pipehill.[10] There was still a headborough for Burntwood, Edial, and Woodhouses in the 1830s; although an officer of Longdon manor, he was nominated by the Burntwood vestry.[11] The township of Burntwood, Edial, and Woodhouses was still summoned to the Longdon leet in 1857.[12]

The constablewick of Pipe cum membris, in existence by the 14th century, covered the same area as the tithing, with the constable elected at the Longdon great court.[13] Even after the division of the tithing in the 1630s, Wall and Pipehill remained part of the constablewick. The constable was still an officer of Longdon manor in the 1830s, but by the later 1820s he too was nominated by the Burntwood vestry.[14]

The lord of Pipe had a three-weekly court in 1299.[15] He still held a court baron in 1838 and apparently in 1857. Its meeting place was recorded as Pipe Hall from 1767.[16]

There was a pinfold in the tithing of Pipe and Wall in 1466.[17] By the late 16th century there was a pinfold at Woodhouses, where the present Woodhouse Lane was known as Pinfold Lane in the late 18th and early 19th century.[18] In 1838 it was stated at the Pipe court that the ancient pinfold in Pipe manor was in decay and that Woodhouses was the most convenient place for a new one.[19]

Part of Ashmore Brook, presumably the Ab-nalls area in Farewell manor, was making presentments at the Farewell view by 1290. At first it formed a tithing with Bourne, evidently in Longdon parish, but by 1341 Ashmore Brook and Bourne presented separately. In the early 1340s Ashmore Brook was represented by two frankpledges and in 1367 by one.[20] It was still a tithing with one frankpledge in 1636.[21]

The estate at Edial and Woodhouses belonging to St. Radegund's chantry in Lichfield cathedral was evidently the main possession of the chantry manor.[22] That manor was within the superior jurisdiction of Longdon manor,[23] but it had its own court baron, records of which survive from 1305.[24] The court met in the Close at Lichfield in 1341 and in the chapel of St. Radegund in the cathedral in the 15th and 16th centuries.[25] In 1577 the court was held at Longdon, the Pagets having acquired both manors.[26] The property of the former chantry still formed a distinct accounting unit in the earlier 1620s.[27]

PARISH GOVERNMENT. As part of the parish of St. Michael, Lichfield, the township of Burntwood, Edial, and Woodhouses had no wardens of its own until the 19th century. With the opening of Christ Church, Burntwood, in 1820 two chapel

[97] S.R.O., D. 150/4/9; above, growth of settlement.
[98] S.R.O., D. 150/5/16.
[99] Below, Hammerwich, econ. hist.
[1] O.S. Map 6", LI. SE. (1888 edn.).
[2] Ibid. (edns. of 1888 and 1924); S.R.O., Q/RDc 102C and D; Barrow and others, *Geol. of Country around Lichfield*, 147.
[3] *Lichfield Dist. Official Guide* (edn. of early 1980s), 59; *Lichfield Mercury*, 7 Mar. 1986, pp. 14–17; Burntwood Libr., Burntwood par. council mins. 3 June, 15 July 1964.
[4] Above, manors.
[5] *Plac. de Quo Warr.* (Rec. Com.), 711.
[6] S.R.O., D. (W.) 1734/2/1/598, mm. 2d., 15; D. (W.) 1734/2/1/603, m. 40.
[7] Ibid. D. (W.) 1734/2/1/604, m. 10; D. (W.) 1734/2/1/606, mm. 29, 31; D. (W.) 1734/2/1/607, m. 4. Pipe was identified as Pipehill in 1574 and 1575: D. (W.) 1734/2/1/598, m. 37; D. (W.) 1734/2/1/623.
[8] Ibid. D. (W.) 1734/2/1/609, mm. 13d., 18.
[9] Ibid. mm. 3, 4d., 10; D. (W.) 1734/2/1/612, m. 6; D. (W.) 1734/2/1/618, f. 2; D. (W.) 1734/2/1/625, f. iv.; D. (W.) 1734/2/1/626, f. 1.
[10] Ibid. D. (W.) 1734/2/1/614, mm. 2, 29d., 31d., 32d.,

33d., 35d., 36d.; D. (W.) 1734/2/1/615; D. (W.) 1734/2/1/723. [11] Ibid. D. 603/J/1/4/15; D. 4045/6/1.
[12] Ibid. D. (W.) 3222/191/30.
[13] *S.H.C.* vii (1), 232; x (1), 110; *S.H.C.* 4th ser. vi. 10; S.R.O., D. (W.) 1734/2/1/598, mm. 35, 46; D. (W.) 1734/2/1/601, m. 15.
[14] S.R.O., D. 603/J/1/4/15; D. 4045/6/1; D. 4045/8/9/90, 96, and 124; below, public services.
[15] S.R.O., D. (W.) 1734/1/4/3A.
[16] Ibid. D. 150/4/1–22; D. (W.) 1734/2/1/760, m. 69; D. (W.) 3222/191/30.
[17] S.R.O., D. (W.) 1734/2/1/598, m. 72.
[18] Ibid. D. (W.) 1734/2/1/617, f. 62; D. (W.) 3222/191/25; above, growth of settlement. [19] S.R.O., D. 150/4/22.
[20] L.J.R.O., D. 30/G 4, mm. 2, 5, 9–10, 12, 15, 17d., 19, 20d., 22. [21] S.R.O., D. (W.) 1734/2/1/385, m. 5.
[22] Above, manors.
[23] S.R.O., D. (W.) 1734/2/1/760, m. 80.
[24] Ibid. D. (W.) 1734/2/1/760.
[25] Ibid. mm. 14, 73, 82, 97–9.
[26] Ibid. D. (W.) 1734/2/1/610, mm. 3, 6.
[27] Ibid. D. (W.) 1734/3/3/46.

wardens were appointed; after the creation of a separate parish in 1845 two churchwardens were appointed.[28] There was a sidesman for each of the hamlets of Burntwood, Edial, and Woodhouses by 1637. From 1733 Edial shared a sidesman with Pipehill, but by 1792 it had its own again. The sidesmen ceased to be appointed after 1865.[29]

Each of the hamlets had its own overseer of the poor by 1674.[30] Three separate overseers continued to be appointed until 1700 when the inhabitants agreed that there should be a single overseer, chosen in rotation from Woodhouses, Edial, and Burntwood in that order.[31] By 1813 there were two overseers.[32] A paid assistant was appointed in 1835.[33] By 1824 there was a select vestry, elected for the last time in 1834.[34]

From the late 18th century the overseers owned three cottages at Woodhouses which they used as poorhouses. A meeting of ratepayers of the township in 1838 authorized the guardians of Lichfield poor law union to sell them.[35] Between 1819 and 1829 the overseers paid £4 4s. rent in respect of the workhouse at Norton Canes, presumably in return for being allowed to send paupers there.[36]

Under the Burntwood inclosure award of 1861 the churchwardens and overseers were assigned 4 a. at Ball's Mount for the benefit of the labouring poor, subject to a rent charge of £2. The land was settled on trustees in 1864 and divided into 16 holdings, which were let at a rent of 5s. each. The surplus income was used in aid of the poor rates.[37]

By 1637 a surveyor of the highways was elected for each of the three hamlets.[38] All three surveyors were salaried by the late 19th century.[39]

The township was included in Lichfield poor law union, formed in 1836.[40] It was recognized as a civil parish in the later 19th century,[41] and its name was changed from Burntwood, Edial, and Woodhouses to Burntwood in 1929.[42] In 1969 the meetings of the parish council were transferred from Chase Terrace comprehensive school to the committee room at the newly opened baths.[43]

Having been part of Lichfield rural district, Burntwood became an urban parish in the new Lichfield district in 1974, with its council styled a town council.[44] The council offices were moved in 1983 from the recreation centre to temporary accommodation in Bridge Cross Road at Sankey's Corner and in 1986 into a building there which also contains shops, other offices, and a snooker hall. The building was named Lambourne House in 1987 in memory of Ernie Lambourne, a member of the council 1976–84.[45]

PUBLIC SERVICES. In 1870 a meeting of ratepayers of the township of Burntwood, Edial, and Woodhouses, concerned at the state of drainage in Chasetown, agreed to lay a sewer along Queen Street, discharging into a field.[46] An inspector of nuisances was appointed for the township in 1872.[47] In 1877 an inspecting committee of ratepayers found the sanitary condition of Chasetown 'not very bad': the streets were kept clean, and there was surface sewering. In Chase Terrace and Boney Hay, on the other hand, they found some streets 'a foot deep in mud, ashes, and sewage', and the ratepayers decided to introduce sewering.[48] In 1880 a meeting agreed to undertake the sewerage of those parts of Chasetown not yet served.[49] The drainage of the southern part of Ironstone Road in Chase Terrace was agreed in 1891, from Eastgate Street to Cannock Road.[50]

In the rural part of the township in 1892 the medical officer of health of the district found the sanitary state of Woodhouses 'as bad as it can be'. A particular problem was the scarcity of pure water. The supply came mainly from three roadside wells. The best was only three feet deep, but it was bricked round and covered with wood; the other two were 'mere open holes by the side of the road ... fouled by the wet and all sorts of rubbish being thrown into them'.[51]

In 1898 Chasetown's sewerage was remodelled and a sewage works was opened south of Queen Street on the Hammerwich side of the boundary; it remained in use until the late 1960s.[52] Another works was opened east of Rugeley Road at Chase Terrace in 1906.[53] A sewerage scheme for Burntwood was begun in 1914 and completed in 1919.[54] Water closets were the norm in Chasetown and Chase Terrace by 1920 and in Burntwood by 1925. Water was supplied by the South Staffordshire Waterworks Co. which had built a pumping station in Chor-

[28] Board at W. end of the nave of Christ Church, Burntwood; S.R.O., D. 4045/6/2, 25 Mar. 1847.
[29] L.J.R.O., D. 27/5/3.
[30] S.R.O., D. 150/7/1.
[31] L.J.R.O., D. 110/1.
[32] S.R.O., D. 4045/7/2; D. 4045/8/9/6 and 125.
[33] Ibid. D. 4045/6/1, 30 Mar. 1835.
[34] Ibid. D. 4045/6/1.
[35] Ibid.; D. 4045/7/1 and 2; D. 4045/8/9/35 and 54.
[36] Ibid. D. 4045/7/2.
[37] Ibid. D. 4045/6/2, 30 Jan. 1869 and facing p.; D. 4045/6/3, pp. 58, 73–7; D. 4045/7/3; S.R.O., Q/RDc 102C and D.
[38] L.J.R.O., D. 27/1/2, at end; D. 110/1, reverse pages; S.R.O., D. (W.) 3222/191/1 and 2.
[39] S.R.O., D. 4045/6/3 and 4.
[40] Poor Law Com. Order 1836 forming Lichfield Union (copy in L.J.R.O., D. 77/16/3).
[41] Census, 1881, 1891.
[42] Lichfield Mercury, 12 Oct. 1920, p. 6; 14 Dec. 1928, p. 1.
[43] Ibid. 22 Aug. 1969, p. 17; Burntwood Libr., Burntwood par. council mins. 18 June and 1 Oct. 1969.
[44] Burntwood Libr., Burntwood par. council mins. 5 Dec. 1973, 3 Apr. 1974.
[45] Inf. from the Town Manager and Clerk to the Burntwood Town Council; Lichfield Mercury, 8 May 1987, p. 12; above, plate 40.
[46] S.R.O., D. 4045/6/2, 16 May 1870.
[47] Ibid. 13 and 20 June 1872.
[48] Ibid. D. 4045/6/3, pp. 6, 18–19, 21, 24; Staffs. Advertiser (S. Staffs. edn.), 21 Apr. 1877, p. 5.
[49] S.R.O., D. 4045/6/3, pp. 34–5, 36–9.
[50] Ibid. D. 4045/6/4, 6 Apr. 1891.
[51] Lichfield Union Rural Sanitary Dist. Ann. Rep. of M.O.H. 1892, 12–13 (copy in S.R.O., C/H/1/2/1/3).
[52] Lichfield Mercury, 14 Apr. 1899, p. 6; below, Hammerwich, public services.
[53] Lichfield Mercury, 22 Mar. 1907, p. 7; above, fig. 18.
[54] Lichfield R.D.C. Ann. Rep. of M.O.H. 1914, 10; 1916, 8; 1919, 5 (copies in S.R.O., C/H/1/2/2/25).

ley Road in 1913.[55] Public collection of refuse was started in the parish in 1920.[56] A sewage works was opened in Peter's Lane at Edial in 1930, replacing the works at Chase Terrace.[57]

By 1935 there were 110 council houses in the parish, and slum clearance was in progress. There were 202 council houses by 1938, 50 of them built that year in the Boney Hay part of Chorley Road.[58] Building was resumed after the Second World War, the first new house being opened in Rugeley Road, Chase Terrace, in 1946. The Oakdene estate at Chasetown, begun soon afterwards, was by 1958 the largest council estate in Lichfield rural district.[59]

The area is served by Hammerwich Cottage Hospital, opened in 1882.[60] The Annie Ker Gettings Memorial Home in Bridge Cross Road at Sankey's Corner was opened in 1923 as a district nurses' home. It was named in memory of Annie Ker (d. 1920), who was matron of the cottage hospital for several years until her marriage to J. S. Gettings, a surgeon who worked at the hospital from its opening until shortly before his death in 1928. During the First World War she was commandant of a military ward at the hospital. Much of the cost of building the home was met with money raised to support the military ward and with the Burntwood and Hammerwich Parishes War Fund established in 1919 by Mrs. Gettings' efforts. The home was closed apparently in 1951, and in 1987 the building was used as a wine bar and night club.[61] The Oakdene day centre in Sycamore Road for the elderly and the handicapped was opened in 1988.[62]

A county asylum for pauper lunatics was opened on an estate of over 94 a. on Hobstone Hill north-west of Woodhouses in 1864. It was designed by W. L. Moffatt of Edinburgh. The part then completed consisted of the central block, including a chapel, and the west wing containing the male wards, with a portion partitioned off for female patients.[63] The east wing containing the female wards was completed in 1868.[64] A burial ground was consecrated in 1867 and extended in 1904. It remained in use until the 1920s, and its chapel was demolished in the 1960s.[65] In 1871 there were 491 patients and a staff of 4 officers, 41 attendants and nurses, and 5 artisans.[66] There have been many extensions, notably in the later 1890s and the mid 1930s. A

detached chapel was opened in 1900, and a nurses' home was built in 1914.[67] The name St. Matthew's was adopted in 1947.[68] From 1940 to 1947 there was an emergency hospital on the site for both military and civilian patients; part of the asylum was taken over, and new wards were built in the grounds. The first patients were 242 sick and wounded rescued from the Dunkirk beaches.[69]

Policing was undertaken by the township authorities in the earlier 19th century. Stocks were set up near the Nag's Head inn at Fulfen in 1809.[70] A lock and key for handcuffs were bought in 1823 and a constable's staff in 1832.[71] In December 1829 the select vestry ordered the headborough to 'attend the village of Woodhouses on Sunday evening for the purpose of detecting disorderly people that frequent that quarter'.[72] The constable's activities in 1831–2 included 'routing gypsies at the over end of Burntwood' and 'going round the public houses'; his expenses were paid by the township.[73] In 1871 there was a police constable lodging in Chasetown and another living in Edial.[74] A police station consisting of two houses was built in High Street, Chasetown, about the end of 1873; two constables were living there in 1881. About 1927 the two houses were converted into one, which was occupied by the officer in charge and included office accommodation. A new station was opened in 1963 on a site behind the old building, which was demolished; houses were built there for the sergeant in charge and two other officers.[75] Burntwood had a station in Cannock Road by 1896, and there was another at Chase Terrace by 1912.[76] The Chasetown station is the headquarters of a section covering all three areas.[77]

A fire station was opened in Rugeley Road, Chase Terrace, in 1969.[78]

A gasworks was built south of Queen Street, Chasetown, in 1870 by the Chasetown Gas Co. Ltd. It remained in use until c. 1952.[79] When electricity was introduced at the Cannock Chase Colliery Co.'s no. 2 pit in Chasetown in 1883, the supply was extended to the church, the nearby school, and the manager's house. When the Chasetown Institute was opened in 1888, it too was lit by electricity. In 1922 the colliery company erected street lamps in Chasetown, Chase Terrace, and Boney Hay and supplied

[55] Ibid. *1920*, 5–6; *1925*, 11; *1926*, 10; date on pumping station.
[56] Lichfield R.D.C. *Ann. Rep. of M.O.H. 1920*, 6, 38.
[57] Ibid. *1929*, 9–10.
[58] Ibid. *1935*, 23; *1938*, 23.
[59] *Lichfield Mercury*, 14 June 1946, p. 7; above, growth of settlement.
[60] Below, Hammerwich, public services.
[61] *Staffs. Advertiser*, 21 Apr. 1923, p. 3; *Lichfield Mercury*, 27 Oct. 1922, p. 8; 27 July 1928, p. 4; Lambourne and James, *Burntwood*, 16; *Kelly's Dir. Staffs.* (1884 and edns. to 1928); S.R.O., D. 4430/1/2, pp. 27–8; 3, p. 49; inscription on the Gettings grave in Hammerwich churchyard.
[62] *Lichfield Mercury*, 3 June 1988, p. 3.
[63] D. Budden, *Hist. of St. Matthew's Hosp.* (priv. print. 1989), 9; *Ann. Rep. of Visitors of Staffs. Asylum at Burntwood 1866*, 6 (copy in S.R.O., Q/AIc, box V); O.S. Map 6″, Staffs. LII. SW. (1887 edn.).
[64] Budden, *St. Matthew's Hosp.* 13–17; *Ann. Rep. of Visitors 1868*, 7, 11.
[65] Budden, *St. Matthew's Hosp.* 18; Lich. Dioc. Regy.,

B/A/2i/R, pp. 208–11; U, pp. 617–23.
[66] P.R.O., RG 10/2916.
[67] Budden, *St. Matthew's Hosp.* 54–6, 58, 96–8; *St. Matthew's Hosp., Burntwood, near Lichfield, 1864–1964* (copy in W.S.L.).
[68] Budden, *St. Matthew's Hosp.* 104.
[69] Budden, *St. Matthew's Hosp.* 99–100; *Lichfield Mercury*, 27 Dec. 1946, p. 4.
[70] S.R.O., D. 4045/7/2, 18 Dec. 1813.
[71] Ibid. 11 Apr. 1823; D. 4045/8/9/120.
[72] Ibid. D. 4045/6/1, 13 Dec. 1829.
[73] Ibid. D. 4045/8/9/120.
[74] P.R.O., RG 10/2914–15.
[75] Ibid. RG 11/2773; *Staffs. Advertiser*, 4 Oct. 1873, p. 8; *Cannock Chase Courier*, 5 Dec. 1963, p. 16; inf. from the Chief Constable of Staffs.
[76] *Kelly's Dir. Staffs.* (1896; 1912).
[77] Inf. from the Chief Constable.
[78] *Lichfield Mercury*, 10 Jan. 1969, p. 9.
[79] S.R.O., D. 734/11/1; inf. from Mr. C. Daker of Chasetown.

them with electricity generated at the power station built at no. 5 pit in 1908; it also built substations at Chasetown and Chase Terrace. Whereas the streets of Chasetown had been lit by gas, Chase Terrace and Boney Hay had depended mainly on oil lamps. The electricity was sold to private customers.[80] Lichfield corporation's supply was extended to the eastern part of Burntwood parish in 1927.[81] In 1929 the colliery company transferred its electricity operations to the Chasetown and District Electricity Co. Ltd. which was later taken over by the West Midlands Joint Electricity Authority. The power station at no. 5 pit ceased generating in 1942–3.[82]

The master of Burntwood school was also acting as post master by 1850; letters were carried on foot to and from Lichfield.[83] The master was still keeping the post office in 1854, but in the 1860s Thomas Hodson, a nailer of Norton Lane, kept it.[84] There was a post office at Chasetown by 1868 and one at Chase Terrace by 1884.[85]

In the early 20th century horse-drawn buses ran between Chasetown and Chase Terrace and between the White Swan, Burntwood, and Chasetown. Both services continued until 1924. There were also buses on Fridays from the White Swan to Lichfield. The first motor bus was introduced in 1913 by the London & North Western Railway to run between Brownhills station and Chasetown.[86]

Elizabeth Ball's charitable bequests by will proved 1770 included £100 for building a hearse house on the waste at Fulfen or Burntwood and for buying a hearse for use by the township and by Hammerwich.[87] It is not known whether those intentions were carried out.

CHURCHES. Ecclesiastically Burntwood remained part of the parish of St. Michael, Lichfield, until the 19th century. By the 18th century, however, a large number of people from Burntwood, Edial, and Woodhouses were baptized and buried at Hammerwich chapel.[88] In 1818, encouraged by the formation of the Church Building Society, J. C. Woodhouse, dean of Lichfield cathedral, opened a subscription for building and endowing a church to serve Burntwood, Edial, and Woodhouses. He

pointed out that the inhabitants were so far from the parish church that they rarely went there and were 'exposed to become a prey to the wildest and lowest of the sectaries'. He led the way by giving £100, and some £900 was contributed by the clergy, leading landowners, and principal inhabitants of the area, by the parishioners of St. Michael's, and by the inhabitants of the Close. Over £80 was raised in small subscriptions. A grant of £350 was made by the Church Building Society. Sir Robert Peel gave ½ a. at the junction of the later Church Road and Farewell Lane as the site of the church, and Lord Anglesey gave an adjoining piece of waste. Building began in 1819.[89]

Christ Church was consecrated in 1820, with a perpetual curate nominated by the vicar of St. Mary's, Lichfield.[90] In 1845 it was assigned a parish out of St. Michael's.[91] The perpetual curacy was styled a vicarage in 1868, and the patronage remained with the vicar of St. Mary's until the union of the benefices of St. Mary's and St. Michael's in 1979. It was then transferred to the dean and chapter of Lichfield.[92]

A farmhouse south-west of the church and 7 a. were bought from Sir Robert Peel as a house and glebe for the minister.[93] In 1822 a sum of £2,297 from benefactions and a parliamentary grant was invested to provide an income for him.[94] Around 1830 his annual income averaged £78.[95] In 1851 it consisted of £16 10s. from glebe, £66 13s. from other endowments, £2 from pew rents, and £2 7s. 6d. from fees.[96] In 1860, 1863, and 1876 the Ecclesiastical Commissioners made grants totalling £275 a year.[97] A new vicarage house was built in the early 1970s on part of the ground attached to the first house; that house was demolished, and Canterbury Close was built over its site and garden.[98]

The perpetual curacy was held with that of Hammerwich from 1831, and it became the practice to hold the Sunday services alternately in the morning and the afternoon at each church.[99] The congregation at the afternoon service at Burntwood on Census Sunday 1851 was 90, with a further 29 Sunday school children, the incumbent blaming the bad weather for the fall below the usual number of c. 160.[1] George Poole, appointed in 1852, decided that he should devote himself to the growing population of Burntwood, and he gave up Hammer-

[80] Old Chasetown, 70–4; Kelly's Dir. Staffs. (1924); Lichfield Mercury, 6 Oct. 1922, p. 4.
[81] Lichfield Mercury, 10 June 1927, p. 1; L.J.R.O., D. 127/electric lighting cttee. min. bk. p. 91.
[82] Jnl. Staffs. Ind. Arch. Soc. ix (2), 30; S.R.O., D. 4226/2/3.
[83] P.O. Dir. Staffs. (1850).
[84] Ibid. (1854 and edns. to 1868); P.R.O., RG 9/1973.
[85] P.O. Dir. Staffs. (1868); Kelly's Dir. Staffs. (1884).
[86] Lambourne and James, Burntwood, 7, 24–5, 47; St. John's, Chase Terrace, Centenary, 1886–1986 (copy in W.S.L.); Old Chasetown, 50–5.
[87] P.R.O., PROB 10/2523, will of Eliz. Ball, 1770. Warw. Jan.
[88] S.R.O., D. 3802/1/1.
[89] Ibid. D. 603/K/16/81, letters from J.C. Woodhouse 9 Sept. 1818 and from C. Oakeley 12 Apr. 1819; D. 4520/4, pp. 2–3; Lich. Dioc. Regy., B/A/2i/G, pp. 147–9; board at W. end of the nave.
[90] Lich. Dioc. Regy., B/A/2i/G, pp. 150–64; L.J.R.O.,

B/A/3/Burntwood; board at W. end of the nave.
[91] Lond. Gaz. 6 May 1845, pp. 1358–9.
[92] Lich. Dioc. Ch. Cal. (1869); Lich. Dioc. Dir. (1987/8); Lond. Gaz. 2 Aug. 1979, p. 9798.
[93] L.J.R.O., B/A/15/Burntwood, nos. 276–9; [A. Williams and W. H. Mallett], Staffs. Illustrated (Lichfield, n.d.), 33; Rep. Com. Eccl. Revenues [67], p. 467, H.C. (1835), xxii; Mason, Found Ready, pl. facing p. 19.
[94] L.J.R.O., B/V/6/Burntwood, 1849.
[95] Rep. Com. Eccl. Revenues, 467.
[96] P.R.O., HO 129/377/1/22.
[97] Lond. Gaz. 30 Oct. 1860, pp. 3913–14, 3921–2; 12 June 1863, p. 3023; 20 Nov. 1863, p. 5567; 25 Aug. 1876, pp. 4736–8.
[98] Lichfield Mercury, 22 Sept. 1872, p. 9; inf. from the Revd. D. A. Weaver, priest in charge.
[99] Erdeswick, Staffs. pp. lxxvii–lxxviii (giving the date as 1828; it was in fact 1831: L.J.R.O., B/A/3/Burntwood); Mason, Found Ready, 20; P.O. Dir. Staffs. (1850).
[1] P.R.O., HO 129/377/1.

wich in 1858.[2] About then he started a mission at Chasetown, and he was preaching in the open at Boney Hay in 1883.[3] He introduced the singing of psalms and hymns.[4] He was friendly towards nonconformists, speaking at Primitive Methodist meetings and contributing towards the cost of a new Primitive Methodist chapel.[5] He was an advocate of temperance and became a teetotaller, and he persuaded colliers to speak at temperance meetings in Burntwood and Chasetown.[6] His successor, Richard Weston, vicar 1886–1922,[7] opened an iron mission room in Ogley Hay Road at Boney Hay in 1893; it had been closed by 1924 and was sold in 1927.[8] A parish magazine was started by Weston in 1886 but had lapsed by 1925, when there were plans for reviving it.[9] A mothers' union was formed in 1886.[10] Quarterly collections were introduced in 1888 and weekly offertories in 1909.[11]

In 1889 the Sunday school received 50 bibles and 100 New Testaments from Rowland Hill of Tipton, who distributed copies of the scriptures widely as a memorial to his wife. Fifty New Testaments were received in 1891. By 1900 a Rowland Hill New Testament charity had been formed for the parish, consisting of a capital sum of £10, the interest on which was spent by the vicar and churchwardens on New Testaments. The charity still existed in the mid 1980s.[12] The parish also benefits from several bequests for church purposes: £100 from A. O. Worthington of Maple Hayes by will proved 1918; £100 from Dr. J. B. Spence, superintendent of Burntwood asylum 1881–1924, by will proved 1928; £2,130 from Mrs. S. E. Homer in 1940; and £300 from John Hall of Burntwood by will proved 1948.[13]

CHRIST CHURCH, a building of red brick with stone dressings, was designed in a Gothic style by Joseph Potter the elder of Lichfield. Originally it consisted of a chancel, a nave with a west gallery, and a west tower incorporating an entrance porch and containing a bell.[14] A four-bayed north aisle designed by Stevens & Robinson of Derby was built by subscription in 1869–70 to accommodate the growing congregation. The gallery was removed at the same time, though, Poole wrote, 'not without a struggle'.

He added that 'the new seats are without doors ... Most of the old pews remain.'[15] A clock in memory of Sarah Worthington (d. 1913), wife of A. O. Worthington, was placed in the tower by her children in 1921.[16] A vestry was added at the west end of the north aisle in 1929; W. W. Worthington of Maple Hayes gave £100 towards the cost.[17] The font is dated 1715 and was originally in Hammerwich church.[18]

The churchyard was enlarged by ¼ a. in 1878, ½ a. in 1913, ½ a. in 1942, and ¼ a. in 1959.[19] A lych gate was erected by subscription in 1931 as a memorial to Richard Weston (d. 1929).[20]

In the late 1850s George Poole began holding Sunday evening services in a carpenter's shop in what was to become Chasetown. Soon afterwards the services were transferred to the Colliery school there.[21] A church of St. Anne east of the school was consecrated in 1865. It was built and endowed by J. R. McClean, managing director of the Cannock Chase Colliery Co.; all the sittings were free. In 1876 his widow Anna gave £1,000 to provide an income for keeping the church in repair.[22] The patronage was vested in McClean and his heirs during the term of the colliery company's mining lease, with reversion to the marquess of Anglesey and his heirs as the landlords. The first minister was the founder's nephew, D. S. McClean.[23] A parish was formed out of parts of Burntwood, Hammerwich, and Ogley Hay in 1867 with D. S. McClean as the incumbent.[24] The living was styled a vicarage in 1868.[25] On J. R. McClean's death in 1873 the patronage passed to his son Frank and in 1888 to the vicar of Burntwood, who held it in 1987.[26]

In 1868 the Ecclesiastical Commissioners assigned the incumbent £11 6s. 8d. a year in respect of a benefaction, which they matched with a further £11 6s. 8d.[27] When J. M. Seaton was appointed to succeed D. S. McClean in 1871, the colliery company granted him a personal stipend of £255 on condition that the sittings remained free.[28] When the patronage was transferred in 1888, the Commissioners substituted a stipend of £230 and the vicar's total income was some £293.[29] Initially a house on the Hammerwich side of the township

[2] Mason, *Found Ready*, 17, 20–2.
[3] Ibid. 46, 109; below.
[4] Mason, *Found Ready*, 20–1.
[5] Ibid. 43.
[6] Ibid. 35–9.
[7] S.R.O., D. 4520/4, pp. 7, 104.
[8] *Lichfield Mercury*, 5 May 1893, p. 8; 4 Aug. 1893, p. 7; S.R.O., D. 4520/4, pp. 25, 28, 32, 105–7; O.S. Map 6″, Staffs. LI. SE. (1921 edn.).
[9] S.R.O., D. 4520/4, pp. 6, 107.
[10] Ibid. 7.
[11] S.R.O., D. 4045/6/4, 4 May 1909, 1 Apr. 1910, 21 Apr. 1911, 10 Apr. 1912; D. 4520/4, pp. 21, 24.
[12] Ibid. D. 4520/4, pp. 29, 45–6; *Kelly's Dir. Staffs.* (1900); inf. from Mr. C. Latimer, treasurer to the P.C.C.
[13] *Kelly's Dir. Staffs.*(1924); D. Budden, *Hist. of St. Matthew's Hosp.* (priv. print. 1989), 25–6, 84, 122; S.R.O., D. 4045/3/6, deed of 19 Mar. 1949; D. 4045/9/1/4; D. 4520/5, pp. 52–4; inf. from Mr. Latimer; below, chars. for the poor.
[14] Pevsner, *Staffs.* 83; Lich. Dioc. Regy., B/A/2i/G, p. 152; board at W. end of the nave; above, plate 41.
[15] Mason, *Found Ready*, 59–63; *Staffs. Advertiser*, 15 and 22 Jan. 1870.
[16] *Lichfield Mercury*, 2 Dec. 1949, p. 7; above, Lichfield,

churches (Christ Church).
[17] S.R.O., D. 4520/4, pp. 107–8; 5, p. 58; date on the vestry.
[18] Below, Hammerwich, church.
[19] Lich. Dioc. Regy., B/A/2i/S, p. 212; V, pp. 375, 419–20; X, pp. 28, 375–6; S.R.O., D. 3952/1/60; D. 4045/6/3, p. 17.
[20] *Lichfield Mercury*, 26 June 1931, p. 5.
[21] *Staffs. Advertiser*, 19 Sept. 1868, p. 6; Mason, *Found Ready*, 47–8.
[22] *Staffs. Advertiser*, 16 Sept. 1865, p. 5; *Parish Church of St. Anne, Chasetown* (copy in S.R.O., D. 3952/1/82); S.R.O. 1456/2, pp. 182, 191, 198; 1456/9/1, pp. 59, 68, 70–1.
[23] *Lond. Gaz.* 5 Feb. 1867, p. 625; *Lich. Dioc. Ch. Cal.* (1867); *Staffs. Hist.* viii. 35.
[24] *Lond. Gaz.* 5 Feb. 1867, pp. 625–6; L.J.R.O., B/A/3/ Chasetown.
[25] *Lich. Dioc. Ch. Cal.* (1869).
[26] Ibid. (1888; 1889); *Lich. Dioc. Dir.* (1987/8); S.R.O., D. 4520/4, p. 20.
[27] *Lond. Gaz.* 8 May 1868, p. 2632.
[28] S.R.O. 1456/2, pp. 143–4.
[29] *Lond. Gaz.* 6 July 1888, p. 3699; S.R.O., D. 4520/4, pp. 20–1.

boundary was provided for the incumbent by the colliery company.[30] In 1910 land on the east side of High Street, Chasetown, was conveyed as the site for a vicarage under the will of William Pavier Smith, and to meet that benefaction and another the Ecclesiastical Commissioners granted £399 towards the cost of the house. Building began in 1911.[31] A new house was built on an adjoining site c. 1980.[32]

A church room was opened in High Street in 1908; it was converted into Elim Pentecostal Church in 1984.[33] A parish magazine existed by 1896 but had lapsed by 1920 when there was a proposal to revive it. A magazine was again published from 1938.[34]

The church of ST. ANNE on the south side of Church Street, Chasetown, is a building of polychrome brick with a slate roof and was designed in a Romanesque style by Edward Adams of Westminster.[35] The dedication may have been an allusion to the name of J. R. McClean's wife Anna. The church consists of an apsidal chancel and an aisled nave of four bays, and there is a bell in a cote over the west end. The interior of the apse has marble panels. The chancel is laid with Minton tiles, while the sanctuary is of stone inlaid with alabaster. A Lady chapel was formed in 1960.[36] The west end was reordered in 1985; the end bays of the aisles were formed into rooms on two levels, and a stairway was inserted.[37] A bust of J. R. McClean was installed c. 1947, the cost being met by his descendants.[38] The church claims to be the first in the country to have been lit by electricity, which from 1883 was supplied from the Cannock Chase Colliery Co.'s no. 2 pit. It also claims to be the first to have a bell rung electrically, a device having been fitted in 1938.[39]

The burial ground on the north side of Church Street was originally ¾ a. in area. It was extended in 1897 by ½ a. given by the marquess of Anglesey.[40] Another ½ a. was added in 1928.[41]

In 1883 a committee was formed at Chase Terrace to build a mission room there.[42] The foundation stone of the mission church of ST. JOHN was laid in 1884 by Elizabeth Hussey of Wyrley Grove in Norton Canes, who met much of the cost of building.[43] The church was opened in 1886.[44] It had its own wardens and from 1887 its own magazine.[45] A church room was built in Ironstone Road in 1939,[46] and a 2-a. burial ground in Rugeley Road was consecrated in 1943.[47] St. John's became a district church with

its own minister in 1986.[48] Designed by H. E. Lavender of Walsall,[49] it is a building of brick with stone dressings and consists of a chancel, a nave, and a north-west porch. Originally there was a bell turret on the north side of the roof behind the west gable,[50] but in 1987 the bell hung in a cote on the west front.

ROMAN CATHOLICISM. The Heveninghams and their successors as lords of Pipe, the Simeons and the Welds, were Roman Catholics, at least from the earlier 17th century, and they provided a focus for a small Roman Catholic population in the area.[51] Edward Sprott of Ashmore Brook (d.1591) may have been the man of that name who was one of several laymen arrested at Stafford in 1588 while attending a mass celebrated by Blessed Robert Sutton; like the other laymen he was condemned to death but released on payment of a fine.[52] In 1609 another Edward Sprott, of Bilston Brook, was presented for not attending his parish church.[53] In 1657 five papists were recorded at Pipe Hall, three at Woodhouses, five at Burntwood, and one at Pipehill; they were yeomen, labourers, husbandmen, and tailors.[54] There were nine papists at Woodhouses and Burntwood in 1706, including John Bates, the tenant of Pipe Hall, and his wife and two children; the other five were described as poor.[55] Thomas Bridgewood, a priest serving several Roman Catholic centres in Staffordshire in the early 18th century, was at Pipe Hall in 1718. In 1737 the hall was one of the Midland centres served by the Franciscan Laurence Loraine (alias Thomas Hall).[56]

Edward Weld, having rebuilt Pipe Hall c. 1770, made provision for a resident priest, with Weld paying a stipend of £15 a year and the tenant, William Bates, providing board and lodging.[57] When a new priest, John Kirk, was appointed in 1788, Thomas Weld increased the stipend to £20, but out of it Kirk had 'to find his washing and supply the altar'; board was still provided by the tenant, then Edward Weetman. Kirk remained at Pipe Hall until 1792, and during his time there he enlarged the chapel by the addition of a sanctuary. The chapel was probably on the first floor: a wall between a first-floor bedroom and a smaller room behind retains the outlines of a central arch and two smaller side arches which could have connected the body of the chapel with the sanctuary. The

[30] S.R.O. 1456/2, p. 144; D. 4426/1/12; D. 4426/6/6; O.S. Map 6", Staffs. LVII. NE. (1888 edn.).
[31] Lond. Gaz. 5 Aug. 1910, p. 5690; 31 Mar. 1911, p. 2616; Lich. Dioc. Regy., B/A/2i/V, p. 309; date on the foundation stone.
[32] Inf. from the vicar, the Revd. G. Wooderson.
[33] S.R.O., D. 3952/1/76; D. 3952/2/2; D. 3952/3/1, p. 11; below, prot. nonconformity.
[34] S.R.O., D. 3952/3/1, p. 48; D. 3952/4/2, p. 31 and 24 Jan. 1938; Church of St. Anne, Chasetown.
[35] Staffs. Advertiser, 16 Sept. 1865, p. 5.
[36] Church of St. Anne.
[37] Exhibition of photographs in the church (1987).
[38] S.R.O., D. 3952/1/38.
[39] Jnl. Staffs. Ind. Arch. Soc. ii. 18; The Blackcountryman, ix (3), 56–7; Lichfield Mercury, 15 Oct. 1886, p. 5; Church of St. Anne.
[40] Lich. Dioc. Mag. (1897), 166; S.R.O., D. 4426/3/22.
[41] Lich. Dioc. Regy., B/A/2i/W, pp. 78, 314.
[42] Mason, Found Ready, 109.
[43] Lich. Dioc. Mag. (1884), 139.
[44] Lichfield Mercury, 26 Feb. 1886, p. 5.
[45] St. John's, Chase Terrace, Centenary, 1886–1986 (copy in W.S.L.).
[46] S.R.O., D. 3952/1/72; D. 3952/4/2, 14 Mar. 1939; D. 4137/5/1–7; D. 4137/5/9–11.
[47] Ibid. D. 3952/4/2, 15 June 1942, 1 Mar. 1943; D. 4137/1/1; Lich. Dioc. Regy., B/A/2i/X, pp. 36, 41–4.
[48] St. John's, Chase Terrace.
[49] Lichfield Mercury, 26 Feb. 1886, p. 5.
[50] St. John's, Chase Terrace.
[51] Staffs. Studies, ed. P. Morgan (Keele, 1987), 131; S.H.C. 1915, 375, 380–1; S.H.C. 4th ser. ii. 18; Staffs. Cath. Hist. xviii. 4, 13; xxii. 24–5; Harwood, Lichfield, 472, 534.
[52] Staffs. Cath. Hist. xxiii. 10; above, manors.
[53] S.H.C. 1948–9, 164.
[54] Staffs. Studies, 131.
[55] Staffs. Cath. Hist. xiii. 31.
[56] Staffs. Studies, 132.
[57] Next two paras. based on Staffs. Studies, 132–4.

furnishings probably included an altarpiece depicting the Crucifixion by the Flemish painter Nicolaes de Bruyn (d. 1656).[58]

Nine Roman Catholics were confirmed at Pipe Hall in 1774 and 19 in 1788. About 1790 the congregation included some dozen people from Lichfield. The chapel was closed when the hall was sold in 1800, and in 1801 a mass centre was opened in Lichfield. The Pipe Hall vestments, chalice, and furnishings were transferred to the Lichfield mission, and the Burntwood area was then served by the priest at Lichfield. In the 1840s Lady Fitzgerald of Maple Hayes was a member of the congregation.

The population of the Chasetown area in the later 19th century included a large number of Irish immigrants, and c. 1870 a local group began to raise money to build a Roman Catholic church.[59] Land was bought on the west side of High Street, Chasetown, and building started in 1882. It seems that a mass centre, served by the priest from Lichfield, was opened the same year in a shop. The church, dedicated to St. Joseph, was opened in 1883, and later that year the Chasetown area became a separate mission with its own priest. The church was also used as a school until 1915. A presbytery was completed east of the church in 1884. The church, which fronts on New Street, was designed by G. H. Cox of Birmingham and is a brick building with stone dressings. Originally it consisted of a chancel, a nave of four bays, and a sacristy. A clubroom was added on the north side in the late 1890s. A fifth bay was added at the west end c. 1933, and a choir gallery was erected there; the entrance, previously at the west end, was moved to the south-west corner facing New Street. In 1978 land on the south side of Cannock Road in Burntwood was bought as the site for a church, hall, and presbytery intended to replace the Chasetown buildings.

A service was held at Burntwood asylum every alternate Saturday in 1891.[60] A mass centre was started there during the Second World War, presumably as a result of the opening of an emergency hospital on the site. At first mass was said in the wards, but in 1948, after the closure of the emergency hospital, a hut was converted into a Roman Catholic chapel.[61] From 1982 mass was said in the hospital chapel.

PROTESTANT NONCONFORMITY. A Quaker named Robert Harrison was living in Burntwood in 1680.[62] In 1707 John Derry of Burntwood had his daughter baptized at the Presbyterian meeting house in Longdon.[63] In 1808 William Salt, the Congregational minister at Lichfield, opened a preaching house at Burntwood Green; he found the people there 'as ignorant as heathens – but many disposed to hear the Gospel'.[64] A house at Burntwood Green was registered for worship in 1811, Salt again being involved.[65] In 1819 he registered a chapel there,[66] but its later history is not known.

Two houses at Burntwood were registered for worship by protestant dissenters in 1830 and 1842.[67] In 1846 a house in what became Chase Road was registered for Primitive Methodist worship, and it continued to be used until 1849 when a Primitive Methodist chapel was opened in the same road. The attendances on Census Sunday 1851 were 16 in the afternoon (with 26 Sunday school children) and 25 in the evening; the average congregations were claimed to be respectively 35 and 50. The chapel was replaced in 1875 by one in Cannock Road, now Burntwood Methodist church.[68] A rear extension was built in 1900, and a hall was added in 1983 when the church interior was refurbished also.[69]

The club room at the Queen's hotel in Queen Street, Chasetown, was being used for Wesleyan Methodist meetings in 1860. A site for a Wesleyan chapel at the southern end of High Street was bought in 1863 and the chapel opened in 1864. It was rebuilt on a larger scale in 1884 and later became Trinity Methodist church.[70] Zion's Hill Primitive Methodist chapel further north in High Street was built in 1866. It was closed in 1970, and by 1986 the building was used as a carpet warehouse. The congregation united with that of Trinity, which was renamed Chasetown Methodist church.[71] It was replaced by a new church in Queen's Drive off Queen Street in 1977; the Joseph Rank Benevolent Trustees contributed towards the cost.[72]

The first Primitive Methodist meeting in Chase Terrace was held in a room at the Two Oaks inn. Mount Calvary Primitive Methodist chapel in Princess Street, Chase Terrace, was built in 1870; in 1987 it was Chase Terrace Methodist church.[73] At Boney Hay Wesleyan Methodists, having met in the home of John Howells and his wife, registered a chapel in Rugeley Road in 1879; it was closed in 1970.[74] A Methodist New Connexion chapel was built in Chapel Street, Chase Terrace, by 1883; later renamed Carmel Methodist church, it was closed in 1964 and subsequently demolished.[75]

[58] The ref. ibid. 138 n.30, relating to the painting should read B.A.A., C 1665.
[59] Rest of this section based on M. W. Greenslade, St. Joseph's, Chasetown (Stafford, 1983; copy in W.S.L.).
[60] B.A.A., B 10609.
[61] St. Matthew's Hosp., Burntwood, near Lichfield, 1864–1964 (copy in W.S.L.).
[62] S.R.O., D. 3159/1/1, no. 140.
[63] Ibid. D. 4119, p. [56].
[64] T.S.S.A.H.S. xiii. 60; S.H.C. 4th ser. iii. 17.
[65] S.H.C. 4th ser. iii. 24.
[66] Ibid. 48.
[67] Ibid. 76, 96.
[68] Ibid. 99; C. H. Gregory, Burntwood Past and Present (1953; copy in W.S.L.), stating that the house was used from 1845; P.R.O., HO 129/377/1/22.

[69] Date on extension; Cannock Libr., newspaper cuttings, Burntwood, churches.
[70] The Blackcountryman, ix (3), 57–8; Old Chasetown, 66; G.R.O., Worship Reg. no. 27580.
[71] The Blackcountryman, ix (3), 57–8; S.R.O., D. 3153/152, pp. 8–9; date on the building; inf. from Mr. C. Daker of Chasetown.
[72] Lichfield Mercury, 28 Jan. 1977, p. 9.
[73] Ibid. 12 Sept. 1924, p. 5; inscription on the building (describing it as a school).
[74] Lichfield Mercury, 12 Sept. 1935, p. 10; 5 June 1936, p. 9; G.R.O., Worship Reg. 24734; S.R.O., D. 3153/150, p. 5; O.S. Map 6", Staffs. LI. SE. (1888 edn.); inf. from Mr. Daker.
[75] Lichfield Mercury, 19 June 1959, p. 1; S.R.O., D. 3153/153, pp. 4, 7; O.S. Map 6", Staffs. LI. SE. (1888 edn.).

The Salvation Army had a barracks at Chase Terrace in 1899.[76] Emmanuel Tabernacle in Cannock Road, Chase Terrace, was registered by the Assemblies of God in 1940. The original prefabricated building was replaced in 1962 by the new Emmanuel Pentecostal church on the same site. Its name was changed to Emmanuel Church New Life Centre in 1984.[77] Elim Pentecostal church was opened in 1984 in the former St. Anne's church room in High Street, Chasetown.[78]

EDUCATION. A school board was compulsorily formed for Burntwood civil parish in 1876.[79] The county council reorganized the schools on Hadow lines in 1932. In 1946 or 1947 the two senior schools became secondary modern schools. Comprehensive secondary education was introduced in 1965. In 1977–80 Burntwood became one of the few areas in which the county council adopted a three-tier pattern of schools (first schools for children up to the age of 9, middle schools for children 9–13, and high schools for children 13–18). The intention was to provide a greater flexibility in meeting demand in a district with a rising population. In the mid 1980s, however, a combination of falling school rolls and restraints on local government finance led to several closures or threats of merger or closure. The three-tier system was abandoned in a reorganization of 1988 which gave Burntwood 10 primary schools for children up to the age of 11 and two high schools.[80]

Burntwood Charity (National) school. By will proved 1770 Elizabeth Ball of Castle Bromwich (Warws.) left £600 to build and endow a school at Fulfen, where she owned a farm.[81] From the income a master and mistress were to be paid to teach the elements, knitting, and sewing to poor children of Fulfen, Burntwood, Edial, Woodhouses, and Hammerwich. Books were to be bought for the children as necessary.[82] Miss Ball asked her cousin and heir James Birch to make up any deficiencies in her various charitable bequests.

In 1769 Miss Ball built a schoolroom and a teacher's cottage at the junction of Coulter Lane and the later Church Road. On her death later the same year Birch began to make the stipulated charitable payments. The school had cost £200 to build, and he therefore paid a master a stipend equal to the interest on £400. The money for that and for Miss Ball's other charities in and around Burntwood was drawn from the rent paid by the tenant of the farm at Fulfen. The farm descended from Birch to his son and then to his two grandsons in succession. All of them apparently made regular payments from the rent, but none established a permanent charge on the farm to create an endowed charity.

In 1821 Maj.-Gen. Thomas Birch Reynardson, the second of the grandsons, was paying £20 a year to a schoolmaster appointed by his land agent. The money was handed to the master by the tenant of the farm, who also nominated the 20 or 30 pupils.[83] Each child was given two years' schooling; some stayed longer. All were taught the Catechism. The boys were taught the elements, and the girls reading, sewing (by the master's daughter), and, if their parents demanded it, writing and arithmetic. Each child paid 1s. a year towards fuel for the schoolroom. The executors of Andrew Newton, a Lichfield philanthropist (d. 1806), had given the school £20, the interest on which (18s.) was added to the master's stipend.

Supervision of the school seems to have been lax. By 1821 masters had taken to demanding fees of 4d. a week whenever a pupil was an only child whose parents could afford to pay. In 1809 David Moss, master at least from 1782 until his resignation in 1808, was fined and imprisoned for indecently assaulting girl pupils.[84] In 1792 and 1793 he and Elizabeth Moss were running a boys' boarding school at Burntwood; whether it was a separate venture or an attempt to transform the charity school is not clear.[85] The master in office in 1821 was alleged to suffer from 'certain defects of temper' which rendered him unsuitable as a teacher and deterred parents from using the school. The Charity Commissioners urged Reynardson to establish a properly managed charity.

No formal steps were taken, but Reynardson continued to support the school. In 1833 it had 50 children attending it; 11 boys and 11 girls were taught free and the rest paid fees. At a Sunday school, added in 1820, 44 children were being taught free. The master's income in 1834 was £40.[86] In the mid 1840s 50 children were attending the day school, 21 both the day and Sunday school, and 8 the Sunday school alone. There were a master and a mistress, both salaried.[87]

Reynardson died in 1847,[88] and in 1849 an endowed charity was finally created.[89] In accordance with his wishes his heirs settled the school building in trust with an endowment of £1,000 stock. The building was to be used as a National school for Burntwood, Edial, Fulfen, Woodhouses, and Hammerwich and as a teacher's house. The endowment income was to be used to pay the master up to £20 a year, to keep the

[76] *Lichfield Mercury*, 12 May 1899, p. 7.
[77] G.R.O., Worship Reg. no. 59440; *Lichfield Mercury*, 13 July 1962, p. 7; 3 Feb. 1984, p. 19.
[78] G.R.O., Worship Reg. no. 76510; *Lichfield Mercury*, 18 May 1984, p. 7.
[79] *List of School Boards, 1902* [Cd. 1038], p. 79 (1902), lxxix.
[80] *Lichfield Mercury*, 29 July 1988, p. 12; inf. from Staffs. C.C. Educ. Dept.
[81] Next 4 paras. based on *7th Rep. Com. Char.* 353–5; above, manors (Fulfen).
[82] P.R.O., PROB 10/2523, will of Eliz. Ball, 1770. Warw. Jan. *7th Rep. Com. Char.* 353, wrongly omits reading from

the specified curriculum.
[83] *Digest of Returns to Sel. Cttee. on Educ. of Poor*, H.C. 224, p. 866 (1819), ix (2), wrongly states that the foundation limited the number to 20.
[84] S.R.O., D. 3802/1/1, 21 Oct. 1782; L.J.R.O., D. 30, box labelled 'Schoolmasters (cont.)', testimonial for Wm. Saunders, 28 June 1808; *Staffs. Advertiser*, 15 Apr. 1809.
[85] Below (private schools).
[86] *Educ. Enq. Abstract*, 885; White, *Dir. Staffs.* (1834), 104.
[87] *Nat. Soc. Inquiry, 1846–7*, Staffs. 6–7.
[88] Above, manors (Fulfen).
[89] Next 4 paras. based on *Staffs. Endowed Chars.* 28.

building in repair, and for general school expenses. In 1852 the new incumbent, George Poole, considered the National school 'a pretty roomy cottage'. By 1865 he and his wife were helping to run a night school there.[90]

In 1876, when the school board was set up, the population of Burntwood village itself was still small, and the board's first thought was apparently to acquire the National school, which could accommodate 80 children and was adequate for immediate needs. Poole was in favour of handing the school over, but negotiations failed and a board school was built in the village. The National school was closed at the end of 1878, and the board school was opened in January 1879.[91]

The National school building continued to be used as a Sunday school. During winter months in the 1880s it was also used as a night school, and in the 1890s an art class and young men's improvement classes were held there.[92] In June 1890 the day school was reopened as a higher grade National school with two certificated teachers and 14 pupils. There were 24 children on the books by December, and by 1892 there were 36.[93] The school had closed by 1898.[94] There was probably little local demand for it. The curriculum was limited, and the fees were 4 guineas a year, although reductions were offered for younger siblings.[95] Possibly the building was inadequate: a classroom had apparently been added in 1887,[96] but although an appeal for funds to build a large room was launched in 1888, it was not until 1904 that a room was built.[97]

Under a Scheme of 1898 the building was conveyed for use as an Anglican Sunday school and an undenominational night school for the poor of Burntwood ecclesiastical parish and the part of Chasetown parish in Burntwood civil parish. The trustees were permitted to maintain a lending library and run science and art classes, while the vicar was allowed to use the building for parochial purposes. One third of the charity's net income was allotted to the rector of Hammerwich for his day and Sunday schools; in 1903 the allowance was commuted to £8 a year. In 1905 the charity's gross income was c. £28. The aims of the charity, subsequently renamed the Ball and Birch Reynardson Educational Foundation, were later modified to provide support for an Anglican Sunday school and general educational help for poorer children. A proposal in 1929 to sell the buildings failed as a result of

local opposition, and they continued to be used for the Sunday school and for meetings and social gatherings, mainly connected with the parish church, until c. 1965. In 1987 the former teacher's house was occupied but the rest had been closed and partly demolished. The charity's annual income, c. £50, was disbursed according to the modified trust deeds.[98]

Chasetown county primary school (formerly *the Colliery school*). The Cannock Chase Colliery Co. was formed in February 1859, and by July it was supporting a school, presumably for its workers' children. A schoolroom had been built on the south side of the later Church Street, Chasetown, by 1861,[99] and a Sunday school was also held there.[1] From the mid 1860s, and probably from the beginning, the school took girls and infants as well as boys. There was an evening school by the mid 1860s.[2] The master of the boys' department from 1864 was Elijah Wills, who came direct from Saltley training college (in Aston, Warws., later Birmingham); he retired in 1906 as head of the whole school.[3]

The boys' department began to receive a government grant in 1864 and the girls' in 1866. There were infants in both departments. By 1866 there were c. 140 pupils, the building was becoming overcrowded, and children were being turned away.[4] In 1867 the company built a separate schoolroom for the girls and some of the infants, leaving the original building to the boys and the rest of the infants.[5] By 1873 there were over 400 pupils.[6] Renewed overcrowding was eased slightly in 1875 when the company opened a school at Chase Terrace, but government inspectors continued to demand a separate infants' department, and for several years part of the school's grant was withheld.[7] An infants' schoolroom was finally built in 1881; within a month the new department had an average attendance of over 60.[8]

Until 1875 the school was generally known simply as the Colliery school. From 1875 until 1878 it was the Colliery no. 1 school; it then reverted to its earlier name. It was sometimes known as St. Anne's school.[9] At the end of 1887 the company handed it over to the school board, which reopened it in January 1888 as its no. 3 board school.[10] In 1892 the boys' and girls' departments were merged to form a mixed department. In 1896 the school had an average attendance of over 400.[11] A new infants' school was built on the north side of Church Street in 1912.[12] The mixed department became a junior

[90] Mason, *Found Ready*, 19, 55, and pl. facing p. 160.
[91] Ibid. 23; L.J.R.O., D. 77/16/10, pp. 1, 4, 9, 15, 17, 50; D. 77/16/11, p. 217.
[92] Mason, *Found Ready*, 24, 44, 108; S.R.O., D. 4520/4, pp. 7, 26, 29, 31.
[93] S.R.O., D. 4520/4, pp. 28, 30; *Lich. Dioc. Ch. Cal.* (1891), 156; *Lichfield Mercury*, 2 Jan. 1891, p. 6.
[94] It is not mentioned in the 1898 Scheme.
[95] *Lichfield Mercury*, 30 May 1890, p. 4.
[96] S.R.O., D. 4520/4, pp. 37, 98.
[97] Ibid. pp. 21, 24–5, 29–30; *Lich. Dioc. Mag.* (1889), 134; C. H. Gregory, *Burntwood Past and Present* (Lichfield, 1953).
[98] S.R.O., Charities Index; S.R.O., D. 4520/5, pp. 133–5; Gregory, *Burntwood*; inf. from the Revd. D.A. Weaver, priest in charge of Burntwood.
[99] S.R.O. 1456/2, pp. 3, 12; P.R.O., RG 9/1973, incor-

rectly describing it as a British school.
[1] Mason, *Found Ready*, 48.
[2] e.g. S.R.O., CEL/85/1, pp. 5, 8, 18, 26.
[3] Ibid. CEL/83/2, p. 333; *Lichfield Mercury*, 23 Jan. 1925, p. 8.
[4] S.R.O., CEL/85/1, pp. 1, 32–3; CEL/85/3, p. 1.
[5] Ibid. CEL/85/1, pp. 85–6; CEL/85/3, pp. 53, 57, 99.
[6] Ibid. CEL/85/1, pp. 202–3; ibid. CEL/85/3, pp. 183–4, 186.
[7] Ibid. CEL/85/3, pp. 238, 300, 348, 375.
[8] Ibid. CEL/85/5, p. 1.
[9] *P.O. Dir. Staffs.* (1864 and later edns.); *Kelly's Dir. Staffs.* (1880 and edns. to 1888); L.J.R.O., D. 77/16/12, p. 386.
[10] *Staffs. Advertiser*, 11 June 1887, p. 7; 10 Mar. 1888, p. 7.
[11] S.R.O., CEL/85/4, p. 132; *Kelly's Dir. Staffs.* (1896).
[12] S.R.O., CEL/85/2, pp. 401–2.

school in 1932. It was merged with the infants' school in 1940, and the 19th-century buildings were closed. In 1950 the school had 254 pupils. It became a first school in 1980 and a primary school in 1988.[13]

Chase Terrace county primary school (formerly the Colliery no. 2 school). In 1875 the Cannock Chase Colliery Co. opened its no. 2 school, for 300 children, on Cannock Road, Chase Terrace.[14] In 1878 the company decided that it could no longer afford to maintain it, and the school board took over the management of what then became no. 2 board school. Subsequently, in spite of protests from the ratepayers, the board apparently bought the buildings.[15] The school was enlarged in 1883, and in 1896 it had accommodation for 600 and an average attendance of 500.[16]

In 1907 the county council opened a school for 312 girls and 316 infants in Rugeley Road, Chase Terrace, leaving the Cannock Road buildings as a boys' school. The new school, with two blocks separated by a playground, was one of the first of the so-called 'Staffordshire schools', the architect using verandahs instead of closed corridors in accordance with the education committee's emphasis on adequate ventilation.[17] In 1931 the boys' school was closed because of mining subsidence, and in 1932 the girls' school became a junior mixed school. In 1976, while the buildings were remodelled, the junior school was moved temporarily to new buildings in Chorley Road, Boney Hay. It was moved back to Rugeley Road in 1977 and became a middle school. At the same time the infants' school became a first school.[18] A nursery unit was added to the first school in 1978.[19] In 1988 the middle school was closed and its buildings became an annexe of Chase Terrace High School. The first school became a primary school, retaining its nursery unit.

St. Joseph and St. Theresa R.C. (Aided) junior mixed and infants' school. The church of St. Joseph was opened at Chasetown in 1883, and a school for boys, girls, and infants was started in the building in December with 70 pupils.[20] By 1891 there were 137 on the books. Only 83 were Catholics; it had earlier been claimed that some parents sent children to St. Joseph's when they failed to win prizes at the other Chasetown school or were asked for fees.[21] There was an average attendance of 108 in 1896.[22] In the late 1890s some of the classes were held in the clubroom attached to the church. By 1913 the conditions in which the school was held had been condemned, and in 1914 the founda-

tion stone was laid of a school in High Street dedicated to the memory of Theresa of Lisieux (d. 1897), who had not yet been beatified. It was opened in 1915. In 1940 it became a junior mixed and infants' school. The building was extended in 1957, 1966, 1969, and 1974. Later there was a gradual decline in numbers; in 1983 there were 144 on the roll, fewer than half the number in 1971.[23]

Burntwood no. 1 board school (later Burntwood first school). The school board opened its no. 1 board school in Church Road, Burntwood, in 1879. There was accommodation for 300 children, and a master's house was attached. After a fortnight there were some 200 on the roll. By 1896 the average attendance was 285. The school became a junior school in 1932, a junior mixed and infants' school in 1957, and a first school in 1979. A large extension was built in the early 1960s. The school was closed in 1988.[24]

Schools opened by the county council from the 1930s.[25] Chase Terrace high school in Bridge Cross Road was opened in 1932 as two senior schools on a single site, one for 320 boys and one for 320 girls. In 1946 or 1947 they became secondary modern schools.[26] They were merged in 1961 to form a mixed secondary modern school which became a comprehensive school in 1965 and a high school in 1977.

Boney Hay junior mixed and infants' school in Birch Terrace was opened in 1965. It became a first school in 1977 and was closed in 1988.

Park primary school in Tudor Road, Burntwood, was opened in 1968 as an infants' school. It became a first school in 1979 and a primary school in 1988.

Springhill primary school in Mossbank Avenue, Chasetown, was opened in 1968 as a junior school. It became a middle school in 1979 and a primary school in 1988.

Ridgeway infants' school in Grange Road, on the Hammerwich side of the boundary from Chasetown, was opened in 1969. It became a first school in 1980 and was closed in 1988.

Ridgeway primary school in Grange Road, adjoining the infants' school, was opened in 1970 as a junior school. It became a middle school in 1980 and a primary school in 1988.

Chasetown high school in Pool Road, on the Hammerwich side of the boundary, was opened in 1970 as a comprehensive secondary school. It was extended in 1974 and became a high school in 1980.

Oakdene junior mixed and infants' school in Sycamore Road, Chasetown, was opened in 1972. It became a first school in 1980. By 1983

[13] Ibid. CEL/85/7, pp. 39, 92, 218; inf. from Staffs. C.C. Educ. Dept.
[14] S.R.O. 1456/2, p. 170; S.R.O., CEL/85/3, pp. 222–3, 228; *P.O. Dir. Staffs.* (1876).
[15] L.J.R.O., D. 77/16/10, pp. 451–2, 477, 486; *Staffs. Advertiser*, 9 Feb. 1878, p. 5; 27 July 1878, p. 4; 6 Dec. 1879, p. 7.
[16] L.J.R.O., D. 77/16/11, pp. 30, 50, 134; *Kelly's Dir. Staffs.* (1896).
[17] G. Balfour, *Ten Years of Staffs. Education, 1903–1913* (Stafford, 1913), 86–8, 126; *Staffs. Advertiser*, 13 Apr. 1907, p. 3.
[18] S.R.O., Survey of School Records, 1979; *Staffs. C. C. Record for 1930*, 632–3, 861 (set in S.R.O.); Lambourne and James, *Burntwood*, 33; *Staffs. Advertiser*, 1 Oct. 1932,

p. 4; *Old Chasetown*, 94; inf. from Staffs. C.C. Educ. Dept.
[19] *Lichfield Mercury*, 31 May 1985, p. 8.
[20] P.R.O., ED 7/108/68.
[21] M. W. Greenslade, *St. Joseph's, Chasetown, 1883–1983* (Stafford, 1983), 16; S.R.O., CEL/85/1, pp. 374–5, 387, 392–3, 436–7.
[22] *Kelly's Dir. Staffs.* (1896).
[23] Greenslade, *St. Joseph's*, 17, 19–20, 23–4.
[24] S.R.O., Survey of School Records, 1979; *Lichfield Mercury*, 17 Jan. 1879, p. 5; 13 Feb. 1987, p. 4; *Kelly's Dir. Staffs.* (1896); inf. from Staffs. C.C. Educ. Dept.
[25] The following list is based on S.R.O., Survey of School Records, 1979; inf. from Staffs. C.C. Educ. Dept.
[26] *Staffs. Advertiser*, 1 Oct. 1932, p. 4; S.R.O., CEK/74/1.

part of the building was no longer in use, and in 1985 the school was closed.[27]

Highfields primary school in Elder Lane, Burntwood, was opened in 1974 as a junior mixed and infants' school. It became a first school in 1979 and a primary school in 1988.

Fulfen primary school in Rugeley Road, Burntwood, was opened in 1978 as a middle school and was temporarily accommodated at Chase Terrace high school. It moved into the Rugeley Road buildings in 1979. It became a primary school in 1988.

Boney Hay primary school in Chorley Road was opened as a middle school in 1977 in buildings which had been used in 1976–7 as temporary accommodation for Chase Terrace Junior school. It became a primary school in 1988.

Holly Grove primary school in Holly Grove Lane, Chase Terrace, was opened in 1977 as a first school. It became a primary school in 1988.

PRIVATE SCHOOLS. The 'Borned Wodde' where the antiquary Robert Talbot was teaching a school in 1531 has been identified as Burntwood.[28] It is more likely to have been Brentwood (Essex).

Samuel Johnson opened an academy at Edial Hall in 1735 or 1736. He had abandoned the enterprise by March 1737 when he and David Garrick, one of his pupils, set out from Lichfield to seek their fortune in London.[29] The hall was again being used as a school in 1807.[30]

In 1792 and 1793 David and Elizabeth Moss were running a boys' boarding school at Burntwood. The curriculum was limited to the elements and drawing; the Mosses also offered free dancing lessons and a cold bath, erected 'at a considerable expense' within 20 yards of the school.[31] No more is known of the venture. Moss was master of the charity school, and he may have been trying to change that school's character and discourage poor children from attending it. That may explain why, some time between 1794 and 1797, Francis Barber, Johnson's former servant, thought it worth his while to open a school in Burntwood; it is unlikely that it was more than a dame school. He had apparently abandoned the venture by 1799.[32]

A small boarding school was opened at Burntwood in 1809 and was still being advertised in 1811. The proprietor, J. Child, seems to have specialized in commercial education: extras which he offered included gauging and surveying.[33]

From 1869 dame schools were recorded at Burntwood and Chasetown, while at Chase Terrace in 1871 a dame school was opened in a chapel. In the early 1880s there were two dame schools in Burntwood and two in Chasetown, with between 30 and 40 pupils in all. One of the Chasetown schools was run by a certificated teacher, a former assistant mistress at the Colliery school. In 1883 the school board expressed annoyance that some parents were taking their children from board schools and sending them to her.[34]

H. W. Hambling, after running a short-lived boarding school at Hammerwich, apparently set up in Burntwood in the late 1890s but with no success.[35]

A day and boarding school for dyslexic children was opened by Dr. E. N. Brown at Maple Hayes in 1982. In 1989 it had 120 pupils.[36]

FURTHER EDUCATION. From the early 1870s the Cannock Chase Colliery Co. provided evening classes in colliery working and management at its Chasetown school for its employees.[37] The work was later undertaken by the county council, which was among the first local authorities to appoint a full-time organizer for mining instruction. From 1891 it employed lecturers to give courses at centres in the Staffordshire coalfields. Chasetown was one of the original centres, and thereafter courses were held there regularly.[38]

The 1911 Coal Mines Act, by requiring firemen in most collieries to pass an examination, produced an increased demand for practical instruction. It was partly that demand which led the county council to open a small mining institute in Queen Street, Chasetown, in 1913. The two-storeyed building contained a laboratory, a drawing office, and two lecture rooms. There was test equipment in the basement and also an electricity generator which provided light and power for the building.[39] From 1929 the mining institute was one of three senior centres grouped round a new county mining college at Cannock.[40] It became an annexe of the college (later the Cannock Chase Technical College) in 1962 and was closed in 1987.[41]

By 1896 a local committee was running lectures and classes in practical subjects such as gardening and home nursing at the Chasetown Institute in High Street. It worked in conjunction with the county council's technical instruction committee.[42]

CHARITIES FOR THE POOR. By will of unknown date John Ward of Edial[43] left a rent

[27] Chase Post, 16 Feb. 1984; Lichfield Mercury, 2 Aug. 1985, p. 4.
[28] L. & P. Hen. VIII, v, p. 289 and index; D.N.B.
[29] Reade, Johnsonian Gleanings, vi. 29–54.
[30] Above, manors.
[31] Wolverhampton Chron. 2 Jan. 1793 (ref. kindly supplied by Mr. D. G. Brown of Tamworth).
[32] Reade, Johnsonian Gleanings, ii. 65, 76–7, 79–80; viii. 77–9.
[33] Aris's Birmingham Gaz. 8 May 1809 (inf. supplied by Mr. Brown; Staffs. Advertiser, 6 Jan. 1810; 5 Jan. 1811.
[34] S.R.O., CEL/85/1, pp. 173–4, 368–9; ibid. 3, pp. 115, 168; L.J.R.O., D. 77/16/10, pp. 393, 466–7, 470; ibid. 11, pp. 94, 100, 217.
[35] Kelly's Dir. Staffs. (1900), 68, 817.

[36] Lichfield Mercury, 15 Jan. 1982, p. 9; 18 June 1982, p. 10; 7 Apr. 1989, p. 3.
[37] Jnl. Staffs. Ind. Arch. Soc. ix (2), 59.
[38] e.g. Staffs. C.C. Record for 1892, 21–2; 1902, 345; 1907, 358; 1916, 347.
[39] Balfour, Staffs. Educ. 31; Staffs. Advertiser, 27 Sept. 1913, p. 5.   [40] Hednesford Advertiser, 26 Oct. 1929, p. 5.
[41] Lichfield Mercury, 19 Sept. 1986, p. 7; 20 Feb. 1987, p. 3; inf. from the vice-principal, Cannock Chase Technical Coll.; inf. from Staffs. C.C. Educ. Dept.
[42] Staffs. Advertiser (S. Staffs. edn.), 18 July 1896, p. 7.
[43] Possibly the John Ward who was buried at St. Michael's, Lichfield, 22 Jan. 1642/3: L.J.R.O., D. 27/1/2. Details of the benefactor's identity had been forgotten by the 1780s: Char. Dons. ii. 1128–9.

charge of £1 6s. 8d.; £1 was to be distributed on St. Thomas's Day (21 December) among the poor of Burntwood, Edial, and Woodhouses (15s.) and the poor of Hammerwich (5s.), and the rest was for a sermon at Hammerwich chapel on Whit Sunday. In 1821 the tenant of a farm at Edial chose 30 poor of Burntwood, Edial, and Woodhouses and gave them 6d. each on Christmas Day at Hammerwich chapel. He gave a further 5s. to an inhabitant of Hammerwich who distributed it among the poor there.[44] A Scheme of 1933 provided that three quarters of the net income was to be paid to the vicar of Hammerwich and the rest used for the benefit of the poor. The charity had been lost by 1966.[45]

By will proved 1709 William Cadman of Edial, a tailor, left two 40s. rent charges, one for four sermons a year at Hammerwich chapel and the other to provide doles for the poor of Burntwood, Edial, and Woodhouses at Hammerwich chapel on the Sunday after Christmas and the Sunday after Midsummer. He left his cottage and croft at Edial in reversion to provide two more sermons each year at Hammerwich and to augment the doles to the poor. He did not specify how the income was to be divided, but a trust deed of 1806 assigned £1 a year for the sermons and the rest to the poor. In 1807 the cottage, then derelict, was let with the croft on a 10-year repairing lease at 40s. a year. It was rebuilt with the aid of a bequest from James Watkins, and from 1817 it and the croft were let for £4 10s. a year. The trustees were thus able to distribute £5 10s. a year to the poor.[46] In the 1920s and 1930s the income from the property was £8 a year.[47] A Scheme of 1970 provided that £2 5s. of the income was to be paid for sermons and the rest used for the relief of those in need.[48] In the later 1980s the charity was managed by Burntwood town council, which distributed annually most of the income of between £600 and £700. In 1986–7 the Burntwood and Hammerwich War Fund, established in 1919 to provide a nurses' home, was added to Cadman's charity.[49]

By will proved 1770 Elizabeth Ball of Castle Bromwich (Warws.) left £250 to the poor of Fulfen, Burntwood, Edial, Woodhouses, Hammerwich, and St. Michael's, Lichfield; the money was to be invested and the income distributed annually. A codicil assigned the interest from a further £100 for distribution in Christmas week among the poor of Fulfen,

Burntwood, Burntwood Green, Edial, Woodhouses, Cannock Wood (in Cannock), Gentleshaw (in Longdon), and Hammerwich. The management of her charitable bequests was entrusted to her cousin and heir, James Birch, and to his heirs. They made regular payments in accordance with her wishes but took no steps to establish an endowed charity. In 1821, to cover the bequests, Birch's grandson, Maj.-Gen. Thomas Birch Reynardson, was allowing £14 to the poor out of the rent from his Fulfen estate. A 'respectable inhabitant' from each of the four hamlets of Burntwood, Edial, Woodhouses, and Hammerwich submitted a list of suitable beneficiaries to Thomas Derry, the tenant at Fulfen, received cash from him, and distributed it on Lady Day. In 1821 ninety-three people in the four hamlets received £13 6s. in sums ranging from 1s. to 6s. and the poor of Cannock Wood and Gentleshaw received 14s. in bread; there were complaints that the recipients, although poor, were not always industrious or deserving. The later history of the two bequests is unknown; payments to the poor may have lapsed on Reynardson's death in 1847.[50]

By will proved 1805 James Watkins of Edial left £20 towards the repair or rebuilding of the cottage devised by Cadman. He also left the residue of his personalty, after the payment of legacies and expenses, to the poor of Burntwood, Edial, and Woodhouses. Trustees were to invest the residue, which turned out to be 'somewhat above £100', and to distribute both income and capital at their discretion in sums of up to £5. By 1821 the invested capital had increased to almost £190, and the surviving trustee proposed to use it to establish a Sunday school.[51] What in fact happened is not known.

By will proved 1918 A. O. Worthington of Maple Hayes left £100, the interest to be distributed annually in clothing, food, and coal among the poor of Christ Church parish, Burntwood, on St. Thomas's Day. The charity was still paid in 1986.[52]

By will proved 1928 Dr. J. B. Spence, superintendent of Burntwood asylum 1881–1924, left £100 for the relief of the poor of Christ Church parish, Burntwood, the interest to be distributed in a similar way to that of Worthington's charity. It was still paid in 1986.[53]

Woodhouses benefited under the charity of Theophila Reading of Woodhouses.[54]

[44] 7th Rep. Com. Char. 357–8.
[45] S.R.O., Charities Index.
[46] L.J.R.O., P/C/11, Wm. Cadman (1709); 7th Rep. Com. Char. 355–6. For Watkins see below (this section).
[47] Kelly's Dir. Staffs. (1924; 1940).
[48] S.R.O., Charities Index.
[49] Inf. from the Town Manager and Clerk to the Burntwood Town Council; above, public services.
[50] 7th Rep. Com. Char. 353–5; V.C.H. Staffs. v. 75; above, manors (Fulfen). The benefaction to the poor of St. Michael's, Lichfield, may not have been intended. The probate

copy of the will inserts 'and St. Michael in Lichfield' after the list of hamlets as an afterthought, probably by mistake for 'in St. Michael in Lichfield': P.R.O., PROB 10/2523, will of Eliz. Ball, 1770. Warw. Jan.
[51] L.J.R.O., P/C/11, Jas. Watkins (1805); 7th Rep. Com. Char. 357.
[52] S.R.O., Charities Index; inf. from the Revd. D. A. Weaver, priest in charge of Burntwood.
[53] S.R.O., D. 4045/9/1/4; D. 4520/5, p. 54; inf. from Mr. Weaver.
[54] Below, Hammerwich, chars. for the poor.

CURBOROUGH AND ELMHURST

THE civil parish of Curborough and Elmhurst, north of Lichfield, was formerly a township in St. Chad's parish, Lichfield. It included several detached portions which were transferred by boundary changes in 1879: a farmhouse at Ashmore Brook was added to Burntwood township; Pipehill Farm and the former tollhouse near by were amalgamated with Pipehill township; and 240 a. around Little Pipe were added to Farewell and Chorley civil parish. After the changes Curborough and Elmhurst covered 1,294 a.[55] The detached portions at Ashmore Brook and Pipehill are treated in the present volume respectively under Burntwood and Wall; the detached portion at Little Pipe is reserved for treatment in a later volume.

The northern, eastern, and southern boundaries of Curborough and Elmhurst run along Full, Curborough, and Circuit brooks; the western boundary runs partly along Bilson brook and partly along the Lichfield–Stafford road. The subsoil is Keuper Marl, with a band of Keuper Sandstone along the western boundary. There are stretches of alluvium along Full, Curborough, and Bilson brooks.[56] The soil around Elmhurst hamlet is fine loam over clay; further east it is a mixture of fine and coarse loam.[57] The land lies at its highest in the southwest where Red Brae Farm stands at 387 ft. (118 m.). It falls away steeply on the north to Bilson brook. On the east it slopes down more gently to 246 ft. (75 m.) on the northern boundary near New Farm and to 231 ft. (70 m.) on the eastern boundary.

Thirteen people were assessed for tax in 1327 and 50 in 1380.[58] In the earlier 1530s eight families were recorded at Curborough and ten at Elmhurst.[59] Twenty-six householders in the township were assessed for hearth tax in 1666 and another four were too poor to pay.[60] In 1801 the population, possibly including that of the detached portions, was 174. It had risen to 229 by 1811 and to 250 by 1821.[61] The population, excluding the detached portions, was 197 in 1841, 201 in 1851, 187 in 1861, 211 in 1871, and 203 in 1881.[62] It was 212 in 1891, falling to 170 by 1901. During the 20th century the population fluctuated. It was 196 in 1911, 214 in 1921, 174 in 1931, 219 in 1951, 211 in 1961, and 180 in 1971. In 1981 it was 188.[63]

Curborough derives its name from Old English words meaning 'mill stream' (*cweorn burna*), evidently referring to Curborough brook.[64] The principal settlement presumably lay near Curborough Hall Farm on the road from Stowe in Lichfield: the area around the farmhouse was known as Great Curborough in the early 14th century. Little Curborough centred on Curborough House in Streethay.[65] A bridge over Curborough brook carried a lane running between Curborough Hall Farm and Curborough House. Called Pipe bridge in 1386, it was ruinous in 1489, when both Streethay township and Curborough and Elmhurst township were ordered to repair it.[66] Curborough Hall Farm was built in 1871; an earlier house, Curborough Hall, built in the late 16th or early 17th century, stood to the north. Land to the east provided the endowment for Curborough prebend in Lichfield cathedral and there was a house there, north of the present Field House, by the earlier 16th century.[67] A site near Corporation Farm to the north-west may have been inhabited by the later 17th century.[68] By the late 18th century a farmhouse there was part of the Curborough Hall estate; the present farmhouse dates from the early 19th century. In 1877 the farmland was bought by Lichfield corporation for a sewage works. As Corporation farm, it was sold to the tenant in 1986.[69]

Elmhurst, whose name is derived from Old English words meaning 'elm wood', was an inhabited area in the early 13th century.[70] A hamlet developed along a road to King's Bromley which followed Fox Lane and part of Park Lane.[71] A green, mentioned c. 1300, probably lay at the southern end of Park Lane where the pinfold stood in the early 19th century,[72] and Elmhurst Hall stood to the north-west. There were several houses in the hamlet in the late 18th century, including King's Field House which presumably derived its name from land held there by the Crown in the 14th century.[73] In 1841 the hamlet's population was c. 40, consisting mainly of agricultural labourers and their families. By 1861 it had increased to 57 and included a wheelwright, a clock-case maker, a platelayer, two ropemakers, and a school mistress. The population in 1881 was 72,[74] and a school and a mission room were opened in 1882. In 1980 the school was converted into a village hall.[75]

South-east of Elmhurst hamlet lies an area known as Stychbrook in 1086.[76] The name, which presumably derived from the stream now called Circuit brook, is of uncertain derivation. The area was inhabited by the mid 13th century,

[55] *Census*, 1881, 1891. This article was written in 1987. The people named in footnotes as supplying information are thanked for their help.
[56] Geol. Surv. Map. 1″, drift, sheet 154 (1922 edn.).
[57] Soil Surv. Sheet 3 (1983).
[58] *S.H.C.* vii (1), 234; xvii. 179–80 (date corrected by *S.H.C.* 4th ser. vi. 3 n.). [59] Ibid. 4th ser. viii. 183.
[60] *S.H.C.* 1923, 122–3.
[61] *V.C.H. Staffs.* i. 322.
[62] P.R.O., HO 107/975; HO 107/2014(2); ibid. RG 9/1974; RG 10/2915; RG 11/2774. The 1871 Census return includes 20 people living at 'Railway Crossing', which was in King's Bromley parish; that figure has been omitted from the total given here. [63] *Census*, 1891–1981.
[64] *Eng. Place-Name Elements* (E.P.N.S.), i. 63, 122.

[65] *S.H.C.* ix (1), 44; *S.H.C.* 1913, 20; below, Streethay, introduction.
[66] S.R.O., D. (W.) 1734/2/1/599, m. 10; D. (W.) 1734/2/1/604, m. 5; D. (W.) 1734/2/3/112D.
[67] Below, estates. [68] Below, nonconformity.
[69] S.R.O., D. 4566/97, Packington, deed of 25 Mar. 1780; L.J.R.O., B/A/15/Lichfield, St. Chad, nos. 1140–50; inf. from Mr. J. Lees of Corporation Farm.
[70] *Eng. Place-Name Elements*, i. 277; *S.H.C.* iii (1), 172–3; *S.H.C.* 1939, 105. [71] Above, fig. 1.
[72] S.R.O. 3764/48; below, local govt.
[73] Above, fig. 1; P.R.O., E 199/41/15; L.J.R.O., D. 44/6; S.R.O., D. (W.) 1752/E/7/20.
[74] P.R.O., HO 107/975; ibid. RG 9/1974; RG 11/2774.
[75] Below, church; education. [76] *V.C.H. Staffs.* iv. 42.

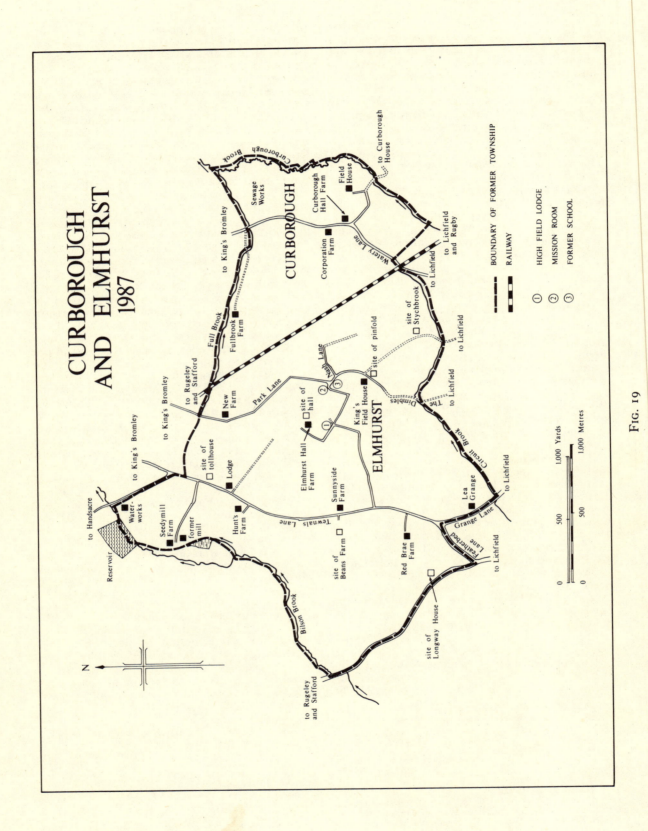

CURBOROUGH
AND ELMHURST
1987

BOUNDARY OF FORMER TOWNSHIP
RAILWAY

① HIGH FIELD LODGE
② MISSION ROOM
③ FORMER SCHOOL

FIG. 19

and Stychbrook green was recorded in the 15th century.[77] The settlement probably lay along a road from Stowe which joined Fox Lane opposite King's Field House.[78] Lea Grange to the west was probably in existence by the 15th century.[79]

West of Elmhurst hamlet on the Stafford road stood Longway House, in existence probably by the mid 17th century and demolished in the 19th century.[80] Three early 19th-century farmhouses stand along Tewnals Lane (Tunalls Lane in 1711),[81] part of the road from Lichfield to Handsacre and King's Bromley: Red Brae Farm (formerly Binns Farm);[82] Sunnyside Farm to the north;[83] and Hunt's Farm further north, which replaced a farmhouse probably of mid 17th-century date.[84]

New Farm, north of Elmhurst hamlet, probably stands on the site of a cottage built between 1813 and 1818; the present farmhouse dates from the later 1870s.[85] Fullbrook Farm to the east was built c. 1835.[86] In the north-west corner of the parish Seedy mill on Bilson brook was in use by the mid 13th century.[87] A pumping station was opened to the north on the Handsacre road in 1938; it serves Hanch reservoir which straddles the boundary with Longdon. A waterworks was built nearby in 1949,[88] and eight houses to the south were built about the same time, presumably for workers there.

The road from Lichfield to Handsacre and King's Bromley was turnpiked in 1729. The route originally left the city along Grange Lane; by order of 1783 it was changed to follow Featherbed Lane.[89] An order was made in 1766 for a tollhouse and a gate at the junction of Tewnals Lane and Featherbed Lane;[90] another order was made in 1782 for a gate near the point where Tewnals Lane divided, one branch going to Handsacre and the other to King's Bromley.[91] By the early 1830s a tollhouse had been built near the latter gate.[92] The 1782 order was presumably connected with the change of route from the city in 1783, evidently leading to the abandonment of the Featherbed Lane gate; a bar was set up near Lea Grange in 1834.[93] The road was disturnpiked in 1870, the tollhouse surviving until the 1940s.[94]

Elmhurst was supplied with electricity by Lichfield corporation from 1932.[95]

ESTATES

An estate centring on *ELMHURST HALL* may have been created by the later 12th century, when Thomas son of Robert held ¼ knight's fee of the bishop of Chester. The fee was almost certainly at Elmhurst, and Thomas may have been Thomas Noel of Ranton: in 1242–3 Richard Puer, whose family were tenants of the Noels, held ¼ knight's fee at Elmhurst.[96] Richard le Child held the fee in 1284–5, together with a fee in Whittington.[97] Richard's heir, whose name is not known, was the holder in 1298. By the early 14th century the heir had been succeeded or replaced by John of Polesworth.[98] Nothing more is known about the estate until 1501, when it was held by William Clerkson, who in that year was succeeded by his son John. John died in 1533, leaving a son Richard.[99] Richard was succeeded in 1552 by his daughter Anne, a minor in the custody of a relative John Otley. John died soon afterwards, and the custody evidently passed to his son Thomas. In 1565 Anne, as wife of Humphrey Everard, tried to recover her inheritance, alienated by the Otleys who claimed that her father had disinherited her.[1] She was unsuccessful, and by 1571 the estate had evidently passed to Simon Biddulph, who then held 4 messuages and 106 a. in Curborough and Elmhurst.[2]

Simon, a Lichfield mercer who was four times bailiff of the city, died in 1580.[3] His heir was his son, also called Simon (d. 1596).[4] His son and heir, another Simon (d. 1632), was also four times bailiff of Lichfield.[5] His son Michael received a coat of arms in 1635 and was M.P. for Lichfield in 1646 and 1648. Probably the first of his family to live at Elmhurst, he died in 1658[6] and was succeeded by his son, another Michael (d. 1666).[7] Michael's heir was his brother Theophilus, a London mercer and silk merchant, who was M.P. for the city of London in 1656–8 and 1659 and for Lichfield in 1661. He was knighted in 1660 and created a baronet in 1664.[8] To gain possession of Elmhurst Hall and its estate, Theophilus bought out Michael Biddulph's servant, Elizabeth Ames. She had been left a life interest by Michael in what Bishop Hacket called his 'base and scandalous will'.[9] Theophilus was succeeded in 1683 by his son Sir Michael, several times M.P. for Lichfield, who

[77] *S.H.C.* 1924, p. 74; S.R.O. 938/151; L.J.R.O., D. 30/VC, palimpsest, ii, f. 9v.
[78] Above, fig. 1; B.L. Maps, O.S.D. 258.
[79] Below, estates.   [80] Ibid.
[81] L.J.R.O., P/C/11, Thurstan Southern (1711).
[82] Below, estates (Longway House).
[83] Date stone on house 'J. T. 1810' (possibly for Joseph Turner: L.J.R.O., D. 29/1/2).
[84] Below, estates.
[85] W.S.L. 37/3/46, deed of 23 June 1818; S.R.O., D. (W.) 1752/E/7/20.
[86] Below, estates.
[87] Below, econ. hist. (mills).   [88] Date stone on buildings.
[89] Above, Lichfield, communications.
[90] L.J.R.O., D. 15/2/2, 5 Apr. 1766; *Aris's Birmingham Gaz.* 19 May 1766.
[91] L.J.R.O., D. 15/2/3, 6 Nov. 1781, 5 Mar. and 6 Aug. 1782.
[92] J. Phillips and W. F. Hutchings, *Map of County of Stafford* (1832); L.J.R.O., B/A/15/Lichfield, St. Chad, no. 1222.
[93] L.J.R.O., D. 15/2/4, 7 Jan. 1834.
[94] Above, Lichfield, communications; inf. from Mr. W. Baskerville of Hunt's Farm.

[95] L.J.R.O., D. 127/electric lighting cttee. min. bk. p. 207a.
[96] *S.H.C.* i. 147, 158; *Bk. of Fees*, ii. 969.
[97] *Feud. Aids*, v. 8.
[98] S.R.O., D. (W.) 1734/J. 2268, f. 1v.
[99] Ibid. (W.) 1734/2/1/604, m. 26d.; D. (W.) 1734/2/1/606, m. 13d.
[1] Ibid. D. (W.) 1734/2/1/609, m. 2; P.R.O., C 78/29/35; C 142/97, no. 72.
[2] W.S.L., S. MS. 326/1. The surname was then spelt Biddle.
[3] Harwood, *Lichfield*, 418, 420; L.J.R.O., D. 27/1/1, f. 1v. His will is in P.R.O., PROB 11/62, ff. 102–103v.
[4] L.J.R.O., D. 27/1/1, f. 9v.
[5] Ibid. f. 8ov.; P.R.O., PROB 11/62, f. 102; Harwood, *Lichfield*, 422–4.
[6] Shaw, *Staffs*. i. 352; *S.H.C.* v (2), 41; *S.H.C.* 1920 and 1922, 85–6; 1948–9, 5. His will is in P.R.O., PROB 11/275, ff. 83–84v.
[7] *Hist. Parl., Commons, 1660–90*, i. 650.
[8] Ibid. 650–1; G.E.C. *Baronetage*, iii. 299–301. His will is in P.R.O., PROB 11/373, ff. 28–30v.
[9] S.R.O., D. 1851/8/30, deed of 23 Mar. 1666/7; Bodl. MS. Tanner 45, f. 181.

was succeeded in 1718 by his son Theophilus (d. 1743).[10] Theophilus had no children, and the baronetcy passed to his uncle's grandson, another Theophilus Biddulph. Under an Act of 1754 Elmhurst Hall and 370 a., some of it in King's Bromley, were sold in 1765 to Samuel Swinfen of Swinfen in Weeford.[11] Samuel died unmarried in 1770 and was succeeded by his brother Thomas, who died in 1784 leaving as heir his son John.[12] From 1765 the hall was let to Maj. St. George Bowles, who moved to Lichfield in 1790.[13]

Francis Perceval Eliot, the writer, apparently attracted to Lichfield by the company of the city's *literati*, moved to Elmhurst Hall as tenant in 1790.[14] The same year he agreed to buy the estate from John Swinfen; it then comprised 352 a.[15] He also acquired the Stychbrook estate, the leasehold of Lea Grange, and the leasehold of land owned by the vicars choral of Lichfield cathedral. Altogether Eliot came to hold over 850 a.[16] He borrowed heavily to buy the estate, which in 1797 he unsuccessfully offered for sale.[17] He later sold Stychbrook to Granville Leveson-Gower, marquess of Stafford, and mortgaged the rest of his holding.[18] By 1800 he was living in Lichfield.[19] In 1808 the 696-a. estate still held by Eliot was put up for sale. John Smith of Fenton in Stoke upon Trent bought the largest part, amounting to 381 a. It included the site of Elmhurst Hall which Eliot had pulled down.[20]

John Smith, sheriff of Staffordshire in 1816, built a new hall at Elmhurst, and died there in 1840.[21] Later the same year his widow Elizabeth and their son Charles let the hall for five years to Isabella, widow of John Campbell, Baron Cawdor.[22] Charles Smith was living at Elmhurst in 1848.[23] In 1856 he sold the estate to Newton John Lane, then living at the hall.[24] Lane died in 1869, and in 1874 his trustees sold Elmhurst to George Fox, a retired Manchester businessman (d. 1894).[25] The hall and 640 a. were sold in 1895 to Henry Mitchell, a Smethwick brewer. Mitchell, who died in 1914, let the hall.[26] In 1918 his executors put the hall and the estate up for sale.[27] There was no buyer for the hall, which was demolished in 1921.[28] In 1922 the estate was sold to Joshua Rymond, possibly acting on behalf of a syndicate. The land was split up, and

in 1923 Rymond sold the site of the hall, the surviving farm buildings, and 30 a. to William Snelson, who converted the stables into a farmhouse, Elmhurst Hall Farm. In 1932 he sold the farm to Patons & Baldwins, wool manufacturers of Halifax (Yorks. W.R.), who established an angora rabbit farm. The farm was closed in 1934, and the farmhouse and land were sold to a local farmer, William White. The property was subsequently sold to James Dawson in 1939 and Arthur Hollinshead in 1956. In 1962 Hollinshead sold the farm, which then covered 32 a., to Mr. Leonard Brookes, the owner in 1987.[29]

In 1658 the house apparently contained only a hall, parlour, dining room, and four or five chambers.[30] It was evidently rebuilt by the younger Michael Biddulph, the hall being assessed for tax on 12 hearths in 1666.[31] The new house, three storeys high with a parapeted roof, was seven bays wide, with the three central bays projecting. It stood on a platform backed by walls, and along the front there was a balustraded terrace with steps down to what was presumably a lawn or pasture ground.[32] In 1744 the ground floor consisted of a hall, three parlours, a drawing room, and a servants' hall.[33] The house was demolished probably in 1804; building materials were still being offered for sale in 1806.[34] John Smith's new house was of brick with stone dressings in an Elizabethan style with a gabled front of seven bays and an off-centre entrance porch. It was probably on the same alignment as the former house, facing north-east, and there was a haha in front of it.[35] In 1894 George Fox let the house to the duke and duchess of Sutherland so that they could entertain the prince of Wales there when he visited Lichfield for the centenary of the Staffordshire Yeomanry.[36] It was demolished in 1921.

A large walled garden on the south side of the house existed by the earlier 1740s, when it was planted with fruit trees. It was probably created for Sir Theophilus Biddulph (d. 1743), a cultivator of flowers,[37] and it apparently included a hot house and a greenhouse in 1808.[38] The walled area survives as an enclosure.

In the later 18th century the hall was approached from the west along a drive from Tewnals Lane. A small lodge on the road existed

[10] *Hist. Parl., Commons, 1660–90*, i. 650; G.E.C. *Baronetage*, iii. 299-301.
[11] *V.C.H. Staffs*. iv. 147; W.S.L. 11/118/2/50; L.J.R.O., D. 44/6.   [12] W.S.L. 135/5/47; *V.C.H. Staffs*. iv. 147.
[13] S.R.O., D. (W.) 1738/C/4/2; *Gent. Mag*. lxx. 801.
[14] *D.N.B.*; *Poetical Works of Anna Seward*, ed. W. Scott (Edinburgh, 1810), ii. 342; W.S.L. 5/49, Wm. Ramsay to F. P. Eliot, 12 Dec. 1779 and 2 Feb. 1781; ibid. Hen. White to F. P. Eliot, 3 Mar. 1786.
[15] W.S.L. 135/6/47; S.R.O., D. (W.) 3222/228/1, pp. 1–2, 8–9; L.J.R.O., D. 15/10/3/10.
[16] S.R.O., D. 615/240/2/8(D), articles of agreement, 2 Apr. 1801.
[17] *Staffs. Advertiser*, 4 Feb. 1797.
[18] S.R.O., D. (W.) 3222/228/1, pp. 11–13, 21–2, 49–53.
[19] *Aris's Birmingham Gaz*. 27 Oct. 1800.
[20] S.R.O., D. 802/12, sale partics. 28 Oct. 1808; D. (W.) 3222/523/27; *V.C.H. Staffs*. viii. 213, 222; below (this section).
[21] S.R.O., D. 3272/1/17/9/3; W.S.L., S. 1902i, f. 65; *Staffs. Advertiser*, 9 May 1840.
[22] S.R.O., D. 3272/1/17/2/3; *Complete Peerage*, iii. 122–3; *Dyott's Diary*, ed. R. W. Jeffery, ii. 350.

[23] L.J.R.O., B/A/15/Lichfield, St. Chad, no. 1215.
[24] Deed in possession of Mr. L. Brookes of Elmhurst Hall Farm.
[25] S.R.O., D. 357/A/19/10; Elmhurst Hall Estate sale cat. 1874 (copy in S.R.O., D. 1083/2); *Lichfield Mercury*, 8 June 1894, p. 7.
[26] Elmhurst Hall Estate sale cat. 1894 (copy in Lichfield Libr.); *Lichfield Mercury*, 20 Sept. 1895, p. 8; *V.C.H. Staffs*. xvii. 117; *Kelly's Dir. Staffs*. (1900 and edns. to 1916).
[27] Elmhurst Hall Estate sale cat. 1918 (in possession of Mr. Brookes).
[28] *Lichfield Mercury*, 1 July 1921, p. 1.
[29] Deeds in possession of Mr. Brookes.
[30] *S.H.C.* 4th ser. v, pp. 108–10.
[31] *S.H.C.* 1923, 123.
[32] Above, plate 43.
[33] *Aris's Birmingham Gaz*. 2 Apr. 1744.
[34] W.S.L., S. MS. 384, p. 64; *Staffs. Advertiser*, 10 May 1806.   [35] Above, plate 44.
[36] *Staffs. Advertiser*, 2 June 1894, p. 4; printed souvenir of visit (copy in L.J.R.O., D. 77/20/12).
[37] *Aris's Birmingham Gaz*. 19 Mar. and 2 Apr. 1744.
[38] W.S.L. 135/11/47.

by 1832.[39] High Field Lodge south of the hall was built in the mid 1870s.[40]

An estate which formed the endowment of *CURBOROUGH PREBEND* in Lichfield cathedral was centred on a house north of the later Field House. The prebend may have been created in the mid 12th century, and in 1200 land in Curborough was held by Walter de Tilbury, a chamberlain of Bishop Muschamp and possibly prebendary of Curborough.[41] By 1415 the estate was known as Curborough Turvile, evidently after Philip de Turvill, prebendary of Curborough 1309–37;[42] by the early 17th century the name had been corrupted to Darvell or Darvile.[43] In 1571 the estate comprised a messuage and 50 a. of inclosed land, besides 25 a. of field land in Lichfield; in 1650 it amounted to 122 a.[44] Under the Cathedrals Act of 1840 the prebendal estate was transferred to the Ecclesiastical Commissioners, who in 1920 sold a house converted out of farm buildings and the land, then only 70 a., to the tenant William Woolley.[45] In 1987 the house, known as Field House, was owned by Mr. P. Owen and the land by Mr. G. Hollinshead of Curborough Hall Farm.[46]

A house existed by 1528 when the prebendary, Rowland Lee, later bishop of Coventry and Lichfield, let it to his sister Isabel.[47] It stood on a moated site.[48] There was evidently a chapel south-east of the house, where there was land called Chapel Yard in 1650. At the same date land called the Bowling Alley was recorded near the house.[49] The house was no longer standing in 1837, and by 1848 farm buildings to the south had been converted into four dwellings, evidently for labourers.[50] The dwellings were altered, probably in the early 20th century, to comprise a farmhouse, dairy, and cottage, themselves converted in the early 1980s into the present Field House.[51]

Dr. Zachary Babington, admitted as prebendary of Curborough in 1584 and later precentor of Lichfield cathedral and diocesan chancellor, created an estate centred on *CURBOROUGH HALL FARM*.[52] He had a house there known as Curborough Hall when he died in 1613.[53] He

was succeeded by his son William (d. *c.* 1625), whose son Zachary, a lawyer, was living at Curborough in 1666 but later moved to Whittington.[54] In 1684 Zachary's son John was living at Curborough.[55] Zachary died in 1688 and John in 1706.[56] John was succeeded by his son Zachary (d. 1745), whose heirs were his three sisters, Catherine wife of Ralph Hawkes, Dorothy wife of Luke Robinson, a Lichfield mercer, and Mary wife of Theophilus Levett, a Lichfield lawyer.[57] A division of the Babington estates was made in 1780 and Curborough Hall went to John Levett, the son of Mary and Theophilus.[58] John died in 1799, and Curborough Hall descended in his family.[59] In 1906 the estate comprised 76 a.[60] In 1925 T. B. P. Levett sold it to William Boston of Brownsfields Farm in Streethay.[61] Boston sold it *c.* 1935 to Herbert Hollinshead, whose son Geoffrey was the owner in 1987.[62]

The present farmhouse was built in 1871.[63] To the north stood a house assessed for tax on 13 hearths in 1666 and probably built for Zachary Babington (d. 1613).[64] It had been demolished by 1848, when its site was known as Old Hall Close.[65] A tablet bearing the Babington coat of arms and the initials Z. B. and W. B., presumably for Zachary Babington (d. 1613) and his son William, was removed to farm buildings where Field House now stands and surmounted the entrance to the dairy; it has since been set on a wall inside Field House.[66] By 1780 another house, New Hall, had been built south of the present farmhouse.[67] It was described as ruinous in 1866 and was demolished presumably afterwards.[68] Surviving farm buildings date from the early 18th century.

By 1640 Lichfield corporation owned 15 a. of inclosed land called the Beenes, later part of an estate known as *BEANS FARM*.[69] In 1718 the tenant, Rowland Turner, who had already built a barn on the land, agreed to construct a farmhouse.[70] The farm, which covered nearly 26 a. in 1776, was sold in 1876 to George Fox of Elmhurst Hall.[71] The farmhouse still existed in 1848[72] but no longer survives.

FULLBROOK FARM in Elmhurst centres

[39] Above, fig. 1; J. Phillips and W. F. Hutchings, *Map of County of Stafford* (1832).
[40] *Staffs. Advertiser*, 12 May 1877, p. 7.
[41] *V.C.H. Staffs.* iii. 141; *Cur. Reg. R.* i. 188; *S.H.C.* 1924, pp. 239–40.
[42] Le Neve, *Fasti, 1300–1541, Coventry and Lichfield*, 27–8; *S.H.C.* xvii. 54.
[43] *S.H.C.* xvi. 208; *S.H.C.* N.S. iii. 57.
[44] W.S.L., S. MS. 326/1; W.S.L., S.D. Pearson 1308.
[45] *V.C.H. Staffs.* iii. 190; Eccl. Com. sale cat. 1920, lot 5 (copy in S.R.O., D. 4566/E); inf. from the Church Com.
[46] Inf. from Mr. Hollinshead.
[47] L.J.R.O., D. 30/C.A. iv, f. 47; *D.N.B.* s.v. Lee, Rowland.
[48] S.R.O., D. 4566/97, Packington, deed of 25 Mar. 1780; L.J.R.O., B/A/15/Lichfield, St. Chad, no. 1083.
[49] W.S.L., S.D. Pearson 1308; L.J.R.O., B/A/15/Lichfield, St. Chad, nos. 1072, 1078.
[50] S.R.O., D. (W.) 1851/10/5; L.J.R.O., B/A/15/Lichfield, St. Chad, no. 1074; P.R.O., HO 107/2014(2).
[51] Inf. from Mr. Hollinshead.
[52] J. Nichols, *Hist. and Antiquities of Leics.* iii (1), 221; *Alum. Oxon. 1500–1714*, i. 52; Le Neve, *Fasti* (1854), i. 594.
[53] *S.H.C.* 1935, 231; W.S.L., S.D. Pearson 1280.
[54] *S.H.C.* v (2), 23; *S.H.C.* 1923, 122; Shaw, *Staffs.* i. 377; *Students admitted to the Inner Temple, 1547–1660*, 322; C. B. Herrup, *The Common Peace*, 94.

[55] W.S.L., S.D. Pearson 1338.
[56] *S.H.C.* v (2), 24; L.J.R.O., P/C/11, John Babington (1706).
[57] Shaw, *Staffs.* ii. 27; Reade, *Johnsonian Gleanings*, iv. 188; S.R.O., D. (W.) 1734/2/1/751, p. 136.
[58] S.R.O., D. 4566/97, Packington, deed of 25 Mar. 1780.
[59] Shaw, *Staffs.* ii. 27. For the family see above, Burntwood, manors (Edial House Farm).
[60] Curborough, Whittington, and Edial sale cat. 1906 (copy in S.R.O., D. 4363/4/5/5).
[61] S.R.O., D. 4566/9, T. B. P. Levett corresp., esp. John German to Hinckley & Brown solicitors, 20 Mar. 1925; *Staffs. Advertiser*, 9 June 1928, p. 2.
[62] Inf. from Mr. Hollinshead.
[63] Date stone on house.
[64] *S.H.C.* 1923, 122.
[65] L.J.R.O., B/A/15/Lichfield, St. Chad, no. 1094.
[66] Inf. from Mr Hollinshead.
[67] S.R.O., D. 4566/97, Packington, deed of 25 Mar. 1780.
[68] L.J.R.O., B/A/15/Lichfield, St. Chad, no. 1096; W.S.L., M. 164.
[69] B.R.L., Homer 150/63B, deed of 24 June 1640.
[70] L.J.R.O., D. 77/5/1, f. 201.
[71] Ibid. D. 77/8/1, pp. 21–2; W.S.L. 37/9/46, declaration of 29 Dec. 1876 with plan.
[72] L.J.R.O., B/A/15/Lichfield, St. Chad, no. 957.

on an estate of 67 a. devised by Richard Walker (d. 1547) to Lichfield corporation to provide an income for the city's grammar school, of which Walker had been master.[73] By 1776 the corporation had added a further 35 a., of which 11 a. lay in King's Bromley.[74] In 1876 it sold the farm, then 94 a., to George Fox of Elmhurst Hall.[75] Enlarged by Fox to 185 a., it remained part of the Elmhurst Hall estate until the early 1920s. In 1962 it was bought by the tenant, Frank Baskerville (d. 1975), whose widow Mary remained the owner in 1987, when Fullbrook Farm was occupied by her son Edward.[76] The brick farmhouse was built *c.* 1835 and was later extended.[77]

In 1502 Sir Humphrey Stanley of Pipe Hall in Burntwood gave land in Elmhurst to Thomas Milley, archdeacon of Coventry. In 1504 Milley made it part of the endowment of an almshouse for poor women in Beacon Street, Lichfield, later known as Dr. Milley's hospital.[78] There was probably a farmhouse there in the mid 17th century.[79] In 1808–9 the farm consisted of a house and *c.* 68 a.[80] and by 1830 was known as *HUNT'S FARM*, probably from a member of the family of Thomas Hunt, who was living in the Tewnals Lane area in 1760.[81] In 1920 the almshouse sold the farm to W. Hollinshead.[82] In 1932 he sold it to George Sandways, who sold it in 1935 to the tenant William Baskerville. Mr. Baskerville and his family still owned the farm in 1987.[83] The present brick farmhouse dates from the early 19th century.

In 1259 the executors of Ralph of Lacock, subdean of Lichfield, gave land in Stychbrook and Elmhurst to St. John the Baptist's hospital in Lichfield for the maintenance of a chantry for Lacock.[84] The estate was known as Stychbrook Grange in the 15th century.[85] In the later 16th century it was 140 a. in extent, being held by Hugh Hill in 1555–6 and Richard Hill in 1575.[86] William Hill was living there in 1641, and in 1652 a lease was made to Zachary Hill and Thomas Whitby.[87] Zachary died in 1656, leaving a son Zachary.[88] In 1692 the lease of what was then called *LEA GRANGE* otherwise Stychbrook Grange was renewed for the same or another Zachary (d. 1714) and Thomas's widow Robinah.[89] In 1723 the house and 105 a. were occupied by a Mr. Whitby; a further 52 a. was held by Zachary's widow.[90] St. John's hospital sold the house and 68 a. in 1921 to the executors of the former tenant, John Scarrat.[91] The farm remained in the Scarrat family until 1965, when it was bought by Ernest Bradbury (d. 1973). His daughters Mrs. Lisa Teal and Mrs. Susan Toon were the owners in 1987.[92]

The name Stychbrook Grange in the 15th century suggests the existence of a house. In 1666 a house there was assessed for tax on 6 hearths, the two lessees (Zachary Hill's widow and Thomas Whitby) being answerable for 3 hearths each.[93] In 1723 the house comprised a square block with a long range to the east.[94] The main block was rebuilt in the early 19th century.[95] The house was originally of three storeys, but the upper storey was removed in the later 1960s when the house was extensively altered.[96] The long range was also rebuilt in the early 19th century as a low two-storeyed range incorporating much re-used material.

An estate centring on the former *LONGWAY HOUSE* was owned by Ralph Chetwynd of Rugeley (d. 1653).[97] His son Charles sold it to Ralph Coton of London, who in turn sold it to Thomas Bearcroft, rector of Walton upon Trent (Derb.). In 1680 Bearcroft left it to his nephew and namesake. It remained in the family until 1761, when it was sold to John Barker, a Lichfield banker (d. 1780). His widow Catherine died in 1803, and it was presumably her executors who in the same year put the estate up for sale as a 69-a. farm.[98] It was evidently bought by John Barker Scott, the continuator of Barker's bank. In 1811 Scott took a lease from the vicars choral of Lichfield cathedral of land called the Bynds, north of Longway House, and amalgamated it with his estate.[99] He was succeeded in 1819 by his daughter Ann, who married William Gresley, later curate of St. Chad's, Lichfield.[1] In 1851 the estate covered 86 a.[2] Gresley was succeeded in 1876 by his brother Maj. Francis Gresley (d. 1880), whose executors owned the farm in 1895.[3] In 1987 it was owned by Mr. J. Borland.

Longway House no longer exists, but a brick barn of the 18th century stands near its site. It was replaced as the farmhouse by Binns Farm (the present Red Brae Farm), built in the later 1810s on an elevated site to the north-east.[4]

[73] W.S.L., S. MS. 326/1; *V.C.H. Staffs.* vi. 159.
[74] L.J.R.O., D. 77/8/1, pp. 11–12.
[75] W.S.L. 37/9/46, declaration of 29 Dec. 1876 with plan; L.J.R.O., D. 127/council min. bk. 1866–82, p. 261.
[76] J. H. Rymond's estate sale cat. 1931 and C. Heeley's estate sale cat. 1935 (copies in Lichfield Libr.); inf. from Mr. Baskerville.
[77] W.S.L. 37/9/46, declaration of 29 Dec. 1876.
[78] L.J.R.O., D. 103/6/28/1; *V.C.H. Staffs.* iii. 276.
[79] L.J.R.O., D. 103/6/15/3.
[80] Ibid. D. 103/6/2, map V; D. 103/6/15/10.
[81] Ibid. D. 103/3/1; W.S.L. 37/3/46, deed of 29 Nov. 1760.
[82] L.J.R.O., D. 103/2/5, 14 Jan 1920.
[83] Inf. from Mr. Baskerville.
[84] *S.H.C.* 1924, pp. 319–20.
[85] L.J.R.O., D. 30/VC, palimpsest, ii, f. 9.
[86] Ibid. D. 88/rentals, 1555–6 and Jan. 1574/5; W.S.L., S. MS. 326/1.
[87] S.R.O., D. (W.) 1734/2/1/614, m. 36.
[88] L.J.R.O., D. 29/1/1, f. 6v.; P.R.O., PROB 11/264, f. 390.
[89] L.J.R.O., D. 15/8/5/1; L.J.R.O., P/C/11, Zachary Hill (1714).

[90] Ibid. D. 88/hosp. land, plan no. 4.
[91] Annotated copy of 1921 sale cat. in S.R.O., D. 4363/A/5/14; *Kelly's Dir. Staffs.* (1900 and edns. to 1940).
[92] Inf. from Mrs. Teal.
[93] *S.H.C.* 1923, 122–3.
[94] L.J.R.O., D. 88/hosp. land, plan no. 4.
[95] Sale partics. 17 Aug. 1815 (copy in S.R.O., D. (W.) 3222/523/64).
[96] Inf. from Mrs. Teal.
[97] *Cal. S.P. Dom.* 1653–4, 234; *S.H.C.* v (2), 83; J. Ogilby, *Britannia* (1675), pl. between pp. 44 and 45.
[98] *S.H.C.* v (2), 83; *Alum. Cantab. to 1751*, i. 117; L.J.R.O., D. 39/1/8; *Aris's Birmingham Gaz.* 9 May 1803; above, Lichfield, econ. hist. (professions).
[99] S.R.O., D. (W.) 3222/271; L.J.R.O., B/A/15/ Lichfield, St. Chad, nos. 966 sqq.; below (vicars choral estate).
[1] *Staffs. Advertiser*, 11 Dec. 1819; *S.H.C.* n.s. i. 151–2.
[2] L.J.R.O., B/A/15/Lichfield. St. Chad, nos. 966 sqq.
[3] *S.H.C.* n.s. i. 151–2; S.R.O., D. 4566/12, copy of 1815 sale cat. and assoc. papers.
[4] B.L. Maps, O.S.D. 258; L.J.R.O., bk. of plans of Mark part etc. 1821, plan [1], no. 48.

A chantry established in Lichfield cathedral for Dean John Yotton (d. 1512) was endowed with land at Stychbrook. At least some of it was apparently administered by the college of chantry priests.[5] After the suppression of chantries in 1548 the land was divided, but John Dyott of Lichfield later re-united it, buying a cottage and a close from John Pilsworth in 1553[6] and a messuage called *STYCHBROOK* and land from Hugh Ensdale in 1568.[7] In 1571 Dyott held the messuage and cottage, 50 a. of enclosed land, and 77 a. in the open fields.[8] He was succeeded in 1578 by his son Anthony (d. 1622), whose son Sir Richard Dyott gave the estate to his third son Matthew.[9] Matthew was succeeded in 1698 by his son John,[10] who died in 1742 leaving the estate in trust for his nephew Thomas Dyott, a Birmingham engraver. It was then 206 a. in area, of which 80 a. lay in Lichfield. In 1771 it passed to Thomas's son John, a resident of Lichfield.[11] In the 1790s it was bought by Francis Eliot of Elmhurst Hall, who in 1801 sold 168 a. at Stychbrook to the marquess of Stafford.[12] By 1848 the owner was the earl of Lichfield.[13] His great-grandson sold the 179-a. estate in 1920 to the tenant Evan Weston (d. 1959).[14] His family retained it until 1973, when the house and 14 a. were sold to Robin Taylor and the remaining 83 a. to Mr. G. Hollinshead of Curborough Hall Farm.[15] A farmhouse was built by John Dyott in the later 1730s.[16] It survived until the later 1970s when it was left uninhabited and allowed to fall down.[17]

The tithes of Curborough and Elmhurst were divided among several prebendaries in Lichfield cathedral.[18] The small tithes were assigned to the vicar of St. Mary's, Lichfield, by Bishop Lloyd in 1694.[19] When the tithes were commuted in 1848, no tithe was payable from 183 a. and prescriptive payments were made for other land.[20] The prebendal shares of the great tithes were then from 170 a. (Prees or Pipa Minor), 157 a. (Curborough), 136 a. (Hansacre), 71 a. (Bishopshull), and 57 a. (Gaia Minor); in addition, tithes from 596 a. were divided among the prebendaries of Freeford, Gaia Major, Hansacre, Stotfold, and Weeford. Tithes from 121 a. were paid to the curate of St. Chad's, Lichfield, to whom they had been granted by the dean in 1842.[21] The dean and chapter, to whom Stotfold prebend had been assigned in 1803, were

awarded a rent charge of £19 16s. 1d. The vicar of St. Mary's was awarded a rent charge of £39 6s. 1d., and the other rent charges, totalling £222 0s. 3d., were payable to the Ecclesiastical Commissioners.

William of Leicester, a canon of Lichfield (d. by 1342), granted the vicars choral of Lichfield cathedral a messuage and land at Stychbrook. In the early 19th century they had 91 a. around Lea Grange, of which 65½ a. lay in Curborough and Elmhurst township and the rest in Lichfield.[22] In the later 1460s the vicars acquired a messuage and pasture called the Bynds, north of Longway House. In the early 19th century they had 23 a. there, which were later sold to the owner of the Longway House estate.[23]

Rents in Elmhurst and Stychbrook were included among the endowments of the chantry of Hugh de Sotby, a canon of Lichfield, established in the cathedral in the mid 13th century.[24] By 1414 the chantry's property in the township consisted of two messuages with a virgate each, three other messuages, and several pieces of land.[25] After the suppression of the chantry in 1548 the estate was acquired by the Paget family, lords of Longdon manor. In 1571 some of the messuages were held of that manor by Simon Biddulph, and they presumably became part of the Elmhurst Hall estate.[26]

ECONOMIC HISTORY. AGRICULTURE. Selions in Curborough and in Elmhurst were recorded c. 1312.[27] Curborough field and Elmhurst field were mentioned in the earlier 1360s, as was Ley field which lay mostly in Lichfield south of Stychbrook.[28] Selions recorded in King's field in 1373 probably lay south of Elmhurst hamlet near King's Field House.[29] Selions near Seedy mill were recorded in the later 14th century.[30] The open fields were evidently enclosed piecemeal. In 1610 Anthony Dyott, the owner of Stychbrook, noted that his open-field land there could be easily inclosed with the consent of other freeholders 'who are very forward for that purpose'.[31]

Crops grown in Elmhurst in 1359 included oats, dredge, maslin, and peas, and the fields were then cropped in rotation.[32] Farming was evidently mixed in the later 17th century,[33] and there may have been an emphasis on pastoral

[5] *Valor Eccl.* (Rec. Com.), iii. 139; Bodl. MS. Top. Staffs. c. 1, f. 3.
[6] S.R.O., D. 661/2/342A and 454; D. (W.) 1734/2/3/112D.
[7] P.R.O., C 3/237, no. 9; *S.H.C.* xiii. 269.
[8] W.S.L., S. MS. 326/1.
[9] S.R.O., D. 661/1/58 and 97; below, Freeford, manor.
[10] L.J.R.O., D. 29/1/1, f. 46v.; S.R.O., D. 661/1/799.
[11] S.R.O., D. 661/2/814; W.S.L. 135/14/47; B.R.L., Homer 150/65.
[12] S.R.O., D. 615/240/2/8(D), articles of agreement of 2 Apr. 1801 and deed of 24 Mar. 1804; above (Elmhurst Hall).
[13] L.J.R.O., B/A/15/Lichfield, St. Chad, no. 1062.
[14] Ibid. D. 88/abstract of title to Stychbrook Farm, 1937; *Lichfield Mercury*, 27 Feb. 1959, p. 6.
[15] Sale cat. 1973 (in possession of Mr. J. Lees of Corporation Farm).
[16] B.R.L. 381700, pp. 73, 92, 137.
[17] *Lichfield Mercury*, 10 Apr. 1981, p. 19 (with photograph of the house).

[18] Para. based on L.J.R.O., B/A/15/Lichfield, St. Chad.
[19] Above, Lichfield, churches.
[20] The area covered in the award included the township's detached portions.
[21] *Lond. Gaz.* 29 Apr. 1842, p. 1169; Lich. Dioc. Regy., Bp.'s Reg. 30, pp. 208–9.
[22] Bodl. MS. Ashmole 1521, p. 43 (2nd nos.); L.J.R.O., D. 30/XXIV, f. 40v.; L.J.R.O., VC/A/21, CC 17529, plan 6.
[23] Bodl. MS. Ashmole 1521, p. 28 (2nd nos.); L.J.R.O., VC/A/21, CC 17529, plan 6.
[24] *S.H.C.* 1924, pp. 70, 73–4.
[25] S.R.O., D. (W.) 1734/2/1/760, m. 120.
[26] W.S.L., S. MS. 326/1.
[27] S.R.O., D. 661/1/597; D. 661/2/595.
[28] *S.H.C.* 1939, 98–9.
[29] S.R.O., D. 661/2/542.
[30] Ibid. D. (W.) 1734/2/1/760, m. 68.
[31] Ibid. D. 661/1/44.   [32] P.R.O., E 199/41/15.
[33] *S.H.C.* 4th ser. v, pp. 112, 125, 148; L.J.R.O., P/C/11, Lawr. Spooner (1667).

farming, notably dairying; there was a dairy at Elmhurst Hall in 1765.[34] Livestock offered for sale by F. P. Eliot of Elmhurst Hall in 1797 included some 30 pedigree cows and heifers, as well as 80 ewes in lamb. At a sale later that year Eliot offered 32 head of cattle, including a cow bred by the experimental breeder John Princep of Croxall (Derb.), over 100 sheep, and several pedigree horses.[35] Equipment for cheese and butter making was among goods offered for sale by a farmer at Elmhurst in 1810 and by one at Curborough in 1811; each had herds of up to 30 cows.[36] George Fox of Elmhurst Hall kept pedigree Shorthorns from the later 1870s. The cattle were provided with purpose-built quarters at New Farm, known as New Building in 1881 and as Shorthorn Buildings in 1918.[37]

Crops were grown on about a third of the 831 ha. (2,053 a.) of farmland returned for Curborough and Elmhurst in 1984. Most of the cultivated land was devoted to wheat and barley, with 23.7 ha. of potatoes; 15.6 ha. at New farm was used for growing fruit, principally strawberries but also raspberries, gooseberries, and blackcurrants. New farm also specialized in pigs, of which it had over 5,000. There were nearly 1,400 head of cattle in the parish, over half of them kept for beef and the rest for milk. Five farms concentrated on dairy products. Sheep in the parish numbered 754.[38]

MILLS. The name Curborough implies a water mill in the Anglo-Saxon period.[39] Curborough mill was recorded in 1298 and 1430, and in 1561 a lane north of the later Field House was called Mill Lane.[40]

Seedy mill on Bilson brook south of Seedymill Farm was recorded in the mid 13th century as 'Synethimilne'.[41] It was probably the mill which William de Aston held in the area in the earlier 14th century. In 1571 Seedy mill was held of the lord of Longdon manor by Sir Walter Aston.[42] By 1628 the owner was Thomas Sprott of Ashmore Brook in Burntwood, and the mill descended with Ashmore Brook until 1812 when it was sold to the tenant John Shaw.[43] Shaw was dead by 1817, and in 1848 the mill was owned by John Smith of Elmhurst Hall.[44] New machinery was installed in 1852.[45] The mill went out of use in the 1930s but still stands.[46]

LOCAL GOVERNMENT. By 1297 Curborough and Elmhurst formed a single township which made presentments at the great court of Longdon manor. In 1327 it was represented by two frankpledges, evidently one for Curborough and the other for Elmhurst.[47] Two frankpledges were still sent in 1604 but one only from 1605.[48] In the mid 18th century the township was known as Elmhurst and Curborough. A headborough was still appointed at the court in 1839.[49] A separate township called Curborough Turvile for the estate of Curborough prebend was represented in 1485 by a frankpledge at the Longdon great court.[50] No other instance of his attendance has been found. There was a constable for Curborough and Elmhurst in 1377.[51] The constable was still chosen at the Longdon court in 1839.[52]

A 'warden of the field of Elmhurst', mentioned in 1560, probably acted as pinner.[53] A pinner was chosen at the Longdon great court in 1637 and until 1763.[54] A pinfold recorded in 1798 may have been the one which in 1824 stood at the southern end of Park Lane.[55] About 1900 the pinfold stood in Fox Lane opposite King's Field House.[56]

Parochially Curborough and Elmhurst were part of St. Chad's, Lichfield. By 1740 the township, described as the country part of the parish, had its own churchwarden, presumably chosen by the inhabitants, who were appointing by 1755. From 1865 two sidesmen were appointed instead.[57] The township organized its own poor relief by 1748, and possibly by 1666.[58] It was placed in Lichfield poor-law union in 1836.[59] As part of Lichfield rural district it became part of the new Lichfield district in 1974.

Curborough and Elmhurst subscribed to the Whittington association for the prosecution of felons, in existence in 1780 and 1828.[60]

CHURCH. A mission served from St. Chad's, Lichfield, had been established at Elmhurst by 1872.[61] Services were probably held in a cottage, also used as a schoolroom, east of Elmhurst Hall. A mission room was opened next to the cottage in 1882. It was provided by George Fox of Elmhurst Hall, who regularly preached to his servants there.[62] Students from Lichfield Theo-

[34] S.R.O., D. (W.) 1738/C/4/2.
[35] Aris's Birmingham Gaz. 30 Jan. 1797; W.S.L. 135/8/47.
[36] Aris's Birmingham Gaz. 12 Mar. 1810; Staffs. Advertiser, 9 Mar. 1811.
[37] Staffs. Advertiser, 7 July 1877, p. 4; P.R.O., RG 11/2774; Elmhurst Hall Estate sale cat. 1918 (copy in possession of Mr. L. Brookes of Elmhurst Hall Farm).
[38] M.A.F.F., agric. returns 1984.
[39] Above, introduction.
[40] S.R.O., D. (W.) 1734/J. 2058; D. (W.) 1734/J. 2268, f. 3; W.S.L., S.D. Pearson 1275.
[41] S.H.C. 1924, p. 75; S.R.O., D. (W.) 1734/2/1/740, m. 123, Elmhurst entry.
[42] S.H.C. xii (1), 91; W.S.L., S. MS. 326/1.
[43] P.R.O., CP 25(2)/484/4 Chas. I, East. no. [25]; S.R.O., D. 833/3/1, deed of 10 July 1734; D. 833/4; above, Burntwood, manors.
[44] Staffs. Advertiser, 1 Mar. 1817; L.J.R.O., B/A/15/ Lichfield, St. Chad, no. 907.   [45] Inscr. on mill stone.
[46] Inf. from Mr. Douthwaite of Seedymill Farm, the present owner.

[47] S.R.O., D. (W.) 1734/2/1/598, mm. 2d., 14d.
[48] Ibid. D. (W.) 1734/2/1/613, mm. 6d., 10d.
[49] Ibid. D. 603/J/1/4/15.
[50] Ibid. D. (W.) 1734/2/1/598, m. 69.
[51] S.H.C. 4th ser. vi. 10.
[52] S.R.O., D. 603/J/1/4/15.
[53] Ibid. D. (W.) 1734/2/1/609, m. 1; above, Lichfield, town govt. (govt. to 1548: manorial courts).
[54] S.R.O., D. (W.) 1511(34)/33; D. (W.) 1734/2/1/733.
[55] Ibid. D. (W.) 1511(34)/33; D. (W.) 1821/5; W.S.L. 47/1/45, f. 22, no. 2052.
[56] O.S. Map 1/2,500, Staffs. LII. 7 (1902 edn.).
[57] Above, Lichfield, parish govt.
[58] S.H.C. 1923, 123; W.S.L., M. 871.
[59] Poor Law Com. Order of 1836 forming Lichfield union (copy in L.J.R.O., D. 77/16/3).
[60] Aris's Birmingham Gaz. 24 Apr. 1780; 30 Jan. 1797; Lichfield Mercury, 1 Feb. 1828.
[61] Lich. Dioc. Ch. Cal. (1872).
[62] Staffs. Advertiser, 18 Mar. 1882, p. 5; Lichfield Mercury, 1 June 1894, p. 10.

logical College and other laymen helped to maintain services in the early 20th century, and in the 1930s and 1940s the services were taken by a lay reader.[63] The room was extended in 1920 by the addition of a chancel, paid for by Mrs. M. Hamer, the tenant at Elmhurst Hall. In 1921 John Mitchell gave the room and an adjoining cottage to St. Chad's parish in memory of his father Henry, formerly of Elmhurst Hall.[64] Fortnightly services were held in 1987.[65]

NONCONFORMITY. The Presbyterian congregation established at Lichfield in the later 17th century was possibly supported by Michael Biddulph of Elmhurst, who was recorded in 1662–3 as being of that persuasion.[66] His brother and heir Sir Theophilus was evidently not a Presbyterian: according to Bishop Hacket it was without his knowledge that a conventicle was held in 1669 in the house of one of his tenants, a man called Hill.[67] The tenant was presumably Zachary Hill of Lea Grange. Three children of Zachary Hill (d. 1714) were baptized by the Presbyterian minister for the area between 1708 and 1714.[68]

Lawrence Spooner, a Curborough yeoman who died in 1661 leaving some of his clothes to poor Baptists, was presumably a Baptist himself. He directed that his body was to be buried in Harpers Croft, south of the later Corporation Farm; his house may have stood on or near the site of the farmhouse.[69] His son, also Lawrence, was a Baptist. A conventicle was held at his house in 1683, and he ministered to local Baptists, apparently including those in Lichfield.[70] In 1707 he was buried near his father.[71]

EDUCATION. A school was held at Elmhurst in 1833, when it had 21 pupils taught by a mistress. It was supported partly by subscription and partly by parents who could afford to pay; the mistress received 3*d.* a week for each child.[72] The children were probably taught in a cottage next to the later mission room; a mistress was living in the cottage by 1874.[73]

A school board for Curborough and Elmhurst was established in 1881, with George Fox of Elmhurst Hall as chairman, and in 1883 a school was opened for 45 children. It was built on land given by Fox on the other side of the road from the mission room. Children paid from 2*d.* to 4*d.* a week according to age.[74] In 1891 fees were abolished for children aged up to 15 years.[75] The school had 17 boys and 25 girls in 1901, and in 1908 the county council added a classroom.[76] From 1931 children aged over 11 years attended schools in Lichfield, but the parents successfully resisted a proposal that the school should be closed because numbers were reduced.[77] In 1953 there were only 14 children on the roll.[78] The school was renamed the Elms county primary school in 1954, and in 1958 was reorganized as a junior mixed and infants' school with *c.* 20 pupils.[79] The school was closed in 1980, and pupils were transferred to Christ Church primary school in Lichfield. The former school building and playing field were bought by the Elmhurst and Curborough Community Association, formed that year, and the building was converted into a village hall.[80]

CHARITIES FOR THE POOR. None known.

FISHERWICK
WITH TAMHORN

FISHERWICK, 2,130 a. (861 ha.) in area, is a civil parish without a village, there being no church, school, shop, or public house.[81] It was formed in 1934 from most of the existing parish of Fisherwick (all but 6 a. of its 1,313 a.), the parish of Tamhorn (793 a.), and a small portion of the parishes of Elford and Wigginton.[82] Fisherwick and Tamhorn were formerly townships in the ancient parish of St. Michael, Lichfield, though detached from the main part of the parish; Tamhorn had become extra-parochial by the 1830s.[83] Fisherwick township occupied the northern part of the present civil parish and Tamhorn the southern part. In addition there

[63] L.J.R.O., D. 29/5/1, pp. 195–6; D. 77/20/8, p. 7.
[64] Ibid. D. 29/4/3; D. 39/2/7–8; plaques in mission room.
[65] *Lichfield Mercury*, 11 Sept. 1987, p. 16.
[66] *S.H.C.* 4th ser. ii. 7; Shaw, *Staffs.* i. 350; *Hist. Parl., Commons, 1660–90,* .i. 650; above, Lichfield, protestant nonconformity.
[67] A. G. Matthews, *Cong. Churches of Staffs.* 73–4 (giving Thomas in error for Theophilus: Bodl. MS. Tanner 44, f. 125).   [68] S.R.O., D. 4119, pp. [56–7].
[69] L.J.R.O., P/C/11, Lawr. Spooner (1667); L.J.R.O., bk. of plans of Mark part etc. 1821, plan [1], no. 187; S.R.O., D. (W.) 1734/2/1/745, p. 250. Mr. J. Lees of Corporation Farm is thanked for help in identifying the burial site.
[70] *Primitive Methodist Mag.* June 1840, p. 205; above, Lichfield, protestant nonconformity.
[71] W.S.L., M. 164, pp. 3–6.
[72] *Educ. Enq. Abstract*, 873.

[73] Elmhurst Hall Estate sale cat. 1874 (copy in S.R.O., D. 1083/2).
[74] S.R.O., CEB/8/1, pp. 1, 4, 28, 69.
[75] Ibid. p. 162.
[76] Ibid. CEH/32/1, 4 Apr. 1901, 8 July 1908.
[77] Ibid. 31 Oct. 1930, 29 Jan. 1931, 15 Apr., 22 Dec. 1932.
[78] Ibid. CEH/32/2, 9 Nov. 1953.
[79] Ibid. 6 Sept. 1954, 23 Jan. 1957, 6 Mar. 1958.
[80] *Lichfield Mercury*, 8 Aug. 1986, p. 3; inf. from Mrs. I. Boughey of Elmhurst.
[81] This article was written in 1985–6. Mr. A. G. Ward, C.B.E., of Fisherwick Park Farm and others named in footnotes are thanked for their help.
[82] Staffs. Review Order, 1934, pp. 63, 67, and map 7 (copy in S.R.O.); *Census*, 1931, 1981. The eastern boundary thereafter ran down the centre of the river Tame.
[83] Below, local govt.

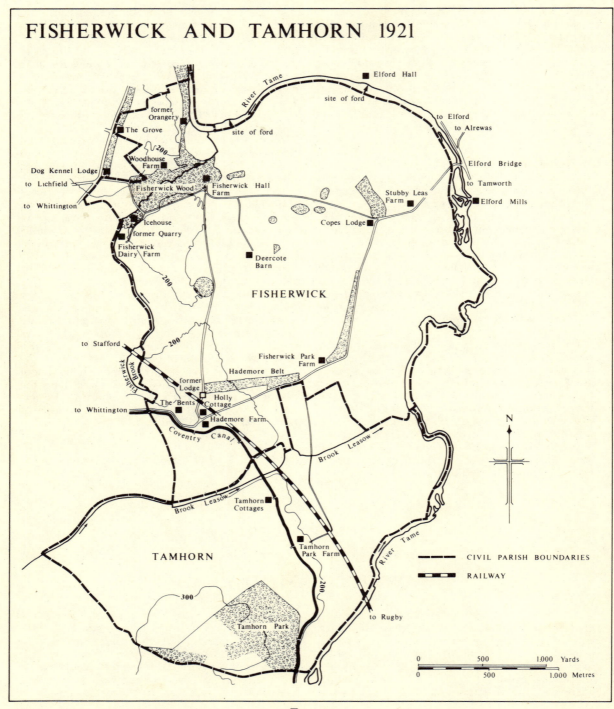

FISHERWICK AND TAMHORN 1921

Elford Hall

River Tame

site of ford

former Orangery

The Grove

site of ford

to Elford

to Alrewas

Woodhouse Farm

200

Elford Bridge

Dog Kennel Lodge

to Tamworth

to Lichfield

Fisherwick Wood

Fisherwick Hall Farm

Stubby Leas Farm

Elford Mills

to Whittington

Copes Lodge

Icehouse

former Quarry

Fisherwick Dairy Farm

200

Deercote Barn

FISHERWICK

to Stafford

200

Fisherwick Park Farm

Hademore Belt

former Lodge

Holly Cottage

The Bents

Fisherwick Brook

to Whittington

Hademore Farm

Coventry Canal

Brook Leasow

N

Brook Leasow

Tamhorn Cottages

Tamhorn Park Farm

River Tame

200

CIVIL PARISH BOUNDARIES

RAILWAY

TAMHORN

300

Tamhorn Park

to Rugby

| 0 | | 500 | | 1,000 Yards |
| 0 | | 500 | | 1,000 Metres |

FIG. 20

were once two other settlements, Timmor on the east and Horton in the Hademore area on the west.

On the north and east the river Tame forms the boundary with Elford. Fisherwick brook, a tributary named in 1571 as Throxsall brook, forms part of the boundary with Whittington on the north-west.[84] Much of the boundary between Fisherwick and Tamhorn followed Brook

Leasow, another tributary of the Tame formerly known as Tamhorn brook.[85] The Keuper Marl underlies the north part of the parish, the Keuper Sandstone the centre, and the Bunter Sandstone the south. There are gravel terraces and alluvium along the Tame; the gravel also extends into the central area, and there has been extensive sand and gravel working in recent years. A band of Boulder Clay runs through the

[84] S.R.O., D. (W.) 1734/2/3/90.

[85] Ibid.; D. (W.) 1734/2/1/600, mm. 9–10; 601, m.23; D. (W.) 1734/2/3/112D, boundaries of Whittington lordship.

north and west parts of the parish and through Tamhorn.[86] The ground slopes up from 191 ft. (58 m.) by the Tame at Elford bridge to 250 ft. (76 m.) on the boundary south-west of Hademore; in the north-west corner of the parish it rises steeply above the river to 200 ft. (61 m.) and on the southern boundary it rises to 300 ft. (91 m.).

A site on the gravel terrace by the Tame in the north may have been occupied some time after *c.* 1900 B.C. during the Neolithic period.[87] There may have been Iron Age settlement west of Fisherwick Park Farm in the centre of the parish *c.* 1000 B.C.[88] An Iron Age site on a terrace by the Tame north of Brook Leasow seems to have been occupied in the 3rd and 2nd centuries B.C.; it is possible that its occupation began in the 4th century B.C. and continued into the 1st century A.D. There was another Iron Age settlement to the south on the opposite side of Brook Leasow.[89] There may have been two other prehistoric settlements near the river in the south-east.[90] The possibly Neolithic site in the north was occupied by a Romano-British farmstead in the 2nd and 3rd centuries A.D. There is no trace of a large house; instead the farm seems to have been worked by labourers living in huts.[91]

Fisherwick and Timmor together formed a township by the late 13th century.[92] Fisherwick, an Old English name meaning the dwelling (*wic*) of the fisherman,[93] does not appear in Domesday Book, but it was the name of a manor by 1167. The medieval hamlet was evidently in the north-west of the township, and the manor house built in the later 16th century stood there.[94] In 1282 the manor included 10 messuages and 9 cottages, and in 1556 it contained 9 messuages and 3 cottages.[95] The settlement, still in existence in the late 17th century, had disappeared by 1760,[96] perhaps as a result of the extension of the park in the late 1750s. In the 1760s and 1770s the hall was rebuilt, the park was greatly improved, and a smaller park·was created north-west of the hall; the home farm was rebuilt in the valley south-west of the hall. After the sale of the estate in 1808 the hall was demolished and the parkland was turned into farmland. The outbuildings of the hall became Fisherwick Hall Farm, while Jenny's Lodge farm, later Fisherwick Park farm, was formed on the south side of the main park. Two other farms, Grove and Woodhouse, were created on the north-western part of the estate.[97]

Timmor in the east of the township existed by 1086.[98] In the 16th century the name became confused with Tamhorn, with such spellings as Tympehorn and Tymhorne.[99] The settlement may have been in decay by 1585 when its bridge and highways were in disrepair.[1] There were at least two houses there in 1635,[2] but by the later 18th century the name was used only for a notional manor, and the sole surviving farm was Stubby Leas.[3] The farm took its name from a close of pasture mentioned in the earlier and mid 16th century.[4] A house there was described in 1584 as lately built.[5] The present house is a double-pile building of the early 18th century, with extensions of the 19th and 20th centuries. It ceased to be a farmhouse after sand and gravel working began in the area in 1967, and since 1980 it has been occupied as a rest home for the elderly.[6]

The township of Fisherwick and Timmor had 6 people assessed for the subsidy of 1327, 7 for that of 1332–3, and 27 for the poll tax of 1380–1.[7] For the subsidy of 1524–5 Fisherwick had 11 people assessed.[8] The muster roll of 1539 contains 15 names for Fisherwick and 5 for Timmor.[9] Nine persons in the township were assessed for hearth tax in 1666.[10] A population of 83 in 1801 had dropped to 73 by 1811, but it had increased, after some fluctuation, to 101 by 1861 and, again with fluctuation, to 129 by 1901.[11] The population was still 129 in 1911 but had risen to 149 by 1921, dropping to 129 again by 1931. The enlarged parish had a population of 153 in 1951, 138 in 1961, and 119 in 1971 and 1981.[12] The estimated population in 1987 was 140.[13]

Tamhorn and Horton formed a township by the late 13th century, with Horton apparently the more important.[14] Both existed by 1086.[15] Tamhorn is an Old English name meaning a bend of the Tame or a horn of land by the Tame.[16] By the later 17th century the settlement consisted only of the manor house, the predecessor of the present Tamhorn Park Farm.[17] Tamhorn Cottages to the north were built as five dwellings for agricultural labourers between 1851 and 1861.[18]

[86] *V.C.H. Staffs.* i, map before p. 1; Geol. Surv. 1", drift, sheet 154 (1922 edn.); *Fisherwick*, ed. C. Smith (B.A.R. Brit. Ser. lxi, 1979), 93; below, econ. hist.
[87] *T.S.S.A.H.S.* x. 11, 20–1.
[88] Ibid. xvi. 8.
[89] *Fisherwick*, ed. Smith, *passim.*
[90] *T.S.S.A.H.S.* xx, map 6.
[91] Ibid. x. 1–19.
[92] Below, local govt.
[93] Ekwall, *Eng. Place-Names.*
[94] *T.S.S.A.H.S.* xx, map 3; below, manors.
[95] *S.H.C.* vi (1), 121; N.R.A., TS. list of Massereene (Staffs.) deeds, no. 29.
[96] *S.H.C.* 1923, 194; Plot, *Staffs.* map; W.S.L. 114/31.
[97] Below, manors; econ. hist.
[98] S.R.O., D. (W.) 1746/P/3; below, manors.
[99] Erdeswick, *Staffs.* 452 n.; *Valor Eccl.* (Rec. Com.), iii. 71; *S.H.C.* xvi. 131; W.S.L., M. 520, p. 35.
[1] S.R.O., D. (W.) 1734/2/1/612, m. 74.
[2] Ibid. D. 661/2/1/1, f. 73.
[3] Above, fig. 1; Shaw, *Staffs.* i. 375.
[4] *Topographer and Genealogist*, i. 335; *S.H.C.* 1912, 194;

P.R.O., C 1/1195, nos. 1–2; C 1/1344, no. 57; P.R.O., STAC 2/3, nos. 261–5.
[5] N.R.A., Massereene (Staffs.) deeds, no. 33.
[6] Inf. from the owner, Mr. J. R. Hughes.
[7] *S.H.C.* vii (1), 232 (corrected by *S.H.C.* 4th ser. vi. 24); x (1), 109; xvii. 175 (date corrected by *S.H.C.* 4th ser. vi. 3–5).
[8] P.R.O., E 179/177/97; E 179/118. Timmor was grouped with Tamhorn and Horton, with 6 names for all three: E 179/118.
[9] *S.H.C.* n.s. iv. 230.
[10] *S.H.C.* 1923, 194.
[11] *V.C.H. Staffs.* i. 322.
[12] *Census*, 1911–81.
[13] Staffs. C.C. *Small Area Population Estimates Mid 1987.*
[14] Below, local govt.
[15] Ekwall, *Eng. Place-Names*; *N. Staffs. Jnl. of Field Studies*, xxi. 3.
[16] Below, manors.
[17] *S.H.C.* 1923, 225; S.R.O., D. (W.) 1746/P/3.
[18] P.R.O., RG 9/1974.

Horton is also an Old English name, meaning a settlement on muddy ground.[19] It was situated on the higher ground in the present Hademore area.[20] There were evidently five houses in Horton in 1635.[21] There was still a house there in the earlier 18th century.[22] It was probably Hademore Farm, now Holly Cottage, a small brick house of that period with an extension of c. 1800.[23] In the later 19th century the present Hademore Farm was built on the opposite side of the road next to the existing outbuildings of the farm. Bents farm to the west existed by 1841, but the farmhouse was unoccupied in 1881.[24] In the later 1980s the Bents was a private dwelling.

The township had 12 people assessed for the subsidy of 1327 and 10 for that of 1332–3.[25] Only two names appear on the muster roll of 1539,[26] and only the tenant of Tamhorn manor house was assessed for hearth tax in 1666.[27] Tamhorn had a population of 10 in 1801 and 5 in 1841. The population was 10 in 1851 and rose to 23 in 1861 after the building of Tamhorn Cottages. Having reached 33 in 1881, it had dropped to 21 by 1891 and 20 by 1901. It was 51 in 1911 and 19 in 1921 and 1931.[28]

Three roads ran north and east from the settlement at Fisherwick to Elford, crossing the Tame by fords which were described in 1766 as often impassable.[29] The most northerly ford lay north-east of Fisherwick Hall and was known as Fisherwick ford in the early 16th century.[30] The second road followed part of an Iron Age track leading to the river.[31] Its ford was known as Elford Hall ford in the 16th century. In 1600 there was a ferry there, and the crossing was known in 1766 as Elford ford or Elford ferry.[32] The third and most southerly road ran through Timmor and crossed the Tame by a ford at Elford mill, known as Broad ford in the 13th century.[33] The road was then known as 'Sropstreteweye', probably meaning the Shrewsbury or Shropshire road.[34] It continued west from Fisherwick to Lichfield via Huddlesford Lane in Whittington, and in the early 16th century it was part of the route from Leicester to Lichfield.[35] In 1599 the road was described as difficult, especially in winter.[36] It still ran through Fisherwick park in 1766, but by then the Leicester–Lichfield route was along the road running east and south of the park to Whittington village.[37] A bridge at Timmor, described as on the highway between Timmor and Whittington, was mentioned in 1585 and 1616.[38] A way through Timmor from 'Penecford' to 'Fenneford' was mentioned in the 13th century. The latter ford was evidently in Tamhorn where there was a ford called the Fenny ford in 1399; it was presumably approached along Fennyford Lane in Tamhorn, mentioned in 1456.[39]

The roads radiating from the former hamlet of Fisherwick ran through Fisherwick park until the later 18th century when they were stopped up under an Act of 1766 as part of Lord Donegall's improvement of the park. In return he built a bridge over the Tame north of Elford mill and assumed responsibility for its maintenance and for the repair of the Whittington road from the bridge as far as Hademore.[40] Built of pink sandstone, the bridge consists of three arches over the main part of the river and an eight-arch flood section to the west. Also in 1766 Lord Donegall granted the lord of Elford and his servants a right of way through the park in a straight line from the gate where the road from Elford ford entered the park, across to Hademore gate. The right covered pedestrians, horses, and carriages but not carts.[41] In 1911 H. F. Paget, as lord of Fisherwick, and his eldest son F. E. H. Paget made an agreement with Lichfield rural district council for the maintenance of the Whittington road. The council took over the work of maintenance during the lifetime of the Pagets, who agreed to pay for it; the liability of the owner of the Fisherwick estate to maintain the road was to remain.[42]

The Coventry Canal, built from the Trent and Mersey Canal at Fradley in Alrewas under an Act of 1785 and completed in 1788,[43] enters the parish at Hademore and runs through Tamhorn. Its line is closely followed by the Trent Valley Railway, opened in 1847 to link London and the north-west via Rugby and Stafford.[44] The railway passes over the Elford–Whittington road at Hademore where there is a level crossing.

A new form of transport caused local excitement in 1910. Claude Grahame-White was twice forced to land his aeroplane in a field by Hademore level crossing during his unsuccessful attempts to win the £10,000 prize offered by the *Daily Mail* for a flight from London to Manchester in under 24 hours. Like his successful rival Louis Paulhan he also landed in Streethay near Trent Valley station.[45]

[19] Ekwall, *Eng. Place-Names.*
[20] See e.g. P.R.O., E 134/3 Jas. I East./19; E 134/3 Jas. I Hil./3 and 4; S.R.O., D. (W.) 1734/2/3/90, bounds of Whittington manor 1571; below, econ. hist. (agric.).
[21] P.R.O., E 134/3 Jas. I Hil./3 and 4; S.R.O., D. 661/21/1/1, f. 73.
[22] S.R.O., D. (W.) 1734/2/1/749, p. 279; D. (W.) 1734/2/1/750, p. 81.
[23] Hademore farm was recorded in 1760: below, econ. hist. (agric.).
[24] Below, econ. hist. (agric.).
[25] *S.H.C.* vii (1), 233; x (1), 105.
[26] *S.H.C.* N.S. iv. 237.
[27] *S.H.C.* 1923, 225.
[28] *V.C.H. Staffs.* i. 323; *Census*, 1911–31.
[29] *C.J.* xxx. 548; Fisherwick Park sale cat. n.d. [1808], plan between pp. 6 and 7 (copy in W.S.L. 115/6/41).
[30] B.R.L., Elford Hall MSS. no. 55.
[31] *Fisherwick*, ed. Smith, 8, 101; *T.S.S.A.H.S.* x. 7, 9.
[32] B.R.L., Elford Hall MSS. nos. 55, 150, 660.
[33] Ibid. no. 12; *S.H.C.* 1924, p. 53; W.S.L. 114/31; *C.J.* xxx. 548.
[34] Bodl. MS. Ashmole 1527, f. 21v.
[35] L.J.R.O., D. 30/VC, B 124 and 126; B.R.L., Elford Hall MSS. no. 555; S.R.O., D. 4566/S, bdle. 74, deed of 30 Apr. 1736; D. (W.) 1734/2/3/90, bounds of Whittington manor.
[36] Below, church.
[37] *C.J.* xxx. 548.
[38] S.R.O., D. (W.) 1734/2/1/612, m. 74; D. (W.) 1734/2/1/613, m. 65.
[39] Ibid. D. (W.) 1734/2/1/599, m. 44; D. (W.) 1734/2/1/603, m. 51; Shaw, *Staffs.* i. 375.
[40] 6 Geo. III, c. 60; *C.J.* xxx. 548, 717; Fisherwick Park sale cat. 1808, p. 11 (copy in S.R.O., D. 661/19/10/18).
[41] B.R.L., Elford Hall MSS. no. 660.
[42] Ibid. no. 1219.
[43] *V.C.H. Staffs.* ii. 292.
[44] Ibid. 308–9.
[45] *Lichfield Mercury*, 29 Apr. 1910, p. 8; 6 May 1910, p. 7; 26 Apr. 1985, pp. 32, 49.

MANORS AND OTHER ESTATES. *FISHERWICK*

FISHERWICK was a manor by 1167, presumably held of the bishop of Coventry whose successors were overlords in the 13th century. Assessed with Horton as 1 hide c. 1255,[46] it remained a member of the bishop's (later the Paget family's) manor of Longdon, being still regarded as such in the early 20th century.[47] A chief rent of £1 9s. 4d. was due from the Fisherwick estate to the lord of Longdon c. 1760; in 1804 a chief rent of £1 18s. 1d. was due from the freehold part of the estate and 10s. 3d. from the small copyhold portion, which was also subject to a payment of double the rent on death or alienation.[48]

In 1167 Fisherwick was held by a member of the Durdent family, which had probably been granted it by Bishop Walter Durdent (1149–59).[49] Roger Durdent held it by 1176.[50] In 1203 William Durdent held half a hide in Fisherwick, but it was claimed by his sister Margery, wife of Hugh de Loges, as her inheritance. William acknowledged the right of Hugh and Margery and thereafter held the land as their tenant. He later held of Margery and her son, another Hugh de Loges, for a rent of 15s. William was succeeded by his brother Nicholas, who did homage to the younger Hugh in 1224. In 1236 Hugh de Loges granted to the bishop the custody and homage of Nicholas's heir, a minor, in return for 50s.[51]

The heir was probably the Roger of Fisherwick who held the manor of the bishop as $\frac{1}{5}$ knight's fee in 1242–3.[52] Roger was presumably the Roger Durdent who was alive in 1276 and whose widow Lucy sued his son Richard Durdent for dower in Fisherwick in 1282.[53] Richard granted the manor for life to his brother Nicholas,[54] who in 1298 held Fisherwick of the bishop as $\frac{1}{4}$ knight's fee for a rent of 15s. and service at the Longdon court every three weeks.[55] Nicholas died between 1321 and 1323.[56]

In 1326 Roger, son of Richard Durdent, and in 1327 John, son of Nicholas Durdent, granted their right in Fisherwick to Roger Hillary.[57] Roger died in 1356 as Sir Roger Hillary, C.J., and the manor passed to his son, also Sir Roger, whose right was challenged by a John Durdent

in or before 1377.[58] The younger Sir Roger died in 1400, and his widow Margaret held Fisherwick until her death in 1411.[59] Sir Roger's heirs were the heirs of his sisters Joan and Elizabeth, and Fisherwick passed to Elizabeth's daughter Elizabeth, widow of John, Lord Clinton.[60] In 1419, however, Robert Cook of Marchington Woodlands, in Hanbury, and his wife Alice, sister and heir of John Durdent, laid claim to Fisherwick. They entered the manor and were accepted by the tenants. The next day they granted it to John Mynors of Uttoxeter, William Mynors, and others, who took possession. Elizabeth challenged the right of John Mynors and the Cooks, and Fisherwick was taken into the king's hands.[61] In 1421 John and William Mynors quitclaimed the manor to Elizabeth and her trustees, but it was not until 1424 that the Crown ordered the escheator to hand it back to the trustees.[62] Meanwhile in 1423 Elizabeth died childless. Fisherwick passed to Margaret, the widow of Frederick Tilney of Boston (Lincs.), as one of the granddaughters and coheirs of Sir Roger Hillary's sister Joan.[63]

Margaret apparently still held the manor in 1440,[64] but by 1441 it had passed to her son Sir Philip Tilney of Boston, who died in 1453.[65] On the division of his property in 1455 Fisherwick was assigned to his second son Robert.[66] Later it passed to Elizabeth, daughter and heir of Sir Philip's son Sir Frederick Tilney of Ashwellthorpe (Norf.). Her first husband was Humphrey Bourchier, killed at the battle of Barnet in 1471, and her second Thomas Howard, created earl of Surrey in 1483 and duke of Norfolk in 1514. She died in 1497. The heir to Fisherwick was her son John Bourchier, Lord Berners, but Howard continued to hold it by the courtesy. A lease of the manor in 1503 was made by both of them.[67] In 1520 Lord Berners sold the reversion after the death of the duke of Norfolk to John (later Sir John) Skeffington of London, a merchant of the Staple.[68] In 1521 the duke and Lord Berners granted the manor outright to Skeffington, who gave the duke an annuity of £26.[69]

Sir John Skeffington died in 1525 with a son William, a minor, as his heir. Fisherwick passed for life to his widow Elizabeth, and in 1527 she

[46] Shaw, *Staffs*. i, app. to Gen. Hist. p. xvi.
[47] B.R.L., Elford Hall MSS. no. 1221.
[48] Ibid. no. 935; Fisherwick Park sale cat. 1804, p. 14 (copy in S.R.O., D. 661/19/10/18).
[49] *S.H.C.* i. 47; *V.C.H. Staffs*. iii. 21.
[50] *S.H.C.* i. 78, 82, 85.
[51] *S.H.C.* iii (1), 76–7, 104; *S.H.C.* 1924, p. 167; *Cur. Reg. R.* xi, p. 300.   [52] *Bk. of Fees*, ii. 969.
[53] W.S.L., S. MS. 332 (ii), p. 77; *S.H.C.* vi (1), 121.
[54] N.R.A., TS. list of Massereene (Staffs.) deeds, no. 3. P.R.O., E 164/17, printed in *Feud. Aids*, v. 8, names Roger Durdent as still holding ¼ fee in Fisherwick in 1284–5.
[55] S.R.O., D. (W.) 1734/J. 2268, f. 1v.
[56] *S.H.C.* ix (1), 87, 110; N.R.A., Massereene (Staffs.) deeds, no. 10.
[57] *Cal. Close*, 1323–7, 551; 1327–30, 91.
[58] *S.H.C.* 1913, 169–70; *Sel. Cases in K.B.* vi (Selden Soc. lxxxii), p. lxvi; P.R.O., C 260/130, no. 20. The younger Roger was probably the Roger Hillary who was knighted in 1336: W. A. Shaw, *Knights of Eng.* ii. 5.
[59] P.R.O., C 137/36, no. 36; C 137/84, no. 36; *Cal. Close*, 1402–5, 216; S.R.O., D. (W.) 1734/2/1/600, m. 31.
[60] Dugdale, *Warws.* (1730), i. 599, 993–4; *V.C.H. Warws.* v. 154; P.R.O., C 137/36, no. 36; S.R.O., D. (W.) 1734/2/1/600, mm. 34, 35d., 36.

[61] *Cal. Inq. Misc.* vii, pp. 343–4; *Cal. Pat.* 1416–22, 253; *S.H.C.* xvii. 73–4; *S.H.C.* n.s. vii. 242–3; W.S.L., M. 520, p. 13.
[62] *Cal. Close*, 1419–22, 192, 197; 1422–9, 99.
[63] P. Thompson, *Hist. and Antiquities of Boston* (1856), 319, 373 and facing pedigree; Erdeswick, *Staffs.* 460 n.; P.R.O., C 139/12, no. 36; S.R.O., D. (W.) 1734/3/2/602, mm. 7, 10.
[64] S.R.O., D. (W.) 1734/2/1/603, mm. 12–13.
[65] Ibid. m. 15; Thompson, *Boston*, 374 and n., pedigree facing p. 373.
[66] *Cal. Close*, 1468–76, pp. 248–9 (adding the date 1456, which is not in the original); Thompson, *Boston*, pedigree facing p. 373.
[67] S.R.O., D. (W.) 1734/2/1/598, m. 67d.; D. (W.) 1734/2/1/604, mm. 10d., 38d.; D. (W.) 1734/2/1/605, mm. 2, 9; W.S.L., M. 520, pp. 14–15; Thompson, *Boston*, 373–4 and pedigree facing p. 373; *Complete Peerage*, ii. 153; ix. 614.
[68] N.R.A., Massereene (Staffs.) deeds, no. 24; S.R.O., D. 260/M/T/2/6; A. B. Beaven, *Aldermen of City of London*, ii. 24.
[69] *S.H.C.* xi. 262–3; Erdeswick, *Staffs.* 460 n.; P.R.O., CP 40/1030, enrolled deeds section, mm. 3–4d.; S.R.O., D. (W.) 1734/2/1/605, mm. 16d., 18–22.

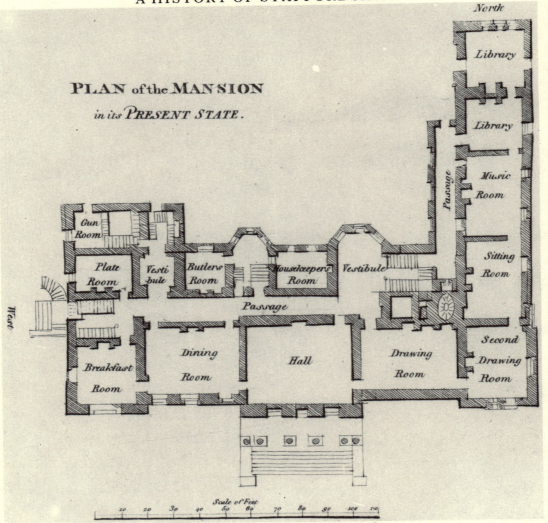

FIG. 21. FISHERWICK HALL IN 1808

and her new husband Sir John Dauncey made a lease of the manor for so long as Dauncey should hold it in right of his wife. He still held it in 1537, but by 1539 he and Elizabeth were divorced and she was taking the profits.[70] She died in 1549, followed by William Skeffington in 1551; his heir was his son John, who came of age in 1556.[71] John gave possession of his estates to his son and heir William in 1587 and died at Fisherwick in 1604.[72] William, who was created a baronet in 1627, died at Fisherwick in 1635 with a son John as his heir.[73] John, who had been knighted in 1624, had his estates sequestrated in 1643 for raising money for Charles I; he compounded in 1650.[74] On his death in 1651 he was succeeded by his son William, who died in 1652.[75] The heir was William's cousin John

Skeffington. In 1654 he married Mary, daughter and heir of Sir John Clotworthy, created Viscount Massereene in 1660. Sir John Skeffington succeeded to the viscountcy and a large Irish estate by special remainder on the death of his father-in-law in 1665. He was elected M.P. for Antrim in 1661 and remained active in the affairs of Ulster. He died in 1695.[76]

Fisherwick then descended with the viscountcy until 1755 when the 5th viscount sold the mortgaged estate to Samuel Swinfen of Swinfen, in Weeford, as trustee of Samuel Hill of Shenstone Park.[77] On Hill's death in 1758 Fisherwick passed to his nephew, Samuel Egerton of Tatton Park (Ches.), who sold it to Samuel Swinfen in 1759.[78] Swinfen sold it in 1761 to Arthur Chichester, earl of Donegall.[79]

[70] P.R.O., C 142/49, no. 44; S.R.O., D. (W.) 1734/2/1/606, mm. 2, 21; S.H.C. 1912, 134–5.
[71] P.R.O., C 142/94, no. 66; N.R.A., Massereene (Staffs.) deeds, no. 29.
[72] P.R.O., C 142/680, no. 12; N.R.A., Massereene (Staffs.) deeds, no. 35.
[73] P.R.O., C 142/600, no. 114; G.E.C. Baronetage, ii. 14.
[74] S.H.C. 1920 and 1922, 52; Cal. Cttee. for Compounding, iii. 2207; W.S.L., S. MS. 339 (transcripts of royalist composition papers), vi, pp. 17, 20.

[75] N.R.A., Massereene (Staffs.) deeds, no. 54; G.E.C. Baronetage, ii. 14.
[76] G.E.C. Baronetage, ii. 14–15; Complete Peerage, viii. 544; D.N.B.
[77] B.R.L., Elford Hall MSS. nos. 1408–10, 1412–15; S.R.O., D. (W.) 1734/F/2/2.
[78] B.R.L., Elford Hall MSS. nos. 1416–19; H. Sanders, Hist. and Antiquities of Shenstone (1794), 294; S.R.O., D. 1016/1/3, burial of 26 Feb. 1758.
[79] B.R.L., Elford Hall MSS. nos. 636, 1421–3; W.S.L. 114/31.

The earl, created Baron Fisherwick in 1790 and earl of Belfast and marquess of Donegall in 1791, rebuilt the hall and remodelled the park. He died in 1799, and under his will Fisherwick, again heavily mortgaged, passed to a younger son, Lord Spencer Chichester.[80] He sold it in 1804 to George Stedman, a potato merchant of Spitalfields (Mdx.). Stedman failed to pay the deposit and was declared bankrupt in 1805; his assignees released their interest in 1807.[81] In 1808 Chichester sold the manorial rights, the hall, and much of the land to R. B. Howard of Ashtead Park (Surr.), lord of Elford. Most of the remainder was bought by Sir Robert Peel of Drayton Bassett.[82]

Howard died in 1818, having demolished Fisherwick Hall. He was succeeded by his daughter Mary, the wife of F. G. Howard (formerly Upton, d. 1846).[83] She died in 1877 and left the Elford and Fisherwick estate to H. F. Paget, son of her cousin F. E. Paget, the rector of Elford. In 1919 Paget put the outlying parts of the estate up for sale, including Fisherwick Hall farm and Stubby Leas farm. He was succeeded in 1935 by his son F. E. H. Paget, who in 1936 gave the manor of Fisherwick and other property in the area to Birmingham corporation; the land was mainly in Elford but included a small amount in Fisherwick. The gift was made to promote 'the healthful recreation of the citizens of Birmingham' and to preserve the rural character of the property.[84] In the later 1980s part of the Fisherwick land was let as a small holding and part was unused woodland.[85]

In the later 16th century John Skeffington built 'a very proper brick house' at Fisherwick.[86] He made it over to his son and heir William in 1587, reserving to himself the little parlour and the chamber and little gallery at the lower end of the house, with access to the kitchen and the cellar.[87] The chamber at the end of the dining room and the 'compas' chamber and square chamber over the hall were mentioned in 1641.[88] The house was assessed for tax on 30 hearths in 1666; there was also 'an old house in Fisherwick park not inhabited' which was assessed on seven hearths and probably stood in the south of the park.[89] A view of the main house in the 1680s shows a three-gabled south range with a central lantern tower and a large bow window at the east end; there was evidently a back wing on the west.[90] Samuel Hill and Samuel Egerton carried out work on the house in 1757 and 1758; Benjamin Wyatt of Weeford and his son William were employed there in 1758.[91]

The house was rebuilt on the same site for Lord Donegall by Lancelot Brown between c. 1766 and c. 1779.[92] The original design evidently provided for four ranges forming a court, with fronts of 180 ft. and 150 ft. The north range was not built, and the west range was finished in a reduced form.[93] The irregular plan of the service corridor behind the main front and the occurrence of two unequal canted bay windows looking into the court suggest that, as in Brown's contemporary rebuilding at Broadlands (Hants), something of the earlier house was retained.[94] The ashlar-faced south front was 11 bays long and three storeys high, and the composition bore a strong resemblance to Brown's first country house at Croome (Worcs.) of the early 1750s. At its centre there was an irregular Corinthian hexastyle portico, bearing the date 1774. The end bays, which projected like towers on the plan but were roofed in line with the adjacent range, had venetian windows on the ground floor.[95]

Behind the portico lay the hall, the largest of the nine principal rooms. It had a floor inlaid with black marble, a scagliola chimney piece, marble pilasters around the walls, scagliola statues in niches, and a richly moulded ceiling. To the west was the main dining room and to the east the principal drawing room. The east range included two more drawing rooms, a second dining room, and two libraries. Many of the rooms had marble fireplaces, some had painted walls, and others were hung with silk. Most of the doors were of mahogany, and the lower sashes of the main rooms on the south front were filled with plate glass.[96] Joseph Rose executed some of the decorative plasterwork, and Joseph Bonomi designed some of the furniture. The ceiling of the principal drawing room incorporated paintings by J. F. Rigaud.[97]

On the first floor there were nine bedrooms and six dressing rooms, besides the housekeeper's bedroom. The attic storey consisted of 18 bedrooms 'with cemented floors'. The basement included the housekeeper's room, the servants' hall, the kitchen, and other offices. A reservoir at the top of the house fed by an engine

[80] *Complete Peerage*, iv. 391–2; W.S.L., M. 761/1/1 and 6.

[81] W.S.L., M. 761/5, deed of 20 June 1807; B.R.L., Elford Hall MSS. no. 737/2; Fisherwick Park sale cat. 1804 (copy in S.R.O., D. 661/19/10/18.

[82] W.S.L., M. 761/9; M. 761/10/1; B.R.L., Elford Hall MSS. nos. 717, 737/19 and 22; Fisherwick Park sale cats. 1808 and n.d. [1808] (copies respectively in S.R.O.. D. 661/19/10/18 and in W.S.L. 115/6/41).

[83] [F. E. Paget], *The Ashtead Estate and its Howard Possessors* (Lichfield, priv. print. 1873), 167, 175–6 (copy in Lichfield Cath. Libr.).

[84] [Paget], *Ashtead Estate*, 176; E. Hill, *Letters to the Elford Flock* (Hythe, [1983]), 53 and pedigree on p. vii; Elford Estate sale cat. 1919 (in the possession of Mr. J. A. Holgate, Fisherwick Hall; copy in W.S.L.); S.R.O. 1070.

[85] Inf. from Mr. A. G. Ward.

[86] Erdeswick, *Staffs.* 461.

[87] N.R.A., Massereene (Staffs.) deeds, no. 35.

[88] Ibid. no. 52.

[89] *S.H.C.* 1923, 194; Plot, *Staffs.* map.

[90] Above, plate 45; W.S.L. 114/31.

[91] B.R.L., Elford Hall MSS. nos. 628, 935; Shaw, *Staffs.* i. 368; H. Colvin, *Biog. Dict. Brit. Architects*, 934–6.

[92] Shaw, *Staffs.* i. 368; D. Stroud, *Capability Brown* (1975), 151; W.S.L., M. 761/8/2. For the background to the rebuilding see *Belfast Nat. Hist. and Philosophical Soc.* 2nd ser. x. 5–21.

[93] Shaw, *Staffs.* i. 368; Fisherwick Park sale cat. n.d. [1808], plan between pp. 2 and 3; W.S.L., Staffs. Views, iv. 200, 202.

[94] *Country Life*, 11 Dec. 1980, pp. 2246–8.

[95] Above, plate 46; Stroud, *Capability Brown*, 57–8 and pl. 7b.

[96] Fisherwick Park sale cat. 1804, p. 4; W.S.L., M. 761/8/2; B.R.L., Elford Hall MSS. no. 819.

[97] G. Beard, *Decorative Plasterwork in Gt. Brit.* 240; *Companion to the Leasowes, Hagley, and Enville, with a sketch of Fisherwick* (1798), 115–16.

supplied water to the rooms requiring it and to water closets on each floor.[98] West of the house Brown built service and stable courts of two storeys in red brick with ashlar-faced archways.[99]

There was a park at Fisherwick, enclosed with a pale, by the late 16th century.[1] Mention was made in 1650 of a little park as well as the main park.[2] About 1660 Sir John Skeffington planted the main park with trees. A one-year lease of the herbage of the park in 1663 stipulated that the tenant was to take care of the young trees, keep deer and rabbits out of the newly paled ground, and destroy the rabbits already in the park; Sir John agreed to reduce the number of deer to 90.[3] By the 1680s the trees had 'grown to a magnitude (for so many together) almost beyond belief' and formed two avenues leading from the house and aligned on Whittington and Tamworth churches.[4] In 1747 the area of the park was 450 a.[5] Samuel Hill and Samuel Egerton enlarged it in 1757 and 1758, evidently to the north-east, and erected a new pale.[6] Lancelot Brown appears to have made a survey in 1757.[7] The area of the park in 1760 was 571 a. Apart from the avenues the main features were then a small lake north-west of the house, formed by damming Fisherwick brook, a large walled kitchen garden north of the lake, and kennels west of the garden.[8]

The public roads through the park were stopped up under an Act of 1766,[9] and Brown was then able to carry out landscaping. He removed the avenues and laid out two drives, one to a lodge at Hademore and the other to Tamworth Gate near Stubby Leas. He planted 10,000 trees, including oaks, elms, planes, and firs; in 1779 Lord Donegall received a medal for planting the greatest number of oaks that year, upwards of 25 a. Several clumps were formed, and a boundary plantation enclosing a ride was made along the south and east sides of the park. A new park of 105 a. extending into Whittington parish was created north of the lake; it too was given a plantation with a ride, and an orangery was built on the high ground above the Tame.[10] The dam supporting the lake was raised so that the lake was lengthened, and towards its west end a five-arched stone bridge was built carrying the approach to the house from Lucas (later Dog Kennel) Lodge on the north-east of the park. Below the dam, on which there was a cascade, a new lake was formed extending to the Tame. On either side of the upper lake there were lawns and shrubberies, partly enclosed by a haha which ran north to the orangery and south to the area by the house;[11] access to the house from the lawn in front was by a tunnel under the carriage road. On the north side of the lake, adjoining the kitchen garden, was a 'ladies' botanical garden' with a Chinese pavilion. Marquees were often erected near the lower lake 'for rustic entertainments'. Spaniels and otter hounds were kept in the kennels. By 1776 there was a new home farm in the valley at the western edge of the main park with a icehouse to the north-east. A deer cot and barn were built where a circle of trees had stood in the centre of the former south-eastern avenue. Jenny's Lodge, consisting of a pair of lodge houses, was erected at the point where that avenue had met the park boundary. It was intended to build a brick wall round the whole park, but only about a mile of it was completed, on the south-east.

By 1808 a scheme had been prepared by J. B. Papworth for reducing the house to 'a residence on a moderate scale' by the retention of the eastern part only.[12] It was not carried out, and R. B. Howard had the house demolished. The sale of materials and fittings had begun by the spring of 1814 and culminated in a four-day sale in May 1816. The portico was sold to 'the architect of Lord Anson', and in 1823 it was erected at the George hotel in Walsall, where it remained until the demolition of the hotel in 1934.[13]

The parks were divided into fields, and there was extensive felling. The boundary plantation and ride in the main park still existed in 1842. The southern end survived as Hademore Belt until the Second World War when most of the timber was cut, the rest being cleared in the late 1940s. The enclosing wall on the south-east still stands, and part of the plantation in the northern park remains. The upper lake was drained, although the earth dam survives. Much of the bed of the lake became woodland, along with much of the silted-up lower lake and the surrounding lawns and shrubberies.[14] The outbuildings of the hall were converted into Fisherwick Hall Farm; the main approach is along the road from Dog Kennel Lodge, and the stone bridge survives to carry it over Fisherwick brook. The kitchen garden with its gardener's house are part of Woodhouse farm, with the orangery turned into a cowshed. The icehouse

[98] Fisherwick Park sale cat. n.d. [1808], pp. 3, 5.
[99] Ibid. p. 3; W.S.L., M. 761/8/2.
[1] N.R.A., Massereene (Staffs.) deeds, no. 36(b).
[2] W.S.L., S. MS. 339 (vi), p. 25.
[3] S.R.O., D. 948/4/5/3.
[4] Plot, Staffs. 209–10 and map; W.S.L. 114/31; W.S.L., S. MS. 454, no. 22.
[5] Aris's Birmingham Gaz. 23 Nov. 1747.
[6] Shaw, Staffs. i. 368; B.R.L., Elford Hall MSS. nos. 628, 935.
[7] J.R.U.L.M., Egerton of Tatton corresp. 2/1/62 and 64 (refs. kindly supplied by Dr. K. M. Goodway of Keele Univ.).
[8] W.S.L. 114/31; Fisherwick Park sale cat. n.d. [1808], pp. 4, 6, and plan between pp. 6 and 7.
[9] Above, introduction. The rest of this para. is based on Companion to the Leasowes, 117-28; W. Marshall, On Planting and Rural Ornament (1803), 305–13; Shaw, Staffs. i. 370; W.S.L., M. 761/8/2; Fisherwick Park sale cat. n.d. [1808],

pp. 4–7 and plan between pp. 6 and 7; S.R.O., D. 661/8/1/3/10; above, plate 47.
[10] For a plan of the orangery dated 1900 see B.R.L., Elford Hall MSS., misc. plans no. 21.
[11] The moated site shown south of the site of the hall on O.S. Map 6″, Staffs. LIII. SW. (1885 edn.) and recorded in V.C.H. Staffs. i. 363, is in fact the remains of the haha.
[12] Fisherwick Park sale cat. 1808, pl. between pp. 8 and 9 and plans between pp. 10 and 11; W. Papworth, John B. Papworth (priv. print. 1879) 21 (ref. kindly supplied by Mr. H. M. Colvin). There is mention of a 'Fisherwick curiosity sale' on 24 Feb. 1800 in the Revd. Henry White's diary: Guildhall Libr., London, MS. H 9.4, no 16.
[13] B.R.L., Elford Hall MSS. no. 819; Gent. Mag. lxxxvi (2), 76 (ref. supplied by Mr. Colvin).
[14] B.L. Maps, O.S.D. 258; C. and J. Greenwood, Map of County of Stafford (1820); L.J.R.O., B/A/15/Fisherwick; B.R.L., Elford Hall MSS. no. 762; inf. from Mr. A. G. Ward.

was demolished *c.* 1980.[15] The eastern lodge house of Jenny's Lodge survives as part of Fisherwick Park Farm, in existence by 1820.[16] Dog Kennel Lodge too has been incorporated into a dwelling house. Hademore Lodge, which was occupied by an agricultural labourer and his family in 1871, was a ruin by 1881,[17] and only the gate piers remain. Copes Lodge, which stands on the site of Tamworth Gate on the east side of the park, was evidently built soon after the sale of 1808.[18]

Fisherwick Hall Farm was bought from the White family *c.* 1930 by Nathan Buxton, who let it to M. H. Meddings. From 1938 the tenants were Buxton's daughter Jessie and her husband John Leese, who eventually became the owners. Their son Mr. T. E. Leese sold it in 1986 to Mr. J. A. Holgate.[19] The Home farm, which became Fisherwick Dairy farm, was still part of the Fisherwick estate in 1842 but was later owned by S. L. Seckham of Beacon Place, Lichfield, and Whittington Old Hall (d. 1901) and his son B. T. Seckham (d. 1925). In 1945 it was sold by Alice Seckham to J. E. and P. Bostock, from whom it passed to the Leese family *c.* 1960. It was sold by Mr. Leese to Robina Properties in 1988.[20]

In 1086 *TIMMOR* was a member of the bishop of Chester's manor of Lichfield (later Longdon) and so continued until at least 1739.[21] It was held of the bishop by Ranulf in 1086.[22] By 1135 it formed part of 1 knight's fee with Freeford and with Fradswell, in Colwich.[23] In 1166 William of Timmor held the fee.[24] He was succeeded by Simon the clerk (also known as *le sage* and *sapiens*) of Lichfield, who seems to have ousted William by judicial combat in 1167–8.[25] He was dead by 1183.[26] His heir was his daughter Parnel *la sage* (also *sapiens*), who married Godard of Timmor and survived him.[27] She was still living in 1240 but had been succeeded by their son William of Timmor apparently by 1241.[28] William was succeeded by his son Hugh between 1263 and 1267.[29] Hugh died between 1290 and 1293 with a son William as his heir.[30] William of Timmor was coroner in 1328, but that year the sheriff was ordered to have a

replacement elected because William was incapacitated by age.[31] His son John had succeeded to Timmor by 1341 and probably by 1333.[32] He is likely to have been the John of Timmor who was a collector of the subsidy in Staffordshire in 1352; he may still have been living in 1373.[33]

The manor passed into the Heronville family of Wednesbury by the marriage of John of Timmor's daughter Alice to John Heronville.[34] Their son Henry, who succeeded his father as lord of Wednesbury in 1403, was already lord of Timmor in 1392 and probably by 1379.[35] He died in 1406 leaving three infant daughters as his heirs, and Timmor passed to his widow Margaret for life.[36] By 1415 the daughters' guardian was John Leventhorp, a member of the royal household, whose son William married Joan, one of the daughters.[37] The other two became nuns in 1419, and their shares passed to William and Joan.[38] William was still alive in 1435, but Joan was the wife of Henry Beaumont by 1439, when she and her new husband were given possession of the manor by the son of the survivor of Henry Heronville's trustees.[39] Again a widow by 1452,[40] Joan was succeeded by her son Sir Henry Beaumont, who was himself succeeded in 1471 by his son John, a minor.[41] In 1499 John leased the manor for 12 years to Thomas Comberford and David Rochford, a Lichfield mercer.[42] He died in 1502, with three infant daughters as his heirs.[43] By a partition of the inheritance in 1540–1 Timmor was allotted to Joan, the eldest daughter, and her husband William Babington.[44] Their son Anthony had succeeded by 1553 and lived until 1580.[45] His son Matthew, however, held the manor by 1577, and probably by 1571 when he owed suit at the Longdon court.[46] In 1578 he conveyed the manor to Samuel Stanley, who granted Anthony an annuity of £20 out of it in 1579.[47] Stanley conveyed the manor to Peter Rosse (or Roos) in 1581,[48] and in 1593 Rosse granted it to William Skeffington and his wife Elizabeth.[49] The manor then descended with the manor of Fisherwick, with which it was granted to Birmingham corporation in 1936.[50]

The Timmor family presumably had a house

[15] Inf. from Mrs. L. Shiel of Fisherwick Dairy Farm.
[16] Below, econ. hist.
[17] P.R.O., RG 10/2915; RG 11/2774.
[18] It is not on the plan in Fisherwick Park sale cat. n.d. [1808], between pp. 6 and 7, but is shown on B.L. Maps, O.S.D. 258 (surv. 1815–17).
[19] Inf. from Mrs. Leese and Mr. Holgate; *Kelly's Dir. Staffs.* (1932; 1940).
[20] L.J.R.O., B/A/15/Fisherwick; S.R.O., D. 4566/D, will of S. L. Seckham and bdle. relating to Fisherwick Dairy Farm; inf. from Mrs. Leese and Mr. Holgate.
[21] S.R.O., D. (W.) 1734/2/1/750, p. 81.
[22] *V.C.H. Staffs.* iv. 43.
[23] *S.H.C.* i. 147.   [24] Ibid. 153.
[25] Ibid. 53–4, 56–7, 60, 78, 114; iii (1), 137, 170; viii (1), 167; Shaw, *Staffs.* i. 175.   [26] *S.H.C.* i. 114.
[27] Ibid. ii (1), 155; iii (1), 100; iv (1), 16; viii (1), 167–8.
[28] W.S.L., M. 520, p. 29; S.R.O., D. 661/2/505; Shaw, *Staffs.* i. 375; *Bk. of Fees*, ii. 955.
[29] *S.H.C.* iv (1), 156; N.R.A., Massereene (Staffs.) deeds, no. 5.
[30] N.R.A., Massereene (Staffs.) deeds, no. 6; *S.H.C.* vi (1), 256.   [31] *Cal. Close*, 1327–30, 253.
[32] *S.H.C.* x (1), 5, 16.
[33] *Cal. Fine R.* 1347–56, 376; *Cal. Pat.* 1364–7, 165; H. Sanders, *Hist. and Antiquities of Shenstone* (1794), 284; Bodl.

MS. Ashmole 855, p. 212.
[34] Erdeswick, *Staffs.* 451; *Cal. Pat.* 1364–7, 165.
[35] *S.H.C.* xiii. 152; xv. 10, 19; N.R.A., Massereene (Staffs.) deeds, nos. 16–18.
[36] J. F. Ede, *Hist. of Wednesbury* (Wednesbury, 1962), 44; N.R.A., Massereene (Staffs.) deeds, no. 20.
[37] Ede, *Wednesbury*, 49.
[38] *Cal. Fine R.* 1413–22, 330.
[39] N.R.A., Massereene (Staffs.) deeds, no. 21; Ede, *Wednesbury*, 50.
[40] *S.H.C.* xi. 247.
[41] Ede, *Wednesbury*, 50–1.
[42] N.R.A., Massereene (Staffs.) deeds, no. 22.
[43] *Cal. Inq. p.m. Hen. VII*, ii, pp. 370–1.
[44] Shaw, *Staffs.* i. 375.
[45] *S.H.C.* n.s. ix. 171; *S.H.C.* 1912, 194; *Collectanea Topographica et Genealogica*, viii. 335; B.R.L., Elford Hall MSS. no. 86; L.J.R.O., D 27/9/5.
[46] S.R.O., D. (W.) 1734/2/1/609, mm. 19, 22; D. (W.) 1734/2/1/612, m. 22; D. (W.) 1734/2/1/738, f. 4; *S.H.C.* xiii. 278.   [47] *S.H.C.* xiv (1), 200–1; W.S.L., M. 520, p. 37.
[48] *S.H.C.* xv. 135; Shaw, *Staffs.* i. 212.
[49] N.R.A., Massereene (Staffs) deeds, no. 39; *S.H.C.* xvi. 131.
[50] Shaw, *Staffs.* i. 375; Erdeswick, *Staffs.* 452 n.; W.S.L., M. 761/8/6; S.R.O. 1070.

at Timmor. William Babington was described as of Timmor in 1539, and he and his wife were probably living there by 1532.[51] Anthony had a house there in the early 1550s.[52] Samuel Stanley was living at Timmor in 1579.[53] The manor house was leased in 1581 to Michael Lowe, the son of a Lichfield mercer and the son-in-law of Simon Biddulph, another Lichfield mercer. A member of the Inner Temple and a chief clerk of King's Bench, Lowe divided his time between the Inner Temple and Timmor until his death in 1593 or 1594.[54] In 1594 William Skeffington leased his manor house and farm called Timmor to Bartholomew Farmer for 10 years.[55] At the end of the 18th century the site of the house was stated to be a moated site 'on the right side of the road between Whittington and Elford, opposite to Fisherwick Park'.[56] That site is no longer identifiable.

TAMHORN was a member of the bishop's manor of Lichfield (later Longdon) in 1086. Assessed as 1 hide *c.* 1255, it continued as a member of Longdon manor until at least the mid 19th century.[57] A chief rent of £1 8s. 8d. was still payable to the lord of Longdon in 1827.[58]

In 1086 Tamhorn was held of the bishop by Nigel de Stafford.[59] A mesne lordship was held in 1166 by Richard de Gresley, probably Nigel's grandson.[60] It remained in the Gresley family until at least 1421.[61]

The terre tenant in 1166 was Robert of Tamhorn,[62] and a man of that name was still active in local administration in 1203.[63] He was probably succeeded soon afterwards by John of Tamhorn, who held ¼ knight's fee in 1242–3.[64] John appears to have been succeeded by Thomas of Tamhorn, who was mentioned several times between 1246 and 1279 and was a verderer of Cannock forest in 1262 and 1271.[65] Thomas's son William, a verderer in 1286, held the ¼ fee in Tamhorn in 1284–5 and was probably the William of Tamhorn living in 1305.[66] His son William was mentioned from 1306 and was probably the William of Tamhorn who was assessed for tax in 1333.[67] Thomas, son of William of Tamhorn, was lord of the manor by

1337[68] and died between 1347 and 1350.[69] He divided the manor in his lifetime, granting two thirds to his elder son William and a third to the younger son Thomas. William evidently predeceased his father since the younger Thomas was described as the elder Thomas's heir in 1350. He was still a minor in 1362 but was of age in 1363.[70] Knighted by 1377, he was M.P. for Staffordshire in that year and 1382 and was sheriff in 1380.[71] In 1399 he and his wife Alice granted the reversion of the manor, should they have no children, to Sir Adam de Peshale of Weston under Lizard.[72] Sir Adam granted the reversion to his daughter Margaret and her husband Richard (later Sir Richard) Mutton in 1406, the Tamhorns' interest being then described as a life interest.[73] Sir Thomas Tamhorn died probably in 1416 or 1417, and Tamhorn passed to the Muttons.[74]

Sir Richard Mutton died in 1418 and Margaret in 1420; their heir was their son William, who came of age in 1436.[75] He died in 1495 or 1496, and Tamhorn passed to his son John, who died in 1500, leaving a life interest in the manor to his cousin Joyce Jake.[76] The Mutton family, which became known as Mytton in the earlier 15th century, had estates elsewhere in Staffordshire, including Weston under Lizard with which Tamhorn descended until 1763. On the division that year of the estates of the earl of Bradford (d. 1762), Tamhorn was assigned to his sister Diana Coote, countess of Mountrath. On her death in 1766 it passed under her will to Lionel Damer, a younger son of Joseph, Baron Milton and later earl of Dorchester, and on Lionel's death in 1807 to his sister Lady Caroline Damer. In 1818 she conveyed the manor in return for an annuity to Lord George Cavendish, the remainder man.[77] He sold the manor and its 713 a. in 1827 to Robert (from 1830 Sir Robert) Peel.[78]

Tamhorn then descended with the Peel baronetcy. Tamhorn Park farm was sold in 1921 to W. J. S. Hughes. It later passed to N. F. Budgen, who sold it in 1949 to H. F. Deakin. In 1964 Deakin sold it to Hoveringham Gravels Ltd., but he continued as tenant jointly with his

[51] B.R.L., Elford Hall MSS. no. 69; below (Merevale abbey estate).
[52] *S.H.C.* 1912, 192.
[53] W.S.L., M. 520, p. 37.
[54] *S.H.C.* xv. 138; Shaw, *Staffs.* i. 375; *Cal. Inner Temple Rec.* ed. F. A. Inderwick, i. 371, 395; N.R.A., Massereene (Staffs.) deeds, no. 39; P.R.O., PROB 11/83, ff. 148v.–155; L.J.R.O., D. 20/1/1, burial of Margt. w. of Mic. Lowe of Timmor, 1 Apr. 1584; above, Lichfield, econ. hist. (professions); chars. for poor.
[55] W.S.L., M. 520, p. 38.
[56] Shaw, *Staffs.* i. 375.
[57] Ibid. 212 and app. to Gen. Hist. p. xvi; S.R.O., D. (W.) 1746/E67, E72–3; B.R.L., Elford Hall MSS. nos. 712, 767, 945; W.S.L. 11/522/32/50, deposition of Peter Birch.
[58] Tamhorn sale cat. 1827, p. 4 (copy in S.R.O., D.(W.) 1746/E55).
[59] *V.C.H. Staffs.* iv. 35, 43.
[60] *S.H.C.* N.S. i. 26–7, 29–30.
[61] *S.H.C.* xii (1), 98–9; S.R.O., D. (W.) 1734/J. 2268, f. iv.; P.R.O., C 138/51, no. 98.
[62] *S.H.C.* i. 42, 147, 156; iii (1), 186.
[63] Ibid. iii (1), 54, 72, 100, 104–6, 109.
[64] *S.H.C.* 1939, 88, 105; *Bk. of Fees*, ii. 968.
[65] *S.H.C.* iv (1), 151, 215; v (1), 136, 145; vi (1), 140.
[66] *Bk. of Fees*, v. 7; *S.H.C.* v (1), 160, 163; Shaw, *Staffs.* i.

162; S.R.O., D. 661/2/472; D. 661/2/512; D. 661/2/588; S.R.O., D. (W.) 1734/J. 2268, f. iv. In 1284–5 he was called William of Handsacre; like John of Tamhorn before him, he then held ¼ fee in Handsacre.
[67] *S.H.C.* vii (1), 145, 233; ix (1), 4–5, 8; x (1), 105; xi. 128; *S.H.C.* 1939, 108; S.R.O., D. 661/1/583.
[68] *S.H.C.* xi. 75, 161; *S.H.C.* 1939, 119.
[69] *S.H.C.* xi. 161; xii (1), 98–9.
[70] Ibid. xii (1), 98–9; xiii. 22; *Cal. Inq. p.m.* xi, p. 390; *Cal. Close*, 1360–4, 505.
[71] *S.H.C.* 1917–18, 123; 1939, 123.
[72] *S.H.C.* ii. 204.
[73] Ibid. 215; ibid. N.S. ii. 93.
[74] P.R.O., C 138/51, no. 98. The date of death is not legible, but a transcript (W.S.L. 81/12/49) implies 1420; Erdeswick, *Staffs.* 450, gives 4 Hen. V (1416–17). In 1418 he was presented for not attending the Longdon view of frankpledge: S.R.O., D. (W.) 1734/2/1/601, mm. 15, 17.
[75] *S.H.C.* N.S. ii. 117–18.
[76] Ibid. 119–24; S.R.O., D. (W.) 1734/2/1/604, mm. 15, 24d.
[77] *V.C.H. Staffs.* iv. 172–3; v. 156; xvii. 170; xx. 67–8; *S.H.C.* iv (2), 95–6; ibid. N.S. ii. 135, 137, 144, 267–8; S.R.O., D. 661/11/2/3/1/11, 18 Mar. 1816; D. (W.) 1746/E41, T10–11.
[78] S.R.O, D. (W.) 1746/E43–4, E89, T11–14.

son D. F. Deakin. In 1980 the firm, by then Hoveringham Group Ltd., sold 470 a. to CIN Industrial Investments Ltd. and the farmhouse with 11 a. to Mr. and Mrs. D. V. Adams. An area of 84 a. in the west was acquired by the Ministry of Defence, having for a long time formed part of the danger area of the rifle ranges at Whittington barracks.[79]

The Tamhorn family presumably had a house at Tamhorn. A house was part of the manor in 1500,[80] and by the late 16th century it was the home of the Astley family. Walter Astley was Edmund Mytton's bailiff at Tamhorn from c. 1590 and was still living there as bailiff in 1605.[81] He was presumably the Walter Astley who was tithingman for Tamhorn by 1603 and continued in the office from year to year until at least 1642.[82] In 1657 the manor house was still held by a Walter Astley, and he or another Walter Astley was assessed on seven hearths there in 1666.[83] A Walter Astley who died in 1710 conveyed the house in 1690 to his son Matthias, and in 1692 Matthias paid £95 1s. 9d. as six months' rent for the manor.[84] He was succeeded in 1725 by a younger son Arthur, who died in 1742 or 1743 with an infant son Matthias as his heir. Matthias was succeeded in 1751 by his uncle Christopher Astley, who was already living at Tamhorn and continued there until his death in 1780.[85] His daughter and heir Mary married her cousin Richard Dyott in 1783.[86] Dyott went to live at Tamhorn, and although he moved to Freeford in 1784, he renewed his lease of the Tamhorn estate in 1785 and 1807 and continued to farm there.[87] On his death in 1813 the lease passed to his brother Gen. William Dyott, who moved to Tamhorn from Lichfield in 1815. Although he soon sublet the farm, he retained the house until 1817.[88] He believed that it was as a result of his persuasion that Peel bought the Tamhorn estate.[89]

The present house, known as Tamhorn Park Farm, dates from the early 18th century and was built as an L-shaped structure with a south entrance front of five bays. In the mid 18th century it was enlarged by a block which squared off the existing house and projects to the east and south; remains of a dovecot are visible on the west side. A large 17th-century barn stands to the south-west. It was originally timber framed, but the walls have been rebuilt in brick, with the east gable in stone.

By c. 1255 *HORTON* was a member of Longdon manor, assessed jointly with Fisherwick as 1 hide.[90] The estate was still part of Longdon manor in 1739.[91]

In 1298 Horton was held of the bishop by William of Tamhorn,[92] and it descended with Tamhorn until the earlier 16th century, being described as a manor in 1496.[93] It was probably the messuage and virgate held of Sir Thomas Tamhorn for life by Henry atte Pole in 1411–12; by 1500 the manor consisted of two messuages and land in Horton.[94] In the earlier 15th century Elizabeth Beauchamp, Baroness Bergavenny, had some interest in Horton: in 1426 and from 1433 to 1435 she was presented by the Horton frankpledge for failing to appear at the Longdon court.[95]

In 1527 John Mytton evidently mortgaged or sold Horton to John Champeneys, from whom it passed to Richard Weston of Brereton, in Rugeley.[96] Richard's son John held it in 1547.[97] In 1560 John Weston's son Richard and his wife conveyed two messuages and land in Horton and its neighbourhood to Thomas Allen, and in 1563 Allen sold two capital messuages in Horton to John Chatterton of Lichfield.[98] The Chatterton family was living in Horton by 1502.[99] John's father William was bailiff to John Mytton, who leased Horton to him. John Chatterton was living there by 1539, and he was bailiff at Tamhorn to Mytton's grandson and heir Edward Mytton and then to Edward's son John until they quarrelled.[1] John Chatterton granted a moiety of Horton to his son Humphrey 'for his preferment in marriage'. In 1589 Humphrey leased the moiety, consisting of a capital messuage and land, to John Skeffington, lord of Fisherwick, for six years; at the same time Humphrey and his wife, with John Chatterton and his wife, mortgaged the house and land to Skeffington's son William.[2] In 1650 the Skeffington estate included a capital messuage and land in Horton.[3] The manor of Horton descended with Fisherwick and was included in F. E. H. Paget's gift to Birmingham corporation in 1936.[4]

[79] Peel Settled Estates sale cat. p. 17 (copy in B.R.L., Elford Hall MSS. no. 1274); letter of 16 May 1918 loose in B.R.L. copy of sale cat.; inf. supplied by Mr. G. J. Dunham, CIN Agricultural Services Ltd.; inf. from Mrs. Adams.
[80] *S.H.C.* xiii. 274; ibid. N.S. ii. 123, 125.
[81] P.R.O., E 134/3 Jas. I Hil./3 and 4.
[82] S.R.O., D. (W.) 1734/2/1/613, mm. 2 sqq.; D. (W.) 1734/2/1/734.
[83] B.R.L., Elford Hall MSS. no. 297; *S.H.C.* 1923, 225.
[84] S.R.O., D. (W.) 1746/T7; D. 4280/D/4, loose sheet; Shaw, *Staffs.* i. 378.
[85] Shaw, *Staffs.* i. 378–9; S.R.O., D. 661/6/1/24, pedigree; D. (W.) 1734/2/1/750, pp. 136–7; D. (W.) 1734/2/1/751, pp. 24–5, 134, 138; D. (W.) 1734/2/1/752, p. 315; L.J.R.O., B/V/7/Whittington, burial of 7 June 1751; B.R.L., Elford Hall MSS. no. 604.
[86] Burke, *Land. Gent.* (1871), i. 383; Jackson, *Lichfield*, 239.
[87] S.R.O., D. 1042/2, f. 64v. and p. 84; D. (W.) 1746/E1, T9; below, Freeford, manor.
[88] S.R.O., D. (W.) 1746/E7, E95, E99; B.R.L., Elford Hall MSS. no. 819; *Dyott's Diary*, ed. R. W. Jeffery, i. 312, 316; ii. 6; S.R.O., D. 661/11/2/3/1/11, 24 Feb. 1815, May 1815, 18 Mar. 1816; below, econ. hist. (hunting, shooting, and fishing).

[89] *Dyott's Diary*, ii. 10–11.
[90] Above (Fisherwick manor).
[91] *S.H.C.* vi (1), 244; S.R.O., D. (W.) 1734/2/1/750, p. 81.
[92] S.R.O., D. (W.) 1734/J. 2268, f. 1v.
[93] Ibid. D. (W.) 1734/2/1/604, m. 15.
[94] N.R.A., Massereene (Staffs.) deeds, no. 28; *S.H.C.* N.S. ii. 123.
[95] S.R.O., D. (W.) 1734/2/1/602, mm. 7, 23–4, 26–7, 29; *Complete Peerage*, ii. 27–9.
[96] *S.H.C.* xi. 267; ibid. N.S. ii. 126–8; *V.C.H. Staffs.* v. 156; P.R.O., E 134/3 Jas. I East./19.
[97] *S.H.C.* xii (1), 199.
[98] Ibid. xiii. 210; N.R.A., Massereene (Staffs.) deeds, no. 31.
[99] S.R.O., D. (W.) 1734/2/1/604, mm. 31 sqq.
[1] Ibid. D. (W.) 1734/2/1/607, m. 4; D. (W.) 1734/2/1/608, m. 2; D. (W.) 1734/2/1/609, mm. 1, 6d.; B.R.L., Elford Hall MSS. nos. 70, 86; P.R.O., E 134/3 Jas. I East./19.
[2] N.R.A., Massereene (Staffs.) deeds, no. 36; P.R.O., E 134/3 Jas. I East./19.
[3] W.S.L., S. MS. 339 (transcripts of royalist composition papers), vi, p. 25.
[4] S.R.O. 1070.

The great and small tithes of Fisherwick and Timmor were divided between the prebendaries of Stotfold and Freeford in Lichfield cathedral. In 1694 the small tithes were granted by Bishop Lloyd to the vicar of St. Mary's, Lichfield. In 1842 Stotfold held those of 1,133 a., Freeford's being limited to 130 a. in the Hademore area. The dean and chapter became the appropriators of the Stotfold tithes in 1803. Freeford prebend was suspended under the Cathedrals Act of 1840 and its tithes were appropriated to the Ecclesiastical Commissioners. In 1842 Stotfold's share was commuted for a rent charge of £284 17s. and Freeford's for one of £42 12s. 6d; the sums included £129 12s. and £11 10s. for the vicar of St. Mary's.[5] There was a tithe barn in Fisherwick in 1388.[6] The prebendary of Stotfold also held the tithes of Tamhorn and Horton. By the mid 17th century he received a customary modus of £1 6s. 8d. for Tamhorn, although the tithes were stated to be worth £12 a year; the modus was still paid in 1827.[7] For Horton the lord of Fisherwick was paying him a modus of £4 c. 1760.[8]

Parnel, the lady of Timmor, gave land there to Merevale abbey (Warws.), and in 1240 her son William confirmed the gift.[9] In 1532 the abbey granted an 80-year lease of its lands in Timmor to William Babington and his wife Mary; it was stipulated that the Babingtons had first to mark out the bounds.[10] In 1553 the estate, which included 6 a. of meadow, was sold by the Crown to two speculators. Three days later they resold it to Anthony Babington, lord of Timmor.[11]

By 1383 land in Timmor had been given for the maintenance of a light before a statue of Our Lady in Elford church. The land was known by then as St. Mary Hay.[12] After the abolition of such lights in 1545 the rent of 3s. 4d. was spent on the general needs of Elford church, but in 1549 the Crown sold the land, described as a close of pasture, to three speculators.[13] In 1594 it was owned by Robert Stamford of Perry Hall in Handsworth, who then agreed to sell it to William Skeffington of Fisherwick.[14]

ECONOMIC HISTORY. AGRICULTURE. The Iron Age settlements on the east side of the parish had hedged and ditched fields and specialized in livestock farming. The open land to the west was probably used for rough grazing,

forestry, and temporary cultivation.[15] The Romano-British farmstead in the north also specialized in stock farming.[16]

Fisherwick does not appear in Domesday Book, but Timmor had land for one ploughteam in 1086 and Tamhorn land for four.[17] Assarting was in progress by the late 13th century. 'New land' in the area in 1298 included 3 a. held by Nicholas Durdent, the lord of Fisherwick.[18] In 1306 there was land in Fisherwick called the Stockyng, a name suggesting an area of cleared woodland.[19]

The fields of Fisherwick were mentioned in 1306, and that year a quitclaim was made of nine selions in the Stockyng.[20] Grazing in the fallow fields of Fisherwick was mentioned in 1561.[21] There were probably two open fields on the south side of the park. In 1589 Fisherwick field there was described as lately turned into pasture and Tithe Barn field adjoining it on the west was described as pasture lately divided into two.[22] In Timmor the fallow and the sown fields were mentioned in the early 15th century.[23] Hademore field, one of the open fields of Whittington, evidently extended into Horton. In 1589 Humphrey Chatterton's Horton estate included 300 a. in the field.[24] In 1635 land called Horton Hademore was part of Sir William Skeffington's demesne, and in the 1640s what were called Hademore fields were part of his Horton estate.[25] In the 1840s Hademore farm had two fields called Tamhorn field and Lower Tamhorn field; they adjoined each other on the Fisherwick side of the boundary with Tamhorn and may once have been part of an open field, perhaps shared by Horton and Tamhorn.[26]

Inclosure of both arable and pasture was in progress in the later Middle Ages. In the late 14th century plots of land in the township of Fisherwick and Timmor were being held in severalty when they should have been common every third year.[27] Similarly in 1414 a croft in the township of Tamhorn and Horton was being held in severalty instead of being common and fallow every third year.[28] Land in Horton called the Bents should have been common from Michaelmas to Candlemas but was held in severalty in 1419.[29] In 1420 and 1421 the lord of Timmor was presented for holding a pasture called Dodsmore inclosed at all times of the year whereas by custom it should have been open from Michaelmas to Lady Day.[30] In 1455

[5] L.J.R.O., B/A/15/Fisherwick; V.C.H. Staffs. iii. 182, 190; above, Lichfield, churches (parochial organization from 1491).
[6] S.R.O., D. (W.) 1734/2/1/599, m. 15; below, econ. hist. (agric.: open fields).
[7] L.J.R.O., D. 30/LV, f. 79; S.R.O., D. (W.) 1746/E55, E79, E81.
[8] B.R.L., Elford Hall MSS. no. 935.
[9] W.S.L., M. 520, p. 29.
[10] N.R.A., Massereene (Staffs.) deeds, no. 26; Valor Eccl. (Rec. Com.), iii. 71.
[11] Cal. Pat. 1547-53, 91; W.S.L., M. 520, pp. 35-6; S.H.C. n.s. x (1), 120-1, 125-7; S.H.C. 1912, 133-4, 191-4; P.R.O., STAC 2/3, nos. 4-6.
[12] S.R.O., D. (W.) 1734/2/1/599, m. 4d.; D. (W.) 1734/2/1/600, m. 28.
[13] S.H.C. 1915, 94; Cal. Pat. 1549-51, 126.
[14] N.R.A., Massereene (Staffs.) deeds, no. 41.
[15] Fisherwick, ed. C. Smith (B.A.R. Brit. Ser. lxi, 1979), 94-103; Current Arch. lxxii (1980), 26-8.
[16] T.S.S.A.H.S. x. 11.
[17] V.C.H. Staffs. iv. 43.
[18] S.R.O., D. (W.) 1734/J. 2268, f. 2v.
[19] N.R.A., TS. list of Massereene (Staffs.) deeds, no. 7; Eng. Place-Name Elements (E.P.N.S.), ii. 156.
[20] S.H.C. vii (1), 161; N.R.A., Massereene (Staffs.) deeds, no. 7.
[21] Below (this section).
[22] N.R.A., Massereene (Staffs.) deeds, no. 36(b).
[23] Ibid. no. 28.
[24] Ibid. no. 36(b). For Whittington's fields see e.g. S.R.O., D. 1124/4.
[25] S.R.O., D. 661/21/1/1, f. 73v.; W.S.L., S. MS. 339, vi, p. 25.
[26] L.J.R.O., B/A/15/Fisherwick, nos. 71-2; W.S.L., M. 761/9; Fisherwick Park sale cat. n.d. [1808], p. 9 and plan between pp. 6 and 7 (copy in W.S.L. 115/6/41).
[27] S.R.O., D. (W.) 1734/2/1/599, mm. 15, 44.
[28] Ibid. D. (W.) 1734/2/1/601, m. 5.
[29] Ibid. m. 20d.
[30] Ibid. mm. 21-2.

Richard Libbere of Timmor was presented for holding a field there in severalty which should have lain open that year.[31] A presentment was made in 1513 of the inclosure of common at Tymhey in Tamhorn.[32] In the middle of the 16th century a group from Fisherwick broke into nine closes belonging to Anthony Babington, the lord of Timmor, and pastured their cattle there.[33]

The process of inclosure was probably by then connected with the growth of sheep farming. In 1561 the Longdon court fixed the stint for sheep on the waste and fallow fields of Fisherwick at 20.[34] Stock farming and dairy farming were evidently important in the 17th century. The security given by Sir John Skeffington for his debts in 1641 included 8 oxen worth £50, 20 milch cows worth £80, 18 calves worth £36, 28 bullocks and heifers worth £98, and 174 sheep worth £73.[35] A John Smith had a dairy farm at Timmor at his death in 1675. There were 24 head of cattle worth £50, and his goods included churns, milk pans, butter pots, and cheese-making equipment. He was also growing blendcorn (mixed wheat and rye).[36] His farm was probably Stubby Leas, the only farm in that part of Fisherwick township in 1760. There were then two other farms in the township, the home farm attached to the hall and Hademore farm.[37] In 1753 there were horses, cattle, and sheep on the 111-a. home farm, with a herdsman paid £14 a year.[38]

Lord Donegall was a keen farmer. A new home farm had been built in the valley south-west of the hall by 1776 when Lancelot Brown contracted to build a barn there. The buildings enclose a large courtyard with the house in the north-west corner; the barn in the main east-west range has pediments over the central door-ways. Lord Donegall had apartments fitted up at the farm in which he normally breakfasted when at Fisherwick in the summer. He bred Long-horns and oxen on the farm and kept horses in the park.[39] In 1804 the stock at the farm included 30 dairy cows, Leicester sheep, and some 50 horses, among them racehorses.[40]

By 1842 there were eight farms in Fisherwick, five of them part of the Fisherwick estate. The home farm, known as Dairy farm by 1841, covered 112 a. and Stubby Leas 319 a.; Hade-more farm, owned by Sir Robert Peel, covered 118 a.[41] New farms had been created after the break-up of the Fisherwick estate. Jenny's Lodge farm had been formed out of much of the parkland by 1820, with one of Brown's lodge houses as part of the two-storey brick farm-house; it was 187 a. in extent in 1842 and belonged to Sir Robert Peel. The name, still in use in 1861, had been changed to Fisherwick Park farm by 1870, when the farm was adver-tised for letting as a 229-a. turnip and sheep farm. In 1881 it had a steam threshing mach-ine.[42] The outbuildings of the hall had by 1834 been converted into the buildings of a farm known as Old Hall farm by 1842 and Fisherwick Hall farm by 1871; it too covered part of the former park and was 245 a. in extent in 1842.[43] By 1834 there was a farm straddling the north-western boundary of the township, with 42 a. in Whittington in 1837 and 86 a. in Fisherwick in 1842; centring on an 18th-century house on the Fisherwick side of the boundary, it was known as Grove farm by 1861.[44] By 1842 the area of the former kitchen garden and botanical garden, together with adjoining land and the gardener's house, was occupied as a 12-a. holding, known as Woodhouse farm by 1861.[45] Bents farm in the south-west corner of the township existed by 1841; it belonged to Charles Neville and was 11 a. in area. It was offered for sale in 1877, and in 1881 the house was unoccupied.[46] The chief crops of the township by the later 1860s were turnips and barley.[47]

About 1680 Walter Astley, the tenant of Tam-horn, was noted for his system of under-drain-ing which used trenches lined with pebbles, filled with faggots, and covered with soil.[48] Richard Dyott, tenant from 1783, became noted for his cultivation of turnips and barley at Tamhorn; he also grew oats and wheat. He sheared 463 sheep there in 1792 and had a flock of 538 in 1813. He also kept cattle and pigs.[49] In 1822 the tenant, John Holmes, was growing barley, wheat, and oats; turnips, cabbages, and peas were mentioned as well in 1827.[50] In 1828 he put up for sale Leicester sheep, cattle includ-ing dairy cows, pigs, and bloodstock; the imple-ments for sale included a six horse-power threshing machine which had been in constant use for fifteen years.[51] The farm was greatly improved in the late 1840s by drainage schemes carried out by Sir Robert Peel.[52] It was adver-tised for letting in 1862 as a turnip and sheep farm.[53] Stock offered for sale in 1892 consisted

[31] Ibid. D. (W.) 1734/2/1/603, m. 48.
[32] Ibid. D. (W.) 1734/2/1/605, m. 3.
[33] *S.H.C.* 1912, 194.
[34] S.R.O., D. (W.) 1734/2/1/609, m. 4d.
[35] N.R.A., Massereene (Staffs.) deeds, no. 52.
[36] *S.H.C.* 4th ser. v, pp. 21, 239–40.
[37] Above, fig. 1; W.S.L. 114/31; B.R.L., Elford Hall MSS. no. 607, p. 1.
[38] B.R.L., Elford Hall MSS. no. 608, p.1.
[39] *Companion to the Leasowes, Hagley, and Enville, with a sketch of Fisherwick* (1789), 118–19; Shaw, *Staffs.* i. 371; W.S.L., M. 761/8/2.
[40] *Staffs. Advertiser,* 7 July 1804.
[41] L.J.R.O., B/A/15/Fisherwick; P.R.O., HO 107/976.
[42] Fisherwick Park sale cat. 1808, pp. 12, 16 (copy in S.R.O, D. 661/19/10/18); B.L. Maps, O.S.D. 258; C. and J. Greenwood, *Map of County of Stafford* (1820); L.J.R.O., B/A/15/Fisherwick; P.R.O., RG 9/1974; RG 10/2915; RG 11/2774; *Staffs. Advertiser,* 5 Mar. 1870, p. 1.
[43] White, *Dir. Staffs.* (1834), 106; L.J.R.O., B/A/15/

Fisherwick; P.R.O., RG 10/2925.
[44] Fisherwick Park sale cat. n.d. [1808], p. 6 and plan between pp. 6 and 7; L.J.R.O., B/A/15/Fisherwick; ibid. Whittington; P.R.O., RG 9/1974; White, *Dir. Staffs.* (1834), 106.
[45] Fisherwick Park sale cat. n.d. [1808], p. 6 and plan between pp. 6 and 7; L.J.R.O., B/A/15/Fisherwick, nos. 9–11; P.R.O., RG 9/1974.
[46] Fisherwick Park sale cat. n.d. [1808], plan between pp. 6 and 7; L.J.R.O., B/A/15/Fisherwick, nos. 54–61; S.R.O., D. (W.) 1746/T20; P.R.O., HO 107/976; ibid. RG 11/2774; *Staffs. Advertiser,* 14 Apr. 1877, p. 1.
[47] *P.O. Dir. Staffs.* (1868).
[48] *V.C.H. Staffs.* vi. 70.
[49] Pitt, *Staffs.* i. 131; S.R.O., D. 661/8/1/3/7.
[50] S.R.O., D. 661/8/1/2/4; Tamhorn Estate sale cat. 1827, p. 4 (copy in S.R.O., D. (W.) 1746/E55).
[51] S.R.O., D. 603/F/3/25/9.
[52] N. Gash, *Sir Robert Peel,* 680–2.
[53] *Staffs. Advertiser,* 20 Dec. 1862, p. 8.

of 695 Shropshire sheep, 89 beasts, and 73 Tamworth pigs.[54] When the farm was sold in 1980 the main crop was barley but some wheat and oats were also grown; only 8 a. were under grass.[55]

Farming in the north-east part of the parish was curtailed by the sand and gravel working which began in 1967.[56] In 1984 five holdings were officially recorded for the parish, together covering 383 ha. (944 a.). One was involved in general cropping, another concentrated on cereals, and a third specialized in pigs and poultry, mainly turkeys; the other two holdings were farmed part-time. The chief crops were barley (178.2 ha.), wheat (99.7 ha.), and sugar beet (40.6 ha.).[57]

Meadowland along the Tame was recorded from the 13th century.[58] There were several dole meadows. Town meadow, mentioned in 1600 and 1753, lay in the north-east of Fisherwick.[59] Goodman's meadow in Timmor south of Elford mill was recorded from 1571 and was shared by Timmor and Whittington.[60] It was still an open meadow in 1823, but by 1842 it belonged to the overseers of Elford and F. G. Howard, owner of the Fisherwick estate, and was leased to the tenant of Stubby Leas farm.[61] Dodsmore meadow, mentioned from the 15th century, was common to Timmor, Tamhorn, and Whittington.[62] Horton too probably had a share, but by the late 16th century Horton Dodsmore, also known as Horton meadow, was held in severalty.[63] Dodsmore survived as a dole meadow into the 20th century. In 1917 there were 16 doles, of which 6½ belonged to Hademore farm, 5½ to the Green farm in Whittington, 1 to Tamhorn Park farm, 2 to Fisherwick Hall farm, and 1 to Manor farm in Harlaston.[64] In 1753 the Tamhorn estate had a dole in Upper Meadow on the Fisherwick estate.[65]

HUNTING, SHOOTING, AND FISHING. In 1344 Roger Hillary was granted free warren in his demesne lands, including Fisherwick and Horton.[66] In 1402 a group of men were accused of breaking into the warren at Fisherwick and taking hares, rabbits, pheasants, and partridges.[67]

In 1311 the lords of Hints, Freeford, Timmor, and Fisherwick quitclaimed to William of Tamhorn all rights in his wood called Tamhorn wood. The transaction was subject to an agreement by which William granted the lord of Freeford right of estover. It was also recognized that both had hunting rights in the wood and that William had the right to inclose the wood provided that wild animals could pass through.[68] In 1405 Sir Adam de Peshale sued the rector of Elford for breaking into his park at Tamhorn and cutting timber there.[69] Tamhorn park, 87 a. in area in 1763 and 98 a. in 1798, was known as Park wood in 1827 when it covered just over 97 a. in the Tamhorn portion of Hopwas Hays wood.[70] There was 'a vast quantity of pheasants' on the Tamhorn estate at the beginning of the 19th century, and Richard Dyott had a keeper there.[71] When Gen. Dyott left Tamhorn in 1817, he retained the shooting rights and often returned to shoot. In September 1824 Robert Peel and his brother William were the general's guests for a day's shooting at Tamhorn.[72] In 1824 John Holmes, the tenant, sent the general an estimate of damage done to his crops by game amounting to £293 8s. 8d.; he added that he said 'nothing for the loss of straw nor of the injury the land is sustaining by being fruitless'.[73] Peel too retained the shooting rights when he leased the estate.[74] The 71 a. of woodland on Tamhorn Park farm in 1918 formed a sporting estate; 59 a. lay in Tamhorn wood.[75]

As the name Fisherwick indicates, the fishing of the Tame was a feature of the life of the area from early times. Nicholas the fisher had land at Timmor in the earlier 13th century, and Henry the fisher lived at Fisherwick in the latter part of the century.[76] The manors of Fisherwick and Timmor each had a fishery attached.[77] In the earlier 13th century Parnel, the lady of Timmor, and Sir William Vernon of Harlaston, in Clifton Campville, acknowledged each other's fishing rights in the Tame between St. Edith's holm in Wigginton, in Tamworth, and Timmor mill.[78] In 1600 William Skeffington of Fisherwick and Sir John Bowes of Elford were disputing fishing and riparian rights. The matter was settled by arbitrators, who awarded to each fishing rights in separate stretches of the river; each was also given the right to water cattle and to fence his bank.[79] About 1760 the Fisherwick estate had an upper and a lower fishery, the first of which was

[54] Lichfield Mercury, 12 Feb. 1892, p. 4.
[55] Inf. from Mr. G. J. Dunham, CIN Agricultural Services Ltd.
[56] Above, introduction; below (industries).
[57] M.A.F.F., agric. returns 1984.
[58] e.g. Shaw, Staffs. i. 375; S.H.C. 1924, p. 53; S.R.O., D. 661/1/585-6, 588; D. 661/2/348 and 494.
[59] B.R.L., Elford Hall MSS. nos. 151, 607.
[60] W.S.L., S. MS. 326/2; W.S.L., M. 761/7; W.S.L. 114/31, no. 39; Fisherwick Park sale cat. n.d. [1808], p. 8 and plan between pp. 6 and 7.
[61] S.R.O., D. 3094/10/1/9; L.J.R.O., B/A/15/Fisherwick, no. 134.
[62] Bodl. MS. Ashmole 1527, f. 21v.; S.R.O., D. (W.) 1734/2/1, m. 22; D. (W.) 1746/E44; D. (W.) 1746/P/2-3; L.J.R.O., D. 15/10/2/35, deeds of 21 Aug. 1639, 10 Dec. 1735; D. 15/10/2/36, deed of 25 Jan. 1660/1; W.S.L., S.D. Pearson 1454, 1457-8, 1490; Fisherwick Park sale cat. n.d. [1808], p. 9 and plan between pp. 6 and 7.
[63] P.R.O., E 134/3 Jas. I East./19; E 134/3 Jas. I Hil./3 and 4.
[64] B.R.L., Elford Hall MSS. no. 1274, list of Dodsmore doles 1917 on back of letter.
[65] Ibid. no. 607, pp. 11-12.
[66] Cal. Chart. R. 1341-1417, 31.
[67] S.H.C. xv. 102.
[68] S.R.O., D. 661/1/583.
[69] S.H.C. xvi. 49
[70] S.R.O., D. (W.) 1746/P/1 and 2; Tamhorn Estate sale cat. 1827, p. 4.
[71] W.S.L. 11/522/32/50, deposition of Ric. Spencer.
[72] e.g. Dyott's Diary, ed. R. W. Jeffery, i. 306, 336; ii. 6, 11; S.R.O., D. 661/11/2/3/1/11, 15 Sept. 1824.
[73] S.R.O., D. 661/8/1/2/4.
[74] Dyott's Diary, ii. 63, 387.
[75] Peel Settled Estates sale cat. 1918, p. 17 (copy in B.R.L., Elford Hall MSS. no. 1274).
[76] Shaw, Staffs. i. 375; N.R.A., Massereene (Staffs.) deeds, no. 2; S.R.O., D. (W.) 1734/J. 2268, f. 2v.
[77] For Fisherwick see e.g. S.H.C. vi (1), 121; xvii. 73; W.S.L., M. 520, pp. 19-20. For Timmor see S.H.C. xiv (1), 212; xv. 135, 138; S.H.C. n.s. x (1), 126.
[78] Shaw, Staffs. i. 375.
[79] B.R.L., Elford Hall MSS. nos. 150-4.

leased out.[80] The sale of the estate to R. B. Howard in 1808 included fishing rights in the Tame.[81]

The part of the river adjoining Tamhorn belonged to the manors of Comberford and Wigginton, in Tamworth, which were sold by the marquess of Bath to the earl of Donegall in 1790 and were included in the sale to R. B. Howard. Fishing rights in the Tamhorn side of the river were claimed by Lionel Damer as lord of Tamhorn and by Christopher Astley and Richard Dyott, his successive tenants there. Dyott also paid rent for the fishing to Lord Bath and his successors, but in 1810 he sought to establish his claim. His succesor, Gen. Dyott, fished an arm of the river on the Tamhorn side in 1814, and Howard took the matter to law. It was decided that the general had the right to fish the arm but no other part of the river. He duly took a lease of the fishing from Howard. Sir Robert Peel, however, revived the claim to fish the Tamhorn side.[82]

F. E. H. Paget's gift of the Elford and Fisherwick estate to Birmingham corporation in 1936 included fisheries in the Tame from Alder mill to Elford bridge, from the bridge to the confluence with Fisherwick brook, and from the confluence to Williford in Whittington.[83]

MILLS. Fisherwick manor included a water mill in 1282.[84] A mill was still in use at Fisherwick in 1753, but it did not survive the subsequent improvements to the park.[85] There was a mill at Timmor in the earlier 13th century when Parnel, lady of Timmor, granted it to Sir William Vernon; it probably stood upstream from Elford mill.[86] Tamhorn manor included a water mill in 1686.[87]

INDUSTRIES. There was extensive salt working by the Iron Age settlers in the area. The salt produced seems to have been transported over considerable distances.[88]

Fisherwick manor included a fulling mill in 1282.[89] A charcoal burner from Tamhorn was buried at Whittington in 1685.[90] Quarrying was in progress before the later 18th century. Fields called Quarry Hill south of Tamhorn Park Farm were recorded in 1763, and there was a disused

quarry there in the early 1880s.[91] There was a quarry in Fisherwick park in 1772 when a Thomas Weston was killed by a fall of marl there, and a stone cutter living at Fisherwick died in 1774.[92] There was a quarry west of Fisherwick Hall in 1776, probably the disused quarry north of the present Dairy Farm.[93] A quarry in the south-west corner of the park in 1804 was still in use in 1842.[94] Sand and gravel working began in 1967 between the Tame and the Elford–Whittington road south of Stubby Leas Farm. By the early 1980s the deposits there had been exhausted and much of the area had been filled in with fuel ash from Lea Hall power station in Rugeley; working had moved to the northern part of the former park.[95] The explosives storage depot belonging to Imperial Chemical Industries plc in the centre of the park area was opened in 1954.[96]

LOCAL GOVERNMENT. By 1293 Fisherwick, Horton, and Tamhorn attended the Longdon manor view of frankpledge, held at Lichfield.[97] Fisherwick and Timmor together formed one tithing by 1297 and Horton and Timmor another.[98] By 1327 Fisherwick and Timmor were represented jointly at the view by three tithingmen (two for Fisherwick and one for Timmor by 1391) and Horton and Tamhorn by two (one for each by 1424).[99] Fisherwick and Timmor were presenting separately by 1468, and Horton and Tamhorn by 1488.[1] Fisherwick still had two tithingmen in 1586 but only one by 1602.[2] Timmor and Horton were still presenting in 1621, but by 1625 one man represented Fisherwick, Timmor, and Horton together. The change probably reflected the fact that all three manors had had the same lord for some years.[3] One tithingman was still elected for all three places jointly in 1642, but by 1713 Fisherwick alone was mentioned.[4] There was still a tithingman for Tamhorn in 1725.[5]

By the 14th century each of the two tithings was also a constablewick.[6] There was a separate constable for Horton in 1418,[7] and each of the four places had its own constable in the late 16th century.[8] From the early 17th century, however, the election of a constable for Fisherwick alone

[80] Ibid. no. 935.
[81] Fisherwick Park sale cat. n.d. [1808], p. 7; Fisherwick Park sale cat. 1808, p. 19.
[82] S.R.O., D. (W.) 3222/522/30–2, 38; S.R.O., D. 661/18/1; D. 1042/2, p. 70; Tamhorn Park sale cat. 1827, MS. note on p. 3 of copy in S.R.O., D. (W.) 1746/E55; B.R.L., Elford Hall MSS. nos. 687, 782, 821–2, 889.
[83] S.R.O. 1070.   [84] S.H.C. vi (1), 121
[85] B.R.L., Elford Hall MSS. no. 605, p. 2.
[86] Shaw, Staffs. i. 375, 404.
[87] S.R.O., D. (W.) 1746/E41, p. 1.
[88] Fisherwick, ed. Smith, 52–7.
[89] S.H.C. vi (1), 121.
[90] L.J.R.O., B/V/7/Whittington, burial of 4 May 1685.
[91] S.R.O., D. (W.) 1746/P/1 and 2; O.S. Map 6″, Staffs. LIX. NW. (1884 edn.).
[92] L.J.R.O., B/V/7/Whittington, burials of 10 Sept. 1772, 27 July 1774.
[93] W.S.L., M. 761/8/2; G. Barrow and others, Memoirs of Geol. Surv., Geol. of Country around Lichfield, 146; O.S. Map 6″, Staffs. LIII. SW. (1925 edn.).
[94] Fisherwick Park sale cat. 1804, p. 6 (copy in S.R.O., D. 661/19/10/18); Fisherwick Park sale cat. n.d. [1808], p. 4 and

plan between pp. 6 and 7; L.J.R.O., B/A/15/Fisherwick, map.
[95] Geographical Mag. liv. 344–6.
[96] Inf. from Mr. A. G. Ward; Lichfield Mercury, 7 Apr. 1989, p. 2.
[97] Plac. de Quo Warr. (Rec. Com.), 711.
[98] S.R.O., D. (W.) 1734/2/1/598, m. 14.
[99] Ibid. m. 2d.; D. (W.) 1734/2/1/599, f. 16v.; D. (W.) 1734/2/1/602, m. 3.
[1] Ibid. D. (W.) 1734/2/1/598, m. 49; D. (W.) 1734/2/1/604, m. 5.
[2] Ibid. D. (W.) 1734/2/1/612, m. 77; D. (W.) 1734/2/1/613, m. 1d.
[3] Ibid. D. (W.) 1734/2/1/613, mm. 91–2 (membranes in wrong order); D. (W.) 1734/2/1/614, m. 3d.; above, manors.
[4] S.R.O., D. (W.) 1734/2/1/734; D. 603/J, Longdon, 14 Oct. 1713.
[5] S.R.O., D. 603/J/7/11/3.
[6] S.H.C. vii (1), 232–3; x (1), 105, 109; S.H.C. 4th ser. vi. 10.
[7] S.R.O., D. (W.) 1734/2/1/601, m. 15.
[8] Ibid. D. (W.) 1734/2/1/612, mm. 24d., 40, 60, 75; P.R.O., E 134/3 Jas. I East./19; E 134/3 Jas. I Hil./3 and 4.

is recorded.[9] A constable was still being appointed at the Longdon court in 1839.[10]

The pinfold of Fisherwick was mentioned several times in the 16th century.[11] A pinner was still being appointed for Fisherwick at the Longdon court in 1839.[12]

Parochially Fisherwick and Tamhorn townships were detached parts of St. Michael's, Lichfield. There was one sidesman for Fisherwick, Horton, and Tamhorn by 1637; Tamhorn had its own from 1817.[13] Tamhorn was still paying church rates in 1833 but was recognized as extra-parochial from the 1830s[14] and as a civil parish from 1858.[15] Fisherwick too was recognized as a civil parish in the later 19th century.[16] Fisherwick was included in Lichfield poor-law union, formed in 1836; Tamhorn was added in 1858.[17] The two parishes were united as the new civil parish of Fisherwick in 1934.[18] Having been part of Lichfield rural district, the parish was included in the new Lichfield district in 1974.

Fisherwick and Tamhorn were covered by the Whittington association for the prosecution of felons, formed by 1780 and still in existence in 1828.[19]

CHURCH. There is no record of any church or chapel at Fisherwick or Tamhorn, but there may have been a graveyard in the 14th century: Robert *ad cimiterium* was assessed for tax in Fisherwick and Timmor in 1327.[20] Because of the distance from their parish church of St. Michael, Lichfield, the inhabitants often attended nearer churches. In 1599 William Skeffington of Fisherwick and his household were licensed by the archbishop of Canterbury to attend Elford church instead of St. Michael's because of the distance between Fisherwick and Lichfield, the poor state of the roads, especially in winter, and the bodily infirmity of Skeffington, his wife, and some of the servants.[21] John Skeffington was married at St. Michael's in 1614, and the family used the church for baptisms and burials in the earlier 17th century.[22] In the late 18th century Lord Donegall had an ornamented pew at Whittington church, although he built a mausoleum at St. Michael's; the pew evidently passed with the Fisherwick estate to R. B. Howard.[23] Baptisms and burials of many other families from Fisherwick are recorded at Whittington from the 1680s.[24] The Astleys of Tamhorn were normally baptized and buried at Whittington in the later 17th and the 18th century, but there was a pew belonging to the Tamhorn estate in St. Michael's in 1827.[25] In the 1880s it was stated that the inhabitants of Fisherwick attended the churches at Whittington and Elford.[26] Officially Fisherwick remained part of St. Michael's until 1967 when it was transferred to Whittington ecclesiastical parish. At the same time Tamhorn, extra-parochial since the 1830s, was added to Whittington.[27]

NONCONFORMITY. Sir John Skeffington, who succeeded to Fisherwick manor in 1652 and died in 1695, was described in the early 1660s as 'a rigid Presbyterian ... his whole alliance Presbyterian'.[28] In 1672 the house of William Palmer of Fisherwick was licensed for Presbyterian teaching,[29] and in 1693 Fisherwick Hall was included in a list of houses licensed for dissenting worship.[30] Robert Travers, the Presbyterian minister for the Lichfield area, baptized a child at Fisherwick in 1701.[31]

EDUCATION. There is no record of any educational establishment in Fisherwick or Tamhorn. By the late 1880s children from the area attended schools at Whittington and Elford.[32]

CHARITIES FOR THE POOR. None known.

[9] S.R.O., D. (W.) 1734/2/1/613, mm. 2, 29; D. (W.) 1734/2/1/614, mm. 3d., 8, 12d.
[10] Ibid. D. 603/J/1/4/15.
[11] Ibid. D. (W.) 1734/2/1/605, m. 3; D. (W.) 1734/2/1/608, m. 1; D. (W.) 1734/2/1/609, m. 1; D. (W.) 1734/2/1/617, f. 33.
[12] Ibid. D. 603/J/1/4/15.
[13] Ibid. D. 27/1/2, at end; D. 27/5/1, f. 33v.
[14] Ibid. D. 27/5/2; S.R.O., D. (W.) 1746/E44, E55, E61, E81, E99; White, *Dir. Staffs.* (1834), 379.
[15] S.R.O., D. 458/1/4, pp. 502, 520; P.R.O., RG 9/1974.
[16] *Census*, 1881, 1891.
[17] Poor Law Com. Order 1836 forming Lichfield union (copy in L.J.R.O., D. 77/16/3); S.R.O., D. 458/A/G/52, pp. 502, 520.
[18] Above, introduction.
[19] *Aris's Birmingham Gaz.* 24 Apr. 1780; 30 Jan. 1797; *Lichfield Mercury*, 1 Feb. 1828.

[20] *S.H.C.* vii (1), 232.
[21] Lambeth Palace Libr., Whitgift's reg. iii, f. 102. The details have kindly been supplied by the librarian, Mr. E. G. W. Bill.
[22] Shaw, *Staffs.* i. 341; L.J.R.O., D. 27/9/5.
[23] Shaw, *Staffs.* i. 378; B.R.L., Elford Hall MSS. no. 819, 5 May 1814; above, Lichfield, churches.
[24] L.J.R.O., B/V/7/Whittington.
[25] Ibid.; Shaw, *Staffs.* i. 378–9; S.R.O., D. (W.) 1746/E81. There are an Astley vault and an Astley tomb in Whittington churchyard NE. of the church.
[26] *Kelly's Dir. Staffs.* (1888 and later edns.).
[27] Lich. Dioc. Regy., Orders in Council, vol. R, p. 272.
[28] *S.H.C.* 4th ser. ii. 28; *Complete Peerage*, viii. 54.
[29] A.G. Matthews, *Cong. Churches of Staffs.* 93; *Calamy Revised*, ed. A. G. Matthews, 473.
[30] L.J.R.O., B/A/12ii.   [31] S.R.O., D. 4119, p. [51].
[32] *Kelly's Dir. Staffs.* (1888 and edns. to 1924).

FREEFORD

FREEFORD, south-east of Lichfield, was formerly a township of 378 a. in St. Michael's parish, Lichfield.[33] Most of it was an estate centred on Freeford Manor, the home of the Dyott family; the rest was centred on Freeford House. In 1934 Freeford became part of the new civil parish of Swinfen and Packington. A boundary change in 1980 transferred 5½ a. around Freeford House to Lichfield, from which 172 a. east of Lichfield Eastern Bypass was added to Swinfen and Packington.[34]

Part of Freeford's north-western boundary follows the upper reaches of Darnford brook; on the east the boundary with Whittington runs along the Tamworth road. The subsoil is Bunter Sandstone and Pebble Beds, except for an area of Keuper Sandstone north of Freeford Manor.[35] The soil is loam.[36] The ground lies at 226 ft. (69 m.) on the boundary with Lichfield by Freeford House; to the south it rises to 259 ft. (79 m.) at Freeford Manor and 328 ft. (100 m.) on the boundary east of Home Farm.

Six people were assessed for tax in 1327 and 13 in 1332–3.[37] Two householders were assessed for hearth tax in 1666.[38] Freeford's population was 27 in 1841, 23 in 1851, 12 in 1861, 15 in 1871, and 54 in 1881.[39] By 1901 it was 100, falling to 75 in 1911 and 59 in 1921. In 1931, when it was last recorded separately, the population was 64.[40]

Freeford derives its name from a ford on the Lichfield–Tamworth road over Darnford brook. The ford was 'free' in the sense that it was open or accessible, presumably in contrast to Darnford, the hidden or secret ford, further downstream in Streethay. A medieval leper hospital stood south of the junction of two roads from Lichfield, on the site later occupied by Freeford House;[41] there was a house next to the hospital's chapel in 1466.[42] A green, mentioned in 1327,[43] may have lain around the road junction. Freeford Manor to the south may stand on or near the site of a medieval house. The site of Freeford Farm to the west, in Lichfield, was settled in the earlier 18th century.[44] In 1837 a cottage was built south of Freeford Manor on the site of Home Farm, itself dating from the later 19th century, and between 1861 and 1871 two cottages were built in Barkers Lane.[45] Sev-

eral houses were built along the Tamworth road and south of Freeford Farm in the 1930s.[46] East of Home Farm the club house for Whittington golf club was built in the early 20th century. A new club house was opened on the Whittington side of the boundary c. 1960 and the old one became a private house, called Lochranza, where commercial dog kennels were later built.[47]

The Lichfield–Tamworth road was turnpiked in 1770 and disturnpiked in 1882. A tollgate east of Darnford brook was removed in 1882, and North Lodge was built on its site.[48] A new stretch of the road was constructed over Lichfield Eastern Bypass, which was opened in 1971.[49] Part of the former road was converted into a compound for lorries using the bypass; two houses were later built near by.

When Lichfield council took an electricity supply from Walsall in 1926, it supplied Freeford free of charge because poles carrying the cable to the city ran across the Dyott estate.[50]

Edward II stopped at Freeford in 1326 before entering Lichfield city.[51]

MANOR AND OTHER ESTATES. In 1086 *FREEFORD* was a member of the bishop of Chester's manor of Lichfield (later Longdon).[52] It was assessed at 3 hides c. 1255.[53] It remained a member of the bishop's (later the Paget family's) manor of Longdon until at least the later 18th century.[54]

Ranulf held the manor of the bishop in 1086. He also held Timmor in Fisherwick, and by 1135 Freeford formed a knight's fee with Timmor and with Fradswell in Colwich.[55] By 1242–3 the lords of Timmor held Freeford as mesne lords, and in the 1260s William of Timmor and his son Hugh granted the terre tenant, Robert of Freeford, freedom of marriage for himself and his heirs.[56] The mesne lordship survived in 1298.[57]

In 1242–3 William of Freeford held the manor as ½ knight's fee.[58] By the 1260s it was held by his son Robert, who was still alive in 1289.[59] William of Freeford held it by 1294 and was still alive in 1332.[60] In 1323 he settled Freeford on his younger son John, who was

---

[33] *Census*, 1901. *V.C.H. Staffs.* i. 329, confuses Freeford with 'Freeford Hamlet' (the adjoining part of Lichfield city). This article was written in 1985. Miss M. B. Dyott of Whittington and Mr. R. B. Dyott of Freeford Manor are thanked for their help.

[34] Lichfield (Parishes) Order 1980, S.I. 1980 no. 387; inf. from the Chief Executive, Lichfield District Council; below, local govt.

[35] Geol. Surv. Map 1″, drift, sheet 154 (1922 edn.).

[36] Soil Surv. Sheet 3 (1983).

[37] *S.H.C.* vii (1), 233; x (1), 109.

[38] *S.H.C.* 1923, 225.

[39] The totals for 1861 and 1871, given in *V.C.H. Staffs.* i. 322, are incorrect, because of confusion between Freeford and the adjoining part of Lichfield city: P.R.O., RG 9/1973; RG 10/2913–14. The 1881 figure is calculated from P.R.O., RG 11/2773.

[40] *Census*, 1911–31.

[41] Below, manor.

[42] L.J.R.O., D. 30/XVIII, f. 18.

[43] *S.H.C.* vii (1), 233.

[44] Below, manor; econ. hist. (agric.).

[45] P.R.O., RG 9/1973; RG 10/2913–14; below, econ. hist. (agric.).

[46] Inf. from Miss M. B. Dyott.

[47] O.S. Map 1/2,500, Staffs. LVIII. 4 (1922 edn.); inf. from the club secretary.

[48] Above, Lichfield, communications; plaque on the lodge.

[49] Above, Lichfield, general hist. (20th century).

[50] L.J.R.O., D. 127/electric lighting cttee. min. bk. pp. 53, 60; above, Lichfield, public services (lighting).

[51] *Cal. Close*, 1323–7, 456.

[52] *V.C.H. Staffs.* iv. 43.

[53] Shaw, *Staffs.* i, app. to Gen. Hist. p. xvi.

[54] Below, local govt.

[55] *V.C.H. Staffs.* iv. 43; *S.H.C.* i. 147.

[56] S.R.O., D. 661/2/505.

[57] Ibid. D. (W.) 1734/J. 2268, f. iv.

[58] *Bk. of Fees*, ii. 968.

[59] *S.H.C.* iv (1), 208; vi (1), 188; S.R.O., D. 661/2/505.

[60] *S.H.C.* vi (1), 297; x (1), 109; S.R.O., D. 661/2/356.

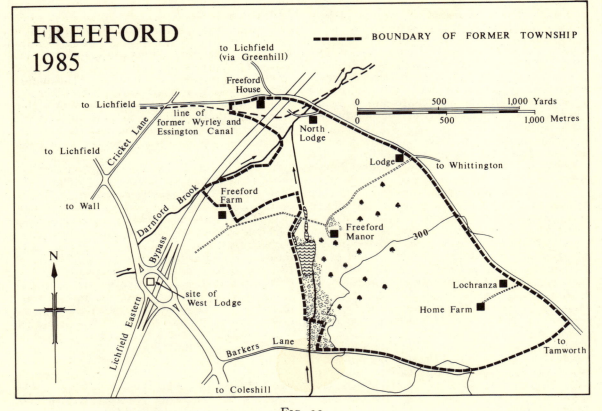

FIG. 22

M.P. for Staffordshire in 1337 and had been knighted by 1338.[61] John died in 1366, leaving three daughters as his heirs.[62] The manor remained divided until it was re-united by John Dyott of Lichfield and his son Anthony between 1563 and 1616.

By the late 14th century a third share of the manor had passed from Margaret, one of Sir John Freeford's daughters, to her daughter Alice and Alice's husband Henry Brown of Lichfield (d. c. 1403). Afterwards it passed to their son John, who was still alive in 1440.[63] His heirs were two daughters, of whom Elizabeth inherited the interest in Freeford. Her daughter Margaret, who was recorded as holding a share of Freeford through her husband John Harcourt of Ranton in 1512 and in her own name in 1514, died in 1522.[64] Her interest passed to her grandson John Harcourt, who let a house and barn at Freeford to John Dyott of Lichfield in 1549. Harcourt died soon after, and his interest in Freeford passed to his son Robert (d. 1558), who left his estate to his mistress Cassandra Cooke and their four sons. In 1584 she and two of the sons conveyed their rights in Freeford to John Dyott's son Anthony.[65]

By 1421 another third of Freeford was held by Sir William Lichfield, evidently as heir of Elizabeth, one of Sir John Freeford's daughters and wife of John Bachecote.[66] William was succeeded in 1446 by his daughter Margaret, wife of Humphrey Stafford of Bishop's Frome (Herefs.).[67] The share evidently passed to Sir William Stafford of Bishop's Frome, whose daughter Margaret married Sir George de Vere. In 1537 Margaret assigned her share to her daughter Elizabeth and Elizabeth's husband Sir Anthony Wingfield.[68] By c. 1600 the share had passed to Jane Kniveton. In 1603 Jane's son William Kniveton conveyed it to Ralph Jarman, a Lichfield innkeeper (d. 1612). In 1616 Jarman's widow Margaret relinquished her rights to Anthony Dyott.[69]

The remaining third share was further divided. One part was held by Thomas Andrews in 1512 and by William Andrews in 1514. In 1563 Humphrey Andrews conveyed it to John Dyott.[70] The other part was held in 1512 by Thomas Swinfen of Swinfen in Weeford and in the later 16th century by William Swinfen. In 1606 John Swinfen sold it to Anthony Dyott's wife Dorothy and their son Richard.[71]

[61] S.R.O., D. 661/2/679; S.H.C. 1911, 98–9; 1917–18, 72–3.
[62] S.R.O., D. 661/2/678; S.H.C. xiii. 59, 63, 171; V.C.H. Warws. iv. 76.
[63] S.H.C. xvii. 296; W.S.L., H.M. Chetwynd 5.
[64] W.S.L., H.M. Chetwynd 5; S.R.O., D. (W.) 1734/2/1/605, mm. 2, 5, 18; S.H.C. 1914, 95.
[65] S.H.C. xvii. 231; S.H.C. 1914, pedigree facing p. 187; S.R.O., D. 661/2/151, 319, 436.
[66] Cal. Pat. 1446–52, 110–11; S.H.C. xiii. 171;

J.R.U.L.M., Ryl. Ch. Phillipps 126.
[67] Cal. Pat. 1446–52, 111.
[68] Complete Peerage, x. 243–4; S.H.C. 1931, 223–4.
[69] S.H.C. xviii (1), 6–7, 10, 13; Shaw, Staffs. i. 30; S.R.O., D. 661/2/109, 112–13; L.J.R.O., D. 27/1/1, f. 37.
[70] S.R.O., D. 661/2/344; D. (W.) 1734/2/1/605, mm. 2, 5; D. (W.) 1734/2/1/612, m. 30; S.H.C. xiii. 228.
[71] S.R.O., D. 661/2/242; D. (W.) 1734/2/1/605, m. 2; P.R.O., C 1/1063, nos. 83–4.

John Dyott, a barrister and three times bailiff of Lichfield, was probably the original of the 'little John Doit of Staffordshire', the boon companion of Shakespeare's Justice Shallow in their youth.[72] He was granted a crest in 1560 and a coat of arms in 1563.[73] He was succeeded in 1578[74] by his son Anthony Dyott, a barrister and M.P. for Lichfield in 1601 and 1603, who died in 1622.[75] He was succeeded by his son Richard, a barrister, who in 1610 had married Dorothy, daughter and heir of Richard Dorrington of Stafford. Knighted in 1635, he was M.P. for Lichfield in the 1620s and in 1640 and a prominent royalist.[76] He was succeeded in 1660 by his son Anthony (d. 1662), another barrister, whose heir was his brother Richard.[77] Richard, who had accompanied Charles II into exile, was elected M.P. for Lichfield in 1667.[78]

On Richard's death in 1677 his son, another Richard, succeeded. He was M.P. for Lichfield in most parliaments 1690–1715 and died in 1719.[79] His heir was his son Richard, the first of the family to live at Freeford rather than Lichfield. He died in 1769 and was succeeded by his son Richard. In 1776 Richard was living at Ashbourne (Derb.) and in 1784 at Leicester, where he died in 1787.[80] He was succeeded by his son Richard, who lived at Freeford from 1784 and was recorder of Lichfield from 1808. He was succeeded in 1813 by his brother Lt.-Gen. William Dyott, a regular soldier who was promoted to full general in 1830. An edition of the diary which William kept from 1781 to 1845 was published in 1907.[81] William was succeeded in 1847 by his son Richard (d. 1891), M.P. for Lichfield 1865–74. Richard was succeeded by Lt.-Col. Richard Burnaby, grandson of William Dyott's sister Lucy. Burnaby, who changed his name to Dyott, was succeeded in 1903 by his grandson Richard (d. 1965). He was followed by his grandson Richard Burnaby Dyott, formerly Shaw, who remained the owner in 1985.[82]

Freeford Manor, known as Freeford Hall until the 1930s,[83] may stand on or near the site of a medieval house. In 1366 Sir John Freeford's widow was granted a licence for an oratory in her house, possibly at Freeford.[84] In the 17th century the Dyott family preferred to live in Lichfield, and in 1719 there was only 'a little house' at Freeford. It was probably incorporated in the brick house which Richard Dyott built there in the early 1730s,[85] improving the site by planting apple, cherry, nectarine, peach, pear, and plum trees next to the house.[86] The house itself was small and had a west front of three bays. A drawing room, later the library, was added on the south in the mid 18th century, and by the late 18th century another large room had been added to it on the east. A two-storey service range on the north side of the house had also been built by the late 18th century. Over the main doorway there was by then an inscription 'Nil nisi bonum, portus amicis', still in place in 1985.[87] The house was approached on the north through a courtyard, whose entrance was flanked by a pair of square buildings.

On gaining possession of the house in 1826 on the death of his brother's widow, William Dyott engaged the architect Joseph Potter the elder of Lichfield to make alterations. The work included resetting the 18th-century main staircase in the south-west corner of the original house and adding bedrooms over the drawing room.[88] The house was further extended and remodelled in 1848–9. The first bay of the 18th-century service wing was rebuilt to restore the symmetry of the west front, and the south front was also made symmetrical. The east wing was given an upper storey and was extended north and east. A shallow stone porch of two storeys was built to emphasize the main west entrance, probably in 1851–2.[89] A bay window was later added on the south side of the library, and in the 20th century various changes were made to the service buildings on the north. The stables north of the house were built in the late 18th or early 19th century, when a kitchen garden nearby was also laid out. The icehouse in the wood south of the house was built in 1842.[90]

There was an enclosed park by the earlier 17th century: in 1646 the estate could not be let because 'the fence is so down and carried away'.[91] The parkland was used for grazing sheep and cattle in the early 18th century,[92] and in the later 1790s it united 'the utility and profits of farming with the pleasurable beauties of the ornamental landscape'.[93] Small plantations of trees were established by William Dyott in the early 19th century.[94] The pool west of the house may have originated as a mill pond in the Middle Ages. In the early 20th century it covered nearly 4 a.[95]

By the later 18th century the main approach

[72] S.R.O., D. 661/1/813(1), pedigree; Harwood, *Lichfield*, 420–1; *2 Hen. IV, iii.* ii; above, plate 22.
[73] *Grantees of Arms* (Harl. Soc. lxvi), 79; *Hist. Parl., Commons, 1660–90,* ii. 251.
[74] L.J.R.O., D. 20/1/1, f. 23.
[75] *Hist. Parl., Commons, 1558–1603,* ii. 72.
[76] *S.H.C.* 1920 and 1922, 23; *Cal. S.P. Dom.* 1628–9, 8; *Alum. Oxon. 1500–1714,* i. 439; S.R.O., D. 661/2/328 and 340; cf. D. 661/1/44.
[77] *Alum. Oxon. 1500–1714,* i. 438; L.J.R.O., D. 20/1/1, ff. 159, 162; S.R.O., D. 661/1/49.
[78] *Hist. Parl., Commons, 1660–90,* ii. 250–1; above, Lichfield, parl. representation.
[79] L.J.R.O., D. 20/1/2, burials of 8 Nov. 1677, 13 May 1719; S.R.O., D. 661/2/173; *S.H.C.* 1920 and 1922, 176.
[80] S.R.O., D. 661/3/3, John Fletcher to Ric. Dyott, 8 July 1776; D. 661/6/2/1, abstract of title to Freeford; D. 1042/2, f. 66; *Gent. Mag.* lvii (1), 90.
[81] S.R.O., D. 1042/2, f. 66v.; Burke, *Land. Gent.* iii (1972), 278; Stringer, *Lichfield*, 97; *Dyott's Diary*, ed. R. W. Jeffery,

i, introduction.
[82] Burke, *Land. Gent.* iii (1972), 278–9; *Lichfield Mercury*, 20 Feb. 1891, pp. 4–5.
[83] S.R.O., D. 661/8/1/2/6; inf. from Miss M. B. Dyott.
[84] *S.H.C.* n.s. viii. 33.
[85] S.R.O., D. 661/2/801, pp. 21, 45; D. 661/21/3, ff. 124v., 126v.
[86] Ibid. D. 661/21/5/1, ff. 1–2.   [87] Above, plate 48.
[88] S.R.O., D. 661/8/1/2/6; D. 661/11/2/3/1/11, 2 Aug., 1 Sept. 1826, 7 Apr. 1827.
[89] Ibid. D. 661/8/1/2/6.
[90] Ibid. D. 661/11/2/3/1/16, 23 Sept. 1842.
[91] Ibid. D. 661/1/33.
[92] Ibid. D. 661/8/1/2/1, pp. [42–3]; Shaw, *Staffs.* i, pl. facing p. 358.
[93] W. Pitt, *General View of Agric. of County of Stafford* (1796), 18; above, plate 48.
[94] S.R.O., D. 661/11/2/3/1/11, 9 Mar. 1819, 20 Mar. 1823, Oct.–Nov. 1826; D. 661/11/2/3/1/13, 8 Dec. 1836, 8 Mar. 1837.   [95] O.S. Map 1/2,500, Staffs. LVIII. 4 (1922 edn.).

to the house was along an avenue from the east, and a lodge on the Tamworth road was renovated in 1839.[96] In the mid 18th century an avenue ran west of the house towards London Road across the recently inclosed part of Old Field.[97] It was replaced as the main approach to the house, probably in the early 1840s, by a road slightly to the north passing near Freeford Farm. A double lodge was built on London Road in 1843. The northern part was demolished before 1900 and the southern in 1958 when London Road was widened.[98] The eastern avenue then became the main approach once more; the lodge there had been rebuilt apparently in the late 19th century. A service road laid out in 1845 joined the Tamworth road at the tollgate replaced in 1882 by North Lodge.[99]

FREEFORD HOUSE occupies the site of the leper hospital of St. Leonard, established by the mid 13th century. The hospital appears to have ceased to function by the later 14th century, and in 1496 its estate was added to that of the almshouse of St. John the Baptist in Lichfield.[1] In 1508 the master of St. John's let a house at Freeford, reserving the former chapel of St. Leonard; that house was presumably part of the St. John's estate in Freeford worth 30s. in 1535.[2] In the early 1720s the estate comprised 18 a.[3] In 1813 the house and land were sold to Jonathan Mallet, evidently the tenant.[4] He died in 1835 leaving his estate to his sisters Harriet (d. 1853)[5] and Mary Ann (d. 1854). Subject to two life interests the estate passed to Mary Ann's great-nephew Thomas Mallet. Thomas was farming at Freeford in 1861[6] and died in 1906 leaving the estate in trust for his wife Lucy (d. 1949). In 1950 her heir or executor, Mrs. Fanny Lear, sold the house to W. G. McKie. He in turn sold it in 1967 to Mr. M. H. L. Farrant, the owner in 1985.

Freeford House is a brick building of the earlier 18th century, joined at right angles to a range which runs east–west along the Tamworth road. That range, of the 16th or 17th century, was timber-framed on a sandstone plinth; most of the timber was replaced by brick at various dates in the 18th and 19th centuries. In the 19th century the range was divided near its west end, presumably to give access to the back of the house. The gap was filled with a small house, Princes Villa, in 1892.[7]

The great and small tithes of Freeford belonged to the prebendary of Freeford in Lichfield cathedral. From 1660 or earlier a modus of 11s. 2d. was paid for both sorts, although in the late 1770s the lessee of the prebend made an unsuccessful attempt to have the great tithes paid in kind.[8]

ECONOMIC HISTORY. AGRICULTURE. In 1086 Freeford had land for six ploughteams.[9] About 1330 two open fields were mentioned, Mere field and Nether field.[10] There was evidently some sheepfarming in the late 15th century: a flock of over 100 sheep was mentioned in 1480.[11]

About 1610 the lordship of Freeford consisted of 240 a. of meadow, pasture, and woodland, with Freeford marshes, evidently along Darnford brook, and heathland in Lichfield called Old Field. Crops then grown included oats, rye, white wheat, red wheat, barley, and peas, and there were 14 cows, 10 young beasts, 6 calves, and a bull. Sheepfarming was evidently important: there were 149 wethers 'fat enough for the shambles', and 80 ewes and 60 lambs kept in Town field in Lichfield. The estate was thought to be worth £120 a year, improvable by inclosure, liming, and a good stock of animals.[12]

The inclosure of Old Field in Lichfield in the late 17th and early 18th century added c. 175 a. of arable land to the Dyott estate. It provided land for Old Field (later Freeford) farm, which included 166 a. in Lichfield in the mid 18th century, when there was a farmhouse on the present site. The home farm, which was worked from Freeford Hall and covered 165 a. at the same date, probably included the Bispells estate in Lichfield held by the Dyotts as lessees. A third mid 18th-century farm, Upper (later Home) farm south of Freeford Hall, covered 171 a.[13] On the home farm in 1725 there were 34 cows (10 of them milkers), 4 calves, a bull and 202 sheep. In the 1730s there were c. 400 sheep; by 1750 the flock had increased to nearly 490, and there were then regular sales of sheep and wool.[14] In the 1760s over 300 sheep were sheared each year.[15]

Richard Dyott (d. 1813), who farmed the home farm from 1784 and also farmed at Tamhorn in Fisherwick, was an agricultural improver and was elected president of the Staffordshire Agricultural Society on its establishment in 1800.[16] At Freeford he drained much of the land to create firm pasture. By 1792 he had a flock of 940 sheep and lambs. Nearly 600 sheep were sheared that year, 463 of them at Tamhorn but the rest at Freeford; the breeding ewes numbered 260 and produced 300 lambs a year. In the 1790s sales of fattened sheep and of wool at Freeford averaged £650 a year. Fattened

[96] Above, fig. 1; S.R.O., D. 661/8/1/2/7.
[97] L.J.R.O., D. 44/4; below, econ. hist. (agric.).
[98] S.R.O., D. 661/11/2/3/1/16, 1 Nov. 1841, 10 Aug. 1843; O.S. Map 1/2,500, Staffs. LVIII. 3 (1884, 1902 edns.); inf. from Mr. R. B. Dyott.
[99] S.R.O., D. 661/11/2/3/1/16, 3 Mar. and 1 Apr. 1845; above, introduction.   [1] Below, church.
[2] S.R.O., D. 661/2/51; *Valor Eccl.* (Rec. Com.), iii. 141.
[3] L.J.R.O., D. 88/hosp. land, plan no. 3.
[4] Rest of para. based on deeds in possession of Mr. M. H. L. Farrant of Freeford House.
[5] L.J.R.O., D. 27/1/11, p. 35.
[6] P.R.O., RG 9/1973.
[7] Date stone on house.

[8] L.J.R.O., D. 30/LV, f. 50; S.R.O., D. 661/3/3.
[9] *V.C.H. Staffs.* iv. 43
[10] S.R.O., D. 661/2/696; L.J.R.O., D. 30/VC, B 131.
[11] *S.H.C.* n.s. vi (1), 128.
[12] S.R.O., D. 661/1/44; D. 661/2/340.
[13] *Aris's Birmingham Gaz.* 23 Feb. 1747; S.R.O., D. 661/3/3, Ric. Dyott's answer to John Fletcher's bill of complaint; D. 661/21/5/1, f. 6v.; 1759 map of Old Field (in possession of Mr. R. B. Dyott); above, Lichfield, econ. hist. (agric.).
[14] S.R.O., D. 661/8/1/2/1, pp. [42–3]; D. 661/21/3/1, ff. 123v., 125v., 133v., 160, 162, 164, 170, 172v.
[15] Ibid. D. 661/21/6/1, ff. 2v.–3.
[16] Ibid. D. 661/20/9; D. 1042/2, ff. 65v., 66v.

bullocks and heifers were included in the annual sales, and the stock had been improved by the purchase of heifers from the experimental breeder John Princep of Croxall (Derb.) and of Scotch steers. Only *c.* 30 a. of wheat were grown at Freeford and 70 a. of turnips as winter food for the sheep; the turnips were followed by barley and then grass for one or two years.[17] The Freeford sales continued in the early 19th century; that of 1810, which took place the day after a meeting of the Staffordshire Agricultural Society at Lichfield, included 100 fat ewes, 50 theaves, and several rams, all apparently of the Leicester breed, and 10 blackfaced wethers, 10 Scotch bullocks, 6 cows, and a bull. Some sales also included racehorses.[18]

William Dyott improved the farm buildings and in 1829 bought a haymaking machine, having had trouble with his labourers.[19] In the later 1830s and early 1840s he was growing turnips, swedes, carrots, and mangolds as feed for his cattle and sheep; he also grew some wheat, barley, and potatoes.[20] Freeford farm and Upper farm were let. They were worked together until 1838, when Upper farm was let separately to Joseph Booth, who also farmed as the tenant at Fulfen in Streethay. Because there was no living accommodation at Upper farm, a cottage was built there in 1837 for Booth's use.[21] Richard Dyott (d. 1891) replaced the cottage with a farmhouse for the amalgamated home farm and Upper farm, known as Home farm by 1872.[22] Richard was a pioneer breeder of Shropshire sheep and won prizes with rams at the 1863 and 1865 Royal Shows. The flock was still kept in the late 1920s.[23]

Thomas Baxter, knighted in 1943 for services to agriculture, was lessee of Freeford farm from 1903 to 1927 and of Home farm from 1909 to 1921. In 1917 he farmed 612 a., of which 65 a. were devoted to barley (chiefly for brewing in Lichfield), 55 a. to wheat, 54 a. to swedes, and 15 a. to mangolds. There was four-course rotation of barley (with clover), clover, wheat (or early potatoes), and roots. The potatoes were sold locally, while much of the root crop was used to feed 550 Shropshire sheep, 50 dairy cows, and other cattle. The yearly sale of milk in 1917 was 26,000 gallons. In 1923 Baxter was one of the first farmers in the county to sow sugar beet.[24]

In 1985 the Dyott estate in Freeford and Lichfield comprised some 625 a. with a further 145 a. in Whittington. Farming was chiefly dairying and cattle rearing.[25]

FISHERY AND WARREN. The fishery of a pool at Freeford was reserved when Richard Dyott let the estate in 1632.[26] Carp were turned into ponds there in 1759, and in 1763 ponds were stocked with carp and trout; tench were introduced in 1765.[27] When the pool was drained in 1784 it yielded 80 carp, 3 perch, and 3 pike. In 1785 it was restocked with 200 carp, 200 perch, 100 trout, and 6 pike, and further stockings of trout were made in 1786 and 1787. The pool was enlarged in 1793 and continued to be fished.[28] Soon after 1827 regular fishing seems to have been abandoned, as the pool became increasingly choked.[29]

In 1585 a lessee of Freeford manor was licensed to kill rabbits.[30] Pasture called 'cunneygreays' in the 18th century was presumably the site of a former warren.[31]

MILL. In the early 13th century Roger Gray, son of Simon Gray, granted Thomas Brown a mill at Freeford.[32] A share in a mill there was acquired by Henry son of Walter of Lichfield in the later 13th century.[33] Henry's son Richard later conveyed four parts of the mill, possibly its entirety, to Robert of Freeford.[34] The mill may have stood below the pool west of Freeford Manor.

LOCAL GOVERNMENT. In 1293 Freeford township made presentments at the great court of Longdon manor.[35] In 1327 it sent two frankpledges but only one by 1370. One was still chosen at the Longdon court in 1642.[36] Freeford remained a constituent township of Longdon manor in 1760, when a headborough for Freeford was recorded among the manorial officials.[37] The Dyott family evidently resented the dependency: in the early 1740s Richard Dyott claimed that he had the right to hunt his own land, but he was forced to admit that Freeford was a township only and not a manor and that all rights to game belonged to the earl of Uxbridge as lord of Longdon.[38] About the same time Dyott alleged that courts baron had formerly been held at Freeford but that no court rolls survived, having been 'lost during the Civil Wars'.[39] There was a constable by 1377,[40] and

[17] Pitt, *Gen. View of Agric. of County of Stafford*, 18–19, 48 n., 134, 142–3; *Staffs. Advertiser*, 6 Sept. 1806; S.R.O., D. 1042/2, ff. 65–6 and pp. 73–9.
[18] *Staffs. Advertiser*, 12 Sept. 1804; 6 Sept. 1806; 23 July 1808; 22 July 1809; 21 July 1810; *Aris's Birmingham Gaz.* 16 July 1810.
[19] S.R.O., D. 661/11/2/3/1/11, 2 Sept. 1829; *Dyott's Diary*, i. 380; ii. 61.
[20] S.R.O., D. 661/11/2/3/1/13, 9–11 Aug., 7 Sept. and 5 Oct. 1836, 2 May and 7 June 1837; D. 661/11/2/3/1/16, 19 Jan. and 20 Oct. 1842, 25 June, 23 Aug. and 9 Oct. 1843.
[21] S.R.O., D. 661/8/1/1/3; D. 661/11/2/3/1/13, 27 Oct. 1837; D. 661/11/2/3/1/14, 18 Mar. 1838; P.R.O., HO 107/976.
[22] *Staffs. Advertiser*, 18 May 1872, p. 4.
[23] S.R.O., D. 1042/3; *Lichfield Mercury*, 20 Feb. 1891, p. 5.
[24] R. A. Pepperall, *Sir Thomas Baxter* (Wells, 1950), 51–61, 67–71, 86–7, 101; *Staffs. Advertiser*, 16 June 1917, p. 2; 3 Dec. 1927, p. 2; *V.C.H. Staffs.* vi. 126; *Kelly's Dir. Staffs.*

(1924; 1928); Burke, *Knightage* (1949).
[25] Inf. from Mr. R. B. Dyott.
[26] S.R.O., D. 661/2/139.
[27] Ibid. D. 661/21/3/1, ff. 117v., 118, 177v.; D. 661/21/6/1, f. 27v.
[28] Ibid. D. 1042/2, pp. 70–2.
[29] Ibid. D. 661/11/2/3/1/11, 9 June 1824, [–] May 1827, 18 June 1828.
[30] Ibid. D. 661/1/54.
[31] Ibid. D. 661/8/1/2/1, pp. [42–3].
[32] Ibid. D. 661/2/348 and 494.
[33] Ibid. D. 661/1/576, 578 and 581.
[34] Ibid. D. 661/1/574.
[35] *S.H.C.* vi (1), 244.
[36] S.R.O., D. (W.) 1734/2/1/598, mm. 2d., 14d., 22; D. (W.) 1734/2/1/734.
[37] Ibid. D. (W.) 1511(34)/33–4.
[38] Ibid. D. 603/K/4/3, ff. 63–6.
[39] Ibid. D. 661/2/801, pp. 28, 39.
[40] *S.H.C.* 4th ser. vi. 11.

election to the office at the Longdon great court was recorded by the late 16th century.[41] In the late 1790s it was the practice that the constable was chosen by the head of the Dyott family from among his household.[42]

Parochially Freeford was in St. Michael's parish, Lichfield, and in 1820 it had a sidesman at that church.[43] Freeford, however, had no organization for administering the poor and was regarded as extra-parochial by the late 1790s. It became a civil parish in 1858, and in the same year was placed in Lichfield poor-law union.[44] In 1934 it was joined with the Swinfen and Packington portion of Weeford to form the civil parish of Swinfen and Packington.[45]

Freeford subscribed to the Whittington Association for the Prosecution of Felons, formed by 1780 and surviving in 1828.[46]

CHURCH. Once St. Leonard's hospital was no longer a leper-house, its chapel was evidently used for services by local people. Dean Buckingham included Freeford chapel as part of his intended visitation of Freeford prebend in 1356, giving no indication that it was other than a chapel of ease.[47] At some date in the 15th

century the chapel possessed vestments, books, a cross, a censer, a pyx, and two candlesticks.[48]

Anthony Dyott (d. 1662) and later members of his family were buried in St. Mary's, Lichfield, the church which earlier members had attended as Lichfield residents.[49] It was a tradition by the early 19th century that the burials took place at night,[50] a practice which elsewhere in the country originated in the 17th century.[51] The last burial at St. Mary's was that of Richard Dyott in 1891, after which the Dyotts were buried at Whittington.[52] From at least the later 18th century the inhabitants of Freeford went to Whittington church.[53] In 1983 Freeford was added to the ecclesiastical parish of Whittington, except for the area around Freeford House west of Lichfield Eastern Bypass which was added to St. Michael's, Lichfield.[54]

NONCONFORMITY. None known.

EDUCATION. No evidence.

CHARITIES FOR THE POOR. None known.

HAMMERWICH

THE civil parish of Hammerwich was formerly a township in the south-west corner of the parish of St. Michael, Lichfield.[55] It lay beside Watling Street, which formed the whole of its southern boundary. Formerly 1,779 a. (721 ha.),[56] its area was increased to 2,535 a. (1,027 ha.) in 1934 by the addition of the civil parish of Ogley Hay Rural south of Watling Street.[57] In 1966 the north-west corner of Hammerwich was transferred to the urban district of Aldridge-Brownhills,[58] and in 1980 there were further boundary adjustments with Burntwood, Wall, and Shenstone.[59] This article covers only the area of the former township. It is a district which remains largely rural. There was, however, a considerable increase in population following the opening of a coalmine in the north-west corner of the township in 1849, while in the later 20th century there has been extensive residential development.

The terrain is undulating and rises from 356 ft. (109 m.) on the eastern boundary to 503 ft. (153 m.) in the north-west. The church is a landmark, standing at 485 ft. (148 m.) on a hill top above Hammerwich village centre. North-west of the church the southern end of Overton Lane lies around the 500-ft. (152-metre) contour and is known as the Plateau. The Lower Keuper Sandstone underlies the eastern part of the parish and the Bunter Upper Mottled Sandstone and Pebble Beds the western part. The Eastern Boundary Fault of the Cannock Chase Coalfield runs across the north-west corner. There is Boulder Clay in the east and, with other gravelly drift, in the west.[60] Crane brook, mentioned in 1300, flows out of Chasewater, which was earlier known as Norton Pool, formed as a canal reservoir c. 1798.[61] Black brook, known as Hammerwich Water in the early 19th century,[62] rises at the north end of Hammerwich village

[41] S.R.O., D. (W.) 1734/2/1/612, mm. 25, 40.
[42] Shaw, *Staffs.* i. 361.
[43] Above, Lichfield, parish govt.
[44] Shaw, *Staffs.* i. 361; *Dyott's Diary*, ii. 244; S.R.O., D. 458/1/4, pp. 502, 520.
[45] Staffs. Review Order, 1934, p. 68 (copy in S.R.O.); Lichfield (Parishes) Order 1980, S.I. 1980 no. 387; inf. from Chief Executive, Lichfield District Council.
[46] *Aris's Birmingham Gaz.* 24 Apr. 1780; 30 Jan. 1797; *Lichfield Mercury*, 1 Feb. 1828.
[47] L.J.R.O., D. 30/9/3/3/4.   [48] Ibid. D. 30/9/3/2/4.
[49] Ibid. D. 20/1/1, f. 112; D. 20/1/2, burials of 8 Nov. 1677, 13 May 1719.
[50] *Swinney's Birmingham Chron.* 10 May 1810; *Dyott's Diary*, ii. 230; S.R.O., D. 661/11/2/3/1/16, 13 June 1847.
[51] C. Gittings, *Death, Burial and the Individual in Early Modern England*, 188–9.
[52] *Staffs. Advertiser*, 21 Feb. 1891, p. 5; Clayton, *Cathedral City*, 157–9.

[53] L.J.R.O., B/V/7/Whittington; S.R.O., D. 661/11/2/3/1/13, 18 Dec. 1836.
[54] Lich. Dioc. Regy., Orders in Council, S, p. 40.
[55] This article was written in 1987. Mr. H. Clayton of Lichfield, Mr. I. G. Crossland of Hammerwich, the Revd. J. A. Fielding-Fox, vicar of Hammerwich, Miss S. H. Shaw of Hammerwich, Mr. W. E. Hopkinson, formerly of Hammerwich, and others named in footnotes are thanked for their help.   [56] *V.C.H. Staffs.* i. 323.
[57] Staffs. Review Order, 1934 pp. 10, 67, and map 7 (copy in S.R.O.); *Kelly's Dir. Staffs.* (1936).
[58] West Midlands Order, 1965, S.I. 1965 no. 2139 (copy in S.R.O.); *Census*, 1971.
[59] Lichfield (Parishes) Order 1980, S.I. 1980 no. 387.
[60] Geol. Surv. 1″, drift, sheet 154 (1922 edn.); G. Barrow and others, *Memoirs of Geol. Surv., Geol. of Country around Lichfield*, 141, 147, 177.
[61] Above, Burntwood, introduction.
[62] S.R.O., D. (W.) 3222/191/20; B.L. Maps, O.S.D. 258.

and formed the north-eastern boundary with Burntwood until the change of 1980; it flows into Crane brook at Chesterfield, in the adjoining parish of Shenstone.

Thirty-one people in Hammerwich were assessed for the subsidy of 1327 and 28 for the poll tax of 1380–1.[63] Twenty-four were assessed for hearth tax in 1666.[64] The population of the township was 209 in 1801 and had risen to 270 by 1851. With the development of mining in the area it had reached 991 by 1861 and 1,325 by 1871. The increase then slowed, with many people leaving by the later 1870s because of the depression in the coal trade. The population of 1,391 in 1881 had risen to 1,573 by 1891. It had dropped to 1,546 by 1901.[65] Immigrants included a large number of Irish who settled in the west part of the parish.[66] Numbers had risen to 1,611 by 1911 and 1,772 by 1921, with a fall to 1,638 by 1931. The enlarged parish had a population of 2,285 by 1951 and 2,408 in 1961. Despite the transfer of a populous area in 1966 numbers were 3,538 in 1971 and 4,252 in 1981.[67]

Hammerwich lay within that portion of Cannock forest which became Cannock Chase in the 13th century. Until the later 19th century settlement was concentrated in the eastern part of the township, with the western part remaining heathland. The Old English name Hammerwich means a place (*wic*) by a hill (*hamor*).[68] There may have been two centres of population in the late 11th century, represented by the 'two Hammerwich' of Domesday Book.[69] Eventually there were three centres, Overton mentioned in the late 13th century,[70] Netherton in 1319,[71] and Middleton in 1381.[72] The names Nether town and Middle town were still used in 1871,[73] while Overton remains in use. There was still a green at each in the early 19th century.[74]

Netherton green lay around the junction of Hall Lane with Coppice Lane and with Lion's Den.[75] The continuation of Hall Lane southeast to Watling Street at Muckley Corner was known as Marebath Lane in the late Middle Ages and Marble Lane in the 19th century.[76] Lion's Den, so called by 1881,[77] was earlier known as Elder Lane, a name in use by the late Middle Ages.[78] Hammerwich Hall Farm on Hall Lane existed by the later 17th century and Hammerwich Place Farm in the angle of Hall Lane and Lion's Den by the 18th century.[79]

Middleton green was presumably the open space in the village centre now known as the village green.[80] Farmhouses were built or rebuilt in the central area in the 18th century, and a windmill was built in 1778.[81] In the later 19th century several large houses were built: Hammerwich House dates from *c.* 1870 when it replaced a farmhouse;[82] Fair View (later Blackroot House) was built in the mid 1870s and was then the home of T. B. Wright, the founder of Hospital Sunday;[83] Gartmore was built in the later 1890s by W. G. Leckie, a Walsall saddlery and harness manufacturer;[84] the vicarage house dates from 1894.[85] Hammerwich Square off the southern part of Overton Lane existed by 1871 when several miners were living there,[86] and other houses in that part of Overton Lane are dated 1904 and 1911. Council houses were built there between the two World Wars and *c.* 1960.[87] In the 1980s there has been considerable private residential development in the village centre, including an estate built over the grounds of the demolished Blackroot House.[88]

Overton green lay along Overton Lane between its junction with Pingle Lane and Coppy Nook Lane and was still the name used for that area in 1892.[89] Pingle Lane was mentioned in the earlier 15th century,[90] and Coppy Nook was an inhabited area by 1783.[91] Overton Manor House dates from the mid 18th century, but it has an earlier cellar.[92] The houses in Pingle Lane date from the late 19th century onwards and those in Burntwood Road from the early 20th century onwards.[93] A privately built estate in the triangle formed by Overton Lane, Burntwood Road, and Pingle Lane dates from the later 1980s.

Further north Norton Lane, which marks part of the boundary with Burntwood, was mentioned in 1449.[94] Sterre (or Star) Lane (later Hammerwich Road), running south from Norton Lane and continuing the boundary, was mentioned in 1453.[95] Apple Tree Farm in Hammerwich Road contains part of a small timber-framed building of the 17th century or earlier,

[63] *S.H.C.* vii (1), 232 (corrected by *S.H.C.* 4th ser. vi. 24); *S.H.C.* xvii. 177 (date corrected by *S.H.C.* 4th ser. vi. 3 n.).
[64] *S.H.C.* 1923, 158.
[65] *V.C.H. Staffs.* i. 323; S.R.O., D. 3801/1/1; above, Burntwood, introduction; econ. hist.
[66] P.R.O., RG 11/2775.
[67] *Census*, 1911–81.
[68] Ekwall, *Eng. Place-Names.*   [69] Below, estates.
[70] S.R.O., D. (W.) 1734/J. 2268, f. 2v.
[71] Ibid. D. (W.) 1734/2/2/52.
[72] Ibid. D. (W.) 1734/2/1/378, m. 4d.
[73] P.R.O., RG 10/2915.
[74] S.R.O., D. (W.) 1821/5; D. (W.) 1851(34)/34. All three greens were mentioned in the 1520s: D. (W.) 1734/2/1/604, mm. 29, 32; D. (W.) 1734/2/1/605, m. 19; D. (W.) 1734/2/3/79.
[75] J. Phillips and W. F. Hutchings, *Map of County of Stafford* (1832).
[76] L.J.R.O., D. 30/VC, palimpsest, iii, f. 3; S.R.O., D. 603/H/5/5, no. 2465; S.R.O., Q/RDc 99; P.R.O., RG 10/2915.
[77] P.R.O., RG 11/2775. The name may be connected with Thomas Lyon, who lived at the southern end of the lane by the 1840s: L.J.R.O., B/A/15/Hammerwich, no. 204; P.R.O., HO 107/980.

[78] L.J.R.O., D. 30/VC, palimpsest, iii, ff. 3v.–4; S.R.O., D. (W.) 1821/5.
[79] Below, estates.
[80] S.R.O., D. 4430/1/5, p. 127.
[81] Below, estates; econ. hist.
[82] Below, estates.
[83] Below, public services (cottage hospital).
[84] *Kelly's Dir. Staffs.* (1900); O.S. Map 6", Staffs. LVIII. NW. (1903 edn.); inf. from Mr. H. Clayton.
[85] Below, church.
[86] P.R.O., RG 10/2915.
[87] Below, public services.
[88] e.g. *Lichfield Mercury*, 19 Oct. 1984, p. 30.
[89] S.R.O., D. (W.) 1821/5; below, estates (Overton farm, n. 97).
[90] S.R.O., D. (W.) 1734/2/1/603, m. 17; D. (W.) 1734/J. 2051, dorse.
[91] S.R.O., D. 3802/1/1, 9 Feb. 1783.
[92] Below, estates.
[93] Date stones on houses; O.S. Map 6", Staffs. LVIII. NW. (1938 edn.).
[94] S.R.O., D. (W.) 1734/2/1/603, m. 29.
[95] Ibid. m. 43 (with Sterrecrofte Lane earlier in 1453: m. 40d.); D. (W.) 3222/191/21, pp. 4–5. For the derivation of the name see below, estates (Church Lands char.).

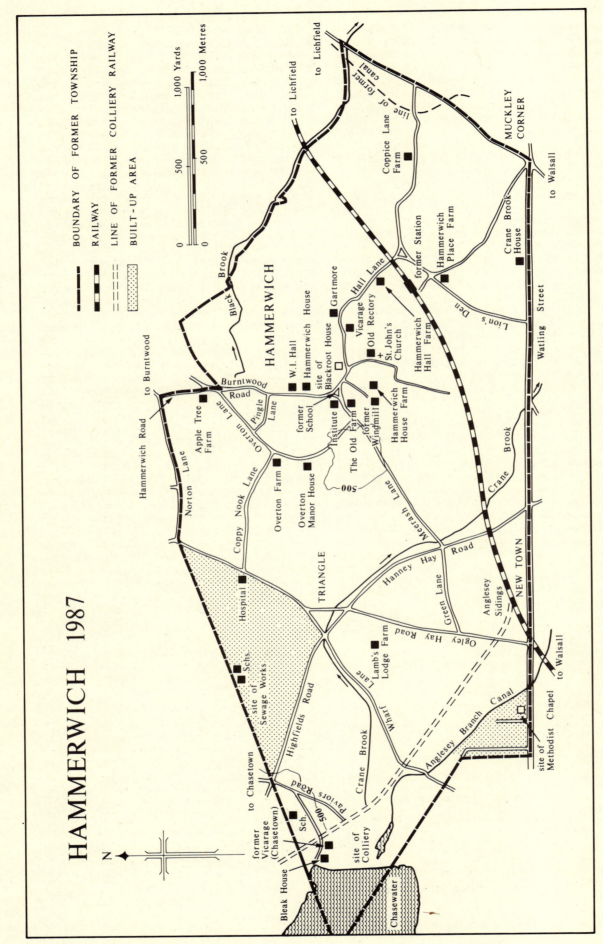

FIG. 23

which was incorporated in the rear wing of the house when it was enlarged in the 18th century.[96]

The south-east corner of the township at Muckley Corner was inhabited by 1775.[97] The farm to the west on Watling Street, later known as Crane Brook House, existed by 1843.[98] Coppice Lane Farm north of Muckley Corner dates from the mid 19th century.[99]

With the inclosure of the heathland in the western part of the township in 1856 under an Act of 1853 new roads were laid out and new settlements appeared. Already in the 18th century a warrener's lodge had been built on the heath.[1] By 1805 there was a cottage with a workshop near the northern end of the reservoir dam;[2] it may have been occupied in connexion with the reservoir. A coalmine was opened to the south in 1849; the cottage was enlarged as the manager's house, which became known as Bleak House, and two pairs of miners' cottages were built nearby.[3] Another house had been built east of Bleak House by 1856; it became the vicarage for St. Anne's, Chasetown, opened in 1865.[4] Building land on Watling Street was advertised for sale in 1854, and by 1861 new settlements of miners were developing in the south-west corner on Watling Street, at New Town to the east along Watling Street, and in the north-west at Pavier's Row and Triangle.[5] Pavier's Row (renamed Pavior's Road in 1962) had been built by 1860 and consisted of 21 cottages belonging to John Pavier of Hammerwich Place Farm.[6] In the early 20th century houses were built along Triangle Road, which was renamed Highfields Road. Building continued there in the years between the two World Wars, and council houses were built at Triangle in 1938.[7] The area on the north side of Watling Street in the west was rebuilt in the years following the Second World War.[8] In the 1960s and earlier 1970s housing estates were built between Highfields Road, Hospital Road, and the Burntwood boundary, building which represents the extension into Hammerwich of the residential development of Burntwood.[9]

The Lichfield–Walsall road on the eastern boundary of the township was turnpiked as far south as Muckley Corner in 1729.[10] The stretch of Watling Street forming the southern boundary of Hammerwich was turnpiked in 1789 to link the Lichfield–Walsall road at Muckley Corner and the Chester road just over the boundary with Norton Canes.[11] In 1838 it was stated that a finger post had once stood where Watling Street crossed that boundary; a cross stood in the area in 1650.[12]

The Wyrley and Essington Canal, opened in 1797, ran through the east of Hammerwich. That stretch was closed in 1954, but for some years it had been used only by maintenance boats.[13] From Norton Pool reservoir a feeder ran through the township into Ogley Hay, linking the reservoir with the canal.[14] It was incorporated in the Anglesey Branch Canal cut in 1850 to link the new colliery with the main canal.[15] The branch became disused with the closure of the last of the Chasetown mines in 1959.[16]

The South Staffordshire Railway was opened through Hammerwich in 1849 with a station at Netherton.[17] There was an immediate rise in the value of property in Hammerwich.[18] The station, having become an unstaffed halt in 1959 or 1960, was closed for goods traffic in 1964 and for passengers in 1965,[19] and the buildings were converted into a private house. A railway linking the colliery with the South Staffordshire Railway at Anglesey Sidings at New Town was built in 1852.[20] The rails had been taken up by 1964.[21]

The Elias Ashmole Ashmall Institute was built in the centre of the village in 1911 in memory of a local farmer who was churchwarden for 34 years and died in 1889. Much of the cost was met by his son-in-law, Sir Richard Cooper, Bt., and the site was given by F. Villiers Forster and Sir Charles Forster. The building was extended in 1972.[22] A women's institute was established in 1920. At first it met at the Ashmall Institute, but in 1936 a W.I. hall was built in Burntwood Road. In 1958 it became the church hall as well.[23] A community centre was opened in 1983 in the former village school.[24] A

[96] Mrs. D. Heathcote of Apple Tree Farm is thanked for her help.
[97] Above, fig. 1.
[98] L.J.R.O., B/A/15/Hammerwich.
[99] Below, estates (property of the Lichfield vicars choral).
[1] Below, econ. hist.
[2] S.R.O., D. (W.) 1511(34)/34; D. (W.) 1821/5; D. 603/H/5/5, no. 2433; L.J.R.O., D. 15/3/1.
[3] Old Chasetown, 58; Jnl. Staffs. Ind. Arch. Soc. ix (2), 2, 58; S.R.O., D. 603/M/1, Landor to Beer, 5 Mar. and 15 June 1850; D. 1456/7, inventory 1855, p. 15; P.R.O., HO 107/2014 (2); below, econ. hist.
[4] S.R.O., Q/RDc 99; above, Burntwood, churches.
[5] Staffs. Advertiser, 24 June 1854, p. 8; 25 Nov. 1854, p. 1; P.R.O., RG 9/1974.
[6] L.J.R.O., Copy Wills, vol. xxxii, f. 231; Lichfield Mercury, 22 Mar. 1889, p. 4. For Pavior's Rd. see S.R.O., D. 4430/1/4, p. 39. Pavier changed his name to Jackson in 1860.
[7] O.S. Map 6", Staffs. LVII. NE. (1903, 1921, and 1938 edns.); Staffs. Advertiser, 29 Feb. 1924, p. 1; below, public services.
S.H.C. 4th ser. xiii. 92; V.C.H. Staffs. ii. 277, 280; L.J.R.O., D. 15/2/3, 3 Feb. 1789.
[12] S.R.O., D. 601/1/788; D. (W.) 3222/191/22.
[13] Above, Lichfield, communications.

[14] L.J.R.O., D. 15/3/1; Phillips and Hutchings, Map of County of Stafford (1832).
[15] D. G. Brown, 'Econ. Dev. of Marquess of Anglesey's Cannock Chase Estate 1842–1891' (Wolverhampton Polytechnic M.A. thesis, 1985), 38, 40; S.R.O., D. 603/M/6/2, Landor to Beer, 30 Oct. 1850. The date of construction is wrongly given as 1840 in V.C.H. Staffs. ii. 296.
[16] S.R.O., D. 4430/1/3, p. 245.
[17] C. R. Clinker, Railways of the West Midlands 1808–1954, 19.
[18] P.O. Dir. Staffs (1850).
[19] S.R.O., D. 4430/1/3, pp. 223, 225, 237; Lichfield Mercury, 23 Oct. 1959, p. 7; C. R. Clinker, Clinker's Reg. of Closed Passenger Stations and Goods Depots, 59, 163.
[20] S.R.O., D. 603/H/5/3, draft letter of 12 Apr. 1849; D. 603/H/6/1, Landor to Beer, 13 Nov. 1851; D. 603/H/6/2, Landor to Beer, 7 Aug. 1853; D. 603/H/7/1/10; D. 603/H/7/3; D. 877/187/2/3; D. 1456/7, pp. 8–9; Brown, 'Cannock Chase Estate', 40; Jnl. Staffs. Ind. Arch. Soc. ix (2), 2, 11; Lond. Gaz. 9 . 1972, p. 8; S.R.O., D. 3802/1/10, p. 14; D. 4430/1/4, p. 14; memorial window to Ashmall in Hammerwich church.
[23] Lichfield Mercury, 21 Feb. 1936, p. 4; St. John's & Hammerwich News (Apr. 1985; set in possession of Mr. I. G. Crossland).
[24] Below, education.

cricket match was played in 1871 between a Hammerwich club and Lichfield (St. Mary's) club, and in 1883 there was a match between Hammerwich and Burntwood, evidently under the auspices of the respective incumbents.[25] A cricket club was formed in 1948 and acquired a ground in Burntwood Road in 1978.[26]

ESTATES. In 1086 the bishop of Chester held two estates in Hammerwich ('due Hameruuich') as part of his manor of Lichfield (later Longdon).[27] They were not subinfeudated as manors but were held of the bishop by freeholders, who paid a fine for a forest offence in 1166–7.[28] Assessed at 2 hides c. 1255, Hammerwich remained part of Longdon manor.[29]

A portion of the area, however, became part of Farewell manor. Bishop Clinton's endowment of the nuns of Farewell priory c. 1140 included ½ hide held by 'Haminch' (probably Hamon) of Hammerwich; half the estate was to be held by the nuns in demesne and half by Haminch's heirs as tenants of the nuns. Henry II, probably in 1155, confirmed the nuns in their possession of a carucate at Hammerwich with villeins, a free man named Hamon the fiddler, the lands of those tenants, and pasture which had belonged to the estate in 1135.[30] The nuns' estate in Hammerwich remained part of Farewell manor, which was granted to the dean and chapter on the priory's suppression in 1527 and to Lord Paget in 1550.[31]

The Stanleys, lords of Pipe in Burntwood, held property in Hammerwich of Longdon manor in the 15th century.[32] A house and lands in Hammerwich descended with Pipe in the 16th century, being held of Farewell manor in 1574 by Christopher Heveningham.[33] George Stanley, a younger son of Thomas Stanley, lord of Pipe, held an estate in Hammerwich of the bishop by 1475 and was described as lord of Hammerwich in the 1480s.[34] He died in 1509, and his son and heir John held three messuages and meadow in Hammerwich at his death in 1534. His home was then at West Bromwich, where the manor was held by his wife. John's son and heir Francis, lord of West Bromwich from 1552, was succeeded by a son George in 1558.[35] In 1574 George Stanley held a house and

land in Hammerwich as part of Farewell manor.[36]

HAMMERWICH HALL, so called by 1741,[37] was the home of William Heath, the son of William Heath of Weeford, by the mid 17th century. He was living in Hammerwich in 1645, and in 1666 he was assessed for tax on eight hearths in the township, the largest assessment there. He died in 1676.[38] The hall and its estate were later the property of Charles Kendall, who was living in Hammerwich by 1727.[39] He was dead by 1734, and his three sisters were his heirs. That year one of them, Theophila, the widow of Job Reading of Woodhouses in Burntwood, sold her third share to Cornelius Reading of Pipehill, evidently her stepson.[40] By his will proved in 1774 Cornelius left most of his property to his son John, whose heir under his will of 1791 was his niece Ann, wife of the Revd. Francis Willington.[41] She was living at Pipehill by 1818. In 1821 Hammerwich Hall was occupied by John Pavier; by 1834 the tenant was his nephew Thomas Pavier.[42] Ann died in 1841 and left Hammerwich Hall to Thomas and his brother John of Hammerwich Place Farm.[43]

By 1843 Thomas was the sole owner of the Hall and its 144-a. farm, although he was no longer living in Hammerwich.[44] In 1860 he settled the reversion of the farm after his death on his daughter Mary.[45] In 1871 he inherited the Wall Hall estate from John; to secure the inheritance he changed his name to Jackson in accordance with the will of his uncle Edward Jackson.[46] Thomas died at Edial, in Burntwood, in 1885.[47] On Mary's death in 1898 Hammerwich Hall farm was divided between the two children of her first and second marriages, J. E. P. Norris and Caroline Brown. They sold it in 1924 to G. H. Holt of Apeton, in Church Eaton. He promptly mortgaged it to R. A. Watkins of Tamworth and George Horne of Stafford. In 1937 they sold it to James Lymer and Reginald Horne, both of Stafford, who sold it in 1947 to Thomas Williams, a coal merchant of Walsall; his father Simeon was already the tenant. Thomas moved there in 1960 and died in 1978. Hammerwich Hall farm passed to his widow Winifred, and after her death in 1987 it was divided among her grandchildren.

In the early 19th century the timber-framed

[25] Staffs. Advertiser, 2 Sept. 1871, p. 2; above, Burntwood, social and cultural activities.
[26] S.R.O., D. 4430/1/4, p. 236; D. 4430/1/6, pp. 196, 236.
[27] V.C.H. Staffs. iv. 42.
[28] S.H.C. i. 48.
[29] Shaw, Staffs. i, app. to Gen. Hist. p. xvi; below, local govt.
[30] V.C.H. Staffs. iii. 223; Dugdale, Mon. iv. 111–12.
[31] V.C.H. Staffs. iii. 166, 224; below, local govt. For the bounds in 1574 see S.R.O., D. (W.) 1734/2/3/57.
[32] S.R.O., D. (W.) 1734/2/1/598, mm. 47–8, 60; D. (W.) 1734/2/1/603, m. 6.
[33] Ibid. D. (W.) 1734/J. 2039.
[34] Ibid. D. (W.) 1734/2/1/598, mm. 45d., 46; S.H.C. 1917–18, 275 n.; S.H.C. 1934 (2), 94.
[35] V.C.H. Staffs. xvii. 16; S.R.O., D. (W.) 1734/2/1/387, m. 15d.; above, Lichfield (cathedral and close: burials and monuments).
[36] S.R.O., D. (W.) 1734/J. 2039.
[37] L.J.R.O., D. 15/11/14/122.

[38] Shaw, Staffs. ii. 25; S.H.C. 1923, 158; S.H.C. 4th ser. ii. 19; H. Sanders, Hist. and Antiquities of Shenstone (1794), 41; L.J.R.O., D. 27/1/1, f. 120v.; below, chars. for the poor.
[39] L.J.R.O., D. 15/11/14/137, deed of 28 Sept. 1727.
[40] Ibid. D. 15/11/14/122. In her will Theophila described Cornelius as her son-in-law: ibid.
[41] L.J.R.O., P/C/11, Cornelius Reading (1774); S.R.O., D. 1317/1/9/1/1/1.
[42] Parson and Bradshaw, Staffs. Dir. (1818); 7th Rep. Com. Char. 357; White, Dir. Staffs. (1834), 107; S.R.O., D. 1317/1/9/1/1/4.
[43] S.R.O., D. 1317/1/9/1/1/3 and 6.
[44] L.J.R.O., B/A/15/Hammerwich.
[45] Rest of para. based on deeds at Hammerwich Hall Farm and at the office of Sharrott, Barnes & Co., solicitors of Lichfield, and on information supplied by Mrs. M. A. Walker of Hammerwich Hall Farm.
[46] Below, Wall, manor.
[47] Lichfield Mercury, 27 Mar. 1885, p. 5, describing him as of Hammerwich Hall.

house had a large block built at its west end. The timber-framed range was demolished to make way for a new house, built in 1960.[48] To the north is a brick barn with a date stone of 1786, and on the opposite side of Hall Lane is a three-bayed timber-framed barn of the 17th century with a later brick extension.

An estate centring on *HAMMERWICH HOUSE* originated in the estate in Hammerwich built up by Simon Biddulph of Lichfield from 1565. By 1574 it included four messuages held of Farewell manor.[49] Simon was succeeded in 1580 by his son Simon, who was followed in 1632 by his son, Michael Biddulph of Elmhurst.[50] In 1636 Michael granted a lease of a house and land at Hammerwich. The house was in decay, and the lessees were to build a new house of two bays, with three bays of other buildings, using the timber from the existing house. In 1655 Michael and his son Michael conveyed the reversion of the Hammerwich estate, including three messuages, after the elder Michael's death to a younger son Theophilus.[51] That death took place in 1658. Theophilus, created a baronet in 1664, was succeeded in 1683 by his son Michael. Sir Michael died in 1718, leaving a farm in Hammerwich and Edial to his wife Elizabeth.[52]

Elizabeth sold the farm to the tenant, Samuel Moor, in 1719, although the conveyance was not completed until 1725. By his will dated 1723 Samuel left the farm to his son Samuel, whose widow Elizabeth held it in 1749. That year, on the marriage of her daughter Elizabeth to Henry Webb of Hammerwich, she settled the reversion on the younger Elizabeth. Between 1781 and 1787 Henry rebuilt the house, and in 1799 he sold it to his son-in-law Thomas Middleton of Hammerwich.[53] By 1749 Henry had inherited from his uncle Henry Webb, a Tamworth innkeeper, another house in Hammerwich, which became his home. He subsequently sold it to Stephen Riley, whose son John Riley of Rugeley (d. 1803) left it in trust to be sold. It too was bought by Thomas Middleton in 1805.[54] In 1824 Middleton conveyed several houses in Hammerwich to his son William.[55] All that property was let, and he and his son were probably living in a farmhouse on the site of the later Hammerwich House. Thomas died in 1839, and in 1843 William owned and occupied the 38-a. farm.[56] In 1861 he was living in retirement at the farm, which was run by his son

William.[57] The elder William died in 1862.[58] His son was living at Torquay (Devon) by 1865 when he settled his Hammerwich estate in trust to be sold.[59]

By 1868 the house, then known as Hammerwich House, was the home of Arthur Hills, a manufacturing chemist with a works nearby in Ogley Hay. He was still living there in 1876,[60] and it was probably in his time that the house was rebuilt. It was offered for sale in 1877 and 1878.[61] By 1880 it was the home of Job Evans, a manufacturer of galvanized iron apparently from Wolverhampton, who put it up for sale with 43 a. in 1895 on leaving the district.[62] It was the home of John Leckie in the later 1890s.[63] In 1901 it was bought by Benjamin Stretton (d. by 1912), whose widow Frances continued to live at Hammerwich House.[64] From 1941 it was used as an annexe by the Birmingham and Midland Hospital for Women at Sparkhill, Birmingham. Mrs. Stretton died in 1944,[65] and in 1945 Hammerwich House was bought by Walsall borough council. It was converted into a girls' remand home, opened in 1946.[66] It later became a children's home. In 1984 the council sold the house, which was reopened in 1985 as a private home for the elderly. In 1988 a nursing unit was added, the house having by then been renamed Hammerwich Hall.[67]

The estate known by the 1860s as *HAMMERWICH HOUSE FARM* was held in the 18th century by the Dolphin family of Shenstone. John Dolphin probably inherited it from his father John (d. 1724). In 1756 the younger John was succeeded by his nephew John Dolphin, who was himself succeeded in 1782 by his son Thomas Vernon Dolphin. In 1802 Thomas sold a house and 90 a. in Hammerwich to William Stubbs, a farmer of Little Wyrley in Norton Canes, who moved to Hammerwich. By 1833 he had left Hammerwich and the farm was occupied by his son William, who was probably working it by 1828. William succeeded his father in 1837.[68] By 1864 he was living in Mill Cottage. He died in 1865, leaving what was by then called Hammerwich House farm to his son Thomas, who had farmed there earlier but had left to farm at Teddesley Hay.[69] In 1857 William had exchanged part of his land with the marquess of Anglesey for Lamb's Lodge and 6 a. adjoining, and by 1863 he had a 49-a. farm centring on the lodge; in his will he left that farm to be sold to pay Thomas's debts.[70] From the

[48] Inf. from Mrs. Walker.
[49] *S.H.C.* xiii. 241, 249, 253, 271, 280, 293; S.R.O., D. (W.) 1734/J. 2039.
[50] For the Biddulph pedigree see above, Curborough and Elmhurst, estates (Elmhurst Hall).
[51] W.S.L., M. 267.
[52] *S.H.C.* 1920 and 1922, 142 n.
[53] S.R.O., D. 1317/1/9/2/1–2; D. 1317/1/14/2/2.
[54] Ibid. D. 1317/1/9/1/3/1–2.
[55] Ibid. D. 1317/1/9/1/4/1.
[56] L.J.R.O., B/A/15/Hammerwich; S.R.O., D. 1317/1/9/2/2.
[57] P.R.O., RG 9/1974; S.R.O., D. 1317/1/9/3/3.
[58] S.R.O., D. 1317/1/9/3/1.
[59] Ibid. D. 1317/1/9/4/1.
[60] *P.O. Dir. Staffs.* (1868; 1876); *Kelly's Dir. Staffs.* (1880); P.R.O., RG 10/2915; O.S. Map 6″, Staffs. LVII. NE. (1887 edn.).
[61] *Staffs. Advertiser*, 24 Feb. 1877, p. 2; 31 Aug. 1878,

p. 8.
[62] *Kelly's Dir. Staffs.* (1880); *Hulley's Dir. Wolverhampton* (1874), 38, 164; *Lichfield Mercury*, 24 May 1895, p. 4; P.R.O., RG 11/2775. Notes by Mrs. M. Allen of Hammerwich on a postcard at Hammerwich House state that the house was built *c.* 1870 by Evans.
[63] *Kelly's Dir. Staffs.* (1900).
[64] Ibid. (1904 and later edns.); notes by Mrs. Allen.
[65] *Lichfield Mercury*, 7 Mar. 1941, p. 7; 7 Apr. 1944, p. 7.
[66] Ibid. 22 Nov. 1946, p. 7.
[67] Ibid. 26 Oct. 1984, p. 46; 10 May 1985, p. 23; 24 June 1988, p. 20; sale cat. (copy in W.S.L.); inf. from Mr. P. McVay, director of the home (1987).
[68] S.R.O., D. 1317/1/14/2/1–4. For the Dolphins see also *V.C.H. Staffs.* xvii. 176–7.
[69] S.R.O., D. 1317/1/14/2/1; D. 1317/1/14/9/5; *P.O. Dir. Staffs.* (1864; 1868).
[70] S.R.O., D. 1317/1/14/2/1; D. 1317/14/7/1; D. 1317/1/14/8/2.

early 1900s Hammerwich House farm was held by J. E. Fawcett and from *c.* 1910 by T. W. Fawcett.[71] It was offered for sale in 1919.[72] By 1924 it was farmed by Edward Fawcett, who sold it in 1959 to Mr. T. J. Bailye, the owner in 1987.[73] The brick farmhouse was described in 1833 as newly built.[74]

The farm known as *HAMMERWICH PLACE FARM* by the 1890s[75] was acquired in the 18th century by the Pavier family.[76] A John Pavier was living at Hammerwich in 1743,[77] and in 1772 a John Pavier was farming 198 a. there.[78] The farm was occupied by another John Pavier in 1834.[79] He lived there until his death in 1871, having changed his name to Jackson in 1860 in order to inherit the Wall Hall estate.[80] By 1920 the farm, 126 a. in extent, was the property of H. A. Russell-Pavier. That year he sold it to Harry Cox, who farmed there until the later 1930s. In 1939 it was sold to Fred Barratt, and the Barratt family owned and occupied the 160-a. farm in 1987.[81] The house dates from the 18th century, but the garden front of three bays with a central doorway was added in the earlier 19th century. The garden has a terrace with statuary at either end. The pond on the opposite side of Hall Lane and the adjoining parkland, decayed by 1987, formed much of the 17-a. estate in John Pavier's occupation in 1843[82] and remained part of the farm.

The farm known as the *OLD FARM* by the 1890s[83] was formerly the endowment of the charity established under the will of Eleanor Alport dated 1727 to benefit eight Staffordshire incumbents. The farm had 72 a. in 1843 and 110 a. in 1921 when the trustees of the charity sold most of it to T. J. Moss. On Moss's death in 1956 it passed to his daughter Mrs. I. M. Bailye, and she and her family occupied the farm in 1987.[84] The house has a brick front range of three rooms, with the date 1767,[85] and a two-roomed back range, probably contemporary.

OVERTON GRANGE was held of Longdon manor in the mid 16th century by William Orme.[86] He probably succeeded Thomas Orme, who was frankpledge for Hammerwich from 1503 until 1528 and may have died *c.* 1539.[87] William was one of the Hammerwich

chapelwardens in 1553.[88] By 1563 he had been succeeded in the property by Fabian Orme, who was living at the Grange in 1571.[89] He was alive in 1590, but by 1597 the Grange was held by his widow.[90] It passed to George Orme, who was living in Hammerwich in 1603 and 1628.[91] A Mrs. Orme was assessed for tax on three hearths in Hammerwich in 1666.[92] In 1574 another house in Hammerwich also called the Grange and lands attached were held of Farewell manor by Thomas Smith.[93]

There were two farms at Overton in 1843. One, known as Overton farm by 1896,[94] had 74 a. and was owned by the Revd. Josiah Webb Flavel.[95] After his death in 1848 the house and 100 a. in Hammerwich and Edial were divided between his sons, the Revd. John Webb Flavel and Thomas William Flavel. Thomas bought his brother's share in 1859, although no conveyance was executed until 1871. In 1884 Thomas's mortgagees put the farm up for sale.[96] By the later 1880s it was occupied by Joseph Pyatt.[97] He was followed *c.* 1905 by Ernest Pyatt and he *c.* 1910 by Sidney Pyatt.[98] Sidney had left by 1940 and sold the farm in 1943 to E. J. Bailey, from whom the house was bought in 1984 by Mr. and Mrs. M. J. Darwin, the farm being divided up.[99] The house dates from *c.* 1900.

The other farm in 1843, 135 a. in extent, was owned by Charles Smith Forster and John Forster, who were evidently the owners by 1837.[1] The Forster family still owned land in Hammerwich in 1911.[2] By the late 1930s the farm was known as Overton Manor farm and was occupied by A. T. Price, who sold it in the 1950s to E. J. Bailey.[3] The house, in 1987 called Overton Manor House, later passed to the Bosworth family, from whom it was bought in 1973 by Mr. and Mrs. L. V. Ray.[4] It is a symmetrical brick house of the mid 18th century with an older stone cellar.[5]

By the later 16th century the tithes of Hammerwich were held by the prebendary of Free-ford in Lichfield cathedral.[6] The small tithes passed from the prebend to the vicar of St. Mary's, Lichfield, as part of the augmentation of that living by Bishop Lloyd in 1694.[7] By the

[71] *Kelly's Dir. Staffs.* (1904 and edns. to 1916).
[72] W.S.L., Sale Cat. H/1/30.
[73] *Kelly's Dir. Staffs.* (1924 and edns. to 1940); *Lichfield Mercury*, 18 Sept. 1959, p. 2; inf. from Mr. T. W. Bailye of the Old Farm.
[74] S.R.O., D. 1317/1/14/2/4.
[75] *Kelly's Dir. Staffs.* (1896).
[76] W.S.L., S. 672, facing p. 226.
[77] S.R.O., D. 4566/B, deed of 17 Feb. 1742/3.
[78] Ibid. D. 3802/8/1.
[79] White, *Dir. Staffs.* (1834), 107.
[80] P.R.O., RG 10/2915; below, Wall, manor.
[81] W.S.L., Sale Cat. H/1/26; *Kelly's Dir. Staffs.* (1924 and later edns.); inf. from Mr. F. Barratt.
[82] L.J.R.O., B/A/15/Hammerwich.
[83] *Kelly's Dir. Staffs.* (1900). It is named as Old Hall ibid. (1896).
[84] *V.C.H. Staffs.* v. 64 (where 1847 should read 1843: L.J.R.O., B/A/15/Hammerwich); inf. from Mrs. Bailye.
[85] Date stone on NE. gable, with initials W.G.
[86] S.R.O., D. (W.) 1734/2/3/79.
[87] Ibid. D. (W.) 1734/2/1/604, mm. 32, 35; D. (W.) 1734/2/1/606, mm. 1d., 25, 28.
[88] *S.H.C.* 1915, 173.
[89] S.R.O., D. (W.) 1734/2/1/609, mm. 11, 12d.; W.S.L., S.

MS. 326/2.
[90] *S.H.C.* 1930, 56, 80; S.R.O., D. (W.) 1734/2/3/112D.
[91] S.R.O., D. (W.) 1734/2/3/112D; *S.H.C.* 1940, 6; 1948-9, 89.
[92] *S.H.C.* 1923, 158.
[93] S.R.O., D. (W.) 1734/J. 2039.
[94] *Kelly's Dir. Staffs.* (1896).
[95] L.J.R.O., B/A/15/Hammerwich.
[96] S.R.O., D. 4566/12, Hammerwich.
[97] *Kelly's Dir. Staffs.* (1888; 1892), showing J. Pyatt at Overton Green; (1896), showing Joseph Pyatt at Overton Farm.
[98] Ibid. (1904; 1908; 1912).
[99] Ibid. (1940); inf. from Mrs. Darwin.
[1] L.J.R.O., B/A/15/Hammerwich; *Staffs. Advertiser*, 29 Apr. 1837, p. 1.
[2] Above, introduction (Elias Ashmole Ashmall Institute).
[3] *Kelly's Dir. Staffs.* (1940); inf. from Mr. T. W. Bailye of the Old Farm.
[4] Inf. from Mr. amd Mrs. Ray.
[5] S. H. Shaw, 'An arch. and hist. survey of the parish of Hammerwich' (Birmingham Univ. B.A. thesis, 1983), 47, states that a third storey was removed in the early 1960s and also describes the former barns there.
[6] Below, church.
[7] Above, Lichfield, churches.

beginning of the 19th century tithes of hay from 'ancient meadow' had been commuted for a customary payment of 1d. a year for each acre.[8] In 1843 the small tithes were commuted for a rent charge of £62 payable to the vicar of St. Mary's and the great tithes for one of £197 payable to the Ecclesiastical Commissioners, to whom the revenues of the prebendary of Free- ford had passed under the Cathedrals Act of 1840.[9] In 1860 the Commissioners assigned their rent charge to the incumbent of the new parish of Hammerwich.[10]

The Church Lands charity originated in property belonging to Hammerwich chapel in the Middle Ages. Land in Hammerwich known in 1295 as 'Chapeleynesmor'[11] was probably part of it. Robert Sterre, who held a house and two selions in Hammerwich of Farewell priory in 1319 and was still living in 1327, was prob- ably the man of that name who left the chapel a rent of 2d. from the selions; by 1377 the rent had been taken into the hands of the prioress.[12] By the early 16th century the chapelwardens held 2 a. of waste in Hammerwich formerly held by Maud Sterre (d. probably c. 1400), and they paid a rent of 12d. for it to the bishop as lord of Longdon.[13] In 1549 the chapel's endowments were listed as a priest's house, a chapelyard, Sterre croft in Hammerwich, and a meadow in Shenstone.[14] The Crown sold the chapel, the chapelyard, and lands in Hammerwich, all de- scribed as concealed lands, to two speculators in 1564.[15] In 1571 the chapelwardens held Sterre croft of Longdon manor for a 12d. rent; it was described as having been 'concealed land and so bought of the prince', presumably by one of the Pagets, the bishop's successors at Longdon.[16] Another estate in Hammerwich consisting of a cottage and ½ a. with 1 a. in Chapel field was held of Lord Paget's manor of Farewell by the inhabitants of Hammerwich in 1574;[17] it had been amalgamated with the chapel's endow- ments by 1716.

In that year Sir Michael Biddulph and others conveyed the chapel, the chapelyard, and lands to trustees. The lands consisted of a croft lately in the possession of the wardens, a meadow in Shenstone, a cottage, what was by then called Star croft, and a meadow, all in Hammerwich, and an acre at the bottom of Chapel Lane, formerly part of Chapel field. The profits were to be used to relieve the inhabitants 'from the payment of taxes and fifteenths thereafter to be due out of the said town' and to repair the church.[18] By the 1790s the income from what were then called the Church Lands was £5 10s.[19] In 1820 the property, 11 a. in extent, consisted of three houses and land in Norton Lane, in- cluding the 7-a. Star croft, another house and other land in Hammerwich, and a 1½-a. field and a piece of land in Shenstone.[20] The rent from Star croft in 1821 was £10 and from the rest £4 4s. The £10 was used for repairs, but when not so required it was banked; the balance in 1821 was £104 16s. The other rents had come to be enjoyed by successive ministers, who apparently regarded the land as glebe; the incumbent still seems to have been receiving them in the 1850s.[21] John Jackson (formerly Pavier) of Hammerwich Place Farm, by will proved 1871, left the trustees £100, the interest to be used for church purposes.[22] There were 10 trustees at the beginning of the 19th century but only eight in 1834.[23] The Church Lands charity remains in the hands of eight trustees, four of them elected by the ratepayers and four co-opted. Half the income is spent on the fabric of the church and half is applied to the general benefit of the inhabitants of Hammerwich. The church re- ceived £1,700 in 1987.[24]

The vicars choral of Lichfield cathedral held property in Hammerwich of Longdon manor in 1463.[25] In 1574 they held a house and a cottage there, closes covering 12 a., and 24½ a. in the open fields; that estate was held of Farewell manor.[26] In 1662 Elias Ashmole became the vicars' tenant in Hammerwich; he renewed the lease in 1673 and was considering a further renewal at the time of his death in 1692.[27] He in turn granted sub-leases in 1669 and 1677.[28] In 1858 the vicars owned 72 a. in Hammerwich, including Coppice Lane farm.[29] They conveyed all their property outside the Close to the Eccle- siastical Commissioners in 1872.[30]

The college of the cathedral chantry chaplains held an estate in Hammerwich by 1469. At the time of the suppression of the college in 1548 its property in Hammerwich consisted of a house and land, which were sold by the Crown to speculators in 1564.[31] It may have been the estate in Hammerwich which the Crown granted to the Savoy hospital in Westminster in 1556; the grant was surrendered in 1558.[32]

Oseney abbey (Oxon.) held a pasture in Ham- merwich by the 16th century, probably as part of its Shenstone estate.[33]

The 'Himersiche' held by the nuns of Blith- bury priory in Mavesyn Ridware, probably in

[8] L.J.R.O., B/A/15/Hammerwich; S.R.O., D. 4250/4.
[9] L.J.R.O., B/A/15/Hammerwich.
[10] Below, church.
[11] L.J.R.O., D. 30/G 4, m. 5.
[12] Ibid.; S.R.O., D. (W.) 1734/2/3/52; S.H.C. vii (1), 232.
[13] J.R.U.L.M., Ryl. Ch. Phillipps 126, dorse; S.R.O., D. (W.) 1734/2/1/601, m. 17.
[14] P.R.O., E 301/43.
[15] Cal. Pat. 1563–6, 62–3.
[16] W.S.L., S. MS. 326/2, m. 6.
[17] S.R.O., D. (W.) 1734/J. 2039.
[18] 7th Rep. Com. Char. 358–9.
[19] Acct. of rents 1789–98 (in possession of Mr. I. G. Crossland).
[20] L.J.R.O., B/A/15/Hammerwich; ibid. Shenstone; B/V/6/Hammerwich, 1820.
[21] 7th Rep. Com. Char. 359; White, Dir. Staffs. (1851), 516;

below, church (income).
[22] L.J.R.O., Copy Wills, xxxii, ff. 246v.–247v.
[23] Harwood, Lichfield, 564; White, Dir. Staffs. (1834), 107.
[24] Inf. from Mr. E. Jarvis, steward and trustee, and from Mr. I. G. Crossland.
[25] S.R.O., D. (W.) 1734/2/1/598, m. 35.
[26] Ibid. D. (W.) 1734/J. 2039.
[27] Elias Ashmole, ed. C. H. Josten, iii. 860; iv. 1339, 1885–8.
[28] Ibid. iii. 1144; iv. 1468.
[29] S.R.O., D. 3802/7/1, f. 7; P.R.O., RG 9/1974.
[30] V.C.H. Staffs. iii. 193.
[31] S.R.O., D. (W.) 1734/2/1/598, m. 52; D. (W.) 3222/525; Cal. Pat. 1563–6, p. 99.
[32] Cal. Pat. 1555–7, 544, 546.
[33] B.R.L. 288210; Valor Eccl. (Rec. Com.), iii. 221.

the later 12th century, has been identified as Hammerwich.[34] The identification seems improbable.

ECONOMIC HISTORY. AGRICULTURE.

In 1086 the two Hammerwich estates consisted of five carucates and were described as waste.[35] By the late 14th century there were at least three open fields. Chapel field extended south and south-east of the church; selions in it were bounded by Crane brook, Watling Street, and Lion's Den.[36] It was mentioned in 1381 and still existed in 1634, but it was inclosed, probably in its entirety, by 1716.[37] It was adjoined by Lightwood field, where selions were bounded by Lion's Den, Watling Street, and Hall Lane c. 1500.[38] Chapel field was also adjoined by Little field, which contained selions bounded by Lion's Den c. 1500 and was still an open field in the earlier 17th century.[39] An open field called Windmill field existed by 1381 and, as Willman field, still existed in 1655.[40] Overton field, mentioned in 1440, was still an open field in 1598.[41] In 1406 John Overton was presented for holding Watte croft in severalty, although it was customary for it to be common every third year; John Webb was presented for the same offence in 1461.[42] Oatcroft field or Oat field was open in 1571 and 1598, but it had evidently been inclosed by 1628 when there was mention of a close or pasture called Oatcroft or Great Oatcroft.[43]

Several plots of 'new land' inclosed from the waste in Hammerwich were held of the bishop in 1298.[44] Land called Cambrell in the portion of Hammerwich within Farewell manor was described in 1589 as recently ploughed from the waste, and the inhabitants were then ordered to repair the hedges and fences round it.[45] In 1599 a similar order was made regarding land lying in the portion within Longdon manor and described as lately inclosed from Cannock heath.[46] Cambrell was evidently part of the land on the heath which by the early 18th century it was customary to inclose and 'lot out' among the inhabitants of Hammerwich; after being cultivated for four or five years the land was thrown open again. The practice came to an end when it

became part of a warren c. 1717.[47] In 1789 the earl of Uxbridge as lord of Longdon granted 11 inhabitants of Hammerwich a 21-year lease of the upper part of a common called Muckley field in the south-east corner of the township at a rent of 2s. an acre. They were permitted to inclose the land and divide it among themselves in proportion to their existing holdings; at the end of the 21 years it was to be thrown open again.[48] During the earlier 19th century, however, it was still cultivated as a number of separate holdings.[49] In 1856 the 670 a. of remaining waste in Hammerwich were inclosed under an Act of 1853. They lay mostly in the west of the township but included Upper and Lower Muckley fields.[50] The inhabitants of Hammerwich also enjoyed common rights in Ogley Hay, an extra-parochial heath south of Watling Street. It was inclosed in 1839 under an Act of 1838.[51]

In 1298 two of the bishop's eight free tenants in Hammerwich owed labour services and pannage as well as rent and suit of court. Henry Wymer, who held 2 virgates, had to send two men to mow the meadow at Williford in Whittington for one day or else pay 8d., and he owed two pigs or 2s. for pannage. Agnes of Overton, who held 1 virgate, had to send one man to mow the lord's meadow for one day or pay 4d., and she owed one pig or 12d.[52] The same services were due from the two holdings in the early 16th century, with carrying services worth 8½d. as well in the case of the second.[53]

In the 14th century six of the c. 30 free tenants on Farewell priory's estate in Hammerwich owed labour services at harvest time.[54] Mowing service, however, had been commuted for payments of between ½d. and 2d. by the early 14th century, and by then six tenants paid between 1¼d. and 3d. for pannage. By 1399 one of the pannage payments had been increased to 2s. but the other five were unchanged. Demesne farming on the priory's Hammerwich estate seems to have ceased by 1419.

Peas and oats were grown at Hammerwich in 1359–60,[55] and rye, peas, and oats were sown there in the later 1370s.[56] Wheat, rye, and barley were grown in the later 17th century, with smaller quantities of hemp and flax.[57] By the late 1860s the main crops were wheat, turnips, and

[34] Dugdale, *Mon.* v. 160; *V.C.H. Staffs.* iii. 220.
[35] *V.C.H. Staffs.* iv. 42.
[36] L.J.R.O., D. 30/VC, palimpsest, iii, ff. 4–5v.; L.J.R.O., B/A/15/Hammerwich, nos. 181, 197.
[37] S.R.O., D. (W.) 1734/2/1/378, m. 7; L.J.R.O., D. 15/11/14/118; *S.H.C.* 1931, 72; below, church.
[38] L.J.R.O., D. 30/VC, palimpsest, iii, ff. 5v.–6; L.J.R.O., B/A/15/Hammerwich, nos. 205–6.
[39] L.J.R.O., D. 15/11/14/113; D. 30/VC, palimpsest, iii, ff. 2v., 3v.–4; L.J.R.O., VC/A/21, CC 162145, i, f. 39; L.J.R.O., B/A/15/Hammerwich, no. 200; S.R.O., D. (W.) 1734/J. 2042.
[40] S.R.O., D. (W.) 1734/2/1/378, m. 7; W.S.L., M. 267, deed of 26 Apr. 1655.
[41] S.R.O., D. (W.) 1734/2/1/603, m. 14; D. (W.) 1734/2/1/671; W.S.L., S. MS. 326/2, mm. 5–6.
[42] S.R.O., D. (W.) 1734/2/1/598, m. 34; D. (W.) 1734/2/1/600, m. 18; L.J.R.O., B/A/15/Hammerwich, nos. 11, 13, 20.
[43] S.R.O., D. (W.) 1734/2/1/401, m. 8; D. (W.) 1734/2/1/617, f. 19; D. (W.) 1734/2/1/671; W.S.L., S. MS. 326/2, mm. 5–6.
[44] S.R.O., D. (W.) 1734/J. 2268, f. 2v.
[45] Ibid. D. (W.) 1734/2/1/393, m. 2.
[46] Ibid. D. (W.) 1734/2/1/674.
[47] S.R.O., D. 260/M/E/429/31, p. 200. The closes included Big Gambrell and Little Gambrell.
[48] Ibid. D. 3802/8/2 (draft).
[49] W.S.L. 47/1/45, ff. 42, 65–6; L.J.R.O., B/A/15/Hammerwich.
[50] 16 & 17 Vic. c. 120 (Local & Personal); S.R.O., Q/RDc 99.
[51] S.R.O., D. 546/1, articles of Jan. 1709/10 and Ogley Hay rentals; White, *Dir. Staffs.* (1834), 106; *S.H.C.* 1941, 18.
[52] S.R.O., D. (W.) 1734/2/1, f. 2v.
[53] J.R.U.L.M., Ryl. Ch. Phillipps 126, dorse. The value of the mowing services for the second tenement is given as 3d.; for the first their value is left blank.
[54] Para. based on information kindly supplied by Dr. F. B. Stitt, formerly Staffordshire county archivist, from S.R.O., D. (W.) 1734/2/1/379; D. (W.) 1734/2/3/52, 54–5.
[55] P.R.O., E 199/41/15.
[56] S.R.O., D. (W.) 1734/J. 2037; S.R.O., D. (W.) 1734/3/3/34 (refs. supplied by Dr. Stitt).
[57] *S.H.C.* 4th ser. v, pp. 104–5, 123, 144, 174–5, 182, 192, 206.

barley.[58] Wheat and oats were advertised for sale at Lamb's Lodge farm in 1894.[59] When Hammerwich Place farm was put up for sale in 1920, it was described as very suitable for growing corn and potatoes.[60] The chief crops in 1984 were barley (140.7 ha. officially recorded), wheat (70.1 ha.), and potatoes (40.6 ha.).[61]

There were two shepherds among Farewell priory's free tenants in Hammerwich in 1318,[62] and sheep farming continued there, with the extensive heathland providing grazing. In the later 17th century most farms combined it with cattle farming.[63] There were four shepherds living in the township in 1861, though only one in 1871.[64] In 1984 the livestock officially recorded consisted of 442 cattle and calves, 1 pig, 1,338 sheep and lambs, and 1,340 poultry birds, mainly hens and pullets.[65]

In 1772 the inhabitants of Hammerwich were suffering extensive damage from moles. That year 15 people entered into a 31-year agreement with Samuel Insley, a Weeford mole catcher, who undertook to destroy the moles and to keep the township free of them. He was to be paid 1d. an acre a year.[66]

PARK AND WARREN. Farewell priory had a park at Hammerwich in the late 1370s.[67]

About 1717 John Lamb, a Lichfield coachmaker, laid out a warren on the Hammerwich part of Cannock Chase, stocking it with rabbits from another warren on the Chase. He built a lodge but later pulled it down and built another on a spur of high ground south of the later Triangle. The inhabitants of Hammerwich, faced with loss of pasture and destruction of their corn, resisted for some five years by digging the rabbits out and killing them. Lamb and his tenant at the lodge overcame their opposition by giving them fair words and the occasional rabbit.[68] By the mid 18th century the warren, held by John Hodgkins, covered several hundred acres. It consisted of 411 burrows, of which 311 had three pairs of rabbits each and 100 eight pairs each.[69] It was one of those destroyed in the attack on the Cannock Chase warrens by inhabitants of the area in the winter of 1753–4. It was restocked and still existed in 1824, when it extended into Burntwood.[70] By 1863, after the inclosure of 1856, the lodge had

become the farmhouse of the 49-a. Lamb's Lodge farm.[71]

WINDMILLS. In 1300 Henry Wymer held a windmill in Hammerwich. It was probably part of the estate in Hammerwich and elsewhere which had been granted to him by Henry Wymer the elder in 1280 and then included four mills.[72] It is the earliest windmill in Staffordshire of which there is definite record.[73] In 1574 a windmill on Brankeley flat in Chapel field formed part of the Hammerwich estate belonging to Farewell manor.[74]

A windmill was built west of the church in 1779 by Thomas Middleton, described as a maltster in 1799 and 1811.[75] He was still working it in 1823, but it was let by 1824 when he conveyed it with the rest of his property in Hammerwich to his son William.[76] By then it was known as Speedwell mill.[77] It was advertised for sale in 1827 with a newly built three-bedroom house adjoining it.[78] It was worked in the earlier 1830s by Thomas Davis.[79] By 1841 it was owned by Elizabeth Benton and worked by John Benton, probably her son. He continued as the miller until his death in 1881,[80] and his widow Elizabeth worked the mill until her own death in 1898.[81] It then ceased grinding and was dismantled in 1908. It was bought by Robert Sanders, the Hammerwich postmaster, who converted it into a house and added a battlemented top to the tower. The house was modernized in 1976–7 and a fibre-glass cupola placed on the tower.[82]

INDUSTRIES. A 'bendwareman', evidently involved with hardware, was living in Hammerwich in 1604.[83] A Hammerwich nailer was mentioned in 1774,[84] and there was a nailer's shop in the later Station Road at Netherton in 1824.[85] There were many nailers in the township in 1841 and 1851, but only two in 1861.[86]

Coal may have been mined in the earlier 17th century. Michael Biddulph's lease of his Hammerwich estate in 1636 included the provision that the lessees were to take a cartload of pit coals to his house at Elmhurst every year at his expense.[87] The 19th-century exploitation of coal in the area began in the north-west corner of Hammerwich. A mine was opened there east of

[58] P.O. Dir. Staffs. (1868).
[59] Lichfield Mercury, 17 Aug. 1894, p. 4.
[60] Sale cat. 1920 (copy in W.S.L.).
[61] M.A.F.F., agric. returns 1984.
[62] S.R.O., D. (W.) 1734/2/3/52.
[63] S.H.C. 4th ser. v, pp. 104–5, 123, 144, 174–5, 182, 192, 206, 271.   [64] P.R.O., RG 9/1974; RG 10/2915.
[65] M.A.F.F., agric. returns 1984.
[66] S.R.O., D. 3802/8/1.
[67] Ibid. D. (W.) 1734/J. 2037.
[68] Ibid. D. 260/M/E/429/31, pp. 184, 200–1; D. 603/K/5/7, list of warrens 1754.
[69] Ibid. D. 260/M/E/429/31, pp. 200–1; D. 603/K/5/7, list of warrens 1754.
[70] D. Hay and others, Albion's Fatal Tree, 220–36; S.R.O., D. (W.) 1511(34)/33, courts of 1770 and 1787; D. (W.) 1821/5; W.S.L. 47/1/45, f. 37; L.J.R.O., D. 15/3/1.
[71] Above, estates (Hammerwich House farm).
[72] S.H.C. vii (1), 74; S.H.C. 1911, 36–7.
[73] Jnl. Staffs. Ind. Arch. Soc. ix (1), 32, which also states that there is record in 1203 of a mill in Blymhill which may have been wind powered.

[74] S.R.O., D. (W.) 1734/J. 2039, rental of Farewell and Chorley 1574.
[75] Ibid. D. 1317/1/9/1/2/2–3; D. 1317/1/9/1/4/1.
[76] Ibid. D. 1317/1/9/2/5; above, estates (Hammerwich House).
[77] S.R.O., D. (W.) 1821/5.
[78] Lichfield Mercury, 23 Nov. 1827.
[79] White, Dir. Staffs. (1834), 107.
[80] P.R.O., HO 107/980; ibid. RG 11/2775; L.J.R.O., B/A/15/Hammerwich; S.R.O., D. 3802/1/10, p. 7.
[81] P.R.O., RG 11/2775; Lichfield Mercury, 18 Mar. 1898, p. 8.
[82] Jnl. Staffs. Ind. Arch. Soc. ix (1), 34; W. A. Seaby and A. C. Smith, Windmills in Staffs. 11, 19; Lichfield & Tamworth Life Mag. ii (1), 19.
[83] S.H.C. 1940, 182; C. H. Pole, An Attempt towards a Glossary of the Archaic and Provincial Words of the County of Stafford (Stratford-upon-Avon, 1880), 8.
[84] S.R.O., D. 603/A/526.
[85] Ibid. D. 603/H/5/3, no. 2433; D. (W.) 1821/5.
[86] P.R.O., HO 107/980 and 2014 (2); ibid. RG 9/1974.
[87] W.S.L., M. 267; above, estates (Hammerwich House).

the dam of Norton Pool in 1849, and in 1850 the Anglesey Branch Canal was cut through the south-west part of the township to connect the mine with the Wyrley and Essington Canal in Ogley Hay. A railway was completed through the same area in 1853, running from the South Staffordshire Railway at New Town to the expanding mining area. The Hammerwich mine was closed in 1856, but the canal and railway continued in use.[88]

There were stonepits north-east of the windmill in the early 1840s, and the stone for St. James's church at Ogley Hay, built in 1850–1, was quarried there. The quarry also supplied the stone for the rebuilding of Hammerwich church in the earlier 1870s.[89] In the earlier 1840s there was a gravel pit straddling the boundary with Burntwood at the north end of the pool dam. Gravel was still being worked on the Hammerwich side in the early 1880s.[90] By then, and probably by the early 1870s, there was a gravel pit on the south side of the canal near Watling Street.[91] By 1915 there was also a sandpit there and another to the north by the railway.[92] Working had spread north to a site off Wharf Lane by 1957,[93] part of which was still worked in 1987. There was a sandpit east of Hammerwich House in the early 1880s.[94] A brickyard was opened near the west end of Highfields Road shortly after the inclosure of 1856.[95] In the early 1880s there was a brickyard south of Norton Lane.[96]

LOCAL GOVERNMENT. In 1293 Hammerwich attended the view of frankpledge for Longdon manor, held at Lichfield.[97] It formed a tithing and by 1327 was represented by a single frankpledge.[98] A headborough was still appointed at the Longdon court in 1728.[99] The part of Hammerwich within Farewell manor was presenting at the Farewell view by 1290. The tithing was represented by two frankpledges, and that was still the number in 1636.[1] There was only one in 1703, and one was still appointed in 1722.[2] Hammerwich was a constablewick by the 14th century, and a constable was still appointed at the Longdon court in 1839.[3]

In 1473 the Longdon court ordered the Hammerwich constable to repair the pound.[4] The Farewell court appointed a pinner for Hammerwich in 1715 and 1722, and one was appointed at the Longdon court in 1839.[5] A pound on the village green was moved to the south-west corner of the green in the mid 19th century to make way for the new school.[6] It was still being maintained in 1896 by the parish council, which that year also appointed a pinner.[7] It was evidently disused by 1900, and in 1907 it was dismantled and the site sold.[8]

Formerly a township in the parish of St. Michael, Lichfield, Hammerwich was recognized as a civil parish by 1871.[9] It was included in Lichfield poor law union, formed in 1836.[10] Having been part of Lichfield rural district, it became part of the new Lichfield district in 1974.

Hammerwich had two chapelwardens by the early 16th century.[11] There were two overseers of the poor by 1832.[12] The parish council appointed a salaried highway surveyor in 1896.[13]

The inclosure award of 1856 assigned 2 a. in Hanney Hay Road to the churchwardens and overseers of the poor for the benefit of the labouring poor, subject to a rent charge of £1 payable to the incumbent.[14] It was divided into plots which were let out, but from 1936 it was let as a single plot.[15] In 1979 the council repossessed the land and in 1980 decided to incorporate it in the adjoining Jubilee Park.[16] The park itself had originated as a 2-a. allotment under the inclosure award for the recreation of the inhabitants of Hammerwich and the neighbourhood.[17]

PUBLIC SERVICES. A sewage works for Chasetown was opened on the Hammerwich side of the boundary with Burntwood in 1898. It was enlarged in 1929–30, when sewers linked with it were laid in Highfields Road and Pavier's Row. It remained in use until the late 1960s, and Oakfield Park was laid out on the site in the mid 1970s.[18] A sewage works was constructed at Triangle in 1899,[19] and another was opened to the south-west off Wharf Lane in 1916.[20] In

[88] Above, introduction; above, Burntwood, econ. hist.
[89] L.J.R.O., B/A/15/Hammerwich, no. 153; G. Barrow and others, *Memoirs of Geol. Surv., Geol. of Country around Lichfield*, 213; White, *Dir. Staffs.* (1851), 574; *Staffs. Advertiser*, 25 July 1874, p. 7; inf. from the Revd. J. A. Fielding-Fox.
[90] L.J.R.O., B/A/15/Burntwood; ibid. Hammerwich; O.S. Map 6″, Staffs. LVII. NE. (1887 edn.).
[91] O.S. Map 6″, Staffs. LVII. NE. (1887 edn.); P.R.O., RG 10/2915, showing sandpit workers living near the site in 1871.
[92] O.S. Map 6″, Staffs. LVII. NE. (1921 edn.).
[93] S.R.O., D. 4430/1/3, pp. 182, 204, 247; D. 4430/1/6, pp. 150, 158.
[94] O.S. Map 6″, Staffs. LVII. NE. (1887 edn.).
[95] S.R.O., D. 3807/7/1, p. 25; S.R.O., Q/RDc 99.
[96] O.S. Map 6″, Staffs. LVIII. NW. (1888 edn.).
[97] *Plac. de Quo Warr.* (Rec. Com.), 711.
[98] S.R.O., D. (W.) 1734/2/1/598, mm. 2d., 14.
[99] Ibid. D. 603/J/7/6/3.
[1] L.J.R.O., D. 30/G 4, mm. 2, 5, 12, 15; S.R.O., D. (W.) 1734/2/1/385, m. 6d.
[2] S.R.O., D. 603/J/5/2/2.
[3] *S.H.C.* 4th ser. vi. 11; S.R.O., D. 603/J/1/4/15.
[4] S.R.O., D. 603/J/13/3/1.

[5] Ibid. D. 603/J/1/4/15; D. 603/J/5/2/2.
[6] Ibid. D. 4430/1/1, p. 145.
[7] Ibid. pp. 4, 6, 10.
[8] Ibid. pp. 145, 150, 154. It is shown on O.S. Map 6″, Staffs. LVIII. NW. (1888 edn.) but not on the 1903 edn.
[9] P.R.O., RG 10/2915.
[10] Poor Law Com. Order 1836 forming Lichfield union (copy in L.J.R.O., D. 77/16/3).
[11] Above, estates (Church Lands char.).
[12] L.J.R.O., D. 27/3/9, 1 Oct. 1832.
[13] S.R.O., D. 4430/1/1, p. 3.
[14] Ibid. Q/RDc 99.
[15] Ibid. D. 4430/1/1, pp. 103–4, 145–6, 153–4, 156–7, 160; D. 4430/1/4, p. 75; D. 4430/2/4.
[16] Ibid. D. 4430/1/6; D. 4430/1/7, pp. 23, 79, 144, 158.
[17] S.R.O., Q/RDc 99.
[18] Above, Burntwood, public services; *Lichfield Mercury*, 18 July 1930, p. 6; S.R.O., D. 4430/1/4, pp. 196, 223; D. 4430/1/6, 9, 37, 41.
[19] *Lichfield Mercury*, 24 Nov. 1899, p. 3; S.R.O., D. 4430/1/1, pp. 76–7, 94.
[20] Lichfield R.D.C. *Ann. Rep. of M.O.H. 1915* (copy in S.R.O., C/H/1/2/2/25), 11; *1916*, 8; O.S. Map 6″, Staffs. LVII. NE. (1921 edn.).

1929 Hammerwich village was connected with the main outfall sewer in Burntwood ready for the opening of a new works in Peter's Lane in Burntwood in 1930.[21] The South Staffordshire Waterworks Co. laid mains at Triangle in 1896 and in the Watling Street and New Town area in 1898 after the wells there had been condemned.[22] It built a pumping station on the Walsall road in the north-east corner of the parish in 1907.[23] The parish council maintained a pump in the centre of Hammerwich village; it was removed apparently c. 1970.[24] Street lighting was introduced in 1923, with electricity supplied by the Cannock Chase Colliery Co.[25]

Twenty-one houses had been built by Lichfield rural district council in Overton Lane and on Watling Street by 1935. Another 10 council houses had been erected in Overton Lane by 1936, and 12 were built at Triangle in 1938.[26] Five more were built in Overton Lane c. 1960.[27] In 1956 six houses in the Hammerwich Square part of Overton Lane were the subject of a compulsory purchase order as unfit for human habitation, and there was slum clearance in Pavier's Row in 1957.[28]

In 1810 Hammerwich began subscribing 1 guinea to the Staffordshire General Infirmary at Stafford and thus became entitled to recommend one inpatient a year and any number of outpatients. From 1811 to 1818 it subscribed 3 guineas.[29] In 1853 Hammerwich had a sick club, attended by a surgeon from Bloxwich, in Walsall.[30] A cottage hospital was opened in Hospital Road in 1882 with two five-bed wards; an isolation ward was added soon afterwards. The cost of building was met by subscription, and the hospital was intended mainly for victims of mining accidents.[31] The prime movers appear to have been Robert Gordon, rector of Hammerwich, and Arthur Sopwith, general manager of the Cannock Chase Colliery Co. The hospital commemorated T. B. Wright, the Birmingham manufacturer who founded Hospital Sunday in 1859 and lived at Fair View in Hammerwich in the mid 1870s. His widow laid the foundation stone of the hospital and later left it £12,000.[32] During the First World War a military ward was added and between 400 and 500 wounded soldiers were treated there.[33] Extensions and improvements were carried out in 1937, including a new operating theatre, and the number of beds was increased from 19 to 25. The cost was met by a bequest of £10,000 from George Hodgkins

(d. 1934), a Brownhills farmer and a member for many years of Brownhills urban district council and Lichfield rural district council.[34] The hospital remained a general hospital until the closure of the operating theatre in 1967, and it then became a hospital for the elderly. In 1981 there was accommodation for 24 patients, and there was also an outpatients' department for physiotherapy and X-ray.[35] Hammerwich House was used as a hospital in the earlier 1940s.[36]

There was a police constable living in Hammerwich in 1851, and a police station had been opened by 1879. By 1896 there was no constable nearer than Burntwood and Muckley Corner, and the one at Muckley Corner was removed that year.[37]

By 1900 a post office had been opened off Mill Lane. It was demolished in 1974, and in 1987 the post office stood east of the green.[38]

By the late 1880s soup was distributed during the winter as a private charity. In the mild winter of 1889–90 the number of distributions dropped to 18, with an average of 120 children and 15 old and sick people benefiting each time. The seven ladies who distributed the soup that winter subscribed £6 7s. 6d. to meet the cost.[39]

CHURCH. Architectural evidence suggests the existence of a chapel at Hammerwich in the 12th century. In 1563 the chapel was described as appropriated to the prebend of Freeford in Lichfield cathedral and within the prebendary's peculiar jurisdiction. In 1549, however, it had been certified as a chantry chapel.[40] The existence of a chapelyard in 1549[41] suggests that the chapel then had burial rights. It had baptismal rights by the early 18th century: its former font, now in Christ Church, Burntwood, is dated 1715.[42] Marriages as well as baptisms and burials were regularly recorded in the first register, dating from 1720. In the 18th century the chapel was also used for baptisms and burials by people from neighbouring areas, especially Burntwood, Edial, and Woodhouses; two residents of Edial also endowed sermons at the chapel.[43] The chapel had its own wardens by the early 16th century.[44]

St. Michael's, Lichfield, was evidently recognized as the mother church by the late 16th century.[45] In 1726, when a new chapelyard was consecrated at Hammerwich, the churchwardens of St. Michael's entered a caveat to pres-

[21] *Lichfield Mercury*, 18 July 1929, p. 6.
[22] S.R.O., D. 4430/1/1, pp. 7, 11; *Lichfield Mercury*, 14 Apr. 1899, p. 6.
[23] Date on building.
[24] S.R.O., D. 4430/1/1, p. 104; D. 4430/1/2, p. 244; D. 4430/1/3, p. 53; *Lichfield & Tamworth Life Mag.* ii (1), 19.
[25] S.R.O., D. 4430/1/2, pp. 45 sqq.
[26] Lichfield R.D.C. *Ann. Rep. of M.O.H. 1935*, 23; *1936*, 23; *1938*, 23–4.
[27] S.R.O., D. 4430/1/3, p. 253.
[28] Lichfield R.D.C. *Ann. Rep. of M.O.H. 1956*, 10; *1959*, 15.
[29] S.R.O., D. 685/12/1.
[30] Ibid. D. 603/M/7/1/10, Somerville to Landor, 3 Feb. 1853; White, *Dir. Staffs.* (1851), 669.
[31] *Lichfield Mercury*, 11 Mar. 1881, p. 5; 20 May 1881, p. 5; *Staffs. Advertiser*, 11 Feb. 1882, p. 7; 7 Feb. 1885, p. 4; *Lich. Dioc. Mag.* (1881), 93.

[32] *Lichfield Mercury*, 11 Mar. 1881, p. 4; 20 May 1881, p. 5; Mason, *Found Ready*, 102–3; *P.O. Dir. Staffs.* (1876).
[33] *Lichfield Mercury*, 21 Apr. 1923, p. 3.
[34] Ibid. 28 Jan. 1938, p. 3.
[35] Ibid. 15 May 1981, p. 13.
[36] Above, estates.
[37] P.R.O., HO 107/2014 (2); *Lichfield Mercury*, 2 May 1879; S.R.O., D. 4430/1/1, pp. 36–7; below, Wall.
[38] S.R.O., D. 3801/1/1, prelim. notes; below, education.
[39] *St. John's & Hammerwich News* (Aug. 1980; copy in possession of Mr. I. G. Crossland).
[40] *S.H.C.* 1915, 173.
[41] Above, estates (Church Lands char.).
[42] W.S.L., Staffs. Views, iv. 239.
[43] S.R.O., D. 3802/1/1.
[44] Above, local govt.
[45] A marriage performed there in 1596 was recorded in the St. Michael's register: L.J.R.O., D. 27/1/1.

erve the rights of their church.[46] Church levies were being paid to St. Michael's by a Hammerwich sidesman by 1733.[47] In 1832, however, while acknowledging St. Michael's as the parish church and Hammerwich as a chapel of ease, the chapelwarden, overseers, and principal inhabitants of Hammerwich imposed conditions on the payment of a levy, including a demand for an allowance for the repair of their own chapel.[48] In 1842 they refused to pay any further church rates to St. Michael's.[49] Hammerwich was described as a parish and its church as a parish church in 1854 when a new parish of Ogley Hay was created and part of Hammerwich was transferred to it.[50] In 1860 the rest of Hammerwich was itself made into a new parish.[51]

During the Middle Ages the curate serving the chapel was presumably appointed by the prebendary of Freeford. As a supposed chantry chapel it passed to the Crown at the Reformation and was sold to two speculators in 1564. It is not clear who thereafter appointed the curates until the 18th century. In 1716 Sir Michael Biddulph and others granted the chapel and its property to a group of trustees (later known as the Church Lands trustees).[52] In 1776 the living was a perpetual curacy with the curate nominated by the trustees.[53] It was styled a vicarage in 1868, a rectory evidently in 1872, and a vicarage again c. 1916.[54] The patronage remains in the hands of the Church Lands trustees.[55]

The curate's stipend was £3 in 1604.[56] In 1646 the committee for plundered ministers granted an augmentation of £40 from the sequestered tithes.[57] Three grants of £200 each were made from Queen Anne's Bounty in 1737, 1758, and 1767, and c. 1770 the money was used to buy 20 a. at Chesterfield, in Shenstone.[58] By will proved in 1770 Elizabeth Ball of Castle Bromwich (Warws.) left £500 in trust; most of the interest was to be used to augment the salary of the minister of Hammerwich provided that there was a service with a sermon in the chapel at least once every Sunday.[59] The living was valued at £60 a year in 1803.[60] A further grant of £200 was made from Queen Anne's Bounty in 1810 and was used to buy 1½ a. at Borrowcop in Lichfield.[61] By 1821 the land at Chesterfield was producing £50 a year and that in Lichfield £9; the income paid to the minister from Elizabeth Ball's bequest was £14 16s. He also received rents from the Church Lands.[62] His total aver-

age income c. 1830 was £45.[63] Another grant of £200 was made from Queen Anne's Bounty in 1844 to meet a benefaction of £300.[64] In the 1850s the minister's average annual income was £65, consisting of £42 from land and houses, £3 from fees, £16 from Elizabeth Ball's charity, and £4 from endowed sermons. There was no income from pew rents: 150 seats belonged to householders and the remainder, some 50, were free.[65] In 1860 the Ecclesiastical Commissioners assigned the incumbent the rent charge of £196 16s. 7d. paid in lieu of great tithes.[66] In 1880 they made a grant of £65 a year and a capital sum of £1,500.[67]

Robert Gordon, incumbent from 1858 to 1890, built himself a house north of the church (later known as the Old Rectory).[68] It was let to his successor C. E. Frossard until the building of the present vicarage in 1894. The cost of the new site, nearly 3 a. in Hall Lane, was met from Queen Anne's Bounty.[69]

From the Middle Ages the chapel had endowments, which were the origin of the Church Lands charity vested in eight trustees. Half of its income is spent on the fabric of the church.[70] By will dated 1558 Sir Philip Draycott of Paynsley, in Draycott in the Moors, left 10s. to Thomas Hanson of Hammerwich to say a trental of masses in the chapel.[71]

Sermons at the chapel were endowed by John Ward of Edial in Burntwood, by will of unknown date, on Whit Sunday, 6s. 8d.; William Heath of Hammerwich (probably William Heath of Hammerwich Hall, d. 1676) by will of unknown date, on Christmas Day and Midsummer Day, 10s. each; William Cadman of Edial by will proved 1709, on the first Sunday after each quarter day, 10s. each, and on the first Sunday of Lent and the first Sunday after the feast of St. James, 25 July, no sums specified but 10s. each by the beginning of the 19th century; and John Silvester of Hammerwich (d.1768) on Palm Sunday and the Sunday following the anniversary of his death on 9 April, 10s. 6d. each. In 1821 the incumbent duly received £5 7s. 8d., but by the 1850s he received only £4 in respect of sermons. Payments were still made from all four bequests in 1933, but Ward's had lapsed by 1966. A Scheme of 1970 provided for a payment of £2 5s. a year in respect of Cadman's.[72]

The perpetual curacy was held in plurality

[46] L.J.R.O., D. 30/9/2/3/28, St. Michael's churchwardens' accts. 1722–7, p. 4.
[47] L.J.R.O., B/C/5/Exhibits/St. Michael's, church levy bk. 1733; ibid. 1784.
[48] L.J.R.O., D. 27/3/9, 1 Oct. 1832.
[49] Ibid. 7 Mar., 3 Nov. 1842.
[50] Lond. Gaz. 9 May 1854, pp. 1440–1.
[51] Ibid. 10 Mar. 1860, p. 1043.
[52] Above, estates.
[53] L.J.R.O., D. 30/9/1/4/20, 39–40; L.J.R.O., B/A/3/ Hammerwich.
[54] Lich. Dioc. Ch. Cal. (1869; 1872; 1917); P.O. Dir. Staffs. (1872); Lich. Dioc. Regy., B/A/33, p. 206.
[55] Lich. Dioc. Dir. (1987/8).   [56] E.H.R. xxvi. 350.
[57] S.H.C. 1915, 100.
[58] C. Hodgson, Account of Augmentation of Small Livings by Governors of Bounty of Queen Anne (1845 edn.), p. ccxcvii; L.J.R.O., B/V/6/Hammerwich, 1820.
[59] 7th Rep. Com. Char. 353, 358–9. For the the rest of the income see below, chars. for the poor.

[60] L.J.R.O., D. 30/9/1/10/1.
[61] Hodgson, Bounty of Queen Anne, p. ccxcvii; L.J.R.O., B/V/6/Hammerwich, 1820.
[62] 7th Rep. Com. Char. 359; above, estates.
[63] Rep. Com. Eccl. Revenues [67], p. 481, H.C. (1835), xxii.
[64] Hodgson, Bounty of Queen Anne, p. ccxcvii; L.J.R.O., B/V/6/Hammerwich, 1849.
[65] S.R.O., D. 3802/3/2.
[66] Lond. Gaz. 30 Oct. 1860, pp. 3913, 3918.
[67] Lich. Dioc. Regy., B/A/2i/S, p. 712.
[68] Inf. from the Revd. J. A. Fielding-Fox; Lichfield Mercury, 31 Jan. 1890, p. 5.
[69] Lichfield Mercury, 11 Aug. 1893, p. 4; P.R.O., C 54/19831, mm. 19–21; O.S. Map 6″, Staffs. LVIII. SW. (1903 edn.).
[70] Above, estates.
[71] S.H.C. 1925, 129–30.
[72] Above (incumbent's income) and below, chars. for the poor; above, Burntwood, chars. for the poor.

with that of Burntwood between 1831 and 1858, and it became the practice to hold the Sunday services alternately in the morning and the afternoon at each church.[73] The congregation at the morning service at Hammerwich on Census Sunday 1851 was 47, with a further 17 Sunday school children. The incumbent commented that when the service was in the afternoon numbers were generally about double.[74]

There was a mission centre at Triangle from c. 1888 to c. 1894[75] and another at Hammerwich hospital from c. 1900 to c. 1949.[76] A parish magazine was started in 1890.[77]

At its demolition in 1872 the church of *ST. JOHN THE BAPTIST* consisted of a small chancel with a north vestry, an aisled nave of three bays with timber arcades and a second north aisle, a west gallery, a south porch, and a timber bell turret at the west end.[78] The walls were of stone, but in the late 18th century, before the addition of the outer north aisle, the north side was timber-framed.[79] The small square chancel and the narrowness of the nave and aisles, which were under a single roof, may indicate a 12th-century date. A new east window was inserted in the chancel in the 14th century; a window on the south side of the chancel in 1777 had been filled in by 1843. By 1777 there was a long low window in the south aisle, and there were two dormers over the nave on the south side; a third dormer had been added at the west end of the south aisle by 1843.[80] The outer north aisle was added after 1816; it had a transeptal roof and a large north window.[81] The vestry was added between 1843 and 1859.[82] The church was repaired in the later 1770s with £50 left by Elizabeth Ball and money raised by subscription.[83] Another £58 8s. 3d. was spent on repairs in 1795.[84]

A new church, opened in 1874, was built of local sandstone in an Early English style to the design of Newman & Belling of London. It consists of an apsidal chancel with a north organ chamber, a nave with a north aisle, a south porch, a west tower with a broach spire, and a north-west vestry. The cost of the rebuilding, just under £3,000, was met by subscription and by £600 from the Church Lands trustees.[85] The

vestry was added in 1883 at the expense of Job Evans of Hammerwich House.[86]

In the early 1550s the chapel had a silver chalice, presumably that recorded in 1549.[87] There is now a chalice of 1729, evidently given by Eleanor Alport.[88] There were two bells in the early 1550s but only one in the late 18th century.[89] That was presumably the bell of 1729 which survived the rebuilding and still hangs in the tower.[90]

The registers date from 1720.[91]

The chapelyard consecrated in 1726 was presumably an extension of that in existence by 1549. The churchyard was extended by ¼ a. in 1864, by just over ¼ a. in 1927, and by 1 a. in 1986.[92]

ROMAN CATHOLICISM. In 1604 there were said to be 'many popish' in Hammerwich.[93] Two married couples there were convicted as popish recusants in 1680.[94] No Roman Catholics were listed at Hammerwich in 1705 and 1706, and in 1767 there was stated to be none there.[95] With a large number of Irish settling in the western part of Hammerwich in the later 19th century a need arose for a Roman Catholic centre. A school was opened at New Town in 1871 and a school-chapel at Chasetown, in Burntwood, in 1883.[96]

PROTESTANT NONCONFORMITY. William Heath of Hammerwich Hall was noted as a Presbyterian in 1662–3.[97]

John Dainty, a coalminer living on Watling Street in the south-west corner of Hammerwich in 1861, was a Primitive Methodist preacher.[98] Mount Pleasant Primitive Methodist chapel on Watling Street in the same area was opened apparently in 1867, the first baptism being in that year.[99] A schoolroom was added to the back of the building in 1926.[1] The chapel, having been renamed Mount Pleasant Methodist church, was closed in 1965, and the society amalgamated with that at Brownhills West. The building was sold to Aldridge-Brownhills urban district council in 1968 and demolished.[2]

[73] Above, Burntwood, churches.
[74] P.R.O., HO 129/377/1/24.
[75] Lich. Dioc. Ch. Cal. (1889; 1894).
[76] Ibid. (1901); Lich. Dioc. Cal. (1949–50).
[77] St. John's & Hammerwich News (Mar. 1980), p. [11]. There is a broken set in the possession of Mr. I. G. Crossland.
[78] S.R.O., D. 3802/4/1; above, plates 52–3. The dedication to St. John was in use by 1860 (Lond. Gaz. 10 Mar. 1860, p. 1043); in the 16th century the dedication was to St. Andrew: J.R.U.L.M., Ryl. Ch. Phillipps 126, dorse; W.S.L., S. MS. 326/2, m. 6; S.R.O., D. (W.) 1734/2/3/112D.
[79] W.S.L., S. MS. 251 (ii), p. 51.
[80] Bodl. G.A. Staffs. 4°, 7, facing p. 564; W.S.L., Staffs. Views, iv. 240.
[81] Bodl. G.A. Staffs. 4°, 7, facing p. 564; Mason, Found Ready, pl. facing p. 96.
[82] W.S.L., Staffs. Views, iv. 240; Lichfield Cath. Libr., Moore and Hinckes drawings, xvi, no. 33.
[83] W.S.L., S. MS. 251 (i), p. 102.
[84] Accts. 1795 (in possession of Mr. Crossland).
[85] S.R.O., D. 3802/4/1; Staffs. Advertiser, 25 July 1874, p. 7; P.O. Dir. Staffs. (1876); above, econ. hist. (industries).
[86] Kelly's Dir. Staffs. (1884).
[87] S.H.C. N.S. vi (i), 181; S.H.C. 1915, 173.
[88] T.B.A.S. lxxiii. 26–7. It is inscribed with the initials E. A.; and see above estates (the Old farm).
[89] S.H.C. N.S. vi (i), 181; S.H.C. 1915, 173; W.S.L., S. MS. 251 (ii), p. 51.
[90] Lichfield & Tamworth Life Mag. ii (1), 19; inf. from Mr. Fielding-Fox.
[91] S.R.O., D. 3802/1.
[92] Lich. Dioc. Ch. Cal. (1865), following p. 80; Lich. Dioc. Regy., B/A/2i/W, pp. 241, 244; Lichfield Mercury, 21 Feb. 1986, p. 41.
[93] E.H.R. xxvi. 350.
[94] B.R.L. 354851, f. 28v.
[95] Staffs. Cath. Hist. xiii. 31; xvii. 22.
[96] Above, introduction; Burntwood, Roman Catholicism.
[97] S.H.C. 4th ser. ii. 19.
[98] P.R.O., RG 9/1974.
[99] Walsall Local Hist. Centre 318/49; O.S. Map 6″, Staffs. LVII. NE. (1887 edn.).
[1] Walsall Local Hist. Centre 318/50, 31 Oct. and 14 Nov. 1925, 16 Jan. 1926.
[2] Ibid. 318/50–2.

Joseph Haycock, a miner living at Triangle in 1861, was a Mormon elder and occasional preacher.[3]

EDUCATION. In the mid 18th century the inhabitants of Hammerwich complained in a petition to Lord Uxbridge that they had been 'for a long time ... quite destitute of a schoolmaster'. The implication is that they had once had a school. For lack of one their children were obliged to go to Lichfield for schooling with resulting expense and 'variety of inconveniences'. The inhabitants therefore resolved to build a schoolhouse, and they asked Lord Uxbridge to allow them to inclose 19 a. of waste near Pipehill as an endowment for the school.[4] He presumably refused since nothing more is heard of the project, and when Elizabeth Ball built a charity school at Burntwood in 1769 she stipulated that Hammerwich children were to be eligible to attend it. Until the mid 19th century it remained the only local school for poor children. After its closure in 1878 the rector of Hammerwich received an annual payment, fixed at £8 in 1903, from its endowment income for his day and Sunday schools.[5]

Ann Willington of Pipehill (d. 1841), the owner of Hammerwich Hall, left the interest from £50 for the support of a Sunday school at Hammerwich.[6] The school had 27 pupils in 1846–7.[7] A Church day school had been established by 1857 in a small room behind a building, later the post office, east of Mill Lane. In the earlier 1860s a mistress was teaching c. 40 pupils.[8] In 1863 the incumbent, Robert Gordon, built a schoolroom at Triangle for c. 50 infants with a mistress's house attached. For several years the Church continued to support the two schools, each under a mistress; the combined attendance averaged c. 70.[9] In 1869 or 1870 the Triangle school apparently became a private-adventure dame school, perhaps in 1869 when several children were moved to the Colliery school in Chasetown.[10]

The Church school in Hammerwich village continued, with c. 40 children, and in 1871 the vestry provided new premises for it in Hall Lane. The building, erected by subscription, contained a schoolroom and a classroom and had accommodation for c. 120 children.[11] By will proved that year John Jackson (formerly Pavier) of Hammerwich Place Farm left the school the income from £100.[12] The establishment was little more than a dame school, but in 1874 a ratepayers' meeting decided on improvements

to enable it to qualify as a public elementary school under the 1870 Act, with the rector and churchwardens as trustees. From 1876 a certificated teacher was employed and the school received a government grant.[13] The change may have been made to forestall the opening of a board school in the village. Hammerwich lay within the district of the Norton-under-Cannock school board, formed in 1876;[14] it is improbable that a board would have tolerated the restricted syllabus and poor teaching which, according to the new teacher, had been provided before her arrival.[15]

The average attendance remained in the 40s until the school board appointed an attendance officer in 1878, when it immediately rose to c. 70.[16] A monitor was appointed in 1878 and pupil teachers from 1879.[17] By the end of 1883 the average attendance was c. 100, and in 1884 it was decided to exclude all children from outside Hammerwich except those living at Muckley Corner. The average attendance promptly dropped to c. 70 but thereafter steadily rose again. By 1888, when a new classroom was added to the building, it was over 100.[18] In 1907 the school was handed over to the county council. Average attendance was then still over 100; in 1930 it was 99.[19] In 1932 the school became a junior mixed and infants' school, with 56 on the register.[20] It became a first school in 1980 and was closed in 1982. The building was reopened as a youth and community centre in 1983.[21]

Chasetown High school in Pool Road, Ridgeway infants' school in Grange Road, and the adjoining Ridgeway primary school are treated under Burntwood.

In 1877 there were at least three dame schools in Hammerwich, that at Triangle and two recently opened. The Triangle school seems to have closed in 1878.[22] In 1871 a Roman Catholic master opened a school in the clubroom of a public house at New Town. By early June several Catholic boys at the Colliery school in Chasetown had left to go to the new school, and within a few weeks there were no Catholic boys remaining at the Colliery school. Nothing further is known of the New Town venture, but by the early 1880s there were again Catholic boys at the Colliery school.[23]

A boarding school, the Old Rectory high school, was opened in the former rectory c. 1895 under local patronage and with the vicar as its visitor. The principal, H. W. Hambling, was described as formerly headmaster of Hong Kong public school and commercial lecturer at St. Joseph's College, Macao. The school was

[3] P.R.O., RG 9/1974.
[4] S.R.O., D. 603/K/5/27 (undated petition to Hen., Lord Uxbridge, succ. 1743, d. 1769).
[5] Above, Burntwood, education.
[6] White, *Dir. Staffs.* (1851), 516.
[7] Nat. Soc. *Inquiry, 1846–7*, Staffs. 4–5.
[8] S.R.O., D. 3801/1/1, notes on hist. of sch.; *Lich. Dioc. Ch. Cal.* (1862; 1863); *Staffs. Advertiser*, 5 Aug. 1871, p. 4; O.S. Map 6″, Staffs. LVIII. SW. (1903 edn.).
[9] *Lich. Dioc. Ch. Cal.* (1864 and edns. to 1870).
[10] S.R.O., CEL/85/3, pp. 108, 113.
[11] Ibid. D. 3801/1/1, notes on hist. of sch.; *Staffs. Advertiser*, 5 Aug. 1871, p. 4.
[12] L.J.R.O., Copy Wills, vol. xxxii, ff. 246–8; *Staffs. Endowed Chars.* 65.

[13] S.R.O., D. 3801/1/1, pp. 1, 14, and notes on hist. of sch.; *Lich. Dioc. Ch. Cal.* (1871 and later edns. to 1875); *P.O. Dir. Staffs.* (1876).
[14] *Kelly's Dir. Staffs.* (1884).
[15] S.R.O., D. 3801/1/1, pp. 2, 4–5, 10.
[16] Ibid. pp. 1, 13, 58–9, 65.
[17] Ibid. pp. 58, 92.
[18] Ibid. pp. 205, 208, 288, 294; *Kelly's Dir. Staffs.* (1892).
[19] S.R.O., D. 3801/1/2, pp. 371, 375–6; *Staffs. C.C. Record for 1930* (copy in S.R.O.), 633.
[20] S.R.O., D. 3801/1/3, pp. 125–6.
[21] *Lichfield Mercury*, 17 Feb. 1984, p. 16; inf. from Staffs. C.C. Educ. Dept.
[22] S.R.O., D. 3801/1/1, pp. 42, 76.
[23] Ibid. CEL/85/1, pp. 178–9, 362.

evidently unsuccessful, and by 1900 Hambling had moved to Burntwood.[24]

CHARITIES FOR THE POOR. William Heath (probably of Hammerwich Hall, d. 1676) bequeathed a rent charge of 40s.; half was for sermons at Hammerwich chapel on Christmas Day and Midsummer Day, and half was for distribution by the overseers among the poor of Hammerwich on those days. In 1821 the tenant paid the minister 20s. for the sermons and distributed 20s. among Hammerwich poor of his own choice.[25]

By will of 1743 Theophila Reading of Woodhouses, in Burntwood, left the interest on £30 for the poor of Hammerwich and Woodhouses.[26] Nothing more is known of the charity.

John Silvester of Hammerwich (d. 1768) left two rent charges of £1 1s. One was for sermons at Hammerwich chapel on Palm Sunday and the Sunday following the anniversary of his death (9 April), and the other was for distribution to the poor of Hammerwich on those days. In 1821 the £2 2s. was being paid as directed.[27] The charity lapsed in 1873 following the sale of the property on which the rents were charged. In 1899, after the parish council had threatened legal action against the purchaser, he paid £1 for that year.

Regular payments seem to have been resumed in 1903, when the vicar waived the payment for sermons and the entire £2 2s. was distributed to the poor.[28]

Elizabeth Ball's charitable bequests by will proved 1770 included 1s. a week for a Sunday bread dole for poor people attending Hammerwich chapel. Her heirs honoured her wishes but took no steps to establish her charities on a formal basis. In 1821 twelve 1d. loaves were distributed to the poor every Sunday, mainly to aged poor attending the chapel or to children of such aged poor as were unable to attend.[29] Nothing more is known of the charity.

By will proved 1871 John Jackson (formerly Pavier) of Hammerwich Place Farm left £100, the interest to be divided each quarter among those Hammerwich poor who were the most regular attenders at the church.[30]

Under a Scheme of 1933 the eleemosynary charities of Heath, Silvester, and Jackson were merged to form Hammerwich Non-Ecclesiastical Charities. In 1987 the sums specified by the donors were being distributed by the vicar.[31]

Hammerwich also benefited from the charity of John Ward of Edial, established by will of unknown date for the poor of Burntwood and Hammerwich.[32]

STREETHAY

WITH FULFEN

STREETHAY, east of Lichfield, was formerly a township in St. Michael's parish, Lichfield, covering 850 a. in the mid 19th century. It was adjoined on the south-east by Fulfen, a township of 240 a., also in St. Michael's.[33] Both Streethay and Fulfen were civil parishes from the later 19th century.[34] Boundary changes in 1879 transferred a detached portion of Farewell and Chorley parish north and east of Curborough House to Streethay and cottages at Darnford from Streethay to Fulfen. As the result of the changes Streethay had an area of 978 a. and Fulfen one of 250 a.[35] Further boundary changes in 1934 established a new civil parish of Streethay of 1,341 a; it comprised 852 a. of the existing parish of Streethay (the other 126 a. being added to Lichfield), 239 a. of Fulfen (the remainder being added to Whittington), 4 a. from Lichfield, and 246 a. from Whittington.[36]

In 1980 the parish lost 61 a. on the west side of Lichfield Eastern Bypass to Lichfield.[37] In 1983 Streethay was amalgamated with Alrewas to form Alrewas with Streethay civil parish.[38] This article deals with Streethay and Fulfen before the boundary changes of the 20th century.

Streethay's western boundary was marked by roads as far as Curborough brook, which it followed before turning east round Curborough House. The eastern boundary followed the line of the Roman Ryknild Street as far as Streethay hamlet, where it turned down Ash Tree Lane and then south to Fulfen brook. Part of Fulfen's boundary with Whittington followed Fulfen brook and Darnford brook.[39]

The subsoil is Keuper Sandstone, and there is an area of Keuper Marl north and north-east of Streethay hamlet. South-east of the hamlet, straddling Trent Valley Road, is a gravel ter-

[24] Kelly's Dir. Staffs. (1896), adverts. p. 81; (1900), 817.
[25] 7th Rep. Com. Char. 357–8.
[26] L.J.R.O., D. 15/11/14/122, will of Theophila Reading.
[27] W.S.L., S. MS. 251 (i), p. 101; 7th Rep. Com. Char. 358.
[28] S.R.O., D. 4430/1/1, pp. 5–121 passim.
[29] 7th Rep. Com. Char. 358; above, church; Burntwood, chars. for poor.
[30] L.J.R.O., Copy Wills, vol. xxxii, ff. 227v., 245, 247v.–248.
[31] S.R.O., Charities Index; inf. from the Revd. J. A. Fielding-Fox.
[32] Above, Burntwood, chars. for poor.

[33] White, Dir. Staffs. (1834), 108; (1851), 517. This article was written mainly in 1986. The people named in footnotes are thanked for their help.
[34] Below, local govt.   [35] Census, 1881–91.
[36] Ibid. 1931; Staffs. Review Order, 1934, pp. 59, 64, and map 7 (copy in S.R.O.).
[37] Lichfield (Parishes) Order 1980, S.I. 1980 no. 387; inf. from the Chief Executive, Lichfield District Council.
[38] S.R.O., D. 4499/1/1, pp. 418, 426.
[39] L.J.R.O., B/A/15/Fulfen; B/A/15/Streethay; S.R.O., D. (W.) 1734/2/3/112D; C. and J. Greenwood, Map of County of Stafford (1820).

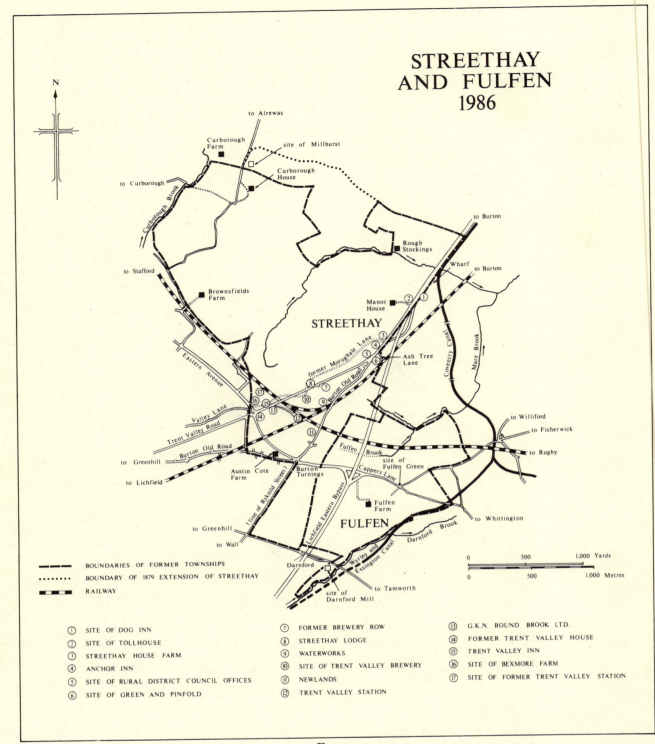

STREETHAY
AND FULFEN
1986

N

to Alrewas

Curborough
Farm

site of Millhurst

Curborough
House

to Curborough

Curborough Brook

to Burton

Rough
Stockings

Wharf   to Burton

to Stafford

Brownsfields
Farm

Manor
House

② ①

Coventry Canal

Mare Brook

STREETHAY

former Morughale Lane

③

Ash Tree
Lane

④

⑤

Burton Old Road

Eastern Avenue

⑥

⑧   ⑦

⑰
⑯ ⑱
Valley Lane   ⑩   ⑨
⑭ ⑬
Trent Valley Road   ⑫

to Williford

to Fisherwick

⑪

to Rugby

Burton Old Road

to Greenhill

Fulfen Brook

site of
Fulfen Green

Cappers Lane

to Lichfield

Austin Cote
Farm

Burton
Turnings

Fulfen
Farm

to Whittington

Lichfield Eastern Bypass

(line of Ryknild Street)

FULFEN

Darnford Brook

to Greenhill

to Wall

Wyrley and Essington Canal

Darnford

0   500   1,000 Yards

0   500   1,000 Metres

site of
Darnford Mill

to Tamworth

— · — · —   BOUNDARIES OF FORMER TOWNSHIPS

· · · · · · · ·   BOUNDARY OF 1879 EXTENSION OF STREETHAY

▮▮▮▮▮▮   RAILWAY

① SITE OF DOG INN
② SITE OF TOLLHOUSE
③ STREETHAY HOUSE FARM
④ ANCHOR INN
⑤ SITE OF RURAL DISTRICT COUNCIL OFFICES
⑥ SITE OF GREEN AND PINFOLD

⑦ FORMER BREWERY ROW
⑧ STREETHAY LODGE
⑨ WATERWORKS
⑩ SITE OF TRENT VALLEY BREWERY
⑪ NEWLANDS
⑫ TRENT VALLEY STATION

⑬ G.K.N. BOUND BROOK LTD.
⑭ FORMER TRENT VALLEY HOUSE
⑮ TRENT VALLEY INN
⑯ SITE OF BEXMORE FARM
⑰ SITE OF FORMER TRENT VALLEY STATION

FIG. 24

race, and along Darnford brook is a stretch of alluvium.[40] The soil is loam.[41] In Streethay hamlet the ground lies between 230 ft. (70 m.) and 246 ft. (75 m.). It rises to 279 ft. (85 m.) in the north-west at Brownsfields Farm and lies at 246 ft. (75 m.) in the north at Curborough House; to the east along Ryknild Street it falls to 204 ft. (65 m.). Fulfen Farm at 250 ft. (76 m.)

stands on a slight rise above low-lying ground. An unnamed stream rises near Streethay's western boundary and passes north of the hamlet to join Mare brook in Whittington.

Twenty-six people were assessed for tax in Streethay and Morughale in 1327 and 37 in 1380. Eight people were assessed in the mid 1520s, and 10 householders were assessed for

[40] Geol. Surv. Map 1″, drift, sheet 154 (1922 edn.).

[41] Soil Surv. Sheet 3 (1983).

hearth tax in 1666.[42] In 1801 Streethay's population numbered 115. In 1841 it was 110 and Fulfen's was 15; the respective figures were 144 and 14 in 1851 and 137 and 10 in 1861. After the 1879 boundary changes the figures were 217 and 38 in 1881, rising to 276 and 43 in 1891. In 1931 they were 252 and 72. After the 1934 boundary changes the population of Streethay civil parish was 263; it had risen to 391 by 1951 but had fallen to 301 by 1961 and 271 by 1971. In 1981 it was 288.[43]

The name Streethay, meaning an enclosure by a Roman road, was recorded in the later 12th century, and the hamlet was evidently settled by the mid 13th century.[44] There was a green in the later 16th century and presumably earlier.[45] The hamlet had an alehouse in 1595.[46] By the later 18th century there were several houses and cottages near the green,[47] including Streethay House Farm, originally **L**-shaped but extended in the early 19th century by the addition of a porch and a large bow on the east. The Anchor inn, north of the green, existed under that name by 1824.[48] The hamlet in 1851 had c. 50 inhabitants, including three railway labourers and their families; by 1881 the number had fallen to c. 40.[49] Prefabricated huts were built south-west of the Anchor in the early 1940s for W.R.A.F. personnel from Fradley airfield in Alrewas. Used as offices by Lichfield rural district council after the Second World War, the buildings were demolished in 1986. Twelve council houses were built on the south side of Burton Old Road in the early 1950s, and a small estate of privately built houses off that road in Dyott Close dates from c. 1960.[50] Eight more houses were built privately on the north side of Trent Valley Road south-west of the district council offices in the 1970s.

The site of Manor House, north of the hamlet, may have been occupied by the mid 13th century.[51] By 1792 an inn called the Dog stood near by on the east side of the Burton road; it survived until the 1840s.[52] To the north the name Rough Stockings, recorded in 1632, indicates an area cleared of trees.[53] A small farmhouse built there probably in the mid 18th century was still occupied by farmworkers in the 1950s but was derelict in 1986.[54]

The lost hamlet of Morughale, south-west of Streethay hamlet, existed by the mid 13th century.[55] The name means a nook of land (*halh*)

bestowed as a morning-gift (*morgen gifu*), referring to the Anglo-Saxon custom by which a man gave land to his bride on the morning after their marriage.[56] The centre of the settlement was presumably somewhere along the former Morughale Lane, the western continuation of which, over the Lichfield boundary, survives as Valley Lane.[57] Until its disappearance in the late 15th century Morughale seems to have been a more important settlement than Streethay. Presentments made at the great court of the bishop's manor of Longdon were invariably entered on the court rolls under the heading of Morughale and Streethay, and the open fields of both hamlets lay principally around Morughale.[58] A charter was dated at Morughale in 1443, but by the late 1480s the hamlet had apparently been deserted.[59] The only inhabited site around Morughale to survive into modern times was Bexmore Farm on the Lichfield boundary.[60]

Brownsfields Farm north-west of Streethay hamlet may have been built or rebuilt in the earlier 17th century. Further north the area around Curborough House was known by 1297 as Little Curborough, evidently to distinguish it from the main settlement of Curborough in the adjoining township. The site of Curborough House has been occupied since at least the later 13th century.[61] Pipe bridge, mentioned in 1386, carried a lane running from Curborough House to Curborough Hall Farm in Curborough and Elmhurst. It was in a ruinous condition in 1489, when both Streethay township and Curborough and Elmhurst township were ordered to repair it.[62]

Fulfen south of Streethay hamlet was mentioned in the mid 12th century.[63] The name means foul marshland, which presumably lay along Fulfen brook. In the mid 13th century Fulfen was styled a vill, and it was later a separate township in Longdon manor.[64] Fulfen Farm was the centre of an estate by the 15th century.[65] A green, recorded in 1435, lay east of Fulfen Farm where the road from Lichfield, Cappers Lane, forked north to Fisherwick and south to Whittington. A cottage by the green was taken down in 1819; others were built to the east probably in the early 19th century.[66]

Darnford at the southern tip of Fulfen township was the site of a mill on Darnford brook by 1243.[67] The name means the hidden or secret ford,[68] presumably in contrast to a more open or

[42] S.H.C. vii (1), 227; xvii. 180 (date corrected by S.H.C. 4th ser. vi. 3 n.); S.H.C. 1923, 211; P.R.O., E 179/77/97.
[43] V.C.H. Staffs. i. 322 (but using P.R.O., HO 107/2014(2) for the 1851 figures); Census, 1871–1981.
[44] Eng. Place-Name Elements (E.P.N.S.), i. 214–15; ii. 161; S.H.C. 1924, p. 165; 1939, 117.
[45] W.S.L. 65/2/41; S.R.O., D. (W.) 1734/2/1/612, m. 14.
[46] S.H.C. 1932, 107.
[47] Above, fig. 1.
[48] W.S.L. 47/1/45, f. 47.
[49] P.R.O., HO 107/2014(2); P.R.O., RG 11/2776.
[50] S.R.O., D. 4499/1/1, p. 31.
[51] Below, estates (Streethay).
[52] S.R.O., D. 603/E/2/190; D. 4566/K, plan of Streethay House Farm estate; P.R.O., HO 107/976; White, Dir. Staffs. (1851), 517.
[53] W.S.L., S. MS. 431, reverse pages, 1632 survey; Eng. Place-Name Elements, ii. 156–7.
[54] S.R.O. 1196/2, deeds of 1 July 1746 and 1 Apr. 1803; inf. from Mrs. K. N. Foden of Streethay House Farm.
[55] S.H.C. 1924, p. 87.

[56] Eng. Place-Name Elements, ii. 43. For variant spellings see S.H.C. iv (1), 258; vi (1), 297; S.H.C. 1924, pp. 82, 88; B.L. Cott. Ch. xxviii. 56; S.R.O., D. 661/1/537, 550, 625, 628; D. (W.) 1734/2/1/598–604.
[57] S.R.O., D. 4566/K, plan of Trent Valley Road; B.L. Maps, O.S.D. 258.
[58] Below, econ. hist. (agric.); local govt.
[59] S.R.O., D. 948/3/62; below, local govt.
[60] Below, estates (Bexmore Farm).
[61] Below, estates; local govt.
[62] S.R.O., D. (W.) 1734/2/1/599, m. 10; D. (W.) 1734/2/1/604, m. 5; D. (W.) 1734/2/3/112D.
[63] S.H.C. 1924, p. 87.
[64] S.R.O., D. 661/2/379; below, local govt.
[65] Below, estates.
[66] S.R.O., D. 661/11/2/3/1/11, 9 Mar. 1819; D. (W.) 1734/2/1/602, m. 28; P.R.O., RG 11/2776; plan of Fulfen estate in 1810 (in possession of Mr. R. B. Dyott of Freeford Manor).
[67] Below, econ. hist. (mill).
[68] Eng. Place-Name Elements, i. 131.

accessible ford at Freeford further upstream. Formerly there were cottages to the north, built in the mid 19th century.[69]

The Roman Ryknild Street entered Streethay in the south-west and ran through the eastern side of the township. It was referred to as Broadway in the earlier 13th century and as Stony Street in 1375.[70] It was joined south of Streethay hamlet by Burton Old Road, a name also given to the stretch of Ryknild Street up to the hamlet. A cross, recorded in the mid 13th century, may have stood at the junction, which was known as Burton Turnings in the mid 19th century.[71] The main route from Lichfield to Burton upon Trent was by Burton Old Road, which was turnpiked in 1729. A tollgate stood near Manor House. An order was made in 1742 for a lodge large enough to take a bed for the keeper, who with his family was to live in a nearby house. A new lodge was built in 1767, on the west side of the road; it was demolished after 1940. Trent Valley Road, providing a more direct route between Lichfield and Burton, was built under an Act of 1832. The Lichfield–Burton road was disturnpiked in 1879. The Lichfield Eastern Bypass, opened in 1971, enters the parish in the south and joins the Lichfield–Burton road north-east of Streethay hamlet.[72]

The Coventry Canal, completed in 1788, runs along the edge of the Burton road north-east of Streethay hamlet, and there was a wharf on the Whittington side of the boundary by 1817.[73] The Wyrley and Essington Canal, opened in 1797 and partly closed in 1954, runs through part of Fulfen.[74] The Trent Valley Railway from Stafford to the Birmingham–London line at Rugby was opened along the south-west side of Streethay in 1847 with a station for Lichfield on the north side of Trent Valley Road. A station master's house was built near by. The South Staffordshire Railway running along the south-east side of Streethay was opened in 1849 with a station, Trent Valley Junction, where the railway crossed Burton Old Road. Both stations were replaced in 1871 by a new one where the lines crossed and the 1847 station was converted into the station master's house.[75]

The opening of Trent Valley Road and of the two railway lines led to the development of the area south-west of Streethay hamlet. The farmhouse at Bexmore became an inn called the Railway tavern, first recorded in 1854.[76] It lost its custom to the Trent Valley hotel (later inn),

built near by on Trent Valley Road in the late 1870s.[77] Trent Valley House opposite the hotel was newly built in 1861.[78] Streethay Lodge on Trent Valley Road east of the Trent Valley railway line was built in the 1850s, apparently for William Leedham (d. 1863), a retired surgeon from Burton upon Trent and an uncle of William Holland of Streethay House Farm.[79] Trent Valley Brewery Co. opened a brewery on the south side of the road in 1877. A row of twelve cottages called Brewery Row was built to the north for its workers; 58 people were living there in 1881. The brewery was demolished in 1970.[80] In 1986 its site was occupied by the premises of Douglas Plant Ltd. and Swan National Leasing. The South Staffordshire Waterworks Co. opened a pumping station east of the brewery in the late 19th century.[81] Council houses on the north side of Trent Valley Road date from the 1950s and privately built houses there from the 1970s.

The area on either side of Trent Valley Road west of the Trent Valley railway was taken into Lichfield in 1934. From 1946 it was developed as a trading and industrial estate and includes a factory opened in 1949 by Bound Brook Bearings (later G.K.N. Bound Brook) Ltd.[82]

ESTATES. An estate known as *STREETHAY* and centring on the later Manor House was held of Longdon manor by Nicholas of Streethay in the mid 13th century.[83] William of Streethay, recorded in 1262 and 1283, had been succeeded by his son Hugh by 1286.[84] Hugh was dead by 1305, leaving a son John, who was alive in 1337.[85] The estate was evidently later held by William of Streethay (d. 1395 or 1396), whose son Philip was still alive in 1418. A John Streethay was recorded in 1469.[86] Later heads of the family were Thomas (d. 1521) and John (d. 1523). John was succeeded by his son Thomas (d. in or before 1538). Thomas's heir was his son Thomas (d. in or before 1540), who was succeeded by his brother John.[87] In 1574 John, described as a gentleman, held 219 a. freehold and copyhold in Streethay.[88] He was succeeded that year by his son Philip.[89] In 1588 Philip held what was called the manor of Streethay, which he sold in 1591 to Richard Pyott, a London alderman whose family were landowners in North Staffordshire.[90]

Richard Pyott died in 1620, leaving a son Richard (d. 1667). The younger Richard, sheriff

[69] P.R.O., RG 9/1973; RG 10/2913–14.
[70] S.R.O., D. 661/1/549; D. (W.) 1734/2/1/598, m. 30.
[71] Ibid. D. 661/1/566; L.J.R.O., B/A/15/Streethay.
[72] L.J.R.O., B/A/15/Streethay, no. 69a; L.J.R.O., D. 15/2/1, 6 May 1742; D. 15/2/2, 3 Mar. and 2 July 1767; above, Lichfield, communications.
[73] V.C.H. Staffs. ii. 292; J. Cary, Inland Navigation (1795), 73–7; Lichfield Mercury, 4 Apr. 1817; L.J.R.O., B/A/15/Whittington, no. 221.
[74] Above, Lichfield, communications.
[75] Ibid.
[76] Below, estates (Bexmore Farm).
[77] P.O. Dir. Staffs. (1876); Kelly's Dir. Staffs. (1880); P.R.O., RG 11/2776.
[78] P.R.O., RG 9/1975.
[79] Ibid.; S.R.O., D. 4566/K, copy will of Wm. Leedham (proved 1864).

[80] P.R.O., RG 11/2776; above, Lichfield, econ. hist. (trades and industries).
[81] O.S. Map. 1/2,500, Staffs. LII. 16 (1902 edn.).
[82] Above, Lichfield, econ. hist. (trades and industries); inscription over main door of factory.
[83] S.H.C. 1939, 117.
[84] Cal. Lib. 1260–7, 97; S.H.C. v (1), 175; S.H.C. 1911, 38–9.
[85] S.R.O., D. 661/2/512; Cal. Close, 1337–9, 101.
[86] S.H.C. xv. 78; S.H.C. 1939, 120; Harwood, Lichfield, 401–2, 405.
[87] Shaw, Staffs. i. 363; S.R.O., D. (W.) 1734/2/1/606, mm. 8d., 25d., 28; above, plate 50.
[88] W.S.L., S. MS. 326/2, m. 4.
[89] L.J.R.O., D. 27/1/1, f. 1; S.R.O., D. (W.) 1734/2/1/635, m. 11; S.H.C. xiii. 255.
[90] S.H.C. xvii. 236; Shaw, Staffs. i. 363.

of Staffordshire in 1635–6, was succeeded by his son John, who was succeeded in 1677 or 1678 by his son Richard (d. 1728). Richard's heir was his son John (d. 1729). John was succeeded by his son Richard, a barrister, who later moved to Chesterfield (Derb.) where his wife Pyarea had property. Richard died childless in 1747, having devised the Streethay estate, subject to his wife's life interest, to a another barrister, Edward Wilmot of Duffield (Derb.).[91]

In 1791 the estate covered 106 a.[92] Edward Wilmot died in 1795, and in 1796 his son Edward sold it to Richard Holland.[93] Richard was the son of William Holland of Rodbaston Hall in Penkridge (d. 1784), who was living at Streethay by 1758 and owned Streethay House Farm.[94] Richard died in 1835, and his son William succeeded to both the Streethay and the Streethay House Farm estates. William was succeeded in 1839 by his son Richard. In 1851 the combined estate, then known as Streethay House farm, covered 250 a.; by 1861 it had been increased to 330 a.[95] In 1869 Richard sold it to his brother William, on whose death in 1887 the estate, mortgaged in 1878, passed to trustees.[96] It was eventually bought in 1920 by Ernest Pyatt, who sold it in 1946 to Mr. R. F. Foden, the owner in 1986 when the estate covered 260 a.[97]

In the Middle Ages the house was surrounded by a double moat. It was rebuilt, probably by the Richard Pyott who succeeded in 1620, in brick with a symmetrical front of three gabled bays; the central bay projected, and over the door was set the coat of arms granted in 1610 to Richard Pyott (d. 1620).[98] In 1666 the house was assessed for tax on 14 hearths. Most of it was demolished in 1792.[99] What survives is apparently the back range of an enclosed courtyard to which a short wing was added. The house was converted into cottages used by farmworkers until the later 20th century, when it was remodelled as the present house. It was bought in 1986 by Maj. R. Conningham.[1]

The remains of the moat round the house were apparently used in the 18th century as a garden feature and as fishponds.[2] A short straight-sided canal was formed on the axis of the house, probably in the late 17th or early 18th century, stretching south-west from the remains of the moat. A stone bath house with a corbelled roof probably of the 17th century stands west of the house.[3] In the early 18th century there was a dovecot in the grounds.[4]

BEXMORE FARM in Morughale originated as a virgate which Bishop Muschamp, 1198–1208, bought from Geoffrey son of Alard and gave to his farrier Robert Ruffus.[5] The bishop evidently made a further grant of land in Morughale to Ruffus.[6] In 1298 two virgates there were held by Robert le Rous, presumably a descendant.[7] About 1300 Robert granted a capital messuage to John son of Henry de la Bourne.[8] The estate passed to the Rugeley family,[9] probably by 1363 when Nicholas son of Richard Rugeley was disputing a half virgate in Morughale.[10] In 1399 Nicholas son of Henry Rugeley held what was called the manor of Morughale.[11] Probably identifiable as Nicholas Rugeley of Hawkesyard in Armitage, and later of Saredon in Shareshill,[12] he left his estate in Morughale to his wife Eleanor, who by 1443 had married Richard Harcourt, lord of Saredon.[13] By 1574 the estate was held by the 'heirs of Harcourt'. It then comprised 58 a. held in severalty and 168 a. in the open fields of Streethay and of Lichfield. Part of the land held in severalty was called Berkesmoor, meaning birch moor, from which the name Bexmore is derived.[14] In 1580 Cassandra Cooke, mistress of Robert Harcourt (d. 1558), and their son John let the estate to Anthony Dyott, the owner of Freeford, who bought at least part of it in 1584.[15] In the early 1750s Richard Dyott let part of the estate in two portions, one of 26 a. with a house and the other of 36 a.[16]

Another part of the estate was evidently acquired by or passed to Sir Theophilus Biddulph, Bt., of Elmhurst, who in 1723 sold it to Thomas Capenhurst of Haunton in Clifton Campville. Capenhurst was living at Bexmore in 1735, when he sold his estate there to Hugh Annerley, also of Haunton. In 1790 Annerley's son Hugh owned 21 a. at Bexmore, together with the farmhouse; he sold the land and house that year to the Revd. Hugh Bailye.[17]

The later descent is unknown until 1849, when the house was owned by a Jane Godwin.[18] In 1851 it was occupied, and may have been owned, by William Sharrod, who farmed 45 a. there. Some time before 1854 he converted the house into an inn, the Railway tavern.[19] He died in 1858, and his son Francis continued to run the inn. After the opening of the Trent Valley

[91] Reade, *Johnsonian Gleanings*, ix. 176–87; Shaw, *Staffs*. i. 363; *Alum. Oxon. 1715–1886*, 1166, 1579; P.R.O., C 12/1211/1.
[92] L.J.R.O., D. 30/Stotfold prebend, plan of 'Hall farm' 1791.
[93] *Staffs. Advertiser*, 8 Aug. 1795; Shaw, *Staffs*. i. 363; S.R.O., D. 783/1/1/1, p. 11.
[94] S.R.O. 1196/3; ibid. D. 4566/K, Holland pedigree; L.J.R.O., D. 27/1/4, p. 144; L.J.R.O., P/C/11, Wm. Holland (1784); *V.C.H. Staffs*. v. 122.
[95] S.R.O., D. 4566/K, will of Wm. Holland (proved 1840); P.R.O., HO 107/2014(2); ibid. RG 9/1975.
[96] *Staffs. Advertiser*, 3 Dec. 1887, p. 7; S.R.O., D. 4566/K, statement re late Wm. Holland, 1888.
[97] Inf. from Mr. and Mrs. Foden.
[98] Shaw, *Staffs*. i. 363; *Grantees of Arms* (Harl. Soc. lxvi), 207; above, plate 51.
[99] *S.H.C.* 1923, 211; W.S.L., Staffs. Views, x. 55.
[1] Inf. from Mrs. Foden and Major Conningham.
[2] Below, econ. hist. (warren and fisheries).

[3] L.J.R.O., B/A/15/Streethay; S.R.O., D. 4566/K, undated [later 19th-cent.] plan of Streethay House farm.
[4] W.S.L., S. 431, demesne acct. 1706.
[5] S.R.O., D. 661/1/545.
[6] Bodl. MS. Ashmole 1527, f. 34v. (2nd charter).
[7] S.R.O., D. (W.) 1734/J. 2268, f. 1v.
[8] Ibid. D. 661/1/614.
[9] Bodl. MS. Ashmole 1527, marginal note on f. 34v.
[10] *S.H.C.* xiii. 32.   [11] S.R.O., D. 661/2/667–8.
[12] *V.C.H. Staffs*. v. 157; W.S.L., S.D. Cooke 161.
[13] *V.C.H. Staffs*. v. 175–6; S.R.O., D. 948/3/62; Bodl. MS. Ashmole 1527, f. 103v.
[14] W.S.L., S. MS. 326/2, m. 4; *Eng. Place-Name Elements*, i. 28–9.   [15] S.R.O., D. 661/2/102; *S.H.C.* xvii. 231.
[16] S.R.O., D. 661/8/1/3/6, 'Mr. Dyott's estate at Streethay'.
[17] L.J.R.O., D. 15/11/14/124, deeds of 25 May 1723, 25 Mar. 1735, 15 Oct. 1790.
[18] L.J.R.O., B/A/15/Streethay, no. 100.
[19] *Staffs. Advertiser*, 18 Feb. 1854, p. 8; P.R.O., HO 107/2014(2); ibid. RG 9/1975.

hotel in the late 1870s, the Railway tavern became a farmhouse again. In 1881 Francis Sharrod ran a 27-a. market garden at Bexmore. He was still alive in 1900, but by 1904 the business had been taken over by his son Thomas.[20] The later history of the estate is unknown. The farmhouse was demolished when Eastern Avenue was laid out in 1972.[21]

Bishop Durdent, 1149–59, granted a tenement in Morughale to his clerk Walter as an augmentation of his prebend in Lichfield cathedral. Bishop Peche in the later 1170s granted the same tenement to Matthew the precentor.[22] In the early 13th century it was held by Hugh of Morughale. Soon afterwards Hugh or his son Hugh, being in debt and 'driven by hunger', sold it to Robert of Hulton.[23] Before 1241 the precentor confirmed Hulton's possession and gave him land called 'Blacknaveriding' to augment the holding.[24] In 1510–11 the lessee was Thomas Harcourt, whose family held Bexmore farm in Morughale with which it was presumably amalgamated.[25]

BROWNSFIELDS FARM apparently took its name from the Brown family of Lichfield. In 1440 the estate of John Brown of Lichfield was divided between his two daughters and coheirs, one of whom, Alice, was the wife of William Rugeley.[26] In 1562 Alice's descendants granted land to Richard Hussey, who in turn sold land called 'Brownes fields' to Michael Lowe of Timmor in Fisherwick and James Weston of Lichfield. Weston died in 1589, and his interest passed to his son Simon; Lowe died in 1593 or 1594, leaving his interest to his son-in-law Edward Bromley.[27] Weston and Bromley sold their shares to Richard Pyott (d. 1620), or his son Richard, of Streethay,[28] and by 1632 Brownsfields was let.[29] When the Pyott estate was broken up in 1796, Brownsfields was bought by a farmer named Oldacres.[30] Thomas Oldacres, the owner in 1834, was succeeded c. 1850 by Edward Oldacres, possibly his son. Edward, who was chaplain to the Lichfield poor-law union, farmed 187 a. at Brownsfields in 1851.[31] By 1861 his cousin Ralph Oldacres was farming there. Ralph's sister Ann bought the farm in 1870. She was declared bankrupt in 1887, and the farm was sold.[32] It was owned by William Boston in 1928,[33] and remained in his family in 1986. The brick farmhouse dates from the ear-

lier 18th century and possibly incorporates an older core.

An estate in Little Curborough centring on *CURBOROUGH HOUSE* originated in a virgate held in the later 13th century by John de Somerville, lord of Wychnor in Tatenhill. John was succeeded in or shortly after 1279 by his son Robert, and Robert in 1297 by his son Edmund.[34] Edmund held the estate as ¼ knight's fee of the bishop as lord of Longdon in 1298. By 1301 he was a clerk and claimed that he held no lay fee.[35] His father apparently had granted an interest in the estate to Sir Ralph de Cromwell on Ralph's marriage to Edmund's aunt Joan in 1292–3,[36] and in the 1320s, after Edmund's death, the estate passed to Sir Ralph's son, also Ralph.[37] Ralph, Baron Cromwell, a descendant, still had an interest in the estate in 1442–3.[38]

John Langton (d. by 1502) had acquired the estate by 1497. His heir was his brother Henry, who was dead by 1540, leaving a son John.[39] John lived in Lichfield and was probably the John Langton who was a member of the 1548 corporation. He was dead by 1560.[40] William Langton, who held 20 a. in Little Curborough with 115 a. in the open fields in 1571, was probably the William Langton who died in 1610, leaving a son John who held the estate in 1623.[41] Its later descent is unknown until 1834, when it was held by John Hanbury, who was lessee of the adjoining estate in Curborough and Elmhurst belonging to Curborough prebend.[42] Hanbury died probably soon after 1851, leaving two daughters as his heirs.[43] The later descent is unknown until 1919, when the estate was bought by Gordon Powell (d. 1966). His son James was the owner in 1986. The estate then covered c. 150 a.[44]

Curborough House, so called in 1851,[45] is a small 18th-century brick farmhouse, enlarged to the south in the same century. In the earlier 19th century it was given a north wing and a new roof, and there was internal remodelling. The remains of a dovecot stand on the east side of the house.[46]

An estate known in 1574 as *MILLHURST*,[47] in the detached part of Farewell and Chorley parish added to Streethay in 1879, originated as part of Henry II's grant of land called Lindhurst to the nuns of Farewell priory.[48] At the priory's dissolution in 1527 the Crown granted its estates

[20] L.J.R.O., B/C/11, vol. iv. 47; below, econ. hist. (agric.).
[21] Above, Lichfield, general hist. (20th century).
[22] *S.H.C.* 1924, pp. 82–3, 87.
[23] Ibid. pp. 88–9; S.R.O., D. 661/1/550 and 552.
[24] S.R.O., D. 661/1/601.
[25] W.S.L., S. MS. 326/2, m. 4.
[26] Ibid. H.M. Chetwynd 5, deed of 24 May 1440; Erdeswick, *Staffs.* 241.
[27] Erdeswick, *Staffs.* 241 n.; P.R.O., PROB 11/83, f. 149v.
[28] W.S.L., S. MS. 431, reverse pages, valuation of Streethay estate.
[29] Ibid., reverse pages, 1632 survey.
[30] S.R.O., D. 783/1/1/1, p. 11.
[31] White, *Dir. Staffs.* (1834), 108; (1851), 517; L.J.R.O., B/A/15/Streethay, no. 41.
[32] P.R.O., HO 107/2014(2); ibid. RG 9/1975; *Staffs. Advertiser*, 19 Mar. 1887, p. 7; 26 Mar. 1887, p. 7.
[33] *Staffs. Advertiser*, 9 June 1928, p. 2.
[34] *S.H.C.* 1911, 172–3, 241.
[35] S.R.O., D. (W.) 1734/J. 2268, f. iv.; *S.H.C.* vii (1),

81–2, 97.
[36] Shaw, *Staffs.* i. 119.
[37] *S.H.C.* ix (1), 75; S.R.O., D. (W.) 1734/J. 2268, f. iv.; *Complete Peerage*, iii. 551 n.
[38] Kent Archives Office, U1475 M207.
[39] S.R.O., D. (W.) 1734/2/1/604, mm. 19, 31d.; D. (W.) 1734/2/1/606, m. 28; D. (W.) 1734/2/1/609, m. 2.
[40] Ibid. D. (W.) 1734/2/1/609, m. 2; P.R.O., C 3/20, no. 61; Harwood, *Lichfield*, 418.
[41] S.R.O., D. (W.) 1734/2/1/612, m. 23; D. (W.) 1734/2/1/613, m. 44d.; W.S.L., S. MS. 326/1; ibid. S.D. Pearson 1282; Shaw, *Staffs.* i. 191.
[42] White, *Dir. Staffs.* (1834), 104; S.R.O., D. (W.) 1851/10/5.
[43] P.R.O., HO 107/2014(2); W.S.L., S. MS. 418(i), p. 27.
[44] Inf. from Mr. Powell.
[45] P.R.O., HO 107/2014(2).
[46] L.J.R.O., B/A/15/Streethay, no. 25.
[47] S.R.O., D. (W.) 1734/J. 2039.
[48] *V.C.H. Staffs.* iii. 223.

to the dean and chapter of Lichfield cathedral for the support of the choristers, and in 1550 the dean and chapter granted them to William Paget, Lord Paget, at fee farm.[49] The tenant at Millhurst in 1574 was William Bird, who held the messuage with 60 a.; his holding had increased to 85 a. by 1591–2.[50] The Bird family remained tenants until the late 18th century.[51] Soon after 1797 the farm, then 121 a., was sold by Henry Paget, earl of Uxbridge, to Fairfax Moresby of Stowe House in Lichfield.[52] By 1819 it was owned by Lord Anson and was part of the 235-a. estate centring on Curborough Farm in Alrewas. It was still part of that estate in 1986.[53] The only building which survives on the site is a ruined brick barn dating from the mid or late 18th century.

About 1170 Geoffrey Peche gave to the nuns of Farewell priory at the behest of his son Richard the service of his man Turstan together with a tenement in Morughale. The grant was evidently a dowry for Geoffrey's daughter Sarah on becoming a nun at Farewell.[54] The nuns received other grants of land in the area, including one which carried a rent charge for the support of a lamp in the priory church.[55]

The tithes of Streethay were divided among several prebendaries of Lichfield cathedral.[56] In 1694 Bishop Lloyd assigned the small tithes to the vicar of St. Mary's, Lichfield.[57] When the tithes were commuted in 1848, the respective prebendal shares of the great tithes were from $399\frac{1}{2}$ a. (Stotfold), 139 a. (Bishops Itchington), 135 a. (Curborough), and $6\frac{1}{2}$ a. (Dernford). The Ecclesiastical Commissioners, as reversioners of the prebends of Gaia Minor and Freeford, then received tithes from 24 a. and 8 a. respectively; the tithe received on behalf of Gaia Minor prebend, however, was restricted to corn and grain, as the tithe of hay was in the form of a prescriptive payment of 2s. The great tithes from a further 75 a. were divided into five parts, assigned to the prebends of Weeford (two parts) and Stotfold, Freeford, and Hansacre (one each). In addition the great tithes from 60 a. had been merged with the land from which they arose and were owned by 15 individuals. The dean and chapter of Lichfield, to whom Stotfold prebend had been assigned in 1803, received a rent charge of £79 4s. The rent charges for the other prebendal tithes were payable to the Ecclesiastical Commissioners: £38 for Curborough, £14 for Bishops Itchington, £7 4s. for Weeford, £5 12s. for Freeford, £3 12s. for Hansacre, and £2 8s. for Gaia Minor. Further rent charges ranging from £7 10s. to 1d. were assigned to the 15 owners of the merged tithes. The vicar of St. Mary's received a rent charge of £52 10s.

William of Fulfen was recorded in 1286 as a free tenant of the bishop as lord of Longdon, and in 1298 Thomas of Fulfen and John of Fulfen were half-virgaters.[58] Thomas Fulfen died in 1422–3 leaving as heir his daughter Agnes, widow of Richard Bertrem,[59] and his estate appears to have been sold; in 1424 it was occupied by Oliver Chatterton whose estate in 1453 was called the manor of *FULFEN*.[60] By 1461 Oliver had been succeeded by his son Roger. In 1498 the owner was Thomas Chatterton, who may have still been alive in 1532–3.[61] It was probably another Thomas Chatterton who died holding Fulfen in 1572 with a son George as his heir.[62] George was succeeded in 1606 by his son Thomas, who in 1637 sold Fulfen to Humphrey Chetham of Turton in Bolton-le-Moors (Lancs.). Chetham may have been acting as a trustee, and in 1638 he and Thomas conveyed the 206-a. estate to Sir Richard Dyott, the owner of Freeford.[63] The estate descended with Freeford until 1919 when it was sold to Gerald Burton (d. 1960). His grandson, Mr. G. A. Burton, was the owner in 1986, when he farmed 202 a. there.[64] The brick farmhouse is of the early 19th century, and some of the farm buildings are of the mid 18th century.

The tithes of Fulfen belonged to the prebendary of Bishops Itchington in Lichfield cathedral. The small tithes were assigned to the vicar of St. Mary's, Lichfield, in 1694. The tithes were commuted in 1839. The prebendary received a rent charge of £53 1s. 11d. and the vicar of St. Mary's one of £17 11s. Eight acres were then tithe free.[65]

In the late 16th century small amounts of land in Streethay were owned by the prebendaries of Bishopshull and Tervin and by St. John's hospital in Lichfield.[66] The vicars choral of Lichfield cathedral held 2 a. of meadow in Streethay in 1298,[67] and in the 15th century they held several small parcels of land in Streethay and Fulfen.[68] In the mid 19th century they still owned $5\frac{1}{2}$ a. in Streethay, north-west of Brownsfields Farm, and $4\frac{1}{2}$ a. in Fulfen, east of Fulfen Farm.[69] The chantry of Canon George Radcliffe in Lichfield cathedral, endowed c. 1460, possessed land in Streethay and Morughale. After the chantry's suppression in 1548 the land was bought by Walter and Edward Leveson, evidently as speculators.[70] Land granted to Halesowen abbey (Worcs.) in 1467 as the endowment of the chantry of Boyce Hampton in the abbey in-

[49] Ibid. iii. 166, 224.
[50] S.R.O., D. (W.) 1734/J. 2039 and 2042.
[51] Ibid. D. 603/E/2/44; D. 603/K/5/15, f. 88.
[52] Ibid. D. 603/H/5/15, Curborough Farm, tenancy of Thos. Goring; D. 1821/3/1.
[53] S.R.O., D. 615/M/1/26; inf. from Mr. J. R. Greaves of Curborough Farm.
[54] B.L. Cott. Ch. xxviii. 56.
[55] L.J.R.O., D. 30/G 4; S.R.O., D. (W.) 1734/2/3/54D.
[56] Para. based on L.J.R.O., B/A/15/Streethay.
[57] Above, Lichfield, churches.
[58] S.R.O., D. (W.) 1734/2/1/598, m. 15; D. (W.) 1734/J. 2268, f. IV.
[59] S.H.C. 1939, 121–2.

[60] Cal. Close, 1422–9, 125; S.R.O., D. 661/2/235.
[61] S.H.C. 1939, 83, 103; S.H.C. 4th ser. viii. 184; S.R.O., D. (W.) 1734/2/1/604, m. 20.
[62] V.C.H. Lancs. v. 98 n.; W.S.L., S. MS. 326/2, m. 4.
[63] S.R.O., D. 661/2/91, 99, 775; P.R.O., WARD 7/29/67.
[64] Lichfield Mercury, 22 Apr. 1960, p. 9; inf. from Mr. Burton.
[65] L.J.R.O., B/A/15/Fulfen.
[66] W.S.L., S. MS. 326/2, m. 4.
[67] S.R.O., D. (W.) 1734/J. 2268, f. IV.
[68] L.J.R.O., D. 30/VC, palimpsest, ii, ff. 13v., 14; iii, f. 20.
[69] L.J.R.O., B/A/15/Fulfen; B/A/15/Streethay.
[70] Cal. Inq. p. m. (Rec. Com.), iv. 297; Cal. Pat. 1549–51, 361.

cluded 8 a. on Streethay's western boundary. At the Dissolution the land probably passed to Sir John Dudley, who acquired the abbey's adjoining land at Pones fields in Lichfield.[71]

ECONOMIC HISTORY. AGRICULTURE. The open fields of Streethay, Morughale, and Fulfen lay south-west of Streethay hamlet. Selions were recorded in the mid 13th century in Cross field and in fields called 'Ruding' and 'Brunehill'. By the earlier 14th century there were five open fields: Cross, Morughale Ridding, Brownhill, Nether Bridge, and Over Bridge.[72] Cross field lay on the north side of Ryknild Street; it presumably took its name from the road junction at Burton Turnings where there may have been a cross.[73] The field was partly inclosed by 1577.[74] Morughale Ridding field, which is presumably the earlier 'Ruding' field, lay north-east of Cross field. In 1397 selions were recorded in Further Mastrudding and Middle Mastrudding, possibly divisions of Morughale Ridding field.[75] At least part of the field had been inclosed by 1580.[76] Brownhill field probably lay on the east side of Ryknild Street near the boundary with Whittington. It was partly inclosed by 1577.[77] Nether Bridge field and Over Bridge field lay to the south on either side of Ryknild Street; the bridge was evidently that which took the road over Fulfen brook.[78] Inclosures in both fields were recorded in 1580–1.[79] Open meadow lay in 1411 along Darnford brook and in 1577 along Fulfen brook.[80]

There were 7 free tenants who held land of the bishop in Streethay and Morughale in 1298: 2 held 2 virgates each, 2 a single virgate, and 3 a half virgate. At Fulfen there were 2 free tenants each holding a half virgate. There were in addition 6 neifs, 5 of whom each held a half virgate of 10 a. with meadow and one a virgate of 20 a. Two of the neifs were also recorded as cottars in Morughale, where they each had a nook, or quarter virgate, as did a third cottar there. Labour services, for which a commuted money payment was allowed, were required from the neifs and cottars and from 4 of the free tenants. For the free tenants the services comprised the carriage of malt, venison, and fresh fish to various of the bishop's manors, carriage of millstones to Lichfield, and mowing the demesne meadow at Williford in Whittington, lifting hay there, and carrying it to Lichfield. The neifs owed the same services, except that they carried corn and malt to Brewood and Haywood in Colwich only; in addition they

owed carriage of building stone from Cannock to Lichfield and elsewhere, carriage of unspecified items to Stowe mill in Lichfield and digging work there, and reaping at Beaudesert in Longdon. The services of the cottars comprised haymaking, driving animals to the bishop's manors, herding pigs from their woodland pannage and driving them to Haywood and Brewood, carriage of hens' eggs to Haywood and Brewood, carriage of millstones, and cleaning the bishop's houses. A cottar, moreover, was obliged to assist the beadle of Longdon manor when distress was taken, and he was liable for service as reeve.[81]

Pannage was levied on the neifs and cottars at the rate of 1d. for each year-old pig and $\frac{1}{2}d$. for each pig under a year old. If a neif had seven pigs, he gave one to the bishop and was thereby released from pannage for the remainder; sows in farrow were exempt from pannage. Items liable to be taken as heriot included the best beast, all stallions, all pigs except one, all hives of bees, whole bacons, an iron-bound cart, a bronze pot, and a complete piece of linen.

By the later 16th century Richard Pyott's Streethay estate, the largest in the township, comprised 219 a. of which 45 a. lay in the open fields.[82] By 1632 his son's estate of over 600 a. comprised 10 holdings, the largest of 134 a. and the others between 71 a. and 31 a., besides 91 a. of open-field land, some of it in Lichfield. By 1688 the estate comprised the home farm, 3 tenanted farms, and 6 smallholdings.[83]

Small acreages of blendcorn, wheat, barley, rye, oats, peas, and beans were grown on the Pyotts' home farm in the early 18th century. Flax was then grown by some of the Pyotts' tenants: nearly 26 a. of it were sown in 1707, and between 1717 and 1724 one tenant received leases of various closes of land of up to 14 a. for growing flax.[84] Turnips were grown at Fulfen in 1707.[85] On the home farm in 1721 there were 10 cows with 4 calves, 20 fat sheep, 50 store sheep, 3 large pigs, and 4 store pigs.[86]

Timber on the Pyotts' estate in 1709 amounted to nearly 1,000 trees and saplings, both oak and ash, chiefly in the northern part.[87] Much was cut down in the 1790s when the estate was broken up.[88] At Fulfen a wood was recorded in 1545.[89] In the late 18th century there was a plantation north-east of Fulfen Farm,[90] and there was still woodland in Fulfen in 1844.[91]

A shepherd was living north of Streethay House Farm in 1861 and 1871, and in the latter year one was living at Brownsfields Farm and one at Fulfen Farm. There was still a shepherd

[71] *Cal. Pat.* 1467–77, 16; W.S.L., S. MS. 326/2, m. 4; above, Lichfield, manor (other eccl. estates).
[72] S.R.O., D. 661/1/547 and 566; D. (W.) 1734/J. 2269.
[73] Ibid. D. 661/8/1/3/6, survey of field land, 1742–3; L.J.R.O., B/A/15/Streethay, nos. 135–7, 139, 141; above, introduction.
[74] S.R.O., D. (W.) 1734/2/1/612, m. 22.
[75] Ibid. D. 661/2/358.
[76] Ibid. D. (W.) 1734/2/1/635, m. 11; D. (W.) 1734/2/1/637, m. 7b.
[77] Ibid. D. 661/8/1/3/6, survey of field land, 1742–3; D. (W.) 1734/2/1/612, m. 21; L.J.R.O., B/A/15/Streethay, no. 148.
[78] S.R.O., D. 661/2/360 and 541; D. 661/8/1/3/6, survey of field land, 1742–3; L.J.R.O., B/A/15/Streethay, nos. 144–5, 156.

[79] S.R.O., D. (W.) 1734/2/1/612, m. 53; D. (W.) 1734/2/1/635, m. 11.
[80] Ibid. D. (W.) 1734/2/1/600, m. 29; D. (W.) 1734/2/1/612, m. 21.
[81] This and the next para. based on S.R.O., D. (W.) 1734/J. 2268, ff. iv.–4.
[82] W.S.L., S. MS. 326/2, mm. 3–4.
[83] Ibid. S. MS. 431.   [84] Ibid.
[85] S.R.O., D. 661/21/4/1, f. 3.
[86] W.S.L., S. MS. 431.
[87] Ibid.
[88] S.R.O., D. 783/1/1/1, p. 11.
[89] Ibid. D. (W.) 1734/2/1/606, m. 36.
[90] Above, fig. 1.
[91] S.R.O., D. 661/11/2/3/1/16, 7 Apr. 1844.

at Fulfen Farm in 1881.[92] Sheep numbered 178 at Streethay House farm in 1887, when there were also 27 milking cows, 36 other cattle, and 13 pigs. The crops then grown on the farm were oats and wheat.[93] At Brownsfields farm in 1928 there were small acreages of wheat, oats, potatoes, mangolds, and swedes, besides a herd of 36 dairy cows.[94] Crops were grown on nearly two-thirds of the 593 ha. (1,465 a.) returned for Streethay civil parish in 1984. Wheat and barley accounted for 350 ha., while potatoes, cabbages, and cauliflowers, grown principally at Fulfen, covered 32 ha. There were over 400 head of cattle in the parish and nearly 500 sheep and lambs, and at Streethay House farm there were 2,600 turkeys.[95]

James Bird, described as a gardener in 1841 and as a market gardener in 1850, had a smallholding centred on Yewtree Cottage (later Austin Cote Farm) in Burton Old Road. It covered 20 a. in 1851.[96] After Bird's death in 1859 the business was taken over by the tenant, John Burton, who farmed 50 a. there as a market gardener in 1861. By 1871 the smallholding appears to have reverted to use as an ordinary farm, Burton and his son George having moved their market-garden business, probably to the nearby Yewtree House in Lichfield.[97] By 1860 Francis Sharrod of Bexmore farm had a market garden of 35 a., reduced to 27 a. by 1881. Sharrod was still in business in 1900 but had been succeeded by his son Thomas by 1904. Thomas apparently discontinued the business.[98] In 1919 George Burton's son Gerald bought Fulfen farm and turned it over to market gardening, specializing in broccoli.[99] Walter Best, who had a smallholding at Newlands in Burton Old Road, claimed to be the largest grower of tomatoes in the district in 1908; he also grew fruit and vegetables and delivered dairy produce. He was still in business in the late 1930s.[1]

WARREN AND FISHERIES. The bishop as lord of Longdon had a warren in Streethay in 1452–3.[2] Land called 'coningray', recorded on the Streethay estate in 1632, was presumably the site of a former warren.[3]

Carp, tench, perch, and eels were put into the moat around the Pyotts' house in 1705. In 1706 the moat and two pools were stocked with 300 carp, and the moat and nearby pools were regularly stocked in the years following. In 1723 the moat contained 250 carp, 40 tench, and an unspecified number of pike, perch, roach, and eels; a pool called Horsemoor pit then had 72 carp, 48 perch, and 3 tench.[4] At Fulfen a pool on the north side of Cappers Lane was fished by the Dyotts of Freeford in 1764, when carp from it were sent to stock a pool at Freeford. The Fulfen pool was itself stocked with carp and tench in the later 1780s; in 1824 it contained carp, tench, trout, and perch. It was still being fished in 1837.[5]

MILL. In 1243 a rent from a mill at Darnford was granted by Geoffrey son of Benet of Lichfield to Reynold de Cleydon, a canon of Lichfield cathedral.[6] In the early 14th century the mill was held by Robert of Rodswell, arch-deacon of Chester, whose heir granted it to William of Freeford and his son Robert.[7] In 1365 Sir John Freeford, William's heir and other son, granted the mill to two chaplains of Lichfield cathedral, one of whom in 1373 transferred it to the chaplain serving a chantry founded by Cleydon.[8] The mill was held by successive chaplains until the suppression of the chantry; a lease made in 1545 was surrendered to the Crown in 1561.[9] In 1610 the mill was held on lease by Anthony Dyott, the owner of Freeford. It was then described as three water mills, presumably under one roof. Dyott bought it from the Crown in 1611, subject to a 40s. fee farm.[10] His family still owned the mill in 1782.[11]

By 1811 the mill was owned by William Dennitts, probably the lessee of Fulfen farm. He sold it that year to George Webb of Hill Ridware, in Mavesyn Ridware. It then comprised three corn mills and a malt mill.[12] Webb constructed a substantial mill pool.[13] By 1818 it had been converted into a paper mill, run by James Webb. The conversion may have taken place by 1815 when a paper maker was living near by at Greenhill in Lichfield.[14] Isaac Newey, presumably a lessee, was running the paper-making business in 1828 and 1841.[15] By 1851 the mill had been converted back to grinding corn, but by 1860 it was used for grinding bones, still its function in 1864.[16] By 1867 ownership had descended to George Webb's great-grand-daughters, Emily Briggs and Mary Gillson. With their husbands they sold it in 1871 to

[92] P.R.O., RG 9/1975; RG 10/2916; RG 11/2776.
[93] S.R.O., D. 4566/K, papers of Wm. Holland, probate valuation of 20 Dec. 1887.
[94] Staffs. Advertiser, 9 June 1928, p. 2.
[95] M.A.F.F., agric. returns 1984.
[96] P.R.O., HO 107/976; HO 107/2014(2); L.J.R.O., B/A/15/Streethay, no. 140; P.O. Dir. Staffs. (1850).
[97] P.R.O., RG 9/1975; RG 10/2913–14, 2916; RG 11/2776; L.J.R.O., B/C/11, vol. v. 108.
[98] P.R.O., RG 9/1975; RG 10/2916; RG 11/2776; P.O. Dir. Staffs. (1860); Kelly's Dir. Staffs. (1900; 1904).
[99] Inf. from Mr. G. A. Burton of Fulfen Farm.
[1] Lomax's Red Bk. (1908), 20; Kelly's Dir. Staffs. (1908 and later edns.); Lichfield Rural Dist. Reg. of Electors, 1924; 1931 (copies in Lichfield Libr.).
[2] S.R.O., D. (W.) 1734/2/1/603, mm. 40, 43.
[3] W.S.L., S. MS. 431, reverse pages, 1632 survey; Eng. Place-Name Elements, i. 106.
[4] W.S.L., S. MS. 431.
[5] S.R.O., D. 661/11/2/3/1/11, 9 June 1824, 30 Aug. 1827; D. 661/11/2/3/1/13, 8 May 1837; D. 661/21/6/1, f. 27v.; D.

1042/2, pp. 70–1; plan of Fulfen estate in 1810 (in possession of Mr. R. B. Dyott of Freeford Manor).
[6] S.H.C. 1924, pp. 96–8.
[7] S.R.O., D. 661/1/658.
[8] Ibid. D. 661/1/660; D. 661/2/369 and 539.
[9] Cat. Anct. D. iii, D 1095.
[10] S.R.O., D. 661/2/340 and 710.
[11] Ibid. D. 661/6/1/19, receipt of 3 Apr. 1782. For a drawing of the mill in 1805 see Bodl. G.A. Staffs. 4°, 7, facing p. 224.
[12] S.R.O., D. 661/6/1/19, abstract of title 1870; D. 661/8/1/1/2.
[13] Ibid. D. 661/6/1/19, deed of 21 Dec. 1811; J. Dewhirst, Map of Lichfield (1836).
[14] B.A.A., reg. of Holy Cross, Lichfield, 1788–1843, reverse pages; Parson and Bradshaw, Staffs. Dir. (1818), 188.
[15] Lichfield Mercury, 8 Feb. 1828; Pigot, Nat. Com. Dir. (1841), 31.
[16] White, Dir. Staffs. (1851), 517; P.O. Dir. Staffs. (1860; 1864).

Richard Dyott of Freeford, who in 1872 redeemed the fee farm.[17] Under Dyott's chairmanship a co-operative of 16 local farmers was established to use the mill for cheese making.[18] It was apparently no longer working in 1881, when the millhouse, a brick building of the early 19th century, was occupied as a farmhouse.[19] The mill has been demolished.

LOCAL GOVERNMENT

The township of Morughale and Streethay made presentments at the great court of Longdon manor in 1297. In 1327 it was represented by two frankpledges, evidently one for each of the constituent settlements: in 1437 the Streethay frankpledge attended the great court, but Morughale was fined for not sending its representative.[20] Two frankpledges were sent in 1457 but one only by the late 1480s, probably an indication that Morughale hamlet was no longer inhabited. The township was still known by the double name in 1642 but by the early 18th century simply as Streethay.[21] There was a constable for Morughale and Streethay by 1377.[22] Election to the office at the Longdon great court was recorded by the later 15th century.[23] A constable was still chosen at the court in 1839.[24]

A township for the area around Curborough House also made presentments at the Longdon great court. Known as Little Curborough in 1297, it was called Curborough Somerville by 1327. In that year it was represented by two frankpledges but by one only in 1375.[25] The inhabitants evidently consisted at that date simply of the owner of the estate and his household: in 1386 it was reported that no frankpledge came because there was no tenant living there. By 1401 the township had ceased to exist separately and any presentments relating to the area were thereafter made by the frankpledges for Morughale and Streethay.[26] In 1436, however, Curborough Somerville again constituted a separate township, which survived at least until 1629.[27]

Fulfen was originally part of Morughale and Streethay township but had become separate by 1486. A single frankpledge attended the Longdon great court until 1499; after that date presentments were again made by the frankpledge for Morughale and Streethay.[28] Fulfen presented separately again in 1578, and a frankpledge was still sent in 1642.[29]

In the earlier 16th century Millhurst and the nearby land of the nuns of Farewell priory formed a township known simply as Curborough. Its frankpledge attended the Farewell manor court and was usually the same man who acted as the Curborough Somerville frankpledge for Longdon manor. It remained a separate township in the early 18th century.[30]

A pinfold at Streethay was mentioned in 1599.[31] In the early 19th century it stood in Ash Tree Lane, then known as Pinfold Lane; it was still there in 1900 but had been removed by 1921.[32] A pinner for Streethay was appointed at the Longdon court in 1728 and until 1839.[33]

Parochially Streethay was part of St. Michael's, Lichfield, and by 1637 it had its own sidesman.[34] There was an overseer of the poor in the late 1720s.[35] Fulfen was claimed as extra-parochial in 1825, probably because it was owned by the Dyotts of Freeford, itself regarded as an extra-parochial area.[36] Although Fulfen was sometimes treated as part of Streethay, as in 1861, it appears to have become a civil parish of itself under an act of 1857.[37] It remained separate until 1934, when it became part of the new Streethay civil parish.[38] Streethay was placed in Lichfield poor-law union from 1836, and Fulfen joined on being recognized as a civil parish.[39] As part of Lichfield rural district Streethay civil parish became part of the new Lichfield district in 1974.

Streethay and Fulfen subscribed to the Whittington association for the prosecution of felons, formed by 1780 and surviving in 1828.[40]

CHURCH

Although Streethay was part of St. Michael's, Lichfield, some inhabitants attended church at Whittington by the late 17th century.[41] In 1983 the part of Fulfen east of Lichfield Eastern Bypass was transferred from St. Michael's to Whittington parish.[42]

NONCONFORMITY

None known.

EDUCATION

No evidence.

CHARITIES FOR THE POOR

None known.

[17] S.R.O., D. 661/6/1/19, abstract of title 1870 and redemption of 19 Feb. 1872.
[18] Ibid. D. 661/19/10/22; *Staffs. Advertiser*, 27 May 1871, p. 2.
[19] P.R.O., RG 11/2773.
[20] S.R.O., D. (W.) 1734/2/1/598, mm. 2d., 14d.; D. (W.) 1734/2/1/603, mm. 3d.–4.
[21] Ibid. D. 603/J/7/6/1, 14 Oct. 1713; D. (W.) 1734/2/1/603, m. 53; D. (W.) 1734/2/1/604, m. 5; D. (W.) 1734/2/1/734.
[22] S.H.C. 4th ser. vi. 10.
[23] S.R.O., D. (W.) 1734/2/1/598, mm. 35, 46, 48, 72.
[24] Ibid. D. 603/J/1/4/15; D. (W.) 1511(34)/33–4.
[25] Ibid. D. (W.) 1734/2/1/598, mm. 2d., 14d., 30d.
[26] Ibid. D. (W.) 1734/2/1/599, mm. 10, 24, 44; D. (W) 1734/2/1/600, mm. 2d., 4, 9; D. (W.) 1734/2/1/601, m. 17.
[27] Ibid. D. (W.) 1734/2/1/603, mm. 1, 3d.; D. (W.) 1734/2/1/721.
[28] Ibid. D. (W.) 1734/2/1/604, mm. 1, 7, 8, 17d., 23, 26d., 30, 43.
[29] Ibid. D. (W.) 1734/2/1/630; D. (W.) 1734/2/1/734.
[30] Ibid. D. 603/J/5/2/2; D. (W.) 1734/2/1/381–5; D. (W.) 1734/2/1/387, m. 6.
[31] Ibid. D. (W.) 1734/2/1/674.
[32] Ibid. D. (W.) 1821/5; W.S.L. 47/1/45, f. 47, no. 2622; O.S. Map 1/2,500, Staffs. LII. 12 (1902 and 1923 edns.).
[33] S.R.O., D. 603/J/1/4/15; D. 603/J/7/6/3.
[34] L.J.R.O., D. 27/1/2, at end of vol.
[35] Ibid. D. 35/bailiffs' accts. 1704–94, p. 120.
[36] Plan of Fulfen estate in 1825 (in possession of Mr. R. B. Dyott of Freeford Manor).
[37] P.R.O., HO 107/2014(2); P.R.O., RG 9/1975; *Census*, 1881–91; *P.O. Dir. Staffs.* (1864), 517.
[38] Above, introduction.
[39] Poor Law Com. Order of 1836 forming Lichfield union (copy in L.J.R.O., D. 77/16/3); *P.O. Dir. Staffs.* (1864), 517.
[40] *Aris's Birmingham Gaz.* 24 Apr. 1780; 30 Jan. 1797; *Lichfield Mercury*, 1 Feb. 1828.
[41] L.J.R.O., B/V/7/Whittington.
[42] Lich. Dioc. Regy., Orders in Council, S, p. 40.

WALL

WITH PIPEHILL

THE civil parish of Wall, south-west of Lichfield, was originally a township in St. Michael's parish, Lichfield, 631 a. in area. It was adjoined on the north by Pipehill, also a township in St. Michael's and partly in the city of Lichfield, covering 580 a.[43] In 1879 a detached portion of Pipehill at Muckley Corner, comprising Muckley Corner hotel and the nearby lime-kilns, was transferred to Wall, while a detached portion of Curborough and Elmhurst township, comprising Pipehill Farm and a former tollhouse, became part of Pipehill. Wall then covered 645 a. and Pipehill 576 a.[44] In 1894 that part of Pipehill township which lay in the city of Lichfield was transferred to the civil parish of St. Michael; the rest of Pipehill was added to Wall, creating a new civil parish of 1,019 a. There were further boundary changes in 1934 when 93 a. of Burntwood parish, including Pipe Grange Farm, Hilltop Farm, and the fish ponds at Maple Hayes, were added to Wall.[45] In 1957 the parish was increased to 1,809 a. (731 ha.) by the addition of 696 a. from Shenstone.[46] In 1980 there were boundary changes with Hammerwich and Shenstone, creating the present civil parish of 1,871 a. (755 ha.).[47] This article deals with Wall and Pipehill according to the boundaries established in 1879, but excluding the Lichfield portion of Pipehill which is treated elsewhere in the volume.

Wall's boundary on the south ran along the line of the Roman Watling Street as far as Manor Farm. It then continued eastwards along what was presumably a medieval road as far as the former Lichfield–Shenstone road, which it followed north-west as far as another Roman road, Ryknild Street. On the south-west Wall's boundary followed the Lichfield–Walsall road to Muckley Corner. An area of waste called Wall Butts on the south side of Watling Street at Muckley Corner was included in the township. Pipehill's boundary on the north followed the upper reaches of Leamonsley (or Pipe) brook.[48] Most of the eastern part of Pipehill township was included in Lichfield city, apparently by the mid 17th century.[49]

The subsoil is Keuper Sandstone with an area of Mottled Sandstone west of Wall hamlet, through which a narrow gravel terrace runs north-west to a point south of Pipehill hamlet where it merges into an area of Boulder Clay.[50] The soil is loam.[51] The upper part of Wall hamlet lies at 370 ft. (114 m.) on the edge of a plateau; the lower part to the south on Watling Street lies some 50 ft. (16 m.) lower. To the north-east on the Lichfield boundary at Aldershawe the land lies at 423 ft. (130 m.), and it is the same level at Pipehill hamlet and at Muckley Corner. Black brook (formerly Hammerwich Water)[52] runs below the gravel terrace west of Wall hamlet. A spring south of Pipe Grange feeds a stream which flows eastwards to Leamonsley brook.[53]

In 1666 Wall had 12 people assessed for hearth tax and Pipehill 10.[54] In 1801 Wall's population was 97 and Pipehill's 95. The figure for Wall was 84 in 1821, 91 in 1841, and 96 in 1851. A fall to 87 by 1861 was followed by rises to 101 by 1871 and 115 by 1881. The figures for Pipehill in 1811, 1821, and 1831, which probably included people living in the Lichfield portion of the township, were respectively 110, 92, and 110. The population, excluding the Lichfield portion, was 94 in 1841, 92 in 1851, 106 in 1861, 98 in 1871, and 119 in 1881.[55] The population of Wall and Pipehill together was 284 in 1901, 306 in 1911, and 330 in 1921; it had fallen to 292 by 1931 and 271 by 1951. The population of the much enlarged civil parish was 397 in 1961, 401 in 1971, and 368 in 1981.[56]

Although flints dating from the Neolithic period have been found at the upper part of Wall hamlet,[57] the first detailed evidence of settlement comes from the 1st century A.D. A Roman fort was probably established at Wall in or soon after 50 A.D. to accommodate Legio XIV, then advancing towards Wales.[58] A fort was certainly built in the area of the upper part of the hamlet later in the 50s or 60s, and Watling Street was constructed to the south in the 70s. A bath house was built on the lower ground south-west of the fort in the late 1st century for use by soldiers; it was later used by the inhabitants of a civilian settlement which developed along Watling Street. In the 2nd century the settlement covered c. 30 a. west of the later Wall Lane. By the 1st or early 2nd century there was a burial area beyond the western end of the settlement.

[43] L.J.R.O., B/A/15/Burntwood. This article was written mainly in 1986. The people named in footnotes as supplying information are thanked for their help.
[44] Census, 1881, 1891; P.R.O., RG 10/2915; RG 11/2775.
[45] Census, 1901; Kelly's Dir. Staffs. (1900); above, Burntwood, introduction. [46] Census, 1961.
[47] Ibid. 1981; Lichfield (Parishes) Order 1980, S.I. 1980 no. 387; inf. from the Chief Executive, Lichfield District Council. [48] Above, Burntwood, introduction.
[49] Above, Lichfield, boundaries and gates.
[50] Geol. Surv. Map 1", drift, sheet 154 (1922 edn.).
[51] Soil Surv. Sheet 3 (1983).
[52] Above, Hammerwich, introduction.
[53] L.J.R.O., D. 88/hosp. land, plan no. 6.
[54] S.H.C. 1923, 163–4.
[55] V.C.H. Staffs. i. 323, 329, where the figures given from 1841 to 1881 are not always correct. The figures given here for those years have been calculated from the original returns (P.R.O., HO 107/980; HO 107/2014(2); ibid. RG 9/1974; RG 10/2915; RG 11/2775). The figures for the detached portion of Curborough and Elmhurst at Pipehill are entered in the Pipehill census returns, except for a family of five which in 1841 was entered in the Curborough and Elmhurst return: P.R.O., HO 107/975.
[56] Census, 1901–81.
[57] T.S.S.A.H.S. viii. 10; xi. 25.
[58] Para. based on articles in T.S.S.A.H.S., esp. vols. ii, viii, xi, xv, xxi, xxiii, and xxv, and on 'Archaeology of Roman Letocetum' (Staffs. C. C. Planning and Development Dept., consultation report, n.d. but 1987; copy in W.S.L.) and Letocetum (National Trust guide bk. 1937 edn.; copy in W.S.L.). For the bath house site see above, plate 55.

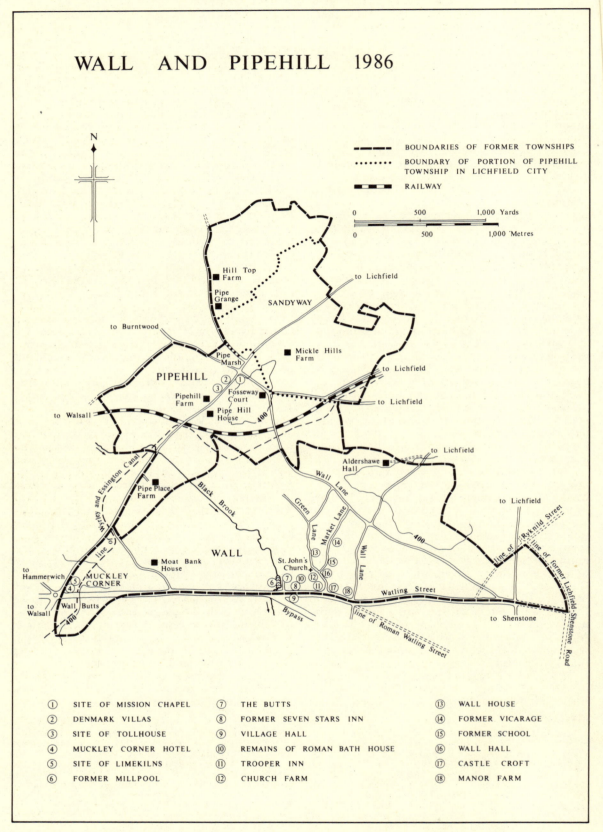

WALL AND PIPEHILL 1986

Legend:
- — — — BOUNDARIES OF FORMER TOWNSHIPS
- · · · · · BOUNDARY OF PORTION OF PIPEHILL TOWNSHIP IN LICHFIELD CITY
- ▮▮▮ RAILWAY

0   500   1,000 Yards
0   500   1,000 Metres

①	SITE OF MISSION CHAPEL	⑦	THE BUTTS	⑬	WALL HOUSE
②	DENMARK VILLAS	⑧	FORMER SEVEN STARS INN	⑭	FORMER VICARAGE
③	SITE OF TOLLHOUSE	⑨	VILLAGE HALL	⑮	FORMER SCHOOL
④	MUCKLEY CORNER HOTEL	⑩	REMAINS OF ROMAN BATH HOUSE	⑯	WALL HALL
⑤	SITE OF LIMEKILNS	⑪	TROOPER INN	⑰	CASTLE CROFT
⑥	FORMER MILLPOOL	⑫	CHURCH FARM	⑱	MANOR FARM

Fig. 25

284

In the late 3rd or early 4th century the eastern part of the settlement, covering *c.* 6 a. between the later Wall Lane and Green Lane and straddling Watling Street, was enclosed with a stone wall surrounded by an earth rampart and ditches. Civilians continued to live inside the settlement and on its outskirts in the late 4th and possibly in the 5th century. The excavated site of the bath house and a museum were conveyed to the National Trust in 1934 and are open to the public under the management of the Historic Buildings and Monuments Commission.

The Roman name for the civilian settlement, *Letocetum*, derived from a Celtic name meaning 'grey wood' and describing the surrounding area. The native population apparently remained Celtic-speaking when the English settled the area, incorporating the Romano-British place name *Luitcoit* in the English name Lichfield.[59] The Celtic tribe of the Cornovii evidently had a shrine outside the Roman fort in the later 1st century A.D. The inversion of stones with pagan motifs in a villa-type building near the bath house may indicate the shrine's conversion to use by Christians, possibly as a house for a community of priests.[60] A bowl and stones with Christian symbols have also been found at Wall.[61]

The name Wall, recorded in the later 12th century,[62] was presumably derived from the physical remains of the Roman civilian settlement. The earliest medieval settlement may have been on the higher ground around Wall House which, though dating mainly from the mid 18th century, is probably on the site of the medieval manor house: manorial rights descended with the house. Wall Hall to the south also dates from the mid 18th century but replaced a house which existed in the later 17th century. The site of Church Farm opposite Wall Hall was occupied by the early 16th century, and there were cottages to the north by the late 18th century.[63] Manor Farm, at the corner of Watling Street and Wall Lane, was built in 1669 as a T-shaped brick house with stone dressings and mullioned windows; originally two storeys high, it was raised in 1844 when additions were made to the rear service wing.[64] It replaced an earlier house.[65]

By the late 18th century several houses on Watling Street west of Manor Farm formed a lower part of the hamlet.[66] An alehouse recorded in 1589 probably stood there.[67] An inn called the Wheatsheaf existed by 1764, and in the 1790s there was one called the Swan, possibly the Wheatsheaf under another name.[68] The Seven Stars, first mentioned in 1776, stood at the west end of the hamlet; it remained an inn until the mid 1920s.[69] The Trooper inn at the corner of Watling Street and Green Lane existed by 1851.[70] In the earlier 1950s ten council houses were built on the road called the Butts,[71] and two privately built houses were added later. Bungalows to the south in what was formerly Shenstone parish were built in 1982. The lower part of the hamlet was relieved of the heavy traffic using Watling Street by the construction of a bypass to the south, completed in 1965.[72]

Aldershawe, a name meaning alder wood, lies ½ mile north-east of Wall hamlet and was inhabited by the early 13th century.[73]

Moat Bank, a mile west of Wall, was evidently a settled area at the end of the 16th century.[74] The name is derived from a rabbit warren there.[75] Lord Henry Paget (later 4th marquess of Anglesey), first master of the South Staffordshire Hunt, established in 1865, built the hunt's first stables and kennels at Moat Bank House, besides establishing a stud for racehorses there. In 1873 the kennels were moved to Fosseway Court in Pipehill.[76]

Muckley Corner on the south-west boundary was so called by 1660, but the name Muckley, meaning the great *leah* (a wood or clearing in woodland), was in use in the mid 13th century.[77] The area was inhabited by the early 18th century.[78] There was evidently an inn there by the 1790s when the Craddock family lived at Muckley Corner House, presumably on the site of the later hotel: James Craddock (d. 1808 or 1809) was both a farmer and a victualler.[79] By the mid 19th century petty sessions were held at the inn, where there was a lock-up. Defendants included people from the developing mining communities in the area, and by the later 1860s sessions were normally held once a month, with another monthly sitting in Shenstone. In 1883 the Muckley Corner sessions were transferred to Brownhills.[80] A police house, possibly over the boundary in Ogley Hay, was advertised for sale or lease in 1873. A police officer was living at Muckley Corner by 1897, presumably in lodgings: he was moved that year because there was no house for him.[81] A police station north of

[59] Above, Lichfield, place name.
[60] *T.S.S.A.H.S.* xxi. 1–11; inf. from Mr. J. Gould of Aldridge.
[61] Above, Lichfield, general hist. (Anglo-Saxon eccl. centre).
[62] *S.H.C.* i. 47.
[63] Above, fig. 1; below, manor.
[64] Plaque formerly over the central doorway but now over the porch, and plaque on west side of house; inf. from Mr. W. J. Ryman of Manor Farm.
[65] Below, manor (Wall).
[66] Above, fig. 1.
[67] *S.H.C.* 1929, 292.
[68] *Aris's Birmingham Gaz.* 22 Oct. 1764; Shaw, *Staffs.* i. 19.
[69] L.J.R.O., D. 27/1/4, burial of 18 Mar. 1776; S.R.O., D. 546/16/8, no. 10; Parson and Bradshaw, *Staffs. Dir.* (1818), 42; *Kelly's Dir. Staffs.* (1880 and edns. to 1924); O.S. Map 6″, Staffs. LVIII. NW. (1888 edn.).
[70] P.R.O., HO 107/2014(2).

[71] *Lichfield Mercury*, 2 July 1954, p. 5.
[72] Local inf.
[73] *Eng. Place-Name Elements* (E.P.N.S.), i. 9; Shaw, *Staffs.* i. 357–8.
[74] Below, manor (Moat Bank House).
[75] Below, econ. hist. (warrens and fishery).
[76] E. S. Mott, *A Mingled Yarn* (1898), 273–4.
[77] *S.H.C.* 1924, p. 297; *Eng. Place-Name Elements*, ii. 18–19, 40; L.J.R.O., D. 127/deed of 17 July 1660.
[78] L.J.R.O., D. 27/1/3, bapt. of 12 Sept. 1716.
[79] S.R.O., D. 3802/1/1, burial of 7 May 1790; L.J.R.O., P/C/11, Jas. Craddock (1809); Parson and Bradshaw, *Staffs. Dir.* (1818), 35.
[80] Mott, *Mingled Yarn*, 2–3; Mason, *Found Ready*, 68–9; *Lichfield Herald*, 5 Oct. 1894 (cutting in S.R.O., D. 4520/5, p. 176); Petty Sessions min. bks. 1866–84 (in possession of Sharrot, Barnes & Co., solicitors of Lichfield).
[81] *Staffs. Advertiser*, 4 Jan. 1873, p. 8; 9 Aug. 1873, p. 1; S.R.O., D. 4430/1/1, p. 36.

Muckley Corner hotel was opened in 1935 and closed in 1971. It then became a private house called Copper's End.[82] There were cottages adjoining the hotel on the north by the late 19th century.[83] One of them may have served as a post office, recorded in 1908 and closed c. 1930.[84] A row of cottages further north on the Lichfield–Walsall road dates from the early 20th century.[85]

Pipehill hamlet lies where the Lichfield–Walsall road crosses one from Burntwood to Lichfield and Wall, formerly an area of waste known as Pipe Marsh.[86] The hamlet was known as Hardwick or Pipe Hardwick in the 14th century, a name still used in the early 17th century and meaning a livestock farm.[87] The site of Pipehill Farm on the south-west edge of the waste was occupied in the mid 14th century and the present farmhouse is partly medieval. Pipe Hill House to the south dates from the mid 18th century but replaces an house in existence by the later 17th century. The site of Pipe Grange north of Pipehill Farm was occupied in the Middle Ages; the present house dates mainly from the 18th and early 19th century. Hill Top Farm to the north was built c. 1800.[88] Pipe Place Farm, south-west of Pipehill hamlet, dates from 1764.[89]

Five families were living at Pipe Marsh in the 1840s, and the number increased with the construction in 1878 of a row of six houses called Denmark Villas.[90] In contrast to Wall hamlet, where most of the working inhabitants were farm labourers in the late 19th century, several Pipehill householders were then artisans: the population of 45 in 1881 included a bricklayer, a carpenter, a boot and shoe maker, a coal miner, and two laundresses.[91]

Fosseway Court east of Pipehill hamlet on the edge of high ground overlooking Lichfield was built probably in the early 19th century by Samuel Hamson, otherwise Bradburne, of Pipe Hill House; either the house itself or a garden feature there was known as Bradburne's Folly in 1836.[92] In 1873 the kennels of the South Staffordshire Hunt were moved from Moat Bank House to Fosseway Court, whose owner, Maj. J. M. Browne, was hunt master; the kennels remained there until the pack was sold in 1885. In 1881 a whipper-in and a groom were living next to the kennels.[93] In 1986 part of the former kennel block was converted into flats.

The Lichfield–Shenstone road which formed part of the eastern boundary of Wall was turnpiked in 1729, and that stretch of the road was replaced in the early 1820s by a new line to the west. The road was disturnpiked in 1875.[94] The Lichfield–Walsall road was also turnpiked in 1729. A tollgate was set up in Pipehill hamlet in 1786, and a tollhouse was built north-east of Pipehill Farm in 1787 and enlarged in 1827.[95] In 1814 a bar was placed across the lane leading to the road from Moat Bank House, and another was set up on Watling Street east of Muckley Corner, where a house was built for the keeper.[96] The Lichfield–Walsall road was disturnpiked in 1879.[97] The Pipehill tollhouse survived as a cottage in 1909 but was removed probably soon afterwards.[98] The roundabout at Muckley Corner was built in the late 1950s.[99]

The Wyrley and Essington Canal, opened in 1797 and closed in 1954,[1] ran through Wall and Pipehill. It passed east of Muckley Corner, where there were limekilns and a wharf by 1845.[2] By the late 19th century there were two other wharves, one north of Muckley Corner served by the lane to Moat Bank House, and the other where the canal passed under the Lichfield–Walsall road south-west of Pipehill.[3] That wharf also adjoined the South Staffordshire Railway, opened from Walsall to Wychnor in Tatenhill in 1849.[4]

Electricity was supplied to Wall by Lichfield corporation from 1927; Pipehill had been connected by 1937.[5] There was a gas supply by 1940.[6] A sewage works was constructed in 1938; most of the parish had been connected by 1947.[7]

A lodge of Oddfellows, established in 1864, met at the Trooper inn in 1876; two other lodges of Oddfellows, one established in 1868 and the other in 1873, met at the Muckley Corner inn and probably drew most of their members from the Ogley Hay and Brownhills area.[8] There was a working men's club in Wall in 1910. It probably met in the village hall on Watling Street, known as the Institute in 1914.[9] A cricket club was formed in 1921, playing on a field in Market Lane owned by Walter Ryman of Manor Farm. It continued to play there in 1986.[10]

MANOR AND OTHER ESTATES. The manor of *WALL* was formed between 1135 and 1166 out of the bishop's manor of Lichfield

[82] Inf. from Mr. Malcolm Lumb, the present owner.
[83] O.S. Map 6", Staffs. LVIII. NW. (1888 edn.).
[84] *Kelly's Dir. Staffs.* (1908 and edns. to 1932).
[85] O.S. Map 1/2,500, Staffs. LVIII. 5 (1923 edn.).
[86] Below, econ. hist. (agric.).
[87] *S.H.C.* n.s. x (1), 17; *S.H.C.* 1913, 137; *Eng. Place-Name Elements*, i. 244.
[88] Below, manor.
[89] Ibid. (Pipe Hill House).
[90] P.R.O., HO 107/980; HO 107/2014(2); date stone on houses. [91] P.R.O., RG 11/2775.
[92] J. Dewhirst, *Map of Lichfield* (1836).
[93] R. Greaves, *Foxhunting in Staffordshire*, 19; P.R.O., RG 11/2775; below, manor (Wall).
[94] B.L. Maps, O.S.D. 258; J. Phillips and W. F. Hutchings, *Map of County of Stafford* (1832); L.J.R.O., D. 15/2/4, 5 Dec. 1820, 2 Oct. 1821, 5 Feb. 1822, 4 Feb. 1823; *Lichfield Mercury*, 14 May 1824; above, Lichfield, communications.
[95] L.J.R.O., D. 15/2/3, 7 Feb., 7 Mar., and 5 Dec. 1786, 4 Sept. 1787; D. 15/2/4, 2 Oct. 1827; W.S.L. 47/1/45, f. 44,

no. 2568; S.R.O.. D. (W.) 1821/5; above, Lichfield, communications.
[96] L.J.R.O., D. 15/2/4, 2 Aug., 6 Sept., and 1 Nov. 1814.
[97] Above, Lichfield, communications.
[98] S.R.O., D. 4430/1/1, p. 168.
[99] Ibid. D. 4430/1/3, pp. 174, 231.
[1] Above, Lichfield, communications.
[2] Below, econ. hist. (trades).
[3] O.S. Map 6", Staffs. LVIII. NW. (1888 edn.).
[4] Above, Lichfield, communications.
[5] *Lichfield Mercury*, 10 June 1927, p. 1; L.J.R.O., D. 127/electric lighting cttee. min. bk., p. 319.
[6] *Kelly's Dir. Staffs.* (1940).
[7] Lichfield R.D.C. *Ann. Rep. of M.O.H.*, 1938, p. 17; 1947, p. 15 (copies in S.R.O., C/H/1/2/2/25).
[8] *Rep. Chief Registrar of Friendly Socs. 1876, App. P*, H.C. 429-1, pp. 404, 411 (1877), lxxvii.
[9] L.J.R.O.. D. 126/acct. bk. 1901-16, p. 184; S.R.O., D. 4566/J, Aldershawe, draft deed of 9 June 1914.
[10] Inf. from Mr. Alan Taylor, chairman of Wall Cricket Club.

(later Longdon). It remained a member of the bishop's (later the Paget family's) manor of Longdon until at least the earlier 19th century.[11]

Rabel Durdent held Wall in 1166 evidently as $\frac{1}{7}$ knight's fee. The manor may have been created for him by Bishop Durdent, 1149–59, presumably a relative; in the early 1150s Rabel was evidently a member of the bishop's household.[12] Robert of Wall, mentioned in the earlier 1190s, was lord in 1227–8,[13] and Ralph was lord in 1235–6.[14] Another Robert was lord in 1242–3, when he held of the bishop $\frac{1}{6}$ knight's fee and a further $\frac{1}{18}$ knight's fee, both at Wall.[15] He may have been the Robert of Wall who held $\frac{1}{16}$ knight's fee there in 1284–5.[16] Hugh of Wall, who held the manor as $\frac{1}{15}$ knight's fee in 1298, was still alive in 1314, but by 1327 he had been succeeded by Ralph, possibly his son.[17] Ralph was dead by 1370 when Ellen, possibly his daughter, was lady of Wall.[18] She and her son Robert were assessed for poll tax in 1380–1.[19] Robert Swinfen, probably Ellen's son, lord in 1388–9 and still alive in 1416–17, was succeeded by his son William Swinfen, otherwise known as William Pipe (d. 1419).[20]

William's heir was his daughter Margaret, who in 1435 married Sir William Vernon of Haddon (Derb.). Sir William was succeeded in 1467 by his son Henry, knighted in 1489 and appointed governor and treasurer to Prince Arthur. Sir Henry was succeeded in 1515 by his son Richard (d. 1516), and Richard by his son George, who was knighted in 1547 and died in 1565.[21] Sir George's heir at Wall was his daughter Margaret, wife of Sir Thomas Stanley of Winwick (Lancs.).[22] Sir Thomas died in 1576, and by 1584 his widow had married William Mather, who held Wall jointly with her. She died in 1596, and Mather evidently acquired Wall from her son Edward (later Sir Edward) Stanley. Mather was still alive in 1607. His son by a second marriage, Ambrose (d. 1625), inherited Wall.[23]

In 1627 Wall was acquired by John Popham of Littlecote (Wilts.) and his wife Mary.[24] In 1634 Popham owned a house and 125 a. at Wall held for life by Elizabeth Mather, the widow of Ambrose Mather, and 274 a. there was held at will by several tenants.[25] In 1636 he sold the manor to Thomas Dutton of Chesterfield and

Francis Erpe of Lynn, both in Shenstone, and to Robert Wood, a London cook. They divided it amongst themselves, Dutton taking a half share which included the principal house, then called Mather's Farm, and Erpe and Wood each taking quarter shares.[26] In 1648 Erpe's widow Lettice sold land at Wall, presumably her husband's share, to Thomas Dutton, and her son John confirmed the sale in 1650.[27] In 1652 Wood's son William, a London barrister, divided his share, selling half to John Marshall, a London cook, and half to Thomas Dutton; in 1658 Marshall sold his portion to Dutton.[28] Having reassembled the manor, Dutton divided it again. He gave a quarter share to William Quinton, probably on William's marriage to his daughter Alice in 1658,[29] and devised on his death in 1689 a quarter share to his grandson Thomas Porter. Dutton's son Edward inherited what remained, except for the manorial fishpool and rabbit warren, both of which were devised to William Quinton.[30]

Edward Dutton, whose share was centred on the later Manor Farm, was succeeded in 1704 by his son Thomas.[31] Thomas was succeeded in 1755 by his brother William, a London draper, whose son Thomas, a London sugar cooper, sold Manor Farm and his share of the manor in 1769 to Ann, widow of Richard Burnes of Aldershawe. In 1777 she gave them to her son John Burnes Floyer.[32] Manor Farm then descended with Aldershawe until 1925, when it was sold to the tenant, Walter Ryman, who was succeeded in 1949 by his son Mr. W. J. Ryman, the owner in 1986.[33]

The share of the manor given to William Quinton centred on what was later known as Wall House. It descended on Quinton's death in 1699 to his son John, who was succeeded in 1714 by his brother Thomas.[34] Thomas died in 1736 and, subject to the life interest of his widow Elizabeth, divided his estate between his daughters Alice, then unmarried, and Anne, the wife of William Jackson, a Lichfield silversmith.[35] Thomas, however, had mortgaged the estate, which evidently through default came to Robert Porter, a Lichfield attorney. Porter had already in 1703 acquired the share bequeathed in 1689 to Thomas Porter, probably his brother.[36] Robert was succeeded in 1744 by his son Shel-

[11] S.H.C. i. 147 (entry for 'Parabel', i.e. Rabel [Durdent]); below, local govt.
[12] S.H.C. i. 47, 147; iii (1), 183.
[13] Ibid. iii (1) 26; iv (1), 70.
[14] S.R.O., D. 546/1/2/3, schedule.
[15] Bk. of Fees, ii. 968, 975.
[16] Feud. Aids, v. 8.
[17] S.R.O., D. (W.) 1734/J. 2268, f. 1v.; H. Sanders, Hist. and Antiquities of Shenstone (1794), 282; S.H.C. vii (1), 233.
[18] S.R.O., D. 714/3; D. (W.) 1734/2/1/598, mm. 22d., 23.
[19] S.H.C. xvii. 178 (date corrected by S.H.C. 4th ser. vi. 3 n.).
[20] S.R.O., D. 546/1/2/3, schedule; J. Nichols, Hist. and Antiquities of County of Leicester, iii (2), pedigree facing p. *982; G. Griffiths, Hist. of Tong, Shropshire (1894), 44.
[21] Nichols, Hist. iii (2), pedigree facing p. *982; Shaw, Staffs. i. 400–1, 404; W. A. Shaw, Knights of Eng. i. 143, 151.
[22] Shaw, Staffs. i. 212; S.R.O., D. (W.) 1734/2/1/609, m. 14.
[23] Nichols, Hist. iii (2), p. *987; Griffiths, Tong, 64; Shaw, Staffs. i. 212; P.R.O., PROB 11/88, f. 318v.

[24] S.R.O., D. 546/1/2/3, schedule, fine of 1627.
[25] Ibid. D. 546/7/2; Nichols, Hist. iii (2), p. 987.
[26] L.J.R.O., D. 15/11/14/130, deeds of 7 June and 10 June 1636.
[27] Ibid. D. 15/11/14/131, deeds of 1 Apr. 1648 and 27 May 1650.
[28] Ibid. D. 15/11/14/132, deeds of 1 Sept. 1652 and 14 Aug. 1658.
[29] For Quinton see below (Moat Bank House).
[30] L.J.R.O., D. 27/1/1, f. 109v.; D. 27/1/3, burial of 3 Dec. 1689; L.J.R.O., P/C/11, Thos. Dutton (1691); P.R.O., PROB 11/284, f. 148v.
[31] L.J.R.O., D. 27/1/3, burial of 2 Feb. 1703/4; S.R.O., D. 546/1/3/2.
[32] L.J.R.O., D. 15/10/1/24, deeds of 28 July 1769 and 16 Aug. 1777; D. 27/1/4, p. 113.
[33] Inf. from Mr. Ryman.
[34] L.J.R.O., D. 27/1/3, burial of 11 Feb. 1698/9; L.J.R.O., P/C/11, Wm. Quinton (1699), John Quinton (1714).
[35] Ibid. P/C/11, Thos. Quinton (1736).
[36] S.R.O., D. 546/1/3/2; D. 546/1/3/10, deed of 15 Dec. 1703; Shaw, Staffs. i. 357.

don, and in 1754 Alice Quinton, then wife of James Garlick, a Lichfield surgeon, confirmed Sheldon's right to her share of the manor.[37] Sheldon died in 1765, leaving as his heirs his sisters Sarah (d. 1776), the widow of Edward Jackson of Wall Hall, and Penelope (d. 1782), a spinster.[38] Penelope died intestate, and her heir was a distant cousin Zachary Hill, a schoolmaster at Anslow in Rolleston, whose son Robert, formerly a Birmingham shoemaker, held the manor in 1808. Robert died in 1812, and the manor, which comprised Wall House with 30 a. in Wall and 12 a. in Shenstone and Moat Bank House with 94 a. in Wall, was sold in two parts in 1813.[39]

Wall House with the accompanying manorial rights was bought by William Mott, a Lichfield lawyer and deputy diocesan registrar.[40] William was succeeded in 1836 by his son John (d. 1869), whose heir was his son William (d. 1887). William's son and heir, the Revd. William Kynaston Mott, died at Wall in 1889. He was succeeded by his nephew, Roger Mott.[41] In 1919 Roger sold Wall House with 5 a. to Capt. Robert Hilton, who sold both house and land in 1920 to Col. (later Brig.-Gen.) Claude Westmacott, then living at Knowle Lodge in Lichfield. Westmacott died in 1948, and the estate was sold to Christina Bather of Lichfield. Following her death in 1984 the house was bought by Mr. Michael Bolland and his wife Janet, the owners in 1986.[42]

Wall House is constructed on a double-pile plan and was presumably built by Sheldon Porter: there is a rainwater head dated 1761 on the south side. Part of the structure and some of the interior panelling, however, are survivals from an early 17th-century house. Both main elevations were originally of three bays in brick with moulded cornices. In the early 19th century the interior was extensively refitted and new kitchens were built on the west.

A messuage and virgate at *ALDERSHAWE* claimed by Nicholas of Wyrley in the later 13th century[43] were probably the estate held there in 1414 by Sir William Newport of Abnalls in Burntwood. He was succeeded in 1415 or 1416 by another William Newport, presumably his son.[44] The later history of the estate is unknown until 1511, when what was probably the same land at Aldershawe was held by a John Hill.[45] In 1571 a later John Hill, of Little Pipe, then a detached portion of Curborough and Elmhurst but later in Farewell, was one of three men who

between them held 120 a. at Aldershawe; the other two were Sir Thomas Stanley, lord of Wall, and Sir Edward Littleton of Pillaton in Penkridge.[46] Sir Edward, who had acquired Abnalls in the 1560s, was evidently the owner of Aldershawe, with Hill his principal tenant: in 1619 Sir Edward's grandson, also called Sir Edward, held 98 a. at Aldershawe, of which 48 a. were tenanted by John Hill of Little Pipe, probably great-grandson of the John Hill of 1511.[47] The Hill family's holding included the site of a house, called Motte house in 1633.[48]

In 1621 Sir Edward Littleton sold a moiety of his land at Aldershawe, formerly held by John Hill, to the tenant John Burnes. Burnes was a Lichfield upholsterer and one of the city bailiffs in 1623–4 and 1632–3.[49] In 1633 Thomas Burnes, a Lichfield mercer and probably John's son, acquired the rest of Aldershawe, including Motte house, from John Hill's son Edward.[50] Thomas was succeeded probably in 1648 by his grandson John, also a Lichfield mercer, who died in 1682, leaving a son Richard (d. 1692).[51] Richard's heir was his son, also Richard, who was succeeded in 1766 by his son John. John became the owner of Manor Farm in Wall in 1777, and as the adopted heir of John Floyer of Longdon he added Floyer to his surname. He died a lunatic in 1817.[52] His heir was his nephew, the Revd. Trevor Burnes Jones, who changed his surname to Floyer. On his death in 1871 Aldershawe passed to his nephew, Edward Corbett of Longnor Hall (Salop.).[53] In 1893 Corbett sold the estate to the tenant, W. B. Harrison, a colliery owner (d. 1912). In 1913 his son W. E. Harrison negotiated the sale of Aldershawe and Manor Farm to Sir Richard Cooper, Bt., who died later the same year. The purchase was completed in 1914 by his son Sir Richard.[54] The estate was broken up in 1925, when the house at Aldershawe was sold with 32 a. to Frank Allen, a cotton and tobacco planter of Rhodesia.[55] In 1946 Aldershawe was bought by Gordon Powell of Curborough House Farm in Streethay. Powell used the stables for training racehorses, and after his death in 1966 the stables, then known as Elkar Stud Racing Stables, were sold with 68 a. separately from the house. In 1983 both the house and the racing stables were bought by Mr. K. H. Fischer, the owner in 1986.[56]

Aldershawe Hall, of brick in Gothic style with timber-framed gables and terra-cotta dressings,

[37] S.R.O., D. 546/1/3/10, deed of 16 Sept. 1754; D. 546/1/4/1.
[38] Ibid. D. 546/1/3/2; L.J.R.O., D. 27/1/4, burials of 11 Aug. 1765, 13 June 1776, 30 Mar. 1782.
[39] S.R.O., D. 546/1/3/2 and 10; D. 546/11/1/1.
[40] Ibid. D. 546/11/1/1; above, Lichfield, econ. hist. (professions).
[41] Burke, *Land. Gent.* (1952), pp. 1835–6; gravestone of W. K. Mott in Wall churchyard.
[42] Deeds in possession of Mr. and Mrs. Bolland.
[43] *S.H.C.* iv (1), 162, 189, 195.
[44] Ibid. xvii. 53; P.R.O., C 138/19, no. 27; above, Burntwood, manors (Abnalls).
[45] *S.H.C.* iii (2), 98; *S.H.C.* n.s. x (1), 116–17; S.R.O., D. (W.) 1734/2/1/604, m. 10d.; D. (W.) 1734/2/1/606, m. 17d.
[46] W.S.L., S. MS. 326/2, m. 5.
[47] L.J.R.O., D. 15/10/1/13, terrier of 9 Dec. 1619; P.R.O.,

C 3/447, no. 75; above, Burntwood, manors (Abnalls).
[48] L.J.R.O., D. 15/10/1/14.
[49] Ibid. D. 15/10/1/13, deed of 3 Oct. 1621; Harwood, *Lichfield*, 425.
[50] L.J.R.O., D. 15/10/1/14; P.R.O., C 3/447, no. 75.
[51] L.J.R.O., D. 20/1/1, f. 125; Sanders, *Shenstone*, 286.
[52] Sanders, *Shenstone*, 143, 286; S.R.O., D. 4566/M, deed of 16 July 1817; *Staffs. Advertiser*, 8 Nov. 1817.
[53] L.J.R.O., D. 15/10/1/3; S.R.O., D. 4566/J, abstract of title to Aldershawe, 1908.
[54] S.R.O., D. 4566/J, abstract of title to Aldershawe, 1908 and 1913, and Cooper papers; *Staffs. Advertiser*, 28 Dec. 1912, p. 9.
[55] S.R.O., D. 4566/J, Aldershawe sale cat. 1925 and letter of 24 Sept. 1926; *Lichfield Mercury*, 8 Feb. 1935, p. 6.
[56] *Lichfield & Tamworth Life Mag.*, June 1972, 17; inf. from Mrs. Fischer.

was built in 1896 to the design of S. Loxton of Walsall and Cannock.[57] It replaced an earlier house, which was an irregular gabled building, probably of the 17th century.[58] On the north and west sides of the hall are pleasure grounds which include pools, grottoes, and plantations probably laid out by Trevor Burnes Floyer. Columns and arches removed from Lichfield cathedral in the 18th century were set up in the grounds, and a small brick chapel was built in 1845.[59] W. B. Harrison, a cricket enthusiast, laid out a cricket ground north of the house over the Lichfield boundary.[60]

Pasture in Wall called Ladyhey owned by the lord of Wall in 1442–3 is probably identifiable as the land with a cottage which the Lichfield guild of St. Mary and St. John the Baptist owned in 1525[61] and which was later called *CHURCH FARM*. The estate passed presumably in 1545 along with other guild land to the trustees of the Lichfield Conduit Lands, who in 1661 held a house and 82 a. in Wall.[62] In the early 19th century the estate covered 50 a., of which 17 a. lay in Wall and the rest in Shenstone.[63] It was sold in 1912 to Walter Ryman of Manor Farm. His son W. J. Ryman sold the house and farm buildings in 1975 to R. G. Goodwin, who converted them into the present Church Farm. Mr. Goodwin remained the owner in 1986.[64]

An estate centred on *HILL TOP FARM* existed by 1720 when it was owned by William Pott (or Potts) of Lichfield. He died probably in 1725, leaving the estate to his nephew John Spateman.[65] It was later divided but was re-united in 1799 by George Addams, a Lichfield wine merchant.[66] Addams, who also owned the nearby Maple Hayes in Burntwood, sold Hill Top in 1803 to Richard Slaney, apparently the tenant. In 1808 Slaney sold it to John Atkinson, who had bought Maple Hayes from Addams in 1804.[67] Hill Top remained part of the Maple Hayes estate in 1986.[68] The farmhouse is a square brick building dating from *c.* 1800.

An estate centred on *MOAT BANK HOUSE* derived from a messuage granted in 1599 by Edward (later Sir Edward) Stanley, the son of Sir Thomas Stanley (d. 1576), to William Quinton and his brother Robert.[69] Robert was

dead by 1619, when William acquired the wardship of Robert's son John.[70] William died in 1630, and the estate evidently passed to John. He was succeeded in 1658 by his son William, who later the same year acquired a share in Wall manor,[71] with which the estate, known as Moat Bank by 1733,[72] descended. When Robert Hill's Wall estate was sold in 1813 what was called Moat Bank House and 94 a. were bought by the tenant Samuel Bradburne, the owner of the Pipe Hill House estate.[73] Samuel (d. by 1834) left Moat Bank to his second son, the Revd. Thomas Bradburne.[74] He was succeeded in 1859 by his nephew John Bradburne, who died in or shortly before 1879, when the house and 11 a. were offered for sale along with Pipe Place Farm.[75] The house was bought in 1980 by Mr. J. R. Alsop, the owner in 1986.[76] Moat Bank House incorporates in a back wing part of a 17th-century building. The main range was built in the later 18th century with its front to the east; a new block, including a staircase, an entrance hall, and a west front, was added in the early 19th century at the south end of the main range.

An estate known as *PIPE GRANGE* by 1377[77] was held of the manor of Longdon by the prior of St. John's hospital, Lichfield, in 1298. The prior's service included stocking the larder of the bishop as lord of Longdon, for which he received a larderer's fee.[78] In the early 18th century the house and adjoining land covered 81 a. and there were a further 137 a. of inclosed and open-field land nearby.[79] In 1921 the hospital sold the house with 14 a. to W. W. Worthington of Maple Hayes.[80] In 1950 it was acquired by the trustees of the Maple Hayes estate, who sold it in 1951 to Walter Boole. He sold it with 3 a. in 1975 to Mr. Nigel Bird, the owner in 1986.[81]

The house was assessed for tax on three hearths in 1666.[82] In the early 18th century it comprised a main block with a small west wing.[83] It was later altered, probably by Cary Butt, a Lichfield surgeon and apothecary, who was living there in 1779; it was then described as 'a low house with two bay windows and two large parlours'.[84] Further alterations were made by Canon Hugh Bailye, chancellor of Lichfield

[57] *Lichfield & Tamworth Life Mag.*, June 1972, 17; [A. Williams and W. H. Mallett], *Mansions and Country Seats of Staffs. and Warws.* (Lichfield, n. d.), 9; *V.C.H. Staffs.* xvii. 282.
[58] *Lichfield & Tamworth Life Mag.*, March/April 1972, 44 (with picture).
[59] Lichfield Cath. Libr., Bridgeman's notes; date stone on chapel.
[60] *Lichfield Mercury*, 3 Nov. 1939, p. 8; O.S. Map Staffs. 1/2,500, LVIII. 2 (1902 edn.).
[61] W.S.L. 50/A 1/56; L.J.R.O., D. 126/cartulary, lease of 1525.
[62] L.J.R.O., D. 16/2/42; above, Lichfield, public services (water supplies).
[63] L.J.R.O., D. 16/5/21, partics. of estate, 1811; L.J.R.O., B/A/15/Burntwood, no. 1050.
[64] Inf. from Mr. Goodwin.
[65] S.R.O., D. 4363/H, will of Wm. Potts, 1724; D. 4363/S/30, deed of 7 Jan. 1719/20; L.J.R.O., D. 88/hosp. land, plan no. 6.
[66] S.R.O., D. 4363/H, articles of agreement 26 Mar. 1798 and deeds of 25 and 26 June 1799.
[67] S.R.O., D. 4363/H, deeds of 29 Oct. 1803 and 26 Mar. 1808; above, Burntwood, manors.
[68] Inf. from the tenant, Mr. J. Hulme.

[69] S.R.O., D. 546/2/1/1.
[70] L.J.R.O., D. 127/deed of 14 Nov. 1619, Wm. Baron Paget to Wm. Quinton.
[71] Ibid. D. 27/1/1, f. 109; D. 27/1/2, burial of 26 Apr. 1630; P.R.O., PROB 11/284, f. 184v.; above (Wall manor).
[72] S.R.O., D. 546/1/3/10, will of Thos. Quinton, 1733.
[73] Ibid. D. 546/11/1/1.
[74] L.J.R.O., D. 27/1/4, bapt. of 3 July 1783; below (Pipe Hill House).
[75] *Alum. Cantab. 1752–1900*, i. 353; sale cat. 1879 (copy in S.R.O., D. 546/18/7).
[76] Inf. from Mr. Alsop.
[77] S.R.O., D. (W.) 1734/2/1/598, m. 32.
[78] Ibid. D. (W.) 1734/J. 2268, f. 2.
[79] L.J.R.O., D. 88/hosp. land, plan no. 6.
[80] Annotated copy of 1921 sale cat. (lot 20) in S.R.O., D. 4363/A/5/14.
[81] Inf. from Mr. Bird.
[82] *S.H.C.* 1923, 163 (s.v. 'Mr. Crowder', who is identifiable as Thos. Crowther of Pipe Grange: Lambeth Palace Libr., Court of Arches, Ee 3, f. 756).
[83] L.J.R.O., D. 88/hosp. land, plan no. 6.
[84] Ibid. D. 88/deed of 1 July 1796; Reade, *Johnsonian Gleanings*, iv. 130–1; viii. 116; *Life and Times of Mrs. Sherwood*, ed. F. J. Harvey Darton, 23.

cathedral, who was the tenant in the 1820s.[85] The house, which is rendered, had a south front of two bays, with Venetian windows to the first floor and semi-circular windows to the attics; a ground-floor room was added on the south probably in the early 20th century. A large drawing room with a bedroom above was added on the east in the later 19th century. A long, single-storeyed rear-wing probably dates from the 18th century. There was a dovecot near the house in 1398.[86]

Land acquired in 1588 and 1593 by Nicholas Bull (d. 1627)[87] was evidently the estate centred on the later *PIPE HILL HOUSE*. His heir may have been Richard Bull (d. by 1655), whose son, also Richard, held land at Pipehill. The younger Richard died in 1660.[88] The Mr. Bull who occupied a house at Pipehill assessed for tax on five hearths in 1666 was presumably the Richard Bull of Pipehill, gentleman, who died in 1671. He was succeeded by his son Thomas, who was dead by 1689 with a son Thomas as his heir.[89] In the early 18th century the estate belonged to another Richard Bull, who sold it to Harvey Green of Lichfield. Green was succeeded in 1721 by his nephew, John Hartwell, a Lichfield cloth manufacturer, who in 1725 sold the estate to Randle Bradburne, a Birmingham ironmonger.[90] Randle's heir was evidently John Bradburne, who in 1751 advertised 200 a. at Pipehill for letting.[91] Most of the estate evidently comprised farmland south of Pipe Hill House and later centred on Pipe Place Farm, built in 1764.[92] John died in 1779 and was succeeded by his illegitimate son Samuel Hamson, otherwise Bradburne.[93] Samuel was still alive in 1824 but dead by 1834 when his widow Ann was living at Fosseway Court in Pipehill.[94] Samuel's son John died in 1834, leaving a son also called John, a minor.[95] John was succeeded in or shortly before 1879 by his son Henry (d. c. 1893). In 1894 an estate of 226 a. centred on Pipe Place Farm was offered for sale.[96] In the 1920s the land was farmed by Walter Ryman of Manor Farm, evidently the owner.[97] The land and Pipe Place Farm remained in his family in 1986. Pipe Hill House, a brick building dating from the mid 18th century, may have been separated from the estate after John Bradburne's death in 1834. It was owned in 1845 by his widow Mary, and in 1871 John's daughter Eliza Bradburne was liv-

ing there.[98] Eliza was still there in 1900 but no longer by 1904, presumably having died.[99] The house was owned by Mrs. Winifred Elms in 1986.

An estate centred on *PIPEHILL FARM* originated as a messuage and 85 a. at Pipehill held by Adam Hardwick (d. 1349).[1] In the 15th century it was held by the Redehill family.[2] Robert Redehill gave it to Canon Thomas Milley, archdeacon of Coventry, who in 1504 included it in his re-endowment of a women's almshouse in Lichfield, later known as Dr. Milley's hospital.[3] By the mid 17th century part of the rent from the farm was 15 horseloads of coal delivered to the hospital on Midsummer Day or 7s. 6d. in lieu. The coal remained part of the rent until the late 18th century.[4] In the early 19th century the estate covered 68 a.[5] In 1920 the hospital sold it to Joseph Hulme (d. 1954),[6] whose daughter, Miss Hilda Hulme, lived at Pipehill Farm in 1986.

Pipehill Farm incorporates in its western corner a bay of a medieval hall with cruck trusses; a cross wing at its south-east end may also be medieval. Beyond the cross wing is an addition which contains early 17th-century panelling on both floors. There are 18th- and 19th-century additions in brick to the north-east, and the cross wing has a Venetian window on the ground floor.

WALL HALL had been built by the later 17th century to replace a house to the south in Castle Croft on Watling Street, owned by the Jackson family of Chesterfield in Shenstone by the late 16th century.[7] In 1666 Henry Jackson was living at Wall Hall, then described as a new house. He was succeeded in 1694 by his son Edward.[8] Edward was succeeded in 1725 by his brother Henry (d. 1727), whose heir was his son Edward (d. 1760). Edward's heir was his brother Thomas, then of Dudley.[9] Thomas was succeeded probably in the early 1780s by his son, also Thomas, master of Dudley grammar school (d. 1794).[10] His successor was presumably Edward Jackson (d. 1830), whose widow Mary held 98 a. in Wall in 1844.[11]

Edward and Mary Jackson shared their home with Richard Croft Chawner, whom they brought up from childhood. Chawner (born 1804), the son of Dr. Rupert Chawner of Burton upon Trent, became a barrister but did not

[85] R. Polwhele, *Reminiscences, in Prose and Verse* (1836), i. 148; *Lichfield Mercury*, 12 and 26 May 1826.
[86] S.R.O., D. (W.) 1734/2/1/599, m. 40.
[87] *S.H.C.* xiii. 297; xv. 184; xvi. 130–1; L.J.R.O., D. 27/1/1, f. 66v.
[88] L.J.R.O., D. 27/1/1, f. 112; D. 103/6/14/1, schedule.
[89] L.J.R.O., P/C/11, Ric. Bull (1671), Thos. Bull (1689); *S.H.C.* 1923, 163.
[90] L.J.R.O., reg. of peculiar wills 1665–1762, ff. 118v.–120 (pencil foliation); B.R.L. Homer 258, deed of 8 June 1725; Reade, *Johnsonian Gleanings*, viii. 128.
[91] *Aris's Birmingham Gaz.* 1 July 1751.
[92] Date stone on house.
[93] L.J.R.O., P/C/11, John Bradburne (1779).
[94] Ibid. Ann Bradburne (1838); W.S.L. 47/1/45, ff. 43–4; S.R.O., D. (W.) 1821/5.
[95] L.J.R.O., D. 27/1/4, bapt. of 23 June 1782; ibid. P/C/11, John Bradburne (1834); W.S.L., S. MS. 384, p. 230.
[96] P.R.O., RG 11/2775; sale cat. 1879 (copy in S.R.O., D. 546/18/7); *Lichfield Mercury*, 24 Aug. 1894, p. 4.
[97] Below, econ. hist. (agric.).

[98] L.J.R.O., B/A/15/Burntwood, no. 868; P.R.O., RG 10/2915; W.S.L., S. MS. 384, p. 230.
[99] *Kelly's Dir. Staffs.* (1900; 1904).
[1] *S.H.C.* xiii. 118, 125.
[2] Ibid. xi. 239; S.R.O., D. (W.) 1734/2/1/600, m. 4d.
[3] L.J.R.O., D. 103/6/28/1; *V.C.H. Staffs.* iii. 276.
[4] L.J.R.O., D. 103/6/14/1, 9, and 12.
[5] Ibid. D. 103/6/2, map II.
[6] Ibid. D. 103/2/5, 10 Mar. 1920; S.R.O., D. 553/1, pp. 82–3; *Lichfield Mercury*, 26 Nov. 1954, p. 7.
[7] Sanders, *Shenstone*, 277–8.
[8] Ibid. 278–9; *S.H.C.* 1923, 164; L.J.R.O., D. 27/1/3, burial of 1 Mar. 1693/4.
[9] L.J.R.O., D. 27/1/3, burial of 16 May 1725; L.J.R.O., P/C/11, Edw. Jackson (1725), Hen. Jackson (1727), Edw. Jackson (1760).
[10] Ibid. P/C/11, Thos. Jackson (1811), enclosing a will of 1780, evidently that of his father Thos.; L.J.R.O., D. 27/1/5, p. 5; Sanders, *Shenstone*, 279; *V.C.H. Worcs.* iv. 521.
[11] S.R.O., D. 4566/J, Aldershawe, abstract of title to Wall farm, 1891; L.J.R.O., B/A/15/Burntwood.

practise, preferring to pursue interests in farming and business. He ran a model farm at Wall Hall and was secretary of the Lichfield (later Lichfield and Midlands Counties) Agricultural Society, probably from its formation in 1838 and certainly from 1842.[12] He was also active in the South Staffordshire Railway Co., the South Staffordshire Waterworks Co., and the Cannock Chase Colliery Co. He moved to Abnalls in Burntwood in the mid 1850s and died there in 1870.[13]

On Mary Jackson's death in 1851[14] the estate passed to Edward's sister-in-law Elizabeth Smith for her life. She died in 1860, and in accordance with Edward's will the estate then passed to John Pavier of Hammerwich Place Farm, son of Edward's sister Mary. John, who changed his name to Jackson to secure the inheritance, was succeeded in 1871 by his brother Thomas Pavier, who also changed his name to Jackson. He was succeeded in 1885 by his sister's grandson, John Jackson Smith of Wolverhampton, who added Jackson to his surname. He died in 1889, leaving a widow Mary, and in 1896 the estate was split up; it then comprised 185 a., of which 97 a. lay in Wall and the rest in Shenstone. The house was presumably bought by Thomas Andrews, who was living there in 1900; it was then called White House. In 1919 the house and 5 a. were bought by Col. George Kay, whose widow in 1942 sold the estate to W. J. Ryman, later of Manor Farm. In 1951 he sold the house and 2 a. to Peter Cutler, who in 1987 sold it to Mr. and Mrs. David Dunger.[15]

Henry Jackson's house, assessed for tax on five hearths in 1666, included in 1695 a hall, a parlour with a chamber over it, and a little parlour.[16] It may partly survive in the east part of Wall Hall, having become the service wing in the mid 18th century. A main range was then built to the west with a central staircase hall with rooms on either side and a west entrance. The enlarged house was presumably built by Edward Jackson (d. 1760); in 1753 he married Sarah, sister of Sheldon Porter of Wall House,[17] which was rebuilt about the same time. Further service rooms and a secondary stair were added to the north end of the house c. 1800, and in the earlier 19th century a new block was added in the angle between the 18th-century ranges. That block comprises a drawing room and entrance hall with rooms above, making a new south-facing front of three storeys with a Doric porch; the ground-floor windows on either side of the porch are formed in segmental bows.[18] Later in the 19th century the front was replastered with decorative architraves. The house in Castle Croft was known as the 'lower house' in 1727, when it included a 'house place' (perhaps an open hall), and great and little parlours.[19] Part of the building survived in the earlier 1790s, but it was then much decayed.[20]

The tithes of Wall belonged to the prebendaries of Prees (or Pipa Minor), Stotfold, and Weeford in Lichfield cathedral, and those of Pipehill to the prebendaries of Freeford, Hansacre, Pipa Minor, Stotfold, and Weeford.[21] The dean and chapter became the appropriators of the Stotfold tithes in 1803.[22] In 1694 Bishop Lloyd assigned the small tithes to the vicar of St. Mary's, Lichfield.[23] By the 1840s parts of both areas were exempt, in some cases in return for a prescriptive payment. The great tithes were commuted in 1845 for rent charges of £41 18s. 7d. to the dean and chapter (for tithes due to Stotfold from 193 a. in Wall and part of 71 a. in Pipehill) and £125 3s. ½d. to the Ecclesiastical Commissioners (Weeford from 331 a. in Wall and 502 a. and part of 71 a. in Pipehill, Pipa Minor from 102 a. in Pipehill and 90 a. in Wall, and Freeford and Hansacre from part of 71 a. in Pipehill). The vicar of St. Mary's was awarded £17 5s. for the small tithes of Pipehill but nothing for those of Wall.

In 1364 John Hardwick, a vicar choral of Lichfield cathedral whose family lived at Pipehill, was licensed by the Crown to endow a chantry at the altar of St. Catherine in the cathedral. The endowment included property in 'Pipe Lichfield', probably Pipehill.[24] By the 1440s the prebendary of Pipa Parva held pastures in Wall called Newland and Muckleys.[25] The vicars choral owned land in Wall in 1535.[26]

The endowments of a school at Kingsbury (Warws.) established in 1686 included 5 a. east of Pipe Place Farm. The school still owned the land in 1879.[27]

ECONOMIC HISTORY. AGRICULTURE. Assarting at Aldershawe is suggested by a rudding recorded there in the 13th century.[28] Three open fields at Wall were recorded in the early 17th century: Shaw field on either side of Green Lane, Little field on either side of Market Lane, and Street field (shared with the inhabitants of Chesterfield in Shenstone) east of the hamlet along Watling Street.[29] The Butts, lying on the west side of the hamlet, was arable by the late

[12] L.J.R.O., D. 109/Lowe's Char., draft affidavits 1841; *Staffs. Advertiser*, 1 Oct. 1842, p. 4; 17 Sept. 1870, p. 4.
[13] *The Blackcountryman*, x (4), 26; xi (1), 30; xi (2), 44; xiii (4), 41; above, Burntwood, manors (Abnalls).
[14] L.J.R.O., D. 27/1/11, p. 14.
[15] S.R.O., D. 4566/J, Aldershawe, abstract of title to Wall farm, 1891; sale cat. 1896 (copy in possession of Mr. and Mrs. Dunger); *Lichfield Mercury*, 10 July 1896, p. 4; 24 July 1896, p. 4; *Kelly's Dir. Staffs.* (1896 and later edns.); inf. from Mr. Ryman and Mrs. Dunger.
[16] *S.H.C.* 1923, 164; L.J.R.O., D. 127/inventory of Hen. Jackson, Mar. 1694/5 [17] L.J.R.O., D. 27/1/4, p. 97.
[18] Above, plate 54.
[19] L.J.R.O., P/C/11, Hen. Jackson (1727).
[20] Sanders, *Shenstone*, 277–8.

[21] Para. based on L.J.R.O., B/A/15/Burntwood.
[22] *V.C.H. Staffs.* iii. 182.
[23] Above, Lichfield, churches.
[24] *Cal. Pat.* 1364–7, 48; 1549–51, 361; above (Pipehill Farm).
[25] W.S.L. 50/A 1–2/56.
[26] *Valor Eccl.* (Rec. Com.), iii. 136, 138.
[27] *V.C.H. Warws.* ii. 368; L.J.R.O., B/A/15/Burntwood, nos. 863–5, 873; sale cat. 1879 (copy in S.R.O., D. 546/18/7).
[28] Sanders, *Shenstone*, 282 (where 'Licholvefrudwig' is evidently a misreading; the name occurs as 'Lychulfrudyns' in 1347: Bodl. MS. Ashmole 855, p. 214).
[29] L.J.R.O., B/A/15/Burntwood; L.J.R.O., D. 15/10/1/20; S.R.O., D. (W.) 1734/2/1/643.

16th century.[30] Pipehill had its own fields. Pipe field, mentioned in 1358 and lying partly in Edial in Burntwood, was still open in 1705.[31] Ash field, mentioned in 1393 and lying in the Lichfield part of Pipehill, was still open in 1651.[32] Mickehill field, south of Ash field and also lying mostly in the Lichfield part of Pipehill, was mentioned in 1577 and was still open in 1639.[33]

In the 1440s most of the income received by the lord of Wall for land in the manor held on lease came from pasture.[34] An area of waste near Moat Bank House survived in the late 17th century, and nearly 20 a. of waste south of Muckley Corner survived as Wall Butts common in the mid 19th century.[35] Pipe Marsh, an area of waste around which Pipehill hamlet grew, was mentioned in the later 14th century and covered 14 a. in the early 19th.[36] There was meadow along Black brook in the early 19th century.[37] Land called Goosemoor near the northern boundary of Pipehill in the mid 19th century may have been used as a feeding ground for geese.[38]

Livestock farming at Pipehill in the Middle Ages is suggested by the early name for the hamlet, Hardwick, and by the requirement on the tenant of Pipe Grange to supply the bishop's larder.[39] The overburdening of common pasture at Aldershawe led in 1370 to the imposition of a stint of 100 sheep, 6 oxen, 4 cows, and 4 heifers for each virgater.[40] The wool sent by the bailiff of the lord of Wall to a fuller in Tamworth in 1448–9 was probably from sheep at Wall.[41] Each inhabitant at Wall in 1580 was evidently allowed to pasture only 5 sheep for each acre held, while at Pipehill in 1586 the limit for cottagers was 10 sheep and for non-residents 6.[42] John Quinton had a flock of 200 sheep in 1658.[43] In the early 18th century land called Danwell Flat (Dunningham Flat in the mid 19th century) on the east side of Wall Lane straddling the boundary between Wall and Pipehill was a sheepwalk.[44] Turnips were grown in Wall in the late 18th century as food for sheep.[45]

Pastoral farming remained important in the 19th and early 20th century. Of 141 a. of titheable land around Wall hamlet in 1808, 50 a. were pasture and a further 33 a. were devoted to hay and clover; land devoted to cereals comprised 20 a. of wheat, 13 a. of barley, and 3 a. of oats; 22 a. were fallow.[46] One farmer in Wall in the early 19th century established a pedigree flock of Blackfaced sheep crossed with New Leicester

and Southdown rams; another at Pipe Place farm in the later 19th century bred Shropshire sheep.[47] In 1917 Walter Ryman, who farmed 353 a. at Manor farm, had a flock of 400 Shropshires, 50 head of cattle, and 70 pigs. Sixty-five acres were then devoted to clover, 21 a. to swedes, 12 a. to turnips and kale, and 8 a. to mangolds, mostly to provide feed for the animals; other crops included 44 a. of oats, 43 a. of wheat, and 85 a. of potatoes. Ryman became noted for his potatoes, and by 1928, when farming some 600 a. which included Pipe Place farm, he was producing over 2,000 tons a year from 200 a.; the potatoes were sold to markets in the Black Country and at Derby. The potato fields were manured by large flocks of Shropshires and Dorset Downs. Ryman was also noted for his pedigree herd of pigs, for whose feed 20 a. were devoted to mixed barley and oats. Other crops grown by Ryman in 1928 were 120 a. of wheat, 30 a. of oats, and 20 a. of roots.[48]

Crops were grown on 564 ha. (1,393 a.) of the 673.5 ha. (1,664 a.) of farmland returned for Wall civil parish in 1984. Over half the cultivated land was devoted to barley, with sugar beet, potatoes, and wheat also being grown; cabbages, cauliflowers, and brussels sprouts were grown on nearly 41 ha. There was one dairy farm, and the animals recorded were 450 cattle, 886 pigs, and 276 sheep.[49]

WARRENS AND FISHERY. There was a manorial warren in 1448, when rabbits from it were taken to Nether Seal (Leics.), a manor also owned by the lord of Wall.[50] The warren presumably lay near Moat Bank House, whose name derives from a warren built in the medieval form of an embankment with a protective ditch; there was land called 'coneygree' near the house in 1733.[51] There was presumably a warren at Aldershawe in 1420 when 100 rabbits belonging to William Newport were stolen there.[52] There was a fishpool in 1685 in Mill Lane at the west end of Wall hamlet.[53]

MILL. Mill field was recorded in 1456.[54] The fishpool in Mill Lane was evidently a mill pool.

TRADES. A tobacco cutter named Daniel Reading lived at Pipehill in the early 1700s. He was a Quaker and had an interest in land in the Quaker territory of New Jersey, whence the tobacco may have come. At his death in 1704 he had £8 worth of goods in a tobacco house, comprising

[30] S.R.O., D. (W.) 1734/2/1/646.
[31] Above, Burntwood, econ. hist. (agric.).
[32] S.R.O., D. (W.) 1734/2/1/599, m. 30; D. (W.) 1734/2/1/603, m. 6; B.R.L. Homer 96.
[33] S.R.O., D. (W.) 1734/2/1/629, m. 3; D. (W.) 1734/2/1/614, m. 35d.
[34] W.S.L. 50/A 1–2/56.
[35] L.J.R.O., P/C/11, Thos. Dutton (1691); L.J.R.O., B/A/15/Burntwood, nos. 1099, 1102.
[36] S.R.O., D. (W.) 1734/2/1/598, m. 30; W.S.L. 47/1/45, f. 45.
[37] S.R.O., D. 546/16/7.
[38] L.J.R.O., B/A/15/Burntwood, nos. 949–50, 960–1.
[39] Above, introduction; manor.
[40] Sanders, Shenstone, 283–4.
[41] W.S.L. 50/A 2/56.
[42] S.R.O., D. (W.) 1734/2/1/634, m. 7 (cancelled entry); D. (W.) 1734/2/1/646.

[43] S.H.C. 4th ser. v, pp. 113–14.
[44] L.J.R.O., B/A/15/Burntwood, nos. 1141–5; L.J.R.O., D. 77/5/1, f. 210.
[45] L.J.R.O., D. 88/hosp. land, appendix to plan no. 6; Aris's Birmingham Gaz. 13 Nov. 1797.
[46] S.R.O., D. 546/16/2 and 7.
[47] Staffs. Advertiser, 14 Aug. 1813; sale cat. 1879 (copy in S.R.O., D. 546/18/7).
[48] Staffs. Advertiser, 21 July 1917, p. 2; 11 Feb. 1928, p. 2; R. A. Pepperall, Biography of Sir Thomas Baxter (Wells, 1950), 68.
[49] M.A.F.F., agric. returns 1984.
[50] W.S.L. 50/A 1–2/56.
[51] L.J.R.O., P/C/11, Thos. Dutton (1691); S.R.O., D. 546/1/3/10, will of Thos. Quinton, 1733.
[52] S.H.C. xvii. 72.
[53] L.J.R.O., P/C/11, Thos. Dutton (1691).
[54] S.R.O., D. (W.) 1734/2/1/603, m. 51.

an engine, press, mill, dyer, two pairs of scales, and cut and uncut tobacco.[55]

There were limekilns and a wharf on the Wyrley and Essington Canal at Muckley Corner by 1845. The kilns were run by Strongitharm & Cooper, a partnership which evidently included George Strongitharm, who had a limeworks at Daw End in Rushall.[56] George and Horatio Stongitharm ran the Muckley Corner business in the 1860s and 1870s. The Daw End Lime Co. ran it in the 1880s and 1890s. The kilns apparently ceased working in the mid 1890s.[57]

Sand was dug at the southern edge of Wall Butts in the early 1880s. Working had ceased by the early 1920s, when there was another sand pit to the north-east on the south side of Watling Street.[58]

LOCAL GOVERNMENT. Wall and Pipehill attended Longdon manor's view of frankpledge, forming part of a tithing which also included Edial, Woodhouses, and Burntwood. In the late 1630s Wall and Pipehill became separate tithings, each with one frankpledge. A headborough was still appointed for each of them at the Longdon court in 1839. By the 14th century Wall and Pipehill were part of the constablewick of Pipe cum membris.[59]

The lord of Wall had his own court by the 1480s. It was presumably a court baron, like that held by the lord of Pipe in Burntwood. It was last recorded in 1713 when a court leet was held at Wall together with a court baron, although no court leet matters were recorded.[60]

There was a pinfold for Pipe and Wall by 1466, probably east of Pipehill hamlet near Mickle Hills Farm, where one stood in 1598.[61] The name Pinfold Croft recorded at Wall in 1693 suggests the existence of a pinfold at some time.[62] A pinner was chosen by Wall manor court in 1713, and in 1839 one for Wall was listed among the officers of Longdon manor.[63] In the late 19th century a pinfold stood at the junction of Watling Street and the road called the Butts.[64]

As part of St. Michael's, Lichfield, Wall had a sidesman in 1637, but in 1638, 1640, and the mid 1660s only a Pipehill sidesman was recorded; by 1733 there were sidesmen for both places. Their appointment continued after Wall parish was created in 1845, but the practice was

discontinued in 1866.[65] There was an overseer of the poor for Wall and one for Pipehill c. 1805.[66] A new civil parish of Wall, including part of Pipehill, was created in 1894.[67] As part of Lichfield rural district Wall civil parish became part of the new Lichfield district in 1974.

Wall and Pipehill were included in Lichfield poor-law union formed in 1836.[68]

CHURCH. A graveyard was recorded at Aldershawe in the mid 13th century.[69] It was presumably used by the inhabitants of the area as a field cemetery. The general burial place, however, was evidently at St. Michael's, Lichfield, which became the parish church for the area.[70] By the 1730s some parishioners, notably from Pipehill, were baptized and buried at Hammerwich chapel.[71]

A church was built at Wall in 1843 on land given by John Mott of Wall House.[72] In 1845 a new parish was formed out of St. Michael's for Wall and the part of Pipehill outside the city of Lichfield.[73] The living, the patronage of which was vested in the incumbent of St. Michael's,[74] was styled a vicarage in 1868.[75] Since 1951 the benefice has been held in plurality with that of Stonnall, the patronage being exercised alternately by the vicar of Shenstone as patron of Stonnall and by the rector of St. Michael's.[76]

John Mott gave an endowment of £700 in 1843. It was augmented by funds which included £500 left by Robert Hill, probably the owner of Wall House who died in 1812 or a relative. Further money for the endowment was raised by subscription.[77] A tithe rent charge of £6 14s. 8½d. was awarded to the incumbent by the Ecclesiastical Commissioners in 1860, and in 1865 they assigned him a further £50 a year. In 1876 another tithe rent charge of £127 11s. 7d. was awarded,[78] and further augmentations of £25 a year were made in 1910 and 1914.[79] A vicarage house (Littlefield House in 1986), was built in Market Lane in 1863 and sold in 1952, the vicar of the combined benefices living in Stonnall.[80]

The church of *ST. JOHN THE BAPTIST*, built of sandstone probably to a design by George Gilbert Scott,[81] consists of a short chancel, an aisleless nave, and a west tower with a spire. An interior view in 1859 shows box pews, benches in the centre of the nave and a two-

[55] L.J.R.O., P/C/11, Dan. Reading (1704).
[56] L.J.R.O., B/A/15/Burntwood, no. 1014a; White, *Dir. Staffs.* (1851), 579; *V.C.H. Staffs.* xvii. 191–2.
[57] *P.O. Dir. Staffs.* (1860 and later edns.); *Kelly's Dir. Staffs.* (1880 and later edns. to 1896).
[58] O.S. Map 1/2,500, Staffs. LVIII. 5 (1884 edn.); LVIII. 5, 6 (1923 edn.).
[59] Above, Burntwood, local govt.
[60] S.R.O., D. 546/1/2/3; D. 546/7/4.
[61] Ibid. D. (W.) 1734/2/1/598, m. 72; D. (W.) 1734/2/1/671.
[62] L.J.R.O., D. 127/deed of 16 June 1693.
[63] S.R.O., D. 546/1/2/3; D. 603/J/1/4/15.
[64] Sale cat. 1879 (copy in S.R.O., D. 546/18/7); O.S. Map 1/2,500, Staffs. LVIII. 6 (1923 edn.).
[65] Above, Lichfield, parish govt.
[66] S.R.O., D. 4045/7/2.   [67] Above, introduction.
[68] Poor Law Com. Order of 1836 forming Lichfield union (copy in L.J.R.O., D. 77/16/3).

[69] S.R.O., D. 4566/M, deed of Thos. the mason to Rob. son of Godwin, where the word *cimiterium* has been misread and wrongly translated as 'warren' in Sanders, *Shenstone,* 281.
[70] Above, Lichfield, churches (parochial organization).
[71] S.R.O., D. 3802/1/1, bapt. of 9 Aug. 1734, burial of 3 Nov. 1738.
[72] Lich. Dioc. Regy., B/A/2i/M, pp. 381–401.
[73] *Lond. Gaz.* 6 May 1845, pp. 1358–9.
[74] Lich. Dioc. Regy., B/A/32, pp. 156, 169.
[75] *Lich. Dioc. Ch. Cal.* (1869).
[76] Lich. Dioc. Regy., Orders in Council, R, pp. 196–7.
[77] Lich. Dioc. Regy., B/A/2i/M, pp. 379–80, 389–94.
[78] *Lond. Gaz.* 30 Oct. 1860, pp. 3914, 3922; 8 Aug. 1865, p. 3880; 23 June 1876, pp. 3625–6.
[79] Lich. Dioc. Regy., B/A/2i/V, pp. 302, 457.
[80] *Lich. Dioc. Ch. Cal.* (1864), 148; *Lichfield Mercury,* 30 May 1952, p. 7.
[81] Pevsner, *Staffs.* 291; above, plate 55.

decker pulpit on the north side of the chancel arch.[82] In 1892 a peal of tubular bells was installed in the spire, and a clock was placed there in 1920 as a war memorial, the cost being met by subscription.[83] A graveyard was included in William Mott's grant of land for the church and was extended by $\frac{1}{5}$ a. in 1910 and $\frac{1}{4}$ a. in 1926.[84]

A mission chapel was opened at Pipehill in 1889. The site was given by Eliza Bradburne of Pipe Hill House, and the building cost was raised by subscription.[85] Built of brick with a porch and small spire, the chapel continued in use until 1963. It was sold in 1969 and was demolished soon afterwards.[86]

NONCONFORMITY. Elizabeth Rawlins, a widow living at Pipehill, was recorded as a papist in 1657.[87] John Hall (d. 1705), who refused to pay tithes in Wall in 1678, was one of the first members of a Quaker meeting based at Lynn and later at Chesterfield, both in Shenstone. By 1681 the meeting was attended by John Reading of Pipehill Farm. Other Quaker members of the Reading family were Daniel (d. 1704), a tobacco cutter, and his brother Job, a yeoman who moved to a farm at Woodhouses in Burntwood in the 1720s.[88] In 1821 Thomas Hickson registered a house on the site of the later Trooper inn for worship by protestant dissenters.[89]

EDUCATION. A dame school in Wall, which was in union with the diocesan board of education by 1844,[90] was presumably the forerunner of the day and Sunday school which had a paid mistress and over 40 children in the later 1840s.[91] It seems to have been closed soon afterwards.[92] In 1867, largely owing to the efforts of the incumbent William Williams and his wife, a National school was opened in Market Lane on the vicarage grounds; it comprised a schoolroom, a classroom, and a mistress's house. The money for it was raised by subscription, with grants from government and the National Society.[93] Average attendance was over 50 in the later 1890s and had risen to c. 80 in 1911, when the building was enlarged. From 1936 it was a junior school, with senior pupils attending schools in Lichfield. As St. John's Church of England (Controlled) primary school, it was closed in 1978.[94] The buildings were later converted into a house.

By 1829 there was a girls' boarding school at Pipehill run by a Miss Holmes. It was probably long-established: when Elizabeth Gautherot took it over with 10 pupils in 1833, it was described as having existed for many years.[95] In 1841 it occupied a house near the tollhouse on the Lichfield–Walsall road.[96] Another girls' boarding school at Pipehill was opened in 1856 by the Misses Topham; it was presumably the one run in 1864 by Mrs. Henry Topham.[97]

CHARITY FOR THE POOR. In 1860 John Jackson of Wall Hall settled a house in Lichfield in trust, $\frac{1}{6}$ of the income to be paid to the minister of Wall church and $\frac{5}{6}$ to be distributed among the poor of Wall and of part of Shenstone parish. The house was sold in 1962 and the capital invested. The income was £59 in 1986 and distributions continued to be made.[98]

[82] Lichfield Cath. Libr., Moore and Hinckes drawings, xvi, no. 20.
[83] Plaque in church porch.
[84] Lich. Dioc. Regy., B/A/2i/M, p. 389; V, pp. 183, 255; W, p. 211.
[85] P.R.O., C 54/19237, no. 40; *Lichfield Mercury*, 11 Jan. 1889, p. 6.
[86] *Lich. Dioc. Ch. Cal.* (1963; 1964); *Lichfield Mercury*, 5 Sept. 1969, p. 1 (with picture); local inf.
[87] *S.H.C.* 4th ser. ii. 90.
[88] *Staffordshire Studies*, ed. P. Morgan (Keele, 1987), 107–10; L.J.R.O., P/C/11, John Hall (1705); above, econ. hist. (trades).
[89] *S.H.C.* 4th ser. iii. 52; S.R.O., D. 546/16/8, no. 14.
[90] Not in the Lich. Dioc. Board of Educ. *3rd Ann. Rep.*

(Lichfield, 1842) but in *5th Ann. Rep.* (Lichfield, 1844), 27 (copies in W.S.L.).
[91] Nat. Soc. *Inquiry, 1846–7*, Staffs. 6–7; Lich. Dioc. Bd. of Educ. *9th Ann. Rep.* (Lichfield, 1848), 26.
[92] Not in *P.O. Dir. Staffs.* (1850) or White, *Dir. Staffs.* (1851).
[93] *Staffs. Advertiser*, 22 June 1867, p. 7.
[94] *Kelly's Dir. Staffs.* (1896 and edns. to 1912); *Staffs. C.C. Record for 1936*, 905; inf. from Staffs. C.C. Educ. Dept. (1987).
[95] Pigot, *Dir. Birmingham* (1829), 84; *Staffs. Advertiser*, 6 July 1833, p. 1; *Educ. Enq. Abstract*, 885.
[96] P.R.O., HO 107/980.
[97] *Staffs. Advertiser*, 5 July 1856, p. 1; 10 Jan. 1857, p. 1; *P.O. Dir. Staffs.* (1864).
[98] Inf. from Mr. W. J. Ryman of Manor Farm.

INDEX